"The book fills a badly needed hole in the managerial and pedagogical literature, and bridges the gap between recent research literature and practice. It has the potential to promote a revolution in thinking about corporate strategy, much as Porter's *Competitive Strategy* did for business strategy."

Richard A. Bettis
The University of North Carolina at Chapel Hill

"There is nothing this good on (1) Creating corporate advantage through competitive advantage, (2) realizing synergies by sharing resources and appropriating value, or (3) making corporate contributions to value creation through appropriate control systems. The cases are designed to teach themselves. The textual chapters can be used as an independent supplementary text. The book is a masterpiece."

Kathryn Rudie Harrigan
Henry R. Kravis Professor of Business Leadership
Columbia University

"This significant and timely book brings theory together with powerful practical applications. It represents the best synthesis of this important subject now available."

Michael E. Porter
Harvard Business School

CORPORATE STRATEGY

Resources and the Scope of the Firm

CORPORATE STRATEGY
Resources and the Scope of the Firm

▲

David J. Collis
Associate Professor of Business Administration

Cynthia A. Montgomery
John G. McLean Professor of Business Administration

Both of the Graduate School of Business Administration
Harvard University

Irwin
McGraw-Hill

Boston, Massachusetts   Burr Ridge, Illinois   Dubuque, Iowa
Madison, Wisconsin   New York, New York   San Francisco, California   St. Louis, Missouri

Irwin/McGraw-Hill

A Division of The McGraw·Hill Companies

3 4 5 6 7 8 9 0 DOC DOC 9098

ISBN 0–256–17894–1

Irwin Book Team

Publisher: *Rob Zwettler*
Executive editor: *Craig S. Beytien*
Senior developmental editor: *Laura Hurst Spell*
Marketing manager: *Michael Campbell*
Senior project supervisor: *Mary Conzachi*
Senior production supervisor: *Laurie Sander*
Designer: *Crispin Prebys*
Director, Prepress purchasing: *Kimberly Meriwether David*
Compositor: *Douglas & Gayle Ltd.*
Typeface: *10/12 Times Roman*
Printer: *R.R. Donnelley & Sons Company*

Library of Congress Cataloging-in-Publication Data

Collis, David J.
    Corporate strategy : resources and the scope of the firm/David
J. Collis, Cynthia A. Montgomery.
      p. cm.
    Includes index.
    ISBN 0-256-17894-1
    1. Strategic planning.   2. Business planning.   I. Montgomery,
Cynthia A., 1952-   . II. Title.
HD30.28.C6433   1997
    658.4'012—dc20   95–36380

http://www.mhcollege.com

Dedication

▲

For Jill, William, Emma, and Charlotte

and

For Bjørn and Nils

PREFACE

Historically, the strategy field has been broken into two discrete fields of study: business level strategy, focusing on competitive advantage within an industry, and corporate level strategy, focusing on the overall plan for managing a diversified firm. Pedagogically and intellectually, this book is an attempt to bridge the schism between these two levels of analysis, and present a unified treatment of the sources of superior economic performance.

As its subtitle suggests, the book analyzes strategy in terms of "Resources and the Scope of the Firm." At the heart of this view is the idea that *corporate* as well as competitive advantage is based on the unique resources of a firm, and the way those resources are deployed in particular competitive settings. The choice of firm boundaries, and the organizational mechanisms that bring strategy to fruition are also essential, and are examined in similar depth.

The book is primarily designed to address corporate strategy issues, but the view of strategy presented here is dynamic, and integrates both corporate and business levels of analysis. While it recognizes that there are areas of distinction between the two, it also recognizes that there are many important areas of overlap. The presentation traces the growth and development of firms, beginning with single-line businesses and gradually reaching to large diversified and vertically integrated firms. This progression reinforces the inextricable link between corporate and business strategy, thus deepening the traditional understanding of both. It also demonstrates that corporate advantage is usually realized at the business level, through the enhanced performance of individual business units.

A number of insights drawn from two distinct bodies of research: the first is the resource-based view of the firm, which has gained prominence in the field of strategic management; the second is organizational economics, in particular transactions cost analysis and agency theory. Both of these theoretical traditions have made a substantial contribution to the arguments advanced here.

Although it is founded upon established research traditions, the book also includes a substantial amount of material that is not available elsewhere. Most importantly, it introduces a unique approach to corporate strategy that the authors have developed over many years of research, teaching, and consulting on the topic. Ideas such as the "Zone of Value Creation," linking industry and competitive analysis with the resource-based view of the firm, and the "Triangle of Corporate Advantage," a unique framework for the assessment of corporate advantage, are new intellectual developments that are deeply woven into the central thesis of the text.

This book is an outgrowth of a corporate strategy course we developed and have taught at the Harvard Business School for the past five years. The course has attracted a wide range of students, including those who intend to be consultants, investment bankers, or stock analysts, as well as those who will run family businesses, or look to long-term careers as general managers in major industrial or consumer goods firms. This diversity testifies to the fundamental nature of the ideas and to the range of companies and settings to which they apply. In addition, in executive programs, the ideas have also been well received by seasoned managers whose primary objectives are to acquire useful, pragmatic management tools.

▲
The Text

The book contains 8 chapters of text, 27 cases, and 3 supplemental appendixes on related topics. Each chapter is designed to be a discrete intellectual module, and is divided into two sections—Principles and Practice. The Principles sections introduce each topic by describing the relevant theory and supporting empirical research. In the Practice sections, these insights are then incorporated into pragmatic frameworks and tools that can be applied to the case studies and strategic analyses.

Chapter 1 begins with a brief introduction to corporate strategy and introduces the "Triangle of Corporate Strategy," the basic organizing framework for the course. The subsequent chapters then address each element of the framework in depth. As the text proceeds, the material cumulates to an overall picture of how to design and implement an effective corporate strategy.

Chapter 2 provides the essential theory about resources, and how assets and capabilities earn economic rents. The argument is made that superior performance at the business *and* corporate level is ultimately due to the skillful deployment of competitively superior and scarce resources. The critical step of matching a firm's resources with its competitive environment is illustrated in the "Zone of Value Creation."

Chapter 3 addresses a firm's optimal competitive scope in a given industry, and how its pattern of resource deployment can shift over time. In doing so, the chapter examines the forces both inside and outside the firm that cause it to broaden or narrow its scope in order to compete successfully within its industry. Economies of scale and scope are examined in detail, and evaluated against the activities in a firm's value chain.

Chapter 4 addresses the deployment of resources across industries, and the economic rationale for diversified firms. While highly diversified firms have long been considered a class unto themselves, this discussion shows that they, in fact, share much in common with other firms. Most notably, the laws governing performance in diversified firms are not unique, but part of a much more general phenomenon relating to the value of a firm's resources and the attractivenenss of the markets in which it competes.

Up to this point, the book has proceeded as if a firm's boundaries are wholly determined by its environmental opportunities and available resources. Chapter 5 complicates this picture by asking not *whether* a particular activity should be performed, but *where* it should be performed—inside the corporate hierarchy or through some form of market exchange. Arguments from agency theory and transaction cost analysis introduce fundamental questions that challenge the primacy of the organizational hierarchy, and demonstrate the need to consider a range of alternatives before committing to this choice. Here the issues are primarily illustrated in the context of vertically integrated firms.

Chapter 6 addresses the implementation of strategy, and the systems, structures, and processes that allow a hierarchy to function and a strategy to be fully realized. Many failures of corporate strategy are due not to bad ideas, but to poor implementation. This chapter addresses this predicament by linking the organizational design of a firm to the critical elements of its strategy. Special emphasis is given to the role of the corporate office in sharing resources and coordinating the activities of the business.

Chapter 7 shifts from a focus on individual elements to a broader examination of how the Triangle of Corporate Strategy works as a complete and integrated system. Key points from earlier chapters are synthesized, and criteria and methods for the overall evaluation of a corporate strategy are introduced.

Management texts often assume that senior managers are both able and willing to craft corporate strategies that increase the value of a firm. However, recent upheavals in corporate governance reveal that this is not always the case. Chapter 8 discusses the evidence of this phenomenon, and presents several theories that explain why corporate managers do not always act in the interests of shareholders. The chapter concludes with a discussion of the responsibilities that accompany the privilege of formulating and implementing corporate strategy, and the structural forces that have emerged to discipline errant corporate behavior.

▲

Acknowledgments

This book is the result of a five-year intellectual odyssey for the authors. As such, we must acknowledge all the assistance received along the way: colleagues at the Harvard Business School, including the Research Directors who supported and funded our work; other faculty in the Competition and Strategy area, particularly Steve Bradley, Pankaj Ghemawat, Michael Porter, and David Yoffie; our colleagues who allowed us to use their cases in this book, Norm Berg, Rosabeth Kanter, Jay Lorsch, Gary Loveman, Anita McGahan,and Gary Pisano; interested (and interesting) friends outside the area, including George Baker, Nancy Koehn, and Joe Bower; as well as our research associates over the years, Toby Stuart, and Dianna Magnani; and our support staff, "T" Harrison, Michael McCole, Jill Dipmann, and Julie Mundt.

Outside the school, we have learned from those who actively work in the field, and we have benefited greatly from those, too numerous to mention, who have taught and commented on the cases. Personally, we owe a debt to Jay Barney, Richard Rumelt, and Philippe Haspeslagh, for case contributions and for many enlightening conversations. In England, the work of Michael Goold, Andrew Campbell, and Marcus Alexander has paralleled our own. Theirs is the closest to our own approach to corporate strategy, and we (David Collis, in particular) owe much to many valuable discussions. Our thanks also go out to our colleagues who reviewed the final draft of the manuscript for the text: Kathryn Harrigan, Columbia University; Philip Bromiley, University of Minnesota; Richard A. Bettis, University of North Carolina; Sahasranam "Sam" Hariharan, University of Southern California; Marvin Lieberman, University of California, Los Angeles; Ron Sanchez, University of Illinois; and J.L. Stimpert, Michigan State University. And we appreciate the valuable input we received from the following individuals who reviewed the book proposal: Raffi Amit, University of British Columbia; Jay Barney, Texas A&M; Jennifer Bethel, New York University; Philip Bromiley, University of Minnesota; Thomas Brush, Purdue University; Jordi Canals, IESE; Sayan Chatterjee, Case Western Reserve University; Bob de Wit, Erasmus University; David Jemison, University of Texas; Robert Kazanjian, Emory University; Ron Meyer, Rotterdam School of Management; Hugh M. O'Neill, University of North Carolina at Chapel Hill; Nitin Pangarkar, University of Minnesota; Margaret Peteraf, Northwestern University; Laura Poppo, Washington University; Joan E. Ricart, IESE; Bill Richardson, Sheffield Business School; Peter Smith Ring, Loyola Marymount University; Garth Saloner, Stanford University; Richard Schoenberg, Imperial College; Joan Winn, University of Denver; Akbar Zaheer, University of Minnesota; Todd Zenger, Washington University.

Elizabeth Wynne Johnson deserves a special mention for her role in researching, and above all, writing the book. She went way beyond and above the duty of a research associate in helping us complete the book. We are enormously grateful that we found someone who so willingly dedicated herself to our project, and contributed so much.

Finally we each want to thank our families in our own way. Birger Wernerfelt, Cynthia's husband, not only was one of the original contributors to the Resource Based View, but he has personally given us the benefit of his insights throughout the development of this book. David could not have written this book without the loving support of his wife, Jill. She took care of the family's life so that he could concentrate on writing without distraction. And William, Emma, and Charlotte, who accepted an absentee father for so long, can now have the time and attention they deserve.

Brief Contents

Vision, Goals, and Objectives

Resources

Businesses

Structure, Systems, and Processes

Putting It All Together

Index

CONTENTS

▲

CHAPTER 5: ORGANIZATIONAL LIMITS TO FIRM SCOPE   99

▲

CHAPTER 6: MANAGING THE MULTIBUSINESS CORPORATION   127

APPENDIX C: MECHANISMS FOR ACHIEVING CORPORATE COHERENCE   154

▲

CHAPTER 7: CREATING CORPORATE ADVANTAGE   167

▲

CHAPTER 8: CORPORATE GOVERNANCE   179

▲

AN INTRODUCTION TO CORPORATE STRATEGY

▲ THE NEED FOR CORPORATE STRATEGY

Consider the following list of companies: IBM, Westinghouse Electric, Time Warner, American Express, General Motors, Kodak. What do they have in common, besides that they are all well known, all compete in multiple markets, and, in the past, all have enjoyed profits well above the norm for their industries?

More recently, each of them has suffered a reversal of fortune. Between 1983 and 1993, while the index of the S&P 500 nearly tripled, these firms barely maintained their value. A few, including such venerable giants as IBM and Westinghouse, even *destroyed* value during this period (Table 1–1).

Another thing these companies have in common is involuntary CEO turnover. The CEO of each of these firms was replaced in the early 1990s, not necessarily due to poor management skills, but because of the failure of their corporate strategies. Each was unable to develop a strategy that effectively addressed the changing competitive environment or capitalized on the potential benefits of owning a wide set of businesses.

The problems these business leaders wrestled with and failed to remedy were, however, not necessarily of their own making. Corporations, like battleships, have enormous inertia; by the time the pathological consequences of poor strategies appear, things are often badly wrong and the company far off course. This insidiousness does not diminish the importance of formulating and implementing an effective corporate strategy; it increases it. Because the impact of corporate strategy is so pervasive and long lasting, it has more important consequences than most other managerial decisions. Setting corporate strategy, therefore, is a critical task and primary responsibility of, the CEO.

▲ TABLE 1–1   Changes in Market Value at Selected Major U.S. Corporations

	1983	1993
IBM	$74.5 billion	$36.7 billion
Tenneco	5.7	8.1
Westinghouse Electric	4.8	4.6
Time Warner	6.0*	14.5
Digital Equipment	4.1	3.0
American Express	7.0	13.3
General Motors	23.4	38.7
Eastman Kodak	13.0	15.4
TOTAL	138.5	134.3
S&P 500 Index	**164.9**	**460.2**

* Estimated.

The Pressure to Change

Surprisingly, top management has not historically expressed great concern with corporate strategy. Surveys show that managers rank it well down the list of major issues they face, after topics such as managing innovation and organizational change.[1] It is unclear whether this is because most executives believe they have an effective corporate strategy in place, and so are worried only about the details of its implementation, or because corporate executives have been protected from the adverse consequences of the poor performance of their strategies.

Unfortunately, as Table 1–1 shows, senior executives' historic indifference to corporate strategy has not been warranted by the performance of some of their companies. In the past, such results might have had limited repercussions; however, substantial changes in the **market for corporate control** that occurred in the 1980s brought this to an end. Firing the CEO is only one threat that is held over a management that fails to implement an effective corporate strategy. An even more extreme remedy is the corporate takeover. Between 1980 and 1987, 20 percent of all manufacturing assets changed hands in some form of financial transaction.[2]

Indeed, the assumption that the corporate hierarchy is the appropriate governance structure for a set of businesses was seriously challenged during the eighties. In particular, a new form of corporate organization, the leveraged buyout (LBO), appeared during this period to remedy the most pathological corporate portfolios. By the end of the decade it was estimated that LBOs were responsible for 7 percent of United States corporate output.[3]

---

[1]C. Gopinath and R.C. Hoffman, "Research for Strategic Management: The CEO's Perspective," working paper, University of Delaware, Newark, DE, 1992.

[2]Michael G. Rukstadt, "RJR Nabisco and Leveraged Buyouts," Harvard Business School Case No. 9-390-077, 1990. Although a siginficant part of the capital market activity during this period involved the same asset moving from one owner to another.

[3]Ibid.

Other **new organizational forms** also gained prominence during this period. These included employee ownership (see "Avis"); the so-called virtual corporation, in which the command and control hierarchy was replaced by a network of flexible market-based linkages between independent entities;[4] and the explosion in joint ventures and other collaborative arrangements. Another visible change was in the rapid growth of franchising, which reached $700 billion in sales by 1990.[5]

All of this suggests that in the recent past the performance of many traditional corporations has left a lot to be desired. Indeed, the crisis of faith America suffered about its international competitiveness in the eighties reflected its concern for the viability of its corporate giants.[6]

In response, many firms in America (and around the world) embarked on major shakeups to transform their corporate strategies and cultures. Attempts to "restructure, refocus, rationalize, and reengineer" were initiated by aggressive CEOs with the goal of rejuvenating and revitalizing their corporations. The notions of *core competence* and *rightsizing* took root as the solution to fundamental corporate problems (see Appendix A, "Past Approaches to Corporate Strategy"). In practice, however, these approaches often led to only partial solu-

---

Avis

Warren E. Avis founded his car-rental company in 1946. Since that time, the agency has changed hands a total of 11 times. In one 10-year stretch, during the frenzied takeover period of the 1980s, Avis had six different owners. In 1983, then-parent company Norton Simon Inc. was acquired by Esmark, which in turn was acquired by Beatrice Companies in 1984. Beatrice was subsequently taken private in a leveraged buyout orchestrated by Kohlberg Kravis Roberts (KKR). KKR then sold Avis to Wesray Capital Corp. and senior Avis management in 1986.

At Wesray, it was determined that the greatest profit potential would come from an employee stock ownership plan (ESOP) sale. Embraced by workers, the ESOP ended Avis' roller-coaster existence and brought stability to the company.

Throughout its history of merry-go-round ownership, costs had soared and operations lagged. Avis chairman Joseph Vittoria explained: "Every time we'd get a new owner, I'd have to educate them and become adjusted to them." Within a year and a half after being bought by its employees, Avis saw its earnings soar and operating costs decline. As a consequence, the company performed well and achieved growth despite an industry slump. Avis' management credited their employees with improvements that led to superior quality and service management and a 40 percent drop in the number of customer complaints.

After doing time in a variety of hands, Avis achieved its finest performance on its own.

---

[4]William E. Halal, A. Geranmayeh, and J. Pourdehnad, *Internal Markets* (New York: John Wiley & Sons, 1993).
[5]G. Matusky, "The Competitive Edge: How Franchisees Are Teaching the Corporate Elephants to Dance," *Success*, September 1990, pp. 58–65.
[6]Robert E. Hoskisson and M.A. Hitt, *Downscoping: How to Tame the Diversified Firm* (Oxford: Oxford University Press, 1994).

Farcus

by David Waisglass
Gordon Coulthart

**"I think it's time to review our
corporate strategy."**

tions. Kodak, for example, restructured three times in five years around a competency in imaging before CEO Kay Whitmore was replaced. Despite all the frenetic activity of the 1980s and early 1990s, therefore, a host of corporate strategy problems remain.

The Story Today: "No There, There"

In 1990, we embarked on a field research project to assess **the state of corporate strategy** in a number of leading companies. In particular, we wanted to know if the individual parts of a firm were integrated into a coherent whole and how the competitiveness of a firm's individual units was affected by their presence in the larger corporation. The study involved on-site interviews with executives in over 40 firms.

A harsh truth emerged from this research: In more than half of the companies we studied, corporate management could not effectively articulate how their firms added value to the businesses in their corporate portfolios. To borrow from Gertrude Stein, when we went in search of corporate strategy, we often found that "there was no there, there."

When asked if he had analyzed the break-up value of his firm, one chief financial officer replied: "Yes. We look at that very carefully, about once a quarter. I honestly do not believe that the pieces would be worth more separately than they are together." Despite the fact that this was a highly visible related-diversified company, none of its senior managers advanced the case that the firm enhanced the competitiveness of its units to such a degree that they definitely would be worth more together than apart.

A corporate officer in a well-known consumer products company gave this historic perspective: "[Our firm] has traditionally placed a heavy emphasis on growing the top line. So long as we have been able to do this, and do it profitably, we have not spent a lot of effort on rationalizing the firm as a whole." In his view, the firm was operating with a deadweight of inefficiency that one day, perhaps soon, would need to be addressed. Until then, the mandate was simply "grow."

As these remarks illustrate, despite the radical shifts of the 1980s and 1990s, corporate leadership still often does not provide the kind of strategic direction that welds a company together or creates substantial value over the long run. To do so, leadership needs a clear idea of what corporate strategy involves and, in particular, what characterizes an effective corporate strategy. This is the challenge we undertake in this book.

PRINCIPLES

▲ WHAT IS CORPORATE STRATEGY?

There are many definitions of corporate strategy. Originally the term was used to describe the pattern of decisions that determined a company's goals, produced the principal policies for achieving these goals, and defined the range of businesses the company was to pursue.[7] Taken literally, this would mean that corporate strategy addressed any and every strategic issue facing a company, from Motorola's entry into the cellular telephone market, to the decision by a restaurant owner to introduce an "all you can eat" buffet.

Over time a distinction came to be made between **business-level strategy**—the issue of how to build a sustainable competitive advantage in a discrete and identifiable market—and **corporate-level strategy**—"the overall plan for a diversified company."[8] This distinction led to the development of a number of valuable analytical frameworks and techniques that were applicable to each level of strategy (see Appendixes A and B). The bifurcation, however, downplayed the many important areas of overlap between the levels, and impeded their integration.

This book introduces a more inclusive definition of corporate strategy:

Corporate strategy is the way a company creates value through the configuration and coordination of its multimarket activities.

This definition has three important aspects. The first is the emphasis on **value creation** as the ultimate purpose of corporate strategy. (See "Value Creation.") The second is the focus on the multimarket scope of the corporation (**configuration**), including its product, geographic, and vertical boundaries. The third is the emphasis on how the firm manages the activities and businesses that lie within the corporate hierarchy (**coordination**). This recognizes the importance of both the implementation and formulation of corporate strategy.

It is important to underscore that this definition, in contrast to past treatments, does not restrict the relevance of corporate strategy solely to large diversified firms (see "Do Universities Need Corporate Strategies?"). Implicitly or explicitly, organizations of every size make choices about the range of markets in which they will compete and how they will manage those activities. Corporate strategy issues, therefore, are as pertinent and important to a small manufacturing firm debating whether to employ its own salespeople or use third-party distributors as they are to Westinghouse Electric trying to decide whether it should acquire CBS, Inc.

Moreover, the definition recognizes that corporate strategy involves far more than the operation of corporate headquarters. Regardless of the type of strategy a firm is pursuing, most of its value will ultimately be realized in the business units, through their enhanced ability to

---

[7]Kenneth R. Andrews, *The Concept of Corporate Strategy* (Burr Ridge, IL.: Dow-Jones, Irwin, 1971).

[8]Michael E. Porter, "From Competitive Advantage to Corporate Strategy," *Harvard Business Review*, May–June 1987, pp. 43–59.

Value Creation

We start from the premise that the purpose of corporate strategy is value creation. Whether that value is completely appropriated by stockholders or whether it is shared with other stakeholders is the decision of those who control the corporation (see also Chapter 8). For example, until recently the majority of the U.K.'s Wellcome PLC, the world's 20th largest pharmaceutical company, was owned by a charitable foundation that is a dedicated supporter of medical research. We will not debate how the value created by a corporate strategy should be distributed, but we will observe that if no value is created, there is nothing to distribute to stockholders, let alone share with other stakeholders.

produce and deliver goods and services to customers.[9] Thus, for a corporation to create value—to justify its existence as a multibusiness entity—it must be able, in some way, to contribute to the competitive advantage of its businesses. Corporate strategy, therefore, draws on an understanding of business strategy, just as it, in turn, informs that analysis. Its focus is on the **relationship between the whole and the parts of the firm**, in particular on whether individual business units are made better or worse by their presence in the corporation.

Do Universities Need Corporate Strategies?

The tendency is to perceive most organizations as single business entities when in fact they are often much more complex. Nearly all the organizations you can think of harbor a myriad of intriguing scope issues. Consider, for example, universities.

Although they may be thought of simply as institutions of higher learning, universities house a number of distinct units. There may be a business school or a medical school; perhaps a university publisher; perhaps a football or basketball team. Each of these has its own customers and staff and its own external reference group—each, implicitly or not, has its own way of competing. However, each is also affected by its membership in the broader university: the individual units share a campus, the university's reputation, a central budgeting system, and so forth. The resulting interrelationships affect the operation of the individual units in many ways, large and small. Anyone who doubts this should consider whether any of the units would be better off as independent entities outside the university.

Although these linkages usually remain in the background, they can quickly come to the fore, and often do over issues of resource allocation. Heated debates, for example, can erupt over questions of cross-subsidization—whether the wealthier units should support the poorer ones, or whether endowments should be held at the school or university level. Questions of standards also generate vigorous debate. One might ask, for example, whether a world-class university should close down a weak academic department or, conversely, invest to bring it up to an appropriate standard. At their core, questions such as these are ones of corporate strategy.

---

[9]Ibid.

PRACTICE

▲ Figure 1–1   The Triangle of Corporate Strategy

▲ A FRAMEWORK FOR CORPORATE STRATEGY

Our framework starts from the empirical observation that there is **no one right corporate strategy**. There is not even a taxonomy of a limited number of generic corporate strategies that can be identified as leading to success. Instead, an effective corporate strategy is a consistent set of five elements that together as a system lead to a corporate advantage that creates economic value (Figure 1–1).

The three sides of the triangle—**resources**; **businesses**; and **structure, systems, and processes**—are the foundations of corporate strategy. When aligned in pursuit of a **vision**, and motivated by appropriate **goals and objectives**, the system can produce a **corporate advantage,** which justifies the firm's existence as a multibusiness entity.

Vision

> *The last thing IBM needs right now is a vision.*
> Lou Gerstner, newly appointed CEO of IBM

> *It's that vision thing.*
> George Bush, Former President of the United States

8

Doubters notwithstanding, the discussion of corporate strategy necessarily begins with vision. Its positioning in the center of the triangle (Figure 1–1) reflects its central role in the formulation and implementation of corporate strategy.[10]

It has been said that "if you don't know where you are going, any road can take you there." The ability to articulate a coherent vision is the best indication that a firm, in fact, *has* a corporate strategy. Indeed, one of the strongest findings of our research was that successful corporations were those that could articulate a coherent vision and were committed to fulfill that vision over an extended period of time.

Crucial to the vision is a sense of purpose that can challenge and motivate employees. When the vision captures the **contribution the company is making to society**, it can provide meaning and fulfillment to employees who carry out the work of the firm.

A powerful vision should continually stretch the corporation's capabilities. For many companies, therefore, the overarching vision is captured in an **ambitious aspiration**, the time frame of which may be ill-defined and distant.[11] In the 1920s, Ford wanted to put "a car in every home"; in the 1980s, Apple looked toward the future and saw "a computer in every home." By the 1990s, Bill Gates had gone further yet: "a computer on every desk, and in every home, running on Microsoft software." Each of these simple expressions offers a compelling statement that guides behavior within the firm. Each also defines the broad domain in which the firm will operate.

Importantly, defining the **domain** is primarily concerned with setting the boundaries of the firm—with describing what businesses the corporation will *not* go into—more than with identifying exactly which businesses it *will* compete in.[12] Within those broad bounds, managers will have the autonomy to operate without the distraction of looking outside the domain or the interference of being told precisely where to compete. Thus, a corporate vision should describe, in fairly loose and qualitative terms, the boundary beyond which it will not operate. Motorola's "portable communications" vision describes a sense of what businesses the company will operate in without, for example, being specific as to whether or not liquid crystal displays are part of that domain.

Often, visions also describe the **ethical values** a corporation will adhere to in the conduct of its business. Called the *mission* in some companies, this part of a vision usually reflects the code of behavior by which employees are governed. In a reasonably homogeneous and stable society, these statements are often quite similar across firms. Nonetheless, statements like "serving the customer" and "treating all stakeholders with fairness and respect" can be highly motivating, and, if implemented in an unusual way, can be a differentiating feature in some firms.

Goals and Objectives

If the vision describes what the corporation wishes to become in many years' time, an effective corporate strategy must also have a set of shorter-term goals and objectives. These will serve as milestones on the path to the fulfillment of the vision. Goals and objectives will more immediately motivate employees because they are closer at hand and so can be seen to

---

[10]Andrew Campbell, M. Devine, and D. Young, *A Sense of Mission* (London: The Economist Books Limited, 1990).

[11]C.K. Prahalad and G. Hamel, "Strategic Intent," *Harvard Business Review*, May–June 1989, pp. 63-77.

[12]R. Simons, *Levers of Control* (Boston, Harvard Business School Press, 1995).

be achievable. Further, both should represent targets the corporation must meet if the vision is to be feasible.

Objectives refer to specific **short- and medium-term quantitative targets**, such as "sustain a 40 percent debt/equity ratio" or "achieve gamma six quality by 1999." Goals, on the other hand, refer to **qualitative intentions** in the same time frame, such as "improve new product development capabilities" or "become a global organization."

By providing an immediate challenge to employees, goals and objectives can become powerful incentives that support a formal reward structure. Indeed, many companies use some version of an annual corporate challenge, such as "improve productivity by 7 percent," to supplement the normal incentive scheme and focus attention on particular activities or targets.

While the vision itself may evolve through time, and always appear on the horizon, goals and objectives are important strategic hurdles. Repeated failures to meet goals and objectives imply a threat both to the feasibility of the corporate strategy and to the motivation of employees. On the route to "encircling Caterpillar," Komatsu, among other things, had to build a presence outside Japan and license state-of-the-art technology. Had it not met these goals, Komatsu not only may have failed to "encircle Caterpillar," it may not have survived. Thus, goals and objectives should always be in line with the vision, but should be less of a stretch than the vision itself.

Resources

This book articulates a concept of corporate strategy that rests on the resources—the **assets, skills, and capabilities**—of the firm.

Resources are the critical building blocks of strategy because they determine not what a firm *wants to do*, but what it *can do*. They are the durable stocks that determine competitive advantage at the business unit level, and so must underlie effective corporate strategies. Resources are also the critical dimension that can distinguish one firm from another. If all firms had identical resources, all could pursue the same strategy, and the basis for corporate advantage would disappear.[13] This, however, is not the case when there are important resource differences among firms.

Moreover, resources determine the range of market opportunities that are appropriate for a firm and so have a major impact on firm scope. The most valuable resources are those that enable a firm to compete successfully in more than one market. IBM's reputation and customer list, built in the computer mainframe business, enabled it to gain dominance in the PC industry, even though it was a late entrant and did not have the best technology. Similarly, Emerson Electric's efficient production processes and skills in assembling small electric motors supported its success in a number of different markets.

Identifying, building, and deploying valuable resources, therefore, are critical aspects of corporate strategy because it is resources that are the ultimate source of value creation both within and across businesses.

---

[13]Jay Barney made this point eloquently in "Firm Resources and Sustained Competitive Advantage," *Journal of Management,* 1991, pp. 99-120.

Businesses

The "business" side of the triangle refers to the industries in which a firm operates, as well as to the competitive strategy it adopts in each.

Industry choice is critical to the long-term success of a corporate strategy. It has repeatedly been demonstrated that the best predictor of firm performance is the profitability of the industries in which it competes.[14] This is true not only for single business firms, but for firms that operate in multiple businesses. The underlying economics of the industries in which a firm competes, therefore, will play an instrumental role in its performance.

The set of industries in which a firm operates also influences the extent to which it will be able to share resources across its businesses. The notion of relatedness, for example, which has underpinned corporate strategic thinking for 30 years, may be used as a surrogate for a firm's ability to create synergy among its businesses. Thus, it would be expected that an ice-cream manufacturer like Ben & Jerry's could compete successfully in frozen yogurt. In contrast, a firm that competes in aerospace and insurance would be expected to have few opportunities for cross-fertilization. (Although that has not deterred either General Motors or ITT from trying to do so!)

The particular competitive strategy a firm pursues in each industry also has an impact on corporate performance. While it may be unusual to find a corporation that pursues exactly the same source of competitive advantage in every one of its businesses, it is important to recognize that a corporation's resources are often only valuable when applied to similar generic strategies. For example, following a low-cost strategy in personal computers and a differentiation strategy in mainframes may well be futile: The key success factors for each strategy are so different that a firm striving to achieve both is unlikely to succeed in either.

Thus, an analysis of a firm's businesses should include the stand-alone profit potential and the competitive strategy the firm will adopt in each, as well as opportunities that exist for cross-fertilization.

Structure, Systems, and Processes

The structure, systems, and processes of a firm determine how the organization controls and coordinates the activities of its various business units and staff functions. **Structure** refers to the way the corporation is divided into discrete units. It describes the formal organization chart that delineates the allocation of authority inside the corporate hierarchy. **Systems** are the set of formal policies and routines that govern organizational behavior. They are the set of rules that define how tasks, from strategic planning to personnel evaluations, are to be fulfilled. **Processes** describe the informal elements of an organization's activities. The network of personal relationships that accompany the flow of work inside a company, for example, can be just as influential on behavior as any formal procedures.

In a complex firm, corporate managers rarely can or should make all the critical business unit decisions. Instead, they influence delegated decision making through the careful design of the context in which business-unit managers operate. Even the most decentralized

---

[14]Richard P. Rumelt, "How Much Does Industry Matter?" *Strategic Management Journal*, March 1991, pp. 167–85; Cynthia A. Montgomery and Birger Wernerfelt, "Diversification, Ricardian Rents, and Tobin's," *Rand Journal of Economics*, Winter 1988, pp. 623–32, and R. Schmalensee, "Do Markets Differ Much?" *American Economic Review*, 1985, pp. 341–51.

corporations, therefore, impose some organizational requirements on their businesses, whether it be financial reporting, capital expenditure budgeting, or human resource management. In turn, these policies have important direct and indirect influences on the decisions made in the businesses, as managers follow the rules and respond to the incentives set by the corporate office.[15]

In establishing a firm's infrastructure, corporate managers have a wide array of organizational mechanisms at their disposal, from the formal boxes in an organization chart to the more subtle elements of corporate culture and style. Because every corporate strategy is different, there is not one optimal set of structures, systems, and processes. Rather, as Alfred Chandler long ago noted, *structure follows strategy*.[16] In other words, a firm's internal design should flow from its strategy and be customized to fit the resources and businesses of the particular firm. In fact, an inappropriate design often causes the failure of otherwise well-constructed corporate strategies.

Corporate Advantage

An effective corporate strategy results from a harmonious combination of the previously discussed five elements. The elements work together as a system **to create value through multimarket activity**; that is, to yield a corporate advantage. Although some value may be created at the corporate level itself—through a lower cost of capital, for example—as discussed earlier, most corporate advantages are realized at the business-unit level, where individual businesses use the benefits of corporate affiliation to outperform their rivals in a particular industry.

Michael Goold and colleagues suggested three questions a firm should ask to test whether or not it possesses a corporate advantage.[17] A modified version of those questions is presented here, in order of increasing difficulty, and can be applied to every business a company owns or is considering acquiring:

- ▲ Does ownership of the business create benefit somewhere in the corporation?
- ▲ Are these benefits greater than the cost of corporate overhead?
- ▲ Does the corporation create more value than any other possible corporate parent or alternative governance structure?

The first of these questions simply asks whether benefits are created anywhere in the corporation through the firm's ownership of the business. Generally, these would occur within the business itself, through the transfer of resources from other business units or from the corporate level. In some circumstances, the benefits appear elsewhere in the corporation. The merger between the pharmaceutical giant, Merck, and Medco, a leading drug distributor, may be such an example. Even if Merck cannot improve the distributor's performance (in fact, Merck's ownership may even harm the distributor by inducing other pharmaceutical companies to supply competitors), it may, nevertheless, benefit from the guaranteed market for its drugs and improved information about customers.

---

[15]Joseph H. Bower, *Managing the Resource Allocation Process* (Cambridge, MA: Harvard University Press, 1970).
[16]Alfred D. Chandler, *Strategy and Structure* (Cambridge, MA: MIT Press, 1962).
[17]M.C. Goold, A. Campbell, and M. Alexander, *Corporate-Level Strategy* (New York: John Wiley & Sons, 1994).

The second question recognizes that enhancing the competitiveness of a business unit is not sufficient justification for corporate ownership. Whatever they are, the benefits of corporate ownership do not come costlessly. No matter how small the corporate office, or how little intervention there is in the daily affairs of the divisions, the extra layer of management incurs costs and delays and dampens incentives. To justify ownership these costs must be less than the benefits created.

The third question is a very strenuous test to pass. It implies that the corporation must be an optimum owner for a business. Many firms add value to their businesses and so appear to justify their corporate ownership. However, if other companies could add more value to the businesses, and are willing to pay a correspondingly high price to do so, keeping those businesses in the corporate portfolio would be inconsistent with value maximization. Moreover, the firm might be able to realize much of the value of its resources through market contracts with independent entities. Justifying ownership of a business, therefore, requires that the value created be greater than that which could be achieved operating the business outside the corporate hierarchy. The retailer JC Penney must have understood this when it decided to outsource the running of its catalog business. Although there was value created by JC Penney offering a catalog, managing it within the corporate infrastructure created less value than operating it as a separate unit.

Managers often find this third test hard to accept. In particular, they often resist selling profitable businesses to which they have demonstrably added value for some time. Nonetheless, a strict interpretation of corporate advantage and the maximization of firm value implies that they should do so.

Enduring Logic

We stated that there is no one right strategy to create corporate advantage. The variety of resources that can generate competitive advantage across multiple businesses, the breadth of industries available to operate in, and the numerous organizational design parameters that shape decisions inside the corporation all make single prescriptions impossible. However, there is an enduring logic that all great corporate strategies have in common. This relates to the quality of the individual items of the triangle; the way those elements work together as a system; and the fit of the whole with the evolving external environment.

In contrast, some corporate strategies fail because of weaknesses in **individual elements** of the strategy. For example, a firm may lack valuable resources, its portfolio of businesses may be in industries that are fundamentally unattractive, or its organizational design may be too interventionist and bureaucratic, given the tasks that need to be accomplished. The firm may also lack a vision or its goals and objectives may not delineate a viable expansion path.

A company may also fail because the elements of its corporate strategy are not in **alignment**, that is, they do not form a coherent whole. For example, a firm's resources may not make an important contribution to competitive advantage in its businesses, its organizational design may prevent the sharing of valuable corporate resources across businesses, or its goals and objectives may not lead to the fulfillment of the company's vision.

Finally, corporate strategies may fail because they do not adapt to the changing **external environment**. Shifts in consumer demand, technology, or channels of distribution, for example, may invalidate previously secure strategies and require dramatic alterations in corporate scope or organization.

In practice, just as most business units are not market leaders, many corporations will not be able to demonstrate that they possess a corporate advantage that extends across all their businesses. The challenge then becomes one of developing a strategy to achieve this goal, just as single businesses develop strategies to improve their market positions. This may involve many steps, including developing a new vision, reconfiguring the corporate portfolio to focus on businesses that are a better match with the firm's resources, upgrading those resources, or modifying the firm's organizational systems and structure. In the following chapters, we will explore these opportunities and their ramifications for corporate advantage.

Despite those pitfalls, there are countless examples of companies that have developed powerful corporate strategies. This book contains examples of several such companies that have started with very little and turned it into something quite remarkable. Their accomplishments, in many respects, offer the purest examples of what superior corporate strategy is all about.

▲ THE ROAD AHEAD

Having introduced the triangle of corporate strategy as the overall framework for the book, we will devote Chapters 2–6 to examining the individual elements in detail. Following this we return to the whole, and evaluate how the triangle operates as a system. As we intergrate the pieces, we are able to identify the patterns that typify successful corporate strategies.

This development of ideas is reflected in the sequence of the accompanying cases. Mirroring the growth of many firms, these progress from straightforward single businesses, to firms that are grappling with intriguing questions of scope within an industry, to very large organizations that face complex diversification or vertical integration issues.

The final chapter of the book returns to the pressing need for effective corporate strategies, and the governance mechanisms that are in place to monitor and evaluate progress toward this goal. At issue here is the question of who bears responsibility for corporate strategy, and how the competing interests of various stakeholders should be reconciled.

▲ RECOMMENDED READINGS

Andrews, K.R. *The Concept of Corporate Strategy.* Illinois: Burr Ridge: Dow Jones–Irwin, 1971.

Ansoff , H.I. *Corporate Strategy: An Analytic Approach to Business Policy for Growth and Expansion.* New York: McGraw-Hill, 1965.

Boston Consulting Group. *The Product Portfolio Concept. Perspective 66.* Boston: Boston Consulting Group, Inc., 1970.

Campbell, A., M. Devine, and D. Young. *A Sense of Mission.* London: The Economist Books Limited, 1990.

Copeland, T., T. Koller, and J. Murrin. *Valuation: Measuring and Managing the Value of Companies.* New York: John Wiley & Sons, 1990.

Goold, M.C., and A. Campbell. *Strategies and Styles.* Oxford: Blackwell, 1987.

Goold, M.C., A. Campbell, and M. Alexander. *Corporate-Level Strategy.* New York: John Wiley & Sons, 1994.

Haspeslagh, P. "Portfolio Planning: Uses and Limits." *Harvard Business Review,* May–June 1982, pp. 58–73.

Hoskisson, R.E., and M.A. Hitt. *Downscoping: How to Tame the Diversified Firm.* Oxford: Oxford University Press, 1994.

McTaggart, J.M., P.W. Kontes, and M.C. Mankins. *The Value Imperative.* New York: Free Press, 1994.

Mintzberg, H. *The Rise and Fall of Strategic Planning.* New York: Free Press, 1994.

Peters, T.J., and R.H. Waterman, Jr. *In Search of Excellence.* New York: Warner Books, 1982.

Porter, M.E. "From Competitive Advantage to Corporate Strategy." *Harvard Business Review*, May–June 1987, pp. 43–59.

Prahalad, C.K., and G. Hamel. "The Core Competence of the Corporation." *Harvard Business Review*, May–June 1990, pp. 79–91.

APPENDIX

A

PAST APPROACHES TO CORPORATE STRATEGY

The analysis of corporate strategy described in this book builds on previous approaches to the subject (see Figure A–1). Much of this work deserves study, not only because it is still used in companies today, but also because it provides the conceptual foundation for a number of tools and techniques. There is not enough space here to provide an exhaustive account of each of these contributions, but we highlight several that have had a lasting impact.[1]

▲ THE CONCEPT OF CORPORATE STRATEGY

Among the most important of the early contributions to corporate strategy was a body of work produced in the 1960s and 1970s by Kenneth Andrews, C. Roland Christensen, and their colleagues in Harvard Business School's business policy group.[2] At a time when management thinking was oriented toward individual functions such as marketing, production, and finance, these scholars articulated the concept of strategy as a holistic way of thinking about a firm.

With respect to strategy in multibusiness firms, Andrew et al identified corporate strategy as defining the businesses in which a company will compete, "preferably in a way that focuses resources to convert distinctive competence into competitive advantage."

Although enormously valuable as a conceptual framework, this treatment did not lay out an explicit methodology for demonstrating how distinctive competence translated into com-

---

[1]The early part of this appendix draws heavily on the Introduction (pp. xi-xii) from *Strategy, Seeking and Securing Competitive Advantage*, edited by Cynthia A. Montgomery and Michael E. Porter, (Boston, MA: Harvard Business Review Book, 1991.)
[2]This critical groundwork was laid in E.P. Learned, C. Roland Christensen, and Kenneth Andrews, *Business Policy: Text and Cases* (Burr Ridge, IL: Irwin, 1965). See also, Kenneth R. Andrews, *The Concept of Corporate Strategy* (Burr Ridge, IL: Dow Jones-Irwin, 1971).

▲ FIGURE A–1 Perspectives on Corporate Strategy

Perspective	Concept of Corporate Strategy	Organization Structure	Diversification	Portfolio Planning	Value-Based	Generic Corporate Strategies	Resource-Based View
Representative author(s)	Ansoff 1965 Andrews 1971	Chandler 1962 Bower 1970 Vancil 1978 1978	Wrigley 1970 Rumelt 1974 Montgomery 1985 Hill 1988	BCG 1968 Haspeslagh 1982	Jensen 1985 Schmalensee 1985 Copeland 1990 Rumelt 1991	Porter 1987 Goold & Campbell 1987 McKinsey 1989	Wernerfelt 1984 Dierickx and Cool 1989 Barney 1991
Date	1960s	1960s and 1970s	1970s	1970s	1980s	1980s	1980s
Concern	General management role	Organization structure	Extent and mode of diversification	Resource allocation	Corporate contribution to SBU performance	Source of corporate advantage	Firm idiosyncrasy and growth
Contribution	Early statement of corporate and competitive strategy	Structure follows strategy, "fit," decentralization	Set of businesses as strategic variable, "synergy"	Portfolio management	Limited evidence of corporate value; market for corporate control	Typology of corporate advantage	Tangible and intangible assets and capabilities
Output	Corporate vision, distinctive competence, SWOT analysis	M-form multidivisional structure	Measure of relatedness, analysis of performance	Growth/share matrix	Free cash flow, value-based strategy	Corporate role	Characteristics of valuable resources

petitive advantage at the business unit level. In particular, because the approach was conceptual rather than analytical, it could not address the underlying economics of corporate advantage, and what specifically made the whole more than the sum of the parts.

Nonetheless, the work of Andrews and Christensen, along with that of others such as Igor Ansoff, and Peter F. Drucker,[3] propelled the notion of strategy into the forefront of management practice. Since then, there have been many advances and refinements in both the practice and theory of strategy. It is a tribute to the soundness of this original work that it can encompass, and indeed has led to, many of these developments.

▲ ORGANIZATION STRUCTURE AND DIVERSIFICATION

At the same time that Andrews and his colleagues were developing their ideas on strategy formulation, Alfred D. Chandler was studying the corporation's organizational structure.[4] His seminal work demonstrated that the multidivisional structure (M-form) allowed corporations to control an extensive array of separate businesses. During the 1960s and 1970s, there was widespread adoption of the M-form as many U.S. and European corporations moved to multidivisional structures of discrete strategic business units (SBUs). This trend, along with the emergence of conglomerates in the 1960s, stimulated research on the performance implications of diversification. (See Chapter 4.)

The rise in multibusiness firms also brought to the fore issues of managing diversified companies. For the first time, corporate executives found themselves responsible for business units with which they were unfamiliar. As a result, they had extreme difficulty in deciding how to allocate corporate funds among the various businesses. Into this gap came portfolio planning.

▲ PORTFOLIO PLANNING

The major source of ideas about corporate strategy shifted from the academic world to management consulting firms. Specialist firms, such as the Boston Consulting Group (BCG), emerged to challenge the strategy practices of the traditional management consulting firms. Indeed, BCG was responsible for the first analytic breakthrough in corporate strategy formulation in the 1970s. Their so-called **growth/share matrix**, best known for its cow and dog metaphors (see Figure A–2), became a primary tool for resource allocation in diversified companies.

The two dimensions of the matrix were industry growth rate, which attempted to capture the potential cash usage of a business, and relative market share, which was a surrogate for overall competitive strength and hence the cash generation potential of a business. Mapping the location of a company's businesses in this matrix by sizing each according to its asset or revenue base gave a picture of the flow of financial resources in the corporation (see the General Foods example in Figure A–3).

A fast-growing business with low relative market share would require a lot of cash to grow; because of uncertainty about their future performance, businesses in this quadrant were called *question marks*. Conversely, a business with high relative market share in a slow-growing industry would be very profitable and would require little reinvestment. Since this

---

[3]For an extended history of strategic planning in general, see H. Mintzberg, *The Rise and Fall of Strategic Planning* (New York: The Free Press, 1994).
[4]Alfred D. Chandler, *Strategy and Structure* (Cambridge, MA: MIT Press, 1962).

▲ FIGURE A–2   The Boston Consulting Group Growth/Share Matrix

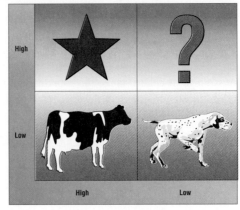

**Annual real
rate of market
growth**

Relative Market Share

Source: The Boston Consulting Group, Inc. "The Product Portfolio," *Perspectives* (Boston, MA: Boston Consulting Group, Inc., 1970).

implied it would throw off a lot of cash, businesses in this quadrant of the matrix were called *cash cows*. *Dogs* were to be found in the lower-right quadrant, at a competitive disadvantage and with little hope of changing that position because of the slow industry growth. In principle, the best strategy for this last category of business was divestment or harvesting. The top-left quadrant contained the *stars*—businesses that were users of cash today because of their rapid growth, but whose dominant market position warranted investing in for the time when industry growth slowed and the business became the next corporate cash cow.

The first prescription of the matrix concerned resource allocation. Dogs would receive no investment unless they could demonstrate a very rapid payback. In contrast, stars would receive funding even though their current profitability might be low or negative. The second prescription was for the CEO to balance the portfolio of business among the quadrants so that the corporation would grow faster than GNP and be neither a net user nor generator of cash.

Such prescriptions allowed corporate executives to regain control of the strategic planning and capital budgeting processes. A CEO could then deal with capital requests from the divisions with a particular bias in mind—to harvest the dogs, milk the cash cows, invest in the stars, or give the question marks a chance to become stars before the industry growth rate slowed. He or she could also trade businesses in and out of the portfolio to achieve the desired balance. As a result, portfolio planning had been adopted by over half of the largest companies surveyed in the early eighties.[5]

However, the prescriptions of portfolio planning assumed that corporations needed to be internally self-financing. In practice, there is no rationale for such a policy when the capital market is efficient. Moreover, portfolio planning largely ignored the relatedness of the business in the matrix and did not address the question of how the corporation added value to completely unrelated businesses. A semiconductor business could, in principle, balance

[5]Philippe Haspeslagh, "Portfolio Planning: Uses and Limits," *Harvard Business Review*, May–June 1982, pp. 58–73.

▲ FIGURE A–3   Growth Share Matrix for General Foods Corporation, 1980–1982

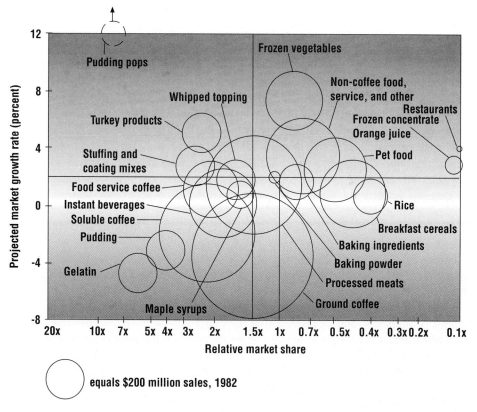

Source: Reprinted with the permission of The Free Press, an imprint of Simon & Schuster Inc. from Corporate Strategy Analysis, by Marcus C. Bogue and Elwood S. Buffa. Copyright © 1986 by The Free Press.

a cash cow steel business in a corporate portfolio just as well as a fast-growing steel mini-mill business.

As a consequence of these limitations, portfolio planning went out of fashion. What remains of portfolio planning is the notion of treating businesses differently according to their position in the portfolio. A market leader in a slow-growth business should perform differently than a follower in a high-growth business, and to expect the same performance of each would be a mistake. Used not as a mechanistic device for resource allocation and portfolio decisions, but rather as a guide for how to consider each division's strategic issues, portfolio planning can still be a valuable tool in corporate planning.

▲ VALUE-BASED STRATEGY

During the1980s, developments in the capital markets, and opportunities to profit from revitalizing underperforming corporations gave rise to the corporate raiders and leveraged buyout firms. Their activities highlighted the underperformance of many large diversified corporations, and led to several sensational takeovers such as RJR Nabisco. As a result of this pressure, corporate executives increasingly focused their attention on the stockmarket valuation of their firms.

To help them, a number of consulting firms developed approaches to value-based management. These adopted the objective of **maximizing shareholder value**. In a diversified company, this involved imputing a stock market price for each business unit. Most commonly, this was done by applying the industry average price/earnings ratio to the business' reported earnings. These estimates were then compared to the value projected for the ongoing operation of the business. When the imputed capital market value was higher than the internal valuation, the recommendation was to either improve the operational efficiency of the business, or to sell the unit.[6] (see Figure A–4.)

More generally, value-based strategy advocated a holistic approach to managing for shareholder value. Arguing that free cash flow was the correct measure of shareholder value, it emphasized careful measurement of the cash flow consequences of any strategic or operating decision. Importantly, those cash flows were to be discounted at the *business-specific* weighted average cost of capital. It was recommended that the resulting calculation of **economic value added** (EVA) be incorporated into the incentive scheme of all corporate and business unit executives.

Embracing value-based strategy was helpful as a means to discipline managers by directly linking the consequences of their actions to shareholder value. At the business unit level, it often resulted in the cancellation of investment projects and the rationalization of product lines that generated negative EVA. At the corporate level, it led to the sale of many underperforming business units and the restriction on investment in other marginal businesses.

Value-based strategy focused management's attention on the prudent management of a firm's capital. Moreover, the techniques were consistent with the need to continually improve a company's stock price. As a consequence, the idea of value-based planning had much appeal and its ideas were adopted by a number of innovative companies, including Marriott, PepsiCo, and Walt Disney.[7]

Despite these advantages, value-based planning was not a panacea. First, the approach required the accurate projection of cash flows from each business. However, these projections were only as good as the ability of managers to accurately measure the financial consequences of competitive position. Incorrect estimates of future returns from a business or investment easily invalidated the whole approach. Second, the implicit assumption of value-based strategy was that all business units and all investment proposals were self-contained. It was usually expected that divesting a business or curtailing an investment project would have no financial repercussions elsewhere in the corporation. This assumption of independence ignored the many linkages and interrelationships that often existed across businesses and among investments. Third, strict financial measurement of many long-term investments, particularly in intangible assets, was impossible. Indeed, value-based strategy is best at improving the efficient utilization of existing assets rather than developing long-term strategic initiatives.

---

[6]T. Copeland, T. Koller, and J. Murrin, *Valuation: Measuring and Managing the Value of Companies* (New York: John Wiley & Sons, 1990).

[7]J.M MacTaggart, P.W. Kontes, and M.C. Mankins, *The Value Imperative*, (New York: The Free Press, 1994).

▲ FIGURE A–4   Framework for Assessing Restructuring Opportunities

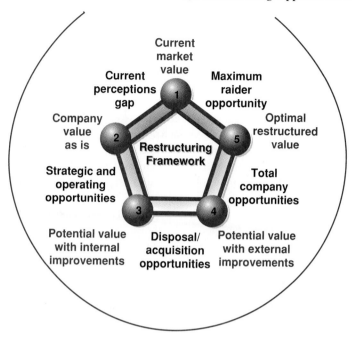

Source: T. Copeland, T. Koller, and J. Murrin. *Valuation: Measuring and Managing the Value of Companies* (New York: John Wiley & Sons, 1990).

▲ GENERIC CORPORATE STRATEGIES

The 1980s highlighted the failure of many very visible diversification strategies, such as Exxon entering the office products market and Coca-Cola acquiring Columbia Pictures. As a result, the notion that "sticking to the knitting"[8] might be the most desirable corporate strategy was widely promulgated. Indeed, by the late 1980s, many managers were struggling to justify the existence of their multibusiness corporations.

Into this void came the development of generic strategies that classified corporate strategies according to the ways in which value was created. Following the success of his notion of generic strategies at the business unit level, Michael Porter identified four types of corporate strategy. These lay along a continuum of increasing corporate involvement in the operation of the business units.[9]

Two of Porter's archetype corporate strategies, **portfolio management** and **restructuring**, could be applied in corporations whose businesses were essentially unrelated. A firm following a portfolio management strategy added little real value to its units because they were run autonomously with minimal corporate involvement. Its logic, therefore, depended on the firm's ability to identify and acquire companies that were undervalued, and on its willingness to sell any unit for an opportunistically high price. In contrast, the restructuring strat-

---

[8]T.J. Peters and R.H. Waterman, Jr., *In Search of Excellence* (New York: Warner Books, 1982).
[9]Michael E. Porter, "From Competitive Advantage to Corporate Strategy," *Harvard Business Review*, May–June 1987, pp. 43–59.

egy required the corporate office to act as more than just a banker and reviewer of individual business units. Restructurers fundamentally changed underperforming companies and so created value by altering strategy, replacing management, improving efficiency, and so forth.

The remaining two strategies, **transferring skills** and **sharing activities**, could only be used in companies where the businesses were related to some degree. Transferring skills involved disseminating a particular capability, such as consumer marketing, across multiple business units. This had the potential to create significant value when the transferred skills improved the competitive positions of the units.

The strategy that involved the most intervention, sharing activities, literally required that business units shared an important function, such as research and development, a distribution channel, or a component manufacturing facility. Ideally, the scale economies that were generated in the shared activities, contributed to the competitive advantage of each business unit. By necessity, however, the configuration of the function, and the allocation of its use, required some level of coordinated decision making.

The consulting firm, McKinsey and Company, also addressed corporate strategy from the headquarters perspective. They identified nine roles for the corporate office that could potentially create value. These, for example, included the roles of *coach* and *orchestrator* whereby the abilities and accumulated experience of corporate executives could be used to train, motivate, and coordinate the behavior of divisional managers.[10]

These ideas had barely gained currency when the focus of research and managerial practice shifted from the corporate office itself to the resources and capabilities of the firm as a whole.

▲ RESOURCE-BASED VIEW

Reminiscent of the original work by Andrews on distinctive competence, in 1990, C.K. Prahalad and Gary Hamel introduced the enormously influential notion of **core competence** to the managerial audience.[11] As described by Prahalad and Hamel, core competence was a capability or skill that provided the thread running through a firm's businesses, weaving them together into a coherent whole.

The idea that a core competence uniquely defined a firm and was the source of value creation was intuitively appealing. Managers in multibusiness firms began to conceive of their firms as portfolios of competencies, not just as portfolios of businesses. Their role, therefore, was to nurture these competencies and deploy them into the businesses. This perspective suggested a new, viable, and important role for CEOs that resonated with executives, particularly after the pressures they had felt in the 1980s.

However, the initial discussion left out much of the detail regarding how to develop a corporate strategy based on core competence. Thus, meaningful application of the core competence notion was difficult because of the generality of its level of analysis and the absence of specific prescriptions.

---

[10]McKinsey and Company, Inc., "What Is the Right Role for a Corporate Parent?" 1989.
[11]C.K. Prahalad and G. Hamel, "The Core Competence of the Corporation," *Harvard Business Review,* May–June 1990, pp. 79–91.

As a result, advances in corporate strategy in the nineties shifted back to the academic arena with the articulation of the **resource-based view of the firm**. This more broadly and accurately defines the assets that can function as core competences and lays out the conditions under which they can be sources of value in multiple businesses. The resource-based theory underpins the treatment of corporate strategy in this book.

RESOURCES AND RENTS

▲ INTRODUCTION

This chapter draws on a theory called the resource-based view of the firm (RBV).[1] Though relatively new to the field of strategic management, it addresses some of the most fundamental questions of business-unit strategy: Why is one firm different from another? Why is one firm more profitable than another? What makes a competitive advantage sustainable? It also provides a powerful explanation of firm scope, and diversified expansion in particular.

One of the great strengths of the resource-based approach is that it explains why a firm possesses both a competitive advantage in a single business and a corporate advantage that extends across many businesses. The approach unifies the treatment of corporate- and business-level strategy, and facilitates strategic analysis at both levels.

The chapter begins with a brief review of industry analysis and competitive positioning. In this context, the resource-based view is introduced and applied to business-unit strategy. Doing so establishes a rigorous foundation for the analysis of resources that is later extended to more complex settings. This way of proceeding also assists in the development of a dynamic view of the firm, starting with small, focused businesses and progressing to very large, complex organizations.

---

[1]Portions of this chapter draw heavily from "Resources: The Essence of Corporate Advantage," Harvard Business School Note No. 792-064, 1992. See also, Collis, David J. and Montgomery, Cynthia A., "Competing on Resources: Strategy in the 1990s," *Harvard Business Review*, July–August 1995, pp. 118–128.

PRINCIPLES

▲ BUSINESS-UNIT STRATEGY

In a world of perfect competition, products are homogeneous. There are countless buyers and sellers, all of whom have access to complete and timely information, and none of whom can influence the price of the goods they buy or sell. In such a world, there is no need for strategy, nor any benefit from having one.

Most markets, however, are not perfectly competitive; they have a number of imperfections or asymmetries. Either the number of sellers or buyers is limited, the products are heterogeneous, the information flows are flawed, or a firm is advantaged by possessing an input that is nonreproducible or in limited supply. A carefully crafted strategy can help a firm exploit the market inefficiencies that exist in these imperfectly competitive settings and, therefore, can play an essential role in maximizing its profits.

In such situations, strategy fulfills two vital purposes.[2] One is the **external positioning** of a firm relative to its competitors in a given industry. By adroitly matching a firm's strengths and weaknesses to market threats and opportunities, effective strategy creates a competitive advantage and allows the firm to earn superior profits. An essential part of formulating any strategy, therefore, requires an understanding of the environment in which the firm competes.

The second purpose of strategy is the **internal alignment** of all a firm's activities and investments.[3] Because strategy clearly articulates a product's market position, the firm's activities in all functions from R&D to marketing can be made consistent with each other. Similarly, investments can be chosen that reinforce each other and cumulate over time in the creation of new and better competitive advantages.

Every firm's profitability can be disaggregated into two components: the industry average level of profitability, and divergence from that average attributable to the competitive advantage (or disadvantage) that the firm's strategy produces within the industry. A widely used approach to analyzing both industry profitability and competitive advantage was developed by Michael Porter.[4] His framework for **industry analysis** (the so-called five forces) is a systematic methodology for examining the impact of industry structure on firm performance. Drawing on industrial organization economics, Porter argued that the long-run average profitability of industries differs as a function of five forces: the threat of new entrants, the power of buyers and suppliers, the intensity of rivalry within the industry, and the threat of substitute products or services. He also showed that the structure of an industry "has a strong influence in determining the competitive rules of the game as well as the strategies potentially available to the firm."

Porter went on to describe a set of **generic strategies** a firm could use to overcome or exploit industry forces and achieve a competitive advantage vis-à-vis its rivals through low cost or differentiation. The effective implementation of either of these strategies with a broad or narrow scope requires a set of organizational arrangements that support the key success factors behind the strategy. Across generic strategies, the pattern of these arrangements

---

[2]This critical groundwork was laid by E.P. Learned, C. Roland Christensen, and Kenneth Andrews, *Business Policy: Text and Cases* (Burr Ridge, IL: Irwin, 1965).

[3]Strategy implies *choice* of product market position, not the efficiency with which that choice is implemented. Michael E. Porter, "What Is Strategy?" *Harvard Business Review*, November–December 1996, pp. 61–78.

[4]Michael E. Porter, *Competitive Strategy* (New York: Free Press, 1980).

differs in predictable ways so that their pursuit is mutually exclusive (for more detail see Appendix B: "Business Strategy and Industry Analysis").

Industry-level profits in part are sustained by **entry barriers** that make it difficult for new competitors to enter an industry. Similarly, profitable strategic groups within an industry are protected by **mobility barriers** that make it difficult for firms pursuing one source of competitive advantage to move to another.[5] Within an industry or strategic group, the superior performance of any one firm must be similarly protected by factors that make it difficult for rivals to duplicate its advantage. Richard Rumelt called such impediments to the imitation of what a firm has, or does, **isolating mechanisms**—the Great Wall around a *sustainable* competitive advantage.[6] Studying these phenomena gave rise to an new area of inquiry: the resource-based view of the firm.[7]

Stocks and Flows

In addressing the roots of sustainable competitive advantage, the resource-based view emphasizes the **stocks** of assets and capabilities (resources) a firm possesses. By doing so, the RBV offers a different, more dynamic, perspective on competitive advantage than an analysis of current **flows** of revenues and expenses might suggest. While flows are transitory and can be adjusted instantaneously, stock levels carry over from period to period and only accumulate slowly over time (see "The Bathtub Metaphor"). As an explanation for *enduring* advantage, therefore, stocks are more important than current flows.

To understand the difference between stocks and flows, consider a firm that has a well-established brand name. A flow analysis of competitive advantage would reveal that it did indeed earn higher profits because it spent less on advertising and received higher prices than competitors. But the reason a new competitor cannot successfully replicate this strategy—spending little on advertising and charging a high price—is that it does not have a comparable brand reputation. In this example, it is the stock of brand-name recognition that makes firms different and so sustains a leader's competitive advantage.[8] Stocks, therefore, underlie a firm's ability to generate profit and sustain durable firm differences (strategic asymmetries).

Flows are nonetheless important in themselves. The activities a firm pursues and the resource investments it makes in the current period are determined by the strategy it is pursuing. Further, many flows accumulate over time into highly valued resource stocks. For example, the continued performance of certain activities, such as launching new products, can result in the development of a unique capability in product development. Thus, while most expenditure flows are expensed on the income statement, many in fact represent long-term investments in the firm's most critical capabilities.

---

[5]Richard E. Caves and M.E. Porter, "From Entry Barriers to Mobility Barriers: Conjectural Decisions and Contrived Deterrence to New Competition," *Quarterly Journal of Economics*, May 1977, pp. 241–61.
[6]Richard P. Rumelt, "Theory, Strategy, and Entrepreneurship," in *The Competitive Challenge*, ed. D.J. Teece (Cambridge, MA: Ballinger, 1987), pp. 137–158.
[7]This term was first introduced in 1984 by Birger Wernefelt, "A Resource-Based View of the Firm," *Strategic Managment Journal*, 1984, pp. 171–180.
[8]Stocks and flows are duals of one another. While the stock of brand recognition determines the flow of advertising expenditures required each period, the expenditures determine how the stock level alters over time.

The Bathtub Metaphor

The fundamental distinction between stocks and flows may be illustrated by the "bathtub" metaphor: at any moment in time, the stock of water is indicated by the level of water in the tub; it is the cumulative result of flows of water into the tub (through the tap) and out of it (through a leak). In the example of R&D, the amount of water in the tub represents the stock of know-how at a particular point in time, whereas current R&D spending is represented by the water flowing in through the tap; the fact that know-how depreciates over time is represented by the flow of water leaking through the hole in the tub. A crucial point illustrated by the bathtub metaphor is that while flows can be adjusted instantaneously, stocks cannot. It takes a consistent pattern of resource flows to accumulate a desired change in strategic asset stocks.

Source: Ingemar Dierickx and K. Cool, "Asset Stock Accumulation and Sustainability of Competitive Advantage," *Management Science*, 1989, pp. 1504-11.

▲ RESOURCES

The premise of the resource-based view is that firms differ in fundamental ways because each firm possesses a unique bundle of tangible and some intangible assets and organizational capabilities—what we call resources.

Because many of these assets and capabilities cannot be accumulated instantaneously, a firm's choice of strategy is constrained by its current stock of resources and the speed at which it can acquire or accumulate new ones. Without asymmetries in resource stocks, and constraints on the rate of change, any firm could elect to follow any strategy it wished. As a result, successful strategies would be very quickly imitated and profits rapidly driven to zero. Resources, therefore, are the substance of strategy, the very essence of sustainable competitive advantage.

What Are Resources?

Resources come in many forms, from common factor inputs that are widely available and easily purchased in arms-length transactions, to highly differentiated resources, like brand names, that are developed over many years and are very difficult to replicate.

Resources can be classified into three broad categories: tangible assets, intangible assets, and organizational capabilities.

Tangible assets are the easiest to value and often are the only resources that appear on a firm's balance sheet. They include real estate, production facilities, and raw materials, among others. Although tangible resources may be essential to a firm's strategy, because of their standard nature they rarely are a source of competitive advantage. There are, of course, notable exceptions. The mundane, twisted copper telephone and coaxial cable wires that link your house to the outside world are now highly prized as the on-ramp to the information superhighway. Real estate locations adjacent to popular tourist sites are also one-of-a-kind resources that may support unusual profits.

Intangible assets include such things as company reputations, brand names, cultures, technological knowledge, patents and trademarks, and accumulated learning and experience. These assets often play important roles in competitive advantage (or disadvantage) and firm value (see "Gerber Products Co."). Intangible assets also have the important property of not being consumed in usage. Indeed, if applied judiciously, some intangible assets can grow with use, rather than shrink. For this reason, they can provide a valuable base for diversified expansion.

Organizational capabilities are not factor inputs like tangible and intangible assets; they are complex combinations of assets, people, and processes that organizations use to transform inputs into outputs. Applied to the firm's physical production technology, these organizational routines govern the efficiency of the firm's activities. Finely honed capabilities can be a source of competitive advantage. They enable a firm to take the same factor inputs as rivals and convert them into products and services, either with greater efficiency in the process or greater quality in the output.

The list of organizational capabilities includes a set of abilities describing efficiency and effectiveness—faster, more responsive, higher quality, and so forth—that can be found in any one of the firm's activities, from product development, to marketing, to manufacturing. Over the last several decades, some Japanese automobile companies, for example, have developed a number of outstanding organizational capabilities.[9] The first was in low cost, "lean" manufacturing, next in high-quality production, and most recently in fast product development. These organizational capabilities generated important efficiency advantages, particularly against foreign rival, and played major roles in the competitiveness of these firms.[10]

Gerber Products Co.

Few firms can boast the kind of brand recognition and loyalty enjoyed by one company in particular, one that made its name as a purveyor of much sought-after foods like strained peas and pureed squash. When it comes time to feed their own children, generations of American parents, themselves raised on Gerber baby food, wouldn't buy anything else. The firm has a 65-year history and commands more than 70 percent of the U.S. baby food market.

When Gerber was acquired by Sandoz Ltd., a Swiss pharmaceutical firm, in 1994, its tangible net worth, including its plants and inventory, was less than $300 million. One might wonder why Sandoz was willing to pay $3.7 billion for the firm—almost 33 times Gerber's annual profits.

The answer lies in Gerber's intangible assets: its brand name, reputation, and considerable expanse of supermarket shelf space. These are the assets Gerber's competitors have vied for decades to imitate, with little success. Someday one of them may come up with a new winning formula, but up until now, displacing the comfort and security that adults experience when buying Gerber has indeed proven difficult.

---

[9]Carliss Y. Baldwin and Kim B. Clark, "Capabilities, Time Horizons and Investment: New Perspectives on Capital Budgeting," Harvard Business School mimeograph, 1990.

[10]Teece, Pisano, and Shuen made an important distinction between static and dynamic routines. Static routines embody the "capacity to replicate certain previously performed tasks." In a stable environment, these can be an important source of competitive advantage. Dynamic routines, on the other hand, are "directed at establishing new competences," and thus enable a firm to adapt to changing strategic demands. (David J. Teece, G. Pisano, and A. Shuen, "Dynamic Capabilities and Strategic Management," working paper, revised 1994). Such resources are not, however, the "ultimate" capability, since there are always higher-order dynamic routines of the "learning to learn" variety (David J. Collis, "How Valuable Are Organizational Capabilities?" *Strategic Management Journal*, Special Issue, Winter 1994; pp. 143–152).

Although the resource-based view of the firm allows for the systematic assessment of these internal elements of strategy, it is important to stress that an analysis of the resources themselves can only take place in the context of the firm's **competitive environment** (see "Resources and Product Market Strategy").

What Makes Resources Valuable?

Although the notion that resources underpin the sustainability of competitive advantage is simple, companies often have a hard time identifying and evaluating their own resources, assessing whether they are strengths or weaknesses, and understanding whether they can be sources of sustainable competitive advantage.

Indeed, as firms evaluate the set of resources they possess, they will find a mixed bag. Some lucky firms will own "crown jewels"—resources that long term can be the basis for successful strategies. Some will find that their resources are actually liabilities. IBM's mainframe culture of "big iron," for example, which had served it well for nearly 40 years, became a liability by the late eighties. Yet other firms might discover that some of their resources are not markedly better than those of competitors or are not particularly highly valued by consumers. The challenge for managers is to understand what distinguishes valuable from pedestrian resources and to use that knowledge to craft strategies that generate an enduring competitive advantage.

Historically, attempts to evaluate resources often resembled inward looking exercises that lacked critical objectivity. The resource-based view added discipline to this subjective process by bringing back into the analysis the external perspective of the industry context and competitive dynamics. As shown in Figure 2–1, the value of a firm's resources lies in the complex interplay between the firm and its competitive environment along the dimensions of **demand**, **scarcity**, and **appropriability**. Value is created in the intersection of the three sets: when a resource is demanded by customers, when it cannot be replicated by competitors, and when the profits it generates are captured by the firm.[11]

Resources and Product Market Strategy

It is important to remember that owning a valuable resource does not permit the firm to sit back and clip dividend checks. Valuable resources will only reap the profits they can theoretically generate if they are applied in an effective product market strategy. Traditional strategy formulation—that is, externally positioning the firm to capitalize on its strengths and minimize its weaknesses—remains essential to realizing competitive advantage. Moreover, the firm still has to deploy its resources in the optimal way and correctly align all its activities in pursuit of its chosen source of competitive advantage. If the strategy is ill-conceived or unsustainable, the value of the firm will suffer, as will the value of most of its resources.

The connection between the competitive product market strategy of a firm and the resource strategy that supports it is ongoing and reciprocal: valuable resources help build strong strategies; strong strategies help build valuable resources.

---

[11]For a related view on sustainability, see Pankaj Ghemawat, *Commitment* (New York: Free Press, 1991) chapter 4.

▲ FIGURE 2–1   The Value Creation Zone

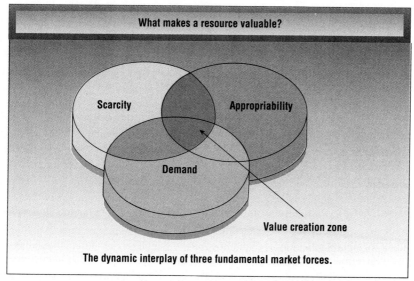

Source: David J. Collis and Cynthia A. Montgomery, "Competing on Resources: Strategy in the 1990s."
Harvard Business Review, July-August 1995.

*Some genius invented the Oreo—we're just
living off the inheritance.*

Ross Johnson, CEO of RJR Nabisco[12]

Customer Demand   The first determinant of resource value is found in the product market.
A valuable resource must contribute to the **fulfillment of a customer's needs**, at a price the
customer is willing to pay. At any given time, that price will be determined by customer preferences, available alternatives (including substitute products), and the supply of related or
complementary goods.[13] These structural forces change over time as consumer preferences
and competitive offerings evolve. Therefore, firms must continually reassess the attractiveness of the industries in which they compete, and the degree to which their resources meet
current and projected needs.

For example, recognizing that generic cigarettes caused a shift in customers' willingness
to pay for branded tobacco products, Philip Morris cut the price of its Marlboro cigarettes by
nearly 25 percent in April 1993. The move demonstrated the firm's recognition of the change
in consumer demand for one of its primary resources, the Marlboro brand name. (Indeed, one
study indicated that over a period of three years, all the world's leading tobacco brands declined sharply in value: Marlboro dropped 27 percent to $33 billion; Camel, 70 percent to
$1.6 billion; and Winston, 73 percent to $2.3 billion.[14])

---

[12]Bryan Burrough and John Helyar, *Barbarians at the Gate: The Fall of RJR Nabisco* (New York: Harper and
Row, 1990).
[13]Adam M. Brandenburger and H.W. Stuart, "Value-Based Business Strategy," *Journal of Economics and
Management Strategy,* Vol. 5, No. 1, Spring 1996, pp. 5–24.
[14]Alexandra Ourosoff, "When the Smoke Clears," *Financial World,* June 21, 1994, pp. 38–42.

It is important to keep in mind that many resources are in fact detrimental to the satisfaction of customer demands. A poor location, for example, can detract from a restaurant's appeal to consumers. Similarly, a reputation for uneven quality or service can reduce the likelihood of repeat business for any firm.

In addressing customer demand, resources are only valuable if they meet customers' needs better than those of their competitors. Even though a resource may be necessary to the implementation of a strategy, if it does not distinguish the firm's product offerings or ways of doing business, it will not be a source of competitive advantage. Cocoa beans, for example, may be a necessary input for chocolate manufacturers, but they do not lead to important product differences. An analysis of a firm's resources has to involve more than just an internal assessment of which activities the firm performs well. It is only when resources contribute to **competitive superiority** in the product market that they will be valuable.

To demonstrate this, it is necessary to show how a firm's resource stock is translated into specific measures of competitive advantage. Figure 2–2, for example, shows the resources that give Wal-Mart an edge over its rivals. Noted alongside each resource is the quantitative measure of the product market advantage it supports.

Demand for a particular resource, and hence the value of that resource, is also very sensitive to the possibility of **substitution**. Porter's five forces analysis highlighted the threat substitute products may pose to an industry's profitability—for example, the way fax machines reduced the demand for overnight delivery services. Even when demand for an end product remains high, competitors can substitute alternative resources for the production of a similar offering. People's Express learned this lesson the hard way. After People's built a dedicated physical infrastructure to offer low-cost flights, the major airlines responded by using their computer reservation systems and skills in yield management to offer correspondingly low rates with their existing fleet configurations. Ultimately, this configuration of resources proved superior in meeting that consumer need, and People's was forced into bankruptcy.

In summary, enduring demand for the good or service a resource generates is a necessary condition for the resource itself to be valuable. However, it is not a sufficient condition. For that, a firm must have an advantage, and a resource, that others do not have and find difficult to replicate.

Resource Scarcity The second essential requirement for a resource to be valuable, therefore, is that it be in short supply. If the resource is plentifully available, any competitor could acquire it and so replicate the firm's competitive advantage.[15] Indeed, by definition, resources that yield a competitive advantage must be uncommon. Therefore, an analysis of a firm's resources must include a critical assessment of whether the firm's resources are unusual when compared to those of its competitors. For this, the term *distinctive competence*, rather than core competence, is more appropriate. To be a source of *sustainable* competitive advantage, however, the rarity of the resource must persist over time.

Inimitability is, therefore, at the heart of value creation because it limits competition. Possessing a resource that competitors can readily copy will only generate temporary value—it cannot be the basis of a long-run strategy.[16] There are four characteristics that make

---

[15]Jay Barney, "Firm Resources and Sustained Competitive Advantage," *Journal of Management*, 1991, pp. 99–120.

[16]Richard Rumelt (1987 op. cit) made this point in "Theory, Strategy, and Entrepreneurship". The characteristics of inimitability are the isolating mechanisms referred to earlier—"impediments to the ex-post imitative dissipation of entrepreneurial rents."

▲ FIGURE 2–2   Wal-Mart's Resource-Based Advantage in 1984
Competitive Advantage

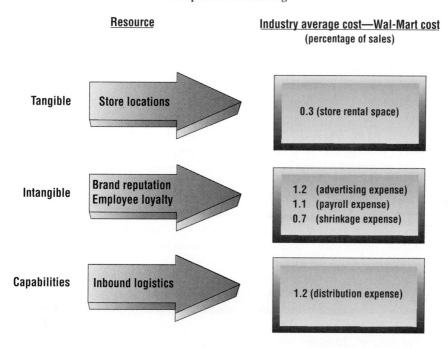

*Each percentage point advantage is worth $500 million in net income to Wal-Mart
Source: Ghemawat, Pankaj, "Wal-Mart Stores' Discount Operations," Harvard Business School case number 9-387-018.

resources difficult to imitate. Resources that play a central role in a firm's strategy should possess at least one of these.

The first category comprises *physically unique* resources that by definition are virtually impossible to copy. A magnificent real estate location, mineral rights, or legally protected drug patents simply cannot be imitated. Although it is tempting to think of most resources as falling into this category, on closer inspection, few do. Even resources that appear to be one of a kind often subsequently prove to be inimitable. Xerox fell into this trap in the seventies when it believed that no one else could ever replicate its reprographic capabilities. Canon proved otherwise, and the seventies turned into the "Lost Decade" for Xerox as its market leadership in photocopiers fell to Canon.

Many more resources are difficult to imitate because of what economists call *path dependency* in their accumulation.[17] These are resources that cannot be instantaneously acquired, but rather must be built over time in ways that are difficult to accelerate. Coca Cola's brand-name recognition, for example, was not built, and cannot be replicated, just by spending hundreds of millions of dollars on advertising. Rather, it comes from the experiences consumers

---

[17]The discussion of path dependency and causal ambiguity follows Dierickx and Cool, "Asset Stock Accumulation," 1989, op. cit.

associate with drinking Coke over the years; to match it would take the passage of time and the accumulation of another set of experiences drinking the new cola. Similarly, crash R&D programs, where many scientists work in parallel, often cannot replicate the results of programs whose problems have been solved sequentially. This need to recreate the path that predecessors took protects the first mover by delaying imitation.

The third source of inimitability is *causal ambiguity*. This implies that potential replicators either cannot disentangle what the truly valuable resource is, or cannot identify the precise recipe for duplicating it. For example, what is the resource that enables so many of Fidelity's mutual funds to outperform the market? Is it just the skilled fund managers, or is it the training of those managers? Or the team approach of managers and stock analysts? Or the advocacy method for picking stocks? Or the incentive schemes that the company employs? And if a senior executive left Fidelity for another company, could he or she take away the knowledge in a set of written blueprints?

Causally ambiguous resources are often organizational capabilities. They are embedded in complex social structures and interactions and may even depend on the personality of a few exceptional individuals. As Delta and United try to mimic Southwest Air's successful low-cost strategy, for example, the most difficult thing they will have to copy is not the planes, the routes, or the fast gate turnaround. These are readily observable and, in principle, easily duplicated. The most difficult thing to copy or surpass will be Southwest's culture of fun, family, frugality, and focus, because no one can quite identify what it is or how it arose.

The last source of inimitability is *economic deterrence*. This occurs when a market leader's competitors have the capability to replicate its resources but, because of limited market size, choose not to do so. This is most likely when strategies are built around large capital investments, such as complex continuous process machines, that are scale sensitive and specific to a given market. When such assets cannot be redeployed—that is, they are sunk in a given market—they represent a credible commitment that the firm will stay in the market and fight any competitor that attempts to replicate the investment. Faced with such a threat, potential imitators may choose not to duplicate the resource when the market is too small to profitably support two players the size of the incumbent.[18]

Although it may be tempting to think of imitability as an either/or condition, more often it is a matter of degree—a question of time and difficulty. The characteristics discussed above often do not prevent imitation; they make it more difficult, or more uncertain. Figure 2–3 captures this by illustrating the range of resource imitability.

Resources may be even more valuable when there are multiple barriers to imitation. For example, a reputation for high-quality, innovative products may involve path dependencies as well as causal ambiguity. It is also worth noting that the very qualities that make resources difficult to imitate may also make them difficult for the firm itself to reproduce or change.

Commenting on why he liked the Walt Disney Company as an investment, Warren Buffet explained, "because the Mouse does not have an agent."[19]

Appropriability   Even if a resource is fulfilling a consumer demand and is in short supply, there still remains a question about the **distribution of profit:** Who actually captures the profits created by a resource?

---

[18]For an excellent discussion, see Pankaj Ghemawat, *Commitment* (New York: Free Press, 1991).
[19]*The Harbus*, March 25, 1996, p. 12.

▲ FIGURE 2–3   Resource Imitability

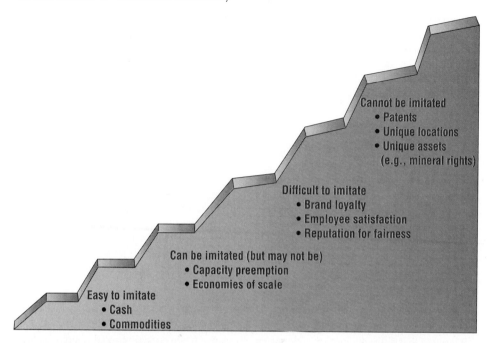

Cannot be imitated
- Patents
- Unique locations
- Unique assets
  (e.g., mineral rights)

Difficult to imitate
- Brand loyalty
- Employee satisfaction
- Reputation for fairness

Can be imitated (but may not be)
- Capacity preemption
- Economies of scale

Easy to imitate
- Cash
- Commodities

Source: Cynthia A. Montgomery, "Resources: the Essence of Corporate Advantage," Harvard Business School Case N1-792-064.

It is a mistake to think that profits automatically flow to a firm's legal owners (the providers of capital). Rather, one must consider who has the property rights to a firm's critical resources; how obvious it is which resources generate profits; and other factors that influence the bargaining power of the relevant stakeholders. (See "Opportunity Costs".)

Generally, if the source of value creation is obvious, and property rights to the critical resources are clearly established, profits will flow to the **owner of the resources**, be it the firm itself, or an external party. For this reason, firms are more likely to appropriate profits from resources they develop themselves, rather than from those they purchase in the market. Warren Buffet, for example, recognized the value of the Walt Disney Company owning the copyright to Mickey Mouse.

In contrast, the explosion in the number of leveraged buyout firms in the 1980's illustrates the delicate issues concerning the ownership of resources by a firm or its employees. One critical resource of such firms was the contacts and relationships they held in the investment banking community. Unfortunately, for many firms, this resource was often vested in the individuals "doing the deals," not in the firm itself. These people could, and often did, trade their skills by establishing their own LBO funds, or by moving to another firm where they could reap a greater share of the profit their resource (skills) generated.

For many firms, the most difficult situations to assess are those where property rights are not clear, or where resources are employed in combination, making it difficult to identify the individual contribution of each. Such situations give rise to bargaining among a host of parties,

When identifying which of a firm's resources are its source of profit, accountants define profit as the difference between the total revenue and total costs that appear on an income statement. Economists use a different definition. They define **economic profit** as the difference between revenue and the opportunity cost of employing all the various resources. This proves to be a crucial distinction.

Opportunity costs consider the alternative ways a resource could be employed. When a firm uses a resource in a given application, it incurs an opportunity cost that is equal to the maximum amount the resource could have earned in its next best employment. This distinction is particularly important when a firm makes significant use of assets whose book value deviates from the market value of the assets. For example, a retailer that owns land in highly sought-after locations should recognize the true cost of those properties— the amount anyone else would pay to rent them—and take care not to confuse the rents earned as a landowner with the profits made as a retailer. If the valuable resources are the locations and the retailer does not charge itself the true cost of those locations, then the retailing business may show a total accounting profit even if the company is actually a poor retailer, but a fortuitous landowner.

which can include customers, distributors, partners, and suppliers, as well as the firm's own employees. (See "Employees and Rent Generation.") Many joint venture partners, for example, have found that difficult questions of appropriation arise when contracts and property rights are not iron-clad.[20]

More generally, whenever a firm earns substantial profits, there is always great pressure to pay them out in the form of abnormal payments for inputs or, equivalently, to dissipate them as slack inside the organization.[21]

Intrinsic Properties of Resources

As the above discussion indicates, most characteristics that affect the value of a resource are determined in the complex interplay within a system of competitors, customers, and suppliers of factor inputs. For this reason, the value of a resource changes as the state of competition and the chosen strategy evolve. Other characteristics of a resource are, however, primarily intrinsic in nature.

Resources differ dramatically in **capacity**, that is, how much a firm has and how long the supply will last. Some resources have fixed levels, while others have a capacity that varies according to how they are used. A stamping machine, for example, has a finite capacity, whereas a brand name or a company's reputation are not bounded in the same way.

It is also important to distinguish between short- and long-term capacity. If a firm's competitive advantage from a resource is to be maintained, the resource itself must not deteriorate and disappear. Only then can resources carry over between periods and so support long-lived strategic asymmetries.

---

[20]David Teece refers to these as co-specialized assets. See D.J. Teece, "Profiting from Technological Innovation: Implications for Integration, Collaboration, Licensing, and Public Policy," in *The Competitive Challenge*, ed. D.J. Teece (Cambridge, MA: Ballinger, 1987), pp. 185-220.
[21]Ghemawat, Pankaj, *Commitment.*

Employees and Rent Generation

In annual reports and end-of-year speeches, management often proclaims that the firm's employees are its most valuable resource. Without denying the importance of the human contribution, it is important to remember that, in the absence of slavery, people are resources that firms must rent, not own. Unlike the assets on a firm's balance sheet, these resources can quit their jobs or attempt to renegotiate their contracts with the firm.

In a reasonably efficient labor market, employees that bring clearly defined talents and skills to a firm should be able to appropriate the value of those resources in personal wages and bonuses. The compensation of skilled athletes, for example, reflects the value they are expected to create for any team. For employees to be a source of economic rent for the firm itself, something must tie them to the firm, or make their skills more valuable in the firm than they would be elsewhere. For example, a firm may appropriate a portion of the rent if it contributes a valuable resource, such as a distribution system, to a management team, so that it would be difficult for the team to leave the firm as a unit and reestablish itself elsewhere. In such settings, when relationship-specific investments tie the parties together, the firm may earn rents not only on resources it owns, but also as a partner of employees who possess valuable resources.

However, resources accumulate *and decay* at different rates. Clearly, the slower the rate of depreciation, the more valuable the resource. Although physical resources, like oil reserves, deplete as they are used, calculating their precise decay rates may be difficult. The task is even more onerous when dealing with intangible resources. Economists have traditionally assigned annual decay rates of .3 and .1, respectively, to a firm's investments in advertising and R&D. In practice, however, judging the **durability** of intangible resources is extraordinarily difficult because their longevity depends heavily on how they are cultivated and on how market demand evolves. The Disney brand, for example, thrived for decades, often of benign neglect, whereas the value of technological knowledge can depreciate rapidly, as the success of different firms in each new generation of semiconductor memories illustrates.

Resources also differ greatly in **specificity**. Some can be used in a variety of applications, and some in only one. Highly fungible resources, such as cash, multipurpose machinery, and general management skills, can be extended across a wide range of markets. More specialized resources, such as expertise in narrow scientific disciplines and secret product formulas, tend to have only limited applications. Consider, for example, the very successful British extermination company, Rentokil. As the firm expanded into plant and garden care, it found itself suddenly burdened by its highly recognizable brand name (read "Rent-to-Kill").

To be the basis for a diversified firm, resources must be fungible to some degree, but specific enough to provide a meaningful advantage in the settings in which they are applied.

Returning to the zone of value creation shown in Figure 2–1, we can now see how the conditions for valuable resources apply (see "How Do You Know if Your Resources Are Valuable?"). The test of demand demonstrates that the resource produces a good or service that customers want, at a price they are willing to pay. The test of scarcity demonstrates that a resource is in short supply and that competitors will not be able to imitate it. Finally, the test of appropriability demonstrates that the firm itself can capture the profits generated by the

How Do You Know if Your Resources Are Valuable?

Demand

Does the resource produce something customers desire, and for which they have a high willingness to pay?

Does the resource contribute to competitive advantage in the product market?

Are there alternative products or resources that provide more value for the customer?

Scarcity

Is the resource rare?

Is it hard to copy?

Appropriability

Who captures the value created by the resource?

competitive advantage the resource provides. Resources that meet these conditions benefit from a substantial zone of value creation; the firm itself is better off when it has an ample supply of such resources, and can apply them across several markets.

It is important to recognize, however, that conditions that affect the value of resources can shift over time, sometimes abruptly. When this happens, the zone of value creation shrinks (or expands). (See "IBM and the PC Business.") Recognizing that this occurs, underscores the importance of a dynamic evaluation of resources, and the role they play in sustaining a firm's competitive (or corporate) advantage.

▲ ECONOMIC RENT

Ultimately the resource-based view argues that all profits can be attributed to the ownership of a scarce resource. Economists interpret these profits as rents accruing to a factor that is in short supply.[22] However, they make an important distinction between two types of economic rent:[23]

- ▲ **Ricardian** or **scarcity rents** are due to valuable factors that are inherently in limited supply. Ricardian rents are due to scarcity.

- ▲ **Schumpeterian** or **entrepreneurial rents** are earned by innovators and occur during the period of time between the introduction of an innovation and its successful diffusion. It is expected that innovations, in time, will be imitated, but until that occurs, the innovator will earn Schumpeterian rents.

---

[22]See, for example, the textbook treatment in H.R. Varian, *Microeconomics Analysis* (New York: Norton, 1978).
[23]Some very insightful articles have been written on strategy, resources, and economic rents. See, for example, K. Conner, "A Historical Comparison of Resource-Based Theory and Five Schools of Thought within Industrial Organization: Do We Have a New Theory of the Firm?" *Journal of Management*, 1991, pp. 333-87; M.A. Peteraf, "The Cornerstones of Competitive Advantage: A Resource-Based View," *Strategic Management Journal*, 1993, pp. 179-91; R. Rumelt, "Theory, Strategy, and Entrepreneurship," and Sidney Winter, "Four Rs of Profitability: Rents, Resources, Routines and Replication," in *Resource-Based and Evolutionary Theories of the Firm: Towards a Synthesis*, ed. C.A. Montgomery (Boston: Kluwer Academic Publishers, 1995), pp. 147-78. These articles also identify "monopoly rents," which accrue to a sole producer that artifically restricts output. While a useful distinction, the question still remains whether the monopoly position is short term or long lived—whether it is due to scarce factors that earn Ricardian or Schumpeterian rents.

IBM and the PC business

In the PC business, which it entered in 1982, IBM's resources—a reputation and brand name, technological know-how, and an organizational capability in product development—initially were extraordinarily valuable. But by the early nineties, the value of those same resources had declined.

Even though demand for PCs had grown exponentially, the **competitive superiority** of the IBM brand was diminished as consumers recognized that many clones were reliable. Similarly, IBM's technological lead was eliminated by the open standard it created, which put everyone on the same footing. Its organizational capability was easily surpassed in new entrepreneurial and highly motivated ventures. Indeed, other resources—low-cost manufacturing skills, design capability, and rapid response—had substituted for IBM's original set of resources as sources of competitive advantage.

The **scarcity** of IBM's resources was also eroded by the flood of clone producers that had 10 years to create their own reputations and develop their own designs. In addition, most profits that were to be made in PCs were **appropriated** by Intel and Microsoft, the two suppliers that owned the valuable technology resources, the microprocessor and operating system, respectively.

The resulting contraction in the value creation zone around IBM's resources was symptomatic of the problems that led to IBM's overall performance problems.

The important distinction between the two is that Ricardian rents are long-lived and Schumpeterian rents are not. Ricardian rents are due to factors that are difficult or impossible to imitate, such as unique geographic locations, complex organizational routines, or long-standing corporate reputations. Schumpeterian rents, on the other hand, are due to innovations that, with the passage of time, will be imitated.

These issues raise a number of fundamental questions for managers. First, assuming a firm is earning economic rent, to what is it due? Second, are the factors more Ricardian or Schumpeterian in nature? Are they the result of an innovation that, with a certain amount of time, competitors will be able to imitate, or is there something about them that makes them inherently difficult to reproduce? Further, is it likely that competitors will introduce innovations that will reduce the value of the resource? When is that likely to occur?

The Sting of Schumpeterian Competition

When the resource-based view was first introduced, the immediate focus was on Ricardian rents and on the kind of resources that generate vast amounts of value over extended periods of time. Not surprisingly, it was soon recognized that while such resources are of critical importance, they are, in fact, relatively rare. Many more resources, and the competitive advantages they confer, are Schumpeterian in nature and can better be described as matters of time and degree (see "Creative Destruction: Inventors, Innovators, and Imitators").

Geoff Waring dramatically illustrated this point in his study of firm-level deviations from industry average profitability (Figure 2–4). Although industries differ somewhat in their speed of convergence, Waring's large sample analysis revealed a remarkable movement to the mean over a six-year period.

Creative Destruction: Inventors, Innovators, and Imitators

Joseph A. Schumpeter, an economist working in the first half of the 20th century, believed strongly that economic life had to be seen as a dynamic process. He distinguished among three important economic functions: **invention**, wherein a novel idea, or model for a new product or process, was developed; **innovation**, wherein that product was commercialized; and, **diffusion**, where competitors successfully imitated the innovation.

Of these, Schumpeter believed the innovator, or entrepreneur, played a particularly important role in economic development. As described by Arnold Heertje, "The gifted few, pioneering in the field of new technologies, new products, and new markets, carry out innovations and, joined some time later by many imitators, they are at the heart of the short and long cycles observed in economic life."*

Schumpeter recognized that entrepreneurs, and innovation, could be found in organizations of any size, not just start-up ventures. They were the people who first gathered the resources to bring an invention, whether a widget or an organizational form, to market, not the inventors. They were also the ones who created profits, not the risk-bearers who provided the necessary capital.

Schumpeter used the term *creative destruction* to describe the life cycle of innovations. In this dynamic perspective, new innovations drive out old ones, and in the process sweep away resources, firms, professions, and the profits of the previous entrepreneurs. Thus, profits ebb and flow in a continual cycle, peaking during the period of innovation and declining, first as imitation becomes widespread, and then as a new innovation is pioneered.

The New Palgrave: A Dictionary of Economics, London, The Macmillan Press Limited, 1987, p. 264.

▲ FIGURE 2–4   Convergence of Firm-Specific Rents

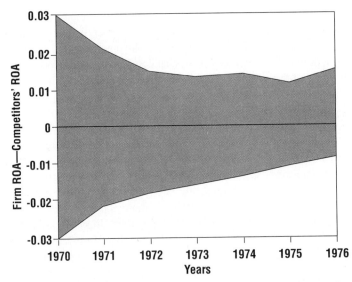

Source: Geoff Waring, "Industry Differences in the Persistence of Firm-Specific Returns," working paper, revised September 16, 1994.

Most firms are engaged in a never-ending struggle for competitive advantage. They cannot merely sit back and collect rents from resources that will effortlessly retain their value. Indeed, most strategies and the resources that support them are under intense competitive pressure from imitators and innovators that will in time erode their value. Given this, managers are well advised to conceive of strategies for confronting that eventuality. Their responsibility is to cultivate their firms' current interests while acting in the present to secure future rent streams.

PRACTICE

▲ RESOURCE-BASED STRATEGY

In addition to developing resources that underpin firm performance at both the business unit and corporate level, a prime responsibility of management is to develop a resource-based strategy. This involves identifying, investing in, upgrading, and leveraging a set of valuable resources.

Identification of Valuable Resources

To craft a resource-based strategy, a firm must first identify and evaluate its resources to find those on which it should base its future competitive (and/or corporate) advantage. This process involves defining the set of resources the firm possesses, and then applying the tests laid out in the principles section to determine which of those (if any) are truly valuable.

In this process, it is important that the firm finds the appropriate level at which to **disaggregate its resources.** Broad categorizations of competences are typically far less helpful than more disaggregated ones that can be directly related to flow measures of competitive advantage. (Figure 2–5 provides such an example.)

Saying that a consumer packaged goods company has good marketing skills, for example, conveys almost no worthwhile information. But dividing marketing skills into subcategories such as brand management that, in turn, can be divided into product-line extensions and cost-effective couponing allows for **data-driven analysis** of whether the firm truly possesses competitive superiority on these dimensions. Evaluating whether Kraft General Foods or Unilever has better consumer marketing skills may be impossible, but analyzing which is more successful at launching product-line extensions is feasible.

Disaggregation is also necessary when developing implications for action. One manufacturer of medical diagnostics test equipment initially defined its core competence as instrumentation. Unfortunately, this intuitively obvious definition was too broad to act upon. By pushing to deeper levels of aggregation, the company came to a powerful insight: its strength in instrumentation was mainly attributable to its competitive superiority in designing the human/machine interface. As a result, the firm decided to hire ergonomists to reinforce that valuable capability and to expand into the faster-growing doctors' office market where the equipment could be operated by medical staff members who were not skilled technicians.

Although disaggregation can be the key to identifying competitively superior resources, sometimes the valuable resource may be a combination of assets and capabilities, none of which is individually superior, but which when combined make a better package. For example,

▲ FIGURE 2–5   Whitbread Restaurants' Resources

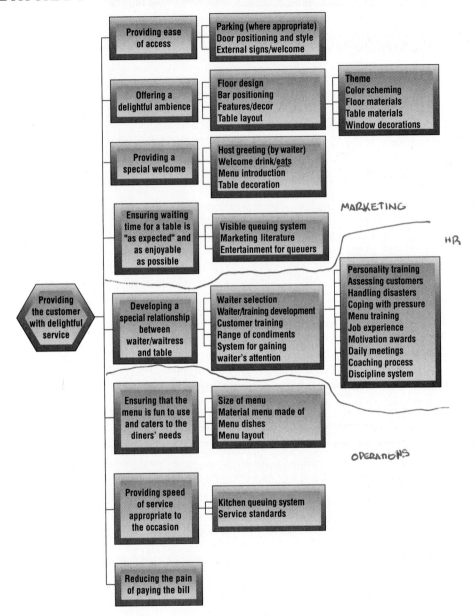

Source: Andrew Campbell and Kathleen Luchs, *Strategic Synergy* (London: Butterworth-Heineman, 1992).

none of the individual components in a Honeywell industrial automation system may be highly distinctive, but the company can still provide the best overall system. This implies that the firm's competitive superiority lies either in the weighted average (although the company doesn't rank first in any resource, on average it may be better than other competitors) or in the company's systems integration capability. This conclusion may be correct, but it should be reached only after careful scrutiny, not instinctively jumped to as a means of short-circuiting a detailed analysis of the individual disaggregated resources.

Investing in Resources

Because all resources depreciate, an effective corporate strategy requires continuous investment to maintain and expand a firm's critical resources. Brand names age unless supported by current advertising expenditures. Technological know-how becomes outdated. Organizational capabilities grow rigid and fail to adapt.[24] Often the investment in key resources will be overseen by corporate management rather than left to divisional managers because it is so critical to the firm's performance.

One of Michael Eisner's first actions as CEO of Disney, for example, was to reassert the company's commitment to animation. He invested $50 million in *Roger Rabbit*, making it the company's first animated feature film hit in many years, and quadrupled the output of animated feature films to one a year—generating successive hits like *Beauty and the Beast, Aladdin,* and *The Lion King.* These rebuilt the Disney brand name and reestablished its competitive superiority with new generations of children and parents. In contrast, Edward Brennan of Sears attempted to build a host of new businesses around its core retailing operations, while failing to reinvest to maintain the health of the core itself.

Importantly, the rents a firm expects to accrue to the resources in which it is investing must not be dissipated in a competitive struggle to acquire them. If many firms see the value in a particular resource, in a reasonably efficient market the price of that resource should reflect its demand. For example, one would not expect any firm bidding for oil reserves to acquire them at below market value unless it was lucky or had private information concerning their value.[25] It may seem that the problem goes away when resources are accumulated internally. However, even when resources such as organizational capabilities are built through internal investments, the profits from them will, in part, depend on the number of competitors who have made similar investments. If many companies develop the same logistics capability, on average none will earn a substantial return on that resource investment.

Investment then, requires careful analysis of a firm's strategic position, and likely competitor investments. A firm can expect a positive return on its investment only when the investment produces a competitively superior resource.[26] Other investments may be necessary to maintain competitive parity, but they will not earn economic rents. As this analysis suggests, choosing which resources to invest in is not a straightforward exercise. It actually raises two of the most difficult trade-offs firms have to face. These are the choices between continuity and adaptability, and between commitment and flexibility.[27]

---

[24]Dorothy Leonard-Barton suggested how core capabilities through time can become core rigidities. "Core Competencies and Core Rigidities: A Paradox in Managing New Product Development," *Strategic Management Journal,* 1992, pp. 111–25.

[25]Jay Barney made this point in "Strategic Factor Markets: Expectations, Luck and Business Strategy," *Management Science,* 1986, pp. 1231–41.

[26]The asymmetry among firms' existing resources is the primary reason all profits are not dissipated in the struggle to acquire resources, even when their value is common knowledge.

[27]For a thorough treatment of these issues, see Ghemawat, *Commitment,* op. cit.

Continuity and Adaptability   When a firm's current resources and those required for future competitive success appear to differ, its management faces a dilemma. Does it stick with the historic resources that have served the firm well in the past, but which may be substituted by other resources and other strategies in the future? Or does it elect to alter its strategy and develop different resources? Or does it choose an intermediate path of wait and see, holding back from investing in either set of resources until the uncertainty has been resolved?

Many firms have faced this quandary. For example, should Sears have adopted the discount retailer format to block Wal-Mart's growth? Or was the firm correct not to follow the example of Atari, which tried (and failed) to develop a new set of resources to accommodate what it saw in the mid-1980s as a shift from video games to personal computing?

Although investing in resources that were valuable historically is easy to justify as the continuation of a successful strategy, the risk is that the investment will lock the firm into an increasingly unfavorable position. Investing in new resources, however, is also risky because it can involve a fundamental change in the organization with no guarantees that the new strategy will be a success; plus, there are the possible costs of cannibalizing existing profitable sales.

For managers, giving up what has worked well in the past for the uncertain possibility of future success from a different strategy can be very difficult. As a consequence, the change is often made too late, when a crisis, brought about by the imminent failure of the original strategy, triggers dramatic action.

Commitment and Flexibility   Many firms solve the dilemma of choosing between stability and change by avoiding commitments to either strategy. Instead of making resource investments that commit them to either strategy, they try to remain sufficiently flexible to be able to choose whichever strategy turns out to be correct at a later date.[28] Although firms should avoid commitments that can economically be deferred, the choice between commitment and flexibility often involves a fundamental trade-off that cannot be avoided and has no general solution.

By committing to a strategy and making irreversible resource investments to support it, a firm is locked into that strategy. This is dangerous if there is uncertainty as to whether or not the strategy is appropriate. But not making the investment is also dangerous because it carries with it the threat of being locked out. By not investing, the firm allows others to preempt it, or, if there are strong path dependencies and the firm fails to make early investments, it may not be able to make later ones. Further, many resources require ongoing investment to stay viable. Once a firm stops a research program, for example, it may be very difficult to restart it later.[29] Similarly, failing to maintain customer relations can make it prohibitively expensive to reenter an industry.

As wrenching as these dilemmas may sound, it is important to recognize the role uncertainty plays in creating the opportunity for strategic gain. If all decisions were made with perfect information from the start, strategies would tend to converge and excess returns might not be possible. Although it is popular to fret about strategic uncertainty, doing so must not obscure its powerful role in creating strategic asymmetries and competitive advantage.[30]

---

[28]Ibid.

[29]Wesley M. Cohen and D. Levinthal, "Absorptive Capacity: A New Perspective on Learning and Innovation," *Administrative Science Quarterly*, March 1990, pp. 128-52.

[30]Jay Barney, "Strategic Factor Markets," addressed the role of expectations and luck in business strategy. P.J. Schoemaker, "Strategy, Complexity, and Economic Rent," *Management Science*, October 1990, pp. 1178-92; and R. Amit and P.J. Schoemaker, "Strategic Assets and Organizational Rent," *Strategic Management Journal*, 1993, pp. 33-46 also provide compelling accounts of the dilemma.

Upgrading Resources

When approached with the kind of systematic rigor implied by the tests described above, the resources of many firms will fail to make the grade. The tests of value are strenuous, and few firms that apply them rigorously will be able to demonstrate conclusively that their resources pass with flying colors. For these firms, doing more of what they are already doing is unlikely to be a sufficient plan for superior performance.

Even those few firms that do possess "crown jewels" have to recognize that the twin threats of Schumpeterian competition—imitation and substitution—make most competitive advantages, and the value of the resources on which they are based, temporary. This challenges firms to struggle ceaselessly to upgrade their resources in a race that has no finish line, or else risk being overwhelmed in the "gale of creative destruction" that Schumpeter described so well.

The quality of a firm's resource base can be upgraded in a number of ways, including: **strengthening existing resources** by increasing their quality; **adding complementary resources** that enhance the firm's position in its existing markets; and **developing new resources** that enable the firm to enter new, more attractive industries.

The Ford Motor Company provides an excellent example of a company that has deliberately moved to strengthen its organizational capabilities in the last decade. Through concerted effort, the firm has made dramatic improvements in quality control and customer service. This was done by reengineering these functions, changing organizational routines, and resetting measurement yardsticks. Intel, on the other hand, has added a new resource, brand identity, to its corporate arsenal: "Intel Inside" is intended to complement the firm's technological base and provide an added degree of protection now that competitors, such as AMD, are imitating its technology, and others, such as Motorola, are using substitute technology.

Upgrading resources is often best done internally. Attempting to acquire the desired resources in a market transaction would generally involve purchasing an entire business, parts of which the firm may have no interest in. Moreover, in an aggressive market for corporate control, unless the company can bring something unique to an acquisition, it is difficult to avoid dissipating the profits it would hope to eventually earn from those resources.

Nucor, a successful U.S. steel company, provides an instructive example of a firm that has sequentially upgraded its resources (see Figure 2–6).[31] In the 1960s, Nucor was a small manufacturer of steel joints. Intent on diversifying out of a very competitive industry, it decided to invest in the new steel minimill technology. Continually improving its manufacturing capabilities as it accumulated experience and opened additional minimills, Nucor was a major player in bar steel by the mid-1980s. As that market became saturated, Nucor decided to apply its new-found continuous process skills to commercialize a new technology: continuous thin slab casting. Success with this technology enabled Nucor to enter the sheet steel market. Its next challenge was to diversify geographically, which it accomplished by opening a joint venture minimill in Southeast Asia. It then took its skill in international management and invested in a Jamaican plant for the direct reduction of iron ore. At each stage, Nucor leveraged its existing capabilities into a new product or process. This required it to master a new skill, which it could then deploy in a new product market.

---

[31]Ghemawat, Pankaj and Standler, Henricus J. III, "Nucor at a Crossroads," Harvard Business School case number 9-793-039.

▲ FIGURE 2–6   Nucor Steel

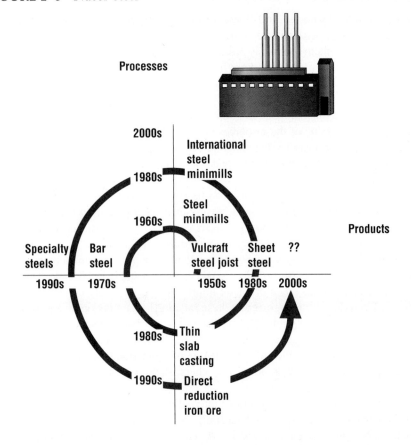

If an incremental strategy to upgrade resources takes on a single challenge each time, while otherwise drawing on existing corporate resources, it can become a remorseless and relatively low-risk process of improvement.

Leveraging Resources

When a firm is not fully employing its valuable resources in its existing markets, the last step in a resource-based strategy is to leverage those resources into other segments or industries where they may create value. Failure to do so would mean that some of the firm's most valuable resources are being underutilized and that, as a consequence, firm value is not being maximized. In many analysts' view, this was the situation at the Walt Disney Company in the years following Walt's death. Not surprisingly, the company was made a takeover target by investors who recognized its underutilized potential.

The leveraging of resources into new markets changes the scope of the firm and represents a transition from business-level to corporate strategy. This critical step is the focus of the next two chapters.

▲ RECOMMENDED READINGS

Amit, R., and P.J. Schoemaker. "Strategic Assets and Organizational Rent." *Strategic Management Journal*, 1993, pp. 33–46.

Barney, J.B. "Firm Resources and Sustained Competitive Advantage." *Journal of Management*, 1991, pp. 99–120.

Barney, J.B. "Organizational Culture: Can It Be a Source of Sustained Competitive Advantage?" *Academy of Management Review*, 1986, pp. 656–65.

Barney, J.B. "Strategic Factor Markets: Expectations, Luck, and Business Strategy." *Management Science*, 1986, pp. 1231–41.

Collis, D.J. "How Valuable Are Organizational Capabilities?" *Strategic Management Journal*, 1994, pp. 143–52.

Collis, D.J. and C. A. Montgomery. "Competing on Resources: Strategy in the 1990s." *Harvard Business Review*, 1995, pp. 118–28.

Conner, K. "A Historical Comparison of Resource-Based Theory and Five Schools of Thought within Industrial Organization: Do We Have a New Theory of the Firm?" *Journal of Management*, 1991, pp. 333–87.

Dierickx, I., and K. Cool. "Asset Stock Accumulation and Sustainability of Competitive Advantage." *Management Science*, 1989, pp. 1504–11.

Ghemawat, P. *Commitment.* New York: Free Press, 1991.

Leonard-Barton, D. "Core Capabilities and Core Rigidities: A Paradox in Managing New Product Development." *Strategic Management Journal*, 1992, pp. 111–25.

Peteraf, M.A. "The Cornerstones of Competitive Advantage: A Resource-Based View." *Strategic Management Journal*, 1993, pp. 179–91.

Porter, M.E. *Competitive Advantage.* New York: Free Press, 1985.

Prahalad, C.K., and G. Hamel. "The Core Competence of the Corporation." *Harvard Business Review*, 1990, pp. 79–91.

Rumelt, R.P. "Theory, Strategy, and Entrepreneurship." In *The Competitive Challenge,* ed. D.J. Teece. Cambridge, MA: Ballinger, 1987.

Schoemaker, P.J. "Strategy, Complexity, and Economic Rent." *Management Science,* October 1990, pp. 1178–92.

Schumpeter, J.A. *The Theory of Economic Development.* Cambridge, MA: Harvard University Press, 1934.

Teece, D.J., G. Pisano, and A. Shuen. "Dynamic Capabilities and Strategic Management." Harvard Business School working paper, revised 1994.

Wernerfelt, B. "A Resource-Based View of the Firm." *Strategic Management Journal,* 1984, pp. 171–80.

Winter, S.G. "Four Rs of Profitability: Rents, Resources, Routines and Replication." In *Resource-Based and Evolutionary Theories of the Firm: Towards a Synthesis,* ed. C.A. Montgomery. Boston: Kluwer Academic Publishers, 1995, pp. 147–78.

BUSINESS STRATEGY AND INDUSTRY ANALYSIS

▲ STRATEGY IDENTIFICATION

The concept of business level strategy was first articulated in the 1960s and 1970s by a number of business policy scholars.[1] Central to their ideas was the notion that firms needed to adopt a unified approach to their activities and resource allocation decisions. Rather than haphazardly allowing each function to pursue its own objectives, a strategy could align all of a firm's functional policies and plans in a coherent pattern, directed toward the fulfillment of the firm's overarching objectives. The value of the strategy, then, would come from eliminating inconsistencies in behavior and making the firm's activities mutually reinforcing.

This notion was depicted in what came to be called the **strategy wheel**. The hub of the wheel was the vision for the firm and the competitive advantage that it sought to achieve. The spokes of the wheel represented the policies and plans of the separate functions. As in a wheel, these emanated from, and were aligned by, the hub. (See Figure B–1).

For a business, defining what is at the hub of its strategy wheel is clearly the most critical part of strategy formulation. To do this—to identify the vision and competitive advantage the firm will pursue, it is necessary to carefully match the company's (**S**)trengths and (**W**)eaknesses to the (**O**)pportunities and (**T**)hreats presented by its environment (see Figure B–2). This approach called **SWOT**, still underlies many contemporary approaches to strategic planning.

---

[1]For example, see E.P. Learned, C. Roland Christensen, and Kenneth Andrews, *Business Policy: Text and Cases* (Burr Ridge, IL: Irwin, 1965); H. Igor Ansoff, *Corporate Strategy: An Analytical Approach to Business Policy for Growth and Expansion* (New York: McGraw-Hill, 1965).

48

▲ FIGURE B–1   The Strategy Wheel

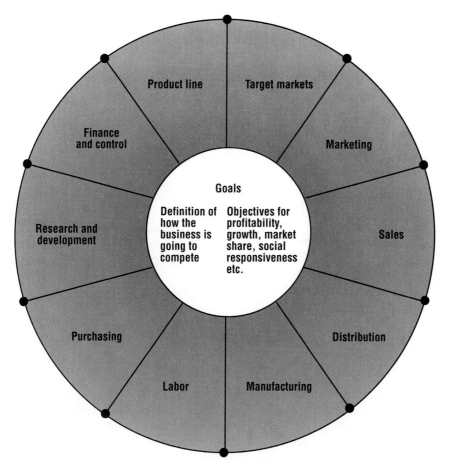

Source: Michael E. Porter, *Competitive Strategy* (New York: Free Press, 1980), pp. xvii.

The central concept here is the notion of *fit* between the unique capabilities of a company and the competitive requirements of an industry. The challenge for management is to choose or create a market position where the company's distinctive competence and resources could produce a competitive advantage.

▲ INDUSTRY ANALYSIS

A rigorous examination of a firm's external environment was systematized in the methodology of industry analysis.[2] Careful industry analysis can help establish whether a particular industry is likely to prove attractive to the average competitor; it can also shed light on profit

---

[2]Substantial portions of this appendix draw on D. Collis and P. Ghemawat, "Industry Analysis: Understanding Industry Structure and Dynamics," in *The Portable MBA in Strategy*, eds. L. Fahey and R.M. Randall (New York: Wiley & Sons, 1994), pp. 171–194.

▲ FIGURE B–2   SWOT Analysis

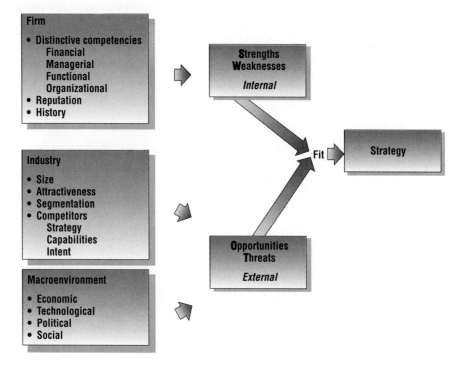

differences among the competitors in that industry. More broadly, industry analysis illuminates the competitive landscape in a way that aids the formulation of effective strategies.

The methodology is most often used to assess the prospects for long-run average industry profitability. As Figure B–3 shows, this can vary widely across industries. A substantial amount of research indicates that the profit potential of an industry is bounded by basic conditions that are largely exogenous, such as the price elasticity of demand and the production technology. The extent to which such profit potential is actually realized by the industry then depends on its internal structure, such as its concentration level, and on the strategies adopted by competitors.

By far the most popular application of these ideas is Michael Porter's "five forces" framework for assessing average industry profitability (see Figure B–4).

The Degree of Rivalry

The intensity of rivalry is the most obvious of the five forces in an industry, and the one that strategists have focused on historically. The structural determinants of the degree of rivalry in a industry are numerous. One set of conditions concerns the number and relative size of competitors. The more concentrated the industry, for example, the more likely it is that competitors will recognize their mutual interdependence and so restrain their rivalry. The presence of a dominant competitor rather than a set of equally balanced competitors also tends to lessen rivalry because the dominant player can set industry prices and discipline defectors. In contrast, equally sized players often compete vigorously to outdo each other and gain advantage.

▲ FIGURE B–3   Profitability by Manufacturing Subsector, 1971-1990.

	Return on Equity	Return on Assets	Return on Sales
Drugs	21.4 %	11.8%	13.1%
Printing and publishing	15.5	7.1	5.5
Food and kindred products	15.2	6.6	3.9
Chemicals and allied products	15.1	7.5	7.2
Petroleum and allied products	13.1	6.5	6.5
Instruments and related products	12.9	7.2	6.9
Industrial chemicals and synthetics	12.9	6.2	6.1
Paper and allied products	12.5	6.0	5.1
Aircraft, guided missiles, and parts	12.4	4.1	3.7
Fabricated metal products	12.3	5.7	3.7
Motor vehicles and equipment	11.6	5.6	3.7
Rubber and misc. plastic products	11.6	5.1	3.4
Electric and electronic equipment	11.5	5.4	4.4
Machinery, except electrical	11.1	5.8	3.4
Stone, clay, and glass products	10.4	4.8	4.0
Textile mill products	9.3	4.3	2.5
Nonferrous metals	8.3	3.9	3.6
Iron and steel	3.9	1.5	1.3

Source: Anita McGahan, "Selected Profitability Data on U.S. Industries and Companies," Harvard Business School 9-792-066,©1992.

A second set of attributes that influence rivalry is related to the industry's basic conditions. In capital-intensive industries, for example, low levels of capacity utilization encourage firms to engage in price competition to fill their plants. More generally, high fixed costs, excess capacity, slow growth, and lack of product differentiation all increase the degree of rivalry.

The degree of rivalry also has behavioral determinants. If competitors have diverse objectives or attach high strategic stakes to their positions in an industry, they are likely to compete aggressively. For example, Cummins Engine, a largely family-owned firm that specializes in diesel engines for trucks, unilaterally cut prices almost in half in the early 1980s to stop Japanese competitors from getting market share, even though this condemned the industry to negative average profitability for nearly a decade.

The Threat of Entry

The key concept in analyzing the threat of entry is entry barriers, which act to prevent an influx of firms into an industry whenever profits, adjusted for the cost of capital, rise above zero. In the restaurant industry, for example, if a new format such as mesquite grilling becomes popular, the limited height of entry barriers allows almost any interested party to open a mesquite grill restaurant, eroding the format's profitability. In contrast, entry barriers exist whenever it is difficult or uneconomic for an outsider to replicate the position of the incumbents.

▲ FIGURE B–4   Elements of Industry Structure

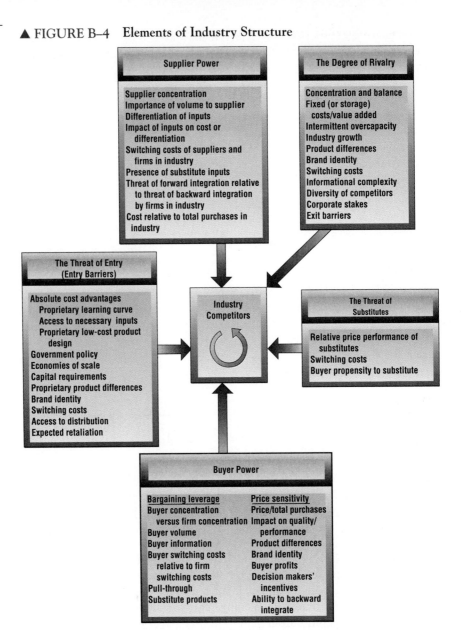

Source: Reprinted with the permission of The Free Press, a division of Simon & Schuster Inc., from *Competitive Strategy: Techniques for Analyzing Industries and Competitors* by Michael E. Porter. Copyright©1980 by The Free Press.

Figure B–4 illustrates that entry barriers can take many different forms. Some barriers reflect intrinsic physical or legal obstacles to entry. It would probably be hard to discover a diamond mine rich enough to justify entry into the diamond industry. Similarly, the existence and efficacy of patents on aspartame (Nutrasweet) and other artificial sweetners have, until recently, impeded entry into that industry.

The most common entry barriers, however, involve the scale and the investment required to enter an industry as an efficient competitor. For example, no one is likely to enter the aluminum industry on an integrated basis, because an efficient integrated facility would cost several billion dollars and account for 5 percent or more of worldwide demand. Similarly, when incumbent firms have well-established brand names and clearly differentiated products, it may be prohibitively expensive for a potential entrant to undertake the marketing campaign necessary for effective introduction of a competing product.

The Threats of Substitutes

The existence of substitutes that perform the same functions as the products or services of the industry being analyzed caps the amount of value an industry can create. When high-fructose corn syrup (HFCS) was replacing sugar as the sweetner in soft drinks, Pepsi and Coca-Cola were willing to switch only when the cost of the HFCS needed to sweeten a can of cola fell below the cost of sugar. The threat of substitution from sugar therefore capped the price of HFCS.

The analysis of the threat of demand-side substitution must focus on the customer function performed, not just on physically similar products. Overnight delivery services, which provide rapid document delivery, must consider facsimile machines to be an important substitute, even though the two use entirely different means to achieve the same end.

Buyer Power

Buyer power allows customers to squeeze industry margins by pressing competitors to reduce prices or to increase the level of service offered without recompense.

Probably the most important determinant of buyer power is the size and concentration of the customers. In its heyday, for example, General Motors (GM) enjoyed enormous bargaining power because it dominated the automobile industry; it regularly threatened its component suppliers with loss of its business. Those suppliers, desperate to avoid losing such a large fraction of their business, often agreed to price or nonprice concessions. GM's bargaining power was also enhanced by other factors, including the extent to which it was informed about suppliers' costs, the credibility of its threat to integrate backward into suppliers' businesses, and the relatively low costs it would incur if it switched suppliers.

It is often useful to distinguish buyer power from the willingness or incentive to use that power. The U.S. government is one of the most powerful buyers in the market by virtue of its size; yet, unfortunately for U.S. taxpayers, it has not historically been one of the most price-sensitive purchasers.

It is necessary to look at a set of behavioral conditions to understand why some firms have the incentive to use their inherent purchasing power. Prime among these conditions is the share of the buyer's cost that is accounted for by the products in question. Purchasing decisions naturally focus on larger-cost items first. Suppliers of incidental products can, therefore, often escape the keenest attention of purchasing agents.

Of almost equal importance is the risk of failure associated with the use of a product. Purchase decisions for items critical to a whole system's operation, such as oil-rig blowout prevention equipment, are usually influenced by such risks of failure, which substantially reduce the buyer's price-sensitivity.

Supplier Power

Supplier power is the mirror image of buyer power. It varies with the size and concentration of suppliers relative to their customers, and with the degree of differentiation in the inputs supplied. The most profitable players involved in the personal computer (PC) industry, for example, are not IBM, Dell, or other manufacturers, but Intel (microprocessors) and Microsoft (operating systems), which have virtual monopolies on the supply of critical components for IBM-compatible PCs.

The acid test of supplier power is whether suppliers are able to set prices that reflect the value of their inputs to the industry and not just their own production costs. Suppliers of many commodity chemicals and other raw materials, for example, manage to pass along cost increases without necessarily possessing supplier power. Their margins may already be very low, and a price increase simply serves to keep them in business at low rates of return. What must be tested instead is whether suppliers are able to extract a substantial portion of the value created in the industries that they serve.

Summary

The inherent attractiveness of an industry—measured by its expected average profitability—is not determined by just one factor. Rather, it reflects the interaction of the competitive forces described above. Using the factors in Figure B–4 as a checklist to determine the strength of each of those competitive forces is, therefore, a critical part of a thorough industry analysis.

▲ GENERIC STRATEGIES

To understand how to achieve a competitive advantage and how to generalize about the relative position of individual firms within an industry, Porter developed the concept of generic strategies, categories of strategy that follow particular patterns. At the business level, Porter identified two basic types of competitive advantage: **low cost and differentiation**. A firm with a successful low cost strategy has the ability to "design, produce, and market a comparable product more efficiently than its competitors."[3] For prices at or near those of competitors, the resulting lower cost translates into superior returns. In the 1970s, for example, Du Pont built a dominant position in the titanium dioxide market by exploiting superior technology, scale economies, and accumulated experience to achieve the low-cost position. Du Pont then nearly doubled its market share, to 60 percent, using aggressive pricing to squeeze out smaller, less efficient competitors.[4]

Differentiation is the "ability to provide unique and superior value to the buyer in terms of product quality, special features, or after-sale service."[5] Differentiation allows a firm to command a premium price, which leads to superior profitability, provided that costs are comparable to those of competitors. Gillette, for example, competes with a differentiation strategy in disposable razors by exploiting its superior technology, reputation, and broad distribution.

---

[3]M. Porter, *The Competitive Advantage of Nations* (New York: Free Press, 1990).
[4]P. Ghemawat, *Commitment* (New York: Free Press, 1991).
[5]M. Porter, *The Competitive Advantage of Nations*.

Although the key success factors of these strategies differ, Porter warns that "any successful strategy must pay close attention to *both* types of advantage while maintaining a clear commitment to superiority on one. A low-cost producer must offer acceptable quality and service to avoid nullifying its cost advantage through the necessity to discount prices, while a differentiator's cost position must not be so far above that of competitors as to offset its price premium."[6]

The other important aspect of strategic choice is **competitive scope**, or the breadth of segments the firm targets within its industry. Serving different segments requires different strategies and calls for different capabilities. Thus, the type and the scope of advantage can be combined into the notion of generic strategies (see Figure B–5).

In the consumer electronics industry, for example, Sony is a broad differentiator, with a well-known brand and successful history of product innovation. Bang and Olufsen, the Scandinavian firm, is a focused differentiator serving only those customers who seek modern Scandinavian design. Matsushita (which sells in the United States under the Panasonic brand) pursues a broad, low-cost strategy, aiming to match Sony's innovations within six months at lower cost. And any number of small Chinese or Malaysian consumer electronics companies use focused, low-cost strategies, producing a limited range of cheaply manufactured items to be sold by mass merchants under private label.

Each of these strategies requires the internal alignment of a set of functional activities in support of the overall objective of the strategy. Across generic strategies, these patterns differ in predictable ways. The idea of generic strategies, therefore, underscores many of the original principles of business strategy. It emphasizes the consistency of a firm's activities and the need to tie each to the firm's overall mission. It also stresses the importance of not getting stuck in the middle—being a little of this and a little of that—and ultimately failing to build a distinctive competence that creates a competitive advantage.

▲ FIGURE B–5   Generic Strategies

Source: Porter, Michael. *The Competitive Advantage of Nations* (New York: The Free Press, 1990), p. 39.

[6]Ibid.

SCALE AND SCOPE WITHIN AN INDUSTRY

▲ INTRODUCTION

Once a firm has chosen a strategy within an industry and identified the valuable resources that will underpin its competitive advantage, the challenge shifts to implementing that strategy: investing in or internally accumulating the required resources and deploying them appropriately in that product market. This may take a number of years, during which time competitors will be pursuing their own strategies. In due course, as investments and other long-term commitments come to fruition, market leaders will emerge, having adopted what turn out to be the winning strategies for the industry. At this juncture, it may appear that, for the triumphant firms, the hard work is over.

On occasion this is so, and the industry proceeds with few perturbations. In such cases, resource barriers lock in competitive positions, external conditions remain stable, and the market experiences a long-term equilibrium. In most cases, however, the environment is not so placid. As Schumpeter warned, it is rare for markets to experience a long term equilibrium with few disturbances. Firms at a competitive disadvantage will be striving to dislodge the market leader. Technology and customer tastes may change and radically alter either supply or demand conditions. Such upheavals disturb industry equilbria, create the need for new resources, and provide opportunities for competitors to craft new strategies that are better suited to the altered industry environment.

The experiences of two companies—Maytag and Iowa Beef—dramatically illustrate the vulnerability of pursuing static single-business strategies in dynamic industry contexts. (See "The Advantages and Limitations of Successful Generic Strategies" I and II.) Each of these firms was once very successful pursuing a classic generic strategy: Maytag as a focused-differentiated

Iowa Beef

Iowa Beef, later known as IBP, entered the U.S. beef industry in 1961, when technological innovations were transforming the industry into a mass-production business and leading to its relocation from the stockyards of Chicago to the cattle-rearing states. By 1980, Iowa Beef was the low-cost leader, running its slaughtering processes at about half the labor cost of its older competitors. Large-scale facilities, highly automated factory line procedures, and integrated transportation enabled Iowa Beef to realize significant economies of scale, yielding it an overall advantage of up to 20 percent of industry average costs.

Although IBP's cost structure remained the best in the industry, competitors narrowed the gap considerably as they made acquisitions to approach IBP's scale and invested in comparable facilities. In addition, the major competitors, ConAgra and Cargill, were diversified into a broader variety of animal proteins and forward integrated into branded products. They also backward integrated into the ownership of feedlots for livestock. At the same time, market demand was changing as the country became more health conscious and the price of chicken dropped sharply in relation to beef. In response, IBP's only strategic move was entry into the pork industry in 1982.

Thus, while its competitors worked to neutralize IBP's distinctive competence and exploited economies of scope though product diversification and vertical integration, IBP held fast to its old ways. Ironically, IBP's overwhelming success in executing a low-cost strategy and its zeal to maintain distinctive capabilities in that race may have been partially responsible for its failure to cultivate a broader resource base and a more dynamic strategy. When floated on the market by former parent Occidental in 1991, IBP was worth less than $800 million, even though its sales were over $9 billion.

Source: Collis, D.J. and Donahue, N., "IBP and the U.S. Meat Industry" Harvard Business School case number 9-391-0068

ducer of laundry equipment, and Iowa Beef as the low-cost beef processor. At the peak of its success, each firm had a distinct advantage relative to its rivals. In time, however, both were challenged by competitors that matched or nearly matched those original advantages while simultaneously benefiting from scope economies that Maytag and Iowa Beef could not duplicate.

These are more than bad-luck tales. They illustrate characteristic challenges that most successful business strategies will face over time. Early market leaders have often specialized and have established a clear advantage either as a differentiator or low-cost producer. To address their disadvantage, in typical Schumpeterian fashion, rivals will attempt to imitate the "winning" strategy, invalidate the leader's advantage by changing the rules of the game, or both. As we will discuss in this chapter, this is often done by exploiting scale or scope economies in an industry. These economies can play an important role in reconfiguring industry structure and transforming competitive strategies.

PRINCIPLES

▲ DIMENSIONS OF SCOPE

The principles that underlie expansion within an industry are similar to those that underlie expansion across industries, the subject of the next chapter. To grasp these ideas, it

The Advantages and Limitations of Successful Generic Strategies II

Maytag

Maytag followed a very different but nonetheless classic generic strategy for many years as a focused differentiated producer. The company enjoyed a reputation as the quality leader in the major home appliance industry for its premium washers and dryers. It succeeded in differentiating its products in terms of durability and reliability, embodying this position in the company's advertisements with "Ol' Lonely," the solitary Maytag repairman who never had any work to do. It also earned number one quality rankings from *Consumer Reports* every year from 1974 to 1983. To capitalize on its perceived differentiation, Maytag typically priced its appliances at a 10–15 percent premium. Accordingly, Maytag's operating structure was geared toward high-quality appliance production.

Over the course of the 10-year period during which Maytag dominated the *Consumer Reports* rankings, the gap in the quality ratings steadily narrowed, while the 10–15 percent price differential remained intact. Partly this was due to the fact that Maytag remained primarily a washer/dryer manufacturer (with some involvement in dishwashers and disposals), while its leading competitors exploited scope economies across a broad line of major home appliances, including dishwashers, refrigerators/freezers, conventional and microwave ovens, ranges, and air conditioners, which they sold under several brands at multiple price points. Meanwhile, as household saturation levels rose steadily for most appliances, overall industry growth slowed.

In time, Maytag chose to broaden its product line, acquiring brands like Magic Chef and Admiral to establish a presence in a broader range of lower-priced appliances. Reputations and cultures clashed, however, as Maytag struggled to raise quality standards in the new acquisitions. And although Maytag stressed that it had anticipated the need to address quality issues in the newly acquired brands, the difficulties associated with doing so showed up in a 40 percent drop in Maytag's stock price, and a decline in its *Consumer Reports* ratings.

Although the timing and implementation of Maytag's actions can be criticized, on a more fundamental level the firm's experience raises questions about a focused differentiated firm's ability to resist broad-scope competitors and then to leverage its own assets and capabilities across a broad line of products. That is, could a firm that had so closely aligned itself with laundry equipment transfer its brand and expertise to ranges and refrigerators when the competitive dynamics demanded it? How long would such a transition take? Questions such as these underscore the need for a dynamic view of business strategy and firm scope.

Source: Collis, D.J. and Donahue, N., "Maytag in 1984" Harvard Business School case number 9-389-055.

---

is helpful to think of the resources that support the initial business as a nucleus within a broader competitive space. Expansion, or contraction, begins from this core and proceeds along three dimensions: **geography, product market, and vertical integration**. The scope of any firm, at any time, can be represented in these three dimensions, whether or not the firm explicitly selected that configuration (Figure 3–1).

It is important to recognize that firms must actively grapple with scope questions throughout their histories, regardless of their size or success. Microsoft's first breakthrough was as a supplier of the DOS PC operating system to computer OEMs. During the eighties, it diversified into the applications software business with the introduction of Excel and Word, deepening its upstream activities in programming and extending its

▲ FIGURE 3–1   The Three Dimensions of Corporate Scope

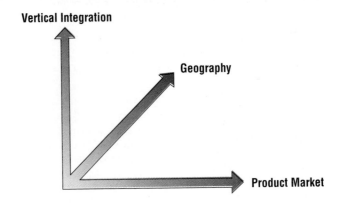

activities downstream by marketing directly to home users. All the while it continued to up-grade its original business, creating Windows to replace DOS and introducing operating systems for networking. Today, the company continues to struggle with issues of scope: backward integrating into the ownership of content for multimedia applications, aggressively expanding overseas, and striving to add new products, as exemplified by its failed takeover of Intuit, the leading provider of tax software.

Too often, firms box themselves into a narrow view of their own opportunities and fail to see alternative directions that may be available. Many costly mistakes could have been avoided if firms, such as Federal Express, had recognized that there are three possible dimensions for expansion. Instead of pouring hundreds of millions of dollars into a failed diversification for the provision of facsimile services in the early eighties, Federal Express could have preempted competitors in the international document delivery business. Instead, when it finally did go global, Federal Express had to incur additional losses in the hundreds of millions of dollars as it struggled to catch up with the entrenched leader, DHL. Conversely, Marks and Spencer's 30-year attempt at international expansion seemed to blind it to valuable diversification opportunities in other retailing segments in the United Kingdom.

Expansion within an Industry

For most firms, expansion begins within their original industry,[1] by vertically integrating, increasing the scale of output, producing closely related products, or entering new geographies. Firms often pursue such expansions proactively, to increase their size and enhance their competitive positions. In other cases, the same moves are taken reactively, to defend a firm's position as others move to exploit scale and scope advantages.

---

[1]The definition of a discrete market or industry is one of the thorniest issues in strategy (D. Abell, *Defining the Business: The Starting Point of Strategic Planning*, Englewood Cliffs, NJ: Prentice-Hall, 1979). There are always some interactive effects (cross-price elasticities) among related industries. Boundaries, therefore, are ultimately defined somewhat arbitrarily, according to similarities among customers, technologies, competitors, and channels of distribution (M.E. Porter, *Competitive Strategy*, New York: Free Press, 1980).

The underlying scale and scope economies in an industry are often apparent to all competitors. For example, the benefits of size are well understood in oil refining.[2] In other cases, the economies may be inherent in an industry, but either not well recognized, or not exploited because firms' attention has been elsewhere. In such situations, creative strategic moves can unlock these latent sources of advantage and dramatically alter industry dynamics. Further, a new sources of scale and scope economies continually arise as economic and technological conditions change. It is therefore important for firms to continually reassess the existence of, and potential to exploit, such economies.

▲ ECONOMIES OF SCALE

When the average cost declines as more units of a good or service are produced, economies of scale exist. These can be found in any one of a firm's activities, from research to service, and have occurred in a wide range of industries.

Single-site economies often occur in physical production processes and are related to the size of the manufacturing unit. When technological scale economies exist, for example, capacity can be increased at a greater rate than the cost of the plant and equipment. The volume of liquid through a pipe, for example, is squared for each doubling in radius, while the area of material from which it is built increases only linearly. Such an effect is pronounced in cement manufacturing, petroleum refining, iron ore reduction, and a host of other processing industries. Economies may also occur in other functions as fixed costs are spread across higher volumes.[3]

Scale also allows specialization, which may be of considerable benefit to a firm. With higher volume production, individual employees can focus their attention on a narrower range of activities and develop or employ more specialized skills. Moreover, highly skilled and expensive labor may only be fully employed when there is sufficient scale of production.

In most industries, dominant firms operate more than one plant or establishment, suggesting there may also be important **multiple-site economies**. These are more likely to be found in R&D and marketing than in the physical production process. Examples include distribution systems and brand names that can be used to sell and distribute products and services from multiple locations. Multiple-site firms may also benefit from economies of risk-spreading and lower capital costs. Finally, larger organizations may be more successful in attracting and holding highly talented people, the cost of which can be spread across a larger volume of output (see "Beaten By Scale").

Scale economies in part determine the maximum number of firms that can compete profitably in an industry. When the **minimum efficient scale** (MES) of production is large in relation to demand, the industry can support relatively few players. Significant multi-site economies also increase the market share each competitor must command to remain viable. Table 3–1 shows estimates of single-site and multiple-site economies in a number of industries and the required share of the U.S. market a firm would need to maintain a competitive cost structure.

---

[2]Alfred D. Chandler, *Scale and Scope* (Cambridge, MA: Harvard University Press, 1990).
[3]F.M. Scherer, *Industrial Market Structure and Economic Performance,* (Boston, M.A.: Houghton Mifflin, 1980), pp. 82–83.

Beaten by Scale:
Taxman and H&R Block in the Tax-Preparation Industry

A contrast between Taxman, Inc., a small, fledgling tax preparation company, and H&R Block illustrates the strategic significance scale effects can have in a rapidly growing service industry.

In the early 1970s, Taxman and H&R Block were competitors in the low-to-middle end of the individual tax-preparation market. Compared to Taxman's 31 offices, H&R Block had 3,286, and its total costs per return were about half of Taxman's. This discrepancy was due primarily to Block's sizeable scale advantages in office management, advertising, and quality assurance (corporate reputation and a year-round presence to stand behind the work it performed). Significantly, within individual offices and across regions, Block had the scale that was necessary to fully employ its highest paid workers. An area manager could oversee five offices, an office manager could oversee numerous tax preparers, and tax preparers could spend all their time doing tax returns, rather than waiting for business to appear or performing less critical operations such as collating and mailing the returns. (Part-time high school students did these tasks.)

As Block's business grew, these advantages increased. Profits were reinvested in the business and used to support additional growth. In time, Block had established a formidable first-mover advantage, building a scale and cost structure that proved increasingly difficult for competitors to thwart or imitate.

▲ TABLE 3–1   The Importance of Scale: Minimum Efficient Plant Sizes

Industry	MES Plant Size as Percentage of U.S. Consumption	Percentage Elevation of Unit Costs (at 1/3 MES)	Number of Plants Needed to Have Not More than a "Slight" Overall Handicap	Share of U.S. Market Required in 1967
Beer brewing	3.4%	5.0%	3–4	10–14%
Cigarettes	6.6	2.2	1–2	6–12
Fabric weaving	0.2	7.6	3–6	1
Paints	1.4	4.4	1	1–2
Petroleum Refining	1.9	4.8	2–3	4–6
Shoes	0.2	1.5	3–6	1
Glass bottles	1.5	11.0	3–4	4–6
Cement	1.7	26.0	1	2
Steel	2.6	11.0	1	3
Bearings	1.4	8.0	3–5	4–7
Refrigerators	14.1	6.5	4–8*	14–20
Storage batteries	1.9	4.6	1	2

*including other appliances

Experience Curve

Whereas economies of scale refer to cost reductions that accompany increases in total current output, a related concept, the **learning**, or **experience curve**, refers to cost reductions that occur as *cumulative* volume rises. Studies have shown that average unit production costs in many industries decline 10 percent to 30 percent with each doubling of cumulated output. Figure 3–2 illustrates the phenomenon in the context of computer chip production.

Although the concept of experience curves emerged out of a manufacturing environment, it is important to note that the underlying logic is also applicable to service firms (see "Saving Lives and Money"). Initially, the effect was attributed to worker learning alone. Later studies identified other factors that contributed to the experience curve, such as ongoing engineering and technical improvements. As a consequence, firms are now more likely to identify broader organizational experience curves for each of their processes.[4]

The important difference between scale and experience effects is that scale, in principle, can be quickly replicated by building a large plant, whereas experience must be built through time.[5] Thus, experience effects are classic examples of path dependency: shortcuts and speeded-up processes often fail. Experience effects also explain why it may be difficult to

▲ FIGURE 3–2   70 Percent Experience Curve for Dynamic RAMs

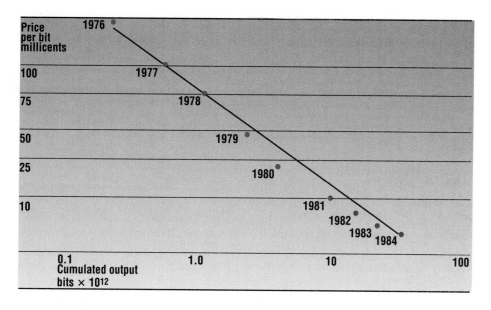

---

[4]D.D. Pattison and C.J. Teplitz, "Are Learning Curves Still Relevant?" *Management Accounting*, February 1989, pp. 37–40
[5]Marvin Lieberman has systematically examined many of the issues of scale and experience within the chemical industry. "The Learning Curve and Pricing in the Chemical Processing Industries," *RAND Journal of Economics*, Summer 1984, pp. 213–28.

Saving Lives and Money: Experience and Its Impact on the Cost of Heart Transplants

In the early 1990s, a multiple regression model was used to analyze the cost patterns associated with 71 heart transplants conducted by a single institution. The model included controls for various preoperative risk factors and differences in individual surgeons' levels of experience. The model predicted that the first heart transplant would cost \$81,297, but would have cost only \$48,431 had it been the 10th. Had it been the 50th, the cost would have been \$25,458.

Arguments already had been made in favor of concentrating certain highly specialized medical procedures in a few facilities. But the findings from this model bolstered an argument to do so based on the cost reduction that would result from exploiting the experience curve at a single hospital.

Source: J. Woods, "The Learning Curve and the Cost of Heart Transplants," *Health Services Research*, June 1992, pp. 219–38.

transfer knowledge across locations even within a firm. To the extent that competence is a function of the firsthand experience of individuals, transfers of knowledge within firms may be as difficult to achieve as those across firms.

Limits to Scale and Experience

Do costs decline indefinitely as scale and experience continue to rise? The answer to this question is no, or industries with sizable scale or experience effects would be dominated by a single firm. Even within the range in which such effects are possible, many are not smooth functions; they occur in discrete steps, often with considerable plateaus in between. Further, physical properties often limit efficiency gains beyond certain levels. Cement kilns, for example, experience unstable internal aerodynamics above 7 million barrels per year capacity.[6] Indeed, in most processes, **diseconomies of scale** set in at some point, and costs *rise* rather than fall as volume increases. This may be due to logistics bottlenecks, coordination costs, or worker motivation problems.

There are also strategic risks to consider. Exploiting scale economies requires considerable investment, often in specialized assets, that firms expect to recoup through cost savings realized over extended periods of time. If tastes change, input prices alter, or competitive strategies shift, these sunk investments may lock a firm into an unattractive strategy and not be recovered. Henry Ford's effort to automate large-scale production of a standard Model T in the mammoth, vertically integrated River Rouge plant, met this unhappy end. When customers flocked to the variety of models General Motors introduced, Ford's highly efficient but rigid production process, which (almost literally) converted iron ore and sand into a finished car, could not manufacture the kind of products customers were demanding. Ford had to shut down the plant for nearly 12 months to retool, and has never regained its leadership position in the U.S. automobile market.

---

[6]This example is taken from F.M. Scherer, *Industrial Market Structure and Economic Performance* (Boston: Houghton Mifflin, 1980), p. 84.

Finally, it is not unusual for the magnitude of scale economies to shift over the life of an industry. As technology evolves and industries mature, scale economies often increase in many activities. However, the reverse can also happen. In the steel industry, for example, minimill technology replaced the traditional vertically integrated mills and substantially reduced industry minimum efficient scale. Moreover, these changes do not necessarily occur evenly across all the activities of a firm. Rather than leading to straightforward increases in firm size, changing scale economies may therefore spark the reconfiguration of an industry and the emergence of specialist producers at particular stages in the vertical chain.

Economies of scale exist when average cost declines as a good or service is produced or sold in larger volume.

Economies of scope exist when the cost of producing and selling multiple products together is lower than the cost of producing and selling the same quantity of goods individually.

▲ ECONOMIES OF SCOPE

The size and scope of a firm is influenced not only by the scale economies of its various activities, but also by the presence of **cost savings *across* functions or units**. Economies of scope exist when "it is less costly to combine two or more product lines *in one firm* than to produce them separately."[7] A classic example of scope economies is a sporting goods chain that sells ski equipment in the winter and tennis equipment in the summer, thus utilizing its physical facilities and its purchasing and sales staffs on a year-round basis.[8]

Economists traditionally believed that, to the extent they existed at all, scope economies would be found primarily in a firm's physical production processes. The notion was that a factory that made television sets would be more efficient if it also made computer monitors. This view, however, has been challenged by recent empirical work. U.S. Census Bureau data for the years 1963–82 reveal an upward trend in firm-level diversification, but a persistent decline in plant-level diversification. Examining this data, Frank Gollop and James Monahan concluded that over time, firms are "shifting toward a more diverse portfolio of increasingly homogeneous plants. Technical economies of scope appear to play little role in explaining the measured increase in [firm-level] diversification."[9]

Even though technical economies of scope are not plentiful, scope economies may be occurring in activities that are not directly related to the physical production process, including research and development, sales and marketing, distribution, transportation, and overhead.[10] When R&D, for example, generates knowledge that is applicable to a range of products, it is subject to economies of scope. (See Figure 3–3.)

[7]John C. Panzar and Robert D. Willig, "Economies of Scope," *American Economic Review*, May 1981, p. 268. The relationship is formally expressed as $C(x+y) < C(x) + C(y)$.
[8]Scope economies have to be distinguished from joint production. It is physically impossible to separately produce lamb and wool from sheep, or hydrogen and oxygen from the electrolysis of water. In contrast, Microsoft can choose whether or not to compete in the spreadsheet and the word processing application businesses.
[9]Frank Gollop and J. Monahan, "A Generalized Index of Diversification: Trends in U.S. Manufacturing," *Review of Economics and Statistics*, 1991, pp. 318–30.
[10]M.L. Streitweiser, "The Extent and Nature of Establishment-Level Diversification in 16 U.S. Manufacturing Industries," *Journal of Law & Economics*, October 1991, pp. 503–34.

The role of intangible resources in scope economies has recently received considerable attention. The value of a firm's reputation, for example, can extend across a range of markets. The individual businesses of a firm like General Electric may well benefit from the corporate reputation for integrity and high quality management. More specifically, by using the same brand name on multiple products, a practice called *umbrella branding*, firms put at risk the future sales of all products as bonds for the quality of each product marketed under that name. By doing so, they can lower the average cost of assuring quality while delivering a powerful message to the customer—a clear benefit of scope.[11]

More generally, scope economies explain the value of truly distinctive corporate competences.[12] These may be the result of large investments and may include routines that embrace tacit knowledge and many years of trial and error. The costs incurred in building such competences can be recovered by applying them to a succession of products or markets over time. Thus, the creation of competences can produce sizable scope economies, and so serve as a valuable source of competitive advantage across multiple products.

In summary, scale and scope economies may conceivably occur in any function, and may be due to tangible or intangible factors. However, it is only when increased volume or the joint production of two or more products by one firm leads to demonstrably lower average costs, superior product quality, or both that expanding the size or scope of the firm produces economic gain.

▲ Figure 3–3   The Advantage of Scope Economies

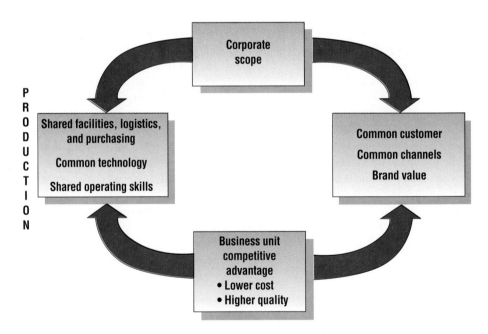

[11]C.A. Montgomery and B. Wernerfelt, "Risk Reduction and Umbrella Branding," *Journal of Business*, 1992, pp. 31–50.
[12]Paul Milgrom and John Roberts, *Economics, Organization, and Management* (Englewood Cliffs, NJ: Prentice Hall, 1992).

▲ OBSTACLES TO EXPLOITING SCALE AND SCOPE

Although the benefits of scale and scope economies can be impressive, they can also be elusive. Simply increasing the volume of a business in no sense guarantees that a firm's cost structure will improve; similarly, combining two related business lines does not mean that product quality will improve or costs will decline.

In some cases, these disappointments are due to poor analysis: some firms simply miscalculate the size of scale or scope benefits that a given strategy may yield.

In other cases, however, the disappointments are due to sheer implementation difficulties. Exploiting scale economies can substantially increase the size of an organization, complicating administrative functions and producing bureaucratic inefficiencies. Scope economies often require profound changes in organizational structure and systems because they depend on sharing of resources and some level of coordination across previously separate units. This places intensive demands on people and their time and introduces inevitable trade-offs and compromises. If the process is mismanaged, net costs may increase rather than decline, and the firm's competitive advantage in each of the products may suffer.[13]

Firms can also fail to exploit scale or scope economies that emerge in an industry because they are locked into a given way of competing. Consider the example of a firm with a leading market position. Over a number of years, it is also likely that the firm developed a set of resources specifically tailored to that strategy. It is likely that the firm's routines, power structure and value system were similarly aligned. Such embedded practices make change difficult for two reasons: they interfere with signals that suggest change is necessary and, in a myriad of ways, impede firms' attempts to do things differently.[14] Thus, while a source of advantage in a firm's initial strategy, these tightly woven systems and processes often constitute "the dark underside of organizational resources," when core capabilities become **core rigidities**.[15]

In such instances, institutionalized capabilities lead to **inertia** (see "Darwin and Sticky Strategies"). This was one of the reasons Maytag resisted moving away from its successful focused differentiation strategy until it was too late. Similarly, IBP's emphasis on scale within a product line made it unlikely that the firm would be the first to assemble a broad product portfolio, and realize the economies of scale it could produce.

These experiences illustrate the double-edged quality of resources: on a firm's ascendancy, they can shield the firm from competition and make it difficult for rivals to close in on its lead; but when a strategy is eventually challenged, they can block the firm's own ability to respond.

---

[13]In Chapter 6 we will describe how firms can structure and organize themselves to realize the benefits of scale and scope without many of the costs that can result.

[14]Richard Rumelt suggests a list of the "five frictions": distorted perception, dulled motivation, failed creative response, action disconnects, and political deadlocks, "Inertia and Transformation" in *Resource-Based and Evolutionary Theories of the Firm: Towards a Synthesis*, Cynthia A. Montgomery, Editor, Boston: Kluwer Academic Press, 1995, pp. 101–132.

[15]D. Leonard-Barton, "Core Capabilities and Core Rigidities: A Paradox in Managing New Product Development," *Strategic Management Journal*, 1992, pp. 111–25.

Darwin and Sticky Strategies

A Darwinian perspective can help us understand firm inertia. Most firms with dominant market positions reached those heights over a number of years. Through experience they developed organizational resources and ways of doing things that proved superior to those of rivals with lesser positions, some of which were forced from the industry. In time, these resources and routines came to embody the firm's competitive advantage and were the very forces that assured its survival. One would not expect, nor necessarily want, such mechanisms to change quickly.

This kind of Darwinian notion is the centerpiece of a stream of research called **population ecology** that applies biological analogies to the growth and survival of populations of firms. As John Freeman explained, this work emphasizes that "all change occurs with friction. Redeploying resources takes

effort, effort that cannot be simultaneously used for productive activity, so change is doubly costly. The more fundamental the change, the more effort it takes." Exogenous shifts, such as new technologies, political upheavals, or dramatic demographic changes, threaten whole populations of incumbent firms that were designed to operate under different conditions. Faced with these challenges, "some organizations adjust; others do not. Failure follows. Opportunity comes with it. That is to say, as existing organizations struggle to deal with this changing world, some succeed and make the adjustment. Others cannot adjust and disappear."

Source: John Freeman, "Business Strategy from the Population Level" in *Resource-Based and Evolutionary Theories of the Firm: Towards a Synthesis*, ed. C.A. Montgomery (Boston: Kluwer Academic Publishers, 1995), pp. 219–50.

PRACTICE

▲ THE SEARCH FOR SCALE AND SCOPE EFFECTS

Managers often refer to economies of scope as synergy, that enticing mathematical equation in which two plus two equals five. Sadly, this concept has been abused and overused in the business press and in managerial plans as well. Experience has exposed countless instances where synergies, once expected, never materialized. The same may be said for scale effects.

Firms often err by expanding into market segments that appear to be related to their existing businesses, but in fact, are quite different. In particular, firms tend to make this mistake when they define relatedness on the basis of product characteristics rather than on resources. Expansion within an industry may sound like an easy route to success, but this enthusiasm often masks the fact that segments in an industry can have different key success factors that prevent the exploitation of scale and scope economies.

Earlier, we identified managerial impediments to the achievement of scale and scope economies. Here, the focus is on the failure of scale and scope effects to materialize because management misjudged them from the start. This often occurs when expansion is based on an impressionistic assessment rather than a more careful analysis of the source and magnitude of expected cost savings.

Identifying Scale and Scope Effects

The fact that scale and scope effects are often difficult to estimate cannot be taken as a license for shoddy analysis. Data-driven analysis of the effects of scale, for example, is possible by comparing cost data between plants of different sizes, or using engineering estimates to simulate the cost of a facility that is different from the current size. Such careful work can go a long way to quantify the extent of scale economies in a business. Similarly, experience curves can be constructed and their slope calculated from data on the past output of a firm or industry.

To evaluate the potential for scope economies between two or more business segments, managers also need a systematic process. This analysis should avoid broad generalities and focus on the specific resources and activities that, through combination, may lead to advantage. The value chain, which divides a firm's activities into discrete processes, provides a useful starting point for such an analysis (see "The Value Chain"). Listing all the discrete activities in the value chains of two businesses or segments under consideration allows for an accurate identification of those that are similar enough to be subject to scope economies.

The potential for scale and scope economies will differ among the various activities, therefore, identifying and isolating those activities where their effect is greatest is an important step. Such activities will either be ones in which a large percentage of the cost structure lies (so that, for example, even a small-scale effect will provide a substantial cost advantage to the largest competitor) or where the magnitude of scale or scope are large.

Using the Value Chain   To understand the use of the value chain as a tool for identifying scope economies, consider the example of an industrial thermostat company that decided to expand into household thermostats. The firm forecast flat growth in its existing markets, but anticipated an increasing demand in the household market. On that basis, it elected to enter the household market, hoping to capture the growing segment.

At first glance, this is a straightforward example of expansion across industry segments. It might appear to be an eminently sensible move: the firm would remain a thermostat producer, only adding an additional product line. Looking closer, however, one can see that the fit between the two businesses was not at all close.

Although the firm was able to leverage some of its technological know-how in entering the new market, R&D was not a critical success factor in household thermostats, nor did it account for a significant portion of the value added in that market. In contrast, design, product appearance, and packaging were significant selling features in household thermostats, but the firm lacked any experience in these activities. The production and distribution of the products also differed markedly. Industrial thermostats were produced to order, with strict tolerances, and sold by an in-house staff of industrial engineers; household thermostats were mass-produced and distributed through a network of industry representatives to mass marketers and plumbing and heating contractors.

The value chains for the two businesses reveal these critical differences (see Figure 3–4). When placed side by side, it is clear that the resources needed to support these businesses are very different, and that there are few possibilities for scale or scope economies. Further, when the company attempted to share activities across the lines, it blurred the boundaries between the businesses and lost sight of the distinct key success factors in each. As a result, the company's profitability not only did not improve, it declined.

To further the analysis of competitive advantage, Michael Porter introduced the value chain as a tool to examine the activities of a business. The value chain disaggregates all of a firm's functions into discrete activities, each of which has its own determinants of cost (called *cost drivers*), and contributes to satisfying different customer needs.

Porter distinguished a firm's support activities from its operational, or primary, activities (see Exhibit 1). The latter contribute directly to production and delivery of a good or service to a customer. The former are the overhead functions that must be performed to keep the operational activities going. Other approaches, such as McKinsey's business system, generate similar if slightly different categories.

In practice, the activities of the firm can be broken down into an almost infinite list. Manufacturing can be subdivided into assembly and machining; machining can be broken down into the discrete stages in the process; and so on. The level of the analysis should depend on the task at hand. A detailed exercise to benchmark a firm's relative cost position, for example, would require the analysis of a far more disaggregated value chain than would an analysis identifying the key success factors of a strategy. Whatever the purpose, however, the activities should be sufficiently disaggregated so that the scale, experience, and scope drivers of cost and differentiation are substantially different among the different activities.

Source: Michael E. Porter, *Competitive Advantage* (New York: Free Press, 1985).

EXHIBIT 1   A Generic Value Chain

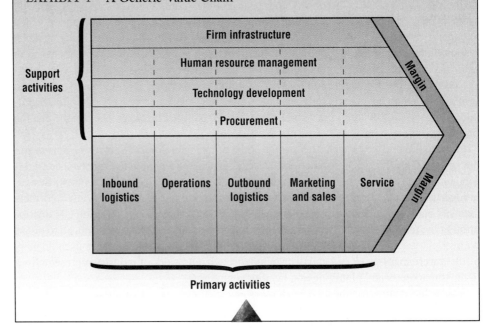

The plight of Maytag in the changing major appliance industry was discussed earlier. This section looks at the industry in more detail and identifies the specific scale and scope advantages that developed as the industry matured.

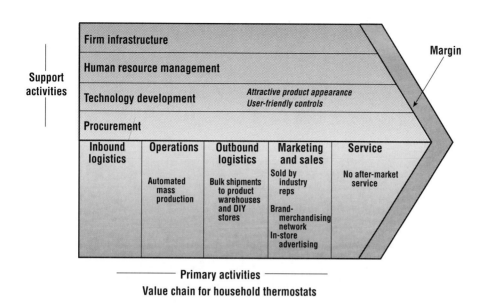

Value chain for household thermostats

Value chain for industrial thermostats

Table 3–2 shows the activities that are performed in the industry, beginning with research and development and extending through customer service. Upstream there are few benefits from being a broad-line producer, except for the possibility of sharing some of the more generic elements of research and design. Scope effects, therefore, are modest at this end of the chain. However, there are considerable scale effects in manufacturing individual appliances. All appliances are produced on separate lines, and the size of the minimum efficient scale plant in every instance is considerable.

▲ TABLE 3–2   Relative Importance of Scale and Scope Economies in the Major Appliance Industry

	R&D	Purchasing	Manufacturing	Distribution	Advertising	Sales	Service	Contract Market
Percentage of cost structure	3%	30%	25%	6%	2%	7%	3%	
Scale within a line	+	+	+++	+	+			
Scope across lines		+		+++	++	+++	+++	+++

Economies of scope are mostly downstream and can only be achieved by sharing costs across multiple products. The volume requirements in these activities are so great that it would be impossible to meet them with a single product line.

Downstream, scope effects are significant. Distribution, branding, sales, and service are all more efficient when done on a large-scale basis across a full line of products.

Figure 3–5 shows the major industry competitors in the mid-1980s. As their different scopes suggest, the firms pursued a variety of strategies. Design and Manufacture (D&M) was a focused private-label producer of dishwashers. It offered no other product and had no downstream capabilities in distribution, sales, or service. Sears, which commanded the largest market share in the industry, did no manufacturing, but sold and serviced a wide line of products under the Kenmore brand. General Electric (GE), on the other hand, manufactured, distributed, and serviced a full appliance line, although it did no retailing. How could these different strategies, and different firm scopes, exist simultaneously in the industry? And, why, as we saw earlier, did Maytag suffer from its narrow focus?

The answer is that each of the successful competitors had access to necessary scale and scope economies throughout the chain, although not always within the boundaries of their own organizations. D&M was large enough to realize significant scale effects in manufacturing dishwashers, but it handed-off at that point to large retailers who had access to downstream scope economies. Sears realized significant scope economies in distribution, sales, and service, while buying in large enough volume to support scale-efficient suppliers. GE manufactured multiple product lines, with scale effects in each, and realized economies of scope in distribution, branding, and service. The companies that were disadvantaged in this scenario, were those who, like Maytag, operated in points of the chain where their competitors had scale or scope economies that they lacked.

At a time when the industry was quite fragmented, Maytag had built a successful differentiation strategy as a narrow-line producer of laundry equipment, a strategy that necessitated the firm's involvement throughout the value chain to preserve its high-quality image. As the industry matured and downstream scope economies emerged, Maytag was slow to see the implications. It recognized too late that its narrow product line and extensive vertical scope would be untenable going forward. At that point, its hasty efforts to acquire a handful of marginal producers in order to fill out its product line proved counterproductive. They brought a host of quality problems (anathema to a differentiated firm) and a string of disappointing results.

▲ Figure 3–5 Map of Home Appliance Industry Players in Product Space

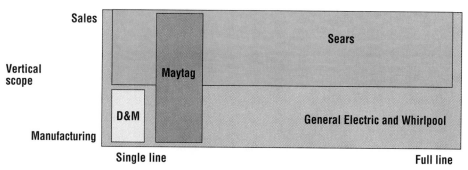

Conclusion

In summary, vague discussions of scale and scope effects are not only unhelpful, they can be very misleading. General statements such as "substantial cost savings are expected in overhead and marketing" are exceedingly difficult to quantify and do not provoke the kinds of questions that help managers expose inconsistencies in their thinking. Rather, systematic analyses and explicit efforts to assess scale and scope benefits are required. As the examples above illustrate, scale and scope economies have no value in the abstract. They create value only when they translate into material advantages for the firm.

RECOMMENDED READINGS

Abell, D. *Defining the Business: The Starting Point of Strategic Planning.* Englewood Cliffs, NJ: Prentice Hall, 1979.

Baumol, W.J., J.C. Panzar, and R.D. Willig. *Contestable Markets and the Theory of Industry Structure.* New York: Harcourt Brace Jovanovich, 1982.

Boston Consulting Group. *Perspectives on Experience.* Boston: Boston Consulting Group, Inc., 1968.

Alfred D. Chandler. *Scale and Scope.* Cambridge, MA: Harvard University Press, 1990.

Ghemawat, P. "Building Strategy on the Experience Curve." *Harvard Business Review,* March–April 1985, pp. 143–49.

Hannan, M.T., and J. Freeman. *Organizational Ecology.* Cambridge, MA: Harvard University Press, 1989.

Leonard-Barton, D. "Core Capabilities and Core Rigidities: A Paradox in Managing New Product Development." *Strategic Management Journal,* 1992, pp. 111–25.

Lieberman, M. B. "The Learning Curve and Pricing in the Chemical Processing Industries." *RAND Journal of Economics,* Summer 1984, pp. 213–28.

Montgomery, C.A., and B. Wernerfelt. "Risk Reduction and Umbrella Branding." *Journal of Business,* 1992, pp. 31–50.

Panzar, J.C., and R. Willig. "Economies of Scope." *American Economic Review,* May 1981, pp. 268–272.

Penrose, E. *The Theory of the Growth of the Firm.* London: Basil Blackwell, 1959.

Porter, M.E. *Competitive Advantage.* New York: Free Press, 1985.

Pratten, C.F. *Economies of Scale in Manufacturing Industry.* Cambridge, England: Cambridge University Press, 1971.

Scherer, F.M. *Industrial Market Structure and Economic Performance.* Boston: Houghton-Mifflin, 1980.

Scherer, F.M., A. Beckenstein, and R.D. Murphy. *The Economics of Multi-Plant Operations: An International Comparisons Study.* Cambridge, MA: Harvard University Press, 1975.

Sutton, J. *Sunk Costs and Market Structure: Price Competition, Advertising, and the Evolution of Concentration.* Boston: MIT Press, 1991.

Teece, D.J. "Economies of Scope and the Scope of the Enterprise." *Journal of Economic Behavior and Organization,* 1980, pp. 223–47.

DIVERSIFIED
EXPANSION

▲ INTRODUCTION

Chapter 3 examined the scale and scope of firms within an industry. This chapter will focus on firms that pursue diversified expansion and choose to compete in multiple distinct product markets.[1]

This order of presentation mirrors the order of expansion many firms follow. For most firms, expansion starts within the core industry, and is undertaken to enhance or protect its position in that market. Then the firm may move outside the initial industry, often tentatively at first, until over the years it becomes considerably more diversified (Figure 4–1).

This chapter begins by addressing the motives and vision behind diversified expansion, and then examines the performance implications of various levels and kinds of diversification. The chapter concludes by discussing alternative modes that firms use to diversify, including internal growth, acquisitions, and alliances.

Guiding Growth

A thousand-mile journey begins with a single step.
Ancient Chinese proverb

Often firms expand within an industry with a minimum of internal disruption. In comparison, expansion into new industries can be considerably more taxing. Now the firm must consider not only how it will compete in one business—its business-level strategy—but also how it will compete across several businesses—its corporate-level strategy.

---

[1]Portions of this chapter draw heavily from C.A. Montgomery, "Corporate Diversification," *Journal of Economic Perspectives*, Summer 1994, pp. 163–78. Copyright 1994, American Economic Association.

▲ FIGURE 4–1   **Pattern of Diversification**

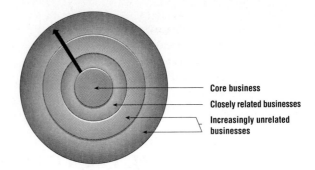

— Core business
— Closely related businesses
— Increasingly unrelated businesses

This transition can be a critical juncture for a firm. Defining a corporate vision and planning for growth across multiple businesses almost by definition demands an open-ended process. The distinction made in Chapter 1 between visions, which point direction, and goals and objectives, which define milestones, is essential in this regard. Richard Normann captured this distinction when he wrote: "Visions are not goals. They are intuitive ideas of reasonable (although in relation to the present state, sometimes highly deviating) future states of the system, which sometimes only exist as subjective ideas nursed by a few discerning and possibly significant actors in the present system"[2] (see "The Growth Idea").

The process through which a vision is nurtured and refined is critical to a firm's long-term success. Locking into a vision prematurely can artificially narrow a firm's opportunities and prevent ongoing learning. On the other hand, failing to solidify a vision as time goes on can result in an unwillingness to make any substantial commitment or a string of actions that are inconsistent with each other. In general, as a firm's experience accumulates, its vision should gain definition. As this is happening, the other elements of the corporate strategy should be taking root. Often by the time the vision itself is well defined and widely agreed to, the primary building blocks of the diversification strategy are in place, and the firm has already gone a considerable distance toward its realization.

PRINCIPLES

▲ WHY DO FIRMS DIVERSIFY?

Firms diversify for many reasons—some inside the firm, and some outside the firm. Edith Penrose referred to these as the external and internal *inducements for growth*.[3]

External inducements are conditions or opportunities in a firm's external environment that draw it into new businesses. These may be attractive opportunities a firm is well positioned to pursue, such as newspapers entering the business of providing on-line information. External inducements can also come in the form of threats, such as a downward shift in demand in a firm's primary market that encourages it to seek its fortunes elsewhere. Defense

---

[2]Richard Normann, *Management for Growth* (New York: John Wiley & Sons, 1977), p. 97.
[3]Edith Penrose, *The Theory of the Growth of the Firm* (London: Basil Blackwell, 1959).

The Growth Idea

Richard Normann made a very useful distinction between what he termed a *business idea* and a *growth idea*. His business idea is analogous to what we have termed *business strategy*; it embodies a firm's means of establishing a competitive advantage within a particular industry.

Normann pointed out that describing a growth idea is far more difficult than describing a business idea. The former involves a process whose outcome is continually changing, best characterized as an emergent process.*

A growth idea begins with a firm's initial endowment of resources and its understanding of the competitive environments it faces or may face in the future. For an established single-business company, these would include everything associated with the business—technology, customers, competitors, and so forth. Going forward, the question for the firm's management is: How should we use what we have to become something different? This query embodies the essence of a growth idea.

Managing a growth idea involves a dynamic process that is quite different from the kind of goal-directed activity that characterizes many mature planning processes. According to Normann: "Planning for growth cannot therefore be derived logically from a well-defined ultimate goal; it can only pro-

ceed step by step. After each step or each measure introduced, the situation must be reconsidered before the next step can be planned or put into effect. Indeed, this kind of planning is characteristic of all learning processes geared to something more than the production of a given final product with the help of some well-known technology, i.e., learning processes aimed at the development of something really new."†

Despite its indistinct nature, it is critical that a vision be linked to concrete and immediate actions. Unless this is done, the vision runs the risk of being "a declaration and nothing more." As these actions are taken, and experience unfolds, each should be scrutinized, not only as an end in itself, but as it relates to the firm's vision and developing strategy.

Due to the complexities involved in positioning or repositioning an entire set of businesses, or developing the resources to support the same, corporate strategies often emerge over a number of years. Even though they may not be born intact, compelling corporate strategies nonetheless are usually forged through such a deliberate and conscientious process.

---

*H. Mintzberg, "Patterns in Strategy Formulation," *Management Science*, 1978, pp. 934–48.
†Normann, *Management for Growth*, p. 97.

---

contractors' recent efforts to deploy their capabilities in private sector businesses illustrate such a shift. As these examples suggest, external inducements can spawn expansion that is *offensive* or *defensive* in nature. The same is true of internal inducements.

Internal inducements are conditions within a firm itself that prompt it to expand. Defensive diversification, for example, may follow a judgment that a firm's skills are not a good match with the developing needs in its market. Although launched as a computer hardware company, Steve Jobs repositioned Next in the software business when it became apparent that the firm could not compete successfully in hardware. Most often, however, internal inducements are offensive in nature and arise from a firm's desire to more fully employ and exploit its resource base. This is the most typical reason firms diversify.

At any given time, most firms have some **excess capacity** in their resource base—resources that are being underutilized. This situation develops for several reasons. First, some resources, intangible resources in particular, grow in both value *and capacity* if used judiciously. Brand names, for example, benefit in this way from ever-widening exposure. Second, resources are often available only in discrete increments; when combined in any given business it is unlikely that all of the resources, such as a specialized piece of test equipment, will simultaneously be used to their full capacity. Third, in the ordinary processes of operation and expansion, firms often generate new resources.[4] While doing audits, for example, Arthur Andersen developed an expertise in information systems, which it in turn leveraged into a huge and profitable consulting practice.

Moreover, many of a firm's most valuable resources are idiosyncratic or deeply embedded in the firm, making it difficult to rent or sell their excess capacity. Other resources may be detachable, but because of high transaction costs or unique characteristics, they are worth more in their present setting than they would be elsewhere. For example, some complex resources, such as corporate R&D laboratories, depend on vital information from many parts of an organization and could not function well if severed from those connections. Such resources are said to be **immobile** because they are nontradable or less valuable to other users;[5] consequently, they remain in the firm. If leveraging these resources into new businesses will increase the firm's total returns, they become a viable basis for diversification.[6]

Obstacles inside and outside the firm often thwart its desire to expand. For example, although an attractive opportunity may beckon, a firm may lack a necessary resource to succeed, or its board of directors may feel the plan for expansion is too risky. Similarly, an otherwise attractive opportunity may be blocked by an external obstacle, such as the presence of an entrenched competitor that would pose a formidable threat to a challenger.

It is important to recognize that the mix of inducements and obstacles a firm faces will influence not only *whether* expansion will occur, but also the direction and method the expansion will take. For example, a firm that identifies an attractive opportunity but faces the obstacle of an insufficient resource base may elect to proceed through a joint venture or merger. Conversely, the firm may decide to forgo that possibility and pursue another alternative, where internal development would be viable. Ultimately, it is the net effect of a firm's inducements and obstacles to expand that shapes its diversification and lays the groundwork for its future profitability.

▲ CHOICE OF BUSINESSES

Matching Resources and Businesses

The essential element behind the successful expansion of a multibusiness firm is the fit between its resources and the product markets in which it may compete. These have been described as "two sides of the same coin":

> Most products require the services of several resources and most resources can be used in several products. By specifying the size of the firm's activity in different product markets, it is possible to infer the minimum necessary resource commitments. Conversely, by specifying a resource profile for a firm, it is possible to find the optimal product market activities.[7]

---

[4]Penrose, *Theory of the Growth of the Firm*.
[5]M.A. Peteraf, "The Cornerstones of Competitive Advantage: A Resource-Based View," *Strategic Management Journal*, 1993, pp.179–91.
[6]The choice between leveraging resources through market contracts or inside the firm is addressed in Chapter 5.
[7]Birger Wernerfelt, "A Resource-Based View of the Firm," *Strategic Management Journal*, 1984, pp. 171–80.

These relationships can be studied through a resource–product matrix, which describes the linkage between a firm's resource and product portfolios (see "Diversification at BIC").

To be the basis for an effective diversification strategy, there must ultimately be a fit between the two so that the **resources contribute to competitive advantage** in the product markets in important ways. This implies that diversification should not be based indiscriminately on any of a firm's resources, but only on those that can be demonstrated to be truly valuable in the new business. It is, for example, easy to argue that one or another of a firm's resources fit an industry; but entry requires creating enough value to overcome customers' switching costs and inertia. Merely imitating competitors or narrowly improving on their offerings is rarely sufficient for successful diversification.

Moreover, when entering a new business, the firm must compete on *all* the resources that are required to produce and deliver the product or service. One great resource does not ensure successful diversification, particularly if the firm is disadvantaged on other dimensions. Anheuser-Busch, for example, discovered this when its Eagle Snacks business, which hoped to leverage the company's distribution and marketing skills, failed to overcome the many resource advantages of Frito-Lay, the entrenched competititor.

Finally, even when the firm's resources could in principle contribute to competitive advantage in a new business, leveraging them into that business must be feasible. Marks & Spencer prided itself on its unparalleled reputation in United Kingdom retailing and its extraordinary domestic supplier network, but neither resource transferred successfully to the Canadian market. Not surprisingly, the factors that prevent resource imitation can also prevent the replication or transfer of resources. The path dependency behind building customer loyalty, for example, can make it difficult to transfer across countries. Companies must, therefore, confirm that their valuable resources can indeed be deployed in new business settings if their diversification strategy is to succeed.

A Sequence of Steps

Although a firm's current resource base often directs its diversified expansion, experience shows that it is neither necessary nor prudent for the firm to consider only its existing resources. Fit between resources and product markets need not always be present at the outset of diversification, if a strategy to develop the missing resources is in place.[8] In following such a plan, firms can balance the exploitation of existing resources with the development of new ones.

Figure 4–2 illustrates how a market opportunity can spur the development of new capabilities. In this case, the matrix represents the planned evolution of the Japanese electronics industry over several decades. In the 1950s, Japan's Ministry of International Trade & Industry (MITI) reportedly identified an attractive opportunity to make electronics industries the leading edge of economic growth in Japan. At the time, however, Japan was 10 to 15 years behind the West in electronics technology and in the manufacture of electronic goods.[9] Recognizing that Japan lacked the requisite skills to compete in the technologically sophisticated segments of the market such as computers, MITI elected to build a base in consumer electronics and to use that as a platform for developing more advanced capabilities.

---

[8]Hamel and Prahalad, for example, made much of the importance of stretch in a firm's strategy, of setting the target well beyond the current capabilities. C.K. Prahalad and Gary Hamel, "Strategic Intent," *Harvard Business Review*, May–June 1989, pp. 63–76.
[9]*Business Week*, December 14, 1981, p. 53.

From rather humble beginnings as a manufacturer of disposable ballpoint pens, the BIC Pen Corporation grew into a leading consumer products firm. Its success was due, in part, to its careful management of diversification.

Exhibit 1 shows BIC's resource and product portfolios in 1974. The firm's skills in plastic injection molding and mass marketing, as well as its well-recognized brand name, all stemmed from its initial involvement in the ballpoint pen industry. In a series of sequential moves, BIC leveraged all three resources in its entries into disposable lighters and razors. Notably, each of these skills was a key success factor in these industries.

After this string of successes, BIC's good judgment appeared to lapse when it decided to enter the pantyhose business. From a product market perspective, it is difficult to argue that the fiercely competitive industry presented an attractive opportunity for expansion. Incumbent players were well established and industry growth was slowing. From a resource perspective, the move was equally disastrous. None of BIC's formidable resources played a valuable role in the industry: the product required a separate distribution system, even within BIC's well-established grocery and drugstore markets;* the BIC brand, recognized for utility and good value, did not transfer well to the fashion-conscious hosiery industry; and BIC's expertise in plastics manufacturing was of no use whatsoever (the hosiery were even sourced from a French company).

In addition to its inability to leverage its existing resources, BIC suffered from a lack of other resources that were instrumental to success in the pantyhose industry. These included a product that met customers' needs (BIC's hosiery were notorious for their poor fit) and a cost-efficient means of producing or procuring that product (BIC's imported hosiery faced stiff import tariffs).

Although BIC's eventual withdrawal from the pantyhose market perhaps came as no surprise, it did come with considerable frustration and great cost. The firm's experience illustrates the challenges even successful diversified firms face in mapping their way forward.

---

*In drug and grocery stores, hosiery distribution required a dedicated service team to replenish stock on a regular basis.

EXHIBIT 1   **Resource-Product Matrix , BIC Pen Corp.**

Resource Market	Plastic injection molding expertise	Mass marketing	Brand name
Disposable pens 1958	●	●	●
Disposable lighters 1973	●	●	●
Disposable razors 1974	●	●	●
Pantyhose 1974			

Adapted from Wernerfelt, "A Resource-Based View of the Firm." Copyright 1984, John Wiley & Sons, Ltd. Reprinted by permission of John Wiley & Sons, Ltd.

Resource / Market	Mass assembly	Consumer marketing	Electronics technology
Semi-conductors	X		X
Consumer electronics	X	X	
Computers			X

Source: Adapted fromWernerfelt, "A Resource-Based View of the Firm." Copyright 1984, John Wiley & Sons, Ltd. Reprinted by permission of John Wiley & Sons, Ltd.

In time, the semiconductor industry would play a particularly important role in carrying out this strategy. Not only would it serve the needs of the consumer electronics firms, but, in turn, it would be supported and nourished by that industry's rapidly growing demand. This symbiotic relationship provided both the cash flows and technical expertise the semiconductor firms needed to pursue more advanced applications. Those were the capabilities that, in time, fostered the development of Japan's four leading computer makers: NEC, Hitachi, Toshiba, and Fujitsu.

Hiroyuki Itami argued that a stepping-stone approach is common in many diversified Japanese firms.[10] In his view, it represents the logical development and deployment of a firm's critical resources through time.

Resources as a Springboard

As the above discussion suggests, the resources of a firm are at the heart of diversified expansion. Ultimately, it is the quantity and quality of a firm's resources that determine its expansion opportunities. Each firm gets its start in *one* industry, and from their beginnings, firms differ in terms of their initial resources and opportunities. Going forward, these differences will have a profound impact on how the firms diversify and on the outcomes they can expect.

As we discussed in Chapter 2, resources differ in their degree of **specificity**. To be the basis for a diversified firm, they must, to some degree, be applicable in more than one business (fungible) but specific enough to provide a competitive advantage in the business in which they are applied.

Specific resources, such as productive skills in biotechnology, may be important to competitive advantage and yield high returns in their initial settings, but often lose value rapidly as they are applied in more distant markets. In contrast, less specific resources, such as teams of general managers or standard milling machines, transfer considerably further, but usually generate lower returns because they are less scarce (Figure 4–3). For example, in countries with well-developed

---

[10]Hiroyuki Itami with T.W. Roehl, *Mobilizing Invisible Assets* (Cambridge, MA: Harvard University Press, 1987).

▲ FIGURE 4–3   Hypothesized Relationship between Diversification Distance and Marginal Rents for Different Degrees of Factor Specificity

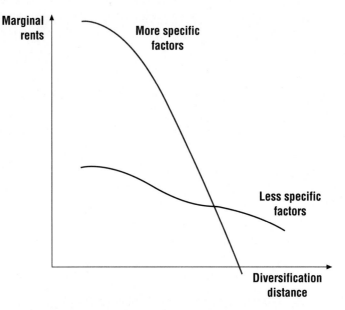

Source: C.A. Montgomery and B. Wernerfelt, "Diversification, Ricardian Rents, and Tobin's *q*," *RAND Journal of Economics*, 1988, pp. 623–32. Copyright©1988. Reprinted by permission of RAND.

capital markets, access to capital is by itself likely to be a poor basis for diversification because of the generic nature of money as a resource. Compared to the number of firms that have had the opportunity to develop general resources, far fewer have had the opportunity to develop specific specialized resources, thus the relative differences in their availability (scarcity) and hence, value.

Given the inherent differences that exist in firms' resource stocks, the optimal level of diversification for each firm will differ. Although all firms should seek to diversify as far as their resources create value (see "Questions to Ask"), the extent of that diversification, and the choice of industries, will differ widely across firms.

Empirical Evidence   Empirical studies have demonstrated the important role resources play in initiating and directing diversified expansion. There is strong evidence, for example, that internally generated diversification emanates from industries in which R&D-to-sales ratios are unusually high, suggesting that technological know-how fuels the effort.[11] Other research has shown that marketing assets and skills are also important drivers of diversified expansion.[12]

Several studies have confirmed that expansion does not occur in random, but in deliberate ways. When expanding, firms tend to diversify into industries that share similar resource characteristics and key success factors. In particular, similarities in R&D intensity, distribution,

[11]D.J. Ravenscraft and F.M. Scherer, *Mergers, Sell-Offs, and Economic Efficiency* (Washington, DC: The Brookings Institution, 1987).
[12]C.A. Montgomery and S. Hariharan, "Diversified Expansion in Large Established Firms," *Journal of Economic Behavior and Organization*, January 1991, pp. 71–89.

Questions to Ask

A few simple questions about a firm's resources and the industries in which it may compete can be a powerful guide in moving from a business unit to a corporate perspective.

Resources

▲ On which of the firm's valuable resources could diversification be based?

▲ Is it likely that those resources would contribute to competitive advantage in another business? Why? Where?

▲ Which resources could be developed further through additional investment or experience?

Businesses

▲ Are there attractive opportunities for expansion?

▲ Could a defensible position be built in the business?

▲ How does the business relate to the firm's existing businesses?

▲ Would additional resources be required?

▲ What are the various ways those resources might be acquired, and at what cost?

Plan

▲ What is the overall plan?

▲ Into which markets, and in what sequence, should diversification take place?

Source: This list of questions draws heavily on Wernerfelt, "Resource-Based View of the Firm."

and marketing channels are significant predictors of the network of industries in which a diversified firm will compete.[13]

Although traditional entry barrier theory emphasized the role incumbents' resources play in restricting entry into highly profitable industries, more recent research has shown that established firms can *vault* their way into such industries if they have the kind of resources and capabilities that are critical to industry success.[14] For these firms, entry barriers do not serve as a deterrent, but as a "gateway,"[15] making available opportunities that would not be accessible to most firms.

Field-based research does reveal, however, that when diversifying, companies often make two systematic miscalculations with respect to resources. First, they tend to *overestimate the transferability of specific resources.* Sears, for example, misjudged the value its customer base and reputation in retailing would bring to the financial services industry. Second, companies tend to *overestimate the value of very general resources in creating competitive advantage in a new market.* General Mills, for example, thought its valuable resource was understanding "the needs and wants of the homemaker," and so diversified unsuccessfully into fashion retailing, toys, jewelry, and clothing during the seventies.

---

[13]Andre Lemelin, "Relatedness in the Patterns of Interindustry Diversification," *Review of Economics and Statistics,* November 1982, pp. 179–98; James M. MacDonald, "R&D and the Direction of Diversification," *Review of Economics and Statistics*, 1985, pp. 583–90; and Farjoun, Moshe, "Beyond Industry Boundries: Human Expertise, Diversification and Resource-related Industry Groups," *Organization Science,* May 1994, pp. 185–199.

[14]This has been proven in studies by George S. Yip, "Gateways to Entry," *Harvard Business Review*, September–October 1982, pp. 85–93; and Montgomery and Hariharan, "Diversified Expansion in Large Established Firms."

[15]This description is from Yip, "Gateways to Entry."

▲ DIVERSIFICATION AND FIRM PERFORMANCE

At any given time, firms are at different places on the path of diversified expansion. Some are just starting out, moving away from their initial businesses. Others are considerably further along, with sets of businesses that may span many industries. Still others are restructuring and divesting businesses. Although the popular press has highlighted recent divestiture activity among large firms, claiming a "return to the core," changes at the margin must not obscure the fact that most of these firms remain remarkably diversified.

When analyzing trends in U.S. manufacturing, for example, Gollop and Monahan concluded that diversification has been "one of the most important structural phenomena" in recent economic activity:

> Diversification has replaced horizontal growth. While pure conglomerate mergers were relatively rare in the immediate postwar era, accounting for 3.2 percent of asset acquisitions in the 1948–53 period, [by 1981, they accounted] for more than 50 percent of merger activity.[16]

Indeed, for the 500 largest U.S. public companies, the evidence suggests that diversification has actually increased recently. (See Table 4–1.) These firms sold $3.7 trillion worth of goods or services in 1992, or approximately 75 percent of the output of all U.S. public companies. These data indicate not only the pervasiveness but also the economic significance of diversification.

▲ TABLE 4–1 Diversification in the Top 500 U.S. Public Companies*

Number of SIC Codes

	1985	1989	1992
Mean	10.65	10.85	10.90

Distribution of Firms

Number of SIC Codes	1985	1989	1992
1	11.8%	12.4%	12.4%
2 or less	18.8	18.4	18.4
3 or less	23.2	22.6	21.8
More than 5	67.6	68.6	69.6
More than 10	42.0	43.6	43.8
More than 20	13.8	14.0	14.0
More than 30	0.6	0.8	0.8

*Data from Compustat PC Plus, April 30,1993. SIC assignments are made by Compustat employees and are primarily at the 4-digit SIC level.

Source: Montgomery, "Corporate Diversification," op. cit. p. 164. Copyright 1994, American Economic Association.

[16]F.M. Gollop and J. Monahan, "A Generalized Index of Diversification: Trends in U.S. Manufacturing," *Review of Economics and Statistics*, 1991, p. 318.

The United States is not the only country in which diversified companies have a significant role in economic activity. Although recent data are difficult to obtain, historical trends indicate that diversification is pronounced in Canada, Japan, the United Kingdom, and other advanced economies.[17] Large conglomerates, often controlled by family groups or government, are also prominent in many developing nations.[18]

Diversification levels may increase or decrease somewhat in the decades ahead, but multibusiness companies will continue to control a majority of corporate assets in many countries. Therefore, comprehending the logic of diversification—what works and what does not—is a critical function of management.

Performance Implications

Many researchers have been eager to examine the performance of diversified firms. Conclusions from this research vary widely depending on who is doing the analysis and on the issues being addressed. Unfortunately, much of the research to date has been conducted in pursuit of an unequivocal conclusion that diversification is either universally good or universally bad. However, as we saw, the phenomenon is far too complex for such a simple answer.

The complexity surrounding the analysis derives from several factors. First, it is difficult to measure diversification in a way that facilitates comparisons across firms. Second, performance is particularly difficult to measure when looking across industries and over very long periods of time. Third, and most important, the relationship between diversification and firm performance is moderated by a host of other variables, notably the quality and quantity of a firm's underlying resources. To evaluate the efficiency of any diversification, therefore, it is essential to consider the resource endowments and business opportunities that were available to a given firm. (See Figure 4-4.) Examining correlations between diversification and performance without considering these underlying conditions can only tell us about the veneer of the relationship, not its inner workings.

Despite these impediments, some notable progress has been made in untangling this very complex relationship. To begin, there is a substantial amount of evidence that diversification and firm performance are negatively correlated when both are measured as continuous, linear variables.[19] Other things being equal, the more diversified the firm, the lower its average profits. Coming upon this result, many have been tempted to conclude that diversification dissipates firm value and is not consistent with profit maximization. However, such a conclusion is not only premature, it is probably wrong.

Consider that a firm at any given time faces a queue of diversification opportunities, ranked from the most to the least profitable. If the firm pursues the opportunities in that order, as any firm should, and *undertakes only projects with a positive net present value*, its *total* accounting

[17]These studies were conducted by R.E. Caves et al. (1980), Goto (1981), Goudie and Meeks (1982), and Utton (1977), respectively. (See recommended readings.)

[18]"Corporate Scope and (Severe) Market Imperfections"—Krishna Palepu and Taran Khanna (working paper #96-051).

[19]Comment, Robert and Jarrell, Gregg A., "Corporate focus and stock returns," *Journal of Financial Economics 37* (1995), pp. 67–87; Berger, Philip G. and Ofek, Eli, "Diversification's effect on firm value," *Journal of Financial Economics 37* (1995), pp. 39–65; and Lang, L.H.P. and Stulz, R.E., "Tobin's q, Corporate Diversification, and Firm Performance," *The Journal of Political Economy*, Vol. 12, No. 6, December 1994, pp. 1248–1280.

▲ FIGURE 4–4   The Relationship between Resources, Businesses, and Profitability

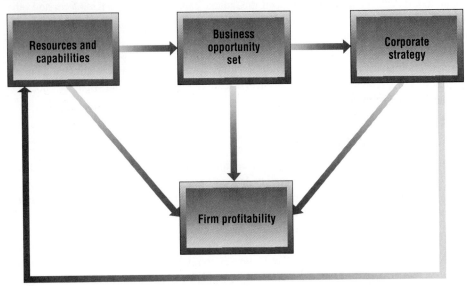

earnings will increase as diversification proceeds, but its *average* accounting earnings will decline. In this scenario, the economic value of the firm will increase as diversification proceeds, so long as expansion stops before undertaking an initiative with a negative net present value. A decline in average accounting earnings, therefore, does not mean that diversification is inconsistent with value maximization.

It is also important to consider that the relationship between diversification and firm performance is not necessarily linear, although most tests have assumed this form. Instead of measuring diversification as a continuous variable, Richard Rumelt used a series of objective and subjective criteria to classify firms into nine categories of diversification.[20] In doing so, he made a critical distinction between what he termed "constrained" and "linked" diversification.

In constrained diversifiers, the majority of a firm's businesses share a set of specialized resources, be they in research, operations, or marketing. Linked diversifiers also have connections across their businesses, but their profiles look quite different. In linked diversifiers, new businesses are added to old by building on a variety of connections, such that each new business is related to at least one other business, but the collection as a whole is virtually unrelated (Figure 4–5).

Using various accounting measures, Rumelt found persistent differences in performance across diversification categories. In particular, constrained diversifiers, those that had grown by building on a central strength or resource, consistently outperformed all

---

[20]Rumelt's nine categories of diversification were single business, dominant constrained, dominant vertical, dominant linked, dominant unrelated, related constrained, related linked, unrelated business, and conglomerate. For a more detailed explanation of the nuances of these categories, see R. Rumelt, *Strategy, Structure, and Economic Performance* (Cambridge, MA: Harvard University Press, 1974).

▲ FIGURE 4–5   Constrained and Linked Diversification

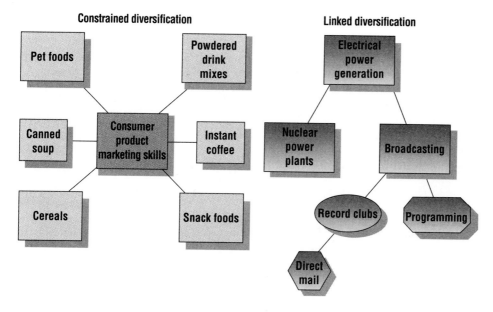

other categories in the sample. Single businesses and linked diversifiers, on average, were middle-of-the-road performers, and unrelated diversifiers were among the worst.[21]

The Importance of the Industry Effect

In addition to replicating Rumelt's results, subsequent research revealed that the firms in Rumelt's sample differed not only in diversification strategy, but also in the type of industries in which they competed, a well-known influence on firm profitability.[22] In particular, it was shown that the industries in which constrained diversifiers competed were, on average, more profitable than those in which other firms competed, while the industries in which unrelated diversifiers competed were, on average, among the least profitable. This finding suggests that the widely observed correlation between different types of diversification and firm performance is, in part, due to the nature and profitability of the industries in which the firms are located.

This result is not surprising. It is likely that firms that came to follow constrained diversification strategies developed valuable resources in their base industries that gave them the means to enter other profitable markets. In contrast, firms that were not so wise or so lucky

---

[21]For example, see: Kurt Christensen and C.A. Montgomery, "Corporate Economic Performance: Diversification Strategy versus Market Structure," *Strategic Management Journal*, October–December 1981, pp. 327–43; D.J. Lecraw, "Diversification Strategy Performance," *Journal of Industrial Economics*, December 1984, pp. 179–98; and P. Rajan Varadarajan and V. Ramanujam, "Diversification and Performance: A Reexamination using a New Two-Dimensional Conceptualization of Diversity in Firms," *Academy of Management Journal*, June 1987, pp. 380–93.

[22]R.A. Bettis, "Performance Differences in Related and Unrelated Diversified Firms," *Strategic Management Journal*, 1981, pp. 379–94; and Christensen and Montgomery, "Corporate Economic Performance."

had to go further to find opportunities that matched their modest skill sets. Typically this would lead them to a high level of diversification in industries that are generally unattractive, with lower levels of profitability.

An important rule of diversified expansion is that firms should seek to enter the most profitable industries in which their resources will give them a competitive advantage. Managers who ignore this precept often suffer in the long run. In the late 1960s, for example, many conglomerates attempted to buy their way into highly profitable industries, without having the resources those industries required. Consequently, for these firms the well-recognized positive relationship between firm and industry profitability was reversed: average firm profits decreased, as industry profits increased.[23] In an absolute sense, such firms were shown to be better off when they stayed in industries that, on average, were less profitable but a better fit with their own relatively pedestrian resources.[24]

Summary

The relationship between diversification and firm performance appears to be curvilinear (Figure 4–6). The most profitable firms are those that have diversified around a set of resources that are specialized enough to confer a meaningful competitive advantage in an attractive industry, yet fungible enough to be applied across several such settings; the least profitable are broadly diversified firms whose strategies are built around very general resources that are applied in a wide variety of industries, but are rarely instrumental to competitive advantage in attractive settings.

▲ FIGURE 4–6   The Relationship between Diversification and Performance

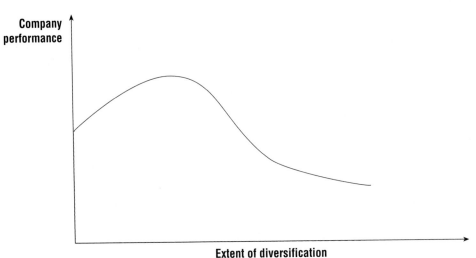

---

[23]C.A. Montgomery and B. Wernerfelt, "Diversification, Ricardian Rents, and Tobin's q," *RAND Journal of Economics*, 1988, pp. 623–32.

[24]Sometimes firms use industry entry as a deliberate means to upgrade their resources. If undertaken thoughtfully and with the recognition that the requisite skills will in fact need to be built or acquired, this can be an effective way to slowly lift a firm out of the doldrums of mediocre industries.

Despite the relative success of the constrained diversification strategy, it does not fit all firms. For any given firm, the appropriate strategy is a function of its own resources and opportunities. While a firm with highly specific resources may maximize its profits at a relatively low level of diversification, another firm with more general resources may need to enter far more markets to maximize its profits and may still produce lower absolute returns.

In light of this evidence, the often-heard adage that firms should stick to their knitting must be interpreted very carefully. Although the foregoing analysis, in effect, supports such advice, arguing that firms should diversify on the basis of what they do well, it also suggests that such strategies will not always result in stellar performance on an absolute basis. In particular, if a firm does its "knitting" with very general resources in pedestrian industries, high profits are unlikely to follow.

Saying that there should be a match between a firm's capabilities and the heights it attempts to scale does not mean that firms with impoverished capabilities are forever relegated to the lowest tier of performers. Rather, it outlines the nature of the challenge such firms face and what they must do to improve their lots. As discussed in Chapter 2 and exemplified in the resource-product matrix, by upgrading their resources, firms can undertake more profitable challenges. However, firms that attempt to shortcut the process and capture the profits without making the requisite investment in resources, are unlikely to succeed.

PRACTICE

▲ MODE OF EXPANSION

Firms can implement their diversification strategies through internal development, acquisitions, mergers, joint ventures, alliances, or contracting with external partners, None of these, however, guarantees easy expansion. Choosing among the various modes involves unavoidable tradeoffs.

Some would argue, for example, that acquiring a company to gain access to the resources needed to compete in an industry is likely to dissipate future profits.[25] Others would cite the difficulties working across organizational boundaries in joint ventures. On the other hand, internal development can be maddeningly slow and rife with uncertainty. In short, each mode of expansion has its own benefits and costs. Thus, a firm must carefully weigh each alternative against its needs and the exigencies of a particular competitive situation.

Such an analysis is complex. Each mode has itself been the focus of numerous and often very insightful studies. As we cannot cover them all, our purpose here is to provide an overview of the most salient issues in choosing a mode of expansion.

▲ MERGERS AND ACQUISITIONS

Buying an existing firm is often seen as the easiest way to diversify. Potentially, it enables the firm to immediately obtain the full set of resources required for competitive advantage within an industry. As with other modes of expansion, acquisition has both benefits and drawbacks that make it more appropriate in some circumstances than in others.

---

[25]Ingemar Dierickx and Karel Cool ("Asset Stock Accumulation and Sustainability of Competitive Advantage," *Management Science,* December 1989, pp. 1504–11), for example, argued that strategic resources are nontradeable assets; that is, they cannot be purchased in a market exchange.

Benefits	Drawbacks
Speed	Cost of acquisition
Access to complementary assets	Unnecessary adjunct businesses
Removal of potential competitor	Organizational clashes may impede integration
Upgrade corporate resources	Major commitment

Benefits

A major advantage of acquisitions is that they can quickly position a firm in a new business. By purchasing an existing player, a firm does not have to take the time to establish its presence or develop for itself the resources it does not already possess. This can be particularly important when the critical resources are difficult to imitate or accumulate. The major pharmaceutical companies, for example, have paid billions of dollars to acquire small biotechnology companies and their technological and manufacturing expertise. Building those capabilities in-house might have taken the drug companies 5 or 10 years, with no guarantee that they could generate the kind of patents or know-how the biotech companies already had.

Acquiring an existing firm also takes a potential competitor out of the market. The internal development required for a firm to reach minimum efficient scale might add substantial capacity to an industry; however, the firm could prevent the increase in rivalry that would result by simply acquiring a competitor that already has the capacity in place. Thus, if the minimum scale of entry would have to be large relative to the market size, acquisition may well be preferred as a means to mitigate intense postacquisition rivalry.

Drawbacks

Despite these advantages, acquisitions can have serious drawbacks. First and foremost, acquisitions can be a very expensive way to enter a market. Premiums of 30 percent or more over current share price are frequently required to close a deal. These prices make it possible that whatever value the acquisition creates will be dissipated in the competition to acquire it.

The high bidder in an acquisition is either a firm with extensive private information about the value of the target; a firm that could create unusual value with the acquisition and, therefore, can afford to pay a very high price; or a firm that has neither of these advantages but simply suffers from the "winner's curse" (being the one who unluckily happened to value the target company higher than everyone else). Excessively high prices are common when firms get carried away in the bidding process, and winning becomes an object of ego satisfaction rather than economics.[26] Unfortunately, there is a good deal of evidence to suggest that this is frequently the case (see "Acquisitions: Rarely a Good Deal for the Acquiring Firm").

In addition to the likelihood of overbidding, acquisitions pose a number of other challenges. Most targets contain bundles of assets and capabilities, only some of which are of

---

[26]To prevent this irrational but common behavior, it is important for acquirers to specify a reservation price above which they will not go, before the bidding begins.

When making an acquisition, managers often lose sight of the fact that acquisitions are purchased in a market—the market for corporate control—that functions reasonably well. Importantly, the going price for a firm reflects not only the value of the firm as a stand-alone concern, but also incorporates the incremental value the market feels the assets would have to a host of potential acquirers. Unless the winning bidder can use the assets in an unusual way, and create value that other bidders could not, it should not expect to earn economic rent on assets it purchases in the market.

Financial economists have looked at this question in some detail. Their research presents a dramatic challenge to firms that hope to use acquisitions as a means to increase firm value. Exhibit 1 shows that acquirers' risk-adjusted stock prices on average decreased significantly when an acquisition was announced. This means that the market thought their stocks were more valuable before than after the acquisitions.

In contrast to acquirers' decline in value, the stock prices of acquired firms (targets), on average, rise significantly when acquisitions are announced. This suggests that the value created in most mergers is captured by the shareholders of the acquired firms.

EXHIBIT 1 Recent Studies of Bidder Cumulative Abnormal Returns (CARs) from Takeover Bids

(t and z statistics, where available, are noted in parenthesis)

Study	Sample Period	Sample Size	Event Window	Bidder CARs	Percent Positive Returns
Panel A: *One- to Four-Day Event Windows*					
Asquith, Bruner & Mullins (1987)	1973–83	(n=343)	(−1,0)	−0.85 %* (t=8.42)	41.1%* (z=−3.35)
Jarrell & Poulson (1988)	1980–86	(n=214)	(−2,+1)	−0.54% (t=−1.38)	n.a.
Jennings & Mazzeo (1987)	1979–85	(n=352)	day 0	−0.8%* (z=−8.11)	37%* (z=−5.08)
Travlos (1987)	1972–81	(n=160)	(1,+1)	−0.70%	n.a.
Variaya & Ferris (1987)	1974–83	(n=96)	(−1,0)	−2.15%* (z=−8.67)	n.a.
You, Caves, Smith & Henry (1986)	1975–84	(n=133)	(−1,+1)	−1.5%	33%* (z=−4.15)
Panel B: *Longer Event Windows*					
Bradley, Desai & Kim (1988)	1981–84	(n=52)	(−5,+5)	−2.9%** (z=−2.79)	35%** (z=−2.33)
Franks, Harris & Mayer (1988)	1980–84	(n=154)	month 0	−0.6%	n.a.

continues

Concluded

(t and z statistics, where available, are noted in parenthesis)

Study	Sample Period	Sample Size	Event Window	Bidder CARs	Percent Positive Returns
Jarrell & Poulsen (1988)	1980–86	(n=215)	(–10,+30)	+0.87% (t=0.99)	n.a.
Singh & Montgomery (1987)	1975–79	(n=105)	(–5,+25)	–1.22%	n.a.
Travlos (1987)	1972–81	(n=160)	(–10, +10)	–.68%	n.a.
You, Caves, Smith & Henry (1986)	1975–84	(n=133)	(–20,+10)	–1.0%	47% (z=–0.78)

*Indicates statistical significance at the .99 confidence level of higher (for a two-tailed test).
**Indicates statistical significance at the .95 confidence level (for a two-tailed test).
Source: Black, Bernard S. "Bidder Overpayment in Takeovers," *Stanford Law Review*, Volume 41, No. 3, February 1989, pp 597-660. Copyright © 1989 by the Board of Trustees of the Leland Stanford Junior University.

interest to the acquirer. Disposing of unwanted assets or maintaining them in the portfolio is often done at significant cost, either in real terms or in management time. "Selling" a unit yet convincing a buyer that it is not "damaged goods" can be difficult, as can untangling systems and people once they have been integrated into a larger corporation.

Postacquisition Integration Process Although these obstacles are serious, a number of acquisitions fail on another account: the postacquisition integration process fails. Integrating an acquired company into a corporation is probably one of the most challenging tasks confronting top management. Michael Porter, for example, found that only 45 percent of acquisitions were still retained by the acquirers seven years later. He interpreted this as evidence of the general failure of the acquisition strategy and process.

Phillipe Haspeslagh and David Jemison have identified four types of integration that vary according to a unit's need for organizational autonomy and strategic interdependence (Figure 4–7).[27]

The easiest mode of integration to manage is **absorption**, whereby an acquirer merely subsumes the acquisition into its existing structures. Typically this occurs when a large firm already active in a business acquires a smaller competitor to increase its overall scale.

When seeking to diversify through acquisition, a more common mode of integration is **preservation**. In this instance, the acquired company is more or less left alone to run itself as a discrete entity. Although easy to achieve operationally, this mode of integration begs the

---

[27]P.C. Haspeslagh and D.B. Jemison, *Managing Acquisitions: Creating Value through Corporate Renewal* (New York: Free Press, 1991), p. 145. The authors found no examples of one type of acquistion—Holding—in their sample. In this type of acquisition, a firm owns several companies in the same business but makes no attempt to integrate them.

▲ FIGURE 4–7   Types of Acquisition Integration Approaches

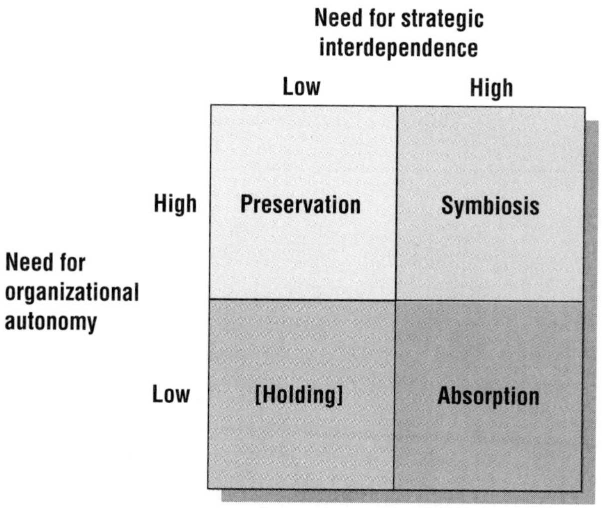

**Need for strategic
interdependence**

	Low	High
High	Preservation	Symbiosis
Low	[Holding]	Absorption

**Need for
organizational
autonomy**

Source: Haspeslagh, Phillipe C. and Jemison, David B. *Managing Acquisitions* (p. 145), The Free Press, 1991.

question of how value will be added to the acquisition. Haspeslagh and Jemison suggest that this mode is more useful as a way to upgrade corporate resources, when the acquiring firm seeks to learn by example from the acquired firm.

Most typically, if an acquirer attempts to inject its resources into an acquired firm, or vice-versa, the integration involves **symbiosis**. In this process, the acquired and acquiring firms are melded together to form a new and different coherent whole. This clearly is the most difficult of the integration modes, and the one on which many acquisitions flounder. Conflicting styles and cultures, a feeling of winners and losers, and operational difficulties in joining systems and people make it extraordinarily difficult to effect this sort of integration.

According to Haspeslagh and Jemison, to work effectively, acquisitions require a gatekeeper who is responsible for managing the interface between the companies. In addition, important decisions have to be made concerning a number of trade-offs, including the speed of integration, equity versus qualification in personnel decisions, operational versus strategic focus in the short term, rationality versus symbolism in decision making, and top-down versus bottom-up decision making.

Many general managers face similar trade-offs in the course of normal operations. In the context of an acquisition, however, these issues can become particularly salient and challenging. As a result, even acquisitions that due diligence suggests are very promising may fail to realize their potential.

▲ INTERNAL DEVELOPMENT

Many companies use another mode of expansion, internal development, as they incrementally exploit corporate resources. As with acquisition, internal development has its pros and cons.

Benefits	Drawbacks
Incremental	Slow
Compatible with culture	Need to build new resources
Encourages intrapreneurship	Adds to industry capacity; subscale entry
Internal investment	Unsuccessful efforts are difficult to recoup

Drawbacks

The drawbacks of internal development are, typically, the opposite of the benefits of acquisition. Most notably, internal development is a slow process as a firm strives to build resources it did not otherwise possess. In its early phases, the development process can put a firm at risk of being subscale, and it can increase rivalry in an industry through the addition of new capacity.

Internal development also introduces the risk that a project will not turn out as planned. Unfortunately, unlike acquisitions, when failure can often be salvaged by selling off the acquired company, investments in an unsuccessful internal development can be very difficult to recoup. For example, Proctor and Gamble never recovered the millions of dollars it spent in advertising its unsuccessful Citrus Hill orange juice. Similarly, Bowmar's hasty decision in the seventies to manufacture its own computer chips left a half-built plant standing idle as the market for its handheld calculators plummeted.

Benefits

While acknowledging the inherent risks of internal development, many firms found it also has benefits. Notably, internal development allows for incremental decision making that can accomodate changing environmental conditions and the learning that may occur within the firm itself. In contrast to acquisitions, where the major commitment is made all at once, internal development can reduce risk by allowing a firm to delay certain of its choices over a longer period of time. Further, in the early stages of an industry life-cycle, internal development may not only be the best choice, it may be the only choice.

Arguably, the greatest benefit of internal development is that it can be an easier, although by no means easy, way to transfer intangible corporate resources into a new business. Employees who understand the firm's culture and embody its tacit collective knowledge can directly deploy those resources in a new context, where they themselves can shape the business from its onset. This suggests that when the resource a firm wants to leverage is an organizational capability, or an intangible asset, the preferred route is internal development.

There are other benefits of internal development. Through in-house expansion, a firm can capture the externalities of a development process, including the learning and experience that accumulate as a business grows. Through time, this tacit know-how can become a valuable resource in its own right and guide further expansion of the firm.

By growing a business internally, management also signals a commitment to developing and leveraging the resources of the firm. This can foster a culture where intrapreneurship can flourish. Experience suggests that the best way to do so is not to create a separate development unit charged with finding new businesses or screening suggestions made by the divisions, but to encourage new business developments in every business, allowing a champion from that unit to carry the project forward. 3M and Rubbermaid, for example, are famed for having such a capability.

▲ ALLIANCES

Alliances of all forms, whether joint ventures, franchises, equity participation, or long-term contractual agreements, are designed to capture the benefits of internal development and acquisition while avoiding the drawbacks of both. To some extent, some alliances are successful in doing so, but many others exhibit a number of weaknesses. It is not possible here to review each type of alliance in detail, but we will make some general observations about the managerial implications they raise.

Benefits	Drawbacks
Access to complementary assets	Lack of control
Speed	Assisting potential competitor
	Questionable long-term viability
	Difficult to integrate learning

Benefits

The objectives of every alliance differ. We will focus on those that are formed to combine complementary resources in order to compete in a new business.[28] These alliances generally occur when one firm has some resources that would be valuable in a new business but needs the assets of another firm to effectively carry out its plan. In the 1970s and 1980s, a number of Japanese firms with high-quality products lacked distribution and service networks to enter the U.S. market. Rather than buying a U.S. company or trying to build the networks themselves, many of these firms entered into alliances that matched their products to a domestic firm's distribution and service networks. Similarly, alliances in the biotechnology industry match the technical know-how of start-up enterprises with the distribution channels of established pharmaceutical companies. Through such alliances, the firms involved are able to assemble the full range of resources they need to compete.

Drawbacks

Although attractive on a number of dimensions, alliances present their own challenges. Issues of control and leadership are near the top of this list. What will each partner contribute? How will those contributions be monitored? Who will set the strategy for the business? If these issues are not resolved at the outset, they can come back to haunt the parties at a later date. There is also the risk, of course, that the alliances may develop in a different direction than originally anticipated, challenging the efficacy of the original assumptions and plans.

---

[28]Alliances have been a topic of much recent writing. We cannot hope to cover all that literature here. Readers are referred to the recommended readings list for a more complete treatment of the issues surrounding alliance formation and management.

The legal structure of an alliance can be helpful in addressing these issues, setting the course and parameters of the exchange. However, there are limits to what can be achieved through legal means. Often, closely aligned business interests can be a more powerful mechanism for resolving disputes between firms and setting and maintaining a common course. Thus, understanding the motivation and incentives of all parties, both in the short and long-run, is critical to the formation of any successful alliance.

In particular, it is important to recognize that the needs and aspirations of partners may change over the life of an alliance, and do so in divergent ways. Predicting what the goals and incentives of the various parties will be under various circumstances is a critical part of effective planning. To the dismay of many U.S. firms, countless of their Japanese partners eventually set up their own distribution networks, ending their alliances with U.S. partners. Other contracts may not end but can become quite problematic over time. Franchising agreements, for example, can be effective in building an organization when there is a high degree of environmental stability and agreement on the strategic direction of the firm. In times of turbulence, however, these contracts can hinder a firm's ability to change and can tie together franchisors and franchisees with asymmetric interests. Pepsi Co. has encountered this many times in its restaurant businesses. Pizza Hut's franchises, for example, resisted the introduction of home delivery, although the franchisor believed it was a strategic necessity.

Many of these experiences highlight the problems of cooperating with a competitor. In the near term, competition between alliance partners is rarely over the product market (since the two are often collaborating on that dimension) but over who gains most from the alliance.[29] In this sense, a firm is considered a "winner" if it is able to upgrade its capabilities faster than its partners or is successful in building the resources it originally lacked. It has been asserted, for example, that Toyota triumphed in the NUMMI joint venture with General Motors because it learned how to build cars in North America; it then went on to build its own plants in Kentucky and Ontario, while GM struggled with how to implement lean production in its other American auto plants.

In their most general terms, then, alliances can be useful in supplementing a firm's resource base; in gaining access to assets and capabilities the firm lacks; or in sharing the costs and risks of a major undertaking. Despite their appeal, many alliances are exceedingly fragile management structures that crumble under the weight of balancing competing objectives and needs. Many alliances, by design or not, are short-lived; others have endured over a number of years and delivered unfailingly on promises envisioned at the start.

▲ RECOMMENDED READINGS

Bettis, R.A. "Performance Differences in Related and Unrelated Diversified Firms." *Strategic Management Journal*, 1981, pp. 379–94.

Caves, R. E., M. Porter, and M. A. Spence, *Competition in the Open Economy: a model applied to Canada.* Cambridge: 1980, Harvard University Press.

Christensen, H. Kurt, and C.A. Montgomery. "Corporate Economic Performance: Diversification Strategy versus Market Structure." *Strategic Management Journal*, October–December 1981, pp. 327–43.

---

[29]Gary Hamel, Yves Doz, and C.K. Prahalad, "Collaborate with Your Competitors—and Win," *Harvard Business Review*, January–February 1989, pp. 133–39.

Goold, M., A. Campbell, and M. Alexander. *Corporate-Level Strategy: Creating Value in the Multibusiness Company.* New York: John Wiley & Sons, 1994.

Goto, A. "Statistical Evidence on the Diversification of Japanese Large Firms." *Journal of Industrial Economics*, March 1981, pp. 271–78.

Goudie, A. W. and Meeks, G. "Diversification by Merger." *Economica*, November 1982, pp 447–59.

Haspeslagh, P.C., and D.B. Jemison. *Managing Acquisitions: Creating Value through Corporate Renewal.* New York: Free Press, 1991.

Itami, H., with T.W. Roehl. *Mobilizing Invisible Assets.* Cambridge, MA: Harvard University Press, 1987.

Kogut, B. "Joint Ventures: Theoretical and Empirical Perspectives." *Strategic Management Journal*, 1988, pp. 319–22.

Lang, L.H.P. and R.E. Stulz, "Tobin's q, Corporate Diversification, and Firm Performance." *Journal of Political Economy*, Vol. 12, No. 6, December 1994, pp. 1248–1280.

Lecraw, D.J. "Diversification Strategy and Performance." *Journal of Industrial Economics*, December 1984, pp. 179–98.

Lemelin, A. "Relatedness in the Patterns of Interindustry Diversification." *Review of Economics and Statistics*, November 1982, pp. 646–57.

MacDonald, J.M. "R&D and the Directions of Diversification." *Review of Economics and Statistics,* November 1985, pp. 583–90.

Montgomery, C.A. "Corporate Diversification." *Journal of Economic Perspectives*, Summer 1994, pp. 163–78.

Montgomery, C.A., and S. Hariharan. "Diversified Expansion in Large Established Firms." *Journal of Economic Behavior and Organization*, January 1991, pp. 71–89.

Montgomery, C.A., and B. Wernerfelt. "Diversification, Ricardian Rents and Tobin's q." *Rand Journal of Economics*, 1988, pp. 623–32.

Normann, R. *Management For Growth.* New York: John Wiley & Sons, 1977.

Penrose, E. *The Theory of the Growth of the Firm.* London: Basil Blackwell, 1959.

Prahalad, C.K., and R. Bettis. "The Dominant Logic: A New Linkage Between Diversity and Performance." *Strategic Management Journal*, 1986, pp. 495–511.

Ravenscraft, D.J., and F.M. Scherer. *Mergers, Sell-Offs, and Economic Efficiency.* Washington, DC: The Brookings Institution, 1987.

Rumelt, R. *Strategy, Structure, and Economic Performance.* Cambridge, MA: Harvard University Press, 1974.

Salter, M., and M.S. Weinhold. *Diversification through Acquisition.* New York: Free Press, 1979.

Teece, D.J. "Towards an Economic Theory of the Multiproduct Firm." *Journal of Economic Behavior and Organization*, 1982, pp. 38–63.

Utton, M.A. "Large Firm Diversification in British Manufacturing Industry." *Economic Journal*, March 1977, pp. 96–113.

Varadarajan, P. Rajan, and V. Ramanujam, "Diversification and Performance: A Reexamination Using a New Two-Dimensional Conceptualization of Diversity in Firms." *Academy of Management Journal*, June 1987, pp. 380–93.

Yip, G. "Gateways to Entry." *Harvard Business Review*, September–October 1982, pp. 85–93.

ORGANIZATIONAL LIMITS TO FIRM SCOPE

▲ INTRODUCTION

Many corporations have pursued the strategy of expansion described in the previous two chapters: starting from a single business, expanding scale and scope within that industry, and then branching out into new markets and geographies. As a result, firms today can be found in an enormous variety of sizes and shapes.

But this raises the question: What are the appropriate boundaries for a particular firm? Although many corporations are still expanding, entering new businesses and markets, and becoming ever larger and more complex, others are reducing the scale and scope of their activities. Not only are they downsizing the number of employees, they are also decreasing the extent of their diversification across businesses and outsourcing a broad range of activities from gardening to legal and computer services.

Perhaps nothing represents this trend better than the "virtual corporation."[1] Such a firm concentrates on developing and maintaining a few "core competences," performing only the activities directly related to those competences. All other activities and businesses are outsourced or licensed to other firms. The athletic shoe company, Nike, for example, employs less than 10,000 people to generate almost $4 billion in revenues. It subcontracts manufacturing to a variety of Far Eastern producers and even relies on outside design houses for many of its product innovations. Nike clothing is supplied by another firm under license.

Such a challenge to the tradition of the fully integrated corporation, and more generally to the wisdom of inexorable corporate expansion, directly questions the limit to the scope of the firm. This chapter addresses that issue by examining which activities and businesses should be retained inside a firm and which should be pursued by other means. To do so, we

---

[1]"The Fall of the Dinosaurs," *Newsweek*, February 8, 1993, pp. 42–53; "The Virtual Corporation," *Business Week*, February 8, 1993, pp. 98–103; "Deconstructing the Computer Industry," *Business Week*, November 23, 1992, pp. 90–100.

explicitly introduce **organizational economics** to the analysis of corporate strategy. The term covers a number of different theories that are currently the focus of much research. Although incomplete in a number of important ways, they represent our best understanding of how to rigorously analyze the organizational determinants of firm boundaries.

PRINCIPLES

▲ SCOPE OF THE FIRM: RESOURCES AND COMPETITIVE ADVANTAGE

One obvious principle determining whether a firm should perform an activity or compete in a business is whether or not the firm possesses resources that provide a competitive advantage in that activity or business. As the previous chapters illustrated, the motivation for geographic expansion and diversification across product markets is that the firm's resources create value in new markets. When the firm's resources generate no unique value in a business, it should not enter that business. This, after all, is why a metal manufacturing company does not compete in the computer industry.

The same argument is also true in the choice of vertical scope. The essential argument for the virtual corporation, for example, is that it should only perform those activities in which the firm's core competences are valuable; all remaining activities should be outsourced to others, just as Nike outsources manufacturing to East Asian companies. More generally, the reason every firm is not vertically integrated into the manufacture of all the materials and equipment it uses, such as telephones, is that their scale would be so low that they would be at a substantial competitive disadvantage if they did so.

Thus, the first determinant of the scope of the firm is simply whether or not the corporation's resources create a competitive advantage in each business or activity. If they do, the firm should consider competing there. If they do not, the firm should not be active in that business unless other reasons require it.

▲ SCOPE OF THE FIRM: MARKET OR HIERARCHY

However, independent of whether there is an underlying economic linkage between businesses or activities, the question still remains: Why should a particular business or activity be performed inside the firm? (See "Questions for Nobel Laureates.")

In the case of diversification, it has to be shown that the best way for a firm to realize value from its resources is to diversify into new businesses itself, rather than just sell or rent its resources to others. Disney, for example, earns substantial income from many different businesses simply by licensing animated characters, such as the Lion King and Pocahontas. It does not need to compete in the fast-food business to appropriate the profits that its characters create from encouraging children to visit a particular restaurant chain.

Similar issues arise in the other two dimensions of scope. With respect to vertical integration, for example, why should Disney own the Disney Stores rather than use franchisees to operate those retail outlets? In the geographic context, why cannot scale economies be exploited by long-term market contracts? Why, for example, should Disney own the largest share of Disneyland Paris, but only choose to receive a management and license fee for operating Tokyo Disneyland for its Japanese owners?

Questions for Nobel Laureates

Delineating firm boundaries may at first sight seem straightforward; however, a closer look reveals that the issue is exceedingly complex. It is at the heart of what economists call the *theory of the firm*, a body of literature that asks fundamental questions about the existence of firms and their ability to achieve things that market transactions alone could not.

Gaining a close understanding of where the lines between markets and firms are drawn is very challenging. Ronald Coase recognized this dilemma in 1937, when he asked, "Why does the entrepreneur not organize one less transaction, or one more?" For this work on the boundaries of firms and other important economic questions, Coase won the Nobel Prize in economics in 1991.

Source: Coase, R., "The Nature of the Firm.," *Economica*, 1937, pp. 386–405.

The choice in each case lies between the two basic forms of economic organization—the **market** and the **hierarchy**. In the former, the price system is used to coordinate the flow of goods and services across separate legal entities. In the latter, goods and services are produced and exchanged within the confines of a firm. Although some activities, such as buying commodities, are very straightforward and easily accomplished through arm's-length market exchanges, the costs of using the price mechanism for others, such as printing a daily newspaper, can be much higher. Organizational economics, therefore, argues that activities should be performed inside the firm, rather than accessed on a market, when administering the activity within the corporate hierarchy is more efficient than conducting it through a market exchange (see "To Print or Not to Print?").

To understand this trade-off, organizational economists examine a basic unit of economic analysis called a **transaction**, which occurs when "a good or service is transferred across a technologically separable interface."[2] For each transaction they then compare the relative costs and benefits of the market and the hierarchy. The costs surrounding a transaction include both the direct costs in producing the good or service and the indirect governance costs associated with completing the transaction, such as the time spent negotiating and enforcing terms of the arrangement. The benefits include the speed and efficiency with which decisions are made, as well as the quality of those decisions.

> The corporate hierarchy will be efficient when it can be shown to be the organizational arrangement that minimizes the sum of production and governance costs. **Production costs** are the direct costs incurred in the physical production and exchange of the item subject to the transaction. **Governance costs** include costs of negotiating, writing, monitoring, enforcing, and possibly also bonding to the terms of the organizational agreement.

Historically, it was believed that production costs were the primary drivers of firm boundaries. An often-cited example was the iron and steel industry, where hot metal was produced in blast furnaces and transported in molten form to an adjacent location to be cast into shapes. The two processes were nearly always owned by the same firm because, it was argued, it would be inefficient for one firm to produce the metal and then let it cool before selling it to another firm to reheat before casting.

---

[2]Oliver E. Williamson, "The Economics of Organization: The Transaction Cost Approach," *American Journal of Sociology*, November 1981, pp. 548–77.

To Print or Not to Print?

There is a substantial difference between local daily newspaper and weekly magazine publishers in their ownership of printing presses. The former generally own their own presses. The latter rarely do so, preferring to contract with outside printers for the production of their magazines. Why should this significant difference in scope occur within the same industry?

An obvious reason would seem to be capacity utilization. A weekly magazine, like *Time*, will be printed on the day before publication. This leaves the presses idle for the other six days of the week. In contrast, a local daily newspaper utilizes the presses every night of the week. However, a weekly magazine publisher could, in principle, sell its excess print capacity to others, just as the outside printer does.

One important and valid reason for the vertical integration of newspaper publishers is the difficulty managing the relationship between the publisher and a printer. Few publishers want to be in the printing business—it is a capital-intensive, low-profit business—yet a newspaper publisher has to control its own printing, in part, for fear that it might be held up by a third-party printer at the last moment.

We are all familiar with the cry, "Stop the presses!" as a late-breaking story requires redoing the front page. But if an independent printer owned the presses it could refuse to cooperate unless paid a huge premium. The publisher, with no alternative available that night, might be willing to pay to ensure that the paper had the breaking story on the front page. Other complexities that result from the frequency and time sensitivity of daily newspaper production would lead any market contract between a printer and a publisher to degenerate into continual bickering.

In contrast, it is easier to contract for the printing of a less time-sensitive weekly or monthly magazine. And if performance is unsatisfactory, another printer for the magazine can be sought anywhere in the United States. Unfortunately, a local daily newspaper needs, for obvious logistical reasons, to be published near the town in which it is sold, where the publisher might well find only a single printer capable of printing it.

Such intricate differences explain the different scopes of the two types of publisher and exemplify the complexity surrounding any firm's decision about its scope.

More recently, however, attention has been placed on the governance costs of these transactions. In the case of iron and steel, for example, it would be quite possible to maintain a physical flow of molten metal even if separate firms owned the different processes. It would be far more difficult to solve the contractual problems that would be created by transferring the product across corporate lines. If the end product was of inferior quality, who would bear the blame? Who would have the right to order changes in the blast furnace to adjust quality? If the caster had a production problem, how much should the blast furnace operator be compensated for having to temporarily shut down its operations? What if one firm wanted to invest in expanding capacity but the other did not? Questions such as these abound when two production processes are tightly linked, yet it is nearly impossible to write contracts that cover all future contingencies. Having both processes owned by one firm, therefore, saves the costs of continual disputes arising from the market governance of such a production process.

Typically, the costs and benefits of the market and hierarchy are analyzed in the context of vertical integration. However, the same principle of comparing the costs and benefits of various organizational arrangements applies equally to diversification and geographic expansion.

For example, as David Teece observed, it is only when the contractual costs of selling or renting excess resources are high that firms themselves can justify diversified expansion into new product markets.[3] Similarly, companies should only become multinational when it is more efficient to perform activities in a foreign country themselves rather than renting their resources, such as a brand name, to local firms.[4]

To clarify the factors that determine the choice between the market and the hierarchical organization of production, we next analyze in detail the costs and benefits of each form of organization.[5]

▲ THE MARKET

Benefits of the Market

The argument that the market is the ideal mechanism for the organization of production goes back to Adam Smith. His notion of the "invisible hand" of market forces maximizing the "wealth of nations" has been enshrined in the philosophy of capitalist economies ever since.[6] It has also been formalized in general equilibrium theory, which demonstrates that under certain, rather restrictive conditions, an economy of independent agents will optimize social welfare.[7] While both of these abstract macroeconomic approaches ignore many of the realities of the modern industrial economy, their underlying premises describe the two main advantages of the market economy and, therefore, of the market organization of production.

The first of these advantages is that the market is more efficient at **information processing** than the administrative hierarchy. At the extreme this can be considered as the advantage of the market over the centrally planned economy. In the former, independent agents make decentralized production decisions in response to a set of market prices. In the latter, all production decisions are made by a single centralized planning body after it has received all the relevant information.

Although the market can lead to suboptimal outcomes,[8] as recent history has demonstrated, it is a more efficient processor of the information needed to make production decisions than central planning. A planned economy could, in principle, reach the optimal production plan if the central planner knew the production possibilities of all the firms; however, in practice it would take a lot of time and vast bureaucratic flows of information to achieve this. Indeed, there are many types of information, such as the know-how possessed

---

[3]D.J. Teece, "Towards an Economic Theory of the Multiproduct Firm," *Journal of Economic Behavior and Organization* 3, 1982, pp. 39–63.

[4]J.H. Dunning, "Trade, Location of Economic Activities, and the MNE: A Search for an Eclectic Approach." In *The International Allocation of Economy Activity*, eds. B. Ohlin et al. (London: Holmes and Meier, 1977), pp. 395–419.

[5]We will address later the intermediate forms of organization, such as joint ventures, that are neither pure hierarchies nor pure market exchanges.

[6]Adam Smith, *The Wealth of Nations* (Dublin: Whitestone, 1776).

[7]K. Arrow and G. Debreu, "Existence of Equilibrium for a Competitive Economy," *Econometrica* 22 (1954), pp. 265–90.

[8]The inefficiencies of the market organization of production include duplication of effort, as occurred in the Winchester disk drive industry when too many firms invested in a single market opportunity (W.A. Sahlman and H.H. Stevenson, "Capital Market Myopia," *Journal of Business Venturing* 1985, pp. 7–30), and disequilibrium trades and delays as prices slowly converge on an equilibrium (P. Bolton and J. Farrell, "Decentralisation, Duplication and Delay," *Journal of Political Economy* 98 (1990), pp. 803–26).

by a team of craftspeople, that simply cannot be transferred up the hierarchy.[9] In contrast, the market does not require an expensive infrastructure to administer because all information is combined and made available in a set of market prices. Indeed, before its demise, designers of central planning proposed mimicking the price system to economize on the costs of information processing.

This argues that it is the decentralized and indirect use of information via a price mechanism that is more efficient than an administrative hierarchy as a means of transferring the information needed to make production decisions and allocate resources within the economy. By analogy, using a market system to govern production decisions is often more efficient than having those decisions made within a corporate hierarchy.

The second benefit of the market organization of production relates to **incentives**. When production is carried out by independent owners, each receives all the profits from their own endeavors. Thus, each has the incentive to work as hard and as efficiently as possible. Self-interested behavior, therefore, ensures that the market organization of production benefits from high powered incentives.

In contrast, inefficiencies arise inside the corporate hierarchy because individuals do not receive all the profit they generate. They, therefore, do not have the incentive to maximize corporate profits, but rather to maximize their own welfare. As a result, levels of *ability, effort, and investment* may be lower inside the corporation than in sole proprietorships. Highly skilled workers, for example, may choose to be self-employed because they anticipate earning more money operating their own businesses. Similarly, self-employed workers will probably work harder and take better care of their tools than employees using company tools. Finally, if self-employed salespeople own their customer lists, they will invest more in building and maintaining those lists than if they are employees of a company that owns the list.[10] As a result, lower skill, effort, and investment inside the hierarchy lead to higher production costs. Thus, this perspective argues that the direct production costs of individual proprietors transacting with one another on the market will often be lower than those involving employees inside a corporate hierarchy.

Costs of the Market: Transaction Costs and Market Failure

The original perspective on the scope of the firm, introduced by Coase and called **transaction cost theory** because it took the transaction as the unit of analysis, recognized the intrinsic merits of markets and concentrated on identifying the costs associated with market transactions. It therefore concentrated on identifying the conditions under which markets are very expensive ways to organize transactions, or in the extreme, fail because those costs are so high. Only in that case, transaction cost theory argued, will the corporate hierarchy become the preferred mode of organization.

A classic example of high transaction costs leading to **market failure** was General Motors' relationship with Fisher Body in the 1920s over the supply of car bodies.[11] GM wanted Fisher Body to build a new plant adjacent to a GM car assembly factory. Fisher Body refused, fearing that once the factory was built, GM could credibly threaten to pay little more

---

[9]M. Jensen and W.H. Meckling, "Specific and General Knowledge, and Organization Structure," in *Main Currents in Contract Economics*, eds. L. Werin and H. Wijkander (Oxford: Blackwell, 1991), pp. 251–274.
[10]S. Grossman and O. Hart, "The Costs and Benefits of Ownership: A Theory of Vertical and Lateral Integration," *Journal of Political Economy* 94 (1986), pp. 691–719.
[11]B. Klein, R. Crawford, and A. Alchain, "Vertical Integration, Appropriable Rents, and the Competitive Contracting Process," *Journal of Law and Economics* 21 (1978), pp. 297–326.

than the variable cost of stamping car bodies. At that point, Fisher Body would have no real choice other than to supply GM, because of the costs involved in finding and switching to a new customer (taking out the GM car-body molds, installing new molds, bearing the transportation costs to the new customer's plant, and so forth). Thus, the threat of GM exploiting Fisher Body once it had made the investment led to a market failure. To avoid this, and to have the stamping plant built next door to reduce production costs, GM bought Fisher Body and internalized the transaction inside the firm.[12]

This example illustrates many of the conditions that lead to market failure. Specifically, market relationships fail when they are subject to:

- ▲ Opportunism
- ▲ Asset specificity (small numbers)
- ▲ Uncertainty
- ▲ High Frequency

The premise of transaction cost theory is that because people act in their own self-interest, if the market relationship allows them to do so, they will behave **opportunistically**— that is, they will seek to benefit themselves at the expense of others, just as GM would have taken advantage of Fisher Body (see "Opportunism, Trust, and Reputation"). It is the possibility of firms acting in this way that causes market failure. The other three conditions listed above create the potential for a firm to act opportunistically.

Opportunism, Trust, and Reputation

Transaction cost theory views all individuals as self-interested and, therefore, opportunistic. Although this assumption is common to nearly all of organizational economics, it leaves transaction cost theory vulnerable to criticism. If there can be trust in a relationship, so that both parties believe that even when the possibility to behave opportunistically presents itself, the other party will not do so, then the market form of organization need never fail. If one party unfailingly trusts the other to follow the spirit of a contract they have made, no matter what opportunity for self-interested behavior arises, a market contract can be capable of efficiently organizing transactions.

Although trust is not the universal solution to market failure, it can be important in certain situations. Particularly in less individualistic cultures, such as Japan, trust can be used to explain the existence of markets that transaction theory could not—markets that might in fact be more efficient than hierarchical arrangements. Japanese car manufacturer relationships with their suppliers, for example, are often portrayed in this light and compared favorably to those of U.S. auto manufacturers.

However, behavior that looks like trust can still be observed in societies where everyone is opportunistic. If a company builds a reputation for acting opportunistically, others will not want to do business with it. Thus, a concern for how reputation may affect future profits can deter firms from acting opportunistically, even when they are culturally and psychologically predisposed to do so.

---

[12]Note that there are other solutions to this problem. One is trust—Fisher Body remains independent because it trusts GM not to act opportunistically. The other is reputation. GM does not exploit Fisher Body because if it did so other component suppliers may refuse to do business with it in the future.

Market failure requires **asset specificity**, that is, an asset that is dedicated (specific) to a particular application. In such cases, the party that has made the investment is vulnerable to exploitation because the asset would be worth less in another application. Consider a firm that has customized its production facility to use a particular grade of raw material supplied by only one producer. If the supplier tries to raise the price of the raw material, what alternatives does the buyer have? It can look for a different supplier, but if it does switch it will have to reconfigure its production facility for the new grade of material, which would be expensive. The firm, then, would be prepared to pay an amount equal to the reconfiguration cost, over and above the original price for the raw material, before it would consider switching suppliers.

Types of asset specificity include location, physical, and human capital:[13]

- ▲ **Location specificity** occurs when buyers and sellers locate fixed assets in close proximity to minimize transport and inventory costs.
- ▲ **Physical asset specificity** occurs when one party or both parties to a transaction invest in equipment that is dedicated to a particular, limited use.
- ▲ **Human capital specificity** occurs when employees develop skills that are specialized to a particular relationship or a given organization.

The frequent occurrence of such investments suggests that the phenomenon of asset specificity is actually quite common. Building a power plant next to a coal mine to minimize transport costs is an example of location specificity. Customizing a plant to a particular grade of material is an example of physical specificity. The network of personal relationships that managers develop inside a firm, which makes their working elsewhere less efficient, is an example of human capital specificity.

As Oliver Williamson argued, investments such as these that are specific to an application create a small numbers bargaining problem. After making such an investment, the purchasing firm is unable to negotiate freely and equally with other potential suppliers, as might well have been possible before the investment was made; instead, a firm is locked into buying from only a few suppliers, and often only one. This gives the supplier bargaining power that allows it to act opportunistically and so leads to the market failure.[14]

The obvious solution to the problem of one party acting opportunistically would be to write a contract for the duration of the asset that simply prevents such behavior. Why doesn't Fisher Body just set a contract price for the supply of car bodies that GM cannot renegotiate? This is when the condition of **uncertainty** comes into play. It would be impossible to write a comprehensive long-term contract if the nature of the transaction is such that all possible future eventualities cannot be written down. If the contract would have to cover an enormous number of clauses, such as, "if demand for the product increases 10 percent in less than one month, the supplier is entitled to deliver only 8 percent more product," it becomes prohibitively expensive to write and enforce.[15] The more uncertainties there are, the more difficult it is to write a long-term contract that covers all possible contingencies, and the more likely that the market will fail.

---

[13]O.E. Williamson, *The Economic Institutions of Capitalism* (New York: Free Press, 1985).

[14]Note, however, that asset specificity almost always leads to a bilateral threat of holdup. In principle, Fisher Body could have held up GM, just as easily as GM could hold up Fisher Body. Once GM had negotiated a price with Fisher Body and installed the molds at its factory, Fisher Body could raise the price. GM would be powerless to object because it would have to remove the molds, install them in another supplier, and potentially lose several months of car production. In practice, however, GM's bargaining power would have overwhelmed Fisher Body.

[15]Indeed, given "bounded nationality"—physical limits to what the mind can process—it will most likely be impossible R.M. Cyert, and J.G. March, *A Behavioral Theory of the Firm* (Englewood Cliffs, NJ: Prentice Hall, 1963).

Finally, it is argued that **high transaction frequency** increases the likelihood of market failure. Frequent transactions repeatedly expose a firm to holdup, so that haggling and negotiation occur more often. To eliminate these costs, and remedy the market failure, vertical integration is often necessary. In contrast, for one-time or occasional transactions, such as a public construction project, vertical integration is unlikely.

Many empirical tests have been conducted to demonstrate the validity of transaction cost theory, particularly in the context of vertical integration. For example, asset specificity (measured by the amount of customized engineering required) has been shown to be an important determinant of vertical integration in the auto components industry.[16] Likewise, the link between physical site specificity and ownership, in the cases of electricity generating stations owning their suppliers of coal and alumina smelters owning their suppliers of bauxite, has also been demonstrated.[17] The same research also found evidence of the effects of frequency and uncertainty on the presence of market versus hierarchical arrangements.

In summary, transaction cost theory identifies durable relationships involving asset specificity, uncertainty, and high frequency of transactions as conditions for market failure. Whenever arm's length market exchange for the sale (or purchase) of a good or service fails, a firm will have to establish some form of hierarchical control over the transaction.

Other Sources of Market Failure

Even without the specific investments that are critical to transactions cost theory, there are other situations in which markets fail. One such instance is **inseparability**—the impossibility of separating one resource from others within a firm.[18] For example, vacationers who perceive lodging as an integral part of their Disney World experience are unable to separate their hotel stay from their overall perception of the Disney brand name. To preserve the latter, Disney believes it must operate the former, and so does not contract out the management of its Disneyworld hotels.

Other failures can arise in the **market for information**.[19] When information can be easily conveyed to others, there is still a classic paradox over its sale. Buyers don't want to pay for information without knowing its content, but sellers don't want to reveal their information before being paid. As a result, when individuals or firms have valuable information, such as the location of a new motorway, they often use it themselves rather than selling it on the market.

Other failures arise when information simply cannot be transferred. This is the case of **tacit knowledge**—knowledge that cannot be written down in a set of blueprints or equations.[20] Archetypal examples are riding a bicycle and shooting pool. However much physics you have studied, you cannot actually ride a bike or pocket a pool ball unless you

---

[16]D.J. Teece and K. Monteverde, "Supplier Switching Costs and Vertical Integration in the Automobile Industry," *Bell Journal of Economics* 25 (1979), pp. 833–48; and G. Walker and D. Weber, "A Transaction Cost Approach to Make-or-Buy Decisions," *Administrative Science Quarterly*, September 1984, pp. 373–91.

[17]P. Joskow, "Vertical Integration and Long-Term Contracts: The Case of Coal-Burning Electric Generating Plants," *Journal of Law, Economics, and Organization*, Spring 1985, pp. 33–80; and J. A. Stuckey, *Vertical Integration and Joint Ventures in the Aluminum Industry* (Cambridge, MA: Ballinger, 1987), pp. 185–220.

[18]D.J. Teece, "Economies of Scope and the Scope of the Enterprise," *Journal of Economic Behavior and Organization*, September 1980, pp. 373–91.

[19]K. Arrow, *Economics of Information* (Cambridge, MA: Belknap Press, 1984).

[20]M. Polyani, *Personal Knowledge* (New York: Harper Torchbooks, 1962).

have practiced how to do it. Thus, tacit knowledge is difficult to sell because it cannot be transferred in written form, it can only be recreated by an individual or firm learning the skill for itself.[21]

Resources that involve tacit knowledge, such as a unique consumer marketing capability that resides in a management team, therefore, are particularly vulnerable to market failure. Indeed such informational resources are the basis for many corporate strategies of diversification. David Teece, for example, found that oil companies were more likely to diversify into markets for alternative fuels that shared proprietary know-how.[22]

A final cause of market failure is not due to efficiency considerations, as are all the previous arguments, but to the exercise of **market power**. More specifically, markets can fail when a firm achieves the *vertical foreclosure* of competitors. This was the idea that Rockefeller exploited in building Standard Oil in the late 19th century. His insight was that by controlling the railroad and pipeline transportation of oil, he could squeeze out his competitors in the oil business, a strategy later made illegal by the Sherman Antitrust Act of 1890. Rockefeller first exploited the benefits of the large size of Standard Oil (by 1869, Standard's Cleveland oil refinery was the largest in the world) to gain leverage with the railroads and later with pipelines. By controlling both the oil production and railroad transportation businesses, Rockefeller then locked production-only competitors out of the market. He could then acquire the firms that Standard wanted at distress prices and drive out of the oil business those firms that it did not need. To avoid being foreclosed from the market, competitors would have had to vertically integrate into the transportation of their own oil. Rockefeller's control of oil transportation, therefore, effectively led to the failure of that market.

This is a dramatic example of a phenomenon that by definition can only be found in concentrated industries, or when a dominant player exists.

Summary

Theory can explain the existence and scope of the firm from the perspective of market failure. Recognizing the potential information processing and incentive advantages of markets, it argues that a firm's activities should be limited to those involving transactions for which the costs of market exchange are extremely high. However, it is also possible to explain the boundaries of the firm from the opposite perspective—considering the advantages and disadvantages of the hierarchy.

▲ THE HIERARCHY

Benefits of the Hierarchy

The benefits of the corporate hierarchy, which allow it to efficiently organize transactions when the market fails, lie in the nature of the hierarchical relationship and the unified ownership structure of the firm.[23]

---

[21]Tacit knowledge is an example of path dependency in the accumulation of a resource, and so is often a valuable and inimitable resource (see Chapter 2).

[22]Teece, "Economies of Scope and the Scope of the Enterprise," pp. 223–47.

[23]Note that the hierarchy itself involves a contractual relationship—the employment relation. Thus, the distinguishing aspect of a firm as a "nexus of contracts" is that it defines residual rights of control (who decides what happens when contracts do not precisely specify behavior) and residual property rights (who retains the profits after all participants have received their contractual payments).

Unlike a market relationship, where no one has **authority** over anyone else, inside the firm superiors are vested with the power, both legal and cultural, to tell employees what to do within broad bounds set out by the employment contract and societal norms. Thus, opportunism and the unproductive bargaining that cause the market to fail can be reduced when corporate executives mandate behavior and then monitor subordinates.

Unified ownership also reduces the pursuit of local goals, unambiguously determines a clear corporate goal, and provides easier access to the relevant information needed to settle disputes.[24] Once all profits flow to the corporation, executives may ignore the conflicting incentives of various units, but can maximize corporate profits.

The hierarchy is particularly effective when there is an ongoing need for intense **coordination** among parties to a transaction.[25] This occurs whenever tasks are mutually dependent, so that appropriate actions by each party depend on what others do. It is easiest to see in the design of a complex product that does not have well defined interfaces between components—what Milgrom and Roberts called *design interconnectedness*.[26] Boeing, for example, takes overall design responsibility for an airframe even though much component design and manufacturing is outsourced.

In this context, a hierarchy is more likely to produce the optimal system design rather than one that reflects the sum of the best individual component designs. Moreover, a hierarchy minimizes the continual bargaining over each unit's profit (the share of the pie), that can prevent the best overall design (the size of the pie) from emerging.[27] For example, an independent manufacturer of auto emission catalysts is less likely to suggest a change in the design of the exhaust system if it leads to less use of catalysts.[28] Although these coordination problems do not completely disappear inside the hierarchy, they are usually reduced.

Costs of the Hierarchy

The exercise of authority inside the corporate hierarchy does not come without costs. If it did, the corporation could extend its scope indefinitely through what is called *selective intervention*—letting divisions make all their own decisions except those that require corporatewide coordination.

The costs of the hierarchy include the drawbacks typically associated with the **bureaucracy** of large-scale organizations that impede efficient information processing: the expense of layers of management in the corporate hierarchy; the slowness and inflexibility of

---

[24]Transaction cost theory, somewhat controversially, argues that the hierarchy can monitor and audit behavior at a lower cost than the market (Williamson, *Economic Institutions of Capitalism*, p. 155). Another theoretical perspective within organizational economics, imperfect decision making, examines the circumstances under which hierarchies are preferable because they allow for the overseeing of individuals, who, however well intentioned and thorough their analyses, will occasionally make incorrect decisions (R.K. Sah and J.E. Stiglitz, "Human Fallibility and Economic Organization," *American Economic Review*, May–June 1985, pp. 292–97.

[25]Alchian and Demsetz argued that a firm must exist when coordination involves team production where the effort of each individual cannot be measured (A. Alchian, and H. Demsetz, "Production, Information Costs and Economic Organization," *American Economic Review*, December 1972, pp. 777–95.)

[26]P. Milgrom and J. Roberts, *Economic, Organization and Management* (Englewood Cliffs, NJ: Prentice Hall, 1992).

[27]This is the argument surrounding incomplete contracts. See Grossman and Hart, op. cit (footnote 10).

[28]The argument that firms should vertically integrate to maximize profitability by setting marginal revenue equal to the sum of marginal costs at each stage in the chain, rather than simply the marginal cost of the last player in the chain, is similar. Without vertical integration, profitability in the whole chain is reduced because participants at each stage try to maximize their own profit.

Influence Costs

One set of costs of the hierarchy has recently received a lot of attention. Termed **influence costs**, they are closely related but not identical to agency costs.[29] Their premise is that a lot of activity inside corporations is wastefully directed toward influencing the decisions of the firm in ways that will produce favorable results for the individual involved. The simplest example would be people lobbying to get the biggest office in the building. This sort of activity, while prevalent in large corporations and immediately recognizable as internal office politics, is, of course, pure waste.

Influence costs inside firms do not presume divergent interests between owners and employees or superiors and subordinates. Influence costs will be incurred whenever there is jockeying for position among participants inside an organization. It is competition among peers for the distribution of the wealth available to the workforce, rather than overt conflict between principals and subordinates, that is the concern of influence costs.[30]

bureaucratic decision making; the difficulties corporate executives have in controlling businesses that may have different dominant logics; and the waste incurred in office politics (see "Influence Costs"). All are costs of performing activities inside the firm.

However, probably the greatest costs of the corporate hierarchy involve what are called **agency costs.** These are the costs that arise when individuals act in their own self-interest, rather than acting to maximize corporate performance (see "Agency Costs").[31] Agency costs are therefore prevalent throughout an organization whenever there is a divergence of interests between shareholders and managers,[32] superiors and subordinates, or, as we will use to illustrate, the corporate office and divisional executives.[33]

In its starkest form (the so-called **moral hazard** problem), the argument of agency theory is that because corporate executives do have access to exactly the same information as divisional management and cannot monitor their every action, divisional managers will pursue their own interests. The resulting behavior may involve simply slacking on the job, such as playing golf on Friday afternoons; but it will more likely involve actions, such as divisional managers acting to reach targets that trigger their bonuses even at the expense of corporate profits; fudging the numbers in favor of investments that expand the size of their own divisions; or refusing to transfer a highly regarded executive to another division. Such behavior incurs both direct production costs—resulting, for example, from the lower effort put out by divisional managers and their inappropriate decisions—as well as the governance costs of the

---

[29]P. Milgrom and J. Roberts, *Economics, Organization and Management* (Englewood Cliffs, NJ: Prentice Hall, 1992).

[30]Influence costs have more typically been examined in the context of public policy, where individuals and groups lobby for legislation that favors their own interests.

[31]M. Jensen and W. H. Meckling, "Theory of the Firm," *Journal of Financial Economics* 3, no. 4 (1976), pp. 305–60, and K. M. Eisenhardt, "Agency Theory: An Assessment and Review," *Academy of Management Review* 14, no. 1 (1989), pp. 57–74.

[32]The implications of agency costs between shareholders and managers are examined in the chapter on corporate governance (Chapter 8).

[33]One reason for the divergence of interest between principals and agents is their respective attitudes toward risk. Agents whose careers depend on the performance of the company are typically assumed to be risk averse while principals for whom there is only one investment are typically assumed to be risk neutral.

Agency Costs

Agency costs arise from the failure of the hierarchical relationship between the principal (typically thought of as the owner of the firm) and the agent (typically an employee). They include production costs resulting from self-interested behavior by agents and the governance costs of writing, monitoring, and bonding to any systems put in place to reduce the principal's losses from that behavior.

The underlying conditions for the existence of agency costs are :

▲ **Asymmetric Interests**. Agents act to maximize their personal welfare and do not automatically act in the interest of principals.

▲ **Private Information**. Because principals do not have access to all of the same information as agents, they incur monitoring costs and have difficulty assessing their skill and effort.

▲ **Uncertainty**. Since performance is affected by unpredictable, exogenous events, principals usually cannot accurately reward agents on the observed outcomes of their behavior.

monitoring and control systems, such as budgets, capital expenditure approvals, and HR reviews that are put in place to prevent such behavior. These are costs of the hierarchical mode of organization.

To minimize self-interested behavior that cannot be prevented by direct monitoring (see "Human Nature"), corporate executives usually install an incentive scheme that attempts to align the interests of divisional managers as closely as possible with those of the corporate office. They might, for example, reward divisional managers on the performance of the whole company as well as their own divisions. Such an incentive scheme can reduce, but will never eliminate, the cost of self-interested behavior: the more divisional managers are rewarded on corporate pay, for example, the less incentive they will have to maximize their own divisions' performance. In addition, there are always expenses involved in the design and maintenance of any incentive scheme.

Other agency costs of the corporate hierarchy result from **adverse selection**. This refers to the inability of the firm to select desirable workers when it cannot accurately distinguish their intrinsic quality before hiring them.[34] For example, start-up firms in Silicon Valley would like to hire innovative and entrepreneurial managers. They would even be willing to pay such individuals more than the average salary because they would create more value. However, since companies are limited in their ability to distinguish such workers from less innovative managers before they hire them, they cannot offer to pay those individuals their true worth. Therefore, individuals who know they have desirable skills but cannot credibly convey that information will choose to establish their own businesses, if they are able to do

---

[34]The costs of adverse selection can also lead to market failures. This was demonstrated in a classic article on the market for used cars (G. Akerlof, "The Market for Lemons: Qualitative Uncertainty and the Market Mechanism," *Quarterly Journal of Economics* 84, 1970, pp. 488–500). Most used cars that are for sale will be of poor quality because any owner who knows that his or her car is reliable will choose (select) to keep driving it. Even if owners want to sell, buyers, who cannot accurately determine a car's quality even in an inspection, will be skeptical that it is reliable and so won't pay much for it. This provides another reason for owners of good-quality cars to keep them off the market. In turn, this reduces the average quality of used cars that are sold, so lowering the price a buyer will pay, leading fewer people with good cars to sell them, and so on.

Some critics of agency theory argue that its premises are unrealistic because they are based on a flawed view of human nature.[35] These critics argue that if people are not treated as individualistic, but, at least partly, as altruistic, and if they value things other than money, then a basic assumption of agency theory is violated.

This is not correct. Agency theory assumes nothing more about human nature than that people are calculating rational actors who respond to incentives in order to maximize whatever they value. Agency theory does not specify what individuals value. It is quite possible for individuals to be altruistic. It is also quite feasible in agency theory to have individuals derive pleasure from peer praise, self-esteem, position in the hierarchy, quality of lifestyle, and so forth. All of these variables can be included in the payoffs that individuals seek to maximize.

Although such an argument supports the theory, real life is more complicated because we never know exactly what any particular individual values, nor can incentive systems be fine-tuned to each individual's motivation.

so, knowing that they will earn more than the salary offered.[36] While an incentive scheme, such as giving managers phantom stock in their divisions, rather than a straight salary, will alleviate some of the problem (only those with confidence in their own entrepreneurial skills will seek out such a compensation scheme) it cannot completely eliminate the costs of adverse selection.

Level of Costs.   Agency costs differ dramatically across businesses and activities. They can be limited, however, by installing incentive schemes that align the interests of employees with those of the owner. As we will see, this is more difficult, and more costly, to achieve in some situations than in others.

If the managerial behavior itself, or an outcome measure that is tightly correlated with managerial skills and effort can be **cheaply and accurately monitored**, it will be easy to design an incentive system that produces the desired behavior, and agency costs will be low.[37] The quality of store managers' contributions, for example, can often be accurately measured by their stores' profitability, so that a profit-based incentive scheme ensures that they will not be able to slack without paying the penalty. In contrast, when it is difficult to directly observe the behavior of managers, or use performance of their units as a surrogate, incentive systems will be less effective, and agency costs will be higher. It is notoriously difficult, for example, to assess the effectiveness of an R&D team because the link between their effort and the success of a project is often weak. In this setting, incentive schemes that are too tightly tied to

---

[35]Michael J. Brennan, "Incentives, Rationality, and Society," *Journal of Applied Corporate Finance*, Summer 1994, pp. 31–39.
[36]The critical condition for the existence of adverse selection is asymmetric information. The individual has private information about how entrepreneurial he or she is, which the firm cannot verify. One solution to adverse selection, therefore, involves the individual incurring costs to acquire a "signal" of those dimensions of quality that cannot objectively be evaluated (A.M. Spence, *Market Signalling: Information Transfer in Hiring and Related Processes* [Cambridge, MA: Harvard University Press, 1973]). The fact that most readers of this book are acquiring MBAs partly reflects their desire to learn something about management, but also, in part, reflects the importance of the MBA as a signal of inherent quality.
[37]Eisenhardt, "Agency Theory" op cit; and W.G. Ouchi, "A Conceptual Framework for the Design of Organizational Control Mechanisms," *Management Science* 25 (1979), pp. 833–48.

performance may be demotivating. Not doing so, however, creates slack that allows R&D managers to shirk or pursue their own interests.

When employees' skills and efforts have a **substantial impact on performance**, the absence of an effective incentive system can be particularly costly. The quality of the contribution of senior managers, for example, can dramatically affect their firms' long-run performance. As a result, the costs of any self-interested behavior that does occur may be high. In contrast, even if a night watchman sleeps on the job, it is likely to have little effect on his performance.

Summary

Although hierarchies have the advantage of authority and unified ownership, they inevitably incur agency costs. Theory suggests these costs will be highest when an employee's skill and effort are important, but difficult to measure accurately. It will be under these circumstances that the expense of the hierarchy may limit the scope of the firm.

It is for these reasons that most large corporations, for example, do not have in-house advertising departments. The skill and effort of creative talent is critical to the development of a good advertisement, yet monitoring how effectively creative people work is very difficult. In addition, evaluating the performance of an advertising campaign is hard. Moreover, talented advertising executives have the choice of establishing their own companies. Thus, rather than incur the agency costs of operating an advertising department inside the corporate hierarchy, most corporations, including those like Unilever that once had their own advertising staffs, now employ outside agencies.

▲ CONCLUSION: THE CHOICE BETWEEN MARKET AND HIERARCHY

Neither the market nor the hierarchy is the ideal form of organization. If either was, the economy would be dominated by one firm or made up exclusively of self-employed individuals. Instead, each form of organization has its costs and each has its benefits. (See Figure 5–1.) In most cases, it will be obvious when a business or activity is best conducted inside a firm or on the market. However, there will be many instances when there is neither a clear market failure, nor overwhelmingly high agency costs inside the firm. In such cases, there is ultimately a trade-off between the market and the hierarchy as mechanisms for the organization of production.

The market benefits from high-powered incentives and efficient information processing because individuals receive the profits from their work and respond to decentralized market prices. However, the market can fail when conditions surrounding an exchange lead to high transaction costs or the exercise of market power.

Conversely, the hierarchy is often more effective at coordinating activity because it can define routines and employ authority that workers, within bounds, will obey. However, the hierarchy incurs bureaucratic costs and the agency costs that result from self-interested behavior by subordinates.

The most complex decisions concerning mode of organization often come down to a trade-off between incentives and coordination. When providing high-powered incentives to individuals is important because of the effect their skill and effort has on performance, the market may ultimately be preferred. When there is a need for continual coordination of activities, the hierarchy may be more efficient.

▲ FIGURE 5–1   Cost and Benefit of the Market and Hierarchy

	Market	Hierarchy
Benefits	Informational efficiency High-powered incentives	Authority Coordination
Costs	Transaction costs Market power	Bureaucracy Agency costs

If we array the set of businesses a firm could enter in descending order according to the value the corporate resources create in those businesses, the firm should only consider including within the corporate hierarchy all those where the benefit is greater than the cost (to the left of A in Figure 5–2). However, since the costs of the hierarchy will increase with broadening scope, if for no other reason than the span of control is increasing, while the market transaction costs are more or less independent of firm scope, the organizational boundary of the firm (B) often comes before this point.[38] Indeed, it is usually the comparative costs of administering a business within the hierarchy and on the market that determines the scope of the firm.

Intermediate Forms of Organization

A problem with the analysis so far is the assumption that the choice of organizational form is binary—that the choice is either the market or the hierarchy. In fact, the range of alternatives more closely resembles a long and varied spectrum (see Figure 5–3). At one extreme is the market, which refers to a well-organized spot market where goods and services are bought and sold at arm's length. At the other extreme is the corporate hierarchy where all the activities are ensconced within the legal boundaries of a firm. In between are a variety of alternative ways to organize a given transaction. Some of these, such as joint ventures, more closely resemble the corporate hierarchy. Others, such as long-term market contracts are market-based alternatives, although they differ considerably from spot market transactions. Indeed, Hennart has gone so far as to call these intermediate forms of governance "the swollen middle" to indicate how common they are in practice.[39]

We do not have space to go into the details of all the intermediate organizational forms. In general, these forms, to greater or lesser extent, combine the strengths and weaknesses of the archetypes. Therefore, the principles determining the costs and benefits of the market and hierarchy, as outlined above, remain appropriate for the analysis of intermediate forms and demonstrate that no form of organization is universally superior.

---

[38]In practice, the costs of the hierarchy and the market are not continuous with expansions of scope (as they appear to be in Figure 5–2). Rather, as the previous discussion demonstrated, they vary with each individual business or activity.

[39]Jean-Francois Hennart, "Explaining the Swollen Middle: Why Most Transactions Are a Mix of 'Market' and 'Hierarchy,'" *Organization Science* 4, no. 4, pp. 529–74.

▲ FIGURE 5–2   The Limit to Firm Scope

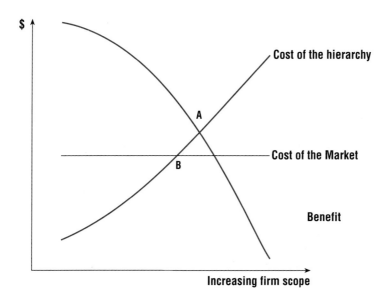

▲ FIGURE 5–3   A Spectrum of Governance Structures

| Spot market exchange | Long-term contracts | Alliances | Joint ventures | Integration |

Williamson, for example, matched governance structures to the attributes of transactions to predict which types of transactions can efficiently employ so-called "mixed modes" of governance. In essence, he predicted that standardized transactions (whatever the frequency) will be handled through the market (classical contracting procedures). In contrast, repeated asset specific investments will be done under the firm hierarchy (unified governance). In between, a host of intermediate solutions will be based on structures, where the autonomy of the parties is maintained (such as joint ventures), or where there are specific third party mechanisms for resolving disputes (for example, arbitration).

PRACTICE

▲ CHOOSING THE SCOPE OF THE FIRM

Although the principles outlined above apply to decisions about the boundary of the firm in all three dimensions of scope, as we said earlier, the ideal place to apply them is to the analysis of vertical integration—the make-or-buy decision. This dimension of scope is currently subject to much examination as firms look to outsource many activities and services that were previously unquestioningly accepted as part of the corporate hierarchy.

Bias to the Market

The underlying premise behind the analysis is that activities should be performed outside rather than inside the firm unless there are compelling reasons to the contrary. The arguments for this bias are the production cost benefits that independent suppliers can exploit, and the governance cost benefits of high-powered incentives and decentralized information processing. The firm inevitably incurs agency costs, so the burden of proof in the analysis of vertical integration will be on justifying why the firm itself should perform a given activity. This principle is contrary to the traditional practice in many large companies for whom the bias was to perform activities in-house. These companies appear to have often overestimated the costs of market exchange while simultaneously overestimating the benefits of the hierarchy.

Today, an increasing number of firms are using market contracting, rather than vertical integration, to coordinate production. One such company is Benetton, the Italian clothing manufacturer.[40] Ninety-nine percent of its knitting, all of its assembly, and most of its finishing are carried out by several hundred small independent contractors, while all its products are sold through independently owned shops. Only a substantial amount of dyeing is done in-house. The whole system is coordinated by a sophisticated management information system system that links stores, production scheduling, and contractors. As a result, Benetton is able to adapt flexibly to uncertain fashion demand without bearing the fixed costs of its own manufacturing capacity.

Given the viability of this model of independent market contracting, the historical bias to perform activities inside the firm can be problematic. Adjusting to the new principle will require a fundamental shift in thinking about the appropriate scope of many companies and a careful assessment of the production and governance costs of the two modes of organization at every stage in their activities (see "When Not to Vertically Integrate").

▲ A DECISION PROCESS

Based on the principles outlined above, we can propose a process that can be applied to decisions about the vertical scope of the firm. The process involves a logical sequence of steps that lead to a conclusion about whether or not a firm should vertically integrate into a particular activity. It should be stressed, however, that issues concerning the organizational boundaries of a firm are some of the most complicated facing the corporate strategist and that there are often no easy answers.

Step 1: Disaggregate the Industry Value Chain

The analysis of vertical integration can only proceed after the industry value chain has been disaggregated into all the production steps that are physically capable of being separated. Too broad a definition of activities can lead firms to compete in an activity simply because of its adjacency to another activity they do perform well. For example, many firms historically developed their own computer programs for production control, arguing that these were integral to their production process. However, outside programs were often found to be better because they were developed by software experts. Determining the appropriate

---

[40]J.L. Heskett, "Benetton Group," Harvard Business School Case no. 396–177.

When Not to Vertically Integrate

There are many fallacies about when vertical integration makes sense. One is that physical linkages in the production process, such as those between different processing stages in an oil refinery, require vertical integration. Although often true because of the need for intense coordination of physically linked processes and specific asset investments, on some occasions such separate processes may be carried out by different firms.

Another fallacy is that it is necessary to backward (or forward) integrate to secure favorable prices in a cyclical industry. This is incorrect. If the firm supplies itself in preference to other customers when supplies are short, it is forgoing the option of charging high prices for those supplies. If it charged itself a transfer price that reflected true market prices, it would find there was no benefit to being integrated.

A third fallacy is that it is good to forward integrate into higher value-added parts of the value chain. This too is often incorrect. Firms want to be in the most profitable part of the value chain, but value-added and profitability often do not correlate. Moreover, a firm's resources do not necessarily allow it to compete successfully in a higher value added business.

A last fallacy is that a firm should backward integrate simply because it is a large purchaser and can exploit manufacturing scale economies. While firms may be above minimum efficient scale for the production of a particular component, specialist outside suppliers who are also above that scale often benefit from efficiencies across a full range of activities, from R&D to service. Further, focused suppliers often are more successful in realizing dynamic innovations.

level of disaggregation of activities is therefore an important prerequisite to analyzing the desired degree of vertical integration.

The intrinsic structural attractiveness of each activity in the industry value chain should then be analyzed. Each can be thought of, at least conceptually, as a discrete business whose profit potential varies according to its underlying structure. In the Australian concrete industry, for example, most of the industry profit is captured in cement production and stone and sand quarrying (see Figure 5–4). More competitive stages of the industry, such as concrete mixing, cover cash costs and provide a fair return on invested capital but create no economic profit.

Having mapped out the separate stages in an industry and determined their expected average profit potential, firms can now apply a set of questions to decide whether or not they should compete in any given stage. The result of decisions made at each stage will determine the overall scope of the firm.

The analysis begins by assuming there are efficiently functioning markets at every stage in the industry value chain. Subsequent steps will address situations where this is not the case.

Step 2: Competitive Advantage

Do you have a competitive advantage in the performance of the activity?

When there are efficient markets, decisions to participate in a given stage of an industry depend simply on whether or not it would be profitable for the firm to do so. That is, could the firm earn a return above its cost of capital? This depends on the fundamental attractiveness of the business and whether or not the firm possesses a competitive advantage that would enable it to make the product (or perform the service) more efficiently than outside suppliers.

▲ FIGURE 5–4   Australian Concrete Industry Value Chain

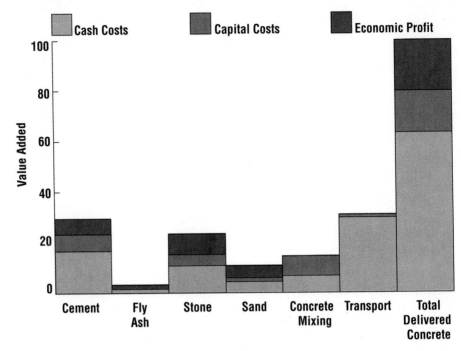

Index: Delivered price of concrete per ton = 100

Source: Adapted from J. A. Stuckey and D. White. "When and When Not to Vertically Integrate," *Sloan Management Review*, Spring 1993, p. 77.

Indeed, when there are perfect markets, the firms that own the valuable resources in an industry should be able to appropriate most of the profit, without having to compete in all stages of the industry. In the personal computer (PC) industry, for example, Intel and Microsoft are able to appropriate a substantial share of industry profits just by providing the microprocessor and the operating system, respectively. They are not vertically integrated into the manufacture and sale of PCs themselves.

This is the argument behind the virtual corporation. Performing only one or two critical activities, while accessing other goods and services from competitive markets, the virtual corporation is presumed to be able to capture most of the profits from an industry and may also use its flexibility and low fixed costs as a source of competitive advantage.

One unusual example of this is Sulzer, a Swiss machinery manufacturer.[41] For many years, Sulzer was the world leader in marine diesel engines, even though it came from a mountainous and landlocked country and did not even make the engines itself. The explanation for Sulzer's success is that it designed the world's most reliable engine. Because the cost of downtime for shipowners is very high, an engine that is more reliable can justify a substantial price premium. Sulzer marketed the merits of its engines to shipowners, provided 24-hour worldwide delivery

---

[41]Richard R. Rawlinson, "Sulzer Brothers Limited," Harvard Business School Case no. 386–021, 1986.

of spare parts, and manufactured only a few of the most critical engine parts. Shipowners then specified Sulzer engines for their vessels, while shipyards, using local contractors to manufacture the remaining parts, installed the engines. In this way, Sulzer was responsible for perhaps 20 percent of the total engine cost. Its design expertise, however, was so valuable that it could make substantial margins while other participants in the value chain made only normal returns.

In many instances, the analysis is more complex because industry profit is not captured by one particular resource or activity. Indeed, profit commonly accrues to a system of assets employed together, for which individual markets do not function adequately or even exist. In these situations, firms might have to extend their scope into markets where they do not necessarily have a competitive advantage to overcome market failures or to exploit the systemic advantages of coordination.

Step 3: Market Failure

Is there a clear market failure? Are the costs of market governance extremely high? Can dominant firms exercise market foreclosure?

Steps 1 and 2 of the analysis explicitly assumed that efficient markets existed at all stages in the industry. When this is not the case, a firm may have to vertically integrate into those activities for which there are no viable markets, just as GM had to acquire Fisher Body. To determine when this is necessary, the firm must examine each activity for conditions that transactions cost theory identifies as leading to high market governance costs and hence to market failure.

Consider, for example, whether a baseball team should own the stadium in which it plays. First, there is a long-term relationship involved. The stadium itself will last up to 80 years (close to the age of Fenway Park, the oldest in major league baseball). Second, the stadium is an **asset that is specific** to the baseball business. Although outdoor concerts could be held there, no other activity could generate the summer attendance that baseball does. Similarly, a team that has built local fan loyalty will be loath to move to another city. Thus, the stadium represents an asset that is committed to one baseball team, and so creates the potential for opportunistic behavior. Once the stadium is built, the team can threaten to pay $1 for the use of the facilities, and the stadium's owner seemingly has no choice but to accept the offer. Conversely, the stadium owner can charge $20 million for a year's usage, and the team seemingly has little option but to pay up.

Given this situation, can a contract be written to prevent opportunism over the life of the stadium? This is problematic given the future **uncertainty**. In principle, it would seem feasible to write a contract that sets a price today and includes an escalator clause. But what if the television contract for baseball quadruples in value? What if the rules of baseball change in 40 years' time and the stadium needs to be expanded? The list of possible contingencies is very long, and writing a foolproof contract is almost impossible. As a consequence, many stadiums, such as Busch Stadium, home of the St. Louis Cardinals, are owned by the teams that play there. Those that are not are usually owned by a municipality that covers the expense through tax revenues.

Transaction costs surrounding the transfer of tacit knowledge will also be high, and so can lead to market failure. When valuable skills or knowledge cannot be written down, firms may have to extend their scope so that knowledge can be directly deployed by those with the relevant experience. In biotechnology, for example, the tacit expertise of researchers is often critical to bringing a manufacturing facility onstream. Because such information cannot be transferred on a market, the R&D function in this case cannot be separated from manufacturing.

In addition, market failures may be due to the exercise of market power. When there are a limited number of firms at any stage in an industry, an opportunity may exist to use their bargaining power to extract profit from upstream or downstream players, or (within legal bounds) to lock out competitors at other stages. This threat can force other firms to vertically integrate into activities in which they do not have a competitive advantage. (See "The Exercise of Market Power.")

Problems with market power can be particularly acute in the case of **cospecialized assets**.[42] These are a set of assets that are specific to each other, yet because of their rarity, each possesses market power. Consider three firms: one owns a patent for a new arthritic drug; another, a specialized (one of a few) biotech manufacturing facility that could make the drug; and a third controls a distribution channel to rheumatologists. Each is a valuable resource, but when deployed in combination, they are likely to create substantially more value than when used separately. The intense bargaining over the profit created by the combination may produce market failure. As a result, cospecialized assets often end up under common ownership, or in joint venture arrangements.[43]

Market failures arising from high transaction costs or the exercise of market power are, in fact, quite common. As a result, they are a major influence on choice of firm scope.

Step 4: Need for Coordination

> Is there an ongoing need for intensive coordination? Are continual and integrated changes required? Is there a distinct interface between activities?

Even if there are no obvious market failures, the benefits that can be achieved from coordination inside the hierarchy might still lead a firm to vertically integrate. Whenever a transaction requires **continual mutual adaptation** by both parties, the benefits of authority and unified ownership may require a firm to perform an activity, even though efficient independent suppliers exist.[44]

Indeed, the argument for maintaining many of the functional activities inside a firm is the ongoing need for coordination. A marketing group may need to change tactics continually and reallocate resources as new products are developed. Similarly, a manufacturing plant may need to adjust output and reschedule production as orders are received, and so on. This simple need to coordinate the response of functional activities to shifting business requirements can lead to prohibitive recontracting costs, and thus justify vertical integration beyond the limited activities the firm performs uniquely well.

Furthermore, performing a coordinated set of activities can give a firm an advantage it does not possess in any single activity. Sharp Corporation, for example, considers itself neither a components supplier nor an end products firm; instead, its advantage comes from its

---

[42]D.J. Teece, "Profiting from Technological Innovation: Implications for Integration, Collaboration, Licensing, and Public Policy," in *The Competitive Challenge* ed. D.J. Teece (Cambridge, MA: Ballinger, 1987), pp. 185–220.
[43]G. Pisano, "The Governance of Innovation: Vertical Integration and Collaborative Arrangements in the Biotechnology Industry," *Research Policy* 1991, pp. 237–49.
[44]A long-term contractual relationship in which both parties stake their reputations on abstaining from self-interested behavior is also a feasible solution. Relationships such as Japanese keiretsu supplier relations that place the long-term relationship above short-term gain can be thought of as pseudo-vertical integration.

The Exercise of Market Power

Pragmatically, the exercise of market power suggests that vertical integration can be valuable as a competitive tool.

First, it can raise *industry entry barriers*. Major trucking firms, for example, are trying to improve their profitability by taking responsibility for the management of customers' logistics. This service is very difficult for smaller firms to provide. As a result, small firms can no longer compete for the transportation business of companies wanting the bundled service.

Second, dominant firms can backward or forward integrate to *offset supplier or buyer power*. Because of their size, even partial integration into an adjacent business can discipline trading partners and keep their profits to a minimum.

Third, a dominant firm may vertically integrate to *pioneer a new market* that otherwise might not be developed. Fragmented downstream firms may be reluctant to make early stage investments that educate customers, if their benefits will spill over to competitors and suppliers. Indeed, as occurred in the introduction of aluminum foil, it was an upstream supplier, Reynolds, who made the necessary investments in market development.

ability to coordinate across these activities. Even though it is not a leading producer of semiconductors, the firm has found that its presence in that business dramatically improves its ability to rapidly introduce innovative consumer electronics products. Other firms that believe their competitive advantages come from the integration of a system of activities, may be similarly reluctant to outsource them.

However, the viability of the market mode of organization, as exemplified by Benetton, forces a careful evaluation of these apparent coordination needs. In most cases, the discriminating factor in favor of the market is whether activities or businesses have **clear interfaces** between them, and behind which each can work without mutual adjustments. Gardening, for example, can easily be outsourced because its operation has no effect on other corporate decisions. In contrast, the design of a new product can rarely be "thrown over the wall" from R&D to manufacturing, but must continually be adjusted to accommodate the needs of both. This blurring of the interface between activities gives rise to the need for explicit coordination, and so may favor the hierarchy.

Step 5: Importance of Incentives

How high are agency costs inside the hierarchy? How much do worker skill and effort affect outcomes? Can an effective incentive scheme be designed? Which is more important: coordination or high-powered incentives?

Achieving the benefits of coordination inside the corporate hierarchy often involves a **trade-off** with exploiting the power of market incentives. The presence of agency costs inside the hierarchy can be a compelling argument to limit the scope of the firm's activities. Thus, when skill and effort are critical to the efficient performance of an activity, there is a powerful argument to establish some form of market relationship that exploits high-powered incentives. Although pay for performance schemes inside corporations can go a long way toward mimicking market incentives, they can never completely replicate them, and they also incur monitoring costs.

Often, the organizational limit to the scope of a firm is ultimately determined in this trade-off between coordination and incentives. When coordination needs are high, and when the importance of incentives are low because the contribution of individual effort is immaterial and monitoring is easy, the firm should be vertically integrated. In contrast, if individual effort is critical to performance, and monitoring is difficult, the market is more likely to be the preferred form of organization. Although the balance in trade-off can shift over time, as competitive and technological conditions alter, it remains central to the decision to vertically integrate in cases that have not been resolved by the analyses in the previous steps.

Franchising, one of the fastest-growing forms of corporate organization, is an illustration of this trade-off.[45] Franchises are typically used in geographically dispersed service or retail businesses to provide high powered incentives for individual unit owners (the franchisees). In the retailing environment, this is often necessary because the skill and effort of the store manager are major determinants of how well a store performs. Further, monitoring the operations of hundreds of stores across the country for 12 hours a day would be very expensive. Conversely, there is limited need for coordination because standardization of the product offering provides a clear interface between the store and the franchisor.

For these reasons, a franchise, which is essentially a long-term market contract, is often the preferred arrangement for the governance of the relation between the individual store and a chain (see "Other Explanations for Franchising"). A pure market exchange would probably be inappropriate because there are often asset-specific investments involved (think, for example, of the McDonald's restaurant building, which would require substantial investment to be adapted to another fast-food chain).

However, franchising is not always the ideal organizational arrangement. It can produce misaligned incentives between two independent parties that can lead to a failure. Consider the use of franchising in the soft-drink bottling industry. Pepsico and Coca-Cola earn their profit on the sale of concentrate to the bottler, and so want to sell as much volume as they can. Their interest, therefore, is to introduce a wide variety of soft drinks and to have as broad distribution as possible, including, for example, in every student's dorm room.

The incentives for franchised bottlers are very different. They bear the costs of manufacturing new varieties of soft drink (extra bottling lines, more SKUs in inventory, and so on), and of distributing the bottles and cans to every outlet. Their concern is with the profitability of each line extension, not simply with whether it sells another ounce of concentrate. Thus, there is an inherent conflict between the concentrate producers and their bottler franchisees over decisions such as product line expansions and retail price wars, which are difficult to fully specify in advance.

It was the prevalence of such misaligned incentives that hampered coordination between soft drink producers and bottlers, and led Pepsico and Coca-Cola to buy back many of their bottler franchises in the eighties. However, the balance between coordination and incentives altered over time. The name of the game in the soft-drink industry in the eighties was product proliferation to stimulate market growth and to squeeze out competitors by filling shelf space. Competitors' optimum number of varieties was established, and the soft-drink companies could deintegrate and so capitalize on the incentives of franchised bottlers to improve efficiency. The experience all parties had with the introduction of new

[45]J.A. Brickley, and F.H. Dark. "The Choice of Organizational Form: The Case of Franchising," *Journal of Financial Economics*, 18 (1987), pp. 401–20.

Other Explanations for Franchising

There is another possible explanation for franchising that has much validity in the early years of a franchise organization: resource scarcity.[46]

For many businesses that are suitable for franchising, there are important first mover advantages and scale economies to exploit. The first successful chain of fresh bread bakeries, for example, will build a brand name and lock up desirable locations. There is, therefore, great pressure on new firms in such businesses to grow quickly. Since opening a new location will be expensive and the access to the capital market for a start-up firm is limited, franchising, which uses the franchisee's capital for most investments, facilitates the strategically important rapid expansion.

varieties also made it somewhat easier to write contracts governing the introduction of any new flavors. In turn, this reduced the governance cost surrounding the franchise arrangement and tilted the balance in favor of the market organization of bottling.

Summary

The pragmatic analysis described above suggests that there is a sequential flow to the decision of whether or not to vertically integrate. If the answer to a particular step in the process is to conduct the transaction inside the firm, the analysis can stop there. If the answer to that step is that vertical integration is not required, the analysis can move to the next set of questions. (See Figure 5–5.)

▲ FIGURE 5–5   Choosing the Scope of the Firm

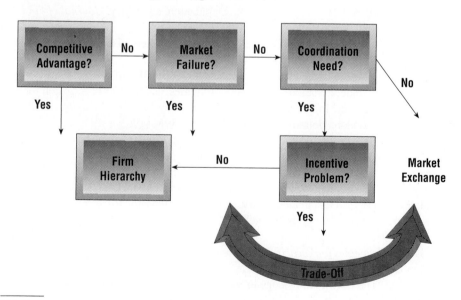

[46]M. Carney and E. Gedajlovic, "Vertical Integration in Franchise Systems: Agency Theory and Resources Explanations," *Strategic Management Journal* 12 (1991), pp. 607–29.

The logic behind the process is that firms should be vertically integrated into those activities where their resources are the source of value creation (Step 2). Even if a firm is not able to earn above-normal returns from an activity, it should still be performed inside the firm if there are asset-specific investments involved or other market failures (Step 3). Even if there are no market failures, an activity should still be performed inside the hierarchy if there are substantial requirements for ongoing coordination (Step 4). Failing that, or if there is a need for high-powered incentives, then the activity should be performed by an independent firm (Step 5).

Even though we began this section by arguing that the default assumption should be to perform activities through market exchange, the analysis that provides many justifications for performing activities inside the corporate hierarchy. It should come as no surprise, given the prevalence of the corporate form of organization, that the traditional hierarchical mode of governance is indeed efficient in many circumstances.

Careful analysis along the lines laid out above will probably lead to a reduction in the vertical scope of most corporations. The simple fact is that too many firms have inherited a particular vertical scope from an era of higher market governance costs and of greater desire for corporate size and control. Starting from the assumption that the market is the preferred arrangement of production will lead to the continuing outsourcing of many corporate activities.

▲ RECOMMENDED READINGS

Akerlof, G. "The Market for Lemons: Qualitative Uncertainty and the Market Mechanism." *Quarterly Journal of Economics*, 1970, pp. 488–500.

Arrow, K. *Economics of Information.* Cambridge, MA: Belknap Press, 1984.

Baumol, W.J., J. Panzer, and R. Willig. *Contestable Markets and the Theory of Industry Structure.* New York: Harcourt Brace Jovanovich, 1982.

Bolton, P., and Farrell, J. "Decentralisation, Duplication, and Delay." *Journal of Political Economy*, 1990, pp. 803–26.

Christensen, C. "The Rigid Disk Drive: A History of Commercial and Technological Turbulence." *Business History Review*, 1993, pp. 531–88.

Coase, R. "The Nature of the Firm." *Economica*, 1937, pp. 386–405.

Dunning, J.H. "Trade, Location of Economic Activities, and the MNE: A Search for an Eclectic Approach." In *The International Allocation of Economic Activity,* eds. B. Ohlin et al, London: Holmes and Meier, 1977, pp. 395–419.

Eisenhardt, K.M. "Agency Theory: An Assessment and Review." *Academy of Management Review*, January 1989, pp. 57–74.

Grossman, S., and O. Hart, "The Costs and Benefits of Ownership: A Theory of Vertical and Lateral Integration." *Journal of Political Economy*, 1986, pp. 691–719.

Halal, William E., A. Geranmaueh, and J. Pourdehnad, *Internal Markets: Bringing the Power of Free Enterprise Inside Your Organization*, New York: John Wiley & Sons, 1993.

Harrigan K. *Strategies for Vertical Integration.* Lexington, MA: D.C. Heath & Company, 1983.

Hayek, F.A. "The Use of Knowledge in Society." *American Economic Review*, 1945, pp. 519–30.

Jensen, M., and W.H. Meckling, "Specific and General Knowledge, and Organization Structure" In *Main Currents in Contract Economics*, eds. L. Werin and H. Wijkander, Oxford: Blackwell, 1991.

Jensen, M., and W.H. Mecklin, "Theory of the Firm." *Journal of Financial Economics*, 1976, pp. 305–60.

Joskow, P. "Vertical Integration and Long-Term Contracts: The Case of Coal-Burning Electric Generating Plants." *Journal of Law, Economics, and Organization*, Spring 1985, pp. 33–80.

Klein, B., R. Crawford, and A. Alchian, "Vertical Integration, Appropriable Rents, and the Competitive Contracting Process." *Journal of Law and Economics*, 1978, pp. 297–326.

Marschak, J., and R. Radner, *Economic Theory of Teams*. New Haven: Yale University Press, 1972.

Milgrom, P., and J. Roberts, *Economics, Organization and Management*. Englewood Cliffs, NJ: Prentice Hall, 1992.

Ouchi, W.G. "A Conceptual Framework for the Design of Organization Control Mechanisms." *Management Science*, 1979, pp. 833–48.

Polyani, M. *Personal Knowledge*. New York: Harper Torchbooks, 1962.

Simon, H. *Administrative Behavior*. Macmillan, 1957.

Spence A.M. *Market Signaling: Transfer in Hiring and Related Processes.*, Cambridge, MA: Harvard University Press, 1973.

Stuckey, J.A. *Vertical Integration in the Aluminum Industry.*, Cambridge, MA: Harvard University Press, 1983.

Stuckey, J.A., and D. White, "When and When *not* to Vertically Integrate." *Sloan Management Review*, Spring 1993, pp. 71–83.

Teece, D.J., and K. Monteverde, "Supplier Switching Costs and Vertical Integration in the Automobile Industry." *Bell Journal of Economics*, Spring 1982, pp. 206–213.

Teece, D.J. "Economics of Scope and the Scope of the Enterprise." *Journal of Economic Behavior and Organization*, 1980, pp. 223–47.

Teece, D.J. "Profiting from Technological Innovation: Implications for Integration, Collaboration, Licensing, and Public Policy." In *The Competitive Challenge*, ed. D.J. Teece, Cambridge, MA: Ballinger, 1987, pp. 185–220.

Walker, G., and D. Weber, "A Transaction Cost Approach to Make-or-Buy Decisions." *Administrative Science Quarterly*, September, 1984, pp. 373–91.

Williamson, O.E. *The Economic Institutions of Capitalism*. New York: Free Press, 1985.

Williamson, O.E. *Markets and Hierarchies: Analysis and Antitrust Implications*. Free Press, 1975.

MANAGING THE MULTIBUSINESS CORPORATION

▲ INTRODUCTION

Managing a multibusiness corporation is perhaps the most difficult corporate strategy challenge. Conceptualizing the strategy can be analytically demanding, but putting the mechanisms in place to bring it to fruition and operating the company on a day-to-day basis can be even more challenging.

Part of this struggle comes from difficulties implementing strategy at any level in an organization. A team of executives must be selected and motivated, a dynamic culture created, and so forth. However, executives in charge of corporate strategy face additional challenges unique to multibusiness corporations. In particular, they must both **maintain control** of the diverse and often autonomous set of businesses in the portfolio and **provide coherence** to the entity as a whole. Only by doing so will they create value and justify the firm's existence as a multibusiness corporation.

This chapter addresses the third side of the Corporate Strategy Triangle—the organizational structure, systems, and processes management can use to implement a strategy. The chapter cannot provide a comprehensive guide to organization theory, nor even to the use of particular organizational mechanisms.[1] Rather, it will draw on aspects of relevant theories to illuminate the management of multibusiness firms and the operation of the corporate office in that setting.

---

[1]See, for example, Miles, Robert H., *Macro Organizational Behavior* (Santa Monica, CA: Goodyear Publishing Co., 1980), and, Mintzberg, Henry, *The Structure of Organizations: The Synthesis of the Research* (Englewood Cliffs, NJ: Prentice-Hall, 1978).

PRINCIPLES

▲ THE ADMINISTRATIVE CONTEXT

In managing a multibusiness corporation, senior executives recognize that they cannot make all the decisions in the firm themselves. The sheer number of complex issues in large diversified companies, quite apart from the impossibility of being fully informed of the circumstances surrounding each one, makes it impractical for corporate executives even to make all the critical strategic decisions. In that case, how do such executives "manage" the firm?

In a classic examination of this issue, Joseph Bower studied the capital budgeting process in a large diversified chemical company.[2] Initially, it appeared to him that corporate management was unable to affect even vitally important resource allocation decisions. He noted that nearly all investment proposals were initiated by the divisions, not the corporate office, and that the corporate team evaluating the requests was dependent on the financial projections and market information supplied by the divisions. Further, nearly all the proposals that reached top management were eventually approved.

On closer observation, however, Bower discovered that corporate management did in fact have a very powerful influence on the pattern of corporate investment. By shaping the **administrative context** within which such decisions were made, corporate management's impact was not limited to just the final rubber-stamp approval of an investment; it extended throughout the entire process. Functional managers in the divisions identified investment projects, mid-level managers decided which of the proposed projects they would support, and senior managers approved projects in response to a very complex set of constraints and incentives established by the organization structure, the measurement and reward systems, the strategic planning process, and so forth, which corporate management had put in place.

This principle underlies the management of multibusiness corporations. Corporate executives do not directly make many of the important business-level decisions. Rather, they impact the firm by establishing an administrative context that shapes the definition, championing, and approval of decisions by managers throughout the organization.

Included in the administrative context are all the elements of structure, systems, and processes that influence delegated decision making in large, complex organizations. The McKinsey Seven-S framework—strategy, structure, systems, style, superordinate goals, staff, and symbols[3]—is representative of the many typologies that describe the range of elements senior management uses to implement strategy. As Figure 6–1 indicates, the list of such elements is long and includes both formal and informal aspects.[4]

Designing the Context

Traditionally, two overarching principles have governed the design of the administrative context. The first is the principle of **internal alignment**, the simple notion that each ele-

---

[2]Joseph H. Bower, *Managing the Resource Allocation Process* (Cambridge, MA: Harvard University Press, 1970).

[3]Pascale, Richard Tanner and Anthony G. Athos, *The Art of Japanese Management* (New York: Simon and Schuster, 1981).

[4]It is impossible to produce a list of the elements of administrative context that is exhaustive and mutually exclusive. The list presented here is, therefore, illustrative rather than definitive.

▲ FIGURE 6–1 The Elements of Organization Design

Organization Structure	Planning and Control Systems
▲ Organization chart	▲ Strategic planning
▲ Corporate functions	▲ Budgeting
▲ Ad hoc teams	▲ MIS
▲ Conflict resolution mechanisms	▲ Resource allocation, capital budgeting
	▲ Transfer prices

Human Resource Management	Culture and Style
▲ Personnel selection and training	▲ Top management role
▲ Reward/incentive schemes	▲ Culture
▲ Measurement variables	▲ Symbolic actions
	▲ Management style

ment of organizational structure, systems, and processes needs to be designed to reinforce rather than conflict with the signals and motivations provided to managers by other aspects of the administrative context. For example, if the incentive system rewards only divisional performance while the corporate culture attempts to foster cooperative behavior, there will be cognitive dissonance within the organization. Managerial behavior results from the complex interplay of all the organizational elements that affect individual motivations. These must, therefore, be designed as a consistent system so that their impact is interactive and mutually reinforcing.

The second overarching principle governing the design of the administrative context is that of **contingent design**. Organization theory has long recognized that no single design is optimal for every corporation or strategy. Instead, it has argued that the internal characteristics of an effective organization should be contingent upon the tasks it must perform interacting with its environment.[5] For a multibusiness firm, contingency theory suggests that the administrative context should be driven by the other elements of a firm's corporate strategy—its resources and set of businesses. These determine the particular tasks the corporation must fulfill to create value and should, therefore, directly shape the firm's overall design (see Form and Function).

Despite their conceptual power, the principles of internal alignment and contingency theory offer little specific advice about how to design the context for a particular firm that will produce the desired behavior (best decisions) at the lowest possible administrative cost. Neither principle addresses the enormous range of elements that influence managerial behavior or the wide variety of options that firms have when implementing each element, such as a budgeting

[5]J.W. Lorsch and S.A. Allen, *Managing Diversity and Interdependence* (Boston: Harvard Business School, Division of Research, 1973), p. 171. See also P.R. Lawrence and J.W. Lorsch, *Organizations and Environment* (Boston: Harvard Business School, Division of Research, 1967).

▲ 130

Chapter 6
Managing the
Multibusiness
Corporation

Form and Function

C.K. Prahalad and Gary Hamel suggested the analogy of a corporation as a tree (see Figure 6–2).[6] The set of businesses in the corporate portfolio are represented by the branches of the tree, and the corporation's resources are the roots that nurture the tree's growth. Extending the analogy, the firm's organizational structure can be interpreted as the tree's shape, while its systems and processes are the tree's vital biological functions that maintain the efficient functioning of the entire system.

The tree analogy is useful. All trees share the same biological processes of photosynthesis and nutrient extraction, even though the precise form of species differs widely. Similarly, all companies have systems for budgeting, capital expenditures, and compensation, even though their details differ enormously. However, just as the structures and processes of each species of tree are optimized for its particular habitat—trees that grow tall have deep roots; evergreens have thin needles filled with pitch to survive the winter; and so forth—so organizational structures, systems, and processes must be optimized according to each firm's strategy for success in its habitat—the resources it employs and the set of businesses in which it competes.

▲ Figure 6–2   Core Competence Tree for Ciba-Corning Diagnostics

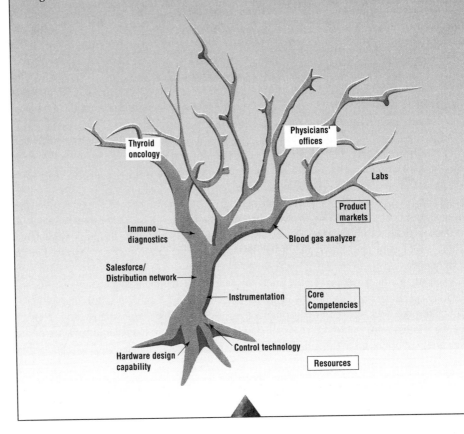

[6]C.K. Prahalad and Gary Hamel, "The Core Competence of the Corporation," *Harvard Business Review* 68, no. 3 (May–June 1990), pp. 79–91.

system. To move beyond these general principles, we need to know specifically how the configuration of a particular structure or system affects managerial behavior and the decisions and costs that result (see Figure 6–3). Modern organizational economics draws on underlying theories to enlighten our understanding of these relationships and so furthers our ability to design effective organizations.

Applying Organizational Economics

Information theory recognizes that there are costs of transferring information within the firm. It also accepts that, because of human limitations, it is infeasible for any individual to assimilate and then act upon all the information that could be cheaply transferred.[7] The challenge, therefore, is to design the administrative context to minimize these costs and circumvent these constraints (see "The Informational Advantage of the Firm").

To achieve this, Jensen and Meckling suggested that the locus of decision-making authority should vary according to the nature of the information being processed.[8] Following Hayek,[9] they argued that there are two types of knowledge: **general knowledge** that can cheaply and easily be transferred up an organizational hierarchy, and **specific knowledge** that is difficult and costly to transfer even with modern information systems. Specific knowledge, which includes, for example, the know-how of skilled craftsmen and experienced managers, is often tacit and so cannot be written down in blueprints or easily communicated to other people.[10] Usually, decisions that depend on this kind of information should be delegated to those who possess the requisite know-how. Only decisions that rest on general knowledge can potentially be made higher up the corporate hierarchy.

Agency theory tempers this view. It argues that, when given decision rights, self-interested managers may act in ways that maximize their own welfare at the expense of the corporate good. As a result, any firm with delegated decision making will incur the adverse consequences of self-interested behavior and the costs of monitoring and control systems intended to deter such behavior. Organizational design must therefore mitigate the agency costs that result from delegated decision making while exploiting the informational cost advantages of delegation.

Drawing on these theories, organizational economics identifies three "rules of the game" that determine behavior inside the firm:[11]

- ▲ The allocation of decision rights.
- ▲ The information structure
- ▲ The set of measurement and reward schemes, or more generally, the incentive structure.

These *organizational rules* collapse the myriad complicated relationships among all elements of the administrative context into a parsimonious but nevertheless comprehensive model of the firm. They identify who will be making a decision, the information that person

[7]Simon, Herbert A., *Administrative Behavior* (New York: The Free Press, 1976). See also Cyert, R. And J. March, *A Behaviorial Theory of the Firm* (Englewood Cliffs, NJ: Prentice-Hall, 1963).
[8]M.C. Jensen and W.H. Meckling, "Specific and General Knowledge, and Organization Structure," In *Main Currents in Contract Economies*, eds. L. Werin and Wijkander. (London: Basil Blackwell, 1991), pp. 251–274.
[9]Hayek, F.A., "The Use of Knowledge in Society," *American Economic Review*, 35, no. 4 (September 1945).
[10]Polyani, M., *Personal Knowledge* (NY: Harper Torch Books, 1962).
[11]Jensen and Meckling (1991).

▲ Figure 6–3   **Strategy Implementation**

The Informational Advantage of the Firm

One argument for the value of diversification is the informational advantage that the corporate hierarchy has over the market.[13] The capital market, for example, may be an inefficient mechanism for the allocation of capital if firms are reticent to release confidential strategic information publicly. In such cases, the corporation, acting as an internal capital market with complete information, may be able to make more efficient investment decisions. The same argument can also be made with respect to the allocation of labor. Since the corporate office will have access to confidential information on employee performance, it can more cheaply and efficiently allocate employees than can the external labor market. These advantages, it is argued, can give validity to multibusiness corporations as economically efficient entities.

Although correct in observing the potentially superior informational characteristics of the hierarchy, proponents fail to recognize the agency costs that can arise with the internal allocation of resources.[14] When not subject to market pressures CEOs can, for example, subsidize poorly performing businesses (see also Chapter 8). Moreover, if the informational advantage of the corporation comes from the rights to confidential information, in principle any firm could own any business. Indeed, one giant conglomerate could efficiently run the whole economy. Clearly, there is a trade-off between the efficiency of internal and external markets as allocators of resources. The availability of information is only one component to be considered in that tradeoff.

will possess, and how he or she will be rewarded for the outcome of the decision. With this information, and knowledge of individual endowments and preferences,[12] one could in principle predict all of a firm's decisions.

In practice, of course, this analysis is impossible to fulfill. One can never isolate and directly measure these three aspects of organizational configuration, nor is there a strict correspondence between the design of particular structures and systems and performance outcomes. While an elegant theoretical description of the firm, this model can never be used pragmatically.

---

[12]These, together with the production possibilities facing the face, are the standard data required for general equilibrium analysis.
[13]Dundas, K.N.M. and P.R. Richardson, "Corporate Strategy and the Concept of Market Failure," *Strategic Management Journal*, 1, no. 2 (April/June 1980), pp. 177-188.
[14]Liebeskind, Julia P., Internal Capital Markets in Diversified Firms: Benefits versus Costs (unpublished manuscript), June 1995.

Nevertheless, the approach does identify the critical parameters that shape managerial behavior. When configuring the more traditional elements of organizational design that can be directly determined by corporate executives—**structure, systems, and processes**—it is, therefore, important to recognize that their effect can be usefully interpreted through their impact on these three rules of the game.

▲ ORGANIZATION STRUCTURE

Formal structure was the traditional concern of organization theory and is probably the element of organization design that has been most studied. Initially much of this research was undertaken with the hope that, for any given strategy, the perfect organization structure could be identified (see "Structure Follows Strategy"). More recently, it has been recognized that organization structures are rarely optimal; rather, the challenge for managers is to identify the structure that best fits the current needs of their corporation.

Structure Follows Strategy

The seminal research on organization structure in multibusiness firms was conducted by the business historian Alfred Chandler. He documented how the rise of the **multidivisional structure (M-form)** in corporate America was a response to the strategy of corporate diversification. Indeed, his observation that "structure follows strategy" was perhaps one of the first statements of contingency theory in the managerial literature.

By studying Du Pont, Sears, General Motors, and Standard Oil, Chandler observed how the traditional functional organization became overloaded when these companies expanded into multiple businesses in the early twentieth century. When this happened, such firms adopted the multidivisional structure in which each division controlled almost the complete set of functional activities for the production, marketing, and delivery of its products.[15] Allowing divisions to take on operating responsibility freed the corporate office to plan strategy and allocate resources among the various businesses. Chandler argued that this partition of the workload solved the information overload problem faced by senior corporate managers when they competed in multiple businesses with a functional organization structure.

Following Chandler's work, there were a host of empirical studies of the adoption of the multidivisional structure in companies around the world.[16] These studies revealed that, although at different rates, most companies in developed countries switched to multidivisional structures as their degree of diversification increased. Empirical studies also verified that corporations improved performance by choosing the appropriate organizational form.[17] Diversified corporations that adopted the multidivisional form, for example, were more profitable than ones that remained functionally organised.

[15]A.D. Chandler, *Strategy and Structure* (Cambridge, MA: MIT Press, 1960).
[16]Channon, D., *The Strategy and Structure of British Enterprise*. (London: MacMillan and Co., 1973); and Pooley-Dyas, G., "Strategy and Structure of French Enterprise," Ph.D. dissertation, Harvard Business School, 1972.
[17]H. Armour and D. Teece, "Organization Structure and Economic Performance: A Test of the Multidivisional Hypothesis," *Bell Journal of Economics* 9 (1976), pp. 106–22; and R.E. Hoskisson, "Multidivisional Structure and Performance," *Academy of Management Journal* 30 (1987), pp. 625–44.

Whatever their differences, most effective organization structures have in common the division of the organization into **discrete subunits that have substantial authority** for their own decisions.

The advantages of such **delegated decision making** are that it allows decisions to be made by those who possess the relevant knowledge, while minimizing the amount of information transfer up the hierarchy. The presence of specific knowledge about competitors, for example, usually explains why it is more effective for divisional, rather than corporate, managers to make operating decisions.

When the corporation is divided into discrete units, each can also be **specialized** to succeed in its own competitive environment.[18] In particular, it can develop and tailor its resources and shape the details of its own organization to fit its unique tasks. For example, the culture of a high-technology division can and should be different from that of a capital-intensive commodity business. Moreover, specialized units that are focused on a particular activity such as distribution, can, through repeated experience, increase their efficiency over time.

It is also expected that the **motivation of managers** who are given control of an entire unit will be high, particularly when they are directly rewarded for the performance of that unit. The alignment of managerial authority with responsibility and rewards, which is possible when decision making is delegated to discrete units, satisfies one of the basic tenets of agency theory and increases organizational efficiency by providing powerful incentives. The resulting sense of ownership also builds managerial commitment, with corresponding increases in effort and initiative.

There are countless variants of organization structures for multibusiness corporations that capitalize on the benefits of discrete subunits (see Figure 6–4). The choice of which to adopt for a particular firm is usually determined by the need to **combine those activities that are most interdependent** in order to minimize the number of informational linkages in the organization and to align authority with responsibility.[19]

The predominant organizational form in multibusiness corporations in the West today is a structure of autonomous and discrete product divisions. This will be the efficient structure when the critical resources and predominant need for integration are located *within the businesses* themselves. However, when the most intense interdependencies are contained *within a function or geographic region*, organizations divided along those dimensions will be more efficient. Many consumer packaged goods companies, for example, are organized around business functions, so that they can realize economies of scale in their critical sales and marketing activities. In contrast, many professional service organizations, such as law and accounting firms, are configured around independent geographic offices so that they can efficiently offer a full range of services to local clients.

Unfortunately, since many diversified firms have important interdependencies along multiple dimensions, there is often no clear-cut structure that is appropriate. Adopting a functional structure, for example, may lead to problems coordinating product strategy, but a product-division structure may lead to inefficient functional activities, perhaps with multiple

---

[18]In the original research on this topic, Lawrence and Lorsch (*Organization and Environment*, Harvard Business School, 1967) and Lorsch and Allen (*Managing Diversity and Interdependence*, Harvard Business School, 1973) described this as the advantages of differentiation.

[19]Nayyar, P.R. and R.K. Kazanjian, "Organizing to Attain Potential Benefits from Informational Assymetries and Economies of Scope in Related Diversified Firms," *Academy of Management Review* 18 (1993), pp. 735-59.
Antle, R. and J.S. Demski, "The Controlling Principle in Responsibility Accounting," *Accounting Review* LXII (October 1988), pp. 700-718.

▲ Figure 6–4   A Range of Organization Types

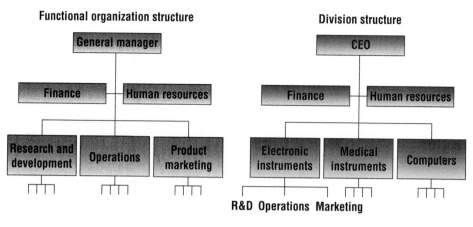

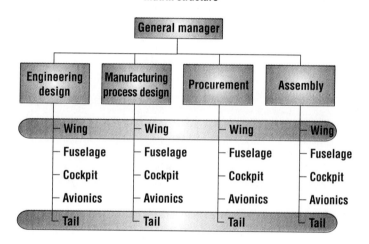

Source: Galbraith, J., *Competing with Flexible Lateral Organizations,* Second Edition
(Reading, MA: Addison-Wesley, 1994), p. 57.

sales forces calling on the same customer. (See "Matrix and Network Organizations" for a discussion of structures designed to simultaneously manage several interdependencies.)

More generally, none of these organization structures will perfectly implement a corporate strategy. Every structure featuring delegated decision making in discrete and differentiated subunits will have drawbacks because of the inherent conflicts that arise in multibusiness corporations over the control of delegated decision making authority and between the differentiation and integration of specialized units.

Ultimately, we have to recognize the **principle of organizational suboptimality**—that no structure is ideal for all firms, nor even for a particular firm at a point in time. Managers should therefore divide the firm into discrete subunits whose activities rely most heavily on one another, and use the other elements of administrative context to support and enhance the chosen structure. In doing so, the firm should be able to offset some of the adverse consequences of the structure while better meeting the overall needs of the strategy.

One structure that promised to solve the trade-off between organizing along different dimensions was the **matrix** organization. In this structure, employees report to two superiors—a function and a division manager, for example; or, in the case of many multinational firms, a division and a country manager. The hope was that these dual reporting structures would accommodate and blend both viewpoints and so provide for the efficient utilization of resources while integrating their deployment across units.[20]

In practice, however, matrix organizations internalized the trade-off in individuals who had to balance the demands of two bosses. The resulting ambiguity and complexity often produced insurmountable problems. Rather than optimally satisfying the needs of both superiors, individuals often ended up satisfying neither.

A more recent innovation in organization structure has been the **network** organization.[21] Rather than using a formal organizational structure, the firm takes on a loose and shifting set of relationships both internally—among teams that, for example, focus on customers or reengineered processes—and externally, with suppliers, customers, and even competitors. The advantages of such a structure are argued to be the flexibility and the adaptability to reconfigure the firm rapidly and cheaply in response to changing circumstances.

The network organization is almost the antithesis of structure; it depends on informal processes to hold the company together. Indeed, in the guise of boundaryless and learning organizations,[22] it suggests that the right set of processes alone can overcome the trade-offs endemic to contemporary organizations.[23] Attractive as this vision is, an exclusive reliance on informal processes can lead to chaos in large, complex companies. Further, network organizations optimistically assume that a context can be generated in which employees act in the best interests of the corporation. In practice, self-interested behavior—the focus of organizational economics—validates the need for the formal aspects of organizational structure and systems, such as incentive schemes.

▲ SYSTEMS AND PROCESSES

Organization structure alone does not define a firm's administrative context. Systems and processes, both formal and informal, influence the incentive structure facing managers, the allocation of decision rights, and the distribution of information inside a firm.

We cannot here discuss the design of all a corporation's systems and processes, from compensation to capital expenditure and strategic planning.[24] Rather, we will focus on how that set of systems and processes can be used to address the two challenges corporate executives

[20]J.R. Galbraith and R.K. Kazanjian, *Strategy Implementation: Structure, Systems and Process* (St. Paul: West Publishing, 1985).

[21]R.G. Eccles, and N. Nohria, eds., *Networks in Organizations* (Boston, MA: Harvard Business School Press, 1992).

[22]Ron Ashkenas, D. Ulrich, T. Jick, and S. Kerr, *The Boundaryless Organization* (San Francisco, CA: Jossey-Bass Publishers, 1995); Peter M. Senge, *The Fifth Discipline* (NY: Doubleday/Currency, 1990); I. Nonaka and H. Takeuchi, *The Knowledge Creating Company* (Oxford: Oxford University Press, 1995).

[23]S. Ghoshal and C.A. Bartlett, "Changing the Role of Top Management: Beyond Structure to Processes," *Harvard Business Review* 73 Jan-Feb 1995, pp. 86–96.

[24]Simons, Robert, *Levers of Control* (Boston, MA: Harvard Business School Press, 1995); and P. Milgrom, and J. Roberts, *Economics, Organization and Management* (Englewood Cliffs, NJ: Prentice-Hall, 1992).

face in managing multibusiness firms—how to maintain **control** over delegated decision making within otherwise autonomous units, and how to provide **coherence** to the corporation by deploying resources across otherwise structurally differentiated units.

Control

Embedded in every organization structure is the need to maintain control over delegated decision making. Agency theory highlights the adverse consequences of delegation and warns that without appropriate systems, the corporate office can quickly lose its ability to determine corporate direction and performance. While independent units must be allowed to operate autonomously as far as possible if they are to maximize their own performance, there must be some measure of corporate control to prevent them pursuing their self-interest to the detriment of the company as a whole.

Historically, discussion of how to balance the trade-off between delegation and control of decision rights focused on a **centralization-decentralization continuum**. This described where control lay between corporate headquarters and the divisions for numerous decisions such as pricing, hiring, facility locations, and so forth. Research, however, revealed that this simple distinction could be quite misleading.[25] For example, a firm could centralize financial policies and retain strategic control at headquarters, but might freely delegate operational control to the divisions. Indeed, there are so many elements to the relationship between the divisions and the corporate office that the whole network of interactions cannot easily be collapsed into a single measure of decentralization. One element of the relationship might be decentralized and another centralized, and the success of a strategy could depend on just such careful differentiation.

More recently, attention has turned to the design of the systems and processes needed to resolve the agency problem created by delegating decision rights. Rather than being concerned with who has the power to make the decision, it recognizes the reality of delegated decision making but suggests important differences in the reward and measurement schemes that can mitigate its adverse effects.

Designing an organization to minimize agency costs is not a simple task. In the case of operating performance, for example, corporate management may have trouble distinguishing between the effects of exogenous industry events and managerial skill and effort on performance. Thus, when evaluating divisional performance, they may not know whether it was due to poor (good) decisions, adverse (positive) exogenous market conditions, or lack of (a lot of) hard work by managers.[26] The difficulty of sorting out these effects may allow divisional managers to act in their own self interest and blame the resulting poor performance on events beyond their control.

To prevent this from occurring, corporate managers can monitor and reward either the outcomes or the behaviors that they observe,[27] depending on which can be correlated more cost

---

[25]Vancil, R.F., *Decentralization: Managerial Ambiguity By Design* (Burr Ridge, IL: Irwin, 1978).

[26]Sophisticated, and probably more realistic, versions of agency theory argue that agency costs are not so much due to slacking but to inappropriate decisions. A division manager, for example, is more likely to propose an investment that generates certain but low returns, rather than an investment in a high-risk, high-return R&D project, even if the expected value of the R&D investment is higher. The personal risk if the project fails (dismissal) is sufficiently great to deter the manager from supporting the higher-expected-value strategy that corporate executives would prefer.

[27]Theoretically, the outcomes or behaviors have to be both observable and legally contractible.

effectively and accurately with the subordinate's skill and effort.[28] If, for example, the current financial results of a bakery are a reasonably accurate measure of how effective management was, then outcome control is appropriate. In a high-technology business, in contrast, short-term financial performance may be a very poor indicator of both underlying strategic position and managerial effectiveness. In that case, a much broader set of variables will need to be evaluated, many of which require qualitative judgments and most of which concern the specific decisions made by managers. (See "Clan Control" for a third type of control.)

This suggests that there will be important differences in organizational systems and processes between firms practicing **outcome control** and **behavior control**.[29] Both rely on delegated decision making, the underlying difference is that outcome control concentrates on monitoring results and behavior control concentrates on prescribing and evaluating actions as means of setting the incentives for subordinates.

Outcome control typically rewards divisional managers on their financial performance. It, therefore, influences divisional decision making indirectly by aligning divisional managers' incentives with corporate goals; it requires little interference by the corporate office in the daily affairs of the division. The archetypal modern example of outcome control is the LBO that holds managers accountable for a limited number of financial targets, usually related to cash flow, but does not intervene in or intensely monitor the means by which those targets are met.

For pure outcome control to be viable, there must be very tight links between effort and skill and financial outcomes, with very little interference from uncertain exogenous events. This implies that outcome control is appropriate in mature, stable, and predictable industries (as opposed to rapidly changing and highly competitive industries); in addition, divisions should be unrelated and self-contained, so that they share few important activities.

Behavior control, in contrast, more directly prescribes and evaluates divisional managers' actions. Typically, this kind of control is practiced by corporations, such as Ford Motor Company, that view themselves as operating companies. Corporate executives rarely make divisional decisions themselves, but will be sufficiently well informed to evaluate divisional managers on those decisions, rather than on just their financial results.

Behavior control is therefore appropriate under different conditions. When judging the actions of divisional executives is possible, behavior control is viable because corporate managers have detailed industry-specific expertise. Perhaps they know to focus on certain operating behaviors that are keys to success in the business, or perhaps asking certain questions allows them to advise on and evaluate appropriate behavior. Second, behavior control can be used when it is difficult to find single summary measures of strategic performance. In some industries, for example, cash flow may be a fair representation of divisional performance, but in many others such simple outcome measures are unreliable. In those cases, corporate managers must continuously monitor a broad range of behaviors and qualitative performance measures to fairly evaluate the performance of divisional managers.

---

[28]Agency theory demonstrates that no incentive scheme can entirely eliminate agency costs. Any scheme is, therefore, what economists call "second best." Prime among these second best solutions is a "tournament." In this, managers are rewarded not for their absolute performance, but for performance relative to their peers. This incentive scheme, would, for example, promote the best-selling regional sales manager to national manager. When all peers are subject to the same exogeneous events, such a scheme controls for the effect of events such as a recession, on performance.

[29]K.M. Eisenhardt, "Control: Organizational and Economical Approaches," *Management Science* 31 (1985), pp. 134–49; and W.G. Ouchi, "A Conceptual Framework for Design of Organization Control Mechanisms," *Management Science* 25 (1979), pp. 833–48.

Clan Control

A third type of control is **clan control.**[30] This type of control may eliminate agency problems inside organizations if subordinates have deeply internalized the goals of the organization. When this happens they interpret their own self-interest in terms of the organization's interests. Examples of this type of control are typically found in nonprofit, religious, and political organizations, whose goals are more ideological than material, and where it is believable that individuals will abdicate their self-interest for a superordinate goal.

Some economic organizations appear to get close to this sort of control system. Cooperatives and small firms run by charismatic entrepeneurs, such as Apple in its early days, are examples. But the occurrence of the sort of messianic purpose that is required for effective clan control is rarely, if ever, found in large multibusiness organizations. Only in cultures in which collectivism rather than individualism is a more accepted philosophy can clan control be expected to solve the control problem for an extended period of time.

Because of the differences between these modes of control, the choice between them is contingent on the other elements of a firm's corporate strategy. Both the set of businesses in which the firm is active (which will, for example, affect the availability of a good outcome measure), and the resources underlying corporate advantage (for example, the particular expertise of senior management) will determine the appropriate method for controlling delegated decision making in a given company. (The Practice section expands on the specific design of the systems required to implement outcome and behavior control.)

Coherence

Merely controlling the operation of autonomous divisions is rarely enough to justify the existence of a corporation as a multibusiness entity. Although units need to be differentiated and specialized if they are to serve their own markets efficiently, valuable resources must also be deployed throughout those units to provide coherence to the corporation. Some degree of integration across otherwise differentiated units is therefore required if the corporate performance is to be more than merely the sum of what the individual divisions could achieve alone.

As described in Chapters 3 and 4, the advantages of corporate coherence can arise in almost all the value-creating activities of a business, and from any of its common assets or capabilities. The specific source of the benefits can be anything from simple economies of scale and experience curve effects, to coordinating product market positions and competitive responses. For example, by using a single corporate sales force, rather than allowing each of its many divisions to have its own, Johnson & Johnson exploits scale efficiencies in providing one-stop shopping to hospitals.

It is tempting to think that autonomous divisions will willingly cooperate to achieve the benefits of corporate coherence. However, there is a limit to the circumstances under which they will do so. Opportunities for integration across divisions that are win/win for all divisions (Pareto optimal) will always be realized (Figure 6–5). However, a purely self-interested

---

[30]W.G. Ouchi, "A Conceptual Framework for Design of Organization Control Mechanisms," *Management Science* 25 (1979), pp. 833–48.

▲ FIGURE 6–5 Cooperation and Corporate Performance

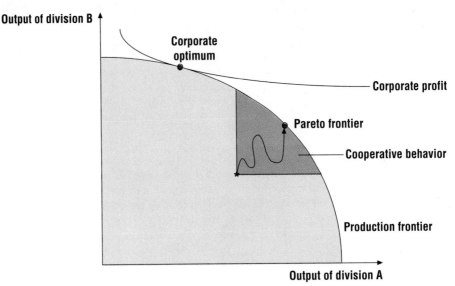

* = Behavior of self-interested divisions.

division will not be able to reach agreement on an action that benefits the corporation as a whole if that gain is accompanied by a loss for any division.

Much can be done by the corporate office to extend the range of issues on which otherwise autonomous divisions will cooperate. Managers, after all, behave in response to their incentives. In principle, therefore, the corporation can create incentives for managers to act in the interests of a broader entity, such as a group of related businesses or the corporation as a whole, by partially rewarding them for the performance of that larger unit.[31] However, there are intrinsic limits to the ability of financial incentives alone to achieve the desired degree of coherence. Managers may now be held accountable for actions beyond their responsibility. The precision of the incentive system will, therefore, decline and agency costs will increase.[32]

To achieve the desired degree of coherence, therefore, corporations not only have to alter incentives, but also employ other systems and processes that potentially supplant divisional autonomy. These mechanisms for leveraging resources throughout the corporation involve the **transfer of skills and resources** and the **coordination of activities**. Transferring skills and resources involves the development and maintenance of a resource or skill that is made available to and then independently used by the different divisions. Coordinating activities involves some degree of direct sharing in the performance of an activity by multiple divisions.

---

[31]The ultimate obstacle to self-interested coordination comes back to the very existence of the corporation as a multibusiness entity. If some form of self-interested behavior could achieve all the desirable cooperation, the firm would not be able to justify its existence.

[32]A.K. Gupta and S. Seshadri, "Horizontal Resource Sharing: A Principal Agent Approach," *Academy of Management Best Papers*, 1994, pp. 37–41. One solution that encourages autonomous divisions to realize the benefits of coherence, even when it is detrimental to a particular unit, is to allow side payments. Informal versions of these payments involving agreements to "scratch your back if you scratch mine" are often implicit inside many companies, but explicit payoffs, such as crediting one division with a negotiated share of another division's profit, are rare.

The transfer of a corporate-level resource requires perhaps the least intervention by the corporate office in divisional affairs. The corporate office takes responsibility for managing the valuable resource, such as a corporate brand name or governance structure, and makes that resource available to the divisions, which can operate more or less freely with it. In transferring skills, the corporate office focuses on improving the quality of the skill and disseminating that knowledge among the divisions. In principle, it is possible to do this with minimal interference in the autonomy of business units because skills can often be used simultaneously by many divisions. At Emerson Electric, for example, manufacturing practices and processes are transferred among divisions without their use in one division precluding their use in another.

Generally speaking, coordinating activities requires more explicit corporate intervention. To compel divisions to give up their autonomy and manage the conflicts that necessarily accompany joint activity requires some form of overt corporate coordination. Although sharing activities, such as purchasing or a sales force, may be the largest and most obvious source of synergy in multibusiness corporations, to a greater or lesser extent the process incurs all the costs that result from divisions losing authority over some of their activities.

Whether transferring skills and resources or coordinating activities across operating units, the pursuit of corporate coherence involves inevitable costs. Not only does it raise the cost of corporate overhead (which must ultimately be borne by the divisions), it can violate the sanctity of divisional differentiation and autonomy (see "Costs of Coherence"). The CEO of a very successful multinational lubricants company, for example, referred to synergy as the "enemy of focus." This is a serious charge. To be of net benefit to the firm, the costs of pursuing coherence must be lower than the benefits it generates, or the strategy is misguided. For managers, the challenge is how to design the systems and processes that create the desired degree of integration at minimal cost.

Costs of Coherence

There are five types of cost incurred when integrating otherwise discrete units.[33]

Compromise costs result from suboptimal decisions. Since two different businesses are sharing some activity or skill, one may be disappointed in the level of service provision. Consider a company, such as Marriott, that maintains hotel chains at several different price points. If the chains share a computer reservation system, one or another may have to compromise, either by paying more for a higher-quality system than it needs or by receiving lower quality service than it desires. No solution is likely to perfectly satisfy all the chains.

Inflexibility costs are those associated with the loss of control over all the business' activities. If one division wishes to switch to just-in-time delivery to improve its production process, it may be impossible to agree to a revised schedule with another division for deliveries from common suppliers. Slower speed of response is another cost of inflexibility.

Coordination costs refer to the time and effort that managers spend working with their peers in other divisions to coordinate joint activities. It simply takes time—in meetings, on the phone, writing memos, and so forth—to reach agreement, and none of that would be incurred if the division alone could decide on all its own activities.

[33]These draw on M. Porter, *Competitive Advantage* (NY: The Free Press, 1985) Chapter 9.

The way to achieve corporate coherence, in contrast, is primarily contingent on the resource that is being deployed across the various businesses. In particular, the choice between transferring a skill and coordinating activities depends on whether the valuable resource can be used simultaneously by several divisions without affecting its employment in each. When a resource is a public good, such as a best demonstrated practice in sales force management, the mechanism used will be the deployment of a skill. However, when the resource is an asset, such as a computer or plant, whose use by one division inevitably leads to conflict with other divisions, the mode chosen must be the coordination of activities. (See Appendix C for a detailed description of mechanisms for achieving coherence.)

▲ SUMMARY: LINKING ADMINISTRATIVE CONTEXT TO PURPOSE

The choice of administrative context for managing a multibusiness corporation is complex and involves a number of difficult trade-offs. However, the guiding principle is that a firm's structure, systems, and processes should flow from its overall strategic vision and the key tasks that must be performed to achieve that vision.

Traditionally, differences in administrative contexts were captured in the dichotomy between corporate strategies of related and unrelated diversification. Generally speaking, unrelated diversifiers were seen as needing organizational designs that separated business units into discrete product divisions with little corporate intervention. In contrast, the prescription for related diversifiers was to adopt functional organizations or have substantial corporate staffs to coordinate divisional activities.[34] As a result, unrelated diversifiers were commonly thought of as requiring decentralized management systems, whereas related diversifiers would need to be considerably more centralized.[35]

More recently, Charles Hill and others have drawn a similar distinction between cooperative corporate strategies, where divisions are related and benefit from sharing with one another, and competitive corporate strategies, where the corporate office merely allocates capital between unrelated product divisions that are in effect competing for that capital.[36]

In our corporate strategy framework, differences (and similarities) among administrative contexts are driven by the resources that firms possess and the businesses in which they compete. It is those aspects of the corporate strategy that largely dictate how a firm will choose to control and integrate the activities of its businesses.

PRACTICE

▲ ROLES OF THE CORPORATE OFFICE

Being a CEO responsible for managing a multibusiness corporation is a task that shares many aspects of any general manager's job. We do not describe that job in this chapter, even though we recognize that in multibusiness corporations, just like any other, having the

---

[34]Norm Berg, "What's Different about Conglomerate Management?" *Harvard Business Review* 47 (1969) pp. 112–120.
[35]Vancil (1978).
[36]Hill et al. (1992).

charismatic leadership and managerial skills of Michael Eisner at Disney or Jack Welch at GE may create as much shareholder value as any particular strategic move Disney or GE could make.[37] Here, we will focus on the unique management challenges of a multibusiness firm and the roles of the corporate office in meeting those challenges.

There are four roles that the corporate office of any public multibusiness company must perform. The first is to articulate and adhere to the **strategy** for the corporation. The second is to act as the **guardian of resources** in the corporation. The third is to fulfill the **general overhead functions** of the corporation, such as the legal reporting requirements. The fourth is to set the **administrative context** for the firm by choosing the structure, systems, and processes to control the various units and achieve coherence across them (see Figure 6–6).

▲ SET STRATEGY

All CEOs have a responsibility to articulate and communicate a strategy for their companies. As described in Chapter 1, this involves the identification of the unique Corporate Strategy Triangle they believe will create a corporate advantage. Here we do not want to reiterate the elements of that triangle; rather, we want to emphasize the importance of an overarching conception for the corporation.

Some believe that this is the most critical aspect of the CEO's task—to identify what Goold, Campbell, and Alexander called the "parenting insight"[38] and what Prahalad and Doz referred to as the "value creation logic,"[39] the differentiating way in which the corporate entity can add value to its businesses. For multibusiness corporations, conceiving this insight can be vital to success. Surfacing the logic that underpins a strategy not only facilitates its implementation but provides a powerful check on the consistency of a firm's actions.

It is important to note that setting corporate strategy does not necessarily involve specifying strategy for each of the business units. The final choice of business unit strategy may be constrained by the corporate strategy, or influenced by the guidance of corporate management, but ultimately the initiation, selection, and commitment to a particular business-unit strategy should ultimately be the responsibilty of its own managers.

▲ RESOURCE GUARDIAN

In Chapter 2 we said that it is the responsibity of the corporate office to develop a resource-based strategy. In that chapter, we focused on the critical task of identifying and investing in a set of valuable resources. However, as resource guardian, the corporate office must also be concerned with the allocation of those resources. Once there is more than one business in the corporate portfolio someone has to decide on the distribution of resources among them. In fact, choosing which businesses to compete in—**portfolio selection**—and which projects to invest in—**capital budgeting**—has been seen as justifying the existence of the multibusiness corporation. It was also the function that portfolio-planning techniques,

---

[37]For useful discussions, see Ghoshal, S. and C.A. Bartlett, "Changing the Role of Top Management: Beyond Structure to Processes," *Harvard Business Review*, Jan.–Feb. 1995. See also Mintzberg, H., *The Nature of Managerial Work.* (NY: Harper & Row, 1973).

[38]Goold, M.C., M. Alexander, and A. Campbell, *Corporate Level Strategy: Creating Value in the Multibusiness Company* (NY: John Wiley & Sons, 1994).

[39]Prahalad, C.K. and Yves L. Doz, "CEO: A Visible Hand in Wealth Creation?" (preliminary draft) Sept. 1995.

▲ FIGURE 6–6   Roles of the Corporate Office

- **Set strategy**
- **Guardian of resources**
- **General overhead functions**
- **Set administrative context**

introduced in the seventies (see Appendix A), were intended to fulfill, along with the more traditional tools of capital expenditure, long-term planning, and annual budgets.

The challenge of resource allocation at the corporate level is twofold. The first is to ensure that while allocating resources to divisions on a project by project basis, the performance of the corporation as a whole is optimized. What may seem to be a good investment to a particular division may in fact weaken the overall position of a company. The corporate office is the entity charged with maintaining overall performance and so has to balance a holistic perspective with the more narrow interests of individual product divisions. Second, in providing for the sustainable growth of the corporation, the challenge is to allocate resources in a way that maintains a balance between short-term profitability and long-term growth.

Unfortunately, because of the intrinsic trade-offs among these different objectives, there will never be easy recipes for achieving a balance in allocating the corporation's resources. Nor are simplistic pictorial representations of the portfolio adequate to capture the complexity of the trade-offs. Only a multidimensional assessment of the strategic and financial consequences of different investment patterns can lead to effective resource allocation decisions over time.

▲ GENERAL OVERHEAD FUNCTIONS

Every firm must conform with regulations concerning the **legal reporting requirements** of its particular governance structure—incorporated, partnership, publicly quoted, and so forth. These requirements are for both taxation and capital market purposes and involve the IRS, the SEC, and external auditors. If nothing else, therefore, the aggregation and reporting of consolidated financial results for the various businesses of a corporation has to be performed at the corporate level. Every company will have a corporate staff to fulfill these reporting tasks and to oversee the performance of the reporting activity in the divisions.

Other corporate functions that verge on being required include activities such as public relations, external communications, government relations, and corporate giving. These activities are pure overhead costs of doing business as a public company; rarely are they important sources of value creation for a corporation. Beyond the attempt to perform these functions as efficiently and accurately as possible, little more remains to be said, as few things differentiate these activities across corporations.

Many corporations also centralize the treasury function or computer operations, such as payroll and benefits administration, at the corporate level, or maintain all their lawyers in a corporate staff function. Such corporate units are not performing public company functions; they are acting as service providers of **scalable overhead functions** for the divisions. This is a perfectly valid role for a corporate center to perform if it is a more cost-effective provider of those services than either the divisions themselves or an outside supplier.

Some firms are beginning to apply exactly this market test to corporate activities that involve the provision of overhead services. As a result, they are structuring some corporate functions to be arm's-length suppliers to divisions that are allowed to choose whether or not to use the services provided by the corporate unit. This imposes a market discipline and allows the divisions to choose the level of service appropriate for them. As a corollary, the corporate unit is often allowed to compete for outside business. This not only demonstrates that the unit is cost effective, but also increases its scale.

The result of this approach has been the **outsourcing** of many corporate services, such as data processing and legal affairs, when third-party suppliers are found to be more efficient and responsive than an internally focused corporate unit. In addition, the approach has led to the **decentralizing** of many overhead functions to the divisions. For example, as part of restructuring at ABB, the European electrical equipment company, Chairman Percy Barnevik dealt with corporate functions according to a "30/30/30/10 rule"—30 percent of the employees were laid off because their activities were outsourced; 30 percent were transferred to divisions as their activities were decentralized; 30 percent moved to units that charged for their services; and only 10 percent remained at headquarters.[40]

Such actions can be entirely appropriate. When it is cheaper to outsource or decentralize an overhead function, or when the service provided by the division or external supplier is more responsive and flexible, there is no longer any reason to maintain a central corporate unit. Outsourcing such opportunities can not only lead to cost reductions, it can force a firm to reconsider the means by which it adds value to its units.

▲ SETTING THE ADMINISTRATIVE CONTEXT

The major influence the corporate office has on the implementation of its corporate strategy is by establishing the administrative context within which delegated decisions are made. As described in the Principles section, the administrative context defines the information structure, the allocation of decision rights, and the incentive structure inside the firm. More pragmatically, in a multibusiness corporation that context is created from the design of the organization structure and the systems and processes used to achieve control and coherence of the units established by that structure.

Structure

As was discussed in the Principles section, organizational designs are rarely ideal for any corporation. No matter how complex the design, every organizational structure will have weaknesses. This does not mean that CEOs should throw up their hands and walk away from structuring their organizations. Rather, it implies that organizational design should be contingent on the immediate task at hand and that managers should be prepared to expect some degree of conflict around, and discomfort within, any organization. Particular designs are not solutions for eternity; rather, they are appropriate at a point in time.

This suggests that a degree of organizational change at reasonable intervals is probably appropriate. The corporation should adopt what currently seems to be the best choice, stick with it for a while to give it a chance to affect behavior, and then make changes as circumstances demand. As a simple example, in transformational processes corporations are often

---

[40]Simons, R.L. and C.A. Bartlett, "Asea Brown Boveri," Harvard Business School case number 192-139.

broken into smaller units to improve efficiencies within those units. At a later stage, the units may be recombined under a single manager in order to exploit the underlying synergies among the businesses. No organizational design can achieve both goals simultaneously, so firms choose different structures to achieve these goals *sequentially*.[41]

Control

Corporate control systems are often seen as the necessary evil of large organizations. They prevent abuse of delegated decision-making authority by autonomous divisions (minimize agency costs) but may add interfering layers of bureacracy to the entrepeneurial activities of those divisions. Although the old fashioned "command and control" hierarchy may not be popular today, the corporate office still has a responsibility to monitor and regulate divisional activities. Further, in a more positive light, such systems can be seen as a powerful discipline for divisions, providing the structure within which creativity may take place.

Most multidivisional corporations ultimately employ some form of hierarchical control by a corporate executive, or in very large corporations, by a number of group vice presidents who reduce the span of control of the CEO to whom they report. Control is also exerted through the selection and replacement of senior divisional personnel. For example, choosing a manager with a particular set of skills, such as cost-cutting experience, is a simple way to ensure that a division will attempt to achieve a particular objective. Similarly, replacing the president of a division is the most immediate way to correct unsatisfactory performance.

Yet the most pervasive form of corporate control is the use of a set of systems and processes that continually monitor and regulate the behavior and performance of the divisions. Typically, these are the budgeting, strategic planning, capital expenditure, and measurement and reward schemes installed by corporate managers. Their value lies in setting the incentive structure for managers by defining performance and behavior targets, monitoring progress toward those targets, rewarding and motivating managers to meet the targets, and including mechanisms to intervene when performance deviates from acceptable bounds.

As noted in the Principles section, control systems can be differentiated by an emphasis on outcome or behavior control. Each approach serves different strategic needs and has different organizational requirements.

Implementing Outcome Control. Outcome control is most appropriate when: (1) a single measure of current financial performance, such as cash flow, is a good surrogate for strategic position in a business; (2) when few exogenous influences intervene between managerial behavior and a business outcome; and (3) when a firm's business units have little need for coordination. Outcome control, therefore, is most often found in mature businesses with low technology, where unprecedented competitive changes are rare.

When implementing an outcome control system, the first task is to structure the organization into **autonomous and self-contained business units**. Managers evaluated on outcome control will be improperly incentivized and demotivated if they are held accountable for events and actions beyond their control. The organizational structure, therefore, must align managerial authority and responsibility as closely as possible.

---

[41]Rumelt, Richard P., "Inertia and Transformation." In *Resource-Based and Evolutionary Theories of the Firm: Towards a Synthesis*, ed. C.A. Montgomery (Boston, MA: Kluwer Academic Publishers, 1995), pp. 100–132.

The next step is to select an appropriate performance measure. Most firms use one or very **few financial measures of performance** to evaluate divisional executives. Some focus on measures of accounting profitability, such as return on investment (ROI), while others, more recently, have installed value-based measures.[42] Many of the incentive schemes are highly leveraged so that managers who do exceed their targets are handsomely compensated. In LBO firms, for example, where incentives are tied to equity stakes, managers have the potential to become very wealthy if their buyout succeeds. Even in more traditional corporate hierarchies, the slope of the incentive payment is often very steep, and the size of the bonus payment relative to base salary is large.

When using outcome control, the critical management system is the **annual budget**. The budget sets goals that divisional managers must meet and is often the basis for most interactions between the divisions and the corporate office. To preserve the integrity of the budgeting system, it is particularly important to avoid gaming by divisional managers around their performance targets. This may be done by holding all divisions accountable to one standard, even if external circumstances change, or by locking managers into the division in which they are currently employed so that if they increase profit today at the expense of profit tomorrow, they themselves will bear the consequences of that action. If a particular division does not meet its target over a sustained period, corporate management is likely to replace the unit's managers or sell the division rather than adjust its goal or attempt to assist in a turnaround. In companies that rely on outcome control, corporate managers are simply unlikely to have the level of specific expertise that more active involvement would require.

Due to their limited involvement in divisional affairs, firms that rely on outcome control typically have **small corporate staffs**. **Controllers** fulfill a critical function in these firms and are usually corporate staff employees. Even though they may be assigned to a particular division, they will be independent from divisional management in matters of financial reporting. In fact, they will often be the most powerful managers inside the company, and many of them will become senior corporate executives.

Not surprisingly, the **accounting system** may well be the only uniform system throughout the entire corporation. Since it is important to hold all divisions to a similar standard, it is critical to have one set of accounts that makes assessment fair and comparisons easy. Divisions may choose the format of their own strategic plans, although the emphasis will always be on the financial implications. Capital budgeting will typically impose a tight discipline on the divisions since investment is, in the short run, the enemy of performance. In fact, some of the more extreme exponents of outcome control, like the U.K. conglomerate Hanson, have very low capital spending limits as a direct check on cash flow.

The clearest examples of outcome control are associated with the classic conglomerates, like ITT under Harold Geneen, which evaluated performance and allocated resources on the basis of divisional ROI. Today, many successful corporations, like General Electric, essentially employ outcome control. Although many of these firms may appear to take a more active role in the management of their divisions, a closer look often reveals that the primary relationship between headquarters and the divisions is one of arm's-length monitoring of financial results.

Implementing Behavior Control. Unlike outcome control, behavior control solves the agency problem inside the corporation by directly evaluating the behavior of divisional

---

[42]J.M. MacTaggart, P. Kontes, and M.C. Mankins, *The Value Imperative: Managing for Superior Shareholder Returns* (New York: Free Press, 1994); and Copeland et al. (1990).

managers, not their results. This system of control is particularly appropriate in companies with **complex interdependencies among divisions**, where outcome control is less feasible.

In these companies, corporate managers usually monitor **multiple operating and financial measures of performance**. In particular, attention is paid to critical operating data, such as reject rates, delivery lead times, and conversion statistics. Indeed, corporate managers in companies practicing behavior control may be presented with monthly reports that contain up to 200 line items on divisional performance. Managerial assessment in this setting may be flexible, and involve a number of **quantitative and qualitative goals**. The tradeoffs among these targets may not be fully specified, and the evaluation and incentive scheme may resemble more of an implicit contract than a simple objective target. Short-term financial rewards are often less important as an incentive than long-term career progression in such companies.

In practice, for corporate managers to utilize behavior control effectively, they have to **know the businesses in the portfolio**. As a result, managers often come from within the firm, or at least from the industries in which the firm operates. When this mode of control is working properly, the role of the corporate officers becomes more of a coach than a monitor. They do not necessarily make decisions for divisional managers, but their industry experience allows them to offer advice and critique behavior in a constructive way that improves the decisions of divisional managers. Consequently, although businesses in the corporate portfolio need not produce similar products, they do need to share similar managerial characteristics; that is, have the same "dominant logic."

Not surprisingly, behavior control typically necessitates active corporate involvement in **many management systems**. The strategic and the capital budgeting processes, for example, will often be interactive and involve corporate initiatives because the corporate managers have something of value to contribute. These processes are also likely to be standardized across divisions so that corporate management can readily understand detailed divisional operating and financial data. Business units will usually have a common culture so that managers can move freely and easily among them.

Finally, behavior control often requires a **larger corporate staff** than outcome control, it does not necessarily demand an enormous corporate infrastructure. If corporate managers are familiar with the industries they are overseeing, it is quite possible for them to be adequately informed without a vast support system.

A Blending of Control Systems.   Although the two modes of control are often treated as a dichotomy, they are more accurately portrayed as a range. Most firms use elements of both: corporate offices, for example, often evaluate divisional managers on financial performance, but also monitor and evaluate more specific behaviors. Nevertheless, the contingencies that determine when each type of control is appropriate and the administrative imperatives of each are sufficiently different that corporations do have to choose an emphasis on one or the other.

Coherence

The second set of systems and processes that the corporate office must design to support a given organization structure are those that provide coherence to the activities of the differentiated business units. It has been in this regard that corporate strategy has too often failed. Yet it is exactly this role that is critical to the effective implementation of any corporate strategy. If the corporation cannot be organized to leverage valuable corporate resources across the divisions, it will not be able to justify its existence as a multibusiness corporation.

In the Principles section we suggested that there are two ways to leverage valuable resources across the divisions: transferring skills or resources, and coordination of activities. Transferring resources and skills across businesses can be a powerful way to create value while minimizing the interference in the autonomy of divisions. Many corporations, for example, simply move highly skilled managers among businesses. Others may explicitly replicate the best demonstrated practices in specific functions, such as supply-chain management, within all their businesses.

Other firms may have the potential to exploit their multibusiness nature by *coordinating* activities across businesses. For example, units may jointly purchase common raw materials to take advantage of purchasing scale economies. Others may share a sales force, a common component manufacturing facility, or a joint distribution system. Coordinating activities may not only reduce costs, it can also provide direct benefits to the customer, such as a single point of contact or a clarification of which of the company's many products are most appropriate.

To leverage valuable resources across business units, a firm has to follow either of these approaches to achieve coherence. However, the two are not mutually exclusive; the necessary systems and processes can be customized for each resource that is being shared. Not surprisingly, therefore, many corporations employ both methods as they exploit their corporate advantage.

Transferring Skills.   In transferring resources or skills across divisions where they will be used independently, the corporate office faces two basic decisions, identified by Andrew Campbell.[43] These are **where to develop the resource** (at the corporate or divisional level), and who has **authority over the transfer** of the resource (the corporate office or the divisions).

In choosing between the two approaches for developing a valuable resource, the advantage of centralization in a corporate unit lies in exploiting economies of scale and being of a sufficient size to support specialists. It also avoids the duplication of effort that ensues when multiple divisions make investments in similar resources or skills. This, for example, is why basic R&D is usually concentrated in a corporate unit. Conversely, the amount of experimentation is increased by allowing divisions to individually develop new knowledge, processes, and practices before selecting the best that emerges. In between these extremes lie a range of alternatives, such as nominating individual divisions to take the lead for a particular innovation, in much the way that multinationals select lead countries for developing particular new products or management practices.

When it has been decided where to develop a resource, a choice then has to be made about how much corporate intervention will be involved in transferring that resource or skill across businesses. At one extreme, transfers can be entirely left up to the self-interest of the divisions. Divisions wishing to adopt a best practice, for example, can seek out individuals in other divisions who are identified as possessing state-of-the-art knowledge and ask them to act as temporary consultants. At the other extreme, the corporate office can mandate that all divisions adopt a particular set of policies and practices, which can even be set down in detail in a thick manual of procedures.

It is important to note that companies can choose how to deploy each separate resource or skill differently. Ideally, most would be transferred in a way that does not violate the autonomy of the divisions. The imposition of more centralized procedures should occur only when those with less intervention fail to achieve the desired degree of coherence.

[43]Andrew Campbell and Kathleen Sommers Luchs, *Strategic Synergy* (Oxford: Butterworth: Heinemann Ltd., 1992).

Coordination of Activities. Despite the many benefits of transferring resources across autonomous divisions, some of the most highly valued benefits of synergy can only be achieved by coordinating activities across businesses.

Because introducing coordination to previously stand-alone businesses can be difficult, it is important to first be **selective** about the activities to be coordinated. This is best done at a disaggregated level. Rather than treat all purchasing as a single activity, for example, it can be disaggregated into discrete processes that can be managed differently. Divisions may be given authority to arrange their own logistics and to select vendors, while the corporate purchasing department is only made responsible for approving vendors, establishing standard terms and conditions for suppliers, and negotiating prices.

Activities that are a **large part of the cost structure**, or those that have little impact on the differentiation of an individual division's products, will, therefore, often be coordinated because sharing will bring substantial benefits. At banks, for example, it is the backroom operations that are shared between consumer, commercial, and large business accounts because they involve substantial costs, and subject to scale economies, and their performance is invisible to the customer. Smaller, or more sensitive activities, such as the issuance of credit, are often left under the control of each product line.

Having identified the activities that should be shared, the next step is to choose the mechanism by which coordination will be achieved. Options for doing so can be arrayed along a **hierarchy of coordination**. This extends from actions guided by self-interested behavior to a fomalized process in which a superior is imposed to directly coordinate divisional activities. (See Appendix C, "Mechanisms for Achieving Coordinating Coherence.")

To be sure, introducing coherence to previously autonomous businesses can be difficult because it often requires a change in attitudes and behavior. Nonetheless, as corporations remain under pressure to justify their existence as multibusiness entities, it will be increasingly important for them to take advantage of opportunities for sharing resources.

There are no universal solutions for the process of introducing coherence to an organization, and trade-offs abound (see "Introducing Coordination"). Moreover, all corporations have to be sensitive to their own unique administrative heritage. However, the preferred approach appears to be incremental. By gradually working up from the synergies that are in all divisions' interests, a firm can "pick the low-hanging fruit" first and address the more difficult and contentious issues later. At that point, a firm may have clarified its intentions and built sufficient commitment to the process to impose solutions on those parts of the organization that still resist.

▲ SUMMARY: THE SIZE OF THE CORPORATE OFFICE

Although all corporate offices perform the four roles described above, the implementation is very different across firms. How executives actually manage their organizations will depend fundamentally on the corporate strategy they are pursuing. As a result, the range and nature of the activities carried out at corporate headquarters will be very different and the appropriate size of the headquarters office itself will be radically different (see Figure 6–7).

Research suggests that the average cost of the corporate office is between .66 percent and .75 percent of corporate assets,[44] or perhaps 1 percent of total corporate revenue. This com-

---

[44]T. Copeland, T. Koller, and J. Murrin, *Valuation: Measuring and Managing the Value of Companies* (New York: John Wiley & Sons, 1990).

Introducing Coordination

The corporate role in a transition to more intensive coordination should be to:

▲ *Sell* the benefits by preaching the quantifiable gains that the corporation will make from cooperation and reiterating the importance of optimizing corporate, not divisional, performance.

▲ *Encourage* the mechanisms that are appropriate at each stage in the change process.

▲ *Facilitate* the transition by removing barriers, whether these are organizational structures, or as is often the case, by having the courage to remove high-performing managers who do not accept the process.

▲ *Validate* the outcomes from the new structures. This involves supporting initiatives that come out of these new structures, even if they appear to be inappropriate, and publicly and repeatedly applauding progress.

▲ FIGURE 6–7   Size of Corporate Office in Various Companies

Company	Assets ($ billions)	Employees in Corporate Office
Sharp	16	1,500
Cooper Industries	5	300
Newell	1.5	250
KKR	40	90

pares with the expense of 0.2 percent of asset value that a mutual fund charges for investing in an indexed portfolio of stocks, the 1 percent that on average Vanguard, the low cost provider of mutual funds, charges, and the 0.45 percent that Fidelity, the most successful actively managed mutual fund company charges for its Magellan Fund. Since the corporate office in a multibusiness firm is, if nothing else, acting like a mutual fund, that comparison provides a minimum benchmark.

As a more pragmatic benchmark, U.K. data reveal that the typical multinational consumer goods company employing 50,000 people had a staff of 227, or 0.5 percent of employees, in its head office.[45] This is, however, a purely descriptive statistic. It carries no normative implications. Deciding whether the number is too large or too small requires understanding how to appropriately implement the roles of the corporate office because that number can, as Figure 6–7 shows, vary broadly.

---

[45]D. Young, *The Headquarters Fact Book* (London: Ashridge Strategic Management Centre, 1993).

▲ RECOMMENDED READINGS

Armour, H., and D.J. Teece, "Organization Structure and Economic Performance: A Test of the Multidivisional Hypothesis." *Bell Journal of Economics* (1978), pp. 106–122.

Bartlett, C., and S. Ghoshal. *Managing across Borders.* Boston, MA: Harvard Business School Press, 1989.

Berg, N. "What's Different about Conglomerate Management?" *Harvard Business Review.* 47 (1969), pp. 112–120.

Bower, J.H. *Managing the Resource Allocation Process.* Cambridge, MA: Harvard University Press, 1970.

Campbell, A. "Building Core Skills." In *Strategic Synergy,* eds. A. Campbell and K.S. Luchs. Oxford: Butterworth Heinemen, 1992, pp. 173–197.

Chandler, A.D. *Strategy and Structure.* Cambridge, MA: MIT Press, 1962.

Copeland, T., T. Koller, and J. Murrin. *Valuation: Measuring and Managing the Value of Companies.* New York: John Wiley & Sons, 1990.

Cyert, R., and J. March. *A Behavioral Theory of the Firm.* Englewood Cliffs, NJ: Prentice Hall, 1963.

Eccles, R.G.N., and N. Nohria, eds. *Networks in Organizations.* Boston, MA: Harvard Business School Press, 1992.

Eisenhardt, K.M. "Agency Theory: An Assessment and Review." *Academy of Management Review* (1989), pp. 57–74.

Galbraith, J. R., and R.K. Kazanjian. *Strategy Implementation: Structure, Systems and Process.* St. Paul, MN: West Publishing, 1985.

Goold, M.C., M. Alexander, and A. Campbell. *Corporate-Level Strategy: Creating Value in the Multibusiness Company.* New York: John Wiley & Sons, 1994.

Goold, M.C., and J.J. Quinn. *Strategic Control: Milestones for Long-Term Performance.* London: The Economist Books, 1990.

Gupta, A.K., and S. Seshadri. "Horizontal Resource Sharing: A Principal Agent Approach." *Academy of Management Best Papers,* 1994, pp. 37–41.

Halal, W.E., A. Geranmayeh, and J. Pourdehnad. *Internal Markets: Bringing the Power of Free Enterprise Inside Your Organization.* New York: John Wiley & Sons, 1993.

Hill, C.W.L., M.A. Hitt, and R.E. Hoskisson. "Cooperative versus Competitive Structures in Related and Unrelated Diversified Firms." *Organization Science* (1992), pp. 501–21.

Jensen, M.C., and W.H. Meckling. "Specific and General Knowledge, and Organization Structure." in *Main Currents in Contract Economics,* eds., L. Werin and H. Wijkander. London: Basil Blackwell, 1991, pp. 251–274.

Lawrence, P.R., and Lorsch, J.W. *Organizations and Environment.* Boston: Harvard Business School Press, 1967.

Lorsch, J.W., and Allen, S.A. *Managing Diversity and Interdependence.* Boston: Harvard Business School Press, 1973.

MacTaggart, J.M., P. Kontes, and M.C. Mankins. *The Value Imperative: Managing for Superior Shareholder Returns.* New York: Free Press, 1994.

Miles, Robert H. *Macro Organizational Behavior.* Santa Monica, CA: Goodyear Publishing Co., 1980.

Nayyar, P.R., and R.K. Kazanjian. "Organizing to Attain Potential Benefits from Information Assymetries and Economies of Scope in Related Diversified Firms." *Academy of Management Review* 18 (1993), pp. 735–59.

Nonaka, I., and H. Takeuchi. *The Knowledge Creating Company.* Oxford: Oxford University Press, 1995.

Ouchi, W.G. "A Conceptual Framework for the Design of Organization Control Mechanisms." *Management Science* 25 (1979), pp. 833–48.

Porter, M.E.. "From Competitive Advantage to Corporate Strategy." *Harvard Business Review* 65, no. 3 (May–June 1987), pp. 43–59.

Porter, M.E. *Competitive Advantage.* New York: Free Press, 1985.

Prahalad, C.K., and Yves L. Doz. *The Multinational Mission.* New York: Free Press, 1987.

Simons, R. *Levers of Control.* Boston, MA: Harvard Business School Press, 1995.

Vancil, R.F. *Decentralization: Managerial Ambiguity by Design.* Burr Ridge, IL: Irwin, 1978.

Young, D. *The Headquarters Fact Book.* London: Ashridge Strategic Management Centre, 1993.

MECHANISMS FOR ACHIEVING CORPORATE COHERENCE

The Principles and Practice sections of Chapter 6 outlined an approach to designing the administrative context for a multibusiness corporation. Here, we describe in detail the systems and processes that can be used to effectively achieve coherence in such organizations.

▲ TRANSFERRING RESOURCES AND SKILLS

Transferring resources and skills across organizational units can produce important synergies. At the same time, it often is a relatively low cost, low risk way of achieving coherence.

As we discussed in Chapter 6, the corporate office must decide where a resource should be developed—at the corporate or divisional level—and who should have authority over its transfer. Andrew Campbell has developed a matrix that portrays these options (Figure C–1).

Quadrant 1. Corporate level resources that are the "crown jewels" of a company merit a high degree of corporate involvement in their deployment. To the extent that an umbrella brand name or technical knowledge, for example, is critical to the corporate strategy, the corporate office must be particularly vigilant in overseeing its development and judicious usage. As a result, the optimum way to deploy these resources across businesses is to adopt systems and processes from quadrant 1 of the grid. In particular, the tasks of the corporate office include investing in the valuable resources; making them available to the divisions to use as they want; and maintaining quality control over their usage by the divisions (see "Disney's Crown Jewels").

The corporate office must be in charge of the development of, and investment in, such critical resources. Divisions might well underinvest in these resources because many are

▲ FIGURE C–1   Transferring Resources and Skills

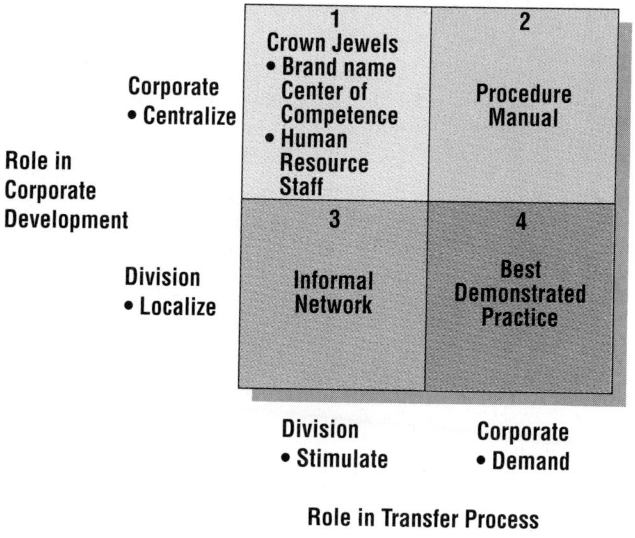

Source: Adapted from Andrew Campbell and Kathleen Sommers Luchs, *Strategic Synergy* (Oxford: Butterworth-Heinemann Ltd., 1992), p. 185.

public goods in which each division wishes to free ride on the investments of others.[1] In the case of R&D, for example, even if divisions will voluntarily pay for a certain amount of central research, the corporation as a whole will often be better off if it spends more than the sum of divisional research requests. Moreover, individual divisions may have conflicting priorities: one division, for example, might want the corporate brand reputation to appeal more to younger consumers, while another division might prefer an older age profile. The corporate office must, therefore, have control over both the level of investment and the specific nature of the resource that is being developed.

Since divisions will ideally regard the crown jewels as vital to their own competitive advantage, they will voluntarily seek transfer of those resources to their businesses. Every division at Disney, for example, wants to use the latest cartoon character in its operations. As a result, divisions can, by and large, be allowed to choose how to deploy the resource in their daily operations. As the cross-firm linkages provide little constraint, if any, on their independent operations, a few specific conflict resolution mechanisms and a strong-minded corporate arbitration policy are often sufficient to resolve divisional differences.

The exception is the need for quality control in the use of the resource. A division may, for example, be tempted to offer poor products to maximize its profits, knowing that they will sell because of the corporation's overall brand name or reputation for technical prowess. To

---

[1]The market for a public good fails because each user has the incentive to underinvest in, or overexploit, the public good. When one firm invests, for example, all other firms benefit, so that the marginal private return to investing is below the social return. Formally, this occurs when the residual rights of control and the residual returns are not vested in the same entity [P. Milgrom and J. Roberts, *Economics, Organization and Management* (Englewood Cliffs, NJ: Prentice Hall, 1992), chap. 9]. The solution is to give one entity (i.e., the corporation) property rights to the public good.

Disney's Crown Jewels

Disney essentially provides its library of cartoon characters as a central resource to otherwise autonomous divisions—theme parks, studio, and consumer products. Disney's chairman, Michael Eisner, invests in one new full-length animated feature film per year, but exactly what the theme park or consumer products divisions do with Simba from the *Lion King* is up to them. Eisner is more concerned with tightly controlling the quality of what the divisions do, rather than with the specifics of the product or service they choose to deliver.

At Disney, coordination among divisions is limited to the marketing function. This prevents conflict between the theme park division's promotion of the *Lion King* at McDonald's and the consumer products division's similar promotion at Wendy's. A marketing calendar is, therefore, used as a coordination device to inform divisions of the programs others are planning. Otherwise, divisions operate autonomously and with no coordination, utilizing, for example, their own pay scales and management systems.

▲ FIGURE C–2   Role in Transfer Process

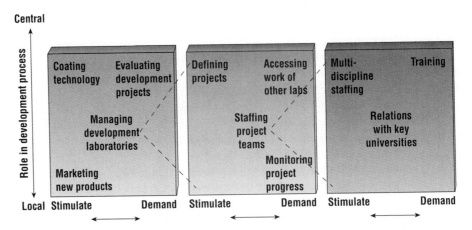

Source: Adapted from Andrew Campbell and Kathleen Sommers Luchs, *Strategic Synergy* (Oxford: Butterworth-Heinemann Ltd., 1992), p. 185.

prevent this degrading of the corporate resource, the corporate office must monitor the quality of divisional activities.

Quadrant 2.   Traditionally the role of the corporate staff functions has fallen in quadrant 2 of the grid. For example, a central staff, such as a manufacturing department, may develop process technologies for divisions to employ and have the authority to interfere in divisional operations to ensure that the manufacturing department's edicts are followed. Staff units in such circumstances have often been viewed as overly interventionist. Bureaucratic and patronizing corporate manufacturing staffs, for example, might establish plant designs that all divisions have to follow, whether or not they are appropriate for their needs.

Operating a staff function in this way is really only necessary for those practices and skills that are absolutely essential to the integrity of the corporation. Accounting and control procedures should probably be operated in this fashion, as, for example, should safety, health, and environmental procedures in chemical companies. Policies should be developed by the corporate center and imposed on divisions only for those activities that, if performed inappropriately, would lead to truly adverse consequences for the company.

Instead, many corporate staffs today are evolving into **centers of competence** (Quadrant 1): central developers of a specific skill or a particular pool of knowledge, such as supply-chain management for batch manufacturing, that can be transferred to divisions as they request it.[2] In this role, corporate staffs can become valuable resources that businesses seek out on their own (see "Core Capabilities at Coopers & Lybrand").[3]

Often the valuable skills that are developed in an organization, such as PepsiCo's consumer marketing know-how, vest in the employees. The easiest way to transfer those skills across the divisions is simply to move people throughout the organization. Indeed, several successful U.S. diversified corporations pursue this approach. General Electric, for example, has created a corporate advantage around the superior managerial skills and knowledge of a cadre of superbly trained people. Although not all firms pursue a corporate strategy based on people as the valuable corporate resource, in those that do the corporate human resources department plays a key role. As such, it exemplifies the modern role of a corporate function as a center of competence (see "Corporate Human Resources").

Quadrants 3 and 4. Rather than having valuable resources developed by a central corporate function, they can instead be developed in the divisions. One division, for example, may build a unique logistics capability; another may have a distinctive competence in high-volume

---

Core Capabilities at Coopers and Lybrand

Coopers and Lybrand identified a number of core capabilities that it felt were required to compete successfully in the audit, tax, and consulting businesses. It made a vice chairman with a small corporate staff responsible for the development of each required expertise and the dissemination of the expertise among the businesses. One of the capabilities identified was client-relationship management.

To become competitively superior at this activity, the vice chairman set up a commit-tee to examine best practices throughout the organization and to make recommendations as to how to improve those practices. Once the committee had completed its investigation, the firm developed a set of policies and practices, written up in a brief manual, for the businesses to adopt. To encourage the implementation of the new policies, the adoption of certain practices, such as creating a lead engagement partner for major clients who used several of the firm's services, was incorporated into individuals' annual goals.

---

[2]R. Eisenstat, "Corporate Staff Work in Divisionalized Corporations," Harvard Business School working paper no. 90-056, May 1990.

[3]This sort of activity by a corporate function needs to be distinguished from its role as a central unit that merely performs a scalable overhead function. A central legal department, for example, is not a valuable corporate resource that gives the firm a corporate advantage in a wide range of businesses.

Corporate Human Resources

The strategic value of the corporate HR function revolves around **the recruitment, training, and career development** of a pool of corporate employees who possess valuable skills that create competitive advantage in the divisions. The brand managers of consumer packaged goods companies, for example, can be thought of in this light. These individuals will be involved in a substantial amount of **personnel transfer** across divisions and often across functions (perhaps 5 to 15 percent of the critical employees will have interdivisional transfers each year) in order to deploy the employees' skills throughout the corporation.

To facilitate corporatewide acceptance of the practice, the corporate HR function must establish a uniform compensation system and also, ideally, a common culture. It also needs training and career development programs that ensure skills truly are competitively superior and up to a common standard throughout the corporation. This gives divisions the confidence not to obstruct transfers of their best employees because they know that a replacement will be of equally high quality.

Since the valuable corporate resource is its people, HR also needs to develop careers that remain within the firm, and promote from within; this also prevents competitors from benefiting from the employees' knowledge. Procter and Gamble, Johnson & Johnson, and Marriott, for example, consider employees as lifetime partners and plan their career paths accordingly.

The synthesis of these organizational requirements is the strategic importance given the HR function by CEOs at companies that develop people as valuable resources. At GE, for example, Jack Welch spends 20 days a year on personnel evaluations of his top 400 managers. At PepsiCo, Wayne Calloway personally interviews proposed candidates for any one of the company's top 600 jobs. At Cooper Industries, Robert Cizik spends nearly a month a year on the company's Management Development and Planning process. These executives view the people in their organizations as critical assets and allocate to them, and their HR roles, the amount of time they deserve.

data processing.[4] The critical task for the corporate office in creating corporate coherence around these resources then becomes ensuring that those skills are transferred around the organization. Typically, this is achieved by either encouraging (Quadrant 3) or mandating (Quadrant 4) the adoption of **best demonstrated practices** throughout the organization. Between these two extremes exist corporate policies that stimulate self-interested divisions to use a resource or skill available elsewhere in the firm, such as regular cross-divisional meetings of particular functional areas, company newsletters that describe breakthrough best practices, or intracompany yellow pages that list individuals who possess a particular expertise.

In summary, practices that facilitate the transfer of resources throughout an organization are many and varied in nature. When used appropriately, they can generate substantial value for a firm, often with modest costs to the organization. In contrast, scope economies that call for coordination of activities across business units tend to challenge firms more and often necessitate

---

[4] While divisional level resources give the division concerned a competitive advantage, they only create a corporate advantage if they can be deployed in other divisions. A purely divisional level competence cannot be the justification for a multibusiness corporation. No matter how valuable a resource is to competitive advantage in a particular division, there must still be mechanisms to deploy it throughout the organization if it is to be the basis for a corporate advantage. A corporate strategy of owning only number 1 or number 2 brands, therefore, is unlikely to be successful if the only resource is the market-leading position of each individual brand.

fundamental changes in organizational infrastructure. However, when relevant and appropriately implemented, the benefits realized from such coordinated activities can be sizable.

▲ COORDINATION OF ACTIVITIES

As discussed in Chapter 6, to achieve the benefits of coordination, a firm should carefully identify the coordination mechanisms that are most appropriate for a given activity. This is done by disaggregating an activity into discrete steps that can be treated separately. For each of these steps, management can choose the coordination mechanism which works best.

Coordination mechanisms range from those that are freely elected by the divisions to those that are imposed on the divisions by corporate management. The **hierarchy of coordination** (Figure C–3) illustrates these possibilities.

At the bottom of the hierarchy are **personal networks** that develop among individuals in different divisions and that can lead to the coordinated sharing of activities. Although such networks of interdivisional contacts are established in the ongoing activities of a firm—in corporate training sessions, planning meetings, and so forth—the corporate office can facilitate the process. For example, annual meetings of divisional presidents or heads of purchasing, at which each presents his or her ideas for coordination opportunities, can be valuable forums for developing such networks.

More structured than personal networks are formal **councils** whose specific agenda is to search out opportunities for cooperation. Many corporations have such groups, under different names, for activities that divisions can profitably share with little compromise, such as stationery purchasing. Indeed, the first step of such a council is often to select those activities that fall into this category and can readily be implemented with the approval of all the interested parties.

The next step up the hierarchy involves the creation of ad hoc **task forces** to address particular coordination needs that have been identified.[5] At this stage, more detailed analysis might be necessary because the ideal solution is no longer immediately visible or agreeable to all concerned. Instead, a team representing all the affected parties investigates possible options and recommends a solution. At this point, the hierarchy begins to diverge from pure divisional self-interest: instead of allowing the divisions to accept or reject the task force's recommendation, the rule might be that a majority vote of the team is sufficient to implement the recommendation. Thus, coordination begins to supplant divisional autonomy.

Moving up the hierarchy, an **integrator** without formal authority to override divisional management may be given responsibility for implementing the sharing of activities across businesses. This is similar to the role of an executive whose job is to coordinate joint purchasing but who has no formal authority over purchasing decisions.

Because of the lack of formal power over decision making, the individual has to have the respect of the operating divisions' management. This implies that the integrator has to be an experienced and successful line executive, not a staff functionary. He or she should also have a broad background and a wide network of contacts within the organization and be an effective resolver of conflicts. To balance divisional conflicts, and to provide the appropriate incentives, the reward scheme for the integrator has to be based on corporate goals and performance.

---

[5]Many corporations use teams as ad hoc mechanisms for reaching major onetime decisions, such as the choice of location of a new, shared manufacturing facility. They are less useful for managing ongoing coordination issues because of the continual intrusion in divisional autonomy.

▲ FIGURE C–3   Coordination Hierarchy

Mode	System	Process
Discrete shared activity	Organization structure	Formalized
Centralized decision maker	Hierarchy	
Prescribed behavior	Manual	
Define responsibilities	Decision grid	
Internalize conflict	Matrix	
Recommendation/persuasion	Integrator	
Team consensus	Task force	
Coordination of information flow	Council	
Bilateral flow of information	Personal network	Self-interested

Source: Adapted from J.R. Galbraith and R.K. Kazajian, "Strategy Implementation: Structures, Systems, Processes" (St. Paul: West Publishing Company, 1978), p. 72.

The explicit allocation of decision-making authority takes place at the next level in the hierarchy. This is captured in McKinsey's notion of a **decision grid** (see Figure C–4); it specifies which divisions and corporate functions have what degree of say in which decisions. The allocation of decision-making rights within a grid varies on a continuum from absolute control, through veto power, to input, and finally to no influence at all.

The decision grid clarifies where the responsibility for shared decisions lies. It does not, however, specify how to resolve conflict when multiple parties are vested with decision-making authority or when those with approval rights disagree. It is, therefore, most useful for demarcating who has no involvement in certain decisions. It does not by itself solve the most difficult and controversial aspects of achieving coordination.

The existence of a written **manual** marks the level in the hierarchy at which divisional discretion is removed. Manuals may eliminate conflict, a direct cost of coordination, but often do so at the expense of both divisional autonomy and, potentially, of finding the best solution to each situation. An example would be transfer pricing between divisions. Lower down the coordination hierarchy, divisions would be allowed to negotiate transfer prices among themselves. With a manual, the way to calculate the transfer price would be prescribed, with no scope for discretion. Doing so is often appropriate for recurring issues that have little effect on corporate performance. In those situations, a manual prevents repeated conflict. For substantive one-time decisions, however, the loss of discretion is more likely to produce a suboptimal decision.

The final step in the hierarchy involves taking away decision-making authority from the business units. This can be achieved through either of two **formal organizational structures.** The first is to give one individual authority over the divisions that share activities. The second is to split off the shared activity into a separate unit with its own management hierarchy. Both eliminate the need for negotiation between divisions to achieve coordination.

In many organizations, the first structural solution is captured in the role of **group vice president.** This person is put in charge of several related businesses with the responsibility and authority for maximizing the performance of the group.[6] It is, therefore, in a group vice

[6]The group vice president role does not necessarily involve coordination responsibilities. It can also be a device to break spans of control in a purely monitoring function. Conglomerates, for example, are frequent users of group vice presidents, but their role is controlling delegated decision making, not coordination.

Figure C–4 Decision Responsibilities for Worldwide TV Business (U.S. and European Relationships)

Legend:
D – Decides
A – Approves
R – Recommends
BC – Business concurrence
TC – Technical concurrence
C – Concurs
I – Initiate
IP – Inputs
* Joint decision
** For U.S. decisions only

	U.S. Electrical Products Division					European Area															Worldwide Management				Corporate Staffs											
						Sovirel							CGISA												Finance											
	Business Development Liscomb	Controller Russell	Business Manager TV Gailey	Manager Manufacturing Frailey	General Manager Dawson	TV Division/Plant Controller Hoflack	TV Production Timbal	TV Sales and Marketing Prestat	Division Manager TV Picot	Technical Director Ayotta	Head of Staff Maurice	President Regis	General Manager CEE McCann	Planning Manager Winkler	Licensing Roederer	Socialist Countries Roederer	Financial Manager Hamer	General Sales Manager Stoff	Deputy Area Manager Wuensch	General Manager Dulude	Staff Marketing and Business Development	Staff Manufacturing and Engineering	Control and Planning	Worldwide Manager Dawson	Treasury	Control	Business and Financial Planning	Manufacturing and Engineering	Technical Staffs	Purchasing	Manufacturing Services	Industrial Relations	Manpower Development	Public Relations	Legal	Government Affairs
Worldwide Resource Allocation 1. Recommend allocation of resources to major new product development programs	R_1	IP	R_1	R_1	R_2	IP	R_1	R_1	R_2	IP	IP	BC				C		IP		BC	R3	IP	IP	D		TC	IP	R/TC	R/TC				IP/TC		TC	
2. Recommend allocation of resources to major process development programs	IP	IP	IP	R_1	R_2	IP	R_1	IP	R_2	IP	IP	BC				C				BC	IP	R3	IP	D		TC	IP	R/TC	R/TC				IP/TC		C	
3. Recommend allocation of resources for major cost reduction programs		IP	IP	R_1	R_2	IP	R_1	IP	R_2	R_1	IP	BC				C			C	BC	IP	R3	IP	D		TC	IP	R/TC	R/TC			C	IP/TC			
4. Determine need, location, and timing for adding or reducing plant capacity		IP	IP	R_1	D*	IP	R_1	IP	R_2	IP	R_2	D*				R	IP	IP		D*	IP	R	IP	D*			TC	IP	R			IP/TC	IP/TC		TC	C**
5. Decide management of production work force (expansion, contraction, assignment)			IP	D	C		R_1		R_2		R_2	D	D							C				C								TC**		IP	TC**	C**
6. Decide on interarea sourcing		IP	IP	R_1	R_2	IP	IP	IP	R_2		R_1	BC	R_2			R_2	IP	IP		BC	IP	IP	R3	D	TC	TC	IP	IP							C	C
7. Decide who maintains existing technologies (e.g., black-and-white, spinning)			IP	R	R		R	IP	R	IP		BC				R				BC	IP	R	IP	D				R/TC								
8. Assign specialized people resources to temporary assignments (e.g., to implement special three-month project)																																				
a. Assign operating personnel (e.g., marketing, manufacturing) to another area			R	R	D/BC		R	R	D/BC	C	C				R	R				BC	C	C		BC									R			
b. Assign technical staff and M&E personnel				R			R			D	C		R		R	R			IP	BC		R		BC				D	D				R			

Source: Christopher Bartlett and M.Y. Yoshino, "Corning Glass Works International (B-1)," Harvard Business School case study no. 381-161.
Note: McKinsey-prepared form as filled out during a decision grid meeting.

president's interest to implement any coordination that benefits the corporation, even if it is at the expense of a single business. Although this has historically been the typical corporate solution, it is not without drawbacks, particularly in terms of diminished divisional autonomy and the concentration of decision-making power in the hands of someone who may be removed from the relevant specific knowledge and overloaded with critical decisions.

The second structural solution begins to approach a **functional organization**: discrete functional units perform common activities for multiple businesses. The argument for this solution is that it recreates the benefits of autonomy, since the shared activity is now a separate, self-contained unit, and so provides the correct incentives, particularly if the new unit sells to outsiders and treats its sister divisions as equal customers. It also facilitates the exploitation of scale economies.

However, this solution also creates its own problems. Creating an organizational unit to perform the shared activity shifts the coordination issue from that between divisions to that between the new unit and each division, particularly when it is set up as an internal market.[7] Yet, as we observed in the Principles section, no organization structure can completely resolve the tension between differentiation and integration,[8] so the coordination issue remains problematic.

Either of these solutions may be appropriate when extensive interdependencies between divisions suggest reconfiguring the organization structure to minimize information processing and coordination costs. However, it is an extreme solution and should probably only be used when other levels in the coordination hierarchy have been tried.

---

[7]Halal et al. (1993).

[8]Proponents of core competence who argue for the creation of independent units responsible for a corporation's "platform products" are, therefore, advocates of an extreme structural solution that is not universally appropriate.

Because most corporations have been structured with a bias toward the autonomy of discrete business units, moving to achieve a higher degree of coherence is often problematic. Any sudden attempt to impose formal integrative structures will most likely be resisted. Conversely, the partial introduction of some limited coordination mechanisms might founder on a lack of perceived commitment to change. Nevertheless, for those activities for which there are real benefits from sharing, the challenge for many corporations is to introduce the appropriate mechanisms that capture those benefits while minimizing the costs.

▲ COORDINATING STRATEGIES

A special case of coordination involves the coordination of divisional strategies. In this situation, the sharing among divisions involves not an internal company activity, but the external customer base or competitors the divisions.

Coordinating Market Positions

When considering whether to coordinate strategies toward the same customers, corporations must decide whether divisions should be allowed to freely compete with one another or should have their spheres of activity clearly demarcated to prevent interdivisional competition. The choice is not simple because there are costs and benefits to each approach.

The advantage of free competition is that it maximizes divisional autonomy and fosters entrepreneurialism in the divisions. PepsiCo, for example, pursues this policy in its restaurant businesses, even though its three quick-service chains consequently compete vigorously with one another. The primary disadvantage of interdivisional competition is that it can lead to the duplication of effort and allow opportunities for coordination to be overlooked. It also eliminates the opportunity to earn oligopolistic profits from coordinating strategies and prices. Marriott, for example, would prefer that its various hotel chains, which are often located close to one another, did *not* compete with one another on price.

Resolving the trade-off primarily depends on whether the market can be proactively segmented. When it can, it makes sense to assign one business to each segment and let each optimize its performance within a segment. GM perfected this strategy under Alfred Sloan with "a car for every purse": each of the divisions was assigned a target market, from luxury (Cadillac), to mass market (Chevrolet), to sporty (Pontiac). Historically, this arrangement worked very profitably until it broke down when the brand images of the divisions became blurred (Figure C–5).

However, it can be impossible to segment the market in an economically meaningful way. In the case of quick-service restaurants, customer segmentation varies from day to day, according to how stomachs feel. In such cases, artificially restricting divisional activities will weaken performance by preventing each from optimizing its own strategy.

The argument for coordination to prevent divisions from cannibalizing each other's sales is also less compelling when competitors are already doing it. The motto here might best be expressed as "do unto yourself what others do unto you." In contrast, preserving discrete market positions is more appropriate when the firm's decision to compete with itself will exacerbate negative externalities, such as increasing the rate of substitution to a lower-profit item. Gillette, for example, was slow to introduce disposable razors because they were less profitable than razor and blade systems.

Figure C–5

Historic and Recent GM Brand Positioning

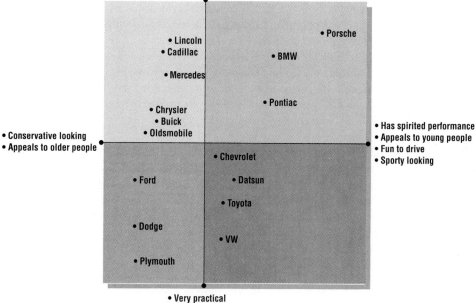

1924 "Touring Car" Price Points

> "A car for every purse, purpose and personality"
> - ▲ Chevrolet: $510
> - ▲ Oldsmobile: $750
> - ▲ Oakland (Pontiac): $945
> - ▲ Buick 4: $965
> - ▲ Buick 6: $1,295
> - ▲ Cadillac: $2,985

1984 Brand Image

Source: *The Wall Street Journal*, March 22, 1984, p. 33.
Reprinted by permission of *The Wall Street Journal*, © 1984 Jones & Company, Inc. All rights reserved worldwide.

Coordinating Multimarket Competition

Multimarket competition occurs whenever a corporation faces the same competitor in more than one market. This raises, at least, the possibility of a coordinated competitive response across markets in order to optimize corporate performance. Examples of multimarket competition abound, from airlines competing with one another on different routes, to consumer packaged goods companies competing with multiple brands across market segments.

There are three fundamental questions raised by multimarket competition. The first is whether such competition stabilizes or intensifies rivalry among the players. The second is how a competitor should allocate its resources across the various markets in which it faces a competitor. The third is how the firm should be organized to capitalize on the opportunities for coordinated response.

Mutual Forbearance. In the heyday of the conglomerates, Corwin Edwards raised a novel concern.[9] His thesis of "mutual forbearance" was that as industry became dominated by conglomerates that competed in a slew of different markets, conglomerates would recognize the futility of competing intensely with one another. Since competition in one market would spill over into all the other markets in which they met, he argued that conglomerates would reach a tacit oligopolistic agreement to maximize profits. This, Edwards believed, represented an important threat to consumer welfare. Conversely, it can be argued that firms that compete in multiple markets are less able to sustain any tacit agreements either because a breakdown in any one market can spill over to all markets or because firms have an incentive to subsidize attacks on competitors across markets.

Early empirical evidence was supportive of the competition-reducing impact of multimarket contact.[10] More recent empirical work has confirmed evidence of a competition-reducing effect from multimarket competition, usually where the markets are different geographies or different product lines with some underlying economic relatedness.[11] In addition, theoretical work, although not conclusive, suggests that mutual forbearance, rather than spoiling, is more likely to occur. Bernheim and Whinston's analysis of repeated games among multimarket competitors formalized the notion that the threat of destroying profit levels across many markets raised the stakes for aggressive action in any one market so high that competitors refrained from undertaking such moves.[12]

Resource Allocation. The second question raised by multimarket competition is how competitors should allocate their resources across the markets in which they compete with one another. This discussion has given rise to a whole host of military metaphors and analogies, since theoretical work on this subject has been limited. These generally start from the assumption that two essentially equivalent competitors are differentially positioned in the various markets, so that each has a "home base" where it is the dominant player.

One proposal for managing the competitive interaction is to attack the competitor's home market. This, it is argued, will force the competitor to respond on terms that cost it dispro-

[9]C.D. Edwards, "Conglomerate Bigness as a Source of Power," in *Business Concentration and Price Policy,* National Bureau of Economic Research (Princeton, NJ: Princeton University Press, 1955).

[10]J.T. Scott, "Multimarket Contact and Economic Performance," *Review of Economics and Statistics* 64 (1982), pp. 368–75.

[11]W.P. Barnett, "Strategic Deterrence among Multiproduct Competitors," *Industrial and Corporate Change* (1993), pp. 249–78; M.D. Gelfand and P.T. Spiller, "Entry Barriers and Multiproduct Oligopolies: Do They Forbear or Spoil?" *International Journal of Industrial Organization,* 5 (1987), pp. 101–23; and A. van Witteloostuijn and M. van Wegberg, "Multimarket Competition: Theory and Evidence," *Journal of Economic Behavior and Organization* 18, (1992), pp. 273–82.

[12]B.D. Bernheim and M.D. Whinston, "Multimarket Contact and Collusive Behavior," *RAND Journal of Economics 2* (1990), pp. 1–26; A. Karnani and B. Wernerfelt, "Multiple Point Competition," *Strategic Management Journal* 6 (1986), pp. 87–96; and M.E. Porter, *Competitive Advantage* (New York: Free Press, 1986).

portionately more. Thus, a specific suggestion is to cut price in a market in which the competitor has a dominant share, but in which the firm in question has only a small share.

An extension of this proposal, which has some support from the mutual forbearance theory, and which has a direct analogy to the cold war, is "mutually assured destruction." The idea is that if each competitor maintains a small market share, "a foothold," in the others' home markets, each possesses a threat to destroy the others' profitability—a "cross parry." This common threat stabilizes competition, since no firm wants to launch an attack that will bring overwhelming retribution on both sides. The pragmatic suggestion is, therefore, that competitors should always try to hold some market share in the others' strong markets and should accommodate a competitor's entry into their home market in order to establish the desirable interlocking market structure (perhaps at an 80/20 division of the market). There are certainly instances where this is how the industry structure has evolved, but definitive proof that it does stabilize competition and raise profits for all competitors has yet to be offered.

However, a very different argument can also be advanced. This position claims that it is better to allocate resources where you are strongest and the competitor weakest. This can be bolstered by asserting that attacks on a competitor's "walled cities" are often the worst strategic moves and that concentration rather than dissipation of resources is the preferable strategy.[13]

Other multimarket resource allocation strategies have also been observed. *Mimetic diversification*—the matching of competitive entry into new markets is frequently found among competitors that already meet in multiple markets. Matsushita's acquisition of MCA after Sony bought Universal Studios is but one example of this sort of behavior. The behavior has an organizational explanation in the incentive structure facing managers when their performance is evaluated against competitors rather than in absolute terms.[14] In such cases, a manager may blindly copy a competitor's moves for fear that he or she might be "punished" for failing to match the competitor's diversification, while knowing that he or she will not look bad if the diversification does fail, provided someone else made the same mistake.

In spite of these varied recommendations, there are some conclusions that can be drawn from these armchair intuitions as to how to coordinate multimarket competition. These hinge on the distinction between whether the markets are economically related or not. If they are related —if there are scale or scope economies linking markets—then markets should be treated as an integrated whole. If, in contrast, the markets are unrelated—as they would be for a conglomerate—any linkage has to be behavioral rather than economic.

More specifically, this suggests that in the case of related markets, a firm should be concerned whenever a multimarket competitor has a strong market share, because that allows the competitor to exploit scale and scope economies. A firm should also be prepared to cross-subsidize an entry into a new market, or into a competitor's strong market, because there is a benefit over and above the return that is earned in the new market alone.

In contrast, if markets are economically unrelated, the firm should treat each one as independent. Entry into one market, or a competitive move in a market where competitors overlap, is only merited if the returns to investment in that one market alone justify the move. There should be no cross-subsidization between markets since there are no spillovers between markets, and firms can quite happily let competitors build dominant positions in other markets since they give the competitor no additional strength in the markets in which the players do meet. The only interconnection between markets that might be justified is to build

---

[13]This idea has roots in some of the earliest writings on military strategy, notably Sun-Tzu's *The Art of War*.
[14]S.T. Knickerbocker, *Oligopolistic Reaction and Multinational Enterprise* (Boston, MA: Harvard Business School Press, 1973).

a toehold in the competitor's stronghold as a way to stabilize competition in all markets where competitors overlap.

Organizing for Multimarket Competition. The following story (possibly apocryphal) illustrates the difficulty of implementing multimarket competition. A major airline divided its pricing group into East and West Coast rooms. One day, the manager for one of the airline's major East Coast hubs was disturbed to find a competitor had cut prices out of the hub. He adjusted prices accordingly and raised some prices he had recently cut at the competitor's hub, in order to signal that he did not want a price war. But it was to no avail. The next day, the competitor came back with even more aggressive price cuts. All attempts to restore pricing rationality failed. On the third day, during an unusually tense cigarette break in the lounge between the East and West Coast rooms, a colleague from the West Coast pricing room asked what the problem was. When told, he countered with, "but didn't you know we cut prices into *his* West Coast hub last week?"

The lesson is that unless the organization is set up, both informationally and managerially, for multimarket competition, the coordination of competitive responses cannot happen. Managing multimarket competitive interaction, therefore, requires an individual to have both responsibility for competitive interaction across multiple markets and the necessary information about the relevant markets. Assigning responsibility is relatively straightforward, although few firms are currently structured this way. A category manager, who is responsible for a set of related brands, at a consumer packaged goods firm is one such example.

The information that is required to coordinate multimarket competition is considerably more complex.[15] In principle, the firm needs to monitor the activities in all the businesses of all the competitors that it meets in at least one market. Even more problematic is structuring the firm to allow for the required cross-subsidization from one business to another. This would involve telling one division manager that it is okay to lose $X million this year by attacking a major competitor in one market "for the good of the firm," while a colleague in another division has his or her profit target raised.

All of this suggests that the theory and the practice of multimarket competition are only just beginning. Theorists have not resolved the way to play the game, and few companies are structured to take advantage of what can, in principle, be the value of exploiting multimarket competition.

---

[15]M.E. Porter, *Competitive Advantage* (New York: Free Press, 1985).

CREATING CORPORATE ADVANTAGE

▲ INTRODUCTION

Chapter 1 introduced the Triangle of Corporate Strategy. The chapters that followed examined individual elements of the triangle in detail from a theoretical as well as a practical perspective, identifying their salient characteristics and respective roles in corporate strategy.

An equally challenging analysis, however, focuses on the triangle itself and how the individual elements relate to one another to create corporate advantage. We will now consider the triangle in its entirety and how a well-constructed corporate strategy can create value for a firm.

Corporate Strategy—The way a company seeks to create value through the configuration and coordination of its multimarket activities.

PRINCIPLES

▲ A SYSTEM OF VALUE CREATION

Effective corporate strategy is not just about having valuable corporate resources, competing in attractive businesses, or having efficient management systems. A great corporate strategy depends not only on the quality of its individual elements, but also, and just as important, on how the elements work together as a whole.

An effective corporate strategy can best be thought of as an **integrated system** in which all elements of the strategy are aligned. Only then will the system as a whole create value and not be pulled apart by internal dissonance. The Triangle of Corporate Strategy captures this logic. Its five elements—vision; goals and objectives; resources; businesses; and structure, systems, and processes—form the foundation of the corporate strategy system. For maximum effect, each element should depend upon and support each of the others, working in a way that is mutually reinforcing. When this occurs, the strategy is said to be *internally consistent*.

Consistency originates with a vision that describes how the system will create value. Out of that vision flows not only the qualities the individual elements should take on but also the linkages that will be required across the individual parts. There are three junctures at which achieving consistency is particularly important but very challenging: in the fit between the firm's resources and its businesses; between the businesses and the organization's structure, systems, and processes; and between the structure, systems, and processes and the firm's resources (Figure 7–1). Consistency across other elements of the triangle is also important but less likely to be a problem.

Consistency between Resources and Businesses

The logic behind the requirement for consistency between a firm's resources and businesses is that the resources should **create a competitive advantage** in the businesses in which a firm competes. To meet this requirement, corporate resources should be evaluated against the key success factors in each business. When doing so, it is important to keep in mind that in order to justify retaining a business, or entering a business, the resources should convey a substantial advantage. Merely having pedestrian resources that could be

▲ FIGURE 7–1   Critical Linkages in the Triangle of Corporate Strategy

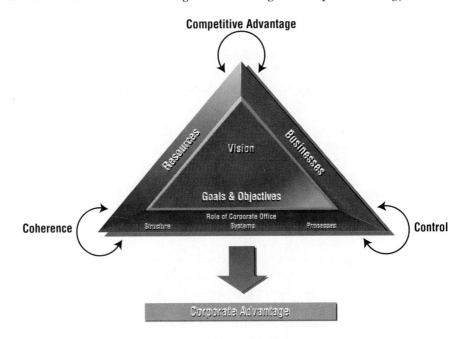

applied in an industry is rarely sufficient to justify entry or to maintain a presence in an attractive industry (see Chapter 4).

Moreover, managers must remember that, regardless of the advantage a particular corporate resource appears to yield, the firm must also compete on all the other resources that are required to produce and deliver the product or service in each business. One great resource does not ensure a successful competitive position, particularly if a firm is disadvantaged on other resource dimensions. Overall, the firm must be confident that its resources give it an advantage against competitors, including those pursuing different strategies based on different corporate strategy triangles.

Consistency between Businesses and Organizational Structure, Systems, and Processes

This consistency requirement concerns the fit between the businesses and the corporate infrastructure. The principle issue here is whether the individual businesses can be effectively **monitored and controlled** under the corporate infrastructure. If the corporate office cannot adequately control its independent businesses, it will never be able to create value.

Consistency between these two sides of the triangle does not require that all the businesses under a corporate umbrella have identical systems and processes, such as personnel policies, MIS systems, or bonus plans. Good corporate strategies can accommodate some organizational differences among divisions. However, a firm's primary operating principles and systems, as well as the experience and capabilities of corporate executives,[1] should apply across the set of businesses in its portfolio (see Chapter 6).

This is necessary for several reasons. First, running multiple systems inside a single organization is very difficult to do. It can thwart the development of efficiency and expertise in any given system, which is likely to cost the firm a critical edge in performance, and it can create confusion at headquarters for corporate executives who must work with a number of business units. Multiple systems can also inhibit, if not prevent, the transfer of managers across divisions, or create interdivisional problems if managers in one unit resent the systems or level of autonomy afforded managers in other divisions.

The obvious solution to this problem may appear to be the separation of businesses that require different modes of control. However, if the separation was as complete as it would need to be, it is unlikely that there would be any value in having the businesses under the same corporate umbrella. Warner-Lambert, for example, operates its chewing gum and pharmaceutical businesses completely separately, even down to having different colored carpets for their offices at headquarters. Not surprisingly, the value from having these businesses within one firm is far from apparent.

When companies enter businesses that are not compatible with their organizational systems, it is rare to find value being created, even if some of their resources could, in principle, contribute to competitive advantage (see "Negative Synergy at Saatchi & Saatchi"). Indeed, such businesses have appropriately been referred to as *value traps*, where the allure of value creation turns into an illusion as the corporate office loses operating control of the businesses.[2]

---

[1]Prahalad, C.K. and R.A. Bettis, "The Dominant Logic: A New Linkage Between Diversity and Performance." *Strategic Management Journal*, November-December 1986, pp. 485-502.
[2]Campbell, A., M. Goold, and M. Alexander, "Corporate Strategy: The Quest for Parenting Advantage." *Harvard Business Review*, March-April 1995, pp. 120-132.

> ## Negative Synergy at Saatchi & Saatchi
>
> In the late 1980s, Saatchi & Saatchi, the world's largest advertising agency and consulting firm, overestimated the generalizability of some of its business systems. Of particular note was the firm's effort to use a budgeting system from its consulting business in its advertising business. The system's inappropriate fit with the latter contributed to Saatchi & Saatchi's eventual downfall.
>
> In consulting, yearly budgeting typically begins with the number of personnel the company wants to employ, because consultants, by and large, generate their own business. In contrast, in advertising budgeting typically starts with estimates of anticipated future revenues from existing clients. This revenue number is then used to determine the number of personnel the agency needs to employ, the floor space required, and so forth to remain profitable.
>
> When Saatchi & Saatchi placed the consulting budgeting system in the notoriously optimistic advertising business, disaster ensued. The advertising agencies predicted their personnel needs would grow dramatically as they gained share in the fast-growing industry. To house this planned growth, they signed long-term leases for additional office space, and fixed costs escalated. Unfortunately, a recession hit the advertising industry, and the expected demand never materialized. Before the damage was over, Saatchi & Saatchi had written off over 350 million pounds to cover losses on unnecessary floor space.

Consistency between Organizational Structure, Systems, and Processes and Resources

The previous consistency requirement concerned the role of structure, systems, and processes in ensuring adequate control over a firm's individual businesses. A firm's structure, systems, and processes must also be designed to enable the firm to achieve **coherence** across those businesses. This is done through the design of an infrastructure that enables a firm's resources to be effectively deployed in its businesses.

As we saw in Chapter 3, scope economies are not vague notions, but realized economic benefits that can occur across functions or units that share value-chain activities or directly benefit from the transfer of corporate capabilities. These cost savings rarely happen spontaneously; instead, they are the result of specific organizational mechanisms that make them a reality. It is for want of such systems and structures that many potential synergies are never realized.

In Figure 7–1, the arrow back to **resources** shows the role of the corporate office in fostering the development and upgrading of valuable resources. Whether or not those resources actually reside at the corporate or divisional level, it is the role of the corporate office to ensure that the desirable type and level of investment in resources is occurring.

▲ A CONTINUUM OF EFFECTIVE CORPORATE STRATEGIES

The consistency requirements outlined also suggest that effective corporate strategies are not a random collection of individual elements but a carefully constructed system of interdependent parts. Despite the attention specific strategies have received in the business press, this does not imply that there is one best type of corporate strategy that fits all firms. Fads and flavors of the month that work for some companies or in some situations pass in time. What endures is the **logic of internally consistent corporate strategies** that are tailored to a given firm's resources and opportunities.

In principle, this suggests there are limitless varieties of successful corporate strategies and that every corporate strategy will have its own unique system. It is important to recognize, however, that there will be patterns among successful strategies since those built around similar types of resources will tend to do things in similar ways. This contingency view suggests that corporate strategies can be usefully arrayed along a continuum that is defined by the *specificity of their underlying resources*, for it is from these that a firm's corporate advantage is derived (Figure 7–2). Usually, the corporate strategies of firms sharing similar positions along the continuum will be more similar than those at greater distances.

Due to fungibility of their resources, corporations pursuing strategies near the general end of the continuum will tend to operate in a wide range of businesses, whereas those near the specialized end will tend to operate in a much narrower set. As we saw in Chapter 6, organizational structures and systems should vary accordingly: firms leveraging specific resources into tightly connected businesses will generally be designed to foster cross-linkages and synergies among units, whereas the infrastructure of firms leveraging general resources into a wide set of businesses will be far simpler and focused on maintaining financial control of independent units (see Table 7–1).

Sharp Corporation's resources and strategy placed it near the specialized end of the continuum. Its strategy was built around its world-class optoelectronics technology that served as a nucleus for its growth and steered, and was steered by, its presence in numerous related product markets. The firm's organization structure was built around key functional activities, the heads of which reported to a small group of top managers. Sharp's success depended critically on its ability to share information and integrate activities throughout the firm; this was achieved through extensive formal and informal coordination mechanisms, including standing committees, task forces, job rotations, and a corporate culture that emphasized team work and shared responsibility. The firm employed approximately 1,500 people in its corporate headquarters, which bolstered the firm's coordination efforts and provided administrative support.

Berkshire Partners was at the other end of the continuum. Its critical resources were its deal-making skills, its track record, and its contacts within the financial community. In 1992, the firm's funds owned 19 businesses in a wide array of virtually unrelated product markets. Each business was structured as a separate legal entity; cross-subsidizations of any kind were

▲ FIGURE 7–2   The Corporate Strategy Continuum

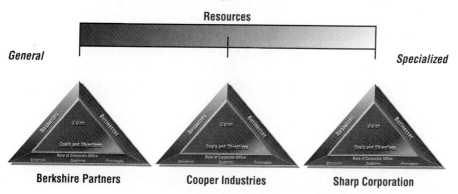

▲ Table 7–1 Corporate Strategies

	Resources	Businesses	Role of Corporate Office	Structure, Systems, and Processes
Sharp	▲ Product development ▲ LCD technology	▲ Consumer electronics ▲ Components	▲ Coordination	▲ Functional structure ▲ Formal integrative devices
Cooper Industries	▲ Cellular manufacturing ▲ Distribution experience	▲ Mature, low-technology manufacturing	▲ Provision of central resources	▲ Management Development and Planning ▲ Manufacturing services unit
Berkshire Partners	▲ Deal-making skills ▲ Contacts	▲ Market leaders ▲ Stable industries ▲ Mid-sized companies	▲ Outcome control outsourced	▲ Nexus of contracts ▲ Equity-based rewards

prohibited; and no efforts were made to exploit operating synergies. Berkshire's control system was based on outcome measures, principally those determined by the businesses' legally enforceable debt covenants. Owner/managers were rewarded with equity, the value of which was determined by external capital markets. To manage this, Berkshire Partners had only 24 people in the head office—5 general partners, 3 junior partners, 10 investment staff, and 6 general staff.

Consistent with its position at the middle of the continuum, Cooper Industries' strategy was built around its cellular manufacturing and distribution management skills—resources that were more specific than Berkshire Partners' yet considerably more fungible than Sharp's. Cooper's divisional structure had 21 strategic business units; these were organized into three synergistic groups to promote opportunities for coordination. The firm's senior managers had extensive operating experience that enabled them to give credible, specific advice to the business-unit managers and to employ an evaluation system (behavior control) that made exceptions for unusual circumstances or events. Cooper's manufacturing services group was instrumental in transferring best-demonstrated practices around the firm and administering the firm's capital budget. In 1988, Cooper maintained a total corporate staff of 317 and had total corporate expenses of $50 million.

The corporate strategies of these firms reflect their very different positions along the resource continuum. The strategies themselves differ dramatically, with few, if any, similar elements within their respective triangles. This is as it should be: the tasks these firms are trying to accomplish are very different, as are the resource bases they are leveraging. Nevertheless, each strategy in itself is a finely tuned system and adds value to the businesses within its fold (Figure 7–3).

Despite the fact that no two strategies will ever look exactly alike, much can be learned by observing a range of strategies along the continuum. Firms can identify others with effective strategies and similar types of resources to serve as role models, while those at greater dis-

▲ FIGURE 7–3   From Corporate to Competitive Advantage

There is not one *best corporate strategy* but there is an enduring logic

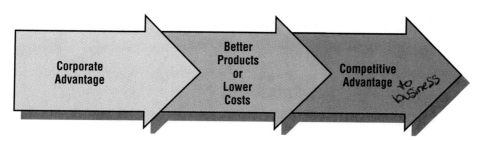

Corporate Advantage → Better Products or Lower Costs → Competitive Advantage to business

tances along the continuum can provide meaningful contrasts. Each in its way can be instructional—one by highlighting similarities, the other by reinforcing differences. Such comparisons compel a firm to clarify its own vision and assess its relative ability to create value in a given way. On close examination, for example, many related diversifiers discover that they are in effect behaving as conglomerates but with larger, and more expensive, corporate staffs. On the other hand, conglomerates may find themselves at a disadvantage relative to leveraged-buyout firms. Like competitive advantage, corporate advantage is relative and should be assessed as such.

PRACTICE

▲ EVALUATING CORPORATE STRATEGY

The fact that there are potentially an unlimited variety of effective corporate strategies does not mean that most corporate strategies are effective. In fact, as we discussed in Chapter 1, an observation of practice suggests just the opposite—that many corporate strategies have serious flaws and do not serve to enhance firm value.

Regardless of a firm's place on the resource continuum, the viability of its corporate strategy, and the likelihood that it will yield a corporate advantage, can be systematically appraised by examining its Corporate Strategy Triangle. We turn now to the question of evaluating corporate strategy in practice. In doing so, we examine the question of how, in the midst of implementation or in advance of implementation, a firm can assess the potential effectiveness of its corporate strategy. Five criteria are particularly helpful in that evaluation: vision, internal consistency, external consistency, feasibility, and corporate advantage.

Vision

▲ Is there a clear and well-articulated corporate vision?

Many firms lack a clear corporate vision, a well-articulated idea about how the company as a whole intends to create value. To provide meaningful direction for a firm, this statement must be more than a platitude. It must convey a sense of the corporate advantage the firm will exploit and be specific enough to guide a firm's actions. Although few firms are without vision statements, far fewer have ones that are truly serviceable.

Other firms confuse what they want to *achieve* with what they want to *become*.[3] In such cases, goals and objectives do not emanate *from* a vision, they drive it. Walt Disney Company, for example, has pursued an annual growth target of 20 percent since 1984. Growth that is mandated in this way often proves not to be tenable in long haul; near-term targets may be met, but they often do not translate into a consistent long-term development path. Being able to suitably describe a firm's vision, and determine that the firm's goals and objectives match it, is a very good test of whether managers have a clear understanding of where the company is heading.

The installation of purpose in place of improvisation and the substitution of planned progress in place of drifting are probably the most demanding functions of the president."[4]

Internal Consistency

▲ Are the elements of the firm's corporate strategy aligned with one another?

▲ Do they form a coherent whole?

The need for internal consistency in corporate strategy was stressed in the Principles section. Firms that work at cross-purposes with themselves are not only inefficient, they often fail to develop or leverage the kind of system that yields important corporate advantages.

Problems in internal consistency are commonplace and reflect the lack of a clear sense of how the firm intends to add value to its businesses. Despite profound differences in resources and business portfolios, for example, most multibusiness firms operate with highly decentralized structures and systems. These infrastructures may be simple to administer and may solve the control problem, but they are not effective in fostering scope economies or deploying resources to create corporate coherence.

To test for consistency, it is prudent to begin with the three critical junctures discussed earlier—competitive advantage; control; and coherence. It is also important to assess the alignment between these elements of strategy and the firm's vision and goals and objectives.

External Consistency

▲ Does the strategy fit with the external environment?

▲ Is the strategy sustainable against changing environmental and competitor strategies?

External consistency requires that a strategy fit with the external environment. Corporations do not act in isolation, but against specific competitors in specific markets. Thus, a strategy must stand up to competitive challenges and be robust to predicted changes in the environment.

These challenges may come at the business-unit level where an analysis of a firm's resource base and relative competitive position are particularly useful. In this regard, it is important to consider whether the key success factors of an industry are changing and whether the strategy anticipates these changes by repositioning the business or investing in resources that will be critical in the future.

Moreover, firms should never forget to assess the underlying attractiveness of the external environment (industries) in which they compete (see Chapter 4). No matter how effective the

---

[3]This insight is due to Seymour Tilles, "How to Evaluate Corporate Strategy," *Harvard Business Review*, July–August 1963, p. 112.
[4]C. Roland Christensen, Kenneth R. Andrews, and Joseph L. Bower, *Business Policy, Text and Cases* (Burr Ridge, IL: Richard D. Irwin, 1973), p. 17.

corporate strategy, if the firm's businesses are tough to make money in, the financial results from the strategy are likely to be poor.

> *When an industry with a reputation for difficult economics meets a manager with a reputation for excellence, it is usually the industry that keeps its reputation intact.*
>
> *Warren Buffet*

Multibusiness firms also face competition at the corporate level from other triangles of corporate strategy. These assaults can directly challenge the logic holding the businesses together and, in doing so, threaten the means through which value is created. For example, a popular premise in the sixties was that firms were better allocators of capital than were banks. As this assumption was challenged by the emergence of new financial instruments and markets, many multibusiness firms functioning primarily as banks scrambled to find new identities. Similarly, as industries mature, many large vertically integrated firms find that they cannot produce the efficiency or rapid response of smaller, focused competitors, and are compelled to "demerge" as ICI has done in the chemical industry. Thus, external analyses must be dynamic and consider the continued viability of the overall strategy.

Feasibility

- ▲ Is the organization being asked to do too much in too short a time?
- ▲ Is the strategy too risky?

Striking the right balance between setting a challenging strategy and overextending an organization is a difficult task. While "stretch" strategies and targets are popular, in advance of implementation, the line between *stretch* and *infeasible* is often unclear.

To evaluate the feasibility of any strategy, it is important to ask whether the firm will have the requisite resources to implement the strategy when it needs them; whether the time frame for the changes is realistic; and whether the firm is capable of implementing changes on multiple fronts simultaneously. These questions can be captured by asking whether the firm's goals and objectives plot a feasible expansion path.

When implementing a strategy, for example, it may first be necessary to uncouple an old strategy.[5] If that strategy has been followed for a number of years, its impact on the organization will be deep and broad, affecting not only the formal systems and structure, but the informal ones as well. The challenges and ramifications of dismantling that system, and the time it will take to do so, must therefore be carefully assessed and planned for.

While firms may have different preferences for risk, the level that is acceptable to each is constrained by its current resources. Every firm must, therefore, evaluate whether its intended path is predicated on the favorable resolution of too many uncertainties. Ultimately, the level of risk intrinsic in the implementation of a strategy must be seen to be realistic.

Strategies that call for fundamental corporate transformation can be particularly difficult to implement because there are rarely blueprints to follow. Bringing the strategy to fruition is likely to involve many unknowns and substantial amounts of time. In such cases, aggressive

---

[5]See John M. Hobbs and Donald F. Heany, "Coupling Strategy to Operating Plans," *Harvard Business Review,* May–June 1977 pp. 119-124.

implementation efforts may not only be costly, they may be ineffective. Gauging the time line for implementing these strategies and finding the appropriate mix of urgency and patience are some of the most challenging tasks managements will face.

Corporate Advantage

▲ Does the strategy truly produce a corporate advantage?

▲ Is value-creation from that advantage ongoing?

Ultimately, the acid test for any corporate strategy is its ability to yield a corporate advantage—to create value through multimarket activity. This advantage is usually realized in the businesses themselves where the benefits of corporate affiliation translate into competitive advantage. In Chapter 1, we suggested three tests of corporate advantage that can be applied to each business. We repeat them here to establish the hurdle that corporate advantage must overcome:

▲ Does ownership of the business create benefits somewhere in the corporation?

▲ Are these benefits greater than the cost of corporate overhead?

▲ Does it create more value than any other possible corporate parent or alternative governance structure?[6]

When evaluating a corporate strategy, it is important to assess not only the *amount* of value it may create, but also the *timing* of when that value creation occurs (see Figure 7–4).

In some companies, the majority of value is added to a business unit in a relatively short time period. This is common, for example, in firms that specialize in business turnarounds, where companies are restructured, plants are rationalized, and product lines are pruned. Once these activities are completed, the corporate resources may generate little additional value in a business. In such cases, the rationale for continued ownership may be difficult to justify, because there is no longer a current corporate advantage. Indeed, Hanson, the archtypical British restructurer, is now splitting itself apart. In contrast, in other firms, such as Sharp, corporate value-added may increase over time as critical resources are shared and scope economies develop, ever deepening the connections among businesses.

As these examples suggest, for many businesses the benefits and costs of corporate membership change over time. In some cases, these changes may be unexpected and occur as a result of changes in the external environment. In others, the pattern of value creation is simply the result of the nature of the corporate resources and the systems through which they are deployed. In all cases, however, it is important to assess a strategy's *ongoing* potential for value creation and to make decisions accordingly.

---

[6]M.C. Goold, A. Campbell, and M. Alexander, *Corporate-Level Strategy* (New York: John Wiley & Sons, 1995).

▲ FIGURE 7–4   Timing of Value Creation

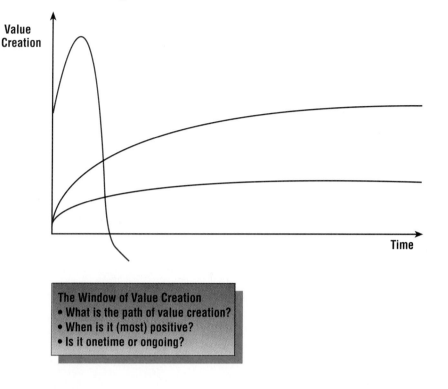

▲ SUMMARY

Although no set of analytical questions can predict with perfect accuracy whether a corporate strategy will be a success, the above criteria provide a powerful means for assessing the viability of a particular strategy, regardless of its location on the resource continuum. When the elements of the Corporate Strategy Triangle are internally and externally consistent, when they are guided by a powerful vision and support a feasible expansion path, the strategy as a whole should create a corporate advantage and truly generate value.

It should be emphasized that developing a corporate strategy is one of the most challenging tasks of management. It requires not only good analytical skills and data, but in-depth knowledge of managerial behavior and systems, as well as intuition and creativity. Without real inspiration and insight, it is rare that any corporate strategy would be remarkable. The challenge for all corporate strategists, therefore, is to develop such an insight and to translate it into a unique and viable Triangle of Corporate Strategy.

CORPORATE GOVERNANCE

▲ INTRODUCTION

The development and implementation of corporate strategy has long been understood to be the responsibility of senior executives. In fulfilling that role, managers have not only been expected to have the appropriate skills and vision to lead a corporation; it was also presumed that they would be stalwart corporate citizens who would discharge those responsibilities with due attention to all stakeholders. Consistent with this view, managers were expected to be above the need for discipline in their conduct, and to act in ways that would require few outside controls.

Despite this optimism, a number of problems in corporate governance emerged over time. In the 1970s, corporate leadership was broadly criticized for not discharging its "social responsibilities"—for polluting the air and waterways, for perpetuating unfair employment practices, and for participating in illegal transactions abroad, among other transgressions. As a result, the U.S. government initiated a series of controls, such as those enacted by the Environmental Protection Agency and the Foreign Corrupt Practices Act.

In the mid-to-late 1980s, the charge against management was a different one: a lack of attention to its fiduciary responsibilities toward shareholders. On the one hand, it was charged that some senior managers have been **inept**. This harkens back to an insightful distinction Peter Drucker made between organizational efficiency (doing things right) and organizational effectiveness (doing the right things). Many of these managers presided over firms that did things right—executed deals correctly, performed sound due diligence and the like—but did the wrong things; by, for example, entering the wrong businesses or failing to adapt to new technologies or global competitive threats. Yet despite their having implemented fundamentally flawed strategies, many of these senior managers were so well entrenched in their positions that they stayed on and continued the same strategies, even as they destroyed shareholder value.

On the other hand, senior executives have been accused of acting in their own **self-interest**, at the expense of the company's shareholders and outside stakeholders. For many years, egregious examples of self-interested behavior went undisciplined by any external constituency. Once again, managers appeared to have total control of corporate governance, and to abuse the privilege.

This chapter examines these failures of corporate governance and the context in which they have occurred.[1] Specifically, the focus is on the mechanisms that determine the allocation of decision making authority in a firm, and, in particular, on whether those mechanisms are sufficiently strong to protect the interests of shareholders. A number of theoretical arguments are introduced, along with a discussion of the checks and balances that are used (with varying degrees of success) to monitor and discipline managerial behavior.

PRINCIPLES

▲ WHY GOVERNANCE FAILS

Agency Problems and Self-Interest

In 1932, Adolph Berle and Gardiner Means noted the consequences of the **separation of ownership and control** when they cautioned against separating the owners (principals) and the managers (agents) of firms.[2] They established the basis for what became known as *agency theory*, a key factor in debates about corporate governance. Chapters 5 and 6 addressed agency problems within a firm and the importance of aligning the interests of managers with the demands of a strategy. Here we examine another set of agency issues: the conflicts that arise between the interests of a firm's owners and its managers. As Morck, Shleifer, and Vishny explained, "When managers hold little equity in the firm and shareholders are too dispersed to enforce value maximization, corporate assets may be deployed to benefit managers rather than shareholders."[3]

These conflicts can lead not only to marginal adjustments in earnings (such as managers paying themselves too much), but to fundamentally wrong strategic choices. How might this occur, and why would managers behave in ways that are not in the interest of the firm's owners? Quite simply, many economists argue, the interests of managers often differ from those of the owners.

Maximizing Growth, Not Earnings. In response to a question about why his firm had not divested more units, a CEO quoted Winston Churchhill: "I did not become prime minister of the British empire to preside over its demise!"

Whereas shareholders (owners) typically want to maximize earnings, managers often want to maximize **firm size**.[4] Ironically, in many cases, this in part has been due to the structure of managers' compensation packages, which have placed a heavy emphasis on firm size.[5] In addition, rewarding employees with job promotions rather than just pay increases necessarily

---

[1]This chapter primarily reflects corporate governance in the Anglo-Saxon context. Governance structures in other countries, particularly Germany and Japan, are noticeably different.

[2]Adolf A. Berle and Gardiner C. Means, *The Modern Corporation and Private Property* (1932).

[3]Randall Morck, A. Shleifer, and R.W. Vishny, "Management Ownership and Market Valuation: An Empirical Analysis," *Journal of Financial Economics*, January–March 1988, pp. 293–315.

[4] Robin Marris, *The Economic Theory of Managerial Capitalism* (New York: Free Press, 1964).

[5]M.C. Jensen and K. Murphy, "Performance Pay and Top Management Incentives," *Journal of Political Economy*, April 1990, pp. 225–64.

creates a need for more jobs within the organization, further compelling managers to push for growth. Finally, managers receive purely social benefits from heading larger firms: in the eyes of their community and fellows, they gain power and prominence as the size of their firms increase. Thus, managers may have an incentive to grow their firms regardless of the long-term profit potential associated with the expansion. Size for the sake of size alone can become the corporate mantra.

Diversifying Risk.   Shareholders want to own a *portfolio of stocks* that together have a desirable risk/return profile. Managers, however, often interpret this objective as applying to their company alone. As a result, they diversify into a number of businesses to reduce total firm risk. The nature of the mistake that arises from this partial view of shareholders' interests can be explained by a closer look at financial economics.

According to the capital asset pricing model, the total risk of any stock can be broken down into two components:

total risk = systematic risk (nondiversifiable) + unsystematic risk (diversifiable)

Systematic risk, called *beta*, describes the variability of a security's return relative to the returns of all other securities in the market; it cannot be diversified away either by a firm or by an individual. Unsystematic, or firm-specific, risk relates to idiosyncratic firm events. It can be reduced, even eliminated, by spreading one's holdings across a variety of firms. The critical question is, How should this diversification be achieved? Should firms provide this service for their shareholders by buying other firms, or should it be left to shareholders to do for themselves?

When firms attempt to reduce unsystematic risk by buying companies with different risk profiles, they often pay a large premium and incur substantial transaction costs at the time of acquisition. Further, these transactions usually involve all of the acquired firm's stock: buying and selling fractions of the whole is rarely done. Consequently, unless a firm can substantially improve the operations of the acquired business, this is likely to be an expensive and clumsy route to risk reduction.

In contrast, in the stock market, where there are many buyers and sellers, fractions of firms can be bought and sold, and transaction costs are relatively low. Individual investors, therefore, can achieve the benefits of diversification by buying a portfolio of stocks or by buying mutual funds run by professional portfolio managers. Consequently, the public markets provide investors with their best opportunity to mitigate risk. Diversification, for the purpose of reducing risk, is not a service that corporations should provide for their shareholders.

Managerial Risk Aversion.   Even though shareholders can efficiently diversify their own portfolios, managers cannot so efficiently diversify their own **employment risk**. As a result, they may pursue diversified expansion as a means of reducing total firm risk and increasing their own job security. For example, U.S. Steel's acquisition of Marathon Oil might be explained by management's feelings of job insecurity as the U.S. steel industry underwent massive downsizing. Diversification for this purpose may improve the lot of managers, but it could prove to be a detriment to shareholders. According to Amihud and Lev, such mergers may be viewed as a form of managerial perquisite intended to decrease the risk associated with managerial human capital. Accordingly, their consequences may be interpreted as an agency cost.[6]

---

[6] Yakov Amihud and B. Lev, "Risk Reduction as a Managerial Motive for Conglomerate Mergers," *Bell Journal of Economics*, Autumn 1981, p. 605–6.

Managerial Self-Preservation. Shleifer and Vishny have suggested another form of managerial perquisite: **management entrenchment.**[7] Entrenchment occurs when managers direct firm expansion in ways that are consistent with their own skills, but not necessarily in the best interests of the firm. For example, this could be done by investing in businesses that require specific knowledge current managers possess, thus increasing their importance to the firm and reducing the likelihood that they would be replaced. When Jim Ketelsen was CEO of the broadly diversified Tenneco in the 1980s, he poured money into the agricultural equipment business where he had spent much of his career. He even spun off the company's oil business to support the cash drain from these marginal investments before he was finally replaced in 1992.

Although one might think that instances of managerial entrenchment are rare, bringing the point a little closer to home may illustrate its prevalence. Imagine being the chief information officer in a company that is considering outsourcing all of its information processing. Would you argue to close the unit that you run, or would you appeal to continue to operate it—perhaps even take in business from outside customers? This drama is repeated daily in every corporation and illustrates the conflicts that can arise when decision makers have private stakes in strategic outcomes.

Managerial Enrichment. Due to the separation of ownership and control, managers may also prefer to unduly enrich themselves rather that maximize shareholders' returns. Because managers may benefit personally from stately headquarters, generous compensation, or extensive retirement packages, while bearing a disproportionately small part of the costs, their incentives to spend corporate funds in these ways will diverge from those of the owners.

Contextual Factors

The issues discussed above are persistent and tend to split the interests of owners and managers. These divergences may explain a fair amount of the diversified expansion undertaken by firms. However, it is also important to consider the context in which such inappropriate expansion may occur. Not all firms are in a position that enables or encourages managers to squander shareholder resources in inappropriate growth or diversification.

Life Cycles and Free Cash Flow. It has been suggested that diversified expansion may be tied to the life cycle of a firm. Young and growing businesses have abundant opportunities to reinvest earnings profitably. As businesses mature, these opportunities often become scarce, and managers may begin to use cash flows from earlier innovative efforts to pursue increasingly far-flung opportunities that are not in the shareholders' interests.[8]

Michael Jensen extended this argument and articulated a theory of **free cash flow:** "cash flow in excess of that required to fund all projects that have positive net present values when discounted at the relevant cost of capital."[9] He maintained that conflicts of interest between shareholders and managers are particularly acute over the payout of free cash flow: "The

---

[7]A. Shleifer and R.W. Vishny, "Management Entrenchment: The Case of Manager-Specific Investments" *Financial Economics*, Vol. 25, November 1989, pp. 123–139.

[8]Dennis C. Mueller, "A Life Cycle Theory of the Firm," *Journal of Industrial Economics*, July 1972, pp. 199–219.

[9]Michael C. Jensen, "Agency Costs of Free Cash Flow, Corporate Finance and Takeovers, *American Economic Review*, May 1986, p. 328.

problem is how to motivate managers to disgorge the cash rather than investing it at below the cost of capital or wasting it on organizational inefficiencies."[10]

Jensen noted that internally funded acquisitions are one way managers spend cash, rather than redistributing it to shareholders:

> [The free cash flow] theory implies managers of firms with unused borrowing power and large free cash flows are more likely to undertake low-benefit or even value-destroying mergers. Diversification programs generally fit this category, and the theory predicts they will generate lower total gains.[11]

To combat this problem, Jensen suggested that debt could play a powerful role in motivating organizational efficiency, particularly in firms that generate large cash flows but have unattractive growth prospects. By paying out cash and taking on debt, a firm effectively bonds its promise to pay out future cash flows. This reduces the resources that are at the top managers' discretion and decreases the likelihood that they will invest in uneconomic projects that satisfy only their self-interest. (See "Eclipse of the Public Corporation.")

Antitrust Enforcement. Many corporations in the United States diversified significantly during the 1960s and 70s, when **antitrust enforcement** was particularly severe.[12] Government authorities disallowed a number of related mergers, and aggressively challenged a host of others. This climate has a profound impact on the number and type of opportunities that were avilable to firms. Related diversification that might have been attractive earlier, and would become so again, was simply made difficult during this time, narrowing the range of options from which firms could choose. Consequently, a large amount of unrelated diversification took place during the period.

Even though most firms at that time had little experience in managing unrelated diversification, there was an optimistic sense that it could be handled with ease, and made profitable for the firm. Conglomerates emerged as a new organizational form, and many managers believed that a well-disciplined team with professional management systems could add value to any business. In due course, experience tempered this view.

Many acquisitions that were consummated during this period were later divested. At the time the diversified expansion was undertaken, however, it could have been the best available opportunity for the firm. Alternatively, management may have made an error in judgment and overestimated their ability to add value to a wide range of businesses. Richard Roll advanced this view as the *hubris hypothesis*.[13]

▲ EVIDENCE OF FAILURES IN GOVERNANCE

Each of the arguments laid out above explains an aspect of management behavior that could result from a separation of ownership and control. To be a real concern for corporate governance, it has to be demonstrated that such behavior is more than a theoretical possibility.

---

[10]Ibid., p. 323.
[11]Ibid., p. 328.
[12]For a discussion of the role of antitrust in diversified expansion, see Andrei Shleifer and Robert Vishny, "Takeovers in the '60s and the '80s: Evidence and Implications," (*Strategic Management Journal*, Vol. 12, 1991), pp 51–59; and Bhagat, A. Shleifer, and R. Vishny, "Hostile Takeovers in the 1980s: The Return to Corporate Specialization," *(Brookings Papers on Economic Activity: Microeconomics 1990*, special issue), pp. 1–84.
[13]Richard Roll, "The hubris hypothesis of corporate takeovers," *Journal of Business*, April 1986, pp. 197–216.

Eclipse of the Public Corporation

In 1989, Michael C. Jensen published a provocative article entitled, "Eclipse of the Public Corporation," in which he argued that in certain sectors of the economy, the historical model of the publicly held corporation had become obsolete. In place of the old model, a new kind of organizational form was emerging to correct the pathologies of the 1960s and 70s that had enabled corporations to waste resources and destroy value. By relying on private debt rather than public equity as the major source of capital, the new form eliminated the basic conflict between owners and managers and fostered greater efficiency in operations, productivity, and shareholder value.

The rise of the LBO association was one of the most prominent manifestations of the trend toward eliminating the separation of owners and managers. By gaining substantial equity stakes in their firms, managers became owners. Moreover, the terms associated with the LBO form worked to impose a tighter discipline on managers. In particular, debt covenants forced managers to distribute cash and to utilize corporate resources wisely to optimize cash flow. Moreover, Jensen argued, high levels of debt forced companies into "crisis mode"—making difficult choices to sell assets that were more highly valued elsewhere and taking necessary, painful steps toward restructuring to promote efficiency sooner than in a corporation with a more traditional capital structure. The idea was to ensure that cash could flow freely to the market, which in turn would allocate the resources to their highest valued use. Only in this way, he argued, would the long-term interests of corporations, shareholders, and society in general be best served.

Importantly, Jensen argued that these new organizations were only appropriate to a specific type of company, or to companies in industries with certain characteristics: slow long-term growth, mature or declining markets, and excess cash. Where this argument did not apply was in the context of rapid-growth, high investment industries such as computer software and biotechnology which consumed cash to fuel growth and R&D. These companies generally were not cushioned by excess cash and were more easily disciplined by external capital markets and competitive forces in their industries.

Source: Jensen, Michael C. "Eclipse of the Public Corporation," *Harvard Business Review*, September-October 1989, pp. 61–74.

While the theories explaining mismanagement are credible, do they really explain a significant amount of corporate activity, or only a few notable outliers? Unfortunately, the empirical evidence suggests that the excesses they describe are neither infrequent nor small.

Managerial Indulgences

By the 1980s, a pattern of the abuse of funds by a number of senior executives had emerged. The spectacle of CEOs enjoying a wealth of expensive perquisites, from country club memberships to the personal use of corporate jets, came to be viewed as evidence that managers were lining their own pockets at the shareholders' expense. Examples also came to light of personal expenses being placed on the corporate tab, and on occasion, CEOs were known to relocate the corporate headquarters to be more convenient to their country homes.

Disillusioned by unimpressive earnings, shareholders became further incensed when they found out how much money CEOs were paying themselves. **CEO compensation**, therefore, became a key factor in producing awareness of suboptimal governance practices. In the

1980s, for example, CEO compensation rose 212 percent, while average earnings per share of the S&P 500 rose only 78 percent.[14] More particularly, CEO compensation was found to be higher when a firm's board was subject to greater control by its CEO.[15]

Entrenched CEOs also reacted to the growing threat of takeover during the 80s. The so-called **golden parachute**—a takeover-activated severance pay contract—was a creation of this period. Golden parachutes were defended on the grounds that they supposedly aligned the incumbent managers' incentives with those of the shareholders. In the event of a hostile bid that would maximize the return to shareholders, the CEO and other top executives would not be motivated to block the acquisition. Critics pointed out that the same terms amounted to a financial incentive to cultivate the likelihood of a takeover. Indeed, there continues to be controversy regarding the actual impact of golden parachutes on management resistance to takeover.[16]

Also during this period, corporations were adopting self-defense mechanisms such as **poison pills**. These too were activated in the event of a hostile takeover attempt and, for example, authorized issuance of preferred stock that shareholders could redeem at a premium after the takeover. The intended effect was to make the company's stock less attractive to potential acquirers—an objective agency theorists suggest may not be in the best interests of shareholders.

Empire Building

Another indication that managers have in fact pursued strategies that are at odds with the interests of their shareholders comes from patterns of acquisitions and divestitures. A substantial number of business units acquired in the late 1960s and early 1970s were later divested.[17] Further, acquisitions were more likely to be followed by divestitures when the target firms were not in businesses highly related to those of the acquiring company.[18]

Another clue can be taken from the stock market's response to the announcements of these acquisitions. A number of studies have shown that, on average, target firms realized substantial benefits, while bidder firms experienced neutral or slightly negative returns.[19] The bulk of these studies did not differentiate among types of acquisition, but some did, and they tended to find evidence that bidding firms in related acquisitions fared better than those in unrelated acquisitions, particularly in more recent years.

Jensen's notion of free cash flow is difficult to operationalize, but some reasonable attempts have been made to do so. Defining free cash flow as operating income before depreciation, less interest expenses, taxes, and preferred and common dividends, one study found returns to the acquirer in tender offers were negatively related to the acquirer's free

[14]*Business Week*, May 6, 1991, pp. 90–112.

[15]Barton K. Boyd, "Board Control and CEO Compensation," *Strategic Management Journal*, June 1994, pp. 335–44.

[16]Harbir Singh and Farid Harianto, "Top Management Tenure, Corporate Ownership Structure and the Magnitude of Golden Parachutes." *Strategic Management Journal*, Vol. 10, Summer 1989, pp. 143–156.

[17]David J. Ravenscraft and F.M. Scherer, *Mergers, Sell-Offs, and Economic Efficiency* (Washington, DC: The Brookings Institutions, 1987); and Steven Kaplan and M.S. Weisbach, "The Success of Acquisitions: Evidence from Divestitures," *Journal of Finance*, March 1992, pp. 107–38.

[18]Kaplan and Weisbach, "The Success of Acquisitions."

[19]M. Bradley, A. Desai, and E.H. Kim, "Synergistics Gains from Corporate Acquisitions and Their Division between Stockholders of Target and Acquiring Firms," *Journal of Financial Economics*, May 1988, pp. 3–40; M.C. Jensen and R.S. Ruback, "The Market for Corporate Control: Scientific Evidence," *Journal of Financial Economics*, April 1983, pp. 5–50; and Roll, "The Hubris Hypothesis."

cash flow.[20] Consistent with Jensen's characterization of firms pursuing ill-founded diversification programs, this result was stronger for firms whose assets were valued lower by the stock market. Another study found evidence corroborating to this effect.[21] In its sample, acquirers who were considered successful after the fact had lower free cash flows at the time of acquisition than those who were later considered unsuccessful. This evidence is consistent with the agency view of corporate diversification.

There is additional supporting evidence from other studies. Ravenscraft and Scherer examined the postmerger performance of diversified firms.[22] Looking at manufacturing mergers from the 1960s and early 1970s, they observed a decline in postmerger accounting profits for firms under new ownership. The problems were most serious following pure conglomerate acquisitions. However, even for "related businesses" and horizontal acquisitions, however, post-acquisition profitability declined relative to pre-merger levels. These findings are consistent with those of Mueller, who found market share losses following horizontal and especially conglomerate mergers.[23]

Rather than looking through the prism of free cash flow, other researchers have tackled these questions by comparing manager-controlled firms with those that are owner-controlled. One study found that manager-controlled firms engaged in more conglomerate acquisitions that owner-controlled firms and in general were more diversified.[24] Two other studies showed that low levels of managerial ownership in bidding firms correlated with lower returns to the acquiring firm.[25] Consistent with the view that managers want to reduce total firm risk, rather than allowing shareholders to do so for themselves, another study found that firms pursue mergers with negatively correlated cash flows.[26]

In light of this evidence, it would seem unwise to conclude that managerial motives or hubris have played no important role in corporate decisions. There are simply too many results that are consistent with those explanations.

PRACTICE

▲ MODERN CORPORATE GOVERNANCE

Historically, senior corporate executives were often able to act in ways described above, with few checks on their behavior. Since the mid-1980s, however, a host of changes have dramatically altered the face of corporate governance and limited managers' freedom of action. Among the most important of these have been changes in the market for corporate control.

---

[20]Larry Lang, R.M. Stulz, and R.A. Walkling, "A Test of the Free Cash Flow Hypothesis: The Case of Bidder Returns," *Journal of Financial Economics*, October 1991, pp. 315–36.

[21]Kaplan and Weisbach, "The Success of Acquisitions."

[22]Ravenscraft and Scherer, *Mergers, Sell-Offs, and Economic Efficiency.*

[23]D.C. Mueller, "Mergers and Market Share," *Review of Economics and Statistics*, May 1985, pp. 259–67.

[24]Y. Amihud and B. Lev, "Risk Reduction as a Managerial Motive for Conglomerate Mergers," *Bell Journal of Economics*, Autumn 1981, pp. 605–17.

[25]W.G. Lewellen, C. Loderer, and A. Rosenfeld, "Merger Decisions and Executive Stock Ownership in Acquiring Firms," *Journal of Accounting and Economics*, April 1985, pp. 209–31; and V.L. You et al., "Mergers and Bidders' Wealth: Managerial and Strategic Factors," in ed. L.G. Thomas, *The Economics of Strategic Planning*, (Boston: Lexington Books, 1986), pp. 201–20.

[26]W.J. Marshall, J.B. Yawitz, and E. Greenberg, "Incentives for Diversification and the Structure of the Conglomerate Firm," *Southern Economic Journal*, July 1984, pp. 1–23.

The Market for Corporate Control

Historically, the market for corporate control was not a threat to managers. Seemingly unfettered growth and diversification was possible, since corporations were not subject to discipline from the capital markets. In particular, for larger corporations, takeovers were not an imminent threat. Analysis has shown that successful takeover bids typically involved at least a 20 percent premium over the original market price, while the associated transaction costs—such as investment banker fees and proxy materials—added another 2 percent. Thus, it was possible for a company to operate at 78 percent efficiency and still not be vulnerable to takeover.

With the stock market boom of the 1980s came the end to the immunity of even the largest firms. Rapidly increasing stock prices appeared to reduce the cost of acquiring with stock, while the availability of debt gave rise to the onslaught of the leveraged buyout (LBO) phenomenon (see Figure 8–1). Over the course of the decade, LBOs not only became increasingly common, they also grew to represent a disproportionately large percentage of the value of all merger and acquisition activity; although LBOs accounted for less than 10 percent of the total number of mergers and acquisitions in 1989, for example, they represented more than 25 percent of their total value.[27]

Because they utilized debt to finance acquisitions, LBOs were free from the size restrictions that had limited takeovers in the past. By the end of the decade, investment banks and LBO partnerships had more than 50 funds, each of which contained at least $100 million in equity capital. On the basis of a 10-to-1 leverage ratio, these funds could make more than a billion dollars' worth of deals each. Suddenly, virtually no company in America was free from the threat of takeover.

Bryan Burrough and John Helyar provided a provocative account of the corporate control contest for RJR Nabisco that took place in October and November of 1988. Several well-known Wall Street financiers took part in the hotly contested struggle around Ross Johnson, RJR's flamboyant president. Burrough and Helyar, who titled their book *Barbarians at the Gate*, described the events as a "huge power struggle," characterized by "brazen displays of ego not seen in American business for decades."[28] The authors claimed the contest would be remembered as "the ultimate story of greed and glory."

Takeover tales are full of color and zest. If one looks closer, however, it is clear that they chronicle an important transition in the history of corporate control. This change has been documented by Paul Hirsch, an organizational sociologist.[29] Most notably, Hirsch showed the remarkable degree of resistance to change that the corporate establishment displayed during this period and the extreme pressure that those outside the corporate mainstream had to apply to overcome that resistance. (See "Hostile Takeovers: Of Villains and Victims.")

In spite of the initial resistance, by the late 1980s acquisitions—even if contested—were an accepted part of the corporate arsenal. As a consequence, the threat to poorly performing or overdiversified companies from the capital market increased remarkably. The market for corporate control, therefore, began to act as a powerful constraint on managerial discretion and ineptness.

---

[27]*Mergers and Acquisitions*, May–June 1990.

[28]Bryan Burrough and John Helyar, *Barbarians at the Gate* (New York: Harper & Row Publishers, 1990).

[29]Paul M. Hirsch, "From Ambushes to Golden Parachutes: Corporate Takeovers as an Instance of Cultural Framing and Institutional Integration," *American Journal of Sociology*, January 1986, pp. 800–37.

▲ FIGURE 8–1   The Leveraged Buyout Market, 1986–1992 ($ millions)

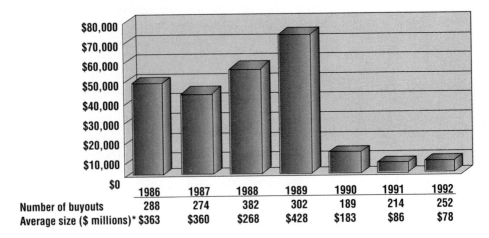

	1986	1987	1988	1989	1990	1991	1992
Number of buyouts	288	274	382	302	189	214	252
Average size ($ millions)*	$363	$360	$268	$428	$183	$86	$78

*of those with values reported

Source: Cynthia A. Montgomery, "Berkshire Partners," Harvard Business School Case No. 391-091.

Institutional Investors

Challenges to corporate control coincided with a profound shift in the patterns of stock ownership. For decades, ownership of public stock has been migrating from fragmented holdings by millions of individuals, to indirect beneficial ownership through large pools of capital, including **mutual funds** and corporate and governmental **pension funds**. In 1988, the combined value of these funds exceeded $1.5 trillion dollars.[30] By 1995, estimates were that these concentrated institutional investors owned 55 percent of all shares in publicly traded U.S. companies.[31] The largest mutual fund company, Fidelity, for example, itself owned over 10 percent of such well known companies as Compaq Computer (see Table 8–1).

By the early 1990s, many institutional investors believed it was difficult to consistently outperform the market. As a result, they placed a significant proportion of their capital in index funds, matching, for example, the S&P 500. When confronting lackluster performance by one of their portfolio companies, they had to retain stock ownership to maintain the market basket of stocks. Moreover, even in their actively traded portfolio, they could not readily sell stock in an under-performing company because their holdings were often so large that any such move could send shock waves through the market.

No longer able to exit by selling stock, and no longer content to loyally follow management's lead in voting their shares, some institutional investors such as CalPERS have become more activist, pressuring underperforming companies to change their strategies.[32]

---

[30]Jay O. Light, "The Privatization of Equity," *Harvard Business Review*, September–October 1989, pp. 62–63.
[31]In France, institutional investors own 70 percent of all shares, and in the United Kingdom they own 75 percent [Jean-Jacques Pic, "Europe's Diverse Corporate Boards—How They Differ from Each Other and the U.S.," *point of view*, Winter 1995, published by Spencer Stuart executive search consultants.]
[32]Albert O. Hirschmann, *Exit, Voice, and Loyalty*, Cambridge: Harvard University Press, 1970.

Sociologist Paul Hirsch applied his discipline's perspective to an analysis of the struggle for corporate control between 1965 and 1985. His conceptualizations convey the drama inherent in these passionately fought, if bloodless, battles. Most importantly, Hirsch's analysis documents the strong social forces that served to protect the status quo, and the nature of change that was required to overcome them.

As Hirsch shows, the earliest hostile takeovers were not initiated by the corporate mainstream, but by renegades who appeared from outside and used unorthodox means to shake up the old order.* Those who brought the change were like foxes—predators who operated on the periphery, like Carl Icahn and T. Boone Pickens—not the corporate lions who defined and operated at the center of the business community.

The language used to describe these events mirrored their timing and the players' status. Initially, when the bidding party was outside the corporate community, accounts of the transactions incorporated violent, "one-way stigmatizations" of bidders, condemning the deviant outsiders as pirates, pariahs, proxy artists, and raiders. Target firms, on the other hand, were portrayed as unfortunate victims, "upstanding citizens placed in the role of 'defenders of the faith'." Language of this nature was used not only by corporate insiders, but was also widely adopted in the business press.

During this period, the corporate mainstream made extraordinary efforts to resist pressures for change. One of its self-defense mechanisms was the poison pill that could be activated in the event of a hostile takeover attempt. Pillars of the corporate establishment even lobbied Congress, pointing out the potential dire consequences of corporate restructuring.

In time, however, these corporate lions themselves became involved in the whole spectrum of takeover activity, first as "white knights" to save their beleaguered fellows, and later as hostile bidders themselves. As this happened, takeovers were increasingly viewed as legitimate business activities. Roles and rules were defined, and the language used to describe the events became more balanced; scenarios of violent conflict gave way to spectator sport analogies and references to corporate soap operas.

As Hirsch explains, the framing of takeovers expanded "from a simple shootout between the forces of good and evil to a less clear-cut morality play." In some cases, criticism shifted from the acquirer to the target firms themselves. If managers were seen as resisting attractive offers, acquisitions were made that they were "feathering their own nests," or seeking sidepayments to soften their own landing.

In summary, after 20 years, both hostile and friendly takeovers were viewed as normal events rather than deviant innovations. Many came to see the activity as serving the best interests of institutions, shareholders, and society in general.

---

* As Hirsch notes, Menzel suggested that early adopters include those cut off from positions of status and centrality and not well integrated into their peer community.

They make specific policy recommendations, lobby for the dismissal of CEOs, and engage in proxy fights with management to prevent the introduction of self-serving corporate policies[33] (see "Governance for Whom?").

---

[33]Shareholder activism has also been stimulated by the perceived trend toward erosion of shareholder rights. As an example, critics point to the Delaware court's support of Time's decision to refuse a takeover bid from Paramount in order to pursue its long-time strategy. Similarly, a number of states have enacted antitakeover laws that shield management from hostile bids.

▲ TABLE 8▲1   Selective Holdings of Fidelity Funds, 1995

	Share of Stock Outstanding
Airborne Freight	14.68%
Lehman Brothers	12.93
RJR Nabisco	12.12
Dell Computer	11.30
Compaq Computer	10.68
OfficeMax	10.37
Bear Stearns	10.04
Caterpillar	8.09
Travelers	7.02
American Express	6.99
Texas Instruments	6.25
Sears Roebuck	6.23
Merrill Lynch	5.83
United Airlines	5.29
American Airlines	5.20
Motorola	5.02

Source: *The Boston Globe*, May 16, 1995.

CalPERS, America's largest state pension fund (over $80 billion in assets), began fighting proxy battles in 1985. Over time, its approach in dealing with management became more systematic, including the formation of a watchdog unit to concentrate specifically on corporate governance. At Zenith, for example, years of consistent losses and the collapse of the company's stock (from the mid-$30s in 1987 to $7 in early 1994) inspired CalPERS to request that nonemployee directors name a leader, whose role would be to counterbalance the authority of the CEO. At Avon Products, CalPERS was behind the establishment of a system of annual meetings with large shareholders. By one account, by the time he resigned in 1994, CalPERS's CEO Dale Hanson had met with 65 CEOs of 56 companies and held dialogues with a multitude of outside directors.[34] The access gained by Hanson, and others like him, was a function of a profound change in the norms surrounding the interactions between shareholders and management.

This process was aided in part by the emergence of **shareholder activists**, who analyze company performance and provide information to institutional investors for use in voting. Because their findings are keenly observed by shareholders, directors, CEOs and their peers, some of these individuals and advisory groups can wield considerable influence (see "Corporate Gadfly").

Beginning in 1990, a series of rulings by the Securities and Exchange Commission (SEC) also contributed to the shift in the balance of power between managers and shareholders. The government made it easier for shareholders to initiate and fight proxy battles, and gave them the right to challenge golden parachutes, request detailed information regarding executive

---

[34]*Business Week*, June 6, 1994, p. 71.

Governance for Whom?

The following statements reflect conflicting perspectives on the validity of maximizing shareholder value:

> The only enforceable discipline that can make corporate management accountable [is maximization of shareholder value].... We need a single standard of economic performance that is simple minded, but effective. (Robert A.G. Monks, founder of Institutional Shareholder Services)

> Maximizing shareholder value is a kind of populism for capitalists. Taken to its extreme, it means that any company whose shares fall below a certain value should be taken over or pulled apart and liquidated like so much scrap metal. This thinking will turn America into a bunch of poor companies with too much debt over the long run. (Louis Lowenstein, Columbia Law School professor)

Few would deny that corporate governance has improved in recent years. Recent changes in governance practices notwithstanding, however, some would argue that the rights of shareholders have been elevated to eclipse all other interests.

For example, Hirsch has pointed out that the discussion of corporate control has reinforced the "image of the corporation as just another liquid asset, easily shifted from one ledger to another."* This development could suggest that the constituency of the firm has narrowed too far. Other stockholders —suppliers, employees, and communities, for example—may have suffered unduly as a result of some of the recent changes.

However, it is important to recognize that many of the recent advantages in governance occurred to overcome the inertia of corporate managements in remedying failing corporate strategies. The difficult choices to downsize, restructure, and rationalize arguably were needed because governance mechanisms had failed in the first place, allowing pathologies to take hold and wreak havoc before they were checked or eliminated. It is critical that governance issues be dealt with proactively to prevent the need for such devastating decisions in the future. Responsible corporate governance is a valuable legacy that today's managers can give to all their stakeholders.

Source: *The Boston Globe*, July 3, 1989.
*Hirsch, "From Ambushes to Golden Parachutes."

compensation, and pursue the formation of a shareholders' independent advisory committee to work with directors on key issues.

Relationship Investing

In the wake of shareholder activism, a trend known as *relationship investing* emerged to formalize a new dynamic between shareholders and management. In 1992, the SEC relaxed federal proxy regulations, allowing institutional investors to combine large ownership stakes with seats on the board, signalling a long-term commitment to supply both capital and management assistance. Supporters hailed such arrangements as a progressive advancement in corporate governance.

Unlike the raiders of the 1980s, relationship investors attempt to intervene before vast amounts of value have been destroyed. Moreover, by establishing a basis for systematic, constructive dialogue between owners and managers, relationship investing represents a step beyond shareholder activism. Shareholders benefit from greater **management accountability**, while management in turn gets **patient capital** and the freedom to focus on

Corporate Gadfly

Once an official in the U.S. Labor Department, Robert A.G. Monks became a leading advocate in the mounting campaign for shareholder rights. He founded Institutional Shareholder Services in 1985 to provide advice to fund managers and analyze proposals from boards of directors. In 1990, he set up an independent spin-off to concentrate on shareholder advocacy. In 1992, Monks established the Lens Fund to look for underperforming S&P 500 companies, using a combination of financial data and *Fortune's* annual surveys on corporate reputations. The Lens Fund sought 3 percent–4 percent stakes in several companies, which it then used as a lever to introduce performance analyses and governance strategies.

Monks gained celebrity status in 1990 when he waged a proxy battle to gain a seat on the board of directors at Sears Roebuck and Co. He warned that the company had to meet its 15 percent ROE target or face restructuring He also advocated separating the jobs of CEO and chairman of the board and reforming board practices. Although Sears defeated Monks's attempt, the publicity surrounding the event heightened public scrutiny of the company's woes. Monks kept the pressure on Sears, which has since enacted a number of the changes that he advocated, such as spinning off financial services, reducing costs, and revamping the retail operations.

the long term.[35] Warren Buffet, chairman of the Berkshire Hathaway Fund, earned fame as a pioneer and prominent practitioner of the relationship investing approach. He realized considerable returns by buying and holding major stakes in corporations, sometimes taking a seat on the board and actively advising management.

Though it breaks down some of the insulation surrounding corporate management, relationship investing is, by itself, not likely to be a panacea for corporate governance. (See "Governance for Whom?"). Critics argue that it might encourage CEOs to spend too much time communicating with large stockholders and not enough time on management. Or worse, the tighter accountability could encourage managerial risk aversion.

▲ THE ROLE OF THE CORPORATE BOARD

The business and affairs of every corporation organized under this chapter shall be managed by or under the direction of a board of directors.

The General Corporation Law of the State of Delaware[36]

Disengaged Directors

In theory and in law, boards of directors exist to represent shareholders and provide a critical check and balance on the management of corporations. In practice, however, when company

---

[35]Long-term patient capital provided by institutional investors has historically characterized the German and Japanese capital markets. Both those countries have long traditions of "dedicated capital," whereby large principal owners maintain long-term investments in companies. In Japan, for example, not only the banks, but also the keiretsu cross-holdings of stock provide long-term capital. Although these systems can be criticized too—for their inability to fund new ventures and slowness in corporate restructuring—and are, today, under pressure as local investors seek higher returns in global markets, they have been identified as a source of advantage for domestic German and Japanese firms (Michael E. Porter, "Investment Behavior and Time Horizon in American Industry: Executive Summary," Harvard Business School, May 13, 1992).

[36]About half of all U.S. public companies are incorporated in Delaware.

performance languished and value-destroying strategies were sustained, these august groups rarely rose to the occasion. In 1971, a major study of corporate governance described directors as "ornaments on a corporate Christmas tree."[37] The positions were often filled by current and retired management, business acquaintances and friends of the CEO, and representatives from banks and law firms who had a financial interest in the continuity of management. Despite their legal obligations, most directors did not see their role as one of protecting shareholders' interests or evaluating the performance of management. Instead, most boards functioned largely as supportive audiences, listening to the plans of CEOs and, on occasion, offering advice and counsel.

Not surprisingly, the impetus to change this comfortable state of affairs did not come from the boards themselves; it came from a number of external sources. Beginning in the 1970s, a series of lawsuits were filed charging firms with corrupt foreign practices (including bribery) and questionable political contributions at home. These suits raised serious questions about the controls that were in place within firms.

Boards also had to confront the realities of the burgeoning market for corporate control. As these contests gained legitimacy, directors were held accountable for maximizing shareholder returns. When *Time* spurned a takeover offer from Paramount and instead merged with Warner, directors were sued for not acting in the best interests of shareholders. (See "The Bad News Board.")

These events, together with the changing patterns of stock ownership, underscored the **fiduciary responsibility** directors have to corporate shareholders and also demonstrated the need for them to actively monitor and evaluate the performance of management. Though it began to happen largely out of self-defense, activism by corporate boards has become one of the most conspicuous manifestations of increasing public pressure on America's companies to change the way they are governed.

The Structure of Good Governance

> *If you had asked me 10 years ago where the next wave of reform would come from,*
> *I would never have guessed it would be the boardroom, but it's happening.*
>
> *A member of the board of directors of Scott Paper Co.,*
> *on the occasion of the board's dismissal of the firm's CEO*

Board Composition.   Structural shifts on corporate boards, such as changing the **ratio of insiders to outsiders**, have made the job of governance easier. Examples of boards stacked with insiders and friends of the CEO are dwindling in number. In the United States, nonmanagement directors now account for 69 percent of the positions on most boards (on average, 9 out of 13) and a majority on most unitary boards in Sweden, Italy, Spain, Belgium, France, and Switzerland[38] (see "Global Trends in Governance"). Board members are also increasingly owning stock in the firms on whose boards they sit, so that their interests are aligned with those of shareholders.

---

[37]M. Mace, Directors: *Myth and Reality* (Boston: Harvard Business School Press, 1971).
[38]England also has unitary boards of directors. Although the proportions of insiders on these boards has decreased, firms seem intent on maintaining a balance between insiders and outsiders. Companies in Germany and Holland have two separate boards. In these two-tier systems, supervisory boards are made up of nonexecutive directors. In Germany, 50 percent of these are shareholders' representatives and 50 percent are workers' or union representatives. Information on European boards is taken from Jean-Jacques Pic, "Europe's Diverse Corporate Boards."

The Bad News Board

In early 1995, Morrison Knudson (MK), a large construction company best known for building the Hoover Dam, found itself in dire financial and legal straits. It had just announced a loss of $174 million for fiscal 1994, and, suspecting problems, the board had forced Chairman and CEO William Agee to step down. A week later, it was discovered that the losses for 1994 in fact were close to $310 million.

When Agee was finally ousted, many wondered how he had held on so long. The answer, according to industry observers, lay primarily in corporate politics. Agee himself had appointed 9 of the board's 10 directors, many of whom knew little or nothing about the construction industry. The CEO went on to forge personal connections with the directors that reportedly went beyond business-related activities.

Agee also frequently replaced senior management, averaging a new chief financial officer and a new president every 18 months. As a result, the board had little choice but to rely primarily on Agee for information. Several board members later claimed that they were kept in the dark regarding the company's true financial situation, or even that they were fed blatantly bad financial information.

The MK story illustrates the power a manipulative CEO can have over a board for an extended period. Although it was two of the directors who eventually demanded a detailed investigation of MK's financial standing, by then the firm's strategic position had deteriorated beyond repair.

Source: Adapted from "The Bad News Board," *Newsweek*, April 3, 1995, p. 46.

Global Trends in Governance

By the early 1990s, changes in the global economy had inspired shareholders in Canada, Europe, and Asia to mirror efforts in the United States to challenge contemporary corporate governance practices. Intensifying global competition for capital inspired fund managers, in particular, to increase the pressure on all corporations to provide better information and expand shareholders' rights.

In Britain, leading regulators and industrialists conducted an 18-month study of corporate governance that culminated in publication of the Cadbury Report in 1992. The report outlined a number of recommendations, including separation of the titles of CEO and chairman, increased power of independent directors on audit and compensation committees, and disclosure of executive salaries. Although the report made such measures vol-

untary, British companies would have to report compliance to the stock exchange. In 1995, three years later, a survey was done of 710 firms, and all reported that they were in full or partial compliance with the 19 points in the Cadbury code of practice. Eighty-nine percent of the top 500 firms now have three or more nonexecutive directors on their boards.*

Even in Japan, investors became disenchanted by the tight relationships between managers and banks and with low dividends and weak earnings. In 1993, a Japanese Justice Ministry committee broke tradition by proposing modest changes in the commercial code to increase corporate accountability to independent auditors and investors.

The Wall Street Journal, European Edition, May 26, 1995.

Board Committees. Having recognized the need for more control over management, most U.S. boards have several standing committees to assist directors with their work. The most helpful of these tend to be the audit and compensation committees, which address critical governance issues where the relevant information is complicated and detailed.[39] Today, on most boards these committees typically consist entirely of outside directors, and so add an element of independence to the oversight of senior executives. As a result, many CEOs no longer determine their own compensation.

Many boards now have nominating committees, both for board members and their CEO, which constrain the previously accepted practice of having CEOs select their own directors and successors. Nonetheless, the influence of such a committee may be limited when compared to that of a dominant chairman/CEO.

Board Actions. In the last decade, more and more boards have taken the lead in initiating corporate change. The most celebrated of these have been in prominent industrial firms, where bitter stand-offs between directors and CEOs have ended with the unceremonious departures of the latter. These actions were often taken after years of poor firm performance and increasing pressure from shareholders. Less visibly, boards are becoming more directly involved in strategy setting, acting proactively to initiate strategic discussions, rather than rubber-stamping management's fully articulated plans.

A number of corporate boards have even generated guidelines to clarify their organizational roles and responsibilities. At General Motors, for example, the board produced a 28-point plan outlining its functions, which included selecting of the chairman/CEO, establishing agenda items for board meetings, defining what constitutes independence for outside directors, and controling over succession planning.[40]

Limitations on the Board's Ability to Govern

Despite these prominent changes, there are still a number of forces that limit the effectiveness of boards. Jay Lorsch, author of *Pawns or Potentates: The Reality of America's Corporate Boards*, identified three of these constraints:

> While [board members] don't see themselves as pawns of management, as did their predecessors of a decade ago, they acknowledge a number of constraints on their ability to govern in a timely and effective manner. Such constraints include their own *available time and knowledge*, a *lack of consensus* about their goals, and the *superior power of management,* particularly the CEO-chairman.[41] (emphasis added)

In the United States, over 80 percent of public companies still have one person fill the roles of chief executive officer and chairman of the board.[42] In such a situation, the person at the helm controls both the agenda and the information flow. Further, most directors have full-time responsibilities in other organizations (63 percent are CEOs of other firms), and positions on other boards. The amount of time they have to focus on issues related to the board is therefore constrained by other obligations.

---

[39]For a more complete discussion, see Jay Lorsch, *Pawns or Potentates* (Boston: Harvard Business School Press, 1989).
[40]*Directors and Boards*, Summer 1994, pp. 5–9.
[41]Lorsch, *Pawns or Potentates*, pp. 1–2.
[42]*Directors and Boards*.

The net effect of these conditions is to limit boards' ability to govern. Without the requisite information, and without the power over those they govern, directors cannot fully discharge the legal responsibilities of their station. Nevertheless, in recent years, corporate boards have played an increasingly active role in corporate governance, and are a force to be reckoned with.

▲ ROLE OF THE CEO

The CEO may be on a shorter leash, but he's a more valuable dog.

Thomas A. Stewart

The clearest casualty in the battle over corporate governance is the old-model CEO, characterized by virtually imperial prerogative. An oft-cited example of the old ways, Edward Brennan at one time filled a multitude of executive positions at Sears, including ones that made him directly accountable to only himself.

As noted earlier, some corporations have begun to separate the positions of CEO and chairman of the board, to increase the autonomy and effectiveness of the board as a check on the CEO's power. This solution is not without controversy; it is unclear whether CEOs will be able to fulfill their leadership roles properly if their authority is compromised. Critics of such splits warn that CEOs may abandon the kind of entrepreneurial activities that are so important to existing corporations.

Many more firms have introduced forms of **incentive compensation** that align the CEO's interest with shareholders. In particular, granting stock options that only have value if the share price improves may solve the intrinsic agency problem. The resulting CEO compensation may be easier to justify, at least from a shareholder perspective.

Chief executives will certainly be called upon to provide more information to shareholders. Given the increase in shareholders' power, it will be in everyone's interests to improve their level of understanding. CEOs also will be encouraged to use boards more effectively, to involve them more substantively in critical corporate strategy decisions, and to make sure they have the information and the incentive to think like owners.

Creating Corporate Advantage

In spite of all these improvements in corporate goverance, CEOs continue to bear ultimate responsibility for the performance of their companies. While this requires them to fulfill a broad range of leadership functions, from maintaining ethical standards to creating a challenging work environment, the CEO's primary task is the establishment or maintenance of corporate purpose, which is codified and implemented through the vehicle of corporate strategy.[43]

Even though boards in particular, and stakeholders more generally, are playing a greater role in strategic decisions, the CEO remains the only person with the knowledge, time, and authority to truly understand the firm's position and develop the appropriate corporate strategy. Others may critique or suggest amendments, but the CEO and his or her team of corporate executives are the ones in a position to initiate and deliver on a strategy.

---

[43]C.R. Christensen, K.R. Andrews and J.L. Bower, *Business Policy: Text and Cases*, Richard D. Irwin: Burr Ridge, Illinois, 1978.

Although there are many conceptual frameworks for CEOs to draw on as they seek to develop a viable corporate strategy, they need to remember that there is not one ideal strategy for all companies. Rather, as this book has described, there is a compelling logic behind all effective strategies that overrides their inherent differences. When CEOs understand the resources of their corporations, the limit to the scope of those resources, and the organizational mechanisms that will release the value therein, they are in the position to develop strategies that will truly build a corporate advantage.

▲ RECOMMENDED READINGS

Bhagat, S., A. Schleifer, and R.W. Vishny, "Hostile Takeovers in the 1980s: The Return to Corporate Specialization," *Brookings Papers on Economic Activity: Microeconomics*, 1990 Special Issue, pp. 1–84.

Finkelstein, S., and D.C. Hambrick. "Chief Executive Compensation: A Study of the Intersection of Markets and Political Processes." *Strategic Management Journal*, March–April 1989, pp. 121–34.

Hirsch, P. "From Ambushes to Golden Parachutes: Corporate Takeovers as an Instance of Cultural Framing and Institutional Integration." *American Journal of Sociology*, January 1986, pp. 800–37.

Jensen, M. C. "Eclipse of the Public Corporation." *Harvard Business Review*, September–October 1989, pp. 61–74.

Jensen, M.C., and R.S. Ruback. "The Market for Corporate Control: Scientific Evidence." *Journal of Financial Economics*, April 1983, pp. 5–50.

Kaplan, S., and M.S. Weisbach. "The Success of Acquisitions: Evidence from Divestitures," *Journal of Finance*, March 1992, pp. 107–38.

Lorsch, J., with E. MacIver. *Pawns or Potentates: The Reality of America's Corporate Boards*. Boston: Harvard Business School Press, 1989.

Mace, M. *Directors: Myth and Reality*. Boston: Harvard Business School Press, 1971.

Monks, R.A.G., and N. Minow. *Corporate Governance*. Cambridge, MA: Blackwell, 1995.

Ravenscraft, D.J., and F.M. Scherer. *Mergers, Sell-Offs, and Economic Efficiency*. Washington, DC: The Brookings Institution, 1987.

Roll, R., "The Hubris Hypothesis of corporate takeovers." *Journal of Business*, Vol. 59, April 1986, pp. 197–216.

Shleifer, A., and R.W. Vishny. "Management Ownership and Market Valuation: An Empirical Analysis." *Journal of Financial Economics*, January–March 1988, pp. 293–315.

Shleifer, A., and R.W. Vishny. "Takeovers in the 60s and the 80s: Evidence and Implications." *Strategic Management Journal*, Winter 1991, pp. 51–59.

THE WALT DISNEY COMPANY (A):
CORPORATE STRATEGY

"It all started with a mouse."

Walt Disney

"I think our biggest achievement to date has been bringing back to life an inherent Disney synergy that enables each part of our business to draw from, build upon, and bolster the others."

Michael Eisner

The Walt Disney Company was founded in 1923 by Walt Disney and his brother Roy with a $500 loan from an uncle (Exhibit 1). Originally a cartoon studio in Hollywood, California, the company had grown by 1987 into a household name throughout the world and an entertainment industry giant with sales of nearly $3 billion (Exhibit 2). Disney competed in a range of industries, including film and television production, theme parks, and consumer products. It now faced the challenge of meeting its stated goal of 20 percent annual growth in earnings per share without violating the culture, traditions, and image of a company which, 22 years after the death of its founder, still strongly reflected Walt's vision and personality.

Professor David J. Collis prepared this case with the assistance of Ellen Holbrook. MBA 1988, and Professor Michael E. Porter.

▲ EXHIBIT 1 Walt Disney Company History

Year	Event	New Business	Exit Business
1901	Walt Disney born		
1923	Walt Disney Productions founded	Cartoons	
1928	Mickey Mouse introduced, "Steamboat Willie" (first sound)		
1929	Mickey Mouse pencil tablets	Consumer products	
1930	Mickey Mouse comic strip	Publications	
	Mickey Mouse book (first book)		
1932	First color cartoon "Flowers and Trees"		
	Established art school		
1933	First record licensed	Records	
	Ingersoll makes first Mickey Mouse watch		
1937	*Snow White and the Seven Dwarfs* (first feature-length cartoon)	Feature-length cartoon	
1940	First public stock offering		
	Disney studio moves to Burbank		
	Fantasia (first stereo sound)		
1944	Educational and Industrial Film Division established	Training films	
1949	"Seal Island" (first true life adventure)		
	Walt Disney Music Co. formed	Music	
1950	*Treasure Island* (first live action)	Live-action movie	
	"One Hour in Wonderland" (first TV show)	TV production	
1952	WED Enterprises founded to design Disneyland		
1953	Buena Vista Distribution Co. formed	Film distribution	
1954	"Disneyland" TV show		
1955	Disneyland opens	Theme park	
	Mickey Mouse Club TV show premieres	TV series	
1957	"Zorro" (first dramatic TV show)	TV syndication	
1963	Audio-Animatronics first used		
1966	Walt Disney dies		
1969	Disney on Parade	Arena shows	
1971	Walt Disney World theme resort opens	Theme resort	
1980	Buena Vista home video	Video	
1982	EPCOT Center opens		
1983	Tokyo Disneyland opens	Overseas theme park	
	The Disney Channel	Cable	
1984	Touchstone (first mature theme) label created	Mature theme movies	
	Arvida purchase	Real estate development	
1986	"Wuzzles" (first Disney television cartoon)		
1987	Disney stores open	Retail stores	
	Arvida sold		Real estate development
	Purchased KHJ-TV	Television station	
	EuroDisneyland announced		
	Wrather Corporation purchased		

▲ EXHIBIT 2   Walt Disney Company Financial Performance ($ millions)

	1940	1945	1950	1955	1960	1965	1970	1975
Sales	2.5	4.6	7.3	24.6	46.4	109.9	167.1	520.0
Net income	(0.1)	0.4	0.7	1.4	(1.3)	11.4	21.8	61.7
Return on sales (%)	(4.0)	8.7	9.6	5.7	(2.8)	10.4	13.0	11.9
Current assets	5	6	9	15	38	44	93	125
Net fixed assets	3	2	2	4	27	40	168	617
Total assets	9	9	11	22	66	88	268	783
Current liabilities	3	2	3	12	21	22	36	74
Long-term debt	—	—	1	0	20	9	2	6
Equity	6	6	6	9	21	53	218	619
Return on equity (%)	(1.7)	6.7	11.7	15.6	(6.2)	21.5	10.0	10.0

	1980	1981	1982	1983	1984	1985	1986	1987
Sales	915	1,005	1,030	1,307	1,452	1,700	2,166	2,876
Net income	135	122	100	93	98	174	247	445
Return on sales (%)	14.8	12.1	9.7	7.1	6.7	10.2	11.4	15.5
Current assets	506	458	262	333	683	767	925	1,462
Net fixed assets	763	1,069	1,673	1,871	1,937	2,001	2,049	2,147
Total assets	1,347	1,610	2,102	2,381	2,739	2,897	3,121	3,806
Current liabilities	145	192	237	238	264	329	436	587
Long-term debt	30	162	409	457	862	823	547	585
Equity	1,075	1,167	1,275	1,401	1,155	1,185	1,419	1,845
Return on equity (%)	12.6	10.5	7.8	6.6	8.5	14.7	17.4	24.1

Business Composition (% of revenue)

	1940	1945	1950	1955	1960	1965	1970	1975
Film/TV	77	67	74	82	50	55	41	22
Theme parks/resorts	—	—	—	—	39	32	49	65
Consumer products	23	33	26	18	11	12	10	14

	1980	1981	1982	1983	1984	1985	1986	1987
Film/TV	18	17	20	13	15	16	21	30
Theme parks/resorts	70	69	70	79	66	62	62	64
Consumer products	12	14	10	9	7	6	5	6
Community development	—	—	—	—	12	16	12	—

▲ COMPANY HISTORY

Walter Elias Disney was born in 1901 and spent most of his youth on a farm in Marceline, Missouri. In 1922, Disney and a friend, Ubbe Iwerks, started a cartoon business, Laugh-O-Grams, which went out of business a year later. Instead of giving up, they moved to Hollywood. In 1923, Walt and his older brother, Roy, teamed up to start The Disney Brothers studio. Walt was the driving force and creative producer, while Roy found the money and managed the administration. For five years they worked on developing cartoon characters and unique animation techniques. One of the first characters to achieve popularity, "Oswald, the Lucky Rabbit," was lost in a contract dispute with the film's distributor because Disney did not own the copyright. After this incident, Disney retained control over the rights to all future characters and ideas his company produced.

In 1928, Disney released the world's first fully synchronized sound cartoon, "Steamboat Willie," which introduced a character that would change the company forever—Mickey Mouse. Drawn by Ubbe Iwerks and using Walt's voice, Mickey's simple but humorous antics pleased audiences of all ages and nationalities. "Steamboat Willie" was distributed to movie theaters throughout the United States, Canada, Europe, and Latin America, and he quickly became an international sensation under various names ("Topolino" in Italy, "Raton Mickey" in Spain, and "Musse Pigg" in Sweden, for example). The first Mickey Mouse product (a pencil tablet) was merchandised under a licensing agreement in 1929 when Walt, short of cash, accepted an offer of $300 from a man in a hotel lobby. That same year, a Mickey Mouse cartoon began appearing in newspapers. The Mickey Mouse Club (organized through movie theaters) had a membership of over a million youngsters by 1932.

By 1937, having already won three Academy Awards, Disney released the world's first full-length, full-color animated feature, *Snow White and the Seven Dwarfs*. The film's characters were used for licensing agreements, while tunes from the film's soundtrack—including "Someday My Prince Will Come" and "Heigh-Ho"—became international hits. Unfortunately, the music rights had been given to a music company in exchange for distribution. Even in 1988, Disney paid a royalty each time it used those songs. Based on the success of *Snow White,* the company set a goal of releasing two or more feature films per year, plus a large number of short subjects. Accordingly, Disney's employment roster grew from 100 to 750 people, and the company moved to its own studio facilities in Burbank. To finance these projects, Walt Disney Productions made its initial public stock offering in 1940.

The next decade brought harder times, precipitated by the box office failure of *Fantasia* (1940) and the war in Europe. Disney Productions survived these problems, in part by diversifying into other business activities, including the production of training and educational films, begun in 1944. Theatrical film-making, however, remained Disney's primary business. In 1949, the Walt Disney Music Company was formed to retain full control over Disney's music copyrights, and top artists such as Perry Como and Dinah Shore recorded Disney tunes.

When television was introduced to the American public after the end of the war, Walt Disney commented:

> It is obvious that television . . . will make a tremendous impact on the world of entertainment and motion pictures . . . . When the time and the occasion are right, we shall play our part and enjoy the proper share of this new activity.

In 1950, Disney's first television special, "One Hour in Wonderland," was broadcast across America, enabling millions of people to watch Disney characters in their living rooms.

Another event was soon to shape the company's destiny. WED Enterprises (using Walt Disney's initials) was founded in 1952 to design Disneyland, an outdoor entertainment park to be built in Anaheim, California. Disney had observed that current amusement parks "were neither amusing nor clean, and offered nothing for Daddy," so he wanted to create a new kind of park—one that was challenging, imaginative, sparkling clean, and would appeal to people of all ages.

WED Enterprises was formed as a separate entity from Disney Productions to provide an environment where Walt and his "imagineers" could dream, design, and build the future Disneyland free of the pressures from film unions and stockholders. Nothing like it had ever been attempted before.

Disney took out millions of dollars in short-term bank loans to finance this new endeavor, and the park became a tremendous financial risk for the company. In 1954, Disney made an agreement with the American Broadcasting Company (ABC) to produce a weekly television show called "Disneyland," in exchange for ABC's help in financing the construction of the park.

Disneyland opened with tremendous fanfare in 1955. Shifting the emphasis from the speed and size of the thrill to the show element, attractions were intended as extensions of the movie experience, with guests taken out of their seats and placed in the middle of the action. In addition to carousels, it boasted roving life-size characters from Disney movies, and fantastic, technically sophisticated rides and attractions. Disneyland continually upgraded its attractions and later on added new exhibits at very little cost to the company through innovative corporate sponsorship programs.

Walt Disney was concerned with achieving excellence in all aspects of park operations, from the attractions to personnel. Initially, the food and merchandise concessions were licensed out to conserve capital, but as Disneyland generated more revenues, the company bought back virtually all the operations inside the park. It also established the Retail Merchandise Division to create its own nonlicensed product specifically for Disneyland. Although Walt Disney Productions initially owned only 34 percent of the park's equity, it was able to buy back the remaining shares within five years.

Also in 1955, Disney premiered the "Mickey Mouse Club" television show, hosted by 24 young "Mouseketeers" and featuring Disney cartoons and short films. Disney then entered the television syndication business when the "Mickey Mouse Club" was syndicated after its network run.

For many years, the company had an agreement with RKO to distribute Disney films both in the United States and abroad. In 1953, however, Disney brought all foreign and domestic distribution functions in-house, forming Buena Vista Distribution. This eliminated the need to pay distribution fees, which were typically one-third of a film's gross revenues, and gave Disney more control.

Having entered live-action motion picture production in 1950 with the release of *Treasure Island,* Disney was releasing an average of three new films per year by the late 1950s. Most were live-action titles, which could be produced at a much faster rate than cartoons; some were animated features like *101 Dalmatians.* The most successful new Disney release of the sixties was *Mary Poppins.* Critics hailed the film for its imagination and advanced special effects, such as cartoon characters dancing with live actors. Newcomer Julie Andrews became a star overnight. By developing his own pool of talent, Walt Disney avoided paying exorbitant salaries. As one writer noted, "Disney himself became the box office attraction—as a producer of a predictable family style and the father of a family of lovable animals." The company also earned millions of dollars by reissuing its old cartoon classics. Every seven or eight years, a film like *Snow White, Dumbo,* or *Bambi* would be taken from the shelf and rereleased in movie theaters to a brand new generation of audiences in what was then called the "Disney Magic Cycle."

With Disneyland still in its infancy, Walt Disney dreamed of starting another theme park. In 1965, he purchased over 27,000 acres of land near Orlando, Florida, on which he planned to build "Walt Disney World" and "EPCOT"—an "experimental prototype community of tomorrow." Walt Disney World was envisioned as a "destination resort"—a place where families could spend their vacations; hence, Florida was chosen for its year-round climate and the accessibility to millions of potential visitors from America and abroad. Unfortunately, Walt Disney was never able to see his dream come to fruition; he died just before Christmas 1966.

The Post–Walt Disney Years, 1967–1984

Roy O. Disney succeeded his brother as chairman, but in order to focus his energies on fulfilling Walt's dreams for Walt Disney World and EPCOT Center, he left much of the decision making for the company's nontheme park activities to other members of management. Long-time Disney employees Donn Tatum and Card Walker were made president and chief operating officer, respectively, in 1968. Walt Disney's son-in-law, Ron Miller, was named executive producer in charge of motion pictures and television.

Disney successfully lobbied to make Disney World separate from local government entities. The creation of Reedy Creek Improvement District by the Florida legislature in 1967 gave Disney full control and responsibility for providing all necessary public services to Walt Disney World. A new engineering and construction division was then established to oversee construction.

Walt Disney World opened in 1971, making headlines the world over. Shortly thereafter, having accomplished much of what his brother originally set out to do, Roy O. Disney died. In its first year of operation, Walt Disney World attracted nearly 11 million visitors and took in gross revenues of $139 million. It had two on-site themed resort hotels, the first hotels operated by Disney. Within a few years, Walt Disney World became the world's number one vacation destination. The Walt Disney Travel Company was formed to work with travel agencies, airlines, and tour companies to stimulate travel to the area. For those who couldn't visit a Disney theme park, Disney came to them. Walt Disney Productions and NBC created the "Disney on Parade" arena show, producing live "traveling" shows in major cities all over the world. Later on, ice shows continued this concept.

In 1976, Disney announced an agreement with the Oriental Land Company to develop a Disney-type amusement park near Tokyo, where 32 million people lived within a 30-mile radius. Tokyo Disneyland would be wholly owned by the Japanese partner, but would be designed and planned by WED Enterprises. Disney would receive 10 percent of the gate receipts and 5 percent of other sales as its royalty and provide consulting services during its operation. The park was weatherproofed because of the variable climate. Apart from differences in the food and language, it looked just like the U.S. parks.

During the late 1960s and 1970s, the output of animated films fell off substantially. Live-action films released during this time included three sequels to the popular film, *The Love Bug,* about a Volkswagen named Herbie. Making sequels was a departure from the company's previous practice. Prior to his death, Walt was quoted as saying, "By nature, I am a born experimenter. I don't believe in sequels. I can't follow popular cycles. I have to move on to new things—there are many new worlds to conquer."

In response to overall movie attendance declines during the late 1970s and early 1980s, Disney decided to launch a new label, "Touchstone," to target the teen/adult market where film going remained high. Touchstone would also share the distribution, promotion, and production overhead of the film division. Nevertheless, its introduction was controversial. Disney ran a full-page newspaper advertisement after the release of *Splash* (the first "Touchstone" movie, which featured partial nudity) to head off criticism.

From 1980 to 1983, the company's financial performance deteriorated (Exhibit 3). The company was incurring heavy costs at the time in order to put finishing touches on EPCOT Center, which opened in 1982. It was also investing in the development of a new cable venture, The Disney Channel, launched in 1983. Film division performance remained erratic. As corporate earnings stagnated and the company's performance was widely criticized, Roy E. Disney (son of Roy O. Disney) resigned from the board of directors in March 1984. In May, Saul Steinberg acquired 12.2 percent of Disney's stock. After making a tender offer with the intention of selling off the separate assets, Steinberg subsequently agreed to sell his stock back to the company at a substantial premium over the market price. Shortly thereafter, Irwin Jacobs purchased a large block of Disney shares and expressed strong interest in buying more.

During the same period, Disney announced plans to make its first acquisition, Arvida Corporation, a real estate development company active in commercial and community housing development. It was felt that Arvida would contribute to the development of the Disney land holdings. In addition, the move was widely interpreted as a way to bolster the firm's takeover defenses. In an unusual maneuver, Sid Bass and other Arvida investors exchanged the real estate company for a substantial ownership share of Disney. Irwin Jacobs then sold his shares to the Bass group of investors. Roy Disney was reinstated to the board and hostile takeover attempts ended.

New Leadership

In October 1984, Michael Eisner, 42, was named Disney's chairman and chief executive officer, and Frank Wells was named president and chief operating officer. Eisner, a former president and chief operating officer of Paramount Pictures, had been associated with such successful films and television shows as *Raiders of the Lost Ark* and *Happy Days*. Wells, a former entertainment lawyer and vice chairman of Warner Brothers, was known for his business acumen and operating management skills. Roy E. Disney was named vice chairman.

In 1986, the company's corporate name was changed from "Walt Disney Productions" to "The Walt Disney Company." The number of reporting business units was reduced by creating fewer, but more extensive, principal businesses. Eisner went outside the company to fill several key management positions. Recruits included several Paramount executives, notably Jeffrey Katzenberg, 33, who became chairman of the motion pictures and television subsidiary, and Rich Frank, its president. Former Marriott chief financial officer, Gary Wilson, was brought in as CFO of Disney in 1985. By 1987, only one of the ten corporate officers and three of the four group executives were Disney veterans.

The company's overall corporate objectives were then outlined: (1) to sustain Disney as the world's premier entertainment company; (2) to maximize shareholder wealth through a target annual growth rate of 20 percent and a 20 percent or greater return on stockholders' equity; (3) to maintain/build the basic integrity of the Disney name and consumer franchise; and (4) to accomplish the above while preserving basic Disney values in terms of quality, fairness, creativity, entrepreneurialism, and teamwork. This was to be achieved by

▲ EXHIBIT 3   Business Performance ($ millions)

	1980	1981	1982	1983	1984	1985	1986	1987
Film and TV								
Sales	161	175	202	165	245	320	512	876
Operating income	52	35	20	(33)	2	34	52	131
Assets	181	184	173	207	313	299	413	483
Capital expenditures	2	4	3	2	24	12	5	16
Theme parks								
Sales	643	692	726	1,031	1,097	1,258	1,524	1,834
Operating income	123	124	128	190	186	255	404	549
Assets	825	1,142	1,809	2,019	2,013	2,088	2,158	2,201
Capital expenditures	158	344	646	288	145	155	160	249
Consumer products								
Sales	110	139	103	111	110	123	130	167
Operating income	52	51	48	57	54	56	72	97
Assets	3	12	7	10	18	15	25	31
Capital expenditures	0	0	0	0	0	0	0	1
Corporate expenses								
G&A	21	36	31	26	60	50	66	70
Interest	(42)	(33)	(15)	14	42	50	40	(20)

1986 Sales Mix ($ millions)

Theme park	
Admission & rides	607
Merchandise	353
Food	284
Lodging	138
Tokyo	137
Film and TV	
Theatrical	146
Television	228
Home video	138
Consumer products	
Character licenses	66
Publications	24
Records/music	30
Educational	10

re-injecting a creative spark into Disney's core businesses (theme parks, filmed entertainment, and consumer products), while expanding their marketing efforts and seeking new areas of opportunity.

▲ THE WALT DISNEY COMPANY IN 1988

The Walt Disney Company in 1988 consisted of three major business segments, Studios, Consumer Products, and Attractions, in addition to a corporate R&D group, a corporate real estate development group, and a corporate administration function. *Walt Disney Studios* was responsible for all the company's films, whether live action or animated, under the Touchstone and Walt Disney labels, as well as all the television shows. It included Buena Vista film distribution, TV syndication, home video, and The Disney Channel. *Disney Consumer Products* was responsible for all of Disney's licensing and joint promotional activities, for Disney books, magazines, and records, and for the sale of Disney products through the theme parks, Disney stores, and mail-order operations. *Walt Disney Attractions* included the theme parks (along with the associated hotels), travel service, and entertainment facilities in the United States, Tokyo, and Europe. *Walt Disney Imagineering* (retitled from WED Enterprises to reflect a combination of imagination and engineering) and its 900 employees were the R&D department for Disney, responsible for generating new attractions, special effects, and facilities for new and existing Disney ventures. They not only developed the ideas, but manufactured and project-managed construction for all the attractions. The *Disney Development Company* was responsible for real estate development projects, including hotels, retail, commercial, and residential.

Walt Disney Studios

In 1987, film box office receipts in the United States and Canada reached an all-time high of $4.25 billion (Exhibit 4). While blockbusters like *Star Wars* might take in $200 million at the box office, industry estimates suggested that out of every ten films made, six lost money, two broke even, and two made a profit. Nevertheless, the number of films released each year had increased from 182 in 1975 to 497 in 1987. These were increasingly being financed by public offerings of film production partnerships.

Successful movies might eventually derive 35–40 percent of their income from domestic box office receipts; 15–20 percent from foreign theatrical rentals; 25–30 percent from home video; and 15–20 percent from sale of broadcast rights to network or cable television. The split of box office receipts between exhibitor, distributor, and the producer and profit participants, like the director and star actor, was based on a complicated series of guarantees, minimums, and formulas. On average, industry experts estimated that exhibitors received 55 percent of a film's gross box office receipts, while distributors received 15 percent and the film's producer and profit participants 30 percent.

Exhibitors (movie theater owners) were becoming increasingly concentrated. By 1987, the 25 largest chains controlled 49 percent of all U.S. screens. Increasingly, these were multiple screens rather than single screens, which gave exhibitors the flexibility to move a strongly performing film from a small to a large theater. With the relaxing of government regulation, studios were again owning movie theaters. Many had been prohibited from doing so

▲ EXHIBIT 4   Film Industry Market Share History

	Share of Box Office (%)					
	1982	1983	1984	1985	1986	1987
Disney	3	3	4	4	10	14
Paramount	14	14	21	11	22	20
Warner Bros.	10	17	19	17	11	13
Orion	3	4	5	6	7	15
Fox	14	21	10	10	8	9
Universal	30	13	8	15	9	7
Tri-Star			5	9	7	6
Columbia	10	14	16	10	10	4
MGM/UA	11	10	7	8	4	4
Total box office ($ billions)	3.4	3.7	4.0	3.7	3.8	4.2
Total attendance (billions)	1.2	1.2	1.2	1.1	1.0	1.1
Total films released*	433	501	520	454	427	497

*Includes reissues.

Source: *Variety*.

since the 1948 Paramount consent decree, which had effectively ended the "studio system" control over exhibitions.

Distribution (the task of getting a film accepted by an exhibitor) was becoming increasingly competitive. Often a distributor had to guarantee a certain budget for promoting and advertising a film before exhibitors would accept it. Larger distributors (mostly the major film studios) with a substantial number of films to offer each year had more leverage with exhibitors and could package less commercial films with blockbusters. Large distributors also benefited from scale economies in advertising and from amortizing the substantial fixed costs of distribution over more output.

The cost of making motion pictures had skyrocketed in the eighties. According to the Motion Picture Association of America (MPAA), the average cost for a major studio to produce a film in 1987 was over $20 million, and the cost of advertising and prints averaged $8.8 million. As recently as 1974, the average film had cost just $2.5 million and $1 million, respectively. Part of the reason for increased costs was that many actors, actresses, and directors could command salaries in excess of $1 million per film, in the belief that they would raise the probability of success. The use of well-known stars, expensive special effects, period costumes, and exotic locations were commonplace. Some studios were successful by holding budgets to less than $8 million and accepting lower, but more certain, revenues from cable TV, home video, and certain types of movie theaters.

New management at Disney Studios had stepped into a troubled situation, but moved rapidly to improve performance. Disney's share of box office had fallen to 4 percent in 1984 (Exhibit 4) and management wrote down $112 million for films and television programs that were underperforming. Previous productions were plagued by high costs, such as the ambitious $30 million special effects film, *Return to Oz*. In order to prevent such problems from happening again, new management held movie budgets to certain target ranges which acted as a "financial box" within which the creative talent had to operate. Management believed that money was no substitute for imagination. Films were closely managed to ensure that they would come in on time and near their target budgets, which were set somewhat below the industry average.

Walt Disney Studios chairman, Jeffrey Katzenberg, set a goal to release 15 to 18 new films per year, up from 2 new releases in 1984. New releases under the Touchstone label were primarily comedies with the amount of sex and violence kept to a minimum. New releases under the Walt Disney label consisted of live-action and animated films with stories and characters designed for a contemporary audience within the constraints of the Disney image for wholesomeness and good storytelling. Disney sought to release a new animated feature every 12–18 months and the animation staff was expanded accordingly. In addition, management planned reissues from Disney's film library, which contained 135 live-action features, 27 animated features, and over 500 short subject films. The cycle of reissuing the animated classics to theaters was shortened to every five years.

Katzenberg was known for his ability to identify good scripts, for his grueling work schedule, and for his persistent pursuit of actors and directors for Disney projects. He had convinced some of Hollywood's best talent from film and television to sign multideal contracts with Disney—without paying them exorbitant salaries. Many were television actors looking to get into films, or film actors whose most recent pictures had been less than spectacular, like Tom Selleck and Bette Midler.

Disney sought to spread the risk of film production by offering shares in limited partnerships. Through Silver Screen Partners II and III, nearly half a billion dollars was raised to expand film and television production activities. The limited partners shared the financial cost of producing a movie, but were residual claimants on the profit stream with a highly leveraged position. Analysts expected returns averaging between 10–15 percent for Silver Screen III. A fourth Silver Screen Partners offering was underway.

The studio returned to prominence in 1986 when Touchstone Films released the successful *Down and Out in Beverly Hills* and *Ruthless People*. By March 1988, Disney was in first place in domestic box office rentals, with a market share of over 30 percent, while the first new animated features developed under the new regime, *Oliver and Company* and *Who Framed Roger Rabbit?* (a collaboration with Steven Spielberg), were to be released later in the year. Nearly all the pictures produced under new management were economic successes.

Home Video   Since 1983, home video had been the fastest growing segment of the film industry. Companies often presold a film's home video rights in order to raise money to cover production costs. A new film would usually be available on home video about six months after its initial theatrical release. In 1987, U.S. videocassette rentals were $4.7 billion, compared to $2.8 billion for outright purchases, up 30 percent from 1986 (Exhibit 5). For the rental market, cassettes might carry a retail price between $80–$90 and would be bought primarily by home video stores which then rented them out to customers for a charge of $2–$3 per night. These stores were often small, poorly capitalized, and carried a limited selection. Nevertheless, a popular film would receive orders for more than 150,000 units from rental outlets. Other videocassettes were priced below $30 in an effort to be affordable to as many consumers as possible.

In 1985, Buena Vista Home Video began experimenting with a "sell-through" pricing strategy for several classic Disney animated titles. In sequence, each title would be released for sale for two years, and then withdrawn for five years. Supported by generous 30–40 percent retailer margins (rather than the industry average 20–30 percent) and ag-

▲ EXHIBIT 5   Videocassette Sales ($ millions)

	1984	1985	1986	1987
Disney	42	90	175	213
Paramount	96	155	210	277
CBS/Fox	128	255	280	252
Warner	110	150	160	210
RCA/Columbia	85	155	205	195
HBO	37	95	145	152
Vestron	48	160	150	143
MCA	66	100	135	142
Other	142	405	700	754
Total	754	1,535	2,160	2,338
VCR household penetration (%)	17.6	27.5	37.2	51.7
Video rental sales ($ millions)	1,834	2,909	4,153	5,193

Source: Paul Kagan Associates.

gressive advertising and promotion campaigns, it proved extremely effective, with orders of nearly three million units for Disney's *Lady and the Tramp*. Touchstone Films remained full-priced and targeted to the rental market. In the fall and winter of 1987, Disney titles accounted for 30 percent of videocassette unit sales. Its dollar revenues were second only to Paramount, which had been extremely successful with the low-priced marketing strategy on titles like *Top Gun* and *Crocodile Dundee*.

Network Television and Syndication   The three major television networks experienced a declining share of television viewership during the 1980s. Growth in the number of independent (non-network-affiliated) television stations, and the proliferation of pay TV and cable channels had provided viewers with other alternatives. These new channels were readily supported by advertisers eager to diversify their media expenditures in the face of high network advertising rates. Recently, the independent television stations had achieved sufficient viewership to buy new shows themselves (called first-run syndication). As each new channel required hours of programming a week, the demand for television programs had been expanding rapidly since the mid-1970s.

Typical industry production costs for a half-hour comedy were about $350,000 and about $100,000 for a game or a talk show. A one-hour action/drama like "Miami Vice" might cost $1 million per show. Over the years, the percentage of each episode's cost covered by the network or first-run syndication had declined to about 80 percent. Producers made up the difference in hopes of earning it back in the rerun syndication market. "The Cosby Show," for example, was syndicated in 1988 for over $4 million per episode. The risks for producers were, however, increasing. Only series which ran for more than 50 episodes were suitable for syndication, but the networks frequently canceled shows in mid-season as they juggled their schedules to boost ratings.

Disney's goal was to establish a major presence in television, entering both the network and first-run syndication business with prime-time shows (primarily comedies) and Saturday morning cartoons. Disney's "Golden Girls" became a network prime-time hit in 1985, but its other efforts for network television met with less spectacular results, as four other shows had poor ratings and were discontinued (Exhibit 6). Disney also developed several new shows for first-run syndication. "Win, Lose or Draw," a game show co-created by Burt Reynolds, did extremely well in the ratings. In 1986, a new Disney anthology series, "The Disney Sunday Movie," returned to prime-time network television on ABC.

In 1985, for the first time ever, Disney successfully premiered two animated children's television cartoons on network Saturday mornings, "Disney's Adventures of Gummi Bears" and "The Wuzzles." Saturday morning children's show competition was intense. Successful television cartoon characters like "The Flintstones" and newer, more contemporary cartoons like "Transformers" vied with "Sesame Street" and the "Muppets" for children's attention. Disney was also having success in first-run syndication of cartoons, with "DuckTales," a series featuring lesser Disney characters Scrooge McDuck and Huey, Dewey, and Louie. In order to save time and money, these shows were partly produced overseas with less detailed animation.

Cable Television   Cable television had been a rapidly growing business for many years, but was still only available to 76 percent of American homes in 1988 (Exhibit 7). The

▲ EXHIBIT 6   Network Television

	1985–86		1986–87		1987–88	
	Series	Hours	Series	Hours	Series	Hours
Prime-time series						
Disney	2	1.5	6	3.5	2	1.5
Universal	11	9	8	6.5	8	7.5
Lorimar-Telepictures	7	5.5	7	5.5	9	6.5
Columbia Pictures TV	6	4	8	4	10	5.5
Stephen J. Cannell	5	5	2	2	5	5
Warner	4	3	8	4	5	3.5
Paramount	7	4.5	5	2.5	5	3.5
Saturday morning animation (1/2 hour)						
Disney	2		2		1	
Hanna-Barbera	4		5		4	
DIC	2		2		4	
TPE	3		3		3	
ITC	—		2		3	
Marvel	2		—		3	
Columbia	—		1		2	
ABC	2		2		1	
Viewing time hours/week		50.2		49.5		
Network share (%)		73		71		

▲ EXHIBIT 7   Cable Television (subscribers in millions)

	1981	1986
Basic services		
WTBS	18.7	41.6
CBN	13.8	35.8
ESPN	12.7	44.3
C-SPAN	10.5	23.0
CNN	9.6	41.6
USA	9.1	39.0
Nickelodeon	5.6	35.8
MTV	—	37.1
Arts & Entertainment	—	27.0
Pay services		
HBO	7.0	15.0
Showtime	2.8	5.3
The Movie Channel	1.7	3.0
Cinemax	.7	4.1
Playboy	.2	.5
Disney	—	3.2
Total pay services		30.2
Total cable households (%)	52	73

Disney Channel became available to cable subscribers in 1983 and was unprofitable in its first year. By 1987, however, it was the fourth-largest pay channel with nearly four million subscribers. It also had the highest subscriber satisfaction rating in the industry and was profitable. Programming, targeted to the entire family, came from the company's own film library, acquisitions of other material, and new original programming. The channel did not typically show Touchstone movies, which had been licensed to Showtime in a five-year deal.

Broadcasting   Regulations preventing television and movie producers from owning exhibition outlets (both movie theaters and television stations) were becoming less stringent. As a consequence, major movie studios like MCA and Warner Brothers began buying interests in TV stations to leverage their programming expertise and assure access to key television markets. Twentieth Century Fox (part of Rupert Murdoch's News Corp.) even purchased the Metromedia Group stations in order to build a rival "fourth network." As of early 1988, Fox provided two evenings of new programs a week which achieved low but respectable ratings.

In 1987, Disney acquired KHJ-TV, Los Angeles' largest independent television station, for $323 million pending approval by the FCC. Disney management thought they could improve KHJ's programming and financial performance. Another Los Angeles television station had recently sold for over $500 million.

Consumer Products

Worldwide licensing was a $50 billion industry of which Disney was responsible for about four percent. Its share of character licensing was substantially higher, reaching 20–25 percent in some categories such as apparel. Disney had more character license agreements than any other company in the world—with over 3,000 worldwide licensees covering over 14,000 products in 50 countries. Major licensees in 1987 included Lorus (Disney watches), Hasbro (plush toys), and Gold Bond Ice Cream (Disney frozen treats). Despite the limited number of product categories as yet unlicensed by Disney, sales were still growing. In particular, there was a major international expansion underway. International sales through 29 country managers were now over one-half of consumer products' sales.

Disney Consumer Products had numerous characters available for licensing, including Mickey Mouse and Donald Duck, and typically licensed only one company in each product category. As an example, a recent initiative had involved licensing Mattel to produce a new preschool line of Disney products. Mattel planned to spend $8–$10 million on a television advertising campaign for the launch.

Disney's licensing group had creative control over the use of the characters once they had appeared in a film, and was quick to exert approval rights. At every stage in the development of a new licensed product, the Consumer Products account executive and the Disney art department had to give their approval. Mickey Mouse, for example, was not allowed to be associated with anything evil or naughty. Substantial alterations to established characters were rare, although they were occasionally redrawn to update their appearance. When Minnie Mouse was modernized in 1986, the redesign was based on what Minnie herself would be like today, rather than changing her character to reflect 1980s attitudes. There was great concern for the judicious use of the characters and with avoiding products or promotional uses of the name where Disney had no expertise or which carried negative connotations (Exhibit 8). Ultimately, appropriateness was a personal perception and approval of any new licensed

▲ EXHIBIT 8   Consumer Research on Company Image

	Attributes (% ranked 1, 2, or 3)
Fun/entertaining	52
Family entertainment	48
Good for whole family	35
Creative/innovative	35
Magic/fantasy	34
Quality	20
Safe/wholesome	18
Traditional values	10
For kids	10
Good value for money	4
Overly expensive	—
Better products than anyone else	—
More than Mickey Mouse	—

products rested with the head of Consumer Products, a 20-year Disney veteran, or sometimes with Eisner himself.

Disney was the world's largest children's record producer and publications licensor. Titles were classics, drawn both from Disney film songs and stories and from other folk stories. Total sales of records were over $10 million a year, and magazine readership was over $1 billion. Disney also competed in educational materials, selling filmstrips and videos on a wide range of subjects to schools. Recently it had licensed Simon & Schuster to distribute and market these materials, believing its size and skill in selling to the school market would benefit performance.

Consumer Products had also traditionally been responsible for promotional activities with other companies. More recently, a corporate emphasis had been placed on these activities, and virtually every division in the company was now involved in joint promotions such as the recent 10-year "strategic alliance" with Sears. Under the terms of this deal, Sears would promote new Disney animated films, sponsor a new studio tour attraction, and establish Disney boutiques within their stores in return for the rights to license new cartoon characters. McDonald's also entered into a year-round series of promotional tie-ins, spending substantial sums on TV advertising with a Cinderella theme in 1987.

In 1987, Disney launched the Disney Stores, a retail entertainment store concept operating outside of the theme parks. Three stores were opened that first year, with additional openings planned for 1988 and a minimum target of 100 stores by the early 1990s. Disney favored retention of full control over the stores, turning down numerous franchise offers. The stores were designed as an entertainment experience as much as a retail outlet, with construction costs about twice the U.S. average. Design features included animated mechanical characters, videos, and music shows, which were changed many times a year to vary the stores' theme.

Only Disney products were sold in the stores, with the staple items being plush toys, videos, and records. Prices were kept comparable to the theme park. Movie and Disney Channel promotional videos ran continuously while there was a direct phone line to place orders for the Disney Channel and to make Disney World reservations. Every guest was greeted courteously (the Disney hallmark) and the level of sales assistance was well above average. All store employees, regardless of geographic location, had to undergo the usual Disney orientation program with training personnel sent out from the Disney University to the stores for that purpose. The stores were profitable, with 300,000 visitors annually, and with sales volumes per square foot three to five times the U.S. average.

Recently combined with the stores was the Disney Family Catalog operation, which had been started in 1985 as Disney's first entry into mail order, selling Disney licensed products. Initially, the catalog was distributed to over eight million people.

Walt Disney Attractions

Total revenues at major theme parks in the United States were about $4 billion in 1987, and amusement park attendance was over 100 million, having grown 30 percent over the last five years. However, some operators were concerned whether these levels could be maintained industrywide (Exhibit 9). One-half of the theme park industry visitors were children or teenagers, and the baby boom generation was passing into adulthood. Admission prices at most parks averaged $17 per person per day, although guest expenditures once inside the park on food, drink, and merchandise were an important source of revenue.

▲ EXHIBIT 9   Major U.S. Theme Parks (attendance in millions)

	1977	1980	1983	1984	1985	1986	1987
Walt Disney World	13.1	13.8	22.7	21.1	33.5	36.4	39.5
Disneyland	10.7	11.5	10.0	9.9			
Knott's Berry Farm	3.9	3.7	3.4	3.2	3.5	3.5	4.0
Sea World, Florida	2.3	3.0	2.8	3.1	3.4	4.0	4.8
Kings Island	2.6	2.5	2.6	2.8	3.0	2.9	3.1
Sea World, California	2.3	2.6	2.9	3.0	3.1	3.1	3.3
Magic Mountain	2.7	1.9	2.6	2.6	2.8	2.8	2.8
Six Flags, Georgia	2.5	2.4	2.4	2.1	2.3	2.4	2.5
Busch Gardens	2.4	3.1	2.9	2.8	2.9	3.0	3.1
Sea World, Ohio	1.3	1.2	1.1	1.0	1.0	1.0	1.2
Universal Studios	3.2	3.7	2.9	2.8	3.3	3.9	4.2
Walt Disney World admission price ($)		13.00	15.00	18.00	19.50	24.50	28.00
Disneyland admission price ($)		9.25	12.00	13.00	16.50	17.95	21.50
Walt Disney World and Disneyland total revenue per guest ($)			32.53	35.39	37.55	42.33	46.55

Source: *Amusement Business.*

By 1988, amusement parks fell into two main categories, according to whether visitors were drawn from the local region or the whole country. As amusement parks were now located within a few hours' drive of every major metropolitan area, 50 percent of those attending parks traveled less than one hundred miles. Bally, with seven "Six Flags" and two other parks, was the leader among such regional parks.

National amusement parks tended to cluster in tourist areas and had become vacation destinations in their own right. Parks like Busch Gardens' "Old Country," near Williamsburg, Virginia, and Knott's "Berry Farm," which featured Snoopy, typically cost several hundred million dollars to construct. Also increasing in popularity were marine attractions, such as Sea World, and film studio tours. MCA, owner of the Universal Studio Tours in California, was spending $120 million to upgrade that tour, and had broken ground for a new location on 414 acres in Orlando, Florida.

Attendance at Disney theme parks in the United States had risen to 39 million by 1987. Disney World was the world's number one destination resort, with guests typically spending several days in the area. Disneyland remained oriented to local residents of Southern California. Both parks found that a substantial portion of their business was from adults and from repeat visitors. The number and variety of rides differentiated them from other amusement parks, which tended to offer only four or five major attractions. Attractions were continually refurbished or replaced ($50 million had been spent to refurbish Fantasyland in 1984), while of the original Disneyland attractions, two-thirds remained in 1988. The newest attractions, costing tens of millions of dollars each, were "Captain EO," a musical space fantasy starring Michael Jackson, which opened at Disneyland in 1986 and was then replicated at Walt Disney World and Tokyo Disneyland, and "Star Tours," created by George Lucas, which opened at Disneyland in 1987.

In Disney parks, visitors were always referred to as guests, employees as the cast, and the park itself as the stage. All cast members, whether permanent or seasonal, received up to four days of training before being allowed on stage. Cast members playing Disney characters had to maintain their performance whenever on stage (a hard task when children teased a character), and were not allowed to eat or drink on stage. Litter was continually swept up by cast members, and the whole stage was washed down each night. Every guest complaint about an employee was thoroughly investigated; consumer reactions and experiences were monitored at all times; every letter received was at the very least acknowledged. Regular surveys of wait times at lines, crowd density along paths, usage of food facilities, etc. were conducted and acted upon.

To build attendance at the parks, new management had for the first time begun national television advertising in 1985. Disney's annual expenditure on theme park advertising was over $35 million in 1988, supported by special events, retail tie-ins, media broadcast events, and other promotional devices. Major advertisers, including Delta Airlines and Coca-Cola, paid for the right to feature Walt Disney World in their own commercials. Restrictions on the number of visitors allowed in the parks were also removed and Disneyland was no longer closed on Mondays for maintenance, which was now performed at other times. The resulting growth in attendance as well as price rises contributed to rapid revenue and profit growth in the theme parks. At the same time, market research showed that guests, who stayed an average of eight hours, felt they received value for money.

Three major new separate entertainment areas were planned for Walt Disney World. "Pleasure Island," set to open in 1988, would feature six nightclubs, restaurants, and shops, and a 10-screen movie theater. Disney thereby hoped to extend the after-dark attractions at the park. "Typhoon Lagoon," opening in 1989, would see Disney's entry into the water park business. It would feature the world's largest wave machine, snorkeling with tropical fish, and waterslides. The most important new gated attraction planned for the United States was the "Disney-MGM Studio Tour" at Walt Disney World. Opening in 1989 at a cost in excess of $400 million, the park would feature fully operational film and television studios where actual productions would take place, as well as recreations of old movie scenes.

The company's most ambitious new venture in the theme park business would be Euro Disneyland. Announced in 1987 after an agreement with the French government, the $2.5 billion attraction and resort complex was set to open in 1992 at a 4,800-acre site 20 miles outside Paris, with 5,000 hotel rooms and projected attendance of 11 million visitors per year. French ownership of the newly formed company would be substantial. Disney would have a minimum 17 percent equity ownership and a long-term management contract—giving it substantial authority to develop and operate the park.

Walt Disney Attractions also operated the hotels and other resort-related businesses around the theme parks. In 1988, this included 2,800 hotel rooms and Lake Buena Vista Village at Walt Disney World. The number of rooms represented 5 percent of tourist hotel rooms in Orlando. While average occupancy rates in the hotel industry hovered around 65 percent, occupancy rates at the Disney-owned hotels averaged about 90 percent. Guests staying at Disney hotels stayed longer and spent more money in the theme parks than those who stayed at non-Disney hotels.

To develop Disney's unused acreage, primarily in Orlando, where only 15 percent of the 43 square miles had been exploited, a new company called the Disney Development Company had been established with Arvida participation in 1984. Most of the assets of

Arvida were, however, divested in 1987 for approximately $400 million. Neither its culture nor its skills in community development fit well with Disney's other activities. Nevertheless, the Disney Development Company proceeded to aggressively expand its activities. At Walt Disney World, a several-thousand room hotel expansion was underway, including a $375 million convention center and hotel complex, and the company's first moderate-priced hotel. In 1988, Disney purchased the Wrather Corporation, which owned the Disneyland Hotel adjacent to Disneyland. Wrather had not reinvested in the facilities and disgruntled guests blamed Disney. A multimillion dollar renovation was planned.

In addition to hotels, other opportunities under consideration for the Walt Disney World property included time share, commercial, and residential developments. The company was also actively exploring new, experimental retail-entertainment complexes that might be expanded across the country. As part of the Wrather acquisition, Disney had obtained the "Queen Mary" ocean liner and "Spruce Goose" aircraft attractions and valuable waterfront acreage in Long Beach, California, which was under consideration for development.

▲ OTHER ENTERTAINMENT COMPANIES

The 1980s had been a decade of entertainment company mergers and acquisitions. Most of the major movie studios, other than Disney, were owned by large conglomerates (Exhibits 10 and 11). Paramount was owned by Gulf+Western; Universal was owned by MCA; and Warner Brothers by Warner Communications, Inc. Columbia Pictures was acquired by Coca-Cola in 1987 and subsequently merged with TriStar.

Warner Communications

Warner Communications, Inc. (WCI) was engaged primarily in the communications and entertainment business through four operating divisions. *Warner Brothers, Inc.* produced and distributed motion pictures and television programs and also manufactured and distributed videocassettes. Warner Brothers, Inc. shared a production studio in Burbank, California, with Columbia Pictures. In animation, Warner produced "Bugs Bunny," "Daffy Duck," and other "Looney Tunes" cartoon characters for television. Its licensing company licensed all these characters for consumer products. *Warner Brothers Records, Inc.* sold records under a dozen proprietary labels, including Warner Brothers, Atlantic, and Electra/Asylum. It also held and distributed the rights to its music. *Warner Publishing, Inc.* published more than 40 comic magazines, including DC comics and *Mad* magazine, sold books, and distributed magazines and books for other publishers. In 1987, *Warner Cable Corp.* owned and operated 101 cable television systems, serving approximately 1.3 million subscribers. Since 1984, WCI owned 45 percent of BHC, Inc. which operated seven television stations in major U.S. markets. By 1986, all of WCI's divisions achieved record profitability, and it acquired the Cable Value Network, a home shopping service, and 50 percent of Gulf+Western's domestic movie theater operations. It considered the purchase of Lorimar, but broke off negotiations early in 1988.

Gulf+Western

Gulf+Western had been a widely diversified conglomerate, but restructured in 1983. The Gulf+Western that then emerged focused on three industries: financial services (The Associates First Capital Corporation); publishing and information services (Simon & Schuster, Prentice

▲ EXHIBIT 10   Entertainment Company Profiles for 1988

Business	Disney	Warner Communications	Gulf+Western (Paramount)	MCA (Universal)	20th Century Fox	Coca-Cola (Columbia)	MGM/UA
Film production	X	X	X	X	X	X	X
Animation	X	X		X			
Film distribution	X	X	X	X	X	X	X
Home video	X	X	X	X	X	X	
TV production	X	X	X	X	X	X	
Children's TV shows	X	X					
TV syndication	X	X	X	X	X	X	
Cable channel	X	X	X	X			
Cable systems		X					
Theater chain		X	X	X		X	X
TV stations	X	X		X			
TV network					X		
Radio				X			
Licensing	X	X		X		X	
Retail/mail order	X			X			
Publishing	X	X	X	X	X		
Music publishing co.	X	X	X				
Records	X	X		X	X	X	
Theme parks	X			X			
Studio tour	X			X			
Amphitheater/stadium			X	X			
Hotels/resorts	X			X			X
Food and beverage			X	X			
Restaurants			X	X			
Real estate	X			X			

Source: Annual reports and other published information.

	1984	1985	1986	1987
Disney				
Sales ($ billions)	1.6	2.0	2.5	2.9
Net income ($ billions)	.10	.17	.25	.45
Return on equity (%)	9.3	14.6	17.4	21.3
P/E ratio	19	15	20	21
ROA (%)	4	6	8	13
Warner Communications				
Sales ($ billions)	2.0	2.2	2.8	3.4
Net income ($ billions)	.01	.1	.14	.26
Return on equity (%)	3.9	19.3	11.7	18
P/E ratio	NMF	20	25	20
ROA (%)	(neg.)	8.5	5.8	8.4
Gulf+Western				
Sales ($ billions)	2.8	3.3	3.8	4.7
Net income ($ billions)	.14	.15	.27	.36
Return on equity (%)	14.2	14.2	12.0	16.9
P/E ratio	8	9	14	13
ROA (%)	3.3	3.7	5.4	7.2
MCA				
Sales ($ billions)	1.7	2.1	2.4	2.6
Net income ($ billions)	.09	.15	.15	.14
Return on equity (%)	7.8	10.7	9.8	8.5
P/E ratio	21	20	23	26
ROA (%)	4.9	6.7	5.8	6.1

Source: *Value Line* (March 11, 1988) and annual reports.

Hall, Pocket Books); and entertainment (Paramount Pictures, Madison Square Garden, and some theater chains). The Associates provided a broad range of consumer and commercial financial services. Simon & Schuster was the leading publisher of school textbooks and distributed paperback and reference books through Prentice Hall. Paramount Pictures produced and distributed films domestically and internationally through a joint venture with MCA. It also produced programming for television networks, pay cable, and home video, and produced the Miss USA and Miss Universe pageants. It owned a 50 percent interest in two chains of movie theaters (co-owned by Warner Communications) and fully owned a large Canadian chain. Gulf+Western also owned 50 percent of the USA Network cable channel (co-owned by MCA). In 1986, each of the three divisions produced record income and all had been profitable since 1983. Paramount Pictures produced 5 of the industry's 10 top-grossing movies in 1986, achieving a 22 percent market share, and ranked as one of the two leading suppliers of programming for network and first-run syndication television.

MCA

MCA, Inc. was a diversified company engaged in the production and distribution of theatrical, television, and home video productions (Universal Pictures and Television); operation of a tour of its motion picture studio (Universal Studios); licensing and merchandising of film properties; manufacture and distribution of recorded music; book publishing (Berkley, G.P. Putnam, and others); design and marketing of toys (LJN); television broadcasting (RKO General); recreation services; and real estate development. The company also owned half of the Cineplex Odeon theater chain and half of the USA Network. Except for LJN toys, all MCA divisions were profitable in 1986. MCA had recently been the subject of takeover speculation.

▲ CORPORATE FUNCTIONS

During his lifetime, Walt Disney had set the strategic direction of the company and initiated or approved every major new development. His philosophy was to create universal timeless family entertainment. A strong believer in the importance of family life, the company was always oriented to fostering an experience that families could enjoy together. As Walt Disney said: "You're dead if you aim only for kids. Adults are only kids grown up, anyway." A reassuring, optimistic reflection of middle America came through in all his work, confirming a belief that things would always turn out right, no matter what the obstacles. Above all, Disney created a warm, safe, family feeling and parents could vicariously enjoy the pleasure their children took from Disney.

To sustain the company's drive and initiative, Walt Disney was forever innovating and challenging the status quo. The huge number of "firsts" that the company could claim were a tribute to the success of this philosophy, but Disney recognized that they were not without risk.

We cannot hit a home run with the bases loaded every time we go to the plate. We also know the only way we can ever get to first base is by constantly going to bat and continuing to swing.

Disney's absolute faith in whatever he undertook led him to put resources behind a good idea, and to stick with it until it could be realized, regardless of the risk to the company. In fact, the inability to raise external funds in the early days had meant that the future of the company rode on each successive film.

Disney attempted to retain control over the complete entertainment experience. Cartoon characters, unlike actors, could be perfectly controlled to avoid any negative imagery. Disneyland had been constructed so that once inside, visitors could never see anything but Disneyland. The need for control rather than short-term profitability was also the driving force behind Disney's acquisition of so much land in Florida. According to Walt:

The one thing I learned from Disneyland [is] to control the environment. Without that we get blamed for things that someone else does. I feel a responsibility to the public that we must control this so-called world and take the blame for what goes on.

Walt Disney placed great emphasis on employee relations. All new employees—including executives—had to go through a basic Disney training program where the values of the company were explained. Stress was placed on teamwork, communication, and cooperation. Employees of all levels were known by their first names (Walt insisted that everyone call him Walt) and a friendly, informal atmosphere pervaded the whole organization. Many workers were lifelong Disney employees and were ardent believers in the Disney dream.

As the business grew, new subsidiaries and divisions were established to manage new activities. Promotions were mainly from within the company ranks and based on seniority, while the corporate office was expanded to control the various businesses. The Disney management style was codified in a series of personnel handbooks, and Disney University was asked to act as a guardian and purveyor of the corporate culture. Company archives were established to preserve its history. Movies were developed according to "what Walt would have done," and an attempt was made to define a Disney style and preserve the Disney legacy.

When Michael Eisner took over as chairman and CEO in October 1984, he was the first outsider to manage Disney. Initial concerns that he would not understand or maintain Disney's culture and reputation faded rapidly. He explicitly stated his belief in and commitment to Disney as "the provider of unique, premium-quality family fun and entertainment." His desire was to build "one unified company across lines of business and across functional disciplines" which treated the Disney values not only as a legacy of the past, but also as a foundation for the future. Eisner mandated a strong commitment to the Disney culture and supported the significant budget of the Disney University.

Eisner viewed "managing creativity" as Disney's most distinctive corporate skill. His concept for managing the company was to foster a constructive tension between the creative and the financial forces as each business aggressively developed its market position. On the one hand, he encouraged expansive and innovative ideas and was very protective of creative efforts in the concept-generation phase of a project. On the other hand, businesses were expected to deliver against well-defined strategic and financial objectives. All businesses, including individual films and television shows, were expected to have the potential for long-run profitability. Nevertheless, spending would be readily approved if creatively necessary. *Roger Rabbit* was rumored to be costing $40–$50 million by its release date. (It went on to be the highest grossing movie released in 1988.)

Eisner and Wells were forever moving around among the different businesses, trying to generate excitement, suggesting new ideas, and challenging executives to justify plans. For example, they each tried to visit Imagineering (whose basic R&D budget, unattached to any specific project, had been restored) at least once a week in order to keep abreast of developments. Eisner often visited the new Disney Stores, offering suggestions for improvement. Under their direction, Disney became more attuned to the marketplace and more receptive to outside suggestions. Five prestigious architects were hired as consultants to advise on the development of the company's European real estate. "Disney Babies" (created in Brazil) were picked up by the publications division and then turned into a merchandise line of toys.

Disney was credited with being one of the "100 best companies" to work for in the United States. Wages and salaries were set to be competitive in each business segment. For senior management, compensation included a base salary, discretionary bonuses allocated according to individual, business unit, and corporate performance, and stock options. The increase in the Disney stock price had made the latter a substantial part of total compensation.

During the three-day training program at Disney University, which all new Disney executives attended, the history and culture of the company, the legacy of Walt Disney, and the basic corporate strategy were discussed. New employees were even expected to be a character at a theme park for one day so that they could develop a sense of pride in the Disney tradition and feel the responsibility that went with the job of caring for people. While there was no formal personnel program to rotate executives through the various divisions, executives did transfer between businesses at the initiation of senior management. While business unit executives were expected to develop their individual businesses, they were also expected to work cooperatively to create unique and distinctive products, as well as to achieve attractive returns for shareholders.

As the business units expanded aggressively after 1984, overlaps among them began to emerge. Promotional campaigns with major corporate sponsors like McDonald's and Kodak in one business needed to be coordinated with similar initiatives by other Disney businesses. The "Disney Sunday Movie" retained a minute's free advertising on each show to promote Disney in some way—but which division should get it? Like many diversified companies, Disney also employed negotiated internal transfer prices for any activity performed by one division for another. Transfer prices were charged, for example, on the use of any Disney film library material by the various divisions. While Eisner and Wells encouraged division executives to resolve conflicts among themselves, they made it clear that they were available to arbitrate difficult issues. Senior management's position was that disputes should be settled quickly and decisively, so that business unit management could get on with their jobs.

Nevertheless, in 1987, a corporate marketing function was installed to stimulate and coordinate corporatewide marketing activities. A marketing calendar was introduced listing the next six months of planned promotional activities by every U.S. division. A monthly meeting of 20 divisional marketing and promotion executives was initiated to discuss interdivisional issues. A library committee was set up which met quarterly to allocate the Disney film library among the theatrical, video, Disney Channel, and TV syndication groups. An in-house media buying group was also established to coordinate media buying for the entire company.

Management also jointly coordinated important future activities. This approach was first used when formulating plans for Snow White's 50th Anniversary in 1987. A meeting of all divisions generated novel ideas, coordinated schedules, and built commitment and excitement for the year's theme. The ongoing arrangements and follow-up were then coordinated by the five-person Corporate Events department. The same format was followed with Mickey Mouse's 60th birthday in 1988.

FUTURE DIRECTIONS

With a growth objective of 20 percent per year and a strong balance sheet and cash flow, Disney executives were looking to identify and experiment with opportunities for future expansion. While continued growth in the core businesses was planned, both internal development and acquisition in new areas were being examined.

The company's criteria for evaluating new businesses included the attractiveness of the business itself, the fit with Disney, the potential returns, and the potential impact on the Disney name and franchise. In the latter regard, the company actively researched its brand image. Choosing which business to enter or acquire remained a critical task for senior management, aided by the corporate planning department, as it sought to follow up on its recent successes.

THE WALT DISNEY COMPANY (B): SUSTAINING GROWTH

Growth becomes tougher as a company gets larger,
but that's what good management is all about.
                    Gary Wilson, former chief financial officer[1]

I think it would be rather clear to anybody what is compatible
and what isn't compatible to the Disney Co.
                    Michael Eisner, chairman & CEO[2]

After 1988, the Walt Disney Company continued to develop new revenue sources, encouraging innovation and aggressively pursuing opportunities for internal as well as external expansion, in order to meet its 20 percent annual EPS growth target. An important part of that expansion took place overseas. Although the projects in which the company invested reflected the corporate assumption that the entertainment industry was unique in its potential for growth, continuing success challenged leadership to maintain its creativity and control across a range of increasingly diverse ventures (Exhibits 1, 2, 3, and 4). Nevertheless, a key focus was the company's growing commitment to being a provider and distributor of entertainment "software."

Research Assistant Elizabeth Wynne Johnson prepared this case under the supervision of Professor David J. Collis. Copyright © 1994 by the President and Fellows of Harvard College.
[1]Geraldine E. Willigan, "The Value-Adding CFO: An Interview with Disney's Gary Wilson," *Harvard Business Review*, January–February 1990, p. 92.
[2]Interview in *Los Angeles Times*, November 12, 1987.

▲ EXHIBIT 1   The Walt Disney Company Financials, 1988–1993 (in millions)

	1993	1992	1991	1990	1989	1988
Sales	$8,529	$7,504	$6,112	$5,757	$4,594	$3,438
Operating income	1,725	1,435	1,165	1,426	1,229	885
Net income	671*	817	637	824	703	522
Return on sales (%)	7.9	10.9	10.3	14.1	15.3	15.2
Earnings per share	1.23	1.52†	4.78	6.00	5.10	3.80
Total assets	11,751	10,862	9,429	8,022	6,657	5,109
Borrowings	2,386	2,222	2,214	1,585	861	436
Stockholders' equity	5,031	4,705	3,871	3,489	3,044	2,359
Return on equity (%)	13‡	19	17	25	26	25

*Before cumulative effect of accounting changes, but including a $515 million pretax loss from investment in Euro Disney.
†Reflects a four-for-one stock split, effective April 1992.
‡Before cumulative effect of account changes.

Results by Business Segment (in millions)

	1993	1992	1991	1990	1989	1988
Theme parks and resorts						
Revenues	$3,441	$3,307	$2,794	$2,933	$2,595	$2,042
Costs and expenses	2,694	2,663	2,248	2,130	1,810	1,477
Operating income	747	644	547	803	785	565
Filmed entertainment						
Revenues	3,673	3,115	2,594	2,250	1,588	1,149
Costs and expenses	3,051	2,607	2,276	1,937	1,331	963
Operating income	622	508	318	313	257	186
Consumer products						
Revenues	1,415	1,082	724	574	411	247
Costs and expenses	1,060	799	494	351	224	113
Operating income	355	283	230	223	187	134
Total number of Disney stores	239	177	113	69	41	13
Corporate expenses (income)						
General and administrative	164	148	161	139	120	96
Interest expense	158	127	105	43	24	6
Investment and interest income	(186)*	(130)	(119)	(81)	(67)	(59)

*Plus $515 million pretax loss from investment in Euro Disney.

▲ EXHIBIT 2   Walt Disney Company: Revenue by Business Segment, 1988–1993 ($ millions)

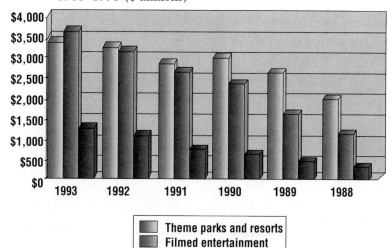

Theme parks and resorts
Filmed entertainment
Consumer products

▲ EXHIBIT 3   What the Walt Disney Company Has and Has Not Done, 1988–1994

Has Done	Has Not Done
Pleasure Island	Third World gate
Typhoon Lagoon	Summer Camp
Animal Kingdom (FL)	Disney Sea (CA)
Euro Disney	Mickey's Kitchen
Hollywood Pictures	CBS
Miramax	Tokyo 2nd gate
Disney Press	Euro Disney 2nd gate
Hyperion	Communication hardware alliance
Hyperion Books for Children	Child care
Disney Adventures magazine	
Family Fun magazine	
Discover magazine	
Childcraft (direct mail)	
Muppet deal	
Hollywood Records	
Disney Vacation Club	
Disney Institute (Celebration)	
Mighty Ducks (Disney Sports Enterprises)	
Corporate Alliances (including Nestle, Coca-Cola, American Express, Delta, and AT&T)	
Disney America	
Beauty and the Beast Broadway production	
New Amsterdam Theater (NY)	
Disney Cruise Line	

▲ EXHIBIT 4   Walt Disney Company Comparative Stock Price Performance, 1988–1993

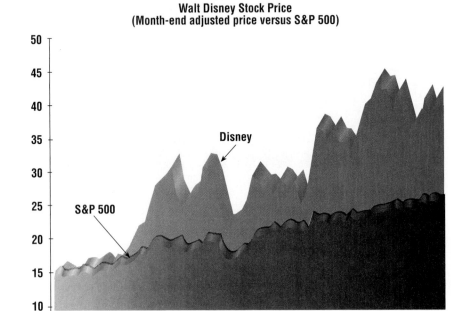

Source: Standard & Poor's, Compustat.

Company chairman and CEO Michael Eisner firmly established himself as keeper of the Disney legacy. He remained faithful to proven Disney ideals of family entertainment, yet identifiable as the driving personality behind the company's continued growth. One observer noted of the company's evolution that "the operative question at Disney no longer seems to be 'What would Walt think?' but 'What does Michael say?'"[3]

▲ THEME PARKS AND RESORTS

The Sun Never Sets on the Disney Empire

Michael Eisner declared 1990 the start of "The Disney Decade": the most accelerated drive toward expansion of theme parks, hotels, and convention space in the company's history. In 1992, on 4,800 acres outside Paris, the company opened Euro Disney, the company's first theme park in Europe (Exhibit 5). In 1993, after considering numerous alternatives for developing new parks, Disney announced its decision to build a park in Virginia based on an American history theme. At each of its existing parks in the United States and Tokyo, Disney added new live shows and Imagineered attractions while stepping up expansion of its hotels and resorts, both to encourage longer stays and to attract major conferences.

---

[3]Richard Sandomir, "Mickey's Man," *Newsday Magazine,* October 21, 1990.

▲ EXHIBIT 5   Geographic Scope of Disney Theme Park Operations in 1993

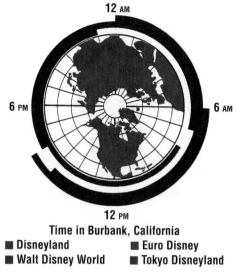

**Throughout the year,
at any given time of day,
a Disney theme park is open.**

12 AM

6 PM   6 AM

12 PM
Time in Burbank, California
■ Disneyland   ■ Euro Disney
■ Walt Disney World   ■ Tokyo Disneyland

Source: The Walt Disney Company.

Euro Disney

Euro Disney was not intended to be a European alternative to the U.S. parks, but rather to develop a market of its own and to build interest in all Disney products. In 1987, international business accounted for 10 percent of Disney's total revenues; by 1992, that figure reached 19 percent.

While Euro Disney was the quintessential Disney theme park, and Disney designed, developed, built, and managed the entire resort, it did not have majority ownership of the business. Fifty-one percent of Euro Disney S.C.A. shares had been sold on several European exchanges, leaving Disney a 49 percent ownership stake. Moreover, although the park cost $4.4 billion to build, infrastructure, attractive financing, and other incentives from the French government, as well as a heavily leveraged financial structure, kept Disney's initial investment cost to $200 million. In return for operating the park, the company would receive 10 percent from ticket sales and 5 percent from merchandise sales, regardless of whether or not the park turned a profit.

The company was adamant about maintaining its adherence to the Disney formula for family recreation, pointing to Tokyo Disneyland as evidence of the formula's universal appeal. Despite important cultural differences, Tokyo Disneyland had defied its critics and performed well, welcoming its 100 millionth guest in 1992. The French were more suspicious, warning of a potential "Cultural Chernobyl,"[4] so Eisner enlisted a former professor of medieval French literature, Robert Fitzpatrick, as the president of Euro Disney to oversee the park's development according to both Disney's specifications and French sensitivities. For

---

[4]*Newsweek,* April 13, 1992. p. 67.

example, Sleeping Beauty's castle became Le Chateau de la Belle au Bois Dormant, to reflect the story's French origin. The project required accommodations on the part of the cast as well as the guests: French cast members were required to submit to the company's insistence on the use of deodorants, for example. Ultimately, Disney gave in on the issue of alcohol in the park, and Euro Disney joined EPCOT Center in making wine available in its restaurants. Overall, Michael Eisner envisioned Euro Disney as a reflection of the dissolution of borders between nations of the European Community. The "cast" at Euro Disney comprised some 85 nationalities and 35 languages, capable of delivering a multinational, multilingual service to the park's guests.

The company had set its attendance target at 11 million visitors in the first year (30,000 visitors each day). Between opening day in April and the end of September 1992, Euro Disney had 7 million visitors. During the summer, attendance was above the projected rate, but the park suffered a downturn as colder weather and rain set in. While Disney had expected that French visitors would account for close to half the market, their attendance fell short of the company's estimates. Foreign visitors to Euro Disney, who came largely from the United Kingdom, Germany, and Italy, were also deterred, as the combination of a weak dollar and high European prices made visits to Disney World more affordable for Europeans than similar trips to Euro Disney.

Although Disney officials publicly emphasized their satisfaction with Euro Disney, the project required considerable fine-tuning. The company lowered prices at its hotels and restaurants in order to make them more affordable, laid off employees, and deferred its management fees for two years. The difficulties resulted in a high-level management shuffle: in September 1992, the company moved Fitzpatrick into the position of chairman, bringing in Philippe Bourguignon, senior vice president of real estate development since 1988, to take over as president. Bourguignon immediately slashed hotel and admission prices and announced plans to cut 950 of 11,100 jobs. He rejected the possibility of closing the park during the winter months. In the meantime, Disney put its plans for expansion, including a studio theme park and water attractions, on hold pending an upturn in the European economy.

In November 1993, Euro Disney S.C.A. announced it had lost in excess of $900 million for the past year and that it would complete a financial restructuring by the spring of 1994. Observers suggested that the involvement of the parent company would be key to sustaining the project financially and to securing the confidence of the banks. One analyst noted the difficulty that Disney would face in allowing the park to go bankrupt: "I'd be amazed if [the company] walked away from such a huge investment. Can they really afford to throw it all away?"[5]

Walt Disney Attractions

Meanwhile, Disney continued aggressive expansion of its U.S. parks. The company had been contemplating two major new projects in California. The first was the proposed development of WESTCOT center, a new $3 billion resort adjacent to Disneyland. The second was Disney Sea, an ocean-themed attraction built around the "Queen Mary" ocean liner and the "Spruce Goose" flying boat. It was to be built on a block of waterfront Long Beach property acquired in a 1988 deal with the Wrather Corporation.

While Disney actively pursued both options, it was generally understood that, ultimately, there would be a choice between the two. The choice would depend on Disney's ability to

---

[5]Richard Cohen, "Euro Disney '93: $900 Million Loss," *The New York Times,* November 11, 1993.

negotiate entitlements and public funding, as well as, the comparative economics of the two projects. An additional concern was the demand on the Imagineers,[6] who were on the verge of being overextended by the call for additions to the existing parks, despite their having increased in number to 2,500 from 400 in 1984. Finally, Disney's Long Beach plans, relying heavily on creating 250 acres of landfill, were subject to the purview of 23 regulatory agencies. Company officials estimated that meeting the regulatory clearances could cost as much as $70 million. The result, after two years of efforts to get past Long Beach regulatory delays, was a corporate decision to abandon the Disney Sea project.

Disney instead decided to focus on WESTCOT, with tentative plans to begin in 1994. The idea was to attract guests for extended vacations at Disneyland, making it a "destination resort" similar to Florida's Disney World. Deteriorating conditions and a lack of public improvements surrounding Disneyland in Anaheim made Disney anxious to get WESTCOT development underway.

The company did not, however, abandon consideration of other theme park locations. Disney had long planned to build a second theme park at Tokyo Disneyland, but its Japanese partner, the Oriental Land Company, had rejected a proposal to build a studio theme park like the MGM Studios in Florida. They were, however, receptive to reviving the Disney Sea project on the waterfront adjacent to Tokyo Disneyland. In addition, the possibility of building a new park elsewhere in the Far East remained under consideration.

In 1993, Disney unveiled its plan for "Disney America," a new theme park and resort with a focus on American history, 30 miles from Washington, D.C., in Virginia. The new park, expected to cost more than $1 billion, was slated to open in 1998. Disney planned to minimize competition with Disney World in Florida by cultivating day-trip visitors and designing the park around American history and culture, in place of the usual cast of Disney characters. As for the subject matter, Disney expressed an intention to present realistic portrayals of American history, including what Eisner described as "painful, disturbing, and agonizing" exhibits on slavery, Native Americans, and the Vietnam War.[7] Virginia's governor pledged his support, and Disney promised to include greenbelts and open spaces to appease concerned neighbors.

Competitors

Behind Disney's principal competitors in the theme park business were some of its most powerful competitors in the entertainment business (Exhibit 6). In 1991, Time-Warner secured 50 percent ownership of Six Flags. Paramount owned five regional theme parks. And MCA, owner of the Universal Studios theme parks in Hollywood, California, and Orlando, Florida, was acquired by Matsushita Electric Industrial Co., Ltd.

In addition to the amusement parks, Paramount's holdings included two professional sports franchises, the New York Knicks (basketball) and the New York Rangers (ice hockey), as well as Madison Square Garden, basic cable networks, and seven TV stations. The company's sales in 1993 were $4 billion. Paramount was acquired by Viacom in 1994, and the two were soon expected to be joined by Blockbuster. Together, sales would reach $12 billion, and assets of $24 billion would include the theme parks, TV, video, cable, films, publishing, and sports.

---

[6]Disney's creative team of engineers who developed ideas and saw them through to construction.
[7]Michelle Singletary and Spencer Hsu, "Disney Says Va. Park Will Be Serious Fun," *The Washington Post,* November 12, 1993.

▲ **EXHIBIT 6** **Entertainment Operations and Assets of Selected Movie and TV Companies in 1994**

	Disney	Matsushita	Paramount (Viacom)	Time-Warner
Movies	X	X	X	X
Library	X	X	X	X
Movie theaters		X	X	X
TV shows	X	X	X	X
TV stations	X			
TV network				
Basic cable		X	X	X
Pay cable	X			X
Cable systems			X	X
Recorded music	X	X		X
Theme parks	X	X	X	X
Sports	X		X	
Publishing	X	X	X	X
Audio players		X		
Video players		X		

Source: Adapted from Standard & Poor's Industry Surveys, *Basic Analysis: Leisure Time* 11 (March 1993).

In 1993, MCA announced plans for a multibillion dollar expansion of its Florida theme park. First opened in 1990, the Florida Universal Studios park was already the third most-visited park in the United States, and fifth in the world. The new "Universal City" would include a second theme park, nighttime entertainment, hotels, and conference facilities. The proposal, a joint venture agreement with Rank Organization PLC, was slated to begin in 1995 and expected to take 10 years to complete. In addition, in January 1994, the company announced that it would open a third Universal Studios theme park in Osaka, Japan, in 1998.

Hotels and Resorts

> *Since we're building more places for people to play, we need more places*
> *for them to stay.*
> *Richard Nunis, president of Walt Disney Attractions[8]*

From 1988, the company's hotel and resorts grew in importance, accounting for one-third of the revenues from the company's Theme Parks and Resorts segment by 1992. Despite general overcapacity in the hospitality industry, the accelerated pace of the Disney Decade spawned an increase in the number of Disney's hotel rooms, from just under 5,000

---

[8]*Annual Report,* 1989, p. 10

in 1988 to over 11,000 in 1993. Nonetheless, at Disney World, Disney only had 15–20 percent of the hotel rooms in the Orlando area, and utilization remained above 80 percent. Emphasis shifted to include construction of more moderately priced hotels, such as the All-Star Music Resort at Disney World, due to open in 1994. With rooms for about $55 per night, it would be Disney's most affordable hotel to date.

During one of his visits to Disney World in the mid-1980s, Eisner was struck by the realization that the complex offered no options for the after-hours crowd. Work began shortly thereafter on the development of an adult-oriented entertainment area. "Pleasure Island" opened in 1989: a six-acre nightlife haven featuring dance clubs, shopping boutiques, and restaurants.

Initially billed as a new family attraction, early performance was below par. The park's general manager Art Levitt felt the park was losing money because it was "just another attraction." Within a year, Disney officially made it an adults-only theme park. Still, the company encountered problems with a number of original ideas. Among the challenges Disney faced were a roller-skating disco that turned out to be dangerous, and a pricing policy of a separate charge for each club that encouraged guests to come to only one club and stay there, leaving other clubs and the streets they had hoped would be teeming with activity empty.

Under Levitt's direction, the park tightened its focus. He got rid of the less successful clubs and replaced them with new ones, and established a single adult-rate admission charge for the entire area. In the evening, the family atmosphere dissipated and the streets held a nightly "New Year's Eve" outdoor celebration. Levitt gave managers monthly "in-costume" duties to keep them in closer touch with guests and more responsive to employees. Managers' experiences in the program were the basis for a variety of improvements in operations: additional food and beverage stations appeared and layout was rearranged to suit waiters', and waitresses' elaborate traffic patterns in the busy clubs. Disney advertised heavily in the local media, cultivating the more than a third of guests who came for a night out from the surrounding Orlando area.

In addition to the creation of Pleasure Island and a new water-based attraction, "Typhoon Lagoon," Disney World grew with the construction of Splash Mountain and the expansion of the Disney–MGM Studios theme park. In California, Disneyland got a new "land" based on the *Roger Rabbit* movie: "Toontown" offered a life-sized cartoon atmosphere, complete with talking manhole covers and dancing dishes. In total the company spent over $1 billion on theme park expansion from 1988 to 1994.

Disney Vacation Club

Disney entered the time-share business in 1991 with its "Disney Vacation Club" in the Lake Buena Vista Resort adjacent to Disney World. The time-share vacation concept, involving the purchase of the right to a specific apartment for a fixed period each year, appealed to regular vacationers. Over the latter half of the 1980s, the time-share business grew into a $400 million annual industry in Central Florida, following entry by high-profile companies like Marriott, Hilton, and ITT Corp. Nevertheless, the industry had acquired a mixed reputation, marred by unethical practices, fraudulent tactics, and unreliable developers.

Disney carefully kept the words "time share" out of its promotional literature, having committed itself to what it considered an original approach to the business.[9] Rather than purchasing rights to a specific apartment, buyers purchased points, which they then used as they pleased: "buying" fewer days in a large family-size apartment or a longer stay in a smaller unit.

---

[9]*Orlando Sentinel,* October 13, 1993, front page, Business.

Although members had a vote in how things were run, as a practical matter, Disney retained management control. Using low-key marketing designed to keep itself above the time-share fray, the Disney Vacation Club signed up more than 7,500 members by 1993. That year, Disney announced plans to build an oceanfront resort at Vero Beach, Florida, its first resort outside a theme park, and pledged to continue building additional time-share sites.

Celebration

In 1991, Eisner announced his plan for the ultimate realization of Walt Disney's dream to create an experimental community. "Celebration" would be a 5,200-acre city just south of Disney World, built over 20 to 25 years, beginning with the construction of family housing and The Workplace, a 3.5 million-square-foot industry showcase where visitors could observe a product being made. The plan also included a proposed "Disney Institute," an educational center where creative minds could come together in adult seminars to share ideas in a campus-like setting. Among the courses to be offered: animation, landscape design, and culinary arts.

Disney negotiated an innovative deal with state environmental officials in order to secure the wetlands permit it needed to begin construction. Disney would compensate for the lost wetlands by purchasing and paying for the restoration and preservation of an environmental haven not far from the site. The deal was one of the most complicated in state history, and the first whereby the state issued a long-term permit for a private development project.

Disney Cruise

Disney's 10-year agreement with Premier Cruise Lines, which gave Premier the right to use Disney characters aboard its ships, expired in March 1994. That year, Disney entered the cruise business as a principal. The family-oriented "Disney Cruise Line" featuring two Disney-designed ships would package 3–4 day cruises with stays at Walt Disney World.

Sports

In line with its commitment to active entertainment, in 1993 the company announced plans for a 100-acre sports complex at Disney World. The president of Walt Disney Attractions linked the decision to Disney's existing sports-friendly resources: "We already have the weather, land, and hotel rooms to host and stage international events. What we're missing . . . are a few key sports facilities."[10] Another Disney executive noted the company's intention to use sports as a means to generating higher attendance and longer stays at its parks.

"Ducks with Pucks"?[11] The stadium move followed Disney's 1992 purchase of an NHL expansion team based in Orange County, California, a few miles from Disneyland in Anaheim. During the 1980s, while other sports soared in popularity among television viewers, professional ice hockey failed to attract a national audience, partly because of the game's often violent nature. Nevertheless, in 1992, the NHL had signed a five-year deal that would

---

[10]Thomas R. King, "Walt Disney World to Build Complex, Stadium to Showcase Amateur Sports," *The Wall Street Journal,* November 22, 1993.
[11]*Business Week,* October 18, 1993.

ensure the network television broadcast of 25 regular season and 37 Stanley Cup games. The league also sought expansion into regions beyond the north-central and northeast quadrants by adding five new franchise teams, including Disney's.

Disney's $50 million purchase decision[12] came at a time when the local city council was still considering the company's $3 billion proposal to build WESTCOT. The expansion would depend on improvements to the area's infrastructure, improvements that could only be funded with major contributions from local government. Nonetheless, Eisner explained the decision to buy the team in terms of the company's overall strategy: "This wasn't done to solve a problem. This was done because this is our home. They have this [arena] you can see from the top of the Matterhorn. To me, it's synergistic."[13]

Inspired by the box office popularity of the movie by the same name, Eisner announced plans to call the team "The Mighty Ducks" after the Disney movie which had taken in $50 million from family-moviegoers. Shortly thereafter came the sequel, *D2: The Champions,* featuring music by Queen, produced by Disney's new Hollywood Records label.

The Mighty Ducks had a natural partner in Disney-owned KCAL-TV, following a trend among media companies toward purchasing sports teams as a source of programming. Nor did the Ducks' prospects end with traditional sports marketing, given the potential for other cross-marketing opportunities. In 1993, 80 percent of the money spent on NHL merchandise went for Duckwear. As one Disney executive noted, the Ducks "opened our eyes to sports as software."

▲ WALT DISNEY STUDIOS

After many years I have learned there is nothing that we absolutely must have. No movie. No property. No project. No deal. What that means is that we go into virtually every negotiation prepared to lose it . . . . We are always prepared to walk away.

Jeffrey Katzenberg[14]

In 1988, the Walt Disney Studios film division had a 19 percent share of the total box office (Exhibit 7). Disney then settled into the role of a market share leader, turning out an increasing number of successful films, including *Beaches* and *Dead Poets' Society,* while maintaining rigid cost-controls in an industry otherwise known for skyrocketing budgets and fiercely independent talent. While the film division grew to comprise three separate studios, Disney, Touchstone, and Hollywood Pictures, output of animated and live-action features under the Disney name continued to account for over half of the studios' revenues and a larger share of its operating income. In addition, Disney distributed films under its Buena Vista International distribution title, garnering profits from an increasing number of studio labels.

Chairman Jeffrey Katzenberg and president Richard Frank held production costs below the industry average, bound by Eisner's insistence that creativity should compensate for dollars, not the other way around. When costs went out of control, as they did in the making of *Dick Tracy,* or actors indulged their temperaments on the set, leadership clamped down. In 1991, the studio suffered a downturn in the cycle, releasing several disappointing live-action

---

[12]Due to the small size of the expense, Eisner was able to bypass the company's board of directors entirely in making the decision to purchase the hockey team.
[13]Maria Cone and Kathryn Harris, "Disney Wins OK to Form Hockey Team in Anaheim," *Los Angeles Times,* December 11, 1992.
[14]Paul Richter, "Disney's Tough Tactics," *Los Angeles Times,* July 8, 1990.

▲ EXHIBIT 7   Film Industry Market Share History, 1988–1993

	Percentage Share of Box Office *(number of films released)*					
	1993	1992	1991	1990	1989	1988
Disney (Buena Vista)	16.3 *(36)*	19.4 *(27)*	13.7 *(23)*	15.5 *(19)*	16.0 *(18)*	19.4 *(18)*
Warner Bros.	18.5 *(37)*	19.8 *(28)*	13.9 *(28)*	13.1 *(26)*	17.4 *(30)*	11.2 *(31)*
20th Century Fox	10.7 *(21)*	14.2 *(24)*	11.6 *(20)*	13.1 *(20)*	6.5 *(17)*	11.6 *(14)*
Columbia	11.2 *(26)*	12.5 *(19)*	9.1 *(14)*	4.9 *(15)*	8.0 *(25)*	3.5 *(19)*
Universal	13.9 *(22)*	11.7 *(22)*	11.0 *(23)*	13.1 *(21)*	16.6 *(19)*	9.8 *(20)*
Paramount	9.3 *(15)*	9.9 *(20)*	12.0 *(21)*	14.9 *(17)*	13.8 *(14)*	15.2 *(19)*
TriStar	6.3 *(13)*	6.6 *(11)*	10.9 *(13)*	9.0 *(19)*	8.0 *(17)*	5.8 *(17)*
New Line	3.4 *(13)*	2.1 *(15)*	4.0 *(18)*	4.4 *(14)*	NA	NA
MGM	1.8 *(12)*	1.2 *(9)*	2.3 *(16)*	2.8 *(15)*	6.3 *(26)*	10.3 *(21)*
Miramax	2.9 *(24)*	1.1 *(20)*	1.4 *(20)*	1.2 *(16)*	NA	NA

Source: *Variety.*

features: *V.I. Warshawski* and the $50 million *Billy Bathgate* among them. That year, Katzenberg penned a 28-page memo urging a return to the company's proven low-cost formula for its live-action films. Discipline prevailed: in 1992, Disney Studios had a net profit margin of 10.9 percent, nearly five times the industry median.[15] In 1993, Disney's profit margin fell to 7.9 percent, but remained well ahead of second-ranked Paramount, with its 4.9 percent margin.

A substantial part of Disney's success came from its quality animated feature films. In the 1980s, vice chairman Roy E. Disney, son of co-founder Roy O. Disney, committed the company to sustaining its emphasis on feature animation. As Michael Eisner remarked, "Roy understood that animation, done right, was magic. And magic is the essence of Disney." The release of *Little Mermaid* in 1990 met the studio's goal of one new animated film per year. It was followed by *Beauty and the Beast* (1991), which became the first animated film ever nominated for an Oscar for Best Picture, and by *Aladdin* (1992). Disney's next three planned animated features would venture away from the classic styles and storylines of their last three hits. *Nightmare before Christmas* was an offbeat Christmas story done with a stop-action "claymation" technique. It would be followed by *The Lion King* (1994) and *Pocahontas* (1995).

In live-action, having once felt the need to apologize publicly for the partial nudity in *Splash,* Disney settled comfortably into the industry mainstream, releasing films like *Pretty Woman* and *Hand That Rocks the Cradle* through its Touchstone studio. Hollywood Pictures was then established in 1990 as the third studio under the Disney umbrella. The new studio enabled Disney to increase its volume of movie output from 8 new films a year in 1988, the most in Disney's history, to an ambitious 50–60 new films in 1994. Since 1989, fewer than half of the Disney's films grossed more than $20 million, and many earned less than half that amount.

---

[15]Elizabeth Comte, "Entertainment and Information," *Forbes,* January 4, 1993, p. 143.

In 1993, Disney acquired Miramax, a small independent production studio making low-budget "art films." Observers called it an unlikely union between a "go by the book" entertainment company and a "shoot from the hip" independent studio headed by Harvey Weinstein.[16] Disney purchased the studio, responsible for the surprise hit *The Crying Game* and other niche-market films, for approximately $65 million. Although the deal reportedly would allow Miramax to retain its autonomy in marketing and advertising, insiders questioned how far Jeffrey Katzenberg would go in not exerting control over the studio's activities. Katzenberg indeed loosened his grip, saying, "I have too many things to accomplish to be involved in every little project."[17] As a safety net, however, Miramax budgets were capped at $12 million; any additional money would have to come from outside investors, while Disney retained the theatrical, video, and other U.S. rights on their films, which included hits like *The Piano*.

Disney continued to finance its film output through limited partnerships that traded a degree of margin for greater earnings stability. Three new partnerships in 1990, one with Touchwood Pacific Partners I for $600 million, would finance film production over several years. When the supply of Japanese capital for the partnerships began to dissipate as the "bubble economy" burst, Disney turned to a $400-million Eurobond offering to finance studio activities.

In 1990, overseas returns made Buena Vista International the number one studio outside the United States, bringing in $500 million from foreign box offices. In 1991, another year of overseas growth led Disney to announce plans to handle its own distribution needs beginning in 1993, replacing Warner Brothers. In addition to reducing costs, the studio viewed development of its own distribution capabilities as a way to further expand its distribution of non-Disney films.

Home Video

As the home video rental and sales industry grew, Disney ranked number one in domestic home video market share every year from 1988 to 1992.

Buena Vista Home Video (BVHV) pioneered the "sell through" approach to marketing videos at low prices (under $30) to the consumer. At 30 million copies, *Aladdin* became the best selling video of all time (followed by Disney's *Beauty and the Beast*) in 1993. Even *Dick Tracy*, which had fallen short of expectations at the box office, sold a record 480,000 units in video rental sales. BVHV broadened the variety of videos it marketed to include music videos, such as *Elvis: The Great Performances*, and *Rocky and Bullwinkle*. BVHV achieved the same market leadership role overseas, with marketing and distribution in all major foreign markets.

Disney also shortened the length of its video rerelease cycle from seven to five years. The success of video marketing techniques gave rise to industry speculation that Disney could be on the verge of cannibalizing itself at the box office. *Pinocchio* was the first animated classic to appear on rerelease at the box office after being available through the video stores. Box office attendance was down, causing some to believe that video availability was harming the market, even for the youngest customers.

[16]Kathy Tyrer, "Disney, Miramax: Odd Couple of Movie Making, Marketing," *Adweek,* May 10, 1993, p. 2.
[17]Ronald Grover, "Jeffrey Katzenberg: No More Mr. Tough Guy?" *Business Week,* January 31, 1994, p. 78

Network Television and Syndication

In the late 1980s, Disney's television studios continued to generate mixed results, with shows like "Carol & Company" (starring Carol Burnett) earning disappointing ratings. In the early 1990s, however, Disney began improving its performance in television. New shows, such as the highly rated "Nurses" and the number one show "Home Improvement," became major hits. In the fall season of 1992, Disney led the industry with the most network situation comedies from any single provider, as well as the most Saturday morning children's programming, including animated programs like "The Little Mermaid," which earned praise for its animation quality.

In domestic syndication, Disney's Buena Vista Television bolstered its position with "The Disney Afternoon," a two-hour block of animated cartoons boasting four of the six top-rated animated shows on syndicated television. The company was also eagerly looking ahead to syndication runs of popular network hits, including "Dinosaurs," that featured characters from Jim Henson Productions, and "Home Improvement."

Disney also expanded its international television production and distribution capabilities. "Disney Club" programs and other Disney-branded shows were produced in 32 countries under Disney's approval. In addition to expanding its western European presence, taking a 25 percent interest in British GMTV, the company signed a 10-year agreement in 1992 to air up to six hours of Disney programming per week in Russia. At latest count, Disney programs could be seen by more than 150 million viewers worldwide, including Poland, the Czech Republic, and Bulgaria.

Cable Television

By 1993, cable access had reached 90 percent of American homes. While the growth rate was slowing, the percentage of TV households subscribing to cable had reached over 61 percent.

By 1992, the Disney Channel had increased its subscriber base to nearly seven million viewers, despite an overall decline in the pay television industry. The company attributed the channel's ability to gain viewers to its blend of programming that appealed directly to the parents as well as children. The channel offered "Jim Henson's Mother Goose" alongside adult-oriented specials like "Paul McCartney: Comin' Home."

Technological advances, still on the horizon in the early 1990s, promised to expand the power of the cable industry. The cable television industry was America's sole operator of a ubiquitous local broadband network. Important developments in optical fiber and video compression technology would greatly increase the capacity of the cable network within the coming decade. Analysts predicted that such profound changes in the capability of cable technology would result in greater returns from existing cable customers and the opportunity to create new business opportunities with new customers.[18]

Broadcasting

In 1989, Disney gave its Los Angeles independent television station, acquired in 1988 for $320 million when it was the area's lowest-rated station, a new format with a unique all-news

---

[18]Barry A. Kaplan, "The Distribution System: Cable Television," from *Communicopia: The Digital Communication Bounty* (Goldman Sachs Investment Research), July 1992, p. 9.

prime-time schedule, and a new identity as KCAL-TV. Its three-hour nightly news format, including the only local broadcast in the L.A.–Orange County market to take a national and international focus, attracted viewers seeking information on the crisis in Kuwait. KCAL-TV also aired the highly rated "Disney Afternoon" and popular syndicated shows like "Live with Regis and Kathie Lee," and it became the exclusive local station for the L.A. Lakers basketball team. In 1991, the station secured the rights to broadcast the L.A. Raiders preseason football games. With Disney's purchase of a National Hockey League franchise, the company gained an additional source of sports programming. By 1992, KCAL-TV was the number two station in the daytime market in L.A., second only to the local ABC-TV network affiliate. The station's prime-time ratings had grown 67 percent since 1989. In 1992, the station began producing local Orange County news updates for CNN, giving KCAL-TV access to 350,000 cable subscribers.

Rumors regularly surfaced that Disney might be in the market to buy a television network. Frequently mentioned as potential targets were NBC, owned by General Electric, and CBS, owned by the Tisch family. Television networks were finding their value in increasing jeopardy, as programming giants became ever more powerful while the networks operated under the constraint of the FCC's Financial Interest and Syndication ("Fin-Syn") rules, which barred them from owning the companies that made and syndicated TV programs. If Disney bought CBS, it would give CBS a valuable source of programming at the same time that it gave Disney ownership of the one distribution channel it was lacking. In 1993, the FCC changed its Fin-Syn rules to allow the networks to have financial equity in 100 percent of the programs they aired, but networks still would not be allowed to syndicate for two years; at the time, the FCC promised that it would reconsider this relaxation of the Fin-Syn rules in the coming years.

Disney Live: On Broadway

I'll be shocked and disappointed if I'm wrong, but I've been wrong before.
Michael Eisner[19]

Late in 1993, Disney unveiled its first Broadway-bound theater production: a staged version of *Beauty and the Beast*. The $10 million show was a hit during its Houston tryout run, and advance ticket sales for the New York debut were strong.

The young director of *Beauty and the Beast*, Jess Roth, age 31, and its choreographer and scenic designer all had agreed to compensation agreements that lacked the potentially lucrative profit-sharing usually associated with a big-budget musical; but all three deemed the experience of working for Disney on a project of this magnitude well worth the financial sacrifice. For Disney's part, if the show proved successful, the company would quickly recoup its estimated $400,000-per-week operating costs. Although notoriously risky, Broadway hits could earn up to $150–200 million in profits. Eisner and Katzenberg were directly involved in the production's development, offering creative guidance, calling for rewrites, and restaging scenes.[20]

In 1994, Disney made a $29 million deal to restore the New Amsterdam Theater on West 42nd Street, giving a substantial boost to the city's beleaguered efforts to reinvigorate the district and giving Disney a permanent home on Broadway. Eisner and Katzenberg commit-

[19]Thomas R. King, "Disney Bets Broadway Beast Is Golden Boy," *The Wall Street Journal,* February 24, 1994, B1.
[20]Ibid

ted to making theater production a long-term stand-alone business. Said Eisner: "Our plans for the New Amsterdam Theater mark our expanding commitment to live entertainment."[21]

▲ CONSUMER PRODUCTS

Our newest customers are born every minute.
Donna Moore, president of Disney Stores

Disney achieved consistent yearly growth in its consumer products division. Promotional efforts hinged on the relationship between the company's theme parks, television, and film releases, while the range of products grew to include store merchandise and book, magazine, and record publishing (Exhibit 8). Disney also established channels of distribution through direct-mail and catalog marketing.

"A Slice of Disney Magic in Every Community"

Disney Stores, first launched in 1987, pioneered the "retail-as-entertainment" concept. The stores consistently generated sales per square foot at twice the average rate for retail. By the end of fiscal year 1993, the number of Disney Stores had grown to more than 200 worldwide, including 3 in Canada, 18 in Europe, and 1 in Japan. The company planned to open 100 more in 1994. The stores were designed to evoke a sense of having stepped onto a Disney soundstage. Customers ("guests") entered through a storefront shaped like a giant reel of film. The stores' merchandise mix included toys and apparel as well as high-end collectors' items aimed at Disney's most grown-up fans, but children were the target consumers.

Disney's success prompted others to enter the themed-store business. By 1994, Time-Warner had opened over 50 Warner Bros. stores. However, although observers regularly spoke of competition among the growing number of themed entertainment stores, Warner Bros.' products were meant to appeal to an adult crowd. Meanwhile, Turner Broadcasting Systems, Inc. opened two stores, featuring merchandise based on MGM and RKO classics like *Gone with the Wind* and the *Wizard of Oz*.

▲ EXHIBIT 8   Consumer Products Revenue Mix, 1988 versus 1992

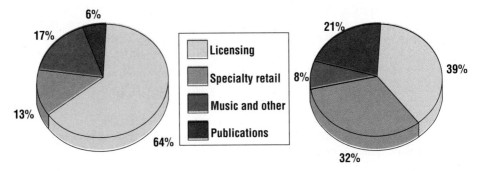

Source: 1992 *Annual Report.*

---

[21]Jeremy Gerard, "Disney's New Dream: 42nd Street Fantasia," *Variety,* February 7–13, 1994, p. 57.

A Mouse in the Kitchen

During one of his many visits to Disney Store locations across the country, Eisner decided that the company needed new ways to draw attention to the expanding Disney presence outside of its theme parks. Recalling discussions within the company regarding entry into the fast-food business, former CFO Gary Wilson said, "[Eisner] felt very strongly. Finally we just said, 'What's wrong with spending $1 million on an Eisner idea?' At least he wasn't spending $100 million."[22]

In 1990, Disney launched Mickey's Kitchen: a fast-food restaurant serving healthy, child-oriented fare such as the meatless Mickey Burger and Jumbo Dumbo Burgers. The first, in California, and the second, in a suburb of Chicago, were opened adjacent to existing Disney Stores with the intention of increasing foot traffic through the stores. Customers dined at tables strategically placed to offer a full view of the colorful merchandise below.

In March 1992, Disney ceased operation at both locations, citing oversaturation of the fast-food business and insurmountable competition from McDonald's. The company had found it could not generate the throughput needed to offer the Disney experience at fast-food prices. Steve Burke, executive vice president of Disney Specialty Retail, explained the closures in terms of strategic priorities:

> We will continue to test new concepts in the Disney Store, but as much as we like Mickey's Kitchen, results to date do not warrant shifting our attention from the larger opportunities we see in retail.

The Muppet Deal

In 1989, Disney entered into a tentative agreement to purchase Jim Henson's Muppet Workshop. For $150–$200 million, Disney was to get the Henson film library and a merchandising agreement, including the Kermit and Miss Piggy characters, both considered appropriate tools for targeting the market of children under three years of age. Jim Henson died not long after the initial agreement was reached, and, in the discord that ensued between Disney and Henson's heirs, the deal collapsed. Nonetheless, Disney in the meantime opened a 3-D Muppet film attraction at Walt Disney World. Despite difficulties relating to the attempted transaction, Disney executives stressed the success of the relationship at the operational level, which included video distribution and the making of a new Muppet movie.

Publishing

Historically, Disney had licensed books and magazines both in the United States and abroad, generating almost $1 billion in retail sales. Having identified publishing as a growth area for the 1990s, Disney began a corporate push that resulted in the creation of three trade publishing units, alongside its existing direct-mail and licensing activities.

Books   In 1990, Disney established the Disney Press, which specialized in children's books featuring Disney characters and partially replaced the previous licensing agreements. In 1991, the company also launched Hyperion Books, an adult trade publishing

---

[22]"Mickey's Man," *Newsday,* October 21, 1990, p. 7.

label. Disney opted to enter the adult publishing market by starting its own operation rather than by acquisition, offsetting newness by assembling a highly experienced staff. The imprint began with no backlist of titles from which to draw. Disney adopted a long-term growth perspective, not expecting its new label to break even for three to five years. Its goal was to grow rapidly by building an eclectic list of titles, avoiding specialization in any one subject. Hyperion published 43 books in 1992, including such titles as *United We Stand*, by H. Ross Perot, and *Hamburger Heaven*, and planned to publish 96 in 1993. Hyperion Books for Children offered titles targeted at children from preschool to young adult, which company officials hoped would be welcomed by the network of outlets already offering Disney Press titles.

Magazines   In 1991, Disney purchased the troubled science-oriented magazine *Discover* for a price in the $7–10 million range. The magazine had been second in the science magazine business behind *Popular Science,* and had been struggling for viability since 1987. It was relaunched after a brief absence from the newsstands. The company publicized its new-improved product on the Disney Channel by running a half-hour program, "*Discover's* 10 Great Unanswered Questions of Science." According to Consumer Products division president Barton K. Boyd, the acquisition fit comfortably in the Disney mix: "*Discover* offers us a variety of excellent opportunities, including international and children's editions, trade and direct response publishing, Disney Channel programming, and exhibits at Disneyland and Walt Disney World."

In 1992, Disney acquired *Family Fun* magazine from its founder Jake Winebaum, a 32-year-old father who got the idea when he noticed that everyone he knew seemed to be having children.[23] The magazine targeted parents of 3- to 12-year-old children, focusing on ideas for family entertainment. Disney's new publication could accommodate joint advertising deals, selling space in both *Family Fun* and *Disney Adventures,* an internally created magazine targeted at children themselves.

While the company's objectives for growth allowed for the possible creation of more niche kids' magazines, Disney did not plan to challenge the giants of the publishing industry. The primary focus would be on building up existing magazines. An executive downplayed the relationship between Disney's vast cross-marketing resources and his work in publishing: "So many people make the mistake of thinking that we're hooked into a deep-pockets situation. Well, there may be deep pockets, but that doesn't mean they're not sewed pretty tight."[24]

▲ HOLLYWOOD RECORDS

Mainstream popular music had represented a rare gap in Disney's entertainment offerings. In the 1980s, industry consolidation had driven the number of competing labels in the $7 billion business down from 30 to only 5 major companies. This consolidation raised the price of acquiring an existing label beyond the acceptable range for Disney; Eisner stated, "I don't believe in acquiring things that are overpriced."[25] But starting his own for less than

---

[23]Dierdre Carmody, "It's His Baby: Publisher Thrives on Family Fun," *New York Times,* February 17, 1992, p. C-4.
[24]"Disney's Skipper Gets His (Donald) Ducks in a Row," *Folio's Publishing News,* July 15, 1992, p. 25.
[25]Richard Turner, "Walt Disney Plans to Launch Record Division," *The Wall Street Journal,* November 19, 1989.

$20 million, the mere cost of making a single Hollywood movie, made sense. In 1989, Disney launched Hollywood Records and named former entertainment lawyer Peter Paterno president.

Unlike Walt Disney Records, which was part of the company's consumer products division, Hollywood Records operated separately under Paterno, who would report directly to Michael Eisner. Hollywood Records plunged into the contemporary music scene, signing bands like WWIII (which featured bondage in its videos) and Roseanne. Paterno quickly bought the rights to the 1970s classic rock band Queen. By the end of 1990, 12 artists had signed contracts with the new label, and Disney had launched a related label, Hollywood BASIC, to specialize in rap.

Although Hollywood Records' 1992 revenues increased threefold over the previous year's, it was largely due to the success of "Classic Queen" and "Queen/Greatest Hits." In 1993, the label failed to produce a release capable of matching the success of the Queen catalog. Steady operating losses led to Paterno's departure in 1993. Although Eisner pledged his continuing support to the label, as of February 1994, Paterno's old position remained open.

▲ CORPORATE

Corporate Imagineer

> *I don't walk past people I don't know and say, "Why didn't you cement over that carpet?" because the next thing you know, it's cemented over. So I have to be very careful about what I throw out and say, because they'll listen to me.*
>
> Michael Eisner. [26]

By 1994, running The Walt Disney Company involved complex issues of management and coordination. Eisner presided over an empire in which decisions had to be made on entertainment questions ranging from scripts to snacks to goal-scoring capability.

Disney's corporate headquarters were located on a 44-acre lot in Burbank, California, and comprised five soundstages and 12 separate facilities. The corporate office, built in 1986 for $75 million, was adorned with massive columns in the shape of the seven dwarfs. In 1991, the company unveiled plans for a significant expansion, deemed necessary in order to accommodate the increasing volume of films and to coordinate the creative activities of a growing staff. In addition to the studio expansion, the plan also called for a new administration building, a Hyperion building, and a technical building. The plans traced back to the company's fundamental source of corporate wisdom: "We want to get back to Walt's original vision of employees working together as a team."

Corporate Control and Management   The company had centralized strategic, financial, and legal functions as well as a small "brand management" function; operations were decentralized. Disney maintained a relatively flat organization structure, with the presidents of Theme Parks and Resorts, Walt Disney Studios, Consumer Products, and Hollywood Records reporting directly to Michael Eisner; other top business managers reported to their respective division presidents.

---

[26]*Newsday*, October 21, 1990.

The decentralized approach to management was controlled in a number of ways: both Eisner and Disney president Frank G. Wells were aggressive "hands-on" managers, frequently visiting and keeping a close eye on the company's diverse businesses; while a Corporate Strategic Planning Department worked closely with Eisner, Wells, division executives, and staff to identify and develop growth opportunities.

Certain key objectives, dictated in broad strokes at the corporate level, established the framework within which new and existing businesses would be considered. The stated objective was to be the top entertainment company in the world by providing entertainment suitable for the whole family. Moreover, the commitment to being a provider of software to the industry was rooted in the company's underlying philosophy: belief in talent and creativity. Beyond those broad outlines, each new business or growth opportunity was considered on an individual basis.

Corporate Alliances   Alliances with major companies were handled exclusively at the corporate level. In recent years, Disney had increased its number of comprehensive agreements; as one executive noted, "[W]e've tried to work with fewer companies of higher quality and have more far-reaching agreements with them . . . . We always go for leaders in their category."[27]

For example, in 1992, Disney expanded its long-term agreement with Mattel, Inc., with whom Disney first allied itself in 1987. Visitors to the "It's a Small World" ride at Disneyland exited directly into a Mattel store featuring Disney-themed merchandise as well as Mattel classics like Barbie. In 1991, Disney's licensing agreement with Mattel yielded 200 million dollars' worth of Mattel's $1.62 billion in sales for that year. Other similar alliances were struck with Nestlé, Delta Airlines, Coca-Cola (soft drinks), AT&T (telephone), and American Express (credit cards).

Synergy   The company's formal mechanism for ensuring horizontal communication was the three-person Synergy Department, whose job was to spend time gathering information on all up-coming projects and developments and to ensure a spread of information across businesses. They accomplished this with the aid of approximately 50 persons total from all the divisions, whose full-time positions typically were in the marketing or special projects areas. It was the divisions' responsibility to identify possible opportunities for synergistic coordination; the Synergy Department would then set up frequent meetings to bring together those individuals in order to establish communication. One executive characterized the nature of the synergy function as self-perpetuating, noting that the more established divisions contributed actively, while newer ones quickly learned to do so.

Starting in 1988, the number of cross-divisional moves by top executives began increasing, largely as a function of the maturity of various businesses. Company policy was that such moves would be the product of mutual decision at both the individual and corporate level. Some recent examples included Steve Burke, the former vice president in the consumer products division who became the COO at Euro Disney, and Mark Pacala, who left Disney Vacation Club to lead the Disney America project. An example of a move from the corporate level to the division level was Linda Warren's switch from the Synergy Department to EPCOT Center.

---

[27]*Los Angeles Times* (Orange County Edition), November 9, 1992, p. D6.

▲ THE EMERGENCE OF MULTIMEDIA

Suppose they threw an interactive party and nobody came?

The Wall Street Journal[28]

It's the product, stupid.

Jeffrey Katzenberg[29]

With the 1990s began a revolution driven by developments in computer software and hardware, consumer electronics, cable, and telecommunications technologies. The developments heralded the emergence of interactive communications, but companies were rapidly moving in a direction for which there existed no navigational tools. Market research proceeded while the capabilities in question—interactive catalog shopping, video-on-demand, and games with other subscribers, for example—remained an untested mystery among consumers. Meanwhile, developers realized only modest revenues from existing interactive technologies, including CD-ROM and on-line computer services.

The lines separating previously unrelated products were nevertheless blurring rapidly, as large companies joined forces to create broad-based multimedia alliances. The trend spanned recording equipment, movie, television and music publishing, cable programming, broadcast networks, cable operation, and telephony (Exhibit 9). With cable systems promising 500 channels in the not-so-distant future, entertainment companies in particular became the focus of alliances or acquisitions to link every step of the chain, from content to delivery and hardware. Newly created alliances included Turner Broadcasting and two production studios, New Line Cinema and Castle Rock Entertainment, Viacom and Paramount Communications, and Bell Atlantic's abortive merger agreement with Tele-Communications, Inc.

In 1994, after Viacom's hard-won victory in the battle for Paramount, Disney became the sole remaining independent studio. Eisner viewed this period of consolidation as an opportunity to remain above the fray, concentrating on software. According to Eisner, "putting money everywhere is a way of admitting you don't know what you're doing."[30] Disney instead put its money into what it did know: the studios stepped up production, with plans to spend more than a billion dollars on TV and film projects in 1993, compared to $606 million in 1992. Moreover, said Eisner, "our company believes in the experience outside the home."[31] As a practical matter, he noted also that the industry was still largely unsure of what products and services would appeal to the consumer, and he questioned the public's appetite for interactive entertainment that would confine them to their televisions. Although Eisner was firm, he was not above being flexible if the issue became one of control: "I'm very worried about the cable world and [the possibility of] one guy getting into the home and being the gatekeeper, [so that] you have to bow and scrape."[32]

---

[28]William M. Bulkeley and John R. Wolke, "Can the Exalted Vision Become a Reality?" *The Wall Street Journal*, October 14, 1993.
[29]Richard Turner and Thomas R. King, "Going It Alone: Disney Stands Aside as Rivals Stampede to Digital Alliance," *The Wall Street Journal*, September 24, 1993, p. A1.
[30]Ibid.
[31]Ibid.
[32]Ibid.

▲EXHIBIT 9   Evolving Integration in Communications

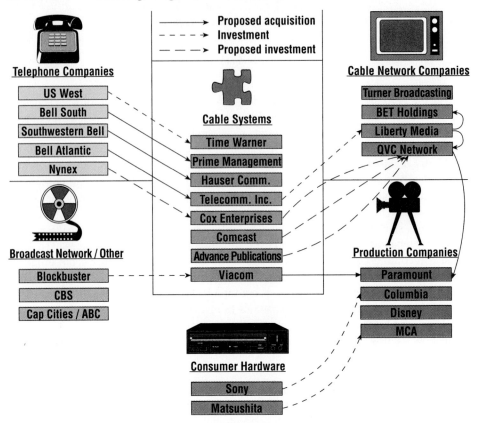

Source: Adapted from Standard & Poor's Industrial Surveys, *Current Analysis: Leisure Time,* November 11,
1993, p. 17.

PORTFOLIO PLANNING AT CIBA-GEIGY AND THE NEWPORT INVESTMENT PROPOSAL

We can [run a diverse set of businesses] because the portfolio tells us what to do.
Heini Lippuner, chairman of the executive committee

From its founding in the mid-eighteenth century through the 1970s, Ciba-Geigy, Ltd., Switzerland's top chemical and pharmaceutical company, had evolved to include chemicals, dyes, pharmaceuticals, crop protection, and animal health businesses. The company had grown profitably by determining overall strategic direction on a largely intuitive basis, relying primarily on case-by-case discussions rather than formal guidelines to determine resource allocation among the multiple businesses.

However, in response to a downturn in financial performance following the second oil crisis in 1979, Ciba-Geigy's then-chairman resolved to change the way the company operated. Initially, this involved a defensive "turnaround" program to remedy the excessive bureaucracy and inflexible operating procedures of a complex functional organization. As these efforts, combined with the relative prosperity of the early 1980s, improved Ciba-Geigy's profitability, the company's turnaround effort shifted from one of defensive reaction to exogenous events, to one of proactive planning for the company's future. As part of this, Ciba-Geigy directly confronted for the first time the issue of corporate strategic planning and looked at introducing portfolio planning to the company. The process involved several years

Research Associate Elizabeth Wynne Johnson prepared this case under the supervision of Professor David J. Collis.

▲ 246

Case 1–3
Portfolio Planning at
Ciba-Geigy and the
Newport Investment
Proposal

of gradually selling the portfolio planning concept to top management as an integral part of the company's first modern strategic plan.

▲ HISTORY OF PORTFOLIO PLANNING AT CIBA-GEIGY

Although portfolio planning models developed by the Boston Consulting Group, General Electric, and Siemens existed (see Exhibit 1) and were initially consulted, Alex Krauer, then deputy chairman of the executive committee (KL) decided in 1982 to develop a customized portfolio planning concept for Ciba-Geigy. He enlisted the help of Hans-Jorg Held as the head of corporate planning. In Held's words, the intention was

> to improve the process of resource allocation and performance assessment. The main idea was to differentiate the businesses—to give them different objectives, different types of managers, and to allow them to adopt the organization structure that was appropriate for each business.

He then added, "We needed a mental map with which to recognize diversity of our businesses in a rigorous, rather than intuitive, way."

Krauer and Held first split up the company into 30 corporate segments that were based on common key success factors and not directly related to the existing organization structure. Each of these segments became a strategic unit, and each was asked to draw up its own strategic plan. Armed with the 30 separate strategic plans, Ciba-Geigy's KL then placed each strategic unit into one of five portfolio categories: development, growth, pillar, core, and niche.[1]

The identification of the five categories was deduced from Krauer and Held's highly pragmatic analysis of Ciba-Geigy's existing businesses. "Looking back," Held reflected, "we really could not have done it any other way." For example, pharmaceuticals, additives, and plant protection were clearly the company's most lucrative performers and would need to receive whatever input was deemed necessary for success. Other businesses, such as pigments and polymers, were more mature and, despite having generated cash on a consistent basis, had been demotivated by years of failing to meet the corporate ROI goal. Yet others, such as Ciba Vision, were growing rapidly and required cash injections to achieve strong market positions.

Having described the corporate portfolio and allocated businesses to categories, portfolio planning then became part of the formal strategic planning system in 1984, and annual strategic meetings with individual divisions were introduced. In August of each year, every unit was required to come before the KL to review its strategic plan; each unit's goals and performance objectives were determined by its role in the portfolio. The KL sought confirmation that assumptions, objectives, and strategies were still valid and resource requirements still the same. Once the KL had reviewed each strategic plan individually, its members would then meet in seclusion to evaluate the portfolio as a whole for overall balance.

With the method for portfolio planning in place, Ciba-Geigy turned its attention to portfolio balance and diversification. To achieve growth and to find uses for the surplus cash that it generated, Ciba-Geigy had entered the seeds business in 1974 with the acquisition of Funk Seeds International.[2] For additional growth, and to respond to what was at the time another

---

[1] A sixth category, "turnaround," was eliminated within a few years.
[2] In part, this acquisition was also intended to bolster the plant protection business at a time when the core pesticides market was predicted to be partly substituted.

▲ EXHIBIT 1   Boston Consulting Group Portfolio Planning Model

▲ 247

Case 1–3
Portfolio Planning at
Ciba-Geigy and the
Newport Investment
Proposal

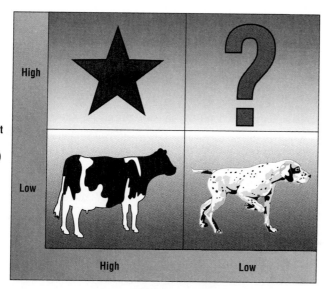

Annual real rate of market growth (percent)

High / Low

Relative market share

High / Low

	High	Low
High	Earnings: High, stable growing Cash flow: Neutral Strategy: Invest for growth	Earnings: Low, unstable growing Cash flow: Negative Strategy: Analyze to determine whether business can be grown into a star, or will degenerate into a dog
Low	Earnings: High, stable Cash flow: High, stable Strategy: Milk	Earnings: Low, unstable Cash flow: Neutral or negative Strategy: Divest

Annual real rate of market growth (percent)

Relative market share

Source: R.B. Grant, *Contemporary Strategy Analysis.* (Oxford: Basil Blackwell, 1987).

prevailing assumption—that the prospects for chemistry were facing maturity—Ciba-Geigy diversified into physical science, acquiring the Spectra-Physics laser company in 1987 and the Toledo weighing instrument company in 1988. Conversely, it divested Airwick, the company's only true consumer products business, in 1985, and Ilford (photographic materials and supplies) in 1988.

▲ 248

Case 1–3
Portfolio Planning at
Ciba-Geigy and the
Newport Investment
Proposal

In 1990, under the direction of Heini Lippuner, chairman of the KL and COO, Ciba-Geigy underwent a major reorganization program to streamline performance and better align the group's functioning with the current social and economic environment. "Vision 2000" dismantled Ciba-Geigy's complex functional structure and replaced it with one built around global product divisions.[3] The new organization was made up of 14 divisions, further subdivided into 33 strategic business units (Exhibits 2, 3, and 4).

One of the first things Lippuner did when he began the transformation process was to review Ciba-Geigy's current portfolio of businesses. He streamlined the group to focus on its core competencies in biology and chemistry, and he divested businesses that did not fit, such as Spectra-Physics (1990), flame retardants and water treatment chemicals, and the Thermoplast and Aminoplast businesses (1993) (Exhibit 5). Looking ahead, he applied a discipline to the group's future composition. To determine whether a business belonged in the portfolio, he identified the following questions: Is the business a provider and/or product of leading-edge knowledge? Is it capable of maintaining an innovative edge? And does it bring synergistic efforts to Ciba-Geigy's current portfolio?

Under Lippuner, corporate planning, and portfolio planning in particular, retained its essential mandate to administer the businesses according to the principles laid out by the five categories. Despite the wide range of remaining businesses, Ciba-Geigy believed both that its competencies wove a "red thread" through the group, justifying its ownership in each case, and that effective management was a matter of each business understanding its role in the portfolio.

▲ PORTFOLIO PLANNING IN 1994

In 1994, portfolio planning took place under the guidance of Verena Laanio. She became head of the four-person corporate planning unit in 1991, after having spent many years in R&D and business development in the agriculture sector. Divisions developed their strategic plans independently. The four-person corporate team was responsible for overseeing the process but did not have formal authority over the 14 separate division managers.

Assessment of Progress

Ciba-Geigy's annual strategic control meetings continued as they had begun in 1984. At these meetings, the executive committee reviewed the key strategies and financial projections of the group and the individual businesses against the strategic plans to determine whether they were on track. That is, had there been shifts in assumptions or the environment, or had objectives been met and/or milestones reached? The KL could decide that a plan required adaptation or that an entirely new plan should be developed. Plan revisions varied in frequency from every two years to every six or seven years.

Portfolio mix issues monitored by the KL focused on growth and profitability relative to competitors, while the KL also evaluated the portfolio as a whole in terms of resource availability and allocation. If, for example, two of the four growth businesses faltered, Ciba-Geigy would most likely buy into another growth business. The goal was to utilize portfolio management as a tool of strategic management.

---

[3]For further information, see "Smashing the Cube: Corporate Transformation at Ciba-Geigy, Ltd.," HBS Case No. 795-041, 1995 (Case 6–6 in this book).

▲ **EXHIBIT 2** Ciba-Geigy, Ltd. Financials, 1983–1993

Previous Accounting System

	1983	1984	1985	1986	1987	1988	1989	1990	1991	1992	1993
Group sales (SFr.m.)	14,741	17,474	18,221	15,955	15,764	17,647	20,608	19,703	21,077	22,204	22,647
Health care								6,953	7,824	8,662	9,220
Agriculture								4,128	4,798	4,817	4,813
Industry								8,622	8,455	8,725	8,614
Net profit (SFr.m.)	776	1,187	1,472	1,161	1,100	1,325	1,557	1,033	1,280	1,520	1,779
As % of sales	5.3	6.8	8.1	7.3	7.0	7.5	7.6	5.2	6.1	6.8	7.9
Operating cash flow (SFr.m.)	1,580	2,050	2,369	2,005	1,958	2,268	2,636	2,120	2,481	2,771	2,564
As % of sales	10.7	11.7	13.0	12.6	12.4	12.9	12.8	10.8	11.8	12.5	11.3
Capital expenditure (SFr.m.)	830	1,007	1,213	1,232	1,368	1,616	1,987	2,058	1,957	1,857	1,739
As % of sales	6	6	7	8	9	9	10	10	9	7	7.7
Depreciation and amortization (SFr.m.)	804	863	897	844	858	943	1,078	1,087	1,201	1,251	1,154
As % of sales	5.4	4.9	4.9	5.3	5.4	5.3	5.2	5.5	5.7	5.6	5.1
Research and development expenditure (SFr.m.)	1,248	1,456	1,674	1,627	1,673	1,797	2,075	2,051	2,185	2,350	2,202
As % of sales	8.5	8.3	9.2	10.2	10.6	10.2	10.1	10.4	10.4	10.6	9.7
Personnel cost (SFr.m.)	4,390	4,893	5,184	4,924	4,842	5,402	6,132	6,275	6,598	6,783	7,053
As % of sales	30	28	28	31	31	31	30	32	31	31	31.2
Number of employees	79,173	81,423	81,012	82,231	86,109	88,757	92,553	94,141	91,665	90,554	87,480
Shareholders' equity (SFr.m.)	12,071	13,921	13,978	14,401	14,188	15,370	16,237	15,454	16,321	18,074	17,080
Key ratios											
Operating profit as % of sales	5.3	6.8	8.1	7.3	7.0	7.5	7.6	5.2	6.1	6.8	10.4
Total debt in % of capitalization	NA	NA	NA	NA	NA	NA	NA	NA	NA	NA	24.7
Current ratio	2.30	2.39	2.43	2.51	2.37	2.19	2.14	1.79	1.79	1.98	2.3
Earnings per share (SFr.)	144.65	221.30	274.40	216.45	205.05	245.40	285.75	185.50	229.90	51.80*	63.8

Note: Due to changeover to International Accounting Standards (IAS) in 1993, the figures for the previous years are not fully comparable.
*After four-for-one stock split.

▲ 250

Case 1–3
Portfolio Planning at
Ciba-Geigy and the
Newport Investment
Proposal

▲ EXHIBIT 3   Ciba-Geigy's Portfolio in 1994: 14 Divisions and 33 Strategic
Business Units

Pillar Businesses	Pharmaceuticals
	Specialties
	Generics
	Plant Protection
	Weed Control
	Disease Control
	Insect Control
	Seed Treatment
	Additives
	Additives for Plastics/Elastomers/Fibers
	Additives for Coat./Rad./Phot.
	Additives for Lubricants
	Additives for PVC Stabilization
Core Businesses	Textile Dyestuffs
	Reactive Dyes
	Wool, Polyamide, and Silk Dyes
	Polyester, Cellulose, Polyacrylonitrile
	Dyeing Auxiliaries
	Chemicals
	Chemtex
	Detergents and Cosmetics
	Paper
	Leather/Fur
	Polymers
	Resins
	Formulated Systems
	Electronic Materials
	Pigments
	High-Performance Pigments
	Classical Pigments
	Dispersions
	Mettler-Toledo
	Laboratory Balances
	Industrial/Retail Weighing
	Analytical and Process Systems
Growth Businesses	Self-Medication
	Zyma
	CCP/USA
	Diagnostics
	Composites
	U.S. Minerals
	Euro Minerals
	Structures and Interiors
	Ciba Vision
	OPTICS (Lenses/Lens Care)
	Ophthalmic Pharmaceuticals
Development Businesses	Seeds, Vaccines
Niche Businesses	Animal Health

▲ EXHIBIT 4   Ciba-Geigy's Organization Structure in 1994

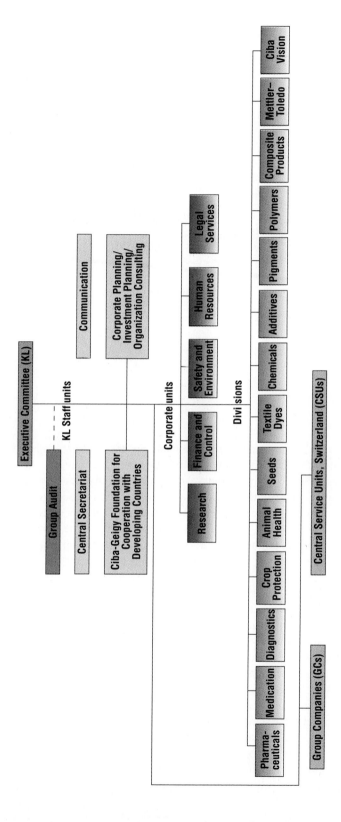

▲ 252

Case 1–3
Portfolio Planning at
Ciba-Geigy and the
Newport Investment
Proposal

▲ EXHIBIT 5   Schematic Representation of Ciba-Geigy's Portfolio in 1994

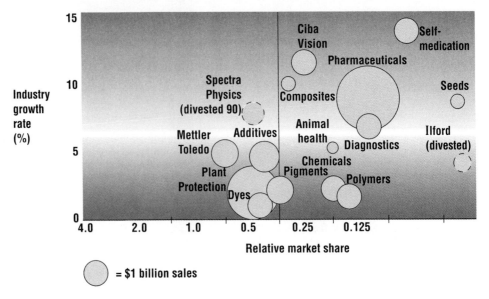

Source: Casewriter estimates.

The Categories

When Laanio assumed leadership of corporate planning, she oversaw adaptation of the existing portfolio categories rather than creation of new ones. The category designations were largely the outgrowth of a business life cycle; accordingly, changes in the category of a business were relatively rare (Exhibit 6). Recent discussion had focused on the composite materials business, where the major aerospace market had been at a standstill for several years. However, the KL decided not to move composites from the growth category. They observed that the market might pick up if oil prices increased or an industrial market finally emerged, and moreover, the business would need support to survive the likely industry consolidation.

The definition of categories was aimed at serving three main functions: first, to serve as a resource allocation device; second, to manage the overall portfolio in terms of cash and growth; and third, to provide management focus on the appropriate key success factors for each stage in the life cycle. In turn, this called for distinct management principles for businesses in the different categories. According to Laanio, the categories served a kind of "liberating" purpose by defining clear boundaries stating what a business was meant to achieve and how it would be measured (Exhibit 7).

Development   A product at the starting point of the life cycle was a "development" project; as such, it would receive careful investment commensurate with Ciba-Geigy's belief in the product's potential and fit with the company. At this stage, however, the level of commitment remained tentative pending a clear demonstration of the product's relation to Ciba-Geigy in terms of its key success factors, profit potential, and growth rate. Corporate planning did not

▲ 253

Case 1–3
Portfolio Planning at
Ciba-Geigy and the
Newport Investment
Proposal

▲ EXHIBIT 6   Business Life Cycle

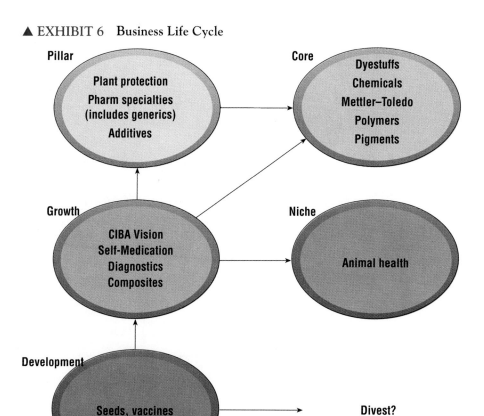

impose preset targets or milestones for its development projects, but in order to move on into the growth category, businesses (e.g., seeds or vaccines) had to meet those criteria within a predetermined period of time and a set limit for total investment or maximum loss.

Growth   The growth category contained those products to which Ciba-Geigy would commit substantial funds in order to build "critical mass." The criteria for inclusion in the growth category included evidence of a large and/or growing market, the potential for innovations that would lead to future profits, and a clear link with Ciba-Geigy's core competencies. Businesses slated for growth in 1994 included self-medication, diagnostics, vision care, and composites.

Pillar   Products that became a key source of profit and cash for the group were labeled pillar businesses, and they included pharmaceuticals, plant protection, and additives. As market leaders, they received high priority in resource allocation and R&D funding and were held to preset targets with the emphasis on promoting market position and internal growth. Ciba-Geigy monitored the pipelines of these businesses annually to ensure a continuing emphasis on innovation.

▲ 254

Case 1–3
Portfolio Planning at
Ciba-Geigy and the
Newport Investment
Proposal

▲ EXHIBIT 7   Hierarchy for Financial Targets

Category	Role	Priority*
Pillar	Substantial contributor to group profitability	1. CAS % of sales RONA 2. Cash flow
Core	Cash provider	1. Cash flow 2. RONA
Growth	Qualitative growth; long-term profitability improvement	1. CAS % of sales RONA 2. Cash flow
Niche	Small pillar	1. CAS % of sales RONA 2. Cash flow
Development project	Development phase	cum. neg. CAS cum. neg. cash flow

*CAS = contribution after services; RONA = return on net assets.
Source: Ciba-Geigy, Ltd.

Niche   The niche category was closely related to the pillar category in terms of basic criteria, and its products were sometimes called "small pillars." They were, however, constrained solely by the size of their market. Animal health, for example, was profitable and a market-share leader, but nevertheless confined to a relatively narrowly defined market segment.

Core   Traditional businesses, such as dyes, polymers, and pigments, had grown large in size and enjoyed significant market share, but competed in mature industries where there was less chance for growth. These "core businesses" were managed primarily for cash. Their principal challenge was to defend their leading market positions, which Ciba-Geigy did by initiating restructuring aimed at maximizing productivity and efficiency. In addition, in making R&D investments, the firm targeted those segments where innovation was rewarded in the marketplace.

The categorization of the SBUs within a division was left up to the divisions themselves, but typically followed lines created by customer groups within the industry or by product category. For example, the additives division placed its SBUs in four distinct categories (Exhibit 3).

Implications of Category Position

Target Setting   All divisions had "stretch" targets for profitability, liquidity, and asset management. However, the priority attached to a division's financial goals was set according to its position in the portfolio (Exhibit 7). Originally, all divisions in a category were assigned the same numeric target for those goals. Laanio came to recognize that to expect the exact same financial performance from divisions in the same category was unrealistic: industry conditions and the strategic position of the divisions varied too greatly. As a consequence, Laanio gave each division its own numeric targets for profitability, cash generation, and asset utilization, and prioritized them according to portfolio category. These financial yardsticks were determined by examining the division's past and projected financial performance, benchmarking competitors' returns from similar businesses (where these could be isolated from a corporation's results), assessing of future industry conditions, and making shareholder value calculations. In general, targets did still vary by category from perhaps a 20 percent RONA in a pillar business to 10 percent in a core business, and perhaps break-even in a growth business.

Compensation   Originally, the performance targets assigned to a division by its position in the portfolio were not linked to management compensation. Pay at Ciba-Geigy, which maintained a traditional Swiss career structure, had largely been determined by position and age. Very limited bonuses were paid, and those that were would be awarded based on managerial judgment rather than on quantitative performance. Under Vision 2000, the compensation package was changed to include result(s)-oriented bonuses and to diminish the automatic link to seniority. Bonuses were paid according to performance against targets that reflected responsibilities: for example, division managers were assessed mainly against divisional performance, corporate managers against corporate performance. For a divisional manager, up to 20 percent of total compensation was then determined by how well the division performed against a divisional RONA (net) target. In 1994, Laanio was still working toward getting the divisional targets more closely aligned with the strategic goals set by the division's position in the portfolio.

Executive Personnel   One of the initial objectives behind the adoption of portfolio planning had been to match executives to portfolio categories. It was argued that the individual required to successfully manage a growth business would be a certain type of manager, very different from the one who would be most effective in a mature core business. Over time, no formal linkage was made between a manager's personality and his divisional assignment, but it was nevertheless believed that choosing among candidates for a senior divisional slot would be indirectly influenced by a judgment about appropriate character traits.

Resource Allocation   In principle, position in the corporate portfolio determined a division's access to capital. Sizable acquisitions, for example, were only permitted for pillar and growth businesses, although exceptions could be made. For capital investment proposals, there was a discrete capital budgeting proposal with authorization limits of up to SFr5 million in the divisional manager, SFr10 million in the KL member responsible for the division, SFr50 million in the KL; all requests above that amount had to go to the board. However, in evaluating an investment proposal, much attention would be given to how the investment fit with the division's position in the portfolio. A core business being managed for cash and return on net assets would find it hard to justify a major investment, particularly since the payback period expected for their investment might be set at two-to-three years and not the seven-to-ten years of a pillar business.

Divisions were expected to have internalized their portfolio goals as a form of self-discipline, so that they would restrict their investment proposals to projects that did not violate their mandate.[4] To this end, portfolio planning was featured in all the company's training programs,

---

[4]As a result, finding a clear example of conflict between portfolio category and investment proposal, for purpose of writing this case, was difficult.

▲ 255

Case 1–3
Portfolio Planning at
Ciba-Geigy and the
Newport Investment
Proposal

▲ 256

Case 1-3
Portfolio Planning at
Ciba-Geigy and the
Newport Investment
Proposal

and every strategic plan would start out with a reference to the businesses' portfolio category. Thus, the terminology and attitudes of portfolio planning had become a "language" of strategic management at all levels of Ciba-Geigy. Nevertheless, it was not intended to be applied mechanically, but rather with a substantial degree of flexibility in interpreting the role of a business within a particular category.

However, the background of resource availability at Ciba-Geigy was changing. Through the 1980s, fueled by the performance of the pharmaceutical division, Ciba-Geigy generated positive free cash flow. Much of this was reinvested in pillar, growth, and development businesses, and in new acquisitions, but the corporation still remained on balance a net cash generator. In the recession of the early 1990s, the performance of the industrial divisions weakened. Just as those divisions recovered, the pharmaceutical business came under cost pressures, particularly in the United States.

▲ PORTFOLIO PLANNING IN ACTION: THE NEWPORT DECISION[5]

In 1993, pigments division head Peter Schutz went before the KL to seek their approval to make a major investment in the comprehensive modernization of a manufacturing plant in Newport, Delaware. The plan would violate portfolio guidelines for investment, so the justification he presented hinged in large part on his vision for the plant's future as a producer of high-quality pigments.

Inherited from a competitor by acquisition in 1984, the Newport plant utilized outdated equipment that initially had been plagued by frequent failures and high maintenance costs, which in turn had resulted in a reduction in capacity and subsequent delivery problems. As a consequence, Ciba-Geigy had experienced losses in revenue and market share in 1988. Although improvement measures had been successful in restoring the division in terms of market share, the Newport plant issue could not be ignored. Looking toward the future, he explained, Ciba-Geigy had three options:

1. Commit to a full investment in the Newport facility, which, for a cost of approximately US$140 million, would bring it up to state-of-the-art standards for productivity, safety, and environmental friendliness, and allow for the manufacture of an additional range of high-quality pigments, known as DPP.

2. Make a limited investment aimed at addressing the current situation by reorganizing and modernizing production. Estimated cost: US$100 million.

3. Close the facility, on the grounds that its existing condition made it an unacceptable risk, both ecologically and financially. Ciba-Geigy could then either: (*a*) relocate to an existing facility in Europe and export to the United States, or (*b*) move production to Ciba-Geigy's plant in Alabama or Louisiana, where the infrastructure was roughly suited to the needs of the pigments division.

The Market for Pigments Pigments were insoluble coloring agents used in printing ink, plastics and synthetic fibers, paints, coating, glass and ceramics. They existed in broad varieties and fetched prices of anywhere between SFr5 to SFr180 per kilogram. All could be

---

[5]Information in this section is partially drawn from a case study by Dr. Peter Donath and Dr. Walter Peter, "Ciba Pigments/Newport: Technologie-, Risiko- un Umweltmanagment," St. Gallen, 1994.

placed in one of the following categories: high-performance pigments (HPP), classical pigments, or dispersions. HPPs were distinguished by their unique resistance to heat and weather conditions and fading, which made then suitable for automobile paints, for example. One such family of pigments, Quinacridone pigments,[6] were currently being produced at Newport.

Ciba-Geigy was the worldwide leader in organic pigments overall, and was a clear number one in HPPs. The company's nearest competitor, BASF, was number one in classical pigments, which, because of their properties, enjoyed high volume use in printing ink. Other major competitors were HOECHST and Dainippon Ink. The total market for pigments in 1994 was estimated at SFr6 billion, with a 2–3 percent growth rate per annum. The principal markets were in Western Europe, North America, South East Asia, and Japan. Following the oil crisis in the 1970s, the industry consolidated and became increasingly competitive, sealed off by high entry- and exit-barriers caused by the need for low-cost, high-quality, and, increasingly, environmentally sound production techniques with consequent high investment requirements. Safety and environmental protection measures consumed more than 10 percent of Ciba-Geigy's total production costs for worldwide pigment production and 15–20 percent of capital expenditures.

On the strength of its innovative products, Ciba-Geigy had achieved steady growth in its pigments business, making pigments a strong performer within the industrial divisions. In 1994, market share was close to 20 percent and revenues reached SFr1.1 billion. Both the pigments division as a whole and the HPP business unit, which contributed roughly half of divisional revenues, were designated core businesses, although HPP had much in common with Ciba-Geigy's pillar businesses. Much of the recent success of the firm's HPP business was due to very profitable products (DPP pigments) not manufactured at Newport, whose patent protection was set to expire in 2000–2002.

By a wide margin, the biggest customers for HPPs were producers of auto paint. Its principal customers were in America and Japan, although over the long term, the division's worldwide revenue potential was seen as split equally among Europe, North America, and the Far East. Currently, U.S. sales accounted for approximately 40 percent of Ciba-Geigy's total sales of HPPs, but 50 percent of DPP sales. Ciba-Geigy viewed having a close relationship with customers as a key to success in the business, and long-term contracts with the expectation of consistent delivery were the norm.

The Newport Plant   Prior to the acquisition of the Newport plant in 1984, Ciba-Geigy did not produce any high-performance pigments in the United States. In 1993, the firm produced at Newport a broad line of mainly Quinacridone pigments, an older line of high-performance pigments. Newport was the only global source for the company's SFr 130 million in sales of Quinacridone pigments.

The Newport plant was a "superfund" site because it continued to produce some pollutants in an already contaminated area. The previous owner was 90 percent responsible for the contamination, but Ciba-Geigy wanted to halt all further site contamination. The proposed investment would cut emissions up to 80 percent and save $2–3 million per annum in materials costs, as well as reduce energy costs by at least 30 percent.

With concerns other than environmental safety foremost on their agendas, many of Ciba-Geigy's pigment clients were not amenable to price increases to cover the cost of

▲257

Case 1–3
Portfolio Planning at
Ciba-Geigy and the
Newport Investment
Proposal

---

[6]Predominantly red pigments, or red with violet and blue tints.

▲ 258

Case 1–3
Portfolio Planning at
Ciba-Geigy and the
Newport Investment
Proposal

environmentally motivated upgrades. However, Ciba-Geigy was the second-largest employer in the state of Delaware, and therefore was under close scrutiny by the local government.

Schultz's task was to prove that the project merited deviation from the division's preset guidelines for resource allocation. According to Ciba-Geigy's portfolio planning guidelines for core businesses, the pigments division was responsible for increasing cash flow (by about [SFr. 50 million] annum) and maintaining 10 percent RONA, its primary and secondary targets, respectively. Schutz produced the results of analysis conducted by his division that showed he would maintain positive cash flow throughout the five-year investment period. At the very worst, he assured the KL, pigment RONA would only dip to 6 percent—and that only during the two worst years. The investment payback period, Schutz concluded, would be about three years.

As the request came under consideration, dissenters voiced their concerns:

Heavy investment in a core business? Ciba-Geigy is a *specialty chemicals* company!

Why would we invest in technology, when we already have manufacturing capacity for these products in Switzerland? and

Was it not Lippuner himself who once said, "We can run this large diversified company, *because the portfolio tells us what to do"*?

MARKS AND SPENCER, LTD. (A)

According to Lord Marks of Broughton, chairman of Marks and Spencer (M&S) from 1916 to 1964, the following five tenets constituted the fundamental operating principles of the firm:

1. To offer our customers a selective range of high-quality, well-designed, and attractive merchandise at reasonable prices.

2. To encourage our suppliers to use the most modern and efficient techniques of production and quality control dictated by the latest discoveries in science and technology.

3. With the cooperation of our suppliers, to enforce the highest standard of quality control.

4. To plan the expansion of our stores for the better display of a widening range of goods and for the convenience of our customers.

5. To foster good human relations with customers, suppliers, and staff.

By applying these guidelines, M&S had grown to be not only the largest and most profitable retail organization in the United Kingdom, but also one of the most admired (Exhibits 1, 2, and 3). According to the *Guinness Book of Records,* in 1988, its flagship store at Marble Arch in London had a turnover of £1,600 ($2,400) per square foot—more than any other department store in the world.

Professor Cynthia A. Montgomery prepared this case. A substantial portion of the presentation is taken from an earlier case (9-375-358) prepared by Ms. Christine Harris, under the direction of Professor Joseph L. Bower. Copyright © 1991 by the President and Fellows of Harvard College.

▲ EXHIBIT 1   Profit and Loss Account, 1984–1988 (£ millions)

Year to March	1984	1985	1986	1987	1988
Sales					
UK					
Clothing	1,326	1,424	1,656	1,869	2,016
Housewares	249	305	377	447	486
Food	1,022	1,171	1,362	1,492	1,671
Total U.K.	2,597	2,900	3,395	3,808	4,173
Europe	74	81	94	119	132
U.S./Canada/Far East	150	175	181	211	180
Other	47	57	64	82	92
Total sales	2,868	3,213	3,734	4,220	4,577
Profit					
U.K.	261	285	351	410	476
Europe	7	7	11	13	19
U.S./Canada/Far East	7	8	9	4	3
Financial	4	4	−5	5	4
Total Pretax profit	279	304	365	425	502

Source: Marks and Spencer, Economic Information Department.

▲ EXHIBIT 2   Consolidated Profit and Loss Account (£ millions)

	1988
Turnover	4,577.6
Cost of sales	3,112.2
Gross profit	1,465.4
Other expenses	951.3
Profit on ordinary activities before profit sharing and taxes	514.1
Profit sharing	12.4
Profit on ordinary activities before taxes	501.7
Tax on profit on ordinary activities	178.4
Profit on ordinary activities after taxes	323.3
Minority interests	—
Profit for the financial year	323.3

Source: Marks and Spencer *Annual Report*.

▲ EXHIBIT 3   **Balance Sheet (£ millions)**

	1988
Fixed assets	
Tangible assets	
Land and buildings	1,840.9
Fixtures, fittings, and equipment	301.3
Assets in the course of construction	8.6
	2,150.8
Investments	—
Net assets of financial activities	81.4
	2,232.2
Current assets	
Stocks	287.9
Debtors	130.4
Investments	15.5
Cash at bank and in hand	276.1
	709.9
Current liabilities	
Creditors: Amounts falling due within one year	623.5
Net current assets/(liabilities) (excl. financial activity)	86.4
Total assets less current liabilities	2,318.6
Creditors: Amounts falling due after more than one year	160.6
Net assets	2,158.0
Capital and reserves	
Called up share capital	666.4
Share premium account	22.2
Revaluation reserve	468.7
Profit and loss account	1,000.7
Shareholder's funds	2,158.0

Source: Marks and Spencer *Annual Report.*

M&S provided a selective range of textiles, housewares, footwear, and food items aimed at rapid turnover. The firm sold all its products exclusively under the St. Michael label. Typically, articles offered the consumer very high quality at moderate, rather than low, prices. This combination of quality and price encouraged customers to associate M&S with good value for their money.

Textile products included women's clothing and lingerie and men's and children's clothing and underwear. Customers could find all their essential clothing at M&S, but few fads or trendy lines. In the United Kingdom, textiles accounted for 48 percent of M&S sales and 55 percent of profits in 1988. Lingerie was a particularly important merchandise group, accounting for a market share in the U.K. of 33 percent. It had even been reported that Princess Diana purchased her underwear from Marks and Spencer.

The food department had separate checkout counters, but there were no barriers separating it from the department store. Among the food offerings were produce, poultry, meat, breads, dairy products, beverages, confectionaries, and prepared foods. M&S also sold a highly regarded line of French wines.

M&S had been described as "the store with a brilliant reputation for pre-cooked meals and food" which had "revolutionized the way the British ate."[1] A streamlined distribution process enabled stores to offer prepared foods that were fresh, not frozen. Specialties included gourmet sandwiches, chicken Kiev, and hand-trimmed Scottish smoked salmon. Somewhat in contrast to the clothing, M&S food was priced in the moderate to high range. Nevertheless, its superior quality appealed to both pensioners and upscale customers. In 1988, food accounted for 40 percent of M&S sales and 33 percent of profits.

M&S sold domestic furnishings, floor coverings, accessories, toiletries, and footwear. In 1988, these products accounted for 12 percent of U.K. sales and profits.

In 1988, M&S operated 289 stores in the United Kingdom, 11 in Europe, and 267 in Canada. In the United States, M&S had 4 small stores in upstate New York that were extensions of the firm's Canadian activities. Buying, merchandising, distribution, quality control, and finance for the U.K. stores were centralized in the firm's headquarters on Baker Street in London. The European and North American operations were managed autonomously with guidance from the U.K.

▲ THE HISTORY OF M&S

The Early Years

The business principles enunciated by Lord Marks had their origins in the experiences of his father, Michael Marks, the founder of M&S. In 1884, the elder Marks, a Polish Jew, began setting up stalls at town markets in northern England. Since he could not converse well in English. he prominently displayed the sign, "Don't Ask the Price—It's a Penny." The slogan proved very popular, and the simplicity of the single fixed-price allowed Marks to give up keeping accounts and to search continually for various high-quality goods that could be sold for a penny. High turnover counterbalanced the low profit margins.

Marks' business flourished, and in 1894, he took Thomas Spencer into partnership. By 1903, when Spencer retired, the company boasted 36 market bazaars and shops. In that year, Marks and Spencer, Ltd. was formed, with control entirely in the Marks and Spencer families. Spencer died in 1905, Michael Marks in 1907. After Marks's death, control of M&S temporarily passed out of family hands.

---

[1] *Courvoisier's Book of the Best,* Ebury Press, 1990.

When the founder's son, Simon Marks (later Lord Marks) regained control of the firm in 1914, it was a national chain with 140 branches. A strong family influence soon returned to M&S. Simon determined overall direction, while his brother-in-law, Israel Sieff (later Lord Sieff), took charge of buying and merchandising. After their deaths, their descendants continued to dominate M&S into the 1980s.

Two outside influences had profound impacts on M&S in the 1920s. First, Chaim Weizmann, the brilliant chemist and famous Zionist leader, encouraged Marks and Sieff in commitments that became cornerstones of the modern M&S. Weizmann interested the pair in the applications and benefits of new technologies and inspired them to regard their business as a social service to both customers and employees. Second, a 1924 visit to the United States allowed Simon Marks to study American chain stores. He returned to England determined to transform M&S into a chain of "superstores" featuring continuous merchandise flow and a central organization acutely sensitive to consumer needs.

M&S went public in 1926 and within 10 years had a branch in every major town in England. Enhanced staff amenities accompanied this rapid growth. The welfare department, founded in 1933, supervised a variety of employee facilities and expanded medical and dental services. Additionally, the firm initiated a pension plan in 1936.

M&S's relations with its suppliers also changed during this period. In 1928, Marks and Spencer registered the "St. Michael" brand name (honoring M&S's founder) and became the first department store in the United Kingdom with the goal of selling only "own brand" merchandise. To assure the highest product quality, M&S insisted on close cooperation with suppliers and stressed using technological advances in materials and production processes. M&S's large orders enabled it to overcome traditional wholesale opposition and to place orders directly with producers.

In the decade following the Second World War, M&S gradually phased out all merchandise not bearing the St. Michael brand, and St. Michael became increasingly identified in consumers' minds with quality and value. Concentrating on a limited product range, M&S developed a dominant position in many textile lines. The food division, which became an important part of the chain's operations in the early 1950s, also had a narrow range.

Operation Simplification—1956

On February 16, 1956, Lord Marks was presented with a budget that exceeded the previous year's by millions of pounds. He launched a companywide campaign to eliminate the burgeoning load of paperwork that appeared chiefly responsible for the rise in overhead. The campaign, "Operation Simplification," aimed at liberating staff, management, and support services from paperwork.
The general principles of Operation Simplification were:

1. *Sensible approximation.* The price of perfection is prohibitive; approximation often suffices and costs less.

2. *Exception reporting.* Events generally occur as arranged, and only exceptions need to be reported.

3. *"Never legislate for exceptions."* Detailed manuals are unnecessary (M&S went from 13 manuals to 2), and local decision making enhances willingness to assume responsibility.

4. *Decategorization.* Those below management and supervisory levels are more useful in a "general staff" category than as specialists.

5. *People can and need to be trusted.* Eliminating checks and controls saves time and money, while improving self-confidence and encouraging a sense of responsibility. Management control is more effectively exercised by selective spot checks.

Lord Marks set a goal of allowing store staff, management, and support services to focus on only one task—increasing sales in pounds sterling. Under the new system, senior executives held full responsibility for profitability; they determined one markup target for food and another for textiles. With margins thus standardized, the selectors focused on finding goods of acceptable quality that would turn over rapidly. Stores then worked to use space to achieve maximum sales of the selected goods.

The campaign, which culminated in a symbolic bonfire of old records, eliminated 26 million pieces of paper per year (120 tons) and reduced the 32,000-person staff by 10,000. Abolishing countless forms and routines freed senior managers from their desks so they could get personally involved in their departments.

Commenting on the drive for simplicity, Lord Sieff wrote:

Both the executives and the merchandisers of the department should *probe* into the goods in the stores with *seeing eyes and a critical mind.* The department supervisor and the [salesperson] are the best sources of information. To depend on statistics is to asphyxiate the dynamic spirit of the business.

A managing director in the foods area illustrated the merits of *probing* with this example:

We get concerned when statistics [are put] on paper because they hide things. For example, suppose I had [this daily] report on sales at [one] store:

	Beginning Stock	Sales	Ending Stock
Item A	100	100	0
Item B	50	20	30

I might conclude that sales of A to B were 5:1 and act accordingly. But if I looked after lunch, I might find that the sales in the morning showed:

	Beginning Stock	Sales	Ending Stock
Item A	100	100	0
Item B	50	10	40

I have to [find out from] the store manager that the proper order is more like 10:1. That's why we distrust statistics and value *probing.*

The emphasis on *probing* became a mainstay of the M&S management philosophy. Much of the information that moved toward top management was judgmental, not numerical. *All* senior executives frequently visited stores and asked store managers and staff very specific questions. For example, an executive might ask a salesperson to evaluate the performance of particular items or comment broadly on recent sales activity. M&S considered these visits valuable two-way communication and thought they provided important opportunities to assess store and managerial performance.

▲ OPERATIONS

Personnel

Point 5 of the general principles of Operation Simplification about eliminating checks and controls of employees reemphasized Marks and Spencer's commitment to the well-being of its workers. Sir Marcus Sieff [later Lord Sieff], Lord Sieff's son, stated the firm's belief:

> You cannot get the goodwill of the people who work for you by changing words such as "canteen" into "dining room," "navvy" to "worker," "office boy" to "junior clerk," and so on, or even just by paying higher wages. In the last analysis, good labor relations comes from workers approving the kind of people they believe their employers to be.

> Good human relations can only develop if top management believes in its importance and then sees that such a philosophy is dynamically implemented . . . . The majority of workers under such conditions take pride in doing a good job. All this results in greater productivity and higher profits. This enables management to provide all those facilities which make for contented and hard-working staff, and to pay better wages based on genuinely increased productivity.[2]

M&S traditionally had a paternalistic relationship with its employees. It viewed itself as a family business with broad responsibility for the welfare of its employees. As Sir Marcus expressed, "People do have troubles, and it is a fundamental part of a good staff policy to give help and advise unobtrusively and speedily when needed."

M&S demonstrated its commitment to employees by offering medical and pension plans that provided well-above-average benefits and by establishing company-financed social and recreational clubs at Baker Street and in each store. In addition, in 1988, the firm's headquarters included a cafeteria that offered heavily subsidized meals and a medical and dental facility that held, among other things, coronary heart disease screenings, health and fitness programs, and dental screenings.

Stores employed a part-time doctor and a personnel manager responsible for the training, placement, and welfare of the employees. Staff amenities included a medical room and nurse, with periodic visits from a dentist and a chiropodist—especially significant to salespeople who spent hours standing; a one-room infirmary; a hairdressing salon; a cloakroom with security lockers; shower and bathroom facilities; a staff refrigerator; a recreation room; and a staff dining room. The dining room provided lunches, coffee, and afternoon tea for nominal charges. The food compared favorably with that served in executive dining rooms. M&S allocated nearly 10 percent of store space to employees and spent £16.2 million in 1988 on welfare and staff amenities.

Retired employees maintained affiliation with Marks and Spencer through Retired Staff Associations of which there were some 30 in the United Kingdom in 1988. These groups were established and run by the retirees but had loose affiliations with M&S stores.

M&S believed that its performance depended on its employees' high productivity and rewarded its staff's hard work with pay and benefits that were well above the average for the industry. Furthermore, M&S regularly promoted employees from within rather than hiring from the outside. Its policies engendered employees' loyalty and trust.

---

[2]Sir Marcus Sieff, 1969 speech.

In the late 1980s, the firm's traditionally paternalistic relationship with employees, in which M&S assumed overwhelming responsibility for their welfare, began to change. There was increased emphasis on self-determination and partnership. M&S encouraged managers to identify their own training and development needs and to be more active in making decisions affecting their careers. The firm provided practical guidelines and support for individual initiatives, including material for foreign language training and guidance to identify and improve personal weaknesses.

Stores

In 1988, M&S divided its 289 U.K. stores into six geographically based divisions, each under a *divisional executive* with responsibility for store operations, building and equipment, transportation, packaging, and real estate. *Personnel, finance,* and *commercial operations controllers* reported to each divisional executive and assisted *store managers* as needed.

Store managers were responsible for sales maximization, cost control, and operational efficiency. Each was assisted by a *personnel manager* who was responsible for the staff, a *deputy general manager* who handled operations, and an *administration manager* who oversaw all systems (e.g., information technology, finance).

Merchandising

Responsibility for handling the flow from suppliers to M&S rested with the merchandise teams. In the textiles area, there were three *executive directors,* one who supervised ladies wear and lingerie, another, menswear and childrens wear, and the other, footwear, gifts, and housewares. Reporting to the executive directors were one or more *divisional directors,* who each supervised several executives. Buying group executives were supported by a team of *merchandise managers, merchandisers,* and *selectors* who were responsible for merchandise ranges, sales estimates, production, packaging, and distribution.

The food division, though more centralized, adhered to the same basic structure and procedures. However, perishability and more rapid turnover required shorter planning horizons and different distribution procedures.

Suppliers

According to Gareth Williams, divisional director of physical distribution, retail systems, and information technology, M&S initiated process control and testing at the point of production: "From factory to sales floor, we are in control of the chain every step of the way."[3] M&S worked closely with approximately 500 food and 350 nonfood independents providing St. Michael merchandise to the firm's specifications. Indeed, Lord Rayner, chairman of the firm since 1984, stated,

> We are involved with suppliers from the raw materials to the finished products. If suppliers don't measure up to our standards of quality, we try to help them. We don't drop them. It's a partnership.[4]

[3]Personal interview, December 12, 1990.
[4]Lord Rayner, personal interview, December 11, 1990.

Some supplier relationships stretched back 40 years or more, and M&S was often responsible for 75 to 90 percent of a supplier's output. Throughout its history, M&S had shared the benefits of its growth and prosperity with suppliers. In return, the firm was able to establish an exceptionally efficient supply base that was capable and willing to meet the firm's very exact standards.

M&S assisted suppliers in designing products and developing innovative production methods. The firm was even able to bring together competing manufacturers to solve logistics problems or work out the details of a new offering. In 1988, M&S employed a large number of scientists, engineers, and support staff who teamed up with merchandising departments and suppliers to establish product specifications and monitor quality.

M&S did not item-buy. In textiles, the firm purchased a substantial portion of the fabrics that external suppliers used to manufacture St. Michael products. The goods were then produced according to an M&S-planned schedule and held until the company requested delivery. Similar policies were adopted in food. For example, M&S worked with a breeder to develop a pig that could be bred for fresh pork, not for bacon. The pigs were sold to farmers who raised them only for M&S. These practices, along with the private label, gave M&S the ability to control specifications and ensured the exclusivity of its products.

In food, Marks and Spencer established the first full-scale cold-chain supply system in the United Kingdom. M&S suppliers prepared food in central kitchens and delivered it to multi-temperature composite warehouse facilities. British Oxygen Corporation or Salserve then transported the goods in a fleet of refrigerated trucks to individual M&S stores. Throughout this process, the temperature of the food did not vary more than one degree Celsius.

Marketing

Marks and Spencer's marketing philosophy, like its personnel policy, developed from traditional antecedents. As Lord Sieff summarized:

> The future of the business depends on quick imaginative study of what the people need—not of what the public can be persuaded to buy. . . . Only in supplying real needs, will a business flourish in the long term. Only by giving the people what on reflection they continue to want, will a business earn the respect of the customer, which is essential to anything more durable than a cheapjack's overnight success. So long as Marks and Spencer continues to study what the people need and efficiently produce it by means of a staff humanely organized, we can meet any economic trend.

Historically, M&S had attempted to maintain one markup percentage for all merchandise. By 1988, the differential markup had been introduced between clothing and food, and the width of the markup bands within each area had expanded. The company sought the same net figures from varying gross margins to accommodate writedowns and other waste. M&S never held sales and reduced the price of merchandise for clearances only. Furthermore, in the United Kingdom, the little advertising it did was limited to the release of information, such as the introduction of a new product line. Executives believed that the products sold themselves and relied largely on word of mouth to tell their story. Also, due to its status in the United Kingdom, M&S received extensive press coverage.

Through the 1970s, M&S stores lacked fitting rooms and sold merchandise on a cash-only basis. For patrons relying on their eyes to select style and size, the stores offered a no-fuss return policy, ensuring that unsuitable purchases could easily be brought back. Although customers could centralize purchases for the purpose of check writing, the firm did not honor credit cards.

In the mid-1980s, M&S introduced fitting rooms and launched a full-scale charge-card operation to make it easier for customers to purchase its goods. Customer response was very favorable. By 1988, there were over 2 million cardholders, and charge-card sales represented 13.4 percent of M&S's U.K. sales. The firm did not honor any other charge card.

Property Base

Unlike Marks and Spencer, many retailers in the United Kingdom sold or leased back their freehold properties to obtain more sites in the early 1980s. When rental rates soared in 1987 and 1988, these retailers struggled to trade profitably in their new sites. Marks and Spencer's retention of freeholds and long leasehold properties protected them from the sharp increases in rental rates and gave them one of the lowest rent/sales ratios in the industry (Exhibit 4).

▲ INTERNATIONALIZATION

In the 1970s, the United Kingdom presented a very difficult presented a very difficult economic environment for retailers. In an effort to help manufacturers compete abroad, the government offered them regional and sector subsidies and devalued the pound sterling. Several M&S executives believed this artificial environment contributed to inefficiency in the manufacturing sector that, when coupled with the rise of aggressive trade unions, led to very high corporate taxes.

In addition, M&S was concerned that it might have reached its natural limits of growth in the United Kingdom. Together, these external and internal circumstances pointed toward expansion abroad. Sir Marcus Sieff, who had become chairman in 1973, gave the reasons for taking M&S overseas:

> First, it is an opportunity for more profit. Given the deteriorating situation in Britain we think Canada can become very important for us. Second, it is a chance to expand British exports. And finally, should things be really bad, it's a lifeline for us abroad.

The Move into Canada

In 1972, M&S had opened four St. Michael Shops in Canada as a 50/50 joint venture with Peoples Department Stores Ltd., a Canadian retailer. At the time, M&S regarded the St. Michael Shops as additional outlets for its U.K. export interests. By 1974, the developing chain consisted of 12 stores.

▲ EXHIBIT 4   Property Costs, 1988–1989

Clothing Retailers	Rent as Percentage of Sales
Marks and Spencer	1.0
Sears	3.0
Next	3.9
Laura Ashley	5.4
Storehouse	5.8
Burton	7.1
Etam	9.1

Source: *County NatWest Woodmac*, "Marks & Spencer: Quality and Value," May 8, 1990.

The nature of M&S's Canadian operations changed dramatically in 1975 when M&S purchased a 55 percent controlling interest in Peoples.[5] In addition to the Peoples Department Store chain, the acquisition gave M&S an interest in Walkers and D'Allaird's, two other retailers Peoples owned.

M&S converted the 46 Walkers stores and the original St. Michael Shops into Marks and Spencer units similar to traditional M&S stores in the United Kingdom. Upper management came largely from Baker Street, and store operating systems were patterned on those in the U.K. Merchandise lines included both textiles and food, a new combination in Canada. All merchandise carried the St. Michael brand name.

In 1977, the Canadian M&S stores incurred a loss of C$6.8 million, due primarily to the clearance of non–St. Michael goods from the stores and the disruption of trading during the change. Management hoped that the entire cost of the changeover had been absorbed and that future returns would be free of substantial nonrecurring costs. However, the M&S outlets continued to show losses until the mid-1980s (Exhibit 5).

These losses were partly due to intense competition, but also reflected some miscalculations by M&S. As the problems became clear, M&S made a number of changes. To accommodate car-borne customers, it relocated a number of stores from downtown shopping districts to enclosed regional malls. In addition, it brought stores in line with Canadian retailers by brightening decor, adding fitting rooms, and promoting fashion items along with the more standard lines. M&S also began to advertise.

Sources of supply were a nagging problem for M&S in Canada. Because of high tariffs on goods entering Canada, M&S departed from its policy of exporting goods from the United Kingdom. By the mid-1980s, over 90 percent of the textiles and 70 percent of the food lines were based on Canadian sources of supply. However, M&S found the quality of these goods to be poor. By 1988, in spite of the high tariffs, products for the Canadian M&S stores were sourced primarily from the U.K. and the Far East.

Peoples and D'Allaird's

Following their acquisition, the D'Allaird's and People chains operated nearly autonomously. D'Allaird's was a highly profitable chain that sold coats, suits, dresses, and sportswear, most of which carried the D'Allaird's label. Target customers were middle-aged women who were extremely loyal to the store. Merchandise was perceived to be of good value, prices were middle-range, and excessive fashion statements were avoided. The chain maintained rigorous fit and quality standards.

The average sale per customer at D'Allaird's was well above Canadian retailing averages. The chain used a limited amount of advertising and offered only two promotional sales a year. D'Allaird's supplied 30 to 35 percent of its merchandise from its own Montreal factory and sourced the remainder from nearly 50 external suppliers. Distribution, inventory, and shrinkage were very tightly controlled.

The stand-alone Peoples department stores, typically located in rural areas, offered a wide range of goods including housewares, textiles, furniture, and some packaged food. The chain competed in the medium- to low-price range, advertising extensively through newspaper flyers and leaflets.

[5]In order to rationalize M&S's Canadian holdings, Peoples then acquired M&S's 50 percent interest in St. Michael Shops. This move left M&S with a controlling interest in Peoples, which now owned the St. Michael Shops.

▲ EXHIBIT 5 Canadian Results (C$ millions)

	1977	1978	1979	1980	1981	1982	1983	1984	1985	1986	1987	1988
Sales												
Marks and Spencer	60.8	65.4	70.0	81.6	93.9	98.7	104.5	111.5	113.3	136.8	158.8	170.9
Peroples	49.7	52.4	26.7	63.5	75.3	85.7	94.9	108.6	122.6	132.1	149.1	152.2
D'Allaird's	20.4	22.9	55.2	34.5	38.7	42.0	51.8	56.6	59.4	67.4	77.5	81.2
Operating profit (Loss)												
Marks and Spencer	(6.8)	(6.5)	(6.9)	(5.8)	(2.9)	(1.4)	(0.8)	0.1	(1.2)	3.2	4.0	0.9
Peoples	3.2	4.1	4.4	3.8	5.3	6.1	6.2	9.3	10.4	7.9	1.5	0.9
D'Allaird's	2.4	2.3	4.0	5.3	5.4	4.6	7.8	7.0	6.3	9.4	11.9	11.1

Source: Marks and Spencer.

Peoples produced more than a decade of stable returns for M&S with little added investment. However, due to increased competition and increasing operating costs, profits dropped sharply in the late 1980s. In response, management took measures to clear unwanted stock and improve information systems.

Entering Continental Europe—1975

In February 1975, M&S opened its first European store on the Boulevard Haussmann in Paris. Later that year, a store was opened in Brussels and another in Lyon. By the close of fiscal 1988, M&S operated 11 stores in Europe. Two additional stores were scheduled to open in Ireland in 1989.

By 1988, all of the European stores were profitable, but the bulk of the profits came from the three capital cities (Paris, Brussels, Dublin). Performance in the smaller provincial stores was less satisfactory. In general, clothing was M&S's most profitable line in Europe. Except in central Paris, the performance of the food offerings was disappointing.

M&S's most concentrated European effort was in France, where it operated eight stores, all serviced by the nearby U.K. supplier network. The French clothing market was roughly the same size as the U.K. market of about £15 billion per year, and people in both countries spent nearly £280 per year on clothing. However, the structures of the respective retailing markets were quite different. In France, independent stores had double the market share of those in the United Kingdom, and hypermarkets[6] held a 17 percent share, compared to a 3 percent share in the United Kingdom. Also, multiple chain stores (multiples) were relatively weaker in France.

This picture began to change in the 1980s. Although the market remained highly fragmented, hypermarkets and multiples gained share at the expense of the independents. The largest multiple chain, C&A, had established nearly 40 stores across France in the previous 15 years, achieving a market share of 1.7 percent in 1987 (Exhibit 6). During this period, revenue growth in department stores was stagnant at best.

Market research in France revealed that M&S merchandise was viewed as somewhat old-fashioned. Customers tended to be older than in the United Kingdom. As in the U.K., however, those who shopped in M&S recognized the store's value, service, and quality (Exhibit 7). Discussing these findings, David Norgrove, head of strategic planning, said,

> Once people come into our stores and get to know us, on the whole, they like what they find. People who don't shop with us don't see the qualities we offer. So the task, among other things, is to encourage more people to come into our stores and to bring the ages of our shoppers down more into the range of our core in the United Kingdom, broadening our market.[7]

By standards of French retailers, M&S stores in France used space intensively. However, by U.K. standards, turnover in the stores was low and trading hours were long. In addition, several of the stores were designed for higher sales than had been realized. The impact of these costs was mitigated by considerable higher gross profit margins in France.

In 1988, a study team evaluated possible expansion plans for France, as well as opportunities in other countries. Economic and retailing conditions differed substantially across European countries (Exhibits 8 and 9). M&S discovered, however, that with few seasonal and

---

[6]Hypermarkets were self-service retail outlets offering a wide range of food and nonfood products at competitive prices. They had selling areas of at least 2,500 square meters and provided ample parking space for customers.
[7]Marks and Spencer, "France: Opportunity and Progress So Far," 1988.

▲ EXHIBIT 6   French Clothing Competitors in 1987

Competitor	Market Share of Clothing Sales (%)
La Redoute	4.3
3 Suisses	3.0
Carrefour	2.1
Leclerc	2.0
Printemps	1.8
C&A	1.7
Auchan	1.7
Nouvelles Galeries	1.6
Monoprix	1.3
Galeries Lafayette	1.1
Euromarche	1.0
Mammouth	1.0
Quelle	0.9
Prisunic	0.7
Pantashop	0.7
Continent	0.7
Kiabi	0.7
Leclerce Textile	0.6
Marks and Spencer	**0.6**

Source: Marks and Spencer, "France: Opportunity and Progress So Far," 1988.

▲ EXHIBIT 7   Perceptions of M&S by the French in 1987 (in percentage)

	Pleasant Place to Shop	High Standard of Service	Good Value for Money	Good-Quality Clothing	Fashionable Clothing	Clothing for Older People
Shoppers	74	61	49	73	24	60
Nonshoppers	33	34	15	52	15	50

Source: Marks and Spencer, "France: Opportunity and Progress So Far," 1988.

cultural exceptions, tastes in clothing were remarkably similar across countries. The firm referred to this phenomenon as the "globalization of fashion." Summer slacks popular in England also did well in southern Spain; the only difference was that they would sell for a longer period in Spain's warm climate. M&S also had to pay close attention to local customs; for example, purple was a funeral color in Spain.

1989	Total Market (£ billions)	£ per Head	Percent Independents
United Kingdom	23	404	25
Belgium	4	405	70
Denmark	2	381	25
France	24	435	45
Greece	2	211	80
Ireland	1	248	50
Italy	32	562	70
Luxembourg	0	402	45
Netherlands	6	405	35
Portugal	2	178	50
Spain	11	291	80
West Germany	34	553	20
Austria	5	623	35
Finland	2	376	30
Iceland	0	678	NA
Norway	2	487	25
Sweden	4	514	20
Switzerland	3	439	35
Cyprus	0	475	NA
Liechtenstein	0	449	NA
Malta	0	210	NA
Turkey	3	57	80
Yugoslavia	1	38	NA
Total West Europe	163	373	
Soviet Union	108	104	NA
Albania	0	61	NA
Bulgaria	1	68	NA
Czechoslovakia	2	91	NA
East Germany	11	117	NA
Hungary	1	63	NA
Poland	1	23	NA
Romania	2	71	NA
Total East Europe	126	211	
Total Europe	289	343	

Source: Marks and Spencer, Economic Information Department.
Note: NA = not available.

▲ EXHIBIT 9   Concentration Levels in Food Retailing

Country	Market Share of Top Five Firms
Norway	81
Denmark	78
Belgium	60
Netherlands	60
United Kingdom	60
Ireland	57
West Germany	51
France	30
Italy	21
United States	20
Greece	15
Spain	15
Portugal	9
Sweden	8

Source: "Ahold and AMS: European Retail Synergy Marketing," *Harvard Business School,* Case #591-054, 1991.

▲ M&S UNDER LORD RAYNER (1984–)

M&S in 1984

In the mid-1980s, some investment analysts were disappointed with M&S's performance. A Scott Goff Layton & Co. report stated:

> In sporting parlance, M&S can be likened to a powerfully built athlete capable of winning a lot more races but never reaching true potential. The reason is the company has always performed well within itself, (but) it has never been pushed beyond three-quarter speed.[8]

Some described the company's performance during this period as "satisfactory, but not exciting." Profit margins had fallen as operating costs increased, partly due to laborious manual control systems and an outdated distribution network.

M&S had recently followed very conservative financial policies, including financing store development (of little more than 2 percent per annum) out of U.K. cash flow. As a result, M&S stores were overcrowded and substandard in appearance.

Lord Rayner was appointed chairman in 1984.[9] He had joined M&S in 1953 and had been appointed to the board in 1967. Rayner had a very close relationship with the Sieff family and was the only nonfamily member to serve as chairman since Simon Marks had developed the modern company.

---

[8]"How Far Is Marks and Spencer a New Investment?" September 1985, p. 7.
[9]A systems expert, Rayner was knighted for his work on defense procurement in the Heath government. In 1983, he became a life peer for his contribution as an informal advisor to Mrs. Margaret Thatcher.

Lord Rayner initiated pivotal changes at Mark and Spencer. Some described these as a "quiet revolution."[10]

Management Development

The new chairman thought exposure to a variety of functional assignments developed well-rounded businesspeople. He encouraged managers to accept cross-functional assignments so that they would appreciate challenges that transcended narrowly defined business responsibilities.

Lord Rayner expected executive and divisional directors to be aware of and participate in every aspect of the firm's development. He met with each group regularly to discuss issues of broad concern to the firm, such as "What are the proper spheres of influence of stores, divisions, and head office?" and "How do we select and develop the leaders of the future?" Weekly meetings in London ensured that all executive directors were informed of specific developments throughout the business. The wide range of questions that Lord Rayner addressed in the annual stockholders' meetings reflected issues with which he expected all executive directors to be familiar (Exhibit 10).

Scrutinies　In service to the prime minister from 1979 to 1982, Rayner headed the government's drive to improve efficiency and eliminate waste in Whitehall.[11] As head of the Efficiency Unit, he initiated a series of *scrutinies* to review government departments, which resulted in managerial reforms.

When he returned to M&S, Lord Rayner instituted a scrutiny process that furthered the firm's dedication to probing. The technique consisted of three elements:

▲ Examination of a specific area of activity, questioning all aspects of the work normally taken for granted.

▲ Proposal of solutions to any problems and recommendations to achieve savings and increased efficiency.

▲ Production of an action plan to ensure implementation of recommendations.

Scrutineers were middle managers. Lord Rayner believed that they were "best equipped and indeed anxious to propose changes and make recommendations to achieve increased efficiency and effectiveness."[12] They were urged not to make the scrutiny a desk study, but to talk to people at all levels and to go outside the company if necessary to gather information.

Following a two-week preparation period, the scrutineer had six weeks to carry out the scrutiny and submit a final report to the chairman and two more weeks to formulate an action plan. Within six months, the scrutineer was to help implement recommendations and file a progress report. A short chain of command ensured a quick response to scrutineers' recommendations.

Since initiating the scrutiny process in 1984, 49 scrutinies had been carried out. Examples of scrutinies included "The Disposal of Below-Specification Merchandise," by A. B. Moore, "Store Display of General Merchandise," by M. Clarkson and R. A. Sadler, "The Causes of Food Waste," by H. F. Eastwood, and "Recruitment and Retention of Store General & Supervisory Staff," by N. A. Instone.

---

[10]Maggie Urry, "St. Michael's Quiet Revolution," *Financial Times,* May 21, 1988.
[11]Location of British government offices.
[12]Lord Rayner, "Back to Basics," speech in May 1990, p. 10.

Mr. Lambert:	Why are we promoting the firm under two names? Who are those other people, D'Allaird's? Surely we are promoting Marks and Spencer. Can we have this altered so that we have one label?
Lord Rayner:	D'Allaird's is a very successful company which you own. Its returns on sales last year were 15 percent, which, I have to tell you, is better than its parent…. [Our Marks and Spencer stores should be] the appropriate copy of the kind of business we know here. [It would not be appropriate] to use an enormously successful asset under a name that people know would be wrong.
Mr. Hoser:	The turnover of the 262 stores [in Canada] was £210 million, which is about one-nineteenth of the U.K. stores. I find that a poor performance on the Canadian stores.
Lord Rayner:	The Marks and Spencer stores are much smaller than the UK stores, with two exceptions. [Furthermore, the levels of trading in the two countries are quite different.] Our stores in Toronto, Canada, for example take C$600 per foot, which is very high in that marketplace…. D'Allaird's are small shops of 3,000 feet and less, so they in no way compare with stores here. Peoples is another kind of chain. It is a store that trades in communities where there are no other stores. It is in Quebec in the main, where these communities are many miles apart…so the cost of operating them in rent and occupancy is low, but equally there are not a lot of people to come and shop there. Until last year when we acquired control and decided to revamp the whole stock and put in modern levels, it had been trading very profitably since we have been associated with it, so we cannot compare England with Canada.
Mrs. Dillon:	Could we compete more actively…on the production of foods that have reduced sugar?…I know that you are very keen on health foods and convenience foods and so on, but in one or two lines we have not quite got it.
Lord Rayner:	We are continually reviewing sugar levels and salt levels. We have, as you have rightly suggested, for many years tried to produce wholesome foods and bring sugar levels down where we think that it is possible and acceptable. There are some products, particularly the St. Michael's brand, where the level of salt and sugar is dictated for reasons of safety. Both, in one form or another, are a form of preservative. But we are very conscious of people's dietary needs and we do, as you know, take the lead. Unfortunately, the last major experiment on calorie-controlled foods was not very successful, but we will try again. I must say that the extra creamy yoghurt is a much faster seller than the one without sugar. But we will continue to try.
Mr. Clark:	Regarding your pajamas, would it be possible, instead of that wretched elastic, to have a cord? I have experienced your otherwise lovely goods, but after eight washes I don't stand up in my pajamas without them falling round my ankles.
Lord Rayner:	Well, I have to tell you that our elasticated waists should stand up to use rather better than you suggest, so I think we had better make a note of your complaint and do a bit of research. We do try cords from time to time. The problem with cords is they get tangled nowadays in washers and they come out, and [people] find it very difficult to put them back in again. I must tell you that I bought some recently in the States with a cord, because they came that way, and I have serious trouble getting them back again.
A Female Shareholder:	I have two very small complaints about your shops…. You have columns with mirrors on four sides, all of which are obscured by rails of clothing. All you see is the top of your head and your feet; you cannot see how the garment looks against you. The other point is that the tag attached to the care label on the garment to stop thieving…obscures the legend about what the article is made of. I have tried to prise it, but I cannot see whether it is cotton or poly-cotton, or whatever.

Lord Rayner: I will deal with the second point first. Of course, we should not apply anything on garments which obscures the labels, so we will certainly investigate that straight away. We only have that in use in 14 stores and we are watching it. We would like not to use them at all, but [stealing] has become a problem nowadays, so we are continuing the experiment to the end of the year.... In the meantime, we will make sure that we do not obscure labels.

On the mirrors, we always seem to get our mirrors wrongly placed. I think part of the problem is the amount of space we have. Certainly in some of our larger stores—one I know well—there are more mirrors in that space. We will have a look again and make sure that, as we work under severe pressures of space, we do leave enough space for customers to see themselves, because we know that it is very important to them.

Source: Marks and Spencer

Finance

Mr. Keith Oates was brought in as finance director from Thyssen-Bornemisza (and earlier, Black and Decker)—the first executive director who did not rise through the ranks. The financial systems installed by Lord Marks were still used but were no longer sufficient. Profit information by business line did not exist, and there were no systematic procedures for allocating corporate costs.

Looking back on this situation, Mr. Oates said, "Some people felt responsible for the gross margin, others for costs. They didn't see the vertical picture." Mr. Richard Greenbury commented, "During those years, we constantly drove sales forward. All the management did was to look at sales. We were not as focused on profitability as we now believe we should have been."[13]

M&S installed new control systems throughout the company. According to Mr. Nigel Colne, then director of store operations, "There is now a far clearer view of how costs are incurred in our business and which group should carry them."[14] This change was consistent with Lord Rayner's desire that managers develop greater awareness of and responsibility for the profit of the firm.

Store managers adopted annual operating plans that included quarterly profit and loss accounts for their stores. Instead of striving only to maximize sales, these managers now could evaluate the cost of various sales programs and their impact on profitability.

The addition of charge-card services in 1985 was another positive change for M&S. Industry observers were sanguine about the charge-card operations. In accordance with lending laws, charge-card interest rates could exceed base rates considerably. With sales of £287 per card per annum, a base of 2 million cards covered fixed operating costs and supported a significant profit contribution. The firm expanded its financial services in 1988 to try a personal loan scheme in which cardholders could borrow unsecured amounts between £500 and £5000 for any purpose.

Information Processing

In the early 1980s, M&S manually audited its over 150,000 stock-keeping units (SKUs) and had a decentralized distribution network. Textiles were held in 50 local warehouses and

[13]Urry, "St. Michael's Quiet Revolution."
[14]Ibid.

J·I·T

considerable (yet cramped) storage spaces in individual stores. For food products, a combination of transport companies, local bakeries, and product suppliers made deliveries to each store.

M&S introduced a state-of-the-art data recovery system in 1986 that enabled it to track sales and inventory electronically. The value of the electronic point-of-sales system (EPOS) was enhanced by a near-complete realignment of product storage and distribution.

Under the new system for textiles, the head office collected information from the stores and placed orders with 12 third-party multiuser warehouses. When stock was needed, M&S notified suppliers who would, if possible, make new deliveries to the warehouses. The maximum benefits from this system came when the supply of textiles was brought into close alignment with demand, thus reducing costly markdowns on slow-selling merchandise and stock-outs on popular items. Although the nature of M&S's primary textile offerings shielded the firm from dramatic swings in style, stock-outs and markdowns significantly impacted the firm's profit.

M&S was confident that, due to its relationship with its suppliers, it could derive much more value from this system than a typical retailer. M&S and some of its key suppliers were forerunners in establishing "flexible response" in retailing. Under this system, data on current sales triggered changes to merchandise in process and altered shipping schedules. This was made easier by the use of part-dyed and part-made-up merchandise, which could be finished in the necessary sizes, colors, and styles as the season progressed. New information technology was intended not only to increase efficiency but also to enable sales assistants to spend more time learning about the merchandise and assessing customers' needs.

Store Refurbishment and Expansion

In 1939, M&S had 234 stores and 2.2 million square feet of total selling space. By 1984, the number of U.K. stores had grown to 272, with a total selling space of 7.2 million square feet. Management acknowledged that expansion efforts had been inadequate to keep pace with the growing range of M&S goods. Stores were cramped and no longer provided a "comfortable and enjoyable shopping experience."

In 1984, Lord Rayner announced the largest development program in the history of the company. During the next four years, M&S modernized all its stores and added satellite stores where space restrictions prohibited the expansion of existing locations. A number of food-only outlets were established as neighborhood stores along with out-of-town and edge-of-town facilities for the convenience of car-borne customers. This £1,600 million effort dovetailed with the introduction of EPOS systems and the conversion of inventory space in stores to sales footage.

The first out-of-town store was opened in October 1986 at the Metro Centre near Gateshead.[15] In 1987, in a joint-site development agreement with Tesco PLC, M&S opened an edge-of-town store at Brookfield Centre in Hertfordshire. The center included parking for nearly 2,000 cars, a petrol station, a restaurant and three other shops. The M&S store had 69,000 square feet of selling space, with 12 room settings showing furniture furnishings, and housewares. M&S planned to have 10 such stores in operation by 1992.

M&S believed that no retail organization competed directly with it on a worldwide basis. However, the firm recognized several competitors in specific product categories and geographic areas. Exhibits 11, 12, and 13 provide information on M&S and its competitors in the United Kingdom.

---

[15]In 1985, when M&S began to pursue out-of-town locations, there were nearly 400 food superstores located in out-of-town or edge-of-town developments. These stores had floor space totaling over 15 million square feet and sales of £6 billion. In addition, there were over 500 self-service superstores, offering a wide range of goods and services, with a footage of 13.5 million square feet and sales of £900 million.

▲ EXHIBIT 11   U.K. Retail Clothing Competitors in 1988

Company	Total Sales (£m)	Clothing Sales (£m)	U.K. Clothing Market Share[a]	Number of Stores	Sales/ Square Feet (£)	Sales/ FTE[b] (£'000s)	Wages/ Sales (%)
Boots	2,590	1,980[c]	NA	1,026[c]	360	35.9	19.6
Burton	1,590	1,498	8.9	1,709	NA	56.7	16.2
Kingfisher	2,172	NA	NA	1,620	NA	61.9	13.1
Marks and Spencer	**4,578**	**2,016[d]**	**15.0**	**283**	**411**	**105.0**	**8.7**
Next	920	582	2.2[g]	665	273	64.7	11.6
Sears PLC	2,360	1,368[e]	13.9[g]	NA	NA	30.8	14.3
Storehouse	1,171	560[f]	5.1	131[f]	166	59.7	14.2

NA = not available.
[a] Source for market share data: *Verdict on Clothing Retailers*, February 1989, p. 24.
[b] FTE = full time equivalent.
[c] BTC only.
[d] U.K. only.
[e] Footwear retailing, specialty retailing, and home shopping.
[f] BhS only.
[g] Excludes mail order.

Source: Goldman Sachs, *UK Retail Handbook*, Summer 1990.

▲ EXHIBIT 12   U.K. Retail Food Competitors in 1988

Company	Total Sales (£m)	Food Sales (£m)	U.K. Food Market Share[a]	Number of Stores	Sales/Square Feet (£)	Sales/FTE[b] (¢'000s)	Wages/ Sales (%)
Argyll Group	3,236	3,230	5.0	952	NA	80.6	9.8
Asda Group	2,577	2,311	5.1	120[d]	9.5[d]	87.1	9.7
Marks and Spencer	4,578	1,671[c]	4.6	283	NA	105.0	8.7
J. Sainsbury	4,792	4,792	11.9	283[e]	14.9[e]	88.5	10.3
Tesco	4,119	4,119	11.5	379	10.4	82.1	9.8

NA = not available
[a] Source for market share data: *Retail Intelligence* (1990), p. 2.38.
[b] FTE = full time equivalent.
[c] U.K. only.
[d] Asda stores only.
[e] J. Sainsbury stores only.

Source: Goldman Sachs, *UK Retail Handbook*, Summer 1990.

Share of Clothing and Footwear Market by Age Group

Age Group	M&S Market Share%
15–24	5.9
25–44	13.9
45–64	21.3
✳ 65+	23.6

Source: *County NatWest Woodmac,* "Marks and Spencer: Quality and Value," May 8, 1990.

BERKSHIRE PARTNERS

I view the [leveraged buyout] as a phase in a company's life.
Carl Ferenbach, general partner, Berkshire Partners

▲ LBO BACKGROUND INFORMATION

A leveraged buyout (LBO) is an acquisition financed using a relatively small contribution of equity. In the 1980s, a typical LBO consisted of 10 percent equity and 90 percent debt.[1] LBO funds or the mergers and acquisitions departments of investment banks usually initiated and arranged the transactions.[2] However, some companies undertook their own LBOs and sought financing from banks and other financial institutions. In the early 1990s, following the collapse of the high-yield market in late 1989, the recession that began in 1990, and the savings and loan and banking crises, the amount of debt financing available for LBOs declined, and equity contributions of 20 percent to 30 percent became the norm.

Within an LBO fund, each company had its own financing. Unlike a corporation, an LBO fund did not cross-subsidize among its companies. This increased the risk of LBOs because an acquired company's cash flow was sometimes inadequate to meet all its requirements. The high debt levels gave firms little leeway before becoming insolvent (Exhibit 1).

---

[1]John Liscio, "The Buyout Bubble," *Barron's,* October 31, 1988.
[2]The term *LBO funds* refers to organizations established for the express purpose of administering LBO transactions.

Research Associate Dianna Magnani prepared this case under the supervision of Professor Cynthia A. Montgomery.

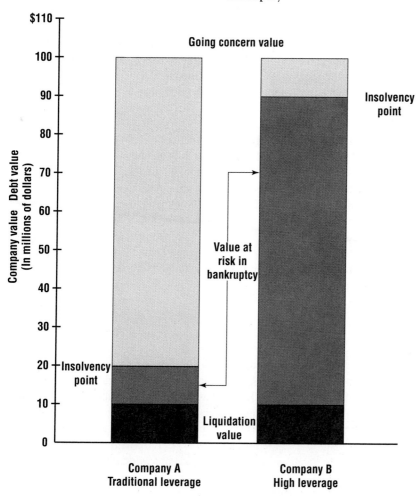

Source: Michael C. Jensen, "Eclipse of the Public Corporation," *Harvard Business Review,* September–October 1989, p. 73.

Commensurate with the high risk, LBOs could generate significant returns for both sellers and buyers of target companies. In situations where target companies were public, share-holders often received significant premiums over the market value for their shares. Similarly, annual returns on LBO equity investments sometimes exceeded 100 percent. Such phenomenal returns, however, became increasingly rare as the 1980s came to a close. Likewise, internal rate of return (IRR) targets declined from about 35 to 40 percent in the 1980s to about 25–30 percent in the early 1990s.

If circumstances were favorable, an LBO could eliminate all its debt in three to eight years. This often involved reducing operating costs, selling assets, and carefully managing expenditures for capital and research and development. When the company had established a pattern of debt reduction and continuing operating income, the LBO fund would most likely sell the company or make a public offering of stock in order to realize any capital appreciation.

During the 1980s, LBOs, were highly popular in the United States. Milton L. Rock, publisher of *Mergers & Acquisitions,* discussed two reasons for the prominence of LBOs: First, the transaction and oversight skills of LBO players had "improved dramatically." Due to this expertise, the risks of highly leveraged buyouts had become more predictable and manageable. Second, economic conditions, including restrained interest rates, low inflation, and tax laws favoring debt relative to equity, had been advantageous. Capital was abundant as the country experienced the largest peacetime expansion in its history. Further, as Rock noted, "The brisk economy created [a] fertile environment for selling assets to accelerate the deleveraging process."[3]

The number and total value of leveraged buyouts increased dramatically from 1980 to 1989. By the end of the decade, there had been 45 LBOs with acquisition values of $1 billion or more, all of which occurred after 1983.[4] The total value of LBOs increased not only in absolute terms but relative to all other mergers and acquisitions. Although LBOs accounted for only 9.9 percent of the mergers and acquisitions in 1989, they represented over one-quarter of the total value of these transactions.[5]

The recession that began in 1990 brought with it tight credit markets and price-competitive product markets. Combined with good public equity new issue markets, these resulted in LBOs being both less frequent and smaller (Exhibits 2 and 3). Accordingly, in the early 1990s, there were fewer LBO funds, and many of those still doing deals were deleveraging their portfolio companies.

Competitors

As the total value of LBOs increased in the 1980s, so did the number of LBO funds competing for investment opportunities. In 1989, there were over 150 leveraged buyout funds operating in the United States—some run by LBO firms, others by investment banks (Exhibit 4). Of these, 12 had $1 billion or more in equity capital available for investments. At least 40 additional funds had $100 million or more. Thus, over 50 funds were capable of performing a billion dollars worth of deals at a debt-equity ratio of 10 to 1. Some funds focused on specific industries or geographic locations, but most invested in a wide range of industries all over the United States.

Some management groups structured and implemented LBOs for their companies. However, debtholders were often more willing to lend in connection with LBO funds that had experience in carrying out transactions and reputations to uphold in the investment community. Furthermore, the partners in LBO funds often invested some of their own money in the buyouts.

As capital for investment became increasingly scarce in the early 1990s, the competition among LBO funds for investor dollars increased dramatically. Whereas an LBO fund managed by people with limited experience could be successful in raising capital in the 1980s, it was much less likely to prosper in the early 1990s. Many funds left the industry, and those that remained worked harder to secure investors, in several instances decreasing their fees and structuring investment terms to be more favorable to investors.

[3]*Mergers & Acquisitions,* November–December 1988.
[4]Ibid. November/December 1987 with updates from May—June 1988–1989.
[5]Ibid., May–June 1990.

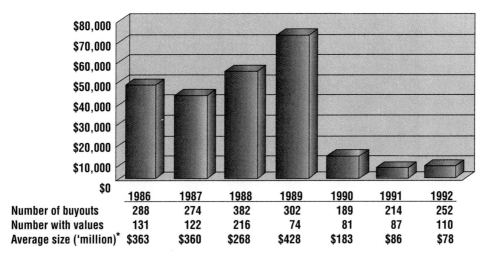

	1986	1987	1988	1989	1990	1991	1992
Number of buyouts	288	274	382	302	189	214	252
Number with values	131	122	216	74	81	87	110
Average size ('million)*	$363	$360	$268	$428	$183	$86	$78

*of those with values

Source: Securities Data Co.

▲ BERKSHIRE PARTNERS

Berkshire Partners (BP), an investment firm, organized its first limited partnership in 1984, a second in 1986, and a third in 1992. The firm's mission was:

> To achieve exceptional rates of return on capital through equity ownership. This is accomplished by investing in a portfolio of midsize companies that meet our investment criteria, including direct investment by management and prudent use of financial leverage. The firm seeks to provide an environment conducive to growth and development for both its portfolio companies and its own staff.

By 1993, BP had five general partners—Bradley M. Bloom, J. Christopher Clifford, Russell L. Epker, Carl Ferenbach, and Richard K. Lubin—and three junior partners. The firm focused on target companies valued between $25 million and $250 million. From 1984–92, Berkshire Partners and its affiliates[6] invested $139.6 million in the acquisition or recapitalization of 30 companies ranging from a jewelry retailer to an automotive parts manufacturer to the largest regional railroad (Exhibit 5).

The firm's main office was in downtown Boston. It was 6,500 square feet and housed all 5 general partners, 3 junior partners, 10 investment staff, and 6 general staff.

The partners felt that the firm's Boston location resulted in direct overhead and salaries (including partners' cash income) that were meaningfully less than those of an investment bank or of the corporate office of a similarly sized conglomerate. The most important source of the partners' income was realized gains on investments.

---

[6]The term *affiliates* refers to Berkshire Partners' two funds and certain current and former employees of Berkshire Partners.

▲ EXHIBIT 3   The 25 Largest Leveraged Buyouts of All Time, 1992

Acquiring Company	Company Taken Private	Value ($ millions)	Year
Kohlberg, Kravis, Roberts & Co.	RJR Nabisco Inc.	$24,716.9	1989
Kohlberg, Kravis, Roberts & Co.	Beatrice Cos. Inc.	6,250.0	1986
Kohlberg, Kravis, Roberts & Co.	Safeway Stores Inc.	5,335.5	1986
Thompson Co.	Southland Corp.	4,004.4	1987
AV Holding Corp.	Borg-Warner Corp. (90%)	3,763.6	1987
Wings Holdings Inc.	NWA Inc.	3,759.6	1989
TF Investments Inc.	Hospital Corp. of America	3,685.8	1989
Kohlberg, Kravis, Roberts & Co.	Owens-Illinois Inc.	3,668.0	1987
FH Acquisition Corp.	Fort Howard Corp.	3,589.3	1988
Macy Acquiring Corp.	R.H. Macy & Co. Inc.	3,501.1	1986
Kiewit-Murdock Investment Corp.	Continental Group Inc.	2,750.0	1984
Hillsborough Holdings Corp.	Jim Walter Corp.	2,436.5	1988
Kelso & Co.	American Standard Inc.	2,431.2	1988
Burlington Holdings. Inc.	Burlington Industries Inc.	2,155.7	1987
HealthTrust Inc.	Hospital Corp. of America (104 hospitals)	2,100.0	1987
IMA Holdings Corp.	American Medical International Inc.	2,001.8	1990
SMG Acquisition Corp.	Supermarkets General Corp.	1,812.6	1987
Kohlberg, Kravis, Roberts & Co.	Duracell Inc.	1,800.0	1988
DMPH Holding Corp.	Del Monte USA	1,775.0	1990
SCI Holdings Inc.	Storer Communications, Inc.	1,772.3	1985
Avis ESOP	Avis Inc.	1,750.0	1987
Private investor group led by Kohlbert, Kravis, Roberts	Union Texas Petroleum Holdings (50%)	1,700.0	1985
L Acquisition Corp.	Lear Siegler Inc.	1,689.4	1987
SIBV/MS Holdings	Jefferson Smurfit Corp.	1,655.5	1989
Aancor Holding Inc.	National Gypsum Co.	1,600.4	1986
Eckerd Holdings Inc.	Jack Eckerd Corp.	1,581.7	1986
FARLEY, Inc.	West Point-Pepperell Inc. (90.2%)	1,561.1	1989

Source: *Mergers & acquisitions,* November–December 1987, updates from May–June 1988, May–June 1989, May–June 1990, May–June 1991, and May–June 1992.

The three limited partnership funds (the Funds) invested primarily in equity securities. Two of them could contribute no more than 20 percent of their total assets to a single portfolio company; the third allowed for a contribution of no more than 30 percent. Institutions purchasing units in any Fund could not directly influence individual investment decisions.

Name of Fund	Size of Fund ($ millions)
Kohlberg, Kravis, Roberts & Co.	$5,600
Forstmann Little & Co.	2,500
Merrill Lynch Capital Partners, Inc.	1,900
Acadia Partners, L.P.	1,600
Thomas H. Lee Equity Co.	1,600
Butler Capital Corp.	1,400
Shearson Lehman Hutton Inc.	1,300
Wasserstein Perella Group Inc.	1,060
Clayton & Dubilier, Inc.	1,000
Continental Equity Corp.	1,000
The First Boston Corp.	1,000
Manufacturers Hanover Trust Co.	1,000
Welsh Carson Anderson & Stowe	910
Blackstone Capital Partners, L.P.	850
Prudential-Bache Interfunding (PBIF)	800
Donaldson, Lufkin & Jenrette Securities Corp.	750
Charterhouse Group International, Inc.	612
First Chicago Venture Capital	600
GKH Partners, L.P.	545
Onex Corp.	500
Chemical Venture Partners	450
Freeman Spogli & Co.	425
BancBoston Capital, Inc.	400
Brooke Partners, L.P.	400
Capital Corp.	400
Golder, Thoma & Cressey	395
Shamrock Holdings, Inc.	350
Boston Ventures Management, Inc.	327
Hellman & Friedman	325
Kenner & Co., Inc.	300
The Jordan Company	300
John Hancock Capital Growth Mgmt., Inc.	295
Narragansett Capital, Inc.	291
Adler & Shaykin	275
Frontenac Co.	254
Allied Capital	200
Berkshire Partners	**200**
Harbour Group	186

continued

▲ **EXHIBIT 4** *continued*

Name of Fund	Size of Fund ($ millions)
Griffin Capital Partners	150
Bain Capital	150
Carl Marks & Co., Inc.	150
Shea, Paschall & Powell	150
The Tribeca Corp.	150
McCown De Leeuw & Co.	138
Castle Harlan, Inc.	125
Centre Partners	120
Alspaugh & Co., Inc.	100
Ardshiel, Inc.	100
Grace Strategic Corp.	100
Bradford Assocs.	100
Dubin Clark & Co., Inc.	100
James A. Matzdorff & Co.	100
MMC Group, Inc.	100
Quincy Partners	100
Weiss, Peck & Greer	100
Zaleski, Sherwood & Co., Inc.	100
Saugatuck Capital Co. Limited Partnerships	93
Piper, Jaffray & Hopwood, Inc.	90
Code, Hennessey & Simmons	82
Cogeneration Capital Assocs., Inc.	75
MST Partners	75
VS&A Communications Partners, L.P.	5
Constitution Capital Corp.	55
Furman Selz Merchant Capital Corp.	55
KD Equities	55
Grubstein Holdings Ltd.	50
The Shansby Group	50
Stoneleigh Acquisition Fund	50
The Charter Group, Inc.	40
Gabelli/Rosenthal & Partners, L.P.	40
J.B. Poindexter & Co.	40
Hamilton Robinson & Co., Inc.	39
Davic Assocs.	38
Leperco Capital Mgmt.	32
First Interstate Venture Capital Corp.	30
Needham & Co., Inc.	30

continued

Name of Fund	Size of Fund ($ millions)
Wedbush Capital Partners	30
Jesup & Lamont Inc.	25
Keystone Venture Capital Mgmt. Co.	25
Leach McMicking & Co.	25
Wharton-Selby Capital partners	25
Barrington Capital Partners	20
D.H. Blair & Co., Inc.	20
Bradford Capital Partners	20
Alex. Brown & Sons, Inc.	20
Equity Dynamics, Inc.	20
Josephberg Grosz & Co., Inc.	20
Eden Hannon & Co.	15
McBain, Rose Partners	15
Signet Investment Banking Co.	15
B.C. Christopher Securities Co.	10
Diehl & Co.	10
Johnsen Securities	10
Pierce Financial Corp.	10
Goldmark	7
MBR Capital Corp.	6
Merchant Banking Group, Ltd.	6
Sutro & Co. Inc.	4
Globus Capital Group, Inc.	3
Raffensperger Hughes & Co.	3
TA Associates	2
Morgan Stanley & Co., Inc.	2
The Robinson-Humphrey Co., Inc.	1

Note: Fund sizes were not available for the following: Advest, Inc.; Andlinger & Co., Inc.; Arc Associates, Inc.; Asset Growth Partners Inc.; Bankers Trust Co.; Beacon Capital Corp.; Bear, Stearns & Co. Inc.; Bourgeois Fils & Co., Inc.; Canadian Imperial Bank of Commerce; Charles Street Securities, Inc.; Chase Manhattan; Chrysler Capital Corp.; Communications Equity Assocs.; Cortec Group, Inc.; Creative Business Strategies; Devries & Co. Inc.; Ditri Assocs., Inc.; DNC Capital Corp.; Dunlevy & Co.; The Dyson-Kissner-Moran Corp.; Equitable Capital Management Corp.; First Allied Corp.; First New England Securities Corp.; First Texas Capital Corp.; Fowler Anthony & Co.; GE Capital; Goldman, Sachs & Co.; Gruss & Co.; Hambrecht & Quist; The Harding Group; Heller Financial, Inc.; Household Commercial Financial Svcs.; IBJ Schroder Bank & Trust; Investcorp International Inc.; Kertes Moss & Co.; Kidd, Kamm & Co.; Kidder, Peabody Group Inc.; Kohlberg & Co.; Mabon, Nugent & Co.; Marine Midland Bank, N.A.; McKinley Allsopp Capital Holdings, Inc.; Milley & Co.; Montrose Capital Corp.; North American Capital Corp.; Odyssey Partners, L.P.; The Omni-Reed Group; Painewebber, Inc.; Alan Patricof Assocs., Inc.; Prudential Capital Corp.; R.A.B. Holdings, Inc.; Solomon Brothers Inc.; Security Pacific National Bank; Sorrento Assocs., Inc.; The Spectrum Group; Sphere Capital Partners; Stanger, Miller, Inc.; Sterling Grace Capital Mgmt.; The Sterling Group; Transcapital Corp.; The Trump Group; Venture Assocs.; Vestar Capital Partners, Inc.; Westinghouse Credit Corp.
Source: *Corporate Finance,* December 1989.

▲ EXHIBIT 5   Berkshire Partners' Portfolio Companies

Investments Fully Realized or Publicly Valued

Carlin Foods Corporation is a manufacturer of premixed food ingredients and vitamin supplements for the dairy, bakery, and food service segments of the food industry. The company was acquired with management from Mallinckrodt, Inc. in 1983 and sold to Bunge Corporation in 1987.

Federal Communications Corporation operates radio stations in Rhode Island and Kentucky. Berkshire Affiliates acquired the stations in conjunction with management in 1983 and sold its interest through a recapitalization organized by management in 1986.

Kelley Manufacturing Company was a domestic manufacturer of wheelbarrows and related goods. The company was liquidated for a loss in 1985 after experiencing a significant decline in its market position resulting from price erosion following a strategic shift by foreign competitors.

Chadwick-Miller Inc. operates book stores under the "Lauriat's" an "Royal Discount Books" names and markets a broad range of imported giftware items to catalog distributors. The company was acquired in connection with management in 1984 and was sold to an investor group, including management, in 1988.

Corhart Refractories Corporation is a manufacturer of specialty, high-wear performance refractory products for use primarily in glass and fiberglass manufacturing applications. The company was acquired in partnership with management from Corning Glass Works Company in 1985 and sold to St. Gobain of France in 1987.

Sterling, Inc. is one of the largest domestic retailers of jewelry with stores primarily located in regional shopping malls nationwide. The company was acquired in conjunction with management in 1985, taken public in 1986, and sold to Ratners Group, plc of the U.K. in 1987.

J. Baker, Inc. is primarily a retailer of footwear operating through licensed shoe department in discount department stores. The company also operates a chain of "one-price" shoe stores under the name "Parade of Shoes." Berkshire Affiliates acquired J. Baker in partnership with management in 1985. The company was taken public in 1986.

Amerace Corporation is a manufacturer of electrical components and highway safety products used by utility, commercial, and industrial customers. Berkshire Affiliates participated in the recapitalization of the company in conjunction with management in 1986. Berkshire Affiliates sold its preferred stock investment in 1987 at face value. In 1989, Amerace was sold to Eagle Industries, Inc.

GS Roofing Products Co., Inc. manufactures and sells roofing products for use in residential and commercial markets. The company was acquired from Imasco Ltd. in 1986. In 1988, Berkshire Affiliates sold its interest through a management-led buyout.

Panache Broadcasting Corporation operates four radio stations in Pennsylvania, Ohio, and Indiana. The stations were acquired in 1987, and Berkshire Affiliates sold its interest to management in 1988 in connection with a recapitalization.

Clean Harbors, Inc. is the largest provider of comprehensive waste management and environmental services in the northeast United States. The company provides these services to governmental, commercial, and industrial customers. Berkshire Affiliates invested in Clean Harbors in 1987, and the company was taken public in 1988.

Wisconsin Central Transportation Corporation owns Wisconsin Central Ltd., the nation's largest regional railroad. Its primary customers are large paper companies. Berkshire Affiliates along with management of the Wisconsin Corporation and other institutional investors acquired the assets of the company from the Soo Line Railroad Company in 1987. The company was taken public in 1991. Berkshire Affiliates sold its interest through a secondary offering in 1992.

Investments Partially Realized or Publicly Valued

United Cape Cod Cranberry Limited Partnership cultivates, processes, and markets cranberries for sale to juice and jelly manufacturers. The company also owns a substantial amount of real estate in Massachusetts. The company's assets were originally acquired with management from Cumberland Farms, Inc. in 1986. Due to financial difficulties, the company liquidated its assets in 1989.

Advanced Drainage Systems, Inc. manufactures high-density corrugated polyethylene pipe and pipe products in 23 plants nationwide. The pipe is used in various drainage applications, including roadway and residential construction, agriculture, recreational sites, and septic field systems. Berkshire Affiliates made an investment in the company in 1988 in conjunction with a recapitalization with management.

Lechmere, Inc. is a New England–based retailer of consumer electronics, home appliances, housewares, and leisure and sporting goods. Lechmere's marketing approach emphasizes a wide assortment of brand name merchandise, low-price guarantees, and innovative store design. Berkshire Affiliates, management, and outside real estate developers acquired the company in 1989 from Dayton Hudson Corporation.

Salem Sportswear, Inc. is a leading company in the design, manufacturing, and marketing of sports apparel licensed by the four major professional sports leagues and many colleges and universities. Berkshire Affiliates and the company's founders made an investment in the company in 1991 in conjunction with a recapitalization.

Private Companies Currently Owned

Black Oak Industries, Inc. (Shepard Clothing Company, Inc.) designs, manufactures, and markets men's tailored clothing consisting of private-label sport coats and suits. The company sells its products to a broad customer base comprised of major department stores, men's specialty stores, general merchandise chains, and discount outlets. The company was acquired in conjunction with management from Hanson Industries, Inc. in 1986.

Marcliff Corporation operates two businesses: one is a manufacturer and supplier of automotive products primarily for the professional and consumer markets; the other is a manufacturer and supplier of specialty incandescent and fluorescent light bulbs. The company was acquired in conjunction with management from American Brands, Inc. in 1987.

Perseus Oil, L.P. was formed for the purpose of acquiring and exploring leased properties in Oklahoma. The company's strategy is to recomplete oil and gas wells on such leases in order to generate enhanced reserves of hydrocarbons.

continued

Image Industries, Inc. is an integrated designated designer, manufacturer, and marketer of residential and commercial carpets. The company markets its products primarily to the medium- and high-end residential market, selling through independent wholesale distributors, retail dealers, and international agents. The company was acquired in 1987 from its founders, who continue to manage the company and own a significant equity interest.

WTI, Inc. through its AFA and Polytek operations, is a leading manufacturer of activated liquid dispensing devices known as trigger sprayers. AFA, located in North Carolina, sells its sprayers to packaging distributors and major consumer product companies. Polytek is located in the Netherlands and markets its products to distributors and consumer product companies in Europe, Asia, and Africa. Berkshire Affiliates made an investment in WTI, Inc. in 1988 in conjunction with a recapitalization including management and other outside investors.

Fresh Start Foods, L.P. is a manufacturer of shortening and bakery products for the fast-food restaurant industry. It is the leading supplier of shortening and the third-largest producer of buns and muffins for the McDonald's system in the United States, and has served McDonald's for over 25 years. The company was acquired in conjunction with management from Sysco Corporation in 1988.

Howard Press, L.P. manufactures business forms and other commercial print products. The company specializes in "contractual printing," and its customers are primarily Fortune 500 companies. Berkshire Affiliates and the company's founder made an investment in the company in 1989 in conjunction with a recapitalization.

Aetna Industries, Inc. is a manufacturer of metal stampings and welded subassemblies used as original equipment in the production of light trucks, vans, utility vehicles, and passenger cars. The company's principal customers are General Motors and Chrysler/Jeep Eagle. In 1989, Aetna Industries was acquired in conjunction with management from an institutional investor.

Xerxes Corporation is a manufacturer of fiberglass reinforced plastic underground storage tanks (550 to 50,000 gallons) for petroleum products. The company also designs and manufactures pollution and process control equipment constructed of fiberglass-reinforced plastic. Xerxes' customers include oil companies, industrial companies, and governmental authorities. The company was acquired in 1989 with management from its founder, who continues to be active in the business.

America's Best Contacts & Eyeglasses, L.P. is a retailer of contact lenses and eyeglasses with 56 stores throughout the United States as of December 1992. Its strategy is to be the price leader, providing high-quality eyewear for a low price. Berkshire Partners acquired the company from the original shareholders, primarily members of the founding family, in 1990.

Loveshaw Corporation is a leading designer, manufacturer, and distributor of corrugated case packaging and marking equipment for the food, beverage, pharmaceutical, paper, and textile industries. Berkshire Affiliates purchased the company in 1990.

Recreation Vehicle Products, Inc. is a manufacturer of air conditioners and awnings for the recreation vehicle industry. Berkshire Affiliates purchased the company from the Coleman Company in conjunction with management in 1991.

Atlas Paper Mills, Ltd. is a manufacturer of tissue products made from 100 percent recycled waste paper. Berkshire Affiliates and the company's founders invested in the company through a recapitalization in 1991.

continued

Papa Gino's Inc. is the largest quick-service pizza and Italian food restaurant chain in New England. Berkshire Affiliates made an investment in Papa Gino's in 1992 in conjunction with a re-capitalization including management and other outside investors.

Gold Coast Beverage Distributors, Inc. is one of the largest beer distributors in the United States. Berkshire affiliates made an investment in Gold Coast in 1992 in conjunction with a recap-italization including management.

Source: Berkshire Partners.

Berkshire Partners, a general partnership, made all acquisition decisions alone. It was also re-sponsible for obtaining and managing investments for the Funds and monitoring portfolio companies after acquisition.

Berkshire Partners' internal responsibilities included investor relations, maintaining an in-vestment strategy, marketing, and general administration and staffing. Externally, the firm cul-tivated relationships with five constituent groups: principals who were selling businesses; the management of target firms; intermediaries, such as investment banks, who provided invest-ment leads; investors in the three Funds; and financiers who provided junior and senior debt for portfolio companies. In addition, members of the firm spent considerable time monitoring and working with portfolio companies. Exhibit 6 presents BP's view of what it could offer each constituency and its means of establishing and maintaining relationships with them.

BP's investment cycle included identifying a business, analyzing it, negotiating terms, ar-ranging financing, closing the transaction, monitoring and working with the business, and achieving liquidity for its investment. For each company, BP thought in terms of a five-year relationship.

Identifying Target Companies

Before founding BP, all five general partners had diverse experience in general manage-ment, turnaround management, commercial and investment banking, and venture capital (Exhibit 7). Their backgrounds had been useful not only in developing skills, but in building business and personal contacts. Berkshire Partners considered these relationships very im-portant. The firm's network, consisting of co-investors in BP's acquisitions, former CEOs of Berkshire companies, investment and commercial bankers, accountants, and lawyers, identi-fied investment opportunities and recommended BP to those needing sponsorship. Through 1992, these connections were instrumental in obtaining 90 percent of Berkshire Partners' ac-quisition leads.

Berkshire Partners only participated in "friendly" bids, that is, those approved by the tar-get companies' boards of directors. The firm selected middle-market[7] companies, typically in high-growth business niches, that had potential to produce significant long-term appreci-ation in shareholder value. Its ideal targets were healthy companies with good management, but it also invested in companies with new teams of management investors in support of plans to reduce operating costs while growing revenues through renewed focus and high levels of customer service.

---

[7]Valued between $25 million and $250 million.

▲ EXHIBIT 6 Marketing Plan

Customers	Product	Price	How Sold	Advertising	Service	Competition
Principals/owners (owners, corporations divesting, other investment groups)	Ability to employ investment capital; financing; proven ability to close; knowledge of business; realistic goals; demonstrated success in prior deals	Not the highest price; reliability; financing	Direct and through intermediaries	Brochure, targeted mailings, seminars, articles	Deal team consulting at firm	Any buyer
Managers	Fair ownership interest; proper capitalization; knowledge of business; commitment to long-term growth and development	30–35 percent IRR to BP; equity return to them	Direct, phone, and mailings	Same as above plus management conference; investment programs for management	Same as above	Any buyer with a management ownership program
Intermediaries (investment banks, regionals, former managers, limited partners)	Market niche (size); history of closing; capital base; relationships	Not the highest price; reliability financing	Direct, phone, and mailings	Same as principals/ owners	Marketing staff and deal team	Any buyer
TBP investors (Fund investors)	Deal flow; mezzanine opportunities; process management (find, evaluate, negotiate, finance, close, monitor, exit); organizational depth	Management fee and override; often preferred return	Direct calling	Same as principals/ owners plus special mailings and annual meeting	Assigned partners and VPs; regular meetings, portfolio updates, annual valuations, deal flow, and investment opportunities reports	LBO firms, venture capital firms
Sources of financing (banks, major insurance companies)	Opportunity to provide junior and senior debt in BP portfolio companies	20% IRR	Direct (relationships)	Same as principals/ owners	Assigned partners and VPs plus deal team	

Source: Berkshire Partners.

General Partners

Bradley M. Bloom, general partner, has invested as a principal in private company acquisitions for over a decade. Previously, Mr. Bloom spent two years with The First National Bank of Boston specializing in secured financing and factoring. Since that time, he has been involved in all aspects of leveraged acquisitions. He received an AB from Harvard college and an MBA from Harvard Business School.

J. Christopher Clifford, general partner, has over 15 years of extensive experience investing in private company acquisitions. Mr. Clifford has actively participated as a principal in numerous middle market company transactions—actively assisting in the companies' acquisition, financing, and development. Earlier in his career, Mr. Clifford was responsible for corporate finance activities in a regional investment banking firm (now a part of Kidder, Peabody). He received a BA from Colgate University and an MBA from Harvard Business School.

Russell L. Epker, general partner, has 14 years of operating experience with Ford Motor Company, Xerox Corporation, and Tyco Laboratories, Inc. As vice president of operations at Tyco, he also directed the company's acquisition program, which resulted in Tyco's growing from $34 million to nearly $600 million in sales during the period 1974–1981. Mr. Epker has over 15 years of extensive experience in the acquisition of private companies. He received a BA from the University of Michigan and an MBA from Harvard Business School.

Carl Ferenbach, general partner, has over 25 years of experience in commercial banking, investment banking, and private company acquisitions. He was formerly a managing director of Merrill Lynch White Weld where he directed the Mergers and Acquisitions Department and led the firm's activities in its first major leveraged buyouts. Mr. Ferenbach is a frequent lecturer and author on the subjects of leveraged acquisitions and corporate governance. He received an AB from Princeton University and an MBA from Harvard Business School.

Richard K. Lubin, general partner, entered the leveraged acquisition business in 1981 after serving as the chief executive officer of FWD Corporation. At FWD Mr. Lubin took over a company with significant losses and quickly returned it to profitability. Prior to FWD, he spent 10 years in management consulting, specializing in the turnarounds of under-performing companies, often assuming an active management role on an interim basis. Mr. Lubin received a BS from the University of Pennsylvania and an MBA from Harvard Business School.

Junior Partners

Jane Brock-Wilson, vice president, has 11 years of diverse experience in manufacturing environments. Prior to joining Berkshire Partners in 1991, Ms. Brock-Wilson was a partner at Bain & Co. where she worked with clients in many industries, including the automotive, automotive supply, textiles, apparel, and waste services industries dealing with critical strategic, operational and marketing issues. Ms. Brock-Wilson received a BS in industrial management from Purdue University and an MBA from Harvard Business School. Prior to her graduate studies, Ms. Brock-Wilson was involved in production management at Raytheon.

continued

▲ EXHIBIT 7   *concluded*

Kevin T. Callaghan, vice president, joined Berkshire Partners in 1987. Mr. Callaghan began his career at Lehman Brothers Kuhn Loeb providing corporate finance and acquisition advisory services to the firm's energy, utility, and industrial clients. Subsequently he worked at Bain & Co., management consultants. Mr. Callaghan received a BS in engineering and management systems from Princeton University and an MBA from Stanford University's Graduate School in Business.

Garth H. Greimann, vice president, joined Berkshire Partners in 1989, after eight years in various positions with The First National Bank of Boston. Mr. Greimann served as vice president of the Bank's Acquisition Finance Division and assisted or led numerous leveraged acquisition transactions involving a broad range of businesses. Previously, Mr. Greimann served in the Bank's Korean and Taiwan offices, where he managed lending activities covering domestic and multinational companies as well as trade finance. He received a BA from Dartmouth College.

Source: Berkshire Partners.

The investment process involved thorough analysis of a company's operations, facilities, management, industry, and competitive and regulatory environments. A partner or a senior member of the investment staff used an extensive checklist to evaluate the target firm's competitiveness and financial strength, the economic characteristics of its industry, and possible deal structures. The partners believed that this formalized screening mechanism was necessary to efficiently process investment opportunities. For every 100 companies brought to BP's attention, the firm ultimately acquired only one.

If a business appeared to be a serious candidate, a deal team consisting of a partner, a vice president, and one or two associates was assigned to evaluate it further. After completing a detailed analysis of the operating characteristics of the business, the deal team developed a financial model driven by cash flow and calculated the expected returns from the proposed investment.

When screening serious candidate firms, one partner generally adopted the role of a skeptic, arguing against the acquisition and alerting the group to the potential downside of the transaction. Berkshire Partners would not commit to an acquisition without the general agreement of its investment staff. Once a company was chosen, the deal team handled the acquisition procedure.

Negotiating and Financing Acquisitions

BP purchased most of its companies through private arrangements that involved, at most, only a handful of potential buyers. When negotiating, the firm emphasized its proven track record in securing financing and working with management and its reputation for fair dealing. From time to time, BP also participated in auction bidding processes. The firm usually was not the highest bidder, even when its bids were successful. Of BP's 30 portfolio companies, 4 were acquired through competitive auctions.

Acquisitions were financed with a combination of equity securities, mezzanine securities (consisting of subordinated debt and preferred stock usually linked with an equity participation), and senior debt. Equity came from BP's Funds, its general and junior partners, some members of its investment staff, and target companies' management (Exhibit 8). Berkshire Partners offered its limited partners opportunities to invest in the mezzanine securities of its

▲ EXHIBIT 8   Ownership Structure

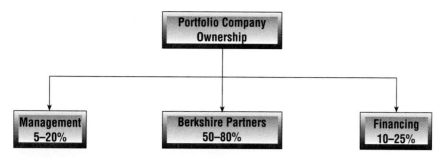

Source: Berkshire Partners.

portfolio companies. Commercial banks and other financial institutions provided the senior debt, based on the collateral value of the company's assets and the amount of annual cash flow from operations that would be available for debt service.

Alongside the three limited partnership funds, the general partners invested a fixed percentage in each transaction. Taken as a whole, this co-investment amounted to a meaningful portion of each fund and represented the principal personal assets of the partners.

The motivation behind the co-investment requirement was twofold: First, an investor's mentality was more beneficial to the limited partners than that of a money manager, second, the general partners could participate directly in the returns generated by their labor. The partners' large personal stakes differentiated BP from many other LBO firms and from public corporations. Whereas the usual requirement for a partnership was a 1 percent equity investment by the general partner, and there was no requirement for a public corporation, BP's general partners contributed about 7 percent of the equity for their LBOs. Carl Ferenbach stated,

> We purchase a significant amount of the equity needed to finance [an] acquisition ourselves, personally. How many senior managers of public corporations make a meaningful purchase of the corporation's common stock each time it makes a new acquisition?[8]

Monitoring Investment

BP argued that stock ownership by management and the need to service and repay a large debt increased a company's efficiency and competitiveness. Managers became much more focused on customers and spent more time developing relationships with suppliers. Equity ownership was a carrot and the large debt load was a stick.

Since BP placed its money and its reputation at stake in each investment, it actively monitored and worked with each firm. Its primary tool was management's five-year business plan on which BP had based its acquisition decision. The partner who had headed the deal team evaluated both financial and operating variables on a monthly or a weekly basis. The variables for each plan were unique to the company being studied. Although BP analyzed the numbers, it did not normally involve itself in the company's day-to-day operations.

Ferenbach stressed the importance of closely monitoring portfolio companies without running them on a daily basis, "We have to be in a position to understand important decisions.... [However], if we're telling management what to do, we're making a mistake."[9]

---

[8]*Harvard Business Review,* letter to the editor, November–December 1989, p. 204.
[9]Personal interview, February 16, 1990.

BP communicated with portfolio company management through monthly management meetings, annual planning meetings, sales meetings, formal board meetings, and numerous phone calls. Berkshire Partners maintained an active dialogue with management on resource allocation questions, such as capital expenditures and levels of working capital. The partners continually considered opportunities to lower a portfolio company's cost of capital. A board consisting of two BP partners, two members of portfolio company management, and one or two industry experts typically directed each acquired company.

Investment Goals

BP believed it created value in portfolio companies by encouraging them to concentrate on long-term growth. It argued that its very acquisition of a company often promoted this goal. Unlike a public company's management, an LBO company's management was responsible to a board that controlled the company. Without concern for reported numbers, management could focus on growth and development strategies.

BP thought it promoted value creation in other ways related to the incentives and guidance that it provided managers of portfolio companies. The firm believed shareholders' interests would best be served when managers had a significant ownership stake in the company they ran. Carl Ferenbach stated,

> When it's a public company and the manager doesn't own much stock, his career often is tied to empire building. When it's a private company and he owns a bunch of stock, and maybe borrowed some money to buy it, he pays a real penalty for empire building.[10]

> As a general manager, you are running your life from an income statement. When you become an owner, you run your life from a balance sheet as well.[11]

Management ownership of BP's portfolio companies consisted of equity purchased at the closing and free and performance-based stock options subject to five-year vesting. The performance incentives were usually based on management's ability to meet the strategic and operating goals it had set in its five-year plans. Berkshire Partners considered its history of successful relationships with management to be a competitive asset.

Investment Record

From 1984–92, Berkshire Partners and its affiliates invested $143.9 million in 31 portfolio companies. The sum of acquisition prices (inclusive of third-party financing) exceeded $1.5 billion.

At the end of 1992, Berkshire Partners had fully or partially realized upon 17 of the 31 companies it had acquired, one of which was liquidated for a loss under BP's control. The 12 fully realized companies, representing $51.0 million in investments by Berkshire Partners and its affiliates, produced annual returns of 79 percent. Each was sold within 21 to 62 months of purchase. The 19 companies Berkshire Partners still owned at the end of 1992 had been acquired in or after 1987 and represented $92.9 million in investments (Exhibit 9).

---

[10]"Roundtable: The Leveraged Buyout Market," *Mergers & Acquisitions,* Summer 1984, p. 36.
[11]"A Discussion of Corporate Restructuring," *Midland Corporate Finance Journal* 2, no. 2 (Summer 1984), p. 48.

▲ EXHIBIT 9   The Berkshire Funds and Affiliates* —Investment Summary as of December 31, 1992 ($000s)

	Purchase Price[†]	Berkshire Affiliates* Cost	Date Acquired	Date of Sale	Total Realized Value
Investments fully realized					
Amerace Corporation	$159,300	$15,000	7/86	9/89	$ 34,441
Carlin Foods Corporation	38,073	1,603	5/84	8/87	7,469
Chadwick-Miller, Inc.	18,200	1,421	10/84	12/88	12,864
Clean Harbors, Inc.	53,000	3,000	8/87 & 8/88	9/89 & 8/90	5,121
Corhart Refractories Corp.	37,300	2,791	5/85	7/87	6,636
Federal Communication Corp.	12,700	778	9/84 & 7/85	12/86	2,445
GS Roofing Products Co	60,000	2,400	12/86	12/88	6,706
J. Baker, Inc.	31,600	2,170	7/85	8/87	27,346
Kelley Manufacturing Company	29,700	4,208	10/84 & 11/85	12/86	71
Panache Broadcasting L.P.	32,000	1,600	3/87	12/88	3,609
Sterling, Inc.	39,100	2,880	6/85	8/87	35,919
Wisconsin Central Transportation Corp.	150,440	6,000	10/87	12/92	31,951
Income from continuing investments		NA			2,305
Subtotal		$50,974			$186,776
Investments partially realized					
Advanced Drainage Systems, Inc.	78,439	5,000	7/88	9/92	7,956
Lechmere, Inc.	120,000	233	10/89	5/91	229
Salem Sportswear, Inc.	24,065	1,500	6/91	6/92	1,708
United Cape Cod Cranberry, L.P.	29,500	390	3/86	12/92	0
					Proposed appraised value at 12/31/92[‡]
Private companies currently owned					
Advanced Drainage Systems, Inc.	$ 78,439	$ 6,662	7/88		37,000
Aetna Industries, Inc.	95,986	7,381	3/89 & 4/91		0
ABC&E	24,000	2,080	4/90		10,000

continued

▲ 299

▲ **EXHIBIT 9** *concluded*

	Purchase Price[†]	Berkshire Affiliates[*] Cost	Date Acquired	Date of Sale	Total Realized Value
Private companies currently owned					
Atlas Paper Mills, Ltd.	19,500	11,545	12/91 & 9/92		9,000
Fresh Start Foods, L.P.	54,653	2,800	11/88		8,259
Howard Press, L.P.	22,893	2,143	7/89		2,143
Image Industries, Inc.	31,500	1,858	6/87		4,000
Lechmere, Inc.	120,000	12,851	10/89		30,000
Loveshaw Corporation	34,500	4,944	8/90 & 11/91		2,472
Marcliff Corporation	27,300	1,688	5187		NA
Papa Gino's Inc.	54,294	8,950	4/92		20,814
Perseus Oil, L.P.	1,240	1,239	5/87–1/89		128
Recreational Vehicle Products, Inc.	31,456	4,800	5/91		10,000
Salem Sportswear, Inc.	29,393	3,812	6/91 & 6/92		27,066
Shepard Clothing Company, Inc.	32,700	1,895	6/86		0
United Cape Cod Cranberry, L.P.	29,500	3,510	3/86		0
WTI, Inc.	49,000	2,700	2/88		8,636
Xerxes Corporation	46,000	7,740	4/89, 9/91 & 3/92	2,000	
Gold Coast Beverage Distributors, Inc.	57,300	4,500	12/92		4,500
Subtotal		$ 92,901			$177,706
Totals		$143,875			$364,482

*Includes The First Berkshire Fund, The Berkshire Fund, Berkshire Partners, and certain employees of Berkshire Partners.
†Includes third-party financing.
‡The general partners of the Funds are required to value the Funds' investments at year end in accordance with generally accepted accounting principles. Many of the investments are carried at cost due to the relatively short period since the investments were made.

SATURN CORPORATION'S MODULE II DECISION

In the spring of 1994, Saturn Corporation was setting sales records by attracting more than 25,000 buyers per month. These results surprised many observers who had predicted an end to the company's growth after a slow first quarter. Since starting production of small cars in 1990, the newest division of General Motors (GM) had increased sales every year, putting 239,000 of its models on the road in 1993. Saturn officials believed there was a long-term opportunity to sell 400,000 to 500,000 cars per year in the U.S. and selected international markets.

To reach these sales levels, however, the company needed to convince GM to finance additional production capacity. Since 1985, GM had spent $3.5 billion to build a dedicated factory and establish the small car brand. Although Saturn earned its first operating profit in 1993, several analysts questioned whether GM could earn an adequate return on its investment. Saturn president Richard "Skip" LeFauve argued that the best way to build profits was by committing to opportunities that leveraged the company's fixed costs of manufacturing and marketing.

LeFauve and other Saturn managers had been reviewing options for a second assembly plant (known as "Module II") with GM since the beginning of the year. One possibility was to expand capacity at Saturn's existing production facilities in Spring Hill, Tennessee. The plant had been constructed between 1986–1990 after GM's management endorsed a "clean sheet" approach for the new nameplate. A second set of options involved refitting one of several GM plants that had been mothballed or was scheduled to close shortly. This approach required a lower fixed investment, but would create additional operating challenges as well as added operating costs.

Research Associate Greg Keller prepared this case under the supervision of Assistant Professor Anita M. McGahan and in consultation with Visiting Professor Arnoldo Hax.

▲ SATURN'S ACHIEVEMENTS

By 1994, Saturn had achieved "cult car" status. Most buyers were aware that the company had been founded to make GM competitive with Japanese imports in the small car market. Advertisements explained how manufacturing and retailing practices had been restructured to improve the overall ownership experience. Saturn's union workers exchanged hourly wages for salaries and bonuses tied to product quality and company profitability. A "no haggle" pricing system and extensive training of salespeople helped build positive relationships with customers. When something did go wrong, the company and its dealers made unprecedented efforts to solve the problem in a positive way. As a result, Saturn regularly earned a place alongside luxury brands in rankings of product quality, dealership satisfaction, and overall customer satisfaction.

Saturn was attracting a new audience for GM. About 45 percent of Saturn owners listed Japanese imports (primarily Toyotas and Hondas) as the car they would have purchased otherwise. Another 30 percent listed Ford and Chrysler models. Further research revealed that Saturn owners had higher than average education levels and household incomes. With a median age of just over 40, the typical Saturn owner was likely to buy four to five more new cars over his or her lifetime than an owner of GM's Cadillac, Buick, or Oldsmobile models (see Exhibit 1).

The company also served as a proving ground for new ideas. On the technical side, for example, Saturn's engine plant was the first to adopt an innovative casting method developed by GM's Technical Center during the mid-1980s. Similarly, the Saturn was the only car with durable thermoplastic panels that covered most of its body. These panels resisted minor damage from rust or dents, and were inexpensive to replace if they were cracked or scraped. At the retail level, the company implemented new approaches to inventory tracking and service management by using information systems to link dealerships with the factory and corporate offices.

Saturn was governed through a team structure that included suppliers, dealers, and union workers. Each member of a Saturn team participated in training programs that emphasized breaking down barriers among people with competing interests. Several Saturn officials said that on the best functioning teams, it was difficult to distinguish members of management from union representatives because of their focus on a common goal.

As a corollary to teamwork, the company committed to exchange what it learned with GM. Saturn's founders had reinforced this objective by including it in the company's mission statement. Information initially spread through corporate meetings, plant visits, and training sessions. In particular, GM's Oldsmobile group tried to incorporate styling features and customer service ideas to appeal to Saturn buyers who wanted larger cars. GM supported the knowledge transfer by promoting engineers and managers from Saturn into other divisions.

Despite these accomplishments, industry observers were divided over whether Saturn could be considered a success. Several Wall Street analysts questioned whether the company could sell more cars without competing with GM's other divisions. They argued that GM should devote its resources to its established car brands. Others believed Saturn should be judged by criteria other than just financial returns. Small cars had never been very profitable, and Saturn was breaking even after three-and-a-half years in production. Moreover, GM relied on Saturn sales to boost the average fuel efficiency of its fleet above the 27.5 mile per gallon threshold required by U.S. law.

▲ The risks for Saturn.

Option 1: Expand at Spring Hill

Locating the Module II site alongside the existing complex was viewed as the least disruptive option for expansion. Excess capacity at the engine systems and body systems factories would supply major components, while the company's current vendors would provide most smaller parts. The increased volume was expected to lower the production costs for these inputs. A second advantage was the presence of trained assembly workers and managers who understood the team management system. These seasoned employees would lead training sessions and could reinforce the lessons by example on the factory floor. Company officials also emphasized the value of informal communication between Module II and the other groups at the Spring Hill complex. They hoped this process would encourage innovation across the sites and reinforce Saturn's team-oriented culture.

UAW vice president Stephen Yokich was not as enthusiastic about the Spring Hill option.[2] He contended that it did not make sense to uproot workers from communities where factories had been shut down or were scheduled to close; GM should be spending any new investment to renovate these plants and retrain local workers. Yokich had been an outspoken critic of Saturn's flexible work rules and had asked to renegotiate the contract on several occasions. This position differed from that of Saturn's local union president, Mike Bennett, who had not given Yokich permission to reopen the agreement. Saturn could expand at Spring Hill without further negotiations, but the Saturn contract could not be applied to another site without the national UAW's approval.

Yokich was particularly interested in renegotiating Saturn's overtime policy. At other GM plants, assembly employees were paid overtime wages for working more than eight hours per day. At Spring Hill, union workers did not have a similar provision, allowing schedules of four 10-hour days per week. Bennett said this flexibility made it easier for Saturn to schedule three shifts per week, while saving the company up to $60 million per year in overtime pay.

Cost had been another deterrent to building Module II next to the existing complex. Constructing a new factory to raise capacity by 178,000 units would require an initial investment of $900 million, an amount GM was reluctant to spend during its turnaround phase. On the other hand, the advantages of lean supply lines and concentrated volumes were expected to reduce variable manufacturing costs to $7,200 per car by 1998,[3] a year after the module would be completed. Variable manufacturing costs currently averaged about $7,600 per car (excluding factory overhead, preproduction expenses, and depreciation charges). An incremental expansion of Spring Hill over a longer period would cost proportionately more per unit of capacity (see Exhibit 2 for a summary of options).

Option 2: Convert an Existing GM Factory

By investing at an existing GM site, Saturn and GM could reduce the initial cost of the project and generate goodwill with the UAW. This choice would signal a commitment to

---

[2]Local unions were covered by an umbrella contract negotiated by the national UAW, but were given flexibility to modify some areas of the agreements through bargaining with local plant managers.
[3]The figures in this paragraph are estimates by the casewriter.

adapt Saturn's management and manufacturing lessons into GM in cooperation with the national union leadership. The process of "Saturnizing" an established plant would also provide vital information about programs and practices that could be transferred to other GM factories. Saturn expected to transfer about 1,500 of its current employees to serve as a core for the new assembly site. Another 1,500 would be recruited from within GM and from UAW rolls of laid-off workers. These additional hires could come from any GM plant, although the applicant pool was likely to include a high concentration of people who had previously worked at the site Saturn chose. Saturn's trainers would lead all employees through classes to emphasize the company's values and initiate the team-building process. Teams would make recommendations on the factory's design, but they would be encouraged to replicate the assembly process at the Spring Hill plant.

Saturn's financial planner attempted to determine the optimal distance between a new site and the Tennessee complex. Many automakers built cars in separate regions to reduce delivery time and transportation expense to dealerships. Saturn weighed these factors against the costs of stretching its supply lines. Any Module II plant would rely on Spring Hill for major components. The company also wanted to avoid having different suppliers for the new site. Expanding on the West Coast had been ruled out, even though this alternative offered advantages for exporting to Asia.

Alternatives to expanding Spring Hill were suggested and explored by Saturn management. One choice was a closed plant in Willow Run, Michigan—20 miles west of GM's Detroit headquarters. This assembly plant had produced larger cars prior to closing in September 1993. Willow Run's local union had negotiated one of the most flexible contracts among GM plants in an attempt to avert a shutdown. This selection would signal a strong symbolic commitment to GM's constituency in the Detroit area. Another possibility was an underutilized Chevrolet Corvette factory in Bowling Green, Kentucky. Proponents said that this location, 50 miles north of Spring Hill via a major highway, would allow Saturn to retain many of its suppliers. Company officials also felt that Bowling Green's proximity would encourage cross-plant communication.

Saturn estimated the costs of converting Willow Run at $850 million, including relocation and training expenses. The facility could be operational in 36 months and would be capable of manufacturing 178,000 cars annually. Bowling Green would require a $900 million investment and would be ready for production within 30–36 months. Because of its smaller size, however, this site's capacity would be limited to 100,000 cars per year. (See Exhibit 2.)

As a prerequisite to converting Willow Run or Bowling Green, the company had to negotiate a separate contract with the UAW. Differences in the contracts at Spring Hill and the new site could lead to variability in the terms and levels of compensation. Assuming some sort of agreement could be reached, Saturn would have to adapt its organizational structure in response to the challenges of coordinating two locations. For example, the company had attempted to push decision making down to the factory floor, but with two plants, the choices made by teams might vary. If these differences were not reconciled over time, the modules might eventually disagree on larger issues, such as choices of suppliers or designs for the cars. Similarly, managing the array of cooperative relationships could be more difficult across two plants, especially if the labor-management partnership deteriorated at either one.

From a marketing and sales perspective, expanding outside of Spring Hill would probably enhance interest in the company. Saturn had attracted the public's attention in the late 1980s and early 1990s by advertising its ambitions to change the way cars were manufactured and

▲ EXHIBIT 2 Saturn's Options for Expansion

| | Option 1:
Expand at Spring Hill | | Option 2:
Convert an Existing
GM Factory | | Option 3:
Source Models from
Another GM Plant | Option 4:
Delay Expansion |
	Full Scale	Low Scale	Willow Run	Bowling Green		
Investment (millions)	$900	$700	$850	$900	$200	NA
Incremental annual capacity	178,000	110,000	178,000	100,000	50,000	NA
Time until onstream	30–36 months	18–24 months	36 months	30–36 months	6 months	NA
Targeted manufacturing costs per car*	$7,200	$7,600	$7,400	$7,300	$6,700 to $7,100 for lower-priced model	NA

*Variable costs per car after start-up at the new facility, including charges for transportation of components from Spring Hill (if applicable); these figures are estimates intended only to illustrate broad trade-offs and are sensitive to assumptions about wage rates, productivity, and design changes.
Source: Casewriter estimates.

sold. Spreading its methods to another production location would be an intriguing second chapter for "The Saturn Story." The potential disadvantage besides higher costs, however, was that any setbacks—such as quality problems or internal tensions—would occur under a spotlight of media attention. If these issues were not resolved to the public's satisfaction, Saturn could lose many of its admirers.

Option 3: Source Models from Another GM Plant

Company officials noted that this option would leverage Saturn's brand equity and sales network. Industry studies showed that customers had such a positive perception of the Saturn name that they would be willing to pay a premium for any car the company sold. Therefore, even though GM was likely to sell a hybrid of the new model through Chevrolet or Pontiac dealerships, Saturn's marketing and customer service would help distinguish the products.

Analysts offered mixed opinions of this option. While the financial details looked positive, some questioned the long-term effect of diluting the Saturn brand. Customer enthusiasm could diminish if the company was seen as deviating from its original goal of doing things differently. The move would also represent a shift in Saturn's mission of "market[ing] vehicles developed and manufactured in the United States," a fact that might be highlighted by the news media.

In addition, these changes would have major implications for the relationships among the various interest groups within and outside the company. Saturn's retailers might not be willing to maintain their "no haggle" pricing approach when a customer could negotiate a lower price for virtually the same car at a Chevrolet or Pontiac dealership. In addition, engineers would be likely to consider the outsourcing choice as an indication that they would eventually be transferred to the centralized NAO design center.

Option 4: Delay Expansion

"We can be profitable without [Module II], but we can be far more profitable over time by having added capacity," said Don Hudler, Saturn's vice president of sales, service, and marketing.[4] David Cole, the director of the University of Michigan's Center for the Study of Automotive Transportation, seconded this opinion while discussing Saturn's labor contract, the need for new products, and the plant expansion decision: "These are all important things that need to be done...but if they're not done in the next six months, it's not the end of the world."[5]

GM and Saturn had been trading proposals regarding Module II since the end of 1993, but no decision had been announced. Analysts suggested three likely reasons for the delays. First, when Saturn began meeting with its parent, GM's decision-making ability was affected by its limited resources. Consequently, GM seemed to focus on other priorities while waiting for its cash balances to recover. Second, Saturn's sales forecasts may have been questioned because of concerns about Chrysler's Neon introduction. The Neon had received strong endorsements from critics and was advertised at $1,000 less than Saturn's base model. Third, GM was pursuing closed-door negotiations with the national UAW to see whether the two sides could reach a compromise related to a Saturn contract for a converted GM facility.

[4]"A Falling Star; Mission Accomplished, Saturn Joins GM's Struggles," *Chicago Tribune*, May 1, 1994, p. 3.
[5]"Saturn Showing Growing Pains," *Gannett News Service*, June 23, 1994.

By June 1994, two of these three constraints had relaxed somewhat. GM's strong performance in the first half of the year generated capital to invest in the car divisions. Saturn had set a sales record in May, while the Neon's momentum had been slowed by a recall shortly after the model's introduction. One source said GM's final decision hinged on the outcome of bargaining with the UAW.

Meanwhile, every month of delay shifted the relative advantages of the options. Each one had a window of opportunity influenced by the required lead time (options 1 and 2) or by the planning processes at other divisions (option 3). In addition, Saturn incurred extra costs related to planning around several different outcomes. Mike Bennett, Saturn's local union president, noted that as the company had adjusted its business plans since 1992, several projects had been postponed or canceled. This process was especially difficult for teams preparing Saturn's international strategy since they did not know what types of new products the company would be able to provide.

▲ GENERAL MOTORS' NORTH AMERICAN AUTOMOTIVE OPERATIONS

GM's North American Automotive Operations (NAO) encompassed seven car and truck lines,[6] as well as numerous components suppliers. In 1993, the group accounted for 70 percent of GM's $134 billion in revenues and contributed $190 million in profits following three consecutive years of negative net income (see Exhibit 3).

The 15 years between 1979 and 1994 had been difficult for NAO divisions. In 1979, GM sold nearly half of all new cars in the United States. By 1993, its share had slipped to under 35 percent. Initial losses were attributable to competition from low-priced Japanese models that offered better fuel economy and superior reliability. In the late 1980s and early 1990s, GM faced increasing competition from its domestic rivals, Ford and Chrysler. These companies had taken steps to improve product development and manufacturing quality that were beginning to pay off.

GM's CEO Roger Smith had pursued a range of plans to revitalize NAO but achieved mixed results during his nine years at the helm. When he retired in August 1990, he told reporters he wanted to be remembered as someone who helped prepare GM for the next decade. He had invested heavily in plant technology and led GM into joint ventures with other automakers. However, he had also presided during the period of NAO's share declines that forced GM to close factories and lay off thousands of union workers.

NAO's problems escalated under Smith's successor, Robert Stempel. The continuing U.S. recession, coupled with increases in labor and benefits expenses, contributed to GM's losses of $2.0 billion in 1990 and $4.5 billion in 1991. In April 1992, the board of directors promoted John F. "Jack" Smith (no relation to Roger) to the presidency and placed John Smale, Procter & Gamble's former CEO, in charge of the GM executive committee. Stempel retained his duties as chief executive but his influence waned. In October of 1992, the board asked Stempel to step down and elevated Smith to CEO. Jack Smith had managed GM's international auto operations during the mid-1980s. His efforts to cut costs and streamline decision making were widely credited for transforming GM-Europe into a consistent profit center. As CEO, he issued a similar blueprint for GM's North American divisions.

---

[6]Buick, Cadillac, and Saturn were strictly car brands, while Chevrolet, Pontiac, and Oldsmobile marketed passenger trucks in addition to cars. GMC Truck, the seventh division, sold larger utility trucks and vans.

▲ EXHIBIT 3   Selected 1993 Financial Results for GM ($000s)

	Total*	North America*	Saturn†
Net sales and revenues	$124,869.9	$97,179.5	$3,000.0
Operating income	NA	NA	$ 100.0
Net income	$ 2,465.8	$ 870.9	NA
Number of employees (000s)	711	547	8

*Covers GM automotive operations and nonautomotive subsidiaries, except for GM Acceptance Corp. (financ-
ing and insurance). Revenues from Automotive Products totaled $107.9 billion in 1993.
†Estimates.
Source: GM 1993 10-K report, casewriter estimates.

By the spring of 1994, NAO had regained profitability. Customers were returning to
showrooms as the U.S. economy rebounded from a long recession. GM's divisions posted
gains of more than 19 percent in the first quarter, while the industry as a whole grew by about
14 percent on a unit basis. Analysts attributed the automaker's better-than-average results to
improved products and a strong yen, which eased price competition from Japanese imports.
Smith also predicted that NAO's share would grow as a result of new product introductions
planned for later in 1994 and 1995.

The Car Divisions

Alfred Sloan organized GM around car divisions in the early 1920s to offer "a car for every
purse and purpose." Chevrolet targeted entry-level buyers, while Pontiac, Oldsmobile, and
Buick offered models that moved progressively up the price scale. Cadillac staked out the high-
end market by providing the largest and most luxurious cars on the road.

From the 1930s to the late 1950s, each of GM's five divisions sold a distinct model. While
the cars shared basic components to save costs, every brand offered a different engine, chassis, and body style to create individual personalities. The corporation began deviating from
this formula in 1959 when it introduced smaller cars that shared "platforms" (i.e., engine and
chassis). This practice became known as "badge engineering." A decade later the company
offered 18 models, many of which differed in only cosmetic features. For instance, the Buick
Skylark, Oldsmobile F-85, Pontiac Tempest, and Chevrolet Chevelle were virtually identical
except for their body panels and upholstery.

Analysts believed GM's increasing reliance on badge engineering and other cost-saving
measures during the late 1960s and early 1970s reflected concerns about antitrust scrutiny by
the U.S. government. The firm had achieved a 50 percent market share and could no longer
aggressively increase sales without the threat of prosecution. Management therefore focused
on increasing profits by taking costs out of the vehicles. Over time, organizational units from
different divisions were merged until their boundaries were indistinguishable. This approach
produced strong financial results until the late 1970s.

In the face of new competitive challenges, GM attempted to revive the divisions' separate
identities under a major reorganization plan in 1984. The company's leaders considered re-
constituting the five divisions, but eventually decided to separate Buick, Oldsmobile, and
Cadillac (BOC) from Chevrolet, Pontiac, and Canadian operations (CPC). One executive recalled, "as we got to looking at the individual areas of expertise..., it was clear that you

couldn't cut them into fives without losing your critical numbers in any one of the capabilities. We finally concluded that two [groups] was as many as you could do."[7]

Saturn was formed outside the BOC/CPC framework to insulate the new division from budget pressure and tensions between brands. This independence was intended to provide flexibility for testing new ideas. Saturn was allowed to produce its own engines and transmissions to infuse the models with a unique feel. New features and styling choices reinforced the claim that Saturn was offering "a different kind of car."

The Turnaround Plan

Starting in 1992, Jack Smith pursued an aggressive plan for improving GM's financial results. Costs were trimmed by shedding layers of management and by following through on plans to close more than 20 assembly factories by 1996. Smith also dismantled the BOC/CPC structure, replacing it with a unified NAO strategy board. This group aimed to eliminate redundancies across divisions by centralizing the design, engineering, and purchasing functions for all brands but Saturn. Smith also announced plans to shrink the number of basic car platforms from 12 to 5, while supplementing the lineup with designs from GM-Europe.

During this transition, several observers predicted that GM would merge Saturn with Oldsmobile or Chevrolet. GM sources denied the rumors, but did not end speculation about the brand's future. Analysts said Saturn could achieve its volume targets by broadening its product line with either larger cars or subcompacts. A more conservative course involved building sales of its current class of products by adding dealerships in the United States and moving into international markets more aggressively. Every option carried implications for Saturn's capacity expansion, as well as for GM's other divisions.

Chevrolet   GM's largest division was leading the NAO recovery during the spring of 1994. First quarter car sales increased 21 percent over the same period in 1993, and the division's truck sales were up 20 percent. Managers said the gains could be attributed to Chevrolet's product "renaissance." The division had recently introduced several redesigned models and was planning to bring out at least five more by the end of the year. These models were part of the first wave of products flowing from the NAO's "common parts" strategy.

As a full-line manufacturer of passenger cars, Chevrolet epitomized GM's difficulties during the past 15 years. General manager Jim Perkins told reporters: "We lost our place in the 80s....We let our products slip."[8] Between 1979 and 1993, Chevy's share of the U.S. car market fell from 20 percent to just under 12 percent.[9] In the interim, the division had made numerous efforts to keep buyers from defecting to imports, especially in the smaller car classes. For example, the division had established the Geo brand of subcompact cars which were produced by NUMMI, a joint venture between GM and Toyota, and by other Japanese manufacturers. These models received better-than-average ratings from auto critics but captured only 8 percent of the small car market. Chevy also pursued entry-level buyers with its Cavalier, a mid-size model that was aggressively priced to compete with smaller imports.

---

[7]Mary Ann Keller, *Rude Awakening: The Rise, Fall, and Struggle for Recovery of General Motors,* p. 110.
[8]"Compact Cars Loom Large for U.S. Makers," *Advertising Age,* April 4, 1994, p. 4.
[9]Chevrolet's share of the combined car and truck market was 16.7 percent in 1993.

When Saturn was introduced, several Chevrolet managers complained that the new brand was cannibalizing their sales. Further research revealed that only about 6 percent of Saturn's buyers listed a Chevy or Geo as a second choice. Moreover, sales trends showed that Chevrolets were most popular in the Midwest and South, while Saturn's core territories were in the East and West.

Chevrolet had recently dropped its "Heartbeat of America" advertising in favor of a more nostalgic "Genuine Chevrolet" theme. Several observers noted that the ads were reminiscent of Saturn's early spots. The first commercial in the campaign showed Chevrolets in slice-of-life scenes from the 1950s to the present. In background, a neighborly voice said:

> You've probably never thought much about it but chances are, at one time or another, you've had a Chevy in your life.... [W]e've always believed what it's all about is finding a car or truck you love, no matter where you are in life or how much you have to spend. It's getting you the safety, comfort, and style you expect, for just a little less than you'd expect to pay. It's being dependable enough to have 36 million people driving around with a Chevy emblem on their front end. It's realizing that while body styles and paint colors may change, the right way to treat a customer doesn't.

Pontiac   Sales gains in 1994 made Pontiac the third-best selling brand in the United States, behind Chevrolet and Ford. General manager John Middlebrook said the division thrived by offering sporty models at a more affordable price than the competing imports. In particular, the brand's two best-sellers, the Grand Am and the Grand Prix, were mid-size models that listed for several thousand dollars less than the Honda Accord and Toyota Camry. First quarter sales of these products increased to 100,000 cars, while the brand as a whole had grown 34 percent to more than 170,000 vehicles versus the same three month period in 1993.

Pontiac's performance had been particularly strong in California, where dealers were experimenting with a "value selling" concept. Cars were packaged with popular features and offered at a "suggested value price" to eliminate haggling. Managers hoped the program would enhance the buying experience by minimizing the need to shop at different dealerships.

National advertising emphasized styling and performance, appealing to a younger group of buyers than traditional GM brands. The median age of ownership was in the mid-40s, comparable to most imports and slightly above Saturn. Pontiac sold cars in the medium, large, and sporty segments. It dropped its small car, the LeMans, in 1993, so dealers relied on a variation of the Chevy Cavalier (sold as a Sunbird) to attract entry-level buyers. Industry sources also speculated that Pontiac would eventually put the LeMans name on a small car imported from one of GM's international divisions.

Oldsmobile   GM's oldest brand was trying to rebuild its base in the mid-range of the divisions. During the mid-1980s, Oldsmobile had sold more than 1,000,000 cars annually. By 1993, however, sales had slipped to under 400,000, prompting analysts to question the brand's viability. In response, Olds' managers committed to remodel after Saturn—a process the media called "Saturnization." Dealers were schooled in team-building and customer service principles. The division also set up a governance board with dealer representatives that endorsed "no haggle" pricing and money-back guarantees.

Oldsmobile received above average reviews on its line of mid-size and larger cars but seemed to have trouble shaking a stodgy image. To reshape this perception, the brand was launching the Aurora, a $32,000 sedan that was designed to challenge the best of the luxury imports. Although Aurora sales would not turn the division around, Olds' marketing staff hoped the car would bring curiosity seekers into showrooms, where they could become familiar with other models and experience the new sales techniques. Olds wanted to attract the same profile of customer as Saturn who might be shopping for a larger vehicle. Oldsmobile offered seven different models, including a minivan and a sport utility vehicle.

Buick   During the 1980s, Olds and Buick models were so similar that some called the cars "OldsmoBuicks." Over the last several years, Buick had distinguished itself by appealing to more conservative tastes. The division's general manager, Ed Mertz, described the brand's image as "distinctive, powerful, and mature." Buick had tested several of the customer service ideas developed by Saturn, but determined that they were not relevant to its target customer population. For example, the division's market research found that most of its buyers liked to bargain over the price. Moreover, Mertz said that Buick's customers generally did not consider import models.

Cadillac   GM's top-of-the-line brand traditionally produced the largest cars on the road. Within the past decade, the division had been challenged by European and Japanese imports that offered new performance and safety features. Cadillac responded by emphasizing product quality. Efforts to improve product and process design earned it a Malcolm Baldrige award in 1990. The first new products following the quality initiative proved popular with critics and customers. The mid-sized, sportier cars showcased Cadillac's ability to integrate technology, style, and comfort, and drew a younger audience (median age of 52) to the brand.

   The LSE, a new model scheduled for 1996, aimed to expand Cadillac's reach in the luxury segment. The smaller sedan and coupe were being developed by a GM-Europe division to give the cars a European look and feel. This design approach also fit Jack Smith's plans to limit the number of platforms GM produced. Cadillac expected the average LSE buyer to be 45 years old and have an income of $75,000.

▲ GM'S COMPETITORS

   Automotive News listed more than 150 car models and over 50 passenger truck lines in the United States. GM marketed about one-quarter of these products and captured 35 percent of the overall market. Ford Motor Company finished second with a 24 percent share, followed by Chrysler (16 percent), Toyota (7 percent), Nissan (5 percent), and Honda (5 percent). Exhibit 4 shows each company's market share by product segment and Exhibit 5 compares 1993 financial results.

Ford

   Like GM, Ford was benefiting from the recent buying surge in the United States. First quarter sales were up about 15 percent over the same period in 1993, largely because of increases in light trucks and cars with newer platforms. In addition, since 1991 the company had added two points to its market share, recapturing the level it held in the late 1970s. These gains let Ford run its plants at close to full capacity, contributing to reduced manufacturing costs for each vehicle.

   The company marketed vehicles under three brands. About four-fifths of the vehicles were sold with the Ford name. Market research showed that customers viewed this line as a close competitor of Chevrolet's in most segments. Other sales were split between the Mercury, a midrange brand, and Lincoln, a close rival of Cadillac and Buick. Analysts noted that the company was seeking ways to improve customer service among its dealers but had not committed to major changes.

Chrysler

The smallest member of the Big Three was riding a wave of new product introductions, which helped build sales by 19 percent in the first quarter of 1994. Chrysler surprised competitors with product development cycles as short as 30 months, roughly half the industry standard. This capability reduced preproduction costs and allowed the company to respond quickly to market conditions. Critics were also impressed with the results. The Neon, a new small car model, won *Automobile Magazine*'s "Car of the Year" honor in 1994, and other recent introductions were frequently mentioned in lists of the top 10 new products. Early in 1994, however, the Neon and a Jeep sport utility vehicle had suffered through recalls that some analysts attributed to the firm's quick product development cycles.

Chrysler had taken advantage of a renewed interest in passenger trucks by offering a strong lineup of minivans, pickups, and four-wheel-drive Jeeps. The products provided high margins and accounted for more than 60 percent of first quarter sales. Cars were sold through four divisions. The Plymouth brand handled low-priced small and mid-size models. Dodge carried some of the same platforms but included sportier features, similar to Pontiac's product line. Eagle, a relatively new brand, targeted import buyers in the middle segment, while the Chrysler name appeared on upper-end models.

Toyota

Japan's largest car manufacturer was a pioneer of continuous improvement in manufacturing processes. By consistently adding new features and enhancing reliability, the company developed a strong reputation for product quality in the small, medium, and sporty categories. Toyota used this credibility to establish the Lexus brand, which was an instant success in the lucrative luxury market. In 1993–94, however, analysts believed that Toyota had been too aggressive in raising its prices. Competing products were matching the brand's features and eroding the company's market share. Consequently, Toyota was trying to reduce manufacturing costs so it would have more flexibility to price its models.

Part of this plan involved steadily increasing the company's production base in North America. This strategy mitigated the pressures of the rising yen, which had raised the automaker's costs. In addition, Toyota's local presence reduced the company's impact on the U.S. trade deficit, helping to defuse nationalist concerns.

Nissan

Nissan, another Japanese automaker, had established U.S. assembly facilities in Smyrna, Tennessee, to produce cars and trucks. Nissan rebounded from a lackluster year in 1993 to post sales gains of over 27 percent in the first quarter of 1994. The recovery was led by increased demand for minivans, pickups, and sport utility vehicles, as well as moderate growth in the company's small and mid-size lines.

▲ **EXHIBIT 4** U.S. Automobile Sales in 1993

4a. Leading Models and Unit Sales

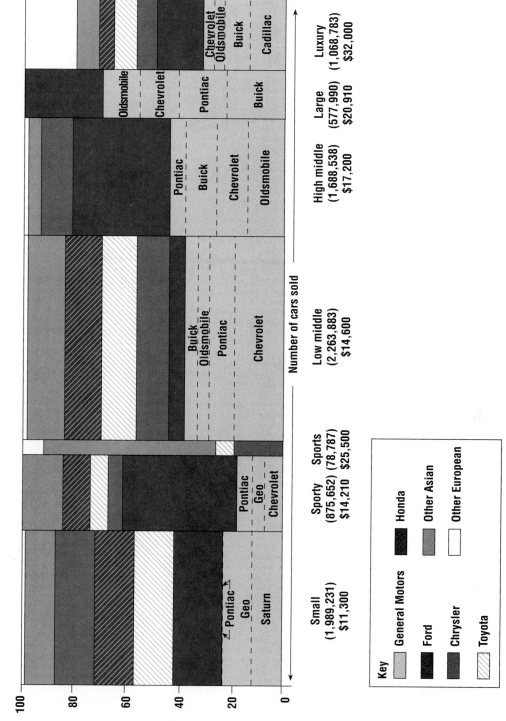

Note: Manufacturer's segment shares often include more than one model (e.g., Chevrolet's Corsica, Beretta, and Cavalier are all classified as low middle cars).

Source: *Automotive News*, J.D. Power & Associates, Casewriter estimates.

continued

▲ EXHIBIT 4   *concluded*

4b. Leading Models and Unit Sales*

Make	1993 Sales
Subcompact	
Ford Escort	269,034
Honda	255,579
Saturn	229,356
Toyota Corolla	193,749
Nissan Sentra	168,846
Total subcompact	2,177,671
Compact	
GM Chevrolet Cavalier	273,617
Ford Tempo	217,644
GM Chevrolet Corisca-Berretta	171,794
Ford Mustang	98,648
GM Pontiac Sunbird	93,233
Total compact	1,255,014
Mid-sized	
Ford Taurus	360,448
Honda Accord	330,030
Toyota Camry	299,737
GM Chevrolet Lumina	219,683
GM Pontiac Grand Am	214,761
Total mid-sized	3,180,006
Large	
Buick LeSabre	149,299
Ford Crown Victoria	101,685
Chrysler Dodge Intrepid	89,127
GM Pontiac Bonneville	88,591
Ford Mercury Grand Marquis	85,195
Total large	892,766
Near luxury	
GM Buick Park Avenue	59,533
BMW 3 series	45,590
Toyota Lexus ES300	35,655
Volvo 940 series	32,495
Volva 800 series	28,367
Total near luxury	300,320
Luxury	
GM Cadillac DeVille	115,650
Ford Lincoln Town Car	110,046
Acura Legend	38,866
GM Cadillac Seville	35,280
Ford Lincoln Mark VIII	31,852
Total luxury	596,372
Specialty	
Mazda MX-5 Miata	21,588
GM Chevrolet Corvette	20,487
GM Dodge Stealth	14,556
Mitsubishi 3000GT	13,006
Ford Mercury Capri	9,723
Total specialty	114,546

*Categories may not exactly match Exhibit 4a due to reclassification.
Source: *Automotive News Market Data Book.*

▲ EXHIBIT 5   Financial Results for Auto Manufacturers ($ millions)

	1993	1992	1991	1990	1989
Chrysler Corp.					
Net sales	42,260	35,501	28,162	29,797	34,922
Cost of sales	32,382	28,740	23,338	23,604	26,629
Selling, general and administrative	4,901	4,350	3,713	3,013	4,058
Operating income	4,977	2,411	1,111	3,180	4,235
Net income	(2,551)	723	(795)	68	359
Working capital	11,356	11,727	9,200	10,764	33,234
Stockholders' equity	6,836	7,538	6,109	6,849	7,233
Total assets	43,830	40,653	43,076	46,374	51,038
Ford Motor Co.					
Net sales	108,521	100,132	88,286	97,650	96,146
Cost of sales	89,887	86,488	76,808	82,165	73,772
Selling, general and administrative	4,968	4,434	3,993	4,000	4,165
Operating income	13,666	9,210	7,485	11,485	18,209
Net income	2,529	(7,385)	(2,258)	860	3,835
Working capital	25,037	25,018	25,027	21,668	20,540
Stockholders' equity	17,032	15,836	23,490	24,038	23,528
Total assets	198,938	180,545	174,429	173,663	60,893
General Motors					
Net sales	133,622	128,533	119,753	122,021	123,212
Cost of sales	106,422	105,064	97,551	96,156	94,683
Selling, general and administrative	14,107	14,434	15,185	14,633	9,925
Operating income	13,093	9,035	7,017	11,232	18,604
Net income	2,467	(23,498)	(4,453)	(1,986)	4,224
Working capital	127,774	124,666	121,627	120,100	121,995
Stockholders' equity	5,597	6,226	27,328	30,047	34,983
Total assets	188,202	191,013	184,326	180,237	173,297
Honda*					
Net sales	35,533	33,059	30,507	24,385	26,433
Cost of sales	25,688	24,083	22,225	17,494	19,274
Selling, general and administrative	7,196	6,373	5,865	4,446	4,427
Operating income	935	1,154	1,041	1,270	1,341
Net income	329	488	541	517	737
Working capital	11,761	11,346	11,475	9,745	9,615
Stockholders' equity	8,913	8,301	7,714	6,864	34,983
Total assets	25,876	23,757	20,946	17,998	17,306
Toyota*					
Net sales	95,428	81,307	71,414	60,084	
Cost of sales	83,610	70,172	59,616	48,883	
Selling, general and administrative	10,118	9,387	8,176	6,999	
Operating income	1,700	1,748	3,622	4,203	
Net income	1,649	1,903	3,126	2,884	
Working capital	42,334	41,443	35,141	33,772	
Stockholders' equity	44,510	37,751	33,174	27,685	
Total assets	87,985	76,662	65,132	55,105	

*Honda's fiscal year ends March 31, Toyota's fiscal year ends June 30.
Source: Annual reports.

Nissan's models received above-average ratings from consumer guides, yet the company was not viewed as a market leader. The recently introduced Altima and Maxima were mid-size models intended to change this perception. The sporty Maxima listed for about $20,000, while the Altima was aimed at budget-conscious customers with a starting price in the $13,000 range.

Honda

Like Toyota, Honda had entered the United States with small, fuel efficient models but gradually moved up-market into higher-margin mid-size and luxury cars. In 1994, the company introduced its first sport utility vehicle but was sourcing the model from another Japanese manufacturer. In contrast to the Big Three manufacturers, Honda had trouble entering the passenger truck segments because its factories were designed to produce smaller cars.

During the first quarter, Honda's sales increased 20 percent following a disappointing 1993. The biggest gains came from the Accord, a mid-size model that had been redesigned for the previous fall. All of Honda's products received above-average ratings in consumer guides for reliability and performance, though the company finished below the industry average in dealer service rankings.

▲ GM IN JUNE 1994

GM's strong sales results continued through the spring of 1994. As Jack Smith prepared for the annual shareholders' meeting, analysts predicted second quarter profits of $1.8 billion, bringing the corporation's total to $2.7 billion for the first half of the year. Smith had succeeded in reducing manufacturing costs by $2,000 per car, and additional changes were expected to produce another $2,000 in savings by 1996. On the sales side, J.D. Power's surveys of customer satisfaction gave GM the highest ratings among domestic car makers. Saturn finished third on the list of all brands, followed by Cadillac (No. 10) and Buick (No. 12).

Keeping up with demand appeared to be GM's most pressing problem. Dealers were compiling customer waiting lists for new platforms, while retooling was taking four to five months at some factories. One analyst estimated that GM lost $65 million to $85 million in pretax profits every month a plant remained idle. The factories also tended to operate at slower speeds during the first months of production to ensure quality. GM executives said the divisions were trying to reduce changeover time to two weeks by the year 2000. Smith addressed the issue of capacity constraints by announcing that GM would convert 13 plants that had been mothballed or were scheduled to close shortly for new production. He had not specified whether these decisions would affect Saturn or the sites its managers were considering.

BANC ONE
CORPORATION, 1989

*It is said that a bank, or any business for that matter, cannot continue
to grow without making radical changes in its philosophy of doing business.
Something has to give. While there is some value in that thinking, it is hardly
an argument for slower growth at Banc One or for revision of a decentralized
management strategy that has worked extremely well for us.[1]*
            John B. McCoy, 1986, Then-president, Banc One Corp.

*My role is chief personnel officer. If I get the right people in the right job,
that's all I have to do.*
            John B. McCoy, 1989, chairman & CEO, Banc One Corp.

John B. McCoy rose from his desk on the 16th floor of Banc One's Columbus headquarters
while the video crew gathered its equipment. He had just finished taping the quarterly
"Chairman's Corner" section of the company news video program. Weeks earlier, on June 29,
1989, Banc One, the largest bank holding company in Ohio and one of the U.S. banking industry's top financial performers, announced that it had beaten five other bidders to purchase
20 of MCorp's failed Texas banks. McCoy had just told employees in his taped message:

> Banking is people. The uncertainty is over for the people of MCorp. The great spirit of Banc
> One will make a difference. We will win back customers and make it work. Our goal is to be
> the biggest and best bank in the state!

Paul S Myers, doctoral candidate, prepared this case under the supervision of Professor Rosabeth Moss Kanter.
Copyright © 1989 by the President and Fellows of Harvard College.
[1]John B. McCoy, "Commentary: Small-Guy Philosophy Drives Top Performance," *Financier,* August 1988, pp.
42–44.

McCoy knew it would be a challenge to transfer Banc One's remarkable success to its largest acquisition, especially at a time when Banc One itself was undergoing major change. With few exceptions, for two decades the company had grown by acquiring small to medium-sized midwestern banks with good performance records in nondilutive, friendly deals. This acquisition comprised 20 banks located in the South; all were insolvent, and their total assets were equal to one-half those of Banc One. Banc One's past success in integrating newly acquired banks derived from its abilities to nurture an "uncommon partnership" with the new bank (called an "affiliate") and to induce better performance from its managers. The "uncommon partnership" balanced autonomous banking decisions based on knowledge of the community at the local level with a strong set of corporate values and operating principles.

Was Banc One entering a new phase that would test McCoy's skill as a general manager and his vision as a corporate leader?

▲ BANC ONE: SUPER-REGIONAL SUPER BANK

In March 1989, before the MCorp purchase, Banc One had 56 affiliate banks with 566 offices, 5 nonbank affiliates (i.e., subsidiaries of Banc One), 18,000 employees, and $23.7 billion in assets. Net income had increased at a compound annual growth rate of 18.39 percent since 1978 (see Exhibit 1). In 1988 Banc One was the most profitable bank holding company as measured by return on average assets among the country's 50 largest banks. Earnings per share and stock price had risen steadily over the preceding decade (see Exhibit 2).

Banc One was primarily a retail bank that focused on offerings loans and other financial services to individual consumers and to small- and medium-sized middle market firms. Its branches operated as "stores," concentrating on product sales to meet income targets. McCoy liked to describe Banc One as similar to McDonald's: "Our stores have a lot in common. We're not selling chicken in one place and steaks in another. We're selling the same thing everywhere." Banc One sought high-margin business in retail and middle market loans, industry diversity, and balanced growth. In 1987 the corporation's net interest margin was 5.8 percent, in contrast to the U.S. regional bank average of 4.41 percent. Banc One also ranked among the 10 largest U.S. banks in both credit card and student lending.

In the corporate segment, Banc One confined its commercial lending to middle market customers primarily in the communities in which its affiliate banks operated. Other than commercial real estate loans at 6 percent of the total loan portfolio, no standard industrial classification of loans represented over 2.5 percent of the loan portfolio. Banc One avoided energy, agriculture, and LDC (less-developed countries) loans, all of which had been sources of serious problems for many U.S. banks. (In late 1987 and early 1988, Banc One eliminated its small, $98 million portfolio of LDC loans through sales and write-offs, thereby strengthening its loan portfolio.) Banc One's significant nonbank activities included trust, leasing, and mortgage operations and extensive data processing.

Banc One's overall goal was to deliver superior customer service while obtaining high financial returns. Member banks prided themselves on treating customers as individuals rather than as mere account numbers. One affiliate president noted, "From the customers' point of view, if you're not delivering that quality personal service, they're not going to stay with you." Banc One believed that its customers saw it as an innovative, fast-paced company always on the leading edge of new products and that customers thus expected to receive from Banc One banks the best products and prices. Advertising emphasized service delivery and specific product offerings equally. Banc One invested steadily in technology R&D to develop new retail products, to improve its competitive lead time, to lower costs, and to generate fee income by

▲ EXHIBIT 1   Selected Financial Data, 1978–1988

Income and Expenses ($ millions)

Year	Total Income	Net Interest Income	Non Interest Income	Non Interest Expense	Income before Securities Transactions	Net Income
1988	$2,734.5	$1,142.0	$452.3	$902.6	$332.9	$340.2
1987	2,384.8	1,092.6	346.6	838.6	227.7	231.5
1986	2,260.6	1,005.2	306.8	757.7	216.0	236.5
1985	2,096.8	869.6	274.1	648.7	198.5	204.5
1984	1,889.2	715.8	227.7	552.3	161.4	162.7
1983	1,457.4	545.8	182.6	454.3	129.2	128.2
1982	1,355.7	460.1	142.3	380.6	101.5	96.6
1981	1,133.3	365.2	107.5	305.8	75.1	73.8
1980	883.9	332.8	87.6	259.0	73.4	73.2
1979	735.0	319.4	70.5	233.3	70.2	69.7
1978	586.4	283.9	60.8	202.6	62.4	62.9
Annual growth,						
1988/87	14.67%	4.52%	30.42%	7.63%	46.20%	46.95%
Compound growth						
5 years	13.41%	15.91%	19.89%	14.72%	20.84%	21.55%
10 years	16.65	14.93	22.22	16.11	18.23	18.39

Balance Sheet ($ millions)

Year	Yearly Average Balances			Year-End Balances		
	Total Assets	Common Equity	Earning Assets	Loans and Leases	Deposits	Primary Capital
1988	$23,484	$1,906	$21,054	$17,325	$19,502	$2,278
1987	21,854	1,650	19,479	15,629	18,176	2,028
1986	20,244	1,437	17,961	14,028	16,741	1,741
1985	17,662	1,223	15,485	12,399	15,480	1,537
1984	15,217	1,008	13,351	10,498	13,348	1,218
1983	12,689	830	11,122	8,346	11,510	1,017
1982	10,783	701	9,300	6,265	8,866	832
1981	8,887	572	7,566	5,371	7,463	683
1980	8,024	523	6,852	4,761	6,602	610
1979	7,410	477	6,354	4,635	6,242	549
1978	6,713	431	5,769	4,057	5,643	494
Annual growth,						
1988/87	7.46%	15.52%	8.09%	10.85%	7.30%	12.33%

continued

▲ **EXHIBIT 1**   *continued*

Balance Sheet ($ millions)

	Yearly Average Balances			Year-End Balances		
Year	Total Assets	Common Equity	Earning Assets	Loans and Leases	Deposits	Primary Capital
Compound growth						
5 years	13.10%	18.09%	13.61%	15.73%	11.12%	17.50%
10 years	13.34	16.03	13.82	15.62	13.20	16.52

Consolidated Condensed Balance Sheet ($ thousands)

	December 31, 1988	December 31, 1987
Assets		
Cash and equivalents	$ 2,191,511	$ 2,172,607
Securities (market value approximates $4,556,300 and $4,417,600 at December 31, 1988 and 1987)	4,624,612	4,453,264
Loans and leases		
Commercial, financial and agricultural	6,992,281	6,337,308
Real estate, construction	765,504	729,408
Real estate, mortgage	2,802,756	2,434,652
Consumer, net	5,450,426	4,858,713
Tax exempt	635,796	726,050
Leases, net	678,024	542,850
Total loans and leases	17,324,787	15,628,981
Reserve for possible loan and lease losses	237,342	216,547
Net loans and leases	17,087,445	15,412,434
Other assets	1,370,086	1,114,978
Total assets	$25,273,654	$23,153,283
Liabilities		
Deposits		
Non-interest bearing	$ 3,363,214	$ 3,487,548
Interest bearing	16,138,542	14,688,528
Total deposits	19,501,756	18,176,076
Short-term borrowings	2,745,559	2,335,800
Long-term borrowings	378,874	327,710
Other liabilities	606,634	511,064
Total liabilities	23,232,823	21,350,650
Preferred stock	25,454	26,353
Common stockholders' equity	2,015,377	1,776,280
Total liabilities, preferred stock and common stockholders' equity	$25,273,654	$23,153,283

continued

Consolidated Condensed Statement Income for the Three Years Ended December 31, 1988
($ thousands, except per share amounts)

	1988	1987	1986
Interest income			
Interest and fees on loans and leases	$1,875,841	$1,651,697	$1,514,010
Interest and dividends on securities	367,831	344,225	332,644
Other interest income	27,806	38,691	73,762
Total interest income	2,271,478	2,034,613	1,920,416
Interest expense			
Interest on deposits	1,013,102	873,128	920,497
Other borrowings	197,923	184,233	168,885
Total interest expense	1,211,025	1,057,361	1,089,382
Net interest income	1,060,453	977,252	831,034
Provision for loan and lease losses	183,422	206,974	146,746
Net interest income after			
provision for loan and lease losses	877,031	770,278	684,288
Other income	463,070	350,149	340,145
Other expenses	902,557	838,619	757,742
Income before income taxes	437,544	281,808	266,691
Income tax provision	97,356	50,312	30,160
Net income	$340,188	$231,496	$236,531
Per common share information			
(amounts reflect the 10% common stock dividend effective February 19, 1988)			
Net income per common share	$2.61	$1.82	$1.92
Weighted average common shares outstanding (000)	129,410	125,123	119,307

Source: Banc One Corporation 1988 *Annual Report.*

providing services to other financial institutions. It used a complex and detailed central financial control system for business planning and performance measurement.

History of Innovations

Banc One could trace its heritage back 121 years to its founding in Columbus, Ohio, as City National Bank (CNB).[2] Its modern history began when John G. McCoy assumed the

---

[2]Portions of this section have been excerpted from the 1982 case "Banc One Corporation and the Home Information Revolution," HBS No. 9-682-091, originally prepared by Dr. Karen Freeze and Professor Richard Rosenbloom.

▲ EXHIBIT 2   Earnings per Share and Stock Price, 1978–1988

Data Per Common Share

Year	Net Income		Income before Securities Transactions	Cash Dividends	Book Value	Stock Price
	Pooled	As Originally Reported				
1988	$2.61	$2.61	$2.57	$.92	$15.59	$22.25
1987	1.82	1.98	1.82	.82	13.91	21.82
1986	1.92	1.94	1.81	.75	12.88	20.80
1985	1.74	1.83	1.75	.63	11.58	21.28
1984	1.48	1.58	1.53	.54	10.12	14.12
1983	1.29	1.41	1.35	.47	9.45	12.90
1982	1.10	1.21	1.17	.40	8.84	12.86
1981	.99	1.10	1.02	.36	8.40	7.89
1980	1.01	.94	1.01	.33	8.06	6.58
1979	.96	.86	.97	.30	7.44	5.05
1978	.88	.75	.87	.25	6.73	4.83
Annual growth,						
1988/87	43.41%	31.82%	41.21%	12.20%	12.08%	1.97%
Compound growth						
5 years	15.14%	13.11%	13.74%	14.38%	10.53%	11.52%
10 years	11.48	13.28	11.44	13.92	8.76	16.50

Common Stock Data (as originally reported)

Year	Average Share Outstdg. (000)	Common Shares Traded (000)	Common Shareholders	Stock Splits & Dividends	Total Market Capital $(mil)	Year-End Price/ Earnings
1988	129,410	42,347	43,892	10%	$2,876	8.5x
1987	105,009	38,297	37,693		2,360	11.0
1986	100,238	21,457	36,855	10%	2,082	10.7
1985	68,254	8,270	24,748	3:2	1,491	11.6
1984	64,673	4,116	24,998	10%	929	8.9
1983	57,031	5,361	21,529	3:2	802	9.1
1982	47,785	2,919	12,974	3:2/10%	655	10.6
1981	34,988	1,466	10,564		301	7.2
1980	34,119	764	8,833	10%	222	7.0
1979	34,245	557	8,709		173	5.9
1978	34,245	535	8,535	10%	165	6.4

Source: Banc One Corporation 1988 *Annual Report*.

presidency upon his father's death in 1958. McCoy made two fundamental decisions: (1) to run "a Tiffany bank rather than a Woolworth's," and (2) in order to achieve that goal, "to hire the best people and then delegate; there wasn't any use of putting you in if you were the finest in the world and then telling you how to do it." For the second decision, his father offered no model; he had made every decision in the bank himself.

John G.'s guiding principle was "to provide financial services to people." He also believed that people choose a bank "because of one word: convenience." To help implement that principle in his first year, he hired John Fisher, a young radio ad man, as head of a newly created advertising department. John G. commissioned him to "find out what the customer wants" and forbade him to learn how to open an account or make a loan. Soon in charge of marketing and public relations, John Fisher created a new image for CNB with slogans like "the loaningest bank in town," "the best all-around bank all around town," and "the good neighborhood bank," featured on a prize-winning billboard ad in 1961. In less than a decade, deposits grew from $140 million to over $400 million.

Fisher's creative vision went beyond ad pitches. Some industry observers credited him with revolutionizing banking by coupling technology with marketing. At John G.'s insistence, since the early 1960s the company had set aside approximately 3 percent of earnings each year for R&D with the hope of identifying ways that technology could improve efficiency and customer service. The company's innovations included introducing the forerunner of the automated teller machine (ATM) in 1969 and in 1972 becoming the first U.S. bank to install ATMs in every branch office. Not all of its innovations took hold. It pioneered efforts, though unsuccessfully, to build a point-of-sale credit card network in 1977 and to introduce at-home banking in 1979.

CNB became the first bank to offer credit cards outside of California by introducing in 1966 the City National BankAmericard (now VISA). This innovation not only provided the bank with profits and industry visibility, but it also helped start the charge card revolution, which changed Americans' spending practices. The company gained additional national exposure in 1976 when Merrill Lynch picked it as the processing arm of its new Cash Management Account (CMA) venture. The CMA accounts permitted customers to use funds from their brokerage accounts via a debit card or checks provided by the bank. This path-breaking alliance helped foment the burgeoning revolution in the U.S. financial services industry.

Driven by the success of its credit cards and its partnership with Merrill Lynch, in the 1970s the company expanded its operations by selling its credit- and debit-card processing expertise to other banks, credit unions, thrifts, finance companies, and brokers. By 1989 Banc One was regarded as a data processing powerhouse.[3] It handled its own 3.2 million cards, over 3.5 million cards for third parties (e.g., credit unions), and supplied the check-clearing and back-office operations for many other banks and financial service firms. In 1989 Banc One's Future Systems Group unveiled Phase I of a new system developed in partnership with Electronic Data Systems (EDS) and Norwest, a Minneapolis bank holding company, to attempt to meet the banking industry's data processing needs for the next 20 years.

At the retail level, Banc One experimented with store concept and design. In Kingsdale, Ohio, the company introduced a full-service banking facility called a "Financial Marketplace" with supermarket hours—open 72 hours a week including Sunday afternoons. The state-of-the-art merchandising system comprised boutiques offering home financing, travel services, trust services, business loan operations, a realtor, and investment services.

---

[3]*The Wall Street Journal,* June 13, 1988, p. B1.

Colorful neon lights identified each separate service area. Interactive (touch-screen) video displays answered customers' questions, and drive-in windows made for quick and easy personal service. Four companies leased boutique space: Banc One Investment Services, Banc One Travel, Nationwide Insurance Corp., and HER realtors. Leasing offered Banc One the advantage of learning how to sell products that banks by law could not provide, while creating awareness of its own investment and travel subsidiaries. It also directly challenged companies such as Sears and American Express that offered a portfolio of financial services. The success of the Kingsdale store led to a second "supermarket," and both were performing well beyond expectations by 1989.

To ensure continuing innovation, Banc One established a "Greenhouse Group" under John Fisher's leadership in June 1989 to create and nurture new ideas outside of the mainstream of the organization. Initial projects included a toll-free, 24-hour-a-day telephone service; interaffiliate check cashing and deposit service; and a home banking service.

Growth through Acquisitions

Limited in growth by Ohio law to one-county branching, City National Bank merged in 1968 with a smaller bank, Farmers Savings and Trust ($55.2 million in deposits), to form a bank holding company, the First Banc Group (FBG). Another Ohio law prohibiting nonbank institutions from including the designation "Bank" in their names dictated the new spelling, "Banc." FBG began acquiring small banks around Ohio. Between 1968 and 1980 it bought 22 banks, each under $100 million in assets.

A decade old in 1977 and still growing rapidly, First Banc Group had 16 members and $1.95 billion in aggregate assets. With FBG's next decade in mind, John G. and his colleagues—including FBG's new president (and John G.'s son) John B. McCoy—began to consider the implications of federal limits on the company's growth. With the entire banking industry in upheaval as it faced challenges from other financial institutions, McCoy and others expected revisions in the law against interstate banking. Anticipating that event, FBG sought a new name unique in the country. At John Fisher's suggestion, they selected "Banc One" and registered the name in every state. The name change took place in October 1979. Thereafter, the holding company would be known as *Banc* One, and each bank as *Bank* One, followed by its location. Thus City National Bank became Bank One of Columbus.

Between 1980 and 1983, Banc One had begun to purchase mid-sized banks in major markets. Previous acquisitions had been in rural and semiurban county seat-type markets. In short order, Banc One bought banks in Cleveland, Akron, Youngstown, and, in June 1983, the $1.6 billion Winters National Bank of Dayton. Winters held assets about one-third the size of those of Banc One.

In 1984 John G. McCoy retired and his son John B. became CEO, in addition to his duties as president; in 1987 John B. became chairman and gave up the presidency. In the meantime, changes in state banking laws that allowed bank holding companies to bank in other states spurred a third phase of Banc One's acquisitions, this time toward purchases of out-of-state larger banks. Looking first to Indiana, Banc One made a purchase about every two weeks in the fall and winter of 1985 and gained six banks. After months of courtship, Banc One announced in May 1986 that it would purchase American Fletcher Bank of Indianapolis. Banc One increased its assets by more than a third overnight because American Fletcher held $4.5 billion in assets and was the second-largest bank in Indiana. This move gave Banc One the largest market share in the state. Shortly after, Banc One made acquisitions in Kentucky, Michigan, and Wisconsin.

Nonbank acquisitions, including a mortgage company and travel agencies, complemented Banc One's operations. Four specialty leasing companies (for photocopiers and telephone switchboards) balanced its retail strategy at the small end of the market. Nonbank holdings accounted for just 7 percent of earnings, not including the card-processing business, which was considered part of the banking operation. This nonbank area, though, was seen as having the most growth potential, perhaps outpacing the rest of the business by 25 percent to 50 percent.

Integration of New Affiliates

Banc One sought successful banks run by managers with proven track records. CEO John B. McCoy commented in 1986 that "the success [of our acquisitions] will be achieved through basically two things: a local management team that knows the market and a similarity between the two organizations' [Banc One's and the acquisition's] products and services." Of the deals that never went through, 80 percent failed because of Banc One's lack of confidence in a potential acquisiton's current management. With rare exceptions, current officers remained in place after a Banc One acquisition. McCoy recounted an often-told story that had become part of the company folklore:

> When my dad was running the bank, the head of the largest bank in Cleveland called and said, "Why don't we take us and Cincinnati and form one bank—we'd be really strong." My dad thought that was a great idea, so the guy came for breakfast to discuss putting the three banks together. As breakfast was being served, Dad asked, "So, what will I do in the new bank?" He was told, "Oh, there wouldn't be any need for you!" That was that. Our issue [when we make acquisitions] is how to *use* current management, not to get rid of it.

Thus, assessment of people was central to acquisition decisions. For example, in the spring of 1989 during the due diligence period in Texas, a team of 20 Banc One analysts and executives from affiliate banks studied MCorp's operations. McCoy recalled:

> Our accounting guy said, "The controls aren't good, but I'm impressed by the people." Then the next guy said something similar. So we went back to focus on the people: why they're here, who the boss is, why they haven't left. When we got comfortable with the people, we went ahead.

McCoy expected the incumbent bank managers to operate the new affiliate profitably and soundly. Banc One put significant pressure on new affiliates to attain higher earnings. It asked each to look at its costs, to improve its proficiency in technology, to expand its loan-making capability, and to professionalize its banking workplace. Banc One had an exceptional track record of improving the performance of its new affiliates. The average acquisition increased its return on assets (ROA) 66 percent. For example, at the time of its acquisition, Winters' (Dayton) return on assets was approximately .7 percent and net income reached $7 million. Five years later, in 1988, ROA was 1.62 percent and earnings hit $32.4 million. American Fletcher had never scored an ROA greater than 1 percent; in just three years with Banc One, its ROA stood at 1.55 percent.

To spur performance improvements, Banc One assigned a "mentor bank" of comparable asset size to share information and expertise with the new bank and to help it build competence in Banc One's products, systems, and operating procedures. Typically, the mentor bank president and various staff members spent, at the beginning, two or three days each month visiting the new affiliate. New member banks also sent their personnel to the mentor affiliate, and to other banks, to learn about such functions as data processing and financial controls. One affiliate president remarked:

The operating culture gets transmitted in part by sharing information between the one with the Banc One culture and the one without. It's easy to see when you have an ROA of .6 percent and the other bank has 1.5 percent that there are [better] ways of doing things that you can learn.

Early in the assimilation of new affiliates, Banc One imposed its powerful financial control system, the Management Information Control System (MICS), as an additional tool to help the banks set and meet performance targets. The MICS tracked all balance sheet and income statement data as well as productivity and loan quality ratios (see Exhibit 3). Affiliates received an inch-thick monthly computer report that included detailed performance results.

Financial discipline was an integral value in the system, and managers placed strong emphasis on the MICS numbers. The system recorded the yearly business plan and financial forecasts for each affiliate. While the original budget stood as a commitment to achieving a stated earnings level, actual results led to revisions in monthly targets. One affiliate manager explained:

> The MICS printout becomes an operating tool for all managers. It doesn't go into a black binder and get hidden away in some drawer. Every month we use it to update our forecasts for the rest of the year. It's the "Banc One Bible." The monthly printout is required reading for all officers and supervisors—those people who make the business forecasts.

MICS brought new affiliates a degree of financial sophistication not typically enjoyed by independent banks. In the words of one financial officer, "MICS helps an affiliate understand itself better. It tells you where you've been, who you are, and where you want to go."

McCoy also found MICS to be a powerful general management tool:

> Everyone is on the same financial system and accounted for the same way. In accounting class at Stanford Business School, we'd look at two banks' [income] statements and they'd be totally different; that left an impression on me. Our practice is to measure everyone the same way. Our other rule is that everyone has access to everyone else's numbers. They can see who is the best, who is the worst. If you see you're the worst, you pick a better bank and see what's happening there. It's friendly peer competition, but not deadly competition. You're in the same company but not competing in the same market.

> Our commercial loan delinquency rate is 2 percent—in the top quartile in the country. Most CEOs would look at that figure and go on to other things. We start there. We list every single bank. We find that some are at 7 percent, some at 1.5 percent. We don't have to call the president with the worst number; he knows the call is coming. If I say to him, "Your loan delinquencies are bad," he would roll his eyes and say, "McCoy, you don't understand my market." He's right; I don't understand his market. But the numbers are there; it's his decision how to learn from someone else with better numbers.

Bringing new affiliates on-line with MICS did not always go without a hitch. For Bank One Dayton (the former Winters Bank), the conversion was difficult, time consuming, and it negatively affected customer service. One manager recalled:

> We spent a lot of time that first year fighting change. Our systems were uprooted and managers viewed that as a big loss because they had spent so much time fighting for it. Lots of turf issues arose. We fought battles from the perspective that those systems were "mine"; we really felt they were trying to take something away from us for no reason. We spent most of our energies trying to maintain what *was* instead of what was going to be.

Despite facing the often frustrating human dilemmas of organizational change, Banc One for the most part smoothly integrated its new acquisitions. Many affiliates gave credit for this success to one element of their new Banc One relationship: the "uncommon partnership."

▲ EXHIBIT 3   Management Information Control System (MICS) "Major Highlights" Summary Data Sheet, February 1989

	FEB ACTUAL	B/(W) PR FCST	B/(W) BGT	FCST F-Y-F	B/(W) FR FCST	B/(W) BGT	PYR 4TH QTR	1ST QTR	2ND QTR	3RD QTR	4TH QTR
					EARNINGS ANALYSIS						
LOAN INT											
LOAN FEES											
INV INC											
INT EXP											
NIM											
PROVISION											
NET FUNDS FNCT											
SERVICE CHGS											
NON-INT INC											
NON-INT EXP											
PRETAX NET											
NET TAX											
NOE											
NET SEC											
NET INCOME											
INCOME											
LOAN YIELD %											
INV YIELD %											
E/A YIELD %											
OVERALL RATE											
NIM %											
FUNDS FNCT %											

continued

▲329

▲ EXHIBIT 3   *concluded*

EARNINGS ANALYSIS

	FEB ACTUAL	B/(W) PR FCST	B/(W) BGT	FCST F-Y-F	B/(W) FR FCST	B/(W) BGT	PYR 4TH QTR	1ST QTR	2ND QTR	3RD QTR	4TH QTR
ROA %											
ROE %											
LOAN QUALITY											
RES RATIO EOM %											
CHG-OFFS/LOANS %											
NPL/LOANS %											
BALANCE SHEET											
LOAN GROWTH %											
DEPOSIT GROWTH %											
LOAN/DEPOSIT %											
LG LIAB DEP %											
EQUITY/ASSETS %											
PRODUCTIVITY											
FTE/MM ASSETS											
DEP'S/OFFICE											
N-I EXP/ASSETS %											
N-I EXP/NOE %											
N-I EXP/REV %											

The Uncommon Partnership

The First Bank Group had adopted "the uncommon partnership" as its slogan, and it became the hallmark of Banc One's relationship with its affiliate banks. McCoy's principle was, "If it involves people, we do it at the local level; if it involves paper, we centralize it." Affiliate autonomy encompassed local lending decisions, pricing based on local market conditions, personnel policies and compensation, and responses to community needs. Such autonomy was "uncommon" in banking. Most holding companies and franchisers imposed a standardized set of rules and practices on their affiliates.

The "uncommon partnership" philosophy was a strong selling point. In one case, Banc One's offer to acquire a bank was $6 per share less than a competitor's; however, target company directors felt that Banc One's uncommon partnership would provide more long-term value to shareholders, so they accepted the lower offer. Treasurer George Meiling explained:

> In the ideal M&A discussion, we don't even talk dollars or price until about the third meeting. We want to get all the social issues and have them understand how it is going to operate. We tell them not to listen to Columbus because we are trying to sell them on the deal. We give them our phone book and have them pick a president of an affiliate they want to talk to. And a lot of banks do it. Our best salespeople are really our presidents.

Banc One tried to bring a number of benefits to newly affiliated banks. While responsibility for traditional banking activities remained with the affiliates, the corporate office in Columbus provided (for a fee) central services including legal, new-product development, and marketing. Affiliation also allowed banks to offer a broad range of products not usually offered by small, independent banks, such as leasing and commercial lending. The Banc One name itself had great value in attracting customers, since the company's reputation for quality service had brought it national recognition. Affiliates gained leverage from the operational and financial resources of a much larger bank. Banc One shared its enormous product R&D experience with them. Affiliates could obtain data that helped them predict which products would be most successful in their local markets. Frank McKinney, chairman of Banc One Indiana, summarized the advantages of Banc One membership this way: "It's like you have a very nice six-cylinder car that gets 18 miles per gallon, and that's the best you can do. So you ask, 'What do we have to do to get 24?' That's why we affiliated."[4] An Ohio affiliate president concluded:

> The uncommon partnership offers our customers the best of both worlds: those local [lending] decisions as well as services not generally offered by a $100 million bank. Because of the uncommon partnership, we're allowed to spend more time with our customers. For example, I don't have my staff bogged down with tracking the changes in regulations. The corporate legal staff does that. We can instead focus on serving the customers.

Work Environment

Along with the uncommon partnership, other aspects of Banc One's work environment had always been determined by top management in Columbus and then diffused throughout the various affiliates. Since the Columbus bank accounted for 50 percent of total company revenue before the 1983 Winters acquisition in Dayton, the operating practices of that bank easily influenced those of the smaller affiliates. But when Dayton became 25 percent of the

---

[4]"Banc One Eases Fears of Wholesale Changes," *Indianapolis Star,* June 12, 1988.

company, and Columbus shrank to 30 percent, John Fisher, now senior vice president, saw the need for some unifying devices:

> I concluded that if this continues, every time we do a merger we'll begin to look a lot more like the new affiliates and less like ourselves. You can just see how if we replicate the mergers, down the road there would be no surviving Banc One operating philosophy or culture. We didn't have a lot of things to give them that would make them look like us. We did have our common name and could offer shared services in data processing. We needed to develop things we could transfer to new affiliates to glue us together as a single organization.

Coincidentally, John B. McCoy had just become CEO. Fisher sensed that McCoy was searching for a platform to call his own, a way to make a distinctive mark on the company that would separate him from his father. He presented to McCoy a "white paper" in October 1984 that proposed quality as that platform. Fisher wrote:

> [Our senior staff] meetings almost invariably, and virtually exclusively, deal with the financial results. Never do they begin by asking about the customer. That's not a criticism of our emphasis on financial performance. It's only a statement of fact about our focus. Our management style is so single-minded, so inward-oriented, that we have become almost totally dependent on financials. We have no other refined management tool to give direction or provide decisions for our business.

To address this concern, Fisher proposed a plan that included establishing a corporate positioning theme, creating a training program for executives, and expanding intracorporate communications through a variety of vehicles.

McCoy acted on Fisher's suggestions. In 1985 Banc One selected as its positioning theme the phrase "Nine Thousand People Who Care," a statement of a goal as much as of common identity. All employees were invited to Columbus to celebrate the announcement of the new slogan at a major rally televised on closed circuit around the state for employees who could not attend. By early 1989, after several acquisitions, the slogan stood at "Eighteen Thousand People Who Care."

The company song captured this theme. McCoy remembered once attending an IBM function with Fisher and hearing IBM's company song. "I said, 'We'd never sing a song in our company.' John Fisher said, 'We will, and I'll have tears in your eyes.' A year later, we had a song." Banc One's broadcast advertising included the song, and employees sang it at various celebrations and company events. In the spring of 1988 McCoy challenged employees to form groups and record their performance of the company song; the winning performers would star in a music video produced for companywide broadcast. Other songs played a part in the Banc One culture as well, as special company events would inspire employees to write a set of lyrics for the occasion. For example, one group of managers sang its own version of "Leaving on a Jet Plane" to Senior Vice President Bill Boardman while he was in the middle of negotiating the Texas acquisition (see Exhibit 4).

One of the most prominent and successful vehicles for transmitting Banc One's values and operating standards was Banc One College. The college was an internal training program originally designed to give senior managers experience working together and to be a catalyst for collaboration and idea exchange among affiliates. The college took participants from their geographically dispersed locations and immersed them in two weeks of intense day and evening experiences. Top executives, including McCoy and Fisher, presented the corporation's operating philosophy and plans. Other classes and presentations honed the managers' problem-solving skills. The college used role playing and "Outward Bound"–type team-building activities to develop trust, sharing, unity, and cooperation.

Banc One Song, 1989

(advertising campaign since 1985)

In our hometown we're proud to be
  The finest bankers there.
And one by one we do our best,
  It's how we show we care.
So when you cross the heartland states
  You'll find us standing strong,
With all of us behind each one
  You'll hear us sing this song. . .

We are Eighteen Thousand People Who Care: BANC ONE;
Yes, we're Eighteen Thousand People
  Who Care about our customers.
Eighteen Thousand People Who Care
  How well we serve.
We're a company, a winning team
Of Eighteen Thousand People Who Care.

Leaving on a Jet Plane

(Banc One version, Spring 1989)

All my bags are packed, I'm ready to go.
I'm standing here on the sixteenth floor,
I hate to return again without a deal.
But the dawn is breakin', it's early morn,
The plane is waitin', I'm ready to board.
I'm Texas-bound and so
It's a hell of a steal.

There's no solution to dilution.
M Bank's pain is Banc One's gain. . .
Their customer will never be the same.
I'm leaving on a jet plane,
Don't know when I'll be back again.
Oh John, I love to go.

College director Beth Luchsinger commented, "Our challenge is to continue fostering innovation while sustaining growth. We use the college as a vehicle to achieve that." While the college's emphasis was always on sharing information and promoting learning between affiliates, conversations with McCoy before each session produced an agenda of specific discussion themes based on current Banc One issues.

Although the semiannual program had a long waiting list of participants, some potential candidates were skeptical about the college. A few considered it a form of brainwashing and refused to attend. On each of these occasions, McCoy contacted these executives and urged them to attend and then report back to him with their evaluation. Three presidents resigned shortly after their two-week experience. Luchsinger reported that each had realized over the two weeks that "this was not the company they wanted to work for. They didn't buy into the philosophy or the way of operating here."

One important by-product of the college was the expanded network of relationships formed by the participants. Annual reunions of all the graduates helped maintain these ties. Most who had attended the college praised this consequence of attending the college. "It was a fantastic experience," extolled one college alum. "I have 24 great friends now that I'm in touch with all the time. I go to reunions, and the network of relationships just grows and grows, which means more and more information is available. You can't get too much information in this business—it just changes too quickly."

Information sharing and idea-exchange were central to Banc One's operating philosophy. Management stressed face-to-face meetings, preferring personal interactions to electronic communications. One Banc One executive, who had spent most of his career with IBM, remarked, "The informality of the organization is unique in banks. I was surprised by the willingness to question procedures. That shows a commitment by the organization to encourage people to think and express their ideas." The annual corporatewide Presidents' Council meetings brought together all the bank presidents to discuss current issues with corporatewide relevance. In addition, the state holding companies held similar Presidents' Council meetings frequently throughout the year. McCoy and other top corporate executives attended these meetings when invited and participated in open discussion forums. One president remarked, "McCoy doesn't have a problem with dissent. He encourages it. People are not shrinking violets in this company."

Many affiliate officers reported calling their peers to inquire about how another had achieved a particularly good performance or solved a problem. Karen Horn, CEO of Bank One Cleveland, a highly experienced bank executive who came to Banc One from the presidency of the Federal Reserve Bank of Cleveland, saw value in this peer exchange:

> When we are dealing with an issue, there are 59 other folks out there that are vaguely in the same business we are that might have good ideas about it. There are also some people in Columbus who might have good ideas about it, and they may be more or less forceful, depending on the situation, in trying to get their ideas implemented. The openness and interchange between the affiliates is one of the enormous strengths of Banc One.

Communication to employees was frequent and detailed. The monthly company newsletter, *The Wire,* reported the latest events, internal organizational changes, promotions, work anniversaries, and assorted items of employee interest. Beginning in 1986, Banc One broadcast systemwide a 30-minute, network-news-style video magazine, *The Quarterly Report.* Local affiliates taped professional-quality reports, and senior managers appeared to answer questions about the past quarter's results and current company issues.

The corporatewide quality program was another unifying force. Bill Bennett, chairman of Bank One Dayton, had developed a formal quality program in response to lapses in quality caused by merging data systems shortly after its acquisition. His hands-on approach included walking around the various banks' facilities, monitoring quality, and encouraging employees to focus on improving customer service. The success of the program in Dayton led to a systemwide, participative quality program under John Fisher's leadership. Included were competitive rankings of affiliates' performance on quality ratings and annual Chairman's Awards for quality leaders. In 1988 some 488 quality teams were addressing issues ranging from the process of sending out a customer statement to the design of a proposed new account.

Awards were abundant. The Chairman's Award was given annually at the Corporate Quality Awards Banquet. "We Care" awards were presented regularly to employees to recognize individual or group contributions to superior customer service; for example, two administrative assistants received "We Care" awards for volunteering to work until 2 AM to draw up a crucial buy/sell agreement by the deadline. In 1988, 210 employees earned this recognition. The most coveted award was the "Blue One" award, given to the banks scoring highest on profitability, credit quality, reserves and liquidity, and productivity. Names and photos of award recipients regularly appeared in *The Wire* (see Exhibit 5).

Other celebrations regularly took place. One particularly enthusiastic event welcomed the new Wisconsin affiliates in 1988. June 13 was declared "Name Change Day," the day when the acquired banks would be called Banc One. The day began with a pancake breakfast served by top executives to all Wisconsin employees. Each employee received a Banc One bag filled with "welcome aboard" gifts, including a T-shirt, cap, and balloons. CEO McCoy and other officials spoke at a rally later in the morning. The employee band played the "Banc One" song while everyone—reading off mimeographed pages—sang along, and all were officially initiated onto the Banc One team.

One of the more controversial aspects of Banc One's culture was its Code of Ethics. Banc One defined ethics as its accountability and responsibility to its depositors and shareholders. When a new bank joined Banc One, each of its employees received a copy of the Code of Ethics that each had to sign attesting knowledge of and agreement with its contents. The code provided guidelines for behavior regarding conflict of interest, personal conduct, and financial affairs (see Exhibit 6). These latter, personal issues raised concerns about violations of privacy and discomfort at the corporation's seeming imposition of a strict morality. Roman Gerber, corporate general counsel, remarked: "To be very frank our code probably goes a bit further than corporate codes go in trying to dictate or guide conduct."

The code also had strict disclosure requirements for officers and directors regarding personal financial obligations. Gerber reported, "This perhaps more than any other piece of the Code of Ethics has been resisted." Some affiliates believed that such disclosure went beyond what an employer was entitled to know. This component of the code was optional for the individual banks. Gerber commented that "rather than just jamming it down their throats, we would rather have them come to understand and come to accept it over time."

Leadership

McCoy described his role and activities this way:

Besides chief personnel officer, my other job is goodwill ambassador. There are times I feel I'm running for office. On the first day in Texas I tried to walk around as many floors as I could, let people see who we are. We had dinners for all the officers; I talked about our philosophy.

McCoy held informal weekly staff meetings (no minutes); in 1989, these included Fisher, Don McWhorter (chairman of Services Corp.), John Westman (CFO), Bill Boardman (SVP

▲ **EXHIBIT 5**   Excerpts from *The Wire*, **July 1989**

We Care Awards

BANK ONE, FREMONT employees **Wendi Jay, Ann King** and **Mary Ann Woessner** assisted in the capture and arrest of a suspected felon to earn their We Care Awards.

In April, a local business contacted the bank and reported two stolen payroll checks. Later that morning a customer asked Wendi to cash a payroll check at the drive-through window.

Wendi recognized the check as one that was stolen and contacted her supervisor, Ann. Ann had the bank's security officer call the police and made note of which direction the customer went after leaving the bank. Meanwhile, Mary Ann, a commercial note teller, got a complete description of the car and its license number and turned this information over to the authorities. The police officer on the scene contacted a police cruiser in the area, and the suspect was apprehended.

We Care Recipients

ANTIGO
Diane Molle, Executive Secretary
Ethel Wenek, Bookkeeper
Sue Zupon, Bookkeeper

CRAWFORDSVILLE
Vicki Lutes, Cashier
Sandy Porter, Loan Clerk

DAYTON
Dan Johnson, Auditor
Carol Chester, Retail Banking
    Administration Specialist

DOVER
Wanda Prysi, Bookkeeping Clerk
Cheryl Morgan, Assistant Branch
    Manager

FREMONT
Wendi Jay, Teller
Ann King, Teller Supervisor
Mary Ann Woessner,
    Commercial Note Teller

INDIANAPOLIS
Peggy Jennings, Cash
    Management Specialist

LAFAYETTE
Cheryl Myers, Customer Service
    Representative
Elizabeth Derringer, Merchant
    Representative

LIMA
Brent Gibson, Branch Manager
Donna Martello, Assistant
    Branch Manager

SIDNEY
Mary Putnam, Teller

STURGIS
Lou Ann James, Teller
Susan Osmun, Teller

PROUD EMPLOYEES — Displaying their We Care Awards are (left to right) Mary Ann Woessner, Ann King and Wendi Jay of BANK ONE, FREMONT.

YOUNGSTOWN
Alice Bovo, Mortgage Loan
    Closer
Obadiah Hall, Credit Processor
Kevin Lamar, Vault Supervisor

SERVICES CORPORATION
Audrey Martin, Authorizations
    Supervisor
David Kocak, Authorizations
    Supervisor
Doug Kirby, Proof Operator
William Tredick, Clerk

New Code of Ethics To Be Distributed

A new BANC ONE CORPORATION Code of Ethics soon will be distributed to all BANK ONE employees.

The brochure has been rewritten to answer questions that have been raised about BANK ONE policies and to better explain certain legal provisions in those policies. The new edition is also written in a more understandable language style.

Because of the importance of the message in the Code of Ethics, all employees will be required to sign a statement acknowledging that they have received the brochure. The statement will be kept in each employee's personnel file.

Acquisitions), and Gerber. Others were invited to discuss particular issues. He also held a monthly policy committee meeting that added the state company heads to the staff meeting group to examine events and results across the company. In addition to chairing meetings of the board of directors, McCoy attended the state Presidents' Council meetings when invited. But he noted that "when things are running well, I don't have to go to a lot of meetings. Because of the strengths of our forecasts and financial systems, we don't do a lot of reviews—only if there is a problem." In fact, McCoy joked, "No one wants to take my phone calls, because they know that I only get called with bad news."

I. Introduction

BANC ONE's success is directly related to customer and investor trust and confidence. We must recognize that our first duty to our customers and to our stockholders is to act in all matters in the manner that merits public trust and confidence. Basic to this obligation is the requirement that every director, officer, and employee conduct their business affairs in strict compliance with all applicable laws and regulations.

For this reason, this Code of Ethics is issued as standards for all directors, officers and employees of BANC ONE. Just as the policies in this Code are not all-inclusive, these policies must be followed in conjunction with good judgment and basic principles of sound banking.

II. Conflict of Interest

The basic policy of BANC ONE is that no director, officer or employee should have any position of interest (either financial or otherwise), make or receive any payment, or engage in any activity which conflicts, or might reasonably conflict, with the proper performance of his or her duties and responsibilities to BANC ONE . . . Each director, officer and employee must manage his or her personal and business affairs so as to avoid situations that might lead to conflict, or even the appearance of a conflict . . .

III. Personal Conduct and Financial Affairs

A. Personal Conduct.   Directors, officers and employees of BANC ONE are expected to conduct their personal and financial affairs on a sound moral, ethical, and legal basis. They are expected to conduct their personal as well as their financial affairs in a manner which (1) is consistent with, and does not violate, basic moral or ethical standards within the community, and (2) recognizes and respects the personal property rights of others. They are also expected to comply with applicable personnel policies of their BANC ONE employer, including those set forth in company personnel manuals, relating to the use, possession, or sale of alcoholic beverages or illegal drugs, to personal appearance, to conduct in the performance of their employment, and to dealing with personnel, customers, and suppliers.

B. Financial Affairs.   Directors, officers and employees shall maintain their personal financial affairs in a manner which is prudent. Officers are required to complete and to submit at least annually to their CEO a questionnaire relative to their compliance with various provisions of the Code of Ethics and legal requirements applicable to them as BANC ONE officers. . .

McCoy relied on Fisher as a confidant and sounding board for a variety of business decisions. He regarded Fisher as the company's "idea man" and believed that Fisher's successful efforts over the years to make Banc One a marketing-driven company were the reason that human resource and quality programs often emanated from the marketing area. McCoy remarked:

> He's a unique individual. He's always coming at you with ideas. John is a good observer of what's going on in the company. He's at the point in his career where he has nothing to lose if he says, "That guy in Dayton is in trouble," or, "There's a problem in Cleveland." I can talk to him. He'll say, "That's dumb. That's right."

Fisher attributed his influence to McCoy's vision and interest in innovations and fresh thought. "The thing that has helped make us unique is the creative flame he has helped nurture," he explained.

Most press accounts as well as investment analyst reports described Banc One as a superior company with talented and dynamic managers. McCoy personally selected people for the top corporate slots, including the state holding company presidents, though he discussed candidates with his key managers individually. Each holding company chose its local bank presidents and officers, though there had not been too many selection decisions due to the usual retention of existing management after acquisitions. According to McCoy, successful managers at Banc One affiliates were entrepreneurial in their outlook toward opportunities, willing to share information and decision-making power with their peers and subordinates, and open to new ideas; they were good at turn-arounds but also able to sustain growth by avoiding major mistakes.

McCoy set a high common standard for managerial performance. According to Fisher, McCoy used "a velvet glove" to motivate the affiliates. He tried to create a work environment that reflected his belief that people are good, bright, and want to do the right things but don't always know what those things are. "The affiliates have a sharing relationship," McCoy remarked. "It's not, 'Hey, you dumb guy.' I'd much rather have a friendly company than an unfriendly one."

Affiliate officers were evaluated on budgeted versus actual earnings (adjusted for events outside of affiliate control) and on ROA. Their bonuses varied as a percentage of total compensation, but were between 10 percent and 50 percent. To earn 100 percent of the bonus, managers had to meet their budget targets and earn a 1.4 percent ROA. There were payoff curves for other combinations of these two variables. Several senior managers acknowledged that while the monetary bonus played a distinct motivational role, it was not the most important factor. According to one affiliate president, friendly competition among the affiliates was the greater incentive:

> No one wants to be on the bottom of the lists. Lots of [senior] people could have moved to different organizations and made more money. But once you get the Banc One spirit in your blood, you can't leave it. You want to win the Blue One award, the Chairman's Award.

Banc One held onto its best managers. One officer reported that while many of his peers frequently received calls from executive search firms, none had been stolen away by other companies. Low turnover meant high retention of experience and knowledge and maintenance of the extensive networks of relationships among the various affiliates. But high standards meant that jobs were not sinecures. In the case of one affiliate bank president with 20 years' service whose job grew too big for him to handle, McCoy reported:

> I told him I'm convinced he can't do [the job], that I've given him a chance for the past year and I must make a change. I said he has two choices: we can get him an outplacement counselor to help him get an outside job or he can become the president of a smaller bank. He chose to take the outside job. It was announced in the company that he simply wanted the job. There was no embarrassment, no cutting him off at the knees. That's the style I want. If everyone feels the hammer is coming right at him, it's harder to get good performance. Of course, if someone breaks the law, they're out the next minute; that's happened.

McCoy believed that leaders came from every level in the company. One effort to emphasize this philosophy proved unworkable. McCoy tried to do away with the proliferation of officer titles at Banc One. Remarked McCoy, "We do a lot of team projects here. There was a junior analyst on the due diligence team in Texas—a great contributor. He was treated as an equal, not as a gofer. If we get a lot of good people on a team, it doesn't matter what their titles are." Focus groups conducted with employees below the officer level agreed with the elimination of titles. Senior managers, however, resisted this change, and McCoy did not force the issue.

Organizational Dilemmas of Growth

In 1987, in response to the complexities of multistate and nonbanking operations, Banc One organized its affiliates into a state holding company structure, with corporate headquarters and staff offices in Columbus (see Exhibit 7). In January 1989, Banc One Ohio had 26 affiliates, including banks in Ohio, Michigan, and Kentucky; Banc One Indiana had 11 affiliates; and Banc One Wisconsin had 19 affiliates. The state holding company structure allowed for future growth, since it could be duplicated as new states were added; it encouraged development of local management talent; and it helped successfully integrate new affiliates.

Sandwiched between the centralized and decentralized features of the Banc One system were some "centralized shared responsibilities": those activities with which central subsidiaries or offices assisted the local banks and holding companies by providing expertise, policy guidelines, and resources for particular products and services. For example, the corporate marketing department assisted affiliates in product development and promotion, and Banc One Services

▲ EXHIBIT 7   Banc One State Holding Company Structure and Corporate Organization, June 1989

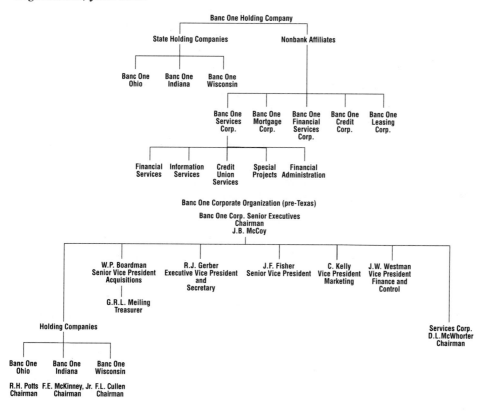

Corporation supplied the data processing/item processing services for all units. In addition, Banc One corporate offices in Columbus, in conjunction with the state holding companies and affiliates, performed financial analyses and forecasting. Mortgages, investment banking, insurance, and leasing were all shared with central nonbank subsidiaries. To add structure and some direction to these "centralized shared responsibilities," Banc One created the Services Corporation in January 1988 to handle operations functions for all of the affiliate banks. These functions included data processing and credit card processing as well as software development and system development to support new products. A year later, in a move that further centralized some operations, the Services Corporation was restructured into five major groups to separate the data processing for information services from that for financial services.

For some affiliates, however, the existence of a more centralized Services organization created tension regarding locus of control. A particularly sore spot was the price that affiliates were charged for central services. Mike Elvir, executive vice president of the Services Corporation, commented:

> This is a source of major irritation. They don't want us to be a profit center. They think it is unfair and makes it hard for them to compete. [The issue of pricing] is raised within the first 20 minutes of almost all dialogues I have with people. Currently our price is based on a market-based price; it is 90 percent of the composite price found. But affiliates still argue. They go out and find one supplier who will give it to them for less. They forget that that same one supplier will not give them all the services they need at such a low price. A lot of energy is wasted on this issue as affiliates try to prove us wrong. McCoy believes that the organization gains a lot by letting affiliates feel they can challenge our pricing. But McCoy and his minions put such a large pressure on increasing margins that the affiliates will never be happy with what we do. This is the cost we pay for the uncommon partnership—as aggravating as it is, I agree with it. The benefits gained from their operating like independent businesspeople outweighs what we lose.

Elvir identified a second trouble spot Banc One had with its affiliates: meeting the needs of diverse entities.

> Regional banks all want autonomy but all require operational support. What is good for one bank is not good for another—a $4.5 million bank in Indiana does not want the same thing as a $700 million bank in Wisconsin. The decisions made are meant to satisfy the majority. Systems need to be common.

This lack of similar needs extended throughout the corporation and raised some crucial questions. Some managers continued to express the concerns voiced by John Fisher in 1983 at the time of the Winters acquisition. How could Banc One maintain a single set of practices and values when the organization's "culture" continued to be diluted with new affiliates, each bringing its own systems, styles, and needs? Craig Kelley, vice president-director/Affiliate Marketing, commented:

> We have created a monster. We have commonality in name, and we share a slogan and a corporate logo. But there are no common operating procedures—not even in how to open an account. For example, there is no common check-cashing system. We have a great franchise system, but customers are not guaranteed that they can cash a check at various Banc One locations—it is up to the whim of local management.
>
> How can we maintain the sense of affiliate self-ownership and impose some commonality, some sense of sameness? So much is driven down to the bank level that there is not a feeling of family; there is not the sense of being a part of something larger. We must put the uncommon partnership aside and say who we are.

Moves away from local autonomy were particularly prominent in two other areas: product line and procurement. In the summer of 1988, Banc One announced a corporatewide uniform product line. After months of discussions involving participants from every Banc One affiliate, the corporate product uniformity committee reduced the number of financial products offered from 63 to 10. New guidelines standardized features, marketing approaches, and product terms and conditions. These changes would make pricing decisions easier, simplify marketing tasks, and streamline operations. For example, uniform products were expected to help solve the marketing problem of creating ads for affiliates, since previously each affiliate had its own way of packaging and selling identical and/or similar services.

At the same time, Banc One extended to the entire organization a central office materials procurement program developed at Banc One Wisconsin. Savings opportunities were estimated at around $5 million annually. Banc One hoped to use its leverage as a $24 billion company to obtain better prices than any individual local unit. McCoy respected the desire of local banks to buy from local suppliers with whom they had long-established relationships, so initially the program was optional. He hoped, however, that the participating banks' bottom-line results would provide incentives for others to join. On this point, one Michigan affiliate president acknowledged that he supported the move to centralized purchasing, with one caveat: The group must serve him at least as well, if not better, than his in-house operations had. "I have the authority," he said assuredly, "to find my own suppliers, if I'm not happy with the job Columbus is doing."

Some affiliate managers saw the movement toward increased centralization and standardization as part of a systematic plan to take away the power of local banks. A few were unconcerned—as long as Banc One continued to leave the banking functions of making loans and accepting deposits to local officials. Nevertheless, managers in Columbus, including John Fisher, saw corporate unity as the paramount concern. Commented Fisher:

> We're here saying, "Hey McCoy, the way to do this baby is to have more central programs. If you don't have central programs, then there is nothing to help you steer." Yet, the other folks out in the field are saying, "You don't need that. We can do all that stuff out here. We don't need corporate ads. We don't need uniform products." McCoy is caught and his two ears are hearing different voices. One group calls for centralization and another wants more autonomy.

▲ THE FUTURE CHALLENGE

In February 1989, *Financial World* magazine named Banc One one of 30 great companies for the 1990s, calling it "the cream of a pack of excellent super-regionals" and noting its "highly innovative products and services" and its skill at "digesting new technology and smaller banks." Despite such accolades, concern at the company over limited future growth of its existing customer base and pressure to maintain its record of superior financial performance had led to conservative actions, such as selling credit card receivables to investors and limiting consumer credit lines, and had intensified Banc One's willingness to make a major acquisition.

In June 1989, Banc One agreed to purchase MCorp's 20 banks for $375 million to $510 million, depending on the banks' financial results, to be paid over five years. The banks' 65 branch offices across the state made up the Deposit Insurance Bridge Bank, which with $13.1 billion in assets was the third-largest Texas bank. The FDIC offered an incentive by agreeing to indemnify all the Bridge Bank's identified and classified nonperforming loans, reducing the asset value of the acquisition by essentially cleaning the balance sheet and leaving only the good assets; it was the third-costliest bailout in FDIC history. The biggest risk in entering

Texas was the future uncertainty of the state's economy. The depressed oil and gas industry had hit the state hard. Even if the depression had bottomed out, any further weakness could hurt the bank's financial performance.

The Bridge Bank purchase was Banc One's first acquisition outside of the Midwest; it involved a large bank, not a small- or medium-sized one. Not only was Bridge Bank unsuccessful and unprofitable, but it was insolvent as well. Unlike all other Banc One acquisitions, Bridge Bank had little strength in the retail or middle market segments. Nor did Bridge Bank lease small ticket items or have a mortgage department. Its focus, and what had led to its downfall, was the commercial lending sector. McCoy commented that there was a major clash of cultures involved, not because of Texas and Ohio styles, but because of loan size: "Ours are $1 million loans; theirs are $50 million."

Banc One named its Chairman McCoy as chairman of Banc One Texas. Thomas Hoaglin, chairman and CEO of Bank One Dayton, was named president and CEO of the new Texas entity. Under Hoaglin's leadership, Dayton was Banc One's top financial performer in 1988, and the bank won a special quality service award that year. While Banc One also planned to name several more senior executives, McCoy told *The Wall Street Journal*, "We found what appeared to us to be good management at the grassroots level, and that's one of the main things that kept our interest in the organization. . . . Believe me, those of us from Columbus don't know much about Texas, so we're going to rely on Texans to run our Texas bank."[5] At the time of purchase, the Bridge Bank had its central headquarters in Dallas directing all major decisions. Banc One was considering changing the organization to a state holding-company-type structure along the lines of the rest of Banc One: separate banks, each with a president and the autonomy to make lending decisions, reporting to a Banc One, Texas headquarters.

Banc One received approval for the purchase on June 29, 1989. McCoy described the days following:

> We were told the Friday before the 4th of July we could go ahead. We sent 80 people selected by the marketing department [down to Texas] on the 4th. On the 5th and 6th of July there were Banc One people in every office. We held training sessions with videos; we gave [our new employees] videos to take home; we had dinners. We told them how we operate. We sent people from Wisconsin and Indiana who told them, "We didn't believe it two years ago either, but this is how we operate."

As McCoy thought about the future, he told a visitor:

> The reason we are in Texas is we think there are really good people [in those banks]. We are buying a $10 billion bank with very capable people. They will question us hard about why we do things the way we do. It will just mean lots and lots of trips for them to our other banks. Success will not happen by my telling them why, but by their going to Indianapolis or Akron and seeing how those banks got their results.

But would Banc One's traditional methods for upgrading people and improving performance work fast enough and effectively enough in the new environment, especially in light of other challenges to the "uncommon partnership"? Should McCoy be considering any new ways for Banc One to meet the challenges ahead?

---

[5] *The Wall Street Journal,* June 29, 1989, p. A6; June 30, 1989, p. A3.

MASCO
CORPORATION (A)

Masco Corporation recorded its 29th consecutive year of earnings growth in 1985. On Wall Street, the firm was gaining a reputation as the "master of the mundane," because of its ability to earn well-above-average profits in consumer industries that were neither high-tech nor glamorous. Included among Masco's brand-name products were Delta, Delex, Peerless, Artistic, and Epic Faucets; Merillat kitchen and bathroom cabinets; Weiser and Baldwin locks and building hardware; Brass-Craft and Plumb Shop plumbing fittings; Thermador and Waste King appliances; and Aqua Glass bath and shower enclosures.

Based on internal sales forecasts, Masco expected to generate nearly $2 billion in excess cash flow from 1985 to 1990. Management planned to use these funds to expand into new consumer product markets, moving beyond the kitchen and bathroom to other areas. The theme was "great products for America's great homes."

In 1986, Masco management was eager to translate this vision into reality. The $14 billion household furniture industry represented the single largest category of products for the home. Masco had to decide whether it represented an attractive area for diversification.

▲ METALWORKING

Masco (originally Masco Screw Products Co.) was founded in December 1929 in Detroit, Michigan, by Alex Manoogian, along with two partners who left during the first year of business. Opening six weeks after Black Tuesday, the day Wall Street collapsed, Masco had a lean start. Manoogian, an Armenian immigrant, saw the firm through this difficult period, in

C. W. Moorman, MBA 1989, and Professor Cynthia A. Montgomery prepared this case, in collaboration with Professor Michael E. Porter. Copyright © 1989 by the President and Fellows of Harvard College.

metalworking capabilities

quality & performance over price

part to gain the financial security he would need to help his tightly knit family escape political and economic oppression in Eastern Europe.

Masco's first products were machined automotive parts sold to the automobile original equipment manufacturers (OEMs). It produced high-volume parts in a business that was highly competitive and cyclical. Able to distinguish itself by superior service in a commodity market, Masco was profitable (although it remained small) through World War II and into the early 1950s.

During the next three decades, Masco built a broad base of metalworking capabilities, including machining; coining; stamping; cold heading; forging; hot heading; powdered metal forging; forming, bending, and shaping; cold and warm extrusion; and heating and welding. These manufacturing processes were supported by metallurgical engineering and technical staffs with substantial experience in product design, tooling and machine design, machine automation, and statistical quality assurance.

Masco believed that the breadth of its metalworking expertise was unparalleled by any other industrial company. Diversification decreased dependence on outside suppliers, while enabling it to offer its customers a single source for finished components, a capability Masco believed would be increasingly valued by its automotive, truck, diesel locomotive, and other industrial customers.

In the mid-1970s, the firm also diversified into specialized metal products for oil, gas, coal, and other natural resource exploration and production. In entering these markets, Masco targeted segments in which quality and performance were more important to the customer than price.

▲ FAUCETS

In 1954, Masco obtained a contract to manufacture parts for an early type of a single-handle faucet. The product met with some initial success, but design problems soon caused it to become a commercial failure. Drawing on his many years of metalworking experience, Alex Manoogian redesigned the faucet and obtained a license to sell the improved version. After trying unsuccessfully to interest several plumbing manufacturers in his patented design, Manoogian set up Delta, his own marketing and sales organization, to distribute the faucet under that name. Sales were made to large wholesale distributors that, in turn, sold to commercial plumbing supply houses.

In 1956, the U.S. faucet industry was highly fragmented, with a general lack of brand recognition, minimal advertising, and a low level of salesperson training. Delta faucets were quickly accepted due to their technical superiority, particularly for kitchen use, where utility and maintenance-free operation were very important. By 1958, sales of Delta faucets had grown to $1,000,000. The company built a new faucet manufacturing plant in 1959 in the small town of Greensburg, Indiana. In 1961, Masco made its first acquisition, Peerless Industries, a manufacturer of plumbing valves and fittings, in order to broaden its manufacturing capabilities in plumbing products. By 1962, sales of faucets totaled $7,000,000 (60 percent of total Masco sales), with an after-tax profit margin of about 10 percent.

Masco gradually broadened the Delta product line and then, in 1971, introduced the Delex line of two-handle faucets. This design, also patented, employed a new type of valve, which eliminated rubber washers, the major cause of faucet failure. The Deltique line, introduced in 1977, was the first of several brands aimed at the upper-end, high-style decorator faucet market.

In the late 1960s, the do-it-yourself (DIY) market was growing faster than the new construction market, and it was somewhat countercyclical to new construction sales. In 1969, Masco introduced a new faucet brand, Peerless, targeted specifically at the DIY market. The Peerless line featured innovative see-through packaging and a no-tools hook-up system, which had broad consumer appeal. DIY products were sold directly to retailers such as hardware stores, home improvement centers, and large chains such as Sears and Kmart. Entering this market required a broadening of Masco's traditional faucet distribution channels, which had consisted mainly of plumbing wholesalers. In 1985, there were more than 40,000 retail outlets for DIY products in the United States, compared with approximately 4,000 plumbing wholesalers.

As the DIY market grew, Masco expanded and refined its Peerless line and entered other DIY markets through several acquisitions. By 1983, DIY product sales accounted for more than 30 percent of Masco's building and home improvement product sales and more than 50 percent of its faucet sales.

In the 1970s, Masco greatly increased its emphasis on marketing. Breaking with industry tradition, it expanded market research, increased advertising, and placed greater emphasis on merchandising and retailer training. In 1975, Masco pioneered the first national television advertising for faucets. By 1981, the firm claimed that it spent more for faucet advertising than all other faucet makers combined. It was the only plumbing-related sponsor of the 1984 Olympics.

Masco also devoted considerable resources to programs for the trade. They included numerous seminars for plumbers and plumbing suppliers to teach them how to install, service, and sell Masco products. The company instituted a "Good/Better/Best" merchandising program for merchants, offering a range of products with varying price points, special packaging, and point-of-sale displays. Masco claimed the best delivery time in the industry, a maximum of 48 hours from order to delivery, made possible by carrying an in-depth factory inventory.

Masco was vertically integrated into the manufacture of key faucet components. Faucet production was highly automated, and labor costs represented about 20 percent of total costs. Purchasing and inventory systems were also automated, and Masco had ongoing programs for cost reduction and value analysis.

By 1985, Masco was the largest U.S. faucet manufacturer, with an estimated 36 percent share of a 25-million-unit market. A small quantity of its faucets were sold in Denmark as Damixa and in Italy as Mariani. Masco also distributed faucets through its 44 percent-owned affiliate, Emco, Ltd. of Canada.

▲ ACQUISITIONS AND CORPORATE GROWTH

Alex Manoogian was Masco's only operating officer when his son, Richard, joined the firm in 1959. Having just graduated from Yale, where he had studied economics, Richard began his career at the Greensburg faucet plant. As the firm's number two manager, Richard was soon responsible for overseeing operations and, most importantly, for reinvesting the profits generated by Delta faucets.

In 1961, with the help of Smith Barney, Masco raised new capital through debt and equity offerings. Added to the cash flow from the faucet operations, these funds supported an aggressive growth program. Masco used these funds to expand its core metal-forming business and to enter new lines of business (see Exhibit 1). Management outlined the firm's mission in the 1978 annual report: "We are a manufacturing company, not financial managers seeking to deploy assets into motion pictures, insurance, fast foods, or other businesses where financial return is the principal criterion. Masco manufactures, at a relatively low unit cost, mass-produced engineered products, utilizing our diverse metalworking capabilities."

▲ EXHIBIT 1   Acquisitions, 1961–1985

Year	Company	Products
1961	Peerless Industries, Inc.	Valves for the plumbing industry
1962	Steel Stamping Company (Name changed to Mascon Toy Corp. in 1964, sold in 1969)	Plastic and metal toys
1964	Nile Faucet Corporation	Single-handle faucets
1965	Gibbs Automatic Molding Company	Plastic components and zinc die-castings
1966	Auto-Flo Company	Air treatment equipment
	Fibercraft Products, Inc.	Air treatment equipment
	Auto-Flo Corporation (Canada)	Air treatment equipment
1967	Molloy Manufacturing Company	Cold extrusions
1968	Burns Companies	Cold extrusions and industrial components
1969	Punchcraft, Inc.	Punches, dies, metal tooling
1970	Century Tool Company	Industrial components
	Keo Cutters, Inc.	Precision drills and cutters
	Commonwealth Industries, Inc.	Heat-treating services
	Trans-Continental Bolt, Co.	Cold-formed industrial components
1971	Electra Corporation	Radio receivers
	Fulton Company	Marine and recreational vehicle products
1972	Exotic Metals, Inc.	Powdered metal industrial components
	Hoffman Die Products, Inc.	Forged golf club heads
	Eskay Screw Products, Inc.	Cold-formed fasteners
1973	Holzer & Company (Germany)	Cold-extruded products
	Davis Manufacturing Company	Brass fittings
	Rupert Manufacturing Company	Specialty products for recreation and transportation
	American Metal Products Corp.	Specialty plumbing and heating products
	Reese Products, Inc.	Specialty products for recreation and transportation
1974	Wilhelm Gebberdt GmbH (Germany)	Commercial and residential air treatment systems
	Rubinetterie Mariani (Italy)	Two-handled faucets for Italian market
1975	Royce Electronics Corporation (sold 51% in 1976; remaining 49% in 1977)	Citizens band and marine transceivers
1976	A-Z International Tool Company	Specialized drilling tools
	Grant Oil Tool Company	Specialized drilling tools
	Dansk Metal & Amaturindustri (Denmark)	Plumbing and heating products
1977	Walker McDonald Manufacturing	Rock-drilling bits
	R&B Manufacturing Company	Tubular metal fabrication

Year	Company	Products
1978	Rieke Corporation (99.8%)	Sealing caps and closures for metal drums and containers
	Compac Corporation (24.5% subsequently increased to 100%)	Commercial insulation facings.
	Flo-Con Systems, Inc.	Slide-gate valve systems for the ferrous metal industry
1979	Arrow Specialty Company	Engines and engine repair parts for oil wells
	Jung-Pumpen GmbH (Germany)	Residential sump pumps
1980	Alup-Kompressoren Pressorun GmbH (Germany)	Air compressors
	Arrow Oil Tools, Inc.	Specialty tools for oil and gas industry
	Lamons Metal Gasket Company	High-performance metal gaskets
1982	Universal Oil Field Services, Inc.	Specialty products for oil and gas industry
	Evans-Aristocrat Industries*	Precision measuring tapes and other products for construction industry
	Baldwin Hardware Manufacturing Corporation	Brass builders' hardware and decorative accessories
	Marvel Metal Products Company	Steel work stations for computers, metal cabinets for copiers
	Foster Oil Field Equipment Company	Oil field products
1983	Brass-Craft Manufacturing*	Plumbing fittings and other products for construction and DIY markets
1984	The Aqua Glass Company	Bathroom products, including bath, shower, and whirlpool units
1985	NI Industries* (Building Products Divisions)	Consumer products including locks, kitchen appliances, faucets, and plumbing fixtures
	Merillat Industries, Inc.	Kitchen and bathroom cabinetry
	Flint & Walling Water Systems	Residential water pumps

*Designates a public company. All other firms were privately owned at the time of acquisition.

In selecting industries to enter, Masco intentionally avoided high-growth ones. Instead, it sought markets in which change had been slow and evolutionary and where competition was more fragmented. When evaluating firms within these industries, Masco stressed that their products should be capable of supporting proprietary market positions. They could include "demonstrably superior design and utility, a unique distribution and/or service capability, or the effective integration of many capabilities which, when combined, [offered] compelling advantages and premium value to the customer."

Most of Masco's acquisitions were privately held firms with strong market positions, often generating profits two to three times higher than typical companies in their industries. Once acquired, Masco generally left the company's management team (which often included the founders) in place, frequently awarding them Masco Corporation stock options. Corporate controls were implemented, but Masco's management felt it was important to "encourage an entrepreneurial management style" with "a minimum of corporate operating constraints." Ordinarily, division heads had only one annual formal meeting with corporate officers and were encouraged to act autonomously. Incentive programs were designed to reward innovation and new product development, as well as above-average performance. Masco took pride in its record of having never lost a management team from any of its acquisitions.

▲ RESTRUCTURING

By the early 1980s, Masco's corporate sales had reached $1 billion. Since its 1929 founding, the company had diversified into three primary areas of business:

- ▲ Building, home improvement, and other: Faucets, plumbing fittings, bathtubs and whirlpools, builders' hardware, steel measuring tapes, venting and ventilating equipment, insulation products, water pumps, weight-distributing hitches, winches, office furniture, brass giftware, plasticware, and scanning monitors.
- ▲ Oil-field and related products: Oil-field equipment and drilling tools.
- ▲ Transportation-related products: Cold-extruded power transmission shafts, precision hot-headed products, special fasteners, gear shift levers, and engine exhaust systems.

According to CEO Richard Manoogian, one by-product of this diversity was that outside observers found the company complex and difficult to understand, causing confusion in the financial community. In the 1960s and early 1970s, Masco stock sold at 150 percent to 200 percent of the Standard & Poor's price-earnings ratio average. Further, Masco's proprietary consumer-related products consistently reported higher growth and higher profits than its cyclical industrial products. Management concluded that it was no longer in the interest of either group to manage them as one company.

Masco undertook a major corporate restructuring in 1984. It transferred industrial products to a newly formed subsidiary, Masco Industries, Inc., with a book value of approximately $440 million, in exchange for $320 million in Masco Industries' subordinated debentures and all of its common stock. Masco Corporation then distributed 42 percent of the shares as a special dividend to its shareholders, making Masco Industries a separate publicly owned company.

Following the restructuring, Masco Corporation would concentrate on proprietary products for the home and family, and Masco Industries would focus on custom-engineered components and specialty industrial products. Each would be free to formulate appropriate goals and strategies for its businesses. Selected income statement and balance sheet information for Masco Industries and Masco Corporation is given in Exhibits 2 and 3.

▲ MASCO CORPORATION IN 1986

In 1986, Masco Corporation's vision was to be the "Procter & Gamble of consumer durables," with its existing brand-name products forming the core of this strategy (Exhibits 4 and 5). Further expansion would be directed to other consumer durables markets in which the firm could compete in differentiated niches.

At the January 1986 National Home Builders' Exhibition, Masco displayed its products in one exhibit—the show's largest display space devoted to a single company. The theme of the exhibit was that Masco's prominent brand-name products had the style, functional appeal, and perceived value necessary to influence consumer buying decisions. The products

▲ EXHIBIT 2

Masco Industries, Inc., and Consolidated Subsidiaries	1985	1984	1983
Net sales*	$ 599,080	$ 544,990	$ 424,920
Net income*	2.900†	23,800	34,430
Total assets*	728,720	535,540	587,770
Shareholders' equity*	105,760	133,530	533,640
Earnings per share	$0.15†	$1.17	—

Masco Corporation and Consolidated Subsidiaries			
	1985	1984	1983
Net sales*	$1,153,960	$ 881,780	$ 753,250
Net income*	164,480	128,730	118,400
Total assets*	1,817,300	1,384,260	1,348,950
Shareholders' equity*	978,970	824,020	774,690
Earnings per share	$2.56	$2.01	$1.92

*In thousands.
†Reflects special charge for oil-field and related operations.

featured were Merillat kitchen and bathroom cabinets; Thermador/Waste King appliances; Brass-Craft plumbing products; Baldwin decorative hardware; Weiser locks and security systems; Aqua Glass tubs, showers, and whirlpools; Auto Flo humidifiers; and Delta, Artistic, and Epic faucets.

In entering new markets, management hoped to leverage its ability to innovate, broadly defined from product design to final sale. Historically, in faucets and metalworking, Masco had spent the equivalent of 2 percent of sales on new product and process development. Technical advancements for these businesses also came from Mechanical Technology, Inc. (MTI), a technology contract research firm in which Masco owned a 37 percent interest. MTI employed over 300 engineers in a variety of disciplines.

Masco also hoped to leverage its manufacturing ability. Dun's *Business Month* noted that the firm was "not only the leader in virtually all its markets, but the most efficient producer" as well. According to that 1986 issue, Masco had been long-regarded as a "state-of-the-art manufacturer" with a heavy investment in specially designed and automated production machinery.

Finally, Masco hoped to leverage its skills in consumer marketing. First initiated in its Delta division, the firm's marketing strategy was built on the concept of "power marketing," defined in Masco's 1985 annual report as "the marshalling of all aspects of the marketing function in a coordinated and focused fashion." The individual functions included market research, merchandising and training, advertising and communication, product development and market segmentation, and product engineering and manufacturing.

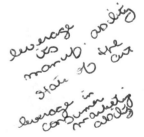

▲ EXHIBIT 3   Masco Corporation Operations by Segment (in thousands)

	Net Sales			Operating Profit			Assets Employed at December 31		
	1985	1984	1983	1985	1984	1983	1985	1984	1983
Operations by industry segment									
Building and home improvement	$1,070,000	$ 769,000	$ 619,000	$210,000	$170,000	$147,000	$797,000	$521,000	$ 473,000
Other specialty products	84,000	113,000	134,000	12,000	15,000	19,000	55,000	62,000	79,000
	$1,154,000	$ 882,000	$ 753,000	$222,000	$185,000	$166,000	$852,000	$583,000	$ 552,000
Segments transferred to Masco									
Oil-field and related products	—	$ 66,000	$ 105,000	—	$ 3,000	$ 1,000	—	—	$ 193,000
Transportation-related	—	138,000	187,000	—	35,000	35,000	—	—	122,000
Other	—	78,000	130,000	—	19,000	23,000	—	—	34,000
	$ —	$ 282,000	$ 422,000	$ —	$ 57,000	$ 59,000	$ —	$ —	$ 449,000
Total	$1,154,000	$1,164,000	$1,175,000	$222,000	$242,000	$225,000	$852,000	$583,000	$1,001,000
Operations by geographic area									
United States	1,039,000	1,050,000	1,040,000	207,000	220,000	201,000	718,000	496,000	857,000
European Common Market	71,000	87,000	104,000	8,000	16,000	18,000	87,000	67,000	112,000
Other foreign countries	44,000	27,000	31,000	7,000	6,000	6,000	47,000	20,000	32,000
Total, as above	$1,154,000	$1,164,000	$1,175,000	$222,000	$242,000	$225,000	$852,000	$583,000	$1,001,000
Other income (expense), net				69,000	(11,000)	(11,000)			
General corporation expense, net				(22,000)	(18,000)	(16,000)			
Income before income taxes				269,000	213,000	198,000			
Net income				$164,480	$128,730	$118,400			
Earnings per share				$ 2.56	$ 2.01	$ 1.92			

▲350

▲ EXHIBIT 4 Products for the Home and Family

Product Category	1985 Sales (millions)	Percent of Total	Products and Markets
Kitchen and bathroom products			
Faucets	$ 303	26%	Delta, Delex, Peerless, Artistic, Epic, Damixa, Mariani, Workforce, and Deltique are well-known domestic and international faucet brands serving all segments of the residential, commercial, and institutional, and DIY markets. Replacement/remodeling and DIY represent more than 60 percent of faucet sales; the balance are sales to new residential and commercial construction. Masco, the largest faucet manufacturer in the world, has an estimated 36 percent share of the 25-million-unit domestic market.
Cabinets	173	15	Merillat manufactures kitchen and bathroom cabinets with a reputation for being the preferred brand of cabinetry among the nation's builders and professional remodeling contractors. Merillat leads the industry in sales, with 6 percent of the $3 billion domestic market. Sales are to the new construction and remodeling markets.
Plumbing specialties	113	10	Brass-Craft is the leading plumbing specialty manufacturer, selling to the wholesale trade under the Brass-Craft name and the Plumb Shop brand at retail to the consumer. The company markets over 4,000 specialty products, including water supplies, hook-ups, fittings, appliance connectors, and toilet and faucet repair items, and enjoys a 50 percent share in its major market.
Other specialty kitchen and bathroom products	184	16	Aqua Glass, Thermador, Waste King, Norris plumbing fixtures, and Trayco are important brand names in their respective markets. Thermador and Waste King are leaders in high-end kitchen appliance products, and Aqua Glass is the leading independent manufacturer of acrylic/gelcoat bathtubs, shower enclosures, whirlpools, and spas.
Total kitchen and bathroom products	$ 773	67%	

continued

▲ EXHIBIT 4 *concluded*

Product Category	1985 Sales (millions)	Percent of Total	Products and Markets
Other specialty building products Builders' hardware	136	12	Weiser and Baldwin manufacture residential and commercial mechanical and electronic lock sets, door knobs, deadbolts, and other builders' hardware. The domestic lock industry is estimated at $900 million, with 55 percent residential and 45 percent commercial. Baldwin is the undisputed market leader in the production of high-end solid brass mortise locks and trim, and Weiser is the largest Canadian and second-largest American producer of medium-priced residential locks.
Air handling and other	161	14	Other leadership market niches include: AMP thermal vent dampers and venting equipment; Auto-Flo humidifiers; Bowers electrical outlet boxes; Compac insulation facings; Gebhardt commercial ventilating products; Evans rules and measuring tapes; and Flint & Walling and Jung water pumps.
Total other specialty building products	297	26	
Total building and home improvement products	1,070	93	
Other specialty consumer products	$ 84	7 %	Reese enjoys a more than 50 percent share of the weight-distributing hitch market for recreational vehicles, and Fulton has an approximate 50 percent share of the boat trailer winch market; Baldwin serves the collectible brass giftware and desk accessory market; and Marvel offers a quality line of computer furniture.
Total products for the home and family	$1,154	100%	

Source: Excerpted from Masco Corp. *Annual Report* 1985.

▲ EXHIBIT 5   Masco Corporation and Consolidated Subsidiaries, as Restated to Reflect Poolings of Interests
(dollar amounts in thousands except as indicated)

| | Net Sales | Income before Taxes | Income Taxes | Net Income | Depreciation and Amortization | Working Capital | Shareholders' Equity | Net Income as a Percent of | | Per Share Data | | Common Shares† |
								Net Sales	Shareholders' Equity*	Net Income††	Average Dividends Paid***	
Growth rates												
5-year	7%	13%	10%	15%	2%	9%	18%	—	—	12%	13%	—
10-year	14	15	13	17	14	16	19	—	—	16	22	—
29-year	18	22	21	23	15	20	20	—	—	20	21	—
Years												
1985	$1,153,960	$268,780	$104,300	$164,480	$34,490	$569,420	$978,970	14.3%	20.0%	$2.56	$.58	64,300
1984	1,164,020	212,810	84,080	128,730	39,210	462,820	824,020	11.1	16.6	2.01	.50	64,150
1983	1,174,690	198,040	79,640	118,400	52,040	561,010	774,690	10.1	19.0	1.92	.44	61,550
1982	922,140	163,410	63,910	99,500	43,940	414,030	623,440	10.8	19.2	1.71	.40	58,150
1981	937,080	162,670	68,050	94,620	38,450	404,950	518,960	10.1	22.2	1.65	.36	56,240
1980	820,500	146,800	64,320	82,480	31,990	366,230	425,830	10.1	23.2	1.44	.32	55,420
1979	780,380	139,020	62,140	76,880	26,550	351,620	355,100	9.9	24.0	1.32	.29	56,780
1978	632,330	120,260	56,590	63,670	19,480	277,000	320,790	10.1	23.7	1.09	.23	57,260
1977	483,040	98,080	45,570	52,510	14,740	206,180	268,690	10.9	23.4	.90	.17	57,250
1976	446,140	91,210	42,400	48,810	10,610	181,330	224,390	10.9	27.2	.83	.11	57,230
1975	325,050	64,210	29,820	34,390	9,370	129,370	179,170	10.6	23.2	.60	.08	57,100
1974	227,150	52,860	24,970	27,890	7,750	104,930	148,300	10.1	22.7	.49	.07	56,950
1973	222,530	44,210	21,900	22,310	6,480	88,000	123,050	10.0	21.8	.41	.06	55,030

continued

▲ **EXHIBIT 5** *concluded*

	Net Sales	Income before Taxes	Income Taxes	Net Income	Depreciation and Amortization	Working Capital	Shareholders' Equity	Net Income as a Percent of Net Sales	Net Income as a Percent of Shareholders' Equity*	Per Share Data Net Income††	Per Share Data Average Dividends Paid†,**	Common Shares†
1972	161,070	34,320	16,980	17,340	4,850	54,500	102,490	10.8	26.3	.33	.04	52,650
1971	119,960	23,360	11,220	12,140	4,310	48,960	66,020	10.1	22.1	.24	.04	50,780
1970	98,000	20,180	9,850	10,330	3,650	44,460	54,980	10.5	22.2	.21	.03	50,250
1969	95,850	21,750	11,770	9,980	2,850	36,260	46,600	10.4	25.8	.20	.03	50,090
1968	85,270	18,660	10,040	8,620	3,080	17,000	38,750	10.1	27.6	.17	.02	49,950
1967	65,180	13,310	6,180	7,130	2,550	14,370	31,200	10.9	27.7	.14	.02	49,720
1966	55,640	12,440	5,770	6,670	1,670	13,240	25,730	12.0	32.9	.14	.02	48,660
1965	43,920	10,010	4,670	5,340	1,220	11,530	20,250	12.2	33.9	.11	.01	48,570
1964	34,530	8,100	3,950	4,150	950	9,620	15,760	12.0	32.7	.09	.01	47,950
1963	27,120	6,160	3,140	3,020	750	7,690	12,690	11.1	28.2	.07	.01	44,980
1962	22,170	4,320	2,160	2,160	810	6,320	10,700	9.7	24.6	.05	.00	44,740
1961	16,120	2,510	1,260	1,250	700	5,050	8,790	7.8	16.1	.03	.00	44,410
1960	15,110	1,960	970	990	860	4,340	7,780	6.6	14.1	.02	.00	44,410
1959	14,950	1,940	960	980	780	3,970	7,060	6.6	15.4	.02	.00	44,410
1958	11,160	1,110	520	590	700	3,220	6,360	5.3	10.1	.01	.00	44,410
1957	11,210	1,030	480	550	620	2,640	5,870	4.9	10.1	.01	.00	38,780

*Based on shareholders' equity as of the beginning of the year.
†After giving effect to 100 percent stock distributions in 1982, 1975, 1971, 1963 and 1961, and 50 percent stock distributions in 1968 and 1967.
††Years 1976 through 1981 include the effect of share dilution.
**Dividends per share have not been adjusted for poolings of interests.
Source: Masco Corporation 1985 *Annual Report*.

Masco's business units were autonomous. To preserve a sense of fluidity, the firm chose not to have a formal organization chart. However, similar businesses were grouped together, under the leadership of a group president, to facilitate communication and exchange. Although Masco did not have specific programs for sharing skills, it encouraged individual managers to exchange ideas and resources across businesses.

In its 1985 annual report, Masco described the following examples of "successful cross-fertilizations":

- ▲ Successful marketing and merchandising programs innovated by Delta, adopted to enhance sales and increase profits at Weiser, Artistic, and Thermador/Waste King.
- ▲ A planned product partnership between Baldwin and Weiser to improve their respective competitive postures in the popularly priced commercial and high-end lock markets.
- ▲ New sophisticated valve mechanisms from the overseas R&D centers incorporated into faucets of Artistic and Waltec (a Canadian affiliate).
- ▲ Expanded corporate R&D activities contributed new products, cost-reduction programs, and numerous advanced technological innovations at many product divisions, including Thermador/Waste King, Weiser, Baldwin, Merillat, and Delta/Peerless.
- ▲ Interdivisional employee promotions.

Metal furniture represented a small percentage of U.S. household furniture, and Masco was not interested in entering this product category. Management believed the more significant opportunities were in wood and upholstered goods that traditionally accounted for a high percentage of household sales. Management thought entry into these product categories would be very attractive if, by leveraging the company's broadly defined management and manufacturing capabilities, the firm could achieve a substantial and profitable position.

CASE
3▴3

THE HOUSEHOLD FURNITURE INDUSTRY IN 1986

Industries dominated by $50–$100 million companies do not have the marketing and advertising resources to command consumer attention, and joint industry efforts always sound good, buy seldom succeed. Americans don't swing gallons of soda pop every year because there are lots of little pop makers. They do so because of Coca-Cola and Pepsico. The same is true for cars and cigarettes. The average tobacco chewer spends more for Levi Garrett Chewing Tobacco every year than does for furniture.

Wesley E. Collins, vice chairman of Universal Furniture Ltd.

[handwritten margin note: highly fragmented / privately owned / 1.9–2.9% growth]

Unlike the highly concentrated soft-drink industry, in 1986 the U.S. household furniture industry consisted of more than 2,500 manufacturing firms with total shipments of more than $14 billion worth of goods. Of these companies, 400 accounted for approximately 80 percent of sales and 19 had sales greater than $100 million. The vast majority were privately owned, including some of the largest ones. Even those firms that were publicly traded often had large blocks of shares held by members of their founding families.

In 1986, industry net profit after taxes as a percentage of sales was in the range of 4 percent (Exhibits 1 and 2). A 1985 Department of Commerce study forecasted that the U.S. furniture market would grow 1.9–2.9 percent annually, in real terms, for the next 15 years. One of the fastest growing segments of the population would be the 35–44 age group, the so-called baby boom generation, the group predicted also to have the greatest need for new furniture in the next five years.

C.W. Moorman, MBA 1989, and Professor Cynthia A. Montgomery prepared this case in collaboration with Professor Michael E. Porter. Copyright © 1989 by the President and Fellows of Harvard College.

▲ EXHIBIT 1   Annual Furniture Sales and Unit Growth (at the manufacturers' level; millions)

	Sales	Change(%)	Producer Price Index Household Furniture (1967 = 100)	Change (%)	Unit Growth (%)
1985	$12,898	7.8	255.7	5.7	2.1
1984	11,965	20.2	242.0	3.1	17.1
1983	9,958	25.4	234.7	2.1	23.3
1982	7,943	(10.1)	229.8	4.8	(14.9)
1981	8,831	1.5	219.2	7.0	(5.5)
1980	8,700	(6.6)	204.8	9.9	(16.5)
1979	9,316	7.6	186.3	7.4	0.2
1978	8,656	10.7	173.5	7.0	3.7
1977	7,819	7.1	162.2	5.7	1.4
1976	7,300	19.2	153.5	4.9	14.3
1975	6,122	(16.4)	146.3	7.1	(23.5)
1974	7,325	6.7	136.6	11.1	(4.4)
1973	6,865	17.5	123.0	4.9	12.6
1972	5,843	18.4	117.3	2.2	16.2
1971	4,934	10.2	114.8	2.9	7.3
1970	4,477	(5.8)	111.6	3.0	(8.8)
1969	4,753	8.2	108.3	4.2	4.0
1968	4,393	12.3	103.9	3.9	8.4
1967	3,912	(1.8)	100.0	3.5	(5.3)

Source: Seidman & Siedman.

Household furniture sales were cyclical and closely tied to broad economic factors such as discretionary income and consumer credit. Since the early 1970s, furniture prices had increased by roughly two-thirds of the Consumer Price Index, yet furniture purchases as a percentage of discretionary income had declined. During this period, consumers were spending an increasing percentage of their discretionary dollars on electronics and appliances.

Household furniture sales were also closely tied to sales of both new and existing homes. They usually lagged new-home sales by one or two years, following purchases for landscaping, window treatment, and appliances. Studies showed that on the sale of one house and the purchase of another, a typical homeowner would retain about one-third of the funds and often use it for new furniture. In 1986, the sales of both new and existing homes were at their highest point since 1978–1979.

The availability of consumer credit was an important factor in furniture sales. In 1984, 64 percent of all furniture was sold on some kind of credit; this figure was much

▲ EXHIBIT 2 Furniture Industry Operating and Profit Ratios (at the manufacturers' level; percentage of net sales)

	Net Sales	Cost of Sales	Selling Expense	Administrative Expense	Other Income (Expense)	Profit Before Taxes	Income Taxes	Net Profit After Taxes
1985	100.00	75.61	11.17	5.36	(0.23)	7.63	3.37	4.25
1984	100.00	76.32	10.66	5.32	(0.42)	7.28	2.89	4.39
1983	100.00	74.55	10.90	6.22	(0.34)	7.98	3.34	4.64
1982	100.00	77.84	11.34	5.81	(0.50)	4.51	2.14	2.37
1981	100.00	78.36	9.83	5.63	(0.80)	5.38	1.97	3.41
1980	100.00	78.40	9.50	5.90	(0.50)	5.70	2.30	3.40
1979	100.00	77.30	9.30	5.00	(0.70)	7.70	3.10	4.60
1978	100.00	77.10	8.80	5.00	(0.50)	8.60	3.60	5.00
1977	100.00	78.10	9.00	5.20	(0.30)	7.40	3.00	4.40
1976	100.00	78.21	9.11	5.02	(0.07)	8.86	3.56	4.03
1975	100.00	82.55	9.25	6.05	(0.85)	1.30	0.85	0.45
1974	100.00	79.35	8.82	5.35	(1.03)	5.45	2.61	2.84
1973	100.00	76.58	8.96	4.99	(0.28)	9.19	4.06	5.13
1972	100.00	76.91	9.79	5.27	0.88	8.91	4.12	4.79
1971	100.00	75.70	10.28	5.19	0.29	9.12	4.29	4.83

Note: Data from 1971 through 1982 based on SFMA Report "Analysis of Operating Ratios."
Source: Salomon Brothers Inc. calculations.

higher at the lower price points. The importance of available, reasonably priced credit was magnified because the purchase of furniture was usually, to quote an industry analyst, a "highly postponable" decision.

There was also an active rental market, both for short periods and for rent-to-own programs. In 1985, it was estimated that 7 percent of the volume of furniture at the retail level was in some kind of rental program.

active rental market

Products

Household furniture could generally be segmented along two dimensions. The first was the primary type of material used in construction, wood (50 percent of domestic shipments), upholstered fabric (35 percent of shipments), metal, or other material. The second dimension was the furniture's use in the home. The two main categories of wooden furniture were case goods (dining room and bedroom furniture) and occasional furniture, such as coffee and end tables. Furniture differed also in style, finish, quality, and price. Most manufacturers targeted a specific niche, but the largest companies produced lines for more than one segment. Volume leaders by product category and price point are given in Exhibit 3.

Design

Design traditionally started at the top of the industry, with most major developments coming from well-recognized industry leaders (e.g., Drexel-Heritage, Henredon, Baker). Middlepriced competitors then adopted their designs for the mass market; "knock-off" products were frequent and rapid. Designs not headed ultimately for the mass market tended to be confined to small, specialized firms.

Manufacturing

Furniture manufacturing in 1986 was a labor-intensive process, with payroll costs accounting for almost 50 percent of value added. Whereas a few of the larger companies, such as Thomasville, had begun to introduce some elements of automation into production, most firms used techniques and equipment that had changed little over many years. Capital investment since 1970 had been primarily to satisfy OSHA and EPA requirements.

labor-intensive little automation

In the late 1980s, several manufacturers had begun to implement CAD/CAM systems, but their costs and those of other high-tech manufacturing improvements limited them to only the largest firms in the industry. Further, the extreme number of style variations and hand-work requirements in upper-end products often worked against automation efforts, although some notable gains had been made. In the mid-1980s, Baker Furniture, a respected high-end producer, installed machinery that could produce in 20 to 30 minutes a parquet table, which formerly had required six to seven hours of hand-routing. Baker also installed high-speed sanders, which reduced finishing costs by providing more even surfaces.

some automation

The major components in wooden furniture production were hardwood lumber; composite wood materials such as particleboard, fiberboard, and hardboard; and finishing supplies such as paint, varnish, and hardware. In upholstered furniture, the primary production components were furniture frames, hardwood lumber, and woven upholstery fabric. The furniture industry purchased a large portion of such materials from outside suppliers. Due

▲ EXHIBIT 3 Volume Leaders by Product Category (1987 estimates)

Bedroom		Dining Room		Occasional	
Henredon	H	Henredon	H	Interco	M–H
Drexel-Heritage	M–H	Drexel-Heritage	H	Pulaski	M
Interco	M–H	Bernhardt	M–H	Lane	L–H
Bassett	M	Interco	M–H	Ashley	L–M
Armstrong	L–H	Armstrong	L–H	Bassett	L
Singer	L–M	Bassett	L–M	Foremost	L
Ladd	L	Singer	L–M	Tandy Corp.	L
		Universal	L–M		

Upholstery		Motion Chairs		Metal Dining	
Henredon	H	La-Z-Boy	M–H	Benchcraft	M
Interco	M–H	Berkline	M	Mohasco	M
Mohasco	L–H	Lane	M	Ladd	L–M
Bassett	L–M	Peoploungers	M	Rachlin	L–M
Klaussner	L	Mohasco	L–H	Douglas	L
Townhouse/		Jackson	L–M	Stoneville	L
Penthouse	L				

Wicker/Rattan		Youth Furniture	
Dixie	M–H	Dixie	M–H
Ayers	L	Lee	L
Alex Vale	M	Kemp	L
O'Asian	H	Bassett	L–M
Fickes Reed	H	Broyhill	L

Price points: L = low; M = medium; H = high.
Source: Industry estimates.

Small firms
had no
economies of
scale
long lead times

to the small size of most furniture manufacturers, few were able to gain leverage or extract significant quantity discounts from suppliers. Long lead times from suppliers creating scheduling difficulties and inflexibilities for most firms.

There was only limited backward integration in the industry. Most upholstered furniture producers purchased their fabric from one of the large textile companies. Hardwoods were available from a large number of sources, including some of the major timber companies. Some of the large wood furniture companies had entered into limited partnerships or built their own production facilities to ensure a supply of composite boards and plywood.

In the early 1980s, manufacturers had begun a limited amount of overseas sourcing. By 1985, most major case goods manufacturers and many upholstery manufacturers were buying some parts from abroad. For low-end firms, imports supplied some completed furniture items that were added to the firms' lines. For upper-end firms, imports provided intricately carved or veneered components at a substantial discount to the price at which they could be manufactured in the United States.

Production planning and product delivery were relatively unsophisticated, in part due to extreme product variety. Deliveries from many producers were often slow and erratic, which created problems at the retail level. In addition, it was common practice to ship different parts of a single order upon completion. For example, in filling an order for a dining room set, the table might be shipped immediately from inventory while the chairs were being built and shipped eight weeks later. In 1986, a few large firms were experimenting with on-line order systems, that provided data on product availability.

Marketing

Most furniture manufacturers marketed their products through furniture retailers. Large companies employed their own commissioned sales force to sell to retailers, whereas smaller companies often relied on independent sales representatives who would handle products from a number of different companies. Sales efforts often revolved around the furniture shows held every April and October in High Point, North Carolina. The shows, offering many manufacturers a way to display their products, were heavily attended by buyers for furniture retailers, and many manufacturers relied on the shows to generate most of their orders for the year.

Total advertising expenditures by manufacturers were estimated to be about 1 percent of sales, with advertising targeted at retailers and interior designers rather than at furniture consumers. The larger manufacturers advertised in magazines such as *Architectural Digest, House and Garden*, and *Home Beautiful*. Retail-level advertising was placed in newspapers and magazines, but was used primarily by the few manufacturers that, like Ethan Allen, had free-standing retail stores.

Brand recognition was relatively low. A survey in the late 1970s found that less than 44 percent of married couples interviewed could name one furniture manufacturer. Among the best-known firms were Baker, Bassett, Drexel-Heritage, Ethan Allen, Henredon, Lane, La-Z-Boy, Pennsylvania House, and Thomasville, all of which sold to the medium to high end of the market.

Channels

In 1986, retail household furniture was distributed through the following channels:

Retail Sales by Channel	
Furniture rental/rent-to-own	4.0%
Design centers/decorator wholesale showrooms	6.0
Major regional chains	8.5
National accounts	9.5
Department stores	12.5
Independent retailers	59.5
	100.0%

Source: Industry interviews

chain stores
FF
+one brand-owned
stores +

galleries

niche stores

The number of furniture stores had declined from $22,000 in 1978 to 16,000 in 1986, largely because of the 1981–1982 recession, which had a severe impact on the entire industry. The mix of furniture stores was also changing. The traditional independent furniture stores, usually with 20,000 square feet or more of retail space, were gradually being replaced by chain operations and specialty stores. In addition, more manufacturers were beginning to open free-standing stores featuring their own products, following the lead of such companies as Ethan Allen and La-Z-Boy.

In 1985, there were 13 furniture store chains with sales of more than $1 million. The largest, Levitz Furniture Corporation, operated large stores and showrooms nationwide. Levitz, which had net income of $27.4 million on $644 million in sales in 1984, sold primarily mid- and lower-priced furniture lines. There were also several large regional chains, including Rhodes and Heilig-Meyers, which were expanding operations. It was predicted that there might be as many as five national chains within 10 years.

The sale of furniture through department stores was in a period of transition. Furniture had historically accounted for a low percentage of most department stores' sales. Between 1978 and 1986, it was estimated that total department store square footage devoted to furniture had declined by more than 35 percent. In the mid-1980s, several department store chains, including Rich's, Macy's, Montgomery Ward, and J.C. Penney, began to develop their own free-standing home furnishings stores, which gave their retailers a much larger area for furniture and avoided the higher rents for mall square footage.

A new method of distribution was the in-store gallery, an arrangement whereby a retailer agreed to allot a certain amount of floor space, typically about 5,000 square feet, for the exclusive display of a particular manufacturer's product line. Galleries had been shown to generate higher sales per square foot and faster inventory turns than conventional space in both independent retail stores and department stores.

A large retailer might feature multiple galleries within one store. By giving a large percentage of space to a small number of manufacturers, retailers substantially reduced their need for fill-in merchandise. Galleries also allowed better coordination of sales and marketing efforts, fewer expenses for billing and sales, faster deliveries, and less inventory risk because of higher turns. *Furniture Today* reported that the following manufacturers had more than 100 in-store galleries in 1986: Norwalk, 327; Pennsylvania House, 322; Broyhill, 230; Drexel-Heritage, 152; Rowe, 150; Thomasville, 114; Fairfield Chair, 110; Brass Bed Co., 104; and Kemp, 103.

Free-standing stores or franchised showcases were those devoted primarily to the merchandise of a single manufacturer. In 1986, there were more than 750 such stores in the United States, including Ethan Allen (300), La-Z-Boy (250), Drexel-Heritage (77), Norwalk (50), King Koil (30), Mersman Waldron (20), Rowe (14), and Thomasville (13).

In addition to stores devoted to a single manufacturer, the number of specialized furniture stores was also increasing. These stores targeted a specific niche—either product type (e.g., sleep shops, dining room, waterbeds) or style (e.g., Scandinavian, contemporary, butcher block). With between 1,500 and 7,000 square feet, they were often located in malls or shopping areas, and many were either owned or franchised by regional or national chains. Some well-known examples included Crate and Barrel and Conran's, which offered moderately priced furniture and accessories with European styling.

Another development in furniture retailing was the arrival in the United States of IKEA in 1985. IKEA was a European contemporary furniture chain and the largest furniture retailer in the world, selling ready-to-assemble as opposed to the assembled furniture sold by most firms. Its product was generally discounted 20–25 percent from assembled contemporary furniture of similar quality. Customers received little sales help and no assistance in assembly. In June 1985, IKEA opened its first store in Philadelphia, totaling some 165,000 square feet. It was reported that the company intended to open as many as 60 stores nationwide.

Competition

In the United States, furniture manufacturing had migrated toward the Southeast where wages were historically below the national average, supplies of hardwood lumber were plentiful, and there was an adequate railroad and highway system. By 1982, North Carolina was the largest U.S. furniture-supplying state, accounting for 28.5 percent of all production.

Geographic concentration was more pronounced among wood then upholstered furniture manufacturers. Upholstered furniture was often bulkier than wooden furniture of the same weight and could not be taken apart ("knocked down") for shipping; thus there was a greater tendency to locate upholstery plants near the end markets. By 1985, wages in the Southeast were no longer substantially below the national average. In addition, the advent of containerized shipping was dramatically changing the economics of domestic and international transportation, generally decreasing costs of shipping furniture products over long distances.

Throughout most of its history, the industry had consisted of numerous companies, each specializing in a limited range of products. There was some indication that this situation might change in the 1960s, when conglomerates and other large firms began buying furniture companies. However, by 1986, many of these companies, including Consolidated Foods, Congoleum, Champion International, Mead, General Housewares, Ludlow, Intermark, Georgia Pacific, Beatrice Foods, Scott Paper, Burlington Industries, and Gulf & Western, had divested themselves of their furniture operations. In most instances, the new owners had been largely unsuccessful in their attempts to "professionalize" the industry. Protracted industry downturns, often on the heels of vigorous upswings, had found firms struggling to deal with overgrown inventories and overbuilt capacity—quite a disappointing scenario for firms that had hoped to earn significant returns from modest strategy changes and from the introduction of modern management practices. Cultural clashes between corporate management and furniture executives also made changes difficult.

The management of most furniture companies in the 1980s was still perceived as unsophisticated. During the previous 50 years, few truly significant changes had occurred in the industry. Wesley Collins of Universal Furniture offered the following commentary:

When everything else in our lives was changing, furniture stood its ground. While we put a man on the moon...furniture put another steak on the backyard grill and muttered, "My God, the price of oak went up again."

When videotape put the home movie camera in the trash can forever, and tape cassettes put the plastic record-maker six feet under, and word processors put typewriters in the closet, and microwave popcorn killed the makers of popcorn poppers...the furniture industry said, "Thanks, but we'll stand pat."

While we sat on our tuffets, the consumer forgot all about us. Our share of consumer expenditures slipped year after year. We lost over 40 percent of the retail furniture space in America, 25 percent of the retailers shut their doors, and department stores discontinued furniture right and left for products that gave them a better ratio of margin and turns per square foot.

In 1986, the top ten U.S. furniture manufacturers together accounted for 22.7 percent of the $13.4 billion U.S. furniture industry. Profit data for the publicity held firms among them are given in Exhibits 4 to 6. In 1986, furniture companies could typically be acquired for 12 to 15 times earnings, although higher and lower multiples had been observed.

There were relatively few large manufacturers, and their strategies varied widely. In 1985, industry market share leaders were Interco (4.1 percent), Mohasco (3.3 percent), Bassett (3.0 percent), Lane Co. (2.3 percent), La-Z-Boy Chair (2.3 percent), Armstrong World (1.8 percent), Ladd Furniture (1.8 percent), Drexel-Heritage (1.7 percent), Universal Furniture (1.2 percent), and Dixie Furniture Companies (1.1 percent). Profiles of these firms are given below.

Interco   Interco, a St. Louis-based consumer products and services conglomerate, owned Ethan Allen and Broyhill. Ethan Allen produced traditional American furniture in the

▲ EXHIBIT 4   Comparative Profits and Expenditures for Selected Publicly Traded Furniture Companies

	Sales*	Cost of Goods Sold*	Selling, General and Administration Expense*	Net Income	Net ROA	Net ROE
Bassett						
1985	$408.5	$310.7	$49.8	$25.0	9.8%	10.9%
1984	398.1	296.8	45.8	30.9	12.7	14.5
1983	341.8	249.6	36.6	32.0	14.3	16.5
Lane						
1985	321.6	200.3	68.6	27.5	15.4	17.6
1984	284.9	177.7	61.3	23.3	15.0	17.1
1983	227.0	141.2	49.2	18.1	13.2	15.0
La-Z-Boy Chair						
1985	282.7	186.2	54.7	21.4	11.7	17.4
1984	254.9	163.2	46.0	23.3	14.9	21.8
1983	197.0	134.0	39.0	12.8	9.8	13.8
Ladd Furniture						
1985	247.5	175.9	33.1	18.4	20.0	32.9
1984	192.7	136.2	25.8	14.8	21.0	36.5
1983	140.8	98.7	17.5	12.3	22.1	67.3
Universal Furniture						
1985	158.0	114.6	23.4	13.1	11.1	18.0
1984	128.2	86.2	22.7	14.1	14.4	22.2
1983	112.2	75.7	20.0	11.1	12.7	21.3

*In millions.
Source: Compustat II.

▲ EXHIBIT 5   1985 Segment Information for Selected Multibusiness Firms
(in millions)

	Sales	Operating Income	Depreciation Expense	Capital Expense	Assets
Interco, Inc.					
Apparel	$907.8	$66.7	$12.0	$13.4	$457.0
General retail merchandising	461.8	32.1	8.3	6.2	234.0
Footwear	558.3	48.5	8.3	8.1	291.3
Furniture	582.8	57.3	14.5	16.2	455.1
Mohasco Corp.					
Carpet	320.3	10.8	8.7	4.2	177.3
Furniture	368.2	26.8	3.9	5.3	141.8
Rental	71.7	13.9	8.5	26.5	65.0
Armstrong World Industries, Inc.					
Floor coverings	854.9	107.1	34.0	56.5	452.0
Furniture	254.3	22.5	6.0	9.7	119.0
Industrial products and other	154.7	23.7	6.0	9.2	101.3
Building products	415.3	62.3	14.3	25.9	235.3

Source: Compustat II.

higher price range and sold it through approximately 300 independently owned Ethan
Allen Galleries. These galleries were backed by five Ethan Allen-owned consolidation
warehouses and five regional distribution centers, which assumed responsibility for the
physical distribution of the firm's products direct to the customer. Ethan Allen operated 24
factories.

Broyhill produced a broad line of bedroom, dining room, and living room furniture in
the medium-price range. It had 20 manufacturing facilities and sold more than 10,000
dealers; it had approximately 230 galleries. Broyhill was rapidly adopting technological
innovation, aided by the know-how and financing of its parent company.

Mohasco   Mohasco Corporation had three major business segments: carpets, furniture manufacturing, and furniture rental, which accounted for 42 percent, 48 percent, and 10 percent,
respectively, of the firm's 1985 sales. Furniture manufacturing consisted of four subsidiaries.
The largest, Mohasco Upholstered Furniture, produced Stratford, Barcalounger, Avon, and
Trend Line products, which included a broad range of motion products, selling from the lower
to upper price ranges. Chromcraft produced casual dining room furniture and medium priced
contract seating and desks. Peters-Revington manufactured midpriced occasional furniture.
Super Sagless produced and supplied mechanisms for motion furniture.

▲ EXHIBIT 6   Revenue and Stock Data for Selected Publicly Traded Firms

Company*	Revenues ($ millions)	Earnings per Share			Stock Price†
		1986E	1985	1984	
American	$ 96.5	$1.20	$1.18	$1.23	16⅛
Bassett	408.5	3.25	3.01	3.67	47½
Bench Craft	106.3	1.25	1.06	0.82	14
Berkline	86.0	1.10	0.50	1.24	15½
Cochrane	27.5	1.60	1.58	1.32	13½
Dresher	31.4	0.79	0.65	0.54	14¾
Flexsteel	125.3	1.50	1.28	1.61	16¾
Henredon	127.4	2.60	2.11	3.05	44
Interco	2,511.0	6.70‡	5.84	4.45	79½
Ladd	247.5	2.15	1.93	1.56	30⅛
Lane	322.0	3.70	3.47	2.98	51
La-Z-Boy	283.0	5.55**	5.00E	4.67	67½
Mohasco	760.0	3.25	2.62	2.60	37¼
Pulaski	74.3	3.25	2.50	2.80	37¾
Rowe	78.6	1.65	1.43	1.48	18⅝
Universal	158.0	2.15	1.64	1.76	34½

*Fiscal years are as follows: Interco, February; La-Z-Boy, April; Berkline, Cochrane, Dresher, Flexsteel, June; Pulaski, October; American, Bassett, Rowe, November.
†As of April 24, 1986.
‡February 1987.
**April 1987.
E=Estimate
Source: *Barron's*, April 28, 1986.

In 1985, Mohasco was emerging from a deep financial slump. Its carpet and furniture businesses, which had suffered losses in the early 1980s, were restructured and returned to profitability by 1985.

Bassett Furniture   Bassett Furniture manufactured a wide range of low- to medium-priced bedroom, dining room, living room, and occasional furniture. The firm sourced some components from the Far East, but continued to manufacture exclusively in the United States. It sold products to dealers through commissioned sales representatives and had 21 galleries operating or under construction. Approximately 24 percent of total sales were to J.C. Penney.

The Lane Company   Lane started as a manufacturer of cedar chests. In the 1960s and 1970s, it acquired seven companies and expanded its line to 2,500 pieces. In 1985, the firm manufactured reclining chairs, cedar chests, case goods, occasional and up-holstered furniture, mostly in the medium-price range. It began producing office furniture in 1980. Major divisions included Action Industries (40 percent of sales) and Lane

Division (30 percent of sales). The company operated 19 plants in four states and sold its products through a nationwide network of independent furniture retailers.

Lane was financially conservative and had not carried debt since 1928. The Lane family and their employees own 35 percent of the company's stock.

La-Z-Boy Chair   With an estimated 22 percent share, La-Z-Boy Chair Company was the largest manufacturer of reclining chairs in the United States, with volume about double that of its nearest rival. Additionally, it held the number two market share in convertible sleepers. The company had 250 Showcase Shoppes, which were independently owned but sold La-Z-Boy products exclusively. La-Z-Boy was also well represented in mass merchandisers and midprice department stores. In 1985, it acquired Burris Industries, a manufacturer of upscale upholstered lines sold through department and furniture stores.

La-Z-Boy operated 11 manufacturing plants and one fabric processing center.

Armstrong World   Armstrong World was a leading manufacturer of interior furnishings, including resilient flooring, ceilings, carpets, and furniture. Its furniture lines included Thomasville and Armstrong World. Thomasville was one of the largest producers of case goods furniture in the United States, offering traditional, contemporary, and transitional lines, sold through major furniture dealers and 114 galleries. In the mid-1980s, Thomasville eliminated approximately 1,000 retail accounts, while offering its gallery customers 5- to 10-day delivery on 85 percent of its merchandise. More than 150 stores were wait-listed for Thomasville galleries. The Armstrong World line offered lower-priced bedroom and occasional furnishings, sold mainly through lower-priced retailers.

Production for Thomasville and Armstrong World included two ready-to assemble furniture plants, second-shift manufacturing, standardized components, and computer production and inventory control.

Ladd Furniture   Ladd Furniture Inc. was created in mid-1981 as a leveraged buyout of Sperry & Hutchinson furniture operations. It manufactured wood, metal, and upholstered furniture for bedrooms, dining rooms, living rooms, and kitchens, mainly in the low-medium to high-medium price range while its Lea Lumber unit manufactured plywood furniture components. Ladd Transportation shipped products for Ladd and others. The company operated 18 plants, 4 of which were completely controlled by computers.

Drexel-Heritage   Drexel-Heritage was owned by New York-based Dominick International, a privately owned holding company. Drexel-Heritage offered a broad range of brand-name wood and upholstered furniture, including the medium- to high-end Drexel brand, the upscale Heritage brand, the upscale Ralph Lauren and Frederick Edward lines of upholstered furniture, and a group of contract products widely used in commercial and government buildings. Drexel and Heritage brands were sold through retail dealerships, with 70 percent of sales going to 77 franchised showcase stores and 152 galleries. Remaining sales were to large, conventional furniture stores, major high-end department stores, and contract accounts. Drexel-Heritage had 10 manufacturing plants, partly supported by seven service plants.

Universal Furniture   Universal Furniture Limited, a British Virgin Islands Company, manufactured popular-priced furniture. Manufacturing operations were located in 10 countries on three continents. The firm's strategy grew out of its initial efforts for supplying dining room furniture to the U.S. market. Designs accomodating a ready-to-assemble concept were created by designers in the United States. Component parts were then fabricated and finished near raw material sources in low-cost labor areas in Southeast Asia. These parts were containerized and shipped to five U.S. assembly plants, which were capable of overnight delivery to major U.S. consumer markets.

Although imports from the Far East were often of uneven quality, industry analysts described Universal as a producer of consistently good-quality, low-cost furniture. The firm had mechanized many hand operations and, in doing so, improved fit and finish and reduced assembly problems. Through a number of acquisitions, Universal expanded its product line to include bedroom and upholstered furniture, as well as metal and wooden dining room furniture.

In the 1980s, Universal added assembly and marketing in Canada, the United Kingdom, and Scandinavia.

Dixie Furniture Companies   The privately held Dixie Furniture Companies included four affiliated units: Dixie, Henry Link, Link-Taylor, and Young-Hinkle. Their products included medium-priced bedroom and dining room furniture; woven wicker bedroom, dining room, and occasional products; solid mahogany eighteenth-century reproductions sold at the upper end of the market; and coordinated furniture for girls' and boys' rooms.

Dixie and its affiliates operated 10 plants and sold through department stores, better quality furniture stores, national accounts, and furniture chains.

Imports

Historically, imports had played a minor role in U.S. furniture sales. Before the 1980s, most imported furniture sold was expensive and limited to contemporary European design or exotic woods. Total imports grew from $1.25 billion in 1981 to $3.31 billion in 1985, with growth principally in lower-priced segments. Exports declined from $643 million in 1981 to $518 million in 1985.

Far Eastern producers increasingly used knock-off product designs along with lower-cost containerized shipping. They also benefited from the use of lumber from defunct rubber plantations, lower taxes on profits, and less government regulation. While European firms lacked some of these advantages and did not have access to hardwoods, they had gained some advantage from the development of flat panel furniture and special types of surface finishes.

Most imported furniture products were either component parts or products that were then used or repackaged by a domestic producer. The $1 billion in furnishings that were sold directly to retailers were primarily lower- and middle-priced products, due to the scale needed for efficient manufacturing and shipping. Also, imports had historically been of lower quality. In the mid-1980s, it was generally believed that imports could not provide sufficient levels of quality and finish to compete with the high-end U.S. manufacturers.

CAT FIGHT IN THE PET FOOD INDUSTRY (A)

"[Pet foods] is an industry waiting for a breakthrough," said Peter Bowen, marketing manager of H.J. Heinz's 9-Lives cat foods.[1] In 1986, virtually all U.S. pet owners purchased commercially produced food for their dogs and cats. However, by the mid-1980's the nation's pet population, consisting of about 50 million dogs and 50 million cats in half of the U.S. households, had entered a period of slow growth. As pet food consumption stabilized at around 10 billion pounds per year, the industry's major players realized that sales increases would most likely follow only from larger "share of stomach."

▲ THE PRODUCT

The vast majority of pet food sales were for cats and dogs. In 1986, dog food sales exceeded $3.2 billion, while cat food sales were about $2.1 billion. Within each of these two broad categories, however, there were different types and flavors of pet food made from many different ingredients including grains, poultry, fish, meat, and animal by-products.

The principal types of pet food were (in order of sales) dry, canned, and moist. Dry pet food, the largest dog and second-largest cat segment in 1986, had a cereal base that was augmented with animal- or plant-based protein, fats, vitamins, and minerals. Dry foods had a low moisture content (5 percent to 15 percent), and therefore did not contain preservatives. Canned food for dogs consisted of meat and meat offal (inedible animal by-products), and for cats it was usually made from fish and fish offal. Canned products typically had a moisture

Research Associate Toby Stuart prepared this case under the supervision of Professor David Collis. Copyright © 1991 by the President and Fellows of Harvard College.
[1]Laura Jereski, "The Nouvelle Pet Food Market," *Marketing & Media Decisions,* February 1985, p. 115.

content of 70 percent to 80 percent. Moist pet food was made from animal by-products, dairy products, fats, oils, soybean products, vitamins, and minerals. These products, with a moisture content of 20 percent to 30 percent, were usually shaped into meat-like chunks or mince that had a pliable consistency, and were packaged in air-tight sachets. The production of moist pet food was specialized and expensive relative to dry or canned food.

Throughout the 1960s and 1970s, pet food sales grew at double-digit rates, in stride with the increasing pet population. However, as the 1980s began, a slowing of new household formation and other demographic trends, such as increasing urbanization, confronted pet food manufacturers with an array of changes. One of the more important of these was that cats were increasingly popular because they were easier to maintain and required less space than dogs, and were therefore better suited to urban living conditions. In 1986, an estimated 26 percent of U.S. households owned cats, compared to 34 percent that had at least one dog. As the composition of pet ownership changed (the cat population increased by 10 million between 1983 and 1986, while the number of dogs remained constant), cat food sales escalated. During the mid-1980s, cat food sales grew at 5 percent to 10 percent per year, compared to 1 percent to 2 percent for dog food.

In addition, economic forces shaped the configuration of pet food consumption. As the economy entered the recession in the early-1980s, private-label and generic products made inroads at the low end of the pet food market, carving out a 25 percent share of dog food sales and a 15 percent share of cat food purchases by 1983. Conversely, as the economy recovered in the mid-1980s, pet food manufacturers introduced a smorgasbord of new products in the premium-priced or gourmet segment, where products were priced about 35 percent higher than mid-range foods. These upscale products, which appealed to pet owners because of their similarity to human food in appearance and composition, began to represent a greater percentage of pet food sales.

Distribution Channels

The principal market for pet foods was the grocery store, which accounted for about 90 percent of pet food sales in the mid-1980s. The other 10 percent of sales were through some 15,000 specialty outlets, including pet stores, breeders, and veterinarians' offices. Typically, specialty stores products were meat- rather than grain-based, and sold at prices comparable to grocery store gourmet brands.

Pet food was the second-largest line for supermarkets, trailing only cereals, and it generally supported high margins. Dry dog food had margins around 13 percent to 15 percent, compared to 15 percent to 17 percent for dry cat food; canned food had margins about 2 percent higher in both dog and cat foods, and the margins on some gourmet products reached 40 percent. To the manufacturer, each percentage of pet food market share was worth about $50 million in sales and $2 million in profits. As new product introductions (particularly in the gourmet segment) proliferated during the mid-1980s, retailers often responded to the additional shelf space requirements by eliminating older product lines. "Pet food is by far the biggest section of our store," said John Gabriel, assistant purchasing director at Tom Thumb-Page, "We wouldn't consider adding more space. If a manufacturer wants to add four new items, they lose four."[2] Retailers typically carried pet food in three price ranges: generic or low-price items, mid-range foods, and gourmet or premium-price products.

---

[2]Deborah Fleishman, "Pet Food: A Deal Driven Market," *Supermarket News,* January 5, 1987, p. 19.

Marketing

There were a number of important factors that motivated purchases of particular brands and types of pet foods, including perceived quality, convenience, and price. Because pet owners considered their animals to be friends and companions, many felt that, through feeding, they were able to give greater attention to their pet's welfare. Often, the higher price tag associated with premium-quality pet foods lessened the guilt that many pet owners felt for being away all day. Most pet owners believed that their pets (especially dogs) enjoyed a varied diet, and therefore often alternated among types and flavors of food. Also, there was a common belief that "crunchy" or dry dog foods were good for the animal's teeth, in addition to supplying roughage to aid in digestion.

Generally, consumers considered pet foods containing more meat rather than fillers or by-products to be of higher quality, and product packaging was found to have a significant effect on consumers' perceptions of product quality. In addition, by the mid-1980s, many gourmet pet foods offered exotic cuisine, such as a mass-marketed dish made in Thailand from hand-cut chunks of seafood in aspic. Discussing the quality of pet food, one author said, "In the world of canned dog food, a smooth consistency is a sign of low quality—lots of cereal. A lumpy, frightening, bloody, stringy horror is a sign of high quality—lots of meat."[3] One grocery store buyer noted, "People look at their pets as family members, and feed their pets whatever they think sounds good," and another added, "When a pet food product looks and smells like something consumers are partial to—like beef stew—they feel more comfortable about feeding it to their pet."[4] Other gourmet products pledged to slim down overweight pets (about 4 out of 10 American dogs were considered to be too heavy), and one even promised to "lower stool volume."

Two other major factors that influenced purchasing decisions were convenience and price. Dry pet food was easiest to serve and did not create a mess. Consumers also showed a preference for smaller cans, especially ones with pop-up tops. Price was also one of the key factors in pet food purchasing decisions, and most new products were backed by television advertisements and coupons.

Advertising and promotions were essential in garnering pet food sales. By the mid-1980s, grocers had grown to expect coupon deals and other merchandising aids, and manufacturers spent roughly equal amounts on promotions and media. Speaking about pet food promotions, one retailer noted, "We don't run any free ads because we don't have to. If [manufacturers] don't offer any ad money, they don't get any ads."[5] However, another retailer added, "If a new product is a major brand, you have to make room for it. There's no way you can refuse such a product because of the big advertising campaign behind it. . . . With the high cost of advertising, manufacturers don't come out with just one item at a time."[6] Because of the high degree of product proliferation during the mid-1980s (in 1985 there were 103 new pet food products introduced, compared with 62 product introductions in 1983), coupled with hyperactive couponing and economic instability, brand loyalty had begun to weaken as consumers were barraged with new-product promotions.

---

[3]Ann Hodgman, "No Wonder They Call Me a Bitch," *The Best American Essays 1990* (New York: Ticknor & Fields, 1990).
[4]Mimi Kmet, "Premium Pet Foods Appeals to Owners," *Supermarket News,* January 4, 1988, p. 13.
[5]Fleishman, *Supermarket News,* p. 19.
[6]Kmet, *Supermarket News,* p. 13.

Sales and Distribution

The major pet food manufacturers had direct sales forces, and most also used food brokers to access additional retailers. Sales were generally made through regional offices, and the physical distribution of food was through regional warehouses. Dry pet food was generally less expensive to ship than moist or canned food because of its low moisture content, although both were distributed through the same warehouses. The major pet food manufacturers all distributed their product through grocery chains and wholesalers, and some, including Ralston Purina, also distributed through feed stores, pet shops, veterinarians, and kennels.

Manufacturing

There were three basic stages involved in pet food production: mixing the ingredients, which was typically done in very large vats; shaping of the product; and packaging the molded product. At the mixing stage, plants usually had separated lines for wet (canned or meat-based food) and dry (cereal-based) product. Also, plants generally had individual lines for bagged and canned foods, and lines were often specialized according to the size of the package, such as 20-pound versus 40-pound bags. Manufacturing lines within a plant were not dedicated to a single product, although plants were sometimes specialized around packaging type, with one facility making only canned or dry food. Capacity utilization was an important element in production costs, and manufacturers sought to keep utilization high. Some plants processed both cat and dog food.

Competition

Seven major companies produced the majority of pet food sold through grocery stores, together accounting for about 75 percent of industry sales in 1986. Each of these seven had substantial consumer products operations outside of pet foods, and many competed in more than one market. The leading competitors were not equally represented in all segments of the pet food industry, although at the industry level competition was tightly concentrated among these companies (Exhibits 1, 2, and 3).

Ralston Purina Beginning as a feed business in 1894, Ralston Purina's founder wanted to "get into a business that fills a need for lots of people, something they need all year around in good times and bad."[7] By 1986, Ralston derived over 90 percent of its profit from branded consumer products, including Purina pet food, Continental Bakery products, Eveready batteries, and Chex Cereal. The company also ran an agri-products subsidiary that produced livestock feed in 14 countries. Ralston was the nation's largest pet food manufacturer, leading the industry with a 28 percent market share, and was the world's largest producer of dry dog and dry and semi-moist cat food. In 1986, Ralston's pet food division was its largest profit center, and was estimated to be one of the more profitable businesses in the grocery industry, with margins of around 20 percent to 25 percent. Comprising one-fourth of Ralston's total sales, the pet food franchise was thought to generate closer to 45 percent of company profits.

In the largely mature dog food category, Ralston focused on the dry segment where it had its category-leading Dog Chow and Puppy Chow brands. Ralston was also the category leader in dry cat food, and had begun to shift additional marketing funds to its cat food lines.

---

[7]Tim Phillips, "Top Ten," *Petfood Industry,* January–February 1990, p. 4.

▲ EXHIBIT 1   Company Market Shares

Year	1985	1984	1983	1982	1981	1980
Ralston Purina	27	27	28	27	28	29
Carnation (Nestlé)	12	11	12	10	11	13
Kal Kan (Mars)	8	9	9	7	7	6
H.J. Heinz	8	7	7	7	7	7
Quaker Oats	7	7	6	8	9	9
Alpo (Grand Met/Liggett Group)	7	6	6	6	6	6
General Foods/Anderson Clayton	7	7	7	8	9	9

▲ EXHIBIT 2   Pet Food Market Share

Company	Percent Share	Sales 1985 ($ m)
Ralston Purina	26.9%	$1,450.1
Carnation (Nestlé)	12.2	659.0
Kal Kan (Mars)	8.4	453.3
Heinz	7.8	422.1
Anderson Clayton	6.6	356.8
Quaker Oats	7.1	383.2
Grand Met USA	7.1	384.9
All others	23.8	1,287.0
Total	100.0%	$5,396.4

Brand	Manufacturer	Market Share	Sales 1985 ($ m)	Ad Spending 1985 ($000)
Cat Food				
Canned				
9-Lives	Heinz	25.0%	$ 266.0	$ 6,191.5
Kal Kan	Kal Kan (Mars)	18.0	189.0	8,355.8
Friskies Buffet	Carnation (Nestlé)	15.5	163.0	6,949.6
Fancy Feast	Carnation (Nestlé)	11.0	114.0	630.3
Purina 100	Ralston Purina	7.0	73.8	
Bright Eyes	Carnation (Nestlé)	2.5	26.4	1,804.2
Puss'n Boots	Quaker Oats	1.6	16.6	
Tabby	Grand Met (USA)			
Unique	Benco		3.9	

continued

▲ EXHIBIT 2   *continued*

Brand	Manufacturer	Market Share	Sales 1985 ($ m)	Ad Spending 1985 ($000)
Friskies	Carnation (Nestlé)		2.3	
All others		18.0	190.7	
Total			$1,050.0	
Dry				
Cat Chow	Ralston Purina	21.5	153.0	13,998.9
Meow Mix	Ralston Purina	12.6	89.3	6,637.5
Friskies	Carnation (Nestlé)	12.4	87.7	5,698.4
9-Lives	Heinz	8.0	56.6	6,662.0
Crave	Kal Kan (Mars)	7.2	51.0	7,164.8
Special Dinners	Ralston Purina	6.7	47.6	106.5
Chef's Blend	Carnation (Nestlé)	5.6	39.6	141.6
Thrive	Ralston Purina	5.4	38.0	236.9
Kitten Chow	Ralston Purina	3.0	21.3	964.5
Alley Cat	Ralston Purina	2.8	20.2	2,440.3
Fish Ahoy	Carnation (Nestlé)		1.7	
All others		14.6	104.0	
Total			$710.0	
Moist				
Tender Vittles	Ralston Purina	48.6	126.0	8,393.7
Happy Cat	Ralston Purina	28.1	72.7	1,353.8
9-Lives/Square Meal	Heinz	14.6	37.8	4,613.2
Moist Meals	Quaker Oats	5.6	14.4	
Moist & Tender	Benco	1.0	2.6	
All others		1.4	3.5	
Total			$259.0	
Dog Food				
Dry				
Dog Chow	Ralston Purina	14.6	256.0	7,228.5
Puppy Chow	Ralston Purina	8.7	153.0	10,802.0
Gravy Train	Gaines	7.3	129.0	7,920.5
Alpo Beef Flavored Dinner	Grand Met USA	5.2	91.0	8,485.2
Dog Meal (Hi-Pro)	Ralston Purina	5.0	88.5	7,197.0
Come 'N Get It	Carnation (Nestlé)	4.8	84.3	305.4

continued

Brand	Manufacturer	Market Share	Sales 1985 ($ m)	Ad Spending 1985 ($000)
Meal Time	Kal Kan (Mars)	3.8	67.2	8,279.5
Chuck Wagon	Ralston Purina	3.0	55.2	8,590.2
Dry Cycle	Gaines	2.5	43.1	971.0
Main Stay	Ralston Purina	2.3	40.7	659.8
Purina Blends	Ralston Purina	2.1	36.4	
Friskies Dinner & Cubes	Carnation (Nestlé)	1.8	32.0	
Fit & Trim	Ralston Purina	1.6	27.4	3,082.0
Praise	Ralston Purina	1.5	26.5	108.6
Hunters Choice	Jim Dandy		11.5	
Jim Dandy Chunk & Ration	Jim Dandy		11.3	435.6
Ken-L Ration Biscuit & Meal	Quaker Oats		8.6	
Sea Dog	Ralston Purina		7.7	831.2
Bow Wow	Piasa		7.3	
Thrive	Ralston Purina		7.1	
Kasco	Piasa		6.0	
Field & Farm	Ralston Purina		4.1	228.2
Blue Mountain	Associated Prod.		2.0	
Vets Nuggets	C.H.B. Foods		1.7	
Strongheart	Beatrice		1.6	
Gaines Meal	Gaines		1.4	
Alamo Brand	Grand Met USA		—	304.5
New Breed	Carnation (Nestlé)	—		
All other		28.1	494.2	
Total			$1,757.0	
Moist				
Gaines Burgers	Gaines	28.0	60.3	1,108.4
Top Choice	Gaines	19.0	40.5	
Ken-L Ration Special Cuts	Quaker Oats	11.9	25.2	
Ken-L Ration Cheeseburger	Quaker Oats	9.0	19.1	
Ken-L Burger (all types)	Quaker Oats	7.0	14.8	
Moist & Meaty	Benco	5.9	12.5	

continued

▲ **EXHIBIT 2**   *continued*

Brand	Manufacturer	Market Share	Sales 1985 ($ m)	Ad Spending 1985 ($000)
Prime/Puppy Choice	Gaines	1.5	3.1	
All others		13.4	28.5	
Total			$212.6	
Snack				
Milk Bone, Flavor Snacks Bonz	Nabisco Brands	38.1	115.0	
Jerky Treats	Heinz	11.3	34.2	2,645.6
Meaty Bones	Heinz	9.1	27.5	4,433.7
Bonz	Ralston Purina	7.8	23.7	326.1
Snausages	Quaker Oats	4.4	13.4	2,688.4
Liv-A-Snaps, Beef-Char-O-Snaps	Grand Met USA	3.9	11.8	701.7
Alpo Jerky	Grand Met USA	3.4	10.4	
Beef Bites	Kal Kan (Mars)	2.6	7.8	
Say Cheese, People Crackers	Hi-Life		1.7	
Recipe	Campbell		1.7	
All others		18.2	54.9	
Total			$302.0	
Canned				
Alpo	Grand Met USA	28.5	245.0	9,814.9
Kal Kan	Kal Kan (Mars)	16.2	140.0	9,387.2
Mighty Dog	Carnation (Nestlé)	12.3	106.0	5,018.4
Cycle	Gaines	7.8	67.4	870.3
Ken-L Rations	Quaker Oats	6.7	57.9	25.9
Skippy Premium	C.H.B. Foods	4.2	36.4	203.0
Recipe	Campbell	2.9	24.8	
Vets	C.H.B. Foods	2.4	21.0	
Cadillac	Cadillac	2.1	18.0	
Strongheart	Beatrice	1.3	11.6	
Skippy	C.H.B. Foods	1.1	9.3	
Blue Mountain	Associated Prod.		8.3	
Twin Pet	Allied Food		7.9	
MPS	Kal Kan (Mars)		6.1	

continued

Brand	Manufacturer	Market Share	Sales 1985 ($ m)	Ad Spending 1985 ($000)
Laddie Boy	Laddie Pet Food		5.4	
Henry Pen	Allied Foods		2.1	
Friskies	Carnation (Nestlé)		2.0	
Tender Chunks Dinners	Quaker Oats		0.5	
All others		8.3	71.5	
Total			$860.0	
Soft-dry				
Kibbles'N Bits 'N Bits	Quaker Oats	44.8	102.0	6,518.8
Tender Chunks	Quaker Oats	28.4	64.7	4,399.0
Moist & Chunky	Ralston Purina	11.5	26.2	
Kibble'N Bits	Quaker Oats			
Dinner Rounds	Campbell	2.1	4.7	
Jim Dandy Tender Moist Chunks	Jim Dandy	1.8	4.0	
Total			$227.5	

Source: *Advertising Age.*

Given its dominant share in the dry segment, Ralston Purina was regarded as the industry leader, and other firms often followed Purina's lead in pricing. The company produced pet food domestically in nine plants located throughout the United States, and distributed its product through a regional warehouse system designed to provide quick turnaround.

In the mid-1980s, Ralston used the large cash-flow generated by its market-leading brands in the dry segment to roll out new products and to pursue market share in the segments that it targeted. Therefore, the company continually shifted its marketing support as it offered new products and line extensions, although all of Ralston's products were advertised under the Purina umbrella brand name. During this time, Ralston had demonstrated that it would aggressively defend its turf and that it could be a predatory competitor. For example, as generic and private-label pet food brands gained market share, Ralston launched marginally advertised dog and cat food brand, Main Stay and Alley Cat, that were nearly competitive with generics in price but carried the Purina brand name. In another instance, Ralston introduced a soft-dry dog food in 1985 called Kibbles & Chunks, a brand name very similar to Quaker Oats' already established Kibbles 'N Bits products. Ralston priced this product about 10 percent below the similarly named Quaker product.

Carnation   Nestlé SA, the Swiss food colossus that ran subsidiaries throughout the food-processing industry, purchased California-based Carnation Foods in 1985. At the time, Carnation primarily had grocery products operations including evaporated milk, instant cocoa mixes, and

▲ EXHIBIT 3 Pet Food Competitor Financials ($'000s)

	1986	1985	1984	1983	1982	1981	1980
Ralston Purina							
Net sales	5,514.6	5,863.9	4,980.1	4,872.4	4,802.6	5,146.4	4,800.1
Net earnings	388.7	256.4	242.7	256.0	69.1	174.8	163.0
Total assets	4,209.9	2,637.3	2,004.2	2,101.2	2,113.8	2,225.9	2,253.9
Shareholders' equity	998.5	924.5	997.5	1,104.1	1,100.1	1,220.6	1,123.4
Pet food sales	1,397.6	1,344.6	1,299.5	1,293.5	1,279.0	1,220.4	1,139.6
Quaker Oats							
Net sales	2,986.6	2,925.6	2,830.9	2,172.4	2,114.7	1,989.8	1,805.8
Net earnings	179.6	156.6	138.7	56.8	96.9	105.2	96.4
Total assets	1,944.5	1,760.3	1,726.5	1,391.9	1,383.3	1,360.3	1,243.3
Shareholders' equity	831.7	786.9	720.1	639.4	630.5	612.6	582.9
Pet food sales	329.2	332.5	305.0	277.4	319.2	297.9	292.8
Nestlé (million SFr)[a]							
Net sales	38,050	42,225					
Net earnings	1,789	1,750					
Total assets	25,095	25,188					
Shareholders' equity	12,201	11,238					
Pet food sales	1,517	1,722					
Carnation							
Net sales				3,365.3	3,382.2	3,354.1	3,362.2
Net earnings				194.8	183.4	172.3	151.9
Total assets				1,748.0	1,712.3	1,645.4	1,993.8
Shareholders' equity				1,184.0	1,105.6	1,014.7	955.1
Pet food sales*				685.3	486.0	482.0	495.5

	1986	1985	1984	1983	1982	1981	1980
Grand Metropolitan[b] (million £)							
Net sales	5,297.3	5,589.5	5,075.0	4,468.8	3,848.5	3,221.2	2,582.6
Net income	273.1	266.2	235.2	200.6	151.4	141.4	122.4
Total assets	2,755.5	2.787.6	2,430.2	2,213.0	2,023.3	2,206.0	1,878.3
Pet food sales ($)*	382.2	384.9	3,105	296.5	270.7	254.0	223.7
H.J. Heinz							
Net sales	4,366.1	4,047.9	3,953.8	3,738.4	3,688.5	3,568.9	2,924.7
Net earnings	301.7	266.0	237.5	192.8	160.8	160.8	131.5
Total assets	2,837.4	2,473.8	2,343.0	2,178.7	2,129.6	2,637.6	1,936.7
Shareholders' equity	1,360.0	1,230.5	1,120.6	1,139.6	1,028.8	944.7	843.8
Pet food sales*	404.5	422.2	392.8	267.8	325.2	300.0	268.8
Anderson Clayton[c]							
Net sales	1,056.5	1,182.2					
Net earnings	16.8	16.5					
Total assets	725.6	743.2					
Shareholders' equity	581.1	569.9					
Pet food sales	323.7	356.8					
General Foods							
Net sales			8,600	8,256	8,351	6,601	5,960
Net earnings			317.1	288.5	200.2	255.4	253
Total assets			4,433	4,310	3,861	3,130	2,979
Shareholders' equity			2,040	1,872	1,626	1,610	983.2
Pet food sales*			350.2	354.5	400.9	387.0	354.2

[a]Nestlé acquired Carnation in 1985.
[b]Grand Met acquired Alpo with Liggett Group i n 1982.
[c]Anderson Clayton acquired General Foods' Gaines division in 1984.
*Pet food sales are estimated from *Advertising Age*.

breakfast drinks. The company also had a pet food division that was strong in canned gourmet and dry cat food with its Friskies and Fancy Feast brands. Carnation also ran a can operation and a milling business. The company operated three plants, all located in the Midwest.

Carnation was the first of the major competitors to begin mass distribution of a gourmet pet food when it introduced Mighty Dog in 1974. This brand grew to capture a large share of the gourmet dog food segment. In the mid-1980s, the company was moving support away from its dry dog entry, Come 'N Get it, to back its upscale and niche brands. For example, in 1983, Carnation relaunched its Fancy Feast gourmet cat food, which it backed with free boxes, coupons, and other advertising and promotional spending that exceeded $45 million. Carnation believed that "The pet food industry is starting to catch up with the trend toward healthier and premium-quality human food."[8] Hugh Chamberlain, Carnation's marketing manager for new products, said, "For more and more people, the pet is becoming a member of the family. As more people become isolated, the pet's importance soars." Chamberlain added that Carnation "followed a Procter & Gamble strategy in marketing. Each brand has to pull its own weight, and generate the profit for its advertising budget."[9]

Kal Kan Foods Purchased in 1969, Kal Kan was a subsidiary of Mars Inc., the Virginia-based, privately held pet food, candy, and rice manufacturer. In 1986, Mars was the world's largest producer of pet foods, with major franchises in Australia, Canada, Europe, and Japan, and with worldwide sales estimated to approach $3 billion. Domestically, the company had particular strengths in canned dog and canned cat food. Although its market share was only 8.4 percent in 1985, Kal Kan was gradually gaining share in the United States. The company had a California headquarters and operated three plants in the United States.

Like Carnation, in the mid-1980s, Kal Kan had begun to shift its emphasis in dog food from it dry Meal Time brand to its canned Kal Kan line. The company entered the gourmet dog segment with four new flavors in 1986 that competed against Carnation's Mighty Dog. Further, the company augmented its support for its canned cat food entries. Mike Nelson, Kal Kan's marketing director, explained the new focus on cat food, "There's a lot of long-term potential for main meal canned cat food—and the cost per share point is much less than in the dog food category."[10] Also, marketing spending levels in cat food were lower than in dog food. Because cats had small appetites, cat food was less price-sensitive than dog food.

Quaker Oats Incorporated as the American Cereal Company in 1901, by 1986 Quaker had grown to become a major player in the packaged food industry and was the leading U.S. manufacturer of hot cereals, pancake mixes, and grain-based snacks. The company manufactured dog food under the Ken-L Ration and Kibbles 'N Bits brand names and cat food under the Puss'N Boots label. In 1986, Quaker operated two domestic and two overseas pet food plants, and distributed its products through a network of regional centers.

Between 1980 and 1985, Quaker Oats' share of the pet food market fell from 8.8 percent to 7.1 percent. The company' loss of share was in part due to the fact that it had major brands in two shrinking dog food segments: Kibbles 'N Bits and Tender Chunks in the soft-dry segment (which had been shrinking since 1975), and Ken-L Ration burgers in the moist category. Consequently, in 1985, Quaker nearly doubled its marketing expenditures in dog food and shifted its support to its dry and canned brands. In cat food, Quaker had two gourmet

[8]Ronald Alsop, "Gourmet Foods Are Going to the Dogs," *The Wall Street Journal,* May 14, 1987.
[9]Jereski, *Marketing & Media Decisions,* pp. 117,123.
[10]Ibid., p. 123.

brands in 1986, but neither one had significant marketing support. Quaker was committed to supporting its dog food brands, where it felt it had the greatest competitive strength.

H.J. Heinz   With 1986 sales of $4.4 billion, Heinz manufactured hundreds of food products on four continents, and operated affiliates such as Weight Watchers International and Ore-Ida Foods. In 1963, Heinz purchased Star Kist, a tuna packer based in California. In 1986, the company operated six pet food plants.

Heinz participated in two pet food segments in 1986. The company's 9-Lives brand, supported by Morris (the cat), was the leading canned cat food, and was available in dry and moist forms as well. By 1985, Heinz had renamed its moist (Square Meal) and dry (Crunchy Meal) cat foods under the 9-Lives brand name. Commensurately, the company increased marketing support for its moist and dry products by $12 million dollars. "We see the line approach as the best way to solidify the 9-Lives business," said Peter Bowen, marketing manager at Heinz, who explained the rationale behind the renaming.[11] The company's only items in dog food were in the dog treats segment.

Anderson Clayton   In 1984, Anderson Clayton, a consumer food and animal feed company, acquired Gaines Pet Foods from General Foods for $156 million plus the assumption of $30 million in debt. During the early-1980s, as rumors circulated that General Foods might exit the pet food industry, the company had attempted to improve Gaines's profitability by cutting ad spending, consolidating manufacturing at two plants (a third one was closed), and reducing marketing personnel. For example, in 1982, General Foods cut ad spending at Gaines to $23 million from $40 million in 1981. As a General Foods division, Gaines had two pet food plants, a pet nutrition center, 12 regional sales offices, and 26 distribution warehouses.

At the time of the Anderson Clayton purchase, Gaines was the nation's second-largest dog food company, with its Gravy Train, Cycle, Gaines Burger, and Top Choice brands. The company was strongest in the semi-moist segment, where its revenues had been falling with the decline in the category. Anderson Clayton increased advertising at Gaines, placing over half its support behind Gravy Train, the company's dry food line. However, the company also backed its semi-moist Gainesburgers with a new flavor introduction in 1984. Gaines also introduced Tast-Tee Chunks in the dog-snack market. The company decided to stay in only dog food and not enter any cat food category.

Alpo Petfoods, Inc.   Grand Met U.S.A., the U.S. Subsidiary of Grand Metropolitan PLC, the United Kingdom–based food, drink, hotel, and retailing conglomerate, purchased Alpo Petfoods in 1982 as part of its acquisition of Liggett Group. Alpo began in 1936 as a single-product enterprise, and grew into one of the nation's largest pet food manufacturers. The company operated five pet food plants located throughout the midwestern states.

In 1986, Alpo was exclusively a dog food company and dominated the canned segment of the market. Alpo expected to garner revenue increases as gourmet sales increased, and in 1985 Alpo more than doubled its annual ad spending to $20 million. In early 1986, the company was prepared to launch Alpo Puppy Food, backed by a $35 million advertising budget. As Alpo considered the introduction of its puppy food, Ralston Purina shifted support behind its Puppy Chow brand, stressing the product's bone-development properties, which were later found to be untrue in a lawsuit filed by Alpo.

---

[11]Ibid., p. 122.

▲ PET FOOD INDUSTRY IN 1986

Between 1984 and 1986, the pet food industry shifted from being a low-profile business to a competitive, deal-driven one. Referring to the situation in pet foods in 1986, one supermarket owner said that it was "a big headache. There are too many sizes and too many varieties."[12] William Johnson, CEO of Heinz Petfood division, added, "There is a pervasive irrationality in the pet food business that is disturbing. People are willing to throw huge amounts of money at a business that is not growing rapidly. It is without a doubt the most difficult consumer products business in the U.S."[13] In mid-1986, the industry structure appeared as though it might change as Anderson Clayton was rumored to be for sale.

---

[12]Fleishman, *Supermarket News,* p. 19.
[13]"Irrationality in the Pet Food Business," *Fortune,* October 8, 1990, p. 136.

ENCLEAN: MALCOLM WADDELL'S STORY (A)

EnClean was established in 1984 in Houston, Texas to provide industrial services to the U.S. process industries. In its early years, EnClean experienced financial success and rapid growth, through both internal growth and acquisitions. The company followed a two-pronged growth strategy, expanding geographically and broadening its service lines. (Exhibits 1, 2, 3, and 4). EnClean's founders, Malcolm Waddell and Tim Tarrillion, took the company public in 1989. Waddell served as chairman and CEO, Tarrillion as president and COO (Exhibit 5).

They continued to grow the organization, and broadened its customer base while extending its activities into environmental services (Exhibit 6). However, the recession and changes in the regulatory environment had their impact on EnClean's business; despite steadily increasing revenues, in fiscal 1992 the company experienced a net loss in excess of $2.5 million.

The following is Malcolm Waddell's personal account of the company's history, culminating in a critical point in the spring of 1993.

▲ PERSONAL HISTORY

Tim and I met at Harvard Business School in 1979. Being the lone Texans up there, we became good friends. Working on a second-year HBS real estate field study together, we found that we had complementary skills. Tim was very good at formulating the overview and setting up strategy and executing. I was good at following up on the details, making

Research Associate Elizabeth Wynne Johnson prepared this case under the supervision of Professor David Collis.

▲ EXHIBIT 1   EnClean Financial Summary ($000), FYE June 30

	1992	1991	1990	As Restated 1989	1988	1987	1986	1985
Revenues	$107,971	$101,190	$62,339	$44,883	$35,911	$20,565	$9,847	$2,628
Cost of goods	67,718	59,552	35,613	27,607	18,590	9,731		
Research and development	NA	NA	NA	2,326	1,989	1,011		
Selling, general and administrative expenses	37,050	31,432	21,188	15,881	10,226	4,774		
Including depreciation and amortization	8,053	5,988	4,086	2,737	2,152	1,207		
Operating income	3,204	10,206	5,537	3,598	2,641	2,228	421	364
Interest	4,389	2,674	2,443	2,216	1,645	1,016		
Income tax expense	45	2,797	1,181	464	205	308		
Net income	$ (2,597)	$ 5,202	$ 2,855	$ 716	$ 366	$ 574	$ (338)	$ 210
Current assets	47,468	32,484	21,398	89,397	8,079			
Net property, plant and equipment	47,348	39,246	40,955	20,977	18,927			
Total assets	$106,793	$ 80,963	$59,343	$30,930	$27,283	$14,196	$9,755	$2,061
Current liabilities	22,727	10,950	14,716	4,653	6,846			
Long-term debt	48,484	30,728	13,973	12,116	14,236	8,672	6,912	898
Including convertible subordinated Debt	47,500	1,500	NA	NA	NA	NA		
Shareholders' equity	$ 34,125	$ 35,921	$30,475	$11,173	$ 4,175	$ 1,257	$ 442	$ 242
Number of employees	1,750	945	896	540	NA	NA		

Industrial	Environmental
Hydroblasting	Liquid-solid separation
• 10,000 psi	• Filter press
• Ultra-high volume (up to 250 gpm)	• Belt press
• 20,000 psi	• Centrifuge
• Ultra-high pressure (35,000 psi) for cleaning and cutting	• Thermal drying
• Kinjet® abrasive cleaning system	• Reverse osmosis
Industrial vacuuming	• Dredging
• Liquid vacuuming	Site remediation
• Dry vacuuming (air moving)	• In situ and clean closure
• Sludge pumping	• Pond and lagoon closure
• Sludge pumping	• PCB extraction
• Power drumming via cyclone	• Bioremediation
Sewer services	• Landfill construction and capping
• Cleaning and vacuuming	Tank service
• Video camera inspection	• Cleaning and sludge removal
• Point repair/grouting	• Unmanned hydraulic dozer
Chemical cleaning	• Waste minimization/product recovery
• Process equipment	• Degassing
• Boilers	• Confined space entry
• Hydraulic oil and lube systems	• Linings
Characterization/TCLP	Analytical services
Catalyst handling	• Hazardous waste
• Removal and screening	• Wastewater/priority pollutants
• Loading	• Groundwater analysis
• Inert entry	• Identification of unknowns
Specialty chemicals	Air monitoring
• Cosmetic/Kinjet® cleaning	• Asbestos, lead, and arsenic
• Degassing/degreasing	• Total hydrocarbons
• Bulk cleaners and detergents	Other environmental services
• Proprietary blends	• Asbestos abatement
• Coal tar liquification	• Emergency response
Industrial coatings	• Heavy metals treatment
• Engineered coating systems	• Lab packs/SQG management
• Epoxy floor systems	
• Secondary containment dike sealants	
• Annual maintenance programs	

sure all the numbers were in place and the deals got done. We also found we were ambitious and had a high tolerance for working long hours. Very importantly, the moral backgrounds of our character were never a question. We never had to worry about either one of us doing something the other would not agree with. In a true partnership, you have to have that element.

▲ **EXHIBIT 3**   EnClean Geographic Spread in 1993

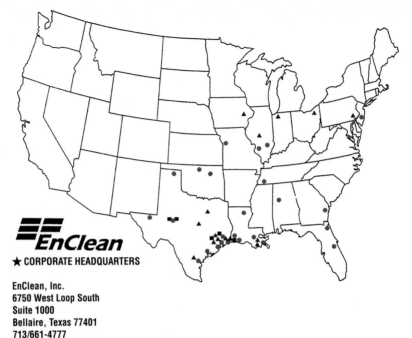

★ **CORPORATE HEADQUARTERS**

EnClean, Inc.
6750 West Loop South
Suite 1000
Bellaire, Texas 77401
713/661-4777

● **SERVICE LOCATIONS**

Beaumont, TX

Borger, TX
Corpus Christi, TX
Decatur, AL
Deer Park, TX
El Paso, TX
Flora, IL

Gonzales, LA
Hitchcock, TX
Jacksonville, FL
Kansas City, MO
La Porte, TX
Memphis, TN
Mitchell, IL
Odessa, TX
Orlando, FL
Point Comfort, TX
Ponca City, OK
Savannah, GA
Sulphur, LA
Swedesboro, NJ
Tulsa, OK
West Monroe, LA

▲ **SUBSIDIARIES**

**Correct Maintenance
Corporation**

Canton, OH
De Witt, IA
Manito, IL
Portage, IN

**EnClean Specialty
Chemicals**

Dallas, TX
Downington, PA
Houma, LA
Houston, TX
Nederland, TX
Reserve, LA
Sulphur, LA

EnClean Environmental Services Group

Carlyss, LA: Separation Technologies
Corpus Christi, TX: Site Remediation
Beaumont, TX: Site Remediation
Houston, TX: Site Remediation
Portage, IN: Environmental Technologies
Austin, TX: Analytical Services

■ **SUPPORT LOCATIONS**

Alvin TX: Catalyst Handling
Alvin, TX: Chemical
Cleaning Services

Alvin, TX: Training Center
Carlyss, LA: Training Center
La Porte, TX: Manufacturing
La Porte, TX: Water Services
Odessa, TX: Accounting
Odessa, TX: Manufacturing

Date	Business	Revenues ($ millions)	Type
January 1984	Texas Catalyst, Inc.	1.3	Asset
October 1985	Parkem Industrial Services, Inc.	10.6	Asset
May 1986	Catalyst Handling Division-Maintech	NA	Asset
August 1987	Maintech Industrial Services	10.0	Asset
November 1989	Correct Maintenance Corporation	8.0	Stock
April 1990	United Water Blasters, Inc.	0.7	Assets
June 1990	Alphachem, Inc.	12.0	Stock
July 1990	Able Industrial Maintenance & Cleaning	2.3	Stock
July 1990	Dynamic Hydra-Blasting	2.5	Asset
November 1990	Challenge Industrial Services, Inc.	1.0	Stock
June 1991	Sizemore Environmental Group	17.5	Stock
July 1991	Orange Environmental Services	2.0	Stock
October 1991	Reduction Technology, Inc.	NA	Assets
February 1992	Escandell Associates	8.7	Stock

In 1979, the two of us wrote down our personal goals and our business goals before we even started. Tim's number one goal was to run his own company. Running my own company was only the second or third on my list. My first goal was to work with Tim Tarrillion, as my partner.

We came back to Houston in 79. Tim went to work for Pace Consultants, a consulting firm to the refining and petrochemical industries, for five years and progressed to the level of manager. When I graduated from HBS, I went to work for Entex, Inc., a diversified gas distribution and oil exploration, drilling and production company, doing mergers and acquisitions. I had been there three years when Tim and I decided we would go out and get something going. We had known that from the day we left Harvard; it was just a question of when.

We thought real estate was where we would make our fortune. I quit my job in May of 1982. Tim couldn't afford to quit; my wife was working outside the home and his wasn't. And he had a child by then. One of us had to be out there full-time. When I was working, I was losing out on real estate opportunities, because somebody else would be there to make the deal and I wasn't. We bought a couple of properties with the idea that we would renovate them or possibly build condominiums. But fortunately, Tim was paying attention to the price of oil, and he knew enough to predict that it was going to go flat. That had serious implications for the real estate market in Houston, so we decided immediately to get out of real estate—which we had gotten into strictly as a means to raise capital—and proceed toward our goal of buying a company.

In October of 1982, we set out to find the needle in the haystack. I went to see the owner of Gibson Guitar, another Harvard MBA, and he told me it would take at least 18 months to find the first company. I told him I didn't want to be unemployed for another 18 months.

▲ **EXHIBIT 5**   Curricula Vitae of Malcolm Waddell and Tim Tarrillion
J. MALCOLM WADDELL
Chairman, CEO

Mr. Waddell is a co-founder of EnClean. He has been the chief executive officer and a director from December 1982 and chairman of the board from December 1987. He served as president of the company from December 1982 until August 1989.

From 1979 until the founding of EnClean, Mr. Waddell worked for Entex, Inc., an energy and natural gas distribution company. He served in its mergers and acquisitions and emerging business ventures group and as an assistant to the executive vice president of the Energy Group. From 1974–77, Mr. Waddell served in various capacities, including chief operating officer and assistant to the president, with The Brinkmann Corporation, a sporting goods manufacturer.

He received a Bachelor of Arts degree in economics and managerial studies from Rice University in 1974 and a Masters of Business Administration degree from Harvard Business School in 1979.

TIM B. TARRILLION
President, Chief Operating Officer

As co-founder and director of the company, Mr. Tarrillion grew EnClean from $1 million/year revenues base in 1984 to over $100 million in annual sales, and expanded EnClean from one location to forty. Mr. Tarrillion acquired and integrated 13 different companies into EnClean's base and was instrumental in raising over $75 million of capital for the company.

From 1979 until 1984, Mr. Tarrillion served as a manager of the Market Analysis Group of Pace Consultants, where he worked with companies in all facets of the energy industry including refineries, petrochemical companies, utilities, gas pipelines, natural gas companies, and governmental institutions. Areas of expertise ranged from technology evaluation, supply/demand/pricing analysis, to strategic planning.

He received a Masters of Chemical Engineering from Rice University in 1974 and a Masters of Business Administration from Harvard Business School in 1979.

Source: Malcolm Waddell.

The First Acquisition

I looked at a lot of small companies, because we were going to be doing it all with leverage, before leveraged buyouts were a big thing. The idea of utilizing leverage came from our real estate background. We planned to use both conventional and owner financing to get a deal done.

You are going to see a lot of marginal deals before you ever see a good deal. Just as we were nearing the end of that 18-month stretch in November 1983, our lawyer called to tell me about one of his clients, a company called Texas Catalyst. Texas Catalyst was about the 23rd or 24th deal we looked at, but of the really good deals we saw, it was only the second. The first was the purchase of a fireplace manufacturing company. We came very close on that one. We spent four or five months investigating it before we decided against it.

The catalyst handling market in the United States was about $50 million—a small part of the industrial service market. Browning-Ferris Industries had a subsidiary that included a catalyst handling business, but it essentially was a cash cow for BFI. Their reputation for service

▲ EXHIBIT 6   EnClean's Revenues/Service Mix

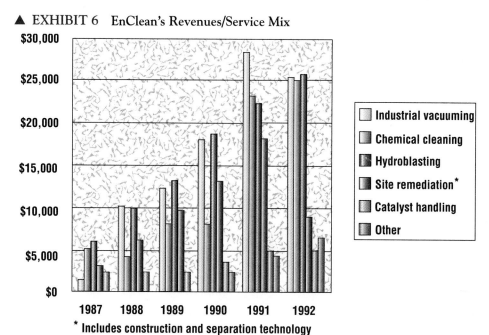

* Includes construction and separation technology

had gone down. Texas Catalyst was established in 1981 by five guys who had left Browning-Ferris. They had a very high penchant for customer service, so they left to start their own catalyst handling company.

By late 1983, this group, along with its outside investors, wanted to sell. They hadn't expected Texas Catalyst to grow to a million dollars in revenues so quickly. They were three field guys and two sales guys, and they had the typical problems of a group starting up: no real management background and very fast growth. The guy who had the most money in it wanted out.

The company had revenues of $1.3 million and made about $300,000 pretax for the year ended January 31, 1984. Tim and I did a leveraged buyout for $1.4 million. We put up about $250,000 of our own, our family's, and four of the original five principals' money, $150,000 of the company's cash, and executed a one million dollar owner-finance note. That was how EnClean was born.

The day before the closing, I was doing the final due diligence when I found a collection of bills stuffed in the president's drawer—unmarked, unpaid. They were bills he said were in dispute, that he had no intention of paying. Nowhere were these bills on the books. By the time I factored those in, we were paying roughly $200,000 too much for this company.

Later that day, our attorney, Tim, and I were in a room together, and I said, "Tim, we are paying $200,000 too much for this company." Our attorney looked at me and said, "At this stage of the game they are not going to take $200,000 less for the company." We had to decide whether we wanted to buy the company or not. Tim looked over at me and he said, "We have to get started somewhere." He asked me if I wanted to try again to find another company. I told him 18 months was long enough. We closed the transaction on January 31, 1984.

My favorite phone call concerning the deal came from the major outside investor we bought out. The day after we closed the deal, he called me up on the phone and asked me how our sales were doing for the month. I said "Hold on, I'll ask James Buckley, our salesman here." I said, "James, how are sales looking this month? Have we got any sales?" He said "No, we don't have any sales. But things are looking great." And the guy on the phone just laughed. "Gee, two Harvard MBA's go and pay $1.4 million for a company that doesn't have any sales."

The Industry

The industry we were in was highly fragmented, and there were several reasons why that was the case. There was a need for entrepreneurialism in what was a very dirty, nitty-gritty, 24-hour-a-day business that required a lot of energy and hands-on management. Another source of the fragmentation was the nature of customer-relations in this business: salesmen call on customers directly to obtain the work, especially large projects, and the service supplier decision is usually made at the local plant level instead of on a regional or corporate level. Labor was the third reason. Union labor employed by the refineries had a tendency to do only their specific task. We had open shop laws in Texas and Louisiana that allowed companies to bring nonunion laborers into a union plant. Those workers would obviously be cheaper, so companies would choose to outsource some of these services. With the capital barriers relatively low and, in many cases, financing available from the equipment manufacturers, many small operators got into the business of providing industrial cleaning services. Over time, they got better at it than the plant personnel because that was all they did—day in and day out.

Texas Catalyst had been doing about 60 percent of its business at the Baytown refinery for Exxon. This is the largest refinery in the United States. I went to talk to Exxon during the due diligence phase of the acquisition, and I asked them why they didn't do this for themselves. Their answer was, "We are in the petroleum products manufacturing business. We are not in the industrial service business. Even if we did utilize your equipment and do it ourselves, we would only be able to keep the equipment busy about half the time, and that would be the half of the time it was broken down."

It was a very competitive business, and low price was one of the key elements. Service was another. Seventy percent of our business was done for the refining and petrochemical industries, about half each. Those two businesses are like night and day, even though they are often divisions of the same companies. They have the same name on the door, but what drives those people, how they operate, and how they think in those plants are totally different.

The chemical plants would pay for and expect quality service. Quality service is defined as on-time, consistent, and safely provided work. We ensured that quality by giving our employees longevity of employment, with benefits and retirement plans so they would stick around and make a career with us. The chemical companies valued workmanship, because they were profit centers and they wanted to get their plants back on line. Unlike the oil refineries that viewed themselves as cost centers and cared more about low price.

EnClean's Early Years

Tim was chief operating officer from day one. He handled all the day-to-day operations. My job was to continue to raise capital, make the acquisitions and handle administration.

Tim had never operated a company in his life, which I think is pretty remarkable. A guy that we knew together at Rice once told me he used to like to play rugby with Tim, because he would just throw the ball to Tim and watch him run. That is very indicative of Tim's personality and his style. I just made sure Tim had a clear playing field and let him run.

We had a true partnership. Tim had to have more salary in the first days, so I got a slightly higher percentage of the equity. I think Tim was paid $60,000 and I was paid $25,000. But once the company grew, our salaries and our bonuses were typically equal, as were the stock option grants. We never let money or greed get in the way of executing the strategy. It was a willingness to supplant one's own personal desires for the benefit of the entity. I knew the long-term payoff to me was always on the equity side. It was never going to be on the debt side, and certainly not on the salary side. I just needed enough to get by.

I tend to get a little emotional about things. If a manager wasn't doing what we wanted, I would want to fire that manager to set the example. Tim was more rational. He was the one asking the question, "Where are we going to get a manager to replace that person?" By talking through our differences, we usually made the right decision. That's why we were a good partnership, we were a good blend.

When we acquired Texas Catalyst, there were about 15 people in the organization, including us. There were 5 sales and management people, and the other 10 were field personnel. The first year, our goal was to maintain a high service level, expand geographically, and broaden our catalyst handling capabilities. We were going to consolidate the catalyst handling market in the United States.

Texas Catalyst had a good reputation for doing $20,000 to $30,000 catalyst jobs which entailed 10-people crews (5 per 12-hour shift) working up to two weeks. Tim and I immediately pushed to expand geographically from our single office near Houston. We were doing some jobs in Oklahoma, and over in the Beaumont/Port Arthur area. Fast response time was very important to our customers. So Texas Catalyst opened an office in the Beaumont/Port Arthur market. Texaco (now Star) and Gulf (now Chevron) became large customers of ours. At the same time, Tim steered the expansion of the product line to include larger catalyst handling projects. He used his marketing and engineering skills to convince Phillips Petroleum and Valero Refining that we could do the catalyst change-outs on residual fuel units. Those jobs generated $400,000 in revenues and required 100-man crews with a crew of 50 on each shift working around the clock for seven days.

Next we started a second service line in Texas Catalyst. About a year into it, we realized that the vacuum trucks were underutilized in the catalyst handling business. Typically the vacuum truck would only be used to pick up small quantities of debris from around the bottom of the reactor, after the catalyst had been dumped out. These trucks were $150,000 pieces of equipment, so we found they could be utilized in the industrial vacuuming segment—particularly in coal-burning utility plants, where ash would build up in fire boxes and need to be removed during outages. We picked up a couple of contract with Texas Utilities Generating Co. to go into their plants and remove the ash. That got us into the dry vacuuming business.

In its first year (ended January 1985), EnClean's sales grew from $1.3 to $1.7 million. By June 1985, it was at $2.5 million annually. Eight hundred thousand of those sales had come from two large residual fuel jobs.

In January of 1985, we didn't have $500,000 to make a first payment on the former Texas Catalyst owners' notes. I walked into a meeting in our attorney's office, where we were supposed to be talking about restructuring the debt. When I got there, the two largest percentage former owners were talking about what they were going to do once they got the company back. I just sat there while they continued to talk about it. Finally I said, "We were supposed to start this meeting about five minutes ago, but there isn't going to be any meeting. We will pay you your checks on Monday when they're due." I took approximately $250,000 of my own personal money and paid off their portion of the notes. The other owners agreed to restructure their debt to allow the company to grow. That money was on top of what I had already put in. Tim didn't have the money or he would have done it, too. Just about everything we had was now in the company. To help cash flow, there were times I didn't cash my paychecks for weeks.

In March of 1985, we had been awarded both residual fuel jobs and needed to secure working capital for this work. I went to our bank when it was in the midst of a buyout. By now the oil business had turned down, so most banks red-lined the refining and petrochemical business. Our own bank would not lend us the money on the receivables on signed contracts. We ended up having to put up more personal money on a CD. In the end, it was another bank, one that didn't know us from Adam, that lent us the money. We thought we would need $90,000 for 60 days, but it turned out we only needed $60,000 for about 30 days. Regardless, payroll on these jobs was met, since we all know payroll is sacred.

The Parkem Acquisition

By 1985, Texas Catalyst had some joint projects, including these residual fuel projects, with other industrial service companies providing complementary services to our two service lines. We also had seen the limit to the market for catalyst handling. We could maybe grow to be a $25 million company, *if* we could consolidate and get half the market. That wasn't going to be big enough for us.

By the time we did our second acquisition, we had decided to turn EnClean into a multiple service company, providing services to multiple industries. We started looking for companies that could provide services that would be complementary to what we already did.

In April of 1985, we wrote five blind letters to owners of hydroblasting (cleaning with high pressure water) and chemical cleaning companies. Parkem Industrial Services, Inc. was the best of the bunch. Phil Parker, the majority owner and CEO, threw our letter in the trash can. His partner and COO, Frank Lamberton, took it out, and we met in early May.

In October 1985, EnClean acquired Parkem for $8.1 million. At that time, Parkem was doing $10.4 million in revenues, making a 15 percent profit pretax. EnClean had two locations; Parkem had eight in Texas, Louisiana, Oklahoma, and Colorado.

We raised about $3 million worth of venture capital. $2.4 million of that was in 12.5 percent preferred stock. At that point in time, the prime rate was around 9.5 percent. The other $600,000 was put in equity which translated into about 50 percent of the equity. We raised the remaining capital, another $5 million from Glenfed Financial Corporation, an asset-based lender, at 2 percent and 2 ¾ percent over prime. We thought we had some cash available in Parkem. But when we got there, thinking we were going to use about a million dollars of their money, we discovered they had paid off all their accounts payable, every single one of them—$1.5 million of accounts payable and the cash to pay them just disappeared. So we had to do some scrambling to be able to get the money for the closing.

We immediately changed Texas Catalyst's name to Parkem. It was a better known name, with a strong reputation for service and more reflective of our overall service capabilities. We consolidated our locations in Beaumont/Port Arthur and retired Messrs. Parker and Lamberton within six months. They were first-stage entrepreneurs who were used to running the business one way—theirs—and could not make the transition to managing as part of a new team. We have found that when you are attempting to combine two previously separate entities there is a conqueror-conquered mentality among the employees that has to be overcome. We immediately got the teams of both companies together to try and understand each other, so we could talk about where we were going.

We were able to keep and develop a lot of the young, very gifted operating managers that had come up through the Parkem organization. They all reported to Tim. At that point, we had nine division managers and two regional managers. A division would be a location like Houston or Beaumont and a region would be the Gulf Coast or the Midwest.

We started cross-selling services to our combined customer base because we realized the customer (especially the purchasing agents) wanted a one-stop shop for industrial services. We immediately started moving services like industrial vacuuming out into the former Parkem divisions. We also began doing catalyst handling work (not previously done by Parkem) out of our Parkem location in the Baton Rouge market, offering the same high-quality service at a low price. Back then, we were still very much oriented towards low price. Both moves started generating internal sales growth.

We made the necessary capital investments. We told division managers we would give them four dry vacuum trucks, because we could finance them. I said if they could get those fully utilized, then we would get them more. They wanted 10 immediately, which would have cost about $1.5 million. They had the 10 within six months.

With 90 percent of our capitalization in the form of debt or quasi-debt (preferred stock), cash flow was always tight. It takes about 40 cents of capital to generate a new dollar of sales, 5 cents to maintain a dollar of sales. So it was a very capital-intensive business. We were able to continue growing the company because we refinanced the company on each acquisition, and were able to borrow on our receivables as they increased with sales.

We would also run pretty hefty cash overdrafts. My controller came from the former Parkem. She didn't like to have any less than a million dollars in the bank. But at that point, we were usually about $300,000 or $400,000 floating negative in our cash. She adapted.

The EnClean Board

We were very fortunate with regard to our board makeup at that time. We had brought Tim's ex-boss from Pace Consultants, whose name was John Matson(now president of Hunt Oil Refining in Alabama). John was growing and maturing as a manager while we were growing and maturing as a company. He was great dealing with operations issues.

Tom Delimitros was our most entrepreneurial director. He had built a company for Baker Hughes Oilfield Services and then become a venture capitalist. I would use Tom to challenge Tim and his major decisions. The two of them were very good against each other. John Jaggers, a high-tech venture capitalist, former corporate finance guy, and HBS classmate, was my main resource for public market finance. His knowledge was invaluable to us as we approached and became a public company. The board expanded again later, as the company continued to grow. As a CEO, having a good board is critical. Each one of our board members played a role.

In 1987, prior to the acquisition of Maintech, EnClean reached $16 million in revenues, with internal growth of 20 percent per annum.

The Maintech Acquisition

By early 1987 we were thinking about acquiring another company. By that time we were paying down debt, the company was cash flow positive, and we were ready to take on the next piece. We were running the company purely for cash flow at this point. We had basically saturated the market with what we had. We could only expand in industrial services one or two ways: by service line or geographically.

Maintech International, Inc. was both an industrial services and a specialty chemical distribution operation. It was the former BFI subsidiary that our Texas Catalysts' group had left in 1981. By 1987, this business had been acquired from BFI by a third party in a leveraged buyout. In the past few years, pre- and post-buyout, they had dwindled from 20 industrial service locations down to only 4. They were doing about $10 million in industrial services, $6 million in specialty chemicals. Around the end of 1986, we got a call from their venture capitalists. They had booted out their CEO, and they wanted to do something. We said we would buy their industrial service facilities, but we were not interested in the specialty chemical operations. The negotiations went back and forth until August of 1987, when we closed the deal.

Maintech Industrial Services was losing money. It was a true turnaround situation, but we needed to get a wounded animal out of the marketplace for the sake of service pricing and to expand our market share. The Maintech acquisition also brought in liquid vacuuming, which gave us an additional industrial service line. We financed the deal as a leveraged buyout. We took on about $3 million worth of debt and issued $1.5 million worth of second-class convertible preferred stock, so we paid $4.5 million for $10 million worth of revenues.

At this point, Tim and I really handled most of the acquisition integration personally. We would go and bring all the parties together. Maintech brought our total up to 13 operating locations. They were up in New Jersey and Memphis, Tennessee, and they had locations overlapping ours down in Texas and Louisiana. We adopted a strategy called connect-the-dots, which meant having service locations within a day's drive of each other to better utilize people and equipment. Right after we bought Maintech, I found another company that would have connected us perfectly up from Memphis through the New Jersey location, giving us Virginia, West Virginia, Ohio, and Kentucky. Unfortunately, the timing wasn't right for either company so we did not move ahead with this deal in 1987. In August 1991, another company, The Brand Companies, acquired this entity.

In the fall of 1987, we were considering a public offering of EnClean stock. We were being courted by the likes of Merrill Lynch, Prudential-Bache, Alex Brown, you name it. Everybody wanted to take us public as an environmental service company. The magic revenue number was $30 million, and revenues were about there. Then, in October of 1987, the stock market crashed. So did any hope of our going public that year.

The following year EnClean maintained its internal 20 percent growth rate. The company had $31 million in revenues in 1988.

The Strategic Planning Process

In addition to the locations we acquired, we also opened several divisions out of internal growth. We had 16 locations by spring of 1988 spread from West Texas to New Jersey. There was a great deal of misinformation and miscommunication, some of which was being spread by people who were the conquerors or the conquered. We also had well-intentioned division managers chasing business opportunities that were too far afield. For example, because of our close ties to Exxon on the Gulf Coast, we were given the chance to bid on the cleanup of the Valdez oil spill. We spent time and resources including trips to Alaska to pursue business clearly outside Tim"s and my vision.

One of my passive investment guys, a venture capitalist, called me up and said he had a friend who wanted to talk to me from Ernst & Young about strategic planning. I said, "Fine, bring him in." I was looking for an answer. I didn't know if this process was the answer, but I knew we needed to do something.

Beginning in May of 1988, Ed Bogle from Ernst & Young came in and started leading our strategic planning process. We began formulating our true strategic plan, beginning with the formulation of our visions, values, and beliefs. Our mission statement outlined our six strategic excellence positions (goals that would differentiate us long-term from our competition), with objectives and individual strategies necessary to execute in order to accomplish those goals (Exhibit 7).

We formalized that process and involved all 16 of the division managers, both regional managers and all the corporate senior management—roughly 30 people (Exhibit 8). We split up into two groups to get both the division managers and corporate managers' input, because you couldn't really run a meeting with 30 people in it.

It was really a revelation, because although people at first looked to see what Tim and I would say, we had everybody's input. The division managers were out there every day in the heat of the battle. Their input became very valuable in developing our key strategic excellence positions. Our belief was that if we could give them a framework to base their decisions on, based on what the priorities of the company were, they would execute strategy. It's the old concept: Can you get out of the desert yourself or does the team always do better? The team always does better, because you bring all the expertise in.

Coming out of this strategic planning exercise, EnClean concentrated on a number of programs and implemented a formal Quality Improvement Process, forming Quality Improvement Teams at each location.

We actually executed off our strategic plan. We wanted to be the quality provider of services, with quality defined in terms of meeting customer requirements. That meant consistent, on-time, safety delivered services, so our customers could get their units up and operating with minimum downtime. Downtime is what costs them money and so do accidents. Some of our customers still had not fully realized that a cheap price is no good if the job is performed unsafely or untimely. The plants were under so much cost or profit pressure that they didn't always remember that.

Safety in particular was very important to us. In 1986, one of our guys went into a small diameter tower and he was cleaning trays up and down, shooting high-pressure hydroblast water between his legs. He came too close and swiped his femoral artery. No one could figure out where he was bleeding from because he was so protected with equipment. They thought he was bleeding from the foot, because the blood was only coming out from his boot. By the time anyone could find the cut, he was almost out of blood.

We set out to be the industry leader in developing a viable safety process. This was, after all, a very dangerous business we were in. We weren't big enough at Texas Catalyst to have a safety director, but when we bought Parkem we started the process in earnest. We had a few early false starts, including hiring someone to be safety director who had 30 years in plant experience but didn't have a pure safety background. But after that, we were guided by two successive safety directors and our operating employees to become the standard for safety in the industry. Most plants weren't big on safety in 1986, but we knew it had to come. It is a big deal today and it was a way to differentiate our service.

Around 1988 we shifted away from the low-cost producer strategy. We created an aura around EnClean based on high-quality service. We formalized our safety and training processes. That fit our belief about where the business ought to go. We got companies, including the refineries to some extent, to buy into that. Our prices were probably 10 percent to 20 percent higher than the rest of the marketplace, but we believed our safety record and turnaround time and hence our total cost was less than competitors. Unfortunately, there

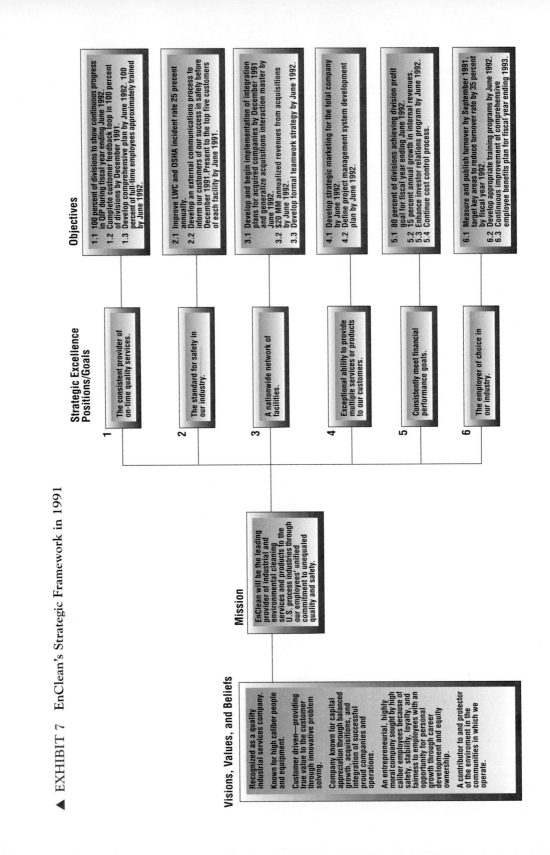

▲ EXHIBIT 7 EnClean's Strategic Framework in 1991

Objectives

1.1 100 percent of divisions to show continuous progress in QIP during fiscal year ending June 1992.
1.2 Complete customer feedback loop in 100 percent of divisions by December 1991.
1.3 Develop comprehensive plan by June 1992. 100 percent of full-time employees approximately trained by June 1992.

2.1 Improve LWC and OSHA incident rate 25 precent annually.
2.2 Develop an external communications process to inform our customers of our success in safety before December 1991. Present to the top five customers of each facility by June 1991.

3.1 Develop and begin implementation of integration plans for acquired companies by December 1991 and generalize acquisitions interaction master by June 1992.
3.2 $20 MM annualized revenues from acquisitions by June 1992.
3.3 Develop formal teamwork strategy by June 1992.

4.1 Develop strategic marketing for the total company by June 1992.
4.2 Define project management system development plan by June 1992.

5.1 80 percent of divisions achieving division profit goal for fiscal year ending June 1992.
5.2 15 percent annual growth in internal revenues.
5.3 Enhance investor relations program by June 1992.
5.4 Continue cost control process.

6.1 Measure and publish turnover by September 1991, target key areas to reduce turnover rate by 35 percent by fiscal year 1992.
6.2 Develop appropriate training programs by June 1992.
6.3 Continuous improvement of comprehensive employee benefits plan for fiscal year ending 1993.

Strategic Excellence Positions/Goals

1 The consistent provider of on-time quality services.

2 The standard for safety in our industry.

3 A nationwide network of facilities.

4 Exceptional ability to provide multiple services or products to our customers.

5 Consistently meet financial performance goals.

6 The employer of choice in our industry.

Mission

EnClean will be the leading provider of industrial and environmental cleaning services and products to the U.S. process industries through our employees' unified commitment to unequaled quality and safety.

Visions, Values, and Beliefs

Recognized as a quality industrial services company.

Known for high caliber people and equipment.

Customer driven—providing true value to the customer through innovative problem solving.

Company known for capital appreciation through balanced growth, acquisitions, and integration of successful proud companies and operations.

An entrepreneurial, highly moral company sought by high caliber employees because of safety, stability, loyalty, and fairness to employees with an opportunity for personal growth through career development and equity ownership.

A contributor to and protector of the enviroment in the communities in which we operate.

▲ EXHIBIT 8 EnClean Organization Chart, 1990

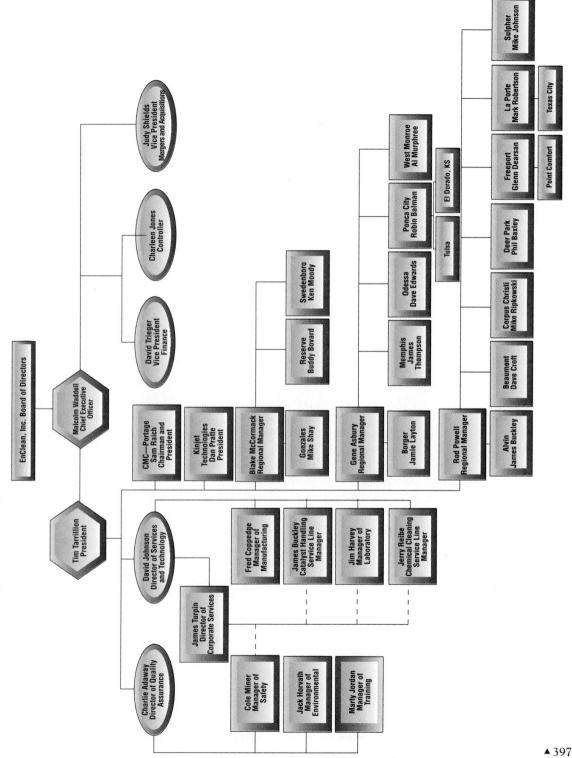

was no way we found to document this fact. Chemicals then became 40 percent and refining 30 percent of our business mix.

By 1988 our accident rates had been cut way back. Lost workday cases fell from around 10 per 100 workers to 1. It was a matter of changing our workers' attitudes. It wouldn't work to tell someone they had to do something; we had to educate them to the point that it became second nature. When you are driving home after a 12-hour shift at 2:00AM and the only light in the whole town turns red, the question is are you going to stop for that light or not? No third party can make you stop. Your attitude has to be that you will stop for that light, no matter how tired you are. That was the way our programs were always designed.

By the time we had four or five companies, our people had different titles for the same job. We simplified our employee standards and created a uniform promotion and grading system, so our employees could see what it would take to move up to the next grade. We also offered our employees a 401K profit-sharing plan, and the majority of them signed on. At the peak, our field operators were sticking around for four years, compared to maybe six months elsewhere. And we had people who started out working as salesmen for a division and ended up running a division.

By April 1989, EnClean had reached $37 million in annual revenues, and was growing quickly both internally and by acquisition. The company benefited from growth in the market itself as well as greater market share. EnClean continued its strategy of rolling out new services under existing names.

Continued Growth: Broadening the Service Lines.

The company continued to expand. The acquisitions provided the locations and the customer base as well as more service lines. The whole point then was to cross-sell existing services while further expanding the nucleus of the company with new service lines. Customers typically have loyalty to the entity they've done business with before. Especially if that company did good work for them. Still, you are only as good as your last job. Companies that botched a job either from an operations or safety perspective in one of those plants didn't get many second chances. Within the industry, there was a high degree of willingness to try new services, especially from companies that had a good reputation for what they did.

In June 1989, we organized our corporate services group to enable us to cross-sell our services throughout our geographic network. For example, in catalyst handling, we centralized the delivery of this service out of the Gulf Coast and were able to offer it throughout all our locations, first by training and supporting our division sales personnel to sell the service and then by providing specialized equipment that came from our corporate services group. We did the same thing with our chemical cleaning service line. The major factors in our business were people and equipment utilization, because that was where the money was made. When the big work came, we rolled people and equipment in from other locations and then rolled them back when the work was done. That allowed us to minimize the amount of staff at a particular location and to maintain high utilization of equipment. Our corporate services group worked essentially the same way. At its peak, the group had as many as 150 people in it.

This group also was responsible for launching new services. Our ultra-high (35,000 psi hydroblasting) and separation technology (dewatering/filtering) service lines were developed in this group, then in turn were rolled out on a systematic basis to our divisions. Our objective with these new services was to deliver them from the central group until enough business and operational expertise built up in a division. Then the service and equipment would be localized.

Some of our local division managers understood how to use the group to leverage their local operations and sell one-stop shopping to their customers. However, asking our salesmen to sell additional service lines took many of our sales people out of their comfort zones, and sales training programs were slow in coming and too infrequent. Also, many of our salesmen were leery about having an outside group deliver a new service to their customers—often out of fear that a poorly performed job might cost them their base hydroblasting or vacuuming business. Finally, on the other side, members of our corporate services group were now working through the divisions rather than working directly for the customer. That undermined the recognition and rewards that customer-contact brought. Furthermore, on the more technical jobs, the lines of authority and responsibility tended to blur: it was the division's customer, but the service expertise and, hence, delivery belonged to the corporate services group. When jobs did go wrong, there was a lot of finger-pointing and resentment.

We were also charging a cost-based transfer price for corporate services. That could be a problem for some divisions on a particular project. In fact, that became the number one internal hassle for the company. Not only for corporate services charged to divisions, but also for what one division charged to another when it sent people or equipment over to help out, because each division or location was a profit center, with incentive pay tied to division performance. This internal transferring was maybe 20 percent of total revenues.

The Public Offering

In April 1989, EnClean completed its initial public offering, raising $7 million at a price of $6 ¾ per share. This was when we adopted the EnClean name. From then on, we would switch companies over to the EnClean name usually within two years.

We went public in 1989 because we needed to refinance the company. We had $20 million in debt. Going public would be a way to boost capital and, at the same time, to have another form of currency to do additional acquisitions. The economy was in a terrible state; we didn't have a whole lot of people interested in doing the offering. One year later, we raised an additional $11 million in a second offering, the proceeds of which were used in part to reduce debt. In July 1991, we raised $46 million in a 7.5 percent convertible subordinated debt offering to take advantage of the low interest rates and to provide us additional capital to grow internally and by acquisitions.

Also in 1989, EnClean acquired Correct Maintenance Corporation (CMC), an industrial and environmental cleaning company based near Chicago, Illinois.

The CMC Acquisition

CMC was a well-established $10 million in revenue company trying to do everything. But when you got right down to it, they primarily did vacuuming and hydroblasting and had several promising new environmental services. EnClean acquired CMC in October 1989 using proceeds from its IPO. Although they were very successful for the first full year, by mid-1991 we knew we had a problem. They saw us as "those boys down in Texas." They were doing well financially because of several large environmental cleaning projects, but they were only paying lip service to integrating into the overall company's facilities' network and sharing those promising environmental service technologies with the rest of EnClean. We attempted to get the local management group to work with Ed Bogle to design and implement a strategic plan for CMC. We kept on the then CFO as heir apparent at CMC, but he never bought into the EnClean strategy. Still, when a guy is making the numbers, do you keep him or not?

In the case of this non-EnClean, noncooperative manager who ran CMC, we kept him around for over two years because of his short-term results and because leadership in all of these companies had to be entrepreneurial by nature. There is no way that steel-making and food-processing customers in Chicago are the same as the refining and petrochemical customers on the Gulf Coast of the United States. We also faced different competitors. Therefore, strong, local management is a must. Still, in this case we paid a high price for leaving this manager in place.

By late 1991, we were losing money at CMC. In December, we replaced CMC's manager with Don Boyd, a chemical engineer/Harvard MBA with a strong operations background. He immediately bought into the multiple services, industrial company concept—including strategic planning with a discipline towards making money. Within about three or four months, he converted the whole organization to operate as part of EnClean. He started to execute a multiple service line strategy, taking our technologies like catalyst handling and selling them in his marketplace, which we hadn't been able to do for almost three years. Don was brand new to EnClean, but he understood where the whole company was going.

The AlphaChem Acquisition

CMC was one of the last industrial service companies bought by EnClean. In May of 1990 EnClean acquired AlphaChem, a specialty chemicals operation.

It was becoming harder and harder for me to find significantly sized industrial cleaning operations. By 1990, our internal growth had slowed down to about 17 percent.

AlphaChem was in the wholesale blending and distribution of bulk chemicals that could be self-applied. The plant would put a tank in; then, instead of calling us out each time they had a drip or a spill on the side of their unit, they would have the materials—primarily soaps or solvents—to handle it with AlphaChem application devices and their own people. We were basically filling up soap dispensers in refineries and chemical and paper plants. We had not previously been a products distribution company.

When we bought AlphaChem we tried to get them to develop and execute their own strategic plan, because they were clearly a different type business than us. Even with Ed Bogle's help, we could not get that group to develop a different strategic plan. They had been at $12 million in revenues for five years. They weren't going anywhere, and their margins were going south from 12 percent to 10 percent, to 9 percent, to 7 percent. Their competition was gaining ground, and they did not have a clear strategy to deal with that. In my opinion, they were stuck on the inside looking out, and they never could figure out what they were supposed to do. Their chosen approach was to adopt EnClean's strategic plan, but our service business was different from AlphaChem's. The group faced many challenges and changes in their marketplace and business, including stricter disposal laws for their customers on the AlphaChem products they used. Faced with these difficulties, the group still was reluctant to plan, but more importantly, they could not sense a new vision for AlphaChem.

▲ CHALLENGES TO CONTINUING GROWTH

As fast as we were growing, we needed additional senior managers besides Tim and me to handle the integration process and develop and execute our strategy. Because of our tight operating margins, we stuck to using our own people, rather than bringing people in from outside. We grew a lot of very bright managers internally. Many of these managers came to us through our acquisitions. In May 1991, Mike Bonem from McKinsey & Co. was brought on to lead our marketing effort, to develop better market data, and to coordinate our sales training and new service line introductions. The only other operating people we brought on to our senior management team from the outside were Don Boyd (December 1991) and D. A. Johnson (January 1992), another Harvard MBA and ex-GEer.

As the number of companies in the EnClean fold increased, we would try to execute planning on an individual division or subsidiary basis and then link that back to the whole strategy. We developed a concept called a weaver, which would be someone from corporate working with an acquired group to weave them into EnClean. It was a part-time position—something we'd ask our people to do in addition to their regular job. For example, our safety director became one of our weavers. Once in there, the weaver had to do the job of getting strategy executed, in a situation where the old leadership of the company was usually against it. In general, those first-stage entrepreneurs didn't like having their strategy dictated from the outside. So the weaver had a difficult job with no real authority over a company, and we never provided them with the proper training on how to do it. As weaving implies, it was an art as much as a science.

Remember each market was unique as we faced customers making local purchasing decisions and different competitors due to fragmentation in the industry. Furthermore, several of our businesses, such as AlphaChem and (later) Sizemore, were different than our traditional industrial service business. There was no easy way to execute planning at the divisional level. The easy solution would seem to have been to assemble all 40 location managers in a strategic planning group. But what you end up with is a convention, not a strategic planning meeting. More than 10 to 12 people in a planning group is too big. It becomes more of a lecture than an interactive process.

Tim and I and our outside consultant were committed to this division planning process. Unfortunately, it was being developed from scratch. I kept asking if there wasn't some off-the-shelf, prepackaged process such as Ernst & Young had for the corporate process. Somebody else had to have faced this same problem. Instead, after several years we ended up with a manual an inch thick that we developed on our own but never implemented. We tried to use quality teams to develop a local marketing and operations planning process, but unlike our corporate process, neither the managers on the quality team nor our uninvolved senior managers bought in. This left our consultant to finish the modules. Bottom line, it was good but it just didn't work.

As we grew, the corporate group was getting further and further removed from the field, and I feel, esoteric in our thinking. Our quality process was a good example of that: quality targeted at customer requirements is a good thing. However, we had some people in there executing quality processes because that's what corporate wanted, but they weren't really doing anything valuable.

The Environmental Services Acquisitions

Altogether, EnClean acquired 14 companies or businesses in a 10-year period of time. The largest came in June of 1991, with the acquisition of Sizemore Environmental Group through a pooling-of-interest. In contrast to EnClean, whose average project size was still around $10,000, Sizemore's average project size was $500,000. By then, EnClean had just begun to add dewatering to its service lines. Dewatering was an environmental cleaning process which squeezed water out of waste streams in order to reduce the quantity of material to be disposed of in scarce, expensive landfills or via costly incineration.

From a strategic point of view, Sizemore looked good on the surface. The dewatering business was something we developed internally in January 1990 as part of our corporate services group, because our customers were asking us to assist them in dealing with their waste streams on site. Prior to Sizemore, we dewatered small 1- to 3-acre pits and ponds created to contain process waste or overflow. We looked at the larger 100+ acre settling ponds and old land farms and saw opportunity. This service was Sizemore's specialty and we could see using them like a corporate services group to roll this service line throughout the geographic network. The environmental market was going great guns at this point.

In February 1992, EnClean expanded its separation technology services with the acquisition of Escandell Associates. Escandell had grown from $1 million in 1988 to $8.6 million at the time of the acquisition. At a price of $12 million in stock, it was the most expensive acquisition in EnClean's history.

When EnClean acquired Escandell, we greatly expanded our dewatering/filtration business. Escandell had some 20 presses, we had 4 or 5. It looked like such a great fit. We didn't have a lot of experts in the filtration service line, and it was growing by leaps and bounds for us. Tom Escandell, the founder of Escandell, had come out of the oil field, where separation technology had been used for years. He looked to us like a natural leader to combine our dewatering operations with his and send this service throughout our network. His company had an extremely good reputation in the marketplace.

He was operating out of one location, highly targeted towards the refining segment, because that's where the oil-based waste streams were. Also, he tended to do much larger-scale projects. Their focus was on the $500,000 four-press jobs, and his people didn't want to worry about the day-to-day pond remediation jobs we were doing. Also operating as a corporate services group unit was a radical adjustment. Selling and assisting divisions rather than selling direct to the end customer caused confusion and animosity between Escandell employees and division personnel.

Land bans had been driving the filter press business to establish specific deadline dates for closing surface impoundments and settling ponds now considered hazardous. The large quantities of aqueous and semisolid waste streams in these enclosures were expensive to dispose of. Hence, compacting or pressing this material reduced waste volume and, in turn, waste disposal costs. Bush delivered his State of the Union address in late January 1992, and I shifted in my seat when I heard him say he was going to look at the environmental laws and might declare a moratorium. Almost all the environmental service deadlines then got pushed back. The big jobs were delayed or postponed. Escandell's base business began to erode, and competition began lowering prices to secure the reduced amount of work that was being contracted.

Losing Control

At the same time that changes in environmental regulations were hurting revenues, the economy continued to be in recession, and industry responded by cutting back further on cleaning and maintenance expenditures. Sizemore, which had made an operating income of 9 percent on revenues of $17 million in fiscal 1991, lost money the following year, even as its revenues grew. In March 1992, EnClean announced a major downturn in profits, and its stock price dropped to 8 (Exhibit 9).

We seemed constantly in a crisis mode from around March 1992. We ran very much afoul of the Peter Principle in some of our management. For example, the manager in charge of our

▲ EXHIBIT 9   EnClean's Stock Price Performance, 1989–1993

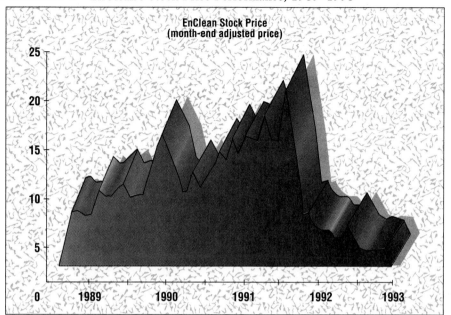

EnClean Stock Price
(month-end adjusted price)

Sizemore operations was the 32-year-old grandson of the founder. We decided to keep him in place to run the company after the acquisition. This gentleman was a bright guy and had been instrumental in the company's rapid growth. However, he did not have the experience to run a $20 million in revenue operation. Our weaver/integrator for this entity was our Gulf Coast industrial service regional manager who had his hands full managing our internal growth in his $20 million revenue region. Furthermore, he had no background in any of Sizemore's businesses. Sizemore's initial results were positive and on target. However, the strategy they executed to continue their growth had nothing to do with the one we had all agreed upon at the outset. They were supposed to expand the environmental, pond remediation side of their business. Instead, they started doing large-scale civil and mechanical contracting—assembling vessels, building towers, that sort of thing.

   We identified early on that Sizemore's cost accounting system needed improvement. Sizemore's management hired a supposedly strong cost accountant, and they were going to make the needed changes themselves under the supposed watchful eye of the EnClean controller.[1] Unfortunately, Sizemore's management didn't have a handle on their costs, and they didn't know where they were on a lot of their projects; then it started to rain...and rain. With no rain delay provisions in their customer contracts we had to absorb all the additional costs. Projects of $1–3 million were losing from $100,000–300,000 at a time. These problems at Sizemore contributed heavily to the debacle in the March quarter of 1992. At the beginning of the quarter, Sizemore estimated that it was on its way to a profit of $200,000; but by the end, they lost about $700,000. On top of this, CMC lost $900,000 in this quarter.

---

[1]Typically, we put smaller acquired companies on our systems. But in the case of larger companies or, like Sizemore, companies in different businesses, we left them on their own systems. We ended up with about five accounting systems in total.

When we reported the loss for the March 1992 quarter, the bottom fell out of the stock. The share price declined more than 50 percent from $17 to $8.

Until March 1992, I had spent the bulk of my time visiting and reviewing potential acquisition candidates and steering the investor relations efforts. After the poor results in that third quarter of fiscal 1992, Tim and I decided no more acquisitions. We had too many things we needed to do internally.

When the numbers in the March quarter surprised us, we were in the process of getting the systems in place that we needed. At that point, we were still relying on many of the subsystems left behind from the original entities. We didn't have a handle on the corporate overhead expense in our company, and we had continued to add to these costs in anticipation of continued internal growth. There was no consolidated income statements or balance sheets coming out on a timely basis.

I demoted the controller, and made Judy Shields, our VP of Mergers and Acquisitions, the controller of the company. Immediately, she and her team of both internal personnel and contract systems people followed through on systematizing all our information. We got comprehensive company reports, cut every way you can imagine: by division, by service line. She also was able to get a handle on equipment utilization, which we had lost track of because our systems couldn't keep up with the growth in service lines. I had Judy report directly to me, and focused our chief financial officer on administration and investor relations. As results continued to miss our expectations, much of the CFO's and my time was taken up with crisis management.

Operationally, Tim was constantly fighting fires. For example, we took Mike Bonem out of marketing, where he was developing a plan for executing the multi–service line strategy. He was suited for that role, but we needed an operating manager at Sizemore. We had to have somebody who could get down there and understand where the numbers were and get that operation turned around. To his credit, Mike and his group had Sizemore turned around within six months. The civil and mechanical operations at Sizemore were discontinued in June 1992. It was a good business decision, but the market saw it as a major divestiture and punished us for it. That took the stock down another notch.

While we were executing our strategy to grow the environmental side of the business, a lot of industrial service guys got disgruntled. Industrial services turned down and went flat because the plants started deferring maintenance. That created a widening gap between contract pricing and what I call spot pricing. Spot prices were what the customer was charged for new project bid work. By early 1993 spot prices were as much as 25 percent below our contract prices. Looking ahead, I knew we'd be facing pressure from our customers to bring our contract prices down. That would have killed us. So when EnClean started having problems, the industrial side blamed the environmental side of the business for our fallback, but the problems were on both sides of our business.

The Brand Companies, a publicly traded industrial and environmental services firm, first contacted EnClean about a possible merger in May of 1992. Brand made a preliminary proposal of $11 a share. EnClean informed Brand's representatives that the company was not for sale and were not willing to entertain Brand's proposal at that price. At that time the stock was trading at around $8. Throughout the following fiscal year, EnClean experienced more unpleasant surprises and declining financial performance. Brand was subsequently merged into Rust International, Inc., an engineering, construction, and environmental consulting services company and a WMX Technologies company. In August 1992, Brand/Rust acquired Naylor Industrial Services, a $15 million competitor to EnClean on the Gulf Coast.

Crisis

By November 1992, Tim and I were convinced that we had to get bigger. We had trimmed SG&A; the problem was the gross profit margins had dropped 10 percentage points, from 43 percent in fiscal 1991 to 33 percent in the December 1992 quarter. The profit margins were down due to competitive pricing and the high fixed cost nature of our business. The only way we were going to survive in that marketplace was by having more revenue at the top, and the only way we were going to do that was by combining companies. We were convinced that to be a publicly traded company, we needed to be at least half a billion dollars in size, but our stock was too low to allow us to go out and acquire any more companies. After consultations with several investment banks, we decided it was unlikely that we could pull off a merger combining three or more parties to reach the revenue target.

By late February 1993, it was obvious that we were going to have a hard time hitting our third quarter 1993 forecast that had just been revised in late December 1992. Revenues were down year over year and gross margins were still under pressure. Shell was a major customer—about 12 percent of our business—and also had been the slowest to react to the downturn in their industry. However, when Shell did start to cut back and lay people off, they hit their outside contractors, including us, with reduced service business. Meanwhile, our people were telling Tim what he wanted to hear: that we weren't losing market share, that the marketplace was down. Yet we were losing salesmen, and we were losing share in some marketplaces as other contractors scrambled to keep their equipment and people busy.

In early March at our regularly scheduled operations meeting, I presented my analysis of the expected third quarter performance shortfall to our senior management. You could have heard a pin drop. None of these guys had any idea, because they were so focused on their own business lines, about how bad things really were or how much money that we might lose in the March 1993 quarter. I gave what Tim later called my hari-kari speech, saying I would quit and leave if that's what it took to turn things around. Tim said that I didn't have to fall on my sword, but added unless we started performing up to expectations one of us would likely be gone in short order. Several of our senior managers, who should have kept this confidential, began spreading the rumor through the organization that I might be going. All of a sudden, I start getting phone calls from operating managers in the field saying, "We hear you're going. Don't go, we want you to stay."

In mid-March, we met with this senior group again in a planning session and agreed on a strategy to move forward, focusing on key issues and execution. Because of discussions at the board level about the possible sale of the company, however, we asked them to put executing this strategy on hold until fiscal 1994. Our managers were operations-oriented people, trained to make decisions and go forward. They didn't understand why they had to sit on their hands, and we couldn't tell them that we were looking at other alternatives. We were starting to lose good people. The philosophical differences between Tim and me became apparent when I watched a $2 million revenue-generating salesman in a $100 million company walk out the door, and Tim simply accepted it.

Around this time, I was fighting off depression: I was staying up nights, fretting. The marketplace had trashed our stock, I wasn't doing any more acquisitions, and I was watching my company slowly dissolve. This is the other side of entrepreneurship.

The board also met in mid-March, and that's where the first strong signs of a split on the board came out. Unlike me, Tim did not appear willing to move forward and execute the very strategy that was the right strategy to execute whether we were acquired or not.

In mid-April, we announced publicly that we expected to report a loss in the third quarter substantially greater than analysts' expectations and that we had engaged an investment banking firm to assist us in exploring various means to return EnClean to profitability and to enhance stockholder value. The loss was greater than we and the board had expected. About this same time, our Gulf Coast regional industrial services manager informed Tim and me that he was leaving the company, destination unknown.

The Secret Meeting

On May 6, 1993, the outside board members held a secret meeting, which they'd never done before. The board, a majority of whose outside members were venture capitalists, was faced with a difficult situation about how to handle the decline of the company. As CEO, I should have continued to add experienced operating managers to the board during the company's growth, but we hadn't. This group had seen two stallions run a good race, but now they had stumbled and gone lame. This board had never shot a stallion before.

A more operations-oriented board would probably have known how to shoot two stallions as opposed to one. But our board chose to shoot one, and the one they chose to shoot, which always surprised me, was Tim. They didn't think Tim would execute, and they believed I would stay no matter how mad I got about the behind-the-back way they had conducted themselves.

My board gave me four parameters. One, Tim could no longer remain the COO of the company. Two, I had to stay. My response was that I didn't know slavery had been reinstated. But they banked on the fact that I would not leave my people in the lurch. And neither would Tim, had they chosen him. The third thing was that the CFO had to go. The fourth was that they left everything else up to me. I was to present a new operating plan for their review at our next board meeting on May 11.

COOPER INDUSTRIES' CORPORATE STRATEGY

The business of Cooper is value-added manufacturing.
Cooper Industries' management philosophy

Manufacturing may not be glamorous, but we know a lot about it.
Robert Cizik, chairman, president, and CEO

Cooper Industries, a company more than 150 years old, spent most of its history as a small but reputable maker of engines and compressors to propel natural gas through pipelines. In the 1960s, the firm's leaders decided to expand the company to lessen its dependence on the capital expenditures of the cyclical natural gas business. During the next 30 years, the company acquired more than 60 manufacturing companies that dramatically increased the size and scope of Cooper Industries (Exhibit 1). Through a process that both insiders and outsiders called "Cooperization," the company welded a group of "independent, over-the-hill companies into a highly efficient, profitable, competitive business."[1]

By 1988, the diversified industrial products company derived $4.3 billion in annual revenues from manufacturing 2 million items. Cooper's products ranged from 10-cent fuses to $3 million turbine compressor sets marketed under an array of brand names, the most famous of which was Crescent wrenches. "We decided a long time ago," said Robert Cizik, chairman, president, and CEO, "that if we could do an outstanding job at the unglamorous part by making necessary products of exceptional quality, then we could be successful indeed."[2]

Research Associate Toby Stuart prepared this case under the supervision of Professor David Collis.
Copyright © 1991 by the President and Fellows of Harvard College.

[1]*Wall Street Transcript,* October 15, 1984, p 75, 590.
[2]*The Houston Post,* August 6, 1989, p. D1.

▲ EXHIBIT 1   Cooper Industries' Acquisitions

Year	Business	Description
1963	Ajax Iron Works	Engines and compressors
1964	Pennsylvania Pump & Compressor Co.	Process compressors
1966	Ken-Tool Manufacturing Co.	Tire-changing tools
1967	Lufkin Rule Co.	Measuring tapes and wooden rules
1968	Crescent Niagara Corp.	Wrenches, pliers, and screwdrivers
1970	Weller Electric Corp.	Electric soldering tools
	Dallas Airmotive, Inc.	Aircraft engine overhaul and service
1971	Howard Industries' Micro Grinder line	Motor-driven hobby tools
1972	Nicholson File Co.	Hand files
1973	Southwest Airmotive Co.	Aircraft engine overhaul and service
	Xcelite Inc.	Screwdrivers, nutdrivers, and pliers
	Nordberg Engine & Parts Services	Engine parts and services
1975	Standard Aircraft Equipment, Inc.	Aircraft engine overhaul and service
1976	J. Wiss & Sons Co.	Scissors, shears, and snips
1978	Dallas Fixed Base Operations	Aircraft engine overhaul and service
1979	Gardner-Denver Co.*	Petroleum drilling and mining equipment
1980	Pinking Shears Corp. Product Line	Pinking shears
	Cannon Manufacturing Corp.	Ball valves
	McDonough's Plumb Tool Line	Hammers, axes, and hatchets
1981	Crouse-Hinds*	Electrical distribution products, traffic control equipment, lighting fixtures, and electronic wire and cable
	Kirsch Co.*	Drapery hardware and window coverings
	Pfaff & Kendall, and Hilldale Co.	Light poles
1982	Sullair Mining Equipment Corp.	Mining equipment
	Escadril Pump Product Line	Hydraulic pumps
	Westinghouse's Lighting Products	Lighting fixtures
	G.E.'s One-Piece Terminal Board Line	Terminal boards
1984	Risdon Corporation	Specialty wire products
	Turner Industries, Inc.	Portable propane torches
	Phalo's Computer Cable Line	Electronic cable
1985	McGraw-Edison Co.*	Electrical power distribution equipment, lighting fixtures, and auto products
	OPI, Inc	Well service pumps
	The Breneman Co.	Roller shades
1987	H.K. Porter, Inc.	Bolt cutters
	Joy Petroleum Equipment and Products*	Pumps and compressors
	Underwriter's Safety Device Division	Fuseholders

Year	Business	Description
	Joy Molded Rubber Products	Electrical connectors
	Joy Industrial Compressor Group*	Air and gas compressors
1988	Wiltshire File Pty. Ltd.	Hand files
	Beswick Division*	Power and electronic fuses
	B.C. Richards & Co. Pty.	Valves
	Macey Mining Services Pty. Ltd.	Electrical connectors
	RTE Corp.*	Electrical power distribution equipment
	Enterprise Engine Aftermarket Business	Engine repair parts

*Indicates transaction price in excess of $50 million.

In early 1989, Cooper Industries tested this philosophy when it launched a $21-a-share, $825 million tender offer for Champion Spark Plug. The Cooper bid trumped a $17.50-a-share bid by Dana Corp., a $4.9 billion auto-parts manufacturer. Although Champion had a well-known brand name and worldwide manufacturing facilities, it faced a shrinking market for spark plugs as the auto industry shifted to smaller engines. In response to the declining market, Champion's aggressive attempts to diversify into other automotive product lines had failed, and 1988 profits had fallen to $24 million. At 25 times 1988 EBIT, Cooper's bid was highly risky.

▲ COMPANY HISTORY

In 1833, Charles and Elias Cooper built an iron foundry in Mount Vernon, Ohio. C&E Cooper evolved in stride with the Industrial Revolution, making first a steam powered Corliss engine that generated power for manufacturing plants and then switching by 1900 to produce natural gas compressors, which pumped gas through pipeline networks to customers. By 1920, Cooper was the recognized leader in pipeline compression equipment. However, another company, Bessemer, manufactured the engines that initially extracted the gas from underground wells. The compatibility of these two companies led to a merger that Cooper initiated in 1929.

By the late 1950s, Cooper-Bessemer was still a small company with about $50 million in annual sales. However, it had developed production expertise and had built a reputation for customer service in the natural gas industry. In 1957, the company elected 38-year-old Gene Miller as president. Miller, an engineer, was also only the second president outside the strong chain of Cooper family influence to lead the company.

In 1958, Cooper suffered a cyclical downturn, during which a corporate raider acquired enough Cooper shares to elect two board members. This experience had a profound impact on Miller, convincing him of the need to diversify. Said Miller, "we shouldn't dare limit ourselves to being engine builders, with perhaps a few sidelines to get us over the rough spots. We had to work toward a radical change in our outlook."[3] Miller planned to guide Cooper through a phase of corporate growth that would put the company in a wider range of product markets. Instrumental to Miller's strategy was growth and diversification through acquisitions.

---

[3]David N. Keller, *Cooper Industries 1933–1983* (Ohio University Press, 1983), p. 98.

To help him achieve these goals Miller enlisted a leader with "current ideas" and expertise in finance. In 1961, Miller recruited Robert Cizik from Standard Oil, to join Cooper as executive assistant for corporate development. Cizik, a midwesterner, had earned a degree in accounting and economics from the University of Connecticut. After briefly working as an accountant, he joined the Air Force during the Korean War. He then entered the Harvard Business School and graduated as a Baker Scholar in 1958.

One of the first items on Miller's and Cizik's agenda was to free top managers and corporate board directors from the restraints of daily operations. To this end, Miller and Cizik formally redesigned Cooper's structure. Under the new system, a small, 10-member policy-making management team headed the company, with a number of operating division managers underneath. Each division manager was responsible for his division's operations and profits and reported directly to President Miller. In the 1965 annual report, Miller called it a "relatively simple, yet highly flexible organizational structure."

To fortify the new structure, Miller and Cizik established clear lines of communication between the parent management team and the divisions, and among the divisions themselves. Cizik also established a uniform accounting system that included comprehensive planning and reporting techniques and capital investment procedures for each division.

In 1965, the company changed its name to Cooper Industries and, in 1967, moved its headquarters to Houston. Cooper was ready to make acquisitions, but would not diversify wildly under the assumption that professional managers can oversee any kind of business, regardless of products, markets, or manufacturing processes. Cizik articulated his opposition to conglomeration. "I believe that to exercise [management control], management must thoroughly understand the company's activities—its production process, products, and markets; the laws that relate to its various activities; and the cultures and customs of the areas in which it operates."[4] Therefore, Cooper's leaders would set limits on the degree of diversification and the timing of their acquisitions. Cooper decided to pursue only companies that exhibited stable earnings, or earnings countercyclical to the oil and gas transmission industry. To ensure consistent earnings, Cooper would focus on products that served basic needs and that were manufactured with mature production technologies. Furthermore, Cooper would seek acquisition candidates that possessed its own strongest assets: it would concentrate on high-quality manufacturing companies preferably with market-leading positions.

Diversification began in 1967 when Cooper acquired the Lufkin Rule Company. Founded in Cleveland, Ohio, in 1869, Lufkin manufactured measuring rules for the lumber industry. By the 1960s, Lufkin was a market leader in measuring tapes and rules and produced premium-quality products used mainly by architects, carpenters, and home "do-it-yourselfers." When Lufkin came up for sale in 1967, Cooper believed the company and its hand-tool business offered exactly the right kind of diversification. Virtually everyone recognized and used hand tools; they were also simple products whose designs and technology changed very slowly in an evolutionary fashion. "Few products are lower tech than a hammer," Cizik once explained.[5] Most important, with few market fluctuations in their sales, hand tools would help Cooper level its cyclical revenues, which were so closely attached to the natural gas industry.

Lufkin also brought to Cooper its recently appointed president, Bill Rector, who envisioned building the world's best hand-tool manufacturing group. Rector proposed adding a "tool basket" group to Cooper, which would be comprised of selected, high-quality, brand leaders joined under modern management. The hand-tool industry was comprised of hundreds

[4]Keller, *Cooper,* p. 244.
[5]*Wall Street Transcript,* October 15, 1984, p. 75, 590.

of small companies, many of them a century old and still under the influence of their founding families. Cizik described these businesses as "third generation companies. . . suffering from a lack of capital investment and effective management."[6] The companies, many of them unprofitable, reinvested minimally and their manufacturing operations were high cost. Additionally, most hand-tool producers had extended their product line beyond their original best-selling items to provide something for everybody. In many instances, a company's money-losing hand tools outnumbered the profitable ones. In 1967, Cooper signed Rector on as a corporate vice president and provided him with capital to develop the tool group.

With Lufkin in place, Cooper quickly acquired two more hand-tool companies. The first, Crescent Niagara Corporation, was one of the most recognized names in the industry and made the well-known Crescent wrench. In 1968, Cooper acquired the unprofitable Crescent Niagara from a small group that had recently bought the company from its family owners. Two years later, Cooper bought Weller Manufacturing Corporation from family owners hoping to retire. Weller, the world's leading manufacturer of soldering tools, operated throughout North and South America and in Europe and gave Cooper's tool group added marketing power.

While retaining their original brand names, the three companies, Lufkin, Crescent, and Weller, were folded into the new tool group, headed by Rector. The tool group revamped the manufacturing operations of the acquisitions, updating processes and equipment and consolidating plants. In some cases, Cooper completely shut down manufacturing sites in the North and opened new plants in the South. The advantages of moving to the South, explained Cizik, were not solely in lower wages or even in new facilities. The key was to "move into an atmosphere where you're able to train your people from scratch. You're not locked into the practices of 20 years ago. You go to South Carolina, and even with the high cost of training and scrappage and breakage that you may have to take for two or three years, you get to a stage where you have a skilled work force doing things without an eye toward history."[7] While implementing manufacturing changes, Cooper also concentrated production on the most profitable and popular hand tools. Tools selling at low rates and most left-handed items were eliminated. At Lufkin alone, Cooper scaled back 3,500 different measuring rules and tapes to 500. In the more drastic case of the Nicholson Company, a maker of saws, rasps, and files that Cooper acquired in 1972, the product count was streamlined from 30,000 to 3,000. Among the products eliminated was a rasp for scraping burned toast.

By 1970, the tool group had set up headquarters in Apex, North Carolina, on the same site where Lufkin had opened a new state-of-the-art manufacturing plant. C. Baker Cunningham, another Harvard Business School graduate who had started at Cooper's corporate planning department in 1970, joined the tool group in 1971 as director of finance and introduced a new computer system to manage inventories, sales, shipping, and billing for all tool products. Also at Apex, the tool group centralized sales and marketing of all the hand tools. As the tool group expanded, it developed a small sales force by retaining only the best people from each acquisition and training them to promote all the products under the Cooper umbrella. After the first three companies had joined the tool group (Lufkin, Crescent, and Weller), the size of the combined sales force was smaller than Lufkin's original team. The consolidated force allowed international salespeople in a country where one brand name was particularly popular to use its leverage to sell other tools in the tool group (Exhibit 2).

---

[6]Sam Fletcher, "Cooper Industries Builds on Merits," *The Houston Post,* August 8, 1990, p. D4.
[7]James Flanigan, "Bob Cizik: He Talks a Good Game—Plays One, Too," *Forbes,* July 8 1979, pp. 100–4

▲ EXHIBIT 2   Advertisement for Cooper's Tool Group

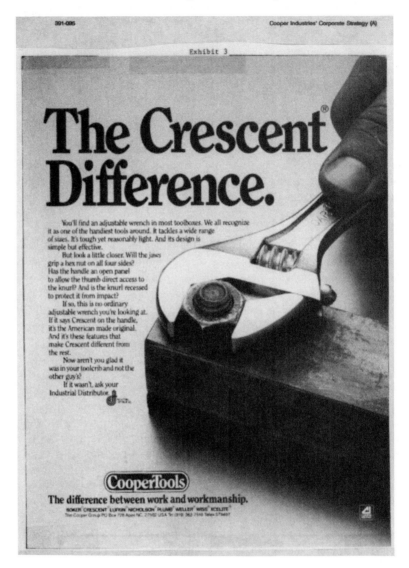

Cooper's early experience with the tool group helped further define its diversification program. Cizik, who by 1969 was chief operating officer, felt that Cooper needed an approach to evaluate acquisitions within its manufacturing focus. Division managers would seek "complementary" acquisitions, defined as logical extensions of Cooper's existing products or markets. The corporate staff, meanwhile, would pursue "diversification" acquisitions. Together these acquisitions would fulfill Cooper's basic corporate growth objective (an increase in pretax earnings per share at a compound rate of 11 percent) and would improve the "quality" of earnings by adding stability. At the same time, Cizik emphasized that the process of building Cooper Industries could involve subtraction as well. "People often think success is measured only by adding, adding, and more adding," said

Cizik. "That's extremely important, but you have to keep examining what you have, and you can't be afraid to get rid of the things that have served their useful time."[8] Cooper divested 33 businesses between 1970 and 1988 (Exhibit 3).

Throughout the 1970s, "complementary" development continued in he tool group with four more acquisitions (Nicholson File in 1972, Xcelite nut runners in 1973, Wiss scissors in 1976, and Plumb hammers in 1980). The most important, Nicholson, was a file and saw maker based in Providence, Rhode Island, whose main asset was its expansive distribution system of independent hardware wholesalers and industrial distributors that reached 53,000 retail outlets in 137 countries. Additionally, at Apex, a quasi-R&D group tested new products and designs for all the group's acquired companies and introduced new hand-tool products under its existing brand names during the 1970s. By 1974, all of Cooper's acquisitions had relocated their manufacturing operations to new plants, mostly in the South. Shortly after, Cooper was recognized as the world's largest and most efficient manufacturer of nonpowered hand tools. At this time, Cizik decided not to enter the electric power-tool industry in the face of Black & Decker's commanding market share.

Besides the complementary mergers in the tool group, Cooper's corporate staff orchestrated an important diversifying acquisition. In 1970, Cooper had quickly followed Lufkin with a second diversification, this time into the aircraft service business. Cooper purchased Dallas Airmotive, a company that repaired and leased jet engines and distributed aircraft parts and supplies. Cooper later supplemented this acquisition with four more air-service companies.

With the "tool basket" well underway and the aircraft service division established, in the early 1970s Cooper's corporate management team turned to the energy division and applied some of its hand-tool strategies there. Specifically, Cooper retrenched and concentrated its resources on compression equipment for oil and gas, where it was the industry leader. In 1976, Cooper purchased Superior, a maker of engines and natural gas compressors that filled the gap between Cooper-Bessemer's largest and smallest products. After the Superior deal, Cooper supplied 40 percent of the horsepower requirements for gas transmission in North America. Concurrently, it stopped producing compressors for petrochemical applications (ethylene, ammonia, nitrogen, oxygen markets, etc.), where Dresser Industries and Carrier dominated the market. This meant reducing the workforce at the original Mount Vernon plant from 1,300 to 250. Cizik reasoned that supporting engineering, development, and service for the multiple applications cost too much. "We could probably have gone ahead and invested $100 million over four to five years for the latest technology. But competitors weren't going to be standing still. I thought we could come out of that and still be third or fourth in many of those lines."[9]

In 1975, in the midst of the oil embargo, Cooper elected Robert Cizik as CEO. Cooper's energy division benefited greatly from the increased activity in the United States that persisted into the early 1980s, and its climbing energy income offset falling hand-tool sales during the simultaneous recession. According to Cizik's vision of a multimarket company, "not everything will be clicking at the same time." However, there will be "movement back and forth between businesses as you need them."[10] Correspondingly, Cooper rerouted the flow of capital expenditures to the energy division.

---

[8]Keller, *Cooper,* p. 157.
[9]Flanigan, *Forbes.*
[10]Keller, *Cooper,* p. 211.

▲ EXHIBIT 3 Cooper Industries' Divestitures

Year	Business	Description
1971	Lufkin Dial Indicators Line	Measuring instruments
1973	Atkins Saw Product Line	Hand and band saws
1974	Ken-Tool Division	Tire changing tools and equipment
1975	C-B Southern	Compressor packaging
1977	Wiss Garden Tool	Garden tools
1978	Danco Division	Plastic tool accessories
1981	Rotor Tool Division	Portable air and electric tool
	Vanguard Studios	Decorative accessories
	Cooper Airmotive	Airmotive engine overhaul and service
1982	Svenska Kirsch AB	Window hardware distributor
	Belden Distribution	Electrical products distributor
	Arrow-Hart Dano	Electrical coils
1983	EDCON	Seismic services
	Traffic Control Products	Traffic lights and systems
1984	Cooper Electronics Division	Electronics production equipment
	Arrow-Hart PPS/PNS Switches	Micro switches
	Belden Bit-Driver	Data transmission equipment
	Worldsbest Industries, Inc.	Infant furniture
1985	Weller Mini-Shop	Motor-driven hobby tools
	Bussmann Process Automation Prod. Line	Automated plating systems
	Chain Link Fence Business	Vinyl coated link fence
	Alex Stuart Design	Office furniture
	Carlton Santee	Real estate development
1986	Onan, Inc.	Portable electric generators
	Boker Knives Product Line	Pocket knives
	Gardner-Denver Company Africa Pty. Ltd.	Mining equipment
	Gleason Reel Division	Cable reels
	Battery, Inc.	Storage batteries
	Clarke	Floor cleaning equipment
1987	McGraw-Edison Service/Controls	Electric motor services/control
	Nicholson Sawblade Product Line	Sawblades
	SPI Lighting Product Line	Indirect office lighting
1988	Hughes W-K-M Do Brazil	Valve service and repair

In 1979, Cooper made its biggest move to date, purchasing Dallas-based Gardner-Denver in what then qualified as one of the 10 largest mergers in U.S. history. A company equal in size to Cooper, Gardner-Denver manufactured machinery for petroleum exploration, mining, and general construction. Cizik described the merger, valued at $635 million, as a "complementary move," involving Cooper in natural gas and petroleum exploration for the first time, and thus filling out Cooper's existing energy division. By adding Gardner-Denver, Cooper now served a range of needs spanning exploration, production, transmission, distribution, and storage for the oil and natural gas industry, and doubled the number of employees, shareholders, and plants.

Gardner-Denver had grown rapidly in the 1960s and 1970s, but was notorious for its lack of planning and cost controls. For example, it had invested heavily in developing a blasthole drill for mining that turned out to be a "gold-plated" white elephant. It was also known as the company that cut prices at just the wrong time, and its sales force, in the words of another industry player, was "looking for nothing but payday and five o'clock."[11]

After the merger, Cizik closed Gardner's Dallas headquarters and moved its corporate functions to Cooper's Houston headquarters. Cooper believed Gardner-Denver's management structure was too centralized and stifled effective decision making at the operational level. Cooper also thought that Gardner's centralized functions were overused. Cizik appraised the situation: "If you try to combine too much under one umbrella, such as consolidating sales into a corporate function, you end up with a lot of people who can't possibly cover such a huge, diverse marketplace, or know much about the plethora of products they're trying to sell."[12] Cooper trimmed Gardner's sales and administrative expenses from the pre-acquisition 16.6 percent of revenues to Cooper's 11.4 percent level. It also cut Gardner-Denver's working capital: Cizik was convinced that inventories and receivables were too high. In a review of Gardner-Denver's products, Cizik spoke about "reclaiming" what was usable. Cooper kept product lines capable of healthy development, eliminating others with little potential.

By the late 1970s, Cooper's acquisition guidelines had evolved to include an additional dimension, acquisition by necessity. When Colorado Fuel & Iron (CF&I), a specialty supplier to Lufkin, stopped production of its 1095 steel, Cooper could find only one other source in the world, a German company offering a much more expensive product. Instead, Cooper bought the CF&I equipment and moved the operations to a newly acquired plant, forming Cooper Steel.

In 1981, as Cooper was in the process of absorbing Gardner-Denver, the company engineered its third diversification (following its move into tools and aircraft service) by capitalizing on an unexpected opportunity to acquire Crouse-Hinds. An electrical products company, Crouse-Hinds had been on Cooper's wish list for years. Subject to a hostile takeover attempt, Crouse-Hinds welcomed Cooper as a white knight, and after a prolonged, acrimonious battle, it joined Cooper on friendly terms. Equal in size to the premerger Cooper or Gardner-Denver, Crouse-Hinds became the core of Cooper's new electrical and electronic business. It was a worldwide producer of electrical plugs and receptacles, fittings, and industrial lighting, and had just acquired Belden, a well-known manufacturer of electronic wire and cable and electrical cords. Together, Crouse-Hinds and Belden increased Cooper's revenues by 50 percent and gave the company a foothold in the "path of power"—the transmission, control, and distribution of electrical energy from the generating plant to the end user.

---

[11]Flanigan, *Forbes.*
[12]Keller, *Cooper,* p. 9.

Describing the acquisition, Cizik said, "This is a true diversification, compared with what I referred to as a complementary move with Gardner-Denver. In that respect it compares to our acquisitions of Lufkin and Dallas Airmotive, except on a much larger scale."[13]

Throughout the electrical industry, Crouse-Hinds was considered one of the best managed companies. Crouse-Hind's CEO, who had joined the company in 1965, stayed on at the helm after the Cooper acquisition until he retired two years later, and Cooper assigned an experienced, younger Crouse-Hinds executive to succeed him.

Many Wall Street analysts criticized this acquisition for reducing Cooper's exposure to the booming oil and gas business. New criticisms of Cooper's ability to service its increasing debt burden were also voiced in 1981 when Cooper acquired Kirsch, the world's largest manufacturer of drapery hardware. In a similar hostile takeover attempt/white knight situation, Cooper had been forced to move quickly to acquire Kirsch, a company it had been eyeing since the 1970s. In fact, Cooper's board gave first approval to purchase Kirsch on the same day that it had closed the Crouse-Hind's deal. Commenting on the action, one investment banker said, "If Cooper had its choice, it probably would have wanted to finish one deal and then work on the other, but the world doesn't wait for you."[14] Kirsch had a customer base similar to Cooper's and employed many of the same manufacturing processes.

Closing out the busy year of 1981, Cooper sold off its airmotive division. Cooper had built its airmotive group into a "decently profitable" unit that it divested at a net profit of $27 million. During the time it was part of Cooper, the unit balanced Cooper's revenue and income stream, but by 1981, Cizik concluded that continued operation of the group conflicted with Cooper's manufacturing-oriented corporate strategy.

Following this period of heavy activity, Cooper repeated its historical pattern of concentrating on digesting recent acquisitions. Said Cizik, "A growing company can outrun its capabilities if it isn't careful to bring up the supply lines. . . .We have to restructure ourselves at a time like this, before we feel comfortable moving out again."[15]

Electricity became Cooper's next target for complementary business-unit development as energy prices slid in the mid-1980s. As one initial skeptic later commented, "I don't know whether Cooper saw the downturn in energy coming, but it eventually proved to be a wise move to diversify and reduce exposure in that area."[16] In 1985, Cooper acquired McGraw-Edison, an electrical company that was put into play by Forstmann Little & Company, a New York firm specializing in leveraged buyouts. Before Forstmann's intentions of a McGraw-Edison buyout were made public, Cizik had approached McGraw's chairman to propose a friendly merger. Cizik, however, was rebuffed; the company was not interested in pursuing a combination. After the Forstmann-McGraw announcement at $59-a-share, Cooper tendered a $65-a-share offer for McGraw-Edison that was eventually accepted.

McGraw-Edison, a leading manufacturer of products for the control and transmission of electrical power, as well as lighting fixtures and fuses, put Cooper at the first stage of electrical power distribution with its transformers, power capacitors, and other products. These connected directly, in the "path of power," to the many secondary electrical power distribution products Cooper had acquired through Crouse-Hinds (for example, circuit breakers, receptacles, and plugs). The "path of power" continued to a third level, the point of consumer use in the home or commercial area, where McGraw's recessed, emergency, and track lighting augmented Crouse-Hind's leading position in the indoor and outdoor lighting market.

---

[13]Keller, *Cooper,* p. 314.
[14]*Wall Street Transcript,* December 13, 1981.
[15]Keller, *Cooper,* p. 339.
[16]*Wall Street Transcript,* March 7, 1988, p. 88, 618.

Following the acquisition, Cooper retained most McGraw senior managers, but began streamlining and consolidating its operations and, in the process, spun off a number of incompatible divisions. Three years later, in 1988, Cooper complemented McGraw's transformer product line with the $324 million acquisition of RTE, a maker of transformers and a supplier of transformer components to Cooper.

At the time of the merger, RTE was fighting a hostile takeover by Mark IV Industries. The company was also suffering from capital constraints resulting from an unsuccessful acquisition program, and Cooper subsequently pumped over $50 million in capital expenditures into the RTE operations. Because of a culture clash with Cooper's "lean and mean" cost structure, many senior managers at RTE left within a year of the acquisition. Cooper consolidated McGraw's and RTE's R&D staffs in one facility and reduced the size of their combined sales force, while also limiting RTE's free-spending habits. In addition, Cooper consolidated computing functions so that RTE's mainframe could be shut down, and eliminated 30 to 40 financial and treasury positions. The RTE restructuring created over $10 million in annual savings for Cooper.

In late 1987, Cooper expanded its existing industrial compressor business with the $140 million purchase of Joy's industrial air and turbo compressor business. After the deal, Cooper eliminated duplicate product lines and suspended manufacture of unprofitable products. It also rationalized manufacturing operations, closing Joy's Indiana plant. Furthermore, Cooper consolidated the two companies' competing distribution channels. The total number of distributors serving the combined company was expected to fall from 160 to 120 over four to five years. However, Cooper would gain leverage with each remaining distributor because it would have a much greater sales volume and a wider product offering.

▲ COOPER'S BUSINESSES IN THE LATE 1980s

In 1988, Cooper was a broadly diversified manufacturer of electrical and general industrial products and energy-related machinery and equipment. U.S.-based Cooper had 1988 revenues of $4.3 billion and over 46,000 employees worldwide, although 85 percent of sales were in North America. The company operated in 3 distinct business segments with 21 separate profit centers (Exhibits 4, 5, 6 and 7).

Electrical and Electronic

The E&E segment was Cooper's largest in 1988, generating one-half of corporate sales and 57 percent of operating profits. Cooper had entered this segment with the 1981 purchase of Crouse-Hinds. By 1988, E&E had four subsegments, each representing quite diverse businesses (Exhibit 7), but all focused on the mature North American market that accounted for over 90 percent of segment sales.

Cooper competed in power transmission and distribution systems with its McGraw-Edison and RTE operations. About 85–90 percent of power system sales were direct to utilities, where the transformers increased and reduced the voltage and channeled the power produced by a generator. Prior to their acquisition by Cooper, McGraw and RTE were roughly tied for third place in the U.S. transformer market, behind GE and Westinghouse. Following the acquisitions, however, Cooper gained a leading market position, despite other consolidations in the industry that reduced the number of major competitors from seven to three. At the consolidated level, the division used the "Cooper Power

▲ **EXHIBIT 4 Cooper Industries' Financials ($000)**

	1988	1987	1986	1985	1984	1983	1982	1981	1980†	1975	1970
Sales	4,258,275	3,585,785	3,433,296	3,067,169	2,029,915	1,850,280	2,393,989	2,866,031	2,335,923	478,066	225,651
Cost of sales	2,904,336	2,430,183	2,301,970	2,070,992	1,357,949	1,250,359	1,642,279	1,864,738	1,555,022	346,291	164,037
Depreciation and amortization	154,650	135,368	127,131	105,815	73,636	67,909	63,816	56,598	46,282	9,571	4,280
Selling and administrative	701,859	622,643	615,943	534,471	368,376	363,101	401,878	429,207	356,749	54,848	29,477
Interest	111,922	86,075	103,080	97,723	20,572	28,460	44,202	56,712	50,320	7,439	3,924
Total costs and expenses	3,872,767	3,274,269	3,148,124	2,809,001	1,820,533	1,709,829	2,152,175	2,407,255	2,008,373	418,149	201,718
Total operating income	385,508	311,516	285,172	258,168	209,382	140,451	241,814	458,776	327,550	59,917	23,933
Income taxes	161,102	137,705	137,450	123,088	102,518	69,282	106,679	217,506	156,120	28,783	11,553
Net income	224,406	173,811	147,722	135,080	106,864	71,169	135,135	284,545*	185,216	31,134	12,380
Long-term debt	1,170,267	884,351	863,615	1,158,310	156,765	175,005	272,888	154,270	301,016	71,030	31,496
Capital expenditures	128,249	100,889	109,497	115,794	68,509	86,237	117,650	128,653	115,414	17,817	7,698
Net plant and equipment	1,115,181	1,016,647	937,741	973,235	685,548	683,318	685,067	624,230	532,025	102,843	47,227
Total assets	4,383,976	3,800,363	3,400,032	3,635,873	1,953,698	1,949,447	2,036,547	2,335,381	2,023,705	369,196	183,926
Shareholders' equity	1,771,712	1,592,912	1,419,946	1,318,001	1,240,143	1,250,649	1,265,646	1,284,899	1,076,407	177,150	100,262
Number of employees	46,300	43,200	40,200	46,000	30,000	30,000	31,000	39,000	37,000	11,262	8,247
Return on year-end assets	5.1%	4.6%	4.3%	3.7%	5.5%	3.7%	6.6%	12.2%	9.2%	8.4%	6.7%
Return on year-end equity	12.7%	10.9%	10.4%	10.2%	8.6%	5.7%	10.7%	22.1%	17.2%	17.6%	12.3%

*Includes gain on the sale of Dallas Airmotive.
†Restated to include Crouse-Hinds on a pooling of interest basis.
‡Includes income from discontinued aircraft service operations.

▲ EXHIBIT 5 Cooper Segment Financials ($000)

	1988	1987	1986	1985	1984	1983	1982	1981	1980*
Electrical and electronic									
Revenues	2,077,522	1,736,446	1,699,708	1,425,463	798,310	768,174	798,440	872,127	825,726
Operating income	307,664	264,657	259,973	225,633	126,166	105,913	90,774	109,397	95,368
Identifiable assets	1,985,361	1,521,455	1,441,857	1,426,135	435,592	430,218	428,290	449,767	439,060
Group return on sales	14.8%	15.2%	15.3%	15.8%	15.8%	13.8%	11.4%	12.5%	11.5%
Group return on assets	15.5%	17.4%	18.0%	15.8%	29.0%	24.6%	21.2%	24.3%	21.7%
Commercial and industrial									
Revenues	1,260,121	1,195,829	1,142,372	927,283	586,453	518,162	489,353	540,812	403,577
Operating income	184,318	171,143	162,675	134,146	98,798	84,581	64,945	92,340	97,518
Identifiable assets	1,006,904	985,528	990,512	1,020,648	495,310	447,390	446,977	479,986	346,318
Group return on sales	14.6%	14.3%	14.2%	14.5%	16.8%	16.3%	13.3%	17.1%	24.2%
Group return on assets	18.3%	17.4%	16.4%	13.1%	19.9%	18.9%	14.5%	19.2%	28.2%
Compression and drilling									
Revenues	912,320	642,825	564,647	691,884	642,926	556,001	1,106,836	1,447,970	1,101,206
Operating income	47,093	(4,529)	(21,865)	11,987	28,266	(4,872)	161,072	341,639	212,442
Identifiable assets	1,177,758	1,131,090	826,675	937,831	928,850	974,111	1,071,732	1,193,762	1,045,832
Group return on sales	5.2%	−0.7%	−3.9%	1.7%	4.4%	−0.9%	14.6%	23.6%	19.3%
Group return on assets	4.0%	−0.4%	−2.6%	1.3%	3.0%	−0.5%	15.0%	28.6%	20.3%

*Restated to include Crouse-Hinds on a pooling of interest basis.

▲419

▲ EXHIBIT 6   Cooper Industries' Comparative Stock Price Performance

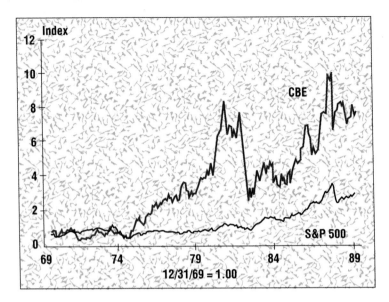

Systems" brand name because its competitors were so well-known, but each of the products maintained the McGraw or RTE brand name. Because these products were sold directly, offering a complete product line that met North American standards provided an important competitive advantage. Furthermore, Cooper's reputation for quality products helped garner sales because of the high costs associated with product failure in such vital systems.

Cooper's lighting division was composed of three formerly independent entities: Crouse-Hinds Lighting and McGraw-Edison's Halo and Metalux subsidiaries. In the mid-1980s, Cooper combined the three businesses and rationalized manufacturing facilities, adopting a focused-factory approach that allowed three underutilized plants to be closed. In 1988, Cooper was in the process of eliminating duplicate administrative functions among the companies and developing a unified market identity through consolidating sales representatives and marketing programs. Cooper also began constructing a showroom to display all of its lighting products and to train architects, designers, and lighting distributors in its full product line.

In the broad and highly fragmented lighting fixture market, Cooper was perhaps the most widely spread manufacturer, participating in fluorescent, high-intensity discharge, and incandescent fixtures. In this industry, the top eight firms had a combined 60 percent market share in 1988, but as the eighth firm represented only 2 percent of the total, the industry was characterized by a large fringe of small producers. Foreign competition was limited because the large size-to-weight ratio of lighting fixtures made transport costs prohibitive. Distributors and manufacturers tended to develop stable, long-term relationships, and, in 1988, Cooper was looking to the day when it could install paperless ordering and invoicing of all Cooper lighting products. Cooper believed that its service level and premium-priced, market-leading products would attract distributors to offer its full product line exclusively or with only one other manufacturer's products.

▲ **EXHIBIT 7** Cooper Industries' Segment Information

	Primary Products	Percent of Revenues	Market Position	Distribution Method
Electrical and Electronic				
Power systems		15		Direct sales
RTE	Transformers		Co-leader	
McGraw-Edison	Distribution switchgear		#1	
Lighting fixtures		12		Distributor
Halo	Incandesent		#2 (Tied)	
Metalux	Flourescent			
Crouse-Hinds	High intensity			
Electronic cables		8		Distributor
Belden	Wire and cable		#1	
Distribution and control		14		
Crouse-Hinds	Electric construction materials		#1	
Arrow-Hart	Distribution equipment		#2	
Bussmann, Beswick	Fuses		#1	
Subtotal		49		
Commercial and industrial				
Automotive aftermarket		10		Distributor
Wagner	Brakes		#1	
	Headlights		#1 (Aftermarket)	
Tools		14		Distributor
Campbell/Lufkin	Nonpower		#1	
Nicholson/Crescent	Hand tools			

continued

▲ EXHIBIT 7 *concluded*

	Primary Products	Percent of Revenues	Market Position	Distribution Method
Window treatments		6		
Kirsch	Drapery hardware		#1	Distributor
Subtotal		30		
Compression and drilling				
Industrial compressors		7		Distributor
Gardner-Denver/Joy	Air compressors		#2 (Tied)	
Energy equipment		13		Direct sales
Cooper Energy Services	Gas compressors		#1	
Gardner-Denver	Drilling equipment		NA	
Demco/WKM	Valves		NA	
Subtotal		20		

Source: Lovett, Mitchell, Webb & Garrison, Inc., September 20, 1989.

In the distribution and control area, Cooper dominated the market with its construction materials division (CMD), the crown jewel of Crouse-Hinds. CMD manufactured protective electrical equipment for hazardous applications. CMD's reputation was so widespread that its products were often included in engineers' design specifications because of its reputation for superior quality.

Cooper's Belden division produced wire and cable used in the electronics industry. Although the cable business was fundamentally low-tech, Belden participated in the more sophisticated end of the product range. Cooper had invested heavily in upgrading Belden's manufacturing facilities. Sales through distributors comprised 75 percent of the division's revenues; the remainder came from the OEM market.

Commercial and Industrial

In the commercial and industrial segment, Cooper participated in the nonpowered hand-tool and window treatment businesses, and in the automotive aftermarket. In the tool group, consolidation of acquisitions was completed and new manufacturing facilities constructed by 1988, and the company held the preeminent market position in most of its tool lines. Cooper's automotive division, consisted of Belden's auto-related cable business and Wagner Lighting and Wagner Brakes, acquired with McGraw-Edison. These businesses serviced the automotive aftermarket, where operating through effective distribution networks was the key to accessing the myriad small car-repair outlets. After revamping its production equipment for quick changeovers, Wagner was positioned to take advantage of Cooper's experience in managing distribution-oriented businesses.

Compression, Drilling, and Energy Equipment

The compression and drilling segment had been Cooper's largest in 1981, generating over 50 percent of revenues and over 60 percent of operating profit. However, the collapse of the energy industry in the early and mid-1980s caused sales of oil and natural gas equipment to fall precipitously. By 1988, this segment accounted for 21 percent of Cooper sales and less than 10 percent of operating income.

The size and breadth of the collapse of the energy industry induced Cooper to take drastic actions. Employment in the compression and drilling segment was reduced by half, as eight plants were closed to control costs and pare down operations. However, Cooper took advantage of the depressed prices in the petroleum industry to make acquisitions that complemented existing products lines. The acquisition of Joy's petroleum equipment business and several smaller mergers increased Cooper's participation in flow control products. Primary competition in this area came from Cameron Iron Works and FMC, while competition for the remaining production and drilling equipment was fragmented.

In the market for natural gas compression equipment, Cooper retained its number one position with the Cooper-Bessemer, Ajax, and Superior product lines. Despite a weak market, the company was optimistic about the prospects for this equipment, as the five competitors consolidated to three.

▲ CORPORATE ROLE

Cooper Industries held increasing shareholder value as a central corporate objective. Management had established a long-term earnings-per-share growth rate target of 5 percent above the rate of inflation and a return on equity objective of 12 percent on top of inflation, reflecting sustainable targets for a "superior" manufacturing company. Furthermore, Cooper targeted 40 percent as a desirable debt to total capital ratio and preferred to finance expansion with cash or convertible preferred stock. These goals were to be achieved in part through a strong corporate emphasis on cash flow; Cooper acted on the motto "cash flow is king." In particular, strong cash flow would allow Cooper to aggressively pursue its acquisition program and meet its earnings growth target. During the 1980s, internal growth generated one-half of total corporate growth, with the other 50 percent arising from acquisitions. Because of Cooper's numerous acquisitions, $1.38 billion of Cooper's total $1.77 billion in stockholders' equity represented goodwill.

A number of guidelines directed Cooper's pursuit of potential acquisitions (Exhibit 8). Cooper sought companies that had stable earnings and had proven manufacturing operations using well-known technologies. Ideally, these products were mature and filled essential needs. Additionally, Cooper looked for companies that served a broad customer base. Finally, Cooper searched for firms with high-quality products that were market leaders with widely recognized brand names. Cooper reviewed about 100 potential acquisitions annually, and signed confidentiality agreements to analyze internal documents for roughly one-half of these. While in principle Cooper would divest any business at the right price, it was not transaction-driven and was unlikely to divest the cores of the company. Cooper discouraged management bids on divisional sell-offs.

In 1988, Cooper derived 16 percent (reaching as high as 20 percent during the previous decade) of its revenues from overseas operations, although almost all of its manufacturing operations were located in the United States. Each of Cooper's divisions had a global responsibility for its operations. Cizik was a strong advocate of improving manufacturing efficiency in the United States, believing that high volume, a cooperative and involved workforce, and technological advantages in the United States were adequate to compete with overseas producers. Consequently, he believed that investing outside the United States was unnecessary if its sole purpose was to achieve lower manufacturing costs.

With each acquisition, Cooper tailored its structure to suit the new configuration of businesses. Management sought to weld synergistic business units under the responsibility of one individual. Therefore, when new companies were acquired, Cooper typically broke them up and combined the pieces with other Cooper divisions to minimize both product transfers between divisions as well as resources shared among business units. Breaking up newly acquired businesses also allowed Cooper to closely examine their parts. For example, when Cooper acquired Wagner Brakes with McGraw-Edison, it separated the brake operations from the automotive lighting business so that it could focus on production difficulties. Only after the problems were ameliorated through manufacturing improvements did Cooper consider reconsolidating the division.

Continuing with its original decentralized operating philosophy, Cooper exercised central control over corporate policy but delegated day-to-day operating decisions to the "semi-autonomous" operating units. Each of the three executive vice presidents (EVPs) was entitled to a staff of one assistant and one secretary, and division heads had no formal relationships with each other. In 1988, Cooper maintained a total corporate staff of 317 that occupied four floors of a Houston office building, and had total corporate expenses of $50 million. Politics played a negligible role at the company and decisions were made quickly. Despite Cooper's decentralized operating philosophy, however, Cizik stressed that "Cooper puts a great deal of emphasis on control—control that's achieved by working as an operating company, not a holding company. To us that means that we just don't buy and sell businesses; we're actively involved in running them. Our corporate management team par-

▲ EXHIBIT 8   Cooper Industries' Acquisition Guidelines

For diversifications:

- Seek acquisitions that exhibit stable earnings or earning patterns that are countercyclical to those we already have.

- Acquire products that serve basic and essential needs and that are derived from proven technologies, thereby contributing to the objective of operating in stable markets with predictable growth.

- Acquire manufacturing companies with products that are of high quality and that are leaders in their markets.

For complementary products:

- Broaden existing product lines.
- Offer opportunities for enhanced earnings through cost management.
- Enhance Cooper's strength in distribution.
- Strengthen a business unit's market position.
- Enjoy widespread brand-name recognition.
- Serve a broad customer base.

Source: Cooper Industries' Management Philosophy.

---

ticipates in every policy decision made in our organization. But at the same time, day-to-day questions are answered at the operational level, and those operations are also heavily involved in determining their own future direction."[17]

Cooper's three senior vice presidents oversaw administrative, financial, and manufacturing consulting functions that were conducted at the corporate level, and they dealt directly with division managers (Exhibit 9). Each division focused primarily on operations. The CEO was removed from daily operating decisions and concentrated on developing the corporate strategy, appraising management performance, and evaluating potential acquisitions and asset dispositions.

Senior Vice President of Finance

Dewain Cross, senior VP of finance, and his department had responsibility for implementing and monitoring corporate standard accounting and control functions at all the divisions. One member of the corporate finance staff tracked each division in detail and was responsible for understanding its financial reports. Corporate finance also had an internal audit staff and a four-person team of manufacturing cost systems experts who were available at the request of division management.

Following acquisitions, Cooper set up reserves to cover anticipated closing costs involved in rationalization. This ensured that division managers incurred no write-offs on their monthly profit and loss statements as they went through the rationalization process. Also, within 30 days after every acquisition, Cooper began to install its own financial and

[17]*Wall Street Transcript,* May 31, 1982, pp. 65, 989.

▲ **EXHIBIT 9** Corporate Organizational Structure, 1988

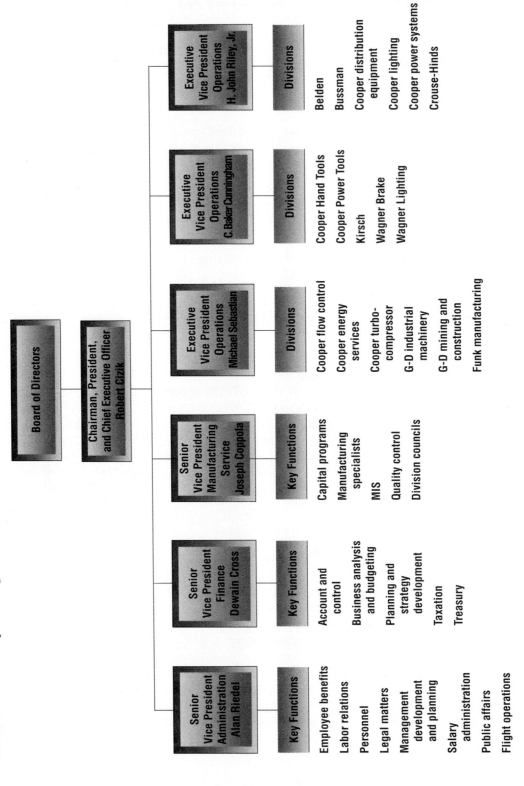

Board of Directors

Chairman, President, and Chief Executive Officer
Robert Cizik

Senior Vice President Administration
Alan Riedel

Key Functions

Employee benefits

Labor relations

Personnel

Legal matters

Management development and planning

Salary administration

Public affairs

Flight operations

Senior Vice President Finance
Dewain Cross

Key Functions

Account and control

Business analysis and budgeting

Planning and strategy development

Taxation

Treasury

Senior Vice President Manufacturing Service
Joseph Coppola

Key Functions

Capital programs

Manufacturing specialists

MIS

Quality control

Division councils

Executive Vice President Operations
Michael Sebastian

Divisions

Cooper flow control

Cooper energy services

Cooper turbo-compressor

G-D industrial machinery

G-D mining and construction

Funk manufacturing

Executive Vice President Operations
C. Baker Cunningham

Divisions

Cooper Hand Tools

Cooper Power Tools

Kirsch

Wagner Brake

Wagner Lighting

Executive Vice President Operations
H. John Riley, Jr.

Divisions

Belden

Bussman

Cooper distribution equipment

Cooper lighting

Cooper power systems

Crouse-Hinds

cost accounting systems on an IBM. As Cross said, "There are only two times to change a business. One is right after you buy it. The second is when it is losing a lot of money. These are the two times when there is the least resistance to change."

All divisions were required to submit Cooper's standard monthly financial report (approximately 150 line items) to corporate headquarters, but they had discretion over how to keep their internal ledgers. Cooper used direct variable cost accounting rather than a full cost absorption system. It also had a large set of internal control guidelines that each division had to follow, such as the number of people required to sign a check above a specified dollar value. Indeed, Cooper's two books of procedures were bigger than its accounting manual.

Because Cooper was extremely cash-conscious, the austerity of Cooper's financial control systems often collided with the systems in place under previous managers. This meant that incumbent managers often left following a Cooper acquisition because they were unable to adjust to the new culture. Cooper tightly controlled working capital and charged divisions interest for its use, although there were no corporate overhead charges or charges for corporate services to divisions. The finance department had central control over treasury and taxation functions so that all divisions effectively maintained a zero-dollar balance in their accounts.

Cross also set guidelines for developing the business-unit strategies that each of the 21 Cooper divisions prepared every three years. Cooper's strategic planning approach was bottom-up: Each profit center developed its own plan under the guidance of its EVP, assisted by Cross's corporate planning and development group, comprised of a staff of seven MBAs. Headquarters was, however, actively involved in strategic planning and all plans had to be presented to and accepted by Cizik and the corporate staff, often after many suggestions and improvements. Cooper only occasionally used outside consultants. In any given year, 7 of the 21 divisions prepared a plan, with new acquisitions formulating their first strategic plan in the year following their acquisition. These comprehensive analyses identified the market, projected market demand, presented an industry overview, and identified types of companies viewed to be desirable acquisition candidates. Separate strategies were developed for each major product line within a division. They elucidated the business unit's view of the competitive situation and outlined strategic options and reasons for the strategies chosen.

Cross, along with the appropriate EVP, also reviewed the annual budget for each division. The annual budgeting process enabled the corporate officers and division managers to agree on short-term performance objectives for each division.

Senior Vice President of Administration

Attorney Alan Riedel, Cooper's senior VP of administration, was the only director inside Cooper besides Cizik. Riedel had as his foremost responsibilities managing the company's legal affairs and establishing and administering personnel policy and benefits programs. He also handled labor relations, shareholder and public relations, and environmental matters, and oversaw the management development and planning (MD&P) program. Cooper maintained a uniform pay scale based on the Hay system. Base salaries throughout the company were similar for employees of corresponding ranks in different divisions, and all were competitive with industry standards. However, bonuses often reached 20–40 percent of base salaries, and were discretionary; division managers had a bonus pool determined by corporate administration that could be awarded largely at their and the EVP's discretion. In addition to salary and bonuses, key managers were granted stock options. With each new acquisition, Riedel's office gradually adjusted pay scales at the acquired division up or down until they reached Cooper's targeted level, with the adjustments taking three to five years. Typically, however, these adjustments were small as pay scales in the industries Cooper participated in tended to be homogeneous. Cooper also required all acquisitions to adopt its standard benefits package for medical insurance and pensions, which could lead to dissatisfaction because it was sometimes conservative relative to the benefits package of the premerger company.

Cooper handled labor relations at the corporate level. Half of Cooper's plants were nonunion; the company maintained a strong union-avoidance policy. Contract renewal and National Labor Relations Board matters were handled by the labor relations staff. Riedel handled antitrust matters, an area particularly important because of Cooper's active acquisition program.

Management development and planning, initiated in 1970, was integral to Cooper's management system. MD&P evaluated organizational effectiveness and individual strengths and weaknesses by focusing on the performance of key managers. Under the program, about 800 division and corporate executives and manager developed qualitative professional development or project-related goals for the forthcoming year. Quantitative goals often reinforced business-unit objectives that were established through the annual budgeting and strategic planning processes. At the end of the year, each employee prepared a progress review worksheet that compared achieved to targeted objectives. Additionally, employees in the program were reviewed by their supervisors. For example, as CEO, Cizik met annually with each executive vice president to review his personal progress, the managerial capabilities in his segment, and the details of necessary future improvements. The objectives for the EVP in the upcoming year, mutually determined at that meeting, became, in Riedel's words, "the road map for action items that are to occur during the year." Similarly, each EVP conducted annual reviews of all of the managers in the division he supervised. While review results were not formally tied to incentive compensation, managers with poor reviews were unlikely to receive substantial bonuses.

Each EVP and senior VP fully embraced MD&P, even though it was extremely time consuming. Cizik noted that "everybody hates the MD&P because it is so much work, but when it is done everyone loves it." The program uncovered existing or potential management gaps and identified people worthy of promotion: it was the method that Cooper used to determine management succession. In addition, the program distinguished candidates for interdivisional transfers, which generally occurred at the higher echelons of the organization; 24 such transfers were made in 1988. Cooper preferred to bring in one of its own people as general manager or controller of a new division, and typically had many personnel requirements in the finance and plant manager areas following an acquisition. MD&P developed an internal pool of people in these areas that could be moved around, but a lack of a sufficient number of such people was often the constraint on further acquisitions. Internal transfers were less frequent in the marketing and sales areas where experience was believed to be business specific. Also, MD&P identified managers who would benefit from corporate-developed management training programs, with courses such as "finance for nonfinancial managers."

Senior Vice President of Manufacturing Services

In 1975, Robert Cizik formed a corporate-level manufacturing services group, chartered to institute manufacturing improvements throughout the company's operating divisions. Cizik felt that "the problem with U.S. manufacturing [was] manufacturing itself."

He promoted Joe Coppola, an operating manager with an engineering background, to lead the new manufacturing group.

In 1988, the manufacturing services group consisted of 14 professionals, all with 10 to 15 years of operations experience, and had an operating budget of $1.8 million. Its staff included experts in facilities, automation, and environmental engineering, and in materials management, quality control, and management information systems. The group had four major objectives: to promote major manufacturing improvements to reach the point of "best value delivered" for the products in each segment; to administer the $200 million 1988 capital expenditure budget; to operate interdivisional councils focused on such aspects of operations as quality control; and, with Riedel's personnel department, to run a manufacturing training program for recent engineering school graduates. The group also published guides on manufacturing issues for the divisions.

The manufacturing services group used benchmarking and cross-referencing to improve production methods and had a bifurcated strategy for introducing the manufacturing improvements. In the case of new acquisitions, the group simply stepped in and worked with EVPs and their operating managers to improve plant efficiency and to transfer Cooper's manufacturing know-how and processes to the new division. In almost every acquisition, Cooper considered the majority of the plants to require production improvements. In contrast, in keeping with Cooper's philosophy, the group maintained a strict policy of never entering an old Cooper division unless they were invited by division managers. There was no charge for their services. Once requested, the group used a three-tiered approach to implementing improvements, acting as a catalyst for change. The first stage was conceptual: the engineering department, assisted by local personnel, determined the ideal configuration for the factory. The process stage followed, designed to show current employees how the new methods would be more efficient than the old ones. This stage typically involved reconfiguring the machinery in the plant for cell rather than batch production. The process stage was heavily communicative: its primary goal was to inculcate factory workers into the new production process, convincing them of its superior efficiency, and would often take two to three years. The final step was the technological stage, during which the group introduced new machinery and technology into the factory. The group spent about 60 percent of its time on acquisitions and 40 percent on existing Cooper divisions.

At all stages of the manufacturing improvement process, the group relied heavily on the participation of local personnel, attempting to give them ownership of the project. The group generally coordinated and directed the three stages, but division employees implemented the changes. Bill Brewer, president of Cooper Power Systems, said of the group, "One of the greatest aspects of Coppola's group is that they are viewed as an extension of our organization. They are constantly called on and are available for concepts and opinions. They have a broader perspective than any one plant can have, and are therefore able to broker success and failure throughout the company."

Coppola's group administered capital expenditures. The capital budget for each division was reached after balancing division requests with available funds and was made consistent with division strategies. Cizik was often involved in the capital budgeting process, making suggestions and amendments to proposals. Corporate headquarters supported all capital and personnel needs that were required to meet division strategies, which often involved sizable investments in newly acquired companies to improve their manufacturing capabilities. Division managers could authorize expenditures up to $100,000; an EVP's approval was needed for expenditures above $100,000; Cizik's signature was required for all projects over $1 million; and the board of directors approved all investments over $5 million.

The manufacturing services group also ran quality, purchasing, traffic, environmental, plant engineering, and technology councils that met four times annually. Each council typically had 12 members, each representing a different operating division, who rotated on an annual basis. For example, in 1984, Cooper established the purchasing council, which soon discovered that some divisions were purchasing steel from the same supplier at different prices. The council then negotiated advantageous prices with various steel companies for all Cooper divisions (Cooper purchased over $100 million of steel annually). In similar instances, the councils allowed managers from different divisions to share information and insights, which helped maximize Cooper's leverage in negotiating with suppliers and vendors.

Finally, the group oversaw a manufacturing training program for entry-level engineering graduates. In 1988, Cooper recruited 16 graduates, primarily from 12 "preferred" midwestern universities. The two-year program consisted of four intensive six-month job rotations; each participant was required to work in at least three of Cooper's four manufacturing subfunctions, as well as to hold a foreman's job. Program graduates were offered supervisory positions, or assignments leading to supervisory and managerial positions.

Executive Vice President of Operations

Each of Cooper's three EVPs headed a worldwide operating segment. Describing his job, H. John Riley, Jr., EVP of the electrical and electronics division, said "Cizik invests a lot of authority in our hands. Each of us functions in a capacity similar to that of the typical chief operating officer. This is what makes the system work." Cooper's EVPs served four major functions. They handled organizational and administrative matters, including selecting key division managers, conducting personnel reviews under the MD&P program, and prioritizing tasks. They also approved all capital expenditures up to $1 million. Second, they worked with the senior VP of finance and division managers to develop the three-year business-unit strategic plans. Likewise they performed strategic planning and analysis at the segment level: they set the long-term strategies for the business segment, and attempted to balance short-term performance with long-term strategic objectives. Third, EVPs located and analyzed potential acquisitions that complemented their segments. As soon as Cooper engineered a complementary acquisition, the appropriate EVP would spend a considerable amount of time on "Cooperizing" the new operating unit. Welding the acquisition with a Cooper division generally required that he make multiple visits to plants and distribution facilities, overseeing the transition while Cooper installed its management systems and culture. EVPs spent approximately 50 percent to 60 percent of their time in the field.

Finally, the EVPs regularly reviewed financial statements, annual budgets, and quarterly forecasts. They received monthly financial statements from each division, which allowed them to roughly compare actual to budgeted performance. EVPs did not focus on any single measure in evaluating a division's performance, but looked at all financial data that would indicate if the strategy was on course, such as sales, profitability, growth, cash flow, and return on assets. These financial data were supplemented with operating data, including order rates, which served as indicators of the level of product demand for the upcoming period, and first-pass line fill, or service-level data, which provided information on the number of orders that could be filled from stock. In many of Cooper's businesses, the ability to immediately fill orders was important for effective distribution, and Cooper maintained first-pass fill targets of 95 percent to 98 percent of orders.

Each EVP had a general management background and had risen through a division within his operating segment. For example, Michael Sebastian, EVP of compression and drilling, was a group manager at Gardner-Denver and joined Cooper when Gardner was acquired. He rose to the EVP position by 1981. Similarly, Riley joined Crouse-Hinds in 1963, became a division head of Crouse-Hinds in 1972, and then was promoted to EVP of Cooper in 1982. Cunningham rose through the tool group to head the commercial and industrial products division.

Except during the Cooperization process, EVPs had a management-by-exception philosophy, seldom intervening in routine division management unless a division suffered prolonged, unsatisfactory performance or violated the boundaries set during the strategic planning process. However, each EVP maintained an ongoing dialogue with his division managers and encouraged them to be up front with problems. Conversations were initiated by either party. In addition to reviews of monthly financial performance, EVPs also advised division managers on resolving particularly difficult operating situations. If unsatisfactory performance continued unattended for a quarter, an EVP would probably request a meeting with division managers to question the methods they had planned to improve the situation. At all times the discussion focused on the steps necessary to comply with the strategy rather than on assigning blame for poor performance. Division managers valued the knowledge, understanding, and support of the EVPs, whom they viewed as extensions of the divisions. Only after extended poor performance would an EVP take direct corrective action.

Chairman, President, and CEO

As chairman, president, and CEO, Robert Cizik developed Cooper's corporate strategy. Initially, his idea that Cooper adopt a manufacturing focus met some resistance. He noted, "I had to argue for five or six years about being a manufacturing company before the others finally accepted it." In 1988, Cizik, Riedel, Cross, and Cunningham had been at Cooper for about 20 years over which time they had developed a team approach, centered on Cizik's strategic vision. At headquarters, Cizik, the three EVPs and the three senior VPs had offices near each other and often met informally to apply their collective talents to problems.

Cizik approved all acquisitions and took charge of investor relations. "Cooper" was used as a brand name only on Wall Street, where Cizik closely interacted with investors and analysts. Cizik was approached by many investment bankers and personally reviewed many of Cooper's acquisition candidates. In particular, he focused on diversifying acquisitions. Because Cooper had few decision makers, the company was able to act quickly on acquisitions, opportunistically undertaking purchases, such as the Kirsch and Crouse-Hinds mergers.

At Cooper, each of the three operating segments had little physical interaction with the other two: divisions in different segments rarely supplied each other, and Cooper did not have a transfer pricing policy. However, if a division in the commercial and industrial segment was building a new plant, for example, it would be expected to purchase Cooper lighting products and construction material. If disputes developed between the divisions about these transactions, Cizik would ask the EVPs of the two operating segments to resolve the conflict.

As CEO, Cizik was not involved in day-to-day operations. His biggest regret was that he no longer had time to visit each plant annually. However, he was always available if a serious problem developed at the operational level, and a telephone conversation with a division manager would bring him up o date on the division's progress. Cizik's involvement with each division became more visionary: his role was to push the frontiers, for example, suggesting to divisions that they expand into Europe. His strategic concepts, such as maintaining "strong brand image," provided focus for divisions. Said Bill Brewer, "Cizik is a very lively participant in the strategy meetings. He makes excellent, directed comments and has a keen sense of the potential of a proposed strategy for success."

Cizik spent an average of 12 days a year on the MD&P process. His participation was essential: he reviewed each EVP and senior VP and their organizations and scrutinized the minutes from the divisional MD&P meetings. He also conducted probing, all-day reviews with each EVP and pushed managers to make difficult personnel decisions under MD&P.

▲ CHAMPION

In January 1989, Champion agreed to a "sweetheart" sale of the company to Dana for $17.50. Dana was a $4.9 billion, Toledo-based manufacturer of power transmission equipment for the automotive original equipment market. At the time of the Dana-Champion announcement, Chinook Partners L.P., a partnership formed by descendants of Champion's founding family, held 35 percent of Champion's stock. The partnership objected to the proposed Dana merger, referring to it as a deal done at "the Toledo Country Club." According to *Business Week,* three weeks after the Dana bid, Cooper "crashed the party" with a $21-a-share tender offer.

At the time of the takeover battle, Champion principally manufactured spark plugs and windshield wipers and derived most of its revenues from sales to spare-parts distributors (Exhibit 10). In early 1989, it had a brand name that was recognized worldwide and was a market leader in spark plugs and wipers (35 percent of Champion's sales were overseas). However, motivated by declines in the spark plug market, Champion had attempted to leverage its internationally recognized brand name by expanding into other automotive product lines. In the most extreme case, the company proposed to penetrate the automotive tool business, although Snap-On, MAC, and Matco had a combined market share of 92 percent. In addition, Champion began licensing its brand name as well as putting it on bought-in parts. These new ventures required significant management and capital outlays, and after a short period of time, most proved unprofitable.

Champion's capital expenditures from 1975 to 1988 were 2 percent of sales, and its overall operating margin was 4.7 percent for 1988. Its U.S. division suffered an operating loss of $6.4 million in 1988, however its Asian-African and European divisions had operating margins of 13.7 percent and 11.6 percent, respectively. *Forbes* described Champion as a "bloated auto parts maker" that, according to industry sources, was manufacturing with 1950s technology. The company had swollen corporate overhead expenses that included the operation of its own fleet of jets.

At the time of the tender offer, Cooper was also considering a $700 million bid for Cameron Iron Works, which manufactured petroleum and natural gas-related equipment, including valves and technically advanced forged products. These product lines would complement Cooper's compression and drilling segment. However, undertaking both acquisitions was likely to send Cooper's debt to total capitalization ratio to the 55 percent to 60 percent range, and Cooper was aware of the risks of attempting both deals. Cizik realized that, in addition to the financial risks, purchasing either or both companies would have profound operational and organizational ramifications for Cooper Industries.

▲ EXHIBIT 10   Champion Spark Plug Financials ($000)

	Dec. 88	Dec. 87	Dec. 86	Dec. 85	Dec. 84	Dec. 83	Dec. 82	Dec. 81	Dec. 80
Sales	738,000	719,900	883,800	829,400	816,500	764,400	783,700	818,600	799,800
Selling, general, and administrative expense	189,600	187,200	213,800	194,200	183,800	178,400	171,900	185,400	190,600
Net income	23,600	19,100	(17,200)	15,200	27,300	27,000	26,800	30,300	36,900
Earnings per share	0.670	0.500	−0.450	0.400	0.710	0.700	0.700	0.790	0.960
Dividends	0.200	0.050	0.200	0.400	0.400	0.400	0.800	0.800	0.800
Total current assets	375,800	462,500	436,700	443,300	398,000	387,200	394,000	421,500	428,100
Net plant, property and equipment	185,500	177,100	194,800	177,800	163,500	163,900	173,400	178,400	181,300
Total assets	575,600	653,000	647,700	640,800	579,300	571,700	590,900	626,000	636,200
Total current liabilities	170,300	202,900	236,100	211,600	165,800	161,000	176,700	183,800	162,900
Long-term debt	13,900	17,500	23,500	29,700	26,000	22,300	23,300	31,400	41,400
Total equity	349,900	387,400	351,800	368,700	359,400	359,500	361,100	384,300	405,900

▲ 433

ASAHI GLASS COMPANY: DIVERSIFICATION STRATEGY

Asahi Glass Company (Asahi Glass), founded in 1907, was the oldest and largest glass manufacturer in Japan and a prominent member of the prestigious Mitsubishi group. After establishing a leading position in the domestic glass industry, the company gradually expanded its range of businesses and its geographic scope through internal growth, acquisitions, and joint ventures. By 1992, Asahi Glass had become a multibusiness, multinational company with consolidated sales exceeding ¥1.3 trillion ($10.5 billion), of which 23 percent were outside Japan (Exhibit 1).

President Hiromichi Seya and other top management of Asahi Glass believed that the company was at a critical juncture in 1993. Adversely affected by Japan's recession, the company's sales had leveled off and net income had dropped in the previous three years. More fundamentally, the company faced a number of vital issues. Its original domestic glass business had matured, while the rapid globalization of its activities into Europe and North America challenged its management practices. The company's diversification into electronics-related business had not met expectations. In the meantime, other opportunities such as "new glass" were appearing on the horizon. In order to continue its pattern of profitable growth into the 21st century, top management had to plan Asahi Glass's future diversification path carefully.

Doctoral candidate Tomo Noda prepared this case under the supervision of Professor David J. Collis.
Copyright © 1994 by the President and Fellows of Harvard College.

▲ EXHIBIT 1 Asahi Glass Company Financial Summary

	Millions of Yen										Millions of Dollars†
	1992	1991	1990	1989	1988	1987	1986	1980	1975	1970†	1992
Consolidated											
Net sales	1,316,789	1,248,083	1,233,908	1,093,033	986,983	862,531	836,446	471,875	241,804	137,393	10,534
Glass and related	739,911	675,191	677,544	579,137	542,543	482,541	479,106	268,936	140,809	94,001	5,919
Chemical	390,139	382,143	371,483†	358,149	313,068	270,272	266,768	177,37	89,559	35,948	3,121
Ceramics and refractories	31,044	32,309	32,199	26,892	22,205	23,585	23,978	17,981	11,433	7,445	248
Electronics	74,155	80,333	80,930	61,545	49,944	36,169	36,230				593
Others	81,540	78,107	71,752	68,310	58,683	49,964	30,364	7,619			652
Gross profit	229,414	246,695	241,836	244,172	215,227	188,504	172,415	111,159	51,377	42,051	1,835
Selling, general, administration	180,492	175,764	164,025	140,208	125,352	116,082	113,990	64,076	40,552	24,409	1,434
Operating income	48,992	21,372	24,498	23,033	13,045	10,231	7,888	47,083	10,825	17,641	391
Income before income tax	49,646	72,895	91,726	115,796	98,203	76,9698	60,954	43,354	1,198	15,228	397
Net income	24,269	37,672	46,864	59,094	46,083	34,928	28,8322	23,254	5,778	10,028	194
Cash	5,689	7,942	4,765	5,619	27,272	3,586	10,253	NA	NA	NA	130
Total assets	1,515,626	1,447,824	1,216,142	1,226,638	1,020,377	932,308	822,961	456,520	366,197	183,751	12,125
Long-term debt	244,488	295,730	193,420	202,361	155,732	142,462	108,296	31,333	112,404	32,029	1,956
Shareholders' equity	596,709	584,930	557,645	515,307	450,692	393,475	328,393	183,878	101,317	67,806	4,774
Return on sales (%)	1.8	3.0	3.8	5.4	4.7	4.0	3.4	4.9	2.4	7.3	1.8
Return on assets (%)	1.6	2.6	3.6	4.8	4.5	3.7	3.5	5.1	1.6	5.5	1.6
Return on equity (%)	4.1	6.4	8.4	11.5	10.2	8.9	8.8	12.6	5.7	14.8	4.1
Nonconsolidated											
Sales	1,011,815	1,022,064	1,018,085	925,931	834,421	721,234	703,408	471,875	241,804	137,393	8,095
Net income	20,484	37,004	40,536	45,076	42,055	32,518	26,389	23,254	5,778	10,028	164
Research and development††	25,475	25,530	26,893	22,893	17,671	15,608	15,174	6,350	3,210	1,745	204

*Numbers for 1970 through 1980 were on a nonconsolidated basis.
†Exchange rate: ¥125/$.
††Consolidated R&D expenditure data was not available.
Source: Asahi Glass Company

▲ 435

▲ COMPANY HISTORY

From Start-Up to World War II

Asahi Glass Company was established by Toshiya Iwasaki, a former chemistry student and nephew of the founder of the Mitsubishi business group (Exhibit 2). Strongly committed to contributing to Japan's industrial success, Iwasaki set himself the goal of establishing a domestic flat (or sheet) glass industry in order to reduce Japan's reliance on imports. Although others, including the government, had failed to manufacture glass commercially, Iwasaki's "pioneer spirit" and "mission to succeed" took on the challenge, and left a lasting legacy in the corporate culture. Having imported the technology, skilled craftsmen, and raw materials from Belgium, Asahi began sheet glass production in 1909. It became Japan's first successful sheet glass manufacturer when in 1912 it made its first profit, a feat not replicated by a competitor until 1920, when a start-up by the Sumitomo group succeeded in the mass production of sheet glass, licensing technology from America. Asahi Glass thus established a dominant position in the domestic market.

Because Japan's economy was still in its infancy, Asahi Glass relied heavily on European soda ash and refractory bricks. When difficulties importing these raw materials arose during the First World War, Asahi Glass began making them in-house. The company later began selling refractory bricks and soda ash to other high-heat furnace users such as steel and cement producers and to chemical companies, respectively. Later, in order to exploit scope economies in raw material usage, Asahi Glass began using raw salt to produce caustic soda (an alkali) in addition to soda ash (Exhibit 3). Therefore, although the vast majority of its revenue still came from glass, Asahi Glass developed technological expertise in ceramics and alkali chemicals.

From World War II to the Oil Crises

As the Japanese economy recovered following World War II and then grew rapidly during the 1950s and 1960s, demand for glass and other construction materials exploded. Since Asahi Glass's three domestic glass plants had survived the war, the company was well positioned to exploit the boom in demand. Indeed the major strategic problem during this period was ensuring that the factories could produce sufficient volume of high-quality output to meet demand. The rapid growth of the market attracted a new entrant, supported by the Mitsui group, in 1958. A "triopoly" then emerged in the domestic flat glass market, with Asahi Glass as the leader.

Flat glass technology changed dramatically in the late 1950s when Pilkington Brothers, a major U.K. glass manufacturer, invented the float glass process. This revolutionary technology involved floating molten glass over the surface of molten tin and annealing it into a strip of sheet glass. Gravity, acting on the upper surfaces of both the tin and the glass, ensured that both sides of the sheet were perfectly flat (Exhibit 4). Because of its technological superiority, all the major glass manufacturers in the world, including Asahi Glass, licensed the float process from Pilkington to preserve their market positions.

The fast-growing television set and automobile industries also boosted postwar demand for glass in Japan. Licensing technologies from Corning Glass Works, Asahi Glass started the production of TV glass bulbs in 1954. It then entered the fabricated automobile (safety) glass business in 1956 drawing on its own technological expertise. By the end of the 1960s, Asahi Glass established the leading domestic position in these two markets.

▲ EXHIBIT 2   Chronological History of Asahi Glass Company

1907	Founded by Toshiya Iwasaki.
1909	Started production of sheet glass for the first time in Japan.
1916	Started production of refractory bricks for in-house use.
1917	Started production of soda ash to provide a raw material for glass.
1932	Started production of caustic soda.
1954	Started production of glass bulbs for TV tubes.
1956	Established Indo-Asahi Glass Co., Ltd. (first overseas entry after WWII).
	Founded Asahi Fiber Glass Co., Ltd. with Owens-Corning Fiber Glass Corp.
	Started automotive fabricated glass operation.
1961	Started production of propylene oxide and propylene glycol (first entry into organic chemical business).
1964	Started production of fluorinated hydrocarbons.
1966	Introduced float glass process from Pilkington Brothers in the U.K.
	Entered into an agency marketing contract with Corning Glass Works Co., Ltd. to sell imported ICs (first entry into electronics-related business).
1972	Established P.T. Asahimas Flat Glass Co., Ltd. in Indonesia.
	Developed fluorinated resin.
1973	Introduced GRC technology from Pilkington Brothers in U.K.
1974	Developed glass delay line in response to request from domestic electric makers.
1975	Developed ion-exchange membranes and chlor alkali process to produce caustic soda.
1976	Established Optrex Corp. with Mitsubishi Electric Co. and started sales and production of liquid crystal displays.
1980	Developed structural ceramics.
1981	Made equity participation in Glaverbel in Belgium and MaasGlas in Holland.
1982	Started full-scale marketing or ophthalmic lenses, frames, and equipment.
1984	Made equity participation in Nippon Carbide Co., Ltd. and ELNA Co., Ltd.
1985	Founded Electronic Products Development Center.
1986	Established Asahi Glass Building Materials to expand building material business.
1987	Founded Asahi Komag Co., Ltd. (a joint venture with Komag of the United States) to manufacture thin-film magnetic disks in Japan.
1988	Established sales companies for sheet glass and building materials in Los Angeles and Hong Kong.
	Established Corning-Asahi Video Products, a joint venture that took over Corning's U.S. facilities for manufacturing TV glass bulbs.
1990	Established Tenneco Soda Ash Joint Venture with Tenneco Minerals to produce natural soda ash in the United States.
	Made equity participation in Splintex and established AS Technology S.A. in Belgium to set up automotive safety glass production capability in Europe.
1990–91	Made equity participation in Glaverbec Inc. in Canada, and Glav-Unionin Czechoslovakia through Glaverbel.
1992	Announced the acquisition of the remaining interests of AFG Industries.

Source: Asahi Glass Company.

▲ EXHIBIT 3   Derivation of Chemical Products

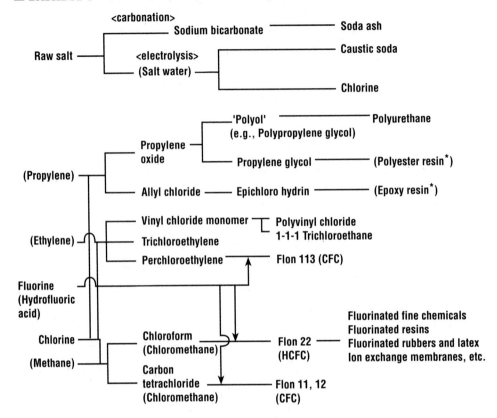

*Asahi Glass did not manufacture polyester resin and epoxy resin itself.
Source: Asahi Glass Company with addition and modification by the author.

▲ EXHIBIT 4   Float Glass Process

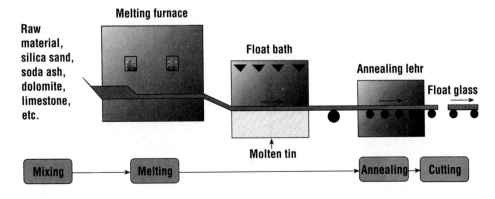

Source: Asahi Glass Company.

In the meantime, searching for additional high-volume opportunities, the company entered into other glass-related businesses. It relied on a Japanese engineer who was sent to live in the United States to gather information. In 1956, it set up a joint venture with Owens-Corning Fiber Glass Corp. to start the production of glass fiber in Japan. In 1964, the company strengthened its borosilicate-glass business (for automobile headlight glass, laboratory ware, and heat-resistant glass houseware) by inviting the equity participation of Corning Glass Works in its subsidiary, Iwaki Glass, in return for Corning's technology.

Asahi Glass also entered the construction materials business. The company already had a strong brand identity within the construction industry, and its wholesalers dealt directly with many builders. Licensing technology from a Swedish firm, Asahi Glass began producing and marketing ALC (autocraved lightweight cement) in Japan in 1962. In 1973, it started the production of GRC (Glass-reinforced cement) with technology licensed from Pilkington Brothers.

Like its glass business, Asahi Glass's chemical business rapidly added new products and market after the war. Because of the existence within the Mitsubishi group of Mitsubishi Kasei, which produced organic chemicals, Asahi Glass initially stuck to alkali and other inorganic chemicals. When a petrochemical industry emerged in Japan in the late 1950s, the company also eschewed becoming a producer of basic petrochemicals such as ethylene and propylene to avoid competition with Mitsubishi Petrochemical. Instead, Asahi Glass focused on alkalis and halogen elements (fluorine, chlorine, bromine, and iodine) as well as their petrochemical additives.

After WWII, Asahi Glass began producing caustic soda using a mercury electrode to perform electrolysis on salt water. Electrolysis not only produced very pure caustic soda, it also yielded chlorine as a by-product (Exhibit 3). Combining chlorine with basic petrochemicals, Asahi Glass started the production of propylene oxide and propylene glycol in 1961, and then established a joint venture with PPG Industries to produce vinyl chloride monomers and chlorinated solvents in 1966. Combining chlorine with natural gas (methane) available near its caustic soda factory, Asahi Glass also began producing chloromethane, which was then used to move into the production of higher value-added chlorofluorocarbons (CFCs). Having developed new applications and new markets for its products, Asahi Glass became a leader in a number of specialty product markets and secured a unique position in the domestic chemical industry.

Throughout this period, Asahi Glass set growth as it primary objective. Top management allowed the divisions to explore new product and geographic market opportunities on the basis of their technological expertise, without obligation to adhere to a given strategic direction.

From the Oil Crises through the Early 1990s

By the early 1970s, Asahi Glass's glass and construction materials business accounted for more than 50 percent of total revenue, and the chemical business for about 40 percent. Although revenue growth had fallen short of management's expectations, profits, which mostly came from the company's leading position in the domestic flat glass market and several niche chemical markets, averaged three times those of the Japanese manufacturing industry.

The two oil crises in the 1970s, however, cast a shadow on the future of the company. As the Japanese economy shifted into a more modest expansion phase, the growth of its basic materials businesses slowed (Exhibit 5). Concerned about this trend, then-president Takeo Sakabe decided in the mid-1970s to begin building an electronics business as the company's "fourth pillar" following glass, chemicals, and ceramics.

▲ EXHIBIT 5   Development of the Japanese Glass Industry

A. Production Trend of Float and Sheet Glass*

(units: 1,000 converted cases†)

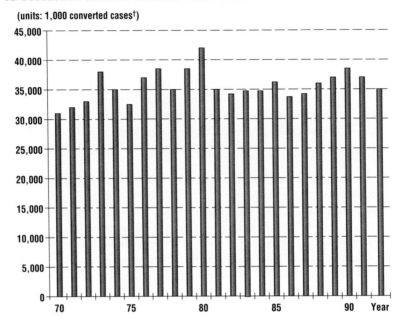

B. Production Trend of Safety Glass††

(units: 1,000 square meters)

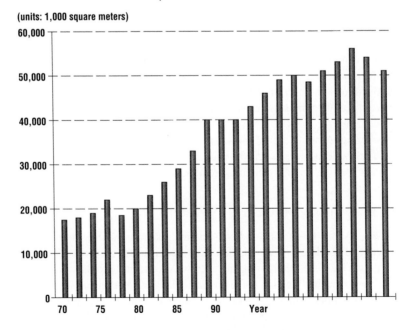

*Including float glass, polished plate glass, sheet glass, and figured glass.
†One converted case equals 9.29m² with 2 mm thickness.
††Including tempered glass and laminated glass for both construction and industrial use.
Source: Flat Glass Association of Japan.

Sakabe focused on electronics because of its growth potential and also because his management had some expertise in it. The company's first foray into the electronics business had been in the mid-1960s, when it formed a relationship with a subsidiary of Corning Glass Works to import and market integrated circuits (ICs). Even after Corning divested its semiconductor business, Asahi Glass continued to distribute ICs, finding new suppliers such as National Semiconductor and Oki Electric. Asahi Glass's other involvement with electronics was through its development of glass delay lines, electronic elements that improved TV picture quality by letting ultrasound signals conduct through glass with some time lag in order to complement video signals. At the request of TV set manufacturers, Asahi Glass's TV glass bulb researchers started research on glass delay lines in 1970 and successfully developed its own technology in 1974.

Top management set a goal of developing electronics to generate 10 percent of the company's revenue within 10 years. They decided to focus resources on areas such as displays, optoelectronics, and components for ICs, where they judged Asahi Glass had the relevant raw materials expertise or processing/fabricating knowledge. Among these areas, management particularly emphasized the development of liquid crystal displays (LCDs),[1] partly as a hedge against the substitution of LCDs for the TV glass bulb business. The company's research group began exploring LCD technology in 1970, and then participated in a cooperative research project sponsored by the Ministry of International Trade and Industry (MITI). Empowered by top management's strategic decision, research was scaled up and led to the formation of a joint venture called Optrex in 1976, in which Asahi Glass owned 60 percent and Mitsubishi Electric 40 percent, to commercialize small-sized LCDs used as the displays in products such as electronic calculators, digital wristwatches, and automotive panels. Optrex soon became Japan's second-largest manufacturer of LCDs, primarily supplying automobile manufacturers.

The Electronics Business Division was established as an independent division in 1982, and was later upgraded to a general division in 1989. In 1984, the company acquired controlling interests in Nippon Carbide Industries Co., and ELNA Co. Nippon Carbide's ceramics processing technology and ELNA's circuit board and aluminum capacitor technology were important for understanding electronics production, although ELNA in particular came with other businesses not necessarily appropriate for Asahi Glass. In addition, by hiring about 50 electrical engineers from the outside, the company established the Electronics Product Development Center at its Central Laboratory in 1985. Since acquisitions and head-hunting were uncommon in Japan, these aggressive moves attracted public attention to the company.

In 1987, Asahi Glass decided to expand its involvement in electronics. In response to an inquiry initiated by Komag Inc., a recently established manufacturer of thin-film disks in California, the company formed a joint venture. Asahi-Komag produced and marketed sputtered thin-film magnetic memory (hard) disks in Japan. Asahi Glass judged that its surface treatment expertise, developed in the glass business, could be applied to the production of disks. Also, it anticipated that glass instead of aluminum would be used as the base material for disks in the future. The joint venture contract was highly detailed in its treatment of technical issues. Small innovations were to be shared freely, "epoch-making" breakthroughs would be cross-licensed, and both parties agreed to limitations on their activities if the venture dissolved. The first shipment from the new factory was made in 1987.

---

[1]LCDs were made up of liquid crystals sandwiched between two glass substrates. The liquid crystals received a charge from an electronic driver to generate the display.

The company's quest for growth was not limited to electronics. In 1981, a new business division was established to develop the optical lens business. While Asahi Glass had been an original equipment manufacturer (OEM) supplier of glass lenses, it decided to become a full-line provider of optical frames and glass and plastic lenses.

While seeking growth by entering these new businesses, Asahi Glass also attempted to strengthen its three traditional businesses by shifting from commodity products to specialty, value-added products. In order to strengthen its position as supplier of materials, the company also expanded into the selected areas of "processing" and assembling" even though such downstream moves sometimes put the company in competition with its own customers.

In the glass and construction materials business, the company further enhanced the design, safety, and energy conservation qualities of its materials, and developed a number of new products including heat-reflective glass and high-insulating double-glazing glass units. In its chemical business, Asahi Glass developed a variety of specialty chemical products, such as foam urethane products for automobile bumpers and seats, fluorinated etching gases used in semiconductor fabrication, and fluropolymer resins for weather-resistant external paints.

Asahi Glass also maintained its lead in the domestic alkali chemical business by developing an ion-exchange membrane production process for caustic soda in 1975. The need for this arose when the government prohibited the use of "mercury process" for caustic soda production after the "Minamata" mercury-poisoning disaster in 1973. Up to 100 engineers were committed to the development project, which combined Asahi Glass's skills in caustic soda production, fluorinated resins as a material for the membrane, and membrane technology itself to commercialize this state-of-the-art process technology. Later, the company applied the ion-exchange membrane technology to develop a hollow fiber membrane for dehumidifiers and hydrogen fuel cells.

The refractories business also evolved into a broader-scope ceramics business. Initially, Asahi Glass explored the possibility of developing temperature-, corrosion-, and wear-resistant ceramics for structural components such as car engines, heat exchangers, and radiators. It established a new division in 1982 to further promote such "structural" ceramics. Later, when a large market for structural ceramics that could be demanded in large quantities failed to emerge, Asahi Glass switched to develop the "functional ceramics" that Kyocera had pioneered. Such functional products were made from fine ceramic compounds according to precise specifications, primarily for use in electronics.

Globalization

After losing its first overseas glass and soda ash plants in China as a result of WWII, Asahi Glass resumed foreign direct investment in 1956. The company accepted the invitation of the Indian government to build a local sheet glass plant primarily to supply the Indian market. It then established a flat glass joint venture with local partners in Thailand in 1964 and in Indonesia in 1972. Both these plants focused on Southeast Asian markets, which were beyond the region of interest to the Western glass companies and protected by local governments. Asahi Glass's policy was to "co-exist" and "co-prosper" with these economies by developing their infant industry, substituting domestic production for imports, and creating employment. While Asahi Glass would send between 5 and 10 Japanese employees to these affiliated plants to provide technical and marketing know-how along with financial support, it delegated all the daily operations to local managers and relied on its local partners for distribution.

Because of economies of scale in float glass production, by the late sixties, the world glass industry was dominated by a few giants, especially Pilkington in the U.K., Saint-Gobain and BSN in France, and PPG in the United States. The increasing automation of the float glass process made it possible for them to operate glass plants without highly skilled labor, so while these firms first entered neighboring regions through exports, increasingly they made foreign direct investments—the Europeans in Africa, Middle East, and Latin America, the Americans in Central America, each establishing their own spheres of influence.

This equilibrium was disturbed in the early 1980s when BSN-Gervais Danone, a French conglomerate, decided to exit the glass business and divest its four unprofitable glass subsidiaries in France, Belgium, Netherlands, and Germany. Because of antitrust regulation, the Continental European glass manufacturers could not bid for BSN plants. Instead, Pilkington purchased the German subsidiary, PPG purchased the French subsidiary, and Asahi Glass bought the Belgian (Glaverbel) and Dutch (Maasglas) subsidiaries. Asahi wanted to acquire the companies in order to learn the European market, access European R&D, and develop the African market. As with its other overseas operations, Asahi Glass retained the management of Glaverbel and MaasGlas and delegated most management decisions to them.

The company's automobile safety glass and TV glass bulb operations also globalized during the 1970s and 1980s as the Japanese automobile and consumer electronics manufacturers started transferring their production facilities, first to Asian countries and then later to the United States and Europe. Following the moves of its customers, Asahi Glass built overseas operations for TV glass bulbs in Singapore in 1979 and in Taiwan in 1980. In the U.S. market, it formed a joint venture with Corning Glass Works that took over the operation of Corning's TV glass bulb facilities in 1988. It also started fabricated automotive glass plants both in Thailand and Indonesia in 1974, and in the United States in 1985.

Similarly, Asahi Glass's chemical business pursued its own globalization strategy. The company started the production of caustic soda and chlorine first in Thailand in 1965. Later, in 1989, it established an integrated operations for caustic soda, chlorovinyl monomers, and polymers in Indonesia. Then in 1990, it formed a join venture with Tenneco Minerals in the United States, its first chemical activity outside Asia, to mine natural soda ash for supply to its local glass plants as well as to outside customers.

▲ BUSINESSES IN 1992

In 1992, 56 percent of Asahi Glass's sales came from glass and related products, 30 percent from chemicals, 6 percent from electronics, 2 percent from ceramics and refractories, and the remainder from other areas (Exhibits 6 and 7).

Glass and Related Products

Three general divisions were responsible for Asahi Glass's glass and related businesses including architectural glass for buildings, glass reinforced cement (GRC) and other construction materials, fabricated glass products for automobiles, and TV glass bulbs. Asahi Glass was not active in fiberoptic cable because in Japan the telecommunication and copper wire companies had won Corning licenses. Nor was Asahi Glass a manufacturer of specialty glass (like Corningware), except through its ownership of Iwaki Glass, because the company had historically sought high-volume industrial markets rather than small consumer markets.

▲ **EXHIBIT 6   Asahi Glass's Major Businesses and Products in 1992**

Area/Sales	Major Products	Major Competition
Glass and related ¥739.911 m (56.2%)	**Architectural glass** Float glass, tempered glass, laminated glass, wired-glass, double-gazing units, mirror	Nippon Sheet Glass, Central Glass, (global) Pilkington Brothers, Saint-Gobain, PPG Industries, Guardian (global)
	Construction materials (a) Glass reinforced cement products, (b) ALC (autocraved lightweight cement)	(a) Matsushita-Denko, Nichiba, Kubota, (b) Asahi Chemicals, Nihon Iyton, Onoda Durox
	Automotive safety glass Laminated safety glass, tempered safety glass	Nippon Sheet Glass, Central Glass, Pilkington Brothers, Saint-Gobain, PPG Industries, Guardian (global)
	CRT glass bulbs TV glass bulbs and other products	Nippon Electric Glass (global) N.V. Philips, Schott, Sam-Sung Corning
	Fine glass and other glass products (a) Ultra-thin glass substrate, (b) conductive glass substrate, (c) photomask glass substrate, (d) borosillicate-glass products, (e) glass fiber	(a) Nippon Sheet Glass, Central Glass, Nippon Electric Glass, (b) Geomatec, Sanyo Cacuum Ind., (c) Shin-Etsu Quartz Products, Toshiba Ceramics, Hoya, (d) Toshiba Glass, (e) Nippon Micro Glass-Wool, Paramount Glass Mfg., Nippon Muki
Chemicals ¥390,139 m (29.6%)	**Alkali chemicals** Soda ash, caustic soda, sodium bicarbonate	Tosoh, Tokuyama Soda, Central Glass Daikin, Showa Denko, Mitsui-DuPont Fluoro Chemicals
	Chloro-chemicals Hydrochloric acid, liquid chlorine, propylene oxide, propylene glycol, polyol, vinyl chloride monomer, polyvinyl chloride (PVCs), epichlorhydrin, chlorinated methane, perchloroethylene, trichroroethylene	FMC, Dow, 3M, ICI, DuPont, ATO Hoechst, Allied (global)

Area/Sales	Major Products	Major Competition
	Fluoro-chemicals	
	CFCs (fluorinated hydrocarbons), fluorinated resins, fluorinated rubbers, specialty materials, coating materials	
Ceramics and refractories ¥31,044 m (2.4%)	(a) Fusion cast refractories, bonded refractories, castable refractories, aluminious cement, (b) fine ceramics (high strength ceramics, low-expansion ceramics, ultrapure aluminum nitride ceramics), ceramic heat exchangers, ceramic blowers, ceramic valves	(a) Shingagawa Refractories, Kurosaki, (b) Kyocera, Toshiba Ceramics
Electronics ¥74,155 m (5.6%)	(a) Semiconductors and semicustom ICs, printed thick-film products, and hybrid ICs, (b) delay lines, delay line modules, (c) aluminum electrolytic capacitors, printed circuit and mounted boards, (d) LCD displays, (e) thin-film magnetic disks	(a) IC trading firms (Ryoyo Electronics etc.), (b) Seiko-KINSEKI, (c) Nichicon, (d) Sharp, Toshiba, Seiko-Epson, Sanyo, Hitachi, Hoshiden, (e) Fuji electric, Showa Denko, Mitsubishi Kasei
Others ¥81,540 m (6.2%)	(a) Ophthalmic and optical products (b) Health and medical products (ultrasonic foamers, purifiers, far-infrared sauna, etc.) (c) FRP (fiber-reinforced plastics) precision-molded products	(a) Hoya, Seiko, Toray Industries

Source: Asahi Glass Company.

▲ EXHIBIT 7   Asahi Glass Company Organization Chart

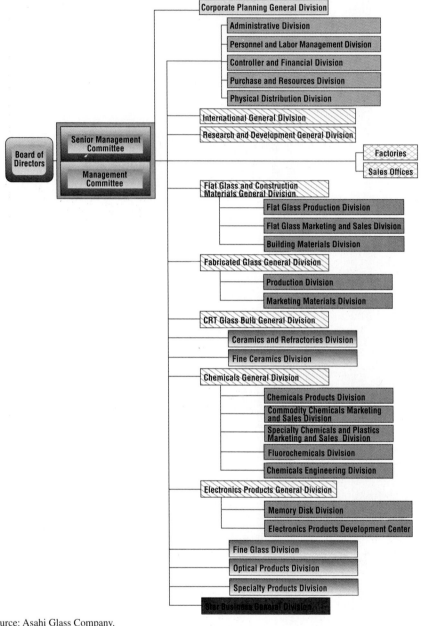

Source: Asahi Glass Company.

Flat glass was the company's biggest generator of sales, and especially of profits. In Japan, Asahi Glass was the dominant supplier with about a 50 percent market share, followed by Nippon Sheet Glass and Central Glass, who held 30 percent and 20 percent of the market, respectively. Nippon Sheet specialized in glass and construction materials business and was putting a new emphasis on fiberoptics. Central Glass, the newest of the three competitors, operated alkali and other chemical businesses as well as glass production (Exhibit 8). The market shares of these companies had remained virtually unchanged since the mid-1960s.

Flat glass was almost exclusively made through the float process. The glass was then transported to wholesalers and dealers who stored, cut, and merchandised the glass directly to customers. In Japan, there were over 400 small-sized, independent wholesalers. Historically, these wholesalers had received financial and technical support from one of the three big manufacturers and had developed a one-to-one relationship to deal only with that manufacturer. Such relationships were also seen in Europe but were not common in the North American markets. Unlike wholesalers, most of the dealers did not have an exclusive relationship with a particular glass manufacturer and could buy from any manufacturer. Sixty percent of Japanese domestic flat glass production went into construction, 30 percent to automobiles, and 10 percent to other industrial uses such as mirrors, display cases, and furniture.

Worldwide, Asahi Glass competed with European and American rivals (Exhibit 9). Pilkington Brothers was a 100-year-old British glass manufacturer which had invented the epoch-making float process technology. In addition to its core glass business which generated 80 percent of its sales, it had diversified into ophthalmics (spectacle lenses, contact lenses, and lens care systems) and insulation materials. For many years, license fees from its float glass process had provided Pilkington with a substantial cash flow. However, the key patents expired in the mid-1980s, and Pilkington's license fees were correspondingly reduced. Saint-Gobain, a French conglomerate, started operations in the 17th century as the royal glassmaker to Louis XIV. About 20 percent of the company's sales were in flat glass and the rest were spread evenly among industrial ceramics, containers, insulation, paperwood, pipe, and related materials. PPG Industries, established in 1883, was also a major paints and chemical producer. In 1992, its three major businesses—glass, paints and coatings, and industrial and specialty chemicals—respectively generated 40 percent, 40 percent, and 20 percent of its total sales. Guardian Industries, the world's fifth-largest glass manufacturer, was a relatively small but fast-growing newcomer, known as a low-cost and aggressive competitor. It had lobbied to include the Japanese domestic sheet glass market in the structural-impediments-to-trade debate between the U.S. and Japanese governments. While some foreign companies, such as PPG Industries, steadily penetrated the Japanese market with local marketing efforts, Guardian argued that the exclusive distribution networks functioned as an effective nontariff barrier.

With a few exceptions, competition in the glass business was seen as friendly but fair. The inherent limitations on transporting flat glass restricted import competition, and the large minimum efficient scale of a float glass plant and the need for distribution usually prevented competitors building plants in each other's major markets. The scale requirement also limited foreign direct investment to one plant per country in developing areas. As the economies of these developing countries expanded, however, it gradually became possible to justify a second plant. For example, Guardian entered into Thailand by building the country's second float glass plant in 1992. In India, Guardian also began to compete with Asahi Glass with its own float glass plant.

Asahi Glass's construction materials business produced wall, ceiling, and floor materials made of glass, cement, ceramics, and composites. In the early 1990s, the demand for its GRC (glass-reinforced cement) fireproof siding boards surged despite the recession in Japan, and Asahi Glass was expanding the production of the material. In addition to selling construction materials, Asahi Glass was also developing systems technologies for construction.

▲ **EXHIBIT 8** Domestic Glass Industry, FY 1992 (millions of yen)

	AGC Group (December 92)	Nippon Sheet Glass (March 93)	Central Glass (March 93)	Nippon Electric Glass (March 93)
Net sales	1,316,789	286,564	203,881	205,170
Operating profit	42,434	6,672	6,310	9,128
Net income	24,269	1,115	495	2,593
Total assets	1,515,626	427,287	239,062	303,941
Shareholders' equity	596,709	150,588	54,232	105,305
Return on sales	1.84%	0.39%	0.24%	1.26%
Return on assets	1.60	0.26	0.21	0.85
Return on equity	4.07	0.74	0.91	2.46
R&D expenditure*	38,000	11,000	6,000	8,500
Employees*	9,924	4,001	2,612	4,518
Glass plants in Japan				
Flat glass	4	3	2	0
Fabricated glass	3	4	2	0
CRT glass bulb	2	0	0	2
Composition of net sales:	Glass & construction: 56% Chemicals: 30% Ceramics: 2% Electronics: 6% Others: 6%	Glass: 66% Building materials & others: 34%	Glass and building materials: 64% Chemical products: 25% Fertilizers: 11%	CRT tubes: 59% Tubing glass: 8% Glass fibers: 12% Other glass: 20% Glass-making machines: 2%

Nonconsolidated.
Source: Asahi Glass Company, annual reports of respective companies.

▲ EXHIBIT 9 Worldwide Glass Industry, FY 1992 (millions of U.S. dollars)

	AGC Group[†] (December 92)	Pilkington[†] (March 93)	PPG (December 92)	Saint-Gobain[†] (December 92)	Guardian[††] (December 92)
Net sales	10,534	4,545	5,814	13,981	1,200
Operating profit	391	155	662	1,212	NA
Profit before tax	397	72	542	722	NA
Net income	192	(35)	319	449	NA
Total assets	12,125	4,368	5,662	17,918	NA
Shareholders' equity	4,774	1,604	2,699	7,357	NA
Return on sales	1.84%	(0.78%)	5.49%	3.21%	NA
Return on assets	1.60	(1.41)	5.63	2.51	NA
Return on equity	4.07	(2.22)	11.82	6.10	NA
R&D expenditure	304	88	221	NA	NA
Employees	9,826	41,600	32,300	104,002	8,000
Float glass production					
Float plants* (total)	29.0	26.5	18.0	17.0	13.0
Asia and Oceania	14.0	4.0	1.0	0.0	2.0
North America	8.0	6.0	13.0	0.0	6.0
Central and South America	0.0	4.5	0.0	1.5	1.0
Europe	7.0	11.0	4.0	15.5	4.0
Others	0.0	1.0	0.0	0.0	0.0
Composition of net sales:	Glass & construction: 56% Chemicals: 30% Ceramics: 2% Electronics: 6% Others: 6%	Glass: 80% Insulation: 3% Vision care: 12% Optronics: 2% Others: 3%	Glass: 37% Coating & resin: 40% chemicals: 19% Others: 4%	Glass: 18% Ceramics: 14% containers: 17% Insulation: 13% Paper-wood: 12% Pipe: 11% Building materials: 9% Fiber reinforcements: 4% Others: 2%	Glass: 80% Photofinishing laboratories: 15% Others: 5%

*As of February 1992 (including float tanks in cold repair and under construction). A joint venture plant operated by two companies was counted as 0.5 plant for each company.
[†]Exchange rates: ¥125/$, $1.7663/£, FF5.2935/$.
[††]Privately held company.
Source: Asahi Glass Company; annual reports of respective companies; *Forbes* "The 400 Largest Private Companies in the U.S.," December 6, 1993.

Fabricated glass involved the additional processing and/or fabricating of flat glass in order to improve safety in products such as automobile windshields. The major flat glass manufacturers were also key players in this market, which had become increasingly global. In 1992, Asahi Glass had a 56 percent market share in the domestic market and a 20 percent world market share.

Glass bulbs for cathode-ray tubes (CRTs) were manufactured in large-scale, specialized plants where molten glass was precision molded, polished, and finished. As unique operational know-how and close coordination with TV set manufacturers was required, only a few major manufacturers of TV glass bulbs remained. Asahi Glass was the market leader with an exceptional quality control record and distinguished technology. It shared the domestic market equally with Nippon Electric Glass, an affiliate of NEC (Exhibit 8). It held about a 30 percent global market share; leading competitors included N. V. Philips in the Netherlands, Schott in Germany, and a joint venture between Samsung (in Korea) and Corning, which covered Southeast Asia. Asahi Glass centrally coordinated the production and distribution of glass bulbs to Japanese and foreign TV set manufacturers from its two domestic and four overseas factories.

Chemicals

Asahi Glass's chemical businesses were handled by the five divisions of the Chemical General Division. The ratio of specialty and fine chemicals to the company's chemical business had steadily increased since the 1970s. The company also sold its chemical engineering expertise, providing, for example, membrane and electrolysis technology and technical assistance to other manufacturers. The bulk of its sales remained in the domestic market for its own use and to other Japanese chemical and manufacturing companies.

Alkali products still constituted the major portion of Asahi Glass's chemical business in 1992, although their relative importance had been gradually declining. As a major consumer itself, Asahi Glass produced 40 percent of the soda ash made in Japan and was also engaged in the joint venture with Tenneco in the United States. It was also the largest domestic producer of caustic soda, with a 46 percent market share, using its efficient, environmentally safe ion-exchange membrane process technology to supply pharmaceuticals, synthetic fiber, and paper and pulp manufacturers. In its commodity chlorine business, including inorganic and organic chlorine derivatives, the company had secured a stable position as the treatment of chlorine required specialized know-how and new entry was difficult. However, chlorinated solvents such as trichloroethylene were suspected of causing health problems, making the future potential of this line of business uncertain. Similarly, although the company was a top producer of fluorochemical products, its chlorofluorocarbons (CFCs), widely used as coolants for refrigerators and air conditioners, were suspected of destroying the earth's ozone layer. As a result, and in accordance with international regulations based on the Montreal Protocol, the company was reducing production of CFCs and investigating environmentally safe alternatives. At the same time, it was allocating resources to develop more value-added products such as fluorinated/fluoropolymer resins, rubbers and films, and pharmaceutical and agricultural intermediates.

Ceramics and Refractories

In 1992, Asahi Glass's Ceramics and Refractory Division offered the capability to provide turnkey high-heat furnaces to industries such as steel, including the design of the furnaces, supply of refractory products themselves, and the construction of the furnace.

The Fine Ceramics Division, which was renamed from Engineering Ceramics in 1988, developed and marketed structural and functional ceramics but remained small relative to Kyocera.

Electronics and Other Businesses

The Electronics General Division supervised and coordinated the company's electronics business activities, including those of the company's relevant subsidiaries and joint ventures such as Optrex, ELNA, Nippon Carbide, and Asahi-Komag. Its major products were IC-related components, glass delay lines, LCD panels, and memory disks, and the majority of these products were sold domestically (Exhibit 10). Optrex, Asahi Glass's LCD joint venture, was increasing production rapidly and was strongly positioned in the market, particularly for automotive LCD panels, although major R&D capital expenditures were required. TFT active-matrix LCD research, for example, had cost $70 million per annum, and a new $200 million facility would soon be built. Asahi-Komag's thin-film magnetic memory (hard) disks were also well accepted in the market because of their superior recording density.

Other divisions included Optical Products, which produced and marketed glass lenses and plastic lenses with fluorine-based nonreflective coatings as well as frames under its own brand name. The Specialty Products Division also sold a number of unique home, health, and medical products. To date the division had developed products such as a face washer based on the company's ultrasonic technology, and hot bath-water purifiers that used the ion-exchange membrane technology. Other products included an egg timer, infrared sauna, and a self-cleaning toilet. The division also produced fiber-reinforced plastic (FRP) for precision plastic parts and marketed them to office automation equipment manufacturers.

▲ ORGANIZATION STRUCTURE AND SYSTEMS

Organization Structure

Asahi Glass had adopted a matrix-like organization structure (Exhibit 7). While physical production and selling activities took place in the factories and sales offices, general management and profit responsibility lay in the divisions, which were in effect given their own balance sheets. As the number of divisions had been growing over time in line with the company's diversification, the company had consolidated 30 divisions into 18 divisions in 1979, and introduced general divisions, one for each of the major product areas, in 1985 to act as sector-level coordinators supervising several functional divisions. In 1993, the company had six general divisions and five independent divisions.

Asahi Glass's product divisions were closely interrelated; many divisions supplied raw materials or end products to other divisions. Transfer prices were not employed between production and sales divisions within the same product division, but were used if product flowed across product divisions, such as soda ash supplied by the Chemical to the Flat Glass General Division.

New business activities that were not obvious fits with existing divisions were concentrated in the Specialty Products Division. This had its roots in a "Corning Center" established in 1960 with the purpose of leveraging the company's technology into consumer markets. Originally the company's IC and LCD developments had been concentrated in this division before being moved out to the joint venture companies or the Electronics Division.

▲ EXHIBIT 10   Asahi Glass's Position in Electronic Businesses

	Asahi Glass's Involvement (Asahi's share)	Major Electronic Products	Sales in 1992	Market Size in 1992 (worldwide)	Relative Position/ Market Share	Major Competitors	Market Growth	Relevance for Asahi Glass's Other Businesses
Electronic Product & Specialty Product General Divisions	Internal divisions	Glass delay lines	¥3 billion	¥12 billion	Among top three	KINSEKI, Matsushita Electronic Component	Flat	Supplier to TV set manufacturers
		Sales of ICs and semicustom ICs	NA	NA	Low share	Ryoyo Electronics, Tokyo Electron, Nissei Sangyo, Ryosan	Very high	
Optrex	Joint venture with Mitsubishi Electric (60%)	Passive-matrix LCDs	¥36.0 billion	¥325.5 billion (including passive- and active-matrix LCDs)	Among top five	Sharp, Seiko Epson, Sanyo, Citizen Watch, Casio Computer	About 10% p.a.	Glass substrate Expertise in chemical compounds
Advanced Display Inc.	Joint venture with Mitsubishi Electric (20%)	TFT active-matrix LCDs	Joint development will be completed by September 1994		No production yet	Sharp, Toshiba, NEC, Hitachi, Hoshiden	30%–40% p.a.	Use of automotive panels
Asahi-Komag	Joint venture with Komag Inc. (40%)	Thin-film magnetic disks	¥10–15 billion	¥60 billion	Among top four	Fuji Electric, Showa Denko, Mitsubishi Kasei	Medium-high	Surface treatment skills (e.g., sputtering) Application of glass to disk substrates
ELNA	Largest shareholder (25%)	Aluminum electrolytic capacitors	¥16.6 billion	¥498 billion (all capacitors)	Among top six in aluminum electrolytic capacitors	Nichicon, Nippon Chemi-con, Murata Manufacturing	Almost flat	Discrete electronics business
		Printed circuits	¥8.4 billion	¥885 billion	NA	Nippon CMK, Hitachi Chemicals, Ibiden	Flat or slight increase	
Nippon Carbide	Largest shareholder (18%)	Electronic materials	¥5 billion (10% of total sales of the company)	NA	NA	Kyocera, Noritake Co., Ltd.	NA	Ceramic processing technology

Source: 1992 annual reports of Asahi Glass, ELNA, and Nippon Carbide. Relative position/market share, market growth, and the numbers for Optrex are estimated by the author

▲452

International activities were coordinated by the International General Division. Since all of Asahi Glass's international subsidiaries were profit centers, and many of them were joint ventures in which Asahi owned only a minority share, the main role of the International Division was liaison between the overseas subsidiaries and the domestic product divisions. It monitored the performance of the overseas subsidiaries and affiliates; helped them in developing business strategies; provided analytic help for new plant decisions; and worked jointly with the divisions for new business development overseas. While Asahi Glass had about 200 Japanese employees overseas, nearly all were divisional personnel who remained assigned to their own division and not to the International Division.

Since Asahi Glass was trying to localize its foreign activities, product divisions only exercised indirect influence on their overseas subsidiaries. While in many cases the company would have a minority board membership and a few employees on assignment at the foreign subsidiaries, they would not dictate day-to-day activities, such as local pricing. Instead, subsidiaries sent monthly financial and operating reports for review and needed approval only for major initiatives such as new plant investment or bond financing. For some of the major subsidiaries such as Glaverbel and AFG Industries, executive meetings were called once every three to four months for Asahi Glass's management to discuss important managerial issues. Otherwise relationships were conducted more informally between relevant personnel on topics such as technology transfer and product development. The exception was the TV bulb glass business. Because Asahi Glass viewed this as a global business, all the foreign subsidiaries, except the Corning joint venture in the United States, were majority-owned and directly controlled by the Product Division. This enabled production, distribution, and pricing decisions to be globally optimized and worldwide performance to be evaluated on an ongoing basis.

R&D and New Product Development

R&D activities were handled by the R&D General Division's research centers and by the Product Division's research laboratories. Of the company's 1,450 researchers, 700 were in the corporate research center, 200 in the separate Corporate Advanced Glass research center, and the remainder in product divisions. However, the Electronics Division laboratory was physically located at the corporate center. The division intended to establish a laboratory on site with its other facilities "when it could afford it."

Corporate R&D was responsible for basic research, the product divisions for new applications. Formal meetings between the two groups took place monthly with the general manager of a product division meeting the heads of the laboratories at the corporate center which were most relevant to his interests. About 70 percent of the corporate R&D expense was borne by the divisions which paid for specific R&D programs, and the remainder was allocated to divisions as a percentage of their sales.

In an attempt to facilitate the product development process and make the company more entrepreneurial, the Star Business General Division hosted "star leader" products. The division had been introduced in 1985, to promote intrapreneurship. Twenty products then under development or investigation were selected and assigned to a leader, usually a champion of the product. The leader was given corporate funding and the authority of a division general manager to accelerate a product's commercialization by taking charge of the entire product development process from R&D through to manufacturing and sales. By 1993, two of those projects (i.e., weather-resistant fluoropolymer paints and thin-film magnetic memory disks) had graduated back to the divisions when they reached ¥10 billion in sales, and six remained active. New projects were chosen from those proposed by the divisions according to their expected future potential size and profitability. Currently Asahi Glass was spending about ¥500 million every year on Star Leader projects, mostly on necessary capital investments.

Human Resource Management

Like other Japanese companies, Asahi Glass hired its future executives for life, and paid executives on a companywide scale that was independent of the business unit they worked for. The company ranked as one of the most desirable manufacturing companies to work for in Japan and recruited graduates from the country's most prestigious universities as well as some executives in their thirties via headhunters. After spending five years in one division, all nontechnical graduate hires would be transferred to a different division. After that, transfers between divisions were the exception rather than the rule, and each business developed its own culture. Senior management, however, tried to encourage cross-cultural transfers and promote a generalist perspective. Moves to subsidiary and joint venture companies also occurred. In 1992, Asahi Glass had 40 employees (mostly R&D personnel) at Asahi-Komag, 70 at Optrex, and 10 at ELNA.

Planning and Resource Allocation

Since 1990 Asahi Glass had been operating under the "Vision 21" long-term plan, whose theme was "Aiming to be a global corporation prospering in the 21st century." The vision saw the company "consolidating our business base further and maintaining expanded equilibrium of our business through harmony of expansion and stability." Objectives for the year 2000 were mainly financial, including targets for nonconsolidated sales of two trillion yen (from one trillion in 1991), profits of 15 percent of sales (from 6 percent), R&D at 5.5 percent of sales (from 3 percent), and for 20 percent of sales to come from products introduced within the last five years. As a tool to measure the company's progress, Asahi Glass employed the concept of "weight value." The company believed it could achieve its objectives by moving into higher value-added businesses and raising the revenue per kilogram of output from ¥100 to ¥150 by the year 2002.

Below the long-term plan was a five-year plan, revised every two to three years, that defined financial goals and resource allocation by division. The strategic planning group decided overall resource availability according to cash flow projections and acceptable debt levels. This was allocated among divisions according to how the company wanted the sales mix to evolve. The five-year plan for 1987, for example, had anticipated electronics becoming 10 percent of corporate sales, and the division had accordingly been absorbing 15–20 percent of the company's R&D in an attempt to reach that share of sales. The one-year budget, revised every six months, was directly linked to these longer-term plans with divisional expenditures for capital and R&D in the budget expected to be set in line with the five-year plan.

Compared to other large Japanese companies, Asahi Glass was known for its top-down management style with a history of many important management decisions having been initiated by the top. The Senior management Committee of the company (the top seven executives) met weekly to review important issues, monitor performance problems in the divisions as identified by the corporate strategic planning group, and approve capital requests over ¥1 billion.

Although top management and the corporate office provided general guidance, they typically did not dictate the strategy for each business. The rule was not to go too far from the core business, as corporate management did not want divisions to "parachute into new areas."

President Seya, Asahi's first president to have come from neither a glass nor an engineering background, strongly believed that for each business unit to be viable it should be allowed to grow in its area of strength and that middle management should take future-oriented initiatives in order to encourage aggressiveness in the organization.

▲ ISSUES FACING ASAHI GLASS IN 1993

In the 1990s, Asahi Glass's performance was badly hurt by the sluggish Japanese economy. In particular, the domestic glass business expected sales and profits to decline for the third consecutive year in 1993.

Accelerated Globalization in Glass

The overseas expansion of the traditional flat glass business was an immediate growth solution for cash-rich Asahi Glass. As the "Iron Curtain" lifted and Eastern European governments started to privatize their glass operations, major global players rushed into this new market. Purchasing former government-owned glass plants and upgrading technologies, Saint-Gobain entered East Germany, Guardian Hungary, and Pilkington Poland. Asahi Glass's Glaverbel subsidiary moved into the former Czechoslovakia in 1991. The growth potential of Asian countries also attracted attention. Guardian built a float plant in Thailand, while Asahi Glass and PPG established a $100 million joint venture in China in 1992.

In the meantime, Asahi Glass's presence in the North American market was enhanced in 1992 when Asahi Glass, jointly with Glaverbel, acquired AFG Industries. AFG was the second-largest glass manufacturer in the United States, with six float glass plants in the United States and one in Canada. When AFG was bought out by its management in 1988, top management of Glaverbel, who had personally known AFG's management and been enthusiastic about the entry into the North American market, persuaded Asahi Glass to invest in the MBO. With PPG Industries and Pilkington, which already owned Libby-Owens-Ford, the second-largest U.S. automotive glass manufacturer, deterred by antitrust regulation, Asahi Glass bid against Saint-Gobain to purchase a 20 percent share of AFG in 1988 with an option to buy the remaining 80 percent shares through 1993. After a heated internal discussion, Asahi Glass decided to exercise that option in June 1992, at a cost of about $1.1 billion.

Such an accelerated globalization of the company, however, challenged Asahi Glass's traditional international practice. Notwithstanding its years of international experience, Asahi Glass was still developing its organizational capabilities outside of Asia. For several years, for example, it had experienced difficulties in coordinating with Glaverbel management before establishing mutual trust. More recently it was Glaverbel that was given responsibility for developing the African, Middle Eastern, and Eastern European markets, rather than the Domestic Glass Division. The larger-scale, worldwide operations would require a higher level of coordination and integration by the headquarters. The full ownership of AFG Industries, in particular, would position Asahi Glass in direct competition with the American glass manufacturers, some of which would in return demand the opening of what was claimed to be the "closed" Japanese glass market. Although overseas expansion in glass looked like an easy way to grow, President Seya was wondering if the company was truly committed to taking a global approach with more integration and coordination of operations.

Slow Growth of Electronics

In Japan, despite its decade-long efforts to develop the business, Asahi Glass was still struggling to establish a firm position in the fast-cycle electronics industry beyond its existing activities. In the LCD business, new thin-film-transistor (TFT) technology had been introduced, and major electronics firms such as Hitachi, Toshiba, and NEC with strong skills in semiconductor manufacturing had entered the now-large market. While Asahi Glass had established a second joint venture with Mitsubishi Electric, Advanced Display Inc., for the manufacture of TFT active-matrix LCDs, Mitsubishi Electric had taken a leading role in this venture with an 80 percent shareholding. Similarly, although Asahi Glass and Komag, Inc. agreed upon a second joint venture for developing thin-film heads for disk drives in 1991, top management realized that the disk head was an "assembly" business, distant from a "materials" business, and that they had stepped into a business in which the company lacked expertise.

Emerging New Glass Opportunities

The emerging opportunities in "new glass" did not come with any clear indication as to what direction the company should take. Although the definition of new glass was yet clear, it was understood to be glass with inherent functions such as selective light transparency, photoconductivity, and electrical insulation or with improved characteristics such as high surface flatness and machinability. Membership in the New Glass Forum, an association established on the initiative of MITI in 1985 to promote information exchanges, ranged from glass manufacturers to chemical, metal, electronics, cable and communications, machinery, and printing companies. The diversity of the membership illustrated the uncertain potential of this new technology. Electrically insulated ultraflat glass substrates for LCDs and memory disks and architectural glass that excluded ultraviolet light were some examples of new glass already under development.

Chairman Furumoto frequently advocated the "restoration of glass." He said, "It was a mistake that the company had termed glass a 'mature' business in the middle 1970s." Under his leadership, Asahi Glass established a Fine Glass Division in 1985 and a New Glass Research Laboratory in 1988, while also taking leadership in the New Glass Forum. Some industry observers viewed the future of the new glass business as rosy, expecting it to reach $20 billion by the turn of the century, and were optimistic about Asahi Glass's capacity to take advantage of it. Others pointed out that the most promising applications for "new glass" would be in the high-technology fields whose competitive environments were far different from the traditional glass business.

Challenge of Combining Technological Expertises

Management believed that in the future it would be important to integrate its various technological expertises if it was to capitalize both on new glass technology and on other growth opportunities. President Seya emphasized that while Asahi Glass had traditionally focused on deepening technological expertise within each of its business areas, he believed that it could combine these expertises to develop unique products. One example was a bilayer glass for automobiles which combined a layer of glass and urethane to improve safety. In 1990, the company agreed with Saint-Gobain to jointly develop it. Another example was a fluoropolymer-coated automotive window glass which repelled water more effectively. Integrating the company's various expertises would, however, not be an easy task, for the company was not used to such coordination, and the cultures of the various divisions often differed.

Revitalizing Corporate Culture

Management recognized that changing the climate of the organization was its biggest challenge. They felt that as the company grew older and larger, its founding "pioneer spirit" had faded away. The company historically had relied on developing new products from its technologies and was not good at developing products that met customer needs. Chairman Furomoto, the first marketing executive to head the company, had been trying to create an entrepreneurial culture in the company where "wind can blow through" the organization across divisions and up and down hierarchies, as well as to promote "market in" customer-focused approaches. His belief was that top management's role was to create an environment that encouraged initiative and innovation.

▲ FUTURE DIRECTION

One morning in the middle of September 1993, President Seya was reviewing the report on the electronics business prepared by the corporate planning staff. The report analyzed the strategic position of its major products, discussed the company's long-term strategy for this business, and proposed several strategic options. These options ranged from the extreme of divestment to another extreme of aggressive investment. While Asahi Glass would benefit if it could establish a strong foothold in this fast-growing business, given the fierce competition, the establishment of such a position would be extremely costly, and its success was not guaranteed. President Seya felt that the discussion around the electronics business was illustrative of the company's dilemma in determining its strategic direction. Whatever action the company would take in this business, it should be aligned with those in other lines of business and consistent with the company's overall direction for the coming decade.

VISICORP 1978–1984

In 1977, Dan Fylstra, a student in the MBA program at the Harvard Business School, wrote a business plan for a newly emerging type of firm, a software publisher. it began:

My fundamental idea is to publish and market software for personal computers in much the same way that books and records are produced and marketed. I plan to solicit software from individual aspiring authors, select and publish specific computer programs based on an analysis of what the market wants, reproduce the programs using audiocassette tapes and ordinary printing, advertise and promote the programs through the personal computer magazine and direct mail, and distribute the programs through the emerging network of retail computer stores, and ultimately through calculator dealers and department stores.

In the fledgling microcomputer industry Fylstra, at 26, was something of an old hand. Having studied computers at MIT, he had been a founding associate editor of *Byte*, the first journal expressly devoted to microcomputer hobbyists, and a founding editor of *Computer Dealer*. Like many technically trained people at that time, he was fascinated by the developing microcomputer industry and was determined to make his career in it.

In early 1978, Fylstra and software writer Peter Jennings formed Personal Software to market programs for the Commodore Pet, Radio Shack, and Apple computers. The first programs offered ware games and an assembler for the 6502 microprocessor. Soon they also offered a chess-playing program by Jennings and a bridge-playing program (Exhibit 1). MicroChess became the largest-selling application program in the still infant microcomputer industry, with over 50,000 units sold by the spring of 1979.

This case was prepared by Professor Richard P. Rumelt with the assistance of Julia Watt. Support for the development of this case was provided by the Price Institute–UCLA Program in Enterpreneurial Studies.
Copyright © 1985 by Richard Rumelt.

PET / TRS-80 / APPLE: Personal Software brings you the finest!!

 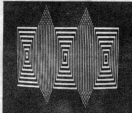 

NEW! THE ELECTRIC PAINTBRUSH by **Ken Anderson** for 4K Level I and II TRS-80s: Create the most dazzling graphics displays you have ever seen with a minimum of effort. *The Electric Paintbrush* is actually a simple 'language' in which you can write 'programs' directing your paintbrush around the screen—drawing lines, turning corners, changing white to black, etc. Once defined, these programs may be called by other programs or repetitively executed, each time varying the parameters of brush movement.

The machine language interpreter executes your programs almost instantaneously, allowing you to create real-time, animated graphics displays. The screen photos above are actually 'snapshots' of the action of a single one-line program over about thirty seconds. Mesmerize your friends with visual effects they've never seen on a TV screen! There's no limit to the variety of exciting and artistic graphics displays you can create with *The Electric Paintbrush*. And it's available now for only **$14.95**

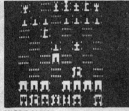  

MICROCHESS is the culmination of two years of chessplaying program development by **Peter Jennings**, author of the famous 1K byte chess program for the KIM-1. MICROCHESS 2.0 for 8K PETs and 6502 APPLEs, in 6502 machine language, offers 8 levels of play to suit everyone from the beginner learning chess to the serious player. It examines positions as many as 6 moves ahead, and includes a chess clock for tournament play. MICROCHESS 1.5 for

4K TRS-80s, in Z-80 machine language, offers 3 levels of play (both Level I and Level II versions are included and can be loaded on any TRS-80 without TBUG). MICROCHESS checks every move for legality and displays the current position on a graphic chessboard. You can play White or Black, set up and play from special board positions, or even watch the computer play against itself! Available now at a special introductory price of only **$19.95**

BRIDGE CHALLENGER by **George Duisman** for 8K PETs, Level II 16K TRS-80s, and 16K APPLEs: You and the dummy play 4 person Contract Bridge against the computer. The program will deal hands at random or according to your criterion for high card points. You can review tricks, swap sides or replay hands when the cards are known. No longer do you need 4 people to play! **$14.95**

STIMULATING SIMULATIONS by **Dr. C.W. Engel** for 8K PETs, 4K Level I and II TRS-80s, and APPLEs with Applesoft II: Ten original simulation games such as Forest Fire, Lost Treasure, Gone Fishing and Diamond Thief, progressing from elementary to quite complex with most suitable for schoolchildren. Includes a 64 page book giving flowcharts, listings and suggested modifications ... **$14.95**

WHERE TO GET IT: Look for the *Personal Software*™ display rack at your local computer store. Nearly 200 dealers throughout the United States, Canada, Europe and Australia now carry the *Personal Software*™ line. (And TRS-80 Microchess is available through all 7,000 Radio Shack® and Tandy Electronics stores!) New dealers are being added at the rate of two every business day. If your local dealer doesn't already carry *Personal Software*™ products, ask him to call us at **(617) 782-5932**. Or you can order direct from us by check, money order or VISA/Master Charge. If you have questions, call us at **(617) 783-0694**. If you know what you want and have your VISA/MC card ready, you can use any phone to

 DIAL TOLL FREE
1-800-325-6400
24 hrs   In Missouri dial 1-800-342-6600   7 days

Or you can mail your order to the address below. To add your name to our mailing list for free literature and announcements of new products, use the reader service card at the back of this magazine.

Personal Software™
P.O. Box 136-B2, Cambridge, MA 02138

Circle 302 on inquiry card

▲ VISICALC

At about the time Personal Software was formed, Dan Bricklin, a student at the Harvard Business School and MIT graduate, was experimenting with the idea of an "electronic blackboard" to take the drudgery out of business calculations. Bricklin imagined a display of numbers linked by rules, with the display responding immediately to any changes. Writing a simple prototype in Basic, Bricklin approached Bob Frankston, a friend he had met while a student at MIT. Frankston, an experienced computer consultant, agreed to help develop a workable version of the program.

Seeking advice from a Harvard faculty member, Bricklin was warned that time sharing systems were already flooded with financial modeling programs. Bricklin was referred to Dan Fylstra, who was known to be interested in new programs. Fylstra liked the concept and gave Bricklin and Frankston an Apple II microcomputer for development, promising to market the product they produced. In January 1979, Bricklin and Frankston formed Software Arts, and continued to work on the project in Frankston's attic.

As the project neared completion, Bricklin and Frankston began to negotiate an agreement with Personal Software concerning the marketing of the program. The contract (Exhibit 2) was signed in April and provided royalties to Software Arts of 435.7 percent of revenues on direct sales and 50 percent of revenues on contract (original equipment manufacturer) sales. In return, Personal Software promised best efforts marketing of the product. The name of the new product, VisiCalc, stood for "visual calculator," and was fashioned in one of the meetings between Fylstra and Frankston.

In May of 1979, Personal Software relocated from Cambridge to Sunnyvale, California, in "Silicon Valley," the center of the growing microcomputer industry. VisiCalc was shown at the West Coast Computer Faire that month and again at the National Computer Conference in New York. Many who saw the program were impressed—VisiCalc was something new under the sun. Industry observer Benjamin Rosen praised the product in the Morgan Stanley *Electronics Letter* saying it was the "software tail that might wag the personal computer dog."

VisiCalc was distributed to the public in October 1979. The original price was $99.50 for the diskette and manual. The response was immediate. Dealers found that computer owners were enthusiastic about a nongame product of general utility. The first month's sales more than repaid the entire year's advances to Software Arts for developments as well as the upfront marketing expenses. As word of the product spread, dealers saw an increasing number of customers buying Apple microcomputers just to run VisiCalc!

VisiCalc was an unprecedented retail "hit" in the microsoftware industry. In 1979, Personal Software's revenues were $882,000, almost all from VisiCalc. In 1980, revenues grew to $3.7 million and the firm showed a profit of $157,000. In 1981, revenues from VisiCalc were approximately $14 million, growing to $22.6 million in 1982. Exhibits 3 and 4 show the financial growth of the company, and Exhibit 5 provides data on the growth and segmentation of the microsoftware industry.

Steven Wozniak, co-founder of Apple Computer, attributed much of his company's rise to the program:

> There were two factors that led to our success—our floppy disk and VisiCalc. Out of the original home computers, which included the TRS-80 [Radio Shack] and the Commodore PET, ours was the only one that had enough memory to run VisiCalc. VisiCalc and the floppy disk sent this company into the number-one position.... After VisiCalc, it was perceived that 90 percent of all Apple IIs sold were going to small businesses. Only 10 percent were going into this home hobby market that we originally thought was going to grow to be billions.

▲ EXHIBIT 2 Excerpts from the Marketing Agreement

Agreement made this 26 day of April 1979 between PERSONAL SOFTWARE, INC., of 22 Weitz Street, Boston, Mass. (hereinafter called "Publisher") and Software Arts, Inc. of 231 Broadway, Arlington, Mass. (hereinafter called "Owner").

1. *Grant of Rights.* The Owner hereby grants Publisher an exclusive worldwide license to copy, publish, sell, license and distribute the following computer software product: VisiCalc (hereinafter called the "Product")…

2. *Term.* The term of this Agreement shall commence on the date hereof and shall, unless sooner terminated, continue until the expiration of the last valid copyright anywhere in the world in the Product or any portion thereof…

6. *Maintenance.* Owner agrees to promptly deliver to Publisher modifications to the Product correcting any errors in the Product of which Publisher notifies the Owner within one year after delivery.… Owner and Publisher agree that due to the nature of complex computer programs such as the Product, Owner cannot warrant the Product to be completely free of errors at present or in the future.

8. *Marketing.* Publisher agrees within a reasonable time after delivery of the Product to it, but in no event later than 90 days from the date of such delivery, that it shall commence the public distribution of the Product, and Publisher agrees to make its best efforts to maximize sales and/or licenses of the Product. All aspects of marketing and distribution of the Product shall be in the Publisher's sole control…Publisher makes no representations or warranty that the Product will be successfully marketed or that any minimum level of sales or licensing will be achieved.

10. *Payments.* (*a*) Publisher shall, except as described in paragraph 10(*b*) hereof, pay to the Owner the amount of thirty-five & 7/10 percent of the Net Sales Price received by it with respect to all sales, leases, licenses or other transactions, pursuant to which copies of the Product are delivered to customers.…(*b*) The Publisher shall pay to the Owner the amount of fifty percent of Net Revenues received by it as a result of sales, leases, licenses, or other transactions pursuant to which the right to sell, lease, or license the Product is granted to a person or entity which assumes primary responsibility for marketing the Product to ultimate consumers and: (*i*) such transaction includes an order for at least 5,000 copies of the Product; or (*ii*) such person or entity is granted the right to reproduce and sell, lease, or license 5,000 or more copies of the Product.…

12. *New Versions.* … Publisher shall have the right, upon written notice to the Owner, to require the Owner to modify the Product for other personal computers than those described in paragraph 1 hereof, and Owner agrees to prepare and deliver to Publisher such new version following receipt, of such request within a reasonable period of time, provided, however, that Publisher pays to the Owner reasonable advances against amounts to be paid on sales on such new versions, that Publisher provides Owner with a personal computer of the type for which such new version is intended for a period reasonably necessary for the development and maintenance of such new version and further provided that Owner shall not be obliged to create such new version based on any request therefore received after December 31, 1980. In addition, Publisher shall have the exclusive right to market any new version of the Product developed by the Owner during the term hereof upon terms and conditions comparable to those contained herein, and the Owner agrees to promptly inform publisher of the availability of such new versions. In the event Publisher desires a specific new version of the Product other than as described above, Publisher shall notify the Owner and give the Owner the opportunity to create such new version under terms an conditions comparable to those provided herein. If Owner is unable or unwilling to so create any new versions of the Product within the time reasonably requested by the Publisher, Publisher shall have the right to create such new version itself following written notice to the Owner specifying a reasonable fixed cost to the Publisher thereof and

such cost shall be applied against any payments due the Owner for the resulting version of the Product hereunder. As used in paragraph 12, the term "new versions" shall mean versions meeting the Specifications for other personal computers as well as changed and improved versions of the Product which can be described by simple addenda to the Specifications.

14. *Trademarks.* Any trademarks used in connection with marketing of the Product shall be the sole property of the Publisher, but in the event of a reversion of rights in the Product to the Owner pursuant to paragraph 16 hereof, the Publisher agrees to transfer title to any such trademarks to the Owner if such trademarks are used solely in connection with the Product....

16. *Reversion to Owner.* If during any period of twelve months following the expiration of three months after delivery to the publisher of the Product, the payments to Owner hereunder do not exceed $1000.00, or if a petition under any bankruptcy or debtors law or a receiver or similar officer is appointed for Publisher and such proceedings or appointment are not promptly terminated and performance of Publisher hereunder does not continue as set forth herein, or in the event of a material breach of any provision hereof by Publisher, which breach is not cured 60 days after written notice thereof to the Publisher, terminate this Agreement and all rights granted to Publisher hereunder shall thereupon automatically revert to Owner except that Publisher may continue to dispose of copies of the Product in inventory at the time of termination unless Owner acquires such inventory form Publisher at the Publisher's cost thereof as then carried on its books....

17. *Default by Owner.* In the event of a material breach by Owner of any provision hereof which breach is not cured 60 days after written notice thereof by Publisher, Publisher may upon written notice to Owner elect to terminate this Agreement, and the rights granted it hereunder shall revert to Owner as provided in paragraph 16 hereof....

Originally we were a home hobby computer. Now, suddenly, small businesses were buying Apple IIs, and they wanted more features....These were all the things that one product, VisiCalc, led to.[1]

Before VisiCalc, many participants in the small computer industry expected that microcomputers would evolve by gradually taking on the power and tasks of minicomputers. In this view, the microcomputers were truncated minicomputers and would gain in speed and power over time until they could run the vast array of software already written for minicomputers. But VisiCalc was a serious application program that had no counterpart in the minicomputer or mainframe world. It performed the functions of financial modeling languages costing $20,000 and more, but did not require that the user learn a language. The program's success was generally attributed to three factors:

1. VisiCalc allowed users with no programming experience to construct quantitative models on the computer. Rather than traditional syntax rules, the program used the metaphor of a spreadsheet and locations on that sheet to structure the pattern of data relationships. As a result, new users could begin to perform useful work on the computer very quickly. Additionally, VisiCalc did not require the user to define the full structure of the model in advance, but encouraged incremental elaboration.

---

[1]Gregg Williams and Rob Moore, interviewers, "The Apple Story," *Byte,* January 1985, pp. 173–74.

▲ **EXHIBIT 3** VisiCorp Financial Results ($000,000)

	Total Revenue	VisiCalc Revenue	Product Develop.	SG&A Expense	Net Income
Total 1979	0.88	NA	0.04	0.44	(0.01)
Total 1980	3.85	NA	0.41	1.29	0.16
1981 Q1	2.62	NA	0.31	0.58	0.20
1981 Q2	4.79	NA	0.52	1.21	0.47
1981 Q3	4.84	NA	0.64	1.04	0.48
1981 Q4	6.55	NA	0.65	1.53	0.72
Total 1981	18.81	NA	2.11	4.36	1.87
1981 Q1	8.48	5.77	0.98	1.70	0.98
1982 Q2	7.61	5.59	1.31	2.14	0.26
1982 Q3	7.58	4.64	1.42	2.38	0.34
1982 Q4	10.05	6.56	1.49	3.31	0.82
Total 1982	33.73	22.56	5.19	9.54	2.40
1983 Q1	11.65	9.35	1.79	2.94	0.78
1983 Q2	12.41	7.60	NA	NA	0.27
1983 Q3	8.00	4.76	3.00	3.81	(0.92)
1983 Q4	8.27	1.87	NA	NA	(1.77)
Total 1983	40.25	23.58	10.07	16.27	(1.65)
1984 Q1	4.00	1.15	2.40	4.02	(3.68)
1984 Q2	8.17	NA	NA	NA	(7.88)

Note: VisiCalc revenues for 1982 estimated by casewriter.

Source: Company records, Regulation A reports, court records, trade journal reports, and casewriter's estimates.

2. VisiCalc exploited the high "visual bandwidth" of the personal computer, providing the user with instant visual response to changes in the model and quickly see the effects of that change. This allowed users to change a number in the model and quickly see the effects of that change.

3. VisiCalc was a general purpose tool, much like a word processor, and did not force any particular problem solution method on the user. Software which purported to "solve" problems had been, in general, much less well received than software which provided a powerful general-purpose tool.

▲ BUILDING VISICORP

As Personal Software grew, Fylstra added management. In the summer, Skip Vaccarello was hired to manage manufacturing and operations; in October, Bill Langenes joined the firm to handle advertising and promotion; and in November, Ed Esber, a Harvard classmate of Fylstra's, came aboard as marketing manager. In the spring of 1980, Mitch Kapor, whom Bob Frankston had met at the Boston Apple User's Group, was hired to manage new products.

▲ EXHIBIT 4   VisiCorp Revenues and Profit History

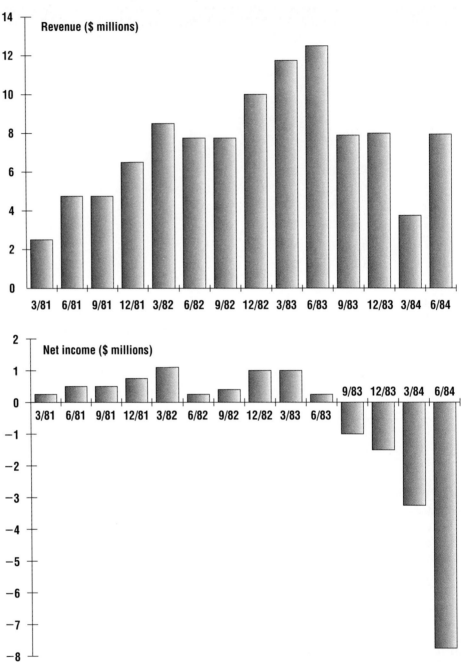

The early success of the company attracted the interest of the venture capital community, and in May of 1980 Personal Software raised $540,000 in return for 30 percent of the stock. The principal outside investors were Arthur Rock (Arthur Rock & Co.) and Venrock Associates (connected with Rockefeller family). Fylstra personally retained 39 percent of the stock and Jennings held 11 percent.

	1981	1982	1983	1984
All microcomputer software publisher revenue ($ millions)		187	398	747
Percent software for IBM PC and PC compatibles		2	13	37
Software sales by channel				
Mail order	31	28	24	17
Retail	58	57	57	57
Direct to corporations	1	3	4	6
Productivity software (%)		33	36	44
Breakdown of type of productivity software				
Wordprocessing (%)	39	36	30	26
Spreadsheet (%)	22	25	15	6
Database (%)	30	29	24	21
Multifunction (%)	0	4	20	37
Other (%)	9	10	10	10

Note: VisiCalc falls in the "Spreadsheet" category, Lotus 1-2-3 in the "Multifunction" category and accounts for most of it.
Source: Alex Brown, IDC, industry analysts, Future Computing, and casewriter's estimates.

After the first-round financing, the board pressed Fylstra to hire an experienced executive to serve as president and chief executive officer. In July, the decision was made to hire 32-year-old Terry Opdendyk for this critical position. Opdendyk had been corporate manager of human resources at Intel, and had previously served as an engineering manager in software development and in the microcomputer systems division of Intel. He was known by Hank Smith, who represented Venrock on the board.

That summer the new management team hammered out the basic product policies for the firm. Games and hobbyist programs now amounted to less than ten percent of revenues. Personal Software, they decided, would move away from the hobbyist market and seek to publish products in each of the five basic "generic" application areas: spreadsheets, word processing, database management, graphics, and communications. It already marketed a simple database manager (CCA/DMS) written by CCA Inc., and would soon add DeskTop Plan (written by Don Williams), a financial planning language. Mitch Kapor had written a statistical analysis program called Tiny Troll while at MIT and was working on a trend analysis and graphics program. To fill the gaps, Personal Software began to seek out authors who could be placed under contract to produce excellent programs in the communications and word processing areas.

While new products were sought, the marketing executives were busy moving the company from its mail-order origins to one that distributed to dealers. This approach soon proved limiting, however, and the company sought distribution through the growing regional software distribution companies. by the end of 1980, the company sold through over 1,000 dealers and regional distributors and used 17 sales representatives. Approximately two-thirds of its revenues derived from direct sales and the remaining one-third from contract or OEM sales.

In the spring of 1981, cumulative sales of VisiCalc reached 100,000 units. Personal Software raised $2.1 million through a second round of venture capital financing. It also added two marketing executives: Roy Folk became product manager and Rich Melman became director of product marketing. Together with Esber, this team developed the concept of a family of products. The company's advertising agency suggested that the identity of that family could be established by extending the use of the "visi" prefix from VisiCalc to the other products. The new line that emerged in May was advertised as "from the same people who brought you VisiCalc" and consisted of:

> *VisiDex:* an automated rolodex filing program (written by Peter Jennings).
>
> *VisiPlot:* charts and graphics (written by Mitch Kapor).
>
> *VisiTrend/VisiPlot:* regressions and time series analysis (written by Mitch Kapor).
>
> *VisiTerm:* communications management (written by Tom Keith).

Subsequently, other programs were added to the series: VisiFile in October 1981, VisiSchedule in February 1982, VisiWord in May 1983, and VisiSpell in June 1983.

Mitch Kapor had left Personal Software in late 1980 and had developed VisiTrend and VisiPlot under contract. Delivered by year end and released in April, the products earned Kapor royalties of almost $500,000 in six months. He explained his position:

> *I had a very attractive contract from my point of view because when that contract was signed in 79 [the same year as Software Arts], people didn't really understand the economics of this business. Today, [1984] software publishers offer 10 or 15 percent royalty contracts; I had a 33 percent contract.[2]*

Concerned about the high royalty rate, Personal Software approached Kapor on the issue and he suggested that he would sell full rights to both programs for $1.2 million. "We also sought rights of first refusal on other software Kapor might develop," Roy Folk recalled, "but Kapor wanted full control over IPL, his pet project." IPL was a concept for a language-based spreadsheet. Because Personal Software already had a fine spreadsheet, and a best efforts marketing clause with Software Arts, it was decided to let IPL go.

Another important event that spring was the secret development work on an IBM version of VisiCalc. Personal Software had been chosen by IBM as one of the three pre-announcement development sites of software for the still unannounced IBM PC. Personal Software executives who saw the machine became convinced that the new IBM machine, scheduled for release in August 1981, would revolutionize personal computing, taking it fully into the corporate world.

▲ BECOMING A DEVELOPMENT COMPANY

Although Dan Fylstra's original vision was of a pure publishing company, several factors led Personal Software to formulate plans to develop its own software. In part, Terry Opdendyk's experience at Intel led him to believe in the efficacy of organized development

---

[2]Quoted by Kevin Goldstein, "1-2-3 Steps Ahead," *Softalk,* February 1984, p. 28.

work rather than the "garage and attic" pattern that was common in the microsoftware industry. In addition, internal development provided a way of avoiding the very high royalties that successful programs generated.

During the spring of 1981, a set of objectives evolved that became broad specifications for a new generation of internally developed software. They were:

▲ *Fast switching.* It was currently difficult to switch from one program to another. For example, someone using VisiCalc might need to make a phone call and need to look up the phone number in their VisiDex file. but to use VisiDex one had to exit VisiCalc, reboot the machine, and then load VisiDex. After looking up the number, the process had to be reversed to return to the spreadsheet. Such a procedure was not an obvious improvement over a manual file system. These considerations led to the need for a way of rapidly switching between programs or tasks.

▲ *Data exchange.* Although Personal Software's products shared a common prefix, they were not fully "integrated." That is, it was not a simple matter to move information from one to the other. Fylstra was convinced that with the right data structures it would be possible to move information between spreadsheets, databases, documents, and graphs easily and quickly.

▲ *Common simple interface.* There were obvious gains to be had in standardizing the ways in which the company's programs displayed and accepted data and commands. In addition to this issue of a "common" interface, Roy Folk argued that ease-of-use would be an increasingly important issue in the industry. As hobbyists were replaced by business users, the winning programs would be those that minimized the time and trouble required to learn to use them effectively.

In July 1981, Xerox announced the Xerox Star Executive Workstation, a new machine using high-resolution "bit-mapped" display, "windows" on the screen to contain separate tasks, and a "mouse" pointing device to simplify the user interface.[3] The ideas behind Star came from the on-going work at Xerox's ivory tower PARC (Palo Alto Research Center), and Apple was known to be working on a scaled-down version of Star (later released as Lisa). Personal Software executives began to examine the windows system to see if it met the three development goals.

Opdendyk knew two talented software engineers working in Texas, Scott Warren and Dennis Abbe, who were independently developing Star-like interfaces. Visiting Sunnyvale, Abbe and Warren "blew our socks off with a demonstration of a Smalltalk implementation on a trash-80 [TRS-80]," one manager recalled. Soon after, a project team was formed to study the question of implementing windows in software on existing machines. The members were Roy Folk (marketing), Bill Coleman (development) and Abbe and Warren, who worked under contract through their firm Rosetta Inc.

The project was code-named Quasar; later the name VisiOn was adopted. Roy Folk recalled that period:

---

[3]Bit-mapped displays required the program to control each point of light on the screen rather than just the placement of characters. The bit-mapped approach gave great control over screen appearance but required substantial extra work from the microprocessor. Windows were rectangular portions of the screen set aside to contain information about a particular task. A mouse was a device that the user pushed across the desktop to control the position of a pointer on the screen.

We really had time to think and plan then. This was, I believe, one of the very few times that an innovative microsoftware product was specified from a marketing point of view. We sat down and defined 16 objectives for the product. It had to work in 128K of memory or less, it had to reside on floppy disks, it had to have rapid response times. We did extensive research on user needs and the psychology of the interface—How much delay will one tolerate on a file save? On a simple keystroke?

We did our homework. At one point we asked whether we really needed windows. could the product work with a simpler split-screen design? Rosetta did a study and discovered that there were things you just couldn't accomplish with that approach.

It took a while, but eventually everyone came on board. Dan [Fylstra] was skeptical about the mouse for almost a year, but he too became a believer.

By November 1981, the team had a simple prototype up and running on an Apple III computer. In December work shifted to a UNIX-VAX environment and the company began the process of staffing and managing a significant engineering development effort. Detailed specifications of the user interface began. Human factors specialists worked with focus groups and software engineers to refine the user interface and product function specifications.

In early 1982, Personal Software changed its corporate name to VisiCorp and in April embarked in earnest on the creation of VisiOn. At that time the product was seen as a mouse-windows environment within which applications programs would run. Although it was expected that outside firms would create applications to run within the VisiOn environment, VisiCorp management was strongly interested in developing its own applications programs for early release.

▲ COMDEX/FALL 1982

When Tom Towers, VisiCorp's new vice president of marketing and sales (hired in Mach 1982), saw the prototype of VisiOn he was astounded at how impressive it was. He argued that the company had a lot to show and should announce and demonstrate the product at Comdex/Fall, the microcomputer industry fall trade show. Others disagreed. Roy Folk, Ed Esber, and David Spencer took their case to Fylstra and Opdendyk, arguing that it was uncertain as to when VisiOn would be ready, that dealers would be angered by announcing a product that might not be ready for almost a year, that there was no upgrade policy in place, that the announcement would hurt the prospects for VisiWord, a new word processor to be released at Comdex/Fall, and that announcement would signal competition. Tom successfully countered, noting the need to generate excitement and the advantages of pre-announcing technology. "In his heart of hearts," Ed Esber explained, "Tom Towers believed that we were IBM and IBM always pre-announces technology, staving off the market."

The demonstration of the VisiOn prototype at Comdex/Fall "astounded the industry," one executive recalled. Many observers found it difficult to believe that the program was actually running on an IBM PC. A frequent comment on the floor of the convention was "Did you see the VisiCorp *movie*?" Bill Gates, the president of Microsoft, speculated that the PC might be simply acting as a terminal for a hidden VAX. Shortly after the show, Portia Isaacson, the president of Future Computing, visited VisiCorp to watch a demonstration of VisiOn. According to employees, she walked around the IBM PC and checked the cables to assure herself that it was really running the program by itself.

The announced system featured a bit-mapped screen that displayed multiple overlapping windows. Using a mouse pointing device, the user could easily and quickly select commands, obtain help, scroll the material within windows, and move data between windows. The promise of moving information from a spreadsheet to a document, graph display, or even to a modem by simply pointing at the data and clicking the mouse was especially powerful. Exhibit 6 shows some of the proposed VisiOn screens.

The announcement of VisiOn definitely "shook up" the microcomputer industry, and established VisiCorp as a strong contender in the competition to define the next generation of software. It also, however, committed the company to the delivery of VisiOn in the summer of 1983.

▲ COMPETITIVE PRESSURES

Another product announced at Comdex/Fall was Lotus 1-2-3, an integrated spreadsheet, graphics, and database program. The program was the brainchild of Mitch Kapor and had evolved from the IPL project he took with him when he left VisiCorp two years earlier. Kapor had used the $1.2 million he received from VisiCorp to found Lotus Development. Raising venture capital, he got software engineer Jonathan Sachs to rework IPL into a combined spreadsheet, database, and graphics product that had the working name of Trio. Trio was originally written in the C language, but Kapor and Sachs abandoned that approach in favor of maximizing the program's performance by writing it directly in assembly language. The end result was Lotus 1-2-3.

Lotus 1-2-3 provided an excellent spreadsheet which, by itself, was a highly competitive product. To that Lotus had added neatly integrated graphics capabilities and a set of simple database functions that operated on spreadsheet information. First shipped in January, by March Lotus 1-2-3 had become the best-selling business software package. For the first six months of 1983, Lotus reported revenues of $12.6 million. In August it went public, raising $27 million and establishing a market value in excess of $200 million.

The effect on VisiCorp was immediate. Revenues from VisiCalc reached their all-time high in January and began to slide downwards thereafter (Exhibit 3).

Reviewers and industry observers agreed that VisiCalc was outclassed by Lotus 1-2-3 and other second-generation spreadsheets like SuperCalc3. While VisiCalc had been one of the first programs on the IBM PC, it had been simply "moved" to the IBM PC rather than redesigned to take advantage of the second-generation hardware it provided. Advanced versions of VisiCalc had been developed by Software Arts for the Apple II and Apple III, but the promised IBM PC version was not yet ready. But even VisiCalc Advanced Version did not provide the integral graphics and database functions of Lotus 1-2-3.

VisiWord, which had been introduced at Comdex/Fall, also faced problems in the market. The product had been conceptually designed by VisiCorp's marketing department and developed under contract by an outside firm. When the results were not satisfactory, an internal development team reworked the product. Unfortunately, the final result did not meet the original performance specifications. Released despite these problems, VisiWord received a number of openly hostile reviews (Exhibit 7).

▲ VisiOn DEVELOPMENT

The positive response to the demonstration of VisiOn convinced management to push ahead at top speed with the VisiOn project. A 52-person development group was formed to move VisiOn from being a prototype to a marketable product. To do this the engineers had to flesh out three layers of software. The deepest was a shell around the operating system that

EXHIBIT 6   VisiOn Screen Display

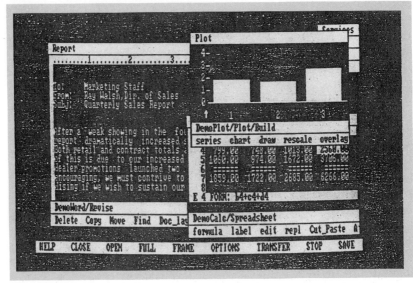

Exhibit 7   Excerpts from Reviews of VisiWord

From Steven Manes, "VisiWord: What You See Is (Almost) What You Get," *PC Magazine,*
November 1983, pp. 579–98:

> *I am not using VisiWord to write this review. A deadline as inflexible as a fixed disk looms. I
> need speed.... I need a nice restful screen that doesn't fry my eyeballs and sear my brain while
> I am working. VisiWord flunks on all counts.*

> *For some reason, VisiWord gives priority to keeping every part of the screen current but the
> part you're working on. You don't actually lose keystrokes; you just don't get to see them for a
> good long while.... To give myself an idea of the snail-like pace of VisiWord, I hit the Enter key
> 20 times at the beginning of a document to get a nice clean screen to work with. I waited an in-
> terminable 15 seconds until VisiWord was ready to acknowledge my presence again.*

> *You can't combine attributes, so if you want something both underlined and boldfaced, or sub-
> scripted and boldfaced, you're out of luck.... And the only way to see which attribute has been
> given an inverse video letter is to move the cursor to it and check the status line....*

> *I don't have to think very hard to think of the many things VisiWord does not do—things like
> footnoting, indexing, multiple windows, and letting you insert non-printing comments in a file.*

From *Infoworld,* May 5, 1984, p. 17:

> *VisiWord has most of the features anyone is likely to need in a word processor. In fact, it comes
> close to some of the dedicated word processors in terms of completeness.... In fact, the only
> serious problem with VisiWord's performance—and some people may find it a crippling one—
> is that it does some things very s-l-o-w-l-y.*

> *The menu structure makes VisiWord easy to learn, but some people may find that it slows them
> down after they become expert.*

handled file management, the display, and created a virtual memory[4] function. One level above that was the VisiOn command system and finally came the applications program itself. The deepest code was done in assembly language, but higher layers were written in C because Bill Coleman, VisiOn development group manager, wanted to make it easy to move the program to other machines when the need arose.

Despite VisiCorp's public promise to have VisiOn ready for release by the summer of 1983, employees close to the project knew that it was not likely to be ready then. The problems in getting the various applications to share memory and swap information were proving unexpectedly difficult. By February it was clear to all that VisiOn would not be ready for release until the fourth quarter. As the pace of development work increased, it also became evident that some of the original design goals could not be met. Roy Folk recalled that

> A critical compromise occurred when the developers said that the release version would only run on a hard-disk system. They estimated that it would take a prohibitive amount of time to hand-work the code to get it to run on a floppy-disk system. I felt that slipping the floppy-disk design goal was a terrible mistake from a marketing point of view. Hard disk systems accounted for only 16 percent of the installed base and Future Computing forecast that they would account for 20 percent of 1984 shipments. If we couldn't release a floppy system we automatically cut ourselves out of most of the market.

Folk lost that battle. Tom Towers and other executives believed that VisiOn's primary market was the corporate world and that hard disks would be ubiquitous there. They argued that the "fast switching" and "data movement" services of VisiOn would not amount to much if the user had to continually swap floppy disks for each new application. Finally, the delay required to compress the program was considered unacceptable.

▲ ORGANIZATIONAL PROBLEMS

In shifting from a software publishing company to a development house, VisiCorp moved the internal focus of attention from its marketing department to engineering. Terry Opdendyk, as CEO and architect of the change, was openly criticized by many disgruntled marketing executives. One former VisiCorp executive recalls that "Terry ignored the marketing side of the house in favor of the development people, but was never able to adequately control the engineering effort." *Infoworld* would later describe this era as a "corporate civil war."[5] According to Ed Esber, "The tragedy is the number of talented people that Opdendyk forced out. A year ago, VisiCorp had a better marketing team than any company in the industry. And its gone."[6] One indication of the problems within VisiCorp was the exit of key executives. The list of the best-known VisiCorp alumni who went on to positions of influence in the industry was impressive:

> Mitch Kapor, project manager for VisiCalc, left November 1980 and went on to found and act as president of Lotus Development Corp.

---

[4]Virtual memory allowed large applications programs to run in machines with smaller amounts of memory. The technique involved swapping chunks of data between disk and fast RAM memory. The advantage was a high degree of machine independence. The disadvantage was that performance of many routine operations became tied to the speed of the disk drive.
[5]Denise Caruso, "Can VisiCorp Come Back?" *Infoworld,* July 2, 1984, pp. 49–51.
[6]Ibid., p. 50.

Ed Esber, executive vice president of marketing, left April 1983 and went on to become president and chief executive officer of Ashton-Tate.

Richard Melman, director of product marketing, left April 1983 and went on to co-found Electronic Arts and, in 1985, was an independent marketing consultant.

Roy Folk, product-marketing manager of VisiOn, left May 1983 and went on to found Paladin Software and in 1985 became executive vice president for marketing and planning at Ashton-Tate.

Don Farrow, regional sales manager, left June 1983 and went on to become the president of Heads-Up-Technology.

Steve Weyl, product manager, left July 1983 and went on to become a vice president of Syntelligence.

David Spencer, director of marketing communications, left in early 1984 and went on to become a vice president with Computerland.

Tom Towers, vice president of marketing and sales, left in early 1984 and went on to become the chief executive officer of Knoware.

▲ SUIT AND COUNTERSUIT

In September of 1983, VisiCorp filed suit against Software Arts, charging breach of contract, seeking an award of $10 million as compensation for lost revenues and lost good will and an additional $50 million in punitive damages. In its complaint, VisiCorp charged that (1) Software Arts had not met its contractual obligations to deliver agreed upon new versions of VisiCalc, (2) that Software Arts allocated its development efforts towards its own proprietary product (TK! Solver) rather than VisiCalc development, and (3) that Software Arts had misrepresented its willingness and ability to develop new versions of VisiCalc. Exhibit 8 provides information on the new versions of VisiCalc requested by VisiCorp and worked on by Software Arts.

Taken by surprise, Software Arts quickly responded with a counterclaim. VisiCorp, it argued, had not used its "best efforts" to market VisiCalc but had instead channeled its profits into the development of VisiOn and VisiOn Calc, programs which built on VisiCalc technology. Furthermore, Software Arts claimed that VisiOn Calc was a "new version" of VisiCalc, within the meaning of paragraph 12 of the 1979 contract (Exhibit 2), and that it had not been offered right of first refusal on its development and that it was due royalties on its sale. VisiCalc claimed, in response, that VisiOn Calc was not a new version of VisiCalc, so that Software Arts was not due any royalties.

▲ THE RELEASE OF VisiOn

Apple released its Lisa computer in the summer of 1983. Priced at $10,000, the machine provided a mouse and windows interface modeled after the Xerox Star and was intended to be Apple's entry into the corporate world. Lisa was hailed as a marvel of interface design, but many users complained that it was slow—that performance had been sacrificed to obtain ease of use.

VisiCorp released VisiOn in December 1983, 13 months after its announcement and 3 months late. It required 2.2 megabytes of hard-disk space and 512K of RAM memory. The pricing was:

▲ EXHIBIT 8   New Versions of VisiCalc Developed by Software Arts as
Requested by VisiCorp

Version	Date Requested	Date Promised	Date Delivered
Tandy III	11–80	6–81	10–81
IBM 156	12–80	7–81	9–91
IBM VAV	2–81	6–82	12–83*
IBM 177-1	2–81	6–82	nd
Apple II VAV	2–81	3–82	8–83
Apple III EV	3–81	8–81	11–81
HP 125	3–81	5–81	10–81
Tandy II EV	7–81	9–81	12–82
Apple III VAV	11–81	6–82	10–82†
DEC VAV	12–81	8–82	nd
Sony	12–81	4–82	2–83
Apple II DOS VAV	7–82	2–83	nd
Tandy IV	7–82	4–83	7–83
TI VAV	10–82	3–83	nd
Wang VAV	2–83	8–83	nd

*VisiCorp claimed this version was unacceptable
†VisiCorp claimed this version contained major bugs
Note: "nd" means the version had not been delivered. VAV refers to VisiCalc Advanced Version. Other versions shown are enhancements of the original product.
Source: *VisiCorp v. Software Arts,* Plaintiffs' Answers to Defendants' Interrogatories (First Set), 12/21/83. This information was provided by VisiCorp in response to legal interrogations and to support its suit. Software Arts did not necessarily agree with this information.

VisiOn Applications Manager	$495
VisiOn Mouse	250
VisiOn Calc (spreadsheet)	395
VisiOn Graph	250
VisiOn Word	375
Total package	$1,765

Together with the computer and hard disk, the cost of installing a VisiOn system was approximately $7,500.

Initial reactions to VisiOn were mixed (Exhibit 9). On the one hand, industry experts praised it as a technical tour de force, calling it the "wave of the future," and the "end of operating systems." On the other hand, beginners tended to find the screen confusing and it was slow, even slower than Lisa. Retailers found that customers compared VisiOn to Lotus 1-2-3 and found it wanting. One Computerland manager recalled that:

A first-time user was simply daunted by the complexity of VisiOn and the investment required to implement it. More experienced users had almost all used or seem Lotus 1-2-3 in action and could not stand the much slower response of VisiOn Calc. It was also common for salespeople *to say that "with Lotus 1-2-3 you got three functions for $495," which meant that with VisiOn you paid almost $600 for each function.*

▲ EXHIBIT 9 Excerpts from a Review of VisiOn

From Thomas Bonoma, "VisiOn: Enough Functionality to Sink a Ship?" *Softalk,* July 1984, pp. 24–32:

VisiOn was conceived in 1982 as the answer to knowledge workers' need for complete functional integration—integration between user, screen, storage, and computation....

Although there are some restrictions on the transfer command, data transfer among VisiOn applications is, for the most part, a miracle of ease. You simply point the mouse to the area of the spreadsheet, report, or whatever it is you want to move, and the transfer is managed automatically. It is even possible, for example, to point to a rectangular block of numbers on a spreadsheet, then point to the graphics screen, and have a bar chart appear. Pure black magic!

With all this functionality underlying every application, you might suspect that VisiOn would be a little slow in operation. It is and it isn't. It's slow in some cases and deadly slow in others.... Moreover, the use of the mouse for everything imaginable means that user sophistication will in large measure determine satisfaction with the system. Even fair typists will likely become inpatient with VisiOn's leave the keyboard, hit a mouse selection, wait, hit a confirmation, wait, wait, choose "done," wait, move back to the keyboard, nope, choose another selection, wait, et cetera style. The option to enter commands at the keyboard instead of via the mouse is not much help on this score. What's going on is that the program is constantly running out to the disk for one thing or another; these disk calls cause delays ranging from half a second to five seconds, and their net effect is to make you wait no matter how you've entered your command.

VisiOn Word is in many ways the star of the system.... Word falls short as a consequence of its being a part of the VisiOn system rather than a stand-alone word processor...the program lacks a certain functionality that a professional writer might demand. There is no provision, for example, for mail-merge, spelling checking, automatic figure numbering, or insertion of graphics.

In summary, the VisiOn system is a milestone in personal computer software. Like many other milestones, it both points the way toward the future and falls far short of it.

Two other events hurt the acceptance of VisiOn. In December 1983, Microsoft announced its intention to offer a new operating environment called "Windows." Scheduled for release by May 1984,[7] Windows would provide a way for existing software to operate within a windows environment. Microsoft said it would be priced between $100 and $250. Secondly, in January Apple released the Macintosh, a $2,500 mouse-and-windows-based machine. Although little software was available for it, the Macintosh received excellent coverage in the media and began to sell extremely well.

No third-party software was available for VisiOn and Fylstra admitted that it would be slow in coming. The development of a VisiOn application required a UNIX-based VAX and VisiOn development tools, which had just been released in December. Fylstra commented that:

---

[7]Microsoft did not release Windows until the spring of 1985. Industry observers coined the term "vaporware" to describe the situation of announced but nonexistentent or only partially developed software.

People have come to expect that applications are going to materialize overnight for these new generation window managers and I don't think that is realistic to expect from software developers. Existing applications just aren't designed to share memory with other applications, and they generally are not designed to use the mouse or graphics as part of the display.[8]

To help boost sales, VisiCorp reduced the price of the VisiOn Applications Manager from $495 to $99 in February, and cut the price of the three application package to $990. Orders increased somewhat, but sales continued to b disappointing.

▲ VISIWAR

In December 1983, Software Arts delivered to VisiCorp the VisiCalc Advanced Version (VAV) for the IBM PC. VisiCorp refused to accept the product, claiming that it was not marketable.

On February 3, 1984, Software Arts filed an amended countersuit. The new charges were that VisiCorp had advertised VisiOn Calc as a superior replacement for VisiCalc. In addition, Software Arts claimed that VisiCorp had released VisiCalc IV, an enhanced version of VisiCalc, without giving Software Arts its contractually guaranteed right of first refusal on the development of the enhancement. Software Arts sought damages which, under Massachusetts law, could amount to as much as $87 million.

With regard to VisiCalc IV, Fylstra defended VisiCorp's actions, explaining that

As a stop-gap measure, VisiCorp acquired the marketing rights to the program called StretchCalc, which was then marketed by MultiSoft Corporation as a separate product, to supplement VisiCalc with graphics capabilities and other functions…although VisiCorp's marketing efforts have resulted in substantial sales of VisiCalc IV with full contractual royalties paid to Software Arts, VisiCorp has not even recovered its advertising costs from the promotion of VisiCalc IV. Moreover, VisiCalc IV's graphics capability competes directly with VisiCorp's VisiTrend/Plot product, which provides stand-along graphics functions and on which VisiCorp pays no royalties.[9]

As Software Arts filed its counterclaim, it simultaneously informed VisiCorp that its refusal to market VAV for the IBM PC, together with other actions, amounted to a breach of the 1979 marketing agreement. Consequently, Software Arts was terminating the agreement and, according to paragraph 16, was entitled to the return of complete rights to the VisiCalc trademark.

Software Arts' initiative coincided with the 1984 Personal Computer Forum, a yearly meeting of industry leaders. At the forum, and in meetings that followed, Software Arts' representatives explained the company's actions and announced its intention to form a "SWAT" team to develop a new version of VisiCalc. Software Arts would market the new program itself. Orders for the new product were taken from OEMs and dealers. Software Arts' plans included a mail-order offer to all registered owners of VisiCalc to trade-up to the new Software Arts version for $99.50.

VisiCorp immediately sought an injunction against Software Arts' planned use of the VisiCalc trademark. However, the U.S. District Court in Boston denied the request. Both companies now claimed the right to the VisiCalc trademark and to the access it provided to the approximately 700,000 VisiCalc users; the dispute would have to be decided in court.

---

[8]Quoted in Ed Scannel, "VisiCorp's Fortunes' Flicker," *Micro-Market World,* March 1984, p. 34.
[9]Affidavit of Daniel H. Fylstra in Support of a Temporary Restraining Order and Preliminary Injunction, *VisiCorp v. Software Arts,* February 12, 1984.

Both Fylstra and Bricklin were quoted in the media as being willing to settle out of court, but no substantive offers were made. "It takes two sides to make a settlement,"[10] Bricklin said. Regarding his counteroffensive, Bricklin added "When someone sues you for a large sum of money you can't sit back and say 'Oh.' You have to do something or else pay $60 million. The legal process involves that you've got to defend yourself."[11]

As the court case developed, the critical issue became the ownership of the trademark. Paragraph 14 (Exhibit 2) stated that

> *Any trademarks used in connection with marketing of the Product shall be the sole property of the Publisher, but in the event of a reversion of rights in the Product to the Owner [Software Arts] pursuant to paragraph 16 hereof, the Publisher agrees to transfer title to any such trademarks to the Owner* **if such trademarks are used solely in connection with the Product.**

VisiCorp's position was that it had registered the trademark "VisiCalc" and had used it in connection with several other products. Consequently, it was argued, the last phrase prevented the trademark's reversion to Software Arts. Bricklin, on the other hand, maintained that the phrase

> *was inserted at the insistence of Daniel Fylstra to protect Personal Software's already existing trademarks....Fylstra expressed his concern to me that these marks not be included among those automatically returned to Software Arts under its reversionary rights upon termination of the 1979 agreement by Software Arts.*[12]

▲ COLLAPSE

In October 1983, Fylstra had predicted that 1984 revenues would top $50 million, a 48 percent increase over 1983 results. At that time, however, third-quarter revenues were barely above the previous year's level—Fylstra was counting on VisiOn to pull the company out of the doldrums. But the continuing decline of VisiCalc and the lukewarm reception given VisiOn began to create financial difficulties. VisiCorp lost $1.7 million in the last quarter of 1983 and lost $3.7 million in the first quarter of 1984.

In May, VisiCorp cut its workforce by 20 percent and announced price cuts of between 30 and 65 percent on most of its software products. VisiCalc's price was cut from $250 to $99 and VisiOn became available on special promotion for $795. The company also announced that it would market a new spreadsheet, FlashCalc, for the Apple II series of computers. FlashCalc was targeted to compete with Multiplan and SuperCalc on the Apple II, and boasted the fastest recalculation and file load times. Lotus 1-2-3 was not available for the Apple II line of computers.

In June, VisiCorp received another round of venture capital from its current set of investors, raising about $2 million on terms reported to be $0.20 per share. At its height, VisiCorp stock had changed hands at $11 per share.

In July, Terry Opdendyk resigned as president and from his position on the board. *Infoworld* quoted Ed Esber as remarking that the move was "about two years overdue."[13] Fylstra assumed the duties of president and soon thereafter Rich Melman, who had once been a marketing executive with VisiCorp. was elected to fill Opdendyk's position on the board.

---

[10]Quoted by Carrie Gottlieb, "S'ware Arts Seeking Market Visibility," *Computer Retail News,* March 19, 1984, p. 14.
[11]Ibid.
[12]Affidavit of Daniel S. Bricklin, *Software Arts v. VisiCorp,* 2/9/84, p. 3.
[13]Denise Caruso, "Opdendyk Leaves VisiCorp," *Infoworld,* July 16, 1984, p. 14.

With Opdendyk gone and losses mounting, Fylstra accelerated the company's contraction in employment and began a systematic program of liquidating assets. In August, the VisiOn technology was sold to control Data Corporation for a rumored $2.5 million. VisiCorp retained the rights to retail marketing of the product. Control Data, in turn, became the developer and planned to use its sales force to sell the product directly to its Fortune 500 clients.

Shortly thereafter, VisiCorp sold its Communications Solutions Inc. (CSI) subsidiary to Control Data, reportedly receiving between $4 and $5 million. CSI had been acquired in May 1983 and its principle product was Access/SNA, a micromainframe communication technology.

In September, after three days of courtroom testimony, VisiCorp and Software Arts agreed to settle their dispute out of court. The terms were

1. VisiCorp agreed to pay Software Arts $500,000 in disputed royalties for past sales of VisiCalc.
2. Software Arts received the VisiCalc trademark. VisiCorp would continue to be able to employ the *visi* prefix but could not market another product using the term *calc* except for FlashCalc.
3. Software Arts promised not to use the term *visi* in any of its future products.
4. Software Arts waived any claim to royalties on FlashCalc and VisiOn Plan (previously VisiOn Calc).
5. The 1979 marketing agreement was formally terminated.

In November, VisiCorp began to ship VisiOn Version 1.2, the last work of the in-house development team. The program was 1.5 times faster than the original, made more use of function keys, and supported more printing functions. It was priced at $495 complete.

In the same month, VisiCorp began work on a plan to merge with Paladin Software. Paladin was a start-up development venture founded by Roy Folk, who had been VisiOn product manager up until May 1983. The merger appeared justified to the board because VisiCorp had been selling assets and was cash rich, but lacked any promising new products to push. Paladin, on the other hand, had an exciting new product under development but had experienced trouble in raising a second round of venture capital.

After much discussion, it was decided that the surviving company, although technically VisiCorp, would be named Paladin. Folk explained that there remained an "image problem" connected with the VisiCorp name, especially in regard to the delays with VisiOn.[14] Fylstra stepped down as president, retaining a position on the board. According to his associates, Fylstra was seeking new entrepreneurial ventures.

▲ POSTMORTEMS

Dan Fylstra: I think the pre-announcement [of VisiOn] hurt a fair amount, but we had a lot of things on our minds....The fact is that VisiOn is the only system that is real. On of the problems we have had to deal with is our reality versus everybody else's promises. Promises are always better than reality.[15]

---

[14]Quoted by Valerie Rice, "VisiCorp Loses Name as Result of Merger with Paladin," *Computer Retail News,* November 19, 1984, p. 6.
[15]Quoted by Denise Caruso, "Can VisiCorp Come Back?," *Infoworld,* July 2, 1984, p. 51.

Our biggest mistake was not finding a way to extract ourselves sooner from the situation with Software Arts. That problem was much larger than any of the problems we were having with VisiOn.[16]

Roy Folk: VisiOn suffered because of the early announcement and because of performance problems. Performance suffered because of the early decision to use a bit-mapped display—a decision we never questioned. In this industry a program can survive errors but not performance problems. Many users never push a program far enough to find its bugs, but performance problems nag at you continually. Good management cannot overcome serious product flaws.

VisiCorp's most serious mistake was letting the relationship with Software Arts sour. In retrospect, we should have found a way to keep VisiCalc alive.

Ed Esber: A lesson to be learned is that it is possible to have very rapid growth in spite of yourself and yet to begin to feel like you controlled that growth, that you made it happen. You have a feeling of invincibility that comes from selling so many units. But there is really very little continuing franchise in this business.

VisiOn was a technological marvel; it still is a marvelous product. The engine [IBM PC] just wasn't powerful enough to carry it. VisiOn didn't sink the company, Lotus 1-2-3 or the lack of a better VisiCalc did.

---

[16]Quoted in "Bloopers, Botches & Blunders of 1984," *Micro Marketworld*, December 1984.

BIRDS EYE AND THE U.K. FROZEN FOOD INDUSTRY (A)

On February 12, 1946, George Muddiman arrived in Liverpool from Canada to take up the job as the first chairman of Birds Eye Foods Ltd. "It was raining," he recalled. "There were no lights on the streets, it was seven o'clock at night and dark. As I looked out of the cab window my heart went into my boots and I thought, 'What have I done? Why have I left Canada to come to this?'"[1]

By the early 1950s, after a host of problems with production, raw materials, and distribution, Birds Eye was firmly established. In 1952, it opened the "Empire's largest quick-frozen food factory" in Great Yarmouth and was set to embark upon a period of continuous expansion. By 1964 the company was able to report that U.K. frozen foods sales for the previous year had grown to £75 million (from a mere £150,000 in 1946) (Exhibits 1a and 1b) with Birds Eye accounting for 70 percent of the market (Exhibit 2).

However, from the late 1960s both return on capital and market share declined as competition in the market intensified. By the retirement of Birds Eye's second chairman, James Parratt ("Mr. Fish Fingers"), at the end of July 1972, the company's fortunes had passed their peak. By 1983 Birds Eye's share of tonnage frozen food sales to the consumer market had shrunk to 18.5 percent.

This case, prepared by Professor David J. Collis, is largely excerpted from Professor Robert M. Grant's case of the same name, © 1985. It also draws on P. Geroski, and T. Vlassopoulos, "The Rise and Fall of a Market Leader: Frozen Foods in the U.K.," *Strategic Management Journal,* vol. 12, © 1991, pp. 467–78; J. Sutton, "Sunk Costs and Market Structure," chapter 8, © 1991; and "Frozen Foodstuffs," The Monopolies and Mergers Commission, © 1974. Copyright © 1992 by the President and Fellows of Harvard College.
[1]W.J. Reader, *Birds Eye Foods Ltd: The Early Days,* © 1963, p. 19.

▲ EXHIBIT 1a   Growth in Volume Sales of Frozen Foods to Households, 1951–1984

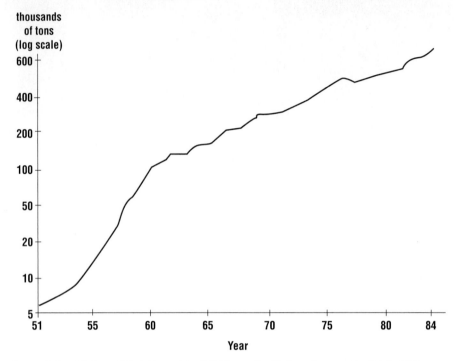

Source: Robert M. Grant, "Birds Eye and the U.K. Frozen Food Industry," case study, © July 1985.

▲ EXHIBIT 1b   U.K. Frozen Food Expenditure, 1967–1982

	At Constant 1975 Prices* (£ million)	Freezer Owners	Nonfreezer Owners	Consumption In-Home	Catering
1967	322	—	—	84%	16%
1973	510	17%	54%	71	29
1974	527	20	50	70	30
1975	500	24	48	72	28
1976	515	30	46	76	24
1977	508	32	43	75	25
1978	514	37	40	77	23
1979	539	40	37	77	23
1980	570	47	32	79	21
1981	593	53	28	81	19
1982	621	59	24	84	16
1983	646	63	21	84	16
1984	692	67	18	85	15

*Sales at current prices deflated by the index of retail food prices.
Source: Birds Eye.

▲ EXHIBIT 2   Market Shares (percent, retail volume basis)

	1966	1970	1974	1978	1982
↓Birds Eye	62	60	45	29	20
⁻ Ross	5	8	6	6	8
↓ Findus	13	13	11	8	4
↗ Own label	—	6	14	21	28
↗Other	20	13	21	35	40

Source: Casewriter.

▲ THE EARLY DEVELOPMENT OF THE FROZEN FOOD INDUSTRY

Quick-freezing arrests the process of decay in perishable foodstuffs and enables fresh foods to be distributed to the consumer, wherever located and at any season.[2] However, the freezing process must be quick to prevent the formation of large ice crystals that damage the cell structure of the food. By the late 1920s, General Foods Corporation was successfully manufacturing and marketing Birds Eye frozen foods in the United States using multi-plate quick freezer developed by Clarence Birdseye.

The establishment of Birds Eye frozen foods in the U.K. was the initiative of Robert Ducas, the chairman of a Kent engineering company, Winget Ltd., who had tried frozen foods in the United States and was impressed by their British potential. In August 1938 Birds Eye Foods Ltd. was incorporated, owned by General Foods Corp., Robert Ducas, and Chivers and Sons Ltd. (a British canner and jam maker).

Birds Eye was not alone in pioneering frozen foods in Britain (Exhibit 3). Commercial quick-freezing had begun in Britain before 1939, initiated by Smedley's (National Canning). In the early years, Smedley's was better established than Birds Eye. Among other leading firms striving to establish viable frozen food businesses were the distributors and marketers of fish, notably Smethurst Ltd., Mudd and Son, and Associated Fisheries Ltd. (through Eskimo Foods Ltd.). A cold storage company, Union International launched "Fropax" frozen foods and Manuel's, an importer and wholesaler of frozen foods, and also obtained the U.K. concession for importing and distributing Findus frozen foods.

By 1942, Unilever had become strongly interested in the Birds Eye business for its value to its subsidiaries MacFisheries (fish), Bachelors Peas (dried peas), and Poulton & Noel, Ltd. (poultry). At a meeting of Unilever's Special committee on February 4, 1942, the guidelines for a frozen food business were established:

> They expected to see the business develop in three main groups of produce—fruit and vegetables, fish, and meat. They hoped to see Birds Eye companies in operation all over the world, and they expected to get together a team of people who could go wherever they were needed to give help with setting up these new companies. They could see that some of their products were likely to be expensive, and they were not against running luxury lines, but in the true tradition

---

[2]Frozen food does not include frozen whole animals or birds, uncooked butcher's meat, or ice cream.

▲ EXHIBIT 3   Early Competitors

	1930s	1940s	1950s	1960s
Birds Eye	1938	1942		Acquired by Unilever
Smethurst		Acquired by Unilever		
Findus	(Manuel's)		1956	1968
Eskimo (Assoc. Fisheries)			Acquired by Nestlé	Acquired by Nestlé
Fropax (Union International)				Merged in 1963
J. Lyons				
Ross Group			1959	1969
Youngs				Acquired by Imperial Group
Smedley's				
Bailey's				
Mudd & Co.				

Source: Casewriter.

of a business founded on the demand of the mass market for everyday products, they hoped that, in general, the business would be built on the large-scale development of certain main products.[3]

In March 1943, when the Second World War was at its height, Unilever acquired Birds Eye Foods. Its task of establishing a frozen food business on any scale in the U.K. was formidable:

> The costs of quick-freezing are high, and it does not pay to freeze any food except the best, that will sell for a price high enough to cover overhead and yield a profit worth having. . . . Next, food must be frozen at the top of its condition or most of the value of the process is lost. That means that something must be done to see that produce is gathered at precisely the right moment and processed, if possible, within hours. For fish, of course, and for some other foods, there can be no control over production, but there must be a highly efficient buying organization.

> When the produce is frozen, there is the problem of keeping it so until it reached the [consumer]. Since many of the products, such as peas, are seasonal, that means keeping them for months in cold storage. On the journey from factory to shop, there must be insulated vehicles. In the shops themselves, there must be cabinets; the shopkeepers must be persuaded to find room, and somebody must finance them—either the shopkeepers themselves or the freezing firms.[4]

One of the first tasks for frozen foods companies was to secure supplies of high-quality raw materials. For vegetables, this was usually achieved through annual contracts with farmers who committed a certain acreage to a processor, such as Birds Eye, in return for a fixed

---

[3]Reader, *Birds Eye Foods Ltd.*, p. 9.
[4]Ibid., p.3.

price per ton according to quality. The processor exercised close control over the crops, supplying the seed, determining planting times, and approving the fertilizer and insecticide used. Technicians monitored the moisture level in the produce to determine the optimal harvesting time and radioed the processing plants, which coordinated the movement of harvesting equipment from farm to farm and the transportation of produce from farm to factory.

Initially, Birds Eye owned most of the harvesting equipment that its growers used. Equipment took the place of manual labor because of the speed with which the crop needed to be harvested before freezing. It remained economical to pick fresh peas manually. Over the years, growers bought their own machines under long-term contracts with Birds Eye, which agreed to repurchase the equipment if the two parties could not agree on an annual acreage contract. Because of the high cost of pea harvesting equipment, farmer cooperatives became the main source of vegetables. By 1974 they were supplying 70 percent of the peas and 60 percent of the beans used for freezing. Many had been supplying Birds Eye continuously for 20 years. As the demand for frozen vegetables grew, the frozen food industry became the single most important customer for green vegetables. In 1975 half of all peas were grown for freezing as were three-quarters of green beans.

The fish used for quick-freezing was whitefish, mainly cod, haddock, halibut, plaice, sole, and coley. Most of it was either bought fresh from dockside auctions or imported from Scandinavia in frozen blocks of fillets for use in fish fingers and other heavily processed items. Some fish, however, was frozen at sea and bought on contract. A typical contract guaranteed to buy a certain proportion of the catch, provided the catch exceeded a certain size, at a price up to 5 percent below the previous month's average auction price. One-third of the total whitefish catch went to freezers by the late 1960s, and contracts were tending to replace the old open auction at fish markets.

In production, the chief problems arose from the concentration of processing into a short time space, the unreliability of machinery, and the lack of skilled labor. Much of the machinery had to be imported from the United States and Canada, and capital costs were high. Over two-thirds of processing costs were fixed, although each plate freezer could be used to freeze any food depending on seasonal demand (Exhibit 4). The location of frozen food processing factories was determined primarily by the source of raw materials. Prepared foods, like desserts or entrees, could be located anywhere. However, for vegetables and fish the industry had to locate on the eastern side of Great Britain, near the vegetable growing areas and the big fishing ports. Peas, for example, needed to be processed within 90 minutes of picking, so processing plants were concentrated in Humberside, Lincolnshire, and East Anglia.

Production problems were small in comparison with those of establishing a national system of distribution. Distribution costs were estimated at between 15 percent and 25 percent of total costs for frozen food.[5] Only a limited capacity existed in public cold stores, used mainly for frozen meat and fish and ice cream, and concentrated near big cities. Cold stores were also expensive. A minimum efficient scale 2.4m ft³ store cost £0.6m in the mid-1960s, and the scale curve on operating expenses was about 80 percent.

The major barrier to the development of the frozen foods industry was, however, the state of retail distribution. During the 1940s and early 1950s, retail distribution was highly fragmented with many small shops and with counter service nearly universal. The structure of

---

[5]K. McClaren, "The Effect of Range Size on Distribution Costs," *International Journal of Physical Distribution and Materials Management* 10., © 1980, pp. 445–56.

▲ EXHIBIT 4   Seasonal Cold Store Occupancy

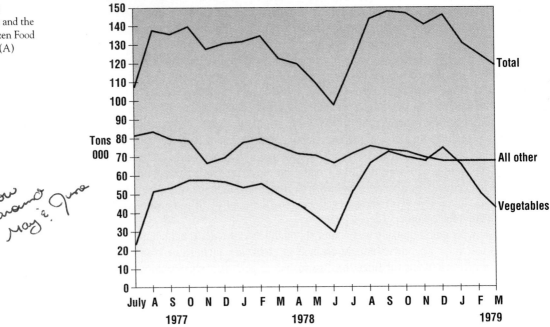

low around June May

Source: Stock records.

retail trade virtually ossified in the early postwar period as a result of food rationing that continued until 1953 and almost eliminated competition among retailers. The chief short-term problem was persuading food retailers to install refrigerated cabinets.

> At an average cost of about £150, a quick frozen food (QFF) cabinet is a big enough outlay to cause the average retailer to think twice about installing one. However, it can be shown that an average-sized cabinet of 10 cu. ft. can be made—without proper siting—to yield an annual turnover of anything between £500 and £1,500. On an average retail margin of 20 percent, a retailer with an annual turnover of, say, £1,000 can net a profit of £200 before servicing and maintenance charges are deducted. Over the 12–15 year life of the cabinet this represents a substantial return on investment.[6]

In the supply of ice cream, the major manufacturers lent cabinets to retailers. The problem of this approach was the enormous capital requirements (equivalent at least to the size of investment in production facilities). In 1953 Birds Eye decided that it would not rent cabinets to retailers. Instead, it persuaded two producers of industrial refrigerators and air-conditioning equipment, Prestcold and Frigidaire, to start the production of "open top" display cabinets suitable for frozen food storage and display. Birds Eye only sought new business with retailers that installed such cabinets.

---

[6]"Frozen Food: Market Prospects," *Retail Business,* Special Report No. 14, © April 1959, p. 83.

With the infrastructure in place, demand for frozen foods expanded. In the beginning, frozen foods were regarded as a luxury, preferred over canned or dried food for their retention of the appearance and flavor of the fresh product. As the price of frozen foods fell, growth increased rapidly, though the price elasticity of demand remained very high and seasonal and annual fluctuations in the consumption of frozen foods were strongly influenced by the price and availability of fresh produce. Between 1956 and 1981, sales increased at an average annual rate of about 15 percent, although the rate of growth of tonnage sales tended to decline over time (Exhibit 1a). From 1956 to 1961 average annual growth was 36 percent, falling to 10.5 percent per annum between 1962 and 1973, and declining again to around 6.9 percent between 1974 and 1980.

Initially, the primary determinant of market size was the number of outlets through which frozen foods expanded rapidly (Exhibit 5), and by 1961, U.K. sales of frozen foods reached the 100,000 ton level. henceforth, frozen food sales were determined much more by consumer demand than by availability and were simulated by the continuous expansion in the range of frozen food available. Lt. Colonel A.E.H. Campbell of the Bunchrew Food Bank of Inverness is credited with marketing the first frozen beefburger in the U.K. in 1949; in 1955 Birds Eye introduced frozen chicken pies, that were followed in the next year by fish fingers. In 1956, Mudd and Sons introduced frozen haddock and chips in a newspaper design carton, and in 1958 it introduced fish-in-sauce in a boil-in-the-bag package. Following this, the late 1950s and 1960s saw a wave of amalgamations in the industry, as a result of which three major U.K. suppliers—Birds Eye, Findus, and Ross—emerged, each owned by a major consumer goods manufacturer (Unilever, Nestlé, and Imperial Group, respectively) (Exhibits 2 and 3).

Developments in Retailing

In the 1960s, developments in food retailing began to influence the frozen food industry. First was the move away from counter service towards self-service (Exhibit 5), which increased vastly the marketing opportunities available to the frozen food processors, including introducing new and novel products and packaging. Second was the emergence of supermarkets and large supermarket chains. In 1960 there were only 367 supermarkets (self-service food shops with 2,000 sq. feet or more floor space). The ability of the supermarket chains to pass on their cost savings to consumers, together with consumers' demand for the wider variety of goods made available by supermarkets were major factors behind increasing concentration in the grocery trade (Exhibit 6).

Many of the major supermarket chains operated central or regional warehouses from which they distributed grocery products to their individual supermarkets. They also began to supply their own brands of frozen foods. Following the introduction by Sainsbury of its own brand of frozen peas (supplied by Findus) in 1967, retailers' brands took an increasing share of retail frozen food sales (Exhibit 2).

The impact of supermarkets in expanding the amount of retail cabinet space available was reinforced towards the end of the 1960s by the introduction of specialist frozen foods stores to serve the increasing number of home freezer owners (Exhibit 1b). To serve this growing market, a new model for frozen food retailing emerged: home freezer centers that combined the sale of home freezers with the sale of large packs of frozen foods (packed for caterers). The retailing of frozen foods by these outlets was characterized by large pack sizes, wide product range, lack of brand consciousness, and low prices. Larger cabinet capacity, usually with back-up storage, enabled freezer centers to require fewer deliveries with larger drops. Their share of frozen food sales was 18 percent in 1978 and 23.5 percent in 1986.

▲ EXHIBIT 5   U.K. Retailing (number of Stores, 000)

	1947	1957	1967	1980
Counter service	143	147	108	50
Self-service	3	4	15	40
Of which, supermarkets	—	1	2	7
Selling frozen food	NA	20	120	87

Source: IFS, Birds Eye, Monopolies & Mergers Commission.

▲ EXHIBIT 6   Shares of Packaged Grocery Sales by Type of Retailer (percent)

	1970	1974	1978	1981
Multiples	49	53	64	70
Cooperatives	19	21	18	17
Voluntary groups	16	14	10	7
Independents	18	13	8	6
Four-firm concentration ratio*	0.26	0.27	0.34	0.42

*Excluding cooperatives.
Source: C. Baden Fuller, Rising Concentration: The U.L. Grocery Trade 1970–82, London Business School ©
1984.

Catering establishments were served by a separate segment of the market that was more
concerned with price than with brand-name recognition and sophisticated product packaging
(Exhibit 1b). A set of independent wholesalers linked manufacturers to caterers for the distribution of all types of food. In 1974, while the combined share of the three major frozen food
producers at retail was over 60 percent, it was less than 30 percent at caterers. Similarly, their
share of home freezer center sales was just over 11 percent.

New Entry

While the early development of the industry had seen a consolidation around three major,
vertically integrated suppliers, there was a wave of new entry in the 1960s and 1970s. For
companies already engaged in food processing, a new technology, blast freezers, could be
purchased "off the shelf" for as little as a few thousand pounds for a small unit. These allowed freezing and packing to occur together and eliminated the need for two separate production processes. While large-scale processing and freezing offered opportunities for
automation and greater division of labor, the cost savings from a greater scale of production
tended to be small.

New entrants to the industry were a diverse group. The Monopolies Commission observed in 1976 that:

A number of new companies have entered the frozen food processing industry during the past 20 years. They include Jus-Rol Ltd. and Primecut Foods Ltd. (then W.B. Wright Provision Ltd.) in 1954, Northray Foods Ltd. (then Northray Farm Products Ltd.) in 1956, Kraft Foods Ltd. (then Brains Frozen Foods Ltd.) in 1963, McCain International Ltd. and Potato and Allied Services Ltd. in 19668, Frozen Quality Ltd. in 1969, Country Range Ltd. and King Harry Foods Ltd. in 1970, White House Foods Ltd. and Fife Growers Ltd. in 1971, and Wold Growers Ltd. in 1974.

Although some of the new entrants have been new enterprises, most have been either established companies or subsidiaries of established companies. In many cases companies already engaged in the production of food have extended their production to include frozen foods. Many of the smaller processors of vegetables and fruit, for example, Northray Foods Ltd., Frozen Quality Ltd., Fife Growers Ltd., and Wold Pea Growers Ltd., originated as agricultural cooperatives. Among the meat companies which have entered frozen food processing are FMC Ltd. (chiefly through its Harris subsidiary), Dalgety Ltd. (chiefly through Dalgety-Buswell Ltd. and Dalgety Frozen Foods Ltd.), and Thos Borthwick & Sons Ltd. (through Freshbake Foods Ltd.). Several fishing and fish merchanting companies have developed the processing of frozen food, notably Associated Fisheries Ltd., J. Marr (Fish Merchants) Ltd. and Chaldur Frozen Fish Co. Ltd.

[Most] companies specialize in one or other of the broad categories of frozen food products, namely vegetables, fish, meat products, and fruit and confectionery. Some smaller companies specialize in a single product only—McCain's output is almost exclusively potato chips and King Harry Foods produces mainly pizzas.[7]

In addition a set of marketing-only companies, such as W.B. Pellew, Harvey & Co. Ltd., and J. Muirhead, emerged. These bought frozen food from other manufacturers and placed their own brand names "Angelus," "Chef's Garden," and "4F" on the products. Independent companies with refrigerated trucks, such as Christian Salvesen, handled their physical distribution needs.

Specialist firms providing storage, freezing, and transportation services also emerged. Public cold storage companies such as Christian Salvesen, Union Cold Storage, and Frigoscandia doubled their amount of cold storage between 1969 and 1973. These companies came to offer not only storage facilities but a comprehensive range of processing, freezing, and distribution services. By 1974, Christian Salvesen's annual freezing capacity was almost one-third of Birds Eye. In 1978, Christian Salvesen processed three-quarters of the vegetables it stored, up from 20 percent in 1969. Services were usually rented under medium-term (multiyear) contracts. Salvesen's fleet of refrigerated trucks operating out of its national network of cold stores was also available for rent, either on long-term contracts or as needed. Sainsbury and marks and Spencer, for example, used Christian Salvesen for some of their refrigerated distribution needs. Other firms specialized in the importing, broking, and distribution of frozen foods. For instance, Frionor and Bonduelle began marketing products imported from their overseas parents, while companies such as Anglo European foods, Snowking Frozen Foods, and Flying Goose specialized in distribution (mainly to the catering trade). Exhibit 7 lists the larger suppliers of frozen foods in 1973.

---

[7]"Report on the Supply of Frozen Foodstuffs," Monopoly and Mergers Commission, HMSO, © 1976, p. 9.

▲ **EXHIBIT 7 The Larger Manufacturers of Frozen Foods and Their Sales of Frozen Foods**

Company	Ultimate Parent Company (if applicable)	Sales of Reference Goods (£ million, 1973)	Main Products	Brand Names
Birds Eye Foods Ltd.	Unilever Ltd.	109.0*	Wide range	Birds Eye, Tempo, Market Day, County Fair
Ross Foods Ltd.	Imperial Group Ltd.	41.5†	Wide range	Ross
Findus Ltd.	Nestle group of companies	41.2	Wide range	Findus
Young's Seafoods Ltd.	Imperial Group Ltd.	21.0†	Shellfish and specialty fish products	Youngs
McCain International Ltd.	McCain Foods Ltd.of Canada	10.1	Chips	McCain, Caterpac, Valley Farms
Associated Fisheries Ltd.		8.8	Fish and fish products	Kingfrost
MacFisheries Ltd.	Unilever Ltd.	7.2*	Fish and fish Products	Kiltie
Henry Telfer Ltd.		7.2	Meat products	Telfer
Kraft Foods Ltd.	Kraftco Corporation, USA	5.4	Meals, pies, faggots, sausages	Krafts, Brains
Ross Poultry Ltd.	Imperial Group Ltd.	4.3†	Poultry products	Buxted, Premier Farm
Northray Foods Ltd.	ITT Corp. of New York	3.6	Vegetable	Northray
Primecut Foods Ltd.	Sardove Ltd.	3.1	Meat and meat products	Primecut
Potato and Allied Services Ltd.	Christian Salvesen Ltd.	2.5	Chips	Distributors' own brands only
Frozen Quality Ltd.		2.4	Vegetables	Froqual
Jus-Rol Ltd.		2.3	Pastry products	Jus-Rol
J.B. Eastwood Ltd.	Fitch Lovell Ltd.	2.1	Poultry portions	Chubby, Kentucky
TW Downs Ltd.	Union International Co., Ltd.	2.1	Portioned meats, poultry, and vegetables	Downs, Ocoma
Brooke Bond Oxo Frozen Foods Ltd.	Brooke Bond Leibig Ltd.	1.8	Poultry, meat, pies	Brooke Farm
Anglian Tendabeef Ltd.		1.4	Meat products	Emborg, Fribo
J. Marr (Fish Merchants) Ltd.		1.1	Fish	Marr, Junella
Scot Bowyers Ltd.	Unigate Ltd.	1.0	Meat products	Scot Bowyers
Unger Meats Ltd.		1.0	Meat products	Unger meats

Source: "Frozen Foodstuffs: A Report on the Supply in the United Kingdom of Frozen Foodstuffs for Human Consumption," Monopolies and Mergers Commission, Great Britain, © 1976, p. 106.

*Excluding frozen foods sales between Unilever subsidiaries.

†Including sales to other subsidiaries of Imperial Foods.

▲ BIRDS EYE

Growth and Market Domination: The 1950s and 1960s

Birds Eye's early history was directed towards establishing an organization that was fully integrated from controlling food production to stocking the retailer's frozen food cabinet. The company was orientated towards the frequent supply of small consumer packs to a large number of small retail stores. The centerpiece of Birds Eye's organization was its national system of distribution, which by 1963 enabled it to directly serve some 93,000 outlets and enabled its tonnage sales to increase at a remarkable 40 percent per annum during the 1950s.

The pioneering role of Birds Eye in the development of the industry was also reflected in its range of innovations. In 1953–54, Birds Eye was instrumental in persuading Prestcold and Frigidaire to design and market an open-top refrigerated display cabinet. it developed a number of food processing and freezing technique—particualrly in the manufacture of fish fingers and beefburgers—and in horticulture, Birds Eye was responsible for improvements in vegetable varieties, cultivation techniques, and harvesting equipment.

By 1960, Birds Eye operated six factories and associated cold stores at Great Yarmouth, Lowestoft, Kirkby, Grimsby, Hull, and Eastbourne. Each factory produced a number of different products in order to utilize manpower and equipment efficiently in the face of seasonal availability of raw materials. Birds Eye's parent, Unilever, through its distribution subsidiary, SPD (Speedy Prompt Delivery), made a heavy investment in cold storage and insulated vehicles.

> SPD was increasingly drawn into the problem. They developed their cold storage capacity and added insulated vehicles to get the goods to shops....Cold storage had increased steadily, with building more and more advanced in their design. Depots were run in close conjunction with SPD and increased to the point where Birds Eye could store about 50,000 tons of frozen food.[8]

By 1974, SPD operated from 42 depots. Birds Eye treated it as an integral part of its own activities, paying for its services at cost and making an annual profit contribution to cover the capital employed by SPD on Birds Eye's behalf. In the few areas that it could not serve cost-effectively, Birds Eye franchised exclusive wholesalers to distribute its frozen foods to retailers.

From the late 1950s, Birds Eye's strategy became more marketing orientated. Having established a national, integrated organization, the company's principal task was to expand sales by introducing new products, promoting consumer awareness of the convenience and value-for-money of frozen foods, and developing consumer recognition of the quality associated with the Birds Eye brand. The introduction of fish fingers in 1955 was followed by beefburgers in 1960 and by a stream of new fish, meat, and dessert products. A product list for 1975 is presented in Exhibit 8. The five biggest-selling products—peas, beans, chips, fish fingers, and beefburgers—accounted for nearly 40 percent of revenue. The introduction of commercial television in 1955 was important to this consumer approach, particularly because until 1958 Birds Eye was the only industry advertiser.

> Birds Eye pioneered frozen foods, with product quality higher than people were used to in processed food and with a personality combining efficiency, hygiene, confidence, and completeness.

---

[8]C. Wilson, Unilever *1945–1965: Challenge and Response in the Post-War Industrial Revolution* London: Cassell, © 1968, pp. 172–73.

▲ EXHIBIT 8 Birds Eye's Retail Product List, August 25, 1975

	Pack Size (oz.)		Pack Size (oz.)
Vegetables		Cod steaks	14, 7
Garden peas	32, 16, 8, 4	Haddock steaks	14, 7
Supreme peas	16, 8	Buttered kipper fillets	10, 6
Petits pois	32, 10	Buttered smoked haddock	7$^{1}/_{2}$
Economy peas	32, 16	Savory fish cakes	4
Peas and baby carrots	8	Cod steaks in batter	7$^{1}/_{2}$
Peas and sweet corn	8	Cod steaks in breadcrumbs	6
Peas and pearl onions	8	Crispy cod fries (handipack)	7
Sliced green beans	32, 16, 8, 4	Cod and chips (handipack)	9
Supreme sprouts	8	Cod in butter sauce	6
Casserole vegetables	8	Cod in sauce, other varieties	6
Broad beans	8, 4	Cod fillets	13, 7$^{1}/_{2}$
Sweet corn	6	Haddock fillets	13, 7$^{1}/_{2}$
Corn on the cob	12	Plaice fillets	13, 7$^{1}/_{2}$
Cauliflower	12	Hake fillets	7$^{1}/_{2}$
Crinkle cut chips	32, 12, 6		
Potato fries	12	**Meats**	
Potato croquettes	6	Beefburgers	48, 16, 8, 4
Potato fritters	8	Minceburgers	8, 4
Tasti-fries	8	American style beefburgers	8
Mushy processed peas	10	Savory rissoles	9, 4$^{1}/_{2}$
Whole french beans	8	Chicken rissoles	4$^{1}/_{2}$
Chopped spinach	8	Brunchies	4
Broccoli	9	Steaklets	11, 5$^{1}/_{2}$
Small onions and white sauce	5	Skinless pork sausages	10, 6$^{1}/_{2}$
Potato waffles	12	Battered bangers	7
Mixed vegetables	4	Gravey and lean roast beef	12, 8, 4
Savory vegetable rice (3 varieties)	8	Gravy and roast chicken	12, 4
		Gravy and roast leg of pork	12, 4
Fish		Shepherds pie	16, 8
Cod fish fingers	36, 16, 10, 6	Faggots, faggot dinner	13, 14
Fish cakes	12, 8, 4	Roast beef dinner	12$^{1}/_{2}$
Salmon fish cakes	4	Roast chicken dinner	11
Economy fish sticks	9, 5–4	Chicken and mushroom casserole	6
Battered fish fingers	9, 4$^{1}/_{2}$	Lamb casserole	6
Cod fillet in batter	—	Braised kidneys in gravy	5
Cod fillets in breadcrumbs	71/2	Beef stew and dumpling	16, 7$^{1}/_{2}$
Breaded plaice fillets	71/2	Minced beef in gravy	16, 6

continued

	Pack Size (oz.)		Pack Size (oz.)
Liver with onion and gravy	5	**Cakes, desserts, and pastries**	
Quarter chicken	9, 8, 7	Mousse certons	9
Four crispy pancake rolls	8	Ripple mousse cartons	—
Special fried rice	8	Mousse tubs	—
Sweet and sour pork in crispy batter	8	Trifle	—
Sweet and sour chicken	8	Lovely	—
Chicken chow mein	8	Melba	—
Prawn curry	9	Cream desserts	—
Beef pie	Serves 3/4, 1	Arctic roll	—
Steak and kidney pie	Serves 2/3, 1	Dairy cream sponge	—
Chicken pie	Serves 2/3, 1	Chocolate (strawberry and blackcurrant)	—
Chicken and mushroom pie	Serves 1	Cheesecake (creams)	—
Minced beef and onion pie	Serves 1	Gateaux	—
Pizza bolognese	8	Puff pastry	13, 7½
Pizza tomato and cheese	8	Short crust pastry	13, 7½
Six sausage rolls	—	Raspberries	8
Two large beef and onion rolls	—	Strawberries	8
Egg, bacon, and cheese flan	—	Florida orange juice and grapefruit juice	—
Danish savory rolls	12,6		

Source: "Frozen Foodstuff: A Report on the Supply in the United Kingdom of Frozen Foodstuffs for Human Consumption," Monopolies and Mergers Commission, Great Britain, © 1976, pp. 100–01.

Birds Eye added values beyond the physical and functional ones that contributed to a clear and likeable personality for the brand.[9]

The company offered discounts on its published trade prices to a number of retailers. The size of discounts depended on the annual turnover of the retailer, the cabinet space allocated to Birds Eye products, and the frequency and size of deliveries. Overall discounts averaged 6 percent of the gross revenues of all retailers. Its "criterion in discount negotiations was to achieve a consistent level of gross profitability from various customers" and the discounts were intended to capture differences in the costs of serving different customers.[10] As a result, large retailers received the highest discounts—over 10 percent of the gross value of their purchases—although these were said to "exceed the cost savings in supplying them."[11]

Throughout the 1950s and 1960s, Birds Eye accounted for over 60 percent of U.K. frozen foods sales on a tonnage basis (Exhibit 2). In terms of the retail market, the company estimated its brand share at over 70 percent by value and around two-thirds by tonnage for

[9]S. King, *Developing New Brands* (London: Pitman © 1973), p. 13.
[10]"Report on the Supply of Frozen Foodstuffs," p. 32.
[11]Ibid.

most of the period. Among the outlets served by Birds Eye, its share of frozen food sales was 75 percent, and some 40,000 retail outlets were served exclusively by Birds Eye. Its top 20 retail customers accounted for nearly a third of total sales.

The success of Birds Eye encouraged it to develop its own sources of raw material. It entered the broiler chicken industry in 1958 and within a few years had built a capacity for producing 6.5 million birds per year at about 20 farms. It sold the farms to Ross Poultry in 1972 in the face of overproduction in the broiler industry and a belief that it was of suboptimal size. In 1965, Birds Eye acquired a majority stake in a fishing company to secure a regular supply of cod. Operating problems coincided with a drop in world fish prices, and Birds Eye sold the assets of the fishing company in 1969.

Competitors

Birds Eye held a substantial competitive advantage over its closest competitors, Ross and Findus, and consistently achieved higher returns on capital employed (on an historic cost basis) than them. In 1974, for example, while Birds Eye's return on capital stood at 15.9 percent, Findus earned 8.9 percent (frozen food only), and Ross Foods earned 4.3 percent (all food businesses) (Exhibit 9). Neither Findus nor Ross tried to innovate or change the structure of the industry. Because they imitated Birds Eye's actions, their advertising expenditures were limited (Exhibit 10). Ross Foods's parent company (Imperial Group) reported to the Monopolies and Mergers Commission that it "considered massive brand support, aimed at achieving dramatic increases in sales, to be far beyond the means of its frozen food companies, and it had never sought to answer Birds Eye's intensive advertising in kind. In 1973 Ross Foods virtually ceased advertising its retail packs since it was not making it more competitive."[12]

Neither competitor was prepared to underprice Birds Eye. Birds Eye's brand leadership was evident in the pattern of pricing behavior observed in the industry. Based on evidence shown in Exhibit 11, the Monopolies and Mergers Commission concluded: "The recommended retail prices of the larger selling retail packs of Birds Eye, Ross Foods, and Findus frozen food have until recently moved broadly in parallel with Birds Eye, more often than not, being the first to change its price."[13] The willingness of the smaller processors to follow Birds Eye was explained by Imperial Foods:

> In supplying frozen foods to retailers for sale under the Ross name, Ross Foods set its prices generally at the same level as those set by Birds Eye. Since Ross Foods only advertises and promotes its products on a very limited scale, it cannot hope to win space in retailers' cabinets and charge prices above those charged by Birds Eye. On the other hand, it cannot afford to undercut Birds Eye's prices to any significant extent.[14]

Ross Ross Foods operated seven factories and supplied a wide range of frozen foods to the retail and catering trades through two national centers and 25 regional depots. Its sister companies in Imperial Group, Ross Poultry, Youngs (fish), an Smedley-HP (meat and vegetables), were autonomous enterprises operating their own distribution networks. The company's market research data showed the Ross brand represented in only 31 percent of

---

[12]Ibid., p.44
[13]Ibid., p.53
[14]Ibid.

▲ **EXHIBIT 9**   Comparative Profitability (pretax return on capital employed, percent)

	1964	1967	1971	1972	1973	1974
Birds Eye	16.2	22.2	19.1	18.4	18.7	15.9
Findus	NA	NA	7.2	5.9	7.2	8.9
Ross	NA	NA	NA	7.6	5.5	4.3
UK manufacturing industry	14.6	12.0	12.5	14.9	17.4	17.4

Source: Robert M. Grant, "Birds Eye and the U.K. Frozen Food Industry," case study, © July 1985.

▲ **EXHIBIT 10**   Advertising and Promotion Expenditures (£ millions)

	1971	1972	1973	1974
Birds Eye				
Sales	88.8	93.2	114.3	132.8
Ads	2.1	2.1	2.8	2.7
Total promotion and advertising	3.8	3.8	4.2	4.5
Ross				
Sales	41.9	49.0	64.2	75.4
Ads	.2	.2	.1	NA
Findus				
Sales	29.0	32.5	43.1	51.5
Ads	.3	.5	.5	.4
Total promotion and advertising	NA	NA	NA	1.6

Source: Casewriter estimates.

grocery outlets in January 1974 compared with 51 percent for Findus and 71 percent for Birds Eye. Ross Foods's brand representation was particularly poor in the supermarket grocery chains, the fastest growing sector of the retail trade, even though Ross had 8,000 refrigerated cabinets exclusively for its own products on free loan to retailers in the mid-1970s. In response, Ross began to focus from the early 1970s on the nonretail sector, particularly "home freezer" packs sold through freezer centers. In 1974 only half of its sales were to the retail market outside freezer centers.

Findus   Formed in 1968 through the merger of four frozen food companies, Findus was a Nestlé subsidiary. Immediately after the merger Findus invested £7 million to expand its production capacity, particularly its two main factories on the East Coast. The company had three other factories and had long-term contracts with Christian Salvesen for some bulk freezing. It distributed products through 52 depots jointly owned with the ice cream company J. Lyons Co. Ltd. Like Ross, Findus used exclusive franchise distribution arrangements with wholesalers to reach areas not covered by its own system. The company provided retailers with one cabinet free out of every eight installed in return for a certain share of display space.

▲ EXHIBIT 11 Changes in the Recommended Retail Prices of Certain Products Supplied by Birds Eye, Findus, and Ross Foods, November 1971 to July 1975*

		Price at Nov.	1971	1972					1973								1974						1975			
			Dec.	Jan.	Apr.	Jun.	Jul.	Oct.	Feb.	Mar.	Apr.	Jun.	Jul.	Sep.	Oct.	Nov.	Feb.	May	Aug.	Sep.	Nov.	Dec.	Feb	Mar.	Apr.	May
Fish	B	19	20			21½			22½	23		25		26½	28½		30						31			32
fingers,	F	19		20			21½		22½	23			25		28	30	31			30			31			32
10 oz.	R	18		19				20½	21½	22			24	26		28	29½		26		26		26			27
Beef	B	20½	22			23½			24½	26½	27½	28½					29½						30			31
burgers,	F	20½		22			23½		24½	26½	27½		28½				29½								30	31
8 oz.	R	20½		22				23½	24½	26½	27½		28½				29½									31
Peas,	B	9½	10		10†							11			9‡		9½	10	11		11½		12½			14
8 oz.	F	9½		10			9½						10½							11½		12½	13½			15
	R	9½		10			9						9½				10	10½	11½		12		12½			14
Sliced	B	11½						12				12½					13		14		16½			16		17
green	F	11½						12½					13		13½	14½	15½			16½		17			18½	19½
bean	R	11½						12					12½				13½		14½		15½					17

Source: "Frozen Foodstuffs: A Report on the Supply in the United Kingdom of Frozen Foodstuffs for Human Consumption," Monopolies and Mergers Commission, Great Britain, © 1976, p. 106.

*B: Birds Eye; F: Findus; R: Ross Foods

‡Weight of pack reduced from 10 oz to 8 oz.

†Weight of pack increased from 8 oz to 10 oz.

Findus, estimating its cost disadvantage against Birds Eye to be 3–5 percent of sales, tried to retain a premium position in the retail market and exited the catering segment in the early 1980s. In 1974, 85 percent of its sales were to the retail segment. It was the supplier of private-label frozen foods to J. Sainsbury and Marks and Spencer, and these sales accounted for almost 20 percent of its revenue.

Deterioration in Birds Eye's Competitive Position during the 1970s

In July 1972, Kenneth Webb, marketing director at Birds Eye since 1959, replaced James Parratt as chairman at a time that, in retrospect, proved to be a watershed in Birds Eye's development. During the early 1970s, Birds Eye's market dominance existed primarily in sales of small retail packs to independent grocers and, to a lesser extent, supermarkets. Birds Eye was poorly represented in some areas: in home freezer centers its share was around 8 percent in 1974 and it had little involvement in retailers' own labels. In the catering sector, Birds Eye's market share by value was about 10 percent in 1973. After the early 1970s, the company's share of tonnage sales fell continuously although the market as a whole continued to expand, albeit at a slower rate (Exhibit 2).

Under the chairmanship of Kenneth Webb, Birds Eye was forced to respond to changes in the market. The orientation of Birds Eye's product range, distribution, and advertising towards small packs for the grocery trade meant that it was slow in responding to the increasing impact of the home freezer. Birds Eye introduced the bulk pack to the retail market in 1972 and followed this with the establishment of County Fair Foods to supply the home freezer centers and anyone else willing to accept a minimum drop size in 1974. County Fair Foods shared production facilities with Birds Eye but had a separate distribution system using Christian Salvesen because of the different requirements of freezer centers with regard to quality, product types, distribution, prices, and promotion. In 1976, Menumaster Ltd. was set up to supply frozen prepared meals to caterers. In the more traditional retail market, the principal aim of Birds Eye was to maintain sales growth, chiefly through extending its product range. During the 1970s the company's dependence upon its traditional big sellers—peas, chips, fish fingers, and beefburgers—was reduced by a constant flow of new products. Particularly important were ready-to-eat meals, desserts, and specialty dishes (i.e., Chinese foods, pizzas).

The growth in the power of large chains in the retail sector encouraged Birds Eye to redirect its marketing efforts. During the 1960s, marketing had been focused almost exclusively on the consumer. During the 1970s, increased attention was devoted to the trade. This shift from consumer marketing to trade marketing required differentiating among individual sectors of the trade and necessitated a closer involvement of the company with major customers, not only in negotiating terms of supply, but also in designing joint promotions. Eight groups were formed to devise tailor-made marketing plans for the 40 or so customers that absorbed three-quarters of Birds Eye's production for the retail trade.[15]

The increased rate of new product launches combined with the new marketing approach led to considerable difficulties in designing an advertising policy, particularly within the limits of the advertising budget. Reviewing market developments over the 12 months to September 1974, Marketing Director Keith Jacobs outlined Birds Eye's advertising approach. For advertising purposes Birds Eye's products would be divided into three groups: lead lines (e.g., fish

[15]*Financial Times,* October 5, 1978.

fingers, peas), support products (e.g., sprouts, sliced beef), and new products.[16] While lead lines required national TV advertising, smaller and newer lines generally required selective exposure where target consumer sectors could be reached at lower cost. As a result, Birds Eye's advertising became more regionally orientated and with greater emphasis on press advertising, especially in women's magazines.

The marketing effort necessary to promote Birds Eye's products in widely different sectors—promoting up-market prepared dishes while expanding into economy packs of commodity products—was difficult to orchestrate. "We will be walking a tightrope," explained Marketing Director Jacobs, "the company's advertising will have two jobs to do: to maintain its image as a basic convenience foods company and to make it credible as a purveyor of, for example, pizzas."

During the 1970s, product and marketing policy also had to take account of changes in the prices and availability of raw materials. The Cod War of 1975 and the fall in the value of sterling created short supplies and high prices of cod and necessitated reformulating and rescheduling advertising campaigns for fish fingers and other cod-based products. It also encouraged the introduction of fish products made from lower-cost fish—"Economy Fish Sticks" in 1974 and "Economy Fish Fingers" in 1977. Cod shortages were accompanied in 1976 and 1977 by vegetable shortages due to drought.

On the production side, the mid-1970s witnessed a program of heavy investment in modernization and rationalization that was designed to exploit efficiency from volume production. Between 1977 and 1980, expenditure on this program amounted to some £20 million. A key feature of the program was the focus of production resources for different product groups at specific factories—fish products at Hull and Grimsby, ready meals at Kirkby and Yarmouth, vegetables at Hull and Lowestoft, and cakes and desserts at Eastbourne—since it was observed that some specialist producers achieved much higher levels of automation.

The quest for lower costs was instrumental in the decision to merge Unilever's two principal frozen product operations, Birds Eye Foods and Walls Ice Cream, into a single company, Birds Eye Walls Ltd. Although the potential for cooperation and the elimination of duplicated functions between Birds Eye and Walls had been identified in the 1960s, the two Unilever subsidiaries had been almost entirely independent prior to the merger. Toward the end of the 1970s, an investment program was aimed at rationalizing the Unicold-Walls distribution network, and on January 1, 1982, Unicold-Walls was transferred to Birds Eye Walls with the intention of speeding the reorganization of distribution and improving coordination. The plan was to complete the reorganization of distribution by early 1985 with a streamlined national network of seven regional distribution centers in operation.

Birds Eye's Restructuring and Quest for Profitability

The efforts made in advertising, new product development, and expanding sales to home freezer outlets were successful in maintaining Birds Eye's brand leadership during the period of intense competitive pressure and unprecedented environmental turbulence of the 1970s, though the decline in share was continuous. In its 1979 annual report, Birds Eye was still able to report that "[f]ew brands in the British grocery market can claim the sort of dominance which Birds Eye has in frozen foods. The best parallel is probably Heinz in canned foods and soups."

---

[16]*Financial Times,* September 12, 1974.

But brand leadership was not a guarantee of growth and prosperity as it had been in the prosperous 1960s. The use of pricing policy to maintain market position and sustain growth meant that frequently the first casualty was profitability. In 1974, in the face of falling sales and sharply rising costs, Birds Eye maintained its advertising budget and cut prices on some major selling products (mainly fish fingers and beefburgers). Though this approach raised sales volume, in July 1975 Chairman Kenneth Webb complained that profit margins had been halved over the previous two years and were currently one-third of the level consistent with the company's heavy investment in manufacturing and distribution facilities. In 1976, the company barely broke even and in 1971 it registered a post-tax loss (Exhibit 12). The outbreak of a price war between supermarkets in 1977 and the increasing share of private labels pressured food manufacturers to give higher discounts and promotional allowance. By the early 1980s, Sainsbury's own brand had over 10 percent of the market, a share greater than that of either Findus or Ross.

The appointment of Mr. Don Angel (then chairman of Wall's Meat) to the chairmanship of Birds Eye early in 1979 came at a time when Birds Eye was again reappraising its strategy in the frozen foods market and embarking upon a period of internal restructuring. Reflecting on the erosion of the company's dominant market position, Don Angel observed that "choices must be made about what the company is best at." Behind this search for a new role was a desire to exploit more effectively the competitive advantages associated with Birds Eye's market leadership and brand recognition. The overriding objective was to restore a satisfactory level of profitability.

▲ EXHIBIT 12 Birds Eye Foods Ltd: Accounts 1972–1979 (£000s)

	1972	1973	1974	1975	1976	1977	1978	1979
Sales	91,838	13,997	132,636	157,142	187,415	212,322	226,308	266,018
Operating profit	2,110	2,875	3,445	4,414	3,453	2,477	6,310	9,352
After-tax profit	1,223	1,465	1,468	1,925	249	(679)	1,094	8,145
Group service charg	NA	NA	NA	NA	NA	5,305	5,527	4,946
Net current assets	15,164	24,717	31,034	32,069	44,792	53,337	59,141	73,165
Stocks	17,479	26,012	29,263	30,983	40,356	52,431	54,317	68,921
Debtors	5,928	10,677	12,124	13,739	17,483	13,523	21,102	28,522
Creditors	4,863	7,484	8,768	9,481	10,592	14,563	15,350	24,573
Capital employed	33,893	42,947	48,993	52,199	90,383	100,004	122,352	132,801

Source: Robert M. Grant, "Birds Eye and the U.K. Frozen Food Industry," case study, © July 1985, p. 13a.

▲ EXHIBIT 1   Tom Bidwell's First Forklift, 1957

The RichardsonSmith Relationship

About the same time Crown began manufacturing forklifts, two industrial designers, Deane Richardson and David Smith, teamed up to form a design consultancy in Columbus, Ohio, 100 miles from New Bremen. They christened the firm RichardsonSmith—soon to be known in the design business as RS. They opened their doors in 1959 and immediately began to hustle for business.

"We started with lists of businesses from the Chambers of Commerce in every town in Ohio," recalled Dave Smith. "Then one of us would go to a town and make 'house calls'—cold. Hopefully that would result in proposals and second visits." Another tactic was the trade show: "We'd go to trade shows—say, a boat show—and follow up with visits to all the manufacturers in the area. By the time we'd talked to 10 of them, we'd sound like we really had something to offer. It was a great way of learning about an industry."

On a house call trip to New Bremen in 1960, Deane Richardson dropped in on Tom Bidwell, who by then had become Crown's director of engineering and manufacturing. "Deane was out trying to drum up some business for his struggling new design firm, and wanted to do a project for us. I was the easiest sell going—we had a new forklift in mind, but I had only $750 available. Fortunately, Deane agreed to do it anyway."

RS made the most of their opportunity. They took on the account and designed a medium-duty, hand-controlled pallet truck for Crown that won a design excellence award from the Industrial Designers Institute in 1963 and gained rapid market acceptance (see Exhibit 2). More importantly, the product attracted attention for Crown and was a critical starting point in building its brand image.

▲ EXHIBIT 2   RichardsonSmith's First Lift Truck, 1963

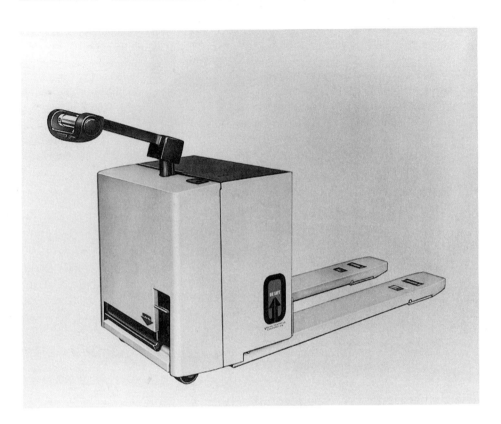

The success of the pallet truck reinforced Bidwell's belief in the value of excellent design. It also became the foundation for a long-term, mutually beneficial relationship between Crown and RS. Crown continued to hire RS exclusively to do the industrial design work on every new product development project, and did not employ any internal industrial designers.

Crown also turned its corporate identity needs over to RS. The designers developed an inclusive program, including the Crown logo and color system, in 1961–62. The program was redone in 1965, and again in 1973.

As Crown grew rapidly, so did RS, becoming one of the world's largest and most respected industrial design consultancies. The companies managed to maintain a close relationship, however. Despite a growing list of clients, RS always treated Crown as a key account. Although other RS people were primary designers for Crown during various periods, Dave Smith provided the continuity and remained intimately involved in most Crown projects. As Tom Bidwell described it: "Dave Smith was so closely involved with our product development efforts that he was more like a Crown employee than a consultant." Indeed, all the RS industrial designers who worked on Crown products were viewed by the Crown engineering group more as partners than as outside consultants. The feeling was mutual. According to Dave Tompkins of RS, who headed the Crown account from 1963 until he left RS in 1977 to start his own firm,

The thing that was so wonderful about Crown is that they cared passionately about how these things looked. The engineers would call us up if they had to make the slightest change. The difference between them and many of our other clients was like night and day.

In particular Tompkins admired Harold Stammen, the senior engineer in product development. "Talk about patience and attention to detail!" Dave Smith called Stammen the "brightest, most creative engineer you'd ever want to know. And completely self-taught." Like Bidwell, Stammen, who had been with the company since its beginnings, enjoyed the challenge of "out-designing the designers." Dave Smith viewed Stammen's role and Bidwell's as essential: "They are the reason we can do what we do. All the Crown engineers care about design, but Bidwell and Stammen are the design conscience of the company." Bidwell was particularly conscious of this role and frequently contemplated who would take it over after he retired. "I'm usually the one who walks around the plants and notices something, like an old nameplate, that needs to be changed. How do you define a system that takes the place of *me*? And then what do you *do* about it?"

Crown's approach to industrial design stood in stark contrast to that of most other industrial companies, who typically hired design consultants to style a product after all the internal engineering was completed. Often design consultants had little say in defining the product concept and were seldom in a position to influence the engineering. With Crown, the situation was quite different. They would call in the RS team as soon as they had a clear idea of a new product target. Both RS's industrial designers and Crown's engineers would assess the user's needs and the competitors' products, from different points of view. Then RS would develop a proposal and work with Crown engineers during product development. According to Don Luebrecht, a senior project engineer who had been with Crown since 1978, this was the secret to Crown design:

> We work together very well. They always listen carefully to us and we always listen carefully to them. Sometimes we have to re-do some of our engineering to accommodate their designs; sometimes they have to change their design recommendations to accommodate our engineering. Sure, there are minor conflicts, but we always manage to work these out. There is always a lot of give-and-take. Of course, they always go home at the end of the day.

Dave Smith had similar views. "For example, many capital goods people, when they get a prototype, don't want you to touch it at all. But at Crown that's no problem. They will do three or four major iterations, because they see the prototype as a three-dimensional drawing to be refined and made better. Only with a prototype can you go through such things as service procedures, testing, careful operator analysis, and project evaluation, and Crown really understands that," (See a list of Crown's major design awards in Exhibit 3.)

The "Pretty Truck" Company

In the late 1960s and 1970s, Crown expanded its line of lift-trucks by introducing a series of new products, all of which were distinguished by innovative design and an unusual level of attention to details. Everything from the shape and color of control levers to the placement of light was carefully considered and designed to enhance the operator's safety, comfort, and efficiency and to improve the truck's appearance as well (see Exhibit 4 for an advertisement reflecting these principles). Because these features promoted operator productivity and reduced the risks of costly accidents, customers were willing to pay a 10 percent price premium for Crown products.

▲ EXHIBIT 3   Crown Equipment Corporation Design Awards

Year	Product	Award
1987	Series SP Stockpicker, Operator's Platform	Selection, Equipment Category, Annual Design Review, *ID* Magazine of International Design
1985	Walkie Trucks, Control Handle	Selection, Equipment Category, Annual Design Review, *ID* Magazine of International Design
1980	Series RR Rider Reach Truck	Industrial Design Excellence Award, Industrial Designers Society of America (IDSA)
1975	Series SC Sit-Down Counterbalanced Rider	Industrial Products and Equipment Design in Steel Award, American Iron & Steel Institute (AISI)
1973	Series RC Stand-Up Counterbalanced Rider	Industrial Products and Equipment Design in Steel Citation, American Iron & Steel (AISI)
	Series WPT Walkie Pallet Truck; Series W, EW, 30 W Walkie Stacker; Series TWR Walkie Rider Tow Tractor; Series RC Stand-Up Counterbalanced Rider	Industry Form (IF) Award, Excellence in Industrial Design Hannover Messe [industry fair]
1972	Series RC Stand-Up Counterbalanced Rider	Selection, Equipment, and Instrumentation Category, Annual Design Review, *ID* Magazine of International Design
1969	Series SP Stockpicker 30W Walkie Stacker	Industry Form (IF) Award, Outstanding Design of an Industrial Product, Hannover Messe
1965	Tow Tractor/Personnel Carrier Pallet Truck W227	Industrial Products Design In Steel Citation, American Iron & Steel Institute (AISI)
1963	First W-Series Pallet Truck	Design Excellence Award, Industrial Designers Institute

A key part of Crown's marketing strategy during this period was to enter segments where the dominant design left something to be desired, or where a niche in the market waited to be filled. In these segments, Crown believed that it could capture market share by being the company that offered a logical and preferred alternative to the competition. In one segment after the other, Crown used this strategy successfully.

By 1972, Crown was making over 100 different models of lift trucks, all in the lighter, 1,500–3,000-pound capacity range, which it sold in 80 countries. Most of its manufacturing was located in Ohio (including its own components' manufacture), but it also had plants in Australia and Ireland. Crown's niche was smaller trucks "that looked nice and won design awards." Other forklift truck companies, most of which competed in the upper range of trucks above 4,000 pounds, ignored Crown, referring to it as the "pretty truck" company.

▲ EXHIBIT 4   Crown Equipment Advertisement

▲ 505

Case 5-3
Crown Equipment
Corporation: Design
Services Strategy

At Crown, our designs predict the future of material handling equipment. They not only look better. They also work better. Every detail is a masterpiece of advanced engineering. Take the design of the 4,000-lb.-capacity walkie pallet truck, for example. The power unit cover is all-steel for rugged durability. It also features the most imitated full-function control handle in the industry. And a uniquely designed battery disconnect lever that helps eliminate exposed cables. You won't find this kind of innovation, expertise and attention to detail anywhere else. And, with a price of **$2,975** *(less battery and charger)*, it is evident that the latest design is also easily affordable. So if you want the most advanced material handling equipment, look closely at Crown. You'll find that tomorrow's technology is already on the job.
Crown Equipment Corp., New Bremen, Ohio 45869 (419) 629-2311

The First Real Choice

In the early seventies Crown's management decided to take on the big companies by developing a new design for a counterbalanced "rider truck," a product segment dominated in the U.S. by Raymond Corporation, which held a 75 percent market share. A standard product in the industry, counterbalanced trucks, quite simply, have a mass of pig iron in the base that keeps them stable when lifting loads of several tons. This truck was bigger than any Crown product yet, having a lift capacity of 4,500 pounds. Dave Tompkins of RichardsonSmith, who had been working with the Crown account for over 10 years, headed the RS contingent. "As with all new products," Tompkins recalled, "Crown began with analyzing everyone else and coming up with what the new truck would have to be. It was like a dot-to-dot drawing, with this information (like head length, turning radius, lift capacity) being the dots." Tompkins and his RS colleagues carried the research further.

> At this time, every other truck had this bizarre condition that, when travelling in reverse, the operator had to turn around and operate the controls from behind his back. We tossed around all sorts of ideas as to what to do about that problem. Then we said, 'in theory, you could stand sideways, and see both forwards and backwards, just by moving your head. But then how would you operate the controls?

Tompkin's team then built a full-scale mock-up and had people of different sizes interact with it. They ran a vision plot to see where blind spots were, and they tested various configurations of a multifunction control system. To accommodate nearly a dozen functions, they developed two controls. The main control lever, for the right hand, moved the forklift forward and backward, up and down. It had two buttons—one for the horn and the other for the tilt mechanism. Steering was controlled by the left hand. When Tompkins offered this radical proposal to Crown, "it took a while to convince them." Bidwell made the final decision to go with it.

The mock-up was moved to New Bremen, and Crown's engineers set to work on the new truck. Eighteen months of engineering and design work followed. For the multifunction control, they first looked at aircraft pistol-grip controls. But when they found out that such controls would cost $250 per unit, RS decided to design it themselves. The result was a sandcast aluminum part. "We got a finished appearance without a big investment in tooling," noted Tompkins. Several other details completed the revolutionary look of the new truck. One was the "dashboard," made of vacuum-molded $1/4$-inch ABS plastic, rather than welded steel. This created a softness and high durability.

The new RC (Rider Counterbalanced) truck, bombarded with criticism by the competition, offered customers their first "real choice" in lift trucks. Within four years, the truck captured a 40 percent market share (see Exhibit 5). Spurred by this success, Crown developed a follow-on rider reach (RR) truck, designed for the narrow aisles that increasingly characterized warehouses and distribution centers. Unlike the counterbalanced trucks, the rider reach had "feet" in the front that kept it in balance. Using the principles developed in the RC, the RR became Crown's showpiece. It won a design award from the Industrial Designers Society of America in 1980, and in 1989 was expected to be in the running for a "Design of the Decade" award (see Exhibit 6).

The TSP Project

With the RR series and other products that followed, Crown evolved from a niche-player and follower to an industry leader with a full product line. Capping off the 1980s was the recently introduced TSP Turret Stockpicker (see Exhibit 7). In just a few months, the TSP, the first of its kind in the United States, had attracted much attention in the industry. It could operate in warehouses with very narrow aisles, and could lift pallet loads of 3,000 pounds up to a height of 40 feet.

▲ EXHIBIT 5   The First Real Choice

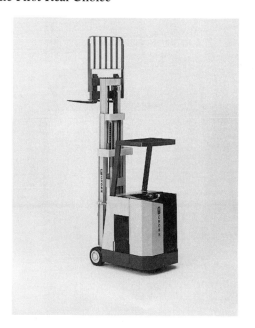

▲ EXHIBIT 6   The First Series RR Truck

▲ EXHIBIT 7   The TSP Turret Stockpicker

The TSP project began in early 1983. (See Appendix 1 for a timeline of the project.) RS designers were brought in within the first few months to assist Crown's product development group with product criteria, appearance, and human factors. Early on it was decided that operator functionality would be a key design objective; since material handling productivity is largely dependent on the operator, the design had to be "operator-friendly." To learn more about how to improve the operator's comfort, safety, and control, Crown engineers and RS designers studied existing European turret-style trucks and other industrial equipment. The team also visited the facilities of key customers to study how current products were used and to interview operators about how they performed their jobs. Ergonomic studies were also conducted. Designers used this information to make preliminary sketches that explored all key design features—for example, the layout of controls. They also built three-dimensional foam models to investigate alternative designs.

These sketches and three-dimensional foam models allowed the team to explore various design concepts relatively quickly. Once the field of choice was narrowed, the Crown-RS team began the difficult task of making firm commitments to specific design details. They had to consider everything from the shape of the control levers to the location of the transmission and drive motor, and to evaluate their collective impact on the overall product.

Don Luebrecht recalled, "We sweated every detail. Nothing was considered 'too minor' to ignore." Design, engineering, manufacturing, service, and marketing were all involved in these choices. After an initial set of design commitments were made, a working prototype was built and tested. The process of revising and refining the design required three more prototype iterations.

In order to ensure that this attention to detail would be matched in final product quality, Crown custom-designed a very large proportion of the TSP's components for manufacture in-house; relatively few off-the-shelf components were used.

Finally, four and a half years after beginning the project, the design was finalized and ready for field testing and manufacturing start-up. The TSP entered the market in late 1988 and was soon in the running for several design awards.

▲ CROWN PEOPLE

Design was not the only factor in Crown's success. Crown's technology too was state-of-the-art, but Crown's top management believed that people were the real key to the company's success.

Crown's talent came not from MBA programs or prestigious engineering schools, but from the villages and farms of the surrounding countryside. Half of Crown employees lived in New Bremen, a town of some 3,000 people situated about 75 miles northwest of Dayton, a city of 200,000 people with a metropolitan area of 800,000 and the nearest major airport. The rest lived within a 40-mile radius, in the small- and medium-sized towns of central Ohio. New Bremen itself housed the county airport. Most of Crown's senior managers had been with the company since its beginnings or shortly thereafter, and most of its employees had spent their working lives at Crown. Many had grown up on family farms. As Don Luebrecht, one of the company's leading project engineers (himself still a practicing farmer), put it: "Farming helps keep your sense—as a user and a fixer—of what's real and what's not."

Many employees had left the area for their education, but then returned to be near their families, or to have "a good place to raise kids." The rural background of the workforce resulted in a stability, a distinctive work ethic, and an individualism that contributed substantially to Crown's culture and the quality of its products. That individualism could be a problem, however, when introducing something so new as a computer-based scheduling system, noted Bidwell with a grin. "We didn't realize that we had an informal communications system that beat our computer. So many people in the company are related to each other that they all think they know what's going on. So they assume they know better than the computer." Eventually management did convince people to start using the computer system, and within a few months it began to take hold.

Good communication among departments and disciplines was an evident characteristic of the company. With most operations located within walking distance of one another, that communication network had developed almost effortlessly. As for the future, there was some concern as to how the communication would operate and how the culture would look when the company doubled in size—management's goal for the next decade.

▲ MANUFACTURING AT CROWN

Australian and German facilities aside, the vast majority of Crown's manufacturing activities were concentrated in the company's enormous New Bremen complex. Located just across the street from the engineering center, the complex consisted of several component fabrication facilities and assembly plants. Within these facilities, the company undertook everything from plastic injection molding and precision machining to chassis welding and body painting. In early 1989 Crown was manufacturing about 80 percent of the components for its products and was building a plant that would begin manufacturing lift-truck motors before the end of the year. Crown's manufacturing engineers were "can-do" people: "Whatever you guys want, we'll make."

Typically, components were fabricated in batches (usually about two weeks' worth at a time) and transported (via Crown lift truck, of course) to the appropriate assembly plant. The need to coordinate the flow of this massive variety of parts was a major challenge for Crown's manufacturing operations. This challenge was augmented by the wide variety of product families and models Crown offered, each of which could be ordered with any number of customized options. Moreover, the cost and size of a finished truck mandated that finished-goods inventories be kept as low as possible. Therefore it was imperative that the assembly operations accommodate a high degree of flexibility. The trucks were generally assembled according to marketing forecast, but customized options were added only after an order commitment was received. Delivery lead time generally averaged around three weeks. To help meet the challenges of coordinating the production of a wide variety of finished models, the company had recently implemented a computerized materials resource planning (MRP) system.

The low volumes and high product variety at Crown made fully automated assembly operations infeasible. Unlike an automobile plant, where each assembly step occurs at a fixed point along a moving assembly line, Crown's assembly operations were designed to accommodate a maximum variety of product and process flow. Trucks were typically assembled in batches of varying size. Each assembly operation (such as installing the seats) took place more or less at the same time for all trucks in a given batch. After a given assembly operation was complete, another operation would begin in the same general work area. At certain points the batch of trucks would be moved to a new work area, but in general, the trucks (especially the largest ones) were moved very little during assembly operations. The sequence of assembly steps was organized so that standard components and subassemblies were attached first, and customizing options were put on later. One of the chief advantages of this production process (over the assembly line) was its flexibility, which made it possible to alter the sequence of products being assembled. For example, if optional parts for a particular order were not ready, the truck or trucks could be set aside (without holding up production of other trucks) until those parts arrived on the line.

▲ THE LIFT TRUCK INDUSTRY

The materials handling industry was born when people started to think of ways to enhance the productivity of the hired hand who lifted stones and bricks, stacked cotton bales or iron pigs, loaded milk cans or flour bags. Various devices using pulleys and levers were invented to assist in the lifting and moving of raw materials, products, and parts. From the simple "dolly," which enabled people to move relatively small but heavy loads around easily, through the highly sophisticated and varied lift trucks that populate late 20th-century factories and warehouses, the industry has followed changing needs and technology.

Lift trucks were powered by gas or electricity—the latter from huge batteries. Gas trucks were used outdoors and in well-ventilated factory areas. Electric trucks, somewhat more expensive than gas, were needed indoors, or wherever air pollution was a problem.

Developments in Warehousing

As the price of land in urban areas became increasingly expensive, warehouses tended to grow up, rather than out. This development required equipment that could help people stack goods on multiple levels of shelves, which might reach up several stories. In the 1950s, the pallet system evolved, which made it possible to store an indefinite number of items in or on large, uniformly sized pallets. This system called for careful tracking, but reduced the handling time of individual parts or materials. It also made possible clear parameters for the designers of materials handling equipment.

As developments in structural materials permitted pallets safely to be stacked ever higher, and space limits resulted in ever narrower aisles, lift truck manufacturers were challenged to provide equipment—like Crown's new TSP—that could maneuver and perform under these conditions.

Because warehouses were no longer predominantly storage areas, but rather distribution centers, this equipment had to be especially flexible, efficient, easy to operate, and reliable.

Little Chips and Big Machines

The manufacturers were also challenged—and had been for many years—by the computer. Some warehouses were fully automated, reducing the need for operators, and mandating the need for robot-operated equipment. In many industries, such as food, bar-codes were becoming ubiquitous, simplifying the work of the operator. Factory applications of lift trucks had changed too, in large part because of automation. In high-labor-cost countries, manufacturers turned to capital-intensive machines to do much of the work previously accomplished by men and women. These machines were often fed by automatic materials handling equipment, from one end of the process to the other. Despite the efforts of industry analysts to predict how the computer would continue to influence and change the industry, long-range product planning was no easy task.

Safety Issues

Another factor was pressing upon Crown and its competitors as the 1980s drew to a close: safety issues. This was especially true in the United States, where the Office of Occupation Safety Hazards had ever-increasing powers and where product liability suits were a major concern. For Crown, the emphasis on operator-safety and comfort was welcome: "We love it!" exclaimed Tom Bidwell, "We've been doing it for thirty years."

▲ COMPETITION AND THE MARKETPLACE IN 1989

At the end of the 1980s, the lift truck industry consisted of some 250 manufacturers worldwide, 25 of which competed directly with Crown. Crown's strongest U.S. competitors were Hyster, Yale, Clark, and Raymond (depending on the type of truck), while Linde of Germany was its chief European competitor. Crown ranked third in sales (all types of trucks included) in the United States, and tenth in the world. Japanese companies such as Toyota, Nissan, and Komatsu, through major players in global market, tended to be stronger in gas and diesel trucks than in Crown's segment, electric trucks. (See Exhibit 8 for selected market share information, and Exhibit 9 for list of international competitors.)

By the end of 1988, Crown was a full-line producer of lift trucks, ranging from the small pallet hand truck (selling for around $500) to the enormous turret stock picker (price tag around $85,000). Within nine product categories, the company offered some 66 different

▲ **EXHIBIT 8** U.S. Market Shares in Selected Product Categories

	1987	1988	1989
Class 1: Electric Motor Rider Trucks*			
Clark	17.0%	16.0%	16.2%
Hyster	14.0	14.4	17.4
Caterpillar	12.3	12.6	13.4
Crown	11.6	11.4	11.5
Toyota	5.7	5.1	5.0
Kalmar AC	4.0	3.2	2.4
Linde/Baker	3.5	4.7	4.5
Nissan	3.1	5.0	5.0
Komatsu	2.3	0.2	2.0
TCM	2.1	1.5	1.2
Schaeff	2.0	2.7	1.0
Drexel	1.8	1.2	1.2
Raymond	1.5	1.4	1.2
Mitsubishi	1.5	1.4	1.4
Class 2: Electric Motor Narrow Aisle Trucks†			
Crown	37.4%	31.0%	30.5%
Raymond	22.8	27.7	26.4
Hyster	7.0	5.8	5.2
Yale	7.0	6.1	6.0
Clark	6.1	6.1	6.3
Linde/Baker	2.8	4.0	4.4
Blue Giant	2.6	3.9	2.6
Lancer Boss	2.2	1.2	1.6
Prime Mover/B.T.	1.8	3.3	4.5
Mitsubishi	1.5	0.7	0.7
Toyota	1.3	0.8	1.0
Big Joe	1.1	1.5	1.9
Drexel	NA	2.3	2.6
Barrett	NA	1.8	2.4
Class 3: Electric Motor Hand Trucks‡			
Crown	20.4%	21.3%	34.2%
Yale	13.9	15.9	16.4
Clark	8.1	6.8	6.8
Prime Mover	6.9	6.8	7.4
Blue Giant	6.8	6.2	4.1
Linde/Baker	5.8	6.5	5.7
Big Joe	4.7	4.7	5.0

	1987	1988	1989
Barrett	4.6	4.9	5.3
Hyster	3.5	0.8	2.1
Multiton	3.5	3.8	2.8
B.T. Lift	1.4	1.8	2.4
Kalmar AC	1.4	0.9	1.1
Raymond	1.4	3.1	3.4

Source: *Dataquest.*
*Counterbalanced riding forklifts.
†RC, RR, TS, TSP models from Crown.
‡Low lift pallet trucks—GPW, PW, PE, PC models from Crown.

▲ EXHIBIT 9   The 10 Largest Lift Truck Manufacturers Worldwide, 1988

	Manufacturer	Country
1.	Balkancar	Bulgaria
2.	Linde-Stihl-Gruppe	West Germany
3.	Toyota	Japan
4.	Hyster	United States
5.	Komatsu	Japan
6.	Clark	United States
7.	Jungheinrich	West Germany
8.	Lansing	Great Britain
9.	BT	Sweden
10.	Crown	United States

trucks. Crown employed 3,800 people worldwide and had annual sales of over $450 million. It held 30 percent of the U.S. market share in lift trucks, and worldwide it ranked tenth among all lift truck manufacturers, both gas- and electric-powered, even through it produced only electric trucks.

In each of its market segments in the United States, Crown enjoyed a leading position in terms of sales revenues. In several product categories (e.g., high-lift stockpickers, walkie stackers), its market share was consistently well over 50 percent. The company had also begun to increase its emphasis on foreign markets. In 1986 it made a major commitment to the European market by opening a subsidiary in Germany, the home of its leading worldwide competitor, Linde-Stihl GmbH. As 1992 and European economic unification loomed nearer, it was clear that the decision was a good one, despite start-up problems. "We wanted the German operation to be *European*," Tom Bidwell explained, "not American. But it is no simple matter to get all of us thinking on the same wavelength."

Success in the marketplace, which transformed Crown from a small, niche-producer of hand trucks to a multinational producer of a full line of lift trucks, created its own set of challenges for top management. As Jim Moran noted,

> The key challenge in this industry is to stay on top. If you look at lift trucks historically, you see that no one has ever sustained market leadership over time. The leaders have always been toppled by someone trying a new approach. For years, we had the luxury of being able to sneak up on market leaders who had become lulled by their own success. Now we've become the market leader that others are gunning for.

Crown's management was particularly concerned that its traditional competitive edge—superior design—would no longer be its exclusive domain. Tom Bidwell noted,

> For years, we have not had to worry. So few companies took design seriously. Unfortunately, our success has shown people just how important good design is. Sooner or later, they're going to start getting serious about design.

This was already beginning to happen. Linde, for example, had recently hired the internationally renowned design firm, Porsche Design Group. Competitors were also beginning, with some success, to copy design features of Crown's products.[3] In one instance, Crown spent three years redesigning the steering-wheel console of one of their older trucks. Within six months of introducing the trucks with the newly designed console, several competitors introduced their own versions. Jim Moran recalled,

> This was a major blow. The new console was supposed to be a critical distinguishing feature on one of our major product lines. The sales force was really excited about it. When competitors began introducing their own versions, it took all the momentum out of sales. It really hurt the morale of our sales force.

The console incident was particularly disturbing given top management's belief that similar design refinements—expeditiously implemented—would become an increasingly important competitive necessity for Crown. For years, the company had emphasized new product development over refinement of existing products. As a result, several of Crown's key products were beginning to age. For example, three of Crown's best-selling W-series High Lift Walkie Trucks, introduced between 1967 and 1971, had essentially remained the same ever since. One of its first walkie stackers had last been upgraded in 1973. The SC Sit-Down Counterbalance truck introduced in 1974 had not been upgraded. From projected orders for 1989, the marketing people sensed that this lack of upgrades on older products was starting to cost them share in some key markets. There were occasional exceptions, however: the SP Stockpickers introduced in the mid-1960s, for example, had received upgrades every five years or so, most recently in the mid-1980s.

The exceptions were neither often nor fast enough for Tom Bidwell. He was frustrated by Crown's inability to do even minor product upgrades in a relatively rapid fashion.

> The minute we talk about a small design change, it seems to turn into a major project. For example, one day while I was walking through the factory, it occurred to me that the nameplate carrying the Crown logo was really getting out of date. It looked 50 years old! I asked RS about redesigning the nameplate. A few months later, I checked back and found out that they were exploring changes in the location of the nameplate. This prompted our engineering department to look at how the nameplate was mounted. Now, RS and our engineering group are exploring a complete redesign of the entire back of the forklift. It's been three years and we still don't have an updated nameplate!

---

[3]Design innovations are notoriously difficult to protect with patents.

Although Bidwell and Moran believed that Crown had to put greater emphasis on upgrading existing products, they also knew it could not ignore major new product development activities. Indeed, as competitors took aim at Crown, and as Crown expanded into growing international markets with different design requirements, it seemed likely that the need for new products would only increase. Bidwell believed that Crown was going to have to become much faster at product development than it had been. In the last decade, Crown had developed only two major new products—the recently introduced TSP stockpicker, and as four-wheel sit-down that was still being tested. The TSP had taken about five years from concept to market, and the four-wheeler was taking just as long. Bidwell was concerned that such long product development lead times would not be acceptable in the future competitive environment. "We need to be able to update our products every one to one and a half years and to introduce a new product every two years."

▲ REEVALUATING THE DESIGN STRATEGY

In addition to the changes in the competitive environment that demanded faster new product development and continuing refinement of existing products, another factor weighed heavily on Bidwell's mind. RichardsonSmith had recently been purchased by Fitch, a highly regarded, British-based design consultancy; after the purchase, the company was renamed Fitch RS. Bidwell wondered whether the new owners understood the special relationship between Crown and its design partner. He was concerned whether FRS, suddenly a very large firm of 500 employees, would be willing or able to do small-scale projects for Crown. He was also concerned about the cost of the consultancy's new prestige: would FRS's services inevitably be much more expensive? Some project engineers also noted that after the acquisition, interaction between the firms had become much more formal. Still, many of the same designers remained at the firm and, most importantly, Dave Smith, although no longer an owner of the firm, was expected to remain at Fitch for at least a few more years.

Several options were considered at this point. To be sure, RS had been Crown's sole design consultant, but there were dozens of other industrial design firms in the United States. Crown could easily find another design consultant. (See Exhibit 10 for the largest U.S. design consultants, with locations.) Crown's reputation for design consciousness, and its $1 million annual design budget, made it an extremely attractive client to many top-notch design houses. Another approach would be to expand the number of design consultants with whom Crown worked. Indeed, many industrial firms preferred relationships with several design consultancies in order to maximize their exposure to different viewpoints and new ideas. Moreover, outside designers could often provide a broad, objective perspective to the problem at hand, unhindered by company traditions and turf issues.

Another option being given serious consideration was the establishment of an in-house design group at Crown. Crown had become large enough and required enough industrial design services to make this option viable. This would entail, according to Bidwell, a group of six to eight designers, the critical mass for this type of endeavor. The internal design group option was attractive for several reasons.

First, communication between industrial design and engineering would likely improve. Rather than having to travel 100 miles between New Bremen and Columbus (the home of Fitch RS), in-house designers and engineers could easily see each other on a daily basis. In addition, an in-house design group could conceivably be integrated more effectively into the entire product development process. With better communication and with tighter integration, product development would presumably proceed faster. And, as the designers gained experience within

▲ EXHIBIT 10   The 10 Largest Product Design Firms in the United States, 1989 (annual fee income in millions)

Firm	Annual Income
Walter Dorwin Teague Associates, New York, Seattle, Los Angeles, Washington, DC	$7.0
Fitch RichardsonSmith, Worthington (OH), Boston	4.8
Designworks/USA, Newbury Park (CA), Troy (MI)	3.5
Design Continuum, Boston	3.3
Henry Dreyfuss Associates, New York	*
GVO, Inc., Palo Alto (CA), Minneapolis	2.8
frogdesign hartmut esslinger, inc., Menlo Park (CA)	2.5
Herbst LaZar Bell Inc., Chicago, Wellesley (MA)	2.5
David O. Chase Design, Inc., Skaneateles (New York)	2.4
Design West, Mission Viejo (CA)	2.2

*Ranked by W&A estimate
Source: Based on a study by Wefler & Associates, Inc., Chicago, IL.

Crown, their in-depth knowledge of every detail of the company's process and product technology would be increasingly valuable. Moreover, an in-house group could efficiently give attention to the smaller tasks involved in the upgrading of existing products.

The in-house design option also contained a number of risks. Maintaining creativity was perhaps the greatest concern. One advantage outside consultants had was their broad exposure to different types of products. Design consultants tended to believe that their creativity was best stimulated by working on diverse projects and did not specialize by industry. It was not uncommon for a top design house to work on products as different as medical instruments and athletic shoes. The working environment of such a firm fostered cross-fertilization and was an ongoing source of new ideas. A critical question was whether Crown, a medium-sized manufacturer of heavy equipment in the Ohio farm country, could create an equivalent environment in an in-house design group. Because they would be working on only one type of product, in-house designers could run the risk of becoming stale.

Providing an attractive environment for an in-house design group would involve gutting and redoing a historic building in the center of New Bremen, about five blocks from the engineering staff. Bidwell estimated the renovation costs at about $120,000. Equipping the studio and model shop with state-of-the-art equipment for designers and model builders would cost another $110,000. Crown's tool shop had a surplus of small machines that would be suitable for the model shop. Each designer, fully burdened, would run about $100,000 annually. Bidwell and Moran had also been discussing the issue of where to locate the group organizationally. If they did decide on an in-house group, should it be under engineering? Marketing? Or should it report directly to Bidwell?

As he pulled into the parking lot of Crown's headquarters, Tom Bidwell recalled his first meeting with Dave Smith, some 30 years ago. In retrospect, that meeting had radically altered the course of Crown's history. This morning's meeting with Dave Smith could mark another turning point. Bidwell hoped that his instincts would serve him as well today as they had at the meeting 30 years ago.

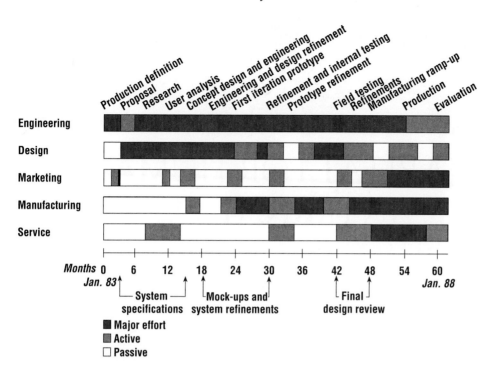

HABITAT FOR HUMANITY INTERNATIONAL

Habitat's goal is to eliminate poverty housing and homelessness from the face of the earth [and]
put the subject of inadequate housing on the hearts and minds of people.

from Habitat's goal statement

When Jeff Snider joined Habitat for Humanity International as executive vice president and chief operating officer in 1990, the not-for-profit organization had experienced a twofold increase in revenues and a nearly threefold increase in house construction since 1988. In his three years on the job, Snider had made considerable improvements in Habitat's organizational structure and control systems, improvements crucial to managing the continued rapid growth that nearly doubled revenues and house construction from 1990 to 1993. In April 1993, Snider recognized that Habitat faced major challenges as it sought to define its mission and strategies amid demands to expand its activities in scale and scope. There were, for example, constituencies within the organization that advocated Habitat's involvement in disaster relief, fighting urban homelessness, and a variety of nonhousing concerns of the poor, such as nutrition, drug prevention, and education. All of these activities departed from Habitat's historical focus on the construction of affordable housing in rural areas.

Snider hoped to initiate a five-year planning process and use it to compel the organization to reconsider its mission and strategies in light of the array of interesting and important opportunities. He wondered what organizational changes would be necessary as Habitat continued to build on its past success, and he questioned whether such changes could be achieved while preserving Habitat's mission-driven spirit and culture. Which of the many pressing social needs should Habitat try to meet, and did the organization have the discipline to say no to any of them? Snider knew that the answers to these questions would determine whether Habitat would continue its remarkable record of performance in the coming years.

Andrew Slavitt, MBA 93, prepared this case under the supervision of Professor Gary Loveman.

▲ HABITAT FOR HUMANITY INTERNATIONAL

Since its modest beginnings on a farm in southern Georgia, Habitat for Humanity grew into an organization that achieved remarkable success, building houses in approximately 850 locations in the United States and Canada and in 40 countries around the world. From its founding in 1976 through April of 1993, Habitat built more than 20,000 houses and planned to build 7,700 during 1993. By other measures, it became an impressively large and strong organization, having achieved considerable media attention due in large part to the active involvement of former President Jimmy Carter. Though driven primarily from a grassroots level, Habitat in 1993 estimated revenues worldwide of $110 million with an active volunteer corps of more than 200,000 (see Exhibit 1).

Habitat's Operating Principles

We don't have any giveaway programs. It's not a charity or benefit. We work side by side with people. We are helping people meet their own needs.... Habitat's key to success is not providing charity, but capital, to worthy families shackled by poverty.

President Jimmy Carter, describing Habitat for Humanity

Habitat operated under several important operating principles that became the central core to its mission:

1. Habitat builds affordable housing for people in need. Houses are not given away, but sold at zero profit with long-term zero interest mortgages. While home costs vary by location, the average house in the United States costs homeowners $35,000, while houses in developing countries average about $2,000.

2. Future Habitat homeowners are required to put in hundreds of hours of "sweat equity," usually on the construction of their house, but often on the construction of others' houses as well.

3. All homeowner payments go into a "Fund for Humanity." These payments are recycled to help pay for the construction of new houses in the community. Outside of the Third World, a portion of all funds raised is set aside for the construction of houses in the Third World, where local communities cannot totally fund Habitat projects on their own.

4. All Habitat projects are originated at a "grassroots" level by people in the community. Habitat never enters a community uninvited.

5. Habitat homeowners are selected at the local level based upon need, willingness to work, and capability to pay for their houses. While minimum monthly income varies by location, a Habitat brochure from the Detroit affiliate suggests $930 as necessary to qualify for a Habitat house. Default rates are estimated to be as low as 1 percent.

6. Habitat accomplishes much of its work through partnership with others. A majority of all labor is donated from the community, as is an increasing percentage of the building materials. All funds for housing construction and operating expenses are privately donated.

7. Habitat is an ecumenical Christian organization, but welcomes everyone to participate in its ministry.

▲ EXHIBIT 1   Habitat for Humanity International, Inc.—Statements of Activity and Changes in Fund Balances, Years Ended December 31, 1992, and 1991 (numbers for 1992 are preliminary)

	Operating Fund			Plant Fund	MacArthur Loan Fund	Annuity Fund	Total, 1992	Total, 1991
	Unrestricted	Restricted	Total					
Support and revenue								
Contributions	$19,808,877	$12,539,333	$32,348,210			$ 95,079	$32,443,289	$22,849,346
Donated assets	2,358,654		2,358,654				2,358,654	1,208,678
Other income—net	687,121		687,121		$ 5,282		692,403	552,611
Total support and revenue	$22,854,652	$12,539,333	$35,393,985		$ 5,282	$ 95,079	$35,494,346	$24,610,635
Expenses								
Program services								
Sponsored program (note 10)	$ 3,846,661	$ 2,833,179	$ 6,679,840				$ 6,679,840	$ 4,975,182
Affiliated program (note 11)	4,780,536	2,670,897	7,451,433				7,487,722	5,343,704
Public awareness and education	2,706,194	322,586	3,028,780				3,028,780	2,755,309
Total program services	$11,333,391	$ 5,826,662	$17,160,053		$ 36,289		$17,196,342	$13,074,195
Supporting services								
Administration	$ 2,956,414		$ 2,956,414				$ 2,956,414	$ 2,462,910
Fund raising	6,144,724		6,144,724				6,144,724	6,375,508
Total supporting services	$ 9,101,138		$ 9,101,138				$ 9,101,138	$ 8,838,418
Total expenses	$20,434,529	$ 5,826,662	$26,261,191		$ 36,289		$26,297,480	$21,912,613

Excess (deficiency) of support and revenue over expenses before capital additions	$ 2,420,123	$ 6,712,671	$ 9,132,794		$ (31,007)	$ 95,079	$ 9,196,866	$ 2,698,022
Capital additions								
Donated assets				$ 103,575			$ 103,575	$ 396,826
Other income—net				(84,333)			(84,333)	11,232
Total capital additions				$ 19,242			$ 19,242	$ 408,058
Excess (deficiency) of support and revenue over expenses after capital additions	$ 2,420,123	$ 6,712,671	$ 9,132,794	19,242	$ (31,007)	$ 95,079	$ 9,216,108	$ 3,106,080
Fund balances at beginning of year	1,715,770	1,540,140	3,255,910	3,714,095	260,760	217,311	7,448,076	4,341,996
Fund balances at end of year	$ 4,135,893	$ 8,252,811	$12,388,704	$ 3,733,337	229,753	312,390	$16,664,184	$ 7,448,076
Operating activities								
Excess (deficiency) of support and revenue over expense after capital additions	$ 2,420,123		$9,132,794	$19,242	$(31,007)	$95,079	$9,216,108	$3,106,080
Items included in excess (deficiency) not affecting cash flows								
Income from donated assets	(2,358,654)		(2,358,654)	(103,575)			(2,462,229)	(1,605,504)
Interest income imputed on mortgages and notes receivable	(43,653)		(43,653)				(43,653)	(45,826)

continued

▲ **EXHIBIT 1** *continued*

	Operating Fund			Plant Fund	MacArthur Loan Fund	Annuity Fund	Total, 1992	Total, 1991
	Unrestricted	Restricted	Total					
Present value discounts on mortgages and affiliated loans receivable	80,462		80,462				80,462	96,549
Interest expense imputed on MacArthur note payable					36,365		36,265	43,550
Depreciation	415,198		415,198				415,198	387,605
Gain/loss on sale of fixes assets				84,333			84,333	56,500
Donated assets used	2,029,477		2,029,477				2,029,477	817,484
Shortage/obsolescence of donated inventory								286,772
Changes in operating assets and liabilities								
(Increase) in marketable securities acquired by gift	(271,278)		(271,278)				(271,278)	(16,421)
(Increase) in accounts receivable	(10,416)		(10,416)				(10,416)	9,233
(Increase)/decrease in notes receivable	(383,324)		(383,324)		188,988		(194,336)	(37,177)

Decrease/(increase) in interfund receivable/payable	89,833	(15,081)	74,752	(85,220)	379	10,089		
(Increase) in face value of mortgages receivable	(65,881)		(65,881)				(65,881)	(144,806)
Decrease in purchased inventory	61,091		61,091				61,091	36,228
(Increase) in prepaid items	(175,782)		(175,782)				(175,782)	(214,885)
Increase in accounts payable	391,747		391,747	7,489		97,938	497,174	407,179
Other items, net	187,798		187,798				187,798	188,853
Net cash provided by operating activities	$ 2,366,741	$ 6,697,590	$ 9,064,231	$ (77,731)	$ 194,625	$ 203,106	$ 9,384,331	$ 3,371,414
Investing activities								
Property additions	$ (294,001)		$ (294,001)	$ (683,587)			$ (977,588)	$ (592,209)
Property sales				358,652			358,652	358,652
Investment purchases		(5,656,118)	(5,656,118)			(556,676)	(6,212,794)	(87,276)
Investment sales						24,765	24,765	
Cash used in investing activities	$ (294,001)	$ (5,656,118)	$ (5,950,119)	$ (324,935)		$ (531,911)	$ (6,806,065)	$ (679,485)
Financing activities								
Proceeds from loans from financial institutions	$				$ (125,000)			$625,000
Proceeds from other borrowings	285,458		285,458				285,458	1,199,050
Principal repayments made	(656,532)		(656,532)				(781,532)	(2,352,717)

continued

▲ EXHIBIT 1 *concluded*

	Operating Fund			Plant Fund	MacArthur Loan Fund	Annuity Fund	Total, 1992	Total, 1991
	Unrestricted	Restricted	Total					
Net cash used in financing activities	$ (37,074)		$ (371,074)		$ (125,000)		(496,074)	$ (538,667)
Transfers								
To plant fund for purchases of property, plant and equipment	$ (402,666)	$ 1,041,472	$ (402,666)		$ 402,666			
Increase/(decrease) in cash and equivalents	$ 1,299,000	$ 1,041,472	$ 2,340,471		$ 69,625	$ (328,805)	$ 2,081,292	$ 2,163,262
Cash and equivalents at beginning of year	1,865,718	1,251,090	3,116,808		144,639	413,801	3,675,248	1,511,986
Cash and equivalents at year end	$ 3,164,718	$ 2,292,562	$ 5,457,280		$ 214,264	$ 5,84,996	$ 5,756,540	$ 3,675,248

Habitat for Humanity International, Inc., Schedules of Functional Expenses, Years Ended December 31, 1992 and 1991 (numbers for 1992 are preliminary)

	Sponsored Program	Affiliated Program	Public Awareness and Education	Administration	Fund-Raising	Total, 1992	Total, 1991
Funds transferred for home-building grants							
Restricted funds	$ 2,833,179	$ 2,733,408				$ 5,566,587	$ 4,833,804
Unrestricted funds	1,900,013	1,400				1,901,413	596,527
Donated assets distributed	811	2,007,993	$207	$20,203	$233	2,029,477	817,484
Salaries and benefits	1,306,910	568,268	1,315,938	673,805	863,936	4,728,857	6,674,659
Professional services	18,254	76,729	1,540,553	174,901	4,819,803	6,630,240	609,175
Travel	178,656	221,111	58,665	59,799	61,343	579,574	249,399
Office supplies and materials	17,018	67,250	47,121	62,649	20,323	214,361	404,854
Printing	4,048	51,505	203,771	233,316	31,901	524,541	351,028
Utilities and telephone	53,898	138,416	58,783	117,718	62,601	431,414	94,914
Insurance	14,791	40,757	14,948	40,097	17,874	128,467	122,842
Interest, service charges, taxes	7,913	45,625	847	8,916	15,994	79,295	286,772
Inventory shortage/obsolesence							
Postage and freight	59,264	171,583	255,337	352,706	165,294	1,004,544	830,131
Repairs and maintenance	13,576	28,180	14,661	39,633	13,703	109,753	114,902
Regional and board meetings	16,287	10,649	10,074	9,618	10,225	56,853	30,850
Rentals	2,384	39,945	15,578	2,098	1,679	61,684	123,120
Leases/equipment not capitalized	33,817	44,640	7,509	133,039	23,130	242,135	230,533
Service agreements	2,852	13,921	5,326	99,324	1,538	122,961	92,956
Depreciation	71,414	94,665	56,467	113,764	78,888	415,198	387,605
Training, recruitment, books	27,483	13,530	7,491	25,775	5,572	79,851	158,436
Discounts on mortgages receivable		68,929				68,929	96,549
Discounts on affiliate loans receivable		11,533				11,533	
Construction supplies	1,172	17,550	130,260	47,880		196,862	
Other	115,865	20,493	32,884	99,040	140,818	409,100	77,216
	$ 6,679,840	$ 7,487,722	$ 3,028,780	$ 2,956,414	$ 6,144,724	$26,297,480	$21,912,613

The Habitat Homeowner

The work of Habitat could perhaps best be understood by looking at the effect it had on people's lives. The following was excerpted from a letter written by a new Habitat homeowner, Irma Cordero:

> Even after a friend had shown me a Habitat newsletter in 1990, I had been reluctant to even apply, because we had been turned down by mortgage companies so many times for not making enough money. Even when Habitat asked me to come in for an interview, I only went to be polite. There was no way I could believe I could own a house on my small salary as a clerk. I don't have the words to tell how I felt when Habitat told me I had been approved. Even as we put in our 500 hours of "sweat equity" it seemed like a dream to me.... Without Habitat, people like me would never be able to have a house of our own. And our children might never learn that they can dream about the same futures as other children who have more.

Millard Fuller, Habitat's president and founder, related this story of another new Habitat homeowner:

> In Oklahoma City, Joe Bell, an elderly gentleman, was the recipient of the first Habitat house. Living with his daughter, he slept on a lumpy couch in the living room. This couch did not convert into a bed; he just crumpled up on it at night. The only place he had to put his meager belongings was behind the couch. The day of Joe's house dedication, he cried when presented with a Bible. He said, "I have never had a home of my own before. I feel just like a king." Since then, two other Habitat houses have been renovated in Joe's neighborhood. It has taken on a completely new look. Where there were weeds in the yards, trash scattered around, screens torn half off, and junk cars parked, there are now neatly mowed lawns, trimmed hedges, and no junk in sight. Homeowners and renters alike have fixed tattered screens and broken steps. They have mended porches and painted houses. And Joe Bell is everywhere, being a good neighbor.

Throughout Habitat, there were countless other stories of the powerful effect the organization had not only on homeowners but on volunteers as well. This caused many who were a part of a Habitat project, on any level, to continue their involvement and act as persuasive spokepersons for Habitat's mission.

Habitat's History

You know, I have never met a person who lived in a house that leaked and they liked it. I have never met a person who lived in a house that didn't have insulation and when the cold days came they couldn't get warm, and they liked it. Have never met a family who lived in a house with great holes in a floor that you could throw a cat through or great holes in the ceiling that you could see the stars through and they liked it. Never! But we have people...living that way. Habitat for Humanity is about changing all that.

Millard Fuller, at a house dedication in 1985,
about why he started Habitat for Humanity

Habitat was founded in 1976 by Millard and Linda Fuller. In 1968, Millard, a highly successful and wealthy businessman and lawyer, and Linda, hi wife, gave up all their worldly possessions and moved to a small Christian community in southern Georgia called Koinonia Farms, where the concept of partnership housing was being practiced. Excited by the potential of this concept, Millard moved with his family in 1973 to Zaire, where he put into practice the concept that later developed into Habitat.

In 1976, based on the operating principles outlined above, Habitat for Humanity was incorporated and operated on a small scale out of Sumter County, Georgia, and in the Third World. In 1978, Habitat started its first affiliate in San Antonio, Texas. Throughout the early 1980s, Habitat, still unknown to most of the world, was a shoestring operation spread out to 14 locations. Millard and Linda did all of the fund raising on their own, realizing several hundred thousand dollars per year.

Involvement of President Carter Habitat's future was changed forever one day in 1984 when Millard met former President Jimmy Carter at his home in Plains, Georgia, a short distance from Habitat's headquarters in Americus. Carter was immediately impressed with Habitat's mission and told Millard to let him know how he could help. Fuller and his board of directors reflected on this generous offer and presented him with a list of 15 requests, including that he sit on the board. Carter called Fuller and agreed to all 15 items on the spot. Speaking of himself and his wife, Rosalynn, Carter said, "We see Habitat as one of today's best *investments* by people who want to help others."

Carter's involvement was the turning point for Habitat, essentially "putting it on the map" and bringing it from a small not-for-profit to a nationally known organization with enormous fund-raising capabilities. By 1986, Habitat's fund raising had jumped to $13.6 million, up from $3.5 million in 1984. Thanks in large part to Carter's involvement, 1993 revenues were expected to be more than 30 times greater than those of 1984.

Jeff Snider and a Shift in Culture In 1990, Habitat's board conducted a search to find a new operational leader for Habitat, allowing Fuller to spend more of his time as chief spokesperson and spiritual leader. Finding the managerial talent pool within Habitat's own senior ranks to be thin, Habitat's board—in a major break from its past—turned to the outside and hired Jeff Snider, a Habitat volunteer in southern California and a former executive of Paula Financial, an insurance holding company, where he had been CEO since 1984.

When Snider arrived at Habitat in Americus, Georgia, to take over the operations, he found an organization virtually void of systems of any sort and led only by the extraordinary vision of Millard Fuller, the power of its mission, and a highly successful direct-mail fund-raising program. Snider saw the choice of a loose structure as contributing to a chaotic feeling in the organization, with potentially dangerous consequences. Despite record levels of building and fund raising, Habitat was mired in financial and human resource management problems. Less visibly, but perhaps more tragically, this lack of organization was hindering Habitat's ability to capitalize on new opportunities.

Snider made several key changes upon arriving at Habitat: (1) bolstering the financial control system; (2) hiring Allan Donaldson, with 25 years of private sector experience, as chief financial officer; (3) replacing the needs-based compensation system with a more traditional, albeit modest, one; (4) trimming administrative staff to reduce annual payroll expenses by more than $1 million; and (5) investing in some basic computer systems. The culture of an organization that had rejected most signs of modernization and professional management was changed forever.

The Habitat Organization

In June 1990 when Snider came to Habitat, he took on the title of executive vice president and chief operating officer, with Fuller retaining the title of president. The two of them sat on and reported jointly to the board of directors. Habitat operated through three divisions:

(1) Habitat Project Worldwide (HPW), which administered the affiliate system and the overseas projects; (2) Habitat Education Ministries (HEM), which ran all the awareness-building program activities (see Exhibit 2 for a partial listing of programs); and (3) Habitat Support Services (HSS), which included support areas such as department, finance, human resources, and information systems (see Exhibit 3 for an organization chart).

The Board of Directors   Habitat's policy was set by the International Board of Directors, which met three times a year. In 1993, it consisted of 27 outside directors, selected by the board, and Fuller and Snider. Board members served a maximum of two 3-year terms.

The Affiliate   Although Habitat's worldwide operations technically were run out of Americus, its real work occurred at the affiliate and project level. Affiliates were responsible for all elements of the Habitat mission. In most instances, they raised their own funds, selected families, completed construction, and collected payments. Affiliates managed the construction of new Habitat houses, which typically took 8 to 12 weeks to complete, with work done only on Saturdays (but with some preparation work done during the week). Volunteers were often retirees, but also included college students, church volunteers, and others from the community, all of whom worked side by side with the Habitat homeowners. Habitat provided a design book for appropriate housing structures, which affiliates modified to suit their local needs.

Each affiliate was required to sign an Affiliate Covenant, agreeing to operate according to Habitat's operating principles. As part of this agreement, each affiliate was requested to tithe 10 percent of the money it had raised in order to support overseas projects in developing countries. In 1992, the tithe from all affiliates totaled $2.2 million.

In the United States and throughout the developed world, Habitat operated through an expanding number of local affiliates. In April 1993, that number totaled 838 in the United States, but was expected to increase to 1,050 by the end of the year. Affiliates ranged in size from those building one house per year to some building approximately 40 per year; the average affiliate built four houses per year. Affiliates operated through five standing committees: Site Selection, Family Selection, Fund Raising, Publicity, and Building. Though virtually all of the labor was volunteer, a growing number of affiliates had full-time staff members—usually an executive director and often a construction manager. Affiliates varied in their degree of sophistication. Many used their own accounting systems and some, quite literally, operated out of the living room of one of the founders. According to a study completed in 1988, the average affiliate had approximately 15 board members and 320 other volunteers.

All Habitat affiliates in the United States were divided into 15 regions, each with a regular director who reported to one of two area directors in Americus. The regional offices schedules conference, provided assistance to new affiliates, reviewed affiliate operations, and attempted to coordinate the activities of all the affiliates within the region.

International Operations   Two-thirds of all Habitat's new houses every year were built overseas, either through sponsored project from money raised in the United States or in self-supporting affiliates.

Sponsored Projects   Habitat sponsored projects throughout Latin America, the Caribbean, across Africa, and into Asia and the Pacific area. The work was accomplished through the partnership of a local committee and Habitat International Partners, expatriates serving three-

▲ EXHIBIT 2   Partial Listing of Habitat for Humanity Programs

House-Raising Week Worldwide/Jimmy Carter Work Projects are annual week-long events planned to bring people together to build houses i partnership with low-income families and to raise global consciousness of the worldwide poverty housing crisis. The Jimmy Carter Work Project takes place in conjunction with House-Raising Week Worldwide. Former President Jimmy Carter and Rosalyn Carter lead a week-long building blitz. Volunteers from around the world travel to the North American Habitat affiliate that is hosting the work project. Both House-Raising Week Worldwide and the Jimmy Carter Work Projects take place in the summer.

Campus Chapters of Habitat for Humanity work in partnership with affiliates to engage educational communities in the full mission of Habitat: fund raising, educational awareness, and house building. Members of campus chapters include students, faculty, staff, and administrators at colleges and universities, technical schools, and high schools.

Global Village Work Camps is a program planned to increase awareness of the worldwide need for durable shelter and to promote brotherhood around the world through short-term work camp experiences. Volunteer work camp participants travel to Habitat for Humanity–sponsored projects in developing countries to build in partnership with local homeowners. Upon their return home, participants are requested to share their experience and spread the news of Habitat in their home communities through speeches and presentations.

International Day of Prayer and Action for Human Habitat is an event sponsored annually by Habitat, usually on the third Sunday in September. it is designed to bring congregations around the world together to raise consciousness of the worldwide poverty housing crisis.

Speakers Bureau provides Habitat for Humanity speakers for any groups that are interested in learning more about Habitat's work. The Bureau serves as a resource center, providing materials and training for Habitat's speakers and maintaining a database of experienced speakers located across the United States and Canada. It also works to develop the ability of affiliates to use speaking engagements to spread their ministry within their local community.

Covenant Church Program is an ongoing commitment between Habitat for Humanity and a participating church or synagogue which involves working together in a practical "hands-on" partnership to eliminate poverty housing. Each congregation pledges financial contributions to Habitat, and agrees to support the ministry through prayer. Beyond that, each congregation determines its own form of commitment.

Habitat World is the educational, informational, and outreach publication of the organization, issued and distributed every two months at no charge, with news about all Habitat projects and related information about affordable housing.

---

year commitments running local projects. In some countries, national organizations responsible for all of Habitat's activities in that country were formed; Habitat granted them money to carry out its mission. Headquarters administered the sponsored projects through three area directors, for Latin America, Asia, and Africa. Because of the lower cost of construction

▲ EXHIBIT 3   Organization Chart, Habitat for Humanity

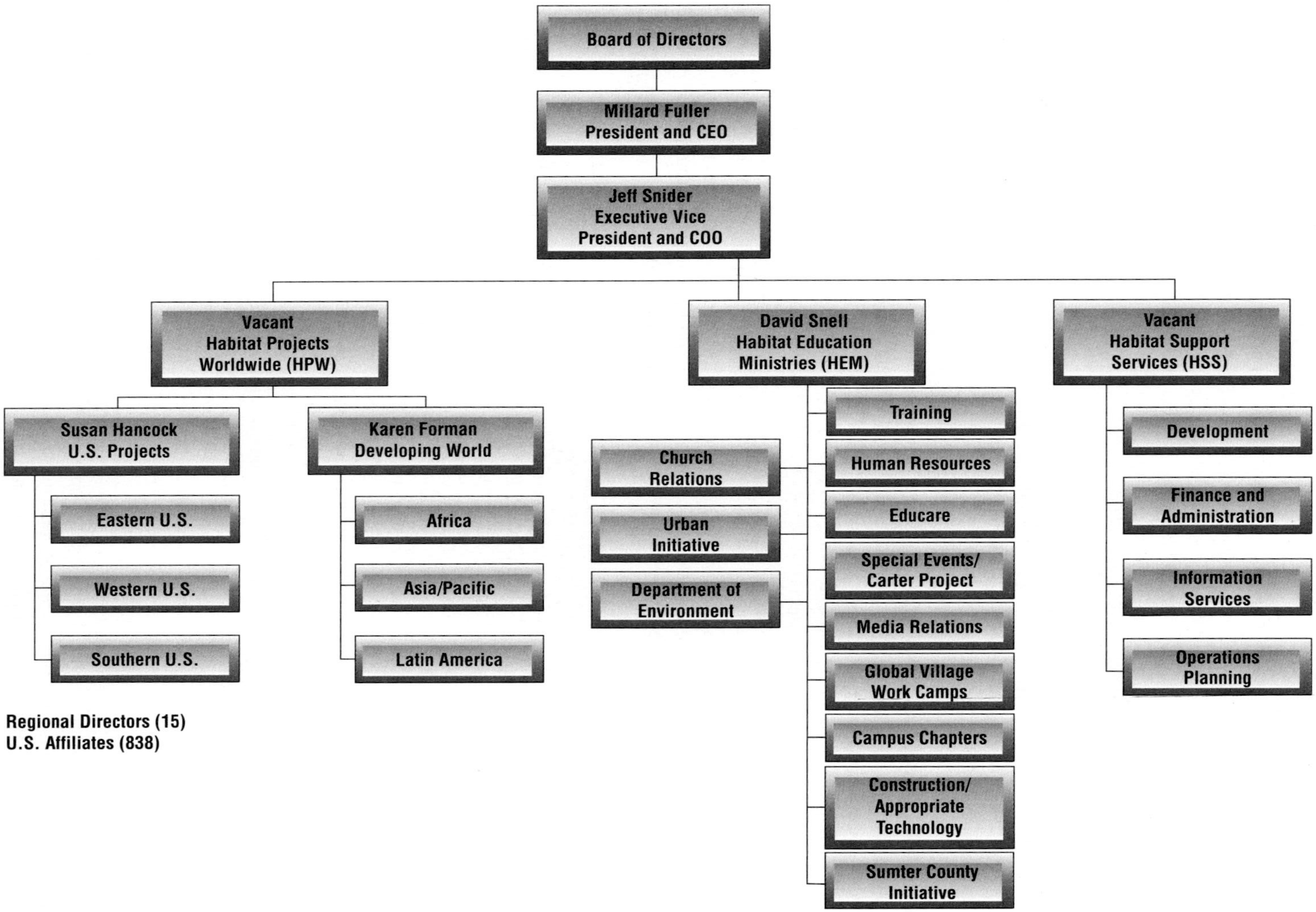

overseas and the simplified regulatory environment, some of Habitat's most successful projects were located outside the United States. In the Mezquital Valley, Mexico, for instance, more than 1,000 houses were completed during the early 1990s.

Overseas Affiliates   Habitat also had active affiliates in Canada, Australia, New Zealand, Poland, and Hungary and in 1993 began operations in England and Northern Ireland.

Education Ministries   "In 1992, a consensus decision was made to take the second mission more seriously," said Bill Odom, director of development—that of putting the housing problem "on the hearts and minds of people everywhere." To tackle a problem as overwhelming as the world's housing crisis, Habitat recognized that it alone would not be able to build every house. Therefore, Snider hired David Snell, a Habitat staff member from several local projects and someone he had worked with at Paula Financial, to lead a concerted effort to raise awareness.

Development   Fund raising is the lifeblood of any nonprofit, just as sales are for a for-profit firm. Habitat had a unique fund-raising style, done on two levels: (1) affiliates were responsible for raising their own funds and were requested to make a contribution to headquarters for International Projects; and (2) headquarters raised money directly for international projects, affiliate programs, and administrative expenses through direct-mail campaigns and personal appeals by Fuller. Fuller's great fund-raising capabilities allowed Habitat to be extremely successful on a grassroots level. Headquarters revenues, which totaled $35 million in 1992, came from more than 800,000 donors. The average check size of a first-time contributor was $28. In 1992, affiliates raised an estimated $65 million through their own fund-raising efforts. In addition, all house payments were made into the Fund for Humanity and reinvested in the community.

Habitat's Growth Trajectory

Habitat completed its 10,000th house in April 1991, 15 years after it had begun operations. By April 1993, it completed its 20,000th house and was expected to complete its 30,000th house early in 1994 (see Exhibit 4 for Habitat's historical growth). Spurred by increased amounts of favorable publicity and the urgent housing need, Habitat's growth was expected to continue as fast as the organization could take it. In 1993, with a backlog of 300 affiliate applications, Habitat added a new affiliate at a rate of close to one every day. In addition to the Carters, President Clinton, Vice President Al Gore, the actor Paul Newman, former Secretary of Housing and Urban Development Jack Kemp, and countless others were seen in newspapers across the country alongside Fuller, wielding the familiar hammer. Hardly a day went by when Habitat was not in the news.

One of the 20 largest home builders in the United States, Habitat expected to become the largest sometime in the 1990s. In the area of addressing the needs of the homeless and underhoused, there was no question that Habitat's growth would not be limited by lack of demand. And, as Habitat became more and more successful, the pressure to grow with the same success rose.

▲ 1993: THE MAJOR CHALLENGES FACING HABITAT

As Snider reviewed the important issues facing Habitat, he realized there were a number of explicit choices it needed to make to decide how to meet the challenges ahead. He also knew that even if he could commit the organization to making these choices, implementing

▲ EXHIBIT 4   Habitat for Humanity's Historical Growth

	1988	1989	1990	1991	1992	1993P
Revenue (in $ millions)						
Headquarters	$10.2	$14.8	$20.7	$24.6	$35.4	$37.8
Affiliates	17.6	29.1	37.0	55.0	65.2	72.0
Total	$27.8	$43.9	$57.7	$79.6	$100.6	$109.8
Number of houses built*						
United States	598	781	1,234	1,862	1,927	2,750
International	707	1,174	2,506	1,875	4,428	4,960
Total	1,305	1,955	3,740	3,737	6,355	7,710
Affiliates	330	445	539	674	814	1,050
Sponsored projects	59	77	105	115	140	160

*Includes houses built or renovated.

them within the context of a nonprofit organization with a grassroots volunteer culture would not be easy. For the purposes of the planning process, he sorted Habitat's challenges into four major areas: (1) balancing growth objectives with Habitat's mission and culture; (2) selecting the right opportunities for growth; (3) mobilizing human resources; and (4) defining a role for headquarters.

1. Balancing Growth Objectives with Habitat's Mission and Culture

Eric Duell, an international partner who had served the organization for six years in Mexico, Haiti, and El Salvador, articulated for many the obvious paradox of Habitat's mission:

> For those not experienced in the construction trade, Habitat has *not* chosen the easiest way to build houses! The easiest way is like the construction companies do it, with paid skilled labor and lots of it. Habitat does not work this way because the ultimate goal is…not the house but the people who participate in the building of that house, the families who will live in that house, the society that they are a part of, and [the volunteers] participating in so many different ways.

Snider thought about the series of goals Habitat had set for itself—to build 30,000 houses per year with revenues of $1 billion by the year 2000, to enjoy name recognition equivalent to that of the Boy Scouts, to be self-sustaining around the globe, and "to eliminate poverty housing." Particularly given Duell's widely accepted comments, Snider wondered if Habitat was ready and willing to make the kind of changes in organization and culture that would be necessary to achieve the goals it had set for itself. "If you look at any of the trend lines…there wasn't a corresponding focus on how you [help] this grassroots organization try to make this vision a reality," Snider commented.

Bruce Gunter, who, in addition to being a member of Habitat's board, was president of Progressive Redevelopment Inc., a nonprofit firm that built low-income housing in Atlanta, wondered if Habitat's operating formula forced it to move too slowly to address the massive need it had set out to address. Even though Habitat in Atlanta was extremely successful as a builder of hope and community through self-reliance and partnership, as Gunter noted, "We have to remember that even when Habitat builds 30 or 40 houses in a neighborhood, there are an estimated 40,000 in need of adequate housing in Atlanta."

Snider had faced resistance to modernizing Habitat's financial and information systems and even stronger resistance to changing human resources policies to help attract and retain professional managers. Habitat's informational materials continued to describe its headquarters as "primarily dependent upon volunteer labor…with an administrative staff…supplemented by long- and short-term volunteers." Snider was aware that many in the organization, including Chairman of the Board Edgar Stoesz and Fuller, felt that as a critical element of Habitat's culture, such practices should not be compromised.

What of more "heretical" ideas to make Habitat into a more professional organization capable of providing the vision and structure necessary for growth? During Snider's tenure, the board was pressed to consider changes that would involve major departures from past practices in the name of helping Habitat grow: moving operations from Americus closer to Atlanta to provide easier access to donors, field operations, and the international organization; accepting government funds and loans; and expanding into areas that had a great need and where Habitat had not been invited. So far, these ideas, which all went against Habitat's culture, were rejected. Snider explained, "with all of these changes, there is the fear, as had been expressed by the board, that 'we risk losing our soul and becoming an institution.'"

Although many in Habitat wanted to preserve the culture of volunteerism and grassroots growth, these same people had difficulty saying no to any opportunity for Habitat to grow still bigger. "Millard wants to keep us just past the realm where reason dominates and faith takes over—while avoiding being foolhardy. He'll say, 'We're going to build 100 houses in a week in Tijuana.' This is what drives a lot of people nuts. But how? With whom? But he doesn't care. 'We're just going to.' What he says becomes self-fulfilling," Snider said. Making reasonable goals, Snider knew, was not entirely consistent with an effort to end the world's housing crisis. Yet, making these goals operational within Habitat's structure was becoming increasingly difficult.

Considering that there were lines Habitat was unwilling to cross to achieve growth, Snider hoped that Habitat could either adjust its goals to fit the organization or adjust the organization to meet its goals. Either choice, he knew, would frustrate Habitat's culture to some degree.

2. Selecting the Right Opportunities for Growth

Our intention has been to build houses as fast as we can and to encourage initiatives to build houses wherever we can.

Millard Fuller, president

Habitat's record in proving that it could make a difference in transforming whole communities gained it access to financial resources beyond its wildest imaginings. Snider knew that there were increasing demands on the organization, both internal and external, to build on its past successes and expand in size and scope. But he was aware of the dangers that faced Habitat as it sought to address a variety of new challenges and focus its mission more broadly. To make his point, Snider prepared for the board a list of goals that Habitat had committed to as an organization (see Exhibit 5). They included 17 far-reaching commitments in the United States, 15 in the developing world, 11 outside the United States in the developed world, 5 in Eastern Europe, and more than 40 other special projects and internal objectives.

All of these commitments required a significant amount of management resources. Snider was concerned that Habitat had not granted priorities to these goals or considered the resources necessary to achieve them.

There were several directions where Habitat was attempting to leverage its strengths. Most prominent were (1) urban homelessness; (2) nonhousing concerns of the poor; and (3) emergency housing. To differing degrees, these were areas in which Habitat had already been involved, but with varying amounts of attention and success.

Urban Homelessness   Habitat's success was largely as an organization serving the working poor in small cities and rural locations. The availability of land, the lack of zoning or government regulations, and the ability to work independently made these areas a more natural fit with Habitat's principles. Yet, rural homelessness did not garner the media attention of the inner-city homeless problem, and Habitat felt increasing pressure to focus its attention on urban areas.

"Invitations from urban centers for Habitat to participate compels the organization to define a response," Snider said, pointing out that solutions to the urban homelessness problem differed from those on which Habitat had built its success. They involved multifamily development, rehabilitations rather than building houses from scratch, a higher degree of interaction with the government, and collaboration with existing urban community development organizations. In addition, Habitat worked with minimal-income families to support home payments, as was consistent with its philosophy of not providing charity. However, the visible problems of urban homelessness and overcrowding affected many without the means to afford a Habitat house and were entangled with such problems as unemployment, drug use, and inadequate job training—problems Habitat was not designed to handle. Snider worried about Habitat's rushing into urban homelessness. "All I think we'd do, with our current operating methods, is add our names to the list of people who can't make it work in the city," he said.

Yet many within Habitat determined that the organization must address its energies to the urban homelessness problems with zeal equal to it applied to rural homelessness. Eric Duell, Habitat's international partner in El Salvador, commented, "The major problems are in the urban slums around the world. But Habitat does 98 percent of its work in rural locations." In an appeal to Habitat's board for more resources to address urban homelessness, Duell wrote:

> Given [Habitat's] desire to "eliminate poverty housing" and "make shelter a matter of conscience," it would naturally seem to follow that [Habitat] would be present or seek to be present wherever poverty housing is an issue. To date this is not so; Habitat for Humanity is a rural housing organization. Habitat's presence in urban centers is noticeably small and in fairness, perhaps legitimately so. Urban programs are reputedly more difficult, expensive, and complicated than rural development. Yet given the staggering statistics of worldwide populations and their growth, given the myriad of urban slums and squatter settlements where squalor best applies does it not follow that [Habitat] is limiting its ministry's impact by not seeking a presence in the world's urban centers?

Urban affiliates continued to open and meet with varying degrees of success as they tried to fit Habitat's operating principles into the more complicated urban environment.[1] However, they worked exclusively with potential homeowners who fit Habitat's selection criteria (i.e., they

---

[1]Much of the success that occurred in urban areas was a result of blitz-building activities, such as the Jimmy Carter Work Projects (see Exhibit 5), where a large block of land could be purchased and enough critical mass built to transform a community.

A Partial List of Activities by Program Area

1. **U.S. Projects**

   a. Projects in all 50 states by 1992

   b. 1,000 U.S. affiliates by 1994

   c. 2,000 U.S. affiliates by 2000

   d. American Indian program 1993

   e. U.S. affiliate tithe reaches $5 million in 1995

   f. Total U.S. affiliate fund raising reaches $200 million in 1995

   g. Urban initiative 1994

   h. Train and deploy 100 U.S. affiliate trainers per year by 1995

   i. Total U.S. house production reaches 9,000 units per year by 2000

   j. Total U.S. affiliate fund raising reaches $800 million in 2000

   k. Sumter County Initiative

   l. Hurricane Andrew

   m. Hurricane Ineki

   n. Justice and Righteousness Fund

   o. Habitat for Homeless Humanity

   p. Habitat for Humanity with Disabilities

   q. Washington, D.C., office in 1993

2. **Two-Thirds World (Developing Countries) Projects**

   a. Projects in 1,000 communities by 1995

   b. Projects in 50 countries by 1996

   c. Projects in 3,000 communities by 2000

   d. National Organizations' 15 countries by 1995

   e. National Organizations' 30 countries by 1997

   f. Urban Project Initiative 1994

   g. Sumter County Honduras Initiative

   h. Global village Work Camps, 100 per year by 1994

   i. Total house production reaches 7,500 per year, 1994

   j. Total house production reaches 20,000 by 2000

   k. International agency funding Malawi, 1992

   l. Regional Office centers Africa, 1992

   m. In-country fund raising reaches $5 million in 1996

   n. House built with revolving funds reach 1,000 units per year 1996

   o. First All National Leadership Conference—Latin America 1993

3. **National Affiliate Projects**

   a. Australia house production reaches 100 per year 1995

   b. Canada house production reaches 150 per year 1995

   c. Hungary house production reaches 100 per year 1994

   d. New Zealand house production reaches 50 per year 1996

   e. Poland house production reaches 20 per year 1994

   f. South Africa house production reaches 50 per year 1995

   g. South Korea house production reaches 20 per year 1995

   h. HFHI cash support to national affiliates levels at $200,000 annually 1994

   i. Canada begins building in Jamaica 1993

   j. England begins construction 1993

   k. Northern Ireland begins construction 1993

4. **Eastern Europe/CIS Projects**

   a. Latvia begins 1995

   b. Romania begins 1994

   c. Albania begins 1995

   d. Bulgaria begins 1995

continued

  e. Russia begins 1995

5. **Campus Chapters**

  a. All U.S. higher educational institutions by 2000

  b. 500 non-U.S. higher educational institutions by 2000

  c. Collegiate Challenge participants at 5,000 by 1994

6. **Global Village Work Camps**

  a. 100 per year by 1994 (1,000 participants)

  b. 200 per year by 1997 (2,000 participants)

  c. Hurricane Andrew work camp support

7. **Habitat World**

  a. Circulation reaches one million households by 1995

8. **Special Projects/Events HFHI**

  a. Jimmy Carter Work Project (JCWP) 1993 Winnipeg

  b. JCWP 1994 American Indian

  c. JCWP 1995 Los Angeles

  d. JCWP 1996 Atlanta Olympic Initiative

  e. Africa Board Meeting 1993

  f. SCI 20/20,000 Project Americus 1993

  g. House number 25,000 Charlotte 1993

  h. HFHI 18th Anniversary Los Angeles 1994

  i. HFHI 20th Anniversary Americus-Atlanta 1996

  j. House number 30,000 1994

  k. House number 50,000 1996

  l. House number 100,000 2000

  m. Overseas board meeting 1996

  n. Overseas board meeting 1999

  o. HFHI 25th Anniversary 2001

9. **Disaster Recovery Projects**

  a. Hurricane Andrew 1992–1995

  b. Hurricane Ineki 1992–1994

  c. Various, unscheduled

10. **Environment Department**

  a. Definition and initiation 1993

11. **Communications**

  a. Electronic Bulletin Board System for U.S. affiliates 1993

12. **Financial Controls**

  a. Selecting a Big Six public accounting partner 1993

  b. Consolidated financial reporting systems U.S. affiliates 1994

  c. Gifts-in-kind (GIK) distribution system

13. **Millard Fuller**

  a. UK–Northern Ireland January 1993

  b. Hawaii, Philippines, South Korea, New Zealand, Australia, Indonesia, India tour February–March 1993

  c. Kampala, Uganda May 1993

  d. Author, *Theology of the Hammer* 1993

14. **Church Relations**

  a. Revival/Day of Prayer and Action

  b. Covenant Church program in 175,000 churches by 2000

15. **Training**

  a. IP Training classes, February, June, and October 1993

  b. Affiliate Executive Director training U.S. 1993

  c. Continuing education—regional events

continued

▲ EXHIBIT 5   *concluded*

Partial List of Policy Topics to Pursue

1. Electronic media (television) policy for fund raising.

2. Licensing agreement policy for fund raising.

3. Establishing direct mail in Europe.

4. International agencies as funding sources.

5. Defining accountability for Affiliate Advisory Council.

6. Defining accountability for Urban Project Council, et al.

7. Defining "senior staff" level for minority and gender balance measurements.

8. Defining a HFHI National Convenant document.

9. Five-year plan process.

---

had a modest income to make minimal house payments). In response to internal and external pressures, Habitat in 1989 established Habitat for Homeless Humanity to attempt to address the needs of the urban homeless not covered by its existing policies. Yet, without the resources to support it in Americus and with attention shifted to other ideas, the effort was considered a failure—dying from inadequate attention and an inability to find a successful way to transfer Habitat's experience into this area.

Nonhousing Concerns of the Poor   In the effort to serve an impoverished community, Habitat could not avoid confronting the many other problems its homeowner families faced. While not a traditional strength, many of Habitat's local volunteers did have backgrounds in other areas of community involvement. And though some said it deterred Habitat from its main mission, others wondered how it was possible to turn away. "Families have other needs. Habitat has to broaden the mission of who we are. We need to work in partnership to help provide these families with their other needs," claimed Kevin Fobbs, president of the Habitat affiliate in Detroit and a new addition to Habitat's board. Because each affiliate supported itself, it was able to establish its own priorities, as long as it abided by the Affiliate Covenant. As a result, many affiliates more broadly defined their role as an outreach organization within their community. Many devoted varying amounts of attention to issues such as hunger, health care, day care, drug prevention, education, and community building. Snider wondered how it would be possible to control the actions of affiliates even if Habitat wanted to.

Emergency Housing   In 1992, on returning from a trip to Africa, Snider was startled to find that, in response to Hurricane Andrew, Fuller had publicly committed Habitat to dedicating its resources to rebuild hundreds of houses in the hurricane-stricken areas. When Snider arrived in Americus, he found virtually the entire headquarters staff, as lean as it was, dedicating its time to relief efforts. Though addressing national emergencies was not part of Habitat's mission and required some special expertise that it did not have, its involvement in the aftermath of Hurricane Andrew garnered an enormous amount of favorable media attention and greatly aided its fund-raising efforts.

Amazingly, although the hurricane wreaked tremendous damage, all 27 Habitat houses in the South Dade area, where the storm hit, were spared. In reaction to the storm, three days after it hit, teams of Habitat volunteers were on the scene helping people with cleanup. In the first few weeks, they provided more than 20,000 hours of labor. Also within days of the disaster, Habitat for Humanity International pledged $1 million for rebuilding in South Florida and launched a direct-mail campaign to raise more money. By early November, it had raised a cash fund totaling $5 million, with another $4 million in commitments of building materials. Habitat planned to construct 100 houses in 1993 and to build or rehabilitate 300 to 500 houses in South Florida and Louisiana in the next two years.

Yet Snider wondered how Habitat would garner the human resources to carry out this project. More important, he worried that nobody, in an organization as people-constrained as Habitat, had stopped to consider what other areas of work would suffer as a consequence of being temporarily put aside. In a similar manner, Fuller led the organization into other areas, with the establishment of a Department of the Environment. "As one of America's largest homebuilders, Habitat for Humanity feels an increasing obligation to acknowledge and address the issues of the environment," said Fuller, who proposed the idea to Habitat's Board. But the department remained unstaffed. "A statement of support for issues of the environment will probably expand the audience of Habitat supporters," Snider admitted. "But how will a focus on the environment leverage a net increase in houses or sensitize more people to the issue of inadequate housing?"

3. Mobilizing Human Resources

Whatever the decisions Habitat made with regard to its growth, Snider knew what without the ability to attract and motivate people within the organization, it would be unable to sustain its growth and continue to serve those who benefited from and participated in its work. Yet Habitat had a staff makeup unlike any other organization Snider had ever seen; it still relied heavily on volunteers and, below the senior management level, was made up largely of people whose greatest assets were their dedication and commitment, rather than specific experience.

Attracting and Motivating Staff and Volunteers   Habitat's headquarters staff was managed by 20 to 25 senior salaried people, earning an average of $30,000 per year, with the highest salary at $50,000. The remainder of the staff included approximately 50 paid employees, who earned an average of $18,000 per year, and approximately 100 volunteers who received a small weekly stipend in a check redeemable at the local grocery store, the Piggly Wiggly. (These checks were known among the staff as "pig checks.") volunteers also received housing and basic insurance coverage once they worked for three months. Snider described the historical staff-recruiting strategy as "inexpensive and inexperienced and fraught with unacknowledged costs."

When Snider arrived in 1990, the compensation system was based entirely on need, not performance. Though he sought and received board approval to replace this system, the human resources system remained characterized by its very modest compensation scale and lack of traditional incentive structures. Although it was never put on paper, Habitat's human resource system relied on several basic premises:

1. The system was designed to enable staff members to pay their bills. All surplus funds were for program expanses.
2. Jobs were defined as broadly as possible to allow people to take more responsibility.
3. Job assignments were constantly changed to fill gaps and create variety.
4. Formal evaluations were used infrequently. Manager were responsible for motivating their staff as they saw fit.
5. There were few salary adjustments (annual or otherwise) or year-end bonuses.

Many of the staff joined Habitat through contact with the work it had done in their communities, and for many, being a part of that mission and the spiritual nature of Habitat's work more than replaced traditional compensation. Still, Snider wondered how the compensation system affected Habitat's ability to attract and motivate good people. He knew the paid staff was motivated by more than money, but he wondered what combination of intangibles and incentives would attract and retain the management talent Habitat needed. When asked for the number one item on his wish list for Habitat, Snider did not hesitate: "talented people."

"What is needed are better coaches in leadership and planning roles in the organization.... The human resource agenda and the need to wrestle with career development planning are central to the pursuit of growing Habitat's management capacity," Snider wrote in a memorandum to the board in February 1993. Three years into the job, Snider still had many high-level positions unfilled or "underfilled." Meanwhile there was very little job stability throughout headquarters and the regional offices. Although everyone acknowledged severe staffing problems, was anyone willing to accept further changes to Habitat's volunteer-oriented human resource policies, including possibly increasing salary levels to attract high-quality managers? When asked, Chairman Stoesz, along with many who had been with Habitat since its early days, showed resistance to major changes to the human resource system. "I will argue that we have a better chance of fulfilling Habitat's mission by the kind of salary scale we are on now than if we were to accept a more commercial scale," remarked Stoesz. Yet Snider and some of the other board members, seeing room for improvement in the system, adamantly disagreed.

Creating Accountability   Snider continually wrestled with how to motivate the headquarters staff in Americus. He wondered what the best way was to hold people in a nonprofit organization accountable for their work and motivate them to increase their productivity.

> Many people choose the NPO environment, having worked in a corporate setting. I first thought this meant the driving consideration to work at Habitat had everything to do with the end beneficiaries—the homeowner family. At times, I wonder if the trade-off had more to do with leaving the corporate concern with accountability and the pressures that go with it. It's like, "You can't tell me what to do. I'm doing something good."

4. Defining a Role for Headquarters

Many affiliates increasingly viewed Habitat's headquarters in Americus as isolated and irrelevant. In fact, there were few points of natural interaction between headquarters and the affiliates. Headquarters provided affiliates with the use of Habitat's name, nonprofit status, training, technical support, information services, some donated materials, and donor lists on request. There was also an affiliate HELP line, set up in 1991 in an attempt to be more responsive to the needs of the affiliates, especially new ones. Maggie Chrisman, a long-time member of Habitat's board of directors, remembers her time with the Phoenix affiliate. "We didn't know [headquarters] existed. Nor did we care. We were just building houses." Chrisman described the relationship in 1993 between the Habitat affiliates and headquarters as being very strained, in large part because of headquarters' increasingly aggressive attempts to solicit donors through its direct-mail campaign. Because the affiliates were self-funded, it had become an issue. "When you start an affiliate, you get a lot of support and help from Americus. but once they get going, [the affiliates] couldn't give a hoot. What they care about is International's attacking their fund-raising turf," says Chrisman.

Snider wondered how best to define Americus's purpose as the organization continued to expand. He acknowledged the complaints that headquarters was losing touch, but pointed to the lack of managerial resources he had to attend to all of the issues Habitat faced around the world. It was also difficult to respond to 800 very disparate voices. As Stoesz, Habitat's chairman, pointed out, "I always tend to think of Habitat as an organization with one founder—Millard. But it's not. Habitat really has 800 founders."

Providing Leadership and Creating a Sustainable Organizational Structure

Habitat is an organization. Millard doesn't buy that. He thinks it's a movement, and I hope it is. But we're also an organization. The organization we have put in place is a weak being. The Habitat paradigm is the most powerful paradigm I know. We need to make our organization worthy of our paradigm.

Edgar Stoesz, chairman of Habitat for Humanity International

In 1993, Habitat's affiliate system was growing at a spiraling rate. From a managerial perspective, the affiliate system was out of control in its existing structure, often with several Habitat affiliates springing up in close proximity to one another. There were already complaints in some areas of affiliates getting in each other's way. Snider wondered what would happen in several years' time when there were 2,000 affiliates; growth was expected to continue at a 30 percent rate for the foreseeable future. What was the optimal structure to allow the affiliates to serve their mission, yet allow Habitat some form of oversight, at least as it pertained to issues of quality assurance and financial control? If affiliates did not pay much attention to Americus now, he wondered about the future. What leverage did headquarters have to influence or lead the affiliates or to increase their effectiveness? How should Habitat work with or retire poor performers?

There were some suggestions that the organization restructure entirely. Specific proposals being considered included rethinking the distinction between affiliates and sponsored projects and creating national organizations in each country and statewide organizations throughout the United States. Such changes would allow Americus to define its role primarily as providing the vision and speaking for the organization. There was a growing sentiment at all levels that Habitat should decentralize and put more people and responsibility in the regional offices. Snider wondered where the economies of scale were and which decision-making functions could be assigned to the regional offices.

Defining Standards   Snider also wondered about measurement systems. To date, Habitat was judged a success if it kept building more houses and raising more money. "The media, perhaps our only public watchdog, continues to concentrate on the anecdotal evidence of Habitat's success," Snider commented. He wondered if that was the best way to judge success. Were there other quantifiable measures that Habitat had overlooked? Should they measure affiliate productivity? In just measuring the number of houses built, would they be leaving out more important quality measures? How much did pursuing quantitative objects minimize the second aspect of Habitat's mission?

Putting Technology to Work   One role that Snider believed Americus could play more effectively was to create and manage information systems. When he joined Habitat, technology was viewed with suspicion and not used in any area other than the direct-mail program.

"When I arrived, we had three volunteers making hard-copy printouts of gifts. A volunteer would take a pair of scissors, cut out the names, and send them in the mail to [the local affiliate where the gift had come from]. It would take three and a half hours every day. Having a computer background, I thought it was a naive form of stewardship," recalled Snider.

Snider described some of the main important roles he believed Information Systems could play at Habitat. "You have a donor base of 800,000. All your revenues come from the donor base. List management is vital. I insisted that the database needs to be bulletproof. I said I will take your excuses away and give you the tools you need." In addition, Snider saw technology as a good way to manage volunteer lists, create common accounting procedures, and standardize operating policies. Interestingly, he found the difficulty of bringing technology and business systems to Habitat as one not from lack of resources but from attitude and culture. "There was this feeling that if we're administratively tool-deprived, somehow there's more integrity in our work," he commented.

▲ THE FIVE-YEAR PLAN: MAINTAINING FOCUS?

In preparing his five-year plan, Snider wondered how useful it was to apply his experience from the private sector in making Habitat's strategic decisions. He wondered to what extent he could think of Habitat's homeowners, volunteers, and affiliates as customers of Americus. Though he knew that it was a difficult and complex exercise in a nonprofit, he recognized the importance of focusing Habitat's thinking. "We need to identify Habitat's stakeholders," he said. "We need to decide who it is we really serve."

Snider believed that the need for resolution of many issues was becoming more and more pressing. Each day that passed without Habitat's making explicit decisions regarding its strategic priorities and organization enabled many of its staff to become more entrenched in their established practices. Perhaps more important, a lack of clear direction made it easier for many affiliates to pursue a wide variety of activities in addition to the construction of affordable homes for people in need. Because Habitat was growing successfully and building more and more houses, Snider expressed concern that "it won't acknowledge the opportunity costs of not making the changes we need to make."

The five-year plan was Snider's first attempt at addressing the macro concerns facing Habitat. He realized the issues confronting him were complex and often even in conflict with one another. He also felt that it was imperative that any recommendations he made be aligned with all of the parties to whom Habitat was accountable. He decided to lay out a worksheet to assist him in sorting through these complex issues (see Exhibit 6).

While hoping that some of the answers would come out of the five-year plan, Snider wondered how an organization empowered to such a large extent by the strength of its mission would react to such a planning document. As he set out to chart Habitat's future, he was not at all interested in academic solutions that would not be accepted or could not be implemented. He needed to reach some decisions, as imperfect as they might be, that could make a real difference.

▲ EXHIBIT 6 Habitat for Humanity Five-Year Plan: Planning Worksheet

Strategic Options	Are We Good at It?	Consistency with Our Past	What Is the Cost? • Human • Financial • Mission	Organizational Implications	What Is the Cost of Not Doing It?	Stakeholder Match: • Homeowners • Donors/Vols. • Affiliates
Grow to projected size						
Expand into urban homelessness						
Define organization's mission more broadly						
Be opportunity driven (hurricanes, environment)						
Restructure affiliate system						

TEXTRON, INC.

In 1952, Textron, Inc., a major textile manufacturer, lost $4 million on sales of $99 million. After making over 75 acquisitions and withdrawing completely from the textile industry, the company earned $44 million (after tax) on sales of $1.13 billion in 1966. Textron's strategy of expansion through acquisition and diversification earned it a reputation as one of the most highly diversified corporations in the United States ("the biggest conglomerate in U.S. history," according to *Fortune*) and the pioneer of the conglomerate form of organization. As *The Wall Street Journal* put it in 1967:

> Textron exemplifies a form of corporate organization so new that only in the past few years have economists coined a name for it. They call it the "conglomerate"—a company that grows, not by internal expansion into product lines related in some way to its original enterprises, but by acquisition of completely unrelated outside businesses.

> Textron is still the conglomerate king. It has been a conglomerate longer than almost any other firm, having started to acquire unrelated businesses in 1953, after spending the previous 30 years as an orthodox textile company. And it is among the very few conglomerates to have abandoned its original business altogether; it sold its last textile operations in 1963.

> All of which raises two questions basic to any consideration of Textron, or of conglomerates generally. Why should anyone want to put together such a hodgepodge in the first place? And

This is a condensation of the original Textron, Inc. (A) and (B) cases, Nos. 368-016 and 368-017, which were prepared by Professor Norman Berg.

how can any group of executives maintain control over such dizzyingly varied businesses, in most of which they can have had no experience?[1]

This case will explore Textron's history, its current businesses in the mid-1960s, its strategy and major operating policies, and the role of the headquarters staff in the administration of the company. It is hoped that this material will make possible at least some preliminary answers to the two questions raised in *The Wall Street Journal* article.

▲ RECENT FINANCIAL PERFORMANCE

Textron's 1966 sales of $1.13 billion and profits of $44 million were 27 percent and 32 percent ahead of 1965, respectively.[2] Both dollar figures were the highest in the company's history. In the *Fortune 500* rankings, the company was 61st in sales, up from 81st in 1965. Return on stockholders' equity had been improving steadily since 1960 and now at 19 percent was the highest in Textron history. for the past five years the annual compound rate of growth had been 18 percent in sales, and 28 percent in earnings per common share, a record matched by very few companies. Ten-year comparisons are shown in Exhibit 1, and recent balance sheets in Exhibit 2.

The balance between growth due to internal expansion and improvements and growth achieved by acquisition was difficult to determine, particularly for an outside observer. The 1966 annual report stated, however, that 85 percent of that year's sales-volume increase had come from increased sales of divisions that were a part of Textron at the beginning of the year. Although some of this increase could be due to small product-line acquisitions made by the divisions during the year, it seemed probable that by far the major part of Textron's growth came from internal sources in 1966. For the five-year period ending in 1966, about three-quarters of each year's sales growth had come from businesses owned at the beginning of the year, with the balance resulting from acquisition growth.[3]

The company's recent performance, together with Wall Street's discovery of conglomerates, led to a dramatic increase in the market price of Textron shares—from a low of about 4 in late 1953 to 20 by the end of 1963 and then to over 80 by the middle of 1967.[4] Most investment analysts took an optimistic view of the future of the company, though some thought the growth potential was fully discounted by the market price of the stock.

The rapid growth of Textron, and the success some other companies had achieved through a strategy of acquisition and diversification, were emphasized in an investment analysis published in May 1966 by Equity Research Associates, Inc.:

> Our analysis indicates that Textron is the second fastest growing (after Litton Industries) of the 70 industrials in the U.S. whose sales are expected to exceed $1 billion in 1966. It is one of the only ten of these companies that we estimate will show (as of the end of 1966) consistent growth at a compound annual rate of better than 10 percent in sales and earnings for the last five years....

---

[1]*The Wall Street Journal*, January 31, 1967.
[2]Comparisons based on restatement of 1965 and 1966 to include sales and earnings of Bostitch, Inc., acquired in 1966.
[3]Textron prospectus, June 8, 1967.
[4]Prices are adjusted to reflect a 2–1 split in early 1966.

▲ **EXHIBIT 1 Textron 10-Year Comparisons (in millions of dollars, except per share amounts)**

	1966	1965	1964	1963	1962	1961	1960	1959	1958	1957
Financial Results										
Net sales	$1,132	$851	$720	$587	$549	$473	$383	$308	$244	$255
Income before federal income taxes	85	59	44	32	27	14	17	17†	11	9
Net income	44	29	22	18	15	11	14	17†	11	9
Depreciation and other noncash charges	20	16	13	11	12	12	10	9	9	8
Net income per common share*	3.53	2.62	2.04	1.71	1.48	1.03	1.47	1.44†	1.15	1.13
Dividends declared per common share	1.10	.93	.80	.70	.63	.63	.63	.60	.50	.50
Financial position at year-end										
Working capital	162	129	125	105	109	115	94	86	61	47
Long-term notes	60	46	58	36	73	90	84	62	54	57
Net properties	123	89	78	63	76	85	81	71	78	80
Common stock equity	234	179	161	146	125	118	110	108	79	63
Common stock equity per share	18.88	16.25	15.08	14.09	12.92	12.08	11.77	11.25	9.11	9.00
Other statistics										
Common shares outstanding at year-end (000)	12,398	11,038	10,699	10,332	9,683	9,807	9,345	9,566	8,699	7,001
Salaries, wages, and employee benefits	407	300	257	228	210	181	136	107	78	76

Note: Per share amounts have been adjusted to reflect the 2-for-1 stock split in 1965. Other figures are as reported in Textron annual reports for the respective years, without retroactive restatement for the pooling of interests with Bostitch, Inc.
*Net income per common share had been calculated on the basis of shares outstanding at the end of each year.
†Including profit of $2,373,000 ($.50 per share) from sale of Textron Electronics, Inc., stock
Source: Textron annual reports.

▲ EXHIBIT 2   Textron Consolidated Balance Sheet (in thousands of dollars)

	December 31, 1966	January 1, 1966
Assets		
Current assets		
Cash	$ 22,859	$ 15,044
Marketable securities		1,683
Accounts receivable (less allowances of $4,552 and $4,068)	138,113	110,378
Inventories, at lower of cost or market		
Finished goods	52,497	52,460
Work in process (less progress payments of $69,180 and $32,464)	96,247	71,938
Raw materials and supplies	47,587	41,549
	196,331	165,947
Prepaid expenses	2,717	2,017
Total current assets	360,020	295,069
Property, plant, and equipment, at cost		
Land and buildings	52,695	44,794
Machinery and equipment	167,195	144,271
	219,890	189,065
Less accumulated depreciation and amortization	96,671	87,740
Total property, plant, and equipment	123,219	101,325
Unamortized debt discount and expense	4,238	5,553
Other assets (including patents, at cost less amortization)	13,144	11,568
	$500,621	$413,515
Liabilities and Shareholders' Equity		
Current liabilities		
Notes payable	$ 12,735	$ 4,900
Accounts payable	59,672	49,573
Accrued expenses and other current liabilities	80,809	55,696
Federal income taxes	30,212	26,917
Current maturities of long-term notes	10,832	8,834
Dividends payable	3,795	
Total current liabilities	198,055	145,920
Long-term notes	59,500	45,790
Other liabilities	6,872	6,545
Shareholders' equity		
Capital stock		
$1.25 convertible preferred	2,130	2,824
Common	3,187	3,164
Capital surplus	100,729	98,633
Earned surplus	145,481	120,804
	251,527	225,425
Less common stock in treasury at cost	15,333	10,165
Total shareholders' equity	236,194	215,260
	$500,621	$413,515

Source: 1966 annual report.

Considering recent growth in both sales and earnings, but giving increased weight to earnings, Litton is growing at about a 35 percent annual rate, Textron is growing at about a 25 percent rate, and FMC is growing at about a 20 percent rate—no other large companies in the U.S. are growing this fast. For the longer term, Litton has predicted $2 billion in sales within four to six years for a 10–15 percent compound annual growth rate, and Textron expects to exceed 10 percent. It is particularly important to note that the three fastest growing large companies in the U.S. are all completely diversified. In fact, only 4 to 10 of the companies (IBM, Eastman Kodak, Monsanto, and Celanese) have as much as 50 percent of their sales in any one product area, and only IBM has less than 33 percent diversification. The moral is clear—if you can't be an IBM, a Xerox, or an Eastman Kodak, and grow by dominating a growth industry, then it is probably best to be a Litton, and FMC, or a Textron.

▲ THE COMPANY

G. William Miller, Textron's president, described the company's strategy to a group of security analysts:

1. As a first priority, we want to make sure that each division is the soundest, best performing operation possible.... We refine and improve in an attempt to make sure that each of our divisions is the best and most efficient producer in its field.

2. Second, we undertake the development of a specific program for expansion, so that the management of each Textron company will be able to employ its full resources in a continuing effort to meet the new market requirements.

3. Our third priority has been acquisitions, where these meet our high standards and contribute to the overall goals of Textron.

   Our future strategy will continue to place special emphasis on management development. We will have great need for highly motivated people who can create growth by applying their skills to translate the new technology into maximum new opportunities for Textron.[5]

In a 1967 address to an industry group, Charles Chapin, vice president, described Textron as follows:

In recent years, there has developed a new type of company of which Textron is one. This new group of business enterprises has been classified under many different names such as multimarket, free-form conglomerate, acquisition type, diversified, and other semantic variations of these. But call them what you may—there is a common theme which may vary in execution from one management to another but, nevertheless, it is still there. The common element of this new management technique is a complete orientation toward total profit as compared with a product or industry orientation....

Textron stands today as a diversified manufacturing company whose principal goal is to produce the highest possible return on its stockholders' equity, both consistently and dependably. Textron has become diversified for the benefit of its stockholders: first, to spread the source of its earnings among a number of different industries which should be subject to different economic cycles and second, to diffuse its investment or exposure of capital in any one area.

---

[5]Remarks to New York Society of Security Analysts, November 7, 1966.

To define Textron in the more conventional terms of principal markets served or products manufactured was not easy because of the diversity of the company. Rupert C. Thompson, Jr., chairman of the board, once said, "We are a pure conglomerate.... We have no part of our original business. We have no principal division. We have no principal product."[6]

Textron did consist of operating divisions, however, and the divisions did manufacture products. In the more prosaic language of the proxy statement, Textron was "a multi-market manufacturing company with sales in the four principal product groups of aerospace, consumer, industrial, and metal products." The 28 divisions included in these groups, and their principal products, are summarized in Exhibit 3. The company operated a total of 110 plants in the United States and 16 plants overseas, and employed about 50,000 people.

Product Group Sales Breakdowns

The 1962–1966 sales and pretax income of Textron's four product groups are shown in Table A. A substantial portion of these sales—39 percent in 1966, up steadily from 27 percent in 1962—was related directly or indirectly to the various agencies of the federal government, primarily to defense programs.

Foreign sales, by export and manufacture, were $95 million in 1966, almost double the amount for the preceding year. Sheaffer Pen and Bostitch, both acquired in 1966, had a total of 10 plants overseas and contributed $17 million to the increase. Textron's foreign sales all stemmed from the domestic divisions rather than separate overseas companies reporting to the corporate level. The policy with regard to international activities was described in the 1966 annual report as one of "planned, steady expansion."

The 28 divisions operated largely independently of each other. Divisions were permitted to buy from or sell to each other if they wished, but only at market terms and prices. With very few exceptions, no division was a significant customer of or supplier to another division with respect to either products or services. Transfers of personnel between divisions were exceedingly rare.

Research and Product Development

In its public statements, the company had been placing increasing emphasis on the importance of research and development in making possible new products. It was stated that 30 percent of the total 1966 sales volume came from products that were not being manufactured by the company five years earlier, and that during this same five-year period an amount equal to 25.8 percent of pretax income had been expended on research and development. Expenditures for company-financed research (several aerospace divisions also participated in government-financed research) totaled $19.5 million in 1966, an increase of 15 percent over 1965. All of the research was done at the division level; there was no corporate-level research facility.

▲ HISTORY

The development of Textron from its inception in 1928 to 1967 can be roughly divided into the following phases. In the period between 1928 and the beginning of World War II, the company expanded slowly within specialized segments of the textile industry. From

---

[6]*Forbes,* December 1, 1967.

Aerospace Group

Bell Aerosystems rocket engines, missile and spacecraft propulsion systems, positive expulsion rocket fuel tanks, inertial guidance and automatic landing systems, vertical lift aircraft, air cushion vehicles, other avionic devices; *Bell Helicopter* military and commercial helicopters, vertical lift aircraft; *Hydraulic Research and Manufacturing* electrohydraulic actuators, control systems, filters; *Accessory Products* pressure regulators, fluid controls, heat exchange equipment, autoclaves; *Dalmo Victor* aerospace antennae systems, electronic warfare systems, magnetic detection systems, electro-optics, automatic test equipment; *Spectrolab/Heliotek* solar cells, electro-optics, solar simulators, space power arrays.

Currently, the most important product included in the Aerospace group in terms of sales is military helicopters, accounting for approximately two-thirds of the sales of this group. Production of military helicopters and repair parts has increased rapidly since 1962 and the Company has followed a policy of subcontracting a substantial portion of this. Company believes that its Bell Helicopter division is one of two largest manufacturers of helicopters for military and commercial use; however, certain of its competitors are substantially larger and more diversified aircraft manufacturers. The Agena rocket engine and missile propulsion systems are also significant products of this group.

Consumer Group

Caroline Foods processed broilers and poultry products; *Hall-Mack* bathroom accessories; *Homelite* chain saws, power lawn mowers, generators, pumps, electric golf carts, in-plant vehicles; *Patterson-Sargent* paints and varnishes; *Randall (Housewares Division)* cooking ware, styled mail boxes, tubular furniture; *Sheaffer* pens and other writing instruments, hearing aids; *Shuron/Continental* eyeglass frames, lenses, cases, ophthalmic machinery; *Speidel* watchbands, identification bracelets, jewelry chains, men's toiletries.

Chain saws, watch bands and writing instruments are the most significant products in this group. The Company believes that its consumer products divisions are among the major domestic manufacturers of chain saws, electric golf carts, certain ophthalmic products, writing instruments, and watchbands.

Industrial Group

Aetna Bearing ball and roller bearings; *Burkart* cushioning materials, polyurethane foam; *Campbell, Wyant and Cannon* gray iron castings for engine blocks, camshafts, brake drums and parts; *Electronic Research* electronic crystals and other frequency control products; *Fanner* chaplets and chills used in casting, electrical line products, service fittings for utilities, malleable iron hardware, plastic products, hand tools, metal abrasives; *MB Electronics* vibration test equipment, environmental test systems, balancing machines, electronic instrumentation; *Randall (Automotive and Appliance Parts Division)* appliance and automobile trim, automobile door frames and body parts; *Spencer Kellogg* chemical products, linseed oil and other oil seed and corn milling products; *Sprague* gas meters and regulators, cylinders, valves and regulators for the liquified petroleum gas industry, marine fittings. *Walker/Parkersburg* underfloor electrical distribution systems, pre-engineered metal buildings.

continued

▲ EXHIBIT 3   *concluded*

Motor vehicle manufacturers are the largest single market for the Company's industrial products and sales to such manufacturers accounted for about one-third of the sales of this group in 1966. Textron's divisions manufacturing gray iron castings, chaplets and chills, interior trim, door frames and body parts, metal abrasive and cushioning materials are among the leading independent manufacturers of such products. The Company's industrial divisions are also leading domestic manufacturers of gas meters and vibration test equipment.

Metal Product Group

Bostitch staplers, staples, stapling hammers, pneumatic nailers, container machinery; *Camcar* cold flow metal parts, fasteners; *Pittsburgh Steel Foundry* aluminum and steel foil mills, heavy duty rolling mills and auxiliary equipment, metallurgical furnaces, steel castings; *Precision Methods and Machines* rolling mill components, precision machining, anti-vibration metal cutters; *Townsend* special fasteners for aerospace, automotive, appliance and construction industries, fastening tools, automatic fastening machines; *Waterbury Farrel* cold heading machines, rolling machines, rolling mills, presses, hobbing machines, precision grinders; *Jones & Lamson* turret lathes, optical comparing and measuring machines.

Textron's divisions are among the leading domestic manufacturers of stapling devices, certain machine tools and metal fasteners. Markets for the products in this group are very diverse and the Company does not believe that sales of this group are dependent upon any single industry.

Source: Proxy statement, 1966.

▲ TABLE A   Product Group Sales, 1962–1966 (in millions of dollars and as a percentage of sales)

	Aerospace		Consumer		Industrial		Metal Product	
	Sales ($m)	Percent of Total	Sales ($m)	Percent of Total	Sales ($m)	Percent of Total	Sales ($m)	Percent of Total
1962	$145	25%	$ 83	14%	$236	41%	$116	20%
1963	198	32	105	17	196	32	119	19
1964	249	33	154	21	200	26	150	20
1965	298	33	184	21	228	26	180	20
1966	463	41	223	20	240	21	206	18

Note: Figures are restated to include Bostitch, Inc., which was acquired September 1, 1966, in a transaction accounted for as a pooling of interests, and reflect the operations of businesses acquired and disposed of generally from the date of acquisition or to the date of disposition, respectively. The 1962 and 1963 sales of the Industrial Product Group include those of the Amerotron (textile) division, which was sold in April 1963. Because of the company's numerous acquisitions and dispositions, the figures shown above in any one year are not necessarily comparable to those of any other.
Source: Textron prospectus, June 8, 1967.

then until about 1950, expansion was very rapid and considerable integration of facilities took place, both primarily by means of acquisitions. From 1950 to 1953, the company withdrew from several stages of the integrated process and became a specialized textile producer again. The first diversification outside the textile industry occurred in 1953, and the 1953–1960 period saw rapid growth and diversification through acquisition. Royal Little, who had guided the company since 1928, retired in 1960, and the period from 1960 to 1967 was one of growth through consolidation of existing activities and the continuing acquisition of new business.

1923 to 1953

The Special Yarns Corp., the predecessor of the firm that is now Textron, was founded by Royal Little in 1923. The original capital consisted of $10,000 Little borrowed on a note endorsed by a friend,[7] and the company began its operations with three employees. Renamed Textron in 1944 after several mergers and changes of name, the company participated in various phases of the textile business through World War II. During the war, however, Little began creating an enterprise that would be completely integrated from raw material to the finished product. Sales expanded from a prewar level of $8 million to $125 million in 1947, largely through the acquisition of existing and admittedly marginal companies. By the end of the 1940s, the acquisition of companies and the integration of their activities was complete, although sales had declined to $68 million in 1949, largely because of depressed conditions in the textile industry.

Unfortunately, the efforts to expand and integrate within the textile industry were considerably less than successful. Two major weaknesses of the strategy soon became apparent: the integrated form of operation did not appear to be feasible in the textile industry, and the textile industry entered a lengthy slump in the late 1940s. According to *Fortune*:

> By the end of 1949 he [Little] had his combine built—and discovered almost immediately that the concept would not work. The company was too big and slow-moving, and could not change the styles of its finished garments fast enough to compete with the hundreds of small dress manufacturers; unlike Textron, they were not tied to the long-term commitments and lead time of a company that wove and finished its own fabrics.[8]

From about the middle of 1950 through the beginning of 1953, Textron carried out a program of withdrawing from the consumer products area of the textile industry and concentrated on the manufacture and sale of greige goods (i.e., basic, undyed fabric). Depressed industry conditions continued, however, with gloomy predictions in spite of the temporary stimulus caused by the Korean War.

1953: Diversification

In 1952, the disappointing results of the integration strategy and the pessimistic textile industry forecasts influenced Little to seek stockholders' approval of a change in the corporate charter that would permit diversification outside the textile industry. On September 30, 1953,

[7]Eliot Farley, who was later credited with having discussed the advantages of creating a "Disassociated Industries" by merging a number of unrelated companies.
[8]"How to Manage a Conglomerate Making…," *Fortune,* April 1964.

in its first diversification move, Textron purchased the Burkart Manufacturing Co. for about $1.8 million. Burkart was described as one of the principal producers of fiber batts and pads for the automotive, furniture, and mattress trades.

Two more companies were purchased, and a jointly owned subsidiary was set up during the next six months; these ventures were all in the electronics and defense industries. In summarizing the diversification plans and progress, the annual report for 1953 noted that

> We are stressing investment in industries directly associated with the aircraft and other vital defense programs. If the current general business recession continues, we believe the government will increase its expenditures in these fields to offset any further substantial drop in consumer spending. Our diversification program as presently constituted should therefore provide us with an excellent hedge against such an eventuality.

Textron's activities during this time, as well as their later all-important three-way merger with the ailing American Woolen Co., the nation's largest woolen and worsted fabrics company, and the Robbins Mills, were summarized as follows by *Forbes:*

> In the late forties, the textile industry went into a prolonged depression from which even the Korean War brought only partial relief. Textron itself was in the red three years out of five between 1949 and 1953. "I didn't see how the textile business could ever be good again in my lifetime," Little says. "But I'd noticed that a few companies like Du Pont and GM made 20 percent on equity, so I said: Why not shoot for that?"

> But Little still had a problem. Textron's total assets were less than $75 million. Its stock sold for less than book value. How was Little going to get the chips he needed to diversify? Paradoxically, he solved the problem by merging two big textile firms. Little wanted American Woolen and Robbins Mills, not for themselves but for their sizable cash reserves, their even more sizable tax losses, and the capital they could bring in through liquidation.[9]

The merger with the American Woolen Co. was a critical step in acquiring the assets needed for Textron's diversification program, as emphasized in a *Wall Street Journal* article:

> American Woolen Company [was] a huge but extremely sick textile company that Textron acquired in 1955 after a bitter proxy fight. Textron eventually sold all American Woolen's plants and figures that, with tax losses and money raised by the plant sales, American Woolen contributed $100 million of capital for Textron to use buying other businesses. Without that infusion, says Royal Little, Textron's founder and the original architect of the conglomerate, Textron could never have become the company it is now.[10]

Because of the tax loss credits, Textron's tax rate was zero as late as 1958, 27 percent by 1961, and did not reach normal levels until 1964.

By the beginning of 1957, roughly 25 acquisitions had been made since the diversification program began in 1953. The rationale underlying the acquisitions was not easy to discern. At a 1957 stockholders' meeting, one woman asked Little a direct and simple question: "Why don't you stop buying new companies and consolidate your gains and grow through what you now have?" The answer to the question was not recorded, and the acquisitions continued.

By the end of 1958, a total of 24 nontextile companies had been purchased and 6 had been disposed of. Nontextile sales reached 75 percent of total sales in 1958, up from zero in 1952 and about 30 percent in 1955. Sales were $244 million, and net earnings $10.8 million, a new high.

---

[9]*Forbes,* December 1, 1965.
[10]*The Wall Street Journal,* January 31, 1967.

One of Textron's largest acquisitions occurred in 1960, when the defense business of Bell Aircraft Co. was purchased for $32 million. *Fortune* commented:

> When Little made his biggest acquisition—Bell Aircraft's defense business—word went around that he had finally been outfoxed. He had become concerned that Textron did not have enough government contracts. Defense was then about 8 percent of sales, most of it done through the Dalmo Victor division, which made airborne radar antennas. Little wanted to raise the figure to at least 20 percent.…In July 1960, Textron concluded a deal for Bell's helicopter division, its rocket and guidance system maker (Bell's Agena engine is the nearest thing to a stock item in big-payload rocketry), and a small manufacturer of servo controls.

> The mistake was supposed to be the price Little had paid: $32 million for a business that in 1959 had earned only $4 million before taxes. However, Textron had put up only about half the purchase price in cash, the remainder being borrowed by Bell Aerospace (as the business was renamed). In any case, the Bell earnings have risen sharply since Textron took over the properties. Thompson says, "We knew we had our objective—25 percent pretax on our investment—from day one." He admits, however, that he and Little had never expected anything like the huge increase in helicopter orders that added $50 million to Textron sales in 1963. Altogether, the Bell companies alone accounted for more than $160 million of corporate sales last year [1963], more than a quarter of the total. Contract backlogs make it probable that these units will increase their sales and profits, despite the current military cutback programs.[11]

1960: A New Management

Royal Little retired as chairman of the board in 1960 and resigned as a director in 1962, upon reaching the age of 65. He was in excellent health at the time and continued with many outside charitable and business activities, including membership on the board of Arthur D. Little, the Boston consulting firm founded by his uncle. He continued to be a major Textron stockholder, with a reported 1 percent of the stock.

The new management team had been hired by Little some years earlier. G. William Miller, who became Textron's president and chief administrative officer in 1960, had left a prominent New York law firm to join Textron in 1956. Rupert C. Thompson, Jr., who became chairman and chief executive officer, had also joined Textron in 1956 as vice chairman of the executive committee and manager of all nontextile operations. Thompson had been one of Textron's bankers and a director for a time and became president in 1957.

In 1967, Little commented on his choice of Thompson to succeed him at Textron:

> The major task we had was to reconceive of the corporate role as managers of capital rather than operators of individual businesses. That was the main reason that I wanted Rupert Thompson to replace me as president. He had been a banker all his life, and therefore knew how to judge people and manage capital. I wanted the corporate level to judge men on their use of capital, not operate individual businesses.[12]

As the number of diversified operations increased, the company had continued to add management personnel at the corporate level; three group vice presidents and a vice president and treasurer were added in 1959 to "strengthen the overall supervision of our diversified businesses." The major change under the new management, however, was a move to a more formal and routine form of management.

---

[11]*Fortune,* April 1964.
[12]Unless otherwise noted, all comments by Little quoted in this case are from an interview conducted in March 1967.

Another step in the program of making the management of the diverse activities more effective was the establishment of a profit improvement program, which still continued in 1967. As *Forbes* put it:

> Thompson's major effort was devoted to a thoroughgoing improvement of Textron's existing operations.

> With Bill Miller in command, Textron launched hundreds of projects, covering everything from inventories to office procedures, in an effort to improve Textron's manufacturing efficiency, reduce its costs, improve its sales volume, and generally tone up its wide-ranging operations.

> The effort paid off and still continues to. Between 1960 and 1964, Textron's pretax earnings rose 162 percent on an 88 percent gain in sales. Despite the rising tax rate, despite the greater number of outstanding shares, Textron was able to post a 39 percent gain in common earnings.[13]

It was during this period that Textron became completely divorced from its original business. The remainder of the textile operations, including the American Woolen properties that had not been previously disposed of, were sold to Deering-Milliken in 1963 for $45 million in cash. The Amerotron Division, as it was then called, was reported to be earning $5 million (before taxes) a year, or 11 percent on its book value, which was considered respectable by textile industry standards, but Textron felt it could use the money to better advantage. Thompson remarked, "I figured that if we invested that $45 million at 26 percent we'd be earning $12 million, not $5 million, and that's exactly what we've done."

▲ FINANCIAL POLICIES

Some indication of the magnitude of the challenges and changes in the financing of Textron is given in Table B. The early growth was financed in large part by expansion of long-term debt. Part of the reason for using debt and paying cash for acquisitions was that Textron stock sold at a relatively low price-earnings multiple of about 7–9 until about 1963, making cash purchases seem more desirable. The low P/E ratio, according to Royal Little, had also been a significant factor in the tendency of the company not to acquire technologically oriented companies, whose stocks generally sold at a much higher multiple than Textron's.

In April 1967, an article appeared in *Barron's*[14] which was critical of the accounting and financial policies of many of the conglomerates. In a subsequent letter to the editor, Joseph Collinson, executive vice president–finance and administration, commented on Textron's policies:

> We do not use "all the liberal accounting techniques"; in fact we use none of those mentioned. For example, Textron has had only one pooling of interests of importance (Bostitch) and that was required by current accounting practices.

> We have had a number of acquisitions for cash in which the purchase price exceeded book value; we have accounted for the full purchase price and have not followed the alternate, less conservative method.

> In connection with acquisitions, Textron has not used convertible securities or preferred stock since 1955. For many years we have made no acquisition in which the price in contingent on

---

[13]*Forbes,* December 1, 1965.
[14]"Day of Reckoning," *Barron's*, April 3, 1967.

▲ TABLE B   Textron Financial Comparisons (in millions of dollars)

	1953	1960	1966
Total assets	$57	$272	$501
Net worth	35	119	236
Long-term debt	5.4	83	60
% of capitalization	13%	41%	20%

Source: Company records.

future earnings. Although we cover a wide range of industries, we have limited our acquisitions to manufacturing companies, avoiding the type of proliferation to which you refer.

Textron common stock is not subject to material dilution; the potential from conversion is less than 5 percent. The only substantial use of unissued shares in an acquisition was for Bostitch in 1966. Other Textron acquisitions for stock have been by the use of treasury shares.

I think you can see that in these areas, at least, Textron does not fit your picture of the typical so-called conglomerate.

With regard to external pressures for growth in earnings per share, however, Collinson commented to the casewriter:

We have to be concerned with increasing our earnings per share, just like everyone else, because that seems to be the way the game is scored in the stock market. The market seems to value increasing earnings per share more than a high return on corporate net worth, so just maintaining a high return on net worth is not enough. In fact, our additions to equity each year from retained earnings mean that we have to keep increasing our absolute level of earnings considerably just to stand still.

▲ ACQUISITION POLICY

Charles Chapin, a vice president who spent much of his time on acquisitions, described some of Textron's acquisition policies in a speech to investment analysts:

Textron classifies its acquisitions in two general categories: these are either a new product or a product line–type acquisition. To be considered as a new product acquisition, the company must have a sales volume of $20 million or more and be in a field in which we do not participate. We have found that a company should have about this sales volume or more to support a proper staff of people to operate the company under our autonomous, decentralized, profit-center–type of organization. Textron does not staff a unit when it is acquired, so it is essential that we acquire good management that will remain.

A product-line acquisition can be almost any size but it must complement one of our present divisions. In a product-line acquisition, we will accept weak management situations or other problems if we feel the division into which it would fit can assimilate the acquisition and solve the problem. It is in this type of acquisition that you most often can expect to achieve the synergistic effect of making 1 and 1 equal 3 that is so widely publicized in acquisition circles.

When a company is first proposed to us as a potential acquisition, we review it to see whether it meets a number of basic criteria, and any company we do acquire must have four characteristics:

1. It must be a manufacturing company.
2. It must be able to meet our return on investment and profit margin standards.
3. It must increase our earnings per share.
4. Its growth potential must be equal to or better than what we expect for Textron as a whole.

In the financial area, we determine first of all if and how we can achieve at least a 25 percent pretax return on the capital we would have to invest. if the company to be acquired has debt and/or preferred stock—then, it is considered as part of our investment. This return does not have to be achieved in the first year of our ownership but we must see how we can achieve it within a reasonable period of time. Presently, we are operating with a return of about 32 percent pretax on our divisional capital, so actually the 25 percent is really more a minimum.

In commenting on the general guidelines that had influenced the type of acquisitions made in recent years, Collinson added:

We have always insisted upon 100 percent ownership of our subsidiaries. Unlike many other companies, we are not interested in joint ventures or in having minority stockholders. Second, we want to buy management with the company. We want profitable companies with good management; we don't have the corporate resources to provide management to poorly managed companies. Third, we have stayed in manufacturing and have avoided the financial or service industries. Fourth, we have generally entered relatively small markets in order to avoid competing head-on with companies like United States Steel or General Motors. We would much prefer to be No. 1 or 2 in a small industry rather than a much smaller company in a large industry.

Another guideline we have followed is to stay out of any regulated industries. We are not interested in those, partly because of the reporting requirements, which may involve the corporation in more reporting than we would like, and partly because the returns are limited. We are moving more and more in the consumer goods direction and away from industries where we have little chance to differentiate our products. We have found that marketing consumer goods is an area in which you can really make money if you do a good job.

Two additional guidelines that had been important, according to Royal Little, were to have not more than 10 percent of the company's net worth in any single business, so as to reduce the risks to the corporation of a decline in that business, and to avoid businesses that tie into each other. He noted that the company had generally avoided the temptation to integrate forward to help an ailing division, and he thought that the only time they had done it had turned out to be a mistake.

Not all of the many acquisitions made turned out well, of course. Various Textron officials frequently emphasized the importance of being willing to sell off divisions that, for one reason or another, did not work out well. Rupert Thompson, for example, told a group of security analysts:

While we have acquired Sheaffer and Bostitch this year, we have disposed of five smaller units [through October 1966]; I think this requires a word of comment. They did not come up to our standards and we did not see a way to make them come up to them. When you acquire a division, you do everything you can to make it a success. When a company does not work out, we try to find a place in another organization where it might fit better. When one is responsible, as we are, for a growth company determined to show continued growth, a realistic attitude is necessary. We are also in the process of consolidating some of our divisions into others, under our refinement program. If we do not acquire any large new companies, I expect we will be down to 22 or 23 companies through this consolidation, so you can see that we are working toward a more and more compact operation.[15]

By the end of 1966, Textron had sold six units that did not meet the company's standards or fit the long-range plans. These six divisions had total sales of about $65 million and produced a return of about 10 percent (pretax) on the capital realized from their sale. Collinson noted that 1966 had been a good time to sell ailing units since business was good and a number of them were making money.

These and additional funds were reinvested into one acquisition that year. This business was reported to be showing about a 20 percent return initially and was expected to improve substantially over the next few years.

▲ CORPORATE ORGANIZATION AND POLICIES

The preceding material provides a basis for answering the questions, "What *is* Textron, and how did it become what it is?" The remainder of the case will address the issue of how the conglomerate works. It describes the nature and role of the corporate headquarters and presents executives' comments on how the corporate staff was able to maintain an effective balance between division autonomy and centralized controlled of Textron's 28 operating units.

Corporate Headquarters

As management described the company in a prospectus:

The operations of the Company and its subsidiaries are conducted by divisions which retain their identity as separate operating units. Each divisional management operates with a high degree of autonomy and is charged with direct responsibility for divisional operations and the achievement of return on investment standards established by Textron's management. Overall supervision, coordination and financial control is maintained by the Company's executive staff located at its principal corporate office in Providence, Rhode Island.

This principal office of the $1.1 billion company consisted of one and a half floors of leased space in a modest downtown office building. The Textron name was nowhere to be found outside of the building, and several pedestrians in the immediate vicinity could not help the visiting researcher find his destination. Once inside, it was necessary to scan the alphabetical directory of the building's tenants, much as one would try to locate a dentist's office, to ascertain that it was indeed the correct building.

The total corporate staff, including secretarial and clerical help, consisted of fewer than 100 people. Only about 20 people had been added in the last five years or so, in spite of the doubling in sales. The executives occupied the outside offices around the 10th floor of the building, and most of the secretarial and clerical employees were in a large central area. Furnishings and office space were remarkably modest.

A corporate organization chart is shown in Exhibit 4. Corporate headquarters maintained contact with and exercised control over the activities of the divisions primarily through the group executives. The task of the group executive was to keep in close touch with the

---

[15]Address to New York Society of Security Analysts, November 7, 1966.

▲ EXHIBIT 4   Corporation Organization Chart

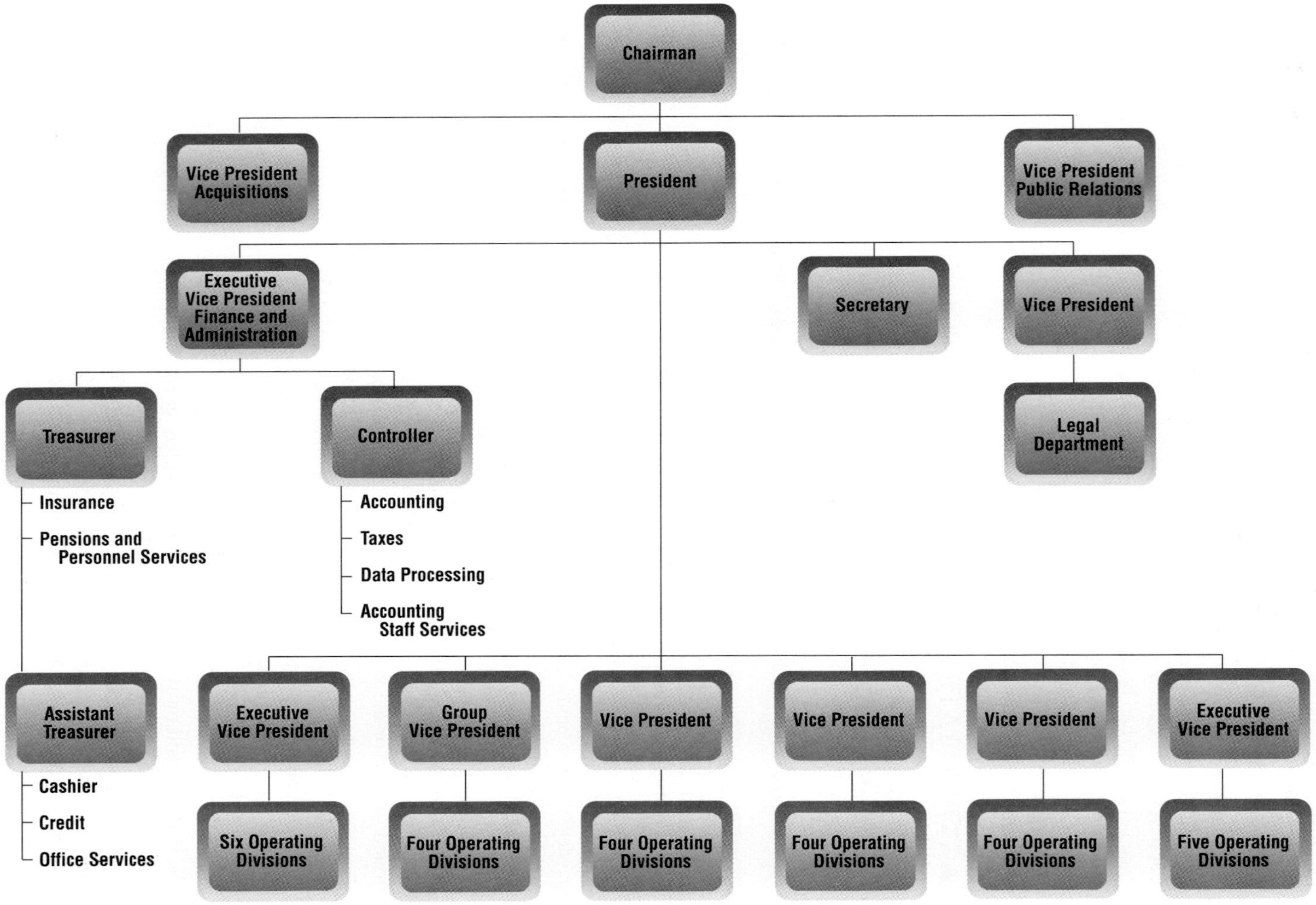

operations of the divisions assigned to him, and to function much as a one-man board of directors for the division president. As G. William Miller described it, the group executive was expected to "control the new use of capital, the selection of top management, and extraordinary expenses, to be aware of any deviations from plan and to pass any special problems up to the board decision."[16] The number of group executives had been stable at five for about the last five years, but a sixth was added in the summer of 1967.

The operating executives at the corporate level had no assistants, assistants to, or staff analysts reporting to them. Every effort had been made to avoid building up a corporate staff that would analyze reports and problems for operating executives or deal with staff counterparts at the division level. The only person at the corporate level responsible for following a specific division was the group executive who had been assigned that responsibility, and aside from the specialized corporate staff services available in areas such as accounting, legal, tax, and data processing, the executive's only formal assistance came from one secretary.

The role of the group executives will be described in more detail in a later section.

Corporate Staff Activities and Responsibilities

A brief description of some headquarters staff units and the administrative procedures they followed in their relationships with the divisions may shed light on the division of responsibility and the working relationships between headquarters and the divisions.

The general administrative procedures governing the relationships between the divisions and the corporate staff were set forth in a remarkably thin administrative manual. Consisting of about 25 partially filled pages, it applied to all domestic and foreign operations. Some of the following material has been extracted from this manual.

Finance and Accounting Trying to make explicit "the keys to this operation," Royal Little said the most important consideration was "to keep a tight rein on the finances and to control the expansion of the divisions. We don't want them to overexpand and let their costs rise in good times, as so many companies in a single business tend to do, and then have to face the problems caused by excess capacity and high costs when conditions change."

Other executives frequently mentioned the importance of careful financial controls, and the financial and accounting procedures were the first activities of the acquired companies to be centralized and coordinated with corporate policies.

Control of cash and capital expenditures was seen as highly important, and the financial policies that facilitated this control were the responsibility of the treasurer's office. To avoid the accumulation of unneeded cash at various locations, and to exercise closer control over division cash expenditures, only minimum cash balances were maintained in the division accounts. All division receipts were deposited in a central Textron account, and disbursements were made to the division accounts by the treasurer's office on an agreed-upon schedule. Opening and closing bank accounts, changing the authorized signers on bank accounts, borrowing money from outside sources, guaranteeing the financial obligations of others, and assigning receivables all required the authorization of the treasurer's office. Divisions could not issue stock or bonds, of course, since they were not separate corporations.

---

[16]*Forbes,* December 1, 1965.

All commitments for the purchase or lease of capital assets required corporate approval. A blanket authorization (typically $25,000 to $100,000) for each division was established by the executive committee at the beginning of each year. Any number of individual projects under $5,000, up to the total amount of the blanket authorization, could be approved by the division president. Requests for approval of projects over $5,000 were submitted to the division's group executive on a standard form. The group executive would generally pass on projects up to about $25,000 if they did not involve policy questions. Other projects might require approval by Miller, Thompson, or the executive committee of the board, depending on the size and nature of the project. There was no capital expenditures committee, and decisions on requests were often made within a few days.

The corporate accounting staff consisted of a controller and four assistants. Two of the assistants were certified public accountants, one was a data processing specialist, and one had considerable experience with various cost systems. This group supervised the routine collection and reporting of accounting information and the changeover of the accounting systems and reporting periods of acquired companies to conform to Textron practices. In addition, they were available to help with special problems of the divisions, and in this respect functioned as a small, internal, management consulting group.

Most of the divisions had, or were planning to acquire, third-generation computers, and the company was moving toward uniformity in equipment and applications and was placing more emphasis on the data transmission capabilities of the new computers. The home office did not have any computer facilities, however, and did not plan to acquire any. According to the 1966 annual report:

> Textron computer activity follows the corporate organizational concept of decentralization, with coordination from the corporate home office. Appropriate equipment is being installed in each location and divisional management is charged with the responsibility for its intelligent and profitable utilization.

Planning and Control   There was no staff unit at the corporate level responsible for planning and control activities for either the divisions or the entire corporation; appropriate line executives had this responsibility. Nor had extensive forms and procedures been set up for this purpose.

Division balance sheets and income statements were submitted monthly on standard forms. These provided the basis for the monthly meetings of the corporate executives (about 20 people in total) to review the performance of the divisions and to highlight the areas that required further investigation. Division presidents were not present at these meetings. One of the most important measures of division performance was the return on division net worth.

The only other major reports submitted regularly for planning and control purposes consisted of financial budgets for the following 12 months, submitted every quarter, and a plan indicating projected sales and earnings for the next five years, submitted annually. Except for the monthly reviews of division performance, there were no major group meetings for planning and control purposes.

The five-year division plans were used as a guide in formulating policies with regard to overall corporate financial planning and the growth to be sought through acquisitions. Specific acquisitions, however, could not be planned long in advance. As Collinson noted, "You can't very well plan three years ahead for what companies you will buy and how you will pay for them. Good acquisitions simply become available, and what we have to do is be clear as to what types of companies, and possibly what specific companies, we would be interested in."

Acquisitions   The corporate-level acquisitions staff consisted of Lon Casler, the vice president–acquisitions, and Charles Chapin, a vice president. These men did not originate all acquisitions, but they did become involved at various stages in every acquisition.

Acquisitions originated from a number of sources within the company. In the case of a small acquisition with products very closely related to an existing division, it was likely that the division manager or the responsible group executive would initiate the contact and carry on some of the analysis and negotiation. Acquisitions of perhaps $25 million or more, or acquisitions in a new line of business would probably originate with the corporate acquisition staff. Many of the largest acquisitions originated with the president, directors, or the chairman of the board. The chairman and the president were said to be aware of all acquisition activity after it had passed a certain stage, and the tax, legal, and accounting sections were kept informed and invariably brought in to help on all acquisitions.

Potential acquisitions were ordinarily brought to the attention of the company by brokers, investment bankers, banks, and friends. In some instances companies were sought out, and occasionally companies that wished to be considered for purchase contacted Textron. In addition, files were kept on companies that Textron felt it might some day be interested in acquiring.

Divisions would evaluate any business that would come under their management if it were acquired, as would the group executives responsible. One group executive stated that he had been involved in a number of purchases and sales of businesses, but that he sought help from others in the organization for specific aspects of the transactions and always kept the acquisitions staff and corporate officers completely informed of the plans and negotiations.

Other Policies and Practices

Approximately 75 percent of the hourly employees of the domestic Textron plants were represented by at least one union, and it was estimated that the company had more than 80 separate labor contracts with various unions and locals at any one time. The corporate policy with regard to union-management relations emphasized the importance of bargaining at a division rather than a corporate level. As stated in the corporate administrative manual:

> It is a principal corporate policy that all collective bargaining is conducted by the Division at the local level, avoiding under all circumstances any implication of Textron in the bargaining or negotiating process. Any attempt by union negotiators to include Textron in the negotiations or to bargain on the basis of Textron's overall size or profitability must be summarily rejected. In this area, particularly, each Division is and must be self-sustaining. It is also corporate policy in the collective bargaining area to assure at all times the preservation of management's right to manage.

There were very few corporatewide personnel policies; these were largely the responsibility of the individual divisions. Pension plans for the hourly employees of the various divisions were kept separate, for example, but were administered from headquarters. No attempt had been made to merge these plans into an overall Textron plan, or to establish corporatewide uniform job titles or salary classifications. Many of the pension plans for salaried employees, however, had been merged into a single Textron plan, and some common policies on fringe benefits for this group had also been established.

Division presidents had the authority to approve annual salaries of $15,000 or less and to hire new employees below this level, but approval by the group executive was required for salary or employment changes above the $15,000 level.

For routine items of only local significance, divisions used local legal counsel. Such matters generally included labor questions, filing of patents and trademarks, collection of receivables, and so forth. The corporate legal department became involved only in matters of significance to the entire corporation.

Federal, state, and local income and franchise taxes were the responsibility of the corporate tax department, as were any tax matters requiring data from more than one division. All other taxes were the responsibility of the divisions.

A limited amount of centralized purchasing of widely used items and materials was done, but the divisions were free to use the service or not, as they wished. No records were kept at the corporate headquarters on either the suppliers or the customers of the various divisions.

Corporate Staff: Size and Succession

Observers often remarked on the extremely small size of the Textron corporate staff in relation to the company's size and diversity. It was often presented as evidence of either genius or folly, depending upon the observer's opinion of conglomerates in general and Textron in particular. Reliance on such a small corporate staff was thought by some to be particularly risky under less favorable economic conditions, and they noted that Textron had never had to weather a significant national economic slump.

Regardless, company officials attached a great deal of importance to restricting the growth of the corporate staff. Royal Little, commenting on Textron's approach to managing its diversified activities, said:

> A key concept is that we have a very minimum of home staff. It consists almost entirely of line managers and clerical personnel, with virtually no staff helping the line managers. We have no R&D section or manufacturing section or marketing section, for example. With our collection of businesses, what would they be? Neither do we have any corporate labor relations officer or staff. We want the unions to bargain separately in each of our divisions, and we will not send any corporate representatives to any labor negotiations.

> We do have a finance section, a legal section, an accounting section, a small acquisitions staff, and some public relations staff. Our total home office charges, through, excluding corporate capital charges, are remarkably small[17] for a corporation our size. Obviously, if you buy a business earning 8 percent on sales and right away deduct 3 percent of that for home office charges, as some of the big corporations do, you have reduced their profitability substantially.

None of the group executives or corporate officers had come form the divisions. Some executives thought that this was not a matter of design and would probably change in the future if it appeared that someone in a division would be more useful at the corporate level. Royal Little, however, considered the separation quite important:

---

[17]Casewriter's estimate: about 0.25 percent of sales. Estimate based on aggregate direct remuneration, plus other benefits set aside or accrued during 1966, of $1.5 million for all of the directors and officers (June 8, 1967, prospectus); plus a very rough estimate of another $1.5 million for all other home office charges, excluding capital charges.

One of the keys to our success has been our approach to organization. We have no promotion up to the corporate level from the division ranks; all of our corporate men have come into the company from the outside. In addition, we have an outside board of directors (currently 13 in total) except for our three top officers. This gives us two independent levels of checks on the operations.

Many of the division managers wouldn't want to move to the corporate level anyway, because they are presidents of their own operations and some of them make more money than some of the corporate officers do. More importantly, though, if we are going to manage the capital entrusted to us most efficiently, it is essential to maintain the independent review of an outside corporate group and an outside board! We don't have any committees of division managers voting on each other's projects, either; that would just end up with everybody doing favors for each other.

With respect to the corporate organization, Collinson commented:

Our present structure, which we have had from the late fifties, seems to work well, and I think we will continue like this for quite a while. We have just added a sixth group executive, and would be glad to add another if we could find the right man. I think the ideal number of divisions for each man to supervise is around four or five, and six or seven group executives is not too many to have reporting to Mr. Miller.

Even though our sales have been growing rapidly, we have been stable at around 25 to 28 divisions for some time. It is easier to increase the size of the individual divisions reporting to each group executive than it is to increase the number of divisions reporting to him. Because of this, we are constantly in a process of trying to consolidate small divisions and product-line acquisitions into other divisions in order to keep the total number of divisions from increasing.

Role of the Group Executive

According to Collinson, the group executives' responsibilities required a good deal of travel. Each group executive was responsible for the operations of four to six divisions; by spending an average of three or four days a week visiting the plants, he could keep in close touch with the operations. Collinson added that there was also a lot of contact by telephone, and that they all tried to rely on verbal communications rather than written memos as much as possible.

The researcher also had the opportunity to talk several times with Robert Grant, a group vice president responsible for the operations of the Sheaffer Pen, Shuron/Continental, Speidel, Electronic Research, and MB Electronics divisions, concerning the role of the group executive.

The youngest of the group executives, Grant had received his MBA degree from the Harvard Business School in 1950. He had been hired by Royal Little in 1960, when Textron was contemplating expansion into the drug field, because he had had considerable experience in acquisition work with Plough, Inc., a "baby conglomerate" with a number of drug and household products. Textron later decided against attempting to build a drug business from scratch, but Grant stayed on as a group executive to supervise several divisions. he later became a vice president and was promoted to group vice president in 1967. During his time at Textron, he had been involved with 10 different companies.

In discussing the role of the group executive, Grant said:

The principal way in which we can help our division is simply to study the various areas within the business, learn what they are doing and why, and determine what areas might be improved. After a while you find out that there are problems which frequently reoccur in the functional areas and there are the less usual projects such as moving a plant or putting up a new building, or acquiring a product line or small company to add to the division, and that it is not necessary to have spent your life in the industry in order to help. Our role is to be a general business consultant, not an industry expert.

In making suggestions and recommendations, I am careful to remember and to communicate that there may be much that I don't know about the specific industry and the company, and that I may make some mistakes in facts and assumptions. What I try to do is to present worthwhile recommendations, and suggest that we get together to talk about them. An answer I will not accept, however, is simply that something can't be done, with the only reason being that I "don't know the industry." If we can't do something, I want to have the reasons explained to me.

It is also important to begin dealing with other managers within the division, and not just the division manager. You can really be misled—and you cannot be of as much value—if all of your information comes from just one channel, and it is essential to deal with more than one person. A key to being able to do this is to have the division manager recognize that you are his friend and that you and he are on the same team. If he feels that you are looking for ammunition to use against him in order to make yourself look good, then it won't work at all, because he will try very hard to prevent you from becoming deeply involved with the business and from meeting with anyone unless he is also present.

There is no sense in limiting your involvement with the divisions to a periodic look at the balance sheets and P&L statements. You have to get involved and help out early, or in times of difficulty your troubles will just become bigger. Besides, a manager could hide or be unaware of problems for quite a while unless the supervisor is familiar with their operations. In addition, you will not be aware of lost opportunities if you don't learn as much as possible about the division and its business. It would also be difficult to set goals for the people. I think you have to become deeply involved, but to recognize that the division people will always be the experts in their operations.

Incentive Compensation

Textron executives felt that an essential aspect of their approach to managing the company's diversified and decentralized activities was a provision for incentive compensation based on performance. Both Thompson and Miller stressed the importance of Textron's incentive compensation plans. In 1967, three such plans were in effect: a divisional net worth compensation plan, a corporate officers' return-on-equity incentive plan, and a separate plan covering Miller and Thompson.

The division plan was by far the largest of the three, in terms of total dollar amounts paid out and the number of people directly covered or influenced. It included everybody who would "significantly affect profits," classifying participants into four groups on the basis of their positions. For the division presidents—the A group—incentive compensation ranged from 0 percent to 100 percent of base salary depending on the division's return on net worth; for example, the president might receive no incentive compensation if the division's return were 10 percent, and 100 percent if division return were 60 percent. The B group consisted of the top vice presidents in the division; their maximum incentive payment was 75 percent. The C group, with a maximum incentive payment of 50 percent, comprised the other vice presidents and the controllers and treasurers. The D group included personnel such as chief engineers, sales managers, directors of manufacturing or purchasing, and so on. The maximum incentive compensation for the D group was 25 percent.

In all cases, the incentive compensate paid was directly proportional to the division return on net worth and the base salary of the participant. Collinson stated, however, that adjustments were made for particular divisions to allow for unusual investment bases with regard to industry standards or unusual factors affecting profits. Once these specific ground rules were established for a given division, they were rarely changed. He added that the presidents of some of the profitable divisions consistently earned incentive payments of more than 50 percent of their base salaries, and that in virtually any year the payments would range from 0 percent to 100 percent.

Executives often mentioned that this form of incentive compensation made it easier to oversee the activities of a number of diverse divisions, because it acted as a strong stimulus to increasing profits and as a deterrent to building up overhead expenses or accumulating excess assets. It was felt to be an effective motivating mechanism as well as a means for facilitating the transfer of capital to the most productive uses possible within the corporation.

Collinson acknowledged that there was always a possibility that division managers would overemphasize short-run profits at the expense of long-run position, but he did not think this was a serious problem because of the close familiarity of the group executives with the activities of the divisions.

The incentive compensation plan for key employees of the corporate office, as selected annually by management, resulted in payments of $115,000 in 1966 to the 13 officers who were covered by the plan. The direct compensation of this group (before incentive compensation) was about $550,000 in that year. The incentive paid was directly related to the amount by which the corporate pretax return on common equity exceeded 10 percent and to the participant's base salary.

Thompson and Miller, with base salaries of $120,000 and $90,000 respectively, did not participate in this plan in 1966, but were covered by individual incentive compensation agreements. They were to receive that proportion of base salary (not to exceed 100 percent) equal to $3\frac{1}{3}$ times the corporate (pretax) percentage return on common equity.

There were no stock option plans available for executives, although such plans had been used in the past. The only options still outstanding (fewer than 4,000) had been granted as a result of substituting options on Textron stock for options already existing on Bostitch stock at the time of its acquisition.

▲ ADVANTAGES OF THE CONGLOMERATE FORM

Diversified, acquisition-minded conglomerates like Textron had attracted a great deal of attention in the mid-1960s. Some parties were interested in restricting their activities, others in imitating them. For both groups, a key question was how corporate management and resources contributed to the operations of the acquired companies. For example, during the 1964 congressional hearings on economic concentration, in which Textron was described as "practically a textbook example of a merger-created conglomerate," the following dialogue took place between Mr. Houghton, a witness who just finished testifying on Textron and a few other conglomerates, and Senator Hart, chairman of the subcommittee:

Senator Hart: Mr. Houghton, thank you very much. We have heard a great deal about conglomerates, but you added something for the record that we have not heard before; at least I have not been aware of it. You have shown us graphically what the merger movement means in terms of specific companies and the lack of any apparent connection in many of these acquisitions. Now, how can conglomerate acquisitions representing expansion into new and unrelated industries make for greater efficiency?

Mr. Houghton: I think that is the basic question that we all ask. I think to analyze it one must break down the problem into two parts. In what respect do companies gain scale advantages and to what extent do they gain scale efficiencies? Now, scale advantage is good for the company, but not necessarily good for other companies or good for the economy. It is difficult and without probing into the details of some of these corporate expansions, it is very unwise to draw conclusions as to how efficient they might be. Some of them haven't been profitable, and this has been noted very widely in the trade press. That is the ultimate test of efficiency; about the only one we have is the profit rate until we dig in and look at some of the cost data.... I suppose some organizations feel that they give a thrust to growth by expanding and taking over what they might consider underdeveloped companies. Whether the whole is greater than the sum of its parts is very difficult to determine.[18]

Several Textron executives interviewed for this case were asked about the nature of the corporate contribution in a conglomerate. Collinson felt that one of Textron's major contributions to the operations of the companies it acquired consisted of additional financial resources. Many acquisitions were companies that had good opportunities for expansion but had outgrown their own resources and were either unable or unwilling to seek alternative forms of financing.

Another important strength was the ability of the corporate headquarters to provide an incentive to the acquired companies to do more planning, and to assist them in this without imposing upon them a complicated or expensive standardized planning procedure. Collinson noted that it is easy for companies to fall into a pattern of not planing their activities very carefully, especially if they have been sufficiently profitable and are not required to present formal plans to a board of directors.

Robert Grant explained Textron's ability to improve the operations of its acquired businesses as follows: "The important added factors involve the application of professional business skills, the addition of new levels of enthusiasm and imagination, and, of course, the availability of substantial financial resources." He emphasized strongly that a critical strength Textron provided was a generalized business knowledge and set of skills that could be highly useful i specific situations. He felt that significant improvements often resulted from the addition of a broad business perspective to the good but also frequently narrow viewpoint of the division management:

> The real thing that we are contributing is a generalized business knowledge, and not expert knowledge about specific products and marketing. The division people will always know more about their own business than we will here at the corporate level. Our contribution stems from being more expert in more generalized business procedures and knowledge.

At a broader level, Grant felt that significant improvements often came from developing new combinations of products or finding new markets for the products and technology of the acquired company. An outsider could sometimes suggest attractive markets very different from those that long-time participants in the business normally think of. As an example of a new combination of products that he was currently seeking, Grant said, "I

---

[18]U.S. Congress, Senate Committee on the Judiciary, Hearings on Economic Concentration, Part I (1964), overall and conglomerate aspects.

would be delighted to find another company with perhaps $5 million in sales with a product that we could sell along with Sheaffer pens. Each company would probably have about 15 percent marketing expenses, and by putting them together, we could save a substantial amount of this charge."

Grant emphasized that it was important for Textron to avoid getting involved in businesses in which success did not hinge on additional financial resources and generalized business skills, Textron's principal strengths. He gave as an example the fiberglass boat business in which the company had been involved for a number of years, and which had been one of his first responsibilities:

Generally speaking, anybody can build a fiberglass boat by hand, and all the money and management skills in the world don't help you guild it very much more cheaply than that. It is still basically a hand-craft operation. A small operator can sell on the weekends, have his wife keep the books, and run a lower-cost operation than we can. This may be changing gradually, but it certainly was not a business for us to be in in the early sixties. It makes much more sense to buy a company for which a quarter of a million dollar machine might reduce your costs just a bit, especially if others in the industry are unwilling or unable to make the same investment.

Along the same line I think it is also important for us to study carefully before we acquire high-technology businesses, since we don't have specific high technological skills at corporate headquarters to help companies of this sort. It has been my experience that if you don't really understand the business and don't have a good feel for the product and the industry, you never will feel comfortable in dealing with the division, because you will have to accept most of what is said at face value. If we were to attempt to manage a number of high-technology businesses, it would be essential to have experts in technology at the corporate level.

In a low-technology business, by contrast, virtually anyone can learn 85 percent of what there is to know about the business in a matter of months, rather than in a period of years. It might take you another 10 years to learn the remaining 15 percent, but combining your other knowledge with what you learn about a specific business is the really valuable aspect of our management. It is our general business experience and skills and the outside viewpoint that is essential, not a detailed knowledge of that specific business. I sincerely feel that at least half of the companies in the United States are poorly managed and that their operations could be improved considerably by the addition of the resources, management skills, and incentives a company like ours can offer. The principal part of these improvements would probably come in the first three years and would certainly taper off after five years, but the improvement would be significant.

Royal Little described Textron's contributions to its acquired companies as follows:

Our companies do better after we have acquired them because we are adding that intangible called business judgment. This is not the same as what many companies try to do, which is to drastically improve the businesses they buy. That is a fatal mistake. The assumption there is that you are smarter than the people that have been in the business, that you can improve the operations of the company greatly by coming in and making lots of changes. Our approach is different. We try to create the proper incentives for the people, provide some money if they need it, and help them on some of the business matters, but we don't meddle too much in the internal affairs of the division. The great temptation is to think that you are smarter than the people in the company that you have acquired and that you know more about their business than they do.

G. William Miller described the advantages of the conglomerate form to a group of financial analysts in 1966:

Our conglomerate form of nonrelated diversification is a powerful weapon in our plans for continued growth and an increasingly higher return on shareholders' investment. The conglomerate organization and philosophy of free, wide-ranging operations have considerable advantages in meeting the challenges of the last part of the 20th century and the coming structure of the 21st century. There are a number of reasons for this. One is the tremendous growth of technology that has made it imperative that companies take a new look at their charters, what they're trying to accomplish. It is necessary for managements to think far more in functional terms than in the past and not be wedded to narrow product identification. Otherwise, they will miss the opportunity to participate in new markets. and will be threatened constantly by the obsolescence of their products, which is bound to take place as scientific skills continue to increase.

The conglomerate form has grown in response to changing economic forces, changing patterns of management, and changing technology. The managements which have recognized this have increasingly become conglomerate in form, whether or not they yet admit it or realize it. This is the trend we think you'll be seeing more and more.

Charles Chapin commented on the conglomerate philosophy as follows:

Diversification is one more step in the process of the professionalization of management that has advanced so rapidly in this country since World War II. It represents the search for a new business structure which will provide a means of survival for the corporation beyond the life cycle of a single industry, just as the corporate form of management provided a means of survival of a business beyond the life cycle of individual ownership.

Rupert Thompson had also commented at various times on the nature and advantages of being a conglomerate, although he much preferred to use the term *multimarket*. *The Wall Street Journal* quoted him as saying, "The function of corporate management is to produce the maximum return on stockholders' money. The conglomerate is the best vehicle for doing that because it can put its money wherever it will work most efficiently."[19] And *Forbes* reported the following remarks:

It doesn't make any difference what type of products make up Textron so long as they meet our goals. Basically, Textron shouldn't be regarded as a manufacturing operation at all, but as a management concept like Litton or FMC. That's the secret of our success and that's where our basic strength lies....

Except for the problem of acquiring management, there is no limit to how far we can go with this type of organization.[20]

---

[19]*The Wall Street Journal,* January 31, 1967.
[20]*Forbes,* December 1, 1965.

PEPSICO'S RESTAURANTS

In early 1992, Wayne Calloway, PepsiCo's chairman and CEO, along with the presidents of each of the company's restaurants and Ken Stevens, the senior vice president of strategic planning, was evaluating two opportunities to expand PepsiCo's restaurant businesses—Carts of Colorado, a $7 million manufacturers and merchandiser of mobile food carts and kiosks, and California Pizza Kitchen, a $34 million restaurant chain in the casual dining segment. The issues before them included whether to pursue these companies, and, if so, how the relationships might be structured, given PepsiCo's large organization and decentralized management approach.

[handwritten margin notes: ① whether to pursue ② how to structure relationship]

▲ PEPSI-COLA COMPANY: THE EARLY YEARS

Pepsi-Cola, a combination of Pepsi-Cola syrup and carbonated water, was invented in the 1890s by Caleb D. Bradham, a southern druggist. When he discovered how much his soda fountain customers liked his beverage, he began to sell it in bottles and to barrel the syrup for other soda fountain operators. Bradham's business, Pepsi-Cola Company, grew quickly. By 1907, its annual syrup production exceeded one million gallons.

After two bankruptcies, one caused by escalating sugar prices due to rationing during World War I and the other caused by the Great Depression, Pepsi-Cola, under a new owner, changed its selling strategy. In 1933, the company doubled the size of its bottles to 12 ounces while lowering the price of a bottle to a nickel, the same price as 6 ounces of Coca-Cola. Depression-weary customers were ready for a bargain and Pepsi-Cola sales increased dramatically.

Research Associate Diana Magnani prepared this case under the supervision of Professor Cynthia Montgomery.

By the end of the 1940s, higher sugar prices meant that Pepsi-Cola could no longer maintain its nickel price. Alfred N. Steele, a former marketing executive for Coca-Cola, who became Pepsi-Cola's president and CEO in 1950, moved the company away from the low-price strategy and launched an extensive marketing campaign to boost the company's image. Customers were urged to "Be sociable, have a Pepsi." With the help of actress Joan Crawford, Steele's wife, Pepsi took on a stylish, even glamorous, image. The strategy was successful—Pepsi-Cola's profits increased to $14.2 million in 1960 from a postwar low of $1.3 million in 1950.

▲ PEPSICO UNDER DONALD KENDALL

Donald M. Kendall, an amateur boxing champion and star football tackle in his youth, became Pepsi-Cola's CEO in 1963. He quickly replaced some of Steele's top managers and reorganized the company so that his "Whiz Team" was in control. Outsiders were also brought into the fold, including Andrall E. Pearson, a veteran management consultant and partner from McKinsey & Co., who became president and chief operating officer, and Vic Bonomo from California's United Vinters whose primary task was to "rebuild the soft-drink [segment] a-round organization rather than personalities."[1] Pearson himself brought several others to the company, recruiting a dozen or so top people from corporations like General Foods and from consulting firms like McKinsey.

A 1980 Business Week article asserted that under the leadership of Kendall and Pearson, the cultural emphasis at PepsiCo changed dramatically from "passivity to aggressivity":

Once the company was content in its No. 2 spot, offering Pepsi as a cheaper alternative to Coca-Cola. But today, a new employee at PepsiCo quickly learns that beating the competition, whether outside or inside the company, is the surest path to success.... Because winning is the key value at Pepsi, losing has its penalties. Consistent runners-up find their jobs gone. Employees know they must win merely to stay in place—and must devastate the competition to get ahead.[2]

John Sculley, who was president of the firm's U.S. beverage operations at the time and who later went on to become CEO of Apple Computer, said that "careers [at PepsiCo] ride on tenths of a market share point." He described managers at the company as the kind of people who "would rather be in the Marines than in the Army." The company encouraged interdepartmental sports competitions and, according to Sculley, "the more competitive it [became], the more we [enjoyed] it."[3]

According to *Business Week,* Kendall himself set a constant example of the kind of "ingenuity and dedication to work he [expected] from his staff."[4] Once when the roads were impassable because of snow, Kendall used a snowmobile to get to work. Pearson, too, earned a reputation for his firmness and loyalty to the company. In 1980, *Fortune* magazine listed him as one of the "10 toughest bosses" in corporate America, stating that his subordinates may have "[hated] his guts at times, but if they [survived] and [succeeded] they [reveled] in the challenge of operating on the fast track."[5]

[1]J.C. Louis, and Harvey Z. Yazijian, *The Cola Wars; The Story of the Global Corporate Battle between the Coca-Cola Company and PepsiCo, Inc.,* (New York; Everest House, ©1980), p. 147.
[2]"The Hard-to-Change Values That Spell Success or Failure," *Business Week,* October 27, 1980, p 148.
[3]Ibid., pp. 151 and 154.
[4]Ibid., p. 154.
[5]Hugh D. Menzies, "The Ten Toughest Bosses," *Fortune,* April 21, 1980, p. 148.

Kendall encouraged managers to take risks, boldly stating, "If you go through your career and never make a mistake, you've never tried anything worthwhile."[6] The corporate office set strategy and maintained financial control, but left operating decisions to its energetic and industrious division managers who were eager to take charge. For example, as head of the $4.6 billion soft drinks segment in the mid-1980s, Roger Enrico arranged for pop star Michael Jackson to shoot a Pepsi commercial at a record $5 million fee and told Kendall about the agreement only a few hours before the contract was to be signed.

Believing that snack chips went well with soda, Kendall merged Pepsi-Cola, which had sales of about $450 million, with Frito-Lay Company, a $184 million snack foods concern, in 1965. The combined company, named PepsiCo, then purchased Pizza Hut, a fast-food pizza chain, and Taco Bell, the largest Mexican fast-food chain, in the late 1970s, partly to have more outlets for its fountain business. The company also bought a van line, a motor freight company, and a sporting goods manufacturer during this period only to sell them off toward the end of Kendall's tenure as CEO (Exhibit 1).

▲ PEPSICO'S CONTINUED GROWTH UNDER WAYNE CALLOWAY

Kendall's choice of a successor was Wayne Calloway. Prior to his promotion to chairman and CEO in 1986, Calloway had held nine positions at PepsiCo with responsibilities in finance, marketing, and operations. Most recently, he had been president of Frito-Lay from 1976 to 1983.

The Organization

The PepsiCo organization had eight major parts: Pepsi-Cola North America, Pepsi-Cola International, Frito-Lay, Inc., PepsiCo Foods International, Pizza Hut Worldwide, Taco Bell Worldwide, Kentucky Fried Chicken Corporation, and PepsiCo Food Systems Worldwide. The heads of most of these businesses reported directly to Calloway (Exhibit 2).

In many ways Calloway carried on in Kendall's tradition. Some of his colleagues described him as "tough as nails"[7] and like Kendall, he was known for "[packing] the company with workaholics and then [expecting] a lot of them."[8] Senior managers described Calloway as a great communicator who was extraordinarily consistent. Steven Reinemund, president of Pizza Hut, remarked: "Wayne has never told me to do or not to do something. But he challenges my thought process, and often suggests people I might want to talk to about a particular issue."[9] Calloway challenged his managers to be innovative and was known for saying, "If it ain't broke, fix it anyway."

PepsiCo flourished under Calloway. When asked by a Fortune magazine reporter to what he attributed PepsiCo's outstanding performance during his tenure, Calloway responded, "the three Ps, 'people, people, people.'" The reporter, Brian Dumain, commented:

Ah, touchy-feely management? Anything but. Behind Calloway's alluring, alliterative slogan lies the country's most sophisticated and comprehensive system for turning bright young people into strong managers. Says [Calloway]: "We take eagles and teach them to fly in formation."[10]

---

[6]Ibid., p. 86.
[7]Dumain, p. 78.
[8]Michael J. McCarthy, "Pepsi Is Going Better with Its Fast Foods and Frito-Lay Snacks," *The Wall Street Journal,* June 13, 1991, sec. A, p. 8.
[9]Personal interview, June 11, 1993.
[10]Dumain, p. 78.

▲ EXHIBIT 1   Selected Events in PepsiCo's History, 1965–1991

1965	Pepsi-Cola Company merged with Frito-Lay Company. Combined company named PepsiCo.
1968	Acquired North American Van Lines, a leading interstate trucking company.
1970–72	Acquired Wilson Sporting Goods Co.
1972–73	Acquired Rheingold Corp.
1974	Sold Rheingold's brewing operations and changed Rheingold Corp's name to United Beverages, Inc.
1976	Acquired Lee Way Motor Freight, Inc.
1977	Acquired Pizza Hut, Inc. for $300 million.
1978	Acquired Taco Bell for approximately $148 million.
1984	Sold Lee Way Motor Freight, Inc.
1985	Acquired bottling subsidiary of Allegheny Beverage Corp. for $160 million.
1985	Sold North American Van Lines for $376 million. Sold Wilson sporting Goods for $134 million in cash and Wilson 10 percent cumulative preferred stock.
1986	Acquired MEI Corp., its third-largest bottler, for approximately $591 million. Acquired Seven-Up International for about $246 million. Acquired Kentucky Fried Chicken for approximately $840 million.
1987	Sold La Petite Boulangerie for approximately $15 million. Acquired 20 percent equity investment in Pepsi-Cola General Bottlers Inc. for approximately $177 million.
1988	Acquired Calny, Inc., the largest owner of Taco Bell franchises. Acquired bottling operations of Grand Metropolitan Inc. for approximately $705 million.
1989	Acquired U.S. franchised bottling operations of General Cinema Corp. for $1.77 billion. Acquired all of the capital stock of Smith Crisps Ltd. and Walker Crisps Holding Ltd., two U.K. snack food companies for $1.34 million.
1990	Acquired more than 70 percent of Sabritas S.A. de C.V., Mexico's largest cookie maker, for approximately $300 million.
1991	Formed joint venture with Thomas J. Lipton Co. to develop and market new tea-based beverages and to expand distribution of existing Lipton ready-to-drink products.

Source: PepsiCo.

A senior PepsiCo executive observed that, consistent with its emphasis on people, the company backed people, not projects, in its resource allocation decisions, and these decisions were made quickly. For example, one restaurant president remarked that, on a Sunday, Calloway gave his approval for a $100 million dollar acquisition even though no other executive supported the proposal at the time.

To evaluate and reward managers, PepsiCo used a two-phase system. First, managers sat down with those who reported directly to them in order to review the latter's performance and establish standards for the coming year. Next, Calloway joined the upper-level management and representatives from personnel and together, they reviewed the perfor-

▲ EXHIBIT 2 Organization Chart, 1992

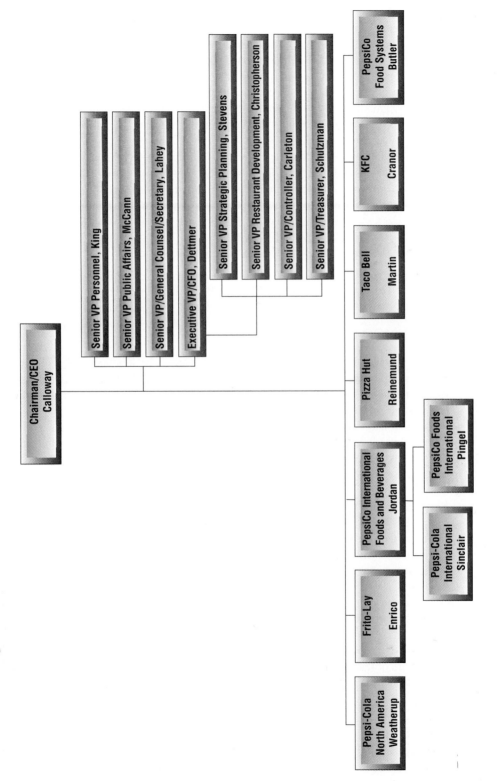

mance of the 550 top-level managers. Based on these discussions, some managers were asked to remain in their present positions, and others were promoted—either to another division, or within their present division to a more challenging position or a different functional area. PepsiCo afforded managers the opportunity to move within and across the various PepsiCo businesses so that they could tackle a broad array of challenges. For example, Roger Enrico was in marketing at Frito-Lay and, after a number of other assignments, became president of Worldwide beverages and then chairman and CEO of Frito-Lay. This kind of movement was very common. In Calloway's view, "different experiences [made] great managers."[11]

give shares *act like owners*

In 1989, PepsiCo was the first major U.S. corporation to offer all of its 300,000 employees a stock option plan, granting them yearly options on shares equivalent (at the then price) to 10 percent of their compensation.[12] In Calloway's view, the purpose of the program was to empower employees and encourage them to "act like [owners], not [hired hands]."[13] By pushing power further down in the already decentralized organization, Calloway hoped to build a sense of identification with PepsiCo within the divisions and to underscore the importance of individual initiative. He argued:

> Unlike General Electric or IBM we don't just win a couple of big contracts each year and make $50 billion.... We have to win them one pizza at a time, one bag of chips, every day.[14]

▲ PEPSICO'S BUSINESSES

Calloway was determined to continue Kendall's legacy of doubling sales every five years and boosting earnings growth. In his first five years at PepsiCo's helm, sales doubled, income from continuing operations grew at a compound rate of more than 20 percent, and the company's value on the stock market tripled (Exhibit 3).

PepsiCo had three segments—soft drinks, snack foods, and restaurants. Together, they generated nearly $20 billion in sales in 1991. Calloway viewed PepsiCo as having three flagships and explained that the company invested according to where it believed it could achieve the highest returns (Exhibit 4).

Soft Drinks   Soft drinks represented 35 percent of PepsiCo's sales and 39 percent of its operating profits in 1991. With four of the top-selling U.S. soft drinks (Pepsi, Diet Pepsi, Caffeine Free Diet Pepsi, and Mountain Dew), the company held nearly a third of the $47 billion U.S. soft drink market. Internationally, PepsiCo's share of the $11 billion market was about 15 percent.

Under Calloway, PepsiCo spent $4.6 billion to acquire several of its franchised bottlers, including some its largest ones. It also acquired the international operations of Seven-Up, the third-largest soft drink operation outside the United States, for $246 million.

Snack Foods.   With top-selling brands, such as Doritos, Lay's, Fritos, and Ruffles, Frito-Lay's share of the $10 billion U.S. snack chips market was nearly half, and PepsiCo Foods International's (PFI) share of the $13 billion international snack chips market was about

---

[11]Ibid., p. 80.
[12]"Can Wayne Calloway Handle the Pepsi Challenge?" *Business Week,* January 27, 1992, p. 90.
[13]Ibid., p. 90.
[14]Ibid., p. 91.

one-quarter. In 1989, PepsiCo purchased two U.K. snack companies—Smith Crisps, Ltd. and Walker Crisps, Ltd.—for $1.34 billion, becoming the leading snack food company in Europe. The following year, it acquired 70 percent of Empresas Gamesa, Mexico's largest cookie maker, for about $300 million. Snack foods accounted for 29 percent of PepsiCo's sales and 35 percent of its operating profits in 1991.

Restaurants   In 1986, PepsiCo purchased Kentucky Fried Chicken. Combined with Pizza Hut and Taco Bell, the purchase made PepsiCo the international leader in number of restaurant units. In 1991, PepsiCo's restaurant segment attained the highest revenue of the company's three segments, surpassing soft drinks for the first time. That year, restaurant sales and operating profits were 36 percent and 26 percent of the total, respectively. Senior management believed PepsiCo's reputation and willingness to move people within and across divisions gave it a competitive advantage in restaurants.

In the early 1990s, each of PepsiCo three chains was the leader in its segment: Pizza Hut had one-quarter of the $16 billion U.S. pizza category, Taco Bell had 70 percent of the $3.5 billion U.S. quick service Mexican-style restaurant category, and Kentucky Fried Chicken had half of the $6.5 billion quick service chicken restaurant category (Exhibit 5). Internationally, Pizza Hut and Kentucky Fried Chicken were very strong; Taco Bell had only a few international units, but was looking to increase its international presence.

Although it successfully expanded its large chains, PepsiCo had difficulty expanding La Petite Boulangerie, a three-unit bakery chain it had purchased in 1982. PepsiCo had envisioned opening hundreds of units beyond the chain's San Francisco, California, home base, but stopped at fewer than 150. Calloway explained, "We made all the mistakes a big dumb company will make. For example, our overhead was enough for 8,000 units when we had only 40. We learned a great deal from that experience and are determined not to do that again."[15] PepsiCo sold La Petite Boulangerie in 1987, taking a $13 million loss.

In the late 1980s, Coca-Cola initiated an aggressive advertising campaign to convince restaurant operators to buy Coca-Cola's fountain syrup. Coca-Cola's main argument was that restaurants that bought syrup from Pepsi-Cola were, albeit indirectly, helping one of their toughest restaurant competitors. Largely as a result of Coca-Cola's campaign, Pepsi-Cola lost the Burger King and Wendy's accounts in 1991, and its volume growth in soft drinks that year was only a small fraction of the industry's volume growth.

▲ PEPSICO'S RESTAURANTS AND THE RESTAURANT INDUSTRY

The U.S. food-service industry had sales of about $250 billion in 1991, and industry experts expected sales to double in the following 10 years. PepsiCo identified the following eight segments within the industry (see Exhibit 6).

Don Christopherson, a senior vice president at PepsiCo, described each segment as being "a rung on a ladder." He believed that each rung had its own set of key success factors and that the skills required to compete in each were not easily transferable across rungs. All three of PepsiCo's restaurant chains were considered quick service, even though Pizza Hut staff waited on customers at their tables.

---

[15]Personal interview, February 16, 1993.

▲ EXHIBIT 3   PepsiCo, Inc. and Subsidiaries Selected Financial Data (in $ millions except per share and employee amounts, unaudited)

| | Growth Rates | | | | | | | |
| | Compounded | | Annual | | | | | |
	10-Year 1981–91	5-Year 1986–91	1-Year 1990–91	1991[a]	1990	1989	1988[b]	1987
Summary of operations								
Net sales	12.8%	16.8%	10.1%	$19,607.9	$17,802.7	$15,242.4	$12,533.2	$11,018.1
Cost of sales and operating expenses				17,485.0	15,628.9	13,459.5	11,184.0	9,890.5
Interest expense				615.9	688.5	609.6	344.2	294.6
Interest income				(163.3)	(182.1)	(177.2)	(122.2)	(112.6)
				17,937.5	16,135.3	13,891.9	11,406.0	10,072.5
Income from continuing operations before income taxes	13.2	19.3	0.2	1,670.3	1,667.4	1,350.5	1,127.2	945.6
Provision for income taxes				590.1	576.8	449.1	365.0	340.5
Income from continuing operations	14.9	18.4	(0.1)	1,080.2	1,090.6	901.4	762.2	605.1
Net income	13.8	18.7	0.3	1,080.2	1,076.9	901.4	762.2	594.8
Income per share from continuing operations	15.5	18.0	(1.5)	1.35	1.37	1.13	0.97	0.77
Net income per share	14.1	18.4	—	1.35	1.35	1.13	0.97	0.76
Cash dividends declared per share	11.3	17.1	20.1	0.460	0.383	0.320	0.267	0.223
Average shares and equivalents outstanding				802.5	798.7	796.0	790	4 789.3
Cash flow data[c]								
Net cash provided by continuing operations	16.8	14.9	15.2	2,430.3	2,110.0	1,885.9	1,894.5	1,334.5
Acquisitions and investments in affiliates for cash				640.9	630.6	3,296.6	1,415.5	371.5
Purchases of property, plant, and equipment for cash	13.4	11.2	23.5	1,457.8	1,180.1	943.8	725.8	770.5
Cash dividends paid	10.5	16.4	16.8	343.2	293.9	241.9	199.0	172.0

Year-end position								
Total assets	16.8	18.5	9.5	18,775.1	17,143.4	15,126.7	11,135.3	9,022.7
Long-term debt[d]	25.5	24.3	32.3	7,806.2	5,899.6	6,076.5	2,656.0	2,579.2
Total debt[d]	20.8	22.9	6.8	8,034.4	7,526.1	6,942.8	4,107.0	3,225.1
Shareholders' equity				5,545.4	4,904.2	3,891.1	3,161.0	2,508.6
Per share	14.0	21.6	13.0	7.03	6.22	4.92	4.01	3.21
Market price per share	23.4	31.0	31.1	33.75	25.75	21.375	13.125	11.25
Shares outstanding				789.1	788.4	791.1	788.4	781.2
Employees	10.9	9.6	9.7	338,000	308,000	266,000	235,000	225,000
Statistics								
Return on average shareholders' equity[e]				20.7%	24.8%	25.6%	26.9%	26.5%
Historical cost net debt ratio[f]				47	47	51	37	35
Market net debt ratio[g]				19	22	24	20	18

All share and per share amounts reflect three-for-one stock splits in 1990 and 1986.

[a] Included $170.0 in unusual charges ($119.8 after-tax or $0.15 per share).

[b] Fiscal years 1988 and 1983 each consisted of 53 weeks. Normally, fiscal years consist of 52 weeks; however, because the fiscal years ends on the last Saturday in December, a week is added every five or six years.

[c] Cash flows from other investing and financing activities, which are not presented, are an integral part of total cash flow activity.

[d] Long-term debt includes the nonrecourse obligation. Total debt includes short-term borrowing and long-term debt.

[e] The return on average shareholders' equity is calculated using income from continuing operations.

[f] The historical cost net debt ratio represents net debt, which is total debt reduced by the nonrecourse obligation and the pro forma remittance of offshore investment portfolios, as a percent of capital employed (net debt, other liabilities and deferred credits, deferred income taxes, and shareholders' equity).

[g] The market net debt ratio represents net debt (see note f) as a percent of net debt plus the market value of equity, based on the year-end stock price.

▲ EXHIBIT 4 Results by Industry Segment

	Net Sales			Operating Profits*			Identifiable Assets		
	1991	1990	1989	1991	1990	1989	1991	1990	1989
Industry segments									
Soft drinks United States	$5,171.5	$5,034.5	$4,623.3	$ 746.2	$ 673.8	$ 577.6			
International	1,743.7	1,488.5	1,153.4	117.1	93.8	98.6			
	6,915.2	6,523.0	5,776.7	863.3	767.6	676.2	$ 6,832.6	$ 6,465.2	$ 6,198.1
Snack foods United States	3,737.9	3,471.5	3,211.3	616.6	732.3	667.8			
International	1,827.9	1,582.5	1,003.7	171.0	202.1	137.4			
	5,565.8	5,054.0	4,215.0	787.6	934.4	805.2	4,114.3	3,892.4	3,310.0
Restaurants United States	6,258.4	5,540.9	4,684.8	479.4	447.2	356.5			
International	868.5	684.8	565.9	96.2	75.2	57.8			
	7,126.9	6,225.7	5,250.7	575.6	522.4	414.3	4,254.2	3,448.9	3,070.6
Total United States	15,167.8	14,046.9	12,519.4	1,842.2	1,853.3	1,601.9			
International	4,440.1	3,755.9	2,723.0	384.3	371.1	293.8			
Total	$19,607.9	$17,802.7	$15,242.4	$2,226.5	$2,224.4	$1,895.7	$15,201.1	$13,806.5	$12,578.7
Geographic areas									
United States	$15,167.8	$14,046.9	$12,519.4	$1,842.2	$1,853.3	$1,601.9	$10,777.8	$9,980.7	$9,593.4
Europe	1,486.0	1,344.7	771.7	61.8	108.5	53.8	2,367.3	2,255.2	1,767.2
Canada and Mexico	1,434.7	1,089.2	899.0	198.7	164.2	117.1	917.3	689.5	409.5
Other	1,519.4	1,321.9	1,052.3	123.8	98.4	122.9	1,138.7	881.1	808.6
							15,201.1	13,806.5	12,578.7
Corporate assets							3,574.0	3,336.9	2,548.0
Total	$19,607.9	$17,802.7	$15,242.4	2,226.5	2,224.4	1,895.7	$18,775.1	$17,143.4	$15,126.7
Interest and other corporate expenses, net*				(566.2)	(557.0)	(545.2)			
Income from continuing operations before income taxes				$1,670.3	$1,667.4	$1,350.5			

(dollars in millions, except per share data)

*Unusual Items: Profits for the years presented included several unusual charges and credits, resulting in a 1991 total charge of $170.0 ($119.8 after-tax or $0.15 per share), a 1990 net credit of $35.2 ($4.2 charge after-tax or $0.01 per share) and a 1989 net credit of $4.4 ($1.8 after-tax). The unusual items were as follows:

Soft drinks: 1990 included $10.5 in domestic charges for receivables exposures related to highly leveraged retail customers. 1989 included a $32.5 credit resulting from a decision to retain a bottling operation in Japan previously held for sale and a $12.3 reorganization charge to decentralize international operations.

Snack foods: 1991 included $127.0 in charges consisting of a $91.4 domestic restructuring charge to streamline operations, as well as a $35.6 international restructuring charge, consisting of $23.6 to streamline operations in the United Kingdom and $12.0 to dispose of or reduce ownership in a small, unprofitable business. 1990 included $10.6 in domestic charges for receivables exposures related to highly leveraged retail customers. 1989 included a $6.6 reorganization charge to decentralize domestic operations and a $4.3 credit resulting from a decision to retain a domestic cookie production facility previously held for sale.

Restaurants: 1991 included $43.0 in charges at KFC consisting of domestic and international restructuring charges of $32.8 and $1.2, respectively, to streamline operations and a $9.0 domestic charge related to a delay in the national roll-out of the new Skinfree Crispy chicken product. 1990 included a $17.6 charge for closure of certain underperforming restaurants as follows: $9.0 at Pizza Hut, $4.0 at Taco Bell, and $4.8 ($0.6 internationally) at KFC. 1990 also included Pizza Hut charges of $8.0 to consolidate domestic field operations and $2.4 to relocate international headquarters. 1989 included reorganization charges of $8.0 at KFC and $5.5 at Taco Bell to consolidate domestic field operations.

Corporate: 1990 included a $118.2 gain from an initial public stock offering by PepsiCo's KFC joint venture in Japan, an $18.0 charge for accelerated contributions to the PepsiCo Foundation and a $15.9 charge to reduce the carrying value of a Pizza Hut International joint venture investment.

Results by Industry Segment

	Capital Spending			Depreciation and Amortization Expense		
	1991	1990	1989	1991	1990	1989
Soft drinks	$425.8	$334.1	$267.8	$393.2	$338.1	$306.3
Snack foods	406.0	381.6	257.9	253.5	232.5	189.3
Restaurants	648.4	460.6	424.6	379.6	306.5	269.9
Corporate	4.1	21.9	9.2	8.2	6.9	6.5
	$1,484.3	$1,198.2	$959.5	$1,034.5	$884.0	$772.0

Results by Restaurant Chain

	Net Sales			Operating Profits*		
	1991	1990	1989	1991	1990	1989
Pizza Hut	$3,258.3	$2,949.9	$2,453.5	$314.5	$245.9	$205.5
Taco Bell	2,038.1	1,745.5	1,465.9	180.6	149.6	109.4
KFC	1,830.5	1,530.3	1,331.3	80.5	126.9	99.4
	$7,126.9	$6,225.7	$5,250.7	$575.6	$522.4	$414.3

*Unusual items are noted above.

▲ EXHIBIT 5   Restaurant Unit and Sales Growth

Number of System Units Worldwide (year-end 1986–1991)*				
Year	Pizza Hut	Taco Bell	KFC	Total
1986	5,646	2,443	6,575	14,664
1987	6,210	2,738	7,522	16,470
1988	6,662	2,930	7,761	17,353
1989	7,502	3,125	7,948	18,575
1990	8,220	3,349	8,187	19,756
1991	8,837	3,670	8,480	20,987
Five-year compounded annual growth rate				
	9.4%	8.5%	5.2%	7.4%

*Units include kiosks and other special concepts.

Number of System Units Worldwide (year-end 1991)				
Year	Pizza Hut	Taco Bell	KFC	Total
United States				
Company	4,012	2,118	1,870	8,000
Franchise	3,252	1,498	3,186	7,936
Total	7,264	3,616	5,056	15,936
International				
Company	343	29	562	934
Joint venture	341	—	457	798
Franchise	889	25	2,405	3,319
Total	1,573	54	3,424	5,051
Total worldwide	8,837	3,670	8,480	20,987

Average U.S. System Sales Per Unit (in $ thousands)*							
	1986	1987	1988	1989	1990	1991	Five-Year% Growth[†]
PH	$468	$490	$520	$570	$607	$613	5.5
TB	560	579	589	686	771	814	7.8
KFC	529	558	597	607	650	675	5.0

*Excludes sales from kiosks and other special concepts.
[†]These are compounded annual growth rates.

Worldwide System Sales (in $ billions)							
	1986	1987	1988	1989	1990	1991	Five-Year % Growth*
Pizza Hut	$2.5	$2.9	$3.4	$4.1	$4.9	$5.3	16.2
Taco Bell	1.3	1.5	1.6	2.1	2.4	2.8	16.6
KFC	3.5	4.1	5.0	5.4	5.8	6.2	12.1
Total	$7.3	$8.5	$10.0	$11.6	$13.1	$14.3	14.4

*These are compounded annual growth rates.

PepsiCo's strategic planners believed that quick service restaurants would remain the largest segment over the following decade. They had identified several major industry trends. First, they believed that simplicity and convenience were becoming increasingly important as people worked longer hours and had less leisure time. Second, they thought that, due to economic pressures and an overall decline in consumer interest in prestige and status, consumers would look for value. Third, they identified variety as a significant trend, remarking that growth in ethnic product categories tended to reflect the increasing diversity of the U.S. population. Finally, they believed that the health and nutrition trend that had begun in the 1980s would continue as the population aged. Based on this analysis, PepsiCo thought the quick service, casual dining, and take-out segments would be attractive opportunities for investment.

Pizza Hut

Pizza Hut was founded in 1958 by Dan and Frank Carney, two college students. Their first restaurant, located in Wichita, Kansas, across from their family's grocery store, was extraordinarily successful. The company grew rapidly, went public in 1969, and became the world's largest pizza chain, in terms of both sales and units, in 1971.

PepsiCo purchased the 3,100-unit chain in 1977 for $300 million. At that time, Pizza Hut was a quick service, eat-in/carryout family-style operation, characterized by distinctive red-roofed, freestanding units. The typical restaurant was open from 11 AM to midnight and had seating for 60 to 90 customers. The average check per customer was about $5.

Facing increasing competition from regional chains, Pizza Hut experienced a sharp decline in market share in the late 1970s. Its introduction of thick crust, deep-dish pan pizza in 1980 contributed to the chain's turnaround. By 1983, pan pizza generated half of Pizza Hut's sales. That year, the chain rolled out the 6-inch Personal Pan Pizza which significantly increased its business at lunchtime, traditionally the slowest period at pizza chains.

In 1984, Pizza Hut was concerned with the rapid rise of Domino's Pizza, a $626 million chain focusing on delivery, and with a slowdown in its own eat-in business, which accounted for more than two-thirds of its sales. In response, Pizza Hut launched its own delivery business in 1985. Allan Huston, who had 14 years' experience in manufacturing and distribution in Frito Lay and Pepsi Cola, joined Pizza Hut in 1986 as general manager for delivery. In his first few years, Huston faced a number of challenges, including resistance from many franchisees who were concerned that delivery might cannibalize their eat-in business. Huston made several changes to the original concept, and, in late 1987, the delivery business reached profitability. A year later, it accounted for more than one-quarter of Pizza Hut's sales growth and half of its profit growth at the store level.

The development and roll out of delivery took place under the leadership of Steven Reinemund, who became president and CEO of Pizza Hut in 1986. The addition of delivery service was the first step toward the repositioning of Pizza Hut into pizza distribution, rather than just the pizza restaurant business. This meant expansion into nontraditional locations, such as airports, amusement parks, stadiums, and school lunchrooms—using freestanding kiosks. By early 1992, the traditional eat-in business accounted for only about one-third of Pizza Hut's U.S. sales.

In 1991, the chain considered offering two new concepts—one in quick service, the other in casual dining. In quick service, Pizza Hut planned to open a 700-square-foot double drive-through and carry-out Italian fast-food concept, called Fastino's, in Wichita. Fastino's would

▲ EXHIBIT 6   Food-Service Revenue by Channel

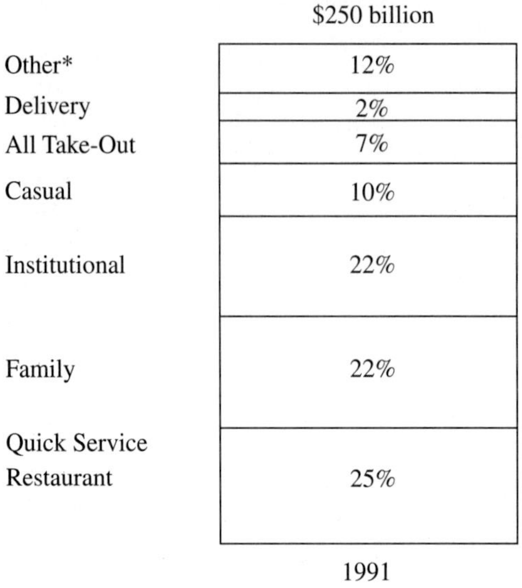

$250 billion

Other*	12%
Delivery	2%
All Take-Out	7%
Casual	10%
Institutional	22%
Family	22%
Quick Service Restaurant	25%

1991

*Other includes White Tablecloth and Hotel/Bars.

Fastino

Pizza
Hut
Cafe

offer a limited menu of pasta and pizza products, ranging in price from $.79 for a slice of pizza to $2.99 for fettucine alfredo and $3.79 for lasagna, which it promised to serve in less than 60 seconds. Pizza Hut planned to expand Fastino's quickly if it was successful in test markets.

In casual dining, Pizza Hut was planning to open Pizza Hut Cafe. To do so, Reinemund sought the help of a food-service management group in Wichita. He stated:

We looked around for a year and a half, and we realized we had a lot to learn about the mid-scale segment. We needed people to come in and break the mold of our thinking. We knew enough to know what we didn't know.[16]

The 185-seat prototype would feature contemporary decor and its menu would include pasta dishes, sandwiches served on focaccia bread, and desserts. Single entrees would be priced under $6.00 and family-sized portions would be available. Pizza Hut expected a cafe concept to generate $1.2 million in sales compared with $700,000 for a traditional unit, and it had visions of expanding such a concept to 100 U.S. markets.

Describing Pizza Hut's two new concepts, Reinemund commented:

Our competitors are doing only one thing; they're all specialists. They do either delivery or carry-out or dine-in. In order for us to succeed, we must do a number of big things well; we're a generalist.[17]

---

[16]Paul Frumkin, and Theresa Howard, "The Future of Pizza Hut: Diversification," *Nation's Restaurant News* 25, no. 45 (November 18, 1991), p. 70.
[17]Ibid., p. 70.

Taco Bell

In 1963, Glen W. Bell Jr. opened the first Taco Bell, a Mexican fast-food restaurant, in Los Angeles, California, after spending several years refining his concept. Soon, he hired Robert L. McKay to help him franchise his operation. By 1969, when Taco Bell went public, it had some 325 franchised and about a dozen company-owned restaurant. In 1970, sales were $6 million, and earnings were about $150,000.

When PepsiCo bought Taco Bell in 1978, it was the country's largest chain of quick service Mexican restaurants, selling tacos, tostadas, and burritos. The 860-unit chain was concentrated in the West and Southwest, mostly in California and Texas, and had recently entered the Midwest. PepsiCo planned to increase the number of outlets rapidly, bringing Taco Bell into the East and Northwest.

The chain did grow in size over the next few years, but sales were slumping and profits were losing steam when John Martin, former president of Burger Chef, Hardee's Food Systems, and La Petite Boulangerie, took over as CEO and president in 1983. He described Taco Bell at the time as "deficient in literally every part of how it did business,"[18] No new products had been added for 10 years, restaurants were small and had little or no seating, and employees had little training.

Martin quickly added new products—including Mexican pizza, soft-shell tacos, and fajitas—and remodeled the restaurants, introducing drive-through windows, brightening decor, and increasing seating capacity. Next, he launched a full-scale effort to turn Taco Bell from a low-tech, labor-intensive operation into a fast-food *retailer*. The change in concept involved a shift in focus—from production to customer service.

One of his first major programs to transform the chain from a food manufacturer to a food retailer was called K-minus. This program reduced the size of the average Taco Bell kitchen from 70 percent of a restaurant to only 30 percent. Purchasing prepared items, such as preshredded lettuce and precooked ground beef, from suppliers not only allowed the chain to increase seating, it allowed employees to spend more of their time interacting with customers. Similarly, an MIS project, called TACO (Total Automation of Company Operations), which networked each store to headquarters, enabled employees to focus more on service and less on paperwork.

Another of Martin's changes was to empower employees at all levels of the organization to make decisions. To support them in their new roles, the chain increased training, redesigned the food preparation process to make it more efficient, and revamped the compensation system to include more performance-based compensation.

Martin also sought to improve the chain's speed of service. An extensive analysis of customers' needs had shown that fast service was very important and that Taco Bell's standard of about 100 seconds was not sufficient. By reformulating some recipes and developing heated holding areas, the company was able to increase peak-hour transaction capacity by 54 percent, while decreasing customer waiting time to 30 seconds.

These changes helped the chain grow steadily, adding about 250 units per year between 1983 and 1988. Despite the growth in units, average sales per unit, the industry barometer of performance, were flat. In an attempt to boost unit sales, Martin tested a "value menu" program throughout the chain in late 1988, slashing prices for a range of basic items. In the first year of the program, the number of customer transactions increased 35 percent and per store sales and profits jumped considerably. By 1991, most Taco Bell units had a three-tier

---

[18]Mary Ann Galante, "Taco Bell: A Ringing Success," *Los Angeles Times,* November 5, 1989, sec. D, Nexis, p. 4.

value menu with items priced at 59¢, 79¢, and 99¢, and the $2.4 billion, 3,300-unit chain was widely heralded as the discount leader in the fast-food industry. That year, Wayne Calloway, described Martin as having achieved "oracle status" at PepsiCo.[19]

In the early 1990s, Martin pursued several areas of growth for Taco Bell. Believing that quick service restaurants, including Taco Bell, made customers "work hard to get their products," Martin set out to reach airports, stadiums, retail stores, colleges, and other non-traditional settings with carts, kiosks, and other downsized modular units. By early 1992, the chain operated about 50 such units and was planning several more.

Franchisees were concerned that these new units would negatively impact their sales. Martin hoped that he could convince them to operate some of the new units in their markets and to view sales on a per market basis as opposed to a per store basis, as, historically, they had been doing.

In addition to increasing Taco Bell's points of distribution, Martin pursued other opportunities, stating:

> If the Taco Bell brand is powerful, why could we not be "Mexican food" period? Why couldn't there be a Taco Bell Grill? Why can't we be in the double drive-through business?…Maybe there are good reasons, but at this point, we're saying, "Why not?"[20]

The Salsa Rio Grill & Salsa Bar, a 115-seat restaurant serving Mexican and Southeastern foods, was Taco Bell's entry into the casual dining segment. Located in suburban Los Angeles, the restaurant served $1.50 char-grilled steak or chicken tacos, a $2.75 chicken and black bean burrito, $4.75 combination platters, and it featured a self-service salsa bar. After about a year, Taco Bell reconverted the grill to a standard Taco Bell, saying that there was a good chance that it would open something similar to the Salsa Rio Grill in the future, though perhaps in a different setting.

In late 1990, as a favor to an acquaintance, Martin paid a short visit to Hot 'N Now, a 77-unit, double drive-through hamburger chain. Hot 'N Now's menu featured a dozen items costing about 39¢ each, and the average transaction was $2.75. Martin was impressed by the chain's small kitchens and inexpensive fare and believed Hot 'N Now would fit well within the Taco Bell organization. Encouraged by Martin's enthusiasm and previous experience as the head of the Hardee's hamburger chain, Calloway agreed to the purchase. Once acquired, Hot 'N Now shared overhead expenses with Taco Bell. As a result, the hamburger chain's overhead fell dramatically from 11–12 percent to 1–2 percent. Martin intended to test the chain in several geographic areas beyond its Michigan home base.

KFC

Kentucky Fried Chicken was founded by Harlan Sanders (the Colonel), who created a recipe for pressure-cooked chicken made with 11 herbs and spices. He sold the chicken at his combination gas station/restaurant/motel, until the location was bypassed by a new interstate highway system in 1956. The Colonel took his recipe on the road, selling some 700 franchises in fewer than nine years and initiating the franchising trend in the fast-food industry.

---

[19]Richard Martin, "Taco Bell Rolls Out New 39-Cent Snack Menu," *Nation's Restaurant News* 25, no. 25 (June 24, 1991), p. 3.
[20]Michael Lev, "Taco Bell Finds Price of Success (59¢)," *The New York Times*, December 17, 1990, D9.

In 1964, when Colonel Sanders was in his mid-70s, he sold his company to a group of investors for $2 million, a lifetime salary, and a position in charge of quality control. Sales nearly doubled in each of the next five years to $200 million, and, in 1970 alone, the chain built almost 500 U.S. units. Under this new ownership, Kentucky Fried Chicken began to expand overseas. The white-bearded Colonel Sanders, wearing his trademark white suit and black string tie, became an international symbol of hospitality.

Heublein, Inc., a packaged goods company with strong brands, purchased the chain in 1971 for $285 million and was, itself, later acquired by tobacco company R.J. Reynolds. When PepsiCo purchased Kentucky Fried Chicken for approximately $840 million in 1986, the chain had a strong international business and was, by far, the largest chicken chain in the world. It was primarily a dinner operation selling freshly prepared fried chicken and extras, such as mashed potatoes with gravy, coleslaw, and biscuits. With this acquisition, PepsiCo's restaurant sales topped $7 billion and its number of units increased to about 14,000. In sales, PepsiCo became second to McDonald's, which had sales of about $11 billion in 1985. In number of outlets, it leapt ahead of McDonald's, which had 9,000 outlets.

John Cranor III became president and CEO of Kentucky Fried Chicken in 1989 after holding various positions in PepsiCo, such as president of Pepsi-Cola USA Fountain Beverage Division and president of PepsiCo's sporting goods manufacturer. At the suggestion of Wayne Calloway, he had learned about the restaurant business from "the ground up," starting as a team member at a Taco Bell restaurant and working in that organization for six months before joining the chicken chain.

Under Cranor's leadership, Kentucky Fried Chicken spent $42 million in restructuring its U.S. and international operations. The chain also invested $50 million in a renovation program to give units fresh paint and more lighting and $20 million in a new computer system to link a unit's cash registers with its kitchen, drive-through window, manager's office, and company headquarters.

As Cranor implemented these structural changes, he launched the chain into nontraditional locations, stating, "The days of our building 600 brand-new full-size restaurants on corner lots in suburbia are over."[21] The first new unit, a 150-square-foot kiosk selling seven items, opened in a General Motors assembly plant in Dayton, Ohio, in 1991. Kyle Craig, president of the chain's U.S. operations, explained that Kentucky Fried Chicken targeted factories with "huge populations" because its products had "tremendous blue-collar appeal."[22] The chain also targeted college campuses because students valued convenience. Cranor's goal was to build 50 more units in 1992 and 200 in 1993.

Since the small units that Cranor wanted to roll out had little space for food preparation, the company developed a portable, ventless fryer and tested several "freezer-to-fryer" products—such as Skinfree Crispy Chicken, Hot Wings, Kentucky Nuggets, and the Monterey Broil Sandwich—throughout the chain. He explained, "We're taking labor from the restaurant and pushing it back up the supply line."[23] In addition to requiring minimal preparation space, the new products were intended to appeal to a more health-conscious customer. Cranor envisioned Kentucky Fried Chicken, renamed KFC in 1990, as reaching beyond fried products to roasted and barbecued chickens and chicken sandwiches.

[21]Peter O. Keegan, "Plotting Domestic Growth through Nontraditional Units," *Nation's Restaurant News* 25, no. 45 (November 18, 1991) p. 94.

[22]"KFC Express," *FoodService Director,* June 15, 1992.

[23]Peter O. Keegan, "KFC Takes Step Back to Move Forward," *Nation's Restaurant News* 25, no. 45 (November 18, 1991), p. 102.

Franchisees, who had always prepared fresh chickens at their units, were reluctant to switch to frozen products. As one franchisee stated, "We don't save enough labor [with a frozen product] to compensate for the extra costs of freight, and processing and freezing it somewhere else."[24] Under pressure from franchisees, the chain canceled the rollout of Skinfree Crispy in 1991 pending formulation of a product with better profit margins. At the same time, it purchased several franchises, including all the restaurants of two of its three largest U.S. franchisees.

Franchisees were also concerned that KFC's increase in points of distribution might negatively impact the traditional business. Under the contracts in place before 1989, KFC franchisees had a 1 1/2 mile protective radius around each restaurant, within which no other KFC unit could locate. In 1989, the company rewrote the contract for those units coming up for renewal. The new contract replaced territorial exclusivity with site-specific arrangements, like those of many other large chains, such as Taco Bell and McDonald's. In 1992, about a quarter of KFC's franchise contracts were site-specific.

▲ COORDINATION ACROSS THE RESTAURANTS

Consistent with PepsiCo's decentralized structure and the emphasis the firm placed on entrepreneurial management, Pizza Hut, Taco Bell, and KFC each operated with a great deal of autonomy. One restaurant CEO remarked, "Calloway really wants to know just three basic pieces of information from us: (1) when we change the top people in our business, (2) when we change our strategy, and (3) what our capital expenditures are."

Very few activities were shared across the chains, and, in most regards, the restaurants operated as stand-alone businesses. One executive said:

> Synergy is a dirty word here. It's a cultural thing at Pepsi that you do it on your own....[But] there is a shared sense of loyalty across the divisions. For example, it is very unlikely that you would find a PepsiCo restaurant pouring another brand of soft drink. It's not a written rule, but how things are done.

Although Calloway structured the restaurant organizations so that "each CEO would wake up in the morning thinking about only one concept," he encouraged the CEOs of the various chains to share their ideas. One restaurant CEO described his relationship with his counterparts at other PepsiCo restaurants as follows:

> Each of us is personally responsible for his business, but we try to take an open view. Of course, we don't give away our trade secrets. Our goal is to try to help each other without hurting ourselves.

Since executives in high- and middle-level management often had recent experience in more than one of PepsiCo's restaurant chains, formal inquiries and exchange of ideas were often unnecessary.

PepsiCo Food Systems

In 1981, PepsiCo created a distribution and supply unit called PepsiCo Food Systems (PFS). Some PepsiCo executives thought PFS would give the restaurants a competitive edge by reducing their supply costs. Others were concerned that coordinating supply and

---

[24]Anna Bell, "The Honeymoon That Never Was," *Restaurant Business,* March 20, 1992, p. 90.

distribution might interfere with the autonomous management style that was so treasured within PepsiCo. Many of those opposed to the establishment of PFS believed that the annual savings would not justify the organization's existence. As one executive bluntly stated: "This kind of coordination is a good, but not a great, idea. It is like knocking over a few gas stations on the way to the bank."

PFS generated cost savings of 10 million dollars in its first year of operation, and increasingly more thereafter. Working with the Great Dane Company, PFS developed specifications for three-compartment trailers to transport dry, refrigerated, and frozen goods. The new trailers took miles out of the existing distribution system and greatly reduced the number of shipments required. By the late 1980s, a technology and data network was in place to link the restaurants with PFS. The network provided 24-hour on-line order-entry capability and inventory and purchasing systems to help restaurants control costs.

In 1991, PFS ranked as the fourth-largest food-service distributor in the United States, servicing more than 12,000 company-owned and franchised Pizza Hut, Taco Bell, and KFC restaurants. PFS president Robert Hunter estimated that this arrangement saved the restaurants between one-half and five points on their food costs, while providing customer-tailored distribution to enhance the chains' competitiveness.

[handwritten: company owned to restaurants]

In contrast to the benefits PFS gained rather swiftly in distribution, its efforts to coordinate purchasing progressed more slowly. The chains had different purchasing criteria for even the most general goods, and coordination was not assigned the same priority by all the chains. In 1987, after a year and a half and three semiannual purchasing meetings, the chains came to an agreement for some joint purchases. Describing the "toilet paper victory," Bob Hunter said: "There was the one-ply school. There was the two-ply school. And there was the 'get it done' school. Finally, the restaurant's vice president of operations said 'Do it!' We did, and we saved them $450,000."[25] Later discussions progressed more rapidly. By 1992, PFS purchased 95 percent of the restaurants' line items, but less than 20 percent of total product costs. The individual chains were reluctant to relinquish control over the purchase of their 20–30 key items. For example, KFC purchased all its own chicken.

[handwritten: chains were reluctant to relinquish control of their key items]

Cost savings notwithstanding, PFS executives found that synergy was often "easier to sell to outsiders than to company insiders." A restaurant CEO gave this view:

[handwritten: * question]

> PFS's achievements are impressive and have benefited the restaurants, but it is important to view them in context. PepsiCo is a growth company. We care about efficiency because efficiency is important for competitiveness. But our focus is on growth. Growth generates profits.

In 1980, about 3,000 KFC franchisees established Kentucky Fried Chicken National Purchasing Cooperative Inc. The Louisville-based company's 1991 sales topped $400 million. In early 1992, a Taco Bell franchisee cooperative joined with its KFC counterpart. At the time, the KFC co-op was claiming it could save restaurants up to $10,000 per year off the amount they would have paid to PFS. PFS disputed this claim and maintained that the cooperative could not match its costs or its service.

[handwritten: so, which is better KFC coop or PFS co-op?]

Pepsi Partners

Another joint effort by the restaurants was a common customer task force, known externally as Pepsi Partners. Pepsi Partners was established in 1991 to coordinate sales to large common customers. These included discount chains, like Wal-Mart, and contract feeders,

[25]Personal interview, June 10, 1993.

[handwritten margin note: how to give customers all three]

like Marriott and ARA, which operated airport and highway concessions where PepsiCo beverages and one or more of the brands were featured. The task force included the person in charge of new concepts for each of the operating divisions (e.g., Frito-Lay, Pepsi-Cola North America, Pizza Hut) and Ken Stevens from PepsiCo headquarters. The task force was felt to be reasonably, though not completely, effective in giving customers a single point of contact with PepsiCo. For example, in some instances, due to preexisting franchise contracts, the task force could not guarantee a customer that each of the three restaurants would be available for a given concession. As the demand for common sites increased, PepsiCo was looking for a more effective mechanism for serving these needs.

Broad-Based Coordination

In the process of working on other assignments within PepsiCo restaurants, some external consultants estimated that Pizza Hut, Taco Bell, and KFC could together save about $100 million annually if they coordinated purchasing more extensively and shared some very general headquarters tasks, such as data management and real estate functions. However, top managers within the restaurants and at corporate headquarters had widely varying views of the potential benefits and costs of increasing coordination.

John Martin, president and CEO of Taco Bell, thought $100 million was a conservative estimate, representing only the "low-hanging fruit." He felt that the most important benefits would come from "reaching higher in the tree" and being more aggressive in driving out duplicate costs. Within his own organization, Martin was establishing systems to treat Taco Bell and Hot 'N Now as brands under a single headquarters unit. The other restaurant CEOs were not convinced that this level of coordination would be prudent for PepsiCo's restaurants as a whole. As one corporate executive explained: "It is always easy to cite the potential cost savings. It is much more difficult to quantify the negative consequences coordination might have on a chain's competitiveness." In this regard, some restaurant managers cited the importance of preserving the ability to marshal resources on the unique challenges facing a chain, such as when Pizza Hut launched its delivery system, or when KFC altered its menu.

[handwritten margin note: Pepsico has a lot of things to consider as is]

[handwritten margin note: Should they do more coordinating?]

In discussing coordination across the restaurant chains, senior corporate executives stressed that joint activity should be initiated by divisions, not headquarters. Division presidents should have the prerogative to decide whether or not a given division would participate in any specific joint activity. As one explained, "Let them sort it out. Eventually, they will. It will make sense. They will get to the right decisions."

▲ DEVELOPMENTS IN THE EARLY 1990s

Carts of Colorado

We are not in the restaurant business. We are in the business of feeding people, and we don't need buildings to do that.[26]

[handwritten margin note: CEO Taco Bell]

John Martin, president and CEO, Taco Bell

In early 1991, John Martin became interested in purchasing Carts of Colorado (COC), a Denver designer, manufacturer, and merchandiser of mobile food carts and kiosks with about $7 million in sales and 100 employees. COC's carts were self-contained units with

---

[26]Jeffrey Leib, *The Denver Post*, February 21, 1992, sec. C, p. 1.

built-in plumbing and electrical systems (Exhibit 7). Basic carts sold for as little as $1,200, and an elaborate cart that could handle a variety of hot and cold foods sold for $65,000 and more.

With a customer list that included Burger King, Coca-Cola Company, Dunkin' Donuts, and Mrs. Fields, COC was one of the fastest-growing private companies in the United States (Exhibit 7). Although carts and kiosks cost only a small fraction of what it would cost to build a restaurant, some generated as much revenue as a typical restaurant. COC's founders, Stan and Dan Gallery, estimated that the 20,000 units they had sold since 1984 were generating about $2 billion in food-service sales annually, with some units having annual sales as high as $1.2 million.

PepsiCo accounted for about 20 percent of COC's 1990 sales. Believing that buying COC would allow PepsiCo to expand its restaurant businesses dramatically, Martin called Wayne Calloway to discuss the idea.

COC's History

I believe business is about location. In the businesses we serve, location is one of the keys to driving sales volume. Our carts and kiosks are able to leverage effectively some powerful trademarks in [many] locations [that were previously unreachable].[27]

Stanley Gallery

Carts of Colorado had its beginning in a business set up by two brothers, Stanley and Daniel Gallery, from Denver, Colorado. Having gained experience in their mother's restaurant, the brothers decided to try their hand in the food-cart business. In 1980, with a credit card cash advance, Stan and Dan set out for New York City where they purchased two carts, each for $1,800.

Calling their business Chicago-Style Sandwiches, the brothers placed a cart near the construction site where Dan had previously worked pouring concrete. With the brand names of their sandwiches placed prominently on their cart, the Gallerys were soon making more money selling Vienna hot dogs and buns, Chicago-style Italian sausages, and beef sandwiches than they had ever made at the family restaurant. Sales for the first cart averaged $400–500 per hour, and the Gallerys quickly set up a second cart.

Encouraged by their early success, Stan and Dan made the minimum payment on their credit cards, brought their sister Debbie into the business, hired a few employees, and bought more carts. By 1984, Chicago-Style Sandwiches had more than 20 carts, and sales were about $3 million. Unfortunately for the Gallerys, local restaurants and an organization for local businesses were concerned that the block-long lines at some of the food carts were hurting their business. Suddenly, their business was "under a microscope": The city of Denver investigated their location permits and the Denver Health Department and the State of Colorado examined their health permits. However, it was not until the Federal Food & Drug Administration (FDA) initiated legal action against them that their operation was in jeopardy.

Stan studied a National Sanitation Foundation (NSF) code book, given to him by the FDA inspector who was handling the case against Chicago-Style Sandwiches. It became clear to him that the carts had to be modified to meet the strict standards. However, their New York cart supplier was not willing to make the necessary changes, and the Gallerys shortly discovered that no supplier of NSF-approved carts existed. Stan developed a plan

---

[27]*PR Newswire,* February 25, 1992, Nexis, p.1.

▲ EXHIBIT 7   Carts of Colorado, Carts and Kiosks

with the owner of a local metalworking shop who agreed to manufacture new carts and modify the existing ones. At Stan's initiative, the carts had nonremovable pan lids that would prevent cross-contamination caused when contaminated lids were placed on clean ones. The new carts did more than meet the current standards: they reached a new standard, Standard 59, developed in part by Stan Gallery. Within five months, the Gallerys were operating the first NSF-approved cart, and the case against them had been dropped.

In the process of making changes to meet the regulations, the Gallerys made other improvements. For example, they redesigned the food preparation area so that the food-cart operator could move from left to right to assemble a sandwich, instead of leaning over one container to reach another. They also made the carts smaller, while increasing their food storage and cooking capacity. Sales volume increased, and Stan and Dan continued to expand their business.

▲ EXHIBIT 8 Carts of Colorado, Selected Financials

	1991	1990	1989	1988	1987	1986	1985
Sales	$7,650,000	$6,372,628	$6,557,736	$6,831,076	$4,892,345	$2,645,533	$880,989
Gross margin	3,341,052	2,502,313	2,115,937	1,875,201	1,298,264	924,514	336,200
S&M	1,415,503	1,315,465	1,048,863	1,951,575	743,525	458,121	227,558
G&A	818,089	810,181	688,425	892,812	429,205	285,484	59,672
Operating income	945,187	576,667	378,649	(969,186)	125,534	180,909	48,970
Interest expense	162,273	95,018	121,114	(183,632)	24,318	26,640	8,490
Income before taxes	695,187	281,649	257,535	(1,152,818)	101,216	154,269	40,480
Income after taxes	695,187	282,149	292,035	(1,065,386)	71,826	154,269	37,096

Source: PepsiCo.

higher profit margin

In 1984, the Gallery brothers established Carts of Colorado to manufacture carts.[28] They sold their first cart, which had cost $700 to build, to a man from California for $5,200. Yet, what proved to be more important than the money they made from this sale was the exposure the Gallerys received. Coca-Cola and Disney inquired about buying carts and, soon, Dan set up deals with both companies.

With COC's sales approaching $5 million in 1987, the Gallerys sold 30 percent of their business to a venture capital firm for $1.3 million in the hope that sales would continue to climb. Stan became vice president of development and engineering, Dan became vice president of marketing. A professional management team stepped in to lead the company. The goal was to double sales within a year to reach $10 million.

Although sales did increase, after a few months, Stan became wary of how the business was being run. The new management team was not able to prevent the majority of COC's distributors from charging unreasonable markups on carts and, in Stan's opinion, was overspending in marketing. Concerned about the company's financial health, Stan hired an outside auditor, who, to everyone's astonishment, estimated COC's midyear loss at $350,000. COC was technically bankrupt, owing $1.25 million to a local savings and loan.

Fortunately for the Gallerys, their savings and loan was taken over by the federal government, which was more concerned with large real estate loans and ignored their relatively small loan. The Gallerys forced COC's new management team out, terminated COC's relationships with distributors, and returned the business to profitability in 60 days. Orders from companies like Pizza Hut kept COC in business in 1989 and focused its interest on restaurant brands.

As their business strengthened, the Gallerys began "pumping money into cart technology." They planned the next generation of carts, "smartcarts," which would be equipped with computers and radio telecommunications, allowing food and beverage vendors to manage sales and inventory from a central location. Also, they purchased their largest competitor, which had sales of $2.5 million, for $65,000 in 1990.

At a meeting in August of 1991, presidents of PepsiCo's divisions along with Ken Stevens and PepsiCo CFO Robert Dettmer discussed the possibility of acquiring or forming a strategic alliance with Carts of Colorado. They believed that COC was not the lowest-cost cart and kiosk manufacturer, but thought it was 18 months ahead of its competitors in terms of engineering and design. Issues raised included whether the existing relationship was sufficient, what COC would bring to PepsiCo, and how a different relationship might be structured.

California Pizza Kitchen

In early 1992, Ken Stevens identified California Pizza Kitchen (CPK), a restaurant chain in the casual dining segment, as a potential PepsiCo acquisition (Exhibit 8). The California-based chain operated 25 restaurants in eight states and was best known for its individual-sized pizza shells topped with offbeat, affordable delicacies, such as barbecued chicken, shrimp with pesto, and rosemary chicken and potatoes (Exhibit 9). This innovative "pizza" accounted for 40 percent of sales, while pasta accounted for 20 percent, salads for 20 percent, and beverages and desserts for the remainder. CPK had about 1,700 employees and annual sales of about $34 million.

---

[28]Their sister Debbie took over the business of managing the vendors who operated existing carts. That business was sold in 1990.

CPK restaurants were typically located in affluent, urban and suburban shopping and entertainment areas and targeted "young, upscale singles and couples, families, and elderly retired people seeking a moderately priced, yet comparable quality, alternative to fine dining restaurants." All menu items cost less than $10, and the average check per person was about $8.50 for lunch and $11 for dinner. Table turnover was nearly double that of the typical casual dining restaurant.

high table turnover

CPK's History

We're not looking for the new food, we're looking for the food you already love and then translating it into pizza.
Larry Flax and Rick Rosenfield, co-founders, CPK

California Pizza Kitchen (CPK) was started by Larry Flax and Rick Rosenfield, two California attorneys. Flax and Rosenfield had met in the early 1970s when they were assistant U.S. attorneys for the Department of Justice. Subsequently, they had run their own law practice, specializing in criminal defense, for 13 years. Weary of their work defending union officials and mob bosses and sharing a passion for cooking, the two set out to open their own restaurant.

The attorneys-turned-restaurateurs were fans of "California pizza"—pizza with exotic toppings, such as goat cheese and duck sausage—which had been popularized by Chef Wolfgang Puck of West Hollywood's trendy Spago restaurant. Flax and Rosenfield intended to create a "Spago for the masses." They leased an 1,800-square-foot space, hired a former Spago chefs as a consultant, borrowed $200,000 in unsecured personal loans, raised $300,000 from friends and associates, and opened their first California Pizza Kitchen in posh Beverly Hills in 1985.

The restaurant was an instant success. However, it was not the Spago-like toppings that were bringing in the crowds, but the new, equally creative, yet less exotic toppings, such as barbecued chicken with sliced red onions. When the consultant from Spago's resisted the move away from duck sausage and other exotic ingredients toward pizza that people "could taste when they saw it on the menu," Flax and Rosenfield fired him and went into the kitchen themselves. They figured, "If it's something that we like, other college-educated people will like it, too."

Sales topped $2 million in 1986, and Flax and Rosenfield opened two more CPKs in Southern California that year. Believing that all upscale neighborhoods had a need for a CPK, they expanded into Atlanta, Georgia, the following year. Initially, they had some difficulty managing the far-away restaurant, but they felt its success was critical to the development of a national chain. After they added management, the location soon turned profitable.

Expansion continued at a brisk pace, with Flax and Rosenfield selecting cities based on their potential to support more than one CPK. by the end of 1990, they had added restaurants in Honolulu (Hawaii), suburban Washington, D.C., Chicago (Illinois), and Las Vegas (Nevada). California, however, remained the company's biggest market, accounting for more than half of the restaurants. "It's tough to beat California as a market," commented Rosenfield. "There's not seasonality here. No snow, no rain. People go out all year round."[29]

Rosenfield attended to the numbers and details, while Flax took responsibility for human relations. However, both loved to cook. After their disagreement with the consultant from Spago, they did most of their own product development. They decided that, instead of hiring chefs, they would hire cooks "who [thought] the highest art form [was]

---

[29]"California Pizza Kitchen, Inc.: Taking Back a Piece of the Pie," *California Business,* November 1990, p. 16.

▲ EXHIBIT 9   California Pizza Kitchen, Inc. and Subsidiaries, Consolidated
Statements of Operations, Fiscal Years Ended June 30, 1991, and
July 1, 1990 (in $ thousands)

	1991	1990
Revenues		
Sales	$33,638	$21,696
Management and license fees	414	183
	34,052	21,879
Costs and expenses		
Cost of sales	17,920	11,379
Operating expenses	8,343	4,993
Depreciation and amortization	1,900	1,132
General and administrative expenses	4,822	3,574
Equity in loss of limited partnerships		
and joint ventures, net	4	154
	32,989	21,232
Operating income	1,063	647
Interest expense, net	260	102
Income before income taxes and		
extraordinary item	803	545
Income taxes	318	279
Income before extraordinary item	485	266
Extraordinary item	226	236
Net income	$ 711	$ 502

Source: PepsiCo.

repetition of what they [had done] before"[30] One of their favorite creations, and a top
seller, was the B.L.T. (bacon, lettuce, and tomato) pizza. It consisted of a crispy shell,
baked with Hormel bacon and tomatoes and topped with lettuce and mayonnaise before
being served. Flax and Rosenfield tested recipes on friends and employees before trying
them in a couple of units and then launching them chainwide. As they added new menu
items, they removed slow sellers.

Over time, the menu expanded to include such foods as white corn tortilla soup and oriental chicken salad with crunchy angel hair pasta. The selection of pizza toppings also
grew. Tuna melt, shrimp-pesto, and thai chicken were just a few of the many additions.
The pizza toppings were so atypical that many customers did not consider CPK to be a
pizza restaurant. A PepsiCo executive concurred, stating, "CPK doesn't sell pizza. It sells
California."

---

[30]"Doing It the American Way: A True Melting Pot," *Nation's Restaurant News* 24, no. 48 (December 3, 1990), p. 11.

SOUP & SALAD

Sedona White Corn Tortilla Soup . . . Imported vine-ripened Italian tomato base with white corn. Southwestern spices and oven-toasted blue corn tortillas. $3.95

Potato Leek Soup . . . Puree of potato and leek with a touch of cream. $3.95

Two In A Bowl . . . Our Sedona White Corn Tortilla Soup and our Potato Leek Soup served side by side in the same bowl. $3.95

Field Greens Salad . . . with an organically-grown seasonal blend of more than a dozen field greens and baby lettuces in a balsamic blend vinaigrette. . . . . $7.50 Half $4.25

Shrimp Louie . . . chilled Canadian Bay shrimp on a bed of mixed leaves with hard-boiled egg, tomato wedges, Mediterranean olives and a tangy homemade Louie dressing, tossed on request. . . . . $8.95 Half $4.95

Mixed Leaf . . . with our Caesar dressing, garlic croutons and shaved romano cheese. . . . . $6.95 Half $3.95

Romaine & Watercress . . . with gorgonzola and walnuts in a balsamic basil vinaigrette. . . . . $6.95 Half $3.95

Chopped Salad . . . with lettuce, basil, salami and cheese in a herb-mustard vinaigrette topped with chilled roast turkey breast, diced tomatoes and sun-dried tomatoes. Chopped garbanzo added upon request . . . . . . $8.50 Half $4.50

Greek Style Salad . . . with mixed greens in a lemon-herb dressing with sweet bellpeppers, Mediterranean olives, mild goat cheese and sun-dried tomatoes. . . $7.95

Oriental Chicken Salad . . . shredded lettuce and crispy angel hair tossed with sliced grilled chicken breast, julienne carrots and scallions in a spicy sweet-and-sour sesame dressing with fresh cilantro. . . . . . . $8.50 Half $4.50

Tuna Salad . . . chilled tuna salad on red leaf lettuce with roma tomato, hard-boiled eggs and slices of chilled red potatoes in an herb-mustard vinaigrette $6.95

Combination Salad . . . consisting of our Oriental chicken salad, mixed leaf salad and tuna salad $8.95

Canadian Bay Shrimp added to any salad $3.00 Half $1.50

PIZZA

All pizzas are wood-fired with the highest quality mozzarella cheese in addition to listed cheeses.
Please specify our traditional or our new honey-wheat dough.

Traditional Cheese . . . with our special homemade tomato sauce. $5.95

Fresh Tomato . . . with fresh sliced tomatoes, garlic and basil. $7.50

B.L.T. . . . with Hormel Bacon and tomatoes, wood-fired, then topped with chilled chopped lettuce tossed with mayonnaise $7.95

The Original BBQ Chicken . . . with barbecued chicken, sliced red onion, cilantro and smoked gouda cheese. $8.95

Southwestern Burrito . . . with grilled chicken breast marinated in lime and herbs, homemade black beans, fire-roasted mild chilies, sweet white onions and cheddar cheese. Served with green tomatillo salsa and sour cream. $8.95

Rosemary Chicken-Potato . . . Chicken roasted with new potatoes, garlic, oregano, rosemary, white wine and lemon $8.95

Caribbean Shrimp . . . with Caribbean-spiced shrimp, Canadian bacon, red and yellow peppers, parmesan, green onions and our spicy Jamaican banana chutney . . $8.95

Mushroom Pepperoni Sausage . . . with mushrooms, Hormel pepperoni, sausage and homemade tomato sauce. $8.50

Vegetarian . . . with broccoli, onions, mushrooms, sun-dried tomatoes, grilled eggplant, fresh oregano and homemade tomato sauce. $8.50

Roasted Garlic Chicken . . . with roasted garlic, grilled chicken, sweet white onion, chopped Italian parsley and garlic-shallot butter $8.95

Shrimp Scampi . . . with shrimp, roasted garlic, sweet white onion, oregano, Italian parsley and a lemon-white wine garlic butter $8.95

Duck Sausage . . . with duck sausage, fresh spinach, sun-dried tomatoes and sweet roasted garlic. $8.95

Two Sausage . . . a combination of mild and spicy Italian sausages on a homemade tomato sauce with red and yellow peppers and sweet white onions (jalapeno peppers added upon request) $8.50

Cajun . . . with Andouille sausage, 3-color peppers, red onion and a spicy Cajun sauce. $8.95

Thai Chicken . . . with pieces of chicken breast marinated in a spicy peanut-ginger and sesame sauce, green onions, bean sprouts, julienned carrots, cilantro and roasted peanuts $8.95

Peking Duck . . . with Peking-style duck breast, wonton fettuccine, seasonal mushrooms, slivered green onions and Hoisin sauce. $8.95

Tandoori Chicken . . . pieces of Tandoori chicken breast (marinated in Indian spices) with zucchini, cilantro and a spicy tomato yogurt curry (try it cheeseless, if you prefer). Mango Chutney served on the side $8.95

Hawaiian . . . with pineapple, Hormel Bacon or Canadian bacon, and homemade tomato sauce $7.95

Grilled Teriyaki Chicken . . . with grilled chicken marinated in an orange teriyaki sauce, red onions, scallions, and sweet peppers $8.95

Shrimp-Pesto . . . with shrimp, fresh tomatoes, Mediterranean olives, sun-dried tomatoes and homemade pesto sauce. $8.95

Goat Cheese . . . with Hormel Bacon, red onions, 3-color peppers, fresh tomatoes and mild goat cheese. $8.95

Mixed Grill Vegetarian . . . mixed grilled vegetables (including zucchini, red onion, red and yellow peppers, and eggplant) with smoked mozzarella and grilled roma tomato sauce $8.95

Five Cheese & Tomato . . . fresh sliced tomatoes, basil leaves, buffalo mozzarella, fontina, smoked gouda, and romano cheeses $8.50

Santa Fe Chicken . . . with pieces of grilled chicken breast marinated in lime and herbs, sauteed onions, and cilantro. Topped with fresh tomato salsa, sour cream and homemade guacamole $8.95

Tuna Melt . . . Our own tuna salad topped with sliced roma tomatoes, sweet white onions and aged cheddar cheese $6.95

Artichoke, Olive & Caper . . . Baby artichoke hearts, Mediterranean olives and capers with our homemade tomato sauce and Italian parsley $8.50
With anchovies $9.50

PASTA

All our pastas are made daily by CPK

Tomato-Herb . . . Spaghetti, Angel Hair or Penne in a fresh herb tomato sauce. $5.95

Bolognese . . . Spaghetti, Linguini or Penne with Bolognese (meat) sauce and grated parmesan. $6.95

Tomato-Basil . . . Spaghetti, Angel Hair or Penne with fresh tomatoes, basil and garlic. $7.95
With mild goat cheese added $8.95

Italian Salsa . . . Spaghetti, Angel Hair or Penne tossed with an Italian Salsa composed of fresh diced Roma tomatoes, basil and garlic $7.95
Primavera (A medley of garden vegetables added) $8.95

Mediterranean . . . Spaghetti, Angel Hair or Penne with diced roma tomatoes, garlic, Mediterranean olives, capers, red wine and fresh Italian herbs $7.95

Carbonara . . . Spaghetti, Angel Hair or Penne with diced bacon, petite peas, cracked black pepper and parmesan cream sauce $8.50

Ginger Black Bean Sauce . . . Angel Hair or Spaghetti with shrimp or chicken, broccoli, and scallions in an Oriental garlic-ginger black bean sauce . . $9.50

Chicken-Tequila . . . Spinach fettuccine with chicken, 3-color peppers, red onion, and fresh cilantro, in a tequila-lime and jalapeno pepper light cream sauce . $8.95

Garlic Cream . . . Fettuccine in a mild garlic cream sauce with grated parmesan and Italian parsley $7.95
With mushrooms added $8.50

Vegetable Marsala-Marinara . . . Spaghetti or Penne in a fresh herb tomato and marsala wine sauce with fresh garden vegetables, parmesan cheese $8.95

Broccoli/Sun-Dried Tomato . . . Fusilli (corkscrew), ... or Spaghetti with fresh broccoli, browned garlic, sun-dried tomatoes, olive oil . . . thyme and parmesan cheese $7.95
With fresh tomatoes added $8.95

Thai Chicken . . . Linguini with pieces of chicken breast, julienned carrots, green onion, cilantro and roasted peanuts in a spicy Thai peanut-ginger sauce topped with fresh bean sprouts. $8.95

Garlic Cream with Chicken or Shrimp . . . Linguini with shrimp or chicken and Italian parsley in a mild garlic parmesan cream sauce. $9.50

Marsala-Marinara with Chicken or Shrimp . . . Linguini with shrimp or chicken, mushrooms, fresh basil and Marsala wine, in our homemade marinara sauce with parmesan cheese $9.50

Grilled Sausage and Pepper . . . Penne or . . . . with slices of grilled spicy sweet Italian sausage, sauteed mild white onion, red and yellow peppers, and parmesan cheese in our homemade tomato herb sauce $9.50

GRILLED ITEMS

We suggest grilled items as an accompaniment to pasta or salad

Grilled Breast of Chicken . . . Boneless breast of chicken marinated in herbs and white wine. $5.50

Grilled Italian Sausage . . . your choice of mild Sicilian or spicy sweet, or a combination of the two. $4.50

▲ 595

Flax and Rosenfield wanted customers to have a "white-cloth" dining experience and developed an extensive training program to ensure a high level of service. When a new restaurant opened, its entire staff underwent two weeks of training where they were "taught an attitude" and "educated in human behavior." This initial training was followed by frequent refresher courses.

The chain offered job security and promoted employees at all levels of the organization. For example, dishwashers became pizza cooks, pizza cooks became pasta cooks, servers became server trainers, and food servers became assistant restaurant managers. Many of the company's top people had been promoted from within the organization. For example, CPK's first waitress became the vice president of training, and a former waiter and cook became a vice president of operations.

Restaurants ranged from 1,800 to 4,000 square feet and had from 70 to 200 seats. A typical unit cost $1 million to $2 million to launch and took about eight months to open from the signing of the lease. Decor was stylish and contemporary—black and yellow signs, black formica tables, white-tiled floors, and indoor palm trees. The center of each restaurant featured a large display cooking area with an imported Italian wood-burning stove that cooked pizzas in three minutes.

CPK limited its advertising to store openings, but it received an avalanche of free press because of its distinctive menu, its fast-paced growth, and the unusual backgrounds of its co-founders. The owners believed they had a loyal customer base and that many new customers had been referred to CPK by friends.

Most of CPK's 25 restaurants in early 1992 were company owned, but 4 were joint ventures or franchises: 2 locations in Chicago were operated by a limited partnership, co-owned by Rick's brother, Neal Rosenfield; and the 2 in Las Vegas were franchised. Flax and Rosenfield had been hesitant to franchise the concept, but believed that having two restaurants in the luxurious Mirage and Golden Nugget hotels would give CPK both national and international exposure. In its first year, the 4,000-square-foot Mirage unit had sales of $5.5 million, compared to $3 million for a typical unit.

In early 1992, when PepsiCo became interested in CPK, the owners were on the verge of taking their company public. Capital constraints had been limiting their ability to expand the chain, and they hoped to raise $30 million in a public stock offering. Flax and Rosenfield wanted to remain as managers; as Flax stated, "It would kill me to sell now for $100 million and sit on the sidelines and watch somebody else either destroy it or do great with it."[31] The owners had chosen underwriters and were putting the final touches on their proposed public offering when PepsiCo contacted them. Although they were ready to take their company public, Flax and Rosenfield wanted to hear what PepsiCo had in mind.

this will take a lot of convincing

How will CPK compete w/ Pizza Hut Cafe Fastino & Salsa Rio Grill concepts?

what does PepsiCo bring to these?

what about experience w/ La Petit?

---

[31]Michael Barrier, "Designer Pizza at Off-the-Rack Prices," *Nation's Business,* March 1991, p. 14.

CODMAN & SHURTLEFF, INC.:
PLANNING AND CONTROL SYSTEM

"This revision combines our results from January to April with the preliminary estimates supplied by each department for the remainder of the year. Of course, there are still a lot of unknown factors to weigh in, but this will give you some idea of our preliminary updated forecast."

As the board members reviewed the document provided to them by Gus Fleites, vice president of Information and Control at Codman & Shurtleff, Roy Black, president, addressed the six men sitting at the conference table: "This revised forecast leaves us with a big stretch. We are almost two million dollars short of our profit objective for the year. As we discussed last week, we are estimating sales to be $1.1 million above original forecast. This is due in part to the early introduction of the new Chest Drainage Unit. However, three major factors that we didn't foresee last September will affect our profit plan estimates for the remainder of the year.

First, there's the currency issue: our hedging has partially protected us, but the continued rapid deterioration of the dollar has pushed our costs up on European specialty instruments. Although this has improved Codman's competitive market position in Europe, those profits accrue to the European company and are not reflected in this forecast. Second, we have an unfavorable mix variance; and finally, we will have to absorb inventory variances due to higher than anticipated start-up costs of our recently combined manufacturing operations.

"When do we have to take the figures to Corporate?" asked Chuck Dunn, vice president of Business Development.

Professor Robert Simons prepared this case.

"Wednesday of next week," replied Black, "so we have to settle this by Monday. That gives us only tomorrow and the weekend to wrap up the June budget revision. I know that each of you has worked on these estimates, but I think that the next look will be critical to achieving our profit objective."

"Bob, do you have anything you can give us?"

Bob Dick, vice president of Marketing, shook his head, "I've been working with my people looking at price and mix. At the moment, we can't realistically get more price. Most of the mix variance for the balance of the year will be due to increased sales of products that we are handling under the new distribution agreement. The mix for the remainder of the year may change, but with 2,700 active products in the catalogue, I don't want to move too far from our original projections. My expenses are cut right to the bone. Further cuts will mean letting staff go."

Black nodded his head in agreement. "Chuck, you and I should meet to review our Research and Development priorities. I know that Herb Stolzer will want to spend time reviewing the status of our programs. I think we should be sure that we have cut back to reflect our spending to date. I wouldn't be surprised if we could find another $400,000 without jeopardizing our long-term programs."

"Well it seems our work is cut out for us. The rest of you keep working on this. Excluding R&D, we need at least another $500,000 before we start drawing down our contingency fund. Let's meet here tomorrow at two o'clock and see where we stand."

▲ CODMAN & SHURTLEFF, INC.

Codman & Shurtleff, Inc., a subsidiary of Johnson & Johnson, was established in 1838 in Boston by Thomas Codman to design and fashion surgical instruments. The company developed surgical instrument kits for use in Army field hospitals during the Civil War and issued its first catalogue in 1860. After the turn of the century, Codman & Shurtleff specialized in working with orthopaedic surgeons and with pioneers in the field of neurosurgery.

In 1986, Codman & Shurtleff supplied hospitals and surgeons worldwide with over 2,700 products for surgery, including instruments, equipment, implants, surgical disposables, fiber-optic light sources and cables, surgical head lamps, surgical microscopes, coagulators, and electronic pain control simulators and electrodes. These products involved advanced technologies from the fields of metallurgy, electronics, and optics.

Codman & Shurtleff operated three manufacturing locations in Randolph, New Bedford, and Southbridge, Massachusetts, and a distribution facility in Avon, Massachusetts. The company employed 800 people in the United States.

In 1964, Codman & Shurtleff was acquired by Johnson & Johnson, Inc., as an addition to its professional products business. Johnson & Johnson operated manufacturing subsidiaries in 46 countries, sold its products in most countries of the world, and employed 75,000 people worldwide. 1985 sales were $6.4 billion with before tax profits of $900 million (Exhibit 1).

Roy Black had been president of Codman & Shurtleff since 1983. In his 25 years with Johnson & Johnson, Black had spent 18 years with Codman, primarily in the Marketing Department. He had also worked at Ethicon and Surgikos. He described his job:

> This is a tough business to manage because it is so complex. We rely heavily on the neurosurgeons for ideas in product generation and for the testing and ultimate acceptance of our products. We have to stay in close contact with the leading neurosurgeons around the world. For example, last week I returned from a tour of the Pacific rim. During the trip, I visited eight Johnson & Johnson/Codman affiliates and 25 neurosurgeons.

Johnson & Johnson and Subsidiaries, Consolidated Statement of
Earnings and Retained Earnings

Dollars in Millions, Except per Share Figures(Note 1)	1985	1984	1983
Revenues			
Sales to customers	$6,421.3	$6,124.5	$5,972.9
Other revenues			
Interest income	107.3	84.5	82.9
Royalties and miscellaneous	48.1	38.0	49.4
Total revenues	$6,576.7	$6,247.0	$6,105.2
Costs and expenses			
Cost of products sold	$2,594.2	$2,469.4	$2,471.8
Selling, distribution, and administrative expenses	2,516.0	2,488.4	2,352.9
Research expense	471.1	421.2	405.1
Interest expense	74.8	86.1	88.3
Interest expense capitalized	(28.9)	(35.0)	(36.9)
Other expenses including nonrecurring charges (Note 2)	50.3	61.8	99.9
Total costs and expenses	$5,677.5	$5,491.9	$5,381.1
Earnings before provision for taxes on income	$ 899.2	$ 755.1	$ 724.1
Provision for taxes on income (Note 8)	285.5	240.6	235.1
Net earnings	$ 613.7	$ 514.5	$ 489.0
Retained earnings at beginning of period	$3,119.1	$2,814.5	$2,540.1
Cash dividends paid (per share: 1985, $2.175; 1984, $1.175; 1983, $1.075)	(233.2)	(219.9)	(204.6)
Retained earnings at end of period	$3,449.6	$3,119.1	$2,824.5
Net earnings per share	$ 3.36	$ 2.75	$ 2.57

Segments of Business (dollars in millions)				Percent Increase (decrease)	
	1985	1984	1983	1985 vs. 1984	1984 vs. 1983
Sales to customers (2)					
Consumer					
Domestic	$1,656.0	$1,588.3	$1,502.5	4.3%	5.7%
International	1,118.5	1,161.4	1,185.3	(3.7)	(2.0)
Total	$2,774.5	$1,749.7	$2,687.8	.9%	2.3%
Professional					
Domestic	$1,553.9	1,429.3	1,465.5	8.7	(2.5)
International	653.1	626.1	620.3	4.3	.9
Total	$2,207.0	$2,055.4	$2,085.8	7.4	(1.5)

continued

▲ EXHIBIT 1   *concluded*

Dollars in Millions, Except per Share Figures(Note 1)	1985	1984	1983	1985 vs. 1984	1984 vs. 1983
Pharmaceutical					
Domestic	$ 780.0	$ 718.3	$ 642.5	8.6	11.8
International	659.8	601.1	556.8	9.8	8.0
Total	$1,439.8	$1,319.4	$1,199.3	9.1	10.0
Worldwide total	$6,421.3	$6,124.5	$5,972.9	4.8%	2.5%
Operating profit					
Consumer	$ 408.7	$ 323.4	$ 422.7	26.4%	(23.5)%
Professional	149.2	118.7	120.0	25.7	(1.1)
Pharmaceutical	461.1	440.4	358.4	4.7	22.9
Segments total	$1,019.0	$ 882.5	$ 901.1	15.5	(2.1)
Expense not allocated to segments (3)	(119.8)	(127.4)	(177.0)		
Earnings before taxes on income	$ 889.2	$ 755.1	$ 724.1	19.1%	4.3%
Identifiable assets at year-end					
Consumer	$1,616.2	$1,560.1	$1,535.9	3.6%	1.6%
Professional	1,876.1	1,717.6	1,673.5	9.2	2.6
Pharmaceutical	1,343.8	1,024.3	996.2	31.2	2.8
Segments total	$4,836.1	$4,302.0	$4,205.6	12.4	2.3
General corporate	259.0	239.4	255.9		
Worldwide total	$5,095.1	$4,541.4	$4,461.5	12.2%	1.8%

At the same time, we are forced to push technological innovation to reduce costs. This is a matter of survival. In the past, we concentrated on producing superior quality goods, and the market was willing to pay whatever it took to get the best. But the environment has changed; the shift has been massive. We are trying to adapt to a situation where doctors and hospitals are under severe pressure to be more efficient and cost-effective.

We compete in 12 major product groups. Since our markets are so competitive, the business is very price sensitive. The only way we can take price is to offer unique products with cost-in-use benefits to the professional user.

Since the introduction of DRG costing[1] by hospitals in 1983, industry volume has been off approximately 20 percent. We have condensed 14 locations to 4 and have reduced staff levels by over 20 percent. There have also been some cuts in R&D, although our goal is to maintain research spending at near double the historical Codman level.

---

[1]On October 1, 1983, Medicare reimbursement to hospitals changed from a cost-plus system to a fixed-rate system as called for in the 1983 Social Security refinancing legislation. The new system was called "prospective payment" because rates were set in advance of treatment according to which of 467 "diagnostic-related groups" (or DRGs) a patient was deemed to fall into. This change in reimbursement philosophy caused major cost-control problems for the nation's 5,800 acute-care hospitals, which received an average of 36 percent of their revenues from Medicare and Medicaid.

Chuck Dunn, vice president of Business Development, had moved three years earlier from Johnson & Johnson Products to join Codman as vice president for Information and Control. During his 24 years with Johnson & Johnson, he had worked with four different marketing divisions as well as the Corporate office. He recalled the process of establishing a new mission statement at Codman,

> When I arrived here, Codman was in the process of defining a more clearly focused mission. Our mission was product oriented, but Johnson & Johnson was oriented by medical specialty. On a matrix, this resulted in missed product opportunities as well as turf problems with other Johnson & Johnson companies.
>
> It took several years of hard work to arrive at a new worldwide mission statement oriented to medical specialty, but this process was very useful in obtaining group consensus. Our worldwide mission is now defined in terms of a primary focus in the neuro-spinal surgery business. This turns out to be a large market and allows better positioning of our products.
>
> In addition to clarifying our planning, we use the mission statement as a screening device. We look carefully at any new R&D project to see if it fits our mission. The same is true for acquisitions.

▲ REPORTING RELATIONSHIPS AT JOHNSON & JOHNSON

In 1985, Johnson & Johnson comprised 155 autonomous susdiaries operating in three health care markets: consumer products, pharmaceutical products, and professional products. Exhibit 2 provides details of the business operations of the company.

Johnson & Johnson was managed on a decentralized basis as described in the following excerpt from the 1985 Annual Report,

> The Company is organized on the principles of decentralized management and conducts its business through operating subsidiaries which are themselves, for the most part, integral, autonomous operations. Direct responsibility for each company lies with its operating management, headed by the president, general manager or managing director who reports directly or through a Company group chairman to a member of the Executive Committee. In line with this policy of decentralization, each internal subsidiary is, with some exceptions, managed by citizens of the country where it is located.

Roy Black at Codman and Shurtleff reported directly to Herbert Stolzer at Johnson & Johnson headquarters in New Brunswick, New Jersey. Mr. Stolzer, 59, was a member of the executive committee of Johnson & Johnson with responsibility for 16 operating companies in addition to Codman and Shurtleff (Exhibit 3). Stolzer had worked for Johnson & Johnson for 35 years with engineering, manufacturing, and senior management experience in Johnson & Johnson Products and at the corporate office.

The senior policy and decision-making group at Johnson & Johnson was the executive committee comprising the chairman, president, chief financial officer, vice president of administration, and eight executive committee members with responsibilities for company sectors. The 155 business units of the company were organized in sectors based primarily on products (e.g., consumer, pharmaceutical, professional) and secondarily on geographic markets.

▲ FIVE- AND TEN-YEAR PLANS AT JOHNSON & JOHNSON

Each operating company within Johnson & Johnson was responsible for preparing its own plans and strategies. David Clare, president of Johnson & Johnson, believed that this was one of the key elements in their success. "Our success is due to three basic tenets: a basic

▲ EXHIBIT 2 Johnson & Johnson Business Operations

Chicopee—Chicopee develops and manufactures products for use by other Johnson & Johnson affiliates, in addition to a wide variety of fabrics that are sold to a broad range of commercial and industrial customers. Chicopee's consumer products include disposable diapers for the private-label market segment.

Codman—Codman & Shurtleff, Inc., supplies hospitals and surgeons worldwide with a broad line of products including instruments, equipment, implants, surgical disposables, fiber-optic light sources and cables, surgical head lamps, surgical microscopes, and electronic pain control stimulators and electrodes.

Critikon—Critikon, Inc., provides products used in the operating room and other critical care areas of the hospital. Intravenous catheters, infusion pumps and controllers, I.V. sets, filters and devices for monitoring blood pressure, cardiac output, and oxygen are among its products.

Devro—Edible natural protein sausage casings made by Devro companies in the United States, Canada, Scotland, and Australia are used by food processors throughout the world to produce pure, uniform, high-quality sausages and meat snacks.

Ethicon—Ethican, Inc., provides products for precise wound closure, including sutures, ligatures, mechanical wound closure instruments, and related products. Ethicon makes its own surgical needles and provides thousands of needle-suture combinations to the surgeon.

Iolab—Iolab Corporation manufactures intraocular lenses for implantation in the eye to replace the natural lens after cataract surgery, as well as instruments and other products used in ophthalmic microsurgery.

Janssen—Janssen Pharmaceutica Inc. facilitates availability in the U.S. of original research developments of Janssen Pharmaceutica N.V. of Belgium. Its products include Sufenta, Innovar, Sublimaze, and Inapsine, injectable products used in anesthesiology; Nizoral and Monistat i.v. for systemic fungal pathogens; Nizoral Cream 2 percent topical antifungal; Vermox, an anthelmintic, and Imodium, an antidiarrheal.

Johnson & Johnson Baby Products Company—The Johnson & Johnson Baby Products Company produces the familiar line of consumer baby products, including powder, shampoo, oil, wash cloths, lotion, and others. Additional products include educational materials and toys to aid in infant development, Sundown sunscreen and Affinity shampoo and conditioner.

Johnson & Johnson Cardiovascular—Johnson & Johnson Cardiovascular manufacturers and markets cardiovascular products used in open heart surgery that include Hancock heart valves, vascular grafts, Maxima hollow fiber oxygenators, Intersept blood filters, and cardiotomy reservoirs.

Johnson & Johnson Dental Products Company—The Dental Products Company serves dental practitioners throughout the world with an extensive line of orthodontic, preventive, and restorative products. The company also provides dental laboratories with a broad line of crown and bridge materials, including the high-strength ceramic Cerestore system.

Johnson & Johnson Hospital Services—Johnson & Johnson Hospital Services Company develops and implements corporate marketing programs on behalf of Johnson & Johnson professional companies. These programs make it easier to do business with Johnson & Johnson and respond to the needs of hospitals, multihospital systems, alternative sites, and distributors to reduce costs. Programs include Corporate Contracts and the Coact On-Line Procurement System.

Johnson & Johnson Products, Inc.—Johnson & Johnson Products' Health Care Division provides consumers with wound care and oral care products. Its Patient Care Division offers hospitals and physicians a complete line of wound care products. Its Orthopaedic division offers immobilization products. The company also provides products to the athletic market.

Johnson & Johnson Ultrasound—Johnson & Johnson Ultrasound specializes in ultrasound diagnostic imaging equipment. This equipment is used in a wide range of medical diagnoses, including abdominal, cardiovascular, gynecologic, obstetric, pediatric, surgical, neonatal, and veterinary applications.

McNeil Consumer Products Company—McNeil Consumer Products Company's line of Tylenol acetaminophen products includes regular and extra-strength tablets, caplets, and liquid; children's elixir, chewable tablets, drops, and junior strength tablets. Other products include various forms of CoTylenol cold formula, Pediacare cough/cold preparations, Sine-Aid, Maximum-Strength Tylenol Sinus Medication, and Delsym cough relief medicine.

McNeil Pharmaceutical—McNeil Pharmaceutical provides the medical profession with prescription drugs, including analgesics, short- and long-acting tranquilizers, an anti-inflammatory agent, a muscle relaxant, and a digestive enzyme supplement.

Ortho Diagnostic Systems Inc.—Ortho Diagnostic Systems Inc. provides diagnostic systems for the clinical and research laboratory community. Products include instrument and reagent systems for the blood bank, coagulation, and hematology laboratories as well as immunology systems and infectious disease testing kits.

Ortho Pharmaceutical Corporation—Ortho Pharmaceutical Corporation's prescription products for family planning are oral contraceptives and diaphragms. Other products include vaginal antibacterial and antifungal agents. The Advanced Care Products Division markets nonprescription vaginal spermicides for fertility control, in-home pregnancy and ovulation test kits, and an athlete's foot remedy. The Dermatological Division provides dermatologists with products for professional skin care treatment.

Personal Products—Products for feminine hygiene—Stayfree Thin Maxis, Maxi-Pads, Stayfree Silhouettes BodyShape Maxis, Assure & Natural Breathable Panty Liners, Carefree Panty Shields, Surf & Natural Maxishields, Modess Sanitary Napkins, 'o.b.' Tampons, and related products—are the specialty of Personal Products Company. Other consumer products include Coets Cosmetic Squares, Take-off Make-up Remover Cloths, and Shower to Shower Body Powder.

Pitman-Moore—Pitman-Moore, Inc., manufactures and sells an extensive line of biological, diagnostic, and pharmaceutical products for use by veterinarians in treating various disease entities in the pet animal segment of the animal health market. Most notable is Imrab, the only rabies vaccine approved for use in five animal species. Pitman-Moore also supplies vaccines and pharmaceuticals for use in food-producing animals, and it markets surgical products of Johnson & Johnson affiliates applicable to animal health.

Surgikos—Surgikos, Inc., markets an extensive line of Barrier disposable surgical packs and gowns and surgical specialty products for use in major operative procedures. Other major products include Cidex sterilizing and disinfecting solutions for medical equipment, Surgine face masks and head coverings, Microtouch latex surgical gloves, and Neutralon brown surgical gloves for sensitive skin.

Technicare—Technicare Corporation offers physcians products in four of the most important diagnostic imaging fields—computed tomography (CT) scanning, nuclear medicine systems, digital X-ray, and the new field of magnetic resonance (MR).

Vistakon—Vistakon, Inc., develops, manufactures, and distributes soft contact lenses. The company provides contact lens dispensing professionals with daily wear and extended wear lenses for nearsighted and farsighted persons. It also is a major supplier of specialty toric lenses for the correction of astigmatism.

Xanar—Xanar, Inc., specializes in products for laser surgery. Laser surgical devices can be used in general surgery and other surgical specialties to provide an effective, less invasive alternative to traditional techniques. Xanar's products include surgical lasers for gynecology, otolaryngology, dermatology, and podiatry.

▲ EXHIBIT 3   Johnson & Johnson Partial Organization Chart

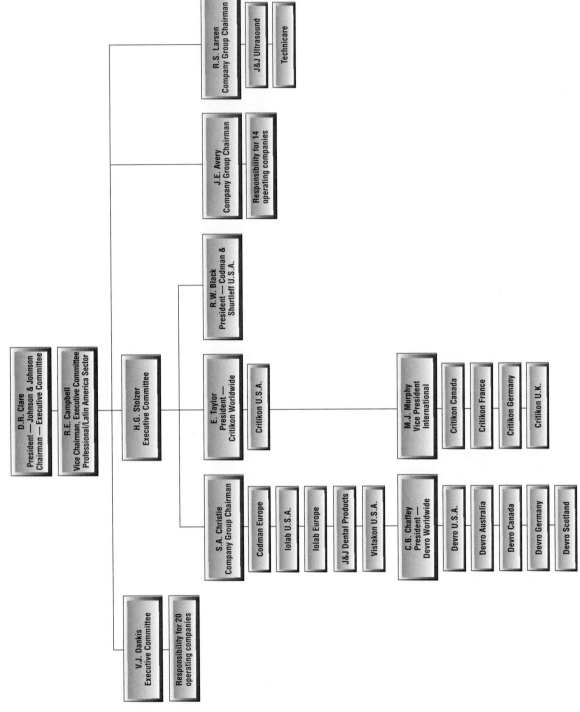

belief in decentralized management, a sense of responsiblity to our key constituents, and a desire to manage for the long term. We have no corporate strategic planning function nor one strategic plan. Our strategic plan is the sum of the strategic plans of our 155 business units."

Each operating company prepared annually a five- and ten-year plan. Financial estimates in these plans were limited to only four numbers: estimated unit sales volume, estimated sales revenue, estimated net income, and estimated return on investment. Accompanying these financial estimates was a narrative description of how these targets would be achieved.

To ensure that managers were committed to the plan that they developed, Johnson & Johnson required that the planning horizon focus on two years only and remain fixed over a five-year period. Thus, in 1983, a budget and second-year forecast was developed for 1984 and 1985 and a strategic plan was developed for the years 1990 and 1995. In each of the years 1984 through 1987, the five- and ten-year plan was redrawn in respect of only years 1990 and 1995. Only in year 1988 would the strategic planning horizon shift five years forward to cover years 1995 and 2000. These two years will then remain the focus of subsequent five- and ten-year plans for the succeeding four years, and so on.

At Codman and Shurtleff, work on the annual five- and ten-year plan commenced each January and took approximately six months to complete. Based on the mission statement, a business plan was developed for each significant segment of the business. For each competitor, the marketing plan included an estimated pro forma income statment (volume, sales, profit) as well as a one-page narrative description of their strategy.

Based on the tentative marketing plan, draft plans were prepared by the other departments including research and development, production, finance, and personnel. The tentative plan was assembled in a binder with sections describing mission, strategies, opportunities and threats, environment, and financial forecasts. This plan was debated, adjusted, and approved over the course of several meetings in May by the Codman board of directors (see Exhibit 4) comprising the president and seven key subordinates.

In June, Herb Stolzer traveled to Boston to preside over the annual review of the five- and ten-year plan. Codman executives considered this a key meeting that could last up to three days. During the meeting Stolzer reviewed the plan, aired his concerns, and challenged the Codman board on assumptions, strategies, and forecasts. A recurring question during the session was, "If your new projection for 1990 is below what you predicted last year, how do you intend to make up the shortfall?"

After this meeting, Roy Black summarized the plan that had been approved by Stolzer in a two-page memorandum that he sent directly to Jim Burke, chairman and chief executive officer of Johnson & Johnson.

Based on the two-page "Burke letters," the five- and ten-year plans for all operating companies were presented by executive committee members and debated and approved at the September meeting of the executive committee in New Brunswick. Company presidents, including Roy Black, were often invited to prepare formal presentations. The discussion in these meetings was described by those in attendance as "very frank," "extremely challenging," and "grilling."

▲ FINANCIAL PLANNING AT JOHNSON & JOHNSON

Financial planning at Johnson & Johnson comprised annual budgets (i.e., profit plans) for the upcoming operating year and a second-year forecast. Budgets were detailed financial documents prepared down to the expense center level for each operating company. The second-year forecast was in a similar format but contained less detail than the budget for the upcoming year.

▲ EXHIBIT 4   Board of Directors

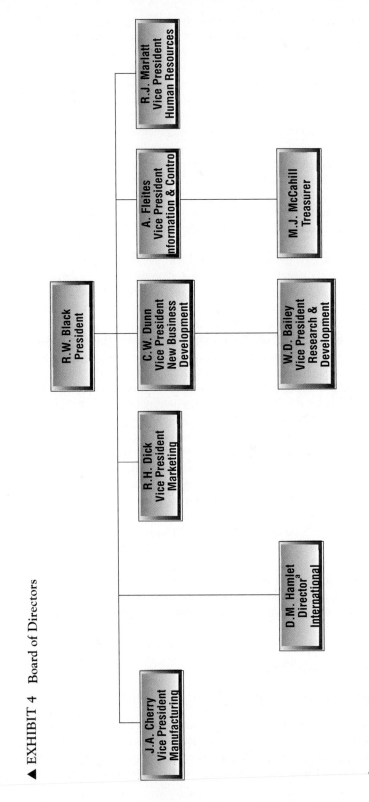

[a]not a board member

Revenues and expenses were budgeted by month. Selected balance sheet items, for example, accounts receivable and inventory, were also budgeted to reflect year-end targets.

Profit plan targets were developed on a bottom-up basis by each operating company by reference to two documents: (1) the approved five- and ten-year plan and (2) the second-year forecast prepared the previous year.

Chuck Dunn described the budgeting process at Codman & Shurtleff,

> We wrote the initial draft of our 1987 profit plan in the Summer of 1986 based on the revision of our five- and ten-year plan. By August, the profit plan is starting to crystallize; we have brought in the support areas such as accounting, quality assurance, R&D, and engineering, to ensure that they "buy in" to the new 1987 profit and marketing plans.

> The first year of the strategic plan is used as a basis for the departments to prepare their own one-year plans for both capital and expense items. The production budget is based on standard costs and nonstandard costs such as development programs and plant consolidations. As for the R&D budget, the project list is always too long, so we are forced to rank the projects. For each project, we look at returns, costs, time expended, sales projections, expected profit, and gross profit percentages as well as support to be supplied to the plants.

> The individual budgets are then consolidated by the Information and Control Department. We look very carefully at how this budget compares with our previous forecasts. For example, the first consolidation of the 1986 profit plan revealed a $2.4 million profit shortfall against the second-year forecast that was developed in 1984 and updated in June 1985. To reconcile this, it was necessary to put on special budget presentations by each department to remove all slack and ensure that our earliest target could be met if possible. The commitment to this process is very strong.

> We are paying more and more attention to our second-year forecast since it forces us to re-examine strategic plans. The second-year forecast is also used as a benchmark for next year's profit plan and, as such, it is used as hindsight to evaluate the forecasting ability and performance of managers.

The procedure for approving the annual profit plan and second-year forecast followed closely the procedures described above for the review of the five- and ten-year plans. During the early fall, Herbert Stolzer reviewed the proposed budget with Roy Black and the Codman & Shurtleff board of directors. Changes in profit commitments from previous forecasts and the overall profitability and tactics of the company were discussed in detail.

After all anticipated revenues and expenses were budgeted, a separate contingency expense line item was added to the budget; the amount of the contingency, changed from year to year, was negotiated between Stolzer and Black based on the perceived uncertainty in achieving budget targets. In 1986, the Codman & Shurtleff contingency was set at $1.1 million.

Stolzer presented the budget for approval at the November meeting of the Johnson & Johnson executive committee.

▲ BUDGET REVISIONS AND REVIEWS

During the year, budget performance was monitored closely. Each week, sales revenue performance figures were sent to Herb Stolzer. In addition, Roy Black sent a monthly management report to Stolzer that included income statement highlights and a summary of key balance sheet figures and ratios. All information was provided with reference to (1) position last month, (2) position this month, and (3) budgeted position. All variances that Black considered significant were explained in a narrative summary.

The accuracy of budget projections was also monitored during the year and formally revised on three occasions. The first of these occasions occurred at the March meeting of the executive committee. Going around the table, each executive committee member was asked to update the committee on his most recent estimates of sales and profits for each operating company for the current year. Herb Stolzer relied on Roy Black to provide this information for Stolzer's review prior to the March meeting.

The "June revision" referred to the revised budget for the current year that was presented to the executive committee in June. The preparation of this revised budget required managers at Codman & Shurtleff and all other Johnson & Johnson companies to rebudget in May for the remainder of the fiscal year. The revision involved rechecking all budget estimates starting with the lowest level expense center as well as revising the second-year forecast when necessary.

The third review of budget projections was the "November update," which was presented to the executive committee at the November meeting concurrently with their consideration of the budget and second-year forecast for the upcoming budget year. The November update focused on results for the 10 months just completed and revised projections for the remaining 2 months. At Codman & Shurtleff, preparation of the November update involved performance estimates from all departments but was not conducted to the same level of detail as the June revision.

▲ CORPORATE VIEW OF THE PLANNING AND CONTROL PROCESS

David Clare, president of Johnson & Johnson,

The sales and profit forecasts are always optimistic in the five- and ten-year plans, but this is OK. We want people to stretch their imagination and think expansively. In these plans we don't anticipate failure; they are a device to open up thinking. There is no penalty for inaccuracies.

The profit plan and second-year forecast are used to run the business and evaluate managers on planning, forecasts, and achievements.

We ask our managers to always include in their plans an account of how and why their estimates have changed over time. That is why we use the five- and ten-year planning concept rather than a moving planning horizon. This allows us to revise our thinking over time and allows for retrospective learning.

If a manager insists on a course of action and we (the executive committee) have misgivings, nine times out of ten we will let him go ahead. If we say, "No," and the answer should have been "Yes," we say, "Don't blame us, it was your job to sell us on the idea and you didn't do that."

Johnson & Johnson is extremely decentralized, but that does not mean that managers are free to challenge as to what they are doing. In the final analysis, managing conflict is what management is all about. Healthy conflict is about *what* is right, not *who* is right.

Our company philosophy is to manage for the long term. We do not use short-term bonus plans. Salary and bonus reviews are entirely subjective and qualitative and are intended to reward effort and give special recognition to those who have performed uniquely. The executive committee reviews salry recommendations for all managers above a certain salary level, but company presidents, such as Roy Black, have full discretion as to how they remunerate their employees.

Herbert Stolzer, executive committee member,

The planning and control systems used in Johnson & Johnson provide real benefits. These systems allow us to find problems and run the business. This is true not only for us at corporate, but also at the operating companies where they are a tremendous tool. Once a year, managers are forced to review their businesses in depth for costs, trends, manufacturing efficiency, marketing plans, and their competitive situation. Programs and action plans result.

You have to force busy people to do this. Otherwise, they will be caught up in day-to-day activities—account visits, riding with salesmen, standing on the manufacturing floor.

Our long-term plans are not meant to be a financial forecast; rather, they are meant to be an objective way of settling aspirations. We never make those numbers—who can forecast sales five or ten years out with unforeseen markets, products, and competitors? Even the accuracy of our two-year forecast is bad. The inaccuracy is an indication of how fast our markets are changing. Our businesses are so diverse, with so many competitors, that it is difficult to forecast out two years.

I visit at least twice a year with each operating company board. We usually spend the better part of a week going over the results, planning issues, strategic plans, and short- and long-term problems. The executive committee, to the best of my knowledge, never issues quantitative performance targets before the bottom-up process begins.

At the executive committee meetings, a lot of argument takes place around strategic planning issues. How fast can we get a business up to higher returns? Are the returns in some businesses too high? Are we moving too fast? However, the outcome is never to go back to the operating company and say we need 8 percent rather than 6 percent. The challenge has already taken place between the executive committee member and the company board. If the EC member is satisfied with the answers provided by the board, that's the end of it.

It happens very rarely that the consolidated budget is unacceptable. Occasionally, we might say, "We really could use some more money." However, in the second review, this may not turn up any extra. If so, that's OK.

Our systems are not used to punish. They are used to try and find and correct problems. Bonuses are not tied to achieving budget targets. They are subjectively determined, although we use whatever objective indicators are available—for example, sales and new product introductions for a marketing vice president.

The key to our whole system is the operating company presidents. We are so decentralized that they define their own destiny. A successful company president needs to be able to stand up to pressure from above. He needs to have the courage to say, "I have spent hours and hours on that forecast and for the long-term health of the company, we have to spend that budget."

Clark Johnson, corporate controller,

At the executive committee review meetings, we always review the past five years before starting on the forecast. We look at volume growth rates—sales growth adjusted for inflation—and discuss problems. Then, we compare growth rate against GNP growth. We keep currency translation out of it. We evaluate foreign subsidiaries in their own currency and compare growth against country specific GNP. We are looking for market share by country. On almost any topic, we start with forecast versus past track record.

The committee never dictates or changes proposals—only challenges ideas. If it becomes clear to the individual presenting that the forecast is not good enough, only that person decides whether a revision is necessary. These discussions can be very frank and sometimes acrimonious. The result of the review may be agreement to present a revision at the next meeting, specific action items to be addressed, or personal feedback to David Clare.

This process cascades down the organization. Executive committee members review and challenge the proposals of company presidents. Company presidents review and challenge the proposals of their vice presidents.

Thursday, May 8, 1986—8:00 pm

Following the Codman & Shurtleff board meeting to discuss the June budget revision on the afternoon of Thursday, May 8 (described at the beginning of the case), Roy Black, Chuck Dunn, Bob Dick, and Gus Fleites worked into the evening going over the list of active R&D projects. Their review focused on R&D projects that had been included in the original 1986 budget. They searched for projects that could be eliminated due to changed market conditions or deferred to 1987 because of unplanned showdowns. After discussing the progress and priority of each major project, Roy Black asked Chuck Dunn to have his staff work the next morning to go over the 40 active projects in detail and look for any savings that could be reflected in the June revision of the budget.

Friday, May 9, 1986—7:45 am

In addition to Chuck Dunn, four people were seated around the table in the small conference room. Bob Sullivan and Gino Lombardo were program managers who reported to Bill Bailey, vice president of Research. John Smith was manager, Technical Development, of the research facility in Southbridge that specialized in microscopes, fiber optics, and light scopes. Gordon Thompson was the research accountant representing the Finance Department.

After coffee was delivered, Chuck closed the door and turned to the others,

> Here's the situation. We are approximately two million short of the June revision pretax profit margin. As you know, our sales volume this year has been good—better than budget, in fact—but a few recent unpredictable events, including unfavorable product mix, and that large variance in the cost of specialty European products, are hurting our profit projection.

> This morning, I want the four of you to look at our original spending projections to see where we stand. For example, we know that R&D underspent $200,000 in the first quarter. Therefore, I think we should take it as a starting point that R&D has $200,000 to give up from its 1986 budget. I know that you can argue that this is just a timing difference, but you know as well as I do that, given the record of the R&D department, this money will probably not be spent this year.

> It's time to get the hopes and dreams out of the R&D list. If we roll up our sleeves, we can probably find $400,000 without sacrificing either our 1986 objectives or our long-term growth.

> We worked late last night looking at the project list and I think it can be done. I have to meet again today at 2:00 with the board and I want to be able to tell them that we can do it. That leaves it up to you to sift through these projects and find that money. We're looking for projects that have stalled and can be put on hold, and some belt-tightening on ongoing work.

After Chuck Dunn had left the group to its work, Gordon led the group through the list of projects. For each project, the group discussed spending to date, problems with the project, and spending needed for the remainder of the year. For each project, Gordon asked if anything could be cut and occasionally asked for points of clarification. On a separate sheet of paper, he kept track of the cuts to which the R&D managers had agreed. He turned to Project 23.

How about 23? You were planning on a pilot run of 100 prototypes this year. Should that still be included in the schedule?

Yes, the project is on track and looks promising. I suppose we could cut the run to 50 without sacrificing our objective. Would anyone have a problem with that?

It's a bad idea. That item has a very high material component and we have a devil of a time getting it at a reasonable price, even for a run of 100. If we cut the volume any more, the unit material cost will double.

O.K., we'll stick with the 100. How about the salesmen's samples? Is there anything there?

If we reduced the number of samples by a third, we could save $20,000. I suppose I could live with that, but I don't know how that will impact the marketing plan. Let me call Bob Dick and see what he thinks.

Gordon kept a running total of the expense reductions as the morning progressed. Dunn stopped in approximately once an hour to ask how the work was coming.

Friday, May 9—2:00 pm

Roy Black opened the meeting, "Gus, do you have the revised budget with the changes we've made? What does it look like?"

As Gus Fleites distributed copies of the budget document to the Codman & Shurtleff board, Chuck Dunn interjected, "Roy, at the moment, we have found $300,000 in R&D. That reflects adjusting our priority list for the rest of the year and cutting the fat out of ongoing projects. As for the last $100,000, we are still working on recasting the numbers to reflect what I call our 'project experience factor.' In other words, I think we can find that $100,000 by recognizing that our projects always take longer than originally planned. My people say that we've cut right to the bone on ongoing programs. The next round of cuts will have to be programs themselves, and we know we don't want to do that."

"We've discussed this before," responded Black, "and I think we all agree on the answer. In the past, we have authorized more projects than we can handle and have drawn the work out over too long a time. The way to go is fewer projects, sooner. It's the only thing that makes sense. Our mission is more focused now and should result in fewer projects. It's unfortunate that Bill Bailey is unavailable this week, but we are going to have to go ahead and make those decisions."

As Fleites briefed the board on the revised budget, Roy Black turned to Bob Dick to discuss inventory carrying costs. "Bob, don't you think that our inventory level is too high on some of our low turnover products? Wouldn't we be better to cut our inventory position and take a higher back order level? With 2,700 products, does it make sense to carry such a large inventory?"

Bob Dick nodded his head in agreement, "You're right, of course, our stocking charges our substantial and we could recover part of our shortfall if we could cut those expenses. But our first concern has to be our level of service to customers."

"Agreed. But perhaps there is room here to provide fast turnaround on a core of critical products and risk back orders on the high-specialty items. The 80/20 rule applies to most of our business. For example, say we offered top service for all our disposables and implants and flagged set-up products for new hospital construction in our catalogue as '90 day delivery' or 'made to order.' We could then concentrate on the fastest possible turnaround for products where that is important and a slower delivery for products that are usually ordered well in advance in any case."

"I think that may be a good tactic. It won't help us for the June revision, but I'll have our market research people look at it and report back next month."

"Good," responded Black, "that just leaves our commercial expenses. We need some donations from each of you. What I am suggesting is that each of you go back to your departments and think in terms of giving up 2 percent of your commercial expenses. If everyone gives up 2 percent, this will give us $500,000. In my opinion, we have to bring the shortfall down to $900,000 before we can draw down part of our contingency fund. We're a long way from the end of the year and it's too early to start drawing down a major portion of the contingency."

Black turned to Bob Marlatt, vice president of Human Resources. "Bob, where do we stand on headcount projections?"

"The early retirement program is set to clear our Corporate Compensation Department next month. That should yield 14 headcount reductions. Otherwise, no changes have been made in our projections through the end of the year. I think that we could all benefit from thinking about opportunities to reduce staff and pay overtime on an as-needed basis to compensate."

Black summed up the discussion,

Well, I think we all know what is needed. Chuck, keep working on that last $100,000. All of you should think in terms of giving up 2 percent on commercial expenses and reducing noncritical headcount. That means that you will have to rank your activities and see what you can lose at the bottom end. Bob, I think that we should go back and look at our marketing plan again to see if we can make any changes to boost revenues.

We need to take a revised budget to Stolzer that is short by no more than $250,000. If necessary, I think we can live with drawing down the contingency to make up the difference.

So, your work is cut out for you. See you back here on Monday. Have a nice weekend! (Laughter all around.)

After the meeting, Roy Black reflected on what had transpired, and his role as an operating manager in Johnson & Johnson.

These meetings are very important. We should always be thinking about such issues, but it is tough when you are constantly fighting fires. The Johnson & Johnson system forces us to stop and really look at where we have been and where we are going.

We know where the problems are. We face them every day. But these meetings force us to think about how we should respond and to look at both the upside and downside of changes in the business. They really get our creative juices flowing.

Some of our managers complain. They say that we are planning and budgeting all the time and that every little change means that they have to go back and rebudget the year and the second-year forecasts. There is also some concern that the financial focus may make us less innovative. But we try to manage this business for the long term. We avoid at all costs actions that will hurt us long term. I believe that Herb Stolzer is in complete agreement on that issue.

It is important to understand what decentralized management is all about. It is unequivocal accountability for what you do. And the Johnson & Johnson system provides that very well.

NEWELL COMPANY: ACQUISITION STRATEGY

*People think we are in the acquisition business, but we're not. We are building a package for the
mass retailer and acquisitions have been a vehicle to build that package.*

Daniel Ferguson, chairman of the board [1]

In 1992, Newell CEO Daniel Ferguson and president William P. Sovey[2] were evaluating
two major acquisition prospects for this broad-range manufacturer of basic home and hardware products. The first was a $600 million deal to buy Sanford—an Illinois-based de-
signer, manufacturer, and marketer of writing instruments, plastic desk accessories, file
storage boxes, and office and school supplies with revenues of $140 million. Despite a
solid history and good management, changes in the office supplies marketplace and a poor
acquisition had hampered Sanford's recent performance. At the same time, Newell was
considering making a bid to buy Levolor—a $180 million well-known manufacturer of
window blinds that was currently performing poorly after a recent leveraged buyout—for
about $70 million.

Given Newell's commitment to meet its goal of 15 percent annual growth in earnings per
share, the decision entailed a considerable risk for the company.

[handwritten: changing office supplies marketplace]

Research Assistant Elizabeth Wynne Johnson prepared this case under the supervision of Professor David J.
Collis. Copyright © 1994 by the President and Fellows of Harvard College. 9-794-066.

[1]Lisa Ann Casey, "Newell Assesses Acquisition," *The Weekly Home Furnishings Newsletter,* 62, no. 49
(December 5, 1988), p. 51.
[2]The following management changes occurred in May of 1992: Daniel Ferguson retired to become chairman of the
board, and William Sovey succeeded him as vice chairman and chief executive officer. Former operating companies president Thomas a. ferguson, Jr. (no relation to Daniel Ferguson), an employee since 1972, became president and chief operating officer.

▲ THE ROOTS OF STRATEGY

Edgar A. Newell bought the assets of a bankrupt manufacturer of brass curtain rods in 1902. At the time, Americans were just beginning the move out of cities to the first suburbs, where people sought homes with extensive windows—both to let light in and to enjoy suburban views. Newell's product, brass extension curtain rods, met with steadily increasing demand from the start.[3]

Newell began by selling its product to small hardware stores, industrial builders, and specialty retailers. As early as 1917, Newell became a regular supplier to the then rapidly growing chain of Woolworth stores, gaining national distribution and a solid reputation among national chain stores.

In 1921, Leonard Ferguson joined the company, becoming a full partner and owner in 1937. His son, Daniel Ferguson, came to Newell after receiving his MBA from Stanford. He became CEO in 1966. At that time, Newell had revenues of $14 million, a limited product range based on curtain rods, and no articulated strategy for the future. Dan Ferguson's first task was to get control of Newell's drapery rod business. The business had been guided by what was essentially a product-line strategy, selling drapery hardware to all channels—including motels, department stores, and in Europe—but lacking anything to differentiate its product. In an effort to overcome this problem, Newell acquired a small window shade manufacturer in 1966.

About this time, Daniel Ferguson attended a Young Presidents' Organization meeting where he heard Stanford professor Bob Katz deliver a speech on strategy. Katz's ideas resonated, but they slipped to the back of Ferguson's mind until months later, when he chanced to meet Katz on a plane. As they talked, Ferguson began to develop a "build on what we do best" philosophy.[4] Already selling extensively to Woolworth's and to Kresge (later Kmart), Ferguson foresaw the trend toward consolidation in the retail business and envisioned a role for Newell:

> We realized we knew how to make a high-volume/low-cost product and we knew how to relate to and sell to a large retail institution—the large mass retailer.[5]

In July of 1967, Ferguson wrote out his strategy for Newell (Exhibits 1 and 2), identifying its focus as the market for hardware and do-it-yourself (DIY) products. The company then made its first nondrapery hardware acquisition in 1969 with Mirra-Cote bath hardware in order to gain penetration into new discount outlets for Newell's existing products. Because Zayre, for example, carried Mirra-Cote bath hardware, it was thought possible for Newell to leverage that relationship to sell other items as well.

Newell Mfg. Co. went public in 1971, receiving a New York Stock Exchange quote in 1978, diluting what remained of the Newell family ownership. Ferguson recalled the decision to go public as one that had to be made "100 percent," putting as much stock as possible up for sale to the public. Access to the capital markets permitted Newell to begin aggressively adding new products by acquisition.

Newell then thrived by following a disciplined and aggressive two-pronged strategy based on acquisitions, acquiring more than 30 businesses in the next 20 years (Exhibit 3). First, it acquired companies that manufactured low-technology, nonseasonal, noncyclical,

[3]William R. Cuthbert, *Newell Companies: A Corporate History*, 1983.
[4]Personal interview with William Sovey, April 23, 1993.
[5]Don Longo, "Ferguson Guides Newell to the Top," *Discount Store News* 28, no. 18 (September 25, 1989), p. 82.

July 1, 1967

STATEMENT OF NEWELL COMPANIES

Newell defines its basic business as that of manufacturing and distributing volume merchandise lines to the volume merchandisers. A combination or package of lines going to the large retailers carries more marketing impact than each line separately, and Newell intends to build its growth through performance and the marketing leverage of this package. This package will also have more economic impact on the financial community both for the securing of financing for future expansion and for the establishment of a market for the Companies' equity securities.

Newell is in a financial position to build the desired package. It has a net worth of approximately 10 million dollars with no long-term debt, and earnings are substantial and growing.

Newell management is professional, young, aggressive, and in excellent control of the basic hardware and shade business. We are aware of the tremendous marketing base, goodwill, and expertise we have in dealing with large merchandisers, and we are dedicated to building growth in earnings for Newell on this solid base.

Daniel C. Feguson
es

Source: Newell Company.

---

nonfashionable products that high-volume retailers would keep on the shelves year in and year out. Then, newly acquired companies underwent a thorough process of streamlining, widely known as "Newellization," focusing on operational efficiency and profitability. The resulting improvements would raise operating margins above 10 percent—the minimum Newell expected from each of its businesses.

As Newell added other businesses to its core line of drapery hardware to assemble a multiproduct offering, it originally adhered to a strategy of consolidation and centralization in order to achieve efficiencies, adopting a functional rather than a divisional organization. For example, Newell used a single sales force to sell all of its products.

Beginning in 1974, however, the company underwent a major organizational transformation. Realizing that a system of centralized marketing was not an effective approach to selling a variety of products, Ferguson led the reorganization of the company into separate divisions, individually responsible for manufacturing and marketing, but centrally controlled by corporate-run administrative, legal, and banking systems. *[handwritten: separate divisions - each responsible for manufacturing and marketing]*

In 1976, Newell established the first modem connection to Wal-Mart for Electronic Data Information (EDI) transfer. By the early 1980s, Newell was more advanced in its computer systems than were most of its retail customers. Top management at retailers was quick to focus on computer linkages as an important asset, a fact which helped "sell" Newell as a supplier.

▲ EXHIBIT 2   Newell Strategy Statement, 1992

Total Newell Strategy

Definition—Newell manufactures and markets staple volume lines to the volume purchaser.

Mission—To increase shareholder value by continuing to build a company with superior EPS growth and ROI, and to earn a reputation for excellence in performance and management.

Basic strategy—To merchandise to the customer goods market a multiproduct offering with superior customer service performance for maximum market leverage.

Financial goals

Return on investment (ROI): 20 percent plus.

Debt: $1/2$ of equity.

Earnings per share growth: 15 percent plus annually.

Source: Newell Company.

By 1992, the Newell Company had revenues of $1.45 billion, distributing primarily to mass retailers and home centers like Home Depot (Exhibit 4). That year, Newell's top 10 customers accounted for 66 percent of its customer sales volume (Exhibit 5). During the same period, roughly 90 percent of Newell's sales were in the United States. In addition to its original line of drapery hardware, Newell offered other hardware products and housewares, which it had first entered with the acquisition of Mirro in 1983, including cookware, specialty glass, and plastic storageware. The company's newest generic business type was home office products (Exhibit 6).

▲ THE ELEMENTS OF STRATEGY

Growth by Acquisition

Profit growth, not sales growth.

Newell Annual Report, 1987

From the corporate headquarters in a white clapboard farmhouse, set in the cornfields on the border of Illinois and Wisconsin, Daniel Ferguson dictated a stringent focus: redirect acquired businesses to focus on their core product, and align them with Newell's core function. He described the process of integrating new companies in the following terms: "2 + 2 do not equal 4. If we do this right, we get *more* than 4."

Chief financial officer Bill Alldredge had the main responsibility for corporate business development. He looked for companies that were underperforming due to high operating costs, preferably with operating margins of less than 10 percent. Newell believed that since the businesses it competed in shared a fundamental similarity, it could quickly compare potential targets' income statements to its own, recognizing, for example, that regardless of how a company was organized, its SG&A expense should never exceed 15 percent.

▲ EXHIBIT 3 Newell's Acquisitions

Company (brand name)	Product Type	Date	Additional Information	Sales in 1990
Renneman	Window shades	1966		
Mirra-Cote	Bathroom hardware	1969		
Bulldog/Dorfile	Hardware and shelving	1971		
EZ-Paintr	Hand-held paint applicators	1973	Sales were approximately $40m prior to acquisition	$83
Counselor	Bathroom scales	1981		*
Judd	Drapery hardware	1982		*
BernzOmatic	Propane and oxygen torches	1982		*
Mirro	Cookware	1983	Mirro and Foley operations combined; brand names including, Rema, Airbrake, and Cushionaire	$234
Foley	Cookware	1984		
Ignitor Products International Inc.	Ignitor products	1985		NA
American Tool Company (Vise-grip)	Wrenches and pliers	1985	Newell acquired a 45% stake	See Mirro/Foley
Enterprise Aluminum Company	Cookware	1986		
Borg	Scales, housewares	1987		*
Anchor Hocking (including Amerock)	Plastic and glassware	1987	Amerock brand in decorative/functional hardware	$270
Wm. E. Wright Company	Home sewing	1987	Sales were $55m prior to acquisition; sold in 1989	NA
Thomas Industries	Hardware (paint applicators)	1988	Newell took 5% stock position in both companies; received paint applicator business in exchange for stock position in Thomas Industries; Vermont America sold to Emerson Electric to prevent takeover by Newell	NA
Vermont American	Tools (power tool accessories)	1988		NA
(WearEver)	Cookware	1989	Cookware division purchased from Nacco industries	See Mirro/Foley
Black & Decker	Tools and hardware	1991	Newell invested $150 m for up to a 15% equity stake	NA
Keene Manufacturing	Office products	1991		
W.T. Rogers	Office products	1991	Deal financed as a pooling of interest	NA
Stuart Hall	Office products	1992	NA	

Note: Listings in italics denote companies in which Newell has taken an equity stake short of acquisition. Mirro/Foley sales in 1990 include WearEver and Enterprise.
*Denotes sales of <$50 million.

▲ **EXHIBIT 4** **Selected Financial Information for Newell Company,**
1977–1991 (000s)

	1991	1990	1989	1988	1987	1986	1985
Net sales	$1,258,958	$1,072,566	$1,122,895	$988,177	$719,687	$401,357	$342,900
Cost of products sold	845,555	748,396	809,025	723,335	532,138	283,221	243,076
Selling, general and admin.	182,226	150,299	149,195	140,544	105,461	71,167	67,293
Depreciation and amortization	44,924	46,548	40,669	39,651	23,531	11,197	8,494
Income taxes	88,411	69,479	60,219	42,951	30,009	20,911	13,979
Net income	↓$ 88,411	$ 101,350	$ 85,363	$ 61,420	$ 37,222	$ 24,009	$ 18,854
Accounts receivable		111,255	120,212	119,967	136,212	56,318	—
Working capital	187,853	194,050	149,360	142,036	185,646	88,241	82,944
Total assets	1,187,460	870,962	871,344	820,001	842,036	335,282	239,003
Long-term debt	176,640	89,286	100,223	152,730	238,382	37,346	34,765
Capital expenditures	59,149	36,599	25,140	27,533	11,068	6,957	9,712
Goodwill	150,353	149,416	138,017	125,631	21,413	19,985	
Stockholders' equity	728,801	508,665	455,818	400,267	354,629	198,009	120,089
Return on invested capital (%)	↑ 20.23	18.51	12.4	17.6	13.8	12.1	12.3
Return on assets (%)	11.4	12.5	10.9	8.5	5.6	7.8	7.2
Earnings per share	↑ 1.81	1.67	1.41	1.01	0.68	0.53	0.49
Average shares outstanding	61,807	60,485	60.058	47,454	46,644	42,816	34,656

1984	1983	1982	1981	1980	1979	1978	1977
$289,540	$236,930	$178,497	$170,389	$138,521	$121,819	$106,115	$97,740
200,962	160,889	118,648	111,871	93,114	81,012	70,892	64,402
59,710	48,776	38,846	36,183	27,406	24,826	21,532	19,078
7,562	5,049	3,403	3,453	2,827	2,188	1,948	1,917
12,488	10,111	8,234	8,665	7,269	6,621	5,994	6,397
$ 14,170	$ 12,985	$ 8,826	$ 9,604	$ 7,820	$ 7,083	$ 4,815	$ 5,837
—	—	—	—	—	—	—	—
74,803	66,443	49,951	36,440	28,426	29,091	25,352	23,225
193,010	125,210	99,016	85,579	72,287	74,196	59,229	—
28,103	28,367	17,584	21,058	15,887	16,040	17,612	11,688
5,552	7,717	2,165	3,645	3,183	2,788	3,229	2,663
106,291	87,370	76,819	51,064	44,014	38,456	33,889	30,735
16.1	NA	NA	NA	NA	NA	NA	NA
6.8	8.2	8.4	9.8	9.5	9.6	9.3	NA
0.39	0.37	0.33	0.38	0.32	NA	NA	NA
34,456	34,180	26,052	25,608	24,874	24,656	NA	NA

▲ EXHIBIT 5   Top 10 Customers in 1992

Customer	Percentage of Newell's Sales
Kmart	11%
Wal-Mart	10
Target	9
Ace Hardware	8
Cotter	7
Home Depot	5
Payless Cashways	5
Price Co.	5
Costco	4
Office Depot	2

Source: Newell Company Report, transcript, December 1992.

▲ EXHIBIT 6   Product Line Profile, 1992 ($millions, approximately)

Cookware	$290	
Glass	170	
Plastics	75	
Bath scales	25	
		$ 560
Office and school stationery	$130	
Office organizers	85	
		$ 215
Cabinet and window hardware	$205	
Paint applicators	105	
Drapery hardware and window shades	100	
Propane torches	40	
Packaged hardware	35	
Shelving	25	
		$ 510
International	40	
		$1,325

Acquisitions were taken over by Newell – president and controller

Ferguson summed it up: "Turnarounds were how we made our living."[6] Beginning immediately after a new acquisition, "Newellization" usually took place in less than 18 months, and often in less than 6 months—typically under the leadership of a new president and controller that Newell brought in from elsewhere in the company. In that time, three categories of standard Newell systems were introduced: accounts payable, sales and order processing, and one of three off-the-shelf manufacturing systems. Corporate teams, composed

[6]Personal interview, April 23, 1993.

of a few company executives acting outside of their existing jobs, were assembled to centralize administration, accounting, and customer-related financial aspects, consolidating their systems into a single corporate computer system in Freeport, Illinois.

Attractive acquisition targets were domestic companies which manufactured staple products under brand names that ranked number one and two in market share. In his back pocket, Daniel Ferguson's successor, William Sovey, carried a handwritten list of such companies. It was his belief that such products virtually owned their space on retailers' shelves, surviving inventory reductions during slow economic times. As one Newell executive noted, "The most important asset in a new acquisition is its shelf space."

In addition, the company also acquired small businesses to round out its existing product lines and reduce the number of competitors in a market. The goal, however, was efficiency rather than pricing power, as the most powerful customers would put a competitor back into business as a counterweight to a dominant supplier. Market rationalization was also a benefit to Newell, because as company president Tom Ferguson noted, "Our worst competitor is one who's sick. That competitor will do anything for cash flow and it'll destroy the market."

Newell's takeover tactics were widely recognized: typically, it began with the taking of an equity stake in a target company, which it would hold for a while before making a full bid. Observers noted that, as a suitor, Newell's overtures were not always welcome, particularly as its reputation for taking a gradual approach to takeover became increasingly widespread. Nonetheless, Newell favored taking minority positions in compatible businesses, noting that in some cases, a minority position in a larger company was preferable to ownership of a product-line with less market power.

Newell's growth strategy was confined almost exclusively to domestic expansion. Newell executives cited the difficulty of replicating their success abroad, given the lack of mass distribution channels and product differences overseas. Beginning in 1990, the company created a position for a senior executive to research opportunities abroad; still, Newell applied a "don't bet the ranch" philosophy to its international activities, preferring to take a minority position with a strong partner with an understanding of foreign culture, in order to learn the market with minimal risk.

Newell exited any business it deemed a "cancer," even divesting businesses with healthy profit margin if they were ill-suited to the company's main focus. Home sewing products, for example, had seemed to fit Newell criteria. The Wm. E. Wright company, a manufacturer of ribbons and home sewing products acquired in 1985 had solid sales and profit performance. But the market for home sewing was in small independent retailers, and the business dwindled out of mass retail channels. Newell sold Wm. E. Wright in 1989, preferring to focus the company's resources on business that better contributed to Newell by making it "more important to the mass retail customer." By 1992, the company was considering selling off some of its smaller business units, even those whose products were distributed through mass retailers, observing that a small business consumed the same amount of senior management time as a large business.

By the early 1990s, the company's growth had a brought about a change in the nature of Newell's criteria for new businesses. Daniel Ferguson explained:

> Back when we had four companies, adding a new one was a big deal. Now adding one more, when we already have 16, is not necessarily going to increase our power. We have to look for a company that is powerful enough in itself to add something to the package.[7]

---

[7]Daniel Ferguson, personal interview, January 28, 1994.

Serving the Mass Retailer

Beginning in the 1970s, the nature of the retail industry changed with the emergence of large-scale mass retailers, whose size gave them considerable power over their suppliers. By 1992, for example, three chains controlled roughly 70 percent of the discount retailer market. At the forefront of this new retail environment was Wal-Mart, whose 33 percent compound growth beginning in 1982 led it to become the nation's largest retailer by 1992. Wal-Mart not only had the influence to dictate the kind and quantity of merchandise shipped to its stores, it also had considerable leverage over price and scheduling, threatening to introduce a competitor to some stores as a way of reducing its supplier switching costs. As a result, manufacturers were forced to respond with greater efficiencies in their warehouse and distribution systems, paring down inventory and eliminating error. As one small manufacturer put it, "They take your guts out,"[8] Even Procter & Gamble, Wal-Mart's largest single supplier with nearly $3 billion in sales to the retailer, was consolidating its selling relationship in order to meet the retailer's demand for a single source of contact.

Newell responded to these pressures by focusing each division on a single goal: furnishing product and service to mass retailers. Customer service was, however, defined as a means to an end. Executives noted that each division was to place primary emphasis on its own profit performance, observing that this would force them to provide superior customer service—not the other way around. In the 1970s, when the industry average for first-pass line-fill (the measure of stock available when an order was received) was 80 percent, Newell's goal was to keep its customers at 95 percent line-fill and 95 percent on-time delivery. As improvements later pushed the industry average higher, Newell's standard rose to nearly 100 percent. It also expanded its activities to include some previously in-store services, such as preticketing.

Newell's goal was to be the "no problem" supplier in the industry. While the company enjoyed a solid reputation for its service—as one executive noted, the frequently asked question in the industry was "Do you ship as well as Newell?"—subpar performance by a newly acquired business could easily damage that reputation. As Daniel Ferguson observed, "The retailer knows Newell by our worst performer, so we can't afford to have one dog in the show."[9] The key was to get the service level in new acquisitions up to Newell's standards as quickly as possible; to that end, the company was willing to carry larger inventories during the early stage following acquisition.

Consistent with its high service level, Newell's pricing was not the lowest in the industry. Rather, it designed its products to fit a certain price point and then delivered consistently, in both product and service quality. Marketing representatives came prepared to show the customer the company's "report card" on several dimensions of service quality as evidence of a product's value, even if prices reflected an apparent 5–10 percent premium.

Newell exploited its size to provide the high-volume retailer with superior service, comprising five key elements: national coverage, on-time delivery, the avoidance of stockouts, computerized EDI and Quick Response inventory supply systems, and program merchandising. However, despite its size and the breadth of products it sold to the mass retailers, Newell maintained distinct identities across its 16 separate divisions (Exhibit 7). Each division president was also the top marketing executive for his product line. The retailer therefore dealt with separate sales teams for each Newell product line it carried, although

Handwritten margin notes:
focus on profits which leads to offering superior customer service (not the other way around)

have to make certain that new acquisitions do not damage reputation

---

[8]"Clout! More and More, Retail Giants Rule the Marketplace," *Business Week,* December 21, 1992, p. 67.
[9]Ibid.

Wal-Mart, for example, would have preferred to deal with a single contact. The same logic underlay the commitment to multiple brand lines; if each product featured its Newell identity prominently, price increases by any one division would likely bring about demands for price cuts in others. The company favored brand-name products rather than manufacturing for private labels, but Newell was willing to make exceptions—as it did for Wal-Mart's Popular Mechanix. In the 1970s, 70 percent of Newell's products were sold under private labels; in 1992, it was down to 30 percent.

EDI / Quick Response

Mass retailers relied on information technology as the foundation of their business. As one observer put it, "the power retailers have figured out a way of converting raw data into insight."[10] As a supplier, Newell had invested heavily in the necessary computer and communications hardware to match its customers' demands. Including the price of software programming, the system had cost $15 million to develop and $3 million per year to operate. However, in the 1980s, Wal-Mart began offering its own electronic communication package, which it provided to smaller suppliers that couldn't develop the systems for themselves.

Newell's top 20 customers place 90 percent of their orders through Electronic Data Interchange (EDI)—the company's sophisticated electronic management system for transmitting purchase orders, invoices, and payments to and from its retail partners across the country (Exhibit 8). Orders and data sent from customers to the company's central computer in Freeport, Illinois were processed and then downloaded to all the divisions. The divisions used this data to schedule their own production and deliveries, allowing retailers to maintain minimal stock levels in line with actual sales.

Along with EDI, Newell developed Quick Response, an electronically monitored inventory restocking system that made it possible for Newell to restock customer warehouses automatically, allowing them to maintain smaller inventories. With Quick Response, Wal-Mart increased its number of yearly inventory turns to 20 from only 6 or 7. Said Newell president Tom Ferguson: ``The whole thing is built on a solid base of performance. By performance, I mean shipping goods and getting them on the counter and keeping the hooks full. That's the name of the game." Newell looked to increasing the number of Quick Response partnerships as part of the company's overall scheme to boost market share (Exhibit 9).

▲ NEWELL'S BUSINESSES

Only the drapery hardware line carried the Newell brand name. Each of Newell's remaining businesses was the product of acquisition, and retained its original brand name.

Hardware   Newell's hardware divisions manufactured DIY products from propane torches to fasteners and miscellaneous fabricated wire products, and were highly successful at utilizing a program-selling approach, offering products in three categories: "good," "better," and "best"—arranged on displays designed to encourage customers to step-up their purchases; within a given display, more expensive items were placed at eye-level, with less expensive alternatives situated below. Also, the displays grouped Newell products to encourage add-on sales through cross-category merchandising. The system worked particularly well in hardware,

---

[10]Ibid., p. 69.

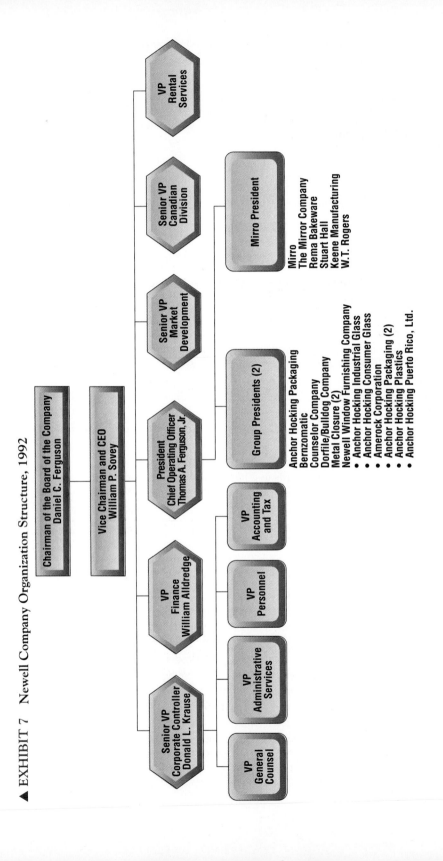

▲ EXHIBIT 7   Newell Company Organization Structure, 1992

Chairman of the Board of the Company
Daniel C. Ferguson

Vice Chairman and CEO
William P. Sovey

President
Chief Operating Officer
Thomas A. Ferguson, Jr.

VP Rental Services

Senior VP Canadian Division

Senior VP Market Development

Senior VP Corporate Controller
Donald L. Krause

VP Finance
William Alldredge

VP General Counsel

VP Administrative Services

VP Personnel

VP Accounting and Tax

Group Presidents (2)

Anchor Hocking Packaging
Bernzomatic
Counselor Company
Dorfile/Bulldog Company
Metal Closure (2)
Newell Window Furnishing Company
• Anchor Hocking Industrial Glass
• Anchor Hocking Consumer Glass
• Amerock Corporation
• Anchor Hocking Packaging (2)
• Anchor Hocking Plastics
• Anchor Hocking Puerto Rico, Ltd.

Mirro President

Mirro
The Mirror Company
Rema Bakeware
Stuart Hall
Keene Manufacturing
W.T. Rogers

▲ EXHIBIT 8   Growth of EDI and Quick Response at Newell (in millions)

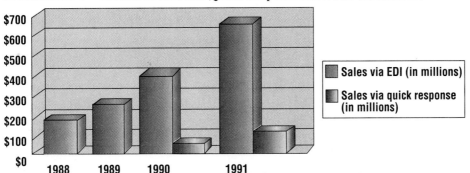

▲ EXHIBIT 9   Quick Response Program

	Mirro	EZ-Paintr	Newell Home Hardware	Anchor Hocking Plastics	Anchor Hocking Glass	Newell Window Furnishings
Wal-Mart	X	X			X	X
Kmart	X	X	X	X	X	X
Target	X	X			X	
Fisher Big Wheel						X
Canadian Tire		X				
Ace Hardware		X				
Coast to Coast		X				
Shopko		X				

Source: Newell Company Annual Report, transcript, December 1992.

where retailers typically carried only one or two brand names in a given category. Hardware product sales were typically stimulated primarily by local promotions and retailer tie-ins, rather than national advertising.

Cookware   In 1983, Newell acquired Mirro, a manufacturer of low-end aluminum cookware sold in supermarkets and discount chains. In the following year, Newell acquired Foley, which, like Mirro, featured lighter-gauge aluminum products coated with SilverStone. Together, Mirro-Foley accounted for 29 percent of the $161.3 million aluminum cookware market. While the two labels were direct competitors, vying for space in the same retail outlets, Newell retained both brand names.

The Foley acquisition offered the opportunity to use the excess capacity from Mirro's aluminum rolling plant in Manitowoc, Wisconsin. Mirro had been selling the excess to its competitors; but with the acquisition of Foley, Newell increased the operating level to 90 percent from 75 percent. And while the industry suffered a 15–17 percent decline that year, Mirro-Foley showed an increase in sales.

In 1986, Newell acquired its biggest competitor for the low-end market, Enterprise Aluminum Company. With that, Newell became the leading cookware manufacturer in the United States. After adding Enterprise to its product line, Newell was able to bring operations at the Manitowoc plant from 90 percent to 100 percent capacity.

Newell's strategy in cookware was to increase its market share with high-volume mass retailers by maintaining differentiated product lines. Unlike hardware stores, which might sell only one brand of paint brush, for example, cookware retailers typically offered a broad selection. The Mirro division alone comprised the brand names Mirro, Foley, Rema, WearEver, AirBake, and CushionAire—relying heavily on in-store advertising and promotions to generate a high inventory turnover for the retailer. In the competition against other suppliers for shelf space, the company took the "good/better/best" approach it learned in hardware and applied it to the housewares business.

Newell's aggressive cost-cutting measures were exemplified by their handling of WearEver, acquired in 1989: WearEver was made profitable through the elimination of its marginal retail accounts and a 40 percent reduction of its previous volume. In 1986, Newell's cookware margins were 9 percent; by 1990, cookware margins were 15 percent.

Glassware   In 1987, Newell took on its biggest challenge to date with the acquisition of Anchor Hocking Corporation. The maker of glassware, hardware, plastic, and packaging products featured two stable brand names: Anchor and Amerock. Although Anchor Hocking had sales of $720.3 million in 1985, compared to Newell's $350 million, Newell targeted it for takeover on the basis of its own vastly stronger profit performance. At the time, Newell was enjoying an 11 percent profit margin, compared to Anchor's 0.5 percent margin.

Following the purchase of Anchor Hocking, two divisions were slated for divestiture: packaging products, which sold closures for glass containers to the food industry, and the food service division, which sold to restaurant chains—neither of which fit neatly with Newell's narrow focus on consumer products for volume purchasers. It was later decided to postpone divestiture of the packaging division. Out of the remaining businesses, Newell created a total of seven separate companies, each leaner and more operationally efficient than the corporation from whence it came. Newell management dismissed a number of high-level Anchor executives, including the chairman, and closed the company's 25 retail stores. They also closed one of three factories, reduced the total number of Anchor Hocking employees from 10,400 to about 9,000, and slashed excess inventory, eliminating 40 percent of Anchor's glass product lines by year end, saving $32.4 million in costs. An additional $12 million was saved by the end of 1987 by centralizing Anchor Hocking's administrative, financial, and computer functions under one roof at Newell's administrative headquarters in Freeport. Finally, Newell reduced the average length of time needed to fill a customer order from 18 to 7 days.

In October of 1992, Newell exited the industrial market with sale of Anchor Hocking Packaging, its $150 million subsidiary, to a French multinational packaging company. In the interim, Newell had acquired another plastic packaging operation for $40 million and consolidated it with Anchor Hocking.

Stanley Works: Seeking a Strong Name in Hardware   After acquiring Anchor Hocking in 1987, Newell went two years without another major acquisition. In 1990, revenues were down 4.5 percent, the first decline in more than a decade. That year, Newell engaged in preliminary merger talks with Stanley Works, a highly respected maker of tools and hardware with sales around $2 billion. Newell professed an interest in a partnership agreement because it lacked a widely recognized hardware brand name. Stanley's leadership immediately sensed the beginnings of a takeover attempt and responded with innovative federal antitrust litigation, with the added support of a separate antitrust action by the Connecticut attorney general.

In the highly publicized dispute that followed, Stanley's chief executive, Richard Ayers, blasted Newell in the press, calling the company "a creeping nuisance."[11] Newell was taken aback by the force of Stanley's protective defenses and eventually relented in October of 1992, citing massive litigation and damage to the company's reputation. Newell CEO William Sovey summarized his view of the dispute by saying, "I would just say that our intentions right along had been friendly. And when we realized that there couldn't be a friendly consummation of any kind of relationship, we decided to withdraw."[12] Newell agreed to sell its current stake of less than 1 percent of Stanley stock and to refrain from buying any more for 10 years.

Black & Decker

> When the market looks at us, I want them to see Newell and Black & Decker
> as a strategic alliance—like NATO.
>
> Daniel Ferguson[13]

In 1991, Newell had also pursued a limited partnership with Black & Decker, another highly respected brand name and manufacturer of power tools and home products that also sold to the same retail channels as Newell. The previous year, Black & Decker had posted $4.6 billion in sales, making it a lofty target for acquisition. Finding capital market conditions unfavorable for financing what would have been a contested bid, Newell negotiated a 10-year standstill agreement with the toolmaker, investing $150 million in convertible preferred stock but agreeing not to exceed its potential (postconversion) 15 percent equity stake.

The Black & Decker stock paid 11 percent per annum after-tax benefits and resulted in an immediate $.05 boost to Newell's EPS, even though the conversion price at $24 was a 60 percent premium over the current Black & Decker share price. Although Newell would be barred from extending its equity ownership for 10 years, the company would get to nominate one of its own as a director to the Black & Decker board of directors.

Office Products   Newell first entered the office products market in 1991, when it acquired two small office supply companies, Keene Manufacturing Co. and W.T. Rogers. The same year, the company also took an 18 percent stake in Stuart Hall, a $126 million manufacturer of paper products for school and office, whose biggest customers were mass retailers, volume drug chains, and supermarkets.

At the time, it was becoming increasingly common for people to work out of their homes, creating the need for office supplies to be sold in retail channels, instead of the traditional wholesale office supply channels that served companies. Early in 1992, Ferguson had estimated that there were already 17 million home offices, and that the number was growing.[14] With that, a new retail trend was emerging: the so-called "office superstores" (Exhibit 10). Many of the people running the new office superstores came directly from mass retail chains,

---

[11]"Stanley Works' Strong Offense Was Best Defense," *The Hartford Courant,* October 19, 1992, p. E1.
[12]Ibid.
[13]Holt Hackney, "Strategic Alliances," *Financial World,* October 29, 1991, p. 20.
[14]Tatiana Pouschine, "The Old-Fashioned Way," *Forbes,* January 6, 1992, p. 68.

▲ EXHIBIT 10   Office Supplies Distribution Shift

Channel	1986 Share	1990 Share	Percent Change
Mass market	5.6%	10.2%	73%
Warehouse clubs	1.9	4.0	111
Office superstores	0.3	7.3	500+
Top 50 dealers	18.2	23.7	30
Small and medium dealers	48.6	34.9	(28)
Other	20.2	15.3	(24)

Source: Newell Company Report, transcript, December 1992.

no guarantee of future growth

and already had experience in doing business with Newell. Still, office superstores were a recent phenomenon, and there was no guarantee as to their future growth.

▲ THE CORPORATE ROLE

Like everything else we do to market to the mass retailer,
the more they see us as an effective partner,
the better the edge we have when a certain product
comes up for review.[15]

Newell maintained centralized administration at the corporate level, making it clear that basic functions—legal and tax issues, benefits, EDI, credit collection, and financial control systems—would be their responsibility. Daniel Ferguson divided the finance job under two corporate executives: the vice president of finance focused on outside asset and liability management, while the controller focused on internal operations. Both positions reported directly to the CEO. Acquisitions were pursued at the corporate level, on the understanding that the various divisions were not to be distracted from their core function: generating profit. Total corporate staff was 260, with about 240 in the administrative headquarters in Freeport and 17 at the corporate headquarters in Beloit. The corporate charge to the divisions was 2 percent of sales.

The divisions were to handle design, manufacturing, marketing, sales, and service, as well as merchandising to the customer. Ferguson stressed the goal of creating lean, efficient contributors to the Newell strategy: "If you have an opportunity to make a product line into a profit unit, the smaller you can make that unit, the more entrepreneurial drive you have."[16] Although Newell encouraged its new businesses to pursue growth, Newell would not permit a division to redefine itself. Each business unit adhered to a specific and disciplined strategy, with permission to develop but not to expand its core product focus. For example, E-Z Paintr made "hand-held paint applicators," that is, paint brushes, not power sprayers or stepladders. Similarly, when the Wright Co. had wanted to add knitting patterns to its product line, the idea was rejected because patterns did no constitute a

---

[15]Hackney, "Stratetic Alliances," p. 20.
[16]Mary Ann Bacher, "The Newell Force in Housewares," *HFD: The Weekly Home Furnishings Newspaper,* January 11, 1988, p. 1 (5).

"volume, staple line." The separate divisions, with the exception of the largest, Mirro, reported to group vice presidents, one level below the company president (Exhibit 7).

Representatives from Newell sought to interface with the retain customer at all levels of management. William Sovey maintained communication with the top people at Wal-Mart and other major customers, as did Newell's president and chief operating officer, Thomas Ferguson. They would discuss issues relating to any of Newell's businesses. Two trade relations executives knew all their retail customers' vice presidents, but they never sold one of Newell's products; as one executive remarked, their job was to sell "Newell." Vested with the duty to run each entity as an entrepreneurial unit, division presidents functioned as their own chief marketing officers. They interfaced directly with their customers and maintained regular contacts with the retail chains' buyers. The company attached great importance to customer relations, frequently inviting buyers for plant visits that, in some communities, served as an occasion for planned celebrations with local officials in attendance. In addition, Newell involved its major customers in a process of shared planning and development.

Newell insisted upon holding customers strictly to the terms it laid out. The company's 2 percent-30-net-45 payment agreements were not negotiable. Acquired companies often had been allowing major customers to pay on 90-day terms; Newell eliminated this practice immediately, which resulted in savings on accounts receivable. Nor did any division president have authorization to allow a cash discount without corporate approval, even to their largest customers, except for preapproved campaigns. To Newell's executives, this "inflexibility" was simply a matter of discipline. The policy defended Newell against the protestations of smaller retailers such as hardware stores, who didn't like to see mass discounters such as Home Depot carrying the same brands for less. Newell also refused to bow to some retailers' demands that it serve them exclusively.

Management incentives both reflected and drove the corporate culture. Salary was based on a uniform system across all divisions, rewarding individuals on the basis of their position and the size of their division. Managers received a base salary that was equal to the industry average, but could look forward to bonuses ranging from a maximum of 33 percent for the most junior manager of a division's 20-person executive team, to 100 percent for division presidents. The expected rate for ROA was standard across all divisions of the company. As Daniel Ferguson noted, "If we can't make 32 percent in a business, we don't want to be in that business." The bonuses were based on division performance alone, and the culture encouraged competition by convening managers for award ceremonies to honor top performers. Stock options, an additional form of incentive made available when the company went public, were made available according to a formula based on salary and position.

Until 1990, the company's system for evaluating yearly bonuses focused exclusively on ROA. The goals were high—beginning at 32.5 percent ROA and reaching the maximum payout at 43.5 percent—and by meeting them, managers achieved spectacular financial results for the company. The company outperformed the S&P, averaging 21 percent ROE over a 10-year period—exceeding its own goal of 20 percent (Exhibit 11). In 1992, Newell was ranked 24th on the Fortune 500 list for highest total return to investors over a 10-year period.

In 1990, Newell altered its bonus structure by adding an additional 30 percent bonus for internal growth on top of existing ROA goals. Although the company had a banner year in terms of profitability, internal growth still lagged. In the first quarter of 1990, Newell's sales were down 5 percent, while earnings leapt 72 percent. Management recognized that, over the long run, the company needed a more sound balance. One top executive noted, "there are years when you can increase earnings more than you increase sales, but you can't do that

▲ **EXHIBIT 11**   Newell Company Comparative Stock Price Performance

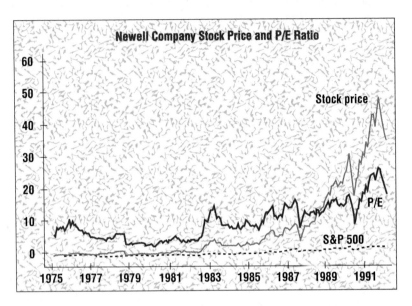

Source: Standard & Poor's, Compustat.

½ from internal growth
½ from acquisitions

year after year." The following year, Newell tried again; this time, the bonus system would be split evenly between ROA and internal growth. Their aim was to wring half of future 15 per-cent yearly sales increases out of internal growth, while the other half would come from ac-quisitions.[17] In 1991, Newell achieved 6 percent internal growth with new products whose purpose was to increase market share with existing customers. Such products included Mirro's colored cookware and Newell Window Furnishings' new miniblind called "Spectrim," which featured a cutting machine built into the brand's store display, making it possible to sell custom-fitted window blinds on a while-you-wait basis.

Given the potential for rewards, demand for positions at Newell was always high. Sovey and Thomas Ferguson sought top management people who would be motivated by success and a lucrative bonus system. Through an intensive application process that only one in ten passed, they screened applicants—mostly mid-level executives from other hardware and cookware companies—for these particular management traits with a personality test. Each newly hired company employee underwent a two-and-a-half-day training program in the Newell corporate culture. The so-called "Newell University" stressed product focus and profit-orientation, the underpinnings of Newellizaton.

Career paths featured frequent transfers and promotions. Among the top 250 managers, the yearly turnover rate was above 10 percent, with one person moving across as many as five divisions. Even division presidents had an average tenure of less than 10 years—a re-flection of the number of acquisitions and the possibility of moving from smaller to larger divisions. Executives generally were responsible for plotting their own career paths. Job openings were publicized within the company; with few exceptions, corporate HR took no

[17]S.J. Heller, *Newell Company Report* (Transcript). Shearson Lehman Brothers, Inc., December 1992.

proactive role in filling them, letting divisional managers choose from among the candidates. Sovey and Ferguson were directly involved in decisions regarding the top 100 people, reaching to one level below division president.

Six times a year, division leaders convened for presidents' meetings. These, in addition to regular encounters at trade shows, kept leadership across divisions apprised as to what was going on elsewhere in the company. Annual management meetings brought together functional VPs for sales and marketing, operations, personnel, control, and customer service from all 16 divisions. Each group had its own two-day meeting, featuring presentations and programs aimed at transferring learning.

Corporate purchasing took place under the direction of a liaison from corporate services. The divisions could get together with one another to establish a contract and coordinate purchasing of shared items. However, the amount of corporate purchasing was limited, and there existed no requirement for intracompany transfers.

To maintain its profit focus, the company adhered to a strict set of monthly financial reviews. Administered by divisional controllers (key members of the management team who also reported directly to the corporate controller as well as to their divisional controller), Newell's financial control system used variable budgeting that adjusted expense items in line with aggregate sales, specifically addressing 30 items. Variances were bracketed, and too many variances would lead to a "brackets meeting." Even if sales were above budget, if the flexed cost numbers showed an unfavorable variance, intervention would follow. While Newell executives stressed that brackets meetings were not intended to be pleasant for the division presidents, they were aimed at identifying and solving the problem. If necessary, the budget would be changed and that division would be strictly held to the adjusted level. Company executives preferred to commit their division heads to a "real budget"—using words like "contract" instead of "plan" and "out of control" instead of "variance."

Operating figures were also collected monthly, on the premise that "If you want it done, you need to measure it." Newell's tightly disciplined approach derived from their conviction that "if each piece is done right, the whole will look after itself." In Daniel Ferguson's words, "We're an operating company, not a holding company." As a consequence, corporate management met with divisional managers regularly throughout the year, with two meetings devoted to budget setting, and at least as many to strategic planning. At least three or four times a year, the two sets of managers would meet at either the corporate farmhouse or the division's headquarters to review the monthly results in person.

▲ SANFORD CORPORATION

Sanford designed, manufactured, and marketed a broad array of markers, pens, and desk supplies for work and school. It was the most profitable company Newell had ever considered as a takeover target. At a price of about $600 million, it also would be the most expensive. Sanford had good management, whose talent for driving the company's growth had been well-noted among industry observers (Exhibit 12). Still, in 1992, Sanford had fewer than ten people at the corporate level, and limited computer systems.

The company focused on creating niche products. "Accent" was number one in the highlighter segment, "Sharpie" led in permanent ink, an "Expo" in dry-erase. New products developed by the company included "Faccent"—a highlighter with ink specially formulated for use on fax paper—and the laundry-proof "Rub-a-Dub" pen for marking clothing. Within Sanford's product line, no one item dominated the company's overall sales volume.

▲ EXHIBIT 12   Selected Financial Information for Sanford Company
(in $ millions)

	1991	1990	1989	1988	1987	1986
Net sales		$138,675	$130,055	$102,376	$83,796	$75,077
Gross profit		72,527	65,746	53,840	45,040	37,221
Operating income		38,476	36,150	30,834	25,543	19,240
Interest expense		115	1,679	1,232	1,095	2,138
Income before taxes		39,413	34,879	30,219	24,979	16,652
Net income		24,152	21,004	17,642	13,092	7,025
Working capital		42,605	22,923	17,599	17,907	13,726
Goodwill		40,344	41,508	42,715	30,202	31,032
Total assets		124,892	103,504	103,381	68,428	62,389
Long-term debt		1,000	2,000	20,500	7,500	14,500
Shareholders' equity		101,308	80,789	61,795	46,590	37,267

Sanford first approached Newell in 1984, when it was making a profit of $4 million on $40 million in sales. Ferguson passed up the opportunity buy the company for $65 million, noting that Sanford offered its products primarily through wholesale stationers, contract stationers, pen wholesalers, and retail outlets; only 2.5 percent of its sales were in the mass market. In the late 1980s, Sanford's management addressed the industry shift toward mass retailers—office "superstores"—by altering their methods of distribution. By 1989, superstores and warehouse clubs commanded 8 percent of Sanford's total volume.

In September 1988, in an effort to upgrade its product line, Sanford had acquired $22 million Sterling Plastics Co., a subsidiary of Borden, Inc., for $31 million. Sterling was a manufacturer of office products in three categories: plastic desk accessories, file storage boxes, and school supplies. With products destined for the same channels of distribution, the Sterling acquisition seemed to fulfill Sanford's centralized shipping needs. However, after its first full year as a subsidiary of Sanford, Sterling had difficulty building a sales base. Sanford attempted to derive value from the acquisition by shifting the manufacturing of some of its component parts to Sterling facilities in order to absorb the excess capacity and create efficiencies; still, the acquisition was hindering Sanford's financial performance. Sterling's sales went down in 1990, causing Sanford's consolidated sales growth rate to be only 7 percent, compared to 27.6 percent in 1989.

▲ LEVOLOR

When Levolor introduced 1-inch mini blinds to America in the early 1970s, it revolutionized what had been a sleepy government and school industry in wide-slat blinds. With the addition of fashion colors, Levolor's sleek Riviera mini blinds gained swift acceptance in homes and offices. The focus of the company was horizontal metal blinds, each custom-made in a choice of almost 200 colors.

To supply the thousand of local decorating shops, regional distributors, and national chains, Levolor opened 22 factories across the country. The largest accounts were Sears,

Montgomery Ward, and distributors, followed by some 6,000 local one- and two-store operations. Business boomed through the 1970s as Levolor dominated the industry. The company slowly added vertical blinds and pleated shades to become a full-line supplier.

Without serious competitors, Levolor had never been concerned about high prices and long delivery times. Though inefficient, the company carried decentralized manufacturing operations and enormous inventories. This gave an opening to more nimble competitors, notably Hunter Douglas, who relied on local fabricators to manufacture and deliver products. As prices became competitive by the mid-1980s, Levolor's margins came under severe pressure.

Until 1987, Levolor had been owned and operated by the Lorentzen family, descendants of the Danish immigrant who began making components for awnings and shades in 1917. The family sold Levolor in a leveraged buyout for $135 million to Dean Witter Capital in 1987. Sales that year were $260 million. Soon after the sale, headquarters moved from New Jersey to California. The company went through a succession of management changes until 1992 when sales bottomed at $180 million (Exhibit 13).

Newell had eyed Levolor as an acquisition for years. When Dean Witter Capital decided to divest Levolor in 1993, Newell stepped in with the high bid of $65 million, recognizing that a significant investment had to be made in the company to consolidate operations.

By this time, Home Depot had become Levolor's leading account, followed by Sears. The top 25 accounts had grown to over 65 percent of volume (Exhibit 14). Distributors had shrunk to 9 percent of sales; small retailers were a declining business. Hunter Douglas was now the industry leader in both sales and new products. Levolor had expanded in stock blinds but continued to rely on custom horizontal blinds, including the trusty Riviera and the newly designed Mark I.

[handwritten margin notes: "operationally inefficient"; "would benefit from Newell's management"; "strong customer base"]

▲ EXHIBIT 13   Selected Financial Information for Levolor (in $ thousands)

	1991	1992
Net sales	181,833	180,335
Gross profit	54,827	49,582
Operating income	8,447	7,279
Net income	(13,383)	(18,118)
Total assets	69,418	63,421

▲ EXHIBIT 14   Levolor Sales by Channel of Distribution

	1990	1991	1992
Direct customers	33%	33%	37%
Home centers	12	20	26
SWAPs	10	10	16
Distributors	26	18	10
Paint/wall covering	7	6	6
Department stores	5	5	3
Other	7	0	2
Total assets	100	100	100

how will Newellization help Sanford and Jewelor?
which will it help more?
what will shareholders think / how to convince?
what are their operating margins? typically Newell looked for operationally inefficient acquisitions
p.623 - what about the trend moving away from private labelling?

SHARP CORPORATION: TECHNOLOGY STRATEGY

Established in 1912, Sharp Corporation owed its name and beginning to the invention of the "Ever-Sharp" mechanical pencil by founder Tokuji Hayakawa. By 1992, with sales of ¥1,518 billion (US$11,497 million) and net income of ¥39 billion (US$296 million),[1] Sharp had grown to include businesses ranging from consumer electronics and information systems to electronic components employing 41,000 people, of whom about 20,000 worked overseas (Exhibit 1).

Rooted in the creed "Sincerity and Creativity," entrepreneurship and technological innovation had always been mainstays of the company. However, Sharp had originally been seen as a second-tier assembler of television sets and home appliances which competed mainly on price, because any new products were quickly imitated by larger competitors, including Matsushita, Hitachi, and Toshiba. A critical turning point came in the early 1970s, when Sharp developed expertise in certain electronic devices, such as specialized integrated circuits (ICs) and liquid crystal displays (LCDs), and used them to develop innovative end products (Exhibit 2). As a result, the company consistently improved its performance so that, by 1992, it was regarded as a world leader in optoelectronics and a premier comprehensive electronics company.

[handwritten: used to compete on price now on innovation]

Doctoral candidate Tomo Noda prepared this case under the supervision of Professor David J. Collis.
[1]Sharp's fiscal year ends March 31.

▲ **EXHIBIT 1** Sharp Corporation—Financial Summary

	Dollar Millions	Japanese Yen (Millions)												
	1992	1992	1991	1990	1989	1988	1987	1986	1985	1980	1975*	1970*	1965*	1960*
Consolidated														
Sales	11,497	1,517,538	1,496,111	1,344,799	1,238,401	1,225,186	1,148,881	1,216,048	1,166,651	514,884	190,185	120,822	30,210	19,922
Gross profit	3,309	436,794	437,232	388,389	315,835	247,253	235,602	283,373	285,511	129,712	27,429	24,130	5,995	5,273
Selling, general, and administration	2,777	366,597	351,185	307,457	262,093	228,584	219,156	239,956	220,067	100,243	22,662	12,501	4,502	2,493
Operating income	531	70,197	86,047	88,932	53,742	20,669	16,446	43,417	65,444	9,469	4,767	11,628	1,493	2,780
Income before tax	629	83,103	99,648	93,511	68,586	43,196	42,831	70,875	78,326	29,596	4,112	8,226	1,070	2,701
Net income	295	39,057	46,918	41,720	29,103	20,341	20,775	35,935	39,903	16,747	2,617	5,271	805	1,429
Total assets	16,270	2,147,690	2,077,030	2,032,598	1,764,662	1,618,625	1,400,352	1,232,747	1,110,153	450,205	168,347	99,673	32,506	14,039
Long-term debt	1,558	205,652	261,639	247,515	196,075	145,787	125,865	128,446	130,394	27,195	13,512	6,420	1,947	0
Shareholders' equity	5,724	755,561	726,763	685,351	534,758	477,925	390,107	379,471	357,891	128,263	38,664	30,540	11,669	5,225
Acquisition of plant and equipment	995	131,373	122,670	116,675	80,722	55,264	59,328	82,042	91,794	39,192	6,881	12,355	NA	1,751
Depreciation and amortization	758	100,107	89,625	75,032	68,449	61,268	58,864	55,451	45,645	15,549	5,936	3,839	805	226
Return on sales (%)		2.57	3.14	3.10	2.35	1.66	1.81	2.96	3.42	3.25	1.38	4.36	2.66	7.17
Return on assets (%)		1.82	2.26	2.05	1.65	1.26	1.48	2.92	3.59	3.72	1.55	5.29	2.48	10.18
Return on equity (%)		5.17	6.46	6.09	5.44	4.26	5.33	9.47	11.15	13.06	6.77	17.26	6.90	27.35
Income per share (yen)		36.61	44.13	39.57	30.65	22.40	28.19	49.01	54.57	31.28	11.08	25.10	6.71	35.73
Dividend per share (yen)		11.00	11.00	11.00	11.00	11.00	11.00	11.00	11.00	7.50	8.25	9.00	6.00	10.70
Number of employees		41,029	36,539	34,017	32,398	29,351	29,346	28,873	28,221	18,743	9,804	15,442	5,591	4,457
Nonconsolidated														
Sales	9,106	1,202,014	1,152,678	1,057,282	992,665	872,707	868,587	955,252	909,581	395,246	190,185	120,822	30,210	19,922
Net income	273	36,063	44,340	37,536	26,232	18,857	20,104	34,735	33,863	12,526	2,617	5,271	805	1,429

*Nonconsolidated; consolidated data for these years are not available.
Source: Sharp Corporation.

Automotive 4" Color LCD TV

"Viewcam" LCD Camcorder

"LCD Museum" Wall-mount Color LCD TV

"Wizard" Electronic Organizer

▲ COMPANY HISTORY

The Era of Tokuji Hayakawa (1912–1970)

Tokuji Hayakawa opened his own small workshop with two employees in 1912, making the snap belt buckle which he had designed himself (Exhibit 3). After three years, Hayakawa invented a mechanical pencil, consisting of a retractable graphite lead in a metal rod, and named it the Ever-Sharp pencil. He introduced assembly line processes, uncommon in Japan at that time, and the business grew rapidly. Unfortunately, the Great Kanto Earthquake of 1923 took everything away from Hayakawa: he lost his wife, two infant sons, many employees, and his workshop.

In 1924, Hayakawa reestablished his company in Osaka with three employees. With radio broadcasting scheduled to begin in Japan the following year, he bought one of the first crystal radio sets imported from the United States and gradually mastered the technology by disassembling this model. The company began to assemble Japan's first domestically produced crystal radio sets in 1925. When, in 1929, several competitors entered the crystal radio market, Hayakawa developed a radio using vacuum tubes that could amplify and receive signals from a wider range. The mass production of this radio, called the Sharp Dyne, and the commencement of its export to South Asia established the company as a leading manufacturer of radios. In 1935, the Hayakawa Metal Works Institute Co. was incorporated with ¥300,000 in capital. The company was renamed Hayakawa Electric Industry Co. (Hayakawa Electric) in 1942.

▲ EXHIBIT 3   Sharp Corporation—Corporate History

1912	Founded by Tokuji Hayakawa in Tokyo. Invented the *snap buckle*.
1915	Invented a *mechanical pencil** named the Ever-Sharp Pencil.
1925	Relocated to Osaka after the Great Kanto Earthquake. Established as Hayakawa Metal Works. Began production of *crystal radio sets*† and components.
1929	Began production of *AC vacuum-tube radio sets*.†
1930	Started export of crystal radios.
1935	Incorporated as Hayakawa Metal Works Institute Co.
1942	Renamed Hayakawa Electric Industry Co.
1953	Developed *black-and-white TV sets*.†
1962	Developed *microwave ovens*.† Established a marketing subsidiary in the United States.
1963	Introduced a multidivisional organization structure.
1964	Developed and began mass production of *all transistor-diode electronic desktop calculator—Compet*.*
1968	Established a marketing subsidiary in Germany.
1970	Established Advanced Development Planning Center (Central Research Laboratories, ELSI Plant and training center) in Tenri, Nara. Renamed Sharp Corporation.
1971	Established Sharp Digital Information Products Inc. Established production companies in Taiwan and Brazil.
1973	Developed *COS electronic calculator incorporating LCD*.* Established a production company in Korea.
1976	Organized New Life committee.
1979	Established Sharp Manufacturing Company of America. Started local production of color TVs in Memphis.
1985	Established Sharp Manufacturing Company of Europe. Established Creative Lifestyle Focus Center in Osaka.
1988	Developed *14-inch TFT color liquid crystal*.*
1990	Established Sharp Laboratories of Europe, Ltd.
1992	Established the Multimedia Systems Research and Development Center.

*World's first.
†Japan's first.

In 1953, in anticipation of the TV era, Hayakawa Electric got a license from RCA to manufacture Japan's first black-and-white TV sets under the Sharp brand name. By 1955, the company was a leading Japanese TV manufacturer with nearly a quarter of the market.[2] This positioned Sharp to grow with the domestic electrical goods market at more than 30 percent each year, as first black-and-white and then color TV sets, refrigerators, washing machines, and air conditioners became household status symbols in Japan. In addition to increasing production capacity and developing market channels for these consumer electronic goods

[2]Hideo Hirayama, *Waga Kaisoroku: Sharp (My Memories on Sharp)* (Tokyo: Denpa Shimbunsha, 1991), p. 52.

and appliances, Hayakawa Electric also introduced Japan's first microwave ovens in 1962 using technology learned while working with Litton, the U.S. innovator in microwave ovens. By 1965, TVs and radios accounted for 53 percent of the company's sales, down from 84 percent in 1960.

Throughout this period, although founder Hayakawa advocated making innovative products that competitors would want to imitate, the company remained primarily an assembler. Its limited size and capital restricted its ability to vertically integrate, and competitors rapidly copied its products. These problems were exacerbated in the mid-1960s when the Japanese economy experienced a severe recession; independent "mom and pop" stores, which had been the dominant distribution channel, coped with the recession by becoming exclusive retailers for large electrical goods producers, such as Matsushita, Toshiba, and Hitachi. Despite its best efforts, Hayakawa Electric was only able to build a distribution network one-seventh the size of Matsushita's and one-third that of Hitachi's and Toshiba's. Because of its smaller distribution network and the continuing imitation of its products. Hayakawa Electric's market share in radios and TVs began to decline.

At the same time, Hayakawa, like many other large electrical products manufacturers, invest in the emerging computer technology industry. In 1961, it established a corporate research laboratory to begin research on computers, solar cells, and microwaves. However, the Ministry of International Trade and Industry (MITI) soon restricted the benefits of its industrial policy for the computer industry to six companies, in effect shutting Hayakawa Electric out of the development of mainframe computers. In order to continue their work, Hayakawa Electric's researchers chose desktop electronic calculators as an alternative target because calculators matched the company's orientation toward the mass consumer market.

The company's refocusing of its computer research led to its introduction of the world's first all transistor-diode electronic desktop calculator, called Compet, in 1964. The Compet weighed 25 kilograms (55 pounds), was 25 centimeters (8.7 inches) thick, and sold for ¥535,000 (about $1,500 at that time), almost as much as a 1,300 cc passenger car. The so-called electronic calculator wars soon followed when Sony, Canon, and then Casio, a leading producer of mechanical calculators, all introduced their own electronic calculators within a few months of one another.

In response, under the direction of Dr. Sasaki, a recently hired outsider who had been a researcher at Bell Laboratories and RCA, Hayakawa Electric introduced the world's first electronic calculators incorporating integrated circuits (ICs) in 1966. These calculators initially used bipolar ICs, which processed commands quickly but consumed much electricity. Dr. Sasaki judged that energy efficiency, not speed, would be critical for consumer electronics and he convinced Hayakawa Electric to switch to a new technology, MOS ICs—because they consumed less electricity and their chip density could easily be increased.[3] By employing MOS ICs supplied by the North American Rockwell Company to make progressively smaller calculators, Sharp quickly assumed a leading position in electronic calculators.

The Era of Akira Saeki (1970–1986)

On a visit to Rockwell in 1969, Mr. Saeki, then senior executive vice president of Hayakawa Electric, was impressed by Rockwell's semiconductor technology that had made the Apollo space mission possible. Although he had spent most of his career in finance and

---

[3]Masahiko Tonedachi, *Dentaku-to-Shinkansen (Electronic Calculators and Super Express Trains: The Arts of the Japanese Advanced Technologies)* (Tokyo: Shinchosha, 1983), p. 75

accounting and did not have a technology background, he was convinced of the semiconductor's potential. Worried about his company's position as an assembler, Saeki also recognized the importance of in-house manufacturing of key components in developing unique products.[4] He repeatedly said, "We can hardly contribute to society if we only make the same products that other manufacturers do…[We need to develop] products which others cannot imitate even if they want to do so."[5]

With the support of President Hayakawa, Saeki proposed canceling the company's participation in the international exhibition scheduled for the following year in Senri, so that the company could build a semiconductor factory in nearby Tenri, instead. Despite the concern of many executives, the company built a C-MOS LSI (large scale integration) plant and a central research laboratory. Investing ¥7,500 million (US$21 million) in the projects (one-quarter of the company's equity), the catchphrase of "Tenri rather than Senri" appeared almost spontaneously in the company as Hayakawa Electric became the 13th semiconductor manufacturer in Japan. Unfortunately, due to a lack of technological expertise, manufacturing yields in the new semiconductor factory were low, and the operation incurred annual losses of ¥400–¥600 (approximately $1.3–$2 million) in its first five years.[6] Only in the mid-1970s did the company's production of C-MOS semiconductors turn profitable.

In January 1970, Hayakawa Electric was renamed Sharp Corporation to reflect the company's brand name and herald its transition from an electrical appliance manufacturer to an electronics company. Mr. Saeki formally assumed the presidency when Tokuji Hayakawa retired from day-to-day operations to become chairman later that year. Competition in electronic desktop calculators then intensified in August 1972, when Casio introduced the revolutionary Casio Mini, a six-digit calculator costing only ¥12,800 (about $40 at that time). Challenged by Casio's low-cost strategy, most firms, including Sony, exited the market.

Stunned by the "Casio Shock" and trying to avoid a price war, a project team sought to develop, by April of 1973, a thinner calculator which would consume less electricity and therefore be truly portable. The team's efforts resulted in the world's thinnest calculator, the LC Mate, which cost ¥26,800, but weighed only 200 grams (0.44 pounds) and was only 2.1 centimeters (0.7 inch) thick. This palm-sized model consumed less than 1/100 of the electricity of conventional fluorescent tube models by incorporating an LCD into a calculator for the first time ever.

LCDs consume little electricity because the liquid crystals themselves do not emit light; rather their molecules are arranged along an electric field, allowing external rays to pass through when voltage is applied. A Sharp engineer had learned about the application of liquid crystals to displays, which had been pioneered by RCA in the late 1960s, while watching a television program about the United States. RCA had since stopped LCD research and exited the business because, Sharp management believed, RCA senior management had seen only a small market for the product at that time.

Sharp soon improved upon the LC Mate, developing a 7-mm-thick electronic calculator using in-house C-MOS LSIs in 1976, and a 1.6-mm version in 1979. The incorporation of photovoltaic cells eliminated the need for an external electricity source, and the introduction

[4]Sharp Corporation, *Seii-to-Soi: Hachijunen no Ayumi (Sincerity and Creativity: The 80-year History of Sharp Corporation)* (Tokyo: Sharp Corp, 1992), p. 42.
[5]Hirayama, p. 79.
[6]Hirayama, p. 85.

of a fully automated chip-on-sheet (COS) manufacturing process contributed to a drastic reduction in product price. As a result of these efforts, Sharp won the Japanese calculator wars and held nearly half of the domestic market share by the end of the 1970s.

Using the same distribution channels and technology developed for calculators, Sharp quickly diversified within the information equipment business in the 1970s. It developed a broad range of office automation products, including microcomputers (1971), electronic cash registers (1971), liquid toner copiers (1972), personal computers (1979), Japanese word processors (1979), and facsimiles (1980).

During the same period, the domestic market for TVs and other appliances was approaching saturation. In response, Sharp abandoned its previous goal of catching up with its rivals in sales volume and concentrated on "distinguishing between where [it could] win and where [it could not], and winning completely in the former."[7] In 1975, a task force proposed introducing "New Life" products to meet the demands of more diversified and sophisticated customers and to actively propose new lifestyles to those consumers. The New Life committee, composed of directors, general managers of business groups, and top managers of sales subsidiaries, was organized to achieve this in 1976. One of the first New Life products was a three-door refrigerator with a freezer at the bottom. This was introduced because customer research had shown that the frequency of use was 80 percent for coolers and 20 percent for freezers. With the cooler at the top, users had to bend less frequently. In addition to functionality, the New Life committee emphasized color and design, which most manufacturers considered to be of secondary importance at that time, and it carefully coordinated these elements across several business groups. With the successful promotion of a series of New Life products, Sharp's appliance business attained annual growth of more 10 percent in the late 1970s and early 1980s, despite the sluggish 3 percent annual growth of the industry as a whole during the period.[8]

Sharp's other achievements during the 1970s, which later led to a strategic thrust to redefine the company as an optoelectronics company, centered on optosemiconductors, which act as converters between light and electricity. Sharp had developed the world's largest solar cells for a lighthouse in 1963, and further research led to the development of solar cells for satellites in 1976. The central R&D laboratory also developed electroluminescent (EL) displays and laser diodes. While the potential of electroluminescence for displays had been known for a long time, most firms had discontinued research in this area because of technological difficulties. Sharp, however, persevered and developed an EL panel in 1978, which was used in space shuttle displays. A few years later, it mass-produced ultra-thin, high-definition EL displays. As for laser diodes, the "optical needle" for compact disks and video disks, Sharp's development of a durable diode in 1981 gained it the leading position in the world market.

The Era of Haruo Tsuji (1986–present)

Sharp's steady growth was interrupted in 1985 by the drastic appreciation of the Japanese yen against the U.S. dollar because of the Plaza Accord. The company's fiscal 1987 nonconsolidated sales dropped by about 10 percent and operating profits by more than 60 percent. In this difficult environment, Haruo Tsuji, a company veteran with extensive experience in the appliance business, assumed the post of president.

---

[7]Comment of Masaki Seki originally cited by Hirayama, p. 93.
[8]H. Takeuchi, K. Sakakibara, T. Kagono, A. Okumura, and I. Nonaka, *Kigyo no JikoKakushin (Self-Renewal of the Japanese Firms)* (Tokyo: Chuokoronsha, 1986), p. 85.

Under Tsuji, Sharp continued its New Life strategy to design products that appealed to different individual tastes. The company introduced new products, such as electronic organizers (i.e., the Wizard in the United States), dual-swing door refrigerators, home-use facsimile machines, and the first combination cordless telephone/answering machines, and furthered its reputation among retailers and customers for user-friendliness.

In addition to experiencing continued success in consumer electronics, Sharp made advances in electronic devices, particularly in LCDs, which it chose to develop in preference to the cathode ray tubes it had always purchased from outside vendors, even for TV sets. Since its first use of LCDs in calculators, Sharp had maintained its leadership in the technology by continuing to develop larger, higher-quality displays. It introduced an alphabetical LCD for calculators in 1979 and a large monochrome LCD for personal computers and word processors in 1983. Using a new thin-film-transistor (TFT) active-matrix technology, it then developed a 3-inch color LCD with faster response and a higher picture quality in 1986, and a 14-inch color TFT LCD in 1988. Based on these LCDs, the company continuously introduced a number of first-in-the-world products, such as a 110-inch color LCD video projector, a 8.6-inch wall-mount LCD monitor (1991), and the "ViewCam" camcorder with a 4-inch color LCD monitor (1992), even though some of these products were initially unprofitable because they only met a small market need.

As Sharp recorded five years of consecutive growth in sales and operating profits to fiscal 1991, its reputation in Japan grew stronger. One corporate image survey showed Sharp climbing from 63rd to 21st in the three years leading up to 1992. Another survey ranked Sharp in 9th position in 1992. In the United States, Sharp was ranked 25th among all companies, U.S. and foreign, in patents filed behind such technological giants as IBM, GM, GE, AT&T, Du Pont, and 3M.[9]

Globalization

Sharp's overseas activities began in 1930, with the export of radios to South Asia. After World War II, Hayakawa Electric rapidly expanded its exports to the United States under the Sharp brand name, starting with transistor radios and then adding black-and-white TV sets in the 1960s (Exhibit 4). It established a wholly owned sales subsidiary in the United States in 1962 and gradually developed a global sales network.

Also, in the early 1970s, in response to cost pressure because of the yen's appreciation, Sharp transferred labor-intensive activities overseas, establishing production companies in Taiwan, Brazil, Korea, and Malaysia. These overseas production facilities were established as joint ventures based on technology licensing rather than as wholly owned subsidiaries. This structure reflected Tokuji Hayakawa's philosophy that his company would not exploit developing countries, but rather prosper with them.

To mitigate U.S. trade frictions, particularly concerning TV sets, Sharp established the Sharp Manufacturing Company of America (SMCA) to produce color TVs in 1979, SMCA steadily expanded its operations, adding LCD production by 1992. Similarly, Sharp Manufacturing Company of U.K., established in 1985, further localized Sharp's overseas operations. Finally, in order to better exploit rapid changes in technology, the company established its first overseas development center in the United States in 1972. In 1990, the company added a research laboratory in the U.K. to conduct basic research in optoelectronics and information processing technologies (e.g., Pan-European translation technology).

localized overseas operations

---

[9]*Business Week,* August 3, 1992, pp. 68–69.

▲ EXHIBIT 4   Sharp Corporation—Exports and Exchange Rates

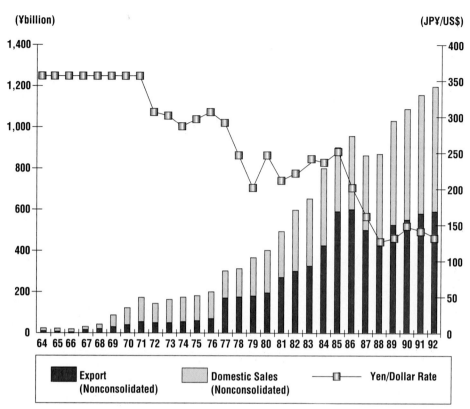

▲ SHARP'S BUSINESSES IN 1992

Sharp products fell into three broad areas: consumer electronics and appliances, information and office automation equipment, and electronic devices (Exhibits 5, 6, and 7).

Consumer Electronics and Appliances

The TV and Video Systems Group was the largest single manufacturing group in the company with sales of about ¥400 billion (25.9 percent of the company's total) in fiscal 1992. The company strove to develop new market niches by applying state-of-the-art LCD technologies to this relatively mature business segment. For example, it introduced 5.6-inch, portable, flat screen, LCD color TVs, only 2 inches deep, which were increasingly installed in cars and used as second or third sets in homes, and LCD projectors, which offered television set picture quality with a 100-inch screen. In preparation for the coming of HDTV, Sharp also developed HDTV projection systems using LCDs and broke a new price point when it introduced a vacuum tube HDTV set in 1992 for ¥1,000,000, a price one-third that of competitors.

The Communication and Audio Systems Group recorded a 40 percent increase in sales between 1989 and 1991 because of its market leadership in combination cordless phone/answering machines, pioneered by Sharp. In 1992, the ¥40 billion facsimiles business held the

▲ EXHIBIT 5   Sharp Corporation—Transition of Business Portfolio (on a nonconsolidated basis)

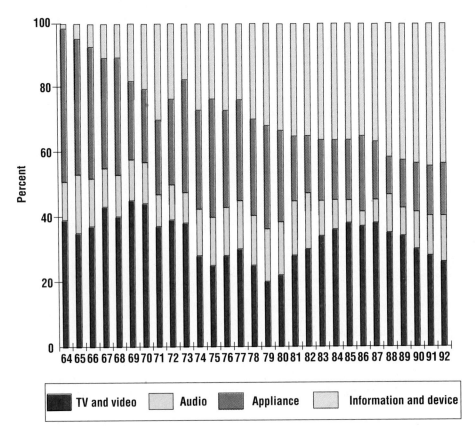

leading share in the U.S. market, having pioneered the move to mass distribution channels. That year, the business was transferred from the Information Equipment Group to this group because top management anticipated the spread of facsimiles to homes and their integration with telephones.

Sales of the Appliance Systems Group amounted to ¥266 billion, or 17.5 percent of the company's total in fiscal 1992. Sharp's New People products, such as a refrigerator with bi-directional doors and a microwave oven with a fuzzy-logic control system, were particularly popular with young people because of their unique functions and appealing designs and colors. However, their share of company sales was declining as the industry matured.

Sharp's major competitors in consumer electronics and appliances fell into three groups based on their original business foci (Exhibit 6). The first group, comprising Hitachi, Toshiba, and Mitsubishi Electric, had started as heavy electric machinery manufacturers and diversified into appliances early in their histories, capitalizing on their strength in electric motors. The second group of competitors, including Matsushita Electric and Sanyo, had been established as appliance manufacturers. Matsushita was the world leader in consumer electronics, well-known for its National brand in Japan and its Panasonic brand overseas. Founded in 1917, it had long dominated the industry because of its unparalleled nationwide retail network (National Shops). Sharp was often compared with Sanyo because it was the same size and was located in the same district; but the two firms differed significantly in their corporate cultures and strategies, with Sanyo regarded primarily as a low-cost player. The third group of competitors, comprising Sony, JVC, Pioneer, Aiwa, and Kenwood, did not produce white goods and concentrated instead on audio-visual products. Sony was particularly well-known for its innovative products and technologies, such as the world's first transistor radios, portable cassette recorders, CD players, and 8-mm camcorders.

Information Systems and Office Automation Equipment

In fiscal 1992, the area of information systems and office automation equipment generated about 23 percent of Sharp's sales. Major products of the Information Systems Group were calculators, electronic organizers, office and personal computers, and Japanese word processors, all of which used displays of one type or the other. The Printing and Reprographic Systems Group produced copiers, scanners, OA peripherals, and associated products. For these products, Sharp concentrated on its color capability, stressing, for example, four-color copiers rather than monochrome ones.

As technology evolved, several firms in such areas as computers, communications equipment, cameras, and appliances entered the information equipment business. Sharp's competitors and market share therefore differed by product market. In electronic calculators and organizers, Sharp had a leading market share and its main competitors were Casio and Canon. In Japanese word processors, where it also had a leading market share, and in personal computers, where it had only a foothold, its main competitors were NEC, Toshiba, Fujitsu, Japan IBM, and Seiko-Epson. Sharp had a strong market position in facsimiles against Matsushita, Ricoh, and Canon, but a smaller share of the plain paper copier market against Ricoh, Canon, Fuji Xerox, and Konica.

Electronic Components/Devices

In the late 1980s and early 1990s, electronic components were the driving force behind Sharp's growth. As a result of aggressive investment, this sector had grown to about 23 percent of total sales in fiscal 1992, as compared with only about 8.0 percent in 1975.

The Integrated Circuits Group was in the semiconductor business. In contrast to larger companies, such as NEC, Toshiba, Hitachi, and Fujitsu, which manufactured commodity chips and aggressively competed on price and processing performance by exploiting scale economies and accumulated learning. Sharp generated 80 percent of its semiconductor sales from customized and semicustomized products. It had applied the C-MOS technology first used for electronic calculators to gate-arrays and microprocessors, and held a 35 percent global market share in masked ROMs (manufacturer-programmed memory chips) used in VCRs, video games such as Nintendo game cassettes, and microwaves.

The Electronics Components Group developed products such as high-frequency satellite transmission components, printed circuit boards, optomagnetic disks, and solar cells. Among these, optoelectronic devices were the most unique to Sharp. Sharp had been the world leader in this segment for eight consecutive years up to 1992,[10] holding dominant global market

---

[10]A survey by Data Quest.

▲ EXHIBIT 6 Sharp Corporation—Current Businesses (overview)

Area	Manufacturing Groups	Consolidated Sales (FY 1992)	Manufacturing Divisions	Major Products	Major Competitors
Consumer electronics	TV and Video systems group	¥393.4 billion (US$2,981 million) 25.9%	• TV Systems Division • LCD Visual Systems Divisions • Video Systems Divisions	Color TVs, TVs with built-in VCRs, video cameras, video camera recorders, LCD color TVs, LCD projectors, personal workstations, video printers, HDTV converters and decoders, etc.	1. Hitachi, Toshiba, Mitsubishi Electric, Fuji Electric (started as heavy electric machinary manufaturers)
	Audio System Group	¥171.6 billion (US$1,300 million) 11.3%	• Audio Equipment Division • Kitchen Appliances Systems Division • Personal Communications Systems Division • Business Communications Systems Divisions	Radio cassette tape recorders, headphone stereos, stereo component systems, CD players, laser disk players, DAT tape decks, car stereo systems, cordless telephones, facsimilies, DAT memory storage systems, optical disk storage systems, etc.	2. Sony, JVC, Pioneer, Aiwa, Kenwood, Akai Electric (Specialized in audio-visual products)
Home appliances	Appliance Systems Group	¥265.7 billion (US$1,850 million) 17.5%	• Refrigeration Systems Division • Kitchen Appliances Systems Division • Air-Conditioning Systems Division • Laundry Systems Division	Central heating and air conditioning systems, kerosene heaters, electric blankets, refrigerators, microwave ovens, dishwashers, washing machines, vacuum cleaners, tele-control systems, electric kitchen tools, etc.	3. Matsushita Electric, Sanyo Electric, NEC Home Electronics, Fujitsu General (started as appliance manufacturers)
Information system and office automation equipment	Information Systems. Group	about ¥350 billion (US$2,640 million) About 23%	• Computer Division • OA Equipment Division • Personal Equipment Division • Calculator Division • Nara Plant	Calculators, electronic organizers, office computers, personal computers, intergrated communication systems, word processors, etc.	Casio, Cannon, NEC, Fujitsu, Toshiba, Hitachi, Mitsubishi Electric, Matsushita

			Products	Competitors
Printing and Reprographic System Group		• Reprography Division • Printer and Scanner Division	Copiers, scanners, POS systems, electronic medical devices, FA systems, CAD systems, OA peripherals, etc.	NETC, Toshiba, Canon, Ricoh, Matsushita Electric, Fuji Xerox, Seiko-Epson, Konica
Electronics components/devices	Integrated Circuits Group	About ¥350 billion (US$2,640 million) About 23%	• Tenri Plant • Fukuyama Plant 1 • Fukuyama Plant 2	LSIs, ICs, gate arrays, LCD drivers, etc. flash memory, masked ROM	NEC, Hitachi, Toshiba, Fujitsu, Matsushita Electric, Sanyo, Mitsubishi Electric, OKI Electric
	Electronic Components Group		• Electronic Components Division • Opto-Electronic Devices Division • Photovoltaics Division	LEDs, semiconductor laser diode units, satellite transmissions, components, electronic tuners, printed circuit boards, solar batteries, optomagnetic disks, optoelectric terminals, etc.	Hitachi, Toshiba, Sanyo Matsushita Electric, Mitsubishi Electric
	Liquid Crystal Display Group		• Nara Plant • Tenri Plant	Passive matrix, LCDs, TFT active matrix LCDs, etc.	Seiko-Epson, Optrex (Asahi Glass & Mitsubishi Electric), Hitachi, Hoshiden, Toshiba, Sanyo, Citizen Watch

*Estimates of the casewriter. (A breakdown of sales and share between information systems and electronic devices was not publicly available.)

EXHIBIT 7 Sharp Corporation—Market Shares for Major Products

Consumer Electronics and Home Appliances

Color TVs (a)		VCRs (a)		Camcorders (a)		Mini Stereo Sets (a)	
1 Matsushita	22.5%	1 Matsushita	25.0%	1 Sony	43.0%	1 Sony	24.0%
2 Toshiba	14.5	2 Toshiba	13.0	2 Matsushita	32.0	2 Pioneer	18.0
3 Sharp	14.5	3 JVC	13.0	3 JVC	10.0	3 Kenwood	16.0
4 Hitachi	10.5	4 Mitsubishi	12.5	4 Hitachi	3.0	4 Matsushita	13.0
5 Sony	10.5	5 **Sharp**	12.0	5 Canon	2.0	5 JVC	11.0

Home Phones (d)		Refrigerators (a)		Air Conditioners (a)		Microwave Ovens (a)	
1 **Sharp**	22.5%	1 Matsushita	22.5%	1 Matsushita	23.0%	1 Matsushita	27.8%
2 Sanyo	18.9	2 Toshiba	18.0	2 Toshiba	18.0	2 **Sharp**	20.4
3 NTT	16.0	3 Hitachi	16.0	3 Hitachi	15.0	3 Hitachi	12.4
4 Matsushita	11.0	4 Sanyo	11.0	4 Mitsubishi	13.0	4 Toshiba	9.2
5 Pioneer Comm.	8.2	5 **Sharp**	8.2	5 Sanyo	11.0	5 Mitsubishi	9.1

Information and Office Systems and ICs

Facsimiles (e)		Plain Paper Copiers (a)		Electronic Calculators (b)		Japanese Wordprocessors (b)	
1 Matsushita	16.2%	1 Ricoh	30.2%	1 Casio	53.5%	1 **Sharp**	19.8%
2 Ricoh	16.0	2 Canon	30.1	2 **Sharp**	39.0	2 Toshiba	15.0
3 Canon	16.0	3 Fuji Xerox	22.1	3 Canon	2.8	3 NEC	12.4
4 **Sharp**	11.0	4 **Sharp**	6.8	4 Sanyo	2.3	4 Fujitsu	12.3
5 NEC	10.0	5 Konica	4.8	5 Toshiba	2.2	5 Matsushita	10.2

Personal Computers (c)		Office Computers (c)		Mainframe Computers (e)		Integrated Circuits (f)	
1 NEC	53.1%	1 NEC	27.3%	1 Fujitsu	25.0%	1 NEC	21.1%
2 Fujitsu	12.7	2 Fujitsu	27.1	2 Japan IBM	23.8	2 Toshiba	17.1
3 Toshiba	10.8	3 Toshiba	9.5	3 Hitachi	18.0	3 Hitachi	13.4
4 Seiko-Epson	8.2	4 Japan IBM	9.0	4 NEC	17.3	4 Fujitsu	12.5
5 Japan IBM	7.05	5 Mitsubishi	8.5	5 Japan Unysis	10.1	5 Mitsubishi	9.5

Notes: The data is based on the survey by "Nihon Keizai Shimbun (The Japan Economic Journal)."

The product's market share is calculated based on (a) its domestic unit shipment, (b) its domestic unit production, (c) its total unit shipment including exports, (d) its domestic sales amount, (e) its domestic production amount, and (f) its total production amount including exports.

Sharp holds the sixth position or below for those products where its names is not listed.

Source: "Nikkei Sangyo Shimbun," June 11, 1992.

▲ EXHIBIT 8   Sharp Corporation—Major Competitors in Consumer Electronics and Appliances (fiscal 1992)

	Sharp	Hitachi	Toshiba	Mitsubishi	Sony	JVC	Pioneer	Matsushita	Sanyo (FY 1991)*
Revenue (¥m)	1,554,920	7,765,545	4,722,383	3,343,271	3,915,396	838,669	613,009	7,449,933	1,615,887
(previous year)	(1,532,571)	(7,736,961)	(4,695,394)	(3,316,243)	(3,690,776)	(926,256)	(599,693)	(6,599,306)	(1,496,085)
Operating profit (¥m)	61,640	352,027	118,460	146,702	166,278	-18,331	57,649	388,957	49,511
	(76,041)	(506,419)	(262,103)	(208,757)	(297,449)	(13,396)	(72,323)	(472,590)	(48,611)
Net income (¥m)	39,057	127,611	39,487	36,074	120,121	1,990	28,469	132,873	16,837
	(46,918)	(230,185)	(120,852)	(79,760)	(116,925)	(16,010)	(34,315)	(225,000)	(17,499)
Total assets (¥m)	2,147,690	8,857,910	5,724,439	3,448,673	4,911,129	664,830	519,294	9,019,707	2,062,575
	(2,077,030)	(8,526,121)	(5,530,370)	(3,318,058)	(4,602,495)	(670,698)	(488,152)	(8,761,143)	(1,998,354)
Shareholders' equity (¥m)	755,561	2,917,951	1,182,050	810,204	1,536,795	309,121	329,670	3,495,867	742,412
	(726,763)	(2,811,141)	(1,178,753)	(792,243)	(1,476,414)	(308,937)	(310,508)	(3,434,747)	(738,212)
R&D expenditures (¥m)**	98,129	411,614	279,200	183,000	240,591	41,000	23,600	418,100	77,237
	(89,351)	(391,898)	(265,300)	(183,000)	(205,787)	(39,288)	(8,080)	(383,912)	(69,531)
Return on sales (%)	2.5	1.6	0.8	1.1	3.1	0.2	4.6	1.8	1.0
	(3.1)	(3.0)	(2.6)	(2.4)	(3.2)	(1.7)	(5.7)	(3.4)	(1.2)
Return on assets (%)	1.8	1.4	0.7	1.0	2.4	0.3	5.5	1.5	0.8
	(2.3)	(2.7)	(2.2)	(2.4)	(2.5)	(2.4)	(7.0)	(2.6)	(0.9)
Return on equity (%)	5.2	4.4	3.3	4.5	7.8	0.6	8.6	3.8	2.3
	(6.5)	(8.2)	(10.3)	(10.1)	(7.9)	(5.2)	(11.1)	(6.6)	(2.4)
Equity ratio (%)	35.2	32.9	20.6	23.5	31.3	46.5	63.5	38.8	36.0
Earning per share (¥)	36.60	36.90	12.00	15.90	293.10	63.00	158.50	60.70	8.60
Dividend per share (¥)	11.00	11.00	10.00	10.00	50.00	7.50	25.00	12.50v	7.50
Employees(¥)**	21,521	82,221	73,714	49,566	18,130	13,561	8,707	47,634	29,638
Retailer network (number of exclusive retailers)	3,800	11,000	12,000	5,500	1,500	N/A	N/A	27,000	4,500

*Sanyo's fiscal year ends on November 30. Fiscal years for other companies end on March 31.

**Nonconsolidated.

Source: *Japan Company Handbook* (Tokyo: Toyo Keizai Inc., 1991 & 1992), and *Kaden Gyokai (Appliance Industry)* (Tokyo: Kyoikusha 1987), p. 88 (for retailer network)..

shares for a number of products, such as 60 percent for electroluminescent displays, 40 percent for laser diodes, and 65 percent for remote control beam receiver units for VCRs, TVs, and other audio visual products.[11]

The Liquid Crystal Display Group was spun off from the Electronic Components Group in 1990. The company's LCD business had grown so remarkably that Sharp was increasingly associated with LCDs. Considered the most promising flat panel display technology in the early 1990s, LCDs were used for a wide range of end products and were expected to replace cathode ray tubes in most applications, including TVs, by the beginning of the 21st century. Worldwide production for LCDs reached ¥299 billion in fiscal 1992, and were predicted to exceed ¥1 trillion (US$7.1 billion) by fiscal 1995 and ¥2 trillion by the turn of the century. Sharp was the largest supplier of LCDs in the world, and its sales of passive-matrix and TFT active-matrix LCDs represented a dominant 40 percent world share. The company was particularly well represented in the most advanced TFT color LCDs. Sharp's major competitors in LCDs included Seiko-Epson, OPTREX (a joint-venture between Asahi Glass and Mitsubishi Electric), Hitachi, Hoshiden, and Toshiba. Despite the huge initial investment and accumulated manufacturing experience required to start an LCD business, several other Japanese companies, such as NEC, Matsushita, and Canon, were also entering the industry. To further strengthen its leading position and obtain a 50 percent world market share in active matrix LCDs by fiscal 1996, Sharp planned to make a capital investment of ¥80 billion (US$ 640 million) in LCD plants between fiscal 1993 and 1995.

already planning to invest in LCD plants [handwritten margin note]

International Business

In 1992, Sharp had 19 sales subsidiaries and 27 manufacturing bases in 18 countries and 4 R&D laboratories in 3 countries. Exports represented 45 percent of company sales in 1992, although their importance was decreasing with the increase in local manufacturing (about 25 percent of total overseas sales in 1992) as Sharp strove to integrate design and manufacturing capabilities in local markets. The geographical composition of exports was 40 percent for North America, 30 percent for Europe, and 30 percent for the rest of the world. Eighty-five percent of exports were final products (92 percent of which were sold under the Sharp brand name), and the rest were components/devices.

▲ ORGANIZATION STRUCTURE

In 1992, Sharp's organization structure shared responsibilities among eight manufacturing groups, five sales and marketing groups, an international business group, a corporate research and development group, and a number of central service groups (Exhibit 9). All of these groups, except the International Business Group, reported directly to the five top managers—the president and the four senior executive vice presidents. The manufacturing groups, the International Business Group, and the sales and marketing groups were profit centers, while the corporate R&D group and central service groups were cost centers. Reconfiguration of this organization structure occurred frequently in response to market and technological changes. Examples were the consolidation of the phone equipment business, which had previously been handled both by the Appliance Systems Group and by the Audio Systems

---

[11]*Business Week,* April29, 1991, pp. 84–85.

▲ EXHIBIT 9   Sharp Corporation—Organization Structure

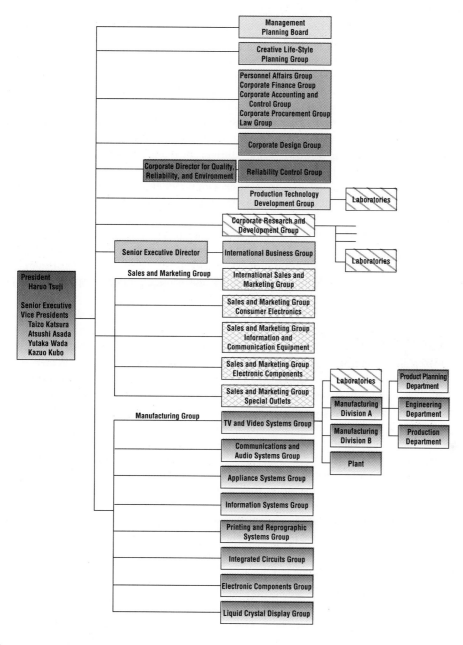

Source: Sharp Corportaion

Group, and the transfer of the facsimile business to the Audio Systems Group. Also, as the company had grown in size and product scope, it had expanded from three to eight manufacturing groups since the early 1980s.

focus towards production

how well this translate to joint venture?

The manufacturing groups were at the core of Sharp's organization structure. The name "manufacturing group" reflected the company's traditional orientation toward production. Each group controlled its domestic production facilities and was responsible for the technical performance of overseas production facilities. It was also in charge of new product development on a worldwide basis. A manufacturing group did not, however, have authority for sales and marketing. Instead, it negotiated sales targets and price levels with domestic sales and marketing groups and overseas sales subsidiaries while assuming overall responsibility for product profitability. Typically, a manufacturing group consisted of its own laboratory, a staff of up to 100 for accounting, purchasing, and other administrative functions, and several product divisions. Each of these in turn comprised several departments, including product planning, engineering, and production. Central to each division was the product planning department which coordinated R&D, manufacturing, and marketing for its products. Located in the manufacturing group, managers in this department met weekly to discuss projects and problems, but spent substantial amounts of time with the marketing groups. The head of the product planning department for the Wizard, for example, spent about two and a half months each year in the U.S. sales subsidiary.

Of the five sales and marketing groups, four were in charge of domestic sales and one was in charge of the international sales of electronic components. The four domestic sales and marketing groups were organized by distribution channel. One sold consumer electronics products through an exclusive network of independent retailers, called Sharp Friend Shops. The second group was responsible for marketing consumer electronic and information equipment to special outlets, such as independent large-volume retailers. The third domestic sales and marketing group distributed communication and information equipment to specialized retailers, such as stationery stores and office equipment retailers. The fourth domestic sales and marketing group marketed electronic devices directly to other manufacturers.

The International Business Group coordinated the company's exports and international activities, acting, for example, as a liaison between sales subsidiaries in the various countries and the manufacturing groups in their twice-yearly transfer price negotiations. Each country's sales subsidiary negotiated independently with the manufacturing groups in order to foster internal competition and resolve the allocation of scarce products. The International Business Group also supervised the overseas sales subsidiaries, which were each independent profit centers, and was responsible for overseas manufacturing, deciding on the location of new manufacturing sites and coordinating production across the company's international TV and VCR factories.

The corporate Research and Development Group was established in 1976 to more effectively coordinate the activities of the manufacturing group laboratories with those of the central research laboratories. It was restructured with the establishment of the Multimedia Systems Research and Development Center in 1992, which prepared the company for computerized fusion of visual and audio information.

In 1992, about 1,500 people worked at the central service groups, engaged in strategic planning, administrative support, and coordinating activities across business groups and subsidiaries.

▲ THE ROLE OF THE CORPORATE OFFICE

Top Management

In 1992, Sharp had about 20 senior directors who, in addition to their individual assignments, coordinated functions across groups. These executives met formally twice a month, attending an executive committee meeting in the morning and a management meeting (called *Keiei Kaigi*) in the afternoon to ratify critical decisions and to discuss the company's future.

In contrast to other large Japanese companies with bottom-up, consensus-building decision-marking styles, Sharp had a tradition of top-down decision making, with most critical decisions being made by a team of top decision makers who complemented one another in personalities and skills. The technological creativity and entrepreneurship of founder Hayakawa was complemented by the administrative skills of Akira Saeki. During his presidency, Saeki benefited from the marketing expertise of Masaki Seki and the technological insights of Dr. Tadashi Sasaki. Haruo Tsuji, well-known for his cosmopolitan marketing sense, was initially assisted by two senior executive vice presidents, Taizo Katsura, who had a background in international, and Dr. Atsushi Asada, who had a background in technology. Tsuji was well-known for frequently walking around business groups and divisions to gather information, and he sometimes provided specific business ideas for new products.

Culture and Business Philosophy

Sharp emphasized its business philosophy and creed (Exhibit 10) and believed its acceptance by employees worldwide was critical to the company's long-term prosperity. The creed was displayed in each office, and employees were asked to commit themselves to its ideals.

Sharp's culture of innovativeness was also enhanced by a feeling of crisis. Hiroshi Nakanishi, the senior manager of the Information Systems Group, who had headed the electronic organizer development project, explained:

> *A strong pressure prevails in our manufacturing divisions. We are always afraid that we might be behind other consumer electronics companies. We also feel threatened by low-cost Asian countries. These pressures continuously force us to expand the range of functions of existing products and think about what will come next.*

Human Resources Management

Like most Japanese companies, Sharp had a paternalistic relationship with its employees, and top management reinforced the view that the company was a family, or community, whose members should cooperate. Employee turnover was very low in accordance with the practice of life-time employment. If a research project or a manufacturing plant closed, researchers and workers were not laid off but transferred elsewhere inside the company. Sharp extended these human resource policies outside Japan: for example, Sharp Manufacturing Company of America celebrated its 10-year anniversary in 1988 with nearly half of its original 230-person workforce.

In the early 1990s, Sharp's performance measurement and reward system was undergoing a gradual transition from an egalitarian seniority system to a merit system in an attempt to motivate employees, particularly young ones who were becoming more individualistic and less loyal to the organization. There were three parts to an employee's reward—salary, bonus, and promotion. Salary was based on three equal criteria—seniority, job type, and performance—although the performance variation was into significant from one individual to the next. The semiannual bonuses, which constituted about one-third of compensation, varied on a forced curve within a range of plus or minus 10 percent among the workers within a job category. Because of the importance of rank in Japanese society, promotion was

▲ EXHIBIT 10   Sharp Corporation—Business Philosophy and Creed

Business Philosophy

We do not seek merely to expand our business volume. Rather, we are dedicated to the use of our unique, innovative technology to contribute to the culture, benefits and welfare of people throughout the world.

It is the intention of our corporation to grow hand-in-hand with our employees, encouraging and aiding them to reach their full potential and improve their standard of living.

Our future prosperity is directly linked to the prosperity of our customers, dealers, and shareholders…indeed, the entire Sharp family.

Business Creed

Sharp Corporation is dedicated to two principal ideals: "Sincerity and Creativity."

By committing ourselves to these ideals, we can derive genuine satisfaction from our work, while making a meaningful contribution to society.

Sincerity is a virtue fundamental to humanity…always be sincere.

Harmony brings strength…trust each other and work together.

Politeness is a merit…always be courteous and respectful.

Creativity promotes progress…remain constantly aware of the need to innovate and improve.

Courage is the basis of a rewarding life…accept every challenge with a positive attitude.

Source: Sharp Corporation.

the most critical element of reward. Most career-track employees were promoted mainly on the basis of seniority and subtle skills, such as teamwork and communication, until they reached a middle management position.

General managers of profit centers were evaluated on their units' performance, although specific criteria varied by group and by division. For example, in 1992, performance criteria for the general manager of the LCD Group included financials, market share, and product availability. For the general manager of the International Business Group, the criteria were primarily financial, but included balanced product sales, employee training, and the cultivation of new distribution channels.

Career-track employees were regularly transferred across manufacturing groups and between functions (e.g., between R&D and marketing and between domestic and overseas operations). In addition, Sharp employed several other personnel schemes to exploit employees' diversity and creativity. The top 3 percent of each rank of researchers were compulsorily transferred between laboratories every three years in a process called "chemicalization." As Tadashi Sasaki said, "It is only hydrochloric acid that is produced when hydrochloric acid is added to hydrochloric acid: while, a new material will come out when hydrochloric acid and something else are blended."[12] Chemicalization was further promoted by the company's aggressive head-hunting and mid-career hiring. Out of 30 board members in 1992, 10 had been scouted or joined the company after extensive experience at another company. Similarly, four of the seven general managers of the Corporate Research and Development Group's laboratories and centers had been recruited from outside Sharp.

[12]Takeuchi, et al., p. 87.

The company's system of in-house job application was also designed to exploit the full potential of its employees (the "right person for the right job") and to promote their creativity and ambition. Every year, the company announced available managerial or staff positions and invited applications from all employees. Those who were interested could apply confidentially—an important condition in Japan, where applying for another job could be interpreted by a supervisor as a sign of disloyalty. Once an application was accepted, divisions could not oppose the transfer. Roughly 100 employees, most of them engineers, moved in this way each year.

Strategic Planning

The Management Planning Board prepared Sharp's overall strategic plans. The planning process consisted of a 10-year vision, a 3-year medium-term plan revised every year, and six-month operating plans, which, in the words of Executive Director Yutaka Iuchi, "existed to be altered." Plan targets for each business group were established mainly in terms of sales, overall profit, and market share. The planning staff then disaggregated the targets and allocated them to individual divisions and products. Financial budgets were made twice a year in parallel with operating plans. The basic rule for capital expenditures was that each profit center could spend its depreciation plus half of its profit after tax. However, each project exceeding ¥5 million had to be authorized by corporate management. In addition to basic financial criteria, such as profit and growth, strategic criteria were considered in approving these capital expenditures.

After plans were set up, they were extensively communicated to all the levels of the organization. The president presented the company's basic management policy in his New Year's address via satellite to middle managers, explaining the company's long-term goals and its annual slogan and strategic objectives. Group general managers then explained the annual goals to their members and outlined detailed strategies for their groups.

In 1992, Sharp's long-term vision was called STAR 21—Strategic and creative minds, Total customer satisfaction, Advanced technology, and Rapid action for the 21st century). Its strategic target was to attain ¥5 trillion consolidated sales by the year 2000, one-third from each of the three areas, consumer electronics and appliances, information systems, and electronic components.

Technology Strategy

Sharp's R&D expenditures had increased steadily, reaching ¥98 billion or 8.2 percent of nonconsolidated sales in fiscal 1992. The company' overall research and development activities were supervised by the Corporate Research and Development Group, which specified research themes and coordinated basic research and product development. The Corporate R&D Group's five laboratories and two R&D centers were engaged in fundamental research looking more than four to five years ahead. They accounted for 10 percent to 15 percent of total R&D expenditures, and employed 800 out of 7,600 total engineers. The manufacturing groups' six laboratories handled product development that would pay off in two to three years and accounted for about 30 percent of corporate R&D. The remaining R&D expenditures were concentrated on more immediate product development in the manufacturing divisions. Careful attention was paid to coordinating activities across the three levels and to promoting the effective transfer of technology between R&D and product development. Once a technology or a product was developed in a laboratory, there was a formal program to transfer that learning to manufacturing groups. Indeed, personnel often followed from the R&D laboratory to the manufacturing group as a technology was commercialized.

The company's overall technology strategy was extensively discussed in a monthly corporate technical strategy meeting at which one division would also present its research plans for approval (Exhibit 11). This meeting was chaired by the general manager of Corporate Research and Development Group and attended by the president, the senior executive vice presidents, the general managers of the manufacturing groups, and the directors of the research laboratories. Prior to this meeting, the laboratory directors met monthly to examine technical matters in detail.

After reviewing the technological capabilities of the company ("technological seeds") and the needs of potential customers ("market needs"), technologies for development were identified where needs existed but seeds did not (Exhibit 12). Decision criteria that determined whether a technology was to be developed in-house included the extent of competition around that technology, the availability of the technology on the outside, the technology's potential to be a source of differentiation to end products, its minimum efficient scale of production, its potential to make Sharp a world leader in an area, the future market size, and its potential to promote valuable learning.

Dr. Asada's view was that "We invest in the technologies which will be the 'nucleus' of the company in the future. Like a nucleus, such technologies should have an explosive power to self-multiply across many products." He continued, "Our guiding principle for investment should be quality not quantity." For example, Sharp's ¥100 billion investment in LCD factories from 1990 to 1992 was based on top management's faith that LCD technology could be leveraged into several end products in the future. Conversely, Sharp had avoided DRAMs, capacitors, and resistors as commodities readily available from competitive suppliers and instead focused on specialties like masked ROMs.

Once it chose to develop a technology, Sharp committed to it for the long term. For example, it pursued LCD research throughout the 1970s, although the market for LCDs did not take off until the 1980s. Similarly, it continued research in gallium arsenide laser diodes long after most competitors had abandoned their research in this area until the first big market for CD players developed in the mid-1980s. Even if a technology seemed to be going nowhere, Sharp continued researching it, though on a very slim budget. For example, it continued its research in solar cells, using the amorphous silica technology it had learned in active-matrix LCDs, although the market for this technology remained tiny. As Dr. Asada noted:

> Unlike the purchaser of real estate who decides which land to buy and which not to buy, technology decisions can hardly set a clear boundary for areas to invest. They are essentially the judgment of possibilities. If the potential of one technology is certain, we are going to assign a large number of researchers. However, even though the other technology has a lot of uncertainties, we cannot stay away from it. In such a case, we let, for example, one researcher study it. If it turns out to have more potential, we will allocate more researchers. If not, and the uncertainties have been resolved, we will stop at that time.

Because of such technological uncertainty, Sharp often maintained small R&D projects on alternative technologies. It was currently researching all possible alternatives to the TFT active-matrix LCD technology, including Ferro LCDs, light-emitting diodes (LED), and plasma and electro-luminescent (EL) displays.

Dr. Hiro Kawamoto, general manager of Corporate Staff Planning and Development at the Tokyo Research Laboratories, also mentioned:

> We do not spend much on basic research. LCDs, MOS ICs, solar cells, semiconductor laser diodes were originally developed elsewhere. But we are prepared to make bets on what we judge

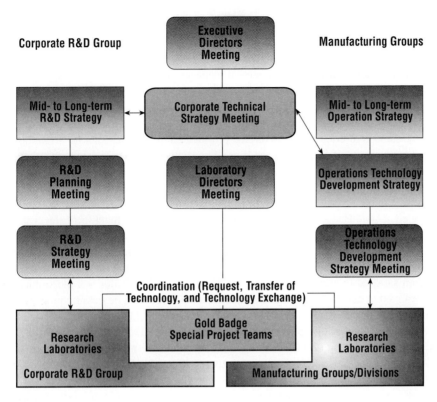

Source: Sharp Corporation.

will be key technologies for the future and commit ourselves to make them work. Our approach is incremental, yet consistent. We make a small start on a technology in response to tiny existing market needs. Engineers work to generate a new product. We earn some money, invest it on R&D, gradually expand activities, thus approaching, over time, a long-term vision. We do not exit from a technology as RCA did from VCRs.... We do not follow the behavior of our rivals, rather purposefully avoiding the "herd behavior." We invest in niches, which might grow up to become grand niches.

look for niches

New Product Development

After the success of the electronic calculators project, Sharp formalized its task-force-based product development process in order to increase development speed and to enhance the effective transfer and integration of technologies among manufacturing groups. To do so, it established a system of Gold Badge projects in 1977. Nearly one-third of the total corporate R&D budget was spent on the 10–15 Gold Badge projects in progress at any time. These were selected at the corporate technical strategy meeting according to whether the product was differentiated and based on original technologies, whether it involved many cross-group linkages, and whether it would be a core of the company's competitiveness. Projects often focused

Gold Badge Projects

need

on areas where technological seeds existed but where Sharp did not offer products that met existing market needs (Exhibit 12).

Once selected, Gold Badge projects were financed by corporate because it was believed that since projects cut across manufacturing groups, no one group would be willing to finance a project alone. Manufacturing groups ultimately paid back half of a project's expenditures when they began to market a product that resulted from the project.

A senior manager at the rank of general manager or higher was chosen to be a project's champion and a middle-level researcher was chosen to be its leader. The leader freely chose his or her 20–40 member staff from the company as a whole. During the one-and-a-half or two-year project period, all project members reported directly to the company president, wore the same gold-color badge as did the president, and were vested with his authority. As such they received top priority for the time of specialists in other divisions that they would not normally have access to. Project members were given wide discretion regarding the way they conducted their project, although the project champion and leader were held accountable for the initial schedule set up at the monthly corporate technical strategy meeting. Once completed, a Gold Badge project was turned over to the relevant manufacturing group.

One successful Gold Badge project was the Wizard electronic organizer. This project was proposed by the Information Systems Group in response to the slowing growth of its core calculator business. Observing that customer needs for data storage and organization, which had been satisfied by stationery such as the Filofax, could be better met electronically, the project aimed to develop a combined calculator and information processing product by integrating several Sharp technologies, such as C-MOS chips, LCD displays, solar cells, and software. Other Gold Badge projects had included a color LCD TV, and HDTV projector with an LCD screen, a magnet-optical disk memory, and an EL display.

Sharp's regular product development activities were coordinated through several committees that cut across manufacturing groups. The New People strategy meeting attended by the president, vice presidents, and the general managers of manufacturing groups and sales and marketing groups discussed both the basic goals of the New People strategy and the details of specific new products using input from the Creative Lifestyle Planning Group. This group conducted market research and surveys with extensive input from the manufacturing groups and overseas sales subsidiaries. Additionally, the Corporate Design Group coordinated design and colors across manufacturing group products.

The components groups were also involved in intense discussions with end product groups to understand their needs. The group general manager of the LCD Group, for example, attended a monthly product development meeting with end product groups.

Operations Strategy

Sharp's domestic manufacturing plants were clustered in seven geographical locations. The LCD plant, for example, was on-site with the semiconductor facility in part because they shared similar production processes. Sharp manufactured a product in Japan until its life cycle had matured and innovations no longer occurred. The manufacturing of nearly all calculators, for example, had been transferred outside of Japan. The company also outsourced components and products, such as CRTs and black-and-white TVs, whenever it saw poor profitability in their production and no potential for technological breakthroughs.

At the corporate level, the Production Technology Development Group developed and integrated the company's process technology. Its group general manager chaired a monthly meeting—attended by the president, senior executive vice presidents, group managers of

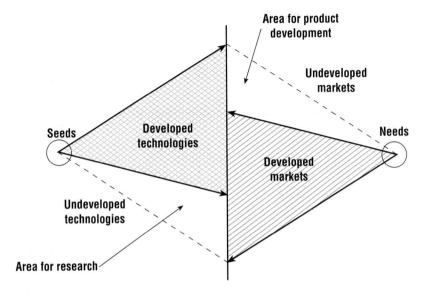

Source: JMA Management Center, ed. *Sharp no Gijutsu Senryaku (Technology Strategy of Sharp)* (Tokyo: JMA, 1986) p. 47.

manufacturing groups, and laboratory directors—to enhance information sharing and technology transfer across plants and laboratories. A similar Quality Group monitored the manufacturing group's product quality and coordinated companywide quality-circle activities.

Internal Coordination

Despite its strategic emphasis on components/devices in the late 1980s and early 1990s, Sharp viewed it as necessary to compete in both end products and devices because improvement in device technologies required continuous feedback on final customer needs. Indeed, Taizo Katsura suggested, "Real value added comes from the link." However, Sharp's involvement in the components business brought about conflicts between component and end product groups. For components also available from outside suppliers, the company took an internal-market approach to resolve such conflicts. The components groups could choose what and to whom they could sell—to the outside customers or the inside end product groups. Similarly, the end product groups had no obligation to purchase from the components groups. They could freely purchase from outside suppliers if the quality or price was better.

All component sales to end product groups took place at an agreed upon transfer price that was normally close to the market price. These transfer prices were determined through intensive discussions at the same time as the six-month operating plans and budgets were set. Prices were, however, renegotiated in response to unexpected changes in the market. According to Yutaka Iuchi, former head of the LCD Group:

no cost advantage in groups (handwritten)

We never sell our LCDs below cost to the other groups. We need profits to fund our vast capital investment expenditures. Even when one of our end product groups and one of our outside customers compete in the same market, for example, in notebook computers, the supply price of our LCDs should be the same for both. If we sell LCDs cheaper and give a cost advantage to our notebook computer division, the division will be spoiled and its long-term competitiveness in the market will decline.

When components were in short supply, as had occurred in LCDs, about 80 percent of which were sold to outside customers, the components groups faced the difficult decision of allocating output between inside and outside customers. In general, this was resolved by giving priority to all customers with whom Sharp expected to have a long-term relationship. Yutaka Iuchi commented:

There were several instances in the past where we had to give some priority to satisfying the demand of our internal groups at the time of supply-demand imbalance. Our group, however, has to maintain a reliable relationship with outside customers. My biggest task is therefore to carefully predict the future demand of LCDs, expand production capacity based on those predictions, and avoid a shortage of our supply capacity.

The timing of the introduction of new components could also be a source of tension because the company's end product groups preferred delaying the availability of new components to competitors if those components enabled them to differentiate their products. Such dilemmas were solved on a case-by-case basis through intensive discussions. In most situations, new components were introduced to both inside and outside customers at the same time. However, the external launch of a few components of substantial strategic importance were deferred after the involvement of the president and senior executive vice presidents.

Transfer prices were also a major issue between the manufacturing groups and sales and marketing groups. Again, Sharp employed an internal market approach. Although it had never happened, the sales and marketing groups could, in principle, refuse to sell a manufacturing group's product if it was of unsatisfactory quality or price. For new products, transfer prices took into account the strategic objective of establishing a competitive position in the market, and both sides were expected to make concessions to reach an agreement.

Transfer prices for exports were determined by direct negotiation between manufacturing groups and overseas sales subsidiaries. Yutaka Wada, senior executive vice president for international business, commented:

Competition is our principle. [The International Business Group] sets up basic rules, but in general, lets sales subsidiaries negotiate directly with manufacturing groups. We do not employ a set transfer pricing approach, such as marginal cost plus a certain mark-up. Such a rule is easy to apply and can be energy-saving. We believe, however, that it would weaken management muscles in the long run.

▲ MAJOR ISSUES FACING SHARP IN 1992

In 1992, Sharp was facing several new challenges. The Japanese economy, which had been overinflated during the late 1980s, entered into recession as the "bubble" burst and stock and land prices declined. As domestic demand for consumer electronics products and information systems fell, Sharp's operating profits declined, though less so than other companies, after five years of growth.

More fundamentally, as Sharp grew in size and scope, it faced increasing technological opportunities and uncertainties. President Tsuji commented:

Technological innovation is more and more accelerated all over the world. Also, its structure is changing drastically, and keeping up with developments in hardware and software is getting increasingly important. In such an environment, it is difficult for one firm to do everything itself. Companies with similar goals need to cooperate to develop new businesses by complementing each other.

In 1992, Sharp was considering two major strategic alliances—one with Intel for flash memories and the other with Apple for pocket-sized portable computers. Flash memory was a high-density, nonvolatile technology which retained stored information even when the power was turned off. As its name suggested, it could be rapidly erased and reprogrammed. As a storage alternative to hard and floppy disks, flash memory was better suited to the consumer marketplace due to its cost-effectiveness, reliability, and performance. In 1992, the market for flash memories was approximately $130 million, 85 percent of which was supplied by Intel, and it was projected to grow to nearly $1.5 billion by 1995. Sharp and Intel planned to jointly design and manufacture flash memories in the future. The partnership would allow Sharp to buy flash memories from Intel for use in its own products or for resale under the Sharp name and to develop new applications for flash memory in its own consumer-oriented markets. In return, Sharp would build a new $500 million plant in Japan that would be the main production base for flash memories for Intel and Sharp in the future.

The Apple and Sharp partnership aimed to jointly develop, manufacture, and market the next generation personal digital assistant (PDA), the Newton, by combining Apple's computer and system software know-how with Sharp's display technologies and expertise in consumer electronics. This alliance was expected to allow Sharp to prepare for the approaching multimedia era.

As Sharp set a goal of becoming a premier "creative-intensive" company in the 21st century, while for the first time relying on external partners for innovation, it faced the challenge of meeting Tsuji's belief that, "As a manufacturing company, Sharp has to contribute to society by developing innovative products that create market demand and fulfill new customer needs."

SMASHING THE CUBE: CORPORATE TRANSFORMATION AT CIBA-GEIGY, LTD.

You can't realize a new strategic direction if you leave your organizational structure as it was in the past.

Heini Lippuner, chairman of the executive committee and chief operating officer[1]

In 1972, a visitor arrived at the imposing headquarters of Ciba-Geigy, Ltd., the Swiss chemical company specializing in pharmaceuticals and a variety of agricultural, industrial, and specialty chemicals. He would later recall his first impressions as he entered the facility:

I was immediately struck by . . . formality as symbolized by large gray stone buildings and stiff uniformed guards in the main lobby. This spacious, opulent lobby was the main passageway for employees to enter the inner compound of office buildings and plants. It had high ceilings, large glass doors, and a few expensive pieces of modern furniture in one corner that served as a waiting area . . . . Upon entering the lobby I was asked by the uniformed guard to check in with another guard, who sat in a glassed-in office. I had to give my name and tell whom I was visiting and where I was from . . . .

My client's secretary arrived in due course and took me up in the elevator and down a long corridor of closed-door offices. Each office had a tiny name plate that could be covered by a hinged metal plate if the occupant wanted to remain anonymous. Above each office door was a lightbulb; some lightbulbs showed red and some green. I asked on a subsequent visit what this meant and was told that if the light is green it is OK to knock, whereas red means that the person does not want to be disturbed under any circumstances.

Research Assistant Elizabeth Wynne Johnson prepared this case under the supervision of Associates Professor David J. Collis.

[1]Carol Kennedy, "Changing the Company Culture at Ciba-Geigy" *Long Range Planning* 26, no. 1 (1993), p. 20.

We went around a corner and down another such corridor and never saw another soul during the entire time.[2]

In 1994, a Harvard Business School professor arrived at the very same spot to conduct some interviews of his own in order to develop a case about Ciba-Geigy's recent corporate transformation. The transformation had reorganized Ciba—formerly split into business divisions, geographical operations, and functions such as production, finance, and legal affairs—into 14 largely autonomous divisions with full global responsibility and 33 strategic business units (Exhibits 1, 2, and 3). Most importantly, the company had set about the creation of a modern corporate culture to serve as the foundation for sustainable growth in the future.

As the professor entered the lobby, he noticed that the guards were wearing cardigans. A 10-foot clown sculpture celebrating a Basel carnival tradition occupied a prominent space in the entry. As the waiting professor wandered over to examine the massive works of modern art that covered the walls, he was approached by an affable and unassuming gentleman who immediately began chatting with him about the company and the case that would eventually be written. Believing the man to be a mid-level executive charged with greeting him, the professor continued to speak amiably as the two made their way past two executives talking in the corridor, one of whom the professor recognized as Ciba's chairman of the board of directors and CEO, Alex Krauer.

Only when the two men arrived at the man's office did the professor realize that his companion was Heini Lippuner, chairman of the executive committee and COO. Following a brief round of introductions, Lippuner began to discuss the nature of his company's recent transformation, addressing the inevitable question: Had Ciba gone far enough in reinventing itself? Or had it gone too far?

▲ HISTORICAL BACKGROUND

In 1758, Johann Rudolf Geigy entered the colonial trade business by peddling Switzerland's dyewoods, drugs, and spices. His company, the Geigy Chemical Corporation, was among the country's pioneers in utilizing technology to overcome its lack of natural resources, to produce chemicals that could be sold in foreign markets. CIBA (Society of Chemical Industry in Basel) was an organic chemical company founded a century later. CIBA and Geigy merged in 1970, when both were firmly established in the specialty chemical business. The resulting entity, Ciba-Geigy, Ltd., comprised a variety of chemical, pharmaceutical, agricultural, and electronics businesses, and had affiliated companies in more than 50 countries. The group maintained its headquarters in Basel, Switzerland, concentrated in the "Stammhaus," a group of multiproduct production, R&D, and administrative facilities that alone employed more than 19,000 of Ciba-Geigy's 88,000 employees.

By the late 1970s, Ciba-Geigy, Ltd. was Switzerland's top multinational drug and chemical company, operating in three distinct sectors: health care, agriculture, and industrial. However, lulled into complacency by years of successful operating performance, Ciba-Geigy had evolved around a complex, three-dimensional organization known as the "cube"—so-named because it was determined on three sides: function, geography, and business. Every major issue had to be reviewed by, and was subject to input from, all three perspectives.

▲ 663

Case 6-6
Smashing the
Cube: Corporate
Transformation
at Ciba-Geigy,
Ltd.

---

[2]Edgar H. Schein, Organizational Culture and Leadership, 2d ed. (San Francisco: Jossey-Bass Publishers, Inc., 1992), pp. 39–40.

▲ EXHIBIT 1 Ciba-Geigy, Ltd. Financials, 1983–1993

	Previous Accounting System										IAS
	1983	1984	1985	1986	1987	1988	1989	1990	1991	1992	1993
Group sales (SFr.m.)	14,741	17,474	18,221	15,955	15,764	17,647	20,608	19,703	21,077	22,204	22,647
Healthcare								6,953	7,824	8,662	9,220
Agriculture								4,128	4,798	4,817	4,813
Industry								8,622	8,455	8,725	8,614
Net profit (SFr.m.)	776	1,187	1,472	1,161	1,100	1,325	1,557	1,033	1,280	1,520	1,779
As % of sales	5.3	6.8	8.1	7.3	7.0	7.5	7.6	5.2	6.1	6.8	7.9
Operating cash flow (SFr.m.)	1,580	2,050	2,369	2,005	1,958	2,268	2,636	2,120	2,481	2,771	2,564
As % of sales	10.7	11.7	13.0	12.6	12.4	12.9	12.8	10.8	11.8	12.5	11.3
Capital expenditure (SFr.m.)	830	1,007	1,213	1,232	1,368	1,616	1,987	2,058	1,957	1,857	1,739
As % of sales	6	6	7	8	9	9	10	10	9	7	8
Depreciation and amortization (SFr.m.)	804	863	897	844	858	943	1,078	1,087	1,201	1,251	1,154
As % of sales	5.4	4.9	4.9	5.3	5.4	5.3	5.2	5.5	5.7	5.6	5.1
Research and development expenditure (SFr.m.)	1,248	1,456	1,674	1,627	1,673	1,797	2,075	2,051	2,185	2,350	2,202
As % of sales	8.5	8.3	9.2	10.2	10.6	10.2	10.1	10.4	10.4	10.6	9.7
Personnel cost (SFr.m.)	4,390	4,893	5,184	4,924	4,842	5,402	6,132	6,275	6,598	6,783	7,063
As % of sales	30	28	28	31	31	31	30	32	31	31	31.2
Number of employees	79,173	81,423	81,012	82,231	86,109	88,757	92,553	94,141	91,665	90,554	87,480
Shareholders' equity (SFr.m.)	12,071	13,921	13,978	14,401	14,188	15,370	16,237	15,454	16,321	18,074	17,080
Key ratios											
Operating profit as % of sales	5.3	6.8	7.3	7.3	7.0	7.5	7.6	5.2	6.1	6.8	10.4
Total debt in % of capitalization	NA	NA	NA	NA	NA	NA	NA	NA	NA	NA	24.7
Current ratio	2.30	2.39	2.43	2.51	2.37	2.15	2.14	1.79	1.79	1.98	2.30
Earnings per share (SFr.m.)	144.65	221.30	274.40	216.45	205.05	245.40	285.75	185.50	229.90	51.80*	63.80

Note: Due to changeover to International Accounting Standards (IAS) in 1993, the figures for the previous years are not fully comparable.
*After four-for-one stock split.

▲ EXHIBIT 2   Ciba-Geigy Organization in 1994

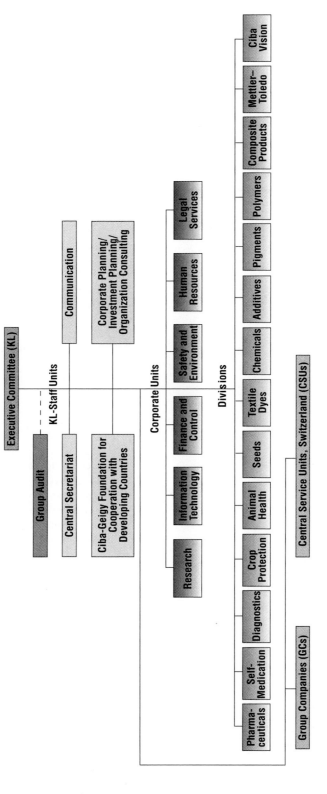

▲ 666

Case 6-6
Smashing the
Cube: Corporate
Transformation
at Ciba-Geigy,
Ltd.

▲ EXHIBIT 3   Ciba's Portfolio in 1994: 14 Divisions and 33 Strategic Business
Units

Pillar Businesses	Pharmaceuticals
	Specialties
	Generics
	Plant Protection
	Weed Control
	Disease Control
	Insect Control
	Seed Treatment
	Additives
	Additives for Plastics/Elastomers/Fibers
	Additives for Coat./Rad./Phot.
	Additives for Lubricants
	Additives for PVC Stabilization
Core Businesses	Textile Dyestuffs
	Reactive Dyes
	Wool, Polyamide, and Silk Dyes
	Polyester, Cellulose, Polyacrilonitrile
	Dyeing Auxiliaries
	Chemicals
	Chemtex
	Detergents and Cosmetics
	Paper
	Leather/Fur
	Polymers
	Resins
	Formulated Materials
	Pigments
	High-Performance Pigments
	Classical Pigments
	Dispersions
	Mettler-Toledo
	Laboratory Balances
	Industrial/Retail Weighing
	Analytical and Process Systems
Growth Businesses	Self-Medication
	Zyma
	CCP/USA
	Diagnostics
	Composites
	U.S. Materials
	Euro Materials
	Structures and Interiors
	Ciba Vision
	OPTICS (Lenses/Lens Care)
	Ophthalmic Pharmaceuticals
Development Businesses	Seeds
Niche Businesses	Animal Health

Originally put into place in the early 1970s after the merger of Ciba and Geigy, on the basis of a McKinsey recommendation, the cube became increasingly unwieldy as the company grew. Bureaucracy slowed the decision-making process on even the simplest issues. Moreover, a "highest common denominator" phenomenon emerged as a result of cultivating a uniform approach across the whole Stammhaus. Businesses with distinct cost structures and key success factors interfered with one another's operating decisions, often causing plans to be upgraded to the point of wasteful inefficiency.

▲ 667

Case 6-6
Smashing the
Cube: Corporate
Transformation
at Ciba-Geigy,
Ltd.

To make the point, Lippuner told a story recalling his own experience as the head of the former dyestuffs and chemicals division. During the mid-1980s, he had wanted to add MRP to improve material flow, and he wanted to use a particular software package that was suited to his division's business requirements. However, the head of the manufacturing function demanded so many modifications, each aimed at meeting the needs of a different business, that the software became "goldplated—a masterpiece of sophistication and maintenance" and of little use to anyone.

In addition to its structural rigidity, Ciba-Geigy's organization and culture were bound by Switzerland's legal and social traditions. A strict signatory bureaucracy required every document with the legal authority of the company to be signed by someone of a specified legal title. In traditional Swiss society, one's legal title in the company, which did not necessarily reflect one's managerial role, bore directly on social status and promotions were published (publicly) yearly.

Despite the company's organizational shortcomings, Ciba-Geigy's balance sheet remained healthy until the second oil crisis in 1979 triggered a downturn in financial performance. In response, the then-chairman initiated a "turnaround" program, introducing methods such as overhead value analysis in an effort to correct the cost structures and asset levels. The turnaround effort brought some improvement, but the basic structure of the cube remained intact. As the 1980s progressed, a booming economy, and a period of prosperity, masked the impact of slow decision-making processes on the company's financial results (Exhibit 1). As a result, pressure to effect change in the system temporarily subsided.

Shifting Ground

> *Ciba-Geigy was like a supertanker, but it needed to be more like a fleet of ships.*
> *We had the benefits of size, but we needed flexibility.*
>
> *Alex Krauer*

By the late 1980s, Ciba-Geigy's environment had begun to change. After years of prosperity and unfettered growth, a recession loomed on the horizon. Recent events had fostered increasingly negative attitudes toward the chemical industry. The rising cost of health care and the conflict surrounding genetic engineering fanned criticism of the pharmaceutical industry. At the same time, the Union Carbide disaster in Bhopal, India, and a 1986 chemical fire at Sandoz (located on the banks of the Rhine opposite Ciba-Geigy) caused a surge of resentment among populations located in areas surrounding the chemical plants. Ciba-Geigy itself had found the regulatory environment in Switzerland so hostile that, some years later, it located a new biochemical plant in France—just the other side of the Rhine. Lippuner remembered, "it was like water building up behind a dam." The company had begun to feel pressure from its own employees. "The rising generation at Ciba-Geigy was full of people who didn't want to leave their beliefs at the door when they came here and pick them up again when they left at 5 PM."

▲ 668

Case 6-6
Smashing the
Cube: Corporate
Transformation
at Ciba-Geigy,
Ltd.

In 1987, Alex Krauer became president and CEO, and in 1988 Heini Lippuner became chairman of the executive committee (KL). Together, they developed a "master plan" for the transformation of Ciba-Geigy (Exhibit 4). At the annual group management meeting (GMM) in 1988, a three-day event with the top 40 managers in the group, Lippuner asked the managers to consider what role Ciba-Geigy should play in the industrial society of the future. He also brought in a "futurologist" who detailed four major revolutions emanating from scientific progress, each of which led in turn to social revolutions. In the heated debates that followed, some managers denied the relevance of the social environment in business calculations, while others warned, "Socialists will walk in on your red carpets!" In the end, an analysis of Ciba-Geigy's recent financial performance convinced the managers that change was indeed necessary.

▲ 1988–1992: SMASHING THE CUBE

In late 1988, Lippuner assembled a multinational "core team" to develop a program of radical culture change: "Vision 2000." In parallel, he formed a think tank composed of younger members of middle and upper management to tap the energies of unorthodox and creative people within the company. With Lippuner serving as a bridge between the core team and the think tank, the former produced a draft of the Vision for presentation to the group's top management at GMM 89. The two-inch thick document detailed the basic strategy: "By striking a balance between our economic, social, and environmental responsibilities, we want to ensure the prosperity of our enterprise beyond the year 2000."

Ciba-Geigy's leadership recognized the need for concrete changes if this new "Vision" was to assume credibility throughout the organization. Said Lippuner, "We must be seen to walk as we talk."[3] Accordingly, they drew up an implementation plan for reforming the company through a progressive series of measures carried out along three axes: portfolio and business strategies, organization and systems, and people and leadership.

Portfolio and Business Strategies   As a part of the transformation process, Lippuner reshaped the group's portfolio in order to focus on core competencies in biology and chemistry. He ended Ciba's diversification venture into physics technology in 1990 with the sale of the Spectra-Physics and Gretag units, and other businesses where Ciba-Geigy's competitive position was weak, such as Ilford photographic materials. The previous year, Ciba-Geigy had acquired Corning's 50 percent share of a medical diagnostics company to become sole owner of Ciba-Corning Diagnostics.

For the remaining businesses, Ciba-Geigy's strategic planning process hinged on the identification of five "categories" of business: development, growth, pillar, core, and niche. Each category carried its own set of implications for performance measurement and resource allocation (Exhibits 3, 5, and 6).[4]

Organization and Systems   At the unveiling of Vision 2000 at GMM 89, Lippuner committed to having a new organization structure by January 1990. Organization 90, the name for the new structure that was arrived at after lengthy deliberations, abolished the cube.

---

[3]Heini Lippuner, "Changing the Corporate Culture—The view of the COO," from *New Winners?—International Panel on Corporate Transformation.*
[4]For further informattion, see Collis, "Portfolio Planning at Ciba-Geigy, Ltd.," HBS Case No. 795-040, 1995 (Case 1–3 in this book).

▲ EXHIBIT 4   "Master Plan" for the Transformation of Ciba-Geigy, 1988

▲ 669

Case 6-6
Smashing the
Cube: Corporate
Transformation
at Ciba-Geigy,
Ltd.

▲ EXHIBIT 5   Schematic Representation of Ciba's Portfolio in 1994

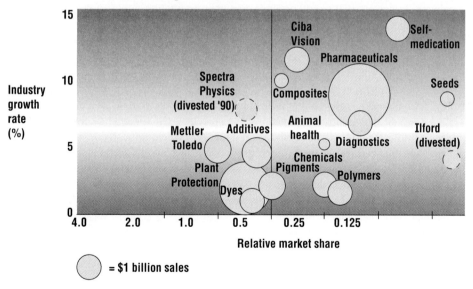

Source: Casewriter estimates.

The three-dimensional matrix was reduced to "one-and-a-half": the principal dimension was business (the global divisions) and the secondary dimension was geography (group company organizations by country). A set of horizontal strategies to define policies across the group were generated and supported by five corporate units (CUs) (see Exhibit 2).

▲ 670

Case 6-6
Smashing the
Cube: Corporate
Transformation
at Ciba-Geigy,
Ltd.

▲ EXHIBIT 6   Hierarchy for Financial Targets

Category	Role	Priority*
Pillar	Substantial contributor to group profitability	1. CAS% of sales RONA 2. Cash flow
Core	Cash provider	1. Cash flow 2. RONA
Growth	Qualitative growth; long-term profitability improvement	1. CAS% of sales RONA 2. Cash flow
Niche	Small pillar	1. CAS% of sales RONA 2. Cash flow
Development project	Development phase	cum. neg. CAS cum. neg. cash flow

*CAS = contribution after services; RONA = return on net assets.

Functions, which had been structured as cost centers, were pushed down into the divisions or consolidated in CUs or central service units (CSUs). Lippuner's principal objective was to create a framework that would produce customer orientation, innovation, and quality.

The product divisions became the principal dimension of the organization matrix and the axis for operating and strategic management of the global business. Global division heads retained direct authority over product strategy and assumed full operating responsibility for the performance of their divisions worldwide. Each division had a separate set of financial objectives specifically suited to its differentiated strategic performance objectives, determined and periodically reviewed by the KL.[5]

As a result of the abolition of functions, the percentage of Ciba-Geigy Switzerland employees working within a division rose from under 60 percent to nearly 75 percent. Before Organization 90, because so many employees were in central functions whose services could not be directly charged for, the divisions had direct control over less than 55 percent of their costs. The rest was determined by allocations of services and corporate infrastructure. Lippuner recalled that, in those days, managers of poorly performing divisions could lay the blame for their results on costs that were beyond their control. With the elimination of the cube, divisions gained control over and accountability for 95 percent of their total costs—including 25 percent directly charged for by the central service units for services rendered. Infrastructure costs now amounted to about 5 percent of total costs.

In every country in which Ciba-Geigy operated, the global product division was to receive support from the group company (GC) head, whose role was to administer the infrastructure and CSUs within the country and act on behalf of the KL to ensure implementation of horizontal policies (Exhibit 7). Previously the GC head had direct operational authority over each

---

[5]Three divisions, diagnostics, Ciba-Vision, and composite products, were headquartered in the United States. The other 11 divisions remained headquartered in Switzerland, although some had moved one or two SBU headquarters outside Switzerland.

▲ EXHIBIT 7   Role of the Group Company Head, 1994

▲671

Case 6-6
Smashing the
Cube: Corporate
Transformation
at Ciba-Geigy,
Ltd.

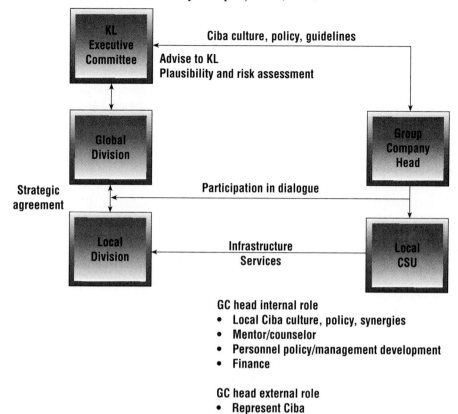

GC head internal role
- Local Ciba culture, policy, synergies
- Mentor/counselor
- Personnel policy/management development
- Finance

GC head external role
- Represent Ciba

of the divisions in the country (and responsibility for their performance); the GC head now assumed the role of "coach" for the divisions in the country, and as an intermediary to facilitate dialogue between the global divisions and local units.

Corporate units (CUs) were "centers of competence" that supported groupwide strategic management by developing and implementing horizontal strategies. The duties and size of the CUs varied according to their specialization (safety and environment, human resources, legal, central research, finance and control). The safety and environment unit, for example, had about 50 people who provided a core of scientific knowledge on issues such as transport, storage, and explosion technique. The CU's role was to interpret and transmit guidelines laid down by the KL, providing training and counseling to line management. They did not, however, have any functional authority over the divisions.

All functions necessary for a division were supposed to be provided by the division itself. However, a certain number of services remained centralized (in the parent company as well as in the group companies) as corporate service units (CSUs). They provided infrastructure and services to the divisions, performing functions that were subject to scale economies, such as running a mainframe computer or performing sophisticated engineering analyses, or those that were inherently shared across divisions, such as maintaining the infrastructure of the Stammhaus. The CSUs billed their services to the divisions at full cost in order to break even at year end, and at competitive prices if they wanted to retain the divisions' business.

▲ 672

Case 6-6
Smashing the
Cube: Corporate
Transformation
at Ciba-Geigy,
Ltd.

If justified by price and/or quality, divisions were ostensibly free to go outside for services offered by the CSUs, although as a practical matter, few did so. Similarly, the CSUs could, under certain circumstances, market their services also outside Ciba-Geigy. For example, the in-house advertising agency was turned into a profit center, with beneficial results. The separation of the CSUs from the CUs facilitated differentiation across divisions, allowing the divisions to choose the level of services and infrastructure appropriate for their individual cost structures.

Although the transformation called for the fundamental reorganization of Ciba-Geigy's businesses into largely autonomous units, the company faced a formidable challenge as it moved to allocate the manufacturing function to the divisions. Previously, many of Ciba-Geigy's plants that had been making a variety of products reported to the manufacturing function. Following the transformation, these plants belonged to separate divisions. In order to cope with this situation, the company allocated most plants to single divisions based on which was the major user. Plants that manufactured products for another business charged break-even transfer prices. Total product costs were set at the beginning of the year, and the group set rules governing how quickly one division could phase out products from another's factory, and how the nonabsorbed costs should be divided. Where this solution was not feasible, Ciba kept multidivisional production units, but set up "plants within the plant," designating particular processes and areas to individual divisions.

Beyond reinventing the structure of the group, Lippuner faced the challenge of reinventing its culture. As he noted, "Formulating a vision and making it operational in a strategic plan is one thing, but it doesn't mean that 90,000 people worldwide will simply change and follow those targets."[6]

People and Leadership   Lippuner's two goals for the people and leadership axis were to flatten the organization, reducing bureaucracy to a minimum, and to transform the culture by replacing management-by-fiat with empowered employees. As Lippuner pointed out, the cube had been in place and had guided employees attitudes with its tight structure for more than 20 years. Moreover, the company had to overcome not only the complacency of the traditional corporate hierarchy, but also the "army" mentality shaped by Switzerland's compulsory national service system with its command and control approach. The transformation aimed to vest all employees with an entrepreneurial role and responsibility within the company, and required a fundamental change in leadership style.

To change the company culture and to push authority down to the level where the relevant knowledge rested, Ciba-Geigy devised its own philosophy of empowerment—"directed autonomy"—with the help of an outside consultant:

$$Empowerment = Direction \times Authority \times Support$$

The elements were *multiplied,* Lippuner explained, because if any one of these was equal to zero, the whole thing would fall apart.

Although many of Ciba-Geigy's managers understood the need for transformation, others resisted. Lippuner had to convince the disgruntled managers that their jobs under the new system were "different," not less important. "The competent managers adapted well to the new system," Lippuner told his guest. Other managers, he explained, who owed their positions to a combination of the growth and the promotion system that were part of the company's history, struggled to adapt: "Those who relied on the hierarchy still feel insecure; we still hear their complaints."

---

[6]Kennedy, p. 20.

At the division level, some of Ciba-Geigy's managers responded to the new freedom by writing their own rule books. After Ciba-Geigy abandoned the practice of imposing corporate guidelines for travel expenses, for example, new written guidelines appeared at the division level. Accustomed to the hierarchical approach, these managers tenaciously clung to the concept of detailed instruction, even if it meant they had to create their own. The problem, Lippuner explained, existed mainly at the middle-management levels that he called the "layer of clay"—where people were either too removed from the upper echelon where the strategy was conceived or too entrenched to be among the younger, more activist element in the company.

To infuse its employees with more entrepreneurial spirit, Ciba-Geigy revamped the promotion and pay system in order to link career advancement and compensation more closely to responsibilities and performance. Traditionally, salary was linked to the executive's title alone, and was determined plus or minus 10 percent within three "salary bands" that increased automatically with age. As part of the reorganization, hierarchical titles were abolished, replacing the three-tiered pay system with one that essentially matched pay to actual job advancement and allowed for differences across divisions. Within the bands, Ciba broke with another long-standing Swiss tradition for managers in Switzerland by establishing a new system of incentive-based pay that paid annual bonuses of − 10 percent to + 20 percent of base salary according to performance on three levels: corporate, divisional, and individual. The relative importance of these levels in calculating an individual's bonus depended on the person's role in the company. "One drawback," noted one HR executive, "is that our people are [now] too preoccupied with incentives."

The transformation process climaxed in the abolition of the signatory bureaucracy in 1993. Ciba-Geigy was one of the first Swiss companies to dispense with this convention, and so dramatic was this break from tradition that the company took out quarter-page ads in Swiss newspapers to inform the public on behalf of the employees who suddenly found themselves stripped of their former status. Similarly, in order to signal his commitment to a total transformation of the company and to reduce costs, in 1991 Lippuner imposed mandatory retirement for all 1,500 employees in Switzerland over the age of 60.

Global dissemination of the Vision 2000 program took place through a series of seminars. The group management meeting was followed by 16 senior management seminars involving 500 key executives, each of whom in turn conducted their own simplified "follow-up" seminars with approximately 5,000 members of middle management. The seminars were divided into three levels of training aimed at distinct levels of management. Training (Vision 2000) for the entire workforce began in Switzerland in 1993, after a year's preparation.

Alternative Approaches to Transformation

Asea Brown Boveri   Immediately following the 1987 merger of two of Europe's largest electrical equipment companies, newly created Asea Brown Boveri's (ABB) new chief operating officer, Percy Barnevik, set about restructuring the company into 1,300 separate operating companies—each one a distinct legal and taxable entity—operating in 140 countries. Barnevik and his 10-person management team created an entirely new organization: a two-dimensional matrix structure that comprised 65 business areas (BAs), which in turn were grouped into business segments on one hand and integrated on a national basis through local holding companies on the other. Corporate functions were dealt with according to the 30/30/30/10 rule: 30 percent were laid off, 30 percent transferred to the divisions, 30 percent charged for, and only 10 percent retained at corporate.

▲ 673

Case 6-6
Smashing the
Cube: Corporate
Transformation
at Ciba-Geigy,
Ltd.

▲ 674

Case 6-6
Smashing the
Cube: Corporate
Transformation
at Ciba-Geigy,
Ltd.

Among the first dimension of the matrix, ABB's activities were clustered into 65 BAs that defined ABB's worldwide product markets. BA managers were responsible for worldwide product and technology strategies. Along the second dimension, each of the 1,300 operating companies was run by a company manager, who was responsible for implementing strategies and meeting annual profitability targets that were set on a regional basis. Regional managers were responsible for all the operating companies within a specific country. This reporting matrix required two bosses for each operating manager. ABB's 11 group vice presidents were the integrating link in the matrix. The role of the group executive management was to maintain a balance between the competing concerns of the strategy-minded business area managers and the operations-minded regional managers.

Barnevik oversaw the functioning of the whole by relying heavily on the data provided by ABACUS, a uniform reporting system for all 1,300 business units. Each month, he reviewed information on 500 different operations—50 business areas, all the major countries, and the key companies in the key countries. Variances prompted closer study to trace the source of the problem. Barnevik's goal, he explained, was to be able to approach his executives armed with complete information, not necessarily to supply operating instructions.

Barnevik explained the challenge facing ABB and his approach to meeting it: "ABB is an organization with three internal contradictions. We want to be global and local, big and small, radically decentralized with centralized reporting and control. If we resolve these contradictions, we create real organizational advantage."[7]

Sandoz Located just a few miles down river from Ciba-Geigy in Basel were the headquarters of Sandoz, one of Ciba's principal competitors in the pharmaceuticals and specialty chemicals business. In anticipation of the EC unification, Sandoz restructured operations in 1989. When the new structure took effect in 1990, the former parent company, Sandoz Ltd., became a holding company, whose role was to provide a framework of overall objectives. The major sectors became separate legal entities—Chemicals, Pharma, Agro, Nutrition, and Seeds—with fully decentralized management responsibility. Services were assigned to the new companies, as were operational elements of the previous corporate functions. Local presidents or national supradivisional organizations took responsibility for functions in countries where Sandoz operated a wide variety of businesses. They provided a link between Sandoz and the local units.

In late 1994, pharmaceuticals and nutrition were the priority areas for Sandoz's management attention. The two sectors were viewed as having further potential for synergies, and were the primary focus for future growth. There was speculation that Sandoz could be considering the possibility of spinning off a division in an effort to better target those areas.

▲ CIBA IN 1994: AFTER THE DUST HAS SETTLED

Ciba—as it was renamed in 1992—retained its identity as a Swiss company, with 51 percent of R&D and 40 percent of production in Switzerland (although only 2 percent of its sales). It operated on a highly differentiated basis in its three business sectors. In 1993, the health care sector generated 40 percent of group sales (and 57 percent of operating income), while the industry and agriculture sectors contributed 39 percent (25 percent) and 21 percent (18 percent), respectively. The operating margins of these three sectors were also different:

---

[7]For further information, see Robert Simons and Christopher Bartlett, "Asea Brown Boveri," HBS Case No. 192-139, 1992.

health care, 16.8 percent; industrial, 7.8 percent; and agricultural, 10.2 percent. Overall, research and development expenditures were around 9–10 percent sales; on pharmaceutical specialties, it was about 15 percent.

For the pharmaceutical business, changes in the health care environment had heightened the level of cost-oriented scrutiny, particularly on the price paid for pharmaceutical products. In the United States, for example, as health maintenance organizations (HMOs) were rapidly replacing private doctors as the primary customers for drugs and other pharmaceutical products, some of Ciba's pharmaceutical competitors were forward integrating into distribution. In 1993, Merck & Company paid $6.6 billion to acquire Medco Containment Services, a mail-order distribution channel. The price was more than two-and-a-half times Medco's sales and 45 times its earnings for fiscal 1993. Similarly high-priced transactions by companies such as SmithKline Beecham and Eli Lilly added to speculation about the landscape of the industry in the future.[8]

The industry and agriculture sectors were cyclical in nature, broadly subject to currency exposure and global economic conditions. In agriculture, the Common Agricultural Policy (CAP) reforms threatened to constrain the profit potential of the agricultural sector in Europe. Most of Ciba's industrial businesses were mature and cost-competitive, but lagging in terms of growth. However, as growth in health care slowed, and agriculture experienced pressures of its own, the industrial division was poised to take advantage of the general economic recovery.

The Business Unit Perspective

Pharmaceuticals   The operational independence that the pharmaceuticals division had enjoyed as a pillar business was largely unchanged by the corporate transformation phase of the early 1990s. However, having launched a number of top sellers during the 1960s and 70s, Ciba's pharmaceuticals division had a maturing portfolio which included products such as Voltaren (a highly successful, no longer exclusive anti-inflammatory drug) and seven other branded products all due to go off patent between 1992 and 1997. Despite its early promise, and the considerable marketing expenditures Ciba made on its behalf, the nicotine patch Habitrol offered only modest growth and profit potential due to a 40 percent reduction in the product's market from 1992 to 1993. Ciba's broad development pipeline featured nine new products slated for introduction to the market during the same period, although none appeared to be blockbuster material.

In the United States, analysts predicted that the pharmaceutical industry leaders would buy up smaller companies in order to secure their positions in the new environment. For its part, Ciba's pharmaceuticals division purchased Fisons' North American over-the-counter business for $115 million plus $25 million for current assets in 1993, gaining two strong brand names: Desenex antifungal and Allerest allergy relief medicine.

To bring concepts such as cost-awareness and customer-sensitivity in-house, where employees still traveled first-class and were headquartered in what was informally dubbed "the Phama Hilton," the pharmaceuticals division imposed a 10 percent cost reduction in 1993. The head of the division noted that cross-divisional transfers that brought managers into his division from Ciba's historically cost-conscious divisions made more sense today than they had before 1990.

---

[8]Anita M. McGahan, "An Outsider's Perspective on the Mergers in Pharmaceuticals," *Harvard Business Review,* November–December 1994, p. 1.

▲ 675

Case 6-6
Smashing the
Cube: Corporate
Transformation
at Ciba-Geigy,
Ltd.

▲ 676

Case 6-6
Smashing the
Cube: Corporate
Transformation
at Ciba-Geigy,
Ltd.

Textile Dyes   Following Organization 90, Ciba's oldest business became its youngest division. Formerly part of Ciba's dyestuffs and chemicals division, textile dyes was split off as a separate division in the early 1990s.

The textile dyes division took aggressive action to respond to market pressures brought on by the recession. With newly transparent accounts, in 1992 the division rationalized plants, cut layers, and became less integrated and more market-driven. The division capitalized on the empowerment measures of Organization 90 to reorganize units and reduce the number of layers below the departmental head from four to two. The delayering was followed by a zero-based budgeting exercise, which eliminated 15–20 percent of costs. In one case, the division eliminated 25 percent of the 200 + employees who were in quality assurance. In another case, having gained control of barge shipping on the Rhine (previously a production function responsibility), the division trimmed its shipping costs substantially. In order to facilitate such rationalizations, Ciba removed the remaining assets of shut-down plants from the divisions' balance sheets after two years. In total, textile dyes was able to focus on its RONA target and cut assets 30 percent, without losing any profit.

Following the reorganization of his division, Hans Gotz, head of the textile dyes division, was asked by the KL to share his expertise on the subject of transformation with other top managers at GM 93. Until that time, he had not been approached by any other division heads wanting to learn from his experience, and Gotz was skeptical of horizontal communication: "We have reached the limit for cross-divisional learning." However, there were cross-divisional meetings of function heads, two to six times a year. And after polymers used CSC Index for a reengineering exercise, three or four Ciba personnel on the project formed a corporate level reengineering team available as part of a CSU to other divisions. Increasingly informal networks were taking shape among the industrial divisions, and in the biological divisions as well.

Gotz was untroubled by the existence of some remaining centralized functions in the CSUs. For example, he was happy to relinquish direct control of purchasing to a designated representative on the corporate purchasing team that sourced all the raw materials for his division. To the extent that one division's interests clashed with those of another in the context of centralized functions, Gotz believed that satisfactory resolution was simply a matter of good negotiating skills.

Pigments   As an industrial division in a maturing business with a low-cost emphasis, the pigments division responded to excesses in its cost structure and competitive threats (particularly from Germany and Japan) by taking advantage of divisional empowerment and decentralization to cultivate a sense of urgency and encourage entrepreneurial behavior.

The division moved out of many functional or multidivisional areas in order to avoid expensive functional service costs as well as corporate overhead. Said pigments division head Peter Schutz, "If different units share the same services, there is always the danger that the common denominator will be at the high end of the potential range." For example, Organization 90 empowered the division to shape its own engineering department and cultivate its own standards—"as good as required," rather than being required by the corporate function to be as good as *possible*. Ultimately, the division reduced capital expenditures by half. The division rebounded from heavy losses in net cash flow in 1990 to a comfortable profit situation by the mid-90s, thus satisfying corporate profitability expectations for a core business.

Encouraged by the cost savings he had been able to achieve, Schutz expressed some frustration with certain remaining limits on his divisional independence, particularly with regard to purchasing of division-specific materials. Purchasing of raw materials represented about one-third of the turnover of the division, making it the division's single largest cost factor. In a mature business, the purchasing of raw materials bore a direct impact on the division's profit performance. As Schutz explained "in the pigments division, the rule of the game is not economies of scale—not supertanker—but specific products from specific suppliers for specific uses." In addition, since some of Ciba's suppliers of pigments intermediates were at the same time competitors in the business *and* customers (e.g., for printing inks or paints), the relationships had to be handled with care and with an overall understanding of the division's strategy. Yet purchasing remained beyond divisional control.

Schutz insisted that profits could be improved if pigments could negotiate its own purchasing deals. "We are operating in an industry with relatively low profit margins, so we must get a better deal. But we are regarded by the suppliers as part of a well-known and comfortably profitable chemical/pharmaceutical company. Pigments represent 5 percent of Ciba's turnover. How can our requirements for low prices and attractive paying conditions influence overall negotiations involving a totally different dimension?" The central purchasing department prepared its negotiations with key suppliers in cooperation with representatives of the pigments division, and the logistic pipelines of central purchasing were coordinated with divisional MRP II systems. Nevertheless, Schutz felt that divisional influence was only "on paper." "The purchasing group ultimately answers to central purchasing, and it is there that their salaries and incentives are determined. The pigments colleagues are not sitting in the drivers' seat."

The pigments division had fully integrated business units outside Switzerland, and they handled the purchasing function on their own. Schutz was aware of the benefits they enjoyed as a result, and he believed that further pressure on divisional margins in the parent company would ultimately oblige Ciba to grant the divisions more autonomy in purchasing.

Overall, Schutz regarded the reorganization as having provided "*the* great chance for the pigments division to recover." And although he viewed the existence of horizontal strategies as a necessary means to prevent Ciba from becoming a holding company, Schutz maintained that in their business approaches and survival strategies, the divisions would continue to have less and less in common with one another. Another division head put it somewhat differently: observing that "horizontal strategies are a constraint on shooting from the hip," he reasoned, "on balance, we have the appropriate degree of horizontal coordination. We can manage ourselves within the confines of the group."

The Corporate Unit Perspective

Human Resources   In the past, human resource management had been the responsibility of the country managers, under the direction of a small corporate unit. The various HR units operated quite independently, and interactions in the HR community were largely driven by the bi-annual, groupwide management development (MD) process, and by the handling of personnel transfers between countries.

Following Organization 90, Stanton Goldberg, vice president–human resources for Ciba-Geigy Corporation in the United States, noted that his position went from being "king" of HR for all the U.S. divisions to being purely advisory, as the divisions established their own HR functions. Still, Goldberg acknowledged, there was a logic behind the control of HR activities by the global product divisions. As Ciba moved toward globalization, top managers would need international experience. Moreover, if global division heads were to be held responsible for performance, it was necessary to give them power over the HR process. At the same time, he noted that the global product divisions' focus was on the top people; as such, they did little to cultivate a significantly higher volume of cross-divisional transfers.

▲ 677

Case 6-6
Smashing the Cube: Corporate Transformation at Ciba-Geigy, Ltd.

▲ 678

Case 6-6
Smashing the
Cube: Corporate
Transformation
at Ciba-Geigy,
Ltd.

To address the new role of HR, the 40-person corporate unit for human resources first attempted to become a "center of competence" for divisional management. With the aim of achieving groupwide acceptance in this role, the corporate unit devised a companywide HR network of all the local HR units. Working with representatives of line management, it developed overarching policies, guidelines, processes, and tools.

By 1993 a mission for corporate HR had been established. A key point was the introduction of a new MD strategy, in which the divisions were to be the driving force behind a global cycle for succession and management development planning. The MD data originated at the local unit level, to be aggregated and compared as it flowed upward through the group companies and the global divisions heads and finally to the executive committee (Exhibit 8). Corporate HR compiled and maintained centralized files on approximately 5,000 top managers and made the information available to the KL. within the pool, the top 1,500 were subject to corporate discretion in succession planning, although proactive intervention was rare.

In 1994, corporate HR introduced a competency model into management training programs. It conceived standard training programs for specific levels of management similar to the traditional "Furigen," Ciba's most elite corporatewide training program, which brought together 120 of the company's newly promoted senior managers for two weeks' education at a hotel retreat in Switzerland. Additionally, there would be regionally operated training programs, and local programs operated by each group company.

In 1994, one corporate HR executive acknowledged, Ciba was still struggling with the adoption of a global approach that would cultivate a sufficient supply of managers who could be moved across businesses and countries. Said one division head, "Our people have no incentive to switch to a new business—there is plenty of room for advancement here." Another division head, however, was disappointed by the small number of cross-divisional transfers. "Such moves work well. Our people are Ciba employees first, division employees second." By his estimate, only two or three of the top fifty people in his division had come from another part of Ciba.

The corporate HR unit also found itself pressing the limits of its resources. In order to strengthen the HR network, it was encouraging group companies to implement their own competence evaluation, training, and development of HR brochures and materials. The corporate unit in Basel was, therefore, characterized by Golberg as a kind of "virtual organization."

Environmental Protection and Safety   Implementation of a groupwide strategy for environmental protection occurred swiftly following Organization 90. Although the upheaval reduced the safety and environmental unit's staff to 50 from 130, many of the displaced members joined divisions and CSUs to perform related functions in plant design and analytics.

Although the corporate unit lost its functional authority in the formal sense as a result of the transformation, it retained the competence it had built since Ciba-Geigy first began addressing the issue of environmental safety much earlier (Exhibit 9). A rhetoric surrounding the vital importance of safety and adhering to strict environmental standards was also ingrained in Ciba's culture. Moreover, the corporate unit retained formal controls in the form of general principles, regulations, and binding guidelines, set by the KL and spelled out in two large volumes. The volumes covered issues such as handling procedures for explosive chemicals. These guidelines were initially developed in consultation with all divisions, though some argued that one or two divisions dominated the discussions.

In lieu of an absolute standard of global uniformity in its environmental protection practices. Ciba implemented "best demonstrated practices" that were determined with the help of outside consultants and subject to regional adjustments. Within this framework, the divisions

▲ **EXHIBIT 8**   Management Development model

▲679

Case 6-6
Smashing the
Cube: Corporate
Transformation
at Ciba-Geigy,
Ltd.

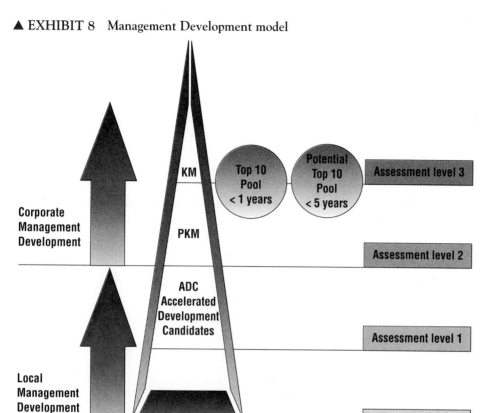

Source: Ciba-Geigy, Ltd.

had full authority to formulate and implement safety and environmental practices. However, if an accident occurred and the KL later determined that Ciba's rules had not been followed, there would be "hell to pay"—at a cost to be determined both by internal executives and, most likely, external attorneys.

Finance   In the late 1980s, after decades of predominantly Swiss ownership, Ciba-Geigy had found itself with limited access to world capital markets. Confronted by an increasingly global marketplace, the company recognized the need to permit unrestricted foreign ownership and to make its financial information more transparent and accessible. As a member of the corporate finance unit put it, "By the late 1980s, we realized that Ciba-Geigy was in danger of missing the boat." As a result, Ciba was the second major Swiss company to open its share register to foreigners, and it changed to international accounting standards (IAS).[9]

Largely aimed at improving relations with foreign investors, the restatement of accounts on an IAS basis boosted 1993 net profits by an additional 6 percent. IAS also simplified the comparison of Ciba's performance relative to its competitors, notably Sandoz and Roche,

---

[9]In 1989, Ciba allowed Americans to buy stock in the company for the first time. In 1990, as part of its campaign to open up communication, the company also initiated a series of roadshows in the United Kingdom, the United States, Japan, and Europe. By 1994, Ciba stock was one-third internationally held.

▲ 680

Case 6-6
Smashing the
Cube: Corporate
Transformation
at Ciba-Geigy,
Ltd.

▲ EXHIBIT 9   Vision 2000 and the Environment

*By striking a balance between our economic, social, and environmental responsibilities
we want to ensure the prosperity of the enterprise beyond the year 2000.*

In environmental terms these goals mean that we aim to:

- Reduce, over time, our environmental impact.
- Save resources with better products and manufacturing processes.
- Streamline product lines which no longer meet today's environmental standards.
- Research, design, and introduce new products and processes which safely fulfill their purposes with as little environmental impact as possible.
- Use natural resources in the most effective way.
- Reduce waste in all forms and dispose safety of all unavoidable waste using state-of-the-art technologies.
- Strengthen environmental consciousness at all levels within the organization.

These are key environmental requirements for all business units.

These guiding principles mean the commitment to long-term sustainable growth—profitable business growth depends on providing products and services which demonstrate superior benefit/risk ratios, reduced resource consumption, and reduced waste per unit.

Source: Ciba-Geigy, Ltd.

both of which had adopted IAS accounting—Roche in 1990 and Sandoz in 1992. The change to IAS allowed the group to establish benchmarks and develop targets on a segment-by-segment basis.

Under the old organization structure, each group company had been required to produce pages of documentation detailing the consolidated results of its various businesses, to be analyzed monthly at the corporate level. After the transformation, each division produced a monthly two-page business report as well as quarterly reports for the KL and the board, but the corporate finance unit typically did not review them in great detail. Nonetheless, each division in every country had to fulfill the standard monthly reporting requirements. In small countries like Ireland, for example, this meant that every month, some divisions had to draw up their accounts for sales of less than $50,000. Moreover, since each division had taken advantage of its autonomy to establish its own controllers' manual, a group company controller now had up to 14 manuals, not one, to deal with.

Beyond regular strategic review meetings, oversight by the KL was limited to quarterly review of divisional reports and monthly divisional sales statistics. The KL reviewed 30-line profit/loss statements, and even fewer items on the balance sheet. The transformation therefore sharply reduced corporate-level analysis of performance figures and decentralized financial accounting responsibility to the divisions, enhancing profit-focus at the division level. However, decentralization and divisional accountability in turn led to a dramatic increase in the number of charge-out items. Even minor costs were charged out, which led to as many as 40,000 service charge transactions in the parent company alone in 1993. One finance executive jokingly pointed out that he was charged by the agricultural division for the use of the toilet down the hall. Observing the financial complexity brought about by divisionalization, managers compared Ciba favorably to ABB, believing they could achieve "80–90 percent of the benefits of being separate entities, without the distraction of having separate finances."

The Group Company Perspective

Consistent with Ciba's overarching focus on divisionalization, the transformation of the role of the group company head gave rise to a number of complicating issues. In countries like Germany, the elimination of the GC head's role in direct operational matters meant a dramatic change in the nature of the job. Under the old organization, a GC head was directly involved in running the businesses in that country, including budgeting, monthly operating results monitoring, and in divisional strategy setting. With the ascendancy of the global product divisions, however, group company managers were forced to relinquish operating authority altogether. Profit performance became the role and responsibility of the global division head.

Although stripped of most of its operational component, the role of the GC head retained a degree of complexity. As the ranking liaison between the global divisions and the local units, they contributed specific knowledge about local conditions, including critical and often sensitive government- and customer-relations issues, and transferred knowledge across all the businesses Ciba was operating in their respective countries (Exhibit 7). They also established countrywide policies, such as determining the average Ciba countrywide pay increase each year. Much of the GC head's role previously had been effected through the existence of informal networks tied to the functions. When the functions were eliminated, the GC head's ability to mediate between the global divisions and the local units became even more important.

In the United States, to some extent, the GC head had already presided over a gradual transformation toward the new form. During the 1980s, for example, in order to compete with other major pharmaceuticals companies in the United States, where higher salaries attracted top talent, Ciba-Geigy Corp. (U.S.) had established divisionalized pay and long-term incentive schemes. In addition to making Ciba more competitive in the U.S. market, the salary and incentive structures also encouraged divisional managers to take greater responsibility. Moreover, noting the diverse set of businesses that resided under the group company umbrella, U.S. Senior Vice President Joe Sullivan insisted, "I couldn't run all the businesses, even if I had that power. They're too diverse, too much to do."

The second major change wrought by the transformation in the group companies, was that the charge for group company activities was reduced from 2 1/2 percent in 1989 to less than 1 percent of divisional sales in 1993, as many functions were pushed into the divisions. Activities that previously had been done by the group company, such as HR, were either moved into the divisions, or made into CUs, or CSUs that charged for their services. After the initial divisionalization of functions, group companies downsized their remaining staff under pressure from the divisions to reduce CSU charges, cutting costs by about a third.

By 1994, the trend began showing signs of reversal. As divisions recognized the cost effectiveness of sharing some activities within a country, they moved functions back to the group company. In the U.K., for example, the group company became the administrative center for two of the divisions. Divisions also came to value the advice of group company managers like J.S. Fraser in the U.K., a senior executive who had previously run the Ilford business worldwide. Cross-divisional functional committees were established by the divisions themselves, sometimes under the chairmanship of the group company head, to conduct quarterly discussions on common issues such as how to handle downsizing or manage a revised budget process.

▲ 681

Case 6-6
Smashing the
Cube: Corporate
Transformation
at Ciba-Geigy,
Ltd.

▲ 682

Case 6-6
Smashing the
Cube: Corporate
Transformation
at Ciba-Geigy,
Ltd.

Finally, local divisions were turning to group company heads to loosen the tight control exerted by some divisional headquarters. One of the division heads noted that, after Organization 90, "the pendulum had swung too far," as divisions took over too many activities, and the Basel divisional headquarters had intervened too much in local divisional activities. In particular, some group company heads felt that the incentive schemes and targets set by the global divisions were too often inappropriate, because conditions varied country by country. Local divisions were increasingly apt to request intervention by the GC head to explain to Basel headquarters why, in a particular country, the division could not be expected to achieve the level of performance that global division management had specified.

Group company heads were particularly troubled by the lack of operational authority in personnel matters. Below the level of a divisional vice president, personnel decisions had previously been almost exclusively the province of the group company. As a result of the reorganization, the global divisions became much more involved in lower-level decisions, inhibiting cross-divisional transfers and causing frustration among the U.S. group company managers who wanted to rotate their best people across divisions in order to broaden their exposure. "Only when the divisions recognize that cross-divisional rotations are a win-win situation," explained Sullivan, "will they cease to be a bone of contention."

Other factors also contributed to the ambiguity that characterized the new GC head's role. For example, in certain countries, the position required only part-time focus and therefore was held in combination with another position: thus in Canada, the group company head spent 90 percent of his time being head of pharmaceuticals. Finally, one effect of reducing the operational authority of GC heads was to compound their resistance to efforts to consolidate some smaller countries under "regional" group company leadership. One example of this was a proposal to consolidate Austria and Germany, which was favored by global product divisions that were adopting more regional strategies, but strongly opposed by Austria's GC head.

The KL Perspective

After the transformation of the company, the eight-member executive committee's role remained the optimization of the company as a whole, and the management of Ciba as an economic entity. Under the old system, the KL's decision-making process was collaborative, with each member, including the chairman of the committee, having an equal say. Each member was designated the "patron" for a particular division, serving as an advocate for its interests but without direct authority or responsibility for the division. The process was deliberative and majority rule prevailed.

The transformation altered the dynamic somewhat by vesting final decision-making authority in the committee chairman. Nevertheless, the KL continued to function on the basis of consensus. Three members served as the liaisons with the technology, finance, and R&D functions; four focused on the divisions and were directly responsible and accountable for their performance. All eight members met every other week; for those responsible for divisions, most of their time was spent at their respective divisions monitoring division performance and operating results.

In addition to periodic review of operating results and, less frequently, direct involvement in a division's strategic planning, the KL reviewed requests for capital expenditures. In line with Organization 90, divisional spending limits had been raised and the number of signatures required on a request cut from as many as 17 to only 4: requests for 5–10m SFr were reviewed by two members of the KL; requests for up to 50m SFr required approval by all eight members. At lower levels, capital expenditures were governed by preset guidelines within the divisions in order to delegate decision making outside the KL.

▲ A WORK IN PROGRESS

Having told the story of their company's efforts to realize a new strategic vision through the implementation of a new organization structure, several Ciba managers turned the question back over to the professor: what did *he* think about the transformation at Ciba-Geigy? As the professor considered his answer, he heeded the words of executive committee chairman Heini Lippuner, who, as the leader of Ciba and one of the principal architects of its transformation, was both optimistic and critical regarding the company's progress:

> We have placed the emphasis on the divisional dimension and structured the functions around that. It is difficult to live in a situation that is neither clearly defined nor one-dimensional, but we will always have to cope with being in a force field. On balance, I believe we are two-thirds of the way there. We are willing to learn from experience and modify our procedures.

▲ 683

Case 6-6
Smashing the
Cube: Corporate
Transformation
at Ciba-Geigy,
Ltd.

BEATRICE COMPANIES— 1985

In early August 1985, the board of directors of Beatrice Cos. (1985 sales of $12.6 billion) convened an emergency meeting to consider the future of James Dutt, the company's president, chairman, and CEO. Dutt, elected chief executive of Beatrice in 1979, had attempted to significantly alter the strategic course of the sprawling conglomerate through a series of acquisitions, divestitures, and corporate reorganizations. However, as Wall Street began to question the viability of Beatrice's new strategy, Dutt was increasingly criticized. At the August board meeting, the directors had to decide not only the fate of James Dutt, but also the future of Beatrice's corporate strategy.

▲ THE EARLY YEARS

George Haskell formed the partnership of Haskell & Bosworth as a wholesale produce dealer in Beatrice, Nebraska, in 1891. After three years of modest success, Haskell entered the dairy processing industry; later, in 1897, Haskell & Bosworth incorporated as the Beatrice Creamery Company, which churned and packaged butter.

Beatrice quickly expanded into the surrounding countryside, buying smaller creameries that were close to raw material sources and shipping the final product to market. In 1905, Beatrice acquired Continental Creamery Co. of Topeka, Kansas. Continental was one of the

---

Research Associate Toby Stuart prepared this case under the supervision of Professor David Collis. Parts of this case draw heavily upon George Baker's paper, "Beatrice: A Study in the Creation & Destruction of Value" (Harvard Business School, April 8, 1991). A subsequent version of this paper was published in the *Journal of Finance* (July 1992, pp. 1081–1119).

oldest dairies and had a strong regional brand in "Meadow Gold," which became the corner-stone of Beatrice's dairy business. At that time, this was the largest merger in the U.S. dairy industry.

In 1927, Beatrice faced financial and management difficulties. William Ferguson, who had succeeded George Haskell as president, decided to sell the firm to National Dairy (later Kraft), at the time the largest dairy company. Ferguson traveled to New York to negotiate the sale price with National Dairy, but National's highest offer of $45.50 a share significantly under-shot Beatrice's over-the-counter price of $60 a share. After negotiations failed to reduce the gap, Ferguson ended talks with National Dairy. The following year, Ferguson retired and the board elected Clinton Haskell, nephew of the company's founder, as president of Beatrice

Haskell had two goals as president of Beatrice. First, he would expand the creamery, fo-cusing on extending processing plants to the East Coast; second, he would diversify into additional product lines within the dairy industry, such as ice cream. Haskell expanded Beatrice mostly by acquiring creameries rather than by constructing new facilities. By the end of 1928, Beatrice had purchased 13 dairy companies, the largest of which was for $1.5 million (Exhibit 1). In stride with these acquisitions, Beatrice's revenues increased from $40 million to $84 million between 1928 and 1930.

In 1930 and 1931, Beatrice acquired an additional 44 dairies. Among these were eastern facilities, such as Carry Ice Cream of Washington, DC, and Maryland Creamery of Baltimore. These purchases established Beatrice, along with National Dairy and Borden, as one of the big three dairy firms. During this time, the dairy industry was consolidating as technological innovations changed the fundamentals of dairy processing. Refrigeration technology coupled with advances in dairy-processing machinery dramatically increased the minimum efficient plant size for dairies. In addition, the federal government introduced a grading system for milk and mandated pasteurization of dairy products, a process of ap-plying sustained heat to milk to eliminate harmful organisms, which meant that more so-phisticated machinery was required to operate a dairy plant.

Beatrice typically acquired small dairy companies and looked for competent incumbent manager who would stay on after the acquisition. The company built market share in a geo-graphic area through selective acquisitions of regional companies. Unlike National Dairy or Borden, Beatrice generally discarded the brand names of its acquisitions. Instead, it pack-aged all of its dairy products under the Meadow Gold logo. As early as 1930, Beatrice adver-tised Meadow Gold in such nationally circulating journals as *Life* and the *Saturday Evening Post*. Another difference between Beatrice and the other large dairies was that National Dairy and Borden focused on the highly urbanized markets, while Beatrice concentrated more heavily on less-populated areas.

In 1931, Beatrice expanded by purchasing a minority stake in Chicago Cold Storage, a re-frigerated-warehousing concern, which operated as a wholly owned subsidiary of Beatrice. The company diversified again in 1938 when it began to distribute frozen foods under the "Birds Eye" label.

The organizational structure that the early Beatrice assumed was decentralized with many geographic divisions and a central office. Each of Beatrice's acquired plants operated as an integrated unit that both processed and distributed its goods. The central office housed the corporate officers and handled all financial, legal, research, advertising, quality control, and general policy formulation activities. Seven district managers linked the field units to the cen-tral office: plant managers reported directly to district managers also located in the field, who in turn reported to corporate. Control laboratories located at each of the major plants moni-tored product quality.

▲ EXHIBIT 1   Number of Acquisitions and Divestitures, 1910–1985

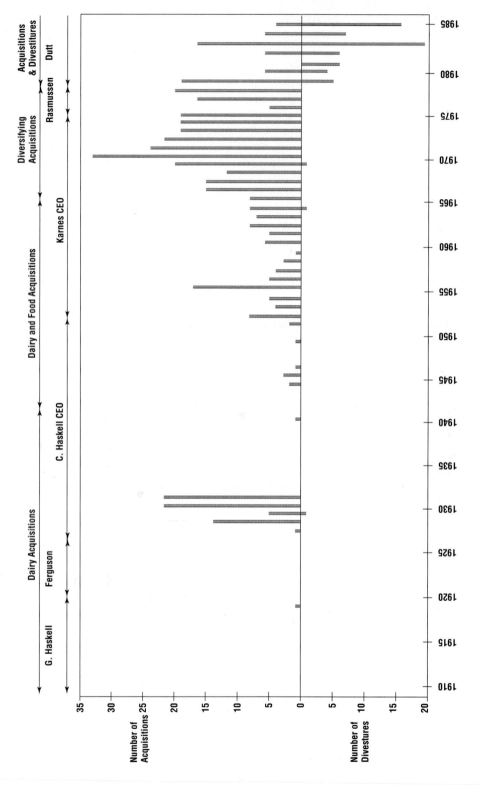

Source: George Baker, "Beatrice: A Study in the Creation and Destruction of Value." Harvard Business School, April 3, 1991.

▲ DIVERSIFICATION: 1940–1976

On November 1, 1943, Beatrice acquired La Choy Food Products of Archbold, Ohio. A maker of Chinese specialty foods, La Choy was Beatrice's first non-dairy-related acquisition. Symbolically, in the company's proxy statement filed for 1945, the board of directors recommended that the company change its name from Beatrice Creamery to Beatrice Foods Co. since "The company had long ceased to be just a creamery."

In 1952, William G. Karnes succeeded Clinton Haskell as Beatrice's president. Karnes was a Northwestern Law School graduate who had served as chief financial officer under Haskell, but had never held an operating position in the company. However, Karnes had been heavily involved in the negotiations for many of Beatrice's previous acquisitions. In the year of his election, Karnes formed a committee, comprised of himself and four other executives, to set long-term objectives for Beatrice. The committee decided to continue Beatrice's strategy of growth through acquisition. In expanding its dairy operations, the committee recommended that Beatrice follow the population shift from the Midwest to the Southeast and Southwest.

In 1953, Beatrice acquired six dairy companies, including Creameries of America, the nation's seventh-largest dairy producer with 1952 revenues of $49 million. Creameries of America had operations in the western states and Hawaii; after the acquisition, Beatrice processed and sold its dairy products from coast to coast. From 1951 to 1961, Beatrice continued expanding its dairy business, participating in about 175 dairy mergers during this period and increasing its sales 136 percent to $539 million in 1961 (Exhibit 2). Beatrice established its first overseas operations in 1961 with the construction of a condensed milk plant in Malaysia. In 1962, it purchased a Belgian dairy.

In the mid-1950s, Congress altered Beatrice's growth strategy when it passed the Celler-Kefauver Act that greatly strengthened Section 7 of the Clayton Act, the existing antitrust law. Following the enactment of Celler-Kefauver, the Federal Trade Commission (FTC) challenged mergers made by large dairy corporations from 1950 to 1956. Among the complaints was one filed against Beatrice for five acquisitions, including the Creameries of America merger. (The FTC also filed antitrust complaints against National Dairy and Borden.) After extensive negotiations, Beatrice agreed to divest certain plants amounting to $27 million in sales and a smaller percentage of its net earnings. In addition, Beatrice accepted a moratorium on all dairy acquisitions for a 10-year period, with the exception of purchases that the FTC approved.

Faced with declining margins in the dairy industry and pressure from the FTC, Karnes decided that Beatrice needed to expand into new industries to maintain its historical earnings growth. Margins in the dairy industry were declining as consolidation intensified competition and as many large grocery store chains backward integrated into dairy processing.

As the FTC reviewed Beatrice's dairy mergers, Karnes led the company into the confectionery business in 1955 with the acquisition of the D.L. Clark Co., a national manufacturer of candy bars. Two years later, Beatrice purchased the Bond Pickle Co. and concurrently established a grocery products division that included its nondairy food operations.

Fueled by the steady cash flow generated by its dairy operations, Beatrice launched an aggressive acquisition campaign in the mid-1960s. Beatrice took its first step toward unrelated diversification in 1964 when it acquired Bloomfield Industries, a manufacturer of institutional food-service equipment for restaurants and hotels. Bloomfield was quickly followed with the $16.9 million acquisition of Stahl Finish and Polyvinyl Chemical in 1965, manufacturers of polymers and raw materials for polishes.

▲ EXHIBIT 2   Beatrice Cos. Financials, 1950–1979

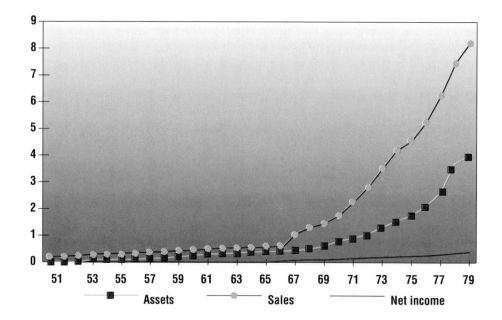

Under Karnes' direction, Beatrice executives analyzed a variety of industries to determine areas for profitable expansion. For example, in 1967, Beatrice conducted a review of the "do-it-yourself market for home consumers" and judged this to be "a very rapid growth and potential profit industry."[1] In the same year, Beatrice purchased Melnor Industries, a manufacturer of do-it-yourself gardening equipment, and followed this acquisition with the purchase of seven additional home products companies in the upcoming two years.

Throughout Karnes' tenure as CEO, Beatrice followed a similar pattern in its acquisitions: after analyzing an industry and orchestrating a first merger, the company followed the beachhead with subsequent purchases in the same business area. Among the list of industries Beatrice expanded into in a similar manner were agricultural products, bakery products, soft-drink bottling, food-service equipment, industrial forging and fabricating, specialty chemicals, recreational vehicles, and graphic arts.

Karnes maintained four guidelines that he steadfastly used to evaluate potential takeover targets. First, Beatrice would pursue only profitable companies in industries growing at a faster rate than food. Second, Karnes only considered producers of branded products; Beatrice was not interested in commodities. Third, only companies judged to possess high-quality managers who were willing to remain in their operating roles after Beatrice gained ownership of the company were acquired. This criterion was extended for overseas acquisitions, where Karnes insisted that managers maintain a 10 to 20 percent equity stake in the target companies. Finally, Karnes only sought small companies compared to Beatrice so that no individual acquisition posed a serious financial risk to the overall company. In making acquisitions, Beatrice preferred not to issue large amounts of debt, instead financing expansion with stock swaps, cash, and lease backs.

[1]Federal Trade Commission, *FTC Decisions,* "Decisions on Beatrice Foods," Docket 8864, July 1975.

Employing these guidelines, Beatrice grew rapidly with 78 acquisitions between 1965 and 1970 (Exhibit 1). Indeed, over $750 million of Beatrice's 1970 sales of $1.83 billion was directly attributable to these purchases. In choosing which companies to acquire within an industry, Beatrice considered the quality of the company's incumbent managers to be the most important single criterion. Particularly when initially entering a new industry, Beatrice pinpointed the company that it desired, and Karnes often became personally involved in negotiating the merger. The vast majority of the companies Beatrice acquired under Karnes were privately held, family-run businesses (of the more than 330 acquisitions made while Karnes was CEO, all but 5 were of privately held firms). Part of the reason for the stress on incumbent managers in Beatrice's first acquisition in a new industry was that these individuals were often valuable sources of future acquisition leads within their industries.

After Beatrice decided on a target company, Karnes would often approach managers four or five times, patiently waiting until they were ready to negotiate. In many cases, there were unusual circumstances at the company prior to the acquisition, such as the death of the company founder. In making acquisitions, Beatrice had a reputation for not being transaction driven: Karnes viewed divestitures very negatively, and throughout his entire tenure as CEO, Beatrice divested only three companies. Beatrice's commitment to growing rather than divesting companies facilitated friendly acquisitions of family-owned businesses.

Under Karnes, Beatrice continued to function in its traditional manner as a decentrally run (and now diversified) company because the companies it acquired usually retained their managers. Every Beatrice division had its own CEO, and division managers possessed the responsibility to hire and fire, promote employees, determine pay scales, purchase supplies, and advertise and promote products. Corporate headquarters, however, retained control over capital expenditures and determined inventory quotas for each division. Headquarters received information about each division through monthly financial reports containing sales and profit data.

Under Karnes, most acquisitions were made individual profit centers when they became part of Beatrice, and Karnes rarely consolidated any of the company's myriad subsidiaries. In addition, Beatrice divisions had very little interaction with one another at the operational level (for example, there were no joint materials purchases, and divisions did not internally source). In 24 annual reports with Karnes as president, not one included the word *synergy*. Corporate headquarters provided each of the hundreds of profit centers with nearly complete manufacturing and marketing autonomy during Karnes's tenure.

Beatrice was liberal in granting funds for capital improvements to its divisions, and target-company managers often agreed to be acquired because Beatrice was known to be generous in providing capital for expansion with few restraints from company headquarters. Corporate headquarters played a bank-like role in loaning capital to divisions. A profit center simply submitted a loan-request form along with its five-year sales, earnings, RONA, and cash-flow numbers, and Beatrice headquarters decided whether to grant the loan, which typically carried a market interest rate, based on the division's historical performance.

Beatrice also installed an incentive system for division managers under which plant managers received a base salary plus a bonus of about 2 percent of plant-level pretax profits. Certain profit center managers were also entitled to stock options under an incentive program instituted in 1957. An additional incentive aspect of the Beatrice system was that every Beatrice corporate officer appointed under Karnes was chosen from within the organization. Divisions therefore served as the training grounds for future corporate officers, and Beatrice regularly held meetings for division leaders at which management problems were discussed and business school professors gave lectures.

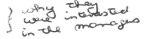
} why they were interested in the managers

▲ THE INTERIM CEO: 1976–1979

William Karnes resigned in 1976 when he reached Beatrice's mandatory retirement age of 65. During Karnes's tenure as president and CEO, Beatrice's annual revenues multiplied from $52 million in 1952 to $5.3 billion in 1976. In that year, Beatrice's return on assets was over 8 percent (Exhibit 3). At the time of his resignation, Beatrice was considered a multinational conglomerate with over 20 percent of its revenues generated overseas.

When Karnes retired, he had left in place what he thought was an adequate succession plan. William Mitchell, an attorney and CFO of Beatrice, was elected chairman and chief operating officer, while Wallace Rasmussen, an operating manager who had ascended to the executive suite through the food segment, was made chief executive officer. Mitchell was said to be Karnes's protege; like Karnes, he was a Northwestern Law School graduate with a background in finance. Rasmussen was 62 years old, and was expected to be a caretaker until he retired at 65 and passed the job of CEO to Mitchell. However, a conflict quickly developed between Mitchell and Rasmussen concerning different opinions over how the company should proceed. While Mitchell felt that Beatrice should focus on digesting its many recent acquisitions, including instituting more thorough reporting structures and tightening control of its roughly 400 profit centers, Rasmussen wanted to aggressively forge ahead with Beatrice's expansion program. The controversy was resolved when Mitchell was "outflanked and outmuscled," and was forced to resign 15 months after accepting his position.[2] James L. Dutt, a 52-year-old operations manager with a background similar to Rasmussen's, replaced Mitchell. According to one ousted executive, in the following months, Rasmussen sought to "clean out anyone who had a close connection to Karnes."[3]

Rasmussen introduced important strategic changes at Beatrice. In 1978, Beatrice made its first substantial acquisition under Rasmussen when it acquired publicly held Tropicana Products Inc. for $490 million (Exhibit 4). This price greatly exceeded the second-highest bid for the company, a $344 million offer from Kellogg Co. In dollar amount, the Tropicana deal was more than six times the size of Beatrice's second-largest acquisition—Samsonite luggage—which Beatrice had purchased for $80 million in 1972. While Tropicana possessed a strong brand name, orange juice was considered by many at Beatrice to be a commodity good, and many also opposed the acquisition because Tropicana competed against the nation's premier marketing companies. One food company executive said of the deal, "With Tropicana, Beatrice not only has to contend with the logistics of distributing the fresh product, but it also now faces the brutal prospect of going head-on with Coca-Cola."[4] In the same year, Beatrice also acquired Culligan International, a make of water softeners, for $50.8 million, and Harman International Industries, a $137 million manufacturer of hi-fi equipment.

While Rasmussen supported Beatrice's decentralized operating philosophy, he began to make some operating changes. For example, the fiscal 1977 annual report stated that Beatrice had created five executive vice president positions to "supervise specific sections of our operations permitting us to concentrate on corporate directions and goals." The company established a pyramid management structure, under which 54 group managers reported to 17

---

[2]Meg Cox and Paul Ingrassia, "Discord at the Top: Beatrice Foods' Board, Officers Split Bitterly in a Battle for Control," *The Wall Street Journal,* May 21, 1976.
[3]"The Man Who Came to Dinner," *Forbes,* February 19, 1979, p. 86.
[4]"Beatrice Foods: Adding Tropicana for a Broader Nationwide Network," *Business Week,* May 15, 1978, p. 114.

▲ EXHIBIT 3   Beatrice Cos. Return on Assets, 1940–1985

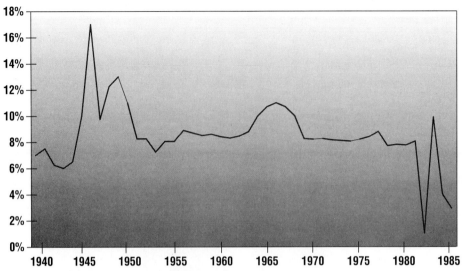

Source: George Baker, "Beatrice: A Study in the Creation and Destruction of Value."

division managers, who in turn reported to one of the five executive vice presidents. Each group manager regularly visited his profit center managers, watching key variables and collecting monthly financial reports that were also reviewed by division managers.

Beatrice also began to emphasize corporate marketing under Rasmussen. Under Karnes, Beatrice had dedicated the vast majority of its advertising expenditures to unmeasured media (coupons, premiums, packaging, and point-of-sale promotions), and even in 1977, $54 million of Beatrice's $76.8 million in ad spending went to unmeasured media. In his letter to shareholders for fiscal 1977, Rasmussen noted, "We have taken a number of steps to strengthen our marketing resources. Special marketing groups now report to each of the five executive vice presidents. These groups give us the flexibility to bolster the marketing activities of individual operating units and to seek out and capitalize on totally new opportunities."

▲ CONTROVERSIAL LEADERSHIP: 1979

Rasmussen reached mandatory retirement age in July 1979, and the board of directors elected James Dutt as his successor in a meeting that came to be known as Beatrice's "boardroom brawl." At the time, the members of the board who worked outside the company purportedly supported Richard Voell, then Beatrice's deputy chairman, as Rasmussen's successor. Rasmussen, however, secretly persuaded all of the inside directors and two outside board members to support Dutt. When Dutt was elected, Voell and two outside directors resigned over the incident.

Dutt began his career at Beatrice in 1947, and had held many domestic and international operating posts. By the time he became CEO in 1979, Beatrice had sales of $8.3 billion and employed 84,000 workers at operations in over 90 countries.

▲ EXHIBIT 4   Beatrice-Related Transactions over $80 Million, 1973–1985

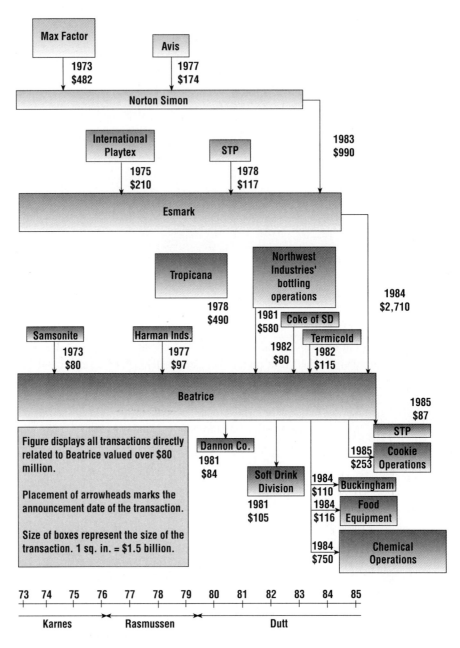

Source: George Baker, "Beatrice: A Study in the Creation and Destruction of Value."

As CEO, one of Dutt's first actions was to move company headquarters from a one-and-one-half-floor office to a five-floor office in a glass tower in downtown Chicago. Dutt's next major step was to streamline Beatrice; he reportedly ranked all of the company's more than

500 subsidiaries according to profitability, and targeted for <u>divestiture</u> those with the lowest return on assets. In 1979, Beatrice began systematically divesting businesses for the first time in its 88-year history. In addition, by 1980, Dutt had come to view international expansion as crucial, complaining about "how exceedingly badly we do in the export business."[5] In 1980, Beatrice signed an agreement with the People's Republic of China that authorized the company to begin a number of joint ventures in China. Domestically, Dutt pushed to expand distribution of Beatrice's many regional products, hoping to roll them out nationally.

Dutt also set out to restructure Beatrice in 1981, forming 10 major divisions to focus the company's 400 profit centers around 10 disparate business areas (Exhibit 5). All subsidiaries which fell outside these areas were also slated for divestiture. By late 1981, Beatrice had divested about 50 companies with roughly $1 billion in sales. Included among the spin-offs were Dannon Yogurt, the largest of Beatrice's early divestitures, which was sold for $84 million; parts of the unprofitable Harman Kardon Inc., a maker of audio equipment; and Beatrice's Royal Crown Soft Drink division, which bottled RC Cola. Many of these companies failed to meet Beatrice's ambitious new financial performance goals. Others were divested because they fell outside the company's core areas, and Beatrice executives, most having risen through the company's food business, felt uncomfortable running some of the less-related subsidiaries. Nonetheless, some core companies were maintained despite their failure to meet Beatrice's ROA target.

In November 1981, Dutt was highly criticized for investing the proceeds of prior divestitures to acquire the Coca-Cola Bottling Division of Northwest Industries. This acquisition continued Beatrice's push into beverages, which began with the Tropicana acquisition. However, the price of Northwest, $580 million, exceeded the book value of the bottler's assets by about $450 million, and represented 22 times 1980 earnings. Many shareholders felt that Beatrice should have done a large stock buyback rather than the acquisition.

Focusing on marketing, in 1982, Dutt established a <u>$25 million corporate marketing</u> fund which could be assigned to operating divisions at his discretion. The fund was designed to support product introductions and geographical expansions that were too costly for individual profit centers. Dutt felt that the fund would enable him to become "closer to the operating end of the business" and would expand his authority in deciding how advertising funds were spent.[6] (Exhibit 6). Beatrice's Swiss Miss division requested support from the marketing fund, and introduced a low-calorie hot-chocolate drink that reached $40 million in sales in its first year and increased Swiss Miss's market share by 50 percent.

▲ STRATEGIC REDIRECTION

At the 1983 annual shareholder's meeting, Dutt unveiled a completely new strategic course for Beatrice, formally abandoning the decentralized management system that the company had employed for its entire history. Justifying this move, Dutt stated, "In the past, our system of small, regional profit centers worked well. But to be competitive and to grow in the future, we need broader product lines, with national marketing and advertising and with national distribution systems." To expand distribution of its product, in 1983, Dutt replaced Beatrice's regional distributors with nationwide food brokers. The centerpiece of Beatrice's new strategy, however, was a "total commitment to marketing." To facilitate this goal,

---

[5]"Beatrice Foods Chief Reins in Growth by Acquisition," *The Wall Street Journal,* July 21, 1980.
[6]Nancy Giges, "Beatrice Has a Big Thirst for Beverages," *Advertising Age,* June 7, 1982, p. 12.

▲ EXHIBIT 5   Business Segment Reorganization, 1981–1985 ($ millions)

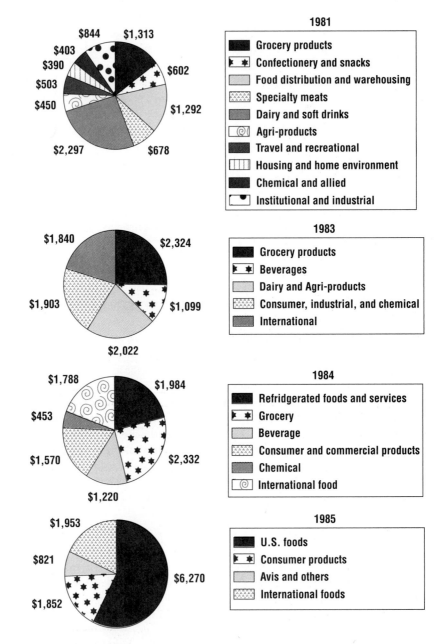

Source: George Baker, "Beatrice: A Study in the Creation and Destruction of Value."

Beatrice underwent a second major realignment, consolidating operations to increase their marketing effectiveness. Dutt again altered the number of its internal divisions to six, explaining, "The result will be much smaller number of free-standing, self-supporting businesses operating in the company's principal marketing areas. These new 'business, of

▲ EXHIBIT 6   Advertising Expenditures

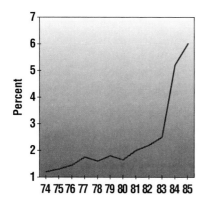

Beatrice's Ad Expenditures

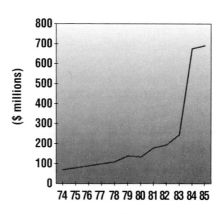

Beatrice's Ad Expenditures

Source: George Baker, "Beatrice: A Study in the Creation and Destruction of Value."

Beatrice' will be larger, cohesive business units"[7] (Exhibit 5). As a component of the reorganization, Beatrice planned to consolidate its 350 profit centers into 50 to 100 divisions. Ultimately, Dutt succeeded in reducing the profit centers to 27 divisions.

To coordinate the division consolidations, Beatrice brought in William Reidy, a former Dart & Kraft executive who helped reorganize Kraft's food operations in the 1970s and who was named senior vice president of strategy at Beatrice. Under the new organization, profit centers that faced common competitors were grouped together. For example, Beatrice consolidated its eight confectionery companies into a single profit center. In another instance, Beatrice combined its Rosarita and Gebhardt Mexican food brands, which formerly had competed against one another, and began to sell all of the division's products under the Rosarita name because of its superior brand recognition.

In addition to the consolidations, Beatrice formed a corporate marketing department under a senior vice president of marketing that focused on taking regional brands national (for example, in 1982, Beatrice's midwestern cheese brand, County Line, spent $142,000 on advertising, compared to the $2.8 million that Kraft spent on its Cracker Barrel line alone). The marketing group's staff was largely recruited from other consumer products marketers, and the new department's mandate was broad, including working with Beatrice's brands on advertising, product development, and market research. Under Dutt's direction, the group reduced the number of advertising agencies that Beatrice used from about 140 to 10, and the corporate office began to set ad spending levels for divisions. Discussing the role of the new group, one advertising executive explained, "We clustered our individual operations into a small number of groups that could effectively exercise their collective marketing muscle, generate synergies, and capitalize on economies of scale."[8] The goal of the new program was

---

[7]Neil R. Gazel, *Beatrice from Buildup through Breakup* (University of Illinois Press, 1990).
[8]Laura Jereski, "Beatrice Make-Over," *Marketing & Media Decisions,* May 1984, p. 75.

to "give us the opportunity to piggyback brands with similar programming objectives and similar demographics."[9]

In reorganizing Beatrice, Dutt hoped to follow the company's competitors, including General Mills, General Foods, and Kraft, in consolidating operations and expanding marketing. These companies had many brands that possessed market share leadership (Exhibit 7). Speaking about Beatrice's competitors, Dutt said, "The degree of sophistication of management and the qualifications of people running the businesses were changing, and we weren't changing with it."[10] To this end, Dutt initiated the "We're Beatrice" corporate advertising campaign that hoped to (unify Beatrice's brands under one logo that had a quality reputation) Beatrice's 1984 annual report noted, "We have begun a television and print campaign, linking Beatrice to our most recognized brands, and we are backing this effort with the largest point-of-sale promotion in our history. We will use this identity on our packaging, signage, trucks, brand advertising, and promotions." Like Nabisco, the company began to place the Beatrice logo on many of its products. Beatrice's umbrella campaign was launched with a $30 million budget, $11 million of which was spent during the 1984 Winter Olympics. Some Beatrice product managers, however, were skeptical of the "We're Beatrice" campaign and worried that efforts to extend the Beatrice umbrella brand to the company's nonfood products was unlikely to garner improved sales. After the campaign, unprompted consumer recognition of the Beatrice name increased threefold to 8 percent.

While Beatrice's corporatewide advertising spending was increased under the new program, competitors often still overspent Beatrice on advertising at the product level. For example, Tropicana spent $12 million on marketing compared to $16 million for Coca-Cola's Minute Maid, and although Beatrice increased support for its (now national) County Line cheese to $2 million, Kraft had a $68 million budget for its cheese items.

Beatrice's continual restructuring came at a short-term price. Corporate net income plummeted from $390 million in 1982 to $43 million in 1983, and in the first quarter of 1983 Beatrice reported its first quarterly loss since before Karnes had become CEO (Exhibit 8). Furthermore, the rapidity and uncertainty of the restructuring left many inside the company confused about the intended direction of the changes. Said one observer, "It is a very different mindset for divisions that operated with a great deal of autonomy. At the moment, no one is quite sure where one's authority begins, and the other's ends."[11] For example, Beatrice divested its candy operations six months after they were consolidated because four of the division's six top managers had left the new profit center. Formerly autonomous chief executives, these four became the equivalent of brand managers after the formation of a single confectionery division.

In May 1984, Beatrice launched a $56-a-share bid for Chicago-based Esmark, with 1983 sales of $4.1 billion. Beatrice finally paid $2.7 billion for Esmark, topping a $2.4 billion Kohlberg Kravis & Roberts–backed leveraged buyout proposal, which had already been accepted by Esmark managers. Esmark, created in 1973, was a holding company that had originally consisted of Swift & Co.'s four major lines of business (food, chemicals, energy, and financial services). In late 1973, Donald Kelly was made president and COO of Esmark, and began to run the company as an investment portfolio, buying and selling over 60 companies before the sale to Beatrice in 1984. Among Esmark's acquisitions were International Playtex,

Handwritten margin notes: "Beatrice co brand"; "underspent competitors on indiv. brands"; "first loss"; "confusing to those in the corp(s)"

---

[9]Ibid., p. 76.
[10]Sue Shellenbarger, "Beatrice Foods Move to Centralize Business," *The Wall Street Journal,* September 27, 1983, p. 1.
[11]Jereski, "Beatrice Make-Over," p. 75.

▲ EXHIBIT 7   Profiles of Beatrice's Major Competitors

Dart & Kraft. In 1980, Kraft Inc. and Dart Industries merged in a $2.5 billion transaction that created a diversified, consumer-oriented company. In the early 1980s, Kraft made mostly dairy- and oil-based products, and had sales of about $7 billion in 1985, and Dart Industries owned Tupperware, West Bend appliances, and Duracell batteries. Even after the formation of Dart & Kraft, the two companies operated largely unmerged.

After the merger, Kraft focused on its food businesses under the leadership of Michael Miles, a former advertising executive and CEO of Kentucky Fried Chicken. In food, Kraft increased its prices while simultaneously raising ad spending to achieve brand leadership. The company also concentrated on volume growth through line extensions and marketing innovations.

General Foods. Postum Cereal Co. was incorporated in 1896 and changed its name to General Foods (GF) in 1929. The company followed a product diversification program that ultimately brought it such brands as Jell-O, Crystal Light, Entenmann's, Oscar Mayer, and Maxwell House. By 1985, GF had revenues of $9 billion and sold food products, primarily dry grocery goods, under about 60 brand names.

In 1985, GF had three major divisions (Oscar Mayer, Worldwide Food, and USA Food) and was reputed to have a swollen corporate bureaucracy that delayed its responsiveness to marketplace changes. While the company had a number of rapidly growing brands, most of these had come from recent acquisitions, and GF relied heavily on sales from mature products such as coffee and frozen vegetables. In mid-1985, Philip Morris acquired General Foods for $5.5 billion.

General Mills. Beginning as a network of flour mills in 1928, General Mills moved from its base in consumer foods into a variety of industries, in the 1960s and 1970s, thus stressing stability as well as growth. General Mill's "balanced diversification" strategy drove the company into toys and games, clothing, jewelry, specialty chemicals, and restaurants, and by the end of this period, the company had significant positions in 13 different industries.

By the late 1970s, General Mills's stock performance had begun to deteriorate (the company's market to book ratio fell from 3.1 in 1973 to 1.4 in 1979). Responding to its devaluation in the stock market, in the early 1980s, General Mills began to consolidate rather then diversify and to stress internal development above acquisitions, particularly in consumer foods (the company's brands included Cherrios, Total, Yoplait, and Bisquick). By 1985, General Mills had exited 7 of the 13 industries that it had formerly held positions in.

Nabisco Brands. Incorporated in 1898, Nabisco had such well-known brands as Oreos, Fig Newtons, and Ritz crackers, although many considered the company unimaginative. In 1981, Nabisco became Nabisco Brands after merging with Standard Brands, a notoriously slow-moving company best known for its Chase & Sanborn coffee and Fleischmann's margarine.

Nabisco Brands shed its stodgy reputation in the early 1980s when the company emerged victorious from "the cookie war." Using its manufacturing ability, expansive distribution network, and advertising clout, Nabisco overwhelmed Procter & Gamble and Frito Lay, both recent entrants into the cookie business. In 1985, RJR Reynolds, the tobacco giant, acquired Nabisco Brands for $4.9 billion.

---

purchased for $210 million in 1975, and Norton Simon, a conglomerate consisting of Avis rental cars and Hunt/Wesson foods, which Esmark had acquired for $990 million in September 1983 (Exhibit 4). Prior to the acquisition, Donald Kelly had announced that he would leave Esmark to form his own investment company along with Roger Briggs,

▲ EXHIBIT 8   Beatrice Companies Financials (in $ millions)

	1985	1984	1983	1982	1981	1980
Net sales	$12,595	$9,327	$9,139	$9,021	$8,773	$8,291
Net earnings	479	433	43	390	304	290
Total assets	10,379	4,464	4,732	4,744	4,237	3,980
Long-term debt	2,587	779	772	759	691	659
Shareholders' equity	2,357	2,028	2,215	2,422	2,484	2,005

	1985		1984		1983	
Segments	Sales	Operating Earnings	Sales	Operating Earnings	Sales	Operating Earnings
U.S. food	$6,270	#372	$4,095	$338	$3,770	$304
Consumer products	1,953	201	948	133	837	117
International food	1,852	101	1,732	105	1,758	124
Avis/other operations	821	64	28	—	33	(1)
Divested businesses	1,699		2,524		2,741	

Esmark's vice chairman. Speaking of the acquisition, one industry observer noted, "Dutt is trying to do an awful lot of diverse things all at one time."[12] Another added, "Beatrice is an acquisition junkie. Every five years it is a different company."[13]

In acquiring Esmark, Beatrice became the largest domestic food company, with over 150 brands in 90 product categories (Exhibit 9). Beatrice's primary goal was to improve its distributional efficiency and its ability to roll out regional brands nationally with the addition of Esmark's Hunt-Wesson national sales force and distribution system. Previously, Beatrice had sold many of its products through regional and national brokers; after the acquisition, all of its dry grocery products would be handled by Hunt-Wesson's 500-person direct sales force and in-house distribution system. Similarly, sales and distribution of Beatrice's Eckrich meats and Esmark's Swift brand could be consolidated. In addition to sales and distribution, Dutt hoped that Hunt-Wesson's research team could be used to hasten Beatrice's new product introduction. Finally, the addition of Esmark would raise Beatrice from the sixteenth to the third-largest domestic advertising spender, establishing Beatrice as one of the world's premier marketers. Speaking of Beatrice's bid for Esmark, Dutt said, "I don't lose. For us, this puts everything into place. It's the final seal on what we've been trying to do."[14] Dutt's determination to achieve his goals for Beatrice was manifested by a cartoon that he kept behind his desk. The cartoon depicted an executive at a broad table surrounded by his management team, and the caption read "All of those opposed, signify by saying 'I quit.'" Following the acquisition, Beatrice again consolidated the number of internal divisions from six to four (Exhibit 5).

---

[12]"Beatrice Begins Offer for Esmark Today in an Attempt to Build Marketing Muscle," *The Wall Street Journal,* May 23, 1984.
[13]Jo Ellen Daily, "Beatrice: An Acquisition Junkie Gets the Shakes," *Business Week,* June 3, 1985, p. 91.
[14]"Beatrice Begins Offer for Esmark."

Brand	Description
Tropicana	• #1 in fresh orange juice
Swift*/Eckrich Meats	• #5 in processed meat
	• $2 billion in meat sales
La Choy	• 18 frozen and 44 canned items
	• #1 in Oriental foods
Hunt*	• #1 in tomato-based products
Culligan	• Industrial/home water processing equipment
Samsonite Corp.	• Full line of hard and soft luggage
	• 41% of business overseas
Coca-Cola Bottling Operations	• Coca-Cola bottlers concentrated in California
Shedd Group	• Largest private-label manufacturer of margarine
Beatrice Candy Operations	• Jolly Rancher/D.L. Clarke/ Red Tulip Chocolates
Playtex International*	• #1 in bras with 16% market share
	• #2 in tampons with 32% market share
	• 6% market share in hosiery
Max Factor*	• In top five in U.S. market share
	• #1 in U.K. and Japan
Somerset*	• #1 premium distilled spirit importer
Avis*	• #2 worldwide market share

*Acquired as part of Esmark.

After the acquisition, Beatrice's debt ballooned to $5.1 billion from $990 million prior to the Esmark takeover. Beatrice planned to reduce its debt load by divesting many of Esmark's businesses over the next two years, amounting to $4 billion in sales and $2 billion in assets. Before the end of 1984, Beatrice had signed agreements to divest its food-service business, its agriproducts and leather operations, its candy divisions, and its chemical operations. The largest of these, Beatrice chemical operations, made high-performance products for many niche markets and was sold for $750 million.

As Beatrice began 1985, the company faced many difficulties. The company's Tropicana subsidiary barely broke even in 1984, as freezes in the Florida citrus belt send fruit prices soaring and as Procter & Gamble introduced Citrus Hill orange juice with a $100 million marketing budget. In addition, while Beatrice's reported earnings reached a healthy $479 million, after subtracting gains from divestitures and restructuring losses, the company netted $259 million in fiscal 1985 compared to $334 million in fiscal 1984. Beatrice's return on assets for 1985 was about 3 percent, down from 8 percent in fiscal 1980, the year Dutt replaced Rasmussen.

Beatrice also faced a management exodus in 1984 and 1985. For example, Fred Rentschler, who had come to Beatrice with the Esmark acquisition, resigned as head of Swift/Hunt-Wesson, citing philosophical conflicts with Beatrice's hand-on management style. Another

micromanager

former Esmark executive commented, "[Beatrice originally] said we would continue to be de-centralized. Then all of a sudden there were phone calls and letters saying, 'Jim [Dutt] does it this way.' I heard his name mentioned more in two months than I heard Kelly's name in six years."[15] Dutt was known to be a very hands-on manager, particularly in the food businesses where he initiated management changes at practically every level of the corporation and became involved in day-to-day operations. By July 1985, 37 of Beatrice's 58 corporate officers in 1979 had left the company; many of them had been fired by Dutt.

In 1985, Beatrice suffered a 20 percent decline in earnings in its fiscal first quarter ended May 31. The company also increased its marketing budget by 25 percent (to a projected $800 million for the year), although many questioned the businesses that received the additional funding (for example, Beatrice committed to spend $70 million sponsoring a professional race car team over the next three years). It was against this backdrop, in August 1985, that James Dutt entered the board meeting to consider the future of him and his corporate strategy, best expressed in his recent letter to shareholders (Exhibit 10).

▲ EXHIBIT 10 Excerpts from James Dutt's Letter to Shareholders, Fiscal 1985 Annual Report

Fiscal 1985 Highlights

- Successfully completed the acquisition of Esmark, Inc. for $2.7 billion.
- Received more than $1.4 billion in proceeds from divesting operations that were not critical to our focus on food and consumer products.
- Substantially increased awareness and marketing value of the Beatrice brand name.
- Simplified the organization and management structure of the company, creating four strong operating segments.

Excerpts

Many of the steps we've taken were dramatic, but necessary for the company to succeed in today's competitive consumer marketplace. All of our actions, both short-term and long-term, are guided by four principles: to make Beatrice the premier worldwide marketer of food and consumer products; to build strong national and international brand franchises; to gain more direct access to our trade customers and the consumers of our products; and to build and develop bigger and better people throughout the organization.

We rapidly accelerated our market-driven strategy during fiscal 1985 with the acquisition of Esmark, Inc. The acquisition was critical to our efforts in developing stronger sales and distribution capabilities and improving our research and development efforts. While we could have developed these products and capabilities internally, we realized that it was more efficient to acquire these strengths. The integration of Esmark has proceeded smoothly, and we have already combined similar businesses into single, larger entities that have greater impact in their respective markets.

With four strong operating segments: U.S. Food, Consumer Products, International Food and Avis/Other Operations, we are now better positioned to respond to and anticipate the needs of the marketplace. At the same time, this structure will allow more efficient management of the company. Each of these segments has the critical mass to truly lead the markets in which it competes.

The "New Beatrice" also has vastly increased marketing clout. As the third largest advertiser in the United States, we have the marketing muscle to establish leadership positions across a broad product range.

---

[15]Daily, "Beatrice: An Acquisition Junkie," p. 92.

ICI AND HANSON (A)

Late in the afternoon on May 14, 1991, Sir Denys Henderson, chairman of ICI (Imperial Chemical Industries), settled down to a cup of tea at ICI's prestigious art deco headquarters at Millbank. He had just discovered that Lord Hanson, co-founder and chairman of Hanson PLC, was the mystery buyer of a 2.8 percent stake in ICI. The pressure was now on Sir Denys to provide the strategy and results that would ward off a full bid for his company. With 1990 sales of £12.9 billion, ICI was Britain's largest manufacturing company and one of its leading centers for R&D, spending £679m. It was also the fourth-largest chemical company in the world with more than half of its operating assets and three-quarters of its sales outside the United Kingdom. However, net profits were £617 million, down from £930 million the year before, principally due to the economic slowdown in ICI's major markets. Return on net assets had similarly declined from 24 percent to 15 percent in 1990 (Exhibit 1).[1]

▲ ICI

Imperial Chemical Industries was founded in 1926 as a merger of the four largest British chemical companies: Brunner, Mond & Co; Nobel Industries; British Dyestuffs Corporation Ltd.; and United Alkali Company Ltd. The dominant partner in the merger was Brunner, Mond, and Sir Alfred Mond became ICI's first chairman and developed much of the firm's business philosophy.

This case is a combined version of two cases, "ICI PLC" (No. 392-088) and "Hanson PLC" (No. 392-087) prepared by Visiting Professor Phillippe Haspeslagh (Copyright © 1992 INSEAD). It was condensed by Professor David Collis with permission from INSEAD.
[1]Du Pont is ranked forth only if Conoco, its energy division, is included.

▲ EXHIBIT 1 ICI Group Financial Record (for the years ended December 31; £ millions)

	1981	1982	1983	184	185	1986	1987	1988	1989	1990
Balance sheet										
Tangible fixed assets	3,342	3,422	3,376	3,629	3,533	3,912	3,750	4,092	4,856	4,947
Investments	433	403	348	442	287	333	417	524	767	483
Current assets	3,363	3,471	3,897	4,853	4,497	4,441	4,620	4,784	5,648	5,369
Total assets	7,138	7,269	7,621	8,924	8,317	8,686	8,787	9,400	11,271	10,799
Current liabilities	1,633	1,933	2,080	2,674	2,503	2,537	2,970	2,990	3,618	3,406
Creditors due after more than one year	1,768	1,504	1,407	1,438	1,284	1,621	1,581	1,764	1,713	1,824
Other liabilities	692	804	792	983	935	863	891	701	926	898
Capital and reserves attributable to parent company	2,955	3,055	3,342	3,829	3,495	3,665	3,445	3,925	5,014	4,671
Turnover and profits										
Turnover, U.K.	2,575	2,848	2,866	3,131	3,011					
Overseas	4,006	4,510	5,390	6,778	7,714					
Total	6,581	7,358	8,256	9,909	10,725	10,136	11,123	11,699	13,171	12,906
Trading profit	348	400	436	440	474	491	464	484	536	525
Depreciation	425	366	693	1,063	978	1,049	1,297	1,470	1,467	1,029
Share of profits less losses of related companies and amounts written off investments	52	39	61	71	56	95	157	162	279	154
Loan intrest	(129)	(135)	(132)	(138)	(143)	(135)	(150)	(160)	(175)	(155)
Taxation	(111)	(92)	(201)	(373)	(308)	(382)	(504)	(540)	(531)	(338)
Net profit attributable to parent company, before extraordinary items	192	145	397	605	552	600	760	881	930	617
Extraodinary items	(6)	—	(19)	(20)	(40)	(43)	—	(44)	127	53
Dividends	(113)	(115)	(147)	(186)	(214)	(238)	(277)	(341)	(381)	(389)
Return on assets										
Profit before loan interest as a percentage of assets employed	9	7	14	20	18	19.4	24.4	26.7	24.2	15.0

Source: ICI Annual Reports.

The chemical industry of the early 20th century was dominated by "heavy" products, such as alkalis and industrial explosives, that were required for the industrial processes of the day. Bruner, Mond had become the biggest alkali producer in the world using a soda ash license from Solvay of Belgium. It had also expanded in the fertilizer business, constructing a large plant on 266 acres in Billingham on the river Tees. The second-strongest partner was Nobel Industries that had grown during World War I by taking advantage of the heavy demand for TNT and ammonium nitrate. United Alkali, on the other hand, had seen its onetime leadership in alkalis largely displaced by the more efficient Solvay process, and British Dyestuffs was overshadowed by German producers in the production of "fine" chemicals such as dyestuffs and pharmaceuticals.

Mergers of chemical companies were common after World War I. In 1920, for example, five U.S. manufacturers producing everything from alkalis to dyes merged to become Allied Chemical and Dye Corporation. The impetus for the ICI merger, however, came from the 1925 formation of IG Farben that grouped the large German firms BASF, Hoechst, Bayer, and Agfa. A corporation of this size posed a formidable threat to the comfortable market-sharing agreements among major British, German, and American producers and sparked the British producers and their government into action. In 1929, ICI negotiated a gentleman's agreement under which foreign competitors would refrain from competing in British Empire markets.

The economic forces behind these mergers consisted of economies of scale in production and vertical integration benefits. For example, in 1927 ICI committed £20 million to developing the Billingham site, a sum exceeding the individual capitalized value of any of the four merging companies. Furthermore, overlapping businesses like soda ash and fertilizers were rationalized, and vertical integration benefits achieved, for example, in the supply of nitrogen and solvents to the group's fertilizer business.

The importance of ties between ICI, the British government, and local communities in the formation and development of the company were also important. At the community level, ICI dominated whole townships, such as Billingham. In response to objections from the Registrar of Companies about the inclusion of the word "Imperial" in the company's name, an outraged Mond and McGowan declared:

> We are "Imperial" in aspect and "Imperial" in name. . . . The developments which this company has in view, we may confidently inform you, will be of enormous value, both from the point of view of national defense and of the economic position of the Empire.[2]

An imperial corporation demanded an imperial corporate headquarters. Within two weeks of ICI's formation, excavators began construction on Millbank, facing the Thames near the Houses of Parliament. The atmosphere inside of the eight-story building was reflected in its main doors: made of cast bronze, they were 20-feet high with panels in bas-relief illustrating the application of science to industry.

The Early Years

ICI began operating in 1927 with five core business groups: alkali products, metals, explosives, dyestuffs, and general chemicals, including chlorine, acids, and synthetic ammonia. Although less advanced than IG Farben in the innovative, "fine" chemicals sector, ICI

---

[2]Ibid; p. 47.

viewed itself as a research-based company. Mond's philosophy was that research should pave the way for industrial progress rather than serve perceived needs. George Pollitt, founding manager of the Billingham plant, explained this policy as follows:

The really lucrative processes are likely to be those manufacturing products which are entirely novel, and it would be unfortunate indeed if research. . .were barred because an investigation indicated there would be no market.[3]

By projecting an image of glamour and offering good pay, ICI was able to attract the best chemists and engineers in Britain. This investment was to pay handsome returns during the ensuing decades, but not in the areas that ICI had initially envisaged. The company's expectations of growing demand for fertilizers had evaporated by the end of the 1920s. With the technology readily available, developing countries had acquired their own ammonia plants—frequently with the help of ICI's competitors. Excess worldwide capacity combined with the falloff in demand for fertilizer in the context of the 1929 depression made ICI's £20 million investment in Billingham increasingly dubious and nearly forced the company into bankruptcy. Moreover, ICI's intensive research into producing oil from coal became increasingly unnecessary with oil discoveries in Texas and the Middle East.

It was ICI's discoveries in plastics that vindicated its research-based strategy. Originally, ICI saw plastics, such as bakelite and cellulite, which had been in existence since the 19th century, mainly as an adjunct to the heavy chemical businesses. Their role was to "serve as a market for the products of other business groupings rather than as a promising field for development in its own right."[4] In 1933, however, two researchers at the alkali group's Winnington plant discovered a waxy solid in a test tube while carrying out high pressure experiments with ethylene. It was polyethylene, a plastic that would subsequently find a host of uses from plastics bags to washbowls to insulation. Then in 1935, researchers in the dyestuffs group discovered another breakthrough plastic, perspex. Following these innovations, in 1938 ICI created a plastics group.

Pharmaceuticals was another business ICI developed through research. In 1936, the company authorized a five-year research program into new remedies and the local manufacture of imported pharmaceuticals. It based this research in the dyestuffs group because of the close affinity in technology between pharmaceuticals and the chemical synthesis used in dyestuffs. ICI was a late entrant to the field, behind the leading German manufacturers as well as domestic companies like Glaxo. With the threat of war and disruption of quinine supplies by Japan, early efforts concentrated on duplicating German research in antimalarial drugs. An offshoot of this antimalarial work was the antiseptic "Hibitane," which as late as the 1980s still ranked as one of ICI's top-selling pharmaceutical products.

Postwar Expansion

Chemicals   In 1945, the prewar cartels were broken up, launching the international chemical industry into a new era of competition. This competition could have been predicted from the economies of large-scale investment inherent in the industry. Given the continuous processes involved, there were "almost unlimited benefits to be gained from building bigger

---

[3]Ibid., p. 55.
[4]Andrew Pettigrew, *The Awakening Giant: Continuity and Change in Imperial Chemical Industries* (Oxford: Basil Blackwell, 1985), p. 259.

plants."[5] Once built, the same economies dictated that the plants be run close to capacity. This, combined with competitors expanding their facilities simultaneously (since patents offered little protection of new processes), led to cyclical overcapacity and compelling reasons for producers to export surplus product.

Another factor at work in the chemical industry during the postwar years was vertical integration, beginning with the raw material petrochemicals for production of plastics known as olefines. ICI was one of the first companies to see the advantages of developing a large in-house olefine production capacity, and started its first olefine cracker in 1951 at the company's Wilton Estate production site.

Wilton Estate dated back to 1943, when the ICI Development Executive Committee decided to base its expansion around a single large, integrated manufacturing site. The 3,500-acre Wilton Estate on the River Tees was acquired for this purpose in 1945, complete with 19th-century mansion. During the 1950s and the early 1960s, ICI built five olefine crackers there, as well as other units such as an aromatic complex to produce raw materials for the plastics Terylene and nylon manufacture. By 1981, a total of £2,000 million in 1981 prices had been invested at Wilton, as compared with total fixed assets valued at £3.34 billion for that year.[6] In addition to plants on the complex itself, the investment included a pipeline to the nearby Billingham plant managed by the agricultural division. Further pipelines were subsequently built to related chemical plants in the northwest of England and central Scotland.

Vertical integration was extended further upstream to naphtha production when ICI acquired a 50 percent stake in a new oil refinery to be built and operated jointly with Phillips Petroleum Company near the Wilton plant in 1964. To complete the chain, ICI set up a consortium with Burmah Oil to begin exploration in the North Sea. In 1979, it created a subsidiary, ICI Petroleum Limited, to consolidate its interests in oil refining and in the exploration and development of oil and gas in the North Sea. The subsidiary also formed partnerships to develop oil and gas reserves in the Gulf of Mexico, offshore California, and in Alberta, Canada.

Plastics   Anticipating growth in demand for plastics, the ICI plastics group became a full division of the company in 1945. Although this division remained small for some years (representing a mere 3 percent of total capital employed in 1952), it continued to be a focal point for research and development, employing 84 technical officers compared with 138 for the much larger alkali and general chemicals units in 1952. Investment in the new division paid off handsomely: in 1975 prices, sales of the plastics division grew from £14 million in 1945 to £150 million in 1965.[7] Moreover, by 1965 new plastics had been added to the product range, including polypropylene and polyester film.

ICI's research with polymers, polyethylene, and perspex led to the development of other plastics. During the early 1950s, Reg Hurd, a researcher in the resins technical service of the dyestuffs division, discovered a method of using polyester resin to produce the world's first nontoxic polyurethane foam. The new product was initially of minor interest to the department. However, by chance Hurd was invited in 1957 to present ICI's new foam at a meeting of the Refrigerated Cargo Research Council. The response to the product as a vastly improved insulation was overwhelming: within two years, ICI was supplying foam to fill cold stores, refrigerated transport, and carbon dioxide tankers.

[5]J. Roeber, *Social Change at Work: The ICI Weekly Staff Agreement* (London: Duckworth, 1975), p. 120.
[6]Ibid., p. 215.
[7]Ibid., p. 262.

Synthetic Fibers   Commercial production of artificial fibers dated back to 1885, when a French inventor, Count Hilaire de Chardonnet, patented an artificial silk made from cellulose nitrate. However, it was Du Pont's invention of nylon, announced in 1938, that marked the take-off of the industry. Recognizing the importance of the discovery, ICI formed a partnership in 1940 to manufacture nylon in Britain with Courtaulds, then the world's largest producer of viscose rayon.

More important to ICI than nylon would be the polyester "Terylene" invented by two researchers at a small company named Calico Printers' Association. ICI became involved in developing the fiber in 1943, and by 1946 had entered into a 20-year licensing agreement with Calico Printers' Association. Commercial sales of Terylene began in 1948, and in 1950 the ICI board authorized construction of a £10 million plant at Wilton with a capacity of 5,000 tons per year. The Wilton plant, controlled by the plastics division, went into production in 1954. ICI's artificial fibers business grew so rapidly that it became a fully fledged fibers division in 1954. Indeed, Terylene proved to be the first and most successful example of polyester, the most widely used synthetic fiber in the world in the 1980s.

Pharmaceuticals   Despite early success in antimalarial drugs, the technical manager of dyestuffs described pharmaceuticals in the early 1950s as "a losing business. . .in the doldrums."[8] ICI continued its in-house research, however, stating, "We're not going to become another company selling Glauber salts—we're going to live and profit by our own discoveries."[9]

The first new pharmaceutical business was anesthetics, a field with few advances since the beginning of the 20th century. Each of the existing compounds had drawbacks, encouraging anesthetists to rely on a mixture of drugs. In 1953, a young ICI chemist named Dr. Suckling discovered a more effective anesthetic, subsequently named "Fluothane." Despite an initial reluctance within the profession, this compound grew to be one of the most widely used anesthetics through the 1980s. The drug also marked a significant change from ICI's earlier inventions in that the research had been focused on a particular target—a perceived market need.

This approach led to the development of ICI's highly profitable series of "beta-blocker" heart drugs. In 1957, the Pharmaceutical Division finally broke free of the de facto control by the dyestuffs division, moving to newly acquired premises at Alderley Park in Cheshire. From the start, research at this new site concentrated on cardiovascular disease, in particular angina pectoris, a heart disease generally treated by increasing the supply of oxygen to the heart.

Attracted by the pharmaceutical division's commitment to the field and its new premises, a senior lecturer from Glasgow University named James Black joined ICI in 1958. Black brought with him a new idea: instead of increasing the supply of oxygen why not "block" the action of adrenaline on the heart? Soon a team of medicinal chemists at Alderly Park developed a drug that produced this effect. In July 1965, just over two-and-a-half years after the first animal trials, ICI's first beta-blocker drug was launched under the name "Inderlin." This led to a series of similar drugs for relieving hypertension, one of which, "Tenormin," was the world's largest-selling heart drug in the 1980s. By this stage, the pharmaceutical division employed 2,500 researchers, evaluating some 10,000 new chemicals every year with a probability that just one of these would achieve commercial success at the end of a development process lasting up to 20 years. By 1990, nearly half of ICI's trading profits came from pharmaceuticals.

---

[8]Ibid., p. 135.
[9]Ibid., p. 136.

Crisis

As chemical companies prospered through the 1960s, many new entrants appeared. U.S. and European oil firms invested massively in downstream chemicals, joined by government-sponsored energy firms in European countries, such as France and Italy, and large Japanese groups, such as Sumitomo and Mitsui. The oil price escalation in the early 1970s and subsequent 1974 recession, while severely affecting demand, barely slowed down the buildup of capacity. On the contrary it prompted some of the oil-producing nations, from Saudi Arabia to Mexico and Norway, to invest in their own feedstock and commodity production.

Facing an overvalued pound and lower domestic growth and higher inflation than its foreign competitors, ICI's ranking in the international chemical industry dropped from first in terms of sales in 1972 to fifth in 1981 behind Du Pont and the three large German companies—Hoechst, BASF, and Bayer. The company responded by improving labor productivity, continuing its traditional focus on technical development, and investing heavily in some of the newer products in which it had a strong position, such as polyethylene, polyester, and crop protection chemicals. At the same time, it tried to reduce its dependence on the British Commonwealth, through investments on the Continent and the acquisition of Atlas Chemicals in the United States. Between 1963 and 1981, its dependence on U.K. sales declined from 52 percent to 39 percent.

Nevertheless, by 1980, four trends had been "slowly developing to convert what some managements had anticipated to be a prospect of prosperity into a scene of catastrophe: feedstock prices increased, technology improved yields, the world economy entered in a prolonged recession, and new sources of product were constructed in hydrocarbon-rich countries."[10] The results were an aggravation of the fundamental imbalance between supply and demand, severe price competition, and massive losses. In Europe and Japan, even the strongest companies operated in the red for several years, and the U.S. chemical industry dipped into negative returns in 1980.

ICI, still dependent on the United Kingdom for 30 percent of its output and having to endure a 20 percent inflation rate as well as an oil-borne rise of the pound against other currencies, was hit particularly hard. In 1981, it sustained losses of £444 million in fibers, £54 million in petrochemicals and plastic, and £30 million in dyestuffs and specialties. To stem this decline and reorient the company, the board of ICI reached into the organization to elect John Harvey-Jones as chairman in April 1982.

Sir John Harvey-Jones

Between 1982 and 1986, John Harvey-Jones, a flamboyant and outspoken leader, transformed ICI. He participated actively in the restructuring of the European commodity business, accelerated internationalization, expanded ICI's presence in specialties, and shifted the technology-driven culture toward a marketing orientation.

Stemming the losses and streamlining the bulk business was a priority. ICI's workforce was reduced to 125,000, 50,000 less than in 1980. In September 1986, the company formed ICI Chemicals and Polymers (C&P), merging its core bulk businesses and separating them from a number of stand-alone specialties businesses. It also reduced the number of organizational

---

[10]Joseph L. Bower, *When Markets Quake: The Management Challenge of Restructuring Industry* (Boston: Harvard Business School Press, 1986), p. 19.

levels from five to three, and eliminated or devolved 80 percent of its central staffs. Furthermore, the company engaged in capacity swaps with BP, exited polyethylene, and put its polyvinylchloride (PVC) interests into a joint venture with Enichem of Italy.

As many of ICI's rivals, Harvey-Jones pushed the company into higher value-added specialties businesses to reduce dependence on cyclical businesses and to build a stable profit base. His motivation for internationalization was equally clear: "The sheer scale of modern businesses is such that almost in every case we need to sell in world markets."[11] Harvey-Jones aimed to "spread ICI's business where the markets of the world were: one-third in Europe, one-third in the Americas, and one-third in the Far East."[12]

Between 1981 and 1987, ICI's sales in industrial businesses fell from 58 percent to 48 percent, while consumer and specialties businesses grew from 23 percent to 37 percent (Exhibit 2). In addition to expanding in pharmaceuticals, the Company pushed ahead in advanced materials, seeds, and the marketing-oriented, decorative paints business. Under the guidance of a newly created corporate acquisition team, the company purchased about 30 companies per year in the 1980s. These included the $750 million acquisition of Beatrice Chemicals that formed the organizational core of the new specialty chemicals and advanced materials businesses; the £500 million Glidden paint acquisition sold by Hanson Trust during its restructuring of SCM; and the 1987 acquisition of Stauffer's. Acquisitions had a significant impact on ICI's international profile: U.K. sales declined from 34 percent to 20 percent between 1981 and 1987, Continental European turnover grew from 14 percent to 39 percent, and American sales from 14 percent to 22 percent.

These strategic shifts were reinforced by even more radical shifts in organizational functioning and company culture. Harvey-Jones had inherited a cumbersome board with 18 executive directors, most of whom were responsible for a single division and interacted with their division's chief executive. He halved the number of board executives and required divisional chief executives to make presentations to the full board. To give the board a more international perspective, he appointed a German insurance executive, in 1982; the chairman of Toshiba, in 1985; and in 1988 Paul Volcker, chairman of the Federal Reserve Board, to the board.

ICI also streamlined corporate headquarters and announced its intention to move out of "imperial" Millbank. Then it organized its businesses internationally, starting with the pharmaceutical division and specialty chemicals businesses in 1983 and the agrochemicals division in 1985. Headquarters of some of these global businesses moved to the Continent, or in the case of the specialty chemicals and advanced materials businesses, to the United States. At the same time, a parallel geographic organization was maintained with nine chief executives representing ICI's interest in the United States, Canada, Australia, India, and other major geographic areas. Despite the considerable complexity this dual organization entailed, including the duplication of accounting and reporting functions, ICI believed it was important to have close contact with local political, economic, and social conditions.

As Harvey-Jones sought to transform the technical and R&D-driven ICI into a market-oriented company, he preserved its focus on the long term. He maintained:

> *What we have to do now is to identify a new market and deliberately aim to meet it by taking bits from all sorts of different technologies and putting them together. And that's a very long-*

---

[11]John Harvey-Jones, *Making It Happen: Reflections on Leadership,* (London: Collins, 1988) p.117.
[12]Ibid., p. 129.

▲ EXHIBIT 2 ICI Trading Profits by Business

	1981	1982	1983	1984	1985	1986	1987	1988	1989	1990
Pharmaceuticals										
Sales	407	516	637	806	936	1,047	1,105	1,172	1,334	1,415
Trading profits	90	138	199	249*	304	311	322	321	399	489
Paints										
Sales	455	500	592	619	692	780	1,293	1,363	1,628	1,639
Trading profits	27	22	26	39*	46	50	96	101	100	108
Other effect products†										
Sales	573	649	803	981**	1,712	1,849	1,944	2,058	2,354	2,321
Trading profits	-30	-18	10	14**	104	182	184	150	69	3
General chemicals										
Sales	1,232	1,386	1,472	1,615*	1,720	1,742	1,884	1,995	2,064	2,000
Trading profits	75	60	107	145*	163	178	220	274	293	153
Petrochemicals and plastics										
Sales	1,746	1,910	2,296	2,778**	3,705	2,809	2,763	2,702	3,001	2,891
Trading profits	-54	-139	-7	138**	146	230	320	416	417	103
Fibers										
Sales	444	464	565	654*	619	624	668	626	704	700
Trading profits	-36	-25	-7	22*	20	58	45	53	27	18
Industrial explosives										
Sales	258	286	301	358	373	329	339	364	414	510
Trading profits	35	33	26	41	35	27	39	48	48	50

continued

▲ **EXHIBIT 2** *concluded*

	1981	1982	1983	1984	1985	1986	1987	1988	1989	1990
Agrochemicals and seeds										
Sales	1,245	1,369	480	635	715	756	901	1,179	1,338	1,362
Trading profits	182	158	54	82	83	29	53	120	152	110
Fertilizers										
Sales	Included	Included	1,027	1,204**	1,100	915	858	814	938	856
Trading profits	above	above	120	136**	79	-17	0	-11	-11	12
Oil										
Sales	1,056	1,160	1,040	1,349	1,107	494				
Trading profits	83	73	93	109	59	20				
Miscellaneous										
Sales	118	94	111	156	175	166	199	224	242	199
Trading profits	0	0	5	9	0	5	20	5	-33	-20

Note: Due to the redefinition of certain businesses in 1985, there are some inconsistencies between the data series for 1984 and 1985. Where these inconsistencies are judged major, they have been marked **; where minor, they are marked *.
†Other effect products consist of colors and fine chemicals, polyurethanes, specialty chemicals, advanced materials, films, and biological products.
Source: ICI annual reports.

haul job. The seeds business, we think, will be a 20-year haul, but we're intellectually sure that by the year 2000 or 2010, the seeds business will have taken over many of the things at present supplied by Fertilizers and Agrochemicals. The development time for a single new product is 10 years, and for a whole new business probably 20 years. The pharmaceutical business, started in 1937, didn't make any money until 1962 and it's now one of our most successful businesses.[13]

Sir Denys Henderson

Sir Denys Henderson, a Scotsman chosen to succeed Harvey-Jones, kept a much lower profile. He carried on the established strategy of internationalization and increased emphasis on specialties. ICI, approaching the peak of a cycle, made record trading profits of £1,470 million in 1988 and £1.47 billion in 1989. In 1990, the board asked Henderson to continue as chairman until 1995.

However, 1990 was a year of deteriorating conditions in the world petrochemical and plastics market, based on the underlying weakness of the economy and the short-run price increase caused by the Gulf War. All the major European producers suffered profit declines during 1990 (Exhibit 3). Even the German "big three" experienced declines in pretax earnings of 37 percent for BASF, 23 percent for Hoechst, and 18 percent for Bayer.[14] U.S. companies such as Dow had seen profits slump on a percentage basis similar to ICI, but there were worse performers such as Exxon Chemicals that saw profits plummet 52 percent.[15]

ICI's trading profit dropped 30 percent to £1,029 in 1990, and its return on net assets employed was 15 percent, compared with returns of between 24 percent and 27 percent from 1987 to 1989. Although performance in pharmaceuticals improved, poor results in the traditional industrial business outweighed this effect. In addition, results in some of the businesses in which ICI had invested significantly, such as advanced materials, were still disappointing. These results prompted the company to question how successful it had been in decreasing its dependence on its cyclical bulk businesses and how proactive it had been in adjusting to the recession. Sir Denys acknowledged that "ICI had spread itself too thin and grown too comfortable during the growth years of the eighties,"[16] and that "Executive directors had failed to keep their fingers firmly on the ICI pulse."[17] Clearly there was a need to reassess the effectiveness and effectiveness and efficiency of each of ICI's businesses.

▲ ICI'S BUSINESSES IN 1991

Pharmaceuticals

By 1990, pharmaceuticals, with profits having grown from £30 million in 1975 to £478 million, was clearly a success story. ICI sales force was one of the strongest in the industry, and the division operated quite independently from the rest of ICI. Nevertheless, ICI ranked only 15th in the industry in terms of sales. Merck, the world leader, with sales of £3.6 billion and around 5 percent of world market share, was almost three times ICI's size.

---

[13]Kennedy, p. 177.
[14]*Chemical Week,* April 3, 1991.
[15]*The Times,* June 3, 1991.
[16]*Business Week,* June 24, 1991.
[17]*Daily Telegraph,* May 16, 1991.

▲ **EXHIBIT 3** Leading Chemical Companies ($ billions)

1990	Sales	Pretax Profit
BASF, Germany	31.20	1.84
Hoechst, Germany	30.02	2.15
Bayer, Germany	27.86	2.25
ICI, U.K.	24.91	1.89
Du Pont, U.S.	22.27	1.50*
Dow Chemical, U.S.	19.77	2.56
Rhône-Poulenc, France	15.48	0.74
Ciba-Geigy, Switzerland	15.46	0.61*
Shell, UK/Netherlands	12.70	1.00*
Elf-Aquitaine, France	10.41	0.98*

*After-tax operating profit.
Source: Financial Times, May 18, 1991, p. 6.

Moreover, the 1989 merger of SmithKline, a U.S. company, and Beecham of the United Kingdom had triggered a wave of consolidation. In the United States, Bristol Myers had merged with Squibb, and Marion with Merrell Dow. Similarly, France's Rhône Poulenc had acquired U.S.'s Rorer.

In addition, ICI's pharmaceutical business approach the 1991 expiration of its U.S. patent on Tenormin, its best-selling heart drug, that accounted for 45 percent of sales. Despite massive expenditure on R&D (£202 million in 1990), ICI expected to launch only two significant drugs in the next five years: Meropenem, an antibiotic, and Casodex, a prostate cancer treatment. The commercial failures of two other drugs, Statil, for diabetes, and Corwin, for congestive heart failure, that the company had expected to become big sellers in the 1990s led to the revamping of R&D procedures. The long-term outlook appeared more encouraging. Mr. Tom McKillop, technical director, stated that 8 promising drugs were in early clinical trials, 10 more in preclinical development, and a "strong flow of compounds coming through from research."[18]

Advanced Materials

ICI had spent significant resources in developing its advanced materials business. The market for advanced materials consisted mainly of advanced composites, resin structures reinforced by fibers such as carbon. Major applications were in the aerospace and defense sector and were expected to develop in sports and leisure, automotive, and industrial. Engineering thermoplastics (ETPs) were one new type of material expected to eventually replace advanced composites since they could simply be stamped into shape, instead of requiring hours to mold.

[18]*Financial Times,* July 9, 1991.

The raw materials used for advanced composites were resins and fibers. These were purchased by intermediate producers who fabricated preimpregnated materials that were then sold to original equipment manufacturers such as Boeing. ICI had bought an intermediate producer, Fiberite, valued at $150 million, in the United States in 1984 as part of its purchase of Beatrice's specialty chemicals business. ICI was believed to have spent a similar amount on establishing one plant in Texas, another in Germany, and a joint venture in Japan. It had also spent £100 million in the 1980s developing polyether sulphone (PES), a nonflammable engineering thermoplastic. ICI expected Fiberite's aerospace customers to buy thermoplastics like PES.

Yet ICI was at a disadvantage in manufacturing preimpregnated materials because it had to buy most of the feedstocks from rival chemical groups. Furthermore, PES had not been successful in the automotive market since General Electric had been able to gain a stranglehold with aggressive marketing. High development costs combined with a slower than expected upturn in the market caused ICI's business to operate at a loss in 1990. At least its competitors were equally unsuccessful: "No one, including General Electric of the U.S., the world leader, is making much money in the field."[19] The director of one European materials business, commenting on the potentially huge market in the next century, had this to say about the industry: "It will be dominated by Japanese companies, because they are the only ones prepared to tolerate years of poor results and losses."[20]

Bulk Chemicals: General Chemicals, Petrochemicals and Plastics

ICI's 1990 results showed that these businesses had remained highly cyclical. Trading profits in general chemicals had halved to £153 million and in petrochemicals and plastics had dropped due to the rising costs of raw materials and the economic slowdown. In addition, ICI's joint venture with Enichem in PVC was adversely affected by surging imports from the United States and Eastern Europe. In petrochemicals and plastics, profitability was squeezed as new capacity, growing competition, and, in some sectors, falling demand made it difficult to compensate for rising costs.

ICI had considered exiting its bulk chemicals business in the mid-1980s, and had actually done so in the United States. However, between 1985 and 1988, its European businesses were sufficiently profitable that the businesses were not divested. In addition, the slow growth of some specialties businesses, such as high-performance films and advanced materials, in which much hope had been placed, made an exit from the bulk business seem unwise. The bulk chemical workforce was cut by 50 percent, however. Partly as a result, performance was significantly better in the recession of the early 1990s then it had been during the previous recession when there was a loss of £30 million.

In petrochemicals, ICI, although a major player, was in competition with oil companies such as Shell and BP that had invested heavily in petrochemicals over the previous 20 years. Both of these groups clearly had the technical expertise to match ICI. Shell, the world's largest petrochemical company, had sales of around £6 billion, dwarfing ICI's sales of around £3 billion. Furthermore, within polypropylene, ICI's was viewed as subscale. It had approached six possible buyers or partners for the business in 1990.[21]

---

[19]"ICI Close to Announcing Its New Look" *Financial Times,* June 7, 1991.
[20]*Financial Times,* July 23, 1991.
[21]*Chemical Week,* June 19, 1991.

Paints

ICI, a manufacturer of paints almost from its inception, had become the world's largest paint manufacturer after having bought Glidden from Hanson Trust for £500 million. During the 1980s, it had expanded its business rapidly by acquisition. It operated in various segments of the paint market: decorative and automotive paints, car refinishes, and can and powder coatings.

The characteristics of the segments in which ICI operated were quite different. Decorative paint was sold to professionals and consumers through retail channels. The product was largely nationally branded in Europe and regionally branded in the United States. ICI distinguished itself by using its Dulux consumer brand across markets where possible. Automotive paints in contrast were R&D intensive and sold to automotive manufacturers. ICI had developed "Aquabase," a nonpolluting water-based paint sold to General Motors and Volvo. The automotive after-market shared characteristics of both: local marketing was important, but so was global R&D and color coding.

ICI was not alone in investing in the coatings market. Akzo, the major Dutch chemicals group, operated in multiple segments. Through acquisitions, it had built a decorative business comparable in size to ICI's in Europe. In the mid-1980s, Williams Holdings, a financial holding company with a philosophy similar to Hanson's, acquired the second and third manufacturers in the United Kingdom, Crown and Berger, and then rationalized the production and distribution facilities. In addition, it acquired some regional companies in the United States. As a result, ICI has a much stronger competitor in the United Kingdom. In the global automotive paints segments, PPG and BASF were clearly the leaders.

Trading profit for the paints group increased from £50 million in 1986 to £96 million in 1987 following the acquisition of Glidden. By 1990, although paint sales volumes were declining slightly, profits had risen to £108 million as ICI cut overhead. For example, in 1990, following acquisitions in North America and Australasia, ICI closed two plants in Canada and Australia.

Agriculture

ICI's agriculture segment consisted of three businesses: agrochemicals, seeds, and fertilizers. Agrochemicals was an R&D-intensive noncyclical business with profitability (including seeds) that had grown rapidly from £9 million in 1986 to £152 million in 1989 on roughly doubled sales of £1,118 million. ICI's U.S. business had been significantly strengthened by the acquisition of Stauffer in 1987. But in 1990, trading profits declined to £110 million. Performance in the United States, Western Europe, and Asia was good, but difficulties in the Middle East due to the Gulf crisis and economic problems in Australia, Latin America, and Eastern Europe contributed to the lower results.

ICI, aiming to capitalize on its bioscience expertise, had entered the seeds business in 1985. By 1990, it was the fifth-largest producer in the world having acquired Contiseed and Edward J. Funk in the United States, and AgroPlant Saatenvertrieb in Germany. The company was optimistic about the seeds business and viewed it as a long-term development. "The territorial expansion of the business has meant a greater international exchange of breeding material. . . . ICI Seeds is well positioned to win a strong global position in hybrid field crops. Its technology also offers options for better management of the environment and the possibility of newer and broader markets for the agricultural industry."[22]

---

[22]Ibid.

Fertilizers, which ICI operated in only a few countries, was characterized by overcapacity in 1990. Losses had occurred in three of the previous five years. ICI sought to exit the business, at least in the United Kingdom.

For some time, ICI had held a 50 percent stake in Tioxide Group PLC, one of the world's leading producers of titanium dioxide, a raw material used in the production of white paint. In December 1990, ICI bought out Cookson, the other 50 percent holder, on the low 1989 multiple of around 2 ½ times earnings, as Cookson attempted to realign its portfolio.

Other Industrial Products

In explosives, ICI was the largest company in the world. Trading profits had increased from £27 million on sales of £329 million in 1986, to £50 million on £510 million in 1990. During 1990, ICI acquired Atlas Powder in the United States and the 30 percent of CXA Ltd. in Canada that it did not already own. Subsequently, it was able to rationalize its business in North America and reinforce its world leadership.

The picture was less rosy for the cyclical fibers business. Due to the economic slowdown and the rising cost of raw materials, trading profits fell from £52 million in 1988 to £18 million in 1990. ICI's response to this situation was: "Continuing research and technology programmes will ensure even better products in the future, while a major restructuring now under way will make for greater market focus and a highly competitive cost base."[23]

▲ RESTRUCTURING AND HANSON INTERVENTION

ICI's 1990 results had focused management attention on the need to further improve profit performance. During the summer of 1990, Henderson asked Mr. Ronnie Hempel, the director responsible for the paints division, to prepare a policy document on management reforms. Hempel was a logical choice since his division had been the first to react to declining sales and returns on capital after 1988. As a result of his work, a new management structure was announced in February 1991 with the aim of refocusing and utilizing resources more efficiently. The chairman commented in the annual report, published in March 1991, as follows:

Priority in the future will be given to those businesses where ICI already has, or can develop, a strong, global position in the three major markets of Europe, North America, and Asia Pacific. We intend to concentrate on Pharmaceutical, Agrochemicals and Seeds, Specialties, Paints, Industrial Chemicals, and Explosives. We are also forming a new Materials Business from most of our existing activities in Advanced Materials, Films, Polyurethanes, Acrylics, and Fibers. By combining ICI's considerable materials skills in this way, we will be better able to adapt to the opportunities that exist in this fast-developing field—much as we have done in recent years on the biotechnology front.

Our businesses in the present ICI portfolio without the same global profit potential will normally not have priority for expansion capital. They will generally be viewed either as cash generators or as candidates for divestment.

Each of the new groupings would be headed by an international chief executive, while the territorial organization would henceforth play a subsidiary role. The divisions would report directly to head office, rather than to the territories. Consistent with the greater emphasis on

---

[23]ICI 1990 *Annual Report,* p. 50.

a divisional form of organization, the international chief executives of the seven divisions would have considerable autonomy. The chief executive of the ailing industrial chemicals division, for example, had capital expenditure authority up to £10 million.

On May 14, 1991, in spite of ICI's restructuring announcements, Smith NewCourt, acting on behalf of Hanson PLC, acquired 20 million shares of ICI, amounting to a 2.8 percent stake. Hanson's timing was seen by the city as splendid: "After a long period of dull performance, the city has become impatient with ICI and its chairman, Sir Denys Henderson." One fund manager commented: "The level of institutional support for ICI's board has never been lower; and the analysts feel misled by promises that the company has eliminated its exposure to business cycles." Henderson, in response, told the *Sunday Times:* "If Hanson is testing the water to feel the temperature, I think it is clear it could get very hot. Maybe too hot at this stage in his long career. We are a well-armed battleship with plenty of missiles and we are prepared to fir them." ICI hired S.G. Warburg and Goldman Sachs, the specialist in defenses, to counter the Hanson threat.

In contrast to ICI, Lord Hanson waited two months until July 26 to make his first public criticism of ICI. Reaffirming that Hanson's own objective was to "create value for our shareholders," he claimed that ICI was "underperforming" and "overmanaged" and that there was "significant scope for enhancing shareholder value," based on his experience with Hanson PLC.

▲ HANSON PLC

For the year ended September 30, 1990, Hanson recorded a turnover of £7.1 billion and a consolidated profit after tax and extraordinary items of £1 billion. This represented a return on employed capital in excess of 40 percent[24] (Exhibit 4). This impressive result capped off a rapid growth in after-tax profits and share price throughout the 1980s (Exhibits 5a and 5b), and included a mere £94 million or so of after-tax profit from sales of businesses and investments.[25]

Hanson PLC businesses spanned the English-speaking world, comprising such businesses as brickworks in Britain, cement works and coal mining in the United States, and various mining interests and chemical plants in Australia. These businesses were organized under one of two corporate offices: U.K. subsidiaries were controlled from Hanson PLC's head office, while U.S. operations came under the purview of Hanson Industries, the group's New Jersey–based subsidiary. Within each corporate group, businesses on both sides of the Atlantic were organized into three major divisions in 1991: consumer, building products, and industrial. Hanson Industries also had a small food division. Exhibit 6 lists Hanson subsidiaries and their activities for each of the major divisions.

Lord Hanson managed the group's U.K. businesses as chairman of Hanson PLC, while Lord White, his co-founder, supervised the U.S. operations as chairman of Hanson Industries. The president and senior vice president of Hanson Industries were also represented on the board of Hanson PLC, but the corporate offices were otherwise independent. White and Hanson kept in touch with one another by telephone on a daily basis, maintaining their close business partnership and the similar management styles that had characterized the group for decades.

---

[24]Estimating capital employed as the mean of the consolidated capital and reserves at the beginning and end average of the accounting year.

[25]Including a rough estimate of after-tax profit from Hanson's sale of its interest in Gold Fields of South Africa, which the company classified amongst ordinary income: "A Balance Sheet for Their Lordships," *The Economist,* July 6, 1991, p. 72.

Sales and income by division for 1990 were as follows:

Division	Sales		Trading Profit	
	£ Millions	Percent	£ Millions	Percent
U.K. activities				
Consumer	2,700	64.8	283	48.9
Building products	942	22.6	146	25.2
Industrial	522	12.6	150	25.9
	4,164		579	
U.S. activities				
Consumer	640	21.3	40	9.6
Building products	565	18.8	66	15.9
Industrial	1,800	59.9	310	74.5
	3,005		416	

Origins of Hanson Trust

In 1943, James Hanson was presented with a half share in the family company, which he joined when the war ended. In 1948 parts of the company, including a national parcel distribution business and bus and coach fleets, were nationalized for a total of £5 million. With Bank of England permission to take £3 million out of the country, James Hanson and his younger brother Bill headed for Canada in search of business ventures. The pair began a road haulage business in Hamilton, Ontario, while continuing to manage the parts of the family company that had escaped nationalization in the United Kingdom. Following Bill's tragic death from stomach cancer in 1954, James Hanson teamed up with White, another Yorkshireman, who had sold advertising space for his father's printing and advertising company. Their first business venture together in the United Kingdom was the Hanson-White Greeting Cards Co. The business was a success, largely due to White's persistent efforts to obtain shelf space at W.H. Smith, one of Britain's largest book and news agency chains.

During the early 1960s, Hanson and White left North America to spend more time in the United Kingdom. After selling their greeting cards company in 1963, along with its name, they began looking for acquisitions. In 1965, they leveraged their ownership of a commercial vehicle distributor into the acquisition of a larger company, the Wiles Group. This acquisition was the start of a series of increasingly ambitious takeovers. By 1971 Hanson and White controlled a small conglomerate engaging in activities as diverse as brickmaking, producing security thread for banknotes, program printing, distributing muck-raking equipment, and renting out pumps. Whereas Hanson contributed the administrative talent, White provided creativity and ambition. Indeed, the omission of White's name when Wiles Group was renamed to Hanson Trust in 1969 was a tribute to his pragmatism rather than a reflection of his status in the partnership.

▲ EXHIBIT 4   Hanson Consolidated Financial Statements (£ millions)*

	1990	1989
Sales turnover	7,153	6,998
Costs and overheads less other income	5,868	5,934
Profit on ordinary activities	1,285	1,064
Taxation	314	251
Profit after taxation	971	813
Extraordinary items	29	288
Profit available for appropriation	1,000	1,101
Fixed assets	5,057	2,414
Tangible	704	957
Investments	5,761	3,371
Current assets	8,993	7,454
Including cash at bank	6,878	5,266
Creditors (due within one year)	4,226	3,269
Total assets less current liabilities	10,528	7,556
Creditors (due after one year)	4,258	4,971
Provisions for liabilities	3,436	1,499
Capital and reserves	2,834	1,086
Sale of business	484	1,298
Sales of investments	179	156
	1,963	2,178
Costs of acquisitions	(661)	(3,285)

*Approved by the board of directors on December 6, 1990.

In 1973, the ever-ambitious White decided to pack his bags and found a new arm of the company in the free-enterprise pastures of the United States. White's new company, Hanson Industries, made its first real acquisition in 1974 of a private commercial fishing company. Seacoast, as the acquisition was renamed, proved to be a savvy purchase: the oil crisis

▲ EXHIBIT 5a   Hanson's Sales and Profit Performance

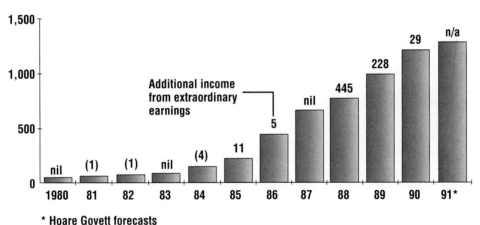

Financial years ending Sept. 30th

Sales
£bn

Ordinary pre-tax profit £m

Additional income
from extraordinary
earnings

* **Hoare Govett forecasts**

Source: "Evaluating Hanson: A Balance Sheet for Their Lordships," *The Economist,* July 6, 1991, p. 73.

produced a steep rise in fish meal prices, and profits rose to $16 million in 1975. In addition, White obtained the services of its previous owner, David Clarke, who rose to the rank of president of Hanson Industries in 1978 and became the chairman's right-hand man. The feed processing industry was, however, highly cyclical and Seacoast was sold in 1984 for its original acquisition price of $32 million.

Larger Acquisitions

The Hanson acquisition program took its first step up in size in 1981, with its $184 million takeover of McDonough, itself a U.S. conglomerate. (See Exhibit 7 for a summary of Hanson's major U.K. and U.S. acquisitions and divestments.) McDonough was followed in 1982 by an acquisition of similar scale in the United Kingdom; the Berec Group, famous for its

▲ EXHIBIT 5b   Hanson's and ICI's Relative Stock Market Performance

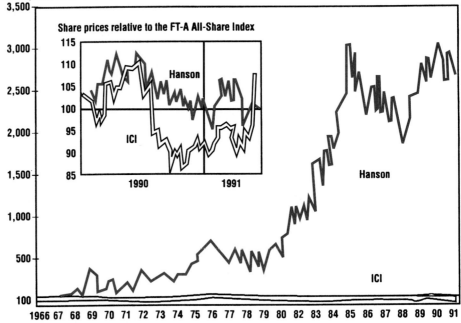

Share prices relative to the FT-A All-Share Index

▲ EXHIBIT 6   Divisional Management and Companies

Consumer		
United Kingdom	Imperial Tobacco Limited	Cigarettes (2d in U.K.), cigars, tobacco
	British Ever Ready	Batteries (1st in U.K.), torches, and cycle lamps
United States	Hanson Housewares	Farberware cookware and small kitchen appliances; vacuum cleaners; clocks and lamps; artificial floral products
	Hanson Recreation	Golf equipment and apparel; physical conditioning and weight training equipment; pool tables and elec-tronic dart games; archery equipment; die-cast toys and model kits

Industrial		
United Kingdom	Lindustries Limited*	Crabtree Electrical, gas meters, health products, other
	Hanson Amalgamated	Construction services, bathroom and household products, Rollalong accommodation units
United States	SCM Chemicals Inc.†	Pigments and related chemicals (titanium dioxide) (3rd in world)

Industrial		
	Hanson Office Products	Manufacturer of office furniture and distributor of office supplies and furniture
	Grove Worldwide Company[†]	Mobile hydraulic and truck-mounted cranes (1st in U.S.); aerial access equipment
	Weber Aircraft Inc.[†]	Aircraft seating, galleys, and lavatories
	Gold Fields Mining Corporation[†]	Gold mining and exploration (10th in U.S.)
	Peabody Holding Company[†]	Coal mining (1st in world)

Building Products		
United Kingdom	ARC limited[†]	Aggregates (1st in U.K.), coated stone and concrete products (2d in U.K.)
	London Brick Company Limited[†]	Fletton bricks (1st in U.K.)
	Butterley Brick Limited[†]	Nonfletton bricks
United States	Hanson Lighting	Residential and commercial fluorescent and incandescent lighting products (4th in U.S.)
	Hanson Building Products	Windows and doors; garden and industrial hand tools; trim; Jacuzzi whirlpool (1st in world), baths, spas, and pumps
	Kaiser cement Corporation[*]	Cement and aggregate products
United States	Newmont Mining Corporation[*]	Gold mining and exploration (49% owned)
	Smith Corona Corporation[*]	Electronic typewriters, personal word processors, and office supplies (48% owned)
	GR Foods, Inc.[*]	Ground Round restaurants; food and agriproducts (49% owned)
Australia	Renison Goldfields	Mining, minerals extraction and exploration (43% owned)

[*]Incorporated in the United States.
[†]Incorporated in Australia
Source: Annual report, 1990.

Ever Ready batteries, joined Hanson's consumer division at a cost of £95 million. Hanson recouped £41 million by selling Berec's West German subsidiary, which had developed the technology for a new battery. Through subsequent cost-reduction efforts, the company increased its margins and realized an operating profit of £45 million in 1990. However, without its German R&D unit, it was reported to have been losing market share to Duracell's alkaline battery.[26]

---

[26]S. Holberon, "Still Limbering Up for the Big One," *Financial Times,* September 18, 1991.

▲ EXHIBIT 7 Acquisitions and Disposals by Hanson

BDH Engineering	**(1973)**	**McDonough**	**(1981)**	**SCM**	**(1986)**
Price	£12.2m	Price	$185	Price	$930m
Disposal		Disposal		Disposals	
1973	£11.0m	1981	$52.5m	1986	$935.0m
				1987	33.6m
				1988	116.0m
				1989	309.0m
				1990	41.5m
					$1,585.1m
Carisbrook	**(1977)**	**UDS**	**(1983)**	**Kaiser**	**(1987)**
Price	$36m	Price	£260m	Price	$250m
Disposals		Disposals		Disposals	
1977	$160.0m	1983	£15.2m	1987	$53.2m
1983	$6.8m	1984	15.3m	1988	221.3m
	$166.8m	1989	231.7m		$274.5m
		1990	0.9m		
			£263.15m		
Hygrade	**(1976)**	**USI**	**(1983)**	**Kidde**	**(1987)**
Price	$32m	Price	$532m	Price	$1.5bn
Disposals		Disposals		Disposals	
1979	$11.5m	1984	$22.5m	1988	$411.9m
1984	14.0m	1985	36.4m	1989	71.6m
1989	140.0m	1986	78.7m	1990	250.7m
	$165.5m	1987	24.5m		$734.2m
		1988	1.9m		
		1989	23.0m		
		1990	13.3m		
			$200.3m		

Intersate United (1978)

Price	$30m
Disposals	
1978	$6.3
1985	93.5m
	$98.9m

Lindustries (1979)

price	£27.9m
Disposals	
1989	£48.0m
1990	1.25m
	£49.25m

Berec (1981)

Price	£95m
Disposals	
1983	£60.m
1989	£1.3m
	£61.3m

London Brick (1984)

Price	£245m
Disposals	
1986	£33.0m

Imperial Group (1984)

Price	£2.5bn
Disposals	
1986	£1,673.0m
1987	23.0m
1988	554.7m
1989	87.7m
1990	1.6m
	£2,340.0m

Stuart Anderson Restaurants (1988)

Price	$20m
Disposals	
1990	$11.4m

Consolidated Gold Fields (1989)

Price	£3.3bn
Disposals	
1989	£614.3m
1990	2,039.75m
	£2,654.05m

Source: Hanson's U.S. annual reports (Form 20-F) 1988–90.

Hanson and White spotted their real gems in 1986: SCM in the United States, and the Imperial Group in the United Kingdom. The takeover of SCM, a 22-company conglomerate, became famous for Hanson Industries' four-and-a-half-month battle to secure it at a price of $930 million. White's timing was perfect: SCM had recently introduced major expansion and restructuring programs, reducing reported profitability through provisions in the accounts with most of the benefits yet to be realized. Expansion had focused on the titanium dioxide business, where SCM had bought three plants for $110 million in early 1984. Although this cyclical industry was in a downturn in 1986, the additional capacity provided an opportunity to profit from a subsequent recovery and price increases. By 1991, this business alone had an estimated value of no less than $2.3 billion. Restructuring had centered on the typewriter operation, including a provision for employee redundancies and refocusing of the product line. Hanson kept the titanium dioxide and typewriter businesses, but progressively disposed of many of the food, paper, and resin subsidiaries for a total of $1,600 million![27] ICI acquired one of these divestments, the U.S. paint manufacturer Glidden, in an auction.

In 1986, Hanson PLC also acquired the Imperial Group for £2.5 billion. by the end of 1990, it had extracted £2.3 billion from sales of Imperial assets, leaving assets valued by Hanson's U.K. broker Hoare Govett at over £1 billion.[28] Not all the benefits came from selling off, however. In Hanson's hands the core tobacco activities doubled their return on assets, albeit at the cost of a small fall in market share. Furthermore, the headcount in manufacturing had fallen from 2,206, October 1985 to 1,200 in September 1990, partly through a £40 million capital investment program and greater efficiency in indirect services.

More recently, Hanson had been more of a seller than a buyer, judging some of the prices too high. Apart from the 1987 $1.7 billion acquisition of Kidde, the 1989 takeover of Consolidated Gold Fields, and a preprivatization bid for Powergen that failed, Hanson had been focusing on its existing portfolio, building up a £6.8 billion cash "war chest." Rumors of Hanson interest had sent scores of company stocks soaring, including BAT, Allied-Lyons, and Blue Circle. Although analysts had pointed to the need for Hanson to make another move, its stake in ICI came as a complete surprise to the market.

Hanson as a Corporate Restructurer

Though Lord Hanson portrayed his company as an industrial manager, the public saw it as a deft practitioner of the age-old principle of buy cheap and sell high. While Lords Hanson and White were still central to the company's ability to identify undervaluation and restructuring opportunities, the Hanson acquisition process had become well honed. There were three phases in the process, each carried out by a distinct team. The first involved selecting the target and executing the deal. Next, a tactical review aimed at significant changes within three months. Finally, a period of strategic analysis set out to create a more productive and profitable company.

Hanson's attention to downside risk meant that takeovers were funded by cash, convertible shares, or regular nonrecourse loans secured on the assets of the target, never by junk bonds. Targets were invariably in "mature" asset-backed industries: In Lord Hanson's terms, "good-quality basic businesses providing essential goods and services."[29] With little exposure to changing fashion or obsolescence through rapidly changing technology, they were

---

[27]Hoare Govett, *Hanson: The U.S. Perspective,* April 1989, p. 9.
[28]*Financial Times,* September 18, 1991.
[29]*The Economist,* April 20, 1985, p. 74.

more salable.[30] Hanson was similarly averse to financial services and "people-intensive" businesses—people, unlike tangible assets, could always walk out the door. It likewise shied away from industries that were capital intensive or required high levels of research and development. Such businesses frequently demanded investments with long payback periods or involved developing "sexy" products that might never succeed.

From an early stage, Hanson sought companies with leading market positions and strong name recognition in their respective industries whose performance could be improved.[31] The importance of the last criterion was underscored by David Clarke, president of Hanson Industries:

> Some people have a mistaken idea about our success in acquisitions. They think that we are simply astute buyers of undervalued assets. They think that it's enough to locate something undervalued, break it apart, sell off the pieces we do not want, keep the rest, and somehow end up with a hefty profit.

> But it's hardly that simple.... When we look at any acquisition, we don't look solely for undervaluation, although of course that is a criterion. We look for a corporation that can respond effectively to our management system as well. We look for a company that needs to be streamlined and that can be readily decentralized. We look for companies in basic industries, with strong cash flow and good managers who can run their businesses under our system.[32]

Alongside the acquisition selection analysis, another team began a tactical management review of the target, looking at how Hanson could run the business more efficiently. In the event that Hanson proceeded with a bid and successfully acquired control, the analysis typically continued for three months with a diagnostic audit. The objective here was to quickly enhance or at least preserve the value of the acquisition. As Alexander, who headed the U.K. team, said, "Three months after we arrive, there must be significant changes—after that, newness is a wasting asset."[33] Immediate goals of this phase included: finding any skeletons in the closet, lifting workforce morale in the wake of acquisition uncertainty; focusing on the core businesses; identifying the jewels in the crown; and identifying new and energetic management.

Strategic analysis was managed by a team under the control of the relevant divisional chairman. This team reaped an incidental psychological benefit from earlier decisions, creating an impression of having saved the survivors from "Hansonization." Nevertheless, changes continued—albeit with a strategic emphasis. After a further analysis of about three months, managers were asked to discuss reorganization. Typical changes included simplifying the organizational structure, increasing accountability and responsibility in the operating divisions through decentralization, and establishing objectives and incentive arrangements.

Hanson PLC as an Industrial Manager

The strategic analysis phase marked the transition to the ongoing management of the Hanson companies. It was this "free-form management," as Lord Hanson called it, that was for him the essence of Hanson. Free-form management rested on a few basic principles.

---

[30]Publicity statement, 1989.
[31]Presentation to U.K. analysts, Monday, June 13, 1988, Whitbread Brewery, London.
[32]Ibid
[33]Hoare Govett, *Hanson as Industrial Manager*, August 1990, p. 9.

The company sought not only to increase shareholder wealth by pursuing earnings growth and return on capital increases, but also to create an organization in which every business manager would act like an owner. This principle was supported by a high level of decentralization and short, well-defined lines of communication. The aim was both to break up centers of power in acquired companies and to return responsibility to the hands of those who added value by "making and selling real things,"[34] providing them with incentives and holding them accountable.

On both sides of the Atlantic, senior management at Hanson's subsidiaries had full authority to make decisions in such areas as manufacturing, marketing, and personnel.[35] Hanson made no pretense of constructing industrial synergies between his far-flung acquisitions, as shown by the operation of two Hanson subsidiaries, Imperial Tobacco Limited and Elizabeth Shaw (a chocolate firm). Both were based in Bristol, England, and delivered goods to newsagents and corner shops throughout the United Kingdom. Hanson was against any sharing of distribution resources on the grounds that any economies of scale would likely be outweighed by "the general sloppiness that would result if each company thought that distribution was the other's problem."[36]

The Role of the London and the New York Head Offices

Hanson Industries headquarters in Iselin boasted a total of 49 executives and 129 corporate employees in 1991, with collective responsibility for controlling about 150 operating units. The story at Grosvenor Place was similar, with some 40 executives at the head office.

Control was implemented through a comprehensive budgetary system. In June of each year individual subsidiaries on both continents prepared budgets covering operating plans, cash flow, and capital expenditure. These were submitted to divisional headquarters in July, which forwarded them to the corporate office in August for approval. Although budgets were expected to be "demanding but realistic," to quote David Clarke,[37] in practice, subsidiary executives were given considerable freedom in setting their objectives.

Tight control over capital investment and cash was a key ingredient of the Hanson formula. Any investment over 500 pounds needed Hanson's personal approval, although in practice he scanned lists of items.[38] At Hanson Industries, capital expenditure in excess of $3,000 required head office approval although White himself had less direct involvement. Nevertheless, operating managers had to be prepared to justify their requests.

In the meantime, the board maintained tight scrutiny of results through a comprehensive reporting system supervised by a small team of highly qualified accountants with professional and industrial experience who were independent of divisional executives. The results of a subsidiary or group of smaller companies were reported on a weekly basis to its chief executive. Monthly accounts were also produced at this level within two weeks after the end of each month and supplemented by more detailed quarterly reports, each for review at the divisional and corporate levels. These formed the subject of regular monthly and ad hoc board meetings with the respective subsidiary and divisional chief executives. Hanson exerted an even tighter grip on cash, which was reported weekly from all operations worldwide.

---

[34]Ibid
[35]J. Byrne, "Hanson, The Dangers of Living by Takeover Alone," *Business Week,* August 15, 1988, p. 47.
[36]"Hanson's Future, The Conglomerate as Antique Dealer," *The Economist,* March 11, 1989, p. 84.
[37]Ibid
[38]Gooding, p. 66; Govett, *Hanson as Industrial Manager*, p. 12.

While Hanson Trust managers were thought to be spurred on by responsibility to run their own company, this responsibility was complemented with a system of performance-based rewards. Commented Bonham:

> If financial control is the safety net, then incentives are the carrot. We reward all divisional and operating management on the basis of profits related to capital employed and that…is our principal measure of performance.

> We define capital employed as fixed assets plus working capital, stock debtors less creditors. This is what management can influence. Because of the centralization of tax and treasury, all financing is treated as part of the equity of the business, cash being regarded as negative equity. To be consistent, profit is measured on an operating, preinterest, pretax basis. The targets we set are independent of the budgets and are based more on a ratchet principle, the aim being to improve performance over the previous year.

> Rewards can be substantial with up to 100 percent of base salary being available for outstanding performance. In addition, managers are encouraged to think like shareholders, and to this end we provide them with share options in order to focus their attention. At last year end, over 1,000 employees were in the program.[39]

Although few denied the impact of Hanson-style management especially on short-term performance, critics were likely to point out that not all earnings came from operating activities. According to estimates by James Capel & Co., one-third of Hanson's 1990 group earnings before tax of £1,285 million was derived from

> fragile, nonoperational sources, much of which has arisen as by-products of the acquisitions policy. Cash deposits and interest income from tax havens are growing features of Hanson's balance sheet, market capitalization, and income statements.[40]

These cash deposits (referred to as Hanson's "war chest") had grown from £1,132 million in 1985 to £6,878 million in 1990. Although this cash was offset by bank loans, debentures, and overdraft and dividend obligations totaling £6,674 million in 1990, it was not used to repay the debt because treasury management was an important source of earnings for Hanson. Hanson's cross-Atlantic revenues allowed the company to keep its deposits in sterling and its debt in dollars. Thus, the company was able to take advantage of the spread in interest rates. For example, during 1990 the average London interbank three-month deposit rate was 6.73 percent higher than the average London Eurodollar three-month rate.

▲ REACTION IN THE CITY

Following the announcement of Hanson's 2.8 percent stake in ICI, there was considerable speculation in the city as to Lord Hanson's motives. Had he brought the stake to test economic and political sentiment behind launching a full bid? Had he bought it hoping to pressure ICI into commencing its own restructuring to raise share prices? Various breakup values of ICI were calculated to look at the economics of a full bid given ICI's current market capitalization of about £9 billion. County NatWest estimated the breakup of ICI at over £12 billion, with pharmaceuticals counting for the lion's share. Estimated breakup values were as follows:

[39]Presentation to U.K. analysts, Monday, June 13, 1988.
[39]James Capel Research, September 1991, p. 3.

Business	£ Millions
Pharmaceuticals	£8,300
Paints	1,150
Other effect products*	700
Tioxide	700
Explosives	550
Agrochemicals	1,550
Bulk chemicals	1,250
Related companies	400
Minorities	− 450
Net debt	− 1,750
Total	£12,400

*Other effect products consist of colors and fine chemicals, polyurethanes, specialty chemicals,
advanced materials, films, and biological products.
Source: "Hanson Lights the Fuse," *Sunday Times*, May 19, 1991.

Several of the businesses were, however, difficult to value. Pharmaceuticals was valued by various stockbrokers at between £5 billion and £8 billion, depending on how ICI's future pipeline of drugs was viewed. Other effect products was very difficult to value given the mix of business. Some estimated the value of the business at £1.4 billion—twice that of County NatWest.

In the short term, there were signs that ICI was recovering well in 1991 in the context of its reorganization, but the longer-term trends in ICI's performance gave cause for concern. During the period between 1965 and 1990, its shares had underperformed the U.K. market by 60 percent. In its peak year of 1989, for example, the company had a net profit after-tax of £930 million. After adjustment for inflation, this was equivalent to ICI's net profit in 1979, the chemical sector's previous cyclical peak year.

Many against Hanson's stake in ICI cited its contribution to the British economy. Though in 1990 Britain had a trade deficit in manufactured goods of £13.7 billion, in chemicals it had a £2.4 billion surplus. ICI was seen as a focal point for U.K. research and development, able to recruit the best science graduates in Britain and elsewhere. As Harry Ewing, Labour MP for Falkirk, said:

> I am horrified at the thought of a takeover. ICI is a well-managed company, with good industrial relations. All that would be put at risk with a bid. The government could not stand by and see a national institution endangered.

Three weeks after the purchase, Sir John Harvey-Jones, the former chairman of ICI, made a passionate appeal against a Hanson bid:

> You cannot compete with Bayer, Hoechst, BASF, Dow, and Du Pont just by making assets sweat. You have to manage international complexity. You have to attract and motivate the best scientists and technologists in the world. You have to nurture relationships with universities throughout the world. You have to invest patient money in support of your view. You have to know the markets of the world and, since chemicals serve every sort of industrial and service outlet, you have to take a consistent view of the long-term future.

It take 10 years of investment and effort to achieve registration in order to sell a drug, and these are 10 years that test the courage, "stickability," and vision of any management. I find nothing in the records of Lords Hanson and White to show their interest or dedication to such a mode of life, or such a style of management. . . . Boosting Ever Ready's return by shutting down research and sponsoring the Derby is not likely to be a blueprint for success in the chemicals industry.

So, what are their alternatives? they can dismember the group and create short-term added shareholder value. This is a lure that I fear may prove irresistible to the institutions and the press. Would this really be a good thing? It isn't an accident that chemicals companies are broadly based across a wide spectrum of technical activities. Most commercial scientific advances are increasingly made not in single fields of specialization, but by collaboration across a number of areas of activity. That at least is the rationale behind the diversity of operations of the world's leading chemical companies[41]

Supporting him, Peter Doyle, ICI's director of research and development, argued that research-intensive businesses like pharmaceuticals and agrochemicals benefited from being part of one chemicals group by sharing common technological tools and making use of each other's discoveries. He cited fungicides as a good example of this exchanges of ideas:

Pyrimidine compounds, used as fungicides for cereals, came originally from pharmaceutical research. Conversely triazole compounds, developed by the agrochemical business, have given pharmaceuticals a potent systemic fungicide.[42]

Another example cited was the development of a biodegradable plastic delivery system by an ICI polymer scientist for Zoladex, a prostate cancer drug.

Such arguments begged the issue of whether ICI was appropriately organized to share the results of its research among businesses. The company had disbanded its corporate laboratory in Runcorn, Merseyside, during the 1960s, distributing the scientists around ICI's operating divisions. Interbusiness communication was achieved through a network of internal scientific committees, but Doyle recognized the need for additional groups to achieve his objective of "corporateness"—ensuring that all parts of the group can make use of good science wherever it arises."[43]

Even more fundamental was the question of whether ICI was receiving enough value from its research. Criticism was levied at ICI's investment of 16 percent of its research budget in advanced materials—a business that continued to lose money and showed little sign of becoming in the short term the new science-based growth industry that ICI had predicted five years earlier. Even the lucrative pharmaceutical business, facing the expiration of the U.S. patent on Tenormin and having only the two new drugs to launch, found its research expenditures had come under attack.

Internally, opinion seemed to be divided among ICI's businesses regarding the importance of being part of a larger group. Spokesmen from the industrial chemicals division cited the strength of the ICI name and historical instances of synergies in research. On the other hand, the specialties business saw its connection with ICI "more a hindrance than a help. It guarded its independence and tried to avoid wasting time with ICI's corporate matters."[44]

---

[41]*Observer,* June 9, 1991.
[42]"An Experiment in Chemical Devence," *Financial Times,* June 20, 1991, p. 13.
[43]Ibid.
[44]"ICI: The Waiting Game," *The Economist,* July 27, 1991.

Questions about Hanson

Having put the spotlight on ICI, Hanson executives soon found their own track record under equal scrutiny. The issues raised ranged from peccadilloes like Lord White's Hanson-financed riding stable to more serious concerns including the lack of shareholder control over Hanson PLC itself (only two nonexecutives were on the board), the importance of financial arbitrages and tax sheltering to Hanson results, and the company's dependence on Lords Hanson and White, both entering their 70s.

THE GENERAL MILLS BOARD AND STRATEGIC PLANNING

*Our biggest assets rest in our Good Will, our merchandising ability, and our efficiency in the use
of publicity. These must be carried into new fields of profit opportunity. Our line of thinking and
experience fits us to exploit projects that have their roots in the soil that grows wheat. We may
follow the trunk of the tree to its utmost tip, but we also should not be averse to grafting
new branches upon it.[1]*

James S. Bell, CEO of Washburn Crosby, the predecessor of General Mills

As he sat in his office the morning of November 30, 1989, General Mills chairman and
CEO Bruce Atwater was pleased. After less than a month of discussions with the largest food
company in the world, Nestlé, S.A., he had a deal. The agreement between the two companies to set up a joint venture in cereals starting in Europe was one of the most significant in
the history of General Mills' international food activities. it was also the most trouble-free set
of negotiations Atwater had ever encountered, especially considering the size and importance
of the joint venture.

The agreement between Nestlé and General Mills called for the creation of Cereal
Partners Worldwide (CPW), a joint venture wholly owned by the two food giants, which
would market and sell General Mills' cereals in Europe and then in other parts of the world
outside of North America. General Mills would provide its vaunted line of cereals, including
Wheaties, Cheerios, Total, and *Kix,* as well as its product technology and marketing expertise. Nestlé had extensive sales and distribution networks in Europe and would ensure entry
into the market for the General Mills products. Nestlé would also provide manufacturing
plants. It made such good sense to Atwater. He explained:

Research Associate James E. Sailer prepared this case under the supervision of Professor Jay W. Lorsch. The case
draws heavily from an earlier case prepared by Professor Michael E. Porter. Copyright © 1991 by the President
and Fellows of Harvard College.
[1]Gray, James, *Business without Boundary: The Story of General Mills,* University of Minnesota Press: 1954.

The Nestlé idea kept coming back to us. Here's a company that wants to be in the cereals business, but has not gained much market share with its own products. They need new products, they need cereal marketing know-how. On the other hand, they have sales operations in each country that are phenomenal. They've got a great name worldwide, and they've got a lot of manufacturing and business know-how. And I know Maucher.

Helmut Maucher, CEO of Nestlé, had responded extremely positively when Atwater had first telephoned him about the possibility of a joint venture on November 6, 1989. Indeed, as the General Mills team found out months after the deal had been consummated, Maucher had been contemplating the same arrangement. After hanging up the phone following Atwater's call, Maucher telephoned Camillo Pagano, a senior vice president at Nestlé, and asked Pagano if he had contracted General Mills without receiving clearance from Maucher. After Pagano assured him that he hadn't, Maucher called Atwater back and confirmed Nestlé's interest. The rest was a whirlwind. Atwater and a top aide flew to Vevey, Switzerland, 4 days later, and the protocol was signed 23 days after Atwater's original phone call to Maucher.

For Atwater, it was an important entry into the international sphere in one of General Mills' core businesses—cereals. The joint venture would be the beginning of a major international cereal business for General Mills.

▲ THE BOARD'S ROLE IN STRATEGIC PLANNING

The General Mills board (see Exhibit 1) met six times a year, typically for less than a day each. The June meeting was a longer meeting set aside to discuss long-range plans. For every regular General Mills board meeting, directors were sent a binder of materials to read. For the long-range planning session, the binder was significantly larger, as management spelled out values, goals, and strategy, and reviewed the company's future business prospects. Emphasis was placed on corporate balance, including the characteristics of the businesses in which General Mills was involved, and financial objectives for the company. The binder was also comprehensive enough to serve in lieu of oral presentations, since the point of the meeting was to receive board members' input, not merely to present the board with information. Atwater explained:

We want questions. We ask for questions. We'd much rather be challenged by the board than we would by the marketplace, and find out we overlooked something.

For Atwater, the board's involvement in strategic planning was not a hierarchical review and approval process. Rather, he wanted input from his directors:

What you learn quickly as a CEO is that you cannot average what your directors say. Directors' opinions on any given subject can be quite diverse, and that diversity is valuable. However, if you average those opinions, you may end up taking the wrong direction or no direction. Management must set the direction, and the board provides input to management's decision process. The board, of course, must endorse the strategic direction of the company.

With both the board and our internal management practice, we view governance as input, as opposed to direction. If governance, meaning input or advice as opposed to direction or supervision, doesn't happen at the board level, it doesn't happen anywhere else. It cascades from the top down through the organization. Every operation has governance issues. We are encouraging our people to think about the differences between governance and supervision.

▲ EXHIBIT 1   General Mills Board of Directors*

H. Brewster Atwater, Jr. (1971), *chairman of the board and chief executive officer, General Mills*

F. Caleb Blodgett (1980), *vice chairman of the board and chief financial and administrative officer, General Mills*

Richard M. Bressler (1984), *chairman of the board and chief executive officer, Burlington Northern Inc.*

Livio D. DeSimone (1989), *executive vice president, information, and imaging technologies sector and corporate services, 3M*

William T. Esrey (1989), *chairman, president, and chief executive officer, United Telecommunications, Inc., and chairman and chief executive officer, US Sprint Communications Company Limited Partnership*

N. Bud Grossman (1980), *chief executive officer, Cogel Management Co.*

Judith Richards Hope (1989), *senior partner, law firm of Paul, Hastings, Janofsky & Walker*

Joe R. Lee (1985), *executive vice president, General Mills, and president, General Mills Restaurants*

Lewis W. Lehr (1979), *chairman of the board and chief executive officer, 3M (retired)*

Gwendolyn A. Newkirk (1975), *professor and chairman of the Department of Consumer Science and Education, University of Nebraska*

William F. Pounds (1979), *professor of management, Alfred P. Sloan School of Management of the Massachusetts Institute of Technology and senior advisor to the Rockefeller Family and Associates*

George Putnam (1981), *chairman, Putnam Management Company, Inc. and chairman and president of each of The Putnam Group of Mutual Funds*

Michael D. Rose (1985), *chairman of the board, president, and chief executive officer, The Promus Companies, Inc.*

Arthur R. Schulze (1986), *vice chairman, General Mills*

Mark H. Willes (1985), *president and chief operating officer, General Mills*

C. Angus Wurtele (1985), *chairman of the board and chief executive officer, The Valspar Corporation*

*Date in parentheses indicates year director was elected to board.

Governance has an advantage, according to Atwater, that supervision does not, and that is direct responsibility for one's decisions. People under supervision follow instructions, and their results, as long as they do what they've been told, are the responsibility of their supervisors. Under a governance structure, each employee is very much responsible for results. Lewis Lehr, a director since 1979, agreed with this point:

A board cannot impose its will. Because once it does, then it is running the company. if the board said, look General Mills, you go over to England, and here's $800 million, and you buy the first company you can buy, we want to be in that market, then from then on, the responsibility for the success of that is the board's and not the management's.

General Mills also used the strategic planning meetings to get the board's opinion on issues and concerns about which management hadn't come to a definite conclusion. Atwater commented:

We discuss issues. The issues tend to be identified by management most of the time. We don't necessarily know how we want to tackle them, but we will bring up places where we are uncomfortable.

▲ GENERAL MILLS THROUGH THE YEARS

The origins of General Mills can be found in the flour mill Cadwallader Washburn took over in the 1860s when he formed the Washburn Crosby Company. As time went on, Washburn Crosby developed, creating the Gold Medal Flour brand in the 1880s, the Betty Crocker character in 1921, and Wheaties, its first ready-to-eat breakfast cereal, in 1924.

In 1928, Washburn Crosby merged with a number of large mills from around the United States to form General Mills. By the 1940s, General Mills had expanded into packaged foods, seeing "practically unlimited" potential "for a food processor with imagination, efficient facilities, and a vigorous advertising and merchandising organization." During World War II, General Mills significantly expanded outside of food for the first time, adding a mechanical division to produce for the war effort.

The postwar 1940s and 1950s saw a rapid period of diversification for General Mills. It first moved into home appliances—using the facilities employed by the mechanical division during the war—followed by industrial electronics, while still pursuing alternatives within food, such as vitamins and other packaged foods. Packaged foods grew to 45 percent of sales and 76 percent of earnings by 1960, in part because General Mills' diversification efforts outside of foods were not successful. The company began posting persistent losses in animal feeds and commercial flour, as well as home appliances and electronics, in the early 1960s.

Divestment in the 1960s

Under retired Air Force general Edwin W. Rawlings, who became president in 1961, General Mills reorganized, divesting operations such as animal feed, electronics, oilseed processing, appliances, refrigerated foods, and industrial flour. Rawlings decided to emphasize growth through the food business, in areas which were more complimentary to General Mills' current product lines. In one such effort in 1961, General Mills tried to expand its cereals into the United Kingdom, but the two-year effort failed, largely because local restrictions on the use of preservatives seriously compromised the quality of General Mills' presweetened cereals.

In 1964, General Mills developed a strategy for worldwide snack foods. This three-pronged strategy was designed to: (*a*) buy snack food operations with conventional store-door or direct delivery systems; (*b*) build a plant to manufacture shaped snacks that had a long shelf life and would be distributed through the company's warehouse distribution system; and (*c*) acquire international snack companies. During the next few years, General Mills acquired Morton's (potato chips) and Tom's Foods (chips, peanuts, and other snacks) in the United States, and a minority interest in Smith's, an international snack company. In 1968, however, the FTC forbade General Mills, for antitrust reasons, from purchasing any more snack companies in the United States. In addition, the FTC action was somewhat restrictive for other domestic food acquisitions. As a General Mills release noted:

> In part because of the FTC agreement, we were unable to build an efficient operating base in snack foods. Broad strategies without an effective operating base are difficult to execute.

General Mills began selling certain segments of its snack operations in 1970, and continued to do so through the mid-1980s. The company retained its presence in savory and cookie snacks in Europe, and in shelf-stable fruit and grain snacks in the United States.

Balancing Growth

While Rawlings led General Mills into divesting from some markets, he also led diversification efforts into others. The conventional wisdom at General Mills by the mid-1960s was that packaged foods wouldn't provide enough growth to meet corporate objectives and the FTC action restricted the company's ability to grow its foods operations through acquisition. Therefore, venture teams were organized to seek entry into new areas. A key focus of these teams was to find branded nonfood consumer products that would benefit from the company's marketing expertise.

In 1965, General Mills purchased Rainbow Crafts, Inc., a toy company. The acquisition was the first of a series of forays into the toy industry, which included the purchase of Kenner Products, Craft Master, and Parker Brothers. Eventually, General Mills became the world's largest toy producer.

In 1968, General Mills entered the fashion market, and continued buying U.S. fashion companies through the 1970s in what management characterized as "above-average margin opportunities, [with] relatively modest product changes, in which marketing and design are the dominant skills, and distribution is generally through the better stores."

General Mills also entered the restaurant business; in 1969, it opened the first of three internally developed Betty Crocker Tree House Restaurant and Bake Shops, a restaurant with table service, bakery take-home food center, and gift shop all under one roof. The following year, General Mills acquired a chain of three seafood restaurants, known as Red Lobster.

In addition, General Mills diversified into the mail-order business, travel agencies, collectibles, and finally, furniture. This expansion, nearly all of it domestic, began toward the end of Rawlings' tenure and continued into the reign of Jim McFarland, who became chairman and CEO in 1969. At its most diversified, General Mills was involved in 13 discrete industry areas.

Divestment in the 1980s

Bruce Atwater became CEO in 1981, when General Mills had focused down to five major industry areas: toys, fashion, specialty retailing, restaurants, and consumer foods. During the late 1970s and early 1980s, the company had good overall growth and performance from its consumer nonfoods operations, especially the Izod line of casual clothes and the Star Wars line of toys. A substantial amount of investment went into these more volatile industries and their success began to change the character of the company. Beginning in 1983–84, the fashion and toys operations experienced severe problems, as earnings from the preppy Izod clothes and Star Wars toys proved unsustainable. General Mills management began to reevaluate the desirability of competing in five diverse industry areas. Ironically, the company also was finding that its packaged foods operations were, in fact, providing higher growth than projected in the late 1960s, when the nonfood diversification began. General Mills decided to exit the volatile and lower-return industries and concentrate on foods and restaurants.

In January 1985, the company announced its intention to divest the toy and fashion groups and later that spring parts of the specialty retailing, restaurant, and consumer foods operations. General Mills then reorganized the company into three industry areas: consumer foods, restaurants, and specialty retailing. To effect the restructuring, General Mills divested 27 businesses that had accounted for approximately 30 percent of total sales and assets in the year of divestiture.

Caleb Blodgett, vice chairman and chief financial and administrative officer since 1985, said General Mills exited the toy and fashion industries in part because they were confusing to shareholders:

From a shareholder point of view since the early 1980s, when people bought General Mills shares, they didn't buy us because they wanted part of a toy business, part of a fashion business, or a wallpaper business. They couldn't understand it. We were forcing a portfolio on them, if you will. If they wanted action in the toy business, they'd sooner make a deliberate step on their own.

Additional issues for General Mills centered around the fact that earnings in the fashion and toy industries were much more volatile and less predictable than foods. In addition, the expected return on investment for these industries was below the expected return for foods and restaurants.

International Operations in the 1980s

Internationally, General Mills also divested its toy and fashion operations and focused its expansion efforts on foods and restaurants. (See Exhibit 2 for international sales statistics.)

The Red Lobster restaurants moved into Canada in fiscal 1984; by 1990, Red Lobster had 61 restaurants there. In 1985, General Mills entered into a joint venture partnership with Jusco, a Japanese retailer, to develop Red Lobster restaurants in Japan. Problems plagued the Japanese effort from the beginning, as the joint venture had difficulty translating the enormously successful Red Lobster domestic experience into success in Japan. First among the difficulties, according to management, was getting a "critical mass" of well-trained Red Lobster staff in each restaurant. By 1990, General Mills was still modestly unprofitable on the Japanese venture, although management was confident most problems had been corrected.

In 1984, General Mills tested three cereal products in France, but found it difficult to achieve distribution at a reasonable price, and the company discontinued its efforts in 1986.

By 1990, this left General Mills with three basic European operations: Smith's Savory Snacks in Belgium, Holland, and France; Biscuitirie Nantaise, the number one sandwich cookie in France; and Pycasa, Spain's leading marketer of frozen precooked entrees. Each of its European companies' products were leaders in their respective markets.

Edward Blood, vice president for strategic planning and analysis, explained management's goals for any operation:

We have high expectations for earnings growth and return on investment. Maybe our expectations are a little higher in that regard than other companies. So we don't make a lot of investments just to make investments. We also have very high expectations for market share. We don't want to be a tiny player in a market segment.

While General Mills had been successful in developing restaurants and snacks in certain international markets, management believed cereals represented another significant international opportunity. General Mills had the products, the cereal technology, and the marketing expertise, but recognized that it didn't have everything, most importantly a strong sales and distribution network, to take advantage of the broad-scale international development of this opportunity. An issue that management faced was how to develop this international cereal opportunity within a reasonable time frame and deliver an adequate return to the company's shareholders.

▲ EXHIBIT 2 General Mills' Domestic and Foreign Sales, Operating Profits, and Identifiable Assets, 1988–1990

	U.S.A.	Foreign
Sales		
1990	$5,796.1	$652.2
1989	5,071.2	549.4
1988	4,474.5	505.1
Operating profits		
1990	655.9	32.2
1989	543.0	37.1
1988	494.1	31.1
Identifiable assets		
1990	2,543.3	329.1
1989	2,181.1	252.7
1988	1,903.2	224.4

In the interest of putting more emphasis on international operations, in September of 1988, Charles Gaillard, who was one of General Mills' most successful operating executives and had formerly been in charge of domestic cereals, was named senior vice president of international foods. At the time, international foods comprised a small segment of General Mills, but Gaillard was given the responsibility of entering the international cereal business.

General Mills immediately entered negotiations to purchase Nabisco's U.K. cereal business—not including its sales and distribution network—but lost in the final round to Rank Hovis McDougall (RHM). Vice Chairman Arthur Schulze explained the sudden flurry of activity:

> In the past, when we looked at doing something with cereals internationally, prior to 1987 and 1988, we thought essentially of de novo entry, requiring distribution and sales organization of some size and some scope, and felt that the prospects of entry were of such risk that we'd probably never be successful. I think that attitude began to change around 87 or 88, when we decided to take the general manager of our domestic cereal business, a man who had run the business in an exceptionally strong way for eight years, and have him become the head of international [operations]. Clearly, part of his assignment was to rethink our ways here.

In January 1989, General Mills began discussing the possibility of a joint venture with RHM, which had a sizable private label cereal business, in addition to its recently acquired Nabisco U.K. operation. After both sides agreed a joint venture wasn't possible, negotiations commenced to discuss a co-packing arrangement, which never materialized because of RHM's decision to put its cereal business up for sale.

The Board's Role in International Strategic Planning

Throughout the 1980s, certain members of the board of General Mills were concerned about the issue of General Mills developing a more meaningful overseas operation. Management did undertake some activities abroad; however, repeated difficulties in various areas, like Red Lobster in Japan and cereals in France, made management hesitant to launch headfirst into another international scheme. Bruce Atwater felt no one was satisfied with the situation:

We were all unhappy. It wasn't that management liked our conclusion, any more than the board did. None of us liked it!

Michael Rose, a General Mills director since 1985, believed that the board kept a quiet but firm pressure on management:

The international issue literally came up at every review of the long-term plans of General Mills, and probably also in the context of reviewing specifically the cereal business. They recognized that international was an opportunity, but one that they found very difficult to take advantage of for reasons that they would set out. The flip side of that being that several of the board members whose company's had significant international experience continued to press on "Don't you think you could rethink that reason."

Of all the General Mills board members, Lew Lehr was the most interested in international expansion. He explained that some of his prodding on international issues did indeed come from his company's success there:

My background was 3M. I know 3M's international operation, and how significant it is to the total business, not only from an earnings standpoint, but from new ideas, new products that could come out from other places, as opposed to the United States.

Having often traveled to Europe in the context of his own company's business, Lehr was puzzled at the lack of General Mills products there. Reports from company officials which cited the lack of a market there didn't jibe with Lehr's own observations of European eating habits. Lehr believed the structure of General Mills' organization led to the relative lack of international involvement. Each division manager was responsible for the sales and marketing of the area which he or she directed. Lehr believed that another office was needed, an office which would be regionally organized in Europe, so that there would be one center which would be aware of international issues, such as personnel, finance, exchange of money, and government regulations. Also, an international coordinator could act to promote international marketing, something on which product managers might not focus their time and attention. Lehr noted:

General Mills was, in my opinion, fragmented. Because of that fragmentation, it appeared to me that no one was pulling this business together, trying to get it started and having focal points in Europe.

Lehr felt it was crucial that General Mills move to international arenas, and believed that "Europe 92" would benefit companies which had a head start with a European operation. Reflecting his concern over the international question, Lehr would discuss his opinions at each June strategy planning meeting:

At each of the strategy meetings, I usually made some remark about their international business. I guess the point that I learned a long time ago in international is that if you want a good market share, you have to keep competition out of balance wherever they are or may be. If you want to sell Cheerios, you'd better control Cheerios worldwide, for fear that the Fijis may develop a Cheerios business and start selling worldwide. It appeared to me that Kellogg's had done that in the breakfast food markets of Europe, and it seemed to me that General Mills had to start someplace, and it would take an investment in order for them to build a market. And it would be costly, because you just can't get market share without making an investment, when you are late in entering a market. So we talked about that.

Lehr described himself as "lighting a little fire" each year at the strategy planning meetings to push for international development. He recounted, laughing:

If we went through one of those sessions, and I didn't ask a question, at the end Bruce would say, "Well, Lew, what are you going to say about international?"

William Pounds, a director since 1979, believed that Lehr's questioning during those sessions was taken seriously by management:

Lew is a person whose opinion people respect, and so the company on several occasions felt obliged to come back in subsequent meetings with an answer to that question. And the answer was always, "Well, we've looked at it, and it turns out that the demand for cereal products outside the United States is not all that great; not very many people in parts of the world other than England and Australia eat a lot of cereal. . .and we are making so much money and we see so much promise in the U.S. market that we don't want to divert assets, because we think that it would not be the wisest use of our money."

Pounds felt the board was satisfied with the responses given by the General Mills management, at least for that year. Invariably, Pounds said, the following year Lehr would ask, "What about now?"

Lehr conscientiously observed his own beliefs regarding the role of directors. He noted the limits inherent in his job as director:

The fine line is between having a director make a contribution, or having a director trying to run the company. And once you cross that line then you have real problems. And that's when, in my opinion, management has to begin to draw back a little bit from the amount of information they bring out at a board meeting. Because once directors start to try to run a company, then they ought to get a different management team because directors should not run companies.

But Lehr did feel his outspokenness on the international issue gave executives at General Mills encouragement to pursue the international issue. According to Lehr, people in General Mills who did believe in pushing overseas knew they had some support, and thus were more likely to continue to press for their agendas. For his part, Lehr stated:

I respected the fact that [management] believed what they believed, because they had a heck of a lot more facts then I did. I hadn't had to suffer through mistakes that had been made, and they did. So I respected their opinions. On the other hand, I think I know some things about the international business that they didn't know because they hadn't been there.

David Kelby, senior vice president and treasurer, described the board's role on the international expansion issue:

I would view the board as being a burr under the saddle. . . .It was there. If you've got a burr under the saddle, if you're a horse, then you want to do something about it.

William Pounds felt that the General Mills board played a significant role in the company:

I think that the General Mills board has worked more effectively than any board I've served on, and I have served on a lot of boards on a lot of good companies. But if I had to pick one as a model, [the General Mills board] works as well as any I know. . . .In this case, the board raised this issue in the mind of management higher than it might have otherwise been. The board didn't tell the management to do it. We didn't say, "We want you to come back with a plan to do something." It wasn't that kind of discussion.

Bruce Atwater believed the board didn't pressure the management on the issue, but instead made management constantly aware that international development was important. He commented:

3M kept Lehr bringing up international

board did not pressure just indicated importance

*What was the board's role in all of this? Did the board set the policy and direct management to ex-
ecute the policy? No. Did the board keep a gentle awareness that we need to be more international? Yes. Would we have done anything differently without the board?…I think we probably
wouldn't have had this quite as much on the front burner without the board.*

The Pursuit of Nestlé

In General Mills' search for alternatives to enter the European cereal market, a joint venture was one of the possibilities. While the cereal market was small outside of the well-developed U.K., it was growing at a double digit rate. And General Mills was behind: Kellogg's
had been selling cereals in Europe before General Mills had been selling cereals in America,
and had over a 50 percent share in every major European country. Knowing General Mills'
lack of certain capabilities had hindered it internationally in the past, Atwater and his team
began to focus more and more on Nestlé as a prospective partner. Art Schulze noted:

*We recognized that Nestlé was trying to enter [the European cereal market]. While our cereal
business was not yet international, we knew we wanted it to be. And Nestlé was, if not a current competitor internationally or in our markets, it was a possible future competitor. Nestlé
also had a very strong sales and distribution network throughout Europe, something we
lacked. So that's how we hit upon Nestlé as a joint venture partner. I think we all saw right
away as "This is the one."*

In the October 1989 board meeting, held in Quebec City, Atwater mentioned the idea to
the board. The topic hadn't been on the board's agenda, but Atwater decided on the spot to
bring it up informally. He told the board "This is our chance," to develop a cereal business in
Europe. The reaction to the idea from the board was positive and immediate—they discussed
the issue for less than 10 minutes. Atwater commented later:

*How can you do something that dramatic in 10 minutes? It takes you 10 minutes to talk about
it, because you've already got all the background from previous discussions.*

The following Monday, Atwater telephoned Maucher and made the arrangements for the
General Mills team to travel to Vevey. After Nestlé officials made a reciprocal visit to
Minneapolis, an agreement on a basic protocol was reached. Three weeks to the day after
Atwater had telephoned Maucher, the General Mills board met via conference call and ap-
proved the protocol of Cereal Partners Worldwide (CPW).

LUKENS INC.: THE MELTERS' COMMITTEE (A)

It was still dark the morning of December 5, 1991, when R. William Van Sant, the new CEO and chairman of Lukens Inc. (Lukens), entered the impressive Georgian mansion that served as the headquarters of Lukens for his first full day on the job. On his desk were several pressing matters, but he was captivated with an idea that a Lukens board member, Frederick R. Dusto, had suggested. Dusto, the former CEO of Harvey Hubbell, Inc. (Hubbell), had described a practice he had utilized as CEO where he would form a special committee of either board members or staff to act as an adversary to major management decisions. Dusto had recommended that Lukens form a similar board committee to evaluate Washington Steel Corporation (Washington) as a potential acquisition. Van Sant thought about this for several days and concluded that forming such a committee had two potential benefits. First, it would bring the board into the heart of the deal and signal to them that under his leadership management wanted to hear what they had to say. Second, Van Sant wanted Washington for Lukens, and was confident that the board would accept the acquisition as zealously as he did if they really investigated its potential.

▲ LUKENS' STRATEGY

Lukens Steel Subsidiary

The headquarters of Lukens was in a small Pennsylvania valley 35 miles west of Philadelphia. Incorporated in Delaware, the company was a diversified Fortune 500 company with sales of $628 million in 1991. Its largest subsidiary, Lukens Steel, accounting for 67.1

Research Associate Alison H. Watson prepared this case under the supervision of Professor Jay W. Lorsch. Copyright © 1993 by the President and Fellows of Harvard College.

[handwritten margin notes: "Superior customer service", "higher-value specialized steel products", "began diversifying '80", "Lukens board more demanding than @ GM"]

percent of total sales in 1991, was just around the corner from Lukens' headquarters. Lukens Steel was a specialized producer of carbon, alloy, and clad plate steel. Using a single 165-ton electric-arc furnace, the company produced its own steel for its plate products. In 1992, Lukens Steel was the third-largest producer of plate steel in the United States, and the largest American producer of alloy plate steel products.

When Van Sant became CEO in December 1991, Lukens Steel's competitive strategy was to provide superior customer service in the production of higher-value specialized steel products. Generally, Lukens Steel received a customer order and then produced steel that met the customer's particular requirements. This strategy was successful because of Lukens Steel's flexible production process, which produced the broadest range of plate sizes and grades in the industry at competitive prices. In addition, Lukens Steel believed it had the highest shipped-on-time performance in the industry. Lukens Steel's ability to meet customers' specific needs better than other steel companies helped protect its market position. In fact, while plate steel demand declined in the 1980s, Lukens Steel's market share in the domestic plate industry increased from 8.1 percent in 1982 to 13.6 percent in 1991.

Strategic Planning

In the early 1980s, the sluggish steel industry prompted Lukens to diversify. Over the next decade it acquired companies that produced highway and industrial safety products, corrosion protection services, and materials-handling products. Lukens also acquired a pipe-coating business, and began operating three short-line railroads. By 1991, nonsteel subsidiaries accounted for 32.9 percent of Lukens' sales.

Under W. R. Wilson, CEO of Lukens from 1980 to 1991 and chairman of the board from 1985 to 1991, the board held nine meetings a year, which included one long-range planning session. Regular board meetings lasted less than a day, while the long-range planning session required a full day. To prepare directors for board meetings, management generally sent them a packet of material containing the meeting agenda, a list of contemplated major capital expenditures, and any other material thought necessary for the meeting. For the long-range planning session, directors were also sent information about the company's strategic direction.

Discussion between management and the directors occurred mostly at board meetings, and thus, some directors believed that Wilson often did not discover their viewpoints until the day of the meeting. Several outside board members described Wilson's leadership as reflecting a more traditional director-management relationship, where management planned and the board approved or disapproved management's proposals. But this did not mean the board was merely rubber-stamping Wilson's agenda. Indeed, the board often exercised its right to say no to management's proposals.

This style of corporate governance continued until the summer of 1991. By then, Lukens' outside board members had become increasingly more involved with its affairs. For example, they decided to reconsider the company's strategy of diversification despite Wilson's opposition to the change. Moreover, they replaced several top managers and chose a new CEO, Van Sant, from their own ranks when Wilson retired. They also created an ad hoc committee of outside directors, chaired by Frederick M. Myers, to meet with Wilson and top management to oversee management's progress on acquisitions that the board thought were of strategic importance.

Van Sant and Washington Steel Corporation

When Van Sant first joined Lukens as a director in 1988, the company was still diversifying. Van Sant remembered proposed growth strategies as often having "no rhyme or reason" for a company dominated by its steel business. These proposals, along with the steel industry's upswing, prompted the Lukens board to reconsider the decision to diversify. Van Sant took this opportunity to approach the board with the possibility of acquiring Washington, a producer of stainless steel sheet. Van Sant was very familiar with Washington's operations, because before becoming a Lukens board member he had been president, CEO, and a director of Blount, Inc., the owner of Washington, from 1979 to 1988.

growth strategies had no rhyme or reason

Washington manufactured rolled stainless sheet and strip and continuous mill plate and was the largest U.S. distributor of rolled stainless steel products. For its fiscal year ending June 1991, the company had sales of $415 million. Similar to Lukens' competitive strategy, Washington produced nonstandard-size products and specialized finishes, focusing on markets in which importers and larger domestic producers were typically not as active.

Washington also specialized

Founded in 1945, Washington continued successfully under two owners until it was purchased by Mercury Stainless Corporation in 1988 for $280 million. The Washington purchase caused Mercury's debt liability to increase to $365 million. Unfortunately, a company strike, a delay in the installation of a new furnace, and the end of a period of high stainless prices left Mercury unable to meet its financial obligations. By the spring of 1991, Mercury had filed for Chapter 11 bankruptcy.

Van Sant was convinced that Lukens should acquire Washington for several reasons. First, both companies used similar technology, yet supplied separate areas of the steel market. This would allow Lukens to grow and build value while staying closely aligned with its steel industry strengths. Second, despite Mercury's bankruptcy, Van Sant judged Washington's management, technology, and products to be very solid. Third, both companies had the same competitive strengths, providing high-quality, nonstandard-size products and specialized finishes. Finally, he thought the two companies would fit together well. They were both medium-size, and Washington's philosophy and marketing strategies parallelled Lukens'.

(1) similar tech, but separate areas of the market (2) solid mgmt, tech, and products (3) same competitive strengths (4) fit well

Although the board showed some interest in acquiring Washington when Van Sant as director presented the possibility in 1989, it was clear to Van Sant that the CEO, W. R. Wilson, did not support the idea. At that time, Wilson still supported the company's strategy of diversification. It was also clear to Van Sant that even if Wilson was amenable to a steel acquisition, he would prefer acquiring another plate manufacturer rather than a sheet and strip producer. In addition, other directors and members of management questioned the asking price for Washington and the soundness of its management and operations. But because the proposal lacked Wilson's support, these issues were not seriously considered.

Three factors moved the Lukens board to investigate Washington as an acquisition. First, by the summer of 1991 the whole board was generally open to switching strategies from diversification to a concentration on steel, even if Wilson was not. Second, in the spring of 1991, Mercury filed for bankruptcy and was put up for sale in October 1991. Third, Van Sant was named CEO and chairman designate in October 1991, a position he assumed on December 4, 1991.

▲ FORMATION OF THE MELTERS' COMMITTEE

Frederick R. Dusto's Involvement

Dusto was flying to the December 1991 Lukens board meeting from his home in Tucson, Arizona. Although Lukens was going through several major changes, he was preoccupied with Van Sant's recommendation to buy Washington. Because the board had been contemplating a switch in long-term strategies for a while, Dusto felt it was not unusual for Van Sant to support a stainless steel company, especially one that had previously reported to Van Sant.

Although Dusto fully trusted Van Sant, he wondered whether the Washington proposal needed a more thorough evaluation by the board. He believed the Lukens staff was still trying to determine what their new CEO's management style was. He thought the staff might not oppose Van Sant if the CEO wanted to acquire Washington. Of course, Dusto knew the staff would review the acquisition and run it past the board. But he wondered whether the kind of discussion and review needed for such a large acquisition would be contemplated.

Because of this concern, Dusto told Van Sant about a practice he had used while CEO at Hubbell. In 1975, Dusto was worried about a Hubbell acquisition because he thought management was too enthusiastic about the deal to enable them to evaluate the potential negatives properly. To facilitate a better review, he asked an outside board member to act as an adversary to the acquisition. Although not particularly pleased with the review, Dusto was pleased with the process, so expanded on it in a later acquisition. This time Dusto had two Hubbell division managers and their staffs take the deal's pro and con sides and debate the issues. Dusto found that such a debate forced a very detailed review of issues associated with the acquisition, including the kind of capital investments needed, the people who were transferable into the acquired company, and legal issues.

Dusto thought the practice of forming an adversarial committee to evaluate major changes in a corporation could be very useful for Lukens' evaluation of Washington. Unlike Hubbell, however, Dusto believed that the special committee formed to evaluate Washington should comprise outside board members instead of management. Dusto thought that Van Sant's new management team might unintentionally fall in line with the new CEO and that a team of outside board members would be more objective.

R. William Van Sant's Involvement

Light started to filter through the blinds of Van Sant's office, signaling that it was time to move on to other matters. For the past two hours, he had spent the mid-December morning thinking about a recent conversation with Dusto. Several days earlier, Dusto had pulled him aside and said:

> Bill, I think we should form a committee and give them the same kind of information that your management team recommending the company has. This committee should take all the data, read it thoroughly, and then raise all the major issues during a meeting with management. I really think that this should be our plan for approaching the Washington question.

In considering the formation of such a committee, Van Sant weighed its benefits against the time and resources needed. He concluded that he had a good chance of pushing the acquisition through without forming the committee. As confident as he was in Washington, however, Van Sant thought of three reasons why he wanted the board to be fully involved in the decision. For one, he wanted 100 percent of the board's support. He was sure that a thorough investigation of the potential synergies between Washington and Lukens would convince them that Washington was an appropriate acquisition.

Second, Van Sant wanted the directors to make an informed decision because the risks were greet and Lukens was going through an unstable period. He believed he needed to make the directors fully aware of all the risks before he went forward with the deal, especially because Washington would be the largest acquisition Lukens had ever made. These risks included a projected increase in the company's debt-to-capital ratio from the current 15 percent to more than 50 percent, the ability to turn a bankrupt company around, the ability of the two companies to merge, competition from Lukens' current customers engaged also in stainless steel making, and Lukens' ability to be successful in the stainless steel market. Finally, there was he general risk of changing the company's strategy from the focus on diversification. A few executives and board members questioned whether it was more prudent for Lukens to continue to diversify.

Besides the risks, Van Sant realized that consideration of the acquisition was occurring during an unstable period for Lukens (Exhibits 1 and 2). For one, Lukens was still experiencing a strike that began on October 1, 1991. This strike plus the general recession in the steel industry caused Lukens a significant loss in the fourth quarter of 1991. Second, the corporate group had reorganized and about 10 key executives had left the company. Their exit and Wilson's departure as CEO caused a void at the top management level. Because of these two events, Van Sant believed the company needed, now more than ever, a unified team behind a decision with such great risks.

Third, Van Sant wanted to establish his style as CEO. He wanted openness, communication, and teamwork between management and the board, and he planned to bring the board into Lukens' strategic planning decisions. He hoped by doing this, he would receive directors' input at an earlier date instead of first learning of their response at board meetings. Van Sant concluded that Dusto's idea of forming a board team to act as an adversary on the Washington acquisition would signal to directors his style of interaction with them.

At the January 4, 1992, board meeting, Van Sant formally proposed to the 12 board members that a committee of outside directors be created to challenge his management team with questions on the Washington acquisition. The proposal was approved, and Van Sant chose 5 outside board members from the 10 who were on the board for the committee: Frederick R. Dusto (chairman of the committee); Frederick M. Myers; William H. Nelson III; Stuart J. Northrop; and W. Paul Tippitt (Exhibit 3). Van Sant called the group the Melters' committee and scheduled a meeting for February 25, 1992 (Melters' meeting), where the committee would challenge management on acquisition issues. It was to begin at 1 PM, but no other time frame was announced. The typical attitude was expressed by John M. Leland, director of business development and communications at Lukens: "We were going to be there, and we were going to stay there until the questions finished."

Because Van Sant felt that all Lukens board members were qualified to participate in the committee, a big concern in choosing members was other time commitments. He wanted to ensure that enough time was devoted for a thorough evaluation. In addition, he wanted to keep the committee small, to ensure that the process was not simply viewed as an additional board meeting. Although board members not chosen for the committee did not request to be on it, Van Sant had decided if any board member asked to be on the committee, he would have included the person on the committee.

▲ EXHIBIT 1   Lukens Inc.—Consolidated Statements of Earnings (dollars in thousands, year-end December 30, 1989, December 29, 1990, and December 28, 1991)

	1989	1990	1991
Net sales	$644,964	$683,644	$628,774
Operating costs and expenses			
Cost of products sold	536,471	563,948	539,578
Selling and administrative expenses	46,685	48,928	52,917
Unusual items			
Gain on sale of assets/subsidiaries	(6,814)	—	—
	$576,342	$612,876	$592,495
Operating earnings	68,622	70,768	36,279
Interest income	—	1,730	2,585
Interest expense	(2,758)	(2,416)	(2,012)
Earnings before income taxes	$ 65,864	$ 70,082	$ 36,852
Income tax expense	24,370	25,930	13,856
Net earnings	$ 41,492	$ 44,152	$ 22,996

Source: Company records.

A few days after the board meeting, Van Sant discussed with his staff the board's decision to form the committee. He described the process he was hoping to develop through the Melters' committee for evaluating Washington. Van Sant asked them whether they liked the idea, and the staff agreed it would be a good approach internally.

▲ RESPONSE TO THE CREATION OF THE MELTERS' COMMITTEE

Management

Van Sant's management team immediately recognized the potential benefits of the Melters' meeting. They viewed it as an audit check and welcomed the additional scrutiny of the $300 million deal. Robert Schaal, senior vice president of Lukens and president and COO of Lukens Steel, commented:

I hoped it would provide a thorough review of the business logic and the strategic significance of the deal, such as why we wanted to stay in steel and go into stainless, by someone who had not been so intimately involved with the numbers.

Management was also confident of its own performance, so it did not fear close scrutiny. In fact, management universally believed that they could answer any question from the Melters' committee, but responded that if they could not, it would still be positively accepted. In the words of John N. Maier, Lukens' controller, "God bless them if they think of something we missed, and it's an important point." Similarly, Schaal remarked, "We were about to

▲ EXHIBIT 2 Lukens Inc.—Consolidated Balance Sheets (dollars in thousands, year-end December 29, 1990 and December 28, 1991)

	1990	1991
Assets		
Current assets		
Cash and cash equivalents	$35,220	$44,387
Short-term investments	—	15,550
Receivables, less allowance of $4,352 in 1991 and $3,563 in 1990	73,848	66,629
Inventories	71,854	74,600
Prepaid expenses and other	3,053	2,764
Total current assets	$183,975	$203,930
Plant and equipment	471,110	503,433
	$471,110	$503,433
Less accumulated depreciation	269,390	292,855
Net plant and equipment	$201,720	$210,578
Other assets	26,224	17,852
Total assets	$411,919	$432,360
Liabilities and Stockholders Investment		
Current liabilities		
Accounts payable	$41,090	$47,159
Accured employment costs	31,615	33,894
Accured income taxes	1,805	22
Other accured expenses	8,542	11,478
Current maturities of long-term debt	4,481	6,625
Total current liabilities	$87,533	$99,178
Long-term debt	54,553	46,637
Other liabilities	10,012	13,626
Deferred income taxes	23,582	24,596
Total liabilities	$175,680	$184,037
Stockholders' investment	263,239	248,323
Total liablities and stockholders' investment	$411,919	$432,360

Source: Company rexcords.

commit Lukens to pay up to $300 million. I was personally sure it was the right decision. But if the board discovered something I missed, then of course I would accept it. It would be suicide if I did not."

▲ EXHIBIT 3   Lukens Inc. Board of Directors

Frederick R. Dusto.* Director since 1983. Former president, CEO, and a director of Harvey Hubbell, Inc. (a manufacturer of electrical products).

Ronald M. Gross. Director since July 1991. Chairman, CEO, and president of ITT Rayonier Inc. (a forest products company producing pulp, chemicals, and lumber).

Nancy Huston Hansen. Director since 1985. Vice president of Evangelical Affairs and director of the Huston Foundation. CEO and director of Hansen Development Corporation (construction and land development).

Wesley J. Howe. Director since 1982. Chairman, director, and former president and CEO of Becton Dickinson and Company (manufacturers of medical and diagnostic products).

Frederick M. Myers.* Director since 1957. Vice chairman of the board, Lukens Inc. Partner of Cain, Hibbard, Myers & Cook (counselors-at-law).

William H. Nelson, III.* Director since 1972. Former executive vice president and a director of Scott Paper Company (a manufacturer of pulp, paper, and forest-related products).

Stuart J. Northrop.* Director since 1982. A director and former chairman and CEO of Huffy Corporation (a manufacturer of bicycles and other sport leisure products).

Robert L. Seaman. Director since 1981. Private consultant. Former vice president of strategic planning for Raytheon Company (a diversified multinatonal corporation).

Harry C. Stonecipher. Director since 1991. Chairman, CEO, and president of Sundstrand Corporation (a manufacturer of aerospace and industrial equipment).

W. Paul Tippett.* Director since 1989. Former director, president, and COO of Springs Industries, Inc. (international manufacturer of finished and industrial fabrics and home furnishings).

R. William Van Sant. Director since 1988. Chairman and CEO of Lukens Inc. Former president, CEO, and a director of Blount, Inc. (a diversified corporation with construction, engineering, manufacturing, and agri-industrial operations).

W. R. Wilson. Director since 1980. Former chairman and CEO of Lukens Inc.

---

*Melters' committee members.
Source: Company records.

While the benefits of such a committee were readily apparent to all executives, the novelty and purpose behind this new idea caused some of these same executives apprehension. First, under the old CEO's leadership this type of interaction would never have occurred, so some were uncertain why the board wanted to do this now. Some executives suspected that the board wanted to ensure that the company was well under control, which, in the words of one executive, "made us feel uncomfortable." Second, some questioned the directors' ability to play devil's advocate against a management team that had spent months on the deal. Third, a few executives wondered whether the outside board members were taking over the company's management. For one thing, Van Sant, who had just been named

CEO, was formerly an outside board member. In addition, the decision to acquire a steel company (a dramatic change from the company's former strategy) was favored by several outside board members. This, combined with the board's increased involvement in company decisions during the previous six months, made some management members question the long-run intentions of the board.

This initial apprehension caused a few executives to make nervous jokes about the name given the committee. One executive stated, "The name conjured up a whole list of images, like they were going to put us into a pot and fry us—melt us under the heat."

The Board

Dusto was pleased with Van Sant's version of the committee. It would be a good way to prevent the Lukens staff from falling behind Van Sant because of his experience with Washington. As chairman of the Melters' committee, Dusto found the board team exceptionally qualified to do a thorough investigation. He was also impressed with Van Sant's internal team put together to evaluate Washington. He noted immediately that the best executives had been taken out of Lukens Steel to evaluate the acquisition. If the committee did their homework, Dusto was confident that the February 25 meeting would be very productive.

Dusto, however, did have three concerns about forming the Melters' committee. One pertained to the proper role of the board:

> You cannot have the board running the company. I don't want the Melters' committee experience to lead to our board always raising "Washington" issues that should not be discussed at the board level.

Dusto's second concern was about the directors not on the Melters' committee. When Van Sant proposed the Melters' committee idea, the board supported it, and Dusto did not think that there were any strong feelings by the nonmembers about the committee. Depending on the board, however, he thought that a division between the committee members and noncommittee members could develop if either side began to oppose the other. Although he was not seriously concerned that a division would develop on the Lukens board, he thought it could be a problem in some companies, depending on the board members and how relations among them developed after holding a meeting like the Melters' meeting.

Third, Dusto wondered how management viewed the creation of the Melters' committee. He knew it represented a further inroad into management decisions by a board that had become increasingly involved in management affairs over the last six months. He remarked:

> I am sure that several members of management wondered with the placement of Van Sant as CEO if outside board members were taking over the company. When the board formed the Melters' committee, I would not have been surprised if they were again wondering what our intentions were.

Myers explained why the board had become so involved and noted a specific example of board activism concerning Washington prior to the creation of the Melters' committee:

> There was a series of things we were concerned about during the period immediately before Wilson's departure. We wanted to make sure that the things we wanted to begin were happening. As a consequence the board was getting into matters more deeply than usual. The board's decision to investigate Washington as a potential acquisition is a good example of the board getting involved. Although in the fall of 1991 several directors were still unclear about their feelings toward Washington, the board as a whole believed, on the basis of preliminary information, that management should move forward on Washington to see if it appeared as attractive as it

*involved b/c
the significant
financial risk* ←

sounded. Thus, we formed an ad hoc committee, which I chaired, to ensure that management proceeded with its investigation of Washington.

Because acquiring Washington posed a significant financial risk to Lukens, several board members expected that their involvement with the company's business would continue into this deal. Although the type of involvement was not set in everyone's mind, most directors wanted to know more about the acquisition before it was approved. Myers commented that Van Sant's proposal of the Melters' committee appeared to satisfy the desire of the board members to have some sort of board evaluation of Washington.

▲ PREPARATION FOR THE MELTERS' COMMITTEE MEETING

Management

John M. Leland, Jr., Lukens' director of business development and communications, was in the basement of corporate headquarters sorting through numerous boxes neatly stacked against the wall. These boxes contained the voluminous materials gathered during the staff's due diligence investigation of Washington. Because Leland's responsibilities at Lukens included managing the acquisition process, Van Sant asked him to put together a package of material that would give the Melters' members enough information to understand the "whole picture" of the potential acquisition. Leland selected information in three main areas: Lukens' strategic direction, an analysis of the stainless steel industry, and an analysis of Washington. This material included a sensitivity chart describing potential changes in the economy, competition, or strategy, and how these would affect Lukens if it acquired Washington. The material also included sales memoranda for Washington. The completed packet of information was about 10 inches thick and color-coded by subject area. Leland included his phone number for any questions and sent the packet to the committee members on February 10, about two weeks before the Melters' meeting.

After putting the information together, Leland was impressed with the minimal amount of time needed for the project. He explained why:

I had been deeply involved with the deal for so long that I actually knew what was in every one of those due diligence boxes. I simply thought about the major pluses and minuses of Washington and put together a packet reflecting these points. I then gave it to my secretary in piles according to how I wanted it color-coded, and she sent it off to be printed. It really was very manageable.

While Leland was preparing the committee members, Van Sant continued to keep the whole board informed on the progress of the acquisition. When he began as CEO, he had decided to send the board members detailed monthly updates on Lukens' activities. He planned to continue this process to ensure that the committee members were not the only ones receiving information on the Washington deal. Furthermore, Van Sant made sure that the Melters' committee information was available to all board members who requested it.

Management had to prepare both the Melters' committee and themselves for the February 25 meeting. But at this stage many on the management team were extremely confident about their ability to answer any questions posed by the Melters' committee. Thus, most did not make special preparations for the meeting. They had reviewed the numbers and other aspects of the deal so many times that they believed they could answer any questions cold.

The Board

Dusto was pleased with the information sent to the Melters' committee. As the Melters' committee chairman, he received no complaints from any of its members about the content or volume of the information. He found the material both manageable and complete in its coverage of issues related to the Washington acquisition. Myers' comments agreed with Dusto's conclusions:

> *The material I received was timely, manageable, and useful for the committee's purpose. It provided us with the basis on which we were able to perform our function as the members of the Melters' committee.*

The committee members did not meet formally as a group prior to February 25. Instead, they prepared individually by setting up meetings with each other or with Lukens management according to their own needs. Dusto started his investigation by going to the Tucson library and researching the technology of stainless steel. Myers prepared independently, explaining that he went through the material the same way he prepared a case in his legal practice.

Some directors also arranged meeting with each other or with management. Dusto participated in several conference calls with other committee members. He wanted to hear their perspectives and ask some questions about issues he did not understand. Likewise, other members called him to ask about the technical aspects of the Washington acquisition.

Dusto elaborated on the committee's objective during the weeks before the Melters' meeting:

> *The objective was to raise all the issues we could to make sure that management had thoroughly evaluated them. We did not intend to evaluate just the short-term financial and legal issues of the acquisition. Instead, we investigated the long-term issues as well, including what type of capital requirements would there be down the road, who would replace the CEO of Washington when the current CEO retired, and how many people at Lukens thoroughly understood Washington's business.*

▲ THE MELTERS' COMMITTEE MEETING

On February 25, 1992, the last of the participants walked into the conference room where the Melters' meeting was to begin at 1 PM. In the room were senior management, lawyers, bankers, middle managers, and the Melters' members. Tables and chairs were arranged in a U shape. One executive described the setting as resembling a courtroom with about 25 management members sitting along the sides of the U, and the five-member Melters' committee sitting at the U's bottom. Except for a short dinner break, the participants were going to be there for the next seven hours.

During the Melters' meeting, the tone remained responsible and serious, and a great amount of interchange occurred. The Melters' members were not embarrassed to ask questions about issues or technology they did not understand. Van Sant, acting as moderator, fielded questions to the appropriate management member. Some answers were oral, while others required blackboards or data sheets. When Van Sant concluded the meeting, he believed that all significant issues concerning the Washington acquisition had been discussed.

The next day the Melters' committee met with the full board. Dusto gave an overview of the Melters' meeting and the committee's recommendation, which was to buy Washington. The board discussed the price and unanimously voted to authorize Van Sant to bid up to $270 million for Washington.

During the next few weeks, Van Sant continued to update the board with more information about the acquisition. This information prompted the board to increase its authorization to $280 million. In a board meeting a week before the bids were due, however, one member who had not been on the Melters' committee argued that Washington should not be lost for $10 million. After some discussion, the rest of the board agreed and authorized Van Sant to bid up to $300 million for Washington. This was $20 million more than the company's successful submitted bid. On March 30, 1992, Lukens announced it was acquiring Washington for $280 million.

INDEX